Economic Analysis of Law in European Legal Scholarship

Volume 8

The purpose of this book series is to publish high quality volumes in the growing field of law and economics research in Europe, from a comprehensive theoretical and practical vantage point. In particular, the series will place great emphasis on foundational and theoretical aspects of economic analysis of law and on interdisciplinary approaches in European Legal Scholarship. Following Nobel laureate Ronald Coase's famous essay "The Problem of Social Cost" (1960) fifty years ago law and economics has become the lingua franca of American jurisprudence. In recent decades, law and economics has also gained widespread popularity in Europe and its influence on Legal Scholarship is growing significantly.

Therefore, the economic analysis of law in European Legal Scholarship academic book series illustrates how law and economics is developing in Europe and what opportunities and problems – both in general and in specific legal fields – are associated with this approach within the legal traditions of European countries. Rather than further exploring economic analysis as such, the main focus of this series lies on the implementation of economic methods in legislation and legal adjudication from a European perspective. It takes into account the particular challenges the European legal systems face. Volumes will address law and economics research in Europe from a critical and comparative viewpoint. The studies in this series are strong and bold narratives of the development of economic analysis of law in European Legal Scholarship. Some are suitable for a very broad readership.

Contributions in this series primarily come from scholars in Europe. The purpose is to provide the next generation of European lawyers with the models and skills needed to understand and improve the economic analysis of law in their own legal field. The series includes monographs focusing on specific topics as well as collections of essays covering specific themes.

More information about this series at http://www.springer.com/series/11927

Georg Miribung

The Agricultural Cooperative in the Framework of the European Cooperative Society

Discussing and Comparing Issues of Cooperative Governance and Finance in Italy and Austria

Springer

Georg Miribung
Faculty of Science and Technology
Free University of Bozen-Bolzano
Bozen, Italy

Economic Analysis of Law in European Legal Scholarship
ISBN 978-3-030-44153-1 ISBN 978-3-030-44154-8 (eBook)
https://doi.org/10.1007/978-3-030-44154-8

This Springer imprint is published by the registered company Springer Nature Switzerland AG.
The registered company address is: Gewerbestrasse 11, 6330 Cham, Switzerland

For Tobias and Klara

Preface

This study is an important component of my academic path, which is linked mainly to the University of Innsbruck in Austria and the Free University of Bozen-Bolzano in Italy. Accordingly, it will come as no surprise that this transnational orientation is reflected in this work. Yet, whereas the research concerning cooperatives was mainly accomplished in Innsbruck, the aspects concerning agricultural law are the results from my research done in Bozen-Bolzano. My interest in carrying out this research was fuelled by the fact that, in the regions where the mentioned universities are located, agricultural cooperatives play an essential role in local development and economic prosperity. In regard to this subject matter, other specific studies have been previously conducted, using methods concerning the sociology of law.[1] The insights obtained from that research have helped to better conceptualise this study and to better discuss the results obtained.

As some readers might know, Bozen-Bolzano is the provincial capital of South Tyrol, a region in the very north of Italy close to Austria, with which it has cultural ties. The chosen approach for this study, which is based on comparative legal techniques, tries to reflect this reality. To do so, it compares legal norms from Italy with those from Austria and attempts to evaluate their differences. This comparison is embedded in a pre-determined legal structure, one pre-determined by European law. Thus, this study considers three legal systems: the European, as well as the Italian and Austrian legal systems. For evaluating those legal norms, this study uses an economic analysis of law. In this way, it takes an interdisciplinary approach.

Doing research on agricultural law is, at least for me, interesting and complex because it encompasses, due to the regulated object, i.e., agriculture, not only public and private law but also a phenomenon whose essence is based on nature. From this perspective, one can affirm that agriculture is the cultivation of nature. Interestingly, whereas all over the world this social and natural phenomenon is similar, if not equal, the juridical approach to it often differs. This is demonstrated by the legal

[1] Miribung (2016).

systems considered in this study and by how they conceive agriculture and, with it, agricultural law. Yet, the study also shows that the differences are often more formal than substantial. Consequently, one of this study's aims is to compare various national and EU norms of agricultural law. This is important because little research has been done on this topic, in particular concerning the Italian and Austrian legal systems. Similarly, it is generally acknowledged that there is little research on cooperative law. This is even truer if one considers comparative legal research. In general, one can affirm, as Professor *Antonio Fici*[2] states, that "comparative legal studies are necessary at least to increase cooperative visibility."[3] One aim of this study is to contribute to this necessity.

That agricultural cooperatives are part of a specific market regulated at the European Union level required a combination of legal methods to develop specific insights into the functioning of agricultural cooperatives. To make comparisons viable, it was necessary to think about what a cooperative might be, primarily from a legal perspective. To this end, I used, as guidelines to define what a cooperative is, newly developed principles that specifically deal with cooperative identity.[4] It is probably the mixture of scientific methods and legal topics, i.e., comparative law and an economic analysis of law, agricultural law and cooperative law, that produces this study's uniqueness.

The period of time I needed to conduct this study and publish it with Springer Publishing House was both professionally and privately challenging and demanding. It was full of joy, especially as my children were in their early years, but also determined by change. Ultimately, this made life, as such, more visible and perceivable. During this period, people came, people went, others entered and then left, like on a ferry. All of them gave, in their unique ways, their support. To all of them—family, friends and acquaintances—I want to express my especial gratitude. One source of particular motivation, especially in moments when things were difficult, came from my children, who due to their simple existence helped to keep me motivated.

This study could not have been accomplished without financial support. In this regard, I am very grateful to *Heiner Nicolussi-Leck*, former president of the administrative organ of the Raiffeisen Federation South Tyrol (RVS), *Paul Gasser* General Manager of RVS, and *Zenone Giacomuzzi* General Manager of Raiffeisen Landesbank Bozen-Bolzano, for their strong financial support. I would like to express my gratitude for their cooperation and for all the opportunities they offered me.

Last, but definitely not least, I am especially grateful to my academic teachers. In Innsbruck, the development of this study was mentored by Professor emeritus *Bernhard Eccher* and Professor *Andreas Schwartze*: thank you for your wise counsel and the sympathetic and valuable guidance. In Bozen-Bolzano, I had the opportunity

[2]University of Molise (Italy).

[3]See Fici (2013), p. 11.

[4]Principles on European Cooperative Law (PECOL).

to be counselled by Professor emeritus *Alberto Germanò*, who, even though not affiliated with my university, critically assessed my findings and helped me to reconsider some aspects, which I otherwise—probably—would not have noticed. I also offer my thanks to Professor *Alberto Germanò*.

I dedicate this study to my children, Tobias and Klara.

Bozen, Italy Georg Miribung

References

Fici A (2013) Pan-European Cooperative Law: where do we stand? SSRN Electron J:1–12. https://doi.org/10.2139/ssrn.2198283

Miribung G (2016) Genossenschaftliche Netzwerke in Südtirol - Versuch einer rechtssoziologischen Betrachtung. In: Ganner M, Voithofer C, Dahlvik J, Fritsche A, Fuchs W, Mayrhofer H, Pohn-Weidinger A (eds) Rechtstatsachenforschung - heute. Tagungsband 2016: Recht & Gesellschaft: Forschungsstand, Perspektiven, Zukunft. Innsbruck University Press, Innsbruck, pp 179–218

Contents

Chapter 1
Research Background

1.1 Aim of This Study

The EU introduced the European Cooperative Society (SCE), i.e., a cooperative with cross-border activities[1] that aims to adapt cooperatives' production structures to the Community dimension, so that, as "groups of companies from different member states",[2] they are not limited solely to meeting local needs,[3] but also those of members living or situated in different EU member states.

The legislative act regulating SCEs, i.e., Council Regulation (EC) No. 1435/2003, of 22 July 2003, on the Statute for a European Cooperative Society (SCE) (henceforth SCE-R[4]), is part of other regulations, such as the Regulation on the Statute for a European company (SE-R)[5] or the proposed Regulation on the Statute for a European Private Company (SPE-R),[6] which draft specific forms of enterprises for capitalist enterprises (SE-R) and small and medium-sized enterprises (SPE-R) in order to provide interested parties with better access to the internal market and, in particular, to promote their cross-border activities. In principle, all these types of companies follow a similar pattern: a strict framework outlined under EU law is combined with the obligation and the possibility of adapting these types of companies specifically to the particular needs of the member states. In contrast to these

---

[1]See recitals 6, 11 and 12 SCE-R.

[2]See recital 3 SCE-R.

[3]See recital 2 SCE-R.

[4]See OJ L 2003/207, 1.

[5]Council Regulation (EC) No. 2157/2001 of 8 October 2001on the Statute for a European company (SE). See OJ L 294/1.

[6]Proposal for a Council Regulation on the statute for a European private company, COM(2008) 396 final, 25.06.2008. See also the proposed directive on single-member private limited liability companies (2014/0120(COD).

G. Miribung, *The Agricultural Cooperative in the Framework of the European Cooperative Society*, Economic Analysis of Law in European Legal Scholarship 8, https://doi.org/10.1007/978-3-030-44154-8_1

regulations, however, the SCE-R contains special rules for membership, which also give the SCE-R its special character. In fact, none of the other regulations has an equivalent set of rules.[7] The concept of members' needs is crucial to the whole discussion conducted in this research, like a sun surrounded by planets. As will be seen,[8] this concept can be described legally in different ways by also allowing a more stringent approach (as determined by Austrian law) or a more open approach (as determined by Italian law). However, the essence is the same and refers to meeting members' 'common economic, social and cultural needs and aspirations'.[9]

The aforementioned pattern implies that a cooperative with cross-border activities is regulated in a very complex way by a hierarchy of norms (as defined in the SCE-R) because national legislation and the SCE regulation's provisions apply.[10] This means that for this study's purposes, EU member states Italy and Austria's laws shall be presented in a comparative manner, particularly rules on cooperatives as laid down in the Italian Civil Code (CC) on one hand and in the Austrian Cooperative Act (*Genossenschaftsgesetz, GenG*) on the other. To varying degrees, these supplement the provisions contained in the SCE-R if cooperative activities are to be carried out across borders within an SCE's framework.

Since the European legislature has employed regulation as a technical means to create law, it is natural to assume that a consistent and coherent framework has been established, one which determines clear rights and duties that are applicable unilaterally throughout the entire European Union (EU).[11] However, as will be explained later,[12] this is only true to a certain extent. In fact, the SCE-R creates a framework of legal norms that strongly interfere with national legislation. As a result, instead of creating a single new type of business organisation, one can assume that there are at least as many different types of SCE as there are EU members. Interestingly, though, and this is what these analyses show, this is not entirely true.

As this study focuses on agricultural cooperatives, it is also necessary to examine whether these national legal systems contain specific legal provisions on agricultural cooperatives. This implies that it is necessary to assess how case law and doctrine conceive agricultural cooperatives.

It generally is proved that agricultural cooperatives are important tools to keep farmers competitive as they try to sell their products in an international market that increasingly has become globalised through the integration of various national markets. Several studies demonstrate the various dynamics of this market integration and its consequences for local farmers, who often operate as small (and not yet medium-sized) enterprises. These studies are typically anchored in the social

---

[7] See Alfandari and Piot (2004). Also consider Cusa (2004), p. 145 et seq.

[8] See Sects. 3.2 and 3.4.

[9] See the International Cooperative Alliance's definition of cooperatives. On this issue, see also Pönkä (2018).

[10] See Art. 8 SCE-R. On this issue, see Sect. 2.4.

[11] See Art. 288 TFEU (Treaty on the Functioning of the European Union).

[12] See Sect. 2.4.

sciences (including economics), but also in law. Many legal topics were addressed from a national perspective, but less from an international and European perspective.[13] Considering European law as it pertains to agricultural cooperatives is, as will be shown, central to the present work. This is, however, not so easy from a legal point of view, because it requires one to compare certain aspects of economic, commercial or private law, and—to complicate things further—agricultural law.

This is particularly challenging for at least two reasons. From a national point of view, agricultural law is generally conceptualised as a cross-cutting subject and is, therefore, not always easy to define as such. In addition, there are different schools of thought at the national level that adopt different approaches to determining what agriculture and agricultural law actually is.[14] It will be shown from a legal point of view that Italy and Austria—the two national legal systems considered here—have used both similar and different approaches to anchor cooperatives in law; the same applies to the notion of agriculture and the subject of agricultural law. This research may partially close this gap.

Thus, it is possible to set up agricultural cooperatives that operate across borders through SCEs. This **study's aim** is to analyse this particular type of SCE by comparing how specific questions arising in this context must be dealt with under the Italian and Austrian legal systems. In this study, the SCE-R is used, therefore, as a tool for the structured analysis of agricultural cooperatives' various aspects. However, a comparison is only meaningful if the results are made comparable on the basis of a previously defined standard. For this purpose, this study uses, on one hand, a cooperative model developed by European legal scholars that defines general guidelines on how a cooperative should function.[15] On the other hand, the results are presented in connection with economic considerations to discuss how efficient rules can be developed.[16] Again, the concept of members' needs is central because it helps differentiate cooperatives from other types of enterprises.

Basically, I use the SCE-R here to analyse agricultural cooperatives' specific problems.[17] Because of personal interest, I focus on governance and financial **issues**. The results ultimately (also) show how an agricultural cooperative can be used as an

---

[13]On these issues, see Van der Sangen (2012), p. 18 et seq.; Ecorys, Wageningen Economic Research (2018), p. 8 et seq.; Amat et al. (2019). See also COPA-COGECA (2015). For a specific literature analysis on legal aspects, see Van der Sangen (2012), 10 et seq.

[14]See Sect. 1.2.2.

[15]See Sect. 1.2.1.

[16]See Sect. 1.3.

[17]However, the SCE-R is not specifically designed as an agricultural cooperative which would not be reasonable and actually possible. In scope and application, it is of a general nature. Yet, it is stressed that the SCE seems more appropriate as a secondary cooperative: that is, a cooperative with other (primary) cooperatives (or companies) as its members. See Fici (2013b), p. 120. The latter are called primary cooperatives and mostly have natural persons as members. One specific argument that favours this assumption is the minimum capital required by Art. 3 para. 2 SCE-R, but this argument alone is not convincing enough. In fact, no specific reason exists to explain why an SCE primarily shall be considered a secondary cooperative.

SCE. These specific issues will be discussed in the second part of this research. But before we analyse these specific questions—which are particularly important to farmers who are part of a modern food production chain—we must clarify what an agricultural cooperative is. Accordingly, part one of this research defines *cooperative* (Sect. 3.2) and how it can be defined as an *agricultural cooperative* (Sects. 3.3 et seq.). This process requires an examination of the legal notions of agriculture, agricultural activities and agricultural entrepreneurs, i.e., farmers. Given the nature of cross-border activities, it also is appropriate to explain how an agricultural cooperative could carry out such activities and whether specific legal aspects exist and should be considered.

All these questions ultimately require a clear—or at least as clear as possible—determination of what shall be compared. Although such a comparison is not an easy undertaking, it is ultimately fruitful because it helps us better understand agricultural law as an area of law which, also because of its economic importance, is anchored in several legislative levels and therefore needs to interact in theory and practice between European requirements and national interests. The fact that national agricultural laws are conceived differently in various member states makes it difficult to develop/implement a uniform approach at the European level. These aspects become visible during this study.

It will become clear that the special character of an agricultural cooperative must be conceived from the national legal order, at least in principle. In fact, in this context, it can also be ascertained that the various legal terms that are relevant here—referring to agriculture, agricultural activity and/or the agricultural entrepreneur/farmer—are determined by national law. These terms, then, also determine the field of activity of an agricultural cooperative. Also in this context, European integration is visible; therefore, these (in principle) national terms relating to content, formalism and systematisation are strongly influenced by European law. Therefore, viewing an agricultural cooperative as an SCE means being aware of various legal rules that often contradict, or are at least inconsistent with, each other. The reasons for this are not only that the SCE-R refers strongly to national law, but also that agricultural law (as a cross-sectional matter) is a rather heterogeneous area of law. This complexity concerns national rules and becomes even stronger if one bears in mind that EU law can also be conceived as a common platform for different legal traditions and approaches.

This study aims to shed light on this jungle of norms. To achieve this, I first analyse and compare the legal frameworks that surround the process of establishing an SCE as an agricultural cooperative in Italy and Austria, then compare and evaluate differing national approaches concerning questions of cooperative governance and finance. As will be seen,[18] to better understand the Austrian legal system, it is also helpful to consider German cooperative law.[19] In addition, as many of the

[18]See Sect. 1.2.1.

[19]This is a common approach when analysing Austrian law in general, and commercial and cooperative law in particular. A reason for this approach is definitely the same language, but also

provisions contained in the SCE-R are similar, if not equal, to those of the SE-R,[20] comments interpreting the provisions of the SE-R are often used as a first indication for interpreting the provisions of the SCE-R. Furthermore, I focused on differences between SCEs and their national counterparts by exploring the content, form and limits of existing law.[21]

The research design is thus ‘vertical’, which implies a top-down study that accounts for EU law and its application in the member states. The research is also ‘horizontal’ in that the set of rules established by EU law in conjunction with the applicable national law is compared with the mere national rules (thus excluding the European perspective). In other words, this requires questioning: What law applies to an Italian/Austrian SCE compared with an Italian/Austrian cooperative? This leads us to the important observation that throughout the regulation, the law of the member state in which the SCE has its registered office applies. Thus, in order to simplify reading, this study generally uses the simple terms ‘applicable national law’ and ‘relevant national law’ instead of the commonly used formula, ‘in accordance with the law of the Member State in which the SCE has its registered office’.

To determine which national law applies, the European legislatures that drafted the SCE-R had to decide whether an SCE should be linked to a legal system based on where the SCE was founded (incorporation theory) or on its headquarters’ location (real seat theory). According to the former, the applicable law is determined by the country where the cooperative is registered. Thus, incorporation theory considers neither the nationality nor the legal residence of the SCE’s members or the members of an SCE’s organs. According to real seat theory, the applicable law is determined by the country in which the cooperative has its headquarters. Hence, the relevant factor is the country where the cooperative has its corporate seat and not the country where it is incorporated.[22]

---

some common developments. A good example is provided by the Austrian Cooperative Act itself, which, when it was introduced in 1873, was based strongly on its German counterpart. See also Sects. 2.1 and 1.2.2.

[20]For a comparison of the options contained therein, see Fici (2010), Appencix 1a.

[21]See Sect. 1.2.1.

[22]See Snaith (2004), p. 37 et seq. For the SE, see Kellerhals and Truten (2002), p. 71; Arnò et al. (2007), p. 26 et seq.; Iengo (2006). Generally, Lutter et al. (2012), p. 69 et seq.; Bianca and Zanardo (2016), p. 206 et seq.; Münkner (2006), p. 17.

The SCE-R contains three specific provisions dealing with this issue: Art. 6 SCE-R, Art. 7 SCE-R and Art. 73 SCE-R. According to Art. 6 SCE-R, an SCE’s registered office must be located within the member state where it has its head office. In addition, the member states may require that an SCE locate its head office and registered office in the same place. In brief, the term “headquarters” refers to the SCE’s effective place of management, whereas the registered office must be located in the member state in which the SCE is registered, according to the law applicable to public limited-liability companies within that member state. As the head office is located in the same member state as the registered office, the law hereby determined corresponds to the law of the actual place of management. As a result, as long as an SCE does not infringe Art. 6 SCE-R, no conflict can arise between the laws determined according to the real seat theory and between laws determined according to the theory of incorporation. See Snaith (2004), p. 38 et seq. Also consider Schöpflin (2018b), p. 1255. In this context, Recital 14 SCE-R states: “In view of the specific

As mentioned above, this study also concentrates on issues of cooperative governance and finance, with many issues discussed in detail. However, it quickly became clear that without strict academic limitations the study's discussions could spiral out of control. Thus, this study does not provide an exhaustive comparison between Italian and Austrian SCEs. Instead, it focuses on the most important differences and similarities between these two entities.[23] To be more precise, I analyse the specific rights and obligations explicitly provided by the SCE-R and examine how they are implemented by national laws, while choosing not to consider in detail the rights and obligations not explicitly mentioned by the SCE-R.[24]

Therefore, this study inevitably contains **gaps**,[25] which might be considered a weakness, as these gaps often concern specific details. For instance, when considering the issue of expelling members of an SCE, it would be interesting to conduct a detailed analysis of the applicable factors to determine how the expulsion process differs between the two legal systems. Moreover, I also ignore issues concerning

---

Community character of an SCE, the 'real seat' arrangement adopted by this Regulation in respect of SCEs is without prejudice to member states' laws and does not pre-empt the choices to be made for other Community texts on company law." Also consider Snaith (2004), p. 40. For the SE, Ringe (2015a), p. 138 et seq.; Urbani (2008), p. 323 et seq. Art. 7 SCE-R defines how an SCE can transfer its registered office to another member state without winding up the SCE or forming a new legal person. It requires publishing a proposal for transfer which contains the details required by the SCE-R. As well as the members of the SCE, this procedure particularly aims to safeguard its creditors and the holders of other rights. See Schöpflin (2018c), p. 1258; Snaith (2004), p. 39. In general, Genco (2006), p. 124 et seq. The SCE-R requires a competent authority in the member state where the SCE has its registered office to issue a "certificate attesting to the completion of the acts and formalities to be accomplished before the transfer." In addition, the member state can allow its authorities to deny the transfer if it is in the public interest, but it must be possible to review this opposition under judicial authority. In addition, if proceedings for winding up (including voluntary winding up), liquidation, insolvency or suspension of payments (or other similar proceedings) have been brought against an SCE, the transfer cannot be carried out. See Art. 7 para. 15 SCE-R. Also consider Snaith (2004), p. 39 et seq.; Schöpflin (2018c), p. 1258 et seq. For the SE, see Ringe (2015b), p. 168 et seq. Next, Art. 73 SCE-R provides an enforcement mechanism if an SCE's headquarters is no longer situated in the same member state as its registered office. According to para. 2, the member state in which the SCE's registered office is situated must take appropriate measures and oblige the SCE to regularise the situation within a specified period. The SCE must then either re-establish its headquarters in the same member state as its registered office or transfer its registered office via the procedure laid down in Art. 7 SCE-R. If the SCE fails to regularise its position, the authorised member state must ensure the SCE is liquidated. The member states have to provide judicial or other appropriate remedy with regard to any established infringement of Art. 6 SCE-R (Art. 73 para. 3 SCE-R). Art. 73 para. 4 SCE-R adds that such a remedy has to have a suspensory effect on the procedures laid down in para. 2 and para. 3 (procedures to oblige the SCE to regularise its situation). For details, see Snaith (2004), p. 39; Schöpflin (2018a), p. 1341 et seq.

[23]I often had to decide whether to continue to pursue details or move forward to preserve the broader picture. In general, I have favoured the latter approach.

[24]Consider in this context Alfandari and Piot (2004), p. 83. Specific rules and restrictions governing the nature of an SCE's business could include national provisions in the banking, insurance or financial services sector. These provisions must be applied in full if an SCE carries out business activity in one of these fields and thus must be considered.

[25]However, this also shall be understood as a call for further specific research.

winding up or bankruptcy[26] and about how employee participation[27] might complement the SCE-R. This study is further limited by the inevitable involvement of other legal rules which are not, strictly speaking, part of agricultural law and/or cooperative law. These rules will be mentioned without further in-depth analysis. In addition, depending on the legal system, sub-national level rules might be addressed.[28] An analysis of SCEs could also consider these rules. However, because of the limited scope of this study, these specific issues will not be discussed.

The study will be conducted using a multifaceted **methodological approach** based on comparative and economic analyses of the law. Because of the various methodologies employed, this study can be considered *interdisciplinary research.*[29] But it is important to stress that the study is still profoundly rooted in law as a field of research, with the economic perspective only supplying specific aspects giving an idea of how, ultimately, the rules should be applied. These matters are only covered as far as necessary.

When conducting any kind of interdisciplinary research, the same research object will be described and analysed from different perspectives.[30] Inevitably, the analyses will use the same or similar notions, albeit with a different content; i.e., the same terms may differ in content, based on the context (i.e., field of research) in which it is used. For example, in the context of ownership, terms may differ in content, as content is determined by the field of research to which a specific term is linked when it is actually used.[31] In order to tackle this problem, *Raiser* stresses that different scientific fields have different aims.[32] Thus, the terms provided by the various scientific fields are also different. Where legal terms refer to values and contain orders, terms taken from sociology, for example, are used to describe things and facts. Thus the reader must bear in mind that the chapters referring to the economic

[26]Further research could concentrate on the civil liability of members of the management, administrative or supervisory organ, specific legal impediments to becoming a member of these organs or the general competence of these organs.

[27]The European legislator adopted a specific directive (Council Directive 2003/72/EC of 22 July 2003, OJ L207/25). On this issue, see Ales (2008), ec.europa.eu/social/main.jsp?catId=707&langId=en&intPageId=213 (15.08.2006) and Marhold (2008), ec.europa.eu/social/main.jsp?catId=707&langId=en&intPageId=213 (01.12.2019). Also consider Kisker (2006), p. 208 et seq.

[28]For example, see Ibáñez (2011).

[29]See Baer (2011), pp. 50 et seq. and 78 et seq. For an example, see Kalss and Schauer (2006).

For a precise introduction to interdisciplinary research methods in law, see Baer (2011), pp. 78 et seq. and 133 et seq. In general Tushnet and Cane (2012); Cane and Kritzer (2013). Also consider Raiser (2011, 2013); Hill and McDonnell (2012), p. 3 et seq.; Fleischer (2000); Denozza (2002), pp. 1 et seq. and 11 et seq.; Richter (2015c); Gallo (2001), p. 13 et seq.; Mattei (1999), p. 505 et seq.; Krimphove (2006), p. 13 et seq.

[30]See Baer (2011), p. 50.

[31]See Sect. 1.3.2.

[32]See Raiser (2011), p. 160 et seq. See also Baer (2011), p. 50 et seq.

perspective also contain specific terms embedded in economic theory (and in particular in new institutional economics).[33]

1.2 About Comparing Agricultural and Cooperative Law: Issues of Method

1.2.1 About Comparative Law

This research focuses on the Italian and Austrian legal systems' diversity concerning cooperatives in general and agricultural cooperatives in particular. To compare the two systems, this study uses comparative law[34] techniques to compare Italian and Austrian agricultural SCEs. Legal science, in the sense of comparative law, is regarded as the science of comparing national legal systems.[35] Accordingly, it is an outward-looking perspective and not an inward-looking perspective. In the latter case, there is only the comparison between old and new national law.[36] With comparative law, conversely, one compares legal norms and then objectively examines the interactions between different legal systems. Thus, differences can be worked out, common features found and similar structures and approaches or methods identified.[37] Then, comparative law is also a matter of finding gaps in the other legal sphere in comparison to one's own. Accordingly, it is also a matter of comparing the applications of the law.[38]

From a conceptual point of view, one can distinguish between a macro- and a micro-comparison. In the former, comparison is done between legal systems or legal cultures according to defined legal circles or families, whereas the latter's object of research involves individual legal rules, judgments or individual legal institutions.[39] The criteria for the legal families are, in particular, legal history, major legal works,

---

[33]Different terms have to be understood in the context of their respective disciplines, and it is inadvisable to apply terms from outside disciplines without outlining their specific context. See Raiser (2011), p. 160 et seq.

[34]For details Zweigert and Kötz (1996), p. 62 et seq. In this context also consider Glenn (2019), p. 423 et seq.; Danneman (2019), p. 393 et seq. Generally, Gallo (2001), p. 3 et seq. and in particular 16 et seq.; Gambaro and Sacco (2014); Mattei (2001); Sacco (1991, 1992); Schlesinger et al. (2009); Gorla (1981); Monateri (2012), Regarding the development of this method in Austria and Italy see Schwenzer (2019) and Grande (2019). See also Guarneri (2003), p. 15 et seq.

[35]See Zweigert et al. (1998), p. 5; Siems (2014), p. 2; Moccia (2005), p. 3 et seq.; Sacco (1994), p. 11 et seq. See also Guarneri (2003), p. 1 et seq.; Gallo (2001), p. 13.

[36]However, overlapping areas exist, e.g., in the internal comparison of a federal state's legal norms.

[37]The valuations hidden behind the law also can be worked out. See Zweigert et al. (1998), p. 5 et seq.; Sacco (1994), p. 11 et seq.; Siems (2014), pp. 2 et seq. and 287 et seq. See also Moccia (2005), p. 12 et seq.

[38]See Siems (2014), p. 3 et seq.; Sacco (1994), p. 19 et seq. See also Moccia (2005), p. 95 et seq.

[39]See Zweigert et al. (1998), p. 5 et seq.

the systematics used, common core elements, common legal methods (e.g., the role of jurisprudence), specific legal branches or norms or a legal cultural background.[40] The legal systems analysed here are part of the Germanic and Roman legal families; they are compared by adding the European perspective.[41]

A core element of comparative law is the functional comparison of laws through which one gains knowledge about the purpose of a foreign legal norm and learns how to deal with specific regulations abroad.[42] Additionally, one evaluates the differences that result from the comparison between one's own norm and the foreign legal norm. It is important to emphasise that the comparison extends beyond pure legal knowledge and allows one to construct common lines of reasoning and essential differences, and to include appropriate evaluations of the differences.[43]

The following steps can be taken during the comparison. First, the applicable legal provisions and/or the relevant case law must be identified. Similarities and differences between these provisions can then be identified. Next, one can identify the different value concepts on which these rules are based. Finally, scholars can evaluate these results with a scientific framework, draw conclusions, and determine how these conclusions might change the legal situation.[44]

Various tasks of comparative law can be derived: among others, this method can fulfil both a mere scientific function and a legislative function.[45] The scientific function helps gaining knowledge about the different functions and structures of law, also because of different legal cultures, and understanding them accordingly. The legislative function supports the legislature as he fulfils his tasks at the national

[40]See Sacco (1994), p. 187 et seq. However, it also should be noted that this formation of the legal circle is fraught with problems. For example, one can ask oneself why civil law should be used as a yardstick. In addition, it can be seen that legal systems often have mixed elements and, therefore, cannot be assigned clearly to just one legal system. It also can be argued that legal norms occasionally are overemphasised in contrast with the application of law. See Guarneri (2003), p. 15 et seq.; Glenn (2019); Zweigert et al. (1998), p. 76 et seq. See also Pargendler (2012).

[41]The methodology of comparative law requires that foreign law must be recognised first and foremost. Accordingly, a basic prerequisite is work on foreign sources. The basic requirement is that the work should be carried out in the original language as often as possible. See Zweigert and Kötz (1996), p. 62 et seq. In this context also consider Glenn (2019), p. 423 et seq.; Danneman (2019), p. 392 et seq. Generally, Gallo (2001), p. 3 et seq. and in particular 16 et seq. Regarding the development of this method in Austria and Italy see Schwenzer (2019); Grande (2019); Guarneri (2003), p. 15 et seq.

[42]See Michaels (2019), p. 348 et seq.; Zweigert and Kötz (1996). Also see Guarneri (2003), p. 10 et seq.; Graziadei (2003), p. 100 et seq.

[43]The essential prerequisite is knowledge of one's own law: Only under these circumstances can the right question be asked. At the same time, the researcher also must be aware that he or she must be careful when using his own terms and thought patterns. See Guarneri (2003), p. 10 et seq.; Zweigert et al. (1998), p. 34 et seq. See also Sacco (1994), pp. 11 et seq. and 24 et seq.

[44]See Siems (2014), p. 13 et seq. See also Guarneri (2003), p. 10 et seq.

[45]Here comparative law serves as an information basis for lawyers and courts. I.e. it is about legal advice and support in the case decision. See Siems (2014), p. 2 et seq. See also Guarneri (2003), p. 10 et seq.

and international levels.[46] Although this research does not perform a legislative function, it nevertheless contains relevant points in this regard. For example, concerning cooperatives, it proved helpful to use a model based on the Principles of European Cooperative Law (PECOL)[47] to compare the rules of the various legal systems (the PECOL generally depict the legal characteristics of a cooperative[48]). With this model, the differences resulting from the comparison can then be evaluated in depth. If one accepts this model as an ideal case, he/she can use any results that deviate from this model to identify possible changes in the law.[49]

The PECOL have been put together by the Study Group on European Cooperative Law (SGECOL) to provide better knowledge of cooperative law.[50] Unlike the Principles of the International Cooperative Alliance (ICA), which are internationally accepted principles about how cooperatives function,[51] the PECOL try to describe cooperative law norms. These norms are the diverse regulations that govern cooperatives. The aim of the PECOL is providing a better understanding of cooperatives and the legal principles on which they are based.[52] Yet, the 'PECOL provisions, in their authors' view, must not be regarded as 'legal principles' in the sense of legal philosophy, but as 'ideal' provisions of cooperative law. Therefore, they will not

---

[46]See Siems (2014), p. 2 et seq.

[47]See Hiez (2017), p. 1 et seq.

[48]See Hiez (2017), p. 11 et seq.

[49]Of course, comparing things is not that easy. See Zweigert and Kötz (1996), p. 33; Danneman (2019), pp. 391 et seq. and 413. Also consider Kalss and Schauer (2006), p. 26. Conducting research into cooperatives first requires defining what a cooperative is. As well as the wide range of different types of SCE which can be found in the EU, one must also bear in mind that cooperative systems within the EU have developed differently and are based on different theoretical concepts (see Sect. 2.2). Thus, it is very difficult to provide a clear definition of a cooperative, at least from a legal standpoint. Instead, one must consider key attributes or features within or outside a legal definition. See Fici (2017), p. 21. This study considers such attributes by utilising the latest insights from a group of leading European scholars, who have worked to identify the common features of cooperatives across the various legal systems of different EU member states. The result are the PECOL. However, this task is a constantly evolving process, and therefore falls outside the scope of this study. Nevertheless, it clearly provides further insights needed to better conceptualise a common cooperative identity.

[50]See Hiez (2017), p. 14 et seq. "SGECOL will use comparative research on cooperative law to explore differences and commonalities across jurisdictions, with a view to considering the feasibility of a ius commune cooperativum." See Study Group on the European Cooperative Law (2012), p. 5. The commission drafting the PECOL is made up of eminent scholars of cooperative law: Gemma Fajardo, Antonio Fici, Hagen Henrÿ, David Hiez, Deolinda Aparícío Meira, Hans Münckner and Ian Snaith. See Hiez (2017), p. 2 et seq. However, this initiative is not new: Since 1982, various European jurists have come together to develop uniform European principles of private law. A famous example is the Lando Commission (originally founded in 1982) and the Principles of European Contract Law (PECL, published in three parts in 1995, 1999 and 2003). See Lando et al. (2019). Since then, numerous such projects have been launched, e.g., in European tort law, European family law, European security law, European company law and European insolvency law. See Zimmermann (2019), p. 588 et seq. See also Adar and Sirena (2013).

[51]See Sect. 2.1.

[52]See Hiez (2017), p. 11 et seq. In this context also consider Ringle (2007).

necessarily reproduce rules (or the 'better' rules) found in the existing cooperative law, although the latter constitutes the main source of inspiration for the drafters. In this sense, the approach taken in the drafting of the PECOL is 'normative' rather than descriptive, in line with the methodology that, in general, SGECOL intends to use in its comparative analysis of cooperative law.'[53]

Based on a structure that takes into account the main cooperatives' organisational issues, the members of the drafting commission analysed their national legal systems and drafted national reports describing how these legal systems dealt with specific issues. Their efforts yielded data on what kinds of legal rules exist, how they are structured and so on. The results were then used to identify shared features and principles, based on existing national law.[54] Yet, the PECOL do not promote further European Union legislation in the area of cooperative law, but instead should function as a coherent body of cooperative law. In particular, it should guide cooperative law expansion and reform throughout Europe by advising legislatures on best practices.[55]

As mentioned, this research's starting point is the Italian and Austrian legal systems' diversity with respect to how cooperatives and agricultural cooperatives are regulated. The national laws in question are contained in the *GenG*, the Austrian trade regulation (*Gewerbeordnung*, *GewO*) and the CC.[56] The conducted analyses are thus anchored in private law, because cooperatives are, first of all, a matter of private law; yet the framework that determines the functioning of these forms of organisations, is strongly influenced by public law, specifically European agricultural law. Accordingly, there are clear interactions between public law and private law.[57] Here, too, the question may arise as to how these interactions function, what interdependencies exist and what differences exist in national law as a result of imposing European law onto national law.[58] From a European point of view, this research therefore considers, in addition to the SCE-R, rules contained in specific

---

[53]See Study Group on the European Cooperative Law (2012), p. 9.

[54]See Hiez (2017), p. 6 et seq. The PECOL contain five chapters which address the following issues: (1) Definition and objectives of cooperatives: This chapter defines cooperatives and their objectives, outlines applicable law, statutes and membership requirements and addresses transactions with members and non-members. (2) Cooperative governance: This chapter contains general principles of governance and open membership and covers the obligations and rights of members, direct member control and governance issues like management and internal control as well as information rights and transparency requirements. (3) Cooperative financial structure: This chapter contains general financial principles, deals with share capital, members' capital contributions, cooperatives' reserves, limited liability and distribution of economic results. (4) Cooperative auditing: This chapter contains general auditing principles and covers the scope and forms of audit, audit entities and auditors, as well as the conclusion of cooperative audits and their effects. (5) Cooperation among cooperatives: This chapter contains general cooperation principles and concentrates on forms of cooperation and social political cooperation.

[55]See Hiez (2017), p. 11 et seq.

[56]For details, see also Sect. 3.2.

[57]See Part I of this study. On this issue, see also Carrozza (2001d), p. 304 et seq.

[58]See Sect. 3.3.3.

regulations—such as Reg. No. 1308[59] or 1307[60]—and, in general, the rules determined by the Common Agricultural Policy (CAP).

The reference to the CAP makes it useful to repeat that my comparison of national cooperative laws also includes agricultural cooperatives and, thus, agricultural law. However, comparing the laws in these sources is a complex task because agricultural law is subject to different approaches. Therefore, as a starting point in this comparison, I refer to the different legal concepts of agriculture.[61] The legal definitions that already exist illustrate the fragmentation of the various concepts.[62] This is true if one compares the approaches adopted by national sources. EU law also offers a similar picture of fragmentation. Especially because of the dynamic nature of relevant terms (decoupling, direct marketing and, finally, new phenomena) conceptual consistency is not possible. Next, agricultural law is cross-sectional,[63] which is a further reason for the difficulties in defining a consistent approach.

1.2.2 About Agricultural Law

Agricultural law presents a mixed picture. There is no question that a systematic structuring of this branch of law would improve clarity and consistency, thereby facilitating legislation and its implementation. I consider two possible ways of determining the subject matter of agricultural law.[64] First, such determination can occur through induction, by which the specific legal norms of a positive legal system can be examined in light of a common core, which can be extended or limited in accordance with the legislature's objectives. This basically corresponds to the

[59]Regulation No. 1308/2013 of the European Parliament and of the Council of 17 December 2013 establishing a common organisation of the markets in agricultural products and repealing Council Regulations (EEC) No 922/72, (EEC) No 234/79, (EC) No 1037/2001 and (EC) No 1234/2007. See OJ L 347/671.

[60]Regulation No 1308/2013 of the European Parliament and of the Council of 17 December 2013 establishing rules for direct payments to farmers under support schemes within the framework of the common agricultural policy and repealing Council Regulation (EC) No 637/2008 and Council Regulation (EC) No 73/2009. See OJ L 347/608.

[61]On this issue, see, among others, Norer (2012), p. 4 et seq.; Norer (2005), p. 37 et seq.; Holzer (2018), p. 31 et seq.; Grimm and Norer (2015), p. 14 et seq.; Bodiguel and Cardwell (2006); Winkler (2018b), p. 164 et seq.; Iannarelli (2007); Germanò and Rook Basile (2014), p. 111 et seq. See also Pernthaler (2007), Leidwein (2007), Welan (2017), Grossi (2016), Budzinowski (2013), Budzinowski (2018), Iannarelli (2013), Costato (2012) and Galloni (2014). In general, Martínez (2018).

[62]See Sect. 3.3.

[63]See Norer (2005), p. 37 et seq.; Norer (2012), p. 6. See also Grimm and Norer (2015), p. 14 et seq.; Norer (2018), p. 114 et seq.; Costato and Russo (2015), p. 3 et seq. See also Rook Basile (1995), p. 19 et seq.

[64]See Norer (2005), p. 141.

approach taken by Austrian doctrine and the Austrian legal system.[65] Second, a strongly codified approach is possible for interpreting the particularities of legal developments in the agricultural sector.[66] Such an approach is based on the *agrarietà* doctrine developed by *Antonio Carrozza*, which roots agricultural law in the biological cycles of plant and animal production by using nature's forces and resources, with resulting products that may be intended for human consumption after processing.[67] The concept of *agrarietà* has strongly influenced French[68] and Italian legislation. In fact, in 2001, *agrarietà* was incorporated into Italian legislation by Decree-Law No. 228 of 18 May 2001, which amended Article 2135 of the Civil Code on the agricultural entrepreneur.[69] The agricultural entrepreneur is assigned activities for land management as well as forestry and animal husbandry, which are directly linked to the management and development of a biological cycle—whether that of a plant or an animal.[70] Additional activities linked to these agricultural activities include the provision of goods and services, such as agri-environmental measures and, in the case of agri-tourism, the use of farm equipment and resources.[71]

The *agrarietà* approach seems particularly interesting because it refers to the given phenomena of reality as the basis for the special rights of agriculture.[72] Furthermore, a distinction is made between a*grarietà territoriale* and *agrarietà non territoriale* to account for soil-independent forms of agricultural production.[73] Yet, for defining agriculture, it is not only the exploitation of biological processes that is decisive but also the fact that it fulfils tasks for society and that the production

---

[65]See Holzer (2018), p. 62 et seq.; Norer (2012), p. 7 et seq.; Holzer (2017). See also Norer (2018).

[66]On this issue, see Norer (2005), p. 76 et seq.

[67]See Carrozza (1988), p. 10 et seq. See also Carrozza (2001d), p. 301 et seq.; Carrozza (2001b), p. 379 et seq.; Carrozza (2001e), p. 712 et seq. See also Winkler (2018b) and Bolognini (2019), p. 305 et seq.

[68]In France, Law No 88-1202 of 30 December 1988 established a definition of agricultural activity, which was inserted as Article L 311-1 into the rural code, the French Code. Agricultural activities are considered to be all activities that serve to manage and exploit a biological cycle of plant and animal life, comprising one or more necessary stages in the course of this cycle, as well as a farmer's activity in the extension of the production process, i.e., in the working, processing and marketing of agricultural products. On this issue, see, among others, Bodiguel and Cardwell (2006).

[69]On this issue, see, among others, Iannarelli (2002b), p. 213 et seq.; Costato (2006). See also Germanò (2019), Lamanna Di Salvo (2003), p. 15 et seq. and Goldoni (2019), p. 372 et seq.

[70]It is an almost literal translation of the definition of agricultural activities introduced by French law.

[71]For details, see Sect. 3.3.1.

[72]See Casadei (2009), p. 329 et seq. See also Winkler (2018b), p. 171 et seq.

[73]See Carrozza (2001a), p. 785 et seq.; Carrozza (2001e), p. 715 et seq.; Costato (2001), p. 142. See also Winkler (2018b), p. 187; Cigarini (1977), p. 694; Winkler (2018a), p. 216; Carrozza (2001e), p. 715 et seq.; Carrozza (2001a), p. 780 et seq.

process is socially organised.[74] Agriculture represents a close link between natural processes and their organisation in the social and economic spheres; it thus determines human activity and behaviour, institutions, and economic and social conditions.[75] We must remember that the biological cycles underpinning the doctrine of *agrarietà* are ultimately unhistorical and repeat themselves over a long period of time, while social processes are integrated into history and change constantly. Thus, *agrarietà* only does justice to agricultural law if the law is not perceived as being static or repetitive, but rather as something changeable; this mutability makes it possible to integrate social factors and biological conditions.[76]

Contrary to the Italian approach, Austrian agricultural law lacks a strict dogma; this fact has prompted scholars to develop definitions and subject-matter provisions.[77] The Austrian legal system contains a number of norms that, according to their content, represent special laws applicable exclusively to agriculture and forestry, such as inheritance law, land reform law, land lease law and agricultural labour law. Accordingly, agricultural law is a special branch of law to which all those norms are assigned that are connected to the peculiar living and economic conditions in agriculture, forestry and their subsidiary branches, as well as to the special relationships which have developed in this environment. Today, the approach defining agricultural law as a special branch of rules dominates German agricultural law.[78] However, especially in Austria from the 1970s onwards, the so-called functional concept of agricultural law developed as an extension of the traditional notion of special law. This functional approach looks for a common core, which can then be extended or limited in accordance with the legislature's objectives.[79] Functional ideas, when applied to agricultural law, include any norm that has specific effects upon agriculture and forestry.[80] This approach analyses those normative structures

---

[74]See also Carrozza (2001c), p. 650 et seq.; Germanò (2016), p. 12; Casadei (2009), p. 332 et seq.

[75]See Germanò (2016), p. 12.

[76]See Winkler (2018b), p. 187; Germanò (2016), p. 12 et seq. Furthermore, it should be noted that criteria for proper law cannot be derived directly from real factors, as mere existence never can justify a determined purpose. It is obvious that real factors do not become decisive for the legal order in their mere factuality, but only in their relation to the meaning of human beings and their behaviour, as well as their spiritual and moral world. From this, it follows that a relationship of derivation cannot exist between the nature of the matter and what is legally normed as 'should', but only a relationship of correspondence in which the requirement of reason for an appropriate regulation results from the elements of the order of reality. See Winkler (2018b), p. 209 et seq.

[77]See Holzer (2018), p. 62 et seq.; Holzer (2017); Norer (2005), p. 120 et seq.; Grimm and Norer (2015), p. 14 et seq.; Norer (2017); Norer (2012), p. 5 et seq.

[78]See Busse (2018) and Norer (2018).

[79]See Holzer (2017); Norer (2005), p. 120 et seq.; Norer (2018), p. 117 et seq.

[80]May it now originate from a legal area shaped by typical agricultural interests or from an area that is predominantly dominated by administrative interests other than those determined by agriculture. It is stressed that with the functional approach, the fragmentation of agricultural law into other legal areas can be countered effectively. These relevant norms, e.g., environmental or planning law norms, are (also) understood as part of agricultural law and summarised under the terms agri-environmental law or agricultural spatial planning law. See Norer (2005), p. 136 et seq.

that make agriculture and forestry the object of legal regulations.[81] The limits of such a system—which ultimately cannot be clearly delimited and is thus open in its systematic references and not closed to other sub-disciplines—are governed by those norms that cover agriculture and forestry in their specific structure of being. It is stressed that the blurred and movable boundaries of this functional notion are countered by the gain of a broad definition of the object corresponding to today's modern necessities.[82]

Regardless of the approach adopted, agricultural law is characterised by numerous legal peculiarities that distinguish it from both general law, and company law. In addition, there are regulations and institutions in the agricultural sector that cannot be found in other sectors of the economy.[83] For agriculture, there are special arrangements for legislation, for the organisation of administration and courts as well as for case law. Accordingly, quite complex agricultural law has arisen at the state and sub-state levels as well as the level of the European Union.[84] In addition, there is the international level, which includes agriculture in the world trade system.[85] These special arrangements are not, however, combined into a single regulatory or systematic unit. In addition to numerous special laws for agriculture, specific regulations permeate the generally applicable laws. At the same time, there are special institutional regulations for agriculture, such as special authorities, self-governing bodies (such as the Chambers of Agriculture), funds from the European Union, special procedural rules for the decision-making processes as determined by Art. 43 of the Treaty on the Functioning of the European Union (*TFEU*), etc.[86]

Agricultural law is not static but, rather, is in a process of constant development and change; this is influenced by two opposing trends. First, certain aspects of

---

[81]This also includes standards that do not constitute a special right, but that generally are valid in their wording, even if, for objective reasons, they are applied almost exclusively in the field of agriculture and forestry. See Norer (2012).

[82]See Norer (2012), p. 7 et seq.; Norer (2018), p. 116; Holzer (1982), p. 306. See also Winkler (2018a), p. 215 et seq.

[83]E.g., tax law, inheritance law. See, e.g., Germanò (2016), p. 177 et seq.; Bäck (2012); Grimm and Norer (2015), p. 4 et seq. On these issues, see also Miribung (2019) and Ferrucci (2011).

[84]See Norer (2005), p. 284 et seq.; Albisinni (2011b), p. 279 et seq.; Albisinni (2011a); Albisinni (2010). See also Rook Basile (1995), p. 75 et seq.

[85]See Holzer (2018), p. 87 et seq.; Norer (2005), p. 276 et seq. In general, Iannarelli (2001), Costato and Russo (2015), p. 105 et seq.

[86]It may come as a surprise that it was not until the twentieth century that the science of law actually recognised agricultural law as a special area of the legal order, and efforts were made to establish and penetrate it scientifically. It is to Giangastone Bolla's credit that he founded agricultural law as a special branch of jurisprudence, and many countries have embraced and built on his work. See Germanò (2017), p. 7 et seq.; Capizzano (1991), p. 25 et seq. Even in former socialist countries, the agricultural law was recognised as a special branch of law. The complexity of agricultural law is not only limited to certain countries—such as Italy, Austria, Germany and the European Union—but also applies to other countries, including Western industrialised countries and Third World countries. It predates its modern application by hundreds of years; during earlier epochs of history, there were special regulations for agriculture (e.g., the leges agrariae in Rome). See Norer (2005), pp. 24 and 212, see also Capizzano (1991), p. 25 et seq.

agricultural law converge and approximate with the law of commercial entrepreneurs,[87] such that agriculture could lose its special legal status and be subject to a legal status common to all businesses. This would cause agriculture to become integrated into society as a whole and, at the same time, would create new forms of production and new ways to organise agricultural holdings. Consequently, the differences between agriculture and the wider economy would become blurry.[88] Under these circumstances, land will no longer be the main factor of production but merely the location of production. Second, agricultural law could not only establish itself as a special law for agriculture, but could even be extended to new regulatory material. In this context, reference should be made to various provisions of agri-economic law and to special provisions of agri-environmental law.[89] All these topics are strongly influenced by European law, which, as a legal system, must be distinguished from national systems, each of which holds different systematisations and conceptualisations about what agriculture is. Various aspects governed by agricultural law are, therefore, not only determined by national rules but also, to a strong extent, by European law. Hence, it seems appropriate to refer to this interplay of rules as a polycentric system.[90]

1.2.3 About Cooperative Law

Similar observations can be made concerning cooperative law, which is the second aspect[91] of this research. National legal sources have never developed independently of other legal systems: As a matter of fact, the *GenG* (adopted in 1873), was initially strongly influenced by the German Cooperative Act from 1867,[92] but it has been amended several times since.[93] Similarly, the Italian Civil Code, which was adopted in 1942 and contains specific norms regarding cooperatives, was also influenced by

[87] Imprenditore commerciale or Gewerbetreibender.

[88] See also Carrozza (2001c), p. 659 et seq.; Costato (2001), p. 142 et seq. Regarding latest developments, see Bolognini (2019), Goldoni (2019) and Iannarelli (2019). Critically, Alessi (2019).

[89] See Norer (2012), p. 18 et seq.; Holzer (2018), p. 87 et seq.; Norer (2005), p. 250 et seq.; Norer (2009), p. 242 et seq.; Magno (2006); Iannarelli (2002a); Adornato (2007); Costato (2004), p. 119 et seq.; Adornato (2004); Costato (2008b); Salaris (2002), p. 72. See also Albisinni (2013), p. 9 et seq.; Di Lauro (2007), p. 584.

[90] See Albisinni (2011b), p. 275 et seq.; Holzer (2018), p. 87 et seq.; Iannarelli (2007). See also Albisinni (2014), pp. 968 et seq. and 971 et seq.; Albisinni (2010), pp. 225 and 234; Vecchione (2004), p. 139 et seq.; Rook Basile (1995), p. 73 et seq.; Alessi (2006), p. 1244 et seq.; Adornato (2004); Costato (2008a), p. 458 et seq.

[91] The first aspect concerns agricultural law.

[92] See Kastner (1986), p. 121. See also Brendel (2011), p. 23 et seq.; Miribung and Reiner (2013), p. 232; Schaschko (2010), p. 41 et seq.

[93] See Tomanek (2014); Miribung and Reiner (2013), p. 231 et seq.

German doctrine.[94] However, the traditions of the cooperative schools of thought, which influence the various rules, differ in part. On the one hand, we have traditions strongly based upon the ideas of *Friedrich Wilhelm Raiffeisen* and *Hermann Schultze-Delitzsch*; on the other hand, there are traditions anchored in the social democratic and labour movement. These different approaches are important for this study because the SCE-R is a compromise based on different traditions.[95] Section 2.1 shortly explains the various developments.

Researching the legal sources of cooperative law is a complex process, but also interesting and challenging. The laws covered in the Italian Civil Code provide a good example here. The specific provisions for cooperatives are complemented by laws drafted for private (*srl*) and public limited-liability companies (*spa*).[96] Conversely, the Austrian legal system provides with the *GenG* a specific and coherent act. Additional laws are only applied if the *GenG* contains a gap that must be closed.[97] Moreover, the development of Austrian law is, to some extent, connected to the development of German law. Therefore, it is helpful to consider German doctrine.

1.2.4 Comparative Law: Limits of This Method

This research shows that the various national solutions regulating cooperatives often can function as examples for statutory provisions of SCEs. In addition, the provisions that national cooperatives (that is, Austrian and Italian cooperatives as opposed to Austrian and Italian SCEs) apply, can be used to identify the specific limits of a given law. In fact, comparing national cooperative law with EU law helps us to better grasp the legal framework that is applicable to an SCE. National law provisions and the issues they deal with are used to consider these very issues in context with the SCE-R. We can thus deepen our understanding of the applicable law.

A solution applied by the SCE-R might be better or worse than the national solution, thus making an SCE more or less attractive compared with a national cooperative. Of course, 'better' and 'worse' are vague terms. In this context, they refer to different levels of flexibility given to those drafting the statute of an SCE or cooperative. In other words, they refer to the degree of statutory freedom when it is

[94]See Cian (1998), p. 218. Also consider Grande (2019), p. 88; Gallo (2001), pp. 196 and 202 et seq.

[95]See Schulze (2004), p. 10 et seq. In general, Münkner (2006), p. 10 et seq.; Engelhardt (1990), p. 10. Also consider Sects. 2.2 and 3.2.

[96]See in this context Art. 2519 CC.

[97]Compare for example Sect. 4.4.3.

used as a tool for enhancing efficiency.[98] This does not imply that increased flexibility is always better, given that certain rules must be used to determine what a cooperative is. At least from a legal perspective, there is no standard definition of what a cooperative is; however, the various legal systems contain similar features, which can be used to derive a standard cooperative identity useful for legal research.[99]

Terminological confusion is typical for comparative law techniques, as specific terms do not always have to have the same definition. This is true for terms in a single national legal system. Terminological issues become more pronounced when one compares different legal systems and are clearer when one better understands the results by applying different scientific disciplines to the research.[100] Yet, different scholars use different terms to translate or explain specific terms; I exclusively use the terms from the SCE-R to translate specific terms from the Italian and Austrian legal systems. Thus, the terminology used by this study deviates to a certain extent from the terminology contained in the English versions of the *GenG* and the Italian Civil Code. For example, while translators use the term 'management board', the SCE-R uses the term 'management organ' instead.[101]

One terminological problem is explicitly solved by the SCE-R. According to Art. 5 SCE-R, the term "statutes of an SCE' shall mean both the instrument of incorporation and, when they are the subject of a separate document, the statutes of the SCE'. Therefore, for the sake of simplicity, the term 'statutes' is used to translate the term 'articles of association', even though both national legal systems differ in the use of these terms.[102]

Another problem is the proper translation of the terms '*Aktiengesellschaft*' (*AG*) or '*società per azioni*' (*spa*) and '*Gesellschaft mit beschränkter Haftung*' (*GmbH*) or '*società a responsabilità limitata*' (*srl*). Again, different scholars use different terms.[103] In addition to the German and Italian acronyms, this study uses the terms 'public limited-liability company' (or simply 'company') and 'private limited-liability company'. The term corporation serves as a generic term.

An additional problem is that the SCE-R allows national legislatures to adopt specific national provisions in order to implement, complement or amend specific provisions of the SCE-R. In the various linguistic versions of the SCE-R, terms are

---

[98]See Faust (2019), p. 834 et seq.; Gelter and Grechenig (2007), p. 40 et seq. Also consider Zweigert and Kötz (1996), p. 46; Krimphove (1998), p. 189. See also Bellantuono (2000, 2016), Marchetti (2000, 2014) and Pardolesi (2015).

[99]See Sect. 3.2.

[100]See Guarneri (2003), pp. 12 et seq. and 119 et seq.; Gallo (2001), p. 46 et seq.; Sacco (1994), p. 27 et seq. On this issue, see Ajani et al. (2007), Pozzo and Timoteo (2008) and Ferreri (2010).

[101]See Art. 36 SCE-R, Sec. 15 of the Austrian Co-operative Act (unofficial translation) and Piacentini (2014), Art. 2409 octies.

[102]See Art. 2521 CC and Sec. 5a GenG.

[103]See Fruehmann and Nagy (2005), which refers to a "stock corporation", and the translation of Art. 2325 of the Italian Civil Code, where the term "company limited by shares" is used. See Piacentini (2014).

sometimes used in ways that do not fully correspond to their use in other languages. An excellent example is Art. 37 para. 1 sent. 2 SCE-R, which refers to a 'managing director'. The German version of the SCE-R uses the term *Geschäftsführer*, while the Italian version refers to an *amministratore delegato*; these terms are different.[104] However, evaluating which is the better or proper term is beyond the scope of this study. Instead, terminology is taken for granted as we focus on the practical consequences that arise from designing Austrian and Italian SCEs. I assume that individuals who consider forming an SCE will first refer to the SCE-R and then consult their own national legal systems for supplementary information. We also suppose that these individuals will not consider any other legal framework.

Similar problems arose with the English translations of provisions and concepts from national agricultural law. A prominent example is the rather general term 'farmer', for which Italian law has two terms: agricultural entrepreneur (*imprenditore agricolo*), according to Art. 2135 CC, and direct farmer or direct cultivator/grower (*coltivatore diretto*), according to Art. 2083 CC. Both terms are linked to entrepreneurial activity. These Italian notions for 'farmer' can be juxtaposed with the concept established by the Austrian legal system, in which the farmer (*Landwirt*) is linked to the *Grundverkehrsgesetze* of the Austrian *Länder*, i.e., the various federal laws dealing generally with the use of agricultural land.[105] Contrary to the Italian concept, the Austrian notion of *Landwirt* does not directly refer to the entrepreneurial aspect of agricultural activity. Interestingly, the various concepts of farmer refer to an agricultural activity carried out primarily by the farmer himself (or members of his family). The concepts strongly resemble the concept of direct farmer as defined by Art. 2083 CC, but as one sees they have a different function or scope. Thus, while there is an official English version of the SCE-R, the corresponding English concepts do not apply to the specific national norms analysed here.

As national concepts may differ slightly in content and context, it does not seem appropriate to use standardised terms for the different national and supranational provisions of agricultural law analysed here. This conclusion is supported by EU law, which defines a farmer both as a *Betriebsinhaber* and an *agricoltore*, while national legislation, as mentioned above, refers to a *Landwirt* and an *imprenditore agricolo* or *coltivatore diretto*. These differences between national terms occur, because different legal systems use different approaches to define agriculture and agricultural activities.

---

[104]See Sect. 4.2.1.1.

[105]On this issue, see Sect. 3.3.2, fn 112 and 144.

1.3 How Can Law Be Considered from an Economic Perspective?

1.3.1 'Economic Analysis of Law' in a Nutshell

Comparing legal rules to each other also requires evaluating them. I do this by considering the PECOL, which describe how a cooperative should function and thus identifies what a cooperative might be. To evaluate the differences that result from the comparison of laws, I also apply efficiency criteria from economic theory and, in particular, specific insights from agricultural economics. The method, which combines economic thinking with the application of legal rules, is called the 'economic analysis of law'.[106] It considers the economic consequences of specific legal rules and regulations and primarily attempts to determine legal solutions that increase welfare or, at least, limit welfare reduction.[107] Those who blend economic and legal analyses tend to promote private contracting. One generally convincing argument for this kind of analysis is its universal approach.[108] Yet, this focus on economic welfare does not mean that considerations like fairness are unimportant. Market participants also consider such ideas and include them in their actions. It is stressed that concepts of fairness usually differ considerably. The same is true for individual motivations to act.[109]

The economic analysis of law thus focuses primarily on the consequences on (economic) welfare. From an economic perspective, legal systems should try, as far as possible, to limit the costs of conflicts that arise between actors in business.[110] In general, private autonomous arrangements (contracts) should be fostered, as they tend to result in an optimal allocation of resources, thus maximising welfare. However, to achieve this optimal allocation of resources, specific behaviours are required, based on the controversial—but nevertheless still central—concept of *homo oeconomicus*, which assumes that participants behave rationally in order to maximise their utility.[111] Thus, it is essential to understand whose utility is perceived

[106]Thus, this study adopts an interdisciplinary approach. See Sect. 1.1.

[107]See Fleischer and Zimmer (2008), p. 9 et seq.; Schäfer and Ott (2012c), p. XXXIII et seq.; Armour et al. (2009c), p. 28 et seq.; Eidenmüller (2005), p. 41 et seq.; Bolten et al. (2007), p. 834 et seq.; Miceli (2004), p. 1 et seq.; Polinsky and Shavell (2007), p. xi; Gallo (1998b), p. 27. Also consider Towfigh (2012), Posner (1996), Posner and Becker (2014) and Mattei and Monti (2001). Generally, Broeusseau (2008) and Fiorentini (1994b). See also Mathis (2019), p. 75 et seq.

[108]See Eidenmüller (2014a), p. 14. Also consider Armour et al. (2009c), p. 14 et seq.; Miceli (2004), p. 3; Craswell et al. (2007), p. 14 et seq.; Armour and Whincop (2001), p. 988. Generally, Leyens (2007), p. 1063 et seq.

[109]See Eidenmüller (2014a), p. 14; Fehr et al. (2007); Fehr and Schmidt (1999); Giudici (2008), p. 4 et seq.

[110]See Eidenmüller (2014a), p. 15; Armour et al. (2009a), p. 35. Also consider Miceli (2004), p. 3; Gallo (1998b), p. 33 et seq.; Giudici (2008), p. 6 et seq.

[111]See Towfigh (2012), p. 27 et seq.; Schäfer and Ott (2012b); Blome-Drees et al. (1998), p. 58; Eidenmüller (2005), p. 28 et seq. This assumption may be arguable because research shows that

because in principle, the utility of a consumer is not the same as the utility that a farmer pursues. The economic aspect of the legislation on agricultural cooperatives will be examined thoroughly in Sect. 3.5.[112]

The economic analysis of law is thus based on the assumption that, in principle, negotiation processes between parties doing business tend to result in economically efficient solutions. Therefore, legal rules must be phrased as options (default provisions).[113] In fact, to allow people to increase their welfare, participants must be allowed to choose (that is to stipulate by contract) the specific regulations that best fit their needs. Accordingly, they should be allowed to deviate from the legal solution proposed by the law. This implies that mandatory cooperative laws (and in general mandatory corporate laws) should be an exception that require specific justification and not the general rule. In other words, the legal framework should support the process of negotiation to allow participants to reduce costs.[114]

One contractual instrument used in agricultural cooperatives is, among others, statutes. These determine the basic terms that shareholders (cooperative members) must observe, but they are also relevant to the relationship with employees and creditors. Moreover, there is a large body of laws that influence the dynamics of these relationships.[115] Some mandatory provisions apply automatically when a specific legal form is used. In other words, there are provisions that are not negotiable. Thus, specific rules are linked to a legal form but are mandatory only within this legal framework. These mandatory provisions are optional only at the meta-level, in which the actors decide to use one specific type of corporation over another.[116]

participants often behave irrationally. Experimental economists and psychologists have proven in recent decades that real people do not always conform to the neoclassical model of homo economicus, which is believed to be fully informed, utility-maximising and rational. In reality, people are exposed to distortions and decision-making errors, especially because it is ultimately impossible to capture and process all relevant information accurately. Furthermore, too much over-optimism often exists, leading to people viewing the probability of others' opportunistic behaviour to be unlikely. Different factors contribute to such bounded rationality, especially availability and representativeness heuristics, or hyperbolic discounting. See, among many, Eidenmüller (2014a), p. 16; Kahneman (1994); monographically Kahneman (2012); Fleischer et al. (2011), p. 12 et seq. Also consider Altmann et al. (2011), p. 63 et seq. See also Schaschko (2010), p. 163 et seq.; Mathis (2019), pp. 28 et seq. and 42 et seq. Nevertheless, there are clear arguments for using this general concept of homo oeconomicus. First, businesspeople generally act rationally because they know what they are doing. Second, it is argued that such an assumption encourages rationality in the long term. See Eidenmüller (2014a), p. 16.

[112]But also Sects. 4.2.3, 4.3.6, 4.4.6 and 5.6.

[113]Rather than mandatory rules.

[114]See Easterbrook and Fischel (1998), p. 15 et seq.; Eidenmüller (2014a), p. 16; Armour et al. (2009c), p. 20; Eidenmüller (2005), p. 63.

[115]See Armour et al. (2009c), p. 19 et seq.; Eidenmüller (2014a), p. 18 et seq. Also consider Schäfer and Ott (2012a), p. 704 et seq.; Giudici (2008), p. 88 et seq.

[116]See Eidenmüller (2014a), p. 18; Armour et al. (2009c), p. 22. Also consider Ribstein (1995), p. 369; Kalss and Schauer (2006), p. 39 et seq. For general information Trebilcock (1997).

Below, I will investigate what is necessary to define the legal form as 'cooperative', including the mandatory provisions that contribute to this definition.[117]

To the contrary, default provisions simplify the process of making a contract, as the actors only have to specify which elements do not follow standard terms.[118] Default provisions should consider those terms that the majority of participants would choose. I borrow from *homo oeconomicus* the assertion that these participants act on a well-informed basis.[119]

A further distinction can be drawn here between default and enabling provisions. Default provisions apply unless participants opt out, while enabling provisions require participants to opt in. I hold that default provisions are presumptive in nature while enabling provisions are permissive.[120] It is worth asking what the advantage of such a distinction might be, as such options often cannot be applied because of high transaction costs,[121] which occur during any economic trade in a market. As these costs are too high, the original regulation is applied even though it might not maximise welfare; moreover, people are often unwilling to exercise their options, as people generally place a higher value on goods that they possess (the endowment effect).[122]

The central question is, when are mandatory provisions justified? Mandatory provisions are often adopted because of some form of contracting failure, i.e., some parties might be exploited by others who are better informed, leading to an inefficient or unfair outcome. In addition, mandatory rules seem to be the best solution to so-called collective action problems (e.g., the prisoners' dilemma).[123] In any case, mandatory provisions are necessary for determining a menu of different standard corporate forms that the actors can choose from when organising their business.[124] In this study, I consider cooperatives as a specific form of enterprise offered by the

---

[117]See Sect. 3.2.

[118]See Armour et al. (2009c), p. 23; Eidenmüller (2014a), p. 18 et seq. Also consider Hansmann (2006); Fleischer (2004), p. 692; Schwartz (1997), p. 105; Cooter et al. (1999), p. 225 et seq.

[119]Alternatively, the law could also provide a 'menu' of different provisions. See Armour et al. (2009c), p. 20 et seq.; Easterbrook and Fischel (1998), p. 34 et seq.; Klausner (1995), p. 839 et seq. Also consider Kalss and Schauer (2006), p. 35 et seq.

[120]See Cheffins (2006), p. 218 et seq.; Bachmann (2008), p. 14 et seq.; Eidenmüller (2005), p. 125 et seq.

[121]See Scarpa (1994). See also Sect. 1.3.2.

[122]See Cheffins (2006), p. 253 et seq.; Eidenmüller (2014a), p. 19; Englerth (2012), p. 188 et seq. Also consider Thaler (1980), Marcin and Nicklisch (2017) and Arlen et al. (2002). Generally, Altmann et al. (2011); Giudici (2008), p. 14 et seq. In this context it has been observed that supervisory organs are more likely to be established if the law contains a default provision but not if the law provides an enabling one. See Eidenmüller (2014a), p. 19.

[123]See Armour et al. (2009c), p. 22; Eidenmüller (2014a), p. 20; Bachmann (2008), p. 12; Schäfer and Ott (2012a), p. 702. Also consider Hardin (1971, 2013); Trebilcock (1997); Armour and Whincop (2001), p. 988 et seq.; Denozza (2002), p. 102 et seq. Clearly, the regulatory environment also shapes the creation of provisions. See Eidenmüller (2014a), p. 21.

[124]These actors can also choose among different jurisdictions. In this context, the general issue of regulatory competition in corporation law is discussed. See Armour et al. (2009c), p. 25 et seq.;

legislature for exercising business activities. For (agricultural) cooperatives, Sects. 3.2 and 3.3 will discuss the content of the legal norms relevant to defining an agricultural cooperative. These analyses include some remarks on producer organisations (PO).

1.3.2 On the Nexus of Contracts and Costs

According to economic theory, private negotiations should lead to efficient solutions. Yet, one can argue that such negotiations will often be impossible to conclude because of very high transaction costs. These are the costs that actors incur when they make economic exchanges (i.e., the cost of participating in a market) and include determining whether a desired good is available, which is the lowest price, and so on (search and information costs). Costs are also incurred when trying to draw up an acceptable agreement (bargaining costs).[125] From an economic perspective, cooperative laws (as in general corporate laws) should determine the parties' implicit will. One can use the theory of *homo oeconomicus* to determine what the parties will do, at least in order to increase their personal welfare. If private agreements cannot be concluded because of high transaction costs, the legal rules used to structure negotiations could facilitate business and thus help increase welfare.[126] This economic thinking allows different legal solutions to be compared. The one which costs least is the most efficient and should be chosen.[127]

Corporations, e.g., cooperatives, comprise an assortment of contracts, such as contracts with shareholders, employees, banks or business partners. In rough terms, these contracts determine a decision making process in the form of a hierarchy, with the aim of allocating resources.[128] This is known as a 'nexus of contracts' or 'nexus for contracts'.[129] One can bundle the various contracts into three types of conflicts that generally arise from the negotiation process in public limited-liability

---

Kirchner et al. (2005). Also consider Kahan and Kamar (2002); Hofinger and Johler (2002); Schäfer and Ott (2012a), p. 723 et seq.; Kalss and Schauer (2006), p. 41 et seq.; Hopt (2016).

[125] See Eidenmüller (2014a), p. 17 et seq.; Armour et al. (2009c), p. 22. Also consider Easterbrook and Fischel (1998), p. 15 et seq.; Eidenmüller (2005), p. 65 et seq.; Gordon (1989); Cooter et al. (1999), p. 234 et seq. In general Trebilcock (1997), Mathis (2019), p. 75 et seq.; Krimphove (2006), p. 10 et seq.

[126] See Eidenmüller (2014a), p. 17 et seq.; Easterbrook and Fischel (1998), p. 15; Eidenmüller (2005), p. 65 et seq.

[127] See Faust (2019), p. 827 et seq. For general information Mattei (1997) and Mattei and Monti (2001).

[128] See Schäfer and Ott (2012a), p. 697. In general, Polo (1994) and Ecchia (1994b).

[129] See Armour et al. (2009c), p. 6; Jensen and Meckling (1976); Fama and Jensen (1983), p. 302; Easterbrook and Fischel (1985), p. 87 et seq.; Alchian and Demsetz (1972), p. 777 et seq. Also consider Adams (1991), p. 14 et seq.

companies.[130] Even though agricultural cooperatives differ from public limited-liability companies, similar relationships also arise in a cooperative.[131] Therefore, my starting point is a **general model** of a modern corporation or public limited-liability company.

A comparative-functional analysis[132] yields five features of a corporation: (1) legal personality, (2) limited liability, (3) transferability of shares, (4) delegation of management and (5) shared ownership by contributors of capital. This last feature implies that the right to control the firm and the right to receive the firm's net asset earnings lie with the capital provider.[133] Apart from the feature of the legal personality, which can only be granted by law, the other four features—limited liability, transferability of shares, delegation of management and ownership of capital providers – can simply be determined by contract.[134]

The general function of corporate law is to determine the structure of corporate forms and the rules that support this structure (ancillary housekeeping rules).[135] Corporate law should help control various conflicts of interest among corporate constituencies. These conflicts can be described by the economic terms 'agency problems' or 'principal-agent problems'.[136] Stiglitz has observed that 'the principal-agent literature is concerned with how one individual, the principal (say an employer), can design a compensation system (contract) which motivates another individual, his agent (say the employee), to act in the principal's interest.'[137] This concept assigns divergent bargaining powers to principals and agents. The principal sets the terms of the contract, which the agent can then accept or reject; yet, the latter cannot make a counterproposal. Now, if all parties are perfectly informed, then the principal-agent problem does not arise. In fact, in such a situation the principal pays

[130]See Armour et al. (2009a), p. 35 et seq.

[131]See Nilsson (2001), p. 331 et seq.; Royer (1999), p. 49 et seq.; Molk (2014), p. 903; Chaddad and Iliopoulos (2013), p. 3 et seq.; Iliopoulos (2014), p. 159 et seq. Also see Armour et al. (2009c), p. 2; Eidenmüller (2014a), p. 8 et seq.; Fama and Jensen (1983), p. 323. See also Sect. 1.3.3.

[132]See Armour et al. (2009c), p. 5 et seq.; Eidenmüller (2014a), p. 5.

[133]See Armour et al. (2009c), p. 5 et seq.; Eidenmüller (2014a), p. 5; Schäfer and Ott (2012a), p. 699; Grossman and Hart (1986); Chaddad and Iliopoulos (2013), p. 5.

[134]See Armour et al. (2009c), p. 19.

[135]It is argued that the primary goal of corporate law is to serve the interests of society as a whole and, more specifically, to aggregate the welfare of those affected by the activity of a specific firm (shareholders, suppliers, employees, customers, etc.). It is argued that maximising shareholder returns ultimately fosters the broader goal of advancing overall social welfare. In fact, as the success of the company also depends on the success of the various stakeholders involved, one can argue that maximising the earnings of the residual claimants and risk bearers (the shareholders), spurs them to ensure that the transactions conducted by the corporation are beneficial to all those involved. See Armour et al. (2009c), p. 28. For other opinions, see fn 111.

[136]See Armour et al. (2009c); Armour et al. (2009a), p. 35. The term "principal-agent problem" was coined by Ross. See Ross (1973). Also consider Eisenhardt (1989); Fama and Jensen (1983), p. 304 et seq.; Blome-Drees et al. (1998), p. 67 et seq. Generally, Cheffins (2012), p. 490 et seq.; Denozza (2002), p. 89 et seq.

[137]See Stiglitz (1989), p. 241.

for precisely what the agent does, and this corresponds precisely to what the principal wants.[138] Thus, a principal-agent relationship exists when an individual—the agent—can make decisions that not only concern his own welfare, but also influence the welfare of another person, the principal. Typical examples of relationships include purchaser and seller, patient and doctor as well as borrower and creditor/lender.[139]

If every participant in such a relationship had complete and free information, there would not be any principal-agent problems. However, in practice, information is not complete. Neither knowledge nor skills are evenly distributed or arbitrarily acquired. As a result, so-called 'information asymmetries'[140] exist, which the agent may use for his own benefit to the detriment of the principal. Deviations from the ideal state of information distribution lead to 'agency costs'.[141]

---

[138] See Steinberg (2010), p. 75 et seq.; Nicklisch and Petersen (2012), p. 121 et seq.; Bolten et al. (2007), p. 842 et seq.; Easterbrook and Fischel (1998), p. 8 et seq. In this context also consider Akerlof (1970).

[139] Whether a person is the agent or principal depends on the situation. In addition, the same person may be a principal in one case and an agent in another.

[140] See Ecchia (1994a).

[141] Three types of cost can be identified. See Picot and Dietl (1993), p. 319 et seq.; Nilsson (2001), p. 334. Also consider Jensen and Meckling (1976); Jensen and Meckling (1979); Barney (1990), p. 209 et seq. The first category is called monitoring expenditures. Here, the principal monitors the behaviour of the agent, which requires resources. The parties (i.e., the principal and the agent) sign a contract, the terms of which the principal controls and enforces. As a second category of costs, bonding expenditures can be addressed; they occur when the agent must reassure the principal that he or she is acting as required. The agent must use resources to provide this guarantee. The last type of cost is called residual losses, which assumes that the agent can, to a certain extent, make independent decisions. As a result, there is a risk that he or she will behave in a way that does not suit the interests of the principal. Even though the principal has the right to any surplus created by the business (residual rights), the agent can manage the business so that this surplus is smaller, thus usurping some of it. As the principal cannot perfectly control the agent, he or she has to accept that the agent may act deceitfully to a certain extent, thus causing him welfare losses. There are trade-offs between these three components. For instance, residual losses may be restricted via higher monitoring and control expenditures, which the agent can reduce with guarantee promises. See Picot and Dietl (1993), p. 320. In this context also consider Aviram (2006), p. 4 et seq. To summarise, the principal-agent problem arises from information asymmetries. Economic theory distinguishes between three types of asymmetric information distribution: hidden characteristics, hidden action and hidden intention. All three have specific and different information advantages for the agent as well as specific coordination problems. They also provide different design possibilities. See Picot and Dietl (1993), p. 320; Nicklisch and Petersen (2012), p. 121 et seq.; Staroßom (2013), p. 100 et seq. Also consider Kräkel (2012), p. 19 et seq. The first type, namely, hidden characteristics, refers to a situation in which the principal does not know the unchangeable or changeable (or at least not changeable for free) characteristics of the agent or the service he/she provides. These characteristics are not known before the contract is stipulated (ex ante), giving the agent an opportunity to deceive the principal. The principal only discovers the true characteristics after the contract has been stipulated. This is the risk of 'adverse selection', which occurs when the wrong partner is chosen. See Picot and Dietl (1993), p. 321. Also consider Akerlof (1970); Stiglitz (1975), p. 292 et seq.; Delbono (1994a); Spence (1981), p. 14 et seq.; Arrow (1973), p. 193 et seq.; Nicklisch and Petersen (2012), p. 128 et seq.; Steinberg (2010), p. 76 et seq. Hidden action, the

As seen, economic theory helps us understand how persons might react to legal norms. It provides theories that describe why some legal solutions are better than others.[142] It is possible to use these concepts to describe contractual relationships and analyse the various legal solutions in terms of efficiency. In fact, specific contractual relationships can be connected to three generic agency problems that firms usually face: (1) the conflict between the owners (shareholders) and managers, (2) the conflict between the majority and minority shareholders and (3) the conflict between the firm itself and other parties, for instance, creditors, employees and customers.[143]

The first conflict arises from the separation of ownership and control.[144] The terms 'owner' or 'ownership'—as defined by the so-called 'new institutional economics' (NIE) and used for economic analysis of the law—are not the same as the terms '*Eigentum*' or '*proprietà*' from the Austrian and Italian legal systems, respectively.[145] The below outlined definition of ownership is based on property rights theory, which, together with principal-agent theory and transactions cost theory,

second type, are information problems that arise after contract stipulation, because the principal cannot evaluate the behaviour of the agent (because of lack of knowledge) or cannot monitor the behaviour of the agent (for practical reasons). In this situation, the principal only knows the result and cannot evaluate to what extent this result is based on the behaviour of the agent or exogenous determinants. If the agent exploits this situation, he or she creates what is called a 'moral hazard'. See Picot and Dietl (1993), p. 322. Also consider Picot (1989), p. 370 et seq.; Delbono (1994b); Eisenhardt (1989), p. 60 et seq.; Grubel (1971); Nicklisch and Petersen (2012), p. 128; Steinberg (2010), p. 76. Lastly, hidden intention describes a situation in which the principal ex ante does not know how the agent is going to behave in the relationship. Unlike hidden action scenarios, the principal will detect the behaviour of the agent. As a result, hidden intention is only a problem in situations where the principal, because of irreversible investments, is in a dependent relationship with the agent. If the agent exploits the relationship, a 'hold up' occurs. See Picot and Dietl (1993), p. 323. Also consider Alchian and Woodward (1987), p. 113 et seq.

[142]The theory of rational choice provides a basis for analysing structures inherent to the principal-agent problem. See van Aaken (2001), p. 149.

[143]See Armour et al. (2009a), p. 35 et seq. Also consider Eidenmüller (2014a), p. 8 et seq.

[144]See Armour et al. (2009a), p. 36; Eidenmüller (2014a), p. 8.

[145]In fact, according to NIE, ownership is much more extensive and refers to all types of rights and duties a person may have in respect of a material or immaterial good. It may also refer to votings rights or political rights. See Bellantuono and Iamiceli (2005), p. 15; Picot and Dietl (1993), p. 308; Tietzel (1981), p. 209. Also consider Blome-Drees et al. (1998), p. 59; Milgrom and Roberts (2005), p. 429 et seq.; Richter (2015b), Mathis (2019), p. 76; Rose-Ackerman (1997). This implies, in the context of a business organisation, that a person may control the organisation and has the right to obtain residual earnings, i.e., the remaining earnings after deduction of all contractual obligations. See Armour et al. (2009c), p. 14; Hansmann (1996), p. 12 et seq.; Chaddad and Iliopoulos (2013), p. 5; Grossman and Hart (1986); Fama and Jensen (1983), p. 302 et seq.; Cheffins (2012), p. 492 et seq.; Armour and Whincop (2001), p. 990. Generally, Miceli (2004), p. 162 et seq. Critically, Stout (2007), p. 804 et seq. Schäfer and Ott also refer in this context to the right to sell the organisation (in full or in part by selling shares. See Schäfer and Ott (2012a), p. 699. "Economists define residual calims as the rights ot the net income generated by the firm, ie, the amount left over after all promised payments to fixed claims holders, including employees, suppliers and debtors. Therefore, residual claimants are considered the residual risk bearers of the firm because net cash flow are uncertain and eventually negative." See Chaddad and Iliopoulos (2013), p. 5.

comprises NIE.[146] A property right includes the authority assigned to a person to choose the final use of a good from among various alternative uses.[147] It protects an individual's ownership of an asset from the attempts of other persons to control the same asset.[148] To be more precise, property rights are assigned to solve problems that can arise from 'incomplete' contracts. The contracts have to be renegotiated in some cases (bargaining).[149] In fact, parties cannot write state-contingent long-term contracts, because they cannot foresee all possible future states. Attempting to determine all possible future states would incur prohibitively high costs. However, this dilemma can be solved by writing contracts *ex ante* that determine adequate

[146]See Picot and Dietl (1993), p. 306 et seq. For general information on NIE consider for example Williamson (1998), Richter et al. (2003), Göbel (2002) and Richter (2015a). Also consider Blome-Drees et al. (1998), p. 57 et seq. The starting point for all these theories is the observations of Ronald Coase, who in 1937 described a company as "a multiplicity of contractual relationships". See Coase (1937). Also consider Kräkel (2012), p. 8 et seq.; Gallo (1998b), p. 36 et seq.; Adams (1991), p. 16 et seq. For details Parisi (1999). Before then, a company was thought of as a black box where resources are used to obtain goods and services. See Hill and McDonnell (2012), p. 2; Cheffins (2012), p. 489 et seq. Generally, Armour and Whincop (2001), p. 987 et seq.; Krimphove (2006), p. 11 et seq.; Garrouste and Saussier (2008).

[147]The term "property right" refers to the fact that the value of a (limited) good depends not only on its physical features but also on the rights and duties linked to it. For example, the value of land depends not just on its location or the composition of the soil, but also how it can be used. Compared to "proprietà" or "Eigentumsrecht", the term "property right" is much more comprehensive inasmuch as it refers to all rights and duties to act linked to a material or immaterial good. In other words, the term "property right" includes all possible duties and rights to act and thus ultimately the complete system of legal and organisational rules (see Picot and Dietl 1993, p. 308) and social norms. See Schmidtchen (1998). Also consider Adams (1991), p. 16 et seq.; Cooter et al. (1999), pp. 83 et seq. and 92 et seq.; Krimphove (2006), p. 29 et seq.; Gallo (1998a), p. 469 et seq. Alchanian stresses that "the rights of individuals to the use of resources (i.e., property rights) in any society are to be construed as supported by the force of etiquette, social custom, ostracism, and formal legally enacted laws, supported by the states' power of violence and punishment. Many of the constraints on the use of what we call private property involve the force of etiquette and social ostracism. The level of noise, the kind of clothes we wear, our intrusion on other people's privacy are restricted not merely by laws backed by police force, but by social acceptance, reciprocity, and voluntary social ostracism for violators of accepted codes of conduct." Alchian (1977), p. 129 et seq. It has also been observed that "property rights are understood as the sanctioned behavioural relations among men that arise from the existence of goods and pertain to their use. These relations specify the norms of behaviour with respect to goods that each and every person must observe in his daily interactions with other persons, or bear the cost of non-observance." See Furubotn and Pejovich (1974), p. 3.

[148]See Alchian (1977); Picot and Dietl (1993), p. 307 et seq.; Furubotn and Pejovich (1974). Also consider Kräkel (2012), p. 44 et seq. Generally, Demsetz (2004); Müller and Tietzel (1999) and Fiorentini (1994a).

[149]"Incomplete contracts, caused mainly by bounded rationality (i.e., limits on the capacity of individuals to process information, deal with complex issues and consider all possible contingencies), difficulties in specifying or measuring performance, and asymmetric information (i.e., when the parties do not have equal access to all information relevant to the contract)" result in transaction costs." See Ortmann and King (2007), p. 53.

governance and control structures.[150] Therefore, because contracts are necessarily incomplete and transactions costs are not nil, property is a key instrument for making and controlling decisions. As a result, assets will be reallocated to those persons who are able to use them to accrue the highest value. If contracts were complete, it would not matter who owned an asset. In fact, it would be possible to use contractual provisions to determine what actions could be carried out and what compensation each party would receive.[151]

Ownership as defined by NIE includes the right to obtain the residual earnings an asset generates. In theory, the owner of a given good is the one who has the incentive to use it effectively. If a person does not have clear property rights, he or she will not have the proper incentive to protect the value of the assets. If they cannot be transferred, the likelihood that the assets are ultimately owned by the persons who will use them most effectively and efficiently will be reduced.[152] Therefore, ownership should be given to those persons who can realise the highest earnings with respect to transaction costs. These are those persons for whom it is most convenient to negotiate with those who are not owners (in other words, those for whom ownership costs less). However, this requires a kind of market for the different forms of corporation.[153] The actors in these markets then choose the organisational form which is most convenient and efficient for achieving their goals.[154]

As seen, diverging interests between parties can lead to a conflict of interests that ultimately produces specific costs. In particular, shareholders incur costs by supervising the directors or management, whereas the latter incur costs by presenting themselves as loyal agents.[155] Depending on the size of a firm (here, an agricultural cooperative), members often manage the business themselves. This can reduce—but never eliminate—these conflicts and associated costs.[156]

This is the economic perspective, whereas my research is rooted in law—this scientific discipline sticks to legal categories like 'duty' and 'liability'. Accordingly, the principal gives specific authority to the agent. The agent is then liable for the acts

---

[150]See Picot and Dietl (1993), p. 327 et seq.; Schäfer and Ott (2012d), p. 687 et seq.; Schwartz (1997), p. 103 et seq.; Denozza (2002), p. 84 et seq. In general Armour et al. (2009a), p. 37 et seq. Also consider Scott (1987) and Macaulay (1963).

[151]See Klein et al. (1978), p. 302 et seq.; Grossman and Hart (1986), p. 693 et seq.; Hart (1988), p. 121 et seq.; Armour et al. (2009c), p. 23; Hart and Moore (1990), p. 1120; Schäfer and Ott (2012d), p. 688 et seq.; Picot and Dietl (1993), p. 312 et seq. Generally Coase (1937); Craswell et al. (2007), p. 68 et seq. Also consider Royer (1999), p. 46 et seq.; Sykuta and Chaddad (1999), p. 72 et seq.; Minguez-Vera et al. (2010), p. 912 et seq. Generally, Gallo (1998b), p. 48 et seq.

[152]See Cook and Iliopoulos (1999), p. 528; Minguez-Vera et al. (2010), p. 912 et seq.; Hansmann (1999), p. 390. Generally, Fama and Jensen (1983). Also consider Aviram (2006), p. 9 et seq.; Adams (1991), p. 18 et seq.; Cooter et al. (1999), p. 155 et seq.

[153]Capital company, cooperative, non-profit company.

[154]See Zoppini (2004), p. 442; Armour et al. (2009c), p. 22 et seq.; Hansmann (1996), p. 22. Also consider Aviram (2006), p. 6 et seq.; Adams (1991), p. 22 et seq. Generally, Ribstein and Kobayashi (1999).

[155]See Jensen and Meckling (1976), p. 349 et seq.

[156]See Sect. 4.2.3.

he/she performs under the authority conferred upon him/her. In addition, the agent has a duty of loyalty.[157]

The second agency conflict stems from potential opposing interests between majority and minority shareholders.[158] To be more precise, the minority shareholders are principals who want to assure that the controlling shareholders, as agents, do not expropriate the minority by making decisions that are not in the minority's interest.[159] Minority shareholders can be particularly vulnerable in closed corporations, because they have no liquid market in which to value their shares and, thus, nowhere to sell them.[160] Share valuation is organised outside capital markets, which means that business valuation methods are applied with significant uncertainties. As a result, an exit at market price is quite difficult. In addition, majority shareholders in closed corporations are not affected by the threat of a public takeover.[161] Instead, specific conflicts arise from the risk of the hidden distribution of profits or other forms of remuneration.[162] Minority stakeholders can also display opportunistic behaviour by using their minority rights to block entrepreneurial decisions and harm the interests of the majority shareholders, who might have made considerable firm-specific investments (due to a required qualified majority).[163]

The last conflict concerns the relationship between the firm—particularly its owners—and third parties. In some circumstances, the firm (in this case, the agent) can exploit or expropriate its creditors, employees and consumers. This problems arises because of limited liability: Shareholders who have only invested a small amount of equity capital can bear losses up to the amount of their investment, despite receiving full benefits from any profits.[164] The problems can occur when the directors are not independent and thus strongly influenced by shareholders. Specific legal instruments can counteract this risk by shifting incentives, and include covenants in loan contracts or liability rules related to shareholders (piercing the corporate veil).[165]

---

[157]See Steinberg (2010), p. 75 et seq.

[158]See Armour et al. (2009a), p. 36. Also consider Eidenmüller (2014a), p. 9 et seq.

[159]See Armour et al. (2009a), p. 36. Also consider Enriques and Volpin (2007), p. 122 et seq.

[160]This is similar to cooperatives. See Sect. 5.6.

[161]See Eidenmüller (2014a), p. 9; Tirole (2006), p. 425 et seq.; Manne (1965), p. 112 et seq.; Bolten et al. (2007), p. 848 et seq.

[162]For instance, transactions concluded with the majority shareholder can give them an advantage to the detriment of the company. Another example would be an extremely high salary given to a majority shareholder who also acts as a member of the management organ. See Eidenmüller (2014a), p. 9. Also consider McCahery and Vermeulen (2008), p. 46.

[163]See Armour et al. (2009a), p. 36; Eidenmüller (2014a), p. 10. Also consider Picot and Dietl (1993), p. 316.

[164]See Armour et al. (2009a), p. 36; Eidenmüller (2014a), p. 11 et seq. Also consider Jensen and Meckling (1976), p. 335 et seq.; Myers (1977).

[165]See Tirole (2006), p. 103 et seq.; Eidenmüller (2014a), p. 12; Hansmann and Kraakman (1991). Also consider Armour et al. (2009b), p. 115 et seq.; Easterbrook and Fischel (1998), p. 35; Manes (1999), p. 85 et seq.; Fleischer (2000), p. 20 et seq.; Schäfer and Ott (2012a), p. 718 et seq. In

1.3.3 Specific Observations on the Cooperatives' Economic Functioning

Cooperatives only partly share the features typical when conducting an efficiency analysis of public limited-liability companies.[166] In addition, they may be compared to closed corporations (i.e., private limited-liability companies) to gain knowledge about the functioning of a cooperative. One example is the transferability of shares in cooperatives. These shares are generally not traded on stock exchanges, which restricts the group of potential members.[167] To a certain extent, this problematic restriction also occurs in closed corporations, making it difficult for shareholders to leave the corporation and cash in their shares. In this case, the necessity for active involvement increases.[168] In addition, the shareholders of public corporations (i.e., public limited-liability companies) are normally better diversified then the shareholders of closed corporations, who tend to invest a significant part of their assets.[169] On the other hand, the transaction costs are generally lower between shareholders in a closed corporation, due to their restricted numbers and strong social ties.[170] These observations are also valid for (agricultural) cooperatives.

As mentioned in Sect. 1.1, a specific distinguishing feature of a cooperative is that it serves its members' specific needs, rather than the remuneration of capital subscribed. For this reason, we must determine which type of cooperative we will analyse. It is possible to distinguish between producers, workers or consumer cooperatives.[171] This distinction implies that different types of cooperatives offer various member benefits. If follows that different types of benefits lead to different incentives to make transactions with the cooperative.[172] This carries consequences for an efficiency assessment of legal rules and inevitably requires restricting this

general Cheng (2014). Different third parties can also be potential conflict partners, for example staff. These problems can be solved via worker cooperatives. Like shareholders of closed corporations, members of a cooperative—and agricultural cooperatives in particular—are generally more interested in the firm in the broadest sense (see Sect. 3.5.2). This is in contrast to shareholders of a public limited-liability company, who may have different investments focusing primarily or even exclusively on returns. See Eidenmüller (2014a), p. 12 et seq. Also consider Easterbrook and Fischel (1998), p. 228 et seq.; Bolten et al. (2007), p. 843.

[166]See Sect. 1.3.2. See also Ziliotti (1994).

[167]See Chaddad and Iliopoulos (2013), p. 6; Bijman et al. (2013), p. 207; Trechter et al. (1997), p. 492 et seq. See also van Bekkum and van Dijk (1997), p. 20 et seq.

[168]See Molk (2014), p. 903 fn 14 and 926 fn 118; Schneiberg (2002), p. 51 et seq.; Nilsson (2001), p. 334; Armour et al. (2009c), p. 15; Eidenmüller (2014b), p. 190. Also consider Holmstrom (1999), p. 412. The problem of exit in a cooperative is discussed in Sects. 3.5.2 and 5.6.

[169]See Molk (2014), p. 927. On this issue, see Tirole (2006), p. 158 et seq.

[170]See Hansmann (1999), p. 397 et seq. Also consider Hansmann (1996), p. 69 et seq.; Dickstein (1991), p. 19 et seq.; Greenberg (1984), p. 184 et seq.; Hoffmann (2006).

[171]See Birchall (2011), p. 3; Laurinkari (1990), p. 5. Also consider Chukwu (1990), p. 15 et seq. Generally, Bijman and Hanisch (2012).

[172]See Fici (2014), p. 151. On these issues, see also Blome-Drees et al. (1998), p. 154 et seq.

study's focus. We chose to concentrate on **agricultural cooperatives as a special type of producer cooperative**. Thus, the farmer's role as a member of a producer cooperative is essential for this research. Two examples are (1) a winegrower who has his harvest processed into wine by a cellar cooperative and then sells the wine and (2) a fruit grower who has his harvest marketed and sold via a cooperative. Conflicts and resolutions over resource allocation, according to economic theory, largely depend on shareholders' (i.e., the members of the agricultural cooperative) interests in monitoring the managing bodies.[173] For various reasons, these interests are generally strongly represented in agricultural cooperatives. In fact, farmers are often deeply affected by how the cooperative functions, particularly in monetary terms. Studies show that these dynamics are less pronounced in credit or social cooperatives, which are therefore also treated as non-profit organisations by various researchers.[174] The different potential agency conflicts have different relevance depending on the type of cooperative considered and its scope. For instance, social cooperatives (which are generally non-profit organisations) face different conflicts from agricultural cooperatives, which are clear profit organisations.[175]

In the previous sub-chapter, I explained the different types of conflicts that might exist between principals, i.e., members of a cooperative, and agents, i.e., the cooperative's managers. All these observations on conflicts, relationships between members, cooperatives, third parties, etc., can be brought together clearly with the help of a model that distinguishes between two types of costs: the costs of market contracting and the costs of ownership.[176] This helps explain briefly some typical problems arising in agricultural cooperatives.[177] The former types of costs generate a positive incentive for firms' patrons to obtain ownership. Patrons are those persons who transact with a firm or enterprise often in different ways: they can purchase its products or sell their supplies to it (i.e., labour or other factors of production).[178]

The first type of costs of market contracting occurs when a firm has market power over a group of its patrons because of economies of scale or other factors.[179] Because

---

[173] See Sect. 1.3.2 and Sect. 3.5.1.

[174] See Thomas (2004). Also consider Hansmann (1996), p. 227 et seq.; Fici (2013a), p. 33 et seq.; Galletti (2006), p. 51 et seq.; Cian (2014), p. 165. In fact, these dynamics are completely different in non-profit versus for-profit organisations. See Steinberg (2010), p. 75 et seq.; Hansmann (2010), p. 63 et seq.; Hansmann (1996), p. 227 et seq.; Fama and Jensen (1983), p. 318 et seq. For specific details see Sacconi and Ottone (2015); Thomsen (2014), p. 17 et seq. Also consider Hansmann (2003). For credit cooperatives, see Grillo (2013), p. 42 et seq. See also Nuhanovic-Ribic et al. (2017), p. 161 et seq.

[175] See Hansmann (1996), p. 120 et seq.; Molk (2014), p. 913 et seq. On these issues, see also Blome-Drees et al. (1998), p. 111 et seq.

[176] Birchall lists the theories that explain the functioning of cooperatives. See Birchall (2011), p. 32 et seq. Also consider Nilsson (1999), p. 458; Aviram (2006), p. 8 et seq.

[177] See also Hansmann (1996), p. 120 et seq.

[178] See Hansmann (1996), p. 12; Hansmann (1988), p. 270.

[179] For example monopoly or severe disparity in information between the contracting parties. See Hansmann (1999), p. 389 et seq.

the firm could exploit this group, incentives are given to assign ownership to them[180]: For example, consumers who could be exploited by a firm with monopolistic power could organise the firm as a consumer cooperative.[181] This case entails farmers who buy their farming equipment from their cooperatives.

While the previous example concerned *ex ante* market power, *ex post* market power, or 'lock-in' is another potential cost of market contracting, incurred after a person becomes an owner of the firm. These problems can arise when two conditions are met. First, the new owner must make substantial transaction-specific investments.[182] Second, these transactions must span a long period of time, becoming complex and unpredictable. As a result, important features of future transactions cannot be determined by the contract in advance and must be determined according to experience. Due to the long-term investment, the new owner will not exit the firm easily in case the latter exploits him or her.[183] A last cost of market contracting is caused by asymmetric information. One of the parties, either the patron or the firm, has better information. For instance, firms often have better knowledge about the quality of the goods they produce.[184] Small farmers are often locked in, because the cooperative is the only vehicle for selling their products on the international market.

The costs of ownership can also be divided into different categories. The first is the cost of monitoring. In order to exercise effective control over a firm's management, patrons must have sufficient information about a firm's operations. They must also communicate effectively amongst each other to exchange information and make decisions so that they can convince the management to run the firm how they want. While monitoring costs can vary considerably, they are likely to be smaller if there are fewer patrons who live close to each other and if the transactions are conducted with the firm on a regular basis.[185] In many cases, rural areas facilitate this proximity, which means that small agricultural cooperatives naturally have an advantage in this respect.

The second type of ownership costs is the costs of collective decision making. As ownership is shared among a group of patrons, a proper method for collective decision making must be determined. Votes are often weighted by the volume of

[180]Market failure can make market contracting particularly costly. In these cases, one way to reduce costs of transacting is to link the purchasing and selling party together through ownership. In other words, the purchaser owns the seller or vice versa. This reduces or even eliminates any conflict of interest between these two parties. In fact, it is these very conflicts of interest which produce the costs of market failure. See Hansmann (1999), p. 389.

[181]See Hansmann (1999), p. 390; Hansmann (1996), p. 24 et seq.

[182]These investments, or more precisely their value, cannot be fully recouped if the relationship with the firm is broken. See Hansmann (1999), p. 391. Also consider Picot and Dietl (1993), p. 316 et seq.

[183]The typical case involves locked-in employees. In this case it may be an advantage to organise the firm as a worker cooperative. Another example are consumer cooperatives. See Hansmann (1999), p. 390 et seq.; Hansmann (1996), p. 25 et seq.

[184]See Hansmann (1999), p. 391; Hansmann (1996), p. 27 et seq.

[185]See Hansmann (1999), p. 391 et seq.; Hansmann (1996), p. 36 et seq.

patronage, i.e., weighted according to a patron's business transactions conducted with the firm. It is important to understand whether the patrons or owners have diverging interests regarding the firm. If they have essentially identical interests, the costs are naturally small. This is quite often the case for agricultural production or supply cooperatives.[186]

The third important type of the costs of ownership is the cost of risk bearing. This is the overall risk of running the enterprise, and this risk is ultimately reflected in the firm's residual earnings and assignable to the owners or patrons.[187] As will be explained in Sect. 3.5, cooperatives have some specific features in this respect that distinguish them from capitalist enterprises.

References

Adams M (1991) Eigentum, Kontrolle und beschränkte Haftung, 1st edn. Wirtschaftsrecht und Wirtschaftspolitik, vol 113. Nomos, Baden-Baden

Adar Y, Sirena P (2013) Principles and rules in the emerging European contract law: from the PECL to the CESL, and beyond. Eur Rev Contract Law 9:1–37. https://doi.org/10.1515/ercl-2013-0001

Adornato F (2004) Di cosa parliamo quando parliamo di agricoltura. Agricoltura Istituzioni Mercati:5–9

Adornato F (2007) Agricoltura a cinquant'anni dal trattato di Roma. Agricoltura Istituzioni Mercati:5–9

Ajani G, Peruginelli G, Sartor G, Tiscornia D (eds) (2007) The multilanguage complexity of European law: methodologies in comparison. Workshop, 17 November 2006, European University Institute, Fiesole, Italy. Information and communications technology. European Press Acad. Publ, Florence

Akerlof GA (1970) The market for "lemons": quality uncertainty and the market mechanism. Q J Econ 84:488–500. https://doi.org/10.2307/1879431

Albisinni F (2010) Istituzioni e regole dell'agricoltura: dopo il trattato di Lisbona. Rivista di diritto agrario:206–247

Albisinni F (2011a) Il diritto agrario europeo dopo Lisbona fra intervento e regolazione: i codici europei dell'agricoltura. Agricoltura-Istituzioni-Mercati:29–52

Albisinni F (2011b) Le peculiarità giuridiche dell'impresa agricola in Italia oggi. In: Accademia dei Georgofili (eds) Le nuove missioni dell'impresa agraria: Giornata di studio, pp 275–293

Albisinni F (2013) La nuova OCM ed i contratti agroalimentari. Rivista di diritto alimentare:4–14

Albisinni F (2014) La definizione di attività agricola nella nuova PAC, tra incentivazione e centralizzazione regolatoria. Rivista Italiana di Diritto Pubblico Communitario XXIV:967–990

Alchian AA (1977) Some economics of property rights. In: Alchian AA, Coase RH (eds) Economic forces at work. Liberty Press, Indianapolis, pp 127–149

Alchian AA, Demsetz H (1972) Production, information costs, and economic organization. Am Econ Rev 62:777–795

Alchian AA, Woodward S (1987) Reflections on the theory of the firm. J Inst Theor Econ (JITE)/ Zeitschrift für die gesamte Staatswissenschaft 143:110–136

[186]See Hansmann (1999), p. 392 et seq.; Hansmann (1996), p. 39 et seq.

[187]See Hansmann (1999), p. 394; Hansmann (1996), p. 44 et seq.

Alessi R (2006) L'impresa agricola. In: Alessi R, Contaldi L, Corapi D, de Donno B (eds) Impresa e società nel diritto comunitario, 2nd edn. Giappichelli, Torino, pp 1234–1274
Alessi R (2019) La ricerca della "specialità" dell'impresa agricola e l'inesorabile tramonto dell'art. 2135 cod. civ. Rivista di diritto agrario:182–196
Alfandari E, Piot B (2004) Die Mitgliedschaft in der SCE. In: Schulze R (ed) Europäische Genossenschaft SCE: Handbuch, 1st edn. Nomos, Baden-Baden, pp 77–90
Altmann S, Falk A, Marklein F (2011) Eingeschränkt rationales Verhalten: Evidenz und Implikationen. In: Fleischer H, Zimmer D, Altmann S (eds) Beitrag der Verhaltensökonomie (Behavioral Economics) zum Handels- und Wirtschaftsrecht. Recht und Wirtschaft, Frankfurt am Main, pp 63–82
Amat L, Chlebicka A, Ferreira I, Montanari F, Sorrentino A, Szabo GG, Traon D, Russo C (2019) Study of the best ways for producer organisations to be formed, carry out their activities and be supported: final report. OPL, Luxembourg
Arlen J, Spitzer M, Talley E (2002) Endowment effects within corporate agency relationships. J Leg Stud 31:1–37. https://doi.org/10.1086/324659
Armour J, Whincop MJ (2001) An economic analysis of shared property in partnership and close corporations law. J Corp Law:73–92. https://doi.org/10.1093/acprof:oso/9780199264353.003.0003
Armour J, Hansmann H, Kraakman RH (2009a) Agency problems and legal strategies. In: Kraakman RH, Armour J, Davies P, Enriques L, Hansmann H, Hertig G, Hopt K, Kanda H, Rock E (eds) The anatomy of corporate law: a comparative and functional approach, 2nd edn. Oxford University Press, Oxford, pp 35–53
Armour J, Hertig G, Kanda H (2009b) Transactions with creditors. In: Kraakman RH, Armour J, Davies P, Enriques L, Hansmann H, Hertig G, Hopt K, Kanda H, Rock E (eds) The anatomy of corporate law: a comparative and functional approach, 2nd edn. Oxford University Press, Oxford, pp 115–152
Armour J, Hansmann H, Kraakman RH (2009c) What is corporate law. In: Kraakman RH, Armour J, Davies P, Enriques L, Hansmann H, Hertig G, Hopt K, Kanda H, Rock E (eds) The anatomy of corporate law: a comparative and functional approach, 2nd edn. Oxford University Press, Oxford, pp 1–34
Arnò G, Cancarini S, Romanelli F (2007) La società europea: La disciplina comunitaria e il suo recepimento in Italia e nei principali stati membri. EGEA, Milano
Arrow KJ (1973) Higher education as a filter. J Public Econ 2:193–216. https://doi.org/10.1016/0047-2727(73)90013-3
Aviram A (2006) A note on economic theories of the firm. SSRN J. https://doi.org/10.2139/ssrn.880435
Bachmann G (2008) Optionsmodelle im Privatrecht. JuristenZeitung 63:11–20. https://doi.org/10.1628/002268808783355591
Bäck E (2012) Anerben- und Höferecht. In: Norer R (ed) Handbuch des Agrarrechts, 2. Aufl. Verlag Österreich, Wien, pp 717–734
Baer S (2011) Rechtssoziologie: Eine Einführung in die interdisziplinäre Rechtsforschung, 1st edn. Nomos-Lehrbuch, Nomos, Baden-Baden
Barney JB (1990) Organizational economics, 1st edn. The Jossey-Bass social and behavioral science series. Jossey-Bass, San Francisco
Bellantuono G (2000) I contratti incompleti nel diritto e nell'economia. Dipartimento di scienze giuridiche, Università di Trento, vol 30. Cedam, Padova
Bellantuono G (2016) The comparative law and economics of energy markets. In: Eisenberg T, Ramello GB (eds) Comparative law and economics. Edward Elgar Publishing, Cheltenham, pp 236–261
Bellantuono G, Iamiceli P (2005) Analisi economica del diritto. UNI service, Trento
Bianca M, Zanardo A (2016) La Società Europea e la Società Cooperativa Europea. In: Pederzini E (ed) Percorsi di diritto societario europeo, 3rd edn. Giappichelli, Torino, pp 177–214

Bijman J, Hanisch M (2012) Developing a typology of cooperatives and producer organisations in Europe. In: Van der Sangen G, Pyykkönen POP, Iliopoulus C, Kühl R, Hagedorn K, Hanisch M, Judis R, Gijselinckx C, Hendrikse G, Hak T, Poppe K, Bijman J (eds) Support for farmers' cooperatives. Wageningen

Bijman J, Hendrikse G, van Oijen A (2013) Accommodating two worlds in one organisation: changing board models in agricultural cooperatives. Manag Decis Econ 34:204–217. https://doi.org/10.1002/mde.2584

Birchall J (2011) People centred businesses: co-operatives, mutuals and the idea of membership. Palgrave Macmillan, Basingstoke

Blome-Drees J, Zerche J, Schmale I (1998) Einführung in die Genossenschaftslehre: Genossenschaftstheorie und Genossenschaftsmanagement. Oldenbourg Wissenschaftsverlag, München

Bodiguel L, Cardwell M (2006) Nuove definizioni di "agricoltura" per un'agricoltura in evoluzione: Francia ed Inghilterra a confronto. Rivista di diritto agrario:149–173

Bolognini S (2019) La "specialità" dell'impresa agricola nel registro delle imprese fra codice civile e legislazione di settore. Rivista di diritto agrario:279–308

Bolten P, Becht M, Röell A (2007) Corporate law and governance. In: Polinsky AM, Shavell S (eds) Handbook of law and economics: volume 2, 1st edn. North Holland, Amsterdam, pp 829–944

Brendel M (2011) Genossenschaftsbewegung in Deutschland - Geschichte und Aktualität. In: Allgeier M (ed) Solidarität, Flexibilität, Selbsthilfe. VS Verlag für Sozialwissenschaften, Wiesbaden, pp 1–36

Broeusseau É (2008) Contracts: from bilateral sets of incentives to the multi-level governance of relations. In: Brousseau E, Glachant J-M (eds) New institutional economics: a guidebook. Cambridge University Press, Cambridge, pp 37–66

Budzinowski R (2013) Il diritto agrario di fronte alle sfide contemporanee. Alcune riflessioni. Agricoltura Istituzioni Mercati:145–155

Budzinowski R (2018) Der Agrarrechtsbegriff aus Sicht der polnischen Agrarrechtswissenschaft. In: Martínez J (ed) Reichweite und Grenzen des Agrarrechts: Gedächtnisschrift für Dr. Wolfgang Winkler, 1st edn. Nomos Verlagsgesellschaft, Baden-Baden, pp 133–150

Busse C (2018) Die Sonderrechtstheorie im Agrarrecht - Konzeptionelle Überlegungen zu ihrer Weiterentwicklung. In: Martínez J (ed) Reichweite und Grenzen des Agrarrechts: Gedächtnisschrift für Dr. Wolfgang Winkler, 1st edn. Nomos Verlagsgesellschaft, Baden-Baden, pp 19–62

Cane P, Kritzer HM (eds) (2013) The Oxford handbook of empirical legal research, reprint. Oxford University Press, Oxford

Capizzano E (1991) Agricoltura, diritto agrario, società: Manuale per la ricerca e l'insegnamento. Cedam, Padova

Carrozza A (1988) Lezioni di diritto agrario I: Elementi di teoria generale. Giuffrè, Milano

Carrozza A (2001a) Agricoltura (teoria generale). In: Massart A, Goldoni M, Sirsi E (eds) Scritti di diritto agrario. Giuffrè, Milano, pp 773–790

Carrozza A (2001b) Diritto agrario "1980". In: Massart A, Goldoni M, Sirsi E (eds) Scritti di diritto agrario. Giuffrè, Milano, pp 361–382

Carrozza A (2001c) La scienza di diritto agrario e il problema dell'oggetto. In: Massart A, Goldoni M, Sirsi E (eds) Scritti di diritto agrario. Giuffrè, Milano, pp 645–662

Carrozza A (2001d) L'autonomia del diritto agrario. In: Massart A, Goldoni M, Sirsi E (eds) Scritti di diritto agrario. Giuffrè, Milano, pp 287–306

Carrozza A (2001e) L'oggetto del diritto agrario. In: Massart A, Goldoni M, Sirsi E (eds) Scritti di diritto agrario. Giuffrè, Milano, pp 705–728

Casadei E (2009) La nozione di impresa agricola dopo la riforma del 2001. Rivista di diritto agrario:309–358

Chaddad F, Iliopoulos C (2013) Control rights, governance, and the costs of ownership in agricultural cooperatives. Agribusiness 29:3–22. https://doi.org/10.1002/agr.21328

Cheffins BR (2006) Company law: theory, structure, and operation. Clarendon Press, Oxford
Cheffins BR (2012) Corporations. In: Tushnet M, Cane P (eds) The Oxford handbook of legal studies. Oxford University Press, Oxford, pp 485–509
Cheng TK (2014) An economic analysis of limited shareholder liability in contractual claims. Berkeley Bus Law J:112–181
Chukwu SC (1990) Economics of the co-operative business enterprise. Theory and practice of self-help promotion Ser. A, Monographs and textbooks, vol 2. Marburg Consult für Selbsthilfeförderung, Marburg
Cian G (1998) Hundert Jahre BGB aus italienischer Sicht. ZEuP:215–225
Cian M (2014) Appunti su scambi mutualistici e traslazioni del rischio d'impresa nelle società cooperative. In: Nappi P, Sgarbanti G, Borghi P, Russo L, Fioravanti C, Agostini C, Manservisi S, Borraccetti M, Rizzioli S (eds) Studi in onore di Luigi Costato: III. Jovene, Napoli, pp 165–174
Cigarini GP (1977) Agrarietà e territorio. Rivista di diritto agrario:688–697
Coase RH (1937) The nature of the firm. Economica 4:386–405. https://doi.org/10.2307/2626876
Cook ML, Iliopoulos C (1999) Beginning to inform the theory of the cooperative firm: emergence of the new generation cooperative. Finn J Bus Econ:525–535
Cooter R, Mattei U, Monateri PG, Pardolesi R, Ulen T (1999) Il mercato delle regole: Analisi economica del diritto civile. Il Mulino, Bologna
COPA-COGECA (2015) Development of agricultural cooperatives in the EU in 2014. http://agricultura.gencat.cat/web/.content/de_departament/de02_estadistiques_observatoris/27_butlletins/02_butlletins_nd/documents_nd/fitxers_estatics_nd/2015/0165_2015_IA_Cooperatives_Cooperatives-UE.pdf. Accessed 5 Dec 2019
Costato L (2001) L'imprenditore agricolo e il mercato. Rivista di diritto agrario:131–143
Costato L (2004) Dal diritto agrario al diritto agroalimentare. Un percorso ricostruttivo. Agricoltura Istituzioni Mercati:119–130
Costato L (2006) L'imprenditore agricolo: novità codicistiche e polemiche retro. Rivista di Diritto Civile:89–100
Costato L (2008a) Attività agricole, sicurezza alimentare e tutela del territorio. Rivista di diritto agrario:451–463
Costato L (2008b) La lezione di Antonio Carrozza (e qualche possibile fraintendimento). Rivista di diritto agrario:15–24
Costato L (2012) I nuovi confini del diritto agrario. Agricoltura Istituzioni Mercati:25–30
Costato L, Russo L (2015) Corso di diritto agrario italiano e comunitario, 4th edn. Giuffrè, Milano
Craswell R, Katz AW, Hermalin BE (2007) Contract law. In: Polinsky AM, Shavell S (eds) Handbook of law and economics, vol 1. Elsevier, Amsterdam, pp 3–138
Cusa E (2004) Die Verwendung des Betriebsergebnisses. In: Schulze R (ed) Europäische Genossenschaft SCE: Handbuch, 1st edn. Nomos, Baden-Baden, pp 123–168
Danneman G (2019) Comparative law: study of similarities and differences? In: Reimann M, Zimmermann R (eds) The Oxford handbook of comparative law, 2nd edn. Oxford University Press, Oxford, pp 390–422
Delbono F (1994a) Adverse selection. In: Zamagni S (ed) Economia politica I, 1. ed. italiana. UTET, Torino, pp 5–6
Delbono F (1994b) Moral hazard. In: Zamagni S (ed) Economia politica I, 1. ed. italiana. UTET, Torino, p 444
Demsetz H (2004) Toward a theory of property rights. In: Geest GD, van den Bergh R (eds) Comparative law and economics, vol I. Elgar, Cheltenham, pp 3–15
Denozza F (2002) Norme efficienti: L'analisi economica delle regole giuridiche. Giuffrè, Milano
Di Lauro A (2007) Scienza, tecnica e diritto agrario: Dialoghi, regole, conflitti. Rivista di diritto agrario:568–587
Dickstein C (1991) The promise and problems of worker cooperatives. J Plann Lit 6:16–33. https://doi.org/10.1177/088541229100600102

Easterbrook FH, Fischel DR (1985) Limited liability and the corporation. Univ Chic Law Rev:89–117

Easterbrook FH, Fischel DR (1998) The economic structure of corporate law, [Repr.]. Harvard University Press, Cambridge

Ecchia G (1994a) Informazione assimetrica. In: Zamagni S (ed) Economia politica I, 1. ed. italiana. UTET, Torino, pp 328–329

Ecchia G (1994b) Teoria dell'impresa. In: Zamagni S (ed) Economia politica I, 1. ed. italiana. UTET, Torino, pp 301–309

Ecorys, Wageningen Economic Research (2018) Study on producer organisations and their activities in the olive oil, beef and veal, arable crops sectors. https://ec.europa.eu/competition/publications/reports/kd0218732enn.pdf. Accessed 26 Nov 2019

Eidenmüller H (2005) Effizienz als Rechtsprinzip: Möglichkeiten und Grenzen der ökonomischen Analyse des Rechts. Univ., Diss.—München, 1994, 3rd edn. Die Einheit der Gesellschaftswissenschaften, vol 90. Mohr-Siebeck, Tübingen

Eidenmüller H (2014a) Analytical framework. In: Bachmann G, Eidenmüller H, Engert A, Fleischer H, Schön W (eds) Regulating the closed corporation. De Gruyter, Berlin, pp 5–27

Eidenmüller H (2014b) Formation, management and transfer of shares. In: Bachmann G, Eidenmüller H, Engert A, Fleischer H, Schön W (eds) Regulating the closed corporation. De Gruyter, Berlin, pp 179–200

Eisenhardt KM (1989) Agency theory: an assessment and review. Acad Manage Rev 14:57–74. https://doi.org/10.2307/258191

Engelhardt WW (1990) Die Genossenschaftsidee als Gestaltungsprinzip. In: Laurinkari J (ed) Genossenschaftswesen: Hand- und Lehrbuch. Oldenbourg, München, pp 10–27

Englerth M (2012) Verhaltensökonomik. In: Towfigh EV, Petersen N (eds) Ökonomische Methoden im Recht: Eine Einführung für Juristen. Mohr Siebeck, Tübingen, pp 165–200

Enriques L, Volpin P (2007) Corporate governance reforms in continental Europe. J Econ Perspect 21:117–140. https://doi.org/10.1257/jep.21.1.117

Fama EF, Jensen MC (1983) Separation of ownership and control. J Law Econ 26:301–325

Faust F (2019) Comparative law and economic analysis of law. In: Reimann M, Zimmermann R (eds) The Oxford handbook of comparative law, 2nd edn. Oxford University Press, Oxford, pp 826–851

Fehr E, Schmidt KM (1999) A theory of fairness, competition, and cooperation. Q J Econ 114:817–868

Fehr E, Klein A, Schmidt KM (2007) Fairness and contract design. Econometrica 75:121–154. https://doi.org/10.1111/j.1468-0262.2007.00734.x

Ferreri S (2010) Falsi amici e trappole giuridiche: Termini contrattuali anglofoni e difficoltà di traduzione. Giappichelli, Torino

Ferrucci N (2011) Il compendio unico. In: Costato L, Germanò A, Rook Basile E (eds) Trattato di diritto agrario: I. UTET, Torino, pp 465–476

Fici A (2010) Mapping of the relevant legislation implementing the SCE regulation in the EU Member States and EEA countries. In: Fici A (ed) Study on the implementation of the Regulation 1435/2003 on the Statute for European Cooperative Society (SCE): Executive Summary and Part I: Synthesis and comparative report. Report drawn up following call tender no ENTR/2009/021 of 23 April from the European Commission, pp 33–80

Fici A (2013a) An introduction to cooperative law. In: Cracogna D, Fici A, Henrÿ H (eds) International handbook of cooperative law. Springer, Berlin, Heidelberg, pp 3–62

Fici A (2013b) The European Cooperative Society. In: Cracogna D, Fici A, Henrÿ H (eds) International handbook of cooperative law. Springer, Berlin, Heidelberg, pp 115–151

Fici A (2014) The essential role of cooperative law. Dovenschmidt Q 2:147–158. https://doi.org/10.5553/DQ/221199812014002004003

Fici A (2017) Definition and objectives of cooperatives. In: Fajardo-García IG, Fici A, Henrÿ H, Hiez D, Meira DMMA, Münkner H-H, Snaith I (eds) Principles of European Cooperative Law: principles, commentaries and national reports. Intersentia, Cambridge, pp 19–45

Fiorentini G (1994a) Diritti di proprietà. In: Zamagni S (ed) Politica economica II. UTET libreria, Torino, pp 163–167
Fiorentini G (1994b) Legge ed economia. In: Zamagni S (ed) Politica economica II. UTET libreria, Torino, pp 352–356
Fleischer H (2000) Grundfragen der ökonomischen Theorie im Gesellschafts- und Kapitalmarktrecht. Zeitschrift für Unternehmens- und Gesellschaftsrecht 30:1–32. https://doi.org/10.1515/zgre.2000.047
Fleischer H (2004) Gesetz und Vertrag als alternative Problemlösungsmodelle im Gesellschaftsrecht. Zeitschrift für das gesamte Handelsrecht und Wirtschaftsrecht:673–707
Fleischer H, Zimmer D (2008) Effizienzorientierung im Handels- und Wirtschaftsrecht: Einführung und Überblick. In: Fleischer H, Zimmer D (eds) Effizienz als Regelungsziel im Handels- und Wirtschaftsrecht. Verl. Recht und Wirtschaft, Frankfurt am Main, pp 9–42
Fleischer H, Schmolke K, Ulrich ZD (2011) Verhaltensökonomik als Forschungsinstrument für das Wirtschaftsrecht. In: Fleischer H, Zimmer D, Altmann S (eds) Beitrag der Verhaltensökonomie (Behavioral Economics) zum Handels- und Wirtschaftsrecht. Recht und Wirtschaft, Frankfurt am Main, pp 9–62
Fruehmann A, Nagy TR (2005) Aktiengesetz: the Austrian stock corporation act; Deutsch/Englisch, bilingual ed. Manz, Wien
Furubotn E, Pejovich S (1974) The new property rights literature. In: Furubotn EG, Pejovich S (eds) Economics of property rights. Ballinger Publishing Co, S.l., pp 1–9
Galletti D (2006) La tutela delle minoranze nella SCE. In: Galletti D, Fici A (eds) La società cooperativa europea: Quali prospettive per la cooperazione italiana? Universita degli Studi di Trento, Trento, pp 48–66
Gallo P (1998a) Introduzione al diritto comparato Vol II: Istituti giuridici. Introduzione al diritto comparato. Giappichelli, Torino
Gallo P (1998b) Introduzione al diritto comparato Vol III: Analisi economica del diritto. Giappichelli, Torino
Gallo P (2001) Introduzione al diritto comparato Vol I: Grandi sistemi giuridici, 2nd edn. Introduzione al diritto comparato. Giappichelli, Torino
Galloni G (2014) L'ampliamento dei confini di diritto agrario: Diritto ambientale e alimentare nel pensiero di Luigi Costato. In: Nappi P, Sgarbanti G, Borghi P, Russo L, Fioravanti C, Agostini C, Manservisi S, Borraccetti M, Rizzioli S (eds) Studi in onore di Luigi Costato: I. Jovene, Napoli, pp 397–406
Gambaro A, Sacco R (2014) Sistemi giuridici comparati, 3rd edn. UTET, Torino
Garrouste P, Saussier S (2008) The theories of the firm. In: Brousseau E, Glachant J-M (eds) New institutional economics: a guidebook. Cambridge University Press, Cambridge, pp 23–36
Gelter M, Grechenig K (2007) Juristischer Diskurs und Rechtsökonomie. Journal für Rechtspolitik 15:30–41. https://doi.org/10.1007/s00730-007-0162-7
Genco R (2006) Le operazioni straordinarie ed il trasferimento di sede della SCE: (Regolamento n 1435/2003 del 22 luglio 2003). In: Galletti D, Fici A (eds) La società cooperativa europea: Quali prospettive per la cooperazione italiana? Universita degli Studi di Trento, Trento, pp 115–136
Germanò A (2016) Manuale di diritto agrario, 8th edn. Giappichelli, Turin
Germanò A (2017) L'istituto di diritto agrario internazionale e comparato. editoriale scientifica, Napoli
Germanò A (2019) Alle "soglie" della formulazione dell'art. 2153 del codice civile del 1942. Diritto agroalimentare:197–238
Germanò A, Rook Basile E (2014) Manuale di diritto agrario comunitario, 3rd edn. Il diritto dell'alimentazione, dell'ambiente e dell'agricoltura. Giappichelli, Torino
Giudici P (2008) La responsabilità civile nel diritto dei mercati finanziari. Il diritto della banca e della borsa, vol 44. Giuffrè, Milano
Glenn HP (2019) Comparative legal families and comparative legal traditions. In: Reimann M, Zimmermann R (eds) The Oxford handbook of comparative law, 2nd edn. Oxford University Press, Oxford, pp 423–441

Göbel E (2002) Neue Institutionenökonomik: Konzeption und betriebswirtschaftliche Anwendungen. Grundwissen der Ökonomik Betriebswirtschaftslehre, vol 2235. Lucius & Lucius, Stuttgart
Goldoni M (2019) L'art. 2135 del codice civile e le esigenze di un ripensamento sul piano sistematico della "specialità" dell'impresa agricola. Rivista di diritto agrario:353–400
Gordon JN (1989) The mandatory structure of corporate law. Columbia Law Rev 89:1549–1598
Gorla G (1981) Diritto comparato e diritto comune europeo. Giuffré, Milano
Grande E (2019) Development of comparative law in Italy. In: Reimann M, Zimmermann R (eds) The Oxford handbook of comparative law, 2nd edn. Oxford University Press, Oxford, pp 87–110
Graziadei M (2003) The functionalist heritage. In: Legrand P, Munday RJC (eds) Comparative legal studies: traditions and transitions. Cambridge University Press, Cambridge, pp 100–128
Greenberg E (1984) Producer cooperatives and democratic theory: the case of plywood firms. In: Jackall R, Levin HM (eds) Worker cooperatives in America. University of California Press, Berkeley [etc.], pp 171–218
Grillo M (2013) Competition rules and the cooperative firm: new wine in old bottles. J Entrep Organ Divers 2:36–53. https://doi.org/10.5947/jeod.2013.003
Grimm C, Norer R (2015) Agrarrecht, 4th edn. Studium und Praxis. C.H. Beck, München
Grossi P (2016) Fattualità del diritto pos-moderno: l'emersione di un diritto 'agrario' in Italia. Diritto agroalimentare:7–28
Grossman SJ, Hart OD (1986) The costs and benefits of ownership: a theory of vertical and lateral integration. J Polit Econ 94:691–719. https://doi.org/10.1086/261404
Grubel HG (1971) Risk, uncertainty and moral hazard. J Risk Insur:99–106
Guarneri A (2003) Lineamenti di diritto comparato. Cedam, Padova
Hansmann H (1988) Ownership of the firm. J Law Econ Organ 4:267–304
Hansmann H (1996) The ownership of enterprise, 1st edn. Belknap Press of Harvard University Press, Cambridge
Hansmann H (1999) Cooperative firms in theory and practice. Liiketaloudellinen aikakauskirja LTA - Finn J Bus Econ:387–403
Hansmann H (2003) The role of trust in nonprofit enterprise. In: Anheier HK, Ben-Ner A (eds) The study of the nonprofit enterprise. Springer US, Boston, pp 115–122
Hansmann H (2010) The economics of nonprofit organizations. In: Hopt KJ, Hippel TV (eds) Comparative corporate governance of non-profit organizations. Cambridge University Press, Cambridge, pp 60–72
Hansmann H, Kraakman RH (1991) The uneasy case for limiting shareholder liability in tort. Yale Law J:1879–1934
Hansmann H, Kraakman RH, Squire RC (2006) Law and the rise of the firm. Harv Law Rev 119:1333–1403
Hardin R (1971) Collective action as an agreeable n-prisoners' dilemma. Behav Sci 16:472–481. https://doi.org/10.1002/bs.3830160507
Hardin R (2013) The free rider problem. In: Edward NZ (ed) The Stanford encyclopedia of philosophy, Spring 2013
Hart OD (1988) Incomplete contracts and the theory of the firm. J Law Econ Organ 4:119–139
Hart O, Moore J (1990) Property rights and the nature of the firm. J Polit Econ 98:1119–1158. https://doi.org/10.1086/261729
Hiez D (2017) Introduction. In: Fajardo-García IG, Fici A, Henrÿ H, Hiez D, Meira DMMA, Münkner H-H, Snaith I (eds) Principles of European Cooperative Law: principles, commentaries and national reports. Intersentia, Cambridge, pp 1–15
Hill CA, McDonnell BH (2012) Introduction: the evolution of the economic analysis of corporate law. In: Hill CA, McDonnell BH (eds) Research handbook on the economics of corporate law. Edward Elgar Publishing, Cheltenham, pp 1–13
Hoffmann EA (2006) Exit and voice: organizational loyalty and dispute resolution strategies. Soc Forces 84:2313–2330. https://doi.org/10.1353/sof.2006.0093

Hofinger H, Johler C (2002) Wettbewerb der genossenschaftlich-nationalen Rechtsformen in der SCE: Auftakt zur Diskussion um die Verweisnormen auf nationale Vorschriften und der Versuch einer attraktiven Gestaltung eines Ausführungsgesetzes für die Stärkung des Wirtschaftsstandorts Österreich. Ziller-Schriften, vol 3. Österr. Genossenschaftsverb. (Schulze-Delitzsch), Wien

Holmstrom B (1999) The future of cooperatives: a corporate perspective. Liiketaloudellinen aikakauskirja LTA - Finn J Bus Econ:404–417

Holzer G (1982) Zum Begriff und Standort des Agrarrechts in der österreichischen Rechtsordnung. Juristische Blätter:300–310

Holzer G (2017) Der funktionale Agrarrechtsbegriff - Erfahrungen und Erkenntnisse. In: Norer R, Holzer G (eds) Agrarrecht: Jahrbuch 2017. Perspektiven des Agrarrechts. Festgabe für Manfried Welan, 1st edn. NWV Verlag, Wien, pp 131–168

Holzer G (2018) Agrarrecht, 4th edn. Studium & Praxis. NWV Verlag, Wien, Graz

Hopt KJ (2016) Directors' duties and shareholders' rights in the European Union: mandatory and/or default rules? SSRN Electron J:1–23. https://doi.org/10.2139/ssrn.2749237

Iannarelli A (2001) Il diritto dell'agricoltura nell'era della globalizzazione. Cacucci, Bari

Iannarelli A (2002a) Il diritto agrario tra profilo globale e profilo locale: spunti sul metodo e sull'oggetto della ricerca. Rivista di diritto agrario:729–753

Iannarelli A (2002b) L'impresa agricola nel sistema agro-industriale. Diritto e giurisprudenza agraria e dell'ambiente:213–219

Iannarelli A (2007) Pluralismo definitorio dell'attività e dell'impresa agricola tra diritto comunitario e diritto interno. Studi sull'integrazione europea:469–495

Iannarelli A (2013) Il divenire del diritto agrario italiano ed europeo tra sviluppi tecnologici e sostenibilità. Rivista di diritto agrario:11–35

Iannarelli A (2019) La parabola della "specialità" dell'impresa agricola dopo il d.lgs. sulle crisi di impresa: considerazioni critiche. Rivista di diritto agrario:197–238

Ibáñez IE (2011) Law applicable to the European Cooperative Society: special reference to the European cooperative established in Spain. Eur Comp Financ Law Rev 8:30–46. https://doi.org/10.1515/ecfr.2011.30

Iengo M (2006) Gli Studi del CNN - Società cooperativa europea - Analisi delle norme applicabili ai sensi dell'articolo 8 del regolamento n. 1435/2003 - Casi e materiali di diritto comunitario di interesse notarile: le società - e.library - Fondazione Italiana del Notariato. Studio n. 9-2006/I. http://elibrary.fondazionenotariato.it/approfondimento.asp?app=21/studiCNN/mi_9_2006_I&mn=3&tipo=3&qn=6. Accessed 21 Nov 2019

Iliopoulos C (2014) Ownership, governance and related trade-offs in agricultural cooperatives. Dovenschmidt Q 2:159–167. https://doi.org/10.5553/DQ/221199812014002004004

Jensen MC, Meckling WH (1976) Theory of the firm: managerial behavior, agency costs and ownership structure. J Financ Econ 3:305–360. https://doi.org/10.1016/0304-405X(76)90026-X

Jensen MC, Meckling WH (1979) Rights and production functions: an application to labor-managed firms and codetermination. J Bus 52:469–506. https://doi.org/10.1086/296060

Kahan M, Kamar E (2002) The myth of state competition in corporate law. Stanford Law Rev 55:679. https://doi.org/10.2307/1229668

Kahneman D (1994) New challenges to the rationality assumption. J Inst Theor Econ (JITE)/ Zeitschrift für die gesamte Staatswissenschaft 150:18–36

Kahneman D (2012) Thinking, fast and slow. Penguin Books, London

Kalss S, Schauer M (2006) Die Reform des Österreichischen Kapitalgesellschaftsrechts: Gutachten. Verhandlungen des Sechzehnten Österreichischen Juristentages Zivilrecht, vol 1. Manz, Wien

Kastner W (1986) Österreichisches Genossenschaftsrecht. In: Patera M (ed) Handbuch des österreichischen Genossenschaftswesens. Orac, Wien, pp 117–232

Kellerhals A, Truten D (2002) The creation of the European company. Tulane Eur Civ Law Forum:71–82

Kirchner C, Painter RW, Kaal WA (2005) Regulatory competition in EU Corporate Law after inspire art: unbundling Delaware's product for Europe. Eur Comp Financ Law Rev 2:159–206. https://doi.org/10.1515/ecfr.2005.2.2.159
Kisker O (2006) Unternehmerische Mitbestimmung in der Europäischen Gesellschaft, der Europäischen Genossenschaft und bei grenzüberschreitender Verschmelzung im Vergleich. Recht der Arbeit:206–213
Klausner M (1995) Corporations, corporate law, and networks of contracts. Va Law Rev 81:757. https://doi.org/10.2307/1073499
Klein B, Crawford RG, Alchian AA (1978) Vertical integration, appropriable rents, and the competitive contracting process. J Law Econ 21:297–326
Kräkel M (2012) Organisation und Management, 5th edn. Neue ökonomische Grundrisse. Mohr Siebeck, Tübingen
Krimphove D (1998) Der Einsatz der ökonomischen Analyse des Rechts als notwendiges Instrument der Europäischen Rechtsvergleichung (Teil I): Dargestellt anhand des Erwerbes vom Nichtberechtigten in den Europäischen Rechtsordnungen. ZfRV:185–204
Krimphove D (2006) Das europäische Sachenrecht: Eine rechtsvergleichende Analyse nach der Komparativen Institutionenökonomik, 1st edn. Europäisches Wirtschaftsrecht (Lohmar, Germany), vol 1. Eul, Lohmar
Lamanna Di Salvo D (2003) La gestione aziendale nelle rilevazioni in partita doppia. WIP, Bari
Lando O, Beale H, Prüm A, Clive E, Zimmermann R (2019) Principles of European Contract Law, Parts I - III: Student edition. Kluwer Law International, [S.l.]
Laurinkari J (1990) Einführung. In: Laurinkari J (ed) Genossenschaftswesen: Hand- und Lehrbuch. Oldenbourg, München, pp 1–10
Leidwein A (2007) Die Internationalisierung des Agrarrechts. In: Österreichische Gesellschaft für Agrar- und Umweltrecht (ed) Agrarrecht im Lichte des öffentlichen Rechts: Festschrift für Univ.-Prof. Dr. Gottfried Holzer zum 60. Geburtstag. NWV, Wien, pp 33–48
Leyens PC (2007) Corporate Governance: Grundsatzfragen und Forschungsperspektiven. JuristenZeitung 62:1061–1072. https://doi.org/10.1628/002268807782717113
Lutter M, Schmidt J, Bayer W (2012) Europäisches Unternehmens- und Kapitalmarktrecht: Grundlagen, Stand und Entwicklung nebst Texten und Materialien, 5th edn. Zeitschrift für Unternehmens- und Gesellschaftsrecht. Sonderheft, T. 1. De Gruyter, Berlin
Macaulay S (1963) Non-contractual relations in business: a preliminary study. Am Sociol Rev:1–23
Magno P (2006) Sul diritto agrario "modernizzato". Rivista di diritto agrario:76–115
Manes P (1999) Il superamento della personalità giuridica: L'esperienza inglese. Le monografie di Contratto e impresa.Serie di diritto comparato, vol 1. Cedam, Padova
Manne HG (1965) Mergers and the market for corporate control. J Polit Econ 73:110–120. https://doi.org/10.1086/259000
Marchetti C (2000) La "nexus of contracts" theory: Teorie e visioni del diritto societario. Studi di diritto privato, vol 88. Giuffrè, Milano
Marchetti C (2014) Il silenzio del contratto: Gli implied terms nel diritto inglese. Giappichelli, Torino
Marcin I, Nicklisch A (2017) Testing the endowment effect for default rules. Discussion Paper Series of the Max Planck Institute for Research on Collective Goods 1:1–39
Martínez J (ed) (2018) Reichweite und Grenzen des Agrarrechts: Gedächtnisschrift für Dr. Wolfgang Winkler, 1st edn. Schriften zum Agrar-, Umwelt- und Verbraucherschutzrecht, v.77. Nomos Verlagsgesellschaft, Baden-Baden
Mathis K (2019) Effizienz statt Gerechtigkeit?: Auf der Suche nach den philosophischen Grundlagen der Ökonomischen Analyse des Rechts, 4th edn. Schriften zur Rechtstheorie, Band 223. Duncker et Humblot GmbH, Berlin
Mattei U (1997) Comparative law and economics. University of Michigan Press, Ann Arbor
Mattei U (1999) Comparative law and economics. In: Bouckaert B, Geest GD (eds) Encyclopedia of law and economics. Edward Elgar, Cheltenham, pp 505–537

Mattei U (2001) The comparative jurisprudence of Schlesinger and Sacco: a study in legal influence. In: Riles A (ed) Rethinking the masters of comparative law. Hart Pub, Oxford, pp 240–256

Mattei U, Monti A (2001) Comparative law and economics: borrowing and resistance. Global Jurist Front 1:1535–1653. https://doi.org/10.2202/1535-1653.1038

McCahery JA, Vermeulen EPM (2008) Corporate governance of non-listed companies. Oxford University Press, Oxford

Miceli TJ (2004) The economic approach to law. Stanford University Press, Stanford

Michaels R (2019) The functional method of comparative law. In: Reimann M, Zimmermann R (eds) The Oxford handbook of comparative law, 2nd edn. Oxford University Press, Oxford, pp 345–389

Milgrom PR, Roberts J (2005) Economia, organizzazione e management I. Il Mulino, Bologna

Minguez-Vera A, Martín-Ugedo JF, Arcas-Lario N (2010) Agency and property rights theories in agricultural cooperatives: evidence from Spain. Span J Agric Res 8:908–924. https://doi.org/10.5424/sjar/2010084-1384

Miribung G (2019) La disciplina dei masi chiusi: analisi delle modifiche apportate all'istituto dalla novella del 2018. Approfondimento del 26 aprile 2019. Giustiziacivile.com:1–13

Miribung G, Reiner E (2013) Austria. In: Cracogna D, Fici A, Henrÿ H (eds) International handbook of cooperative law. Springer, Berlin, Heidelberg, pp 231–250

Moccia L (2005) Comparazione giuridica e diritto europeo. Giuffrè, Milano

Molk P (2014) The puzzling lack of cooperatives. Tulane Law Rev:889–958

Monateri PG (ed) (2012) Methods of comparative law. Research handbooks in comparative law series. Edward Elgar, Cheltenham

Müller C, Tietzel M (1999) Property rights and their partitioning. In: Backhaus JG (ed) The Elgar companion to law and economics. Elgar, Cheltenham, pp 40–52

Münkner H-H (2006) Europäische Genossenschaft (SCE) und Europäische Genossenschaftstradition. Vorträge und Aufsätze des Forschungsvereins für Genossenschaftswesen, vol 30. Eigenverlag des FOG, Wien

Myers SC (1977) Determinants of corporate borrowing. J Financ Econ 5:147–175. https://doi.org/10.1016/0304-405X(77)90015-0

Nicklisch A, Petersen N (2012) Vertragstheorie. In: Towfigh EV, Petersen N (eds) Ökonomische Methoden im Recht: Eine Einführung für Juristen. Mohr Siebeck, Tübingen, pp 117–133

Nilsson J (1999) Co-operative organisational models as reflections of the business environments. Liiketaloudellinen aikakauskirja LTA - Finn J Bus Econ:449–470

Nilsson J (2001) Organisational principles for co-operative firms. Scand J Manage 17:329–356. https://doi.org/10.1016/S0956-5221(01)00010-0

Norer R (2005) Lebendiges Agrarrecht: Entwicklungslinien und Perspektiven des Rechts im ländlichen Raum. Springer, Wien

Norer R (2009) Agrarrecht und Recht des ländlichen Raumes: Orchideenfach oder Zukunftstrend? Zeitschrift für schweizerisches Recht:235–251

Norer R (2012) Agrarrecht: Eine Einführung. In: Norer R (ed) Handbuch des Agrarrechts, 2. Aufl. Verlag Österreich, Wien, pp 3–20

Norer R (2017) Agarrechtliche Sonderrechtstheorie, funktionale Theorie und das Recht des ländlichen Raumes. In: Norer R, Holzer G (eds) Agrarrecht: Jahrbuch 2017. Perspektiven des Agrarrechts. Festgabe für Manfried Welan, 1st edn. NWV Verlag, Wien, pp 169–184

Norer R (2018) Agrarrechtliche Sonderrechtstheorie, funktionale Theorie und das Recht des ländlichen Raums. In: Martínez J (ed) Reichweite und Grenzen des Agrarrechts: Gedächtnisschrift für Dr. Wolfgang Winkler, 1st edn. Nomos Verlagsgesellschaft, Baden-Baden, pp 111–132

Nuhanovic-Ribic S, Tortia EC, Valentinov V (2017) Agricultural co-operatives: struggle for identity. In: Michie J, Blasi JR, Borzaga C (eds) The Oxford handbook of mutual, co-operative, and co-owned business, 1st edn. Oxford University Press, Oxford, pp 158–170

Ortmann GF, King RP (2007) Agricultural cooperatives I: history, theory and problems. Agrekon 46:40–68. https://doi.org/10.1080/03031853.2007.9523760
Pardolesi P (2015) Profili comparatistici di analisi economica del diritto privato. Collana del Dipartimento jonico in sistemi giuridici ed economici del Mediterraneo, vol 13. Cacucci, Bari
Pargendler M (2012) The rise and decline of legal families. Am J Comp Law 60:1043–1074
Parisi F (1999) Coase theorem and transaction cost economics in the law. In: Backhaus JG (ed) The Elgar companion to law and economics. Elgar, Cheltenham, pp 7–39
Pernthaler P (2007) Land- und Forstwirtschaft als Verfassungsbegriff. In: Österreichische Gesellschaft für Agrar- und Umweltrecht (ed) Agrarrecht im Lichte des öffentlichen Rechts: Festschrift für Univ.-Prof. Dr. Gottfried Holzer zum 60. Geburtstag. NWV, Wien, pp 15–32
Piacentini V (2014) Codice civile italiano tradotto in inglese: Parte societaria (Artt. 2325-2510: società per azioni, società a responsabilità limitata, liquidazione, trasformazione, fusione, scissione), 3rd edn. IPSOA, Milano
Picot A (1989) Zur Bedeutung allgemeiner Theorieansätze für die betriebswirtschaftliehe Information und Kommunikation: Der Beitrag der Transaktionskosten-und Principal-Agent-Theorie. In: Kirsch W, Picot A (eds) Die Betriebswirtschaftslehre im Spannungsfeld zwischen Generalisierung und Spezialisierung. Gabler Verlag, Wiesbaden, pp 361–381
Picot A, Dietl H (1993) Neue Institutionenökonomie und Recht. In: Ott C, Schäfer H-B (eds) Ökonomische Analyse des Unternehmensrechts: Beiträge zum 3. Travemünder Symposium zur Ökonomischen Analyse des Rechts. Physica., Heidelberg, pp 306–330
Polinsky AM, Shavell S (eds) (2007) Handbook of law and economics: volume 2, 1st edn. Handbooks in economics, vol 27. North Holland, Amsterdam
Polo M (1994) Teoria dei contratti. In: Zamagni S (ed) Economia politica I, 1. ed. italiana. UTET, Torino, pp 133–141
Pönkä V (2018) The legal nature of cooperative membership. JEOD 7:39–61. https://doi.org/10.5947/jeod.2018.009
Posner EA (1996) Law, economics, and inefficient norms. Univ Pa Law Rev 144:1697–1744. https://doi.org/10.2307/3312637
Posner RA, Becker G (2014) The future of law and economics. Rev Law Econ 10:235–240. https://doi.org/10.1515/rle-2014-0056
Pozzo B, Timoteo M (2008) Europa e linguaggi giuridici. Le lingue del diritto, vol 3. Giuffrè, Milano
Raiser T (2011) Beiträge zur Rechtssoziologie. Nomos, Baden-Baden
Raiser T (2013) Grundlagen der Rechtssoziologie, 6th edn. utb-studi-e-book, vol 2904. Mohr Siebeck, Tübingen
Ribstein LE (1995) Statutory forms for closely held firms: theories and evidence from LLCs. Wash Univ Law Q:369–432
Ribstein LE, Kobayashi BH (1999) Choice of form and network externalities. William Mary Law Rev:79–140. https://doi.org/10.2139/ssrn.163832
Richter R (2015a) Essays on new institutional economics. Springer, Cham
Richter R (2015b) The new institutional economics: its start, its meaning, its prospects. In: Richter R (ed) Essays on new institutional economics. Springer International Publishing, Cham, pp 1–35
Richter R (2015c) The role of law in the new institutional economics in comparison with the economic analysis of law. In: Richter R (ed) Essays on new institutional economics. Springer International Publishing, Cham, pp 77–96
Richter R, Furubotn EG, Streissler M (2003) Neue Institutionenökonomik: Eine Einführung und kritische Würdigung, 3rd edn. Neue ökonomische Grundrisse. Mohr Siebeck, Tübingen
Ringe G (2015a) Art. 7. In: Lutter M, Hommelhoff P, Teichmann C (eds) SE-Kommentar, 2nd edn. Verlag Dr. Otto Schmidt, Köln, pp 135–144
Ringe G (2015b) Art. 8. In: Lutter M, Hommelhoff P, Teichmann C (eds) SE-Kommentar, 2nd edn. Verlag Dr. Otto Schmidt, Köln, pp 145–172

Ringle G (2007) Genossenschaftliche Prinzipien im Spannungsfeld zwischen Tradition und Modernität. Wismarer Diskussionspapiere. Hochsch. Fachbereich Wirtschaft, Wismar
Rook Basile E (1995) Introduzione al diritto agrario. Trittico giuridico. Sezione introduzioni / Collana coordinata da U. De Siervo, G. Iudica, F. Palazzo. Giappichelli, Torino
Rose-Ackerman S (1997) L'inalienabilità e la teoria dei diritti di proprietà. In: Fabbri D, Fiorentini G, Franzoni LA (eds) L'analisi economica del diritto: Un'introduzione. La Nuova Italia Scientifica, Roma, pp 51–74
Ross SA (1973) The economic theory of agency: the principal's problem. Am Econ Rev 63:134–139
Royer J (1999) Cooperative organizational strategies: a neo-institutional digest. J Coop:44–67
Sacco R (1991) Legal formants: a dynamic approach to comparative law (Installment I of II). Am J Comp Law 39:1–34. https://doi.org/10.2307/840669
Sacco R (1992) Che cos'è il diritto comparato. Lo Studio del Diritto, vol 2. Giuffrè, Milano
Sacco R (1994) Introduzione al diritto comparato, 5th edn. Trattato di diritto comparato. UTET, Torino
Sacconi L, Ottone S (eds) (2015) Beni comuni e cooperazione. Studi e ricerche. Il Mulino, Bologna
Salaris F (2002) Autonomia e globalità dell'azienda agraria. Rivista di diritto agrario:54–75
Scarpa C (1994) Costi di transazione. In: Zamagni S (ed) Economia politica I, 1. ed. italiana. UTET, Torino, pp 147–148
Schäfer H-B, Ott C (2012a) Grundstrukturen und -probleme des Unternehmensrechts. In: Schäfer H-B, Ott C (eds) Lehrbuch der ökonomischen Analyse des Zivilrechts. Springer, Berlin, pp 697–729
Schäfer H-B, Ott C (2012b) Homo Oeconomics, Behavioral Economics und Paternalismus. In: Schäfer H-B, Ott C (eds) Lehrbuch der ökonomischen Analyse des Zivilrechts. Springer, Berlin, pp 95–141
Schäfer H-B, Ott C (eds) (2012c) Lehrbuch der ökonomischen Analyse des Zivilrechts, 5. Aufl. 2012. Springer-Lehrbuch. Springer, Berlin, Heidelberg
Schäfer H-B, Ott C (2012d) Vom Vertrag zur Hierarchie. In: Schäfer H-B, Ott C (eds) Lehrbuch der ökonomischen Analyse des Zivilrechts. Springer, Berlin, pp 687–696
Schaschko M (2010) Neugründungen von Genossenschaften in Österreich. Wiener Studien des Forschungsvereins für Genossenschaftswesen, vol 18. Eigenverlag des FOG, Wien
Schlesinger RB, Mattei U, Ruskola T, Gidi A (2009) Schlesinger's comparative law: cases, text, materials, 7th edn. University casebook series. Foundation Press, New York
Schmidtchen D (1998) Funktionen und Schutz von "property rights": Eine ökonomische Analyse. https://www.econstor.eu/bitstream/10419/23100/1/9804prop.pdf. Accessed 21 Nov 2019
Schneiberg M (2002) 2. Organizational heterogeneity and the production of new forms: politics, social movements and mutual companies in American fire insurance, 1900–1930. In: Lounsbury M, Ventresca MJ (eds) Social structure and organizations revisited, vol 19. Emerald, Bingley, pp 39–89
Schöpflin M (2018a) Art. 01. In: Beuthien V, Schöpflin M (eds) Genossenschaftsgesetz: Mit Umwandlungs- und Kartellrecht sowie Statut der Europäischen Genossenschaft, 16th edn. Beck, München, pp 1240–1243
Schöpflin M (2018b) Art. 06. In: Beuthien V, Schöpflin M (eds) Genossenschaftsgesetz: Mit Umwandlungs- und Kartellrecht sowie Statut der Europäischen Genossenschaft, 16th edn. Beck, München, p 1255
Schöpflin M (2018c) Art. 07. In: Beuthien V, Schöpflin M (eds) Genossenschaftsgesetz: Mit Umwandlungs- und Kartellrecht sowie Statut der Europäischen Genossenschaft, 16th edn. Beck, München, pp 1256–1259
Schulze R (2004) Einführung: Die Verordnung über das Statut der Europäischen Genossenschaft. In: Schulze R (ed) Europäische Genossenschaft SCE: Handbuch, 1st edn. Nomos, Baden-Baden, pp 1–18

Schwartz A (1997) Le teorie giuridiche dei contratti e i contratti incompleti. In: Fabbri D, Fiorentini G, Franzoni LA (eds) L'analisi economica del diritto: Un'introduzione. La Nuova Italia Scientifica, Roma, pp 97–126

Schwenzer I (2019) Development of comparative law in Germany, Switzerland and Austria. In: Reimann M, Zimmermann R (eds) The Oxford handbook of comparative law, 2nd edn. Oxford University Press, Oxford, pp 54–86

Scott RE (1987) Conflict and cooperation in long-term contracts. Calif Law Rev:2005–2054. https://doi.org/10.15779/Z38TF07

Siems M (2014) Comparative law. Law in context. Cambridge University Press, Cambridge

Snaith I (2004) Das anwendbare Recht. In: Schulze R (ed) Europäische Genossenschaft SCE: Handbuch, 1st edn. Nomos, Baden-Baden, pp 19–42

Spence AM (1981) Market signaling: informational transfer in hiring and related screening processes, 2nd edn. Harvard economic studies, vol 143. Harvard University Press, Cambridge

Staroßom H (2013) Informationsasymmetrie in der Finanzierung: Das Principal Agent-Problem. In: Staroßom H (ed) Corporate Finance Teil 1. Springer Fachmedien Wiesbaden, Wiesbaden, pp 97–114

Steinberg R (2010) Principal-agent theory and nonprofit accountability. In: Hopt KJ, Hippel TV (eds) Comparative corporate governance of non-profit organizations. Cambridge University Press, Cambridge, pp 73–126

Stiglitz JE (1975) The theory of "screening," education, and the distribution of income. Am Econ Rev 65:283–300

Stiglitz JE (1989) Principal and agent. In: Eatwell J, Milgate M, Newman P (eds) Allocation, information and markets. Palgrave Macmillan UK, London, pp 241–253

Stout LA (2007) The mythical benefits of shareholder control. Va Law Rev:789–809

Study Group on European Cooperative Law (2012) New study group on European Cooperative Law: "principles" project. https://www.euricse.eu/publications/wp-02412-new-study-group-on-european-cooperative-law-principles-project/. Accessed 21 Nov 2019

Sykuta ME, Chaddad F (1999) Putting theories of the firm in their place: a supplemental digest of the new institutional economics. J Coop:68–75

Thaler R (1980) Toward a positive theory of consumer choice. J Econ Behav Organ 1:39–60. https://doi.org/10.1016/0167-2681(80)90051-7

Thomas A (2004) The rise of social cooperatives in Italy. VOLUNTAS: Int J Volunt Nonprofit Org 15:243–263. https://doi.org/10.1023/B:VOLU.0000046280.06580.d8

Thomsen S (2014) Comparative corporate governance of non-profit organizations. Eur Comp Financ Law Rev 11:15–30. https://doi.org/10.1515/ecfr-2014-0015

Tietzel M (1981) Die Ökonomie der property rights: Ein Überblick. Zeitschrift für Wirtschaftspolitik 30

Tirole J (2006) The theory of corporate finance. Princeton University Press, Princeton

Tomanek P (2014) Vor § 1 GenG. In: Dellinger M (ed) Genossenschaftsgesetz samt Nebengesetzen: Kommentar, 2nd edn. LexisNexis ARD Orac, Wien, pp 1–16

Towfigh EV (2012) Das ökonomische Paradigma. In: Towfigh EV, Petersen N (eds) Ökonomische Methoden im Recht: Eine Einführung für Juristen. Mohr Siebeck, Tübingen, pp 23–35

Trebilcock MJ (1997) The limits of freedom of contract, 2nd edn. Harvard University Press, Cambridge

Trechter DD, King RP, Cobia DW, Hartell JG (1997) Case studies of executive compensation in agricultural cooperatives. Rev Agric Econ 19:492–503. https://doi.org/10.2307/1349756

Tushnet M, Cane P (eds) (2012) The Oxford handbook of legal studies. Oxford University Press, Oxford

Urbani A (2008) La problematica della sede sociale e della sede effettiva. In: Capriglione F (ed) La nuova disciplina della società europea. Cedam, Padova, pp 321–342

van Aaken A (2001) Vom Nutzen der ökonomischen Theorie des Rechts für die Rechtsvergleichung. In: Jud B (ed) Prinzipien des Privatrechts und Rechtsvereinheitlichung:

Wiener Tagung, 13. - 16. September 2000. 11. Tagung der Gesellschaft Junger Zivilrechtswissenschaftler e.V. Boorberg, Stuttgart, pp 127–149
van Bekkum O-F, van Dijk G (eds) (1997) Agricultural co-operatives in the European Union: trends and issues on the eve of the 21st century. Onno-Frank van Bekkum, Gert van Dijk (eds); authors: Onno-Frank van Bekkum ... [et al.]. Van Gorcum, Assen, The Netherlands
Van der Sangen G (2012) EU synthesis and comparative analysis report: legal aspects. In: Support for farmers' cooperatives, Wageningen, pp 1–50
Vecchione A (2004) L'imprenditore agricolo. Quaderni del Dipartimento di studi internazionali, Università degli studi di Salerno, Facoltà di giurisprudenza, vol 4. Edizioni scientifiche italiane, Napoli
Welan M (2017) Die Lehre des Rechts an der Universität für Bodenkultur. In: Norer R, Holzer G (eds) Agrarrecht: Jahrbuch 2017. Perspektiven des Agrarrechts. Festgabe für Manfried Welan, 1st edn. NWV Verlag, Wien, pp 105–130
Williamson OE (1998) The economic institutions of capitalism: firms, markets, relational contracting. Free Press, New York
Winkler W (2018a) Agrarrecht - Umweltrecht: Gegensatz oder Ergänzung. In: Martínez J (ed) Reichweite und Grenzen des Agrarrechts: Gedächtnisschrift für Dr. Wolfgang Winkler, 1st edn. Nomos Verlagsgesellschaft, Baden-Baden, pp 211–248
Winkler W (2018b) Agrarrecht, agrarietà und Natur der Sache. In: Martínez J (ed) Reichweite und Grenzen des Agrarrechts: Gedächtnisschrift für Dr. Wolfgang Winkler, 1st edn. Nomos Verlagsgesellschaft, Baden-Baden, pp 159–210
Ziliotti M (1994) Cooperativa, impresa. In: Zamagni S (ed) Economia politica I, 1. ed. italiana. UTET, Torino, pp 144–145
Zimmermann R (2019) Comparative law and the Europeanization of private law. In: Reimann M, Zimmermann R (eds) The Oxford handbook of comparative law, 2nd edn. Oxford University Press, Oxford, pp 557–598
Zoppini A (2004) Il nuovo diritto delle società cooperative: un'analisi economica. Rivista di Diritto Civile:439–450
Zweigert K, Kötz H (1996) Einführung in die Rechtsvergleichung auf dem Gebiete des Privatrechtss, 3rd edn. Mohr, Tübingen
Zweigert K, Kötz H, Di Majo A, Gambaro A, Pozzo B (1998) Introduzione al diritto comparato, Rist. integrata con addenda. Giuffrè, Milano

Part I
The European Cooperative Society (SCE) and Agricultural Cooperatives

Chapter 2
Introducing the SCE

2.1 Cooperation and Cooperatives: From the Equitable Pioneers of Rochdale to the International Cooperative Alliance

Since the SCE is a cooperative with cross-border activities, it is advisable to start examining its discipline by dealing with the cooperative in general. Cooperatives exist in a variety of economic sectors—such as housing, banking, agriculture and other industries—and contribute to meeting the diverse needs of citizens in a changing society. Cooperative members are both shareholders and, simultaneously, employees (workers' cooperatives), producers (producers' cooperatives or resellers' cooperatives) or customers of a cooperative (consumer cooperatives or credit cooperatives).[1]

Cooperatives are, of course, not only a legal phenomenon, but also a social phenomenon that has emerged to meet specific needs.[2] The modern cooperative movement has roots in the eighteenth century, partly because it was generally recognised that organised cooperation could change society and combat inequality and discrimination. Many cooperatives were formed in response to the difficult economic situation at the time and to the complex social problems that influenced the lives of individuals.[3]

[1] See Birchall (2011), p. 4, Paolucci (2012), p. 11, Michie et al. (2017), p. XXIII, Fici (2014), p. 151, Laurinkari (1990), p. 5.

[2] On this issue, see Vella (2010), p. 123 et se. See also Schaschko (2010), p. 79 et seq. Bonfante (2014), p. 33 et seq. In general, Ruggeri (1994).

[3] At that time, many citizens had no voice, either from democratically appointed representation or from a state that protected the common interest. For details, see Bonfante (2014), p. 3 et seq., Brendel (2011), p. 15 et seq., Zamagni (2017), p. 99 et seq., Ianes (2013), p. 17 et seq. See also Morales Gutierrez (2004). In general, Cole (1944), Rabbeno (1915), Shaffer (1999), Fabbri (2011).

G. Miribung, *The Agricultural Cooperative in the Framework of the European Cooperative Society*, Economic Analysis of Law in European Legal Scholarship 8,
https://doi.org/10.1007/978-3-030-44154-8_2

As early as 1750, cheese producers in France worked to set up a producers' cooperative.[4] Similar efforts have been made to establish consumer cooperatives in the United Kingdom. The equitable pioneers of Rochdale (near Manchester) responded to the mentioned economic problems by setting up their own organisation (1844). In a period when the mechanisation of the Industrial Revolution forced more and more skilled workers into poverty, a group of weavers decided to join forces to open their own shop selling food they could not otherwise afford.[5] This initiative is considered to be the first formally modern cooperative, whose influence is still visible today.[6] There were similar initiatives in other countries, e.g., Denmark, where first agricultural cooperatives were founded.[7]

In the territory of present-day Italy,[8] the first cooperatives were formed a decade after those in England and developed mainly (although not exclusively) in the North, where various workers and mutuals associations were active. After the *Albertino* Statute was enacted, the Turin Workers Association opened the Pension Warehouse (1854) to stop the effects of a severe agricultural famine and the resulting rise in prices. Two years later, the first Italian cooperative for production and work, the *Società artistico vetraria di Altare*, was founded, and the number of cooperatives grew in the following years.[9] Then, in 1893, the National Federation of Cooperatives and Mutual was founded.[10]

---

[4]See Vella (2010), p. 44 et seq., See also Birchall (2011), p. 156, Ajates Gonzalez (2018), p. 17 and Zamagni (2017), p. 97 et seq. Other forms of cooperation in agricultural trade followed.

[5]See Vella (2010), p. 34 et seq., Buonocore (1997), p. 27 et seq. See also Fici (2014), p. 150 et seq., Bonfante (2014), p. 14 et seq., Engelhardt (1990), p. 15 et seq., Ianes (2013), p. 18.

[6]See Vella (2010), p. 37 et seq., and 65 et seq. See also Bonfante (2014), p. 14 et seq., Henrÿ (2017). After the great economic depression of the nineteenth century, European countries increasingly regulated the agricultural sector in order to increase yields and introduce new technical innovations. Their initiatives influenced the various ways in which agricultural cooperatives were developed. In some states, cooperatives were imposed by the state authorities and therefore cannot be regarded as self-help organisations. Accordingly, the term cooperative was and is associated with different experiences. See Vella (2010), p. 32 et seq. See also Bonfante (2014), p. 9 et seq., Engelhardt (1990) and Zamagni (2017), p. 99 et seq.

[7]See Vella (2010), p. 54. On this issue, see also Shaffer (1999).

[8]For details, see Fabbri (1979, 2011), Fornasari and Zamagni (1997), Zamagni and Felice (2006).

[9]See Vella (2010), p. 47 et seq., Ianes (2013), p. 22 et seq. Already at that time, cooperatives widely were supported and enriched the political and trade union movement for the emancipation of workers. Cooperation was (and is) viewed as an instrument of non-conflictual inclusion of the subordinate classes in economic development and is, therefore, useful to the entire social organisation. Other interesting initiatives were born in Florence thanks to the activities of some nobles and bourgeois enlightened in 1863 with the Società Cooperativa di Consumo per il Popolo and again, 2 years later, in Como, in which the first Italian cooperative was born with a statute modelled on the principles of Rochdale and drawn up by Francesco Viganò, who travelled around Europe and learned about efforts that already had begun in other countries. See Vella (2010), p. 47 et seq., Ianes (2013), p. 22 et seq.

[10]See Bonfante (2014), p. 8 et seq., Ianes (2013), p. 37 et seq. The league's importance and purpose are evident in that through it, various registered companies had to make their voices heard, laying out their reasoning and common interests on a national level, even if the conservative governments

In addition to the secular-liberal orientation of the early cooperatives,[11] two other forces influenced the cooperative system and caused division within the cooperative movement: the Catholic Church, which concentrated on rural credit and consumer cooperation, and the Socialist movement, which regulated several areas, particularly consumption. The collective involvement of church and government laid the foundation for the division of the Italian sector into red cooperatives (socialist movement) and white cooperatives (Catholic movement).[12]

Well-known representatives of the Italian cooperative movement are Don Lorenzo Guetti, Leone Wollemberg, Don Luigi Cerrutti and, perhaps the most famous, Luigi Luzzati.[13]

The Austrian cooperative movement also has its origins in the nineteenth century. One of the first establishments took place in 1851, the so-called '*Aushilfskasse*' (that is, the first type of cooperative bank); at the same time, the first consumer cooperatives were founded. The first building cooperative dates from 1869.[14]

After the monarchy ended and the First Austrian Republic was established, there was an immediate sharp decline in the cooperative sector. This decline was a consequence of the weak confidence in the economy and the political stability of the now-small state of Austria, which large parts of the business community had not expected to survive. The development of consumer cooperatives, which were in close contact with the Socialist Party and the trade unions, was of great importance for the economy in general and for the development of the cooperative sector.[15] As happened in Italy, the cooperative movement divided into political parties, though in Austria, this division was never as pronounced as it was in Italy.[16]

Important representatives of the Austrian cooperative movement are *Engelbert Kessler*, *Karl Pickert* and *Hermann Ziller*, who were influenced by *F. W. Raiffeisen* and *H. Schulze-Delitzsch*, both known in the German-speaking world and beyond as the two founding fathers of rural, craftsmen and commercial cooperatives.[17]

In 1847, *Raiffeisen* founded the first charitable aid association in Weyerbusch to support the needy rural population. He founded the '*Heddesdorfer Wohlthätigkeitsverein*' in 1852, from which the '*Heddesdorfer*

---

of the late nineteenth century were suspicious of any experience that involved an expansion of democracy.

[11]See Ianes (2013), p. 35 et seq.

[12]See Vella (2010), p. 50, Ianes (2013), p. 37 et seq. See also Morales Gutierrez (2004), p. 50 et seq., Bonfante (2014), p. 40 et seq.

[13]See Vella (2010), p. 50 et seq. and 131 et seq., Ianes (2013), p. 23 et seq. See also Bonfante (2014), p. 8 et seq.

[14]See Tomanek (2014), p. 2 et seq., Miribung and Reiner (2013), p. 213 et seq., Vella (2010), p. 43 et seq.

[15]The first president of the federation was Karl Renner, a socialist who became the first president of the Second Republic of Austria after the Second World War.

[16]See Tomanek (2014), p. 5 et seq., Miribung and Reiner (2013), p. 232.

[17]See Jagschitz Jagschitz et al. (2015), p. 58 et seq.; see also Zamagni (2017), p. 102, Tomanek (2014), p. 3 et seq., Miribung and Reiner (2013), p. 231 et seq., Vella (2010), p. 43 et seq.

Darlehnskassenverein' emerged in 1864. In 1862, a loan fund was established in Anhausen in the Westerwald,[18] which is regarded as the first Raiffeisen cooperative. Raiffeisen followed his loan fund with a central cash office and an association representing cooperatives' specific interests.[19] This system was then successfully adopted in other countries.

At the same time, *Schulze-Delitzsch*, a liberal politician and economist, launched a relief campaign in Delitzsch that benefited the craftsmen in need. Following the principles of self-help, self-administration and self-responsibility, he founded the '*Rohstoffassoziation*' for carpenters and shoemakers in 1847 and the non-profit '*Vorschussverein*' in 1850.[20]

After the First World War, the cooperatives gained importance as they helped rebuild economically destroyed countries.[21] During the fascist period in both Italy and Austria (as well as many other European countries), state-controlled public administration was accompanied by massive restructuring of the state and the economy, which inevitably extended to the cooperative sector, subjecting it to state control.[22] All these structural changes were subsequently reversed after the end of the war.[23]

After the critical period between the two wars, the cooperative movement regained strength and began to grow again. In Italy during the first post-war period, revolutionary attitudes prevailed among the Socialists and Catholics, prompting a drastic separation between Catholic-inspired cooperatives and the League. The Catholics left the League and joined the Italian Cooperative Federation *confcooperative*. Today, the cooperative movement is organized in several federations, some of which distinguish between red and white cooperatives and thus identify their political affiliation.[24]

[18]Anhausen belonged to the joint municipality Heddesdorf, whose mayor was Raiffeisen.

[19]See Brendel (2011), p. 17 et seq., Tomanek (2014), p. 4, Vella (2010), p. 39 et seq., Engelhardt (1990), p. 20 et seq.

[20]See Brendel (2011), p. 17 et seq., Tomanek (2014), p. 3, Vella (2010), p. 39 et seq., Engelhardt (1990), p. 19 et seq. Today, the business area of the three oldest Saxon credit cooperatives belongs to the Volksbank Delitzsch eG.

[21]See Tomanek (2014), p. 5 et seq., Vella (2010), p. 52.

[22]Basically, the fascist regime, in implementing its plan to cancel all other political parties, tried to integrate the reality of cooperation within the system that it created: Controls were activated, and all attempts that seemed to be aimed at operating in a full democracy were discouraged. Fascism imposed adhesion by all cooperatives to the National Cooperative Body, thereby encumbering the companies' social and democratic life and stifling the freedom of economic initiative. See Vella (2010), p. 52 et seq., Brendel (2011), p. 27 et seq., Tomanek (2014), p. 6 et seq. Bonfante (2014), p. 45 et seq., Ianes (2013), p. 48 et seq. and 54 et seq. See also Morales Gutierrez (2004), p. 51 et seq.

[23]See Tomanek (2014), p. 7 et seq., Bonfante (2014), p. 49 et seq., Vella (2010), p. 53, Ianes (2013), p. 61 et seq.

[24]See Ianes (2013), p. 145 et seq. Among the largest are legacoop and confcooperative. As a whole, they represent an important reality for the Italian economy: The cooperative model is effective for both large companies (distribution, construction, insurance/finance and agri-food) and small

Despite this separation, the various cooperative federations have recognised the special value of cooperatives. This common understanding and appreciation is best reflected in the Republican Constitution, Article 45, which recognizes the social value of cooperation and the duty of the State to promote and encourage its growth and to ensure that its character and purpose are safeguarded. This is the cornerstone of Italian cooperative law.[25]

Various legal acts have been created for the implementation of this rule. A number of important legal sources can be noted in addition to the provisions of the Italian Civil Code,[26] such as legislative decree no. 1577 from 14 December 1947,[27] law no. 59 from 31 December 1992, and legislative decree no. 220 from 2 August 2002.[28]

In Austria, significant developments also occurred after World War II. During the Second Republic, the cooperative sector played an important role in the extensive reconstruction efforts; the agricultural cooperatives, mostly the Raiffeisenverband, contributed to this work. This development laid the foundation for the great importance that Raiffeisen still has today in the both the Austrian cooperative system and the entire Austrian economy.[29]

In the 1970s, economic restructuring took place in most cooperative sectors; most of them remained significant—with one important exception: the largest consumer cooperative, '*Konsum*', which was majority owned by the Austrian Federation of Trade Unions, was forced to file for bankruptcy in 1995. This failure not only was a severe blow to the confederation but also had consequences on the law on cooperative auditing.[30]

businesses (fishing, agriculture, tourism, publishing, entertainment, and social and health services). For details, see Vella (2010), p. 97 et seq., Ianes (2013), p. 113 et seq.

[25]See Bonfante (2014), p. 50 et seq., Ianes (2013), p. 64, Buonocore (1997), p. 47 et seq.; on this issue, see also Miribung (2014), Paolucci (2019) and Piras (2017), p. 109.

[26]See Art. 2511 et seq. CC.

[27]So-called lex Basevi. See also, among many, Bonfante (2014), p. 53 et seq. and Buonocore (1997), p. 48 et seq.

[28]Moreover, depending on the type of cooperative, special rules have to be observed. Art. 2520 para. 1 CC refers to the relationship between the general and special provisions, stating: 'cooperatives regulated by a special law are subject to general rules only if compatible.' Various sets of provisions can be distinguished by either the type of good or service produced (e.g., cooperative banks as regulated by legislative decree no. 385 from 1 September 1993) or type of relationship between cooperatives and its members (e.g., worker cooperatives as regulated by law no. 142 from 3 April 2001).

[29]See Tomanek (2014), p. 7 et seq. Building and housing cooperatives gained in importance: they grew until 1955, when the reconstruction ended and a restructuring process reduced the number of such cooperatives. Nonetheless, the importance of the sector remained high. See Tomanek (2014), p. 7 et seq.

[30]The GenRevG (Genossenschaftsrevisionsgesetz—Cooperative Audit Act), which came into force in 1997, introduced new provisions on cooperative accountability and auditing. See Tomanek (2014), p. 8 et seq.

Austria now has three important cooperative associations: the '*Raiffeisenverband*', the '*Österreichischer Genossenschaftsverband*' (*OeGV*) and the '*Österreichischer Verband Gemeinnütiger Bauvereinigungen*' (*GBV*). Some of these associations—in particular, the *Raiffeisenverband*—have considerable political influence.

All these developments led to a collection of legal sources on different aspects of cooperatives. Initially, cooperatives were founded according to the 1852 law on associations (association *patent*), which was replaced by the *GenG* of 1873. This law was based on the cooperative law[31] written by *Hermann Schulze-Delitzsch* (1808–1883) and is still in force, with amendments. In addition, further laws may apply to different types of cooperative, including 'Bankwesengesetz' (*BWG*),[32] 'Wohnungsgemeinnützigkeitsgesetz' (*WGG*),[33] 'Genossenschaftsrevisionsgesetz' (*GenRevG*),[34] 'Genossenschaftsverschmelzungsgesetz' (*GenVG*),[35] 'Genossenschaftsinsolvenzgesetz' (*GenIG*)[36] and 'Genossenschaftsspaltungsgesetz' (*GenSpaltG*).[37]

In general, the various developments in Italy and Austria, in Europe and in the world, have lead to several approaches to defining and describing cooperatives, not only at the regional and international levels but also at the global level. Cooperatives are indeed a global phenomenon. Because of its social implications and therefore importance for society,[38] there have been several attempts to define a common or universal cooperative model.

On the global stage, the ICA, which was founded in 1895 to establish a common identity for cooperatives, played a significant role in this regard.[39] According to the alliance, a cooperative is 'an autonomous association of persons united voluntarily to meet their common economic, social and cultural needs and aspirations through a jointly owned and democratically controlled enterprise.'[40] In 1995, the ICA adopted

---

[31]Adopted in 1867. See Beuthien (2018), p. 3.

[32]The Austrian Federal law on banking.

[33]The Austrian Nonprofit Housing Act.

[34]The Austrian law on cooperative auditing.

[35]The law governing cooperative mergers.

[36]The law governing bankruptcy of cooperatives.

[37]The law governing demerger of cooperatives.

[38]On this issue, see Henrÿ (2017), Pestoff (2017). Also see Bonfante (2014), p. 35 et seq.

[39]See Fici (2013a), p. 4 and in general, among others, Birchall (1997). Also consider Bonfante (2014), p. 16 et seq., Hiez (2017), p. 9 et seq. In general, Ringle (2007).

The ICA describes itself as "an independent, non-governmental organisation established ... to unite, represent and serve co-operatives worldwide." The ICA "... provides a global voice and forum for knowledge, expertise and co-ordinated action for and about co-operatives." See International Co-operative Alliance, What is a co-operative?

[40]See International Co-operative Alliance, What is a co-operative? Co-operatives are businesses owned and run by and for their members. Whether the members are the customers, employees or residents, they have an equal say in what the business does and a share in the profits. See International Co-operative Alliance, What is a co-operative?

a statement on cooperative identity,[41] including specific principles,[42] which served as guidelines for putting the values of cooperatives into practice so that cooperatives can be distinguished from capitalist enterprises.[43]

The principles were developed in 1844 with the Rochdale Cooperative Model, adopted by the ICA in 1937, and remained unchanged until 1966.[44] Between 1980 and 1990, efforts were made to simplify the principles, as world markets were opening up, eventually leading to the establishment of the World Trade Organization (WTO).[45] The principles were amended again in 1995 and adapted to current circumstances.[46] Finally, these principles gained international status in 2002 when they were included in recommendation 193,[47] which was adopted by the International Labour Organisation (ILO).[48] Regional legislation has likewise acknowledged that these cooperative principles are universally accepted.[49]

The first principle is voluntary and open membership. Cooperatives are voluntary organisations. They are open to anyone who can use their services, provided that these persons accept the responsibilities of membership. Moreover, openness implies that there is no gender, social, racial, political and religious discrimination.

---

[41]This statement contains the aforementioned definition as well as cooperative values. Accordingly, co-operatives are based on the values of self-help, self-responsibility, democracy, equality, equity and solidarity. In the tradition of their founders, co-operative members believe in the ethical values of honesty, openness, social responsibility and caring for others. See International Co-operative Alliance, What is a co-operative?

[42]As businesses driven by values other than just profit, co-operatives share internationally agreed principles and act together to build a better world through co-operation. See International Co-operative Alliance, What is a co-operative? ica.coop/en/what-co-operative (22.03.2016). Also consider Henrÿ (2012), p. 55; Hoyt (1996). For details International Co-operative Alliance, Guidance Notes to the Co-operative Principles (2015). Also consider Chukwu (1990), p. 3 et seq. and 10 et seq. On these issues, see also Münkner (1995).

[43]The latest version was adopted in 1995. See International Co-operative Alliance, History of the cooperative movement. Also consider Fici (2013a), p. 21 et seq.

[44]The ICA's principles are based on those developed more than 160 years ago by the Rochdale pioneers. These Rochdale cooperatives' influence, in today's more globalised cooperative movement, remains. Thus, it is true that when discussing the International Cooperative Confederation's principles, one cannot ignore Rochdale's principles to understand the current principles' roots. The principles developed at that time were: (1) member voting on a democratic basis (i.e., one member, one vote); (2) membership is open; (3) equity is provided by patrons; (4) equity ownership as a share of individual patrons is limited; (5) net income is distributed to patrons as patronage refunds on a cost basis; (6) dividend on equity capital is limited; and (7) goods and services are exchanged at market prices. See Bonfante (2014), p. 14 et seq.

[45]It officially commenced on 1 January 1995. For details, see, i.e., Senti and Hilpold (2017).

[46]See Bonfante (2014), p. 16 et seq., Fici (2013a), p. 4 et seq. On this issue, see also Henrÿ (2017), and Münkner (1995).

[47]See International Labour Organisation, R193—Promotion of Cooperatives Recommendation, 2002.

[48]See International Co-operative Alliance, What is a co-operative? Also consider Hiez (2017), p. 9 et seq.; Henrÿ (2013b), p. 98. Henrÿ (2012), p. 47 et seq. and Henrÿ (2013a).

[49]See Art. 6 Droit des sociétés coopératives (Acte uniforme OHADA du 15 décembre 2010). Also consider Henrÿ (2012), p. 46 and Hiez and Tadjudje (2013).

Principle two requires that cooperatives be democratically controlled by their members. Thus, the members actively participate in the decision-making process by electing representatives who are accountable to the members. The principle of 'one member, one vote' is particularly important: accordingly, members have equal voting power irrespective of the amount of capital they have provided.[50]

The third principle concerns members' economic participation by requiring all members to contribute equitably to their cooperative's capital. At least part of this capital must be used as 'common property'. The surplus shall be placed in reserves and used to develop the cooperative, with members only receiving limited compensation from the subscribed capital. These reserves should be at least partly indivisible (i.e., they cannot be allocated to the members, even if the cooperative dissolves).[51] Members should benefit from the cooperative in proportion to the transactions that they conduct with it. In addition, the cooperative should support other activities.

The fourth principle protects autonomy and independence, affirming that a cooperative is an autonomous, self-help organisation controlled by its members. It can enter into agreements with other organisations or raise capital from external sources, on the condition that it does not compromise democratic control by its members.

Principle five governs education, training and information, which the cooperative provides for its members, representatives, managers and employees. Education helps develop the cooperative and provides information to the general public about the nature and benefits of cooperation.

The sixth principle advocates that there be cooperation among cooperatives, requiring that cooperatives should work together through local, regional, national and international structures to effectively serve their members. Cooperation strengthens the cooperative movement.

Finally, principle seven expresses concern for the community, encouraging cooperatives to work towards the sustainable development of their communities. Members are invited to develop and approve the necessary policies to achieve this goal.

All these principles distinguish cooperatives from capitalist companies, which are both organised under private law.

Cooperatives have influential advocates not only at the global level but also at the European level. In the latter sphere, the representative associations of cooperatives, whether in the agricultural or consumer sectors, have always promoted both the cooperative framework and the legal models of cooperatives. They influenced cooperation efforts between various committees, the negotiations over the CAP, and the adoption of the SCE-R. This subject is explained in more detail in Sect. 2.2.

[50]At least in primary cooperatives, whereas principle 2 requires that cooperatives at other levels shall also be organised in a democratic manner. Also consider in this context Sect. 4.4.4.

[51]See Sect. 5.5.

2.2 The Historical Development of the SCE-R

Since their first appearance in modern Europe, cooperatives, unlike other forms of companies, have always cooperated with each other on an international basis to foster and develop shared notions of cooperation. This not only led to the founding of the ICA in 1895,[52] but also the establishment of different European Associations that contributed to developing the Statute for a European Cooperative Society. These associations form the Federation of European Agricultural Cooperatives (CEA), the Federation of Agricultural Cooperatives (COGECA)[53] and Euro Coop,[54] which represents consumer cooperatives. That CEA and COGECA favoured the adoption of the SCE-R underscores the importance of cooperatives for the agricultural sector. Both federations formed special committees to address legal questions concerning cooperatives.[55] Since the establishment of the European (Economic) Community, a specific legal form for cooperatives (based on international or European law) was demanded. Flowing from the proposal for a Statute for a European company (SE),[56] these associations proposed the SCE to establish a new legal form for cross-border activity, rather than trying to harmonise existing national cooperative laws, which were considered too different.[57]

Then, in 1971, COGECA and Euro Coop presented two different proposals to the European Commission. However, instead of crafting its own draft, the Commission focused on its detailed proposal for a European company, provoking fear among the

---

[52]See Sect. 2.1.

[53]For details COPA-COGECA, History.

[54]For details European Community of Consumer Cooperatives, Who we are.

[55]See Schulze (2004), p. 11; See Hagen-Eck (1995), p. 29 et seq. Also consider Schöpflin (2018b), p. 1231.

The CEA was founded in 1948 to represent agricultural cooperatives. It established a working group on cooperative law, which since the 1960s has worked with the European Commission to develop a common cooperative law. COGECA was founded in 1959, after the establishment of the European Economic Community (EEC), by members from the founding members of the EEC and with the aim of representing agricultural cooperatives within the EEC and other institutions. The creation of these interest groups was particularly important for the European agricultural sector. At the time, agricultural products were under competitive pressure from overseas, but there was no unified reaction from the European Community. These different responses led to the disintegration of European agriculture economies, resulting in different costs and pricing levels. To counteract this development, cooperatives and the entire agricultural cooperative system began to foster reintegration within the agricultural sector. See Hagen-Eck (1995), p. 29 et seq. Also consider Fischer (1995), p. 40 et seq.

[56]Based on the observations and thoughts of Thibièrge and Sanders. See Schröder (2010c), p. 21. For details Fischer (1995), p. 23 et seq.; Arnò et al. (2007), p. 4 et seq. and Pellegrini (2008). Also consider Corapi and de Donno (2006), p. 1318 et seq. See also Corapi and Pernazza (2011).

[57]See Hagen-Eck (1995), p. 30 et seq.; Fischer (1995), p. 41. In general, Chirico and Troianiello (2007), p. 18. Also consider Münkner (2006), pp. 5 and 14.

various cooperative federations that, without a specific statute, cooperatives might have a significant competitive disadvantage compared to companies.[58]

In 1975, COGECA, Euro Coop and UGAL (*Union des Groupements d'Achat de l'Alimentation*)[59] submitted another proposal, which contained the standard features of a cooperative, including the promotion mandate, limited liability and the variability of members and capital. This proposal was the first step in deepening cooperation between cooperatives at the European level, allowing cooperatives to enhance cross-border business. One of the main goals of this first draft was to allow cooperatives from different member states to merge. However, this proposal was not adopted.[60]

Then, in the early 1980s, the European Parliament reconsidered the idea of the SCE. It recognized that, among other things, cooperatives addressed employment issues, gave advantages to small and medium enterprises (as compared to larger companies) and accepted various cooperative traditions across the member states. The European Parliament offered two motions for resolution that considered harmonising cooperative laws and proposed a statute for the SCE.[61]

Based on these motions, the Committee on Economic and Monetary Affairs advanced the so-called Mihr Report,[62] which focused on the importance of cooperatives in the European Community. The Mihr Report considered various issues, including the importance of cooperatives for regional development and employment, and proposed the establishment of a European cooperative development fund. The report also stressed that national cooperative laws should be harmonised and repeated the demand for a specific legal form for cooperatives, particularly to boost cross-border cooperation. However, this initiative was also unsuccessful.[63] Nevertheless, it led to a resolution by the European Parliament in 1983, which has been the basis for various initiatives. Yet, none of them have focused on legal issues.[64]

The debates in the European Parliament and the Committee on Economic and Monetary Affairs suggest there was a general mistrust of the cooperative movement. Cooperatives were criticised for receiving preferential treatment over other forms of

[58]See Hagen-Eck (1995), p. 30 et seq.; Schöpflin (2018b), p. 1231. Also consider Münkner (2006), p. 14.

[59]Established in 1963 with the aim of representing retailers. See Independet Retail Europe, About us.

[60]See Hagen-Eck (1995), p. 31 et seq.; Schulze (2004), p. 11; Fischer (1995), p. 42. Also consider Chirico and Troianiello (2007), p. 30 and Münkner (2006), p. 14.

[61]See Hagen-Eck (1995), p. 35 et seq. Also consider Fischer (1995), p. 42.

[62]See MIHR (1982).

[63]Among other things, it was criticised that the report did not address the various legal issues in detail.

[64]See Hagen-Eck (1995), p. 36 et seq.; Fischer (1995), p. 43. Also consider Chirico and Troianiello (2007), p. 19.

companies. Finally, divergent national interests based on different cooperative traditions, hampered further discussions at the European level. Interestingly, the development of a statute for an SCE was strongly linked to the harmonisation of national cooperative laws, which fostered a fear of losing some different national traditions and, thus, the flexibility of the cooperative movement. The discussion about the cooperatives' mandates promoting members' needs—as opposed to concentrating on the needs of the general community—provoked particular concern.[65]

Finally, on 6 March 1992, the European Commission advanced a proposal for the statute of an SCE. This proposal resulted from various developments. First, in 1986, the European Economic and Social Committee, a body with consulting powers, organised a conference on cooperatives, self-help organisations and mutual that recognised the important role of the cooperative sector and addressed the need to establish an alternative, facultative supranational legal framework for cooperative societies. A 1989 conference on the *third sector* in Europe continued this discussion and, in 1990, the European Economic and Social Committee readdressed this issue with its own resolution.[66]

Of particular concern were the needs of various enterprises within the social economy, including maintaining competitiveness among them and improving their access to the common market of the European Union (then, the European Community).[67] Neither the European Economic Interest Grouping (EEIG)[68] nor the re-proposed statute for a European company in 1989 seemed adaptable to the typical features of cooperatives, in particular, prioritising member needs. As a result, the European Economic and Social Committee recommended establishing an alternative legal framework for cooperatives, associations and mutuals, stressing that different statutes had to be drafted for each organisation to protect their specific features.[69]

The European Commission used these recommendations, in a proposal for a statute in March 1992, followed by a proposition by the European Economic and Social Committee in May 1992 that required specific amendments. These were

[65]See Hagen-Eck (1995), p. 38 et seq.; Fischer (1995), p. 44. Also consider Schöpflin (2018b), p. 1231.

[66]See Hagen-Eck (1995), p. 40 et seq.; Schulze (2004), p. 11 et seq.; Fischer (1995), p. 44 et seq. Also consider Münkner (2006), p. 14.

[67]In brief, the European Single Market/Internal Market/Common Market is a distinct market that seeks to guarantee the free movement of goods, capital, services and labour—the 'four freedoms'—within the European Union, where European citizens can choose their place of residence and pursue work, training or entrepreneurial activity freely, without hindrance.

[68]Regulation (EEC) no 2137 adopted in 1985. See Council Regulation (EEC) No 2137/85 of 25 July 1985 of the European Economic Interest Grouping (EEIG), OJ L 1985/199 1.

[69]See Hagen-Eck (1995), p. 40 et seq.; Fischer (1995), p. 44 et seq.

considered in the second draft,[70] proposed in July 1993.[71] In addition, various European cooperative federations, which had formed a coordinating committee, had put forward their own proposal on 12 October 1990, which the Commission incorporated in its 1992 draft.[72]

Notably, until the mid-80s, the adoption of a statute for an SCE was still tied to the idea of harmonising national cooperative laws. This approach has since been dropped, mainly because the discussions surrounding the issue proved cumbersome and difficult because of differences in national traditions and legal forms. Ultimately, it seems the various national federations blocked further discussion.[73] Moreover, after the European Commission's 1985 white paper[74] and the Single European Act of 1986,[75] the attempt to achieve full harmonisation was dropped. The European Commission's new strategy instead focused on minimal harmonisation and the principle of mutual recognition.[76]

Finally, on 22 July 2003, the European legislative bodies adopted Council Regulation no. 1435/2003, creating the SCE as a unique supranational legal form for business organisations. The SCE-R was supplemented by Council Directive 2003/72/EC, which contains specific rules on employee involvement.[77]

---

[70] See Amended proposal for a Council Regulation (EEC) on the statute for a European cooperative society, OJ C 1993/236, 17.

[71] See Hagen-Eck (1995), p. 42; Schulze (2004), p. 11 et seq.; Fischer (1995), p. 45, Schöpflin (2018b), p. 1231 et seq. Also consider Chirico and Troianiello (2007), p. 20 and Münkner (2006), p. 16.

[72] See Hagen-Eck (1995), p. 42; Fischer (1995), p. 45. Also consider Chirico and Troianiello (2007), p. 20.

[73] See Hagen-Eck (1995), p. 43 et seq.; Fischer (1995), p. 45, Schöpflin (2018b), p. 1231. Also consider Lutter et al. (2012), p. 1585; Holthaus and Lehnhoff (2016), p. 45 and Münkner (2006), pp. 6 et seq. and 14 et seq.

[74] See Commission of the European Communities, Completing the Internal Market (1985).

[75] See Single European Act, OJ L 1987/169, 1.

[76] See Hagen-Eck (1995), p. 44 et seq.; Schöpflin (2018b), p. 1231 et seq. In this context also consider Lutter et al. (2012), p. 7 et seq. Generally, Rondinelli (2016).

[77] See OJ L 2003/207, 25. For details Snaith (2006), Fici (2006). Also consider Marano (2006), p. 14 et seq.; Manzini (2006), p. 27 et seq.; Lehner (2009), p. 97 et seq.; Bianca and Zanardo (2016), p. 201 et seq. and Albamonte (2008), p. 316. For the SE, Ficari (2008).

2.3 Council Regulation (EC) N. 1435/2003 Establishing the Statute for a European Cooperative Society (SCE)

The SCE-R has a preamble and nine chapters of provisions located in a total of 80 articles.[78] This preamble contains 20 recitals that provide the background and primary objectives of the SCE-R.[79] One of the main reasons for introducing the SCE-R was to provide cooperatives with a level playing field against for-profit companies. Recital 6 of the SCE-R preamble states 'the Community (. . .) should provide cooperatives (. . .) with adequate legal instruments capable of facilitating the development of their cross-border activities'. It then explicitly states that 'the United Nations has encouraged all governments to ensure a supportive environment in which cooperatives can participate on an equal footing with other forms of enterprise'. The preamble underlines the need for a legal framework that facilitates cross-border cooperation between cooperatives that is unhampered by 'legal and administrative difficulties which should be eliminated in a market without frontiers'.[80] Whether this facilitation of cross-border cooperation ultimately means that an SCE is necessarily obliged to conduct its business with members from different Member States is dealt with in Sect. 3.6.

Recital 13 SCE-R describes the essential aim of the regulation—to allow national cooperatives to operate outside their national territory—and proposes three different ways of establishing an SCE: (1) forming a new one, (2) merging existing national cooperatives or (3) converting a national cooperative into an SCE (without closing down the original cooperative).[81] Similarly, Recital 3 SCE-R acknowledges that 'the legal framework within which business should be carried on in the community is still based largely on national laws'. This situation 'forms a considerable obstacle to the creation of groups of companies from different member states'. Neither the SE nor EEIG suit cooperatives' needs.[82]

[78]Chapter 1 contains general provisions, Chap. 2 deals with the formation of the SCE and contains three sections: Sect. 1 (general), Sect. 2 (formation by merger) and Sect. 3 (conversion of an existing cooperative into an SCE). Chapter 3 contains provisions regarding the structure of the SCE and is divided into 4 sections: Sect. 1 (two-tier system), Sect. 2 (one-tier system), Sect. 3 (rules common to the one-tier and two-tier system) and Sect. 4 (general meeting). Chapter 4 is titled "issue of shares conferring special advantages" and Chap. 5 deals with the allocation of profits. Finally, Chap. 6 contains provisions regarding accounts and consolidated accounts, Chap. 7 deals with winding up, liquidation, insolvency and the cessation of payments, Chap. 8 contains additional and transitional provisions and finally Chap. 9 contains the final provisions.

The articles are divided into numbered paragraphs and non-numbered sub-paragraphs, including lists of items ordered by letter.

[79]See Fici (2013c), p. 118.

[80]See Recital 11 SCE-R. On this issue, see Fleischer (2010), p. 1707 et seq.

[81]Recital 12 SCE-R states: "The introduction of a European legal form for cooperatives, based on common principles but taking their specific features into account, should enable them to operate outside their own national borders in all or part of the territory of the Community."

[82]See Recitals 4 and 5 SCE-R.

SCEs are optional instruments.[83] These instruments are not supposed to replace national cooperative laws nor be used in a compulsory manner to conduct business on an EU scale. Rather, the SCE is the 28th cooperative legal model within the European Union,[84,85] and it has a crucial cross-border requirement that distinguishes it from all other cooperative legal models. This requirement, however, can be easily met and does not relate to the substance of the business.[86]

The European Union legislature did not try to harmonise national cooperative law, but instead attempted to develop an additional instrument to promote the cross-border activities pursued by cooperatives. In the long run, this might lead to the increased use of the cooperative business model, followed by a *de facto* approximation of national cooperative laws.[87] Accordingly, Recital 2 of the SCE-R states that 'the completion of the internal market (. . .) not only (implies) that barriers to trade should be removed, but also that the structures of production should be adapted to the community dimension'.[88]

Whether this regulation will ultimately be successful remains to be seen. As requested by Art. 79 of the SCE-R, the Commission published a 2012 report analysing the success of the SCE-R.[89] However, according to the aims of the SCE-R as outlined in its preamble, this regulation cannot yet be considered entirely

---

Recital 4 states: "The Council has adopted Regulation (EC) No 2157/2001 (9) establishing the legal form of the European Company (SE) according to the general principles of the public limited-liability company (principi generali previsti per le società per azioni.). This is not an instrument which is suited to the specific features of cooperatives."

Recital 5 states: "The European Economic Interest Grouping (EEIG), as provided for in Regulation (EEC) no 2137/85 (10), allows undertakings to promote certain of their activities in common, while nevertheless preserving their independence, but does not meet the specific requirements of cooperative enterprise."

[83]See Recital 20 SCE-R. Also consider Corapi and de Donno (2006), p. 1323 and Chirico and Troianiello (2007), p. 33.

[84]Counted Ante Brexit.

[85]The SCE-R also applies to the European Economic Area. Also consider Fici (2013c), p. 118.

[86]See Sect. 3.6.

[87]See Fici (2013c), p. 131 et seq. Also consider Commission of the European Communities, Communication from the Commission to the Council and the European Parliament, the European Economic and Social Committee and the Committee of the Regions. On the promotion of co-operative societies in Europe, COM (2004) 185 final, 15 eur-lex.europa.eu/legal-content/EN/TXT/?uri=CELEX%3A52004DC0018 (02.02.2017).

[88]Moreover, " for that purpose it is essential that companies of all types the business of which is not limited to satisfying purely local needs should be able to plan and carry out the reorganisation of their business on a Community scale."

[89]See European Commission (2012). For details, see Study on the implementation of the Regulation 1435/2003 on the Statute for European Cooperative Society (SCE) Part I euricse.eu/it/publications/final-study-on-the-implementation-of-the-regulation-14352003-on-the-statute-for-european-cooperative-society-sce-part-i/ (02.02.2017) and Part II euricse.eu/it/publications/final-study-on-the-implementation-of-the-regulation-14352003-on-the-statute-for-european-cooperative-society-sce-part-ii/ (02.02.2017).

successful, even though it has significantly contributed to a common understanding of what a cooperative might be.

The report mentions various reasons for the weaknesses in this business model, including the 30,000 EUR minimum capital requirement for establishing an SCE and a rather complex hierarchy of sources determining the applicable law.[90] This is due to a particular mixture of European and national laws. In principle, regulations like the SCE-R are normative acts that do not need to be implemented by member states. In fact, they 'shall be binding in its entirety and directly applicable in all member states',[91] obliging member states to adopt 'all measures of national law necessary to implement legally binding union acts'.[92] This obligation must be observed whether or not a regulation expressly requires national implementation of the law[93]; yet, the SCE-R also explicitly requires member states to take different measures necessary for its implementation. For instance, Art. 78 para. 1 SCE-R requires making 'such provision as is appropriate to ensure the effective application of this regulation'.[94] In addition, Art. 73 paras. 2 to 5 SCE-R requires that specific measures be taken if Art. 6 SCE-R—which regulates where the registered office must be located—is violated. The significance of these legal rules and, particularly Art. 78 SCE-R, is addressed in the next chapter. Similarly, the next chapter. will discuss Art. 8 SCE-R, which contains a rather complex example of how to determine the applicable law and which explicitly refers to, among others, 'the laws adopted by member states in the implementation of community measures relating specifically to SCEs'. Finally, the SCE-R contains various options for member states, according to which they may adapt specific provisions of the SCE-R, if desired.[95]

The report also contained an in-depth study that compared the different national cooperative laws,[96] highlighting the huge variety of cooperative laws, which differences ranging from minor regulatory aspects to the very nature of cooperatives. In fact, it seems the only shared feature is capital variability. Not all national laws consider cooperatives to be user-owned business organisations or democratic organisations. Significant differences also exist between profit distribution, compulsory

---

[90]See European Commission (2012), p. 7. Also consider Fici (2013b), p. 8 et seq.
Also the preamble of the SCE-R outlines the problem of diversity among national laws with the result of creating a considerable obstacle to cross-border activity of cooperatives. This, moreover, implies a considerable obstacle to the completion of the internal market. See Recital 11 SCE-R. Also consider Fici (2013c), p. 148 et seq.; Krimphove (2010), p. 897 and Holthaus and Lehnhoff (2016), p. 44.

[91]See Art. 288 para. 2 TFEU.

[92]See Art. 291 para. 1 TFEU.

[93]See Bieber and Kotzur (2016), p. 117 et seq. Also consider Chirico and Troianiello (2007), p. 29 et seq.

[94]Art. 78 para. 2 SCE-R requires both that competent authorities be designated according to the meaning of Arts. 7, 21, 29, 30, 54 and 73 and that the commission and the other member states be informed.

[95]See Sect. 2.4. Also consider Fici (2013c), p. 132 et seq.

[96]See fn 89.

allocation to reserves and the devolution of residual assets after dissolution.[97] The limited number of SCEs that existed in 2012 also suggests the SCE-R has met with limited success.[98]

The report's findings contrast with the aims outlined in the preamble to the SCE-R. It must be noted, however, that the SCE-R is justified by the Community's desire to 'ensure equal terms of competition and to contribute to its economic development'. Similarly, communication 2004 no 18 final stresses the need to create legislation that does not give cooperatives preferential treatment, but instead creates a more level playing field for all parties.[99]

Taken together, *Fici* argues that '(. . .) a more flexible SCE-R, not prevalently designed for the aggregation of cooperatives of non-modest size, would have had greater success and contributed more to the cooperative visibility in the common market, especially in those EU countries, where the cooperative movement is less developed, the applicable cooperative law is less suited to cooperatives, and the image of cooperatives is partially obfuscated by the instrumental use of past governments."[100]

We must admit that the SCE-R definitely holds symbolic and political value, and hence has helped to promote cooperatives.[101] The symbolic value of the SCE-R is underlined by a judgement from the European Union's Court of Justice (ECJ), dated 8 September 2011.[102] The case concerned tax exemptions granted by Italian law and their compatibility with EU law. It was questioned whether these benefits might be classified as state aid within the meaning of Art. 107 *TFEU*. While the Court of Justice recognised that tax exemptions generally constitute state aid,[103] it ruled that the measures were compatible with EU law, given the difference between cooperatives and commercial companies. This difference legitimates the more favourable tax treatment given to cooperatives.[104]

---

[97]See Fici (2013c), p. 131. For details Fici (2012) and in general, Study on the implementation of the Regulation 1435/2003 on the Statute for European Cooperative Society (SCE). Interestingly, the cooperative movement does not seem to favour harmonisation. One suggested reason is that EU institutions are not sufficiently familiar with the concept of cooperatives, meaning top-down harmonisation could generate problems. See Fici (2013c), p. 131.

[98]See Commission of the European Communities, Report from the Commission to the Council and the European Parliament, the European Economic and Social Committee and the Committee of the Regions, p. 13.

[99]See Commission of the European Communities, Communication from the Commission to the Council and the European Parliament, the European Economic and Social Committee and the Committee of the Regions, p. 13.

[100]See Fici (2013c), p. 120.

[101]See Fici (2013c), p. 122. Also consider Münkner (2006), p. 28.

[102]See First Chamber 08.09.2011, C-78/08. Also consider Fici (2012), p. 9 et seq.

[103]See First Chamber 08.09.2011, C-78/08 para. 44 et seq. Also consider Germanò (2008).

[104]See First Chamber 08.09.2011, C-78/08 para. 82. The court concludes that "it must therefore be held that producers' and workers' cooperative societies such as those at issue in the main proceedings cannot, in principle, be regarded as being in a comparable factual and legal situation to that of commercial companies – provided, however, that they act in the economic interest of their

The court contributed to a common understanding of cooperatives by extensively using the SCE-R to define a specific cooperative identity, including different general features. According to the ECJ, a particular national treatment of cooperatives can only be justified under EU law if the national cooperative law conforms to the following criteria and statements[105]: (1) cooperative activities should be conducted for the mutual benefit of the members, so that each member can benefit according to his participation in the cooperative, including the transactions he or she makes with it; (2) the principle of the primacy of the individual and disinterested distribution must be observed[106]; (3) cooperatives may not be managed according to the interest of outside investors; (4) control is vested equally according to the principle 'one member, one vote'; (5) reserves are held in common, are non-distributable and must be dedicated to the common interest of the members; (6) as cooperatives have limited access to equity markets, their development therefore depends upon their own capital and credit financing; (7) last, limited interest on loan and share capital makes investment in a cooperative society (because of the lower profit margin) less advantageous than investing in capital companies.[107]

One possible result of this judgment is that national cooperatives, to whom member states wish to grant specific tax treatment, must meet the criteria set out by the SCE-R. This could bring about a *de facto* approximation of national cooperative laws in Europe.[108] In any case, both the SCE-R and the ECJ judgement foster a significantly better understanding of cooperatives. This is important when one considers that 'a balanced society necessitates the existence of strong public and private sectors, as well as a strong cooperative, mutual and the other social and non-governmental sector'.[109] Nevertheless, the fundamental problem of the complex structure of the legal sources remains. This problem will be addressed in the next chapter.

---

members and their relations with members are not purely commercial but personal and individual, the members being actively involved in the running of the business and entitled to equitable distribution of the results of economic performance." See 08.09.2011, C-78/08 para. 61.

[105]See First Chamber 08.09.2011, C-78/08 para. 56 et seq. Also consider Fici (2013c), p. 121 et seq. and Sarti (2012).

[106]Recitals 8 and 10 SCE-R.

[107]In this sense, the Court of Justice states that "it is for the referring court to determine, in the light of all the circumstances of the disputes on which is required to rule whether, on the basis of the criteria set out at paragraphs 55 to 62 above, the producers and workers cooperative societies at issue in the main proceedings are in fact in a comparable situation to that of profit-making companies liable to corporation tax." See First Chamber 08.09.2011, C-78/08 para. 63.

[108]See Fici (2013c), p. 125; Bonfante (2006), p. 10 et seq.; Marano (2006), p. 19 et seq.; Münkner (2006), pp. 5 and 18; Galle (2006), p. 260 and Korte (2012), p. 345 et seq.

[109]See Recommendation 193 2. Similarly, Stieglitz states that his "research showed that one needed to find the balance between markets, government, and other institutions, including not-for-profits and cooperatives, and that the successful countries were those that had found that balance." He adds that "there must be a traditional private sector of the economy, but the two other pillars have not received the attention, which they deserve: the public sector and the social cooperative economy, including mutual societies and not for profits." See Stiglitz (2009), p. 348 and 356.

2.4 The Legal Framework for a National SCE: Which Laws Should Be Applied and How?

The SCE-R contains a rather complex system of sources that focuses on national law. Consequently, an Austrian SCE may be significantly different from an Italian one. In fact, comparing 'Austrian' and 'Italian' SCEs requires first determining which law to apply. This process can expose the rights and obligations that ultimately exist. However, because of the complex hierarchy of norms, which include several references to national law, such a task is not easy. Even though the statute for an SCE has been adopted via regulation, it is more like a skeleton to be fleshed out by national law or statutory provisions. Moreover, there are many areas that are exclusively governed by national law[110]: in this study I not only refer to the rules of the SCE-R and the national rules—which are determined directly (or indirectly) by this regulation—but also to the rules governing agriculture and/or agricultural activities.

Because members have to be from at least two different member states, a minimum of two legal systems must be chosen. Factors like favourable tax laws, insolvency laws or accounting directives affect where an SCE's headquarters will be established. Differences in national cooperative law may also influence this decision; other differences stem from SCE-R itself, which contains references to national laws governing public limited-liability companies. This implies that an SCE may not have to observe the same provisions as a national cooperative.[111]

It is thus essential to analyse and understand the complex system of the hierarchy of norms as determined, first of all, by Art. 8 SCE-R; from a methodological perspective it is important to know that the SCE-R draws a distinction between a general clause and several specific references, which help to define the applicable

---

[110]Consider e.g., Art. 72 SCE-R referring to winding-up, insolvency and similar procedures; consider in this context also Recital 16. According to Recital 16, the SCE-R does not cover specific areas of law such as taxation, competition, intellectual property or insolvency; in these areas the provisions of the member states' laws and Community law must be applied. The same is true for other areas not covered by the SCE-R. Also consider Schulze (2004), p. 14.

Recital 17 SCE-R explains the rules for involving employees in an SCE and describes these provisions as an indissociable complement to the SCE-R to be applied concomitantly. Even though not expressly mentioned (E.g., by Recital 21 SE-R), other social and labour legislation issues are governed by national provisions.

[111]All these possibilities raise the question of whether it is possible to talk about a uniform SCE format, or whether it is more appropriate to talk about as many different formats as there are member states. See Snaith (2004), p. 40 et seq.; Schulze (2004), pp. 12 and 14 et seq.; Iengo (2006). Also consider Münkner (2006), p. 17, Krimphove (2010), p. 893; Galle (2006), p. 257, Korte (2012), p. 345; Fajardo (2012), p. 6 et seq. and Sect. 3.3. For the SE, see Sarcina (2006), p. 748 et seq.

As mentioned in Sect. 2.2, the SCE-R is a result of a compromise between the member states necessary to achieve a common sense solution. This can be best observed when analysing the solution regarding the applicable law.

law. For the latter, a distinction is made between simple references and delegated powers and obligations member states may apply or must observe.[112]

Now, the essential norm for the system of sources used to define the applicable law is contained in Art. 8 of the SCE-R.[113] This general clause establishes a hierarchy of norms, which in principle applies to a wide range of aspects of an SCE, including governance structure, formation and legal personality.[114] Issues regarding employees are addressed by dir. 2003/72/EC.[115] This hierarchy comprises the following five levels[116]: (1) provisions contained in the SCE-R,[117] (2) provisions contained in the statutes of an SCE, where expressly authorised by the SCE-R,[118] (3) laws adopted by member states who implement community measures related to SCEs,[119] (4) laws of member states, which would apply to a cooperative in the member state where the SCE has its registered office,[120] and (5) provisions of the statutes of an SCE, in the same way as in level 4.[121]

The term hierarchy implies that, if there is a contradiction between norms of different levels, the higher norm prevails. Thus the SCE-R is the highest source of law. National law can only be applied in matters that are not regulated or are only

---

[112]Here it is important to note that references to national law in the SCE-R are considered direct references, whether they are in the general clause or specific references. Sachnormverweisung (direct reference) as opposed to Gesamtnormverweisung (comprehensive reference). For the SE, see Brandt and Scheifele (2002), p. 553; Wagner (2002), p. 989; Koke (2005), p. 15; Lächler and Oplustil (2005), p. 384. Different opinion Schröder (2010b), p. 185; Hommelhoff and Teichmann (2015), p. 183 et seq. Also consider Schröder (2010c), p. 35 et seq.

[113]It states: (1) An SCE shall be governed: (a) by this Regulation; (b) where expressly authorised by this Regulation, by the provisions of its statutes; (c) in the case of matters not regulated by this Regulation or, where matters are partly regulated by it, of those aspects not covered by it, by: (i) the laws adopted by member states in the implementation of Community measures relating specifically to SCEs; (ii) the laws of member states which would apply to a cooperative formed in accordance with the law of the Member State in which the SCE has its registered office; (iii) the provisions of its statutes, in the same way as for a cooperative formed in accordance with the law of the Member State in which the SCE has its registered office. (2) If national law provides for specific rules and/or restrictions related to the nature of business carried out by an SCE, or for forms of control by a supervisory authority, that law shall apply in full to the SCE.REG 1435/2003.

[114]Art. 1 para. 5 SCE-R states: "An SCE shall have legal personality." According to Art. 18 para. 1 SCE-R, "an SCE shall acquire legal personality on the day of its registration in the Member State in which it has its registered office, in the register designated by that State in accordance with Article 11(1)."

[115]See Art. 1 para. 6 SCE-R: Employee involvement in an SCE shall be governed by the provisions of Directive 2003/72/EC.

[116]See Lutter et al. (2012), p. 1588 et seq.; Avsec (2009), p. 2. Generally, Sepe (2008), p. 152 et seq.; Chirico and Troianiello (2007), p. 33 et seq. and Arnò et al. (2007), p. 19 et seq.

[117]See Art. 8 para. 1 letter a SCE-R.

[118]See Art. 8 para. 1 letter b SCE-R.

[119]See Art. 8 para. 1 letter c (i) SCE-R.

[120]See Art. 8 para. 1 letter c (ii) SCE-R.

[121]See Art. 8 para. 1 letter c (iii) SCE-R.

partly regulated by the SCE-R.[122] The role of the statutes is limited to some situations that are either expressly authorised by the SCE-R or other situations determined by national law, on the condition that this latter authorises a national cooperative to regulate a certain matter via statutes. In addition to this hierarchy of rules, para. 2 of Art. 8 SCE-R specifies that national law must be applied, if it provides for specific rules and/or restrictions related to the nature of business carried out by an SCE, for example, agricultural business. Similarly, national law concerning enforcement by a supervisory authority must be applied.

The provisions contained in the SCE-R are accorded the highest level and should, in general, not pose interpretive problems.[123] They prevail over statutory provisions and over national law that may be contradictory, regardless of whether the national provisions implement the SCE-R[124] or whether national laws apply to national cooperatives as determined by Art. 8 para. 1 letter c (ii) SCE-R.[125] This category of norms (determined by letter a) also includes provisions that refer to national provisions, for instance Art. 5 para. 3 SCE-R,[126] Art. 12 para. 1 SCE-R,[127] and Art. 10 para. 1 SCE-R.[128] These provisions stem from the legal source as determined by Art. 8 para. 1 letter a SCE-R,[129] and are therefore placed at the highest level, even if they exist in national legal sources.

The provisions of statutes expressly authorised by the SCE-R occupy the second level of the legal hierarchy. The SCE-R differentiates between issues that *must* be regulated by statutory norms and those that *may* be regulated by statutory provisions

---

[122]See Art. 8 para. 1 letter c SCE-R.

[123]This is linked to the principle of priority for European law and entails priority against contradicting national law. In this context consider Schröder (2010b), p. 181 and Sepe (2008), p. 153. This principle is also in line with the definition of a regulation as a legislative act, as contained in Art. 288 TFEU. Accordingly, "a regulation shall have general application. It shall be binding in its entirety and directly applicable in all member states." Art. 8 para. 1 letter a SCE-R is thus declaratory in nature. For the SE, see Brandt and Scheifele (2002), p. 553; Hommelhoff and Teichmann (2015), p. 176.

[124]As determined by Art. 8 para. 1 letter c (i) SCE-R.

[125]See Snaith (2004), p. 19 et seq. In this context also consider Schröder (2010b), p. 181 and Sepe (2008), p. 152 et seq.

[126]It states: "The law for the precautionary supervision applicable in the Member State in which the SCE has its registered office to public limited-liability companies during the phase of the constitution shall apply by analogy to the control of the constitution of the SCE."

[127]It states: "Publication of documents and particulars concerning an SCE which must be made public under this Regulation shall be effected in the manner laid down in the laws of the Member State applicable to public limited-liability companies in which the SCE has its registered office."

[128]It states: "The law applicable, in the Member State where the SCE has its registered office, to public limited-liability companies regulating the content of the letters and documents sent to third parties shall apply by analogy to that SCE. The name of the SCE shall be preceded or followed by the abbreviation 'SCE' and, where appropriate, by the word 'limited'."

[129]For the SE, see Brandt and Scheifele (2002), p. 553; Schröder (2010b), p. 181.

(non-mandatory statutory norms).[130] Art. 36 SCE-R[131] illustrates this point clearly. Accordingly, statutes must contain a provision determining whether an SCE adopts a one- or a two-tier system. Other examples of mandatory norms are Art. 39 para. 4 SCE-R, which concerns the number of members in the supervisory organ; Art. 42 para. 2 subpara. 1 SCE-R, which concerns the number of members of the administrative organ; Art. 45 para. 1 SCE-R, which concerns the term of office for members of the SCE organs; and Art. 48 para. 1 SCE-R, which concerns operations requiring authorisation.

Conversely, the SCE-R allows the statute drafters to define certain statutory provisions—and thus does not obligate the drafters.[132] This is illustrated by Art. 39 para. 2 SCE-R, which concerns appointing members of the first supervisory organ; Art. 42 para. 3 SCE-R, which concerns appointing members of the first administrative organ; Art. 46 para. 1 SCE-R, which addresses the possibility of legal persons being members of the SCE organs; Art. 46 para. 3 SCE-R, which outlines special eligibility conditions for members representing the administrative organ; Art. 50 paras. 1 and SCE-R, which contains rules relating to quorums and decision taking in the SCE organs; and Art. 55 para. 1 SCE-R, which allows a minority of members to call a general meeting. All these rules, however, are not optional, which means that deviation is only possible where expressly authorised, and that the statutes cannot contain supplementary provisions. Art. 8 para. 1 letter b SCE-R grants freedom of contract,[133] which cannot be restricted by national law, as the principle of the priority of EU law prevails. Thus, at this level, the autonomy of freedom of contract is harmonised.[134]

As the provision—as contained in Art. 8 para. 1 letter b SCE-R—only refers to statutory provisions 'expressly authorized by this Regulation', a potential residual gap-filling role of statutory provisions is excluded or, at least, restricted. Self-regulation therefore becomes restricted,[135] and it is further restricted by Art. 11 para. 4 SCE-R, which states that statutes cannot 'conflict at any time with the arrangements for employee involvement which have been so determined'. If so, they have to be amended. Thus, only the provisions of the SCE-R are placed above the provision of the statutes, according to Art. 8 para. 1 letter b SCE-R; however, the

[130]For the SE, see Brandt and Scheifele (2002), p. 555; Habersack, Festschrift für Peter Ulmer zum 70. Geburtstag am 2. Januar 2003 (2003), p. 274 et seq.

[131]Under the conditions laid down by this Regulation an SCE shall comprise:

(b) either a supervisory organ and a management organ (two-tier system) or an administrative organ (one-tier system) depending on the form adopted in the statutes.

[132]Statutory provisions as options. See Fici (2013c), p. 134.

[133]As well as Art. 8 para. 1 letter c (iii) SCE-R.

[134]For the SE, see Schröder (2010b), p. 191. Also consider Raiser (1993), p. 282; Murschitz (2005a), p. 228; Casper (2003), p. 71; Murschitz (2005b), p. 288.

[135]For the SE, see Casper in Habersack 71, Murschitz (2005b), p. 288. This extreme stricture has been criticised by different scholars as it considerably limits the flexibility of an SE's internal structure. National provisions might be more flexible here. See Fleischer (2004), p. 517; Bungert and Beier (2002), p. 2.

SCE-R gives them priority over national law, regardless of whether this law implements the SCE-R—in the broadest sense—or provides specific rules for cooperatives.[136]

Generally, the statutory autonomy of the SCE is highly circumscribed by numerous references to national law, which limits the possibility of a conflict with mandatory national rules. In many cases, the SCE-R provides that statutes only have to respect the mandatory provisions of national law and that certain matters can be regulated by the statutes in cases where national law so permits.[137] Thus, national laws can significantly reduce the autonomy of the SCE-R. This suggests that different national SCEs may ultimately exist. But this result must not be negative as limited uniformity promotes competition between legal systems.[138]

While the provisions in letters a and b of Art. 8 para. 1 SCE-R are quite clear and therefore are not so difficult to apply, letter c, which defines levels 3 to 5 of the hierarchy of sources of law, is more difficult to apply. It contains a general reference to national law.[139] But before analysing the provisions of letter c in detail, some general remarks are in order.

According to Art. 8 para. 1 letter c SCE-R, aspects that are not regulated by or are partly regulated by the SCE-R are regulated by national law, which the member states adopt in order to implement the SCE's regulations. Next, one must consider the laws of the member states when he or she applies to a cooperative formed in accordance with the law of the member state where the SCE has its registered office. Finally, aspects that are not regulated by or are only partly regulated by the SCE-R can be regulated by the statutes of an SCE, just as they are for a cooperative formed in accordance with the law of the member states in which the SCE has its registered office.

These sources apply in two cases: for matters not regulated by the SCE-R or where matters are only partly regulated by it. In the latter case, the areas not covered are regulated according to para. 1 letter c.[140] Thus, to determine the full application of this provision, we must define what 'not regulated' and 'partly regulated' mean. There are two lines of discussion. The first is the extensive interpretation of these words, which argues that national law (as determined by Art. 8 para. 1 letter c SCE-R) applies to an SCE for matters outside the sphere of the SCE-R. This

[136]See Snaith (2004), p. 20. Consider, for instance, Art. 1 para. 2 subpar 3 SCE-R: "Unless otherwise provided by the statutes of the SCE when that SCE is formed, no member shall be liable for more than the amount he/she has subscribed." The result is that an SCE can be set up in the form of an organisation with unlimited liability of members, even though the relevant national law may provide solely for limited liability. For further examples, consider Art. 1 para. 4 SCE-R or Art. 45 para. 1 SCE-R.

[137]For examples in this context, consider Art. 14 para. 1 subpar 2 SCE-R, Art. 65 para. 1 SCE-R or Art. 75 SCE-R.

[138]See Fici (2013c), p. 138 et seq.

[139]In addition, the SCE-R also contains several references throughout the text.

[140]For the SE, see Schröder (2010b), p. 182.

interpretation is arguably supported by the wording 'matters not regulated by this Regulation'.[141]

The second approach is the restrictive interpretation, which argues that this general reference is limited to those matters that reside within a potential sphere of application, even though the SCE-R does not contain (or only partly contains) a specific provision for a certain matter. Two premises support this latter opinion. First, not every matter which will fall under this regulation will have been considered by the drafters of the SCE-R. Second, and probably more importantly, Recitals 16 and 17 define specific areas definitely not covered by the SCE-R.[142]

The second approach is more convincing, given that the EU legislature would not have the competence to regulate matters that do not fall within the regulatory sphere of the SCE-R.[143] Therefore, the terms 'not regulated' and 'partly regulated' refer only to those matters that fall within the genuine sphere of application of the SCE-R. This does not imply, however, that national law automatically has to be applied if the regulation does not contain a specific provision. In fact, there is no regulatory gap in cases where there is deliberate non-regulation. In this case, national law is precluded. In other words, national law here fills the gap and can only be considered as long as the SCE-R does not contain any substantive provision. However, a substantive provision can be given in cases where there is deliberate non-regulation. This argument can be based on the principle of priority of EU law, enshrined in Art. 8 SCE-R. Therefore, national law can only be considered after one determines, on a case-by-case basis, whether the provisions of the SCE-R contain a gap or whether they are exhaustive. The most important criterion here is the intention of the legislature. The recitals of the SCE-R and the preparatory works give particular insight.[144] It is true that closing all gaps by applying national law in a subsidiary fashion would further weaken the already modest uniformity of the SCE and hinder the further development of the law by the ECJ.[145] Nevertheless, in doubtful cases, it seems better to interpret the silence as a gap to be closed by national provisions, rather than as a case of deliberate non-regulation.[146]

[141]See Wagner (2002), p. 988. Also consider Presti (2006), p. 69 et seq.

[142]For the SE, see Brandt and Scheifele (2002), p. 548 et seq.; Jaecks and Schönborn (2003), p. 255; Brandt (2003), p. 1209; Lächler and Oplustil (2005), p. 383 et seq. Also consider Casper (2003), p. 67.

[143]For the SE, see Koke (2005), p. 10; Ebert (2003a), p. 1856.

[144]For the SE, see Schröder (2010b), p. 182. Also consider Maul (1998), p. 13 et seq.; Casper (2003), p. 57; Merkt (1992), p. 657; Hommelhoff and Teichmann (2015), p. 190 et seq.

[145]The interpretation of the SE-R must be pursued autonomously and according to European principles. See Wagner (2002), p. 988 et seq.; Casper (2003), p. 54; Raiser (1993), p. 283.

[146]because of the European legislature aiming to link Community and national law rather than introducing a regulation exclusive to the SCE. On this issue, see Iengo (2006). For the SE, see Schröder (2010b), p. 182. Also consider Rasner (1992), p. 319; Wagner (2002), p. 989.

It is important that Art. 8 SCE-R be read in accordance with Art. 9 SCE-R,[147] which contains the principle of non-discrimination.[148] This is a guiding principle for national legislatures when regulating SCEs and requires treating an SCE 'in every Member State as if it were a cooperative, formed in accordance with the law of the Member State in which it has its registered office'. As a result, national legislatures have to put SCEs on an equal footing with national cooperatives when adopting the implementing law, as requested by Art. 8 para. 1 letter c (i) SCE-R. Furthermore, this principle implies that SCEs have to be treated in the same way as national cooperatives if the SCE-R does not contain specific provisions; hence, specific features have to be determined according to national law, as provided for by Art. 8 para. 1 letter c (ii) SCE-R.

One might ask whether it is possible to treat SCEs better than national cooperatives or whether different national legislatures are obliged to apply (as much as possible) the same rules that they apply to their national cooperatives.[149] The formulation of Art. 9 SCE-R seems quite clear here, obliging member states to treat SCEs the same as national cooperatives. This implies that they may not be treated worse or better.[150] However, this principle allows for better or unequal treatment if it is determined by the regulation itself. In fact, Art. 9 SCE-R states that the requirement of equal treatment is subject to the SCE-R.[151]

These general observations can inform our detailed analysis of Art. 8 para. 1 letter c SCE-R, beginning with the 'laws adopted by Member States in the implementation of Community measures relating specifically to SCEs'. These rules form the third level in the hierarchy of sources. Which laws are meant here has been subject to discussion. It has been argued that this provision only applies to supplementing norms adopted at the supranational level,[152] thus excluding laws adopted to implement the various options. Arguably, special references were added to the SCE-R to fulfil this latter task.[153] Another opinion is more convincing: Accordingly, Art. 8 para. 1 letter c (i) SCE-R refers to the implementing measures adopted by the member states: laws and measures implementing both the SCE-R and directive

[147]It states: "Subject to this Regulation, an SCE shall be treated in every Member State as if it were a cooperative, formed in accordance with the law of the Member State in which it has its registered office."

[148]For the SE, see Schröder (2010a), p. 205. Also consider Bianca and Zanardo (2016), p. 183.

[149]See Fici (2013c), p. 138 et seq.

[150]For the SE, see Schröder (2010a), p. 205; Hommelhoff (2003), p. 277. Other opinion Fici, who argues that better treatment is possible. See Fici (2013c), p. 138 et seq. Also consider Kübler (2003), p. 232 and Albamonte (2008), p. 298.

[151]See Fici (2013c), p. 138 et seq.

[152]For example Council Directive 2003/72/EC of 22 July 2003 supplementing the Statute for a European Cooperative Society with regard to the involvement of employees. For details, see fn 77.

[153]For the SE, see Wagner (2002), p. 989.

2003/72/EC.[154] Art. 8 para. 1 letter c (i) SCE-R, together with Art. 78 para. 1 SCE-R, constitutes the basis for specific acts and measures that implement the SCE-R,[155] with this limitation: they cannot regulate those details already regulated by the SCE-R.[156]

The fourth level in the hierarchy of applicable law contains the 'laws of Member States which would apply to a cooperative formed in accordance with the law of the Member States in which the SCE has its registered office'. This provision provides the main entry point for national law.[157] As a result, national law must be considered in the following cases: (1) if the SCE-R does not contain its own rule; (2) if the SCE-R does not require a rule to be adopted via statutory provisions; and (3) if the SCE-R does not require or allow for a rule adopted by the member states. This provision is therefore crucial to this study.[158]

The fifth and final level refers—again—to the provision of statutes; it is the lowest level on the hierarchy of applicable rules. According to this provision,[159] statutes must be adopted the same as they are for a cooperative formed in accordance with the law of the member state in which the SCE has its registered office. One can now ask whether there are substantial differences between this provision and letter b of Art. 8 SCE-R. In fact, the article may make additional references to an SCE's statutes seem superfluous. Yet, the differences are significant. The second provision

[154]See Fici (2013c), p. 138; Chirico and Troianiello (2007), p. 32 et seq.; Greda (2014), p. 832; Dellinger (2006), p. 570 et seq. For the SE, see Schröder (2010b), p. 184; Brandt and Scheifele (2002), p. 555; Kübler (2003), p. 224.

[155]See Fici (2013c), p. 137. In many cases, implementation has been achieved by amending existing national cooperative law. See Fici (2013c), p. 138.

[156]The European Court of Justice has disapproved of reproducing provisions contained in a regulation within national law. In this context, the European Court of Justice has declared that member states must take all the necessary measures to guarantee the application and effectiveness of European law. As a result, the SCE-R explicitly requires member states to adopt laws which implement (where necessary) the provisions of the SCE. See Snaith (2004), p. 19 et seq.

[157]See Schöpflin (2018a), p. 1260. If the legal system of a member state contains various laws "which would apply to a cooperative formed in accordance with the law of the member state in which the SCE has its registered office," the provisions of the SCE-R can be applied differently. In some member states (for instance France), different types of cooperatives are regulated in different ways. For instance, it must be considered whether the object of a cooperative defines them as consumer cooperative, agricultural cooperative or housing association. In other member states, for example Spain, cooperative law is a matter for local government. See Snaith (2004), p. 20 et seq. and Ibáñez (2011), p. 30.

[158]The references in Art. 8 para. 1 letter c SCE-R not only refer to national law but also judge-made law; in fact, the application of national law to an SCE might need to be supplemented. The aim of the references is to guarantee functional law for an SCE. For the SE, see Schröder (2010b), p. 187; Casper (2003), p. 68; Koke (2005), p. 18 et seq.; Lombardo and Pasotti (2004), p. 179; Hommelhoff and Teichmann (2015), p. 192. Critical, Schulz and Geismair (2001), p. 1079. Moreover, the references are dynamic not static. In other words, the most up-to-date versions of national laws must be applied. For the SE, see Wagner (2002), p. 989; Lächler and Oplustil (2005), p. 385; Raaijmakers (1999), p. 165; Casper (2003), p. 65; Hommelhoff and Teichmann (2015), p. 192.

[159]Art. 8 para. 1 letter c (iii) SCE-R.

highlights that the statutes are relevant as sources of law on two different levels. First, statutory provisions can or must be based on a specific provision of the SCE-R and, consequently, take precedence over national law.[160] Second, freedom of self-regulation can be based on national law.[161] This freedom of self-regulation is thus restricted on a European and national level. The specific degree of limitations ultimately depends on national provisions, whereas freedom of self-regulation as determined by the SCE-R is harmonised.[162]

All these observations relate to the hierarchy of applicable law. In addition, paragraph 2 of Art. 8 SCE-R contains some relevant specifications. Accordingly, the hierarchy of norms established by para. 1 only needs to be applied if national law does not provide specific rules and/or restrictions related to the nature of business carried out by an SCE. The same is true if national law provides for forms of control by a supervisory authority. In both situations, national law fully applies.[163] Unlike national law, as determined by references to Art. 8 para. 1 SCE-R, the scope of this provision is not limited to the law of the member state in which the SCE is registered, but may relate to the place where business is conducted.[164] Specific rules and restrictions related to the nature of business carried out by an SCE could include national provisions for the banking, insurance and/or financial services sectors. These provisions must be applied in full if an SCE carries out business activities in one of these fields.[165]

For the analyses carried out here and, thus, to establish an agricultural cooperative as an SCE, the national regulations and EU laws that determine what is an agricultural cooperative must be considered. First and foremost, we must analyse the norms that define what agricultural activities are. The Italian and Austrian legal systems have developed different approaches to this task, approaches that are also influenced by European law. The European lens reveals that the supposed differences at the national level are formal in nature. In terms of content—that is, the substance of the rules—there are not so many differences.

Having now explained the function of the general clause as contained in Art. 8 SCE-R, the analysis concludes with some observations on the specific references mentioned at the beginning of this chapter, which prevail in respect of the rules determined by the general clause, according to the principle of *lex specialis*.[166] To

---

[160]Art. 8 para. 1 letter b SCE-R.

[161]Art. 8 para. 1 letter c (iii) SCE-R.

[162]For the SE, see Werlauff (2003), p. 89; Hommelhoff in Habersack 276; Wagner (2002), p. 986.

[163]For the SE, see Schröder (2010b), p. 192. Also consider Ebert (2003b), p. 189; Costa and Bilreiro (2003), p. 14 et seq.

[164]See Schöpflin (2018a), p. 1262 et seq.

[165]In this respect, Recital 14 specifies that the SCE-R "does not pre-empt the choices to be made for other Community texts on company law." Also consider Schöpflin (2018a), p. 1262 et seq.

[166]In application of the principle of lex specialis derogat lex generalis. Interestingly, the SCE-R, which is made up of just 80 articles, contains 101 specific references. This raises the question of whether the provisions of this regulation really play a primary role in determining the function of an SCE or whether European and national law play an equal role. See Study on the implementation of

make things a bit complicated, the references are different in nature. *Fici* describes four regularities[167]: (1) the SCE-R determines a rule to be applied, provided that national law does not determine a different rule[168]; (2) the SCE-R provides the option to regulate an issues via statutory provision, on the condition that national law permits or does not contain another specific rule[169]; (3) the SCE-R allows a certain issue to be regulated via statutory provisions 'without prejudice to mandatory provisions of national law'[170]; and (4) the SCE-R allows a statutory provision to be defined in accordance with national law.[171]

Complexity of the analyses is further enhanced, because the references do not all refer to the same branch of national law. For instance, some provisions refer to national cooperative law, whereas others refer to laws applicable to public limited-liability companies.[172] If a choice exists concerning which law to apply, member states generally have the power to dictate a rule that either differs from an SCE provision or acts in addition to an SCE-R rule. In this case, if the option is not exercised, the rule contained in the SCE-R must be observed. In many cases the SCE-R uses wording such as 'a member state may stipulate'.[173]

To sum up, within this category of special references, it is possible to distinguish between (1) simple references and (2) mandatory and non-mandatory options.[174] Regarding the former, one can refer, for example, to the references determined by Art. 8 para. 1 letter c SCE-R: these refer to the entire body of laws, including judge-made laws. For specific regulatory areas, the SCE-R contains general references on national law. Examples include Art. 17 para. 1 SCE-R[175] or Art. 53 SCE-R.[176] Simple references also refer to specific branches of law, for instance, cooperative law or national public limited-liability law. In addition to simple references, the SCE-R contains references that can be grouped as provisions containing an obligation (obligation to act, mandatory options) or an allowance to adopt a measure (empowerment to act, non-mandatory options).[177] These are references in the broadest sense,

2003 on the Statute for European Cooperative /2003 on the Statute for European Cooperative Society (SCE), p. 55. It has been suggested that this approach hampers the effectiveness of the SCE-R. See Fici (2013c), p. 133.

[167]See Fici (2013c), p. 134 et seq.

[168]For example Art. 54 para. 1 SCE-R.

[169]For example Art. 14 para. 1 subpara. 2 or Art. 46 para. 1 subpara. 1 SCE-R.

[170]For example Art. 65 para. 1 SCE-R.

[171]For example Art. 75 para. 1 SCE-R or Art. 46 para. 3 SCE-R.

[172]For example Art. 11 para. 1 SCE-R.

[173]Examples: Art. 6 SCE-R, Art. 37 para. 4 SCE-R, Art. 39 para. 4 SCE-R or Art. 42 para. 2 subpara. 1 SCE-R. See Fici (2013c), p. 134 et seq.

[174]For the SE, see Brandt and Scheifele (2002), p. 552; Lombardo and Pasotti (2004), p. 177; Wagner (2002), p. 987; Hommelhoff and Teichmann (2015), p. 177.

[175]"Subject to this Regulation, the formation of an SCE shall be governed by the law applicable to cooperatives in the Member State in which the SCE establishes its registered office."

[176]Conduct of general meetings.

[177]For the SE, see Lombardo and Pasotti (2004), p. 177.

because once the national legislature has implemented a specific option, it must be considered a simple reference as determined by Art. 8 para. 1 letter c (i) SCE-R.[178] These options can only be implemented by the national legislature. In fact, the SCE-R clearly differentiates between the authority and obligations the drafters and legislatures must consider.[179]

To analyse the SCE-R and to determine differences concerning corporate and financial issues between an Italian and Austrian SCE, the following approach seems most appropriate. First, the rules contained in the SCE-R must be applied. This set of rules includes the specific (101) references contained in the SCE-R. Thus, national law must also be considered in these cases.[180] Next, SCE statutes may regulate a specific issue, provided the SCE-R expressly permits it. Lastly, if any gaps remain, the correct course of action depends on whether the gap has been deliberately left by the legislature. If yes, the applicable law can only be determined according to steps 1 and 2; if not, Art. 8 para. 1 letter c SCE-R applies. If there is any doubt, it seems preferable to assume that a gap has not been left deliberately so as to use national provisions to fill the gap.

Yet nothing has been said about how a cooperative can be designated as an agricultural SCE, i.e., as a particular type of producer cooperative. This issue will be dealt with in Chap. 3 through analyses of national and European law. However, before doing so, it remains to be seen how the two member states, Italy and Austria, have reacted to the possibility of adopting specific acts to introduce the SCE into their legal systems.

2.5 First Considerations on the Application of Reg. 1435/2003 in Austria and Italy's Legal Systems

As explained, Art. 8 para. 1 letter c (i) SCE-R, together with Art. 78 para. 1 SCE-R, comprises the basis for specific acts and measures that implement the SCE-R. The latter contains only a general reference that lacks a narrower application scope. In other words, it merely specifies the principle of effectiveness that was previously addressed by Article 10 ECT and is, therefore, declaratory in nature. Effectiveness here means practical effectiveness and means that all measures contributing to the achievement of the objectives of the Regulation in the country concerned are appropriate.[181] This rather open approach shows that there is room for discretion.

[178]For the SE, see Brandt and Scheifele (2002), p. 553; Lombardo and Pasotti (2004), p. 177 et seq.; Wagner (2002), p. 986 et seq.

[179]See Brandt (2002), p. 992. Also consider Egermann and Heckenthaler (2004), p. 258.

[180]For the SE, see Schröder (2010b), p. 181.

[181]Moreover, it does not mean the entry into force of the regulation itself, as this results from Art. 80 of the SCE-R. The obligation contained therein continues as an obligation to monitor and

Article 78 para. 1 of the SCE-R is intended, first of all, to apply to cases in which the member states feel compelled to take special measures, because certain corporate legal structures do not exist in their national law.[182] These implementing laws must, however, strictly comply with the provisions of the Regulation. This means, for example, that member states must adapt their existing legal system to the provisions on the structure of the SCE in accordance with Art. 36 et seq. of the SCE-R to the extent necessary for its entry into force. In addition, member states may act on the basis of Art. 78 para. 1 SCE-R if measures outside explicit authorisations[183] should become necessary.

Italy and Austria apply these principles differently. While Austria has adopted a specific law, Italy has simply declared via two communications enacted by the ministry of economic development[184] that implementation is not necessary,[185] because its cooperative legislation already offers an adequate legislative framework for the SCE. These communications do not change the legal system, nor do they provide binding legal interpretation.[186]

Concerning the framework an SCE must consider, Ministry for economic development (2006) explains that the existing Italian normative framework also applies to an SCE with no need for further intervention by the legislature. The communication merely acknowledges that the given national legal framework has been applicable to an SCE since 18 August 2006, and it is not necessary to further confirm the binding nature of the national rules. The communication clarifies that the normative rules are already present in the Italian legal system, so the full application of the SCE-R can be based on the existing legal system alone and not account for the communication, which is a mere administrative act.[187] Next, the communication refers to some peculiarities of Italian cooperative law. It confirms that the reference to the provisions adopted for a *spa* not only apply to national cooperatives but also to SCEs. It stresses that the provisions of the SCE-R outline a legal framework inspired by the

intervene; therefore, member states must monitor future compliance with the requirements. See Langhein (2015), p. 966.

[182]The norm addressees are member states, and this refers to all government bodies involved in the implementation of the SCE regulation, particularly the legislature.

[183]As determined by the SCE-R, e.g., see Arts. 42 para. 2 or 47 para. 2 subpara. 2 SCE-R.

[184]A general communication no. 9203 of 30 June 2006, and a specific communication no 57 of 26 March 2007. The latter designates the competent authorities as requested by Art. 70 para. 2 SCE-R.

[185]Likewise Malta. See Fici (2010), p. 45.

[186]Communication no 9203 is interpretive, but ultimately not binding. Considering the nature and purpose of the communication, it has been criticised that it is impossible to meaningfully speak of implementation of SCE regulation, arguing that this is requested by Art. 78 SCE-R or considered by Art. 8 para. 1 letter c (i) SCE-R. This interpretation, however, seems not correct. See Fici and Strano (2010), p. 673. Also consider Ministry for economic development (2006), premessa.

[187]See Ministry for economic development, premessa. Also consider Fici and Strano (2010), p. 673; Chirico and Troianiello (2007), p. 35; Avsec (2009), p. 36.

provisions for the *spa*. The communication then makes some observations about specific provisions of the SCE-R.[188]

The Italian legislature thus has not implemented the SCE-R. This was, from an Italian perspective, not necessary. Consequently, certain options were not applied, even though communication no. 9203 contains observations about some of these.[189] This leads to differences between an Italian SCE and an Italian cooperative. It is rather critically stressed that 'too much reliance has probably been given to the recently reformed company law (2003 reform). And also to the interpretive function, quite important because of the complexity of the sources of the regulation of the SCE, has been delegated to a badly drafted communication, which does not deepen the point in general, but only expresses a few thoughts of scarce relevance, or ventures to suggest interpretations that would require more investigation'.[190]

By contrast, the Austrian legislature had to adopt a different approach and implement the SCE-R with a special law, the *GenRÄG* 2006.[191] This law includes the *Gesetz über das Statut der Europäischen Genossenschaft* (*SCEG*)[192] and indicates modifications of the existing federal law on cooperatives (*GenG*). This law also adapts other laws to make the SCE-R applicable.[193] Thus, the *SCEG* has adapted the existing Austrian legal framework, not only by introducing specific rules that regulate the procedure for establishing an SCE or transferring the registered office of an SCE to another country, but also by adopting specific provisions that govern the structure of an SCE: It has therefore introduced the one-tier system into cooperative law.

References

Ajates Gonzalez R (2018) Farmers' cooperatives and sustainable food systems in Europe. Earthscan Food and Agriculture Ser. Routledge, Milton

Albamonte D (2008) Lo statuto della società cooperativa europea. In: Capriglione F (ed) La nuova disciplina della società europea. Cedam, Padova, pp 295–320

Arnò G, Cancarini S, Romanelli F (2007) La società europea: La disciplina comunitaria e il suo recepimento in Italia e nei principali stati membri. EGEA, Milano

188See Ministry for economic development (2006). Also consider Fici and Strano (2010), p. 673 et seq.; Chirico and Troianiello (2007), p. 35. Also consider Cusa in this context, who refers to the provisions determined for public limited-liability companies. Cusa (2004). Also consider Iengo (2006) and Chirico and Troianiello (2007), p. 35 et seq.

189See Fici and Strano (2010), p. 675 et seq. Also consider Chirico and Troianiello (2007), p. 35.

190See Fici and Strano (2010), p. 676.

191Published 26 June 2006, in the Austrian Bundesgesetzblatz, BGBL L number 100/2006.

192Law on SCEs. The SCEG contains 33 sections, regulating the procedure for establishing an SCE or transferring the registered office of an SCE to another country. It also contains specific provisions governing the structure of an SCE. Sec. 4 SCEG designates the courts of first instance for commercial matters as the authority required by Art. 78 para. 2 SCE-R.

193See Rößl and Reiner (2010).

Avsec F (2009) Die Europäische Genossenschaft innerhalb des europäischen Wirtschaftsraumes. Marburger Beiträge zum Genossenschaftswesen, vol 53. Universität Marburg, Institut für Genossenschaftswesen, Marburg

Beuthien V (2018) Einleitung. In: Beuthien V, Schöpflin M (eds) Genossenschaftsgesetz: Mit Umwandlungs- und Kartellrecht sowie Statut der Europäischen Genossenschaft, 16th edn. Beck, München, pp 1–24

Bianca M, Zanardo A (2016) La Società Europea e la Società Cooperativa Europea. In: Pederzini E (ed) Percorsi di diritto societario europeo, 3rd edn. Giappichelli, Torino, pp 177–214

Birchall J (1997) The international co-operative movement. Manchester University Press, Manchester

Birchall J (2011) People centred businesses: co-operatives, mutuals and the idea of membership. Palgrave Macmillan, Basingstoke

Bieber R, Kotzur M (2016) § 4 Institutionelles System. In: Bieber R, Epiney A, Haag M, Kotzur M (eds) Die Europäische Union: Europarecht und Politik. Nomos, Baden-Baden, pp 101–127

Bonfante G (2006) La società cooperativa europea. In: Galletti D, Fici A (eds) La società cooperativa europea: Quali prospettive per la cooperazione italiana? Universita degli Studi di Trento, Trento, pp 3–12

Bonfante G (ed) (2014) La società cooperativa. Trattato di diritto commerciale. Cedam, Padova

Brandt U (2002) Überlegungen zu einem SE-Ausführungsgesetz. Neue Zeitschrift für Gesellschaftsrecht:991–996

Brandt U (2003) Der Diskussionsentwurf zu einem SE-Ausführungsgesetz. DStR:1208–1215

Brandt U, Scheifele M (2002) Die Europäische Aktiengesellschaft und das anwendbare Recht. DStR:547–555

Brendel M (2011) Genossenschaftsbewegung in Deutschland - Geschichte und Aktualität. In: Allgeier M (ed) Solidarität, Flexibilität, Selbsthilfe. VS Verlag für Sozialwissenschaften, Wiesbaden, pp 1–36

Bungert H, Beier CH (2002) Die Europäische Aktiengesellschaft. EWS - Europäisches Wirtschafts- und Steuerrecht:1–12

Buonocore V (1997) Diritto della cooperazione. Strumenti. Diritto. Il Mulino, Bologna

Casper M (2003) Der Lückenschluß im Statut der Europäischen Aktiengesellschaft. In: Habersack M (ed) Festschrift für Peter Ulmer zum 70. Geburtstag am 2. Januar 2003. De Gruyter, Berlin, pp 51–72

Chirico S, Troianiello P (2007) La società cooperativa europea: Regolamento CE n. 1435/2003. Cooperative e consorzi. IPSOA, Milano

Chukwu SC (1990) Economics of the co-operative business enterprise. Theory and practice of self-help promotion Ser. A, Monographs and textbooks, vol 2. Marburg Consult für Selbsthilfeförderung, Marburg

Cole GDH (1944) A century of co-operation. Georg Allen & Unwin Ltd

Corapi D, de Donno B (2006) Le società in generale. In: Alessi R, Contaldi L, Corapi D, de Donno B (eds) Impresa e società nel diritto comunitario, 2nd edn. Giappichelli, Torino, pp 1275–1324

Corapi D, Pernazza F (2011) La Società europea: Fonti comunitarie e modelli nazionali. Giappichelli, Torino

Costa CTD, Bilreiro AdM (2003) The European company statute. European business law & practice series, vol 19. Kluwer Law International, The Hague

Cusa E (2004) Zur Rechtslage in den Mitgliedsstaaten: Italien. In: Schulze R (ed) Europäische Genossenschaft SCE: Handbuch, 1st edn. Nomos, Baden-Baden, pp 176–183

Dellinger M (2006) Was bringt das GenRÄG 2006? ecolex:570

Ebert S (2003a) Das anwendbare Konzernrecht der Europäischen Aktiengesellschaft. Betriebs-Berater:1854–1860

Ebert S (2003b) The European company on the level playing field of the community. Eur Bus Law Rev:183–192

Egermann C, Heckenthaler S (2004) Der Verwaltungsrat in der Europäischen Gesellschaft (SE) österreichischer Prägung: Überlegungen zu §§ 38 ff SEG. GesRZ:256–266

Engelhardt WW (1990) Die Genossenschaftsidee als Gestaltungsprinzip. In: Laurinkari J (ed) Genossenschaftswesen: Hand- und Lehrbuch. Oldenbourg, München, pp 10–27

European Commission (2012) Report from the Commission to the Council and the European Parliament, the European Economic and Social Committee and the Committee of the Regions. The application of Council Regulation (EC) No 1435/2003 of 22 July 2003 on the Statute for a European Cooperative Society (SCE), COM (2012) 72 final eur-lex.europa.eu/legal-content/EN/TXT/?uri=CELEX%3A52012DC0072. Accessed 29 Dec 2019

Fabbri F (ed) (1979) Il movimento cooperativo nella storia d'Italia, 1854-1975. Feltrinelli, Milano

Fabbri F (2011) L'Italia cooperativa: Centocinquant'anni di storia e di memoria 1861-2011. Ediesse, Roma

Fajardo G (2012) Cooperative finance and cooperative identity. SSRN Electron J:1–12. https://doi.org/10.2139/ssrn.2185328

Ficari L (2008) La partecipazione dei lavoratori nella società europea: Punto d'arrivo o di partenza? In: Capriglione F (ed) La nuova disciplina della società europea. Cedam, Padova, pp 207–234

Fici A (2006) Società cooperative europea e partecipazione dei lavoratori. In: Galletti D, Fici A (eds) La società cooperativa europea: Quali prospettive per la cooperazione italiana? Universita degli Studi di Trento, Trento, pp 137–155

Fici A (2010) Mapping of the relevant legislation implementing the SCE regulation in the EU Member States and EEA countries. In: Fici A (ed) Study on the implementation of the Regulation 1435/2003 on the Statute for European Cooperative Society (SCE): Executive Summary and Part I: Synthesis and comparative report. Report drawn up following call tender no ENTR/2009/021 of 23 April from the European Commission, pp 33–80

Fici A (2012) Cooperative identity and the law. SSRN Electron J. https://doi.org/10.2139/ssrn.2005014

Fici A (2013a) An introduction to cooperative law. In: Cracogna D, Fici A, Henrÿ H (eds) International handbook of cooperative law. Springer, Berlin, Heidelberg, pp 3–62

Fici A (2013b) Pan-European Cooperative Law: where do we stand? SSRN Electron J:1–12. https://doi.org/10.2139/ssrn.2198283

Fici A (2013c) The European Cooperative Society. In: Cracogna D, Fici A, Henrÿ H (eds) International handbook of cooperative law. Springer, Berlin, Heidelberg, pp 115–151

Fici A (2014) The essential role of cooperative law. Dovenschmidt Q 2:147–158. https://doi.org/10.5553/DQ/221199812014002004003

Fici A, Strano C (2010) Italy. In: Fici A (ed) Study on the implementation of the Regulation 1435/2003 on the Statute for European Cooperative Society (SCE): Final Study Part II. National Reports. Report drawn up following call tender no ENTR/2009/021 of 23 April from the European Commission, pp 671–702

Fischer T (1995) Die Europäische Genossenschaft. Univ., Diss.-1995--Münster (Westfalen), 1994. Kooperations- und genossenschaftswissenschaftliche Beiträge, Band 34. Institut für Genossenschaftswesen der Westfälischen Wilhelms-Universität, Münster

Fleischer H (2004) Der Einfluß der Societas Europaea auf die Dogmatik des deutschen Gesellschaftsrechts. Archiv für die civilistische Praxis 204:502–543

Fleischer H (2010) Supranational corporate forms in the European Union: prolegomena to a theory on supranational forms of association. Common Mark Law Rev:1671–1717

Fornasari M, Zamagni V (1997) Il movimento cooperativo in Italia: Un profilo storico-economico (1854-1992). Vallecchi, Firenze

Galle RCJ (2006) The Societas Cooperativa Europea (SCE) and national cooperatives in comparative perspective. Eur Comp Law:225–260

Germanò A (2008) Le agevolazioni fiscali alle cooperative sono aiuti di stato oggetto di autorizzazione della Commissione? Diritto e giurisprudenza agraria, alimentare e dell'ambiente:413–418

Greda C (2014) Statut der Europäischen Genossenschaft. In: Dellinger M (ed) Genossenschaftsgesetz samt Nebengesetzen: Kommentar, 2nd edn. LexisNexis ARD Orac, Wien, pp 829–854

Hagen-Eck R (1995) Die Europäische Genossenschaft. Duncker et Humblot, Berlin
Henrÿ H (2012) Guidelines for cooperative legislation, 3rd edn. International Labour Organization, Geneva
Henrÿ H (2013a) Public international cooperative law. In: Cracogna D, Fici A, Henrÿ H (eds) International handbook of cooperative law. Springer, Berlin, Heidelberg, pp 65–88
Henrÿ H (2013b) The contribution of the ILO to the formation of public international cooperative law. In: Kott S, Droux J (eds) Globalizing social rights. Palgrave Macmillan UK, London, pp 98–114
Henrÿ H (2017) Co-operative principles and co-operative law across the globe. In: Michie J, Blasi JR, Borzaga C (eds) The Oxford handbook of mutual, co-operative, and co-owned business, 1st edn. Oxford University Press, Oxford, pp 39–52
Hiez D (2017) Introduction. In: Fajardo-García IG, Fici A, Henrÿ H, Hiez D, Meira DMMA, Münkner H-H, Snaith I (eds) Principles of European Cooperative Law: principles, commentaries and national reports. Intersentia, Cambridge, pp 1–15
Hiez D, Tadjudje W (2013) The OHADA cooperative regulation. In: Cracogna D, Fici A, Henrÿ H (eds) International handbook of cooperative law. Springer, Berlin, Heidelberg, pp 89–113
Holthaus J, Lehnhoff DJ (2016) Einf. In: Lehnhoff DJ, Holthaus J (eds) Lang/Weidmüller Genossenschaftsgesetz: Gesetz, betreffend die Erwerbs- und Wirtschaftsgenossenschaften mit Erläuterungen zum Umwandlungsgesetz und zur Europäischen Genossenschaft (SCE), 38., neu bearbeitete Auflage. De Gruyter, Berlin, pp 1–54
Hommelhoff P (2003) Satzungsstrenge und Gestaltungsfreiheit in der Europäischen Aktiengesellschaft. In: Habersack M (ed) Festschrift für Peter Ulmer zum 70. Geburtstag am 2. Januar 2003. De Gruyter, Berlin, pp 267–278
Hommelhoff P, Teichmann C (2015) Art. 9. In: Lutter M, Hommelhoff P, Teichmann C (eds) SE-Kommentar, 2nd edn. Verlag Dr. Otto Schmidt, Köln, pp 172–193
Hoyt A (1996) And then there were seven: cooperative principles updated
Ianes A (2013) Introduzione alla storia della cooperazione in Italia (1854-2011): Profilo storico-economico e interpretazione. Università. Rubbettino, Soveria Mannelli
Ibáñez IE (2011) Law applicable to the European Cooperative Society: special reference to the European cooperative established in Spain. Eur Comp Financ Law Rev 8:30–46. https://doi.org/10.1515/ecfr.2011.30
Iengo M (2006) Gli Studi del CNN - Società cooperativa europea - Analisi delle norme applicabili ai sensi dell'articolo 8 del regolamento n. 1435/2003 - Casi e materiali di diritto comunitario di interesse notarile: le società - e.library - Fondazione Italiana del Notariato. Studio n. 9-2006/I. http://elibrary.fondazionenotariato.it/approfondimento.asp?app=21/studiCNN/mi_9_2006_I&mn=3&tipo=3&qn=6. Accessed 21 Nov 2019
International Co-operative Alliance, Guidance Notes to the Co-operative Principles (2015). https://www.ica.coop/en/media/library/research-and-reviews/guidance-notes-cooperative-principles?_ga=2.123262351.52726143.1574094684-1144315335.1574094684. Accessed 18 Nov 2019
Jaecks J, Schönborn AC (2003) Die Europäische Aktiengesellschaft, das Internationale und das deutsche Konzernrecht. Recht der Internationalen Wirtschaft:254–265
Jagschitz F, Rom S, Wiedey J (2015) Gemeinsame Geschichte Österreichischer Genossenschaftsverband (ÖGV) und Konsumverband. In: Brazda J, van Husen R, Rößl D (eds) Perspektiven für die Genossenschaftsidee: Festschrift zum 65. Geburtstag von Verbandsanwalt Professor DDr. Hans Hofinger. EHV Academicpress, Bremen, pp 58–68
Koke C (2005) Die Finanzverfassung der Europäischen Aktiengesellschaft (SE) mit Sitz in Deutschland. Univ., Diss.—Würzburg, 2004. Schriftenreihe zum deutschen und europäischen Gesellschafts- und Wirtschaftsrecht, vol 3. Peter Lang, Frankfurt am Main
Korte O (2012) Die Europäische Genossenschaft (SCE): Analyse der mangelnden Verbreitung dieser supranationalen Rechtsform. In: Baudenbacher C (ed) Aktuelle Entwicklungen des europäischen und internationalen Wirtschaftsrechts. Helbing et Lichtenhahn, Basel, München [u.a.], pp 323–349
Krimphove D (2010) Brauchen wir die Europäische Genossenschaft? EuZW:892–897

Kübler F (2003) Leitungsstrukturen der Aktiengesellschaft und die Umsetzung des SE-Statuts. Zeitschrift für das gesamte Handelsrecht und Wirtschaftsrecht (ZHR):222–234
Lächler C, Oplustil K (2005) Funktion und Umfang des Regelungsbereichs der SE-Verordnung. Neue Zeitschrift für Gesellschaftsrecht:381–388
Langhein G (2015) § 68. In: Lutter M, Hommelhoff P, Teichmann C (eds) SE-Kommentar, 2nd edn. Verlag Dr. Otto Schmidt, Köln, pp 965–969
Laurinkari J (1990) Einführung. In: Laurinkari J (ed) Genossenschaftswesen: Hand- und Lehrbuch. Oldenbourg, München, pp 1–10
Lehner JH (2009) Verschmelzungsvarianten einer Europäischen Genossenschaft (SCE). In: Haslinger M, Kanonier A, Zehetner S (eds) Ein Jurist im Spannungsfeld von Wirtschaft, Technik und Recht: Festschrift für Franz Zehetner zum 60. Geburtstag. NWV, Wien, pp 97–110
Lombardo S, Pasotti P (2004) The Societas Europaea: a network economics approach. Eur Comp Financ Law Rev 1:169–205. https://doi.org/10.1515/ecfr.2004.1.2.169
Lutter M, Schmidt J, Bayer W (2012) Europäisches Unternehmens- und Kapitalmarktrecht: Grundlagen, Stand und Entwicklung nebst Texten und Materialien, 5th edn. Zeitschrift für Unternehmens- und Gesellschaftsrecht. Sonderheft, T. 1. De Gruyter, Berlin
Manzini P (2006) Società Cooperativa Europea e diritto di stabilimento. In: Galletti D, Fici A (eds) La società cooperativa europea: Quali prospettive per la cooperazione italiana? Universita degli Studi di Trento, Trento, pp 27–48
Marano P (2006) La Società Cooperativa Europea nell'ambito delle politiche comunitarie in materia di reti e gruppi d'imprese. In: Galletti D, Fici A (eds) La società cooperativa europea: Quali prospettive per la cooperazione italiana? Universita degli Studi di Trento, Trento, pp 13–26
Maul S (1998) Die faktisch abhängige SE (Societas Europaea) im Schnittpunkt zwischen deutschem und europäischem Recht. Univ., Diss.—Heidelberg, 1997. Europäisches Wirtschaftsrecht, vol 12. Beck, München
Merkt H (1992) Europäische Aktiengesellschaft: Gesetzgebung als Selbstzweck? BB:652
Michie J, Blasi JR, Borzaga C (2017) Introduction an overview. In: Michie J, Blasi JR, Borzaga C (eds) The Oxford handbook of mutual, co-operative, and co-owned business, 1st edn. Oxford University Press, Oxford, pp XXIII–XXXVI
MIHR (1982) http://aei.pitt.edu/62706/1/B2371.pdf. Accessed 25 Oct 2019
Ministry for economic development (2006), Communication no 9203, 30 June 2006, GU no 171 25.07.2006.
Miribung G (2014) Über das genossenschaftliche Eigentum in der italienischen Rechtsordnung. In: Laurinkari J (ed) Genossenschaftswissenschaft zwischen Theorie und Geschichte: Festschrift für Prof. Dr. Johann Brazda zum 60. Geburstag. EHV Academicpress, Bremen, pp 779–791
Miribung G, Reiner E (2013) Austria. In: Cracogna D, Fici A, Henrÿ H (eds) International handbook of cooperative law. Springer, Berlin, Heidelberg, pp 231–250
Morales Gutierrez AC (2004) A comparative synthesis of 20th century agricultural cooperative movements in Europe. J Rural Coop:47–65
Münkner H-H (1995) Chances of co-operatives in the future: contribution to the International Co-operative Alliance centennial 1895 - 1995. Papers and Reports/Institute for Co-operation in Developing Countries, vol 31. Marburg Consult für Selbsthilfeförderung eG, Marburg/Lahn
Münkner H-H (2006) Europäische Genossenschaft (SCE) und Europäische Genossenschaftstradition. Vorträge und Aufsätze des Forschungsvereins für Genossenschaftswesen, vol 30. Eigenverlag des FOG, Wien
Murschitz K (2005a) Die Organstruktur der österreichischen Societas Europaea (SE) und Corporate Governance (CG) (Teil I). GesRZ:227
Murschitz K (2005b) Die Organstruktur der österreichischen Societas Europaea (SE) und Corporate Governance (CG) (Teil II). GesRZ:284
Paolucci LF (2019) Art. 45 Cost. In: Paolucci LF (ed) Codice delle cooperative 2019: Aggiornato con le novità del D.Lgs. n. 14/2019. Maggioli, Santarcangelo di Romagna, Rimini, pp 13–25
Paolucci LF (2012) Definizione e aspetti caratterizzanti. In: Paolucci LF (ed) Le società cooperative. UTET giuridica, Torino, pp 1–23

Pellegrini M (2008) Gli antecedenti storici della società europea. In: Capriglione F (ed) La nuova disciplina della società europea. Cedam, Padova, pp 103–126

Pestoff VA (2017) The social and political dimensions of co-operative enterprises. In: Michie J, Blasi JR, Borzaga C (eds) The Oxford handbook of mutual, co-operative, and co-owned business, 1st edn. Oxford University Press, Oxford, pp 76–94

Piras A (2017) Le società cooperative. In: de Angelis L, Bertacchini E (eds) Diritto commerciale II. Wolters Kluwer; Cedam, Milano, Padova, pp 107–132

Presti G (2006) Le fonti della disciplina e l'organizzazione interna della società cooperative europea. In: Galletti D, Fici A (eds) La società cooperativa europea: Quali prospettive per la cooperazione italiana? Universita degli Studi di Trento, Trento, pp 67–86

Raaijmakers T (1999) The Statute for a European Company: its impact on board structures, and corporate governance in the European Union. Eur Bus Organ Law Rev 5:159–194. https://doi.org/10.1017/S1566752904001594

Rabbeno U (1915) Le società cooperative di produzione, Milano

Raiser T (1993) Die europäische Aktiengesellschaft und die nationalen Aktiengesetze. In: Bierich M (ed) Festschrift für Johannes Semler zum 70. Geburtstag am 28. April 1993: Unternehmen und Unternehmensführung im Recht. De Gruyter, Berlin, pp 277–298

Rasner H (1992) Die Europäische Aktiengesellschaft (SE) – ist sie wünschenswert? Zeitschrift für Unternehmens- und Gesellschaftsrecht 21:314–326. https://doi.org/10.1515/zgre.1992.21.3.314

Ringle G (2007) Genossenschaftliche Prinzipien im Spannungsfeld zwischen Tradition und Modernität. Wismarer Diskussionspapiere. Hochsch. Fachbereich Wirtschaft, Wismar

Rondinelli M (2016) L'armonizzazione nel diritto delle società: evoluzione e prospettive. In: Pederzini E (ed) Percorsi di diritto societario europeo, 3rd edn. Giappichelli, Torino, pp 43–94

Rößl R, Reiner E (2010) Austria. In: Fici A (ed) Study on the implementation of the Regulation 1435/2003 on the Statute for European Cooperative Society (SCE): Final Study Part II. National Reports. Report drawn up following call tender no ENTR/2009/021 of 23 April from the European Commission, pp 325–342

Ruggeri R (1994) Cooperative. In: Zamagni S (ed) Politica economica II. UTET libreria, Torino, pp 113–116

Sarcina A (2006) La Societas Europaea e il consolidamento del sistema societario europea. Europa e Diritto Privato:729–754

Sarti A (2012) L'analisi della Corte di Giustizia sul regime fiscale delle cooperative di produzione a lavoro. Giurisprudenza Commerciale:605–615

Schaschko M (2010) Neugründungen von Genossenschaften in Österreich. Wiener Studien des Forschungsvereins für Genossenschaftswesen, vol 18. Eigenverlag des FOG, Wien

Schöpflin M (2018a) Art. 08. In: Beuthien V, Schöpflin M (eds) Genossenschaftsgesetz: Mit Umwandlungs- und Kartellrecht sowie Statut der Europäischen Genossenschaft, 16th edn. Beck, München, pp 1259–1263

Schöpflin M (2018b) Einl. SCE. In: Beuthien V, Schöpflin M (eds) Genossenschaftsgesetz: Mit Umwandlungs- und Kartellrecht sowie Statut der Europäischen Genossenschaft, 16th edn. Beck, München, pp 1230–1235

Schröder A (2010a) Art. 10. In: Manz G, Mayer B, Schröder A (eds) Europäische Aktiengesellschaft SE: SE, 2nd edn. Nomos, Baden-Baden, pp 204–206

Schröder A (2010b) Art. 9. In: Manz G, Mayer B, Schröder A (eds) Europäische Aktiengesellschaft SE: SE, 2nd edn. Nomos, Baden-Baden, pp 179–204

Schröder A (2010c) Vorbemerkungen. In: Manz G, Mayer B, Schröder A (eds) Europäische Aktiengesellschaft SE: SE, 2nd edn. Nomos, Baden-Baden, pp 21–49

Schulz A, Geismair B (2001) Die Europäische Aktiengesellschaft - Eine kritische Bestandsaufnahme. DStR:1078–1085

Schulze R (2004) Einführung: Die Verordnung über das Statut der Europäischen Genossenschaft. In: Schulze R (ed) Europäische Genossenschaft SCE: Handbuch, 1st edn. Nomos, Baden-Baden, pp 1–18

Senti R, Hilpold P (2017) WTO: System und Funktionsweise der Welthandelsordnung, 2nd edn. Schulthess, Zürich

Sepe M (2008) La cosituzione della società europea nel riferimento alle unità economico-giuridiche nazionali. In: Capriglione F (ed) La nuova disciplina della società europea. Cedam, Padova, pp 145–176

Shaffer J (1999) Historical dictionary of the cooperative movement. Historical dictionaries of religions, philosophies, and movements, vol 26. Scarecrow Press, Lanham

Snaith I (2004) Das anwendbare Recht. In: Schulze R (ed) Europäische Genossenschaft SCE: Handbuch, 1st edn. Nomos, Baden-Baden, pp 19–42

Snaith I (2006) Employee involvement in the European Cooperative Society: a range of stakeholders? Int J Comp Labour Law Ind Relat:213–230

Stiglitz JE (2009) Moving beyond market fundamentalism to a more balanced economy. Ann Public Coop Econ 80:345–360. https://doi.org/10.1111/j.1467-8292.2009.00389.x

Tomanek P (2014) Vor § 1 GenG. In: Dellinger M (ed) Genossenschaftsgesetz samt Nebengesetzen: Kommentar, 2nd edn. LexisNexis ARD Orac, Wien, pp 1–16

Vella M (2010) Oltre il motivo del profitto: Storia, economia, gestione e finanza delle imprese cooperative italiane. Economia sociale, vol 51. Maggioli, Santarcangelo di Romagna, Rimini

Wagner J (2002) Die Bestimmung des auf die SE anwendbaren Rechts. Neue Zeitschrift für Gesellschaftsrecht:985–990

Werlauff E (2003) The SE company – a new common European company from 8 October 2004. Eur Bus Law Rev:85–103

Zamagni V (2017) A worldwide historical perspective on co-operatives and their evolution. In: Michie J, Blasi JR, Borzaga C (eds) The Oxford handbook of mutual, co-operative, and co-owned business, 1st edn. Oxford University Press, Oxford, pp 97–113

Zamagni V, Felice E (2006) Oltre il secolo: Le trasformazioni del sistema cooperativo Legacoop alla fine del secondo millennio. Storia e studi cooperativi. Il Mulino, Bologna

Chapter 3
Defining Agricultural SCEs with Several Steps

3.1 Introduction

The SCE is a cooperative, and in the Italian and Austrian legal systems, provisions on cooperatives in both countries are manifested in the three types of cooperatives, i.e. consumer, worker and service cooperatives. The question arises as to whether and how an Italian or Austrian agricultural cooperative can be set up as an SCE. Though there is a general picture of what a cooperative is, the specific details are conceived differently. This depends not only on different historical developments but also on different approaches, which are based on different political views. Basically, cooperatives can be defined through general principles and legal provisions, which are more precise. However, legal definitions stem from different legal systems and can display significant differences, despite the appearance of similar or identical features.[1]

What, then, is a cooperative from a legal point of view? What seems trivial, especially since cooperatives are among the most popular instruments for enabling entrepreneurial cooperation worldwide and are thus recognised in both developed and less developed countries, is that there is still no precise definition of what a cooperative really is. In general, a cooperative is a firm owned (because of shareholdership) and controlled by the persons who transact with it. These persons are in principle not investors. Hence there is no investor relationship. Instead, the relationship is based on supplying the cooperative, working for it or purchasing its products. Put simply, a cooperative is owned by its suppliers, workers or customers. These groups receive specific advantages, depending on the type of business, and

[1] See Hiez (2017), p. 9 et seq.; Schulze (2004), p. 10 et seq.

G. Miribung, *The Agricultural Cooperative in the Framework of the European Cooperative Society*, Economic Analysis of Law in European Legal Scholarship 8,
https://doi.org/10.1007/978-3-030-44154-8_3

they have control over the enterprise.[2] One definition of a cooperative summarises these observations: 'A cooperative is a user-owned and user-controlled business that distributes the benefits on the basis of use'.[3] This definition contains three elements: First, the persons who own and finance the cooperative are those who use it. Second, the cooperative is controlled by those who use it. Finally, the benefits of the cooperative are distributed to its users on the basis of their use.[4] This return is called 'patronage refund'.[5]

This phenomenon is also described as a People Centred Business,[6] a type of business in which the members use the cooperative to satisfy their own interests. This 'use' must be clearly identified. To put it simply, a person interested in financial services could hardly be interested in the services of a cooperative running an agricultural holding. From a legal point of view, this requires examining whether there are specific rules that link personal interests to the scope of the business—and this in turn requires clearly defining the requirements for those people who wish to become part of the cooperative. It is therefore necessary to define from the outset the group of people who might actually be interested in participating in the cooperative. This connection of people's interests gives rise to specific governance and financial issues, which will be further discussed in Chaps. 4 and 5 of this study.

Still, from a legal point of view, we have not yet fully clarified what an agricultural cooperative is. Since it is agricultural in scope and therefore offers various benefits to the wider community, an agricultural cooperative is not only heavily regulated—to ensure a reliable/healthy food—but also subsidised.[7] Therefore, agricultural cooperatives are not only a matter of private law, but also of public law. In fact, legislatures have enacted various pieces of legislation that help both farmers and agricultural cooperatives stay competitive in a globalised market, for example, by providing them with financial support. Granting financial support, however, requires a clear definition of the object to be promoted so as to prevent abuse. Therefore, a cooperative is determined not only by its scope under private law (including its participating members, the farmers) but also by other norms, which as a rule determine the legal content of the terms agricultural activity and agriculture.

---

[2]See Molk (2014), p. 910; Hansmann (1999), p. 388; Lehmann (2014), p. 36 et seq.; Fici (2017), p. 20 et seq. For details, see Sect. 3.2. For general observations, see Engelhardt (1977).

In contrast, many large-scale enterprises are owned by outside investors. See Molk (2014), p. 901. In this context also consider World Co-operative Monitor 2018.

[3]See Barton (1989), p. 1 et seq. Also consider Ortmann and King (2007), p. 42.

[4]See Barton in Cobia 1 et seq. Also consider Nilsson (2001), p. 341; Ortmann and King (2007), p. 42. Generally, Nilsson (1999).

[5]See Fici (2013a), p. 40 et seq.; Henrÿ (2012), p. 78.

[6]See Birchall (2011).

[7]On this issue, see, among others, Holzer (2018), p. 153 et seq.; Germanò and Rook Basile (2014), p. 127 et seq.; Martinez (2016d), p. 770 et seq.; Vecchione (2009c), p. 353 et seq.; Iannarelli (2001), p. 35 et seq.; Norer (2005), pp. 469 et seq. and 485 et seq.; Götz (2012), p. 11 et seq., Alessi (2006), p. 1255 et seq.

Therefore, this first part begins with a discussion of (1) what a cooperative is,[8] then (2) what agricultural activities are or could be (this is necessary to determine the specific object of an agricultural cooperative),[9] and finally (3) to analyse to what extent and how legal norms can be used to clearly link features of agricultural activities with the object of a cooperative.[10] This last aspect also concerns the involvement of members and the definition of appropriate member policies. This last point is essential for the effectiveness and efficiency of an agricultural cooperative and must therefore be included in a discussion that seeks to clarify what an agricultural cooperative is. This chapter continues with specific insights from economic theory that help explain how agricultural cooperatives function and what clauses they can integrate into their statutes to be effective[11]; finally the notion of "cross-border activities" as a prerequisite for the establishment of the SCE is discussed.[12]

3.2 Explaining the Notion of a Cooperative as Expressed in Reg. 1435/2003 and in Italian and Austrian Legislation

The principles established by the ICA inform how cooperatives function but are clearly too general to define a clear cooperative identity or find an acknowledged legal definition.[13] It is rightly emphasised that a definition cannot cover all the distinguishing features of a cooperative, but that it is also important to read the definition in conjunction with other provisions describing or better explaining its content.[14] To understand the essential function of a cooperative, it is therefore necessary to conduct a step-by-step comparison of the different norms. The PECOL correctly state that a 'definition helps to shape the cooperative identity and thus to distinguish cooperatives from other types of entities(...). However, the importance of a definition must not be overemphasised. In fact, the cooperative

[8]Section 3.2.

[9]Section 3.3.

[10]Section 3.4.

[11]Section 3.5.

[12]Section 3.6.

[13]See Hiez (2017), p. 13. Also consider Beuthien (2007), p. 5; Galle (2006), p. 255; Fici (2010), p. 3 et seq.; Eichwald and Lutz (2011), pp. 41 et seq. and 51. Generally, Ringle (2007), p. 15 et seq.; van Diepenbeek (2007), pp. 13 et seq. and 28 et seq.

This is further complicated by the lack of interest in cooperative law within the international academic community. In fact, cooperative law is primarily discussed among cooperators or cooperative institutions. Nevertheless, there were and are different initiatives that stipulate a legal framework to help provide coherent legislation. These initiatives vary in scope and legal value, and include the SCE-R. See Hiez (2017), p. 14 et seq. Also consider Lehmann (2014), p. 32 et seq.; Krimphove (2010), p. 893; Henrÿ (2012), p. 45 et seq.

[14]See Fici (2017), p. 20 et seq.

identity comprises several aspects and is the result of the overall cooperative regulation, including those provisions dealing with the organisational and financial structure of a cooperative'.[15]

One can ask whether legal rules should determine the identity of a cooperative, as specific elements considered essential for cooperatives in one legal system may not be considered essential in another legal system.[16] For example, a cooperative may focus exclusively on meeting the needs of its members, while other tasks may not be permitted.[17] Conversely, there are cooperatives that provide benefits both to the general public and to their members. An example of this is the social cooperative under Italian law.[18]

Despite these different approaches, it is feasible to define features that are shared by every type of cooperative. The essential elements can be determined with the PECOL. The analysis of national rules also serves to better understand the law applicable to a national SCE (here, an Italian or Austrian one). Therefore, my analyses account for the provisions contained in the SCE-R and supplement them with the Italian and Austrian perspectives. The results are then also discussed in light of the PECOL. But to begin with, one has to consider how the SCE-R deals with the aspect of the definition, because this legal act is the nodal point that holds the different questions together.

The *SCE-R* defines a cooperative in its recitals. They also contain principles that further specify and determine a cooperative's identity. Accordingly, cooperatives are 'primarily groups of persons or legal entities with particular operating principles that are different from those of other economic agents. These include the principles of democratic structure and control and the distribution of the net profit for the financial year on an equitable basis'.[19] To be more precise, the fundamental 'principle of the primacy of the individuals (...) is reflected in the specific rules on membership, resignation and expulsion, where the 'one man, one vote' rule is laid down and the right to vote is vested in the individual, with the implication that members cannot exercise any rights over the assets of the cooperative'.[20] This restriction reflects the principle of disinterested distribution.[21]

---

[15]See Fici (2017), p. 21.

[16]See Henrÿ (2012), p. 45 et seq. Also consider Fici (2013a), p. 16 et seq.; Fici (2012); Hiez (2017), p. 14. Also consider Bonfante (2006), p. 4 et seq. For instance, German law considers the mandatory elements of cooperatives to be: (a) the promotion of members' needs, (b) the secondary status of non-member transactions, (c) statutory freedom, (d) allocation of surplus or profits for transactions conducted between members and the cooperative, (e) the potential for unlimited member liability, and (f) indivisibility of the reserves. See Beuthien (2007), pp. 6 and 16.

[17]For a concise analysis, see Henrÿ, where he discusses cooperatives and the features which distinguish them from social economic enterprises and stock companies. See Henrÿ (2012), p. 30 et seq. Also consider Münkner (2006), p. 12.

[18]On this issue, see Pedri (2017). See also Fici (2014), p. 156 et seq.

[19]See Recital 7 SCE-R.

[20]See Recital 8 SCE-R.

[21]On this issue, see also Pönkä (2018), p. 54 et seq.

When describing the main features of the SCE, Recital 10 stresses that its principal object must be 'the satisfaction of its members' needs and/or the development of their economic and/or social activities'. This complies with the requirement that the activities of an SCE be carried out for the mutual benefit of its members. These benefits shall be allocated according to the participation of the members. This means that 'members of the SCE should also be customers, employees or suppliers or should be otherwise involved in the activities of the SCE'.[22] One refers to this condition as the principle of double quality.[23] Recital 10 adds that membership should not be artificially restricted. We describe this as the principle of open membership. Finally, the distribution of net profit for the financial year must occur in an equitable fashion, and, moreover, interests on share capital have to be limited.[24] The SCE is thus a member-focused, and not an investor-focused, enterprise. It is, therefore, a question of member involvement. This involvement is based on the principle of double quality.

The definition of a cooperative offered by the *Italian legal system* differs, to some degree, from the definition in the SCE-R. One reason is the complexity of Italian legislation dealing with cooperatives. According to this legal system, a cooperative is an autonomous legal form of a company.[25] Italy's legal system contains specific provisions for cooperatives; however, they are scattered among different legal sources. As a result, the Italian legislation on cooperatives is rather complex and fragmentary in nature.[26]

---

[22]See Recital 10 bullet 2 SCE-R.

[23]See Fici (2014), p. 150 et seq.; Schaschko (2010), p. 89 et seq.; Fici (2013a), p. 26; Pönkä (2018), p. 43; Münkner (2015), p. 31 et seq.; Kramer (2006). See also Birchall (2011), p. 205 et seq.

[24]See Recital 7 SCE-R.

[25]Differing from all the other types of business organisations.

[26]In principle, the legal framework determining the functioning of cooperatives can be divided into a group of general provisions and a group of special provisions. General rules are mainly contained in the civil code and have to be applied to all types of cooperatives. However, this basic source of law does not delineate a clear framework. It contains rules specifically adopted for cooperatives (Art. 2511 CC—Art. 2545 octiesdecies CC.), but also refers to provisions to be applied residually, and which have been designed with (capitalistic) companies in mind. In fact, Art. 2519 para. 1 CC declares that, for matters not regulated by the provisions contained in title VI book no 5 of the Italian Civil Code, one has to consider—insofar as these provisions are compatible with cooperatives—the provisions regarding the spa. Alternatively, the provisions adopted for the srl can be applied, depending on the size of the cooperative and contingent on an express choice being formulated in the cooperative's statutes (see Art. 2519 para. 2 CC). The Italian legislator only adapted the existing provisions for the spa, without developing specific provisions for cooperatives. This is true for both the commercial code, enacted in 1882, and the civil code, enacted in 1942, although here fewer references have been provided for. This legislative choice is based on the notion that cooperatives also depend on the rules that govern the markets. It has been criticised that this leads to the imposition of organisation models which primarily pursue a speculative goal at the expense of organisational models which pursue self-organisation. See Bonfante (2014), p. 299 et seq. For details Tatarano (2011), p. 3 et seq. Also consider Zamagni, Per una teoria economico-civile dell'impresa cooperativa, in Mazzoli/Zamagni (Ed), Verso una nuova teoria economica della cooperazione (2005). See also Fauceglia (2019).

The civil code defines a cooperative as a society with variable capital and a mutual purpose that is entered in the register of cooperative societies, according to Art. 2512 para. 2 CC and Art. 223 sexiesdecies of the provisions for the implementation of the present code (prov. impl. CC).[27] The first feature (i.e., variable capital) implies that statutes must not be amended when new members join or old members leave.[28] This feature marks a clear difference to the *spa* and has to be read in conjunction with the principle of open membership (or open door).[29] It also assumes that member numbers can fluctuate.

The other feature refers to the mutual purpose. Even though the Italian definition contains the aim/purpose of a cooperative, the civil code does not explicitly define what this might be. According to case law, the essence of the mutual purpose is determined by the extent to which a cooperative can provide goods, services and/or employment opportunities to its members at conditions more favourable than those provided by the market.[30] Thus, Italian law deals with the principle of double quality. Important in this regard, is also a distinction between a mainly mutual cooperative and other cooperatives, as established by the civil code. These two types of cooperatives mainly differ insofar as the former prevalently conducts business with members and thus may only conduct limited business with non-members, while the latter has more freedom in this regard.[31]

Italian cooperative theory and law, however, not only consider the promotion of member's needs—called internal mutuality—but also permits a mutuality that directly impacts public utility—so-called external mutuality and/or systemic mutuality. This latter type of mutuality is, among others, explained by Art. 2514 CC, which states that, if a mainly mutual cooperative is dissolved, the full residual assets after deducting paid-up capital and dividends must be allocated to mutual funds for

[27]This definition contains a particular feature to help distinguish a cooperative from other legal forms and describes the aim assigned to the cooperative by law. Indeed, the wording "with mutual purpose" is a distinctive and traditional formula of Italian law, referring to the mandate which the SCE regulation or other national laws assign to cooperatives. See Fici (2013b), p. 484. For details Tatarano (2011), p. 82 et seq. See also Piras (2017), p. 110 et seq.; Paolucci (2019a), p. 29 et seq.

[28]Amending statutes requires calling an extraordinary general meeting.

[29]For details, see Sect. 2.1. See also Pönkä (2018), p. 46 et seq.

[30]In other words, an Italian cooperative has to either employ its members (worker cooperatives) or pursue exchanges with its members (consumer cooperatives and production cooperatives). For specific information regarding mandate, membership and similar aspects, see Sect. 3.4.

The law does not specifically limit a cooperative's economic activities, although there are specific rules relating to the nature of business it may conduct. However, these rules apply equally to all legal entities. See Fici and Strano (2010), p. 683; Bonfante (2014), p. 178 et seq.; Paolucci (2019c), p. 64 et seq.

[31]For further information, see Sect. 3.4.1.

the promotion and development of co-operation.[32] This corresponds to the principle of disinterested distribution, which is also mentioned by recital 10 bullet 7 SCE-R.

This second aspect of mutuality clearly demonstrates that the cooperative advantage not only benefits a cooperative's members, but the whole cooperative movement as a whole. This concept, however, is rather general in nature.[33]

Under Italian law, the idea of disinterested distribution is subject to specific rules, such as a specific tax system; it is also an integral part of the specific role that cooperatives are supposed to play in (Italian) society. In this regard, Art. 45 of the Italian Constitution contains this explicit reference: 'the Italian Republic recognises the social function of cooperation with mutual character and without private speculation purposes'. Furthermore, 'the law promotes and favours its growth via the most appropriate means, and insures, with appropriate controls, its character and purposes', implying that the legislature must adopt specific and appropriate legal rules.[34] The application of the principle of disinterested distribution is an important result of this commitment.

Similar to the Italian legal system, *Austrian law* contains specific rules that define what a cooperative is. The legal definition can be found in Sec. 1 para. 1 of the

[32]See Paolucci (2019l), p. 45 et seq.; Paolucci (2019a), p. 33 et seq.; Paolucci (2012b), p. 9 et seq. Also consider Tatarano (2011), p. 62 et seq.; Bonfante (2014), p. 149 et seq. In general, Genco (2014); Ragazzini (1992); Fici (2015), p. 80 et seq. Also consider Sects. 5.3 and 5.5. Similarly, Art. 2545 undecies CC states that if a cooperative is transformed into a company, its assets (at their effective value) must be allocated to mutual funds, after deducting (re-evaluated) subscribed capital and undistributed dividends. As an exception, the law allows increasing non-devolved assets up to the minimum capital necessary to constitute the new company. Also consider Sect. 5.5.

[33]See Paolucci (2012b), p. 9 et seq.; Paolucci (2019a), p. 33 et seq., Law no. 381/1991 addresses social cooperatives, stating that such cooperatives do not pursue a mutual aim but rather promote the general interest of the community. According to Art. 1 para. 1 of this law, "social cooperatives aim to pursue the general interest of the community for the human promotion and social integration of citizens through: (a) the management of social health and education services, (b) the performance of agricultural, industrial, commercial, service or other activities for the working integration of disadvantaged persons." For details consider for example Codini (2007) and Cotronei (2009). In the agricultural sector, for example, this interest includes initiatives that fall within the concept of social farming.

[34]For details see Paolucci (2019k), p. 17 et seq. Also consider Miribung (2014), p. 779 et seq. In line with Art. 45 Cost, Italian cooperatives are subject to public control. Legislative decree no 220/2002 determines the various aspects of this cooperative vigilance. Different forms of control are possible. The ordinary form of control (cooperative revision) basically considers the cooperative's mutual nature, focusing on the effectiveness of membership, the members' contribution to the cooperative's existence (especially by means of transacting with the cooperative), the absence of for-profit aims, eligibility for tax breaks and other benefits and solidity of assets. If irregularities are found via audit, the cooperative must resolve the situation if possible. Otherwise, the supervisory authority can apply different sanctions, including substituting new managers and dissolving the cooperative. The audits are conducted by organisations recognised by the cooperative movement or by the Ministry of Economic Development for Cooperatives. Recognised organisations control all of their associated cooperatives, while the Ministry controls all other cooperatives. Cooperatives are audited every 2 years (ordinary inspections) with the exception of social cooperatives, which are audited every year. Extraordinary inspections are also possible. See Fici and Strano (2010), p. 692 et seq. For details Cusa (2014a). See also Paolucci (2019i).

GenG.[35] Accordingly, cooperatives are 'associations with legal personality and an indeterminate number of members with the principal object to promote their members' business and personal economic activities, such as credit, purchasing, retail, consumer, collecting, utilisation, housing and housing estate cooperatives'. Two aspects are essential: an indeterminate number of members and the promotion of members' activities.

The first feature implies that member numbers can fluctuate. If the competent body (normally the management organ) decides accordingly, new members can easily join and old members can easily leave.[36] As members are also shareholders, this feature implies that the cooperative's capital is dynamic, unlike the relatively static capital of an *AG*, in which a general meeting must be called to make a decision to increase or decrease capital.[37] The Italian definition also refers to this aspect, while the definition provided by the SCE-R is silent.

The second feature is the promotional mandate, the content of which is defined by statutes.[38] It is correct that promoting members' activities is not a cooperative-specific criterion that other legal entities cannot provide. Company shareholders also aim for a certain level promotion: They pool financial resources in order to generate and maximise profits. Therefore, the differences consist in the manner in which promotion must be achieved: the so-called '*naturale Förderung durch Geschäftsverkehr*' ('natural promotion' by means of business transactions) rather than granting dividends.[39] Sec. 1 para. 2 *GenG* specifies that a cooperative's participation in another company must 'serve the statute-like performance of the cooperative's object and not mainly the realization of profit'. Then, according to Sec. 1 para. 3 *GenG*, cooperatives can also pursue the object provided for in Art. 1 para.

---

[35]The Austrian cooperative act was adopted in 1873. See Genossenschaftsgesetz, Austrian Imperial Law Gazette (Reichsgesetzblatt) 1873. It is composed of five main parts with a total of 95 sections. It has been amended several times, most recently in 2006 with a change to cooperative law (Genossenschaftsrechtsänderungsgesetz 2006, [GenRÄG 2006]), in 2008 with a change to company law (Unternehmensrechtsänderungsgesetz 2008 [URÄG 2008]) and finally in 2014 (See Rechnungslegungs-Änderungsgesetz.), 2015 (See Strafrechtsänderungsgesetz.) and 2016 (See Abschlussprüfungsrechts-Änderungsgesetz.).

[36]Open Door Principle. See Sect. 2.1.

[37]For further details, see Sect. 5.2.

[38]It is not a appropriate to define it as a statutory promotional mandate, as the law only requires the mandate—the content is defined by statutes later. For example, the aim of a credit cooperative provides for certain promotion measures, which will definitely not be the same in a production or consumer cooperative, for example. As a result, the promotion mandate as contained in Sec. 1 GenG cannot be considered a valuable substitute for a mandate clearly defined via statutes.

[39]See Dellinger (2014), p. 23.

3 SCE-R.[40] As a result, a cooperative may promote the social activities of its members.[41]

A **comparison** of the definitions contained in the three different legal systems (Italy, Austrian and the European Union) shows that these definitions differ considerably in terms of the formal concepts or formal concepts used, even though they appear to have similar content. In addition, various methods[42] have also been developed to describe the interaction between a cooperative and its members. These differences are caused by definitions that are strongly influenced by path dependency,[43] but also by different systems of legal sources that are used in the various jurisdictions. This latter aspect makes it even more difficult to develop a common approach. This leads to differently shaped legal rules. It is, therefore, no easy task to form a general legal definition of a cooperative. It is, however, what the PECOL want to achieve, among other things.

Accordingly, cooperatives are considered to be legal persons governed by private law with a mandate to conduct economic activity without profit as the ultimate purpose.[44] Sec. 1 para. 1 of the PECOL distinguishes between mutual cooperatives and general interest cooperatives. Mutual cooperatives are defined as conducting

[40]It states: "An SCE shall have as its principal object the satisfaction of its members' needs and/or the development of their economic and social activities, in particular through the conclusion of agreements with them to supply goods or services or to execute work of the kind that the SCE carries out or commissions. An SCE may also have as its object the satisfaction of its members' needs by promoting, in the manner set forth above, their participation in economic activities, in one or more SCEs and/or national cooperatives. An SCE may conduct its activities through a subsidiary."

[41]Until 2008, social activities were admissible as a secondary mandate. See Dellinger (2014), p. 32. It has been correctly observed that the SCE-R allows a principal object (Art. 1 para. 3 SCE-R), which initially went beyond the promotion mandate Austrian cooperatives were allowed to pursue. However, the promotion of social or idealistic aims beyond the economic promotion mandate was allowed only by means of so-called additional transactions. However, in 2008 the GenG was amended to allow social activities as the principal mandate. See Greda (2014), p. 835. For the application of consumer protection law to cooperatives, see Dellinger (2014), p. 31.

[42]As shown below. See Sect. 3.4.

[43]That is, the development of law strongly depends on existing law and rules, verdicts and procedures in a given setting. This makes change difficult, as the existing body of rules is already linked to previous problems which had to be solved. Today, there is a great variety of such paths, because in addition to national law, supranational, international and regional rules have to be observed when developing new laws. See Baer (2011), p. 186 et seq. Also consider Lombardo and Pasotti (2004), p. 193; Leyens (2003), p. 64 et seq.; Roe (2004). Critical, Beyer (2005), p. 5.

[44]The PECOL define a cooperative in Chap. 1, Sec. 1 para. 1.

economic activity mainly in the interest of their members (consumers,[45] providers[46] or workers[47]), while general interest cooperatives mainly conduct their activities in the general interest of the community. Good examples are social cooperatives, as determined by Italian law, and other legal systems.[48] Para. 2 specifies that "profit as the ultimate purpose" (as determined by para. 1) means making profits solely to pay interest, dividends and bonuses that are invested, deposited with or lent to the cooperative or any other person. This notion, however, does not oppose the admission of investor members.[49] Lastly, para. 3 deals with the possibility of conducting economic activity by means of a subsidiary.[50]

The PECOL's definition focuses on the objective pursued by the cooperatives and ignores other characteristics, such as variability of members' capital.[51] It is asserted that the objective is what best distinguishes cooperatives from other legal types of business organisation.[52] As shown, both the Italian and Austrian definitions differ from the PECOL's by referring to the variability of either members or capital. Moreover, the PECOL explicitly refer to profit-making, but broadly applies the concepts of profit and for-profit to include cost savings (as opposed to capital remuneration).[53] Similarly, the SCE-R presumes that the surpluses shall be distributed in accordance with the transactions of the members (recitals 7 and 10, bullet 5).[54] Even though neither the Italian nor the Austrian definitions refer to profit or non-profit–making, the Italian concept in this regard has been appropriately determined by Italian case law. Similarly, the Austrian concept assumes that the idea of cost saving is implicit in the promotion of members' needs under Austrian law.

To summarise, the PECOL refer to two general types of cooperatives and three subtypes of mutual cooperatives.[55] They act in the interest of their members, and agricultural cooperatives can use all variants listed here: For instance, a farmer buys equipment for his holdings from his cooperative and then sells his products through his cooperative, or a farmer could work for his agricultural cooperative. Yet, unlike

[45]The business is managed by the people who use its services.

[46]A producer cooperative comprises producers as members who manage the business. Agricultural marketing cooperatives carry out several related activities concerning the planning of production, cultivation and harvesting, sorting, packaging, transport, storage, food processing, distribution and sales.

[47]The business is managed by the people who work there.

[48]On this issue, see Fici (2017), p. 72 et seq.

[49]See Fici (2017), p. 27. This general definition also applies to secondary or higher degree cooperatives. Fici (2017), p. 22 et seq.

[50]For details, see Fici (2017), p. 32 et seq.

[51]Similar to the SCE-R.

[52]The reference to private law highlights the private nature of cooperatives. See Fici (2017), p. 21.

[53]See Fici (2017), p. 22. The non-profit mandate is given in some national cooperative laws and serves to clearly distinguish between cooperatives and companies. See Fici (2017), p. 22.

[54]Normally by means of patronage refunds. See Sect. 5.3.

[55]These subtypes cover all the different types of cooperative which exist in different sectors of the economy (e.g., agriculture or banking). See Fici (2017), p. 24.

some European legal systems, including the Austrian legal system *GenG*, the PECOL's definition does not contain an explicit reference to the notion of 'members' needs'. The nature of members' needs is based on internal motivation, which cannot be relevant to the cooperative's status as a legal entity.[56] The concept used by the PECOL is therefore closer to the one adopted by the Italian system, and it does not prevent additional objectives from being pursued, for example, altruistic goals.[57] Therefore, this definition is compatible with the concept of disinterested distribution, which the Italian system employs on a partly mandatory basis,[58] while the Austrian system—which is similar to the provisions contained in the SCE-R—leaves it to members' discretion.[59]

Lastly, the PECOL add another type of cooperative, the general interest cooperative.[60] While mutual cooperatives are clearly linked to the traditional model of a cooperative, this second type is more in line with recent developments in European jurisdictions, of which Italian Law No. 381/91 is mentioned here as an example.[61] However, general interest cooperatives might not be accepted in every legal system.[62]

It becomes clear that, while the different definitions of a cooperative focus on different features, they all promote the same core principle: satisfying peoples' needs (which should ultimately reduce costs). Since capitalist companies also focus on people's needs—at least, in the broadest sense[63]—, the main difference between them and cooperatives is that the latter achieves this through the direct involvement

[56]See Fici (2017), p. 25.

[57]It has also been observed that a mutual cooperative may consider ICA principle no 7 (concern for the community) as an additional objective, whereas it is the primary objective for a general interest cooperative. See Fici (2017), p. 31.

[58]See Sects. 5.2 and 5.3.

[59]See Fici (2017), p. 25 et seq. Also consider Sect. 5.5.

[60]The idea behind general interest cooperatives is to use them in the health sector, to provide social services and to offer working integration for disadvantaged people. In addition, they could also provide public services to the community, for instance in the renewable energy field. See Fici (2017), p. 31.

[61]For other examples, see Fici (2017), p. 28 et seq.

[62]For example, German law only knows cooperatives that serve the social and/or cultural interests of their members. There is debate over whether this might ultimately open the door to general interest cooperatives. This type of cooperative might contradict the very essence of a cooperative as it is understood by German scholars. See Fici (2017), p. 30. Also consider Schöpflin (2018a), p. 1241 et seq.; Beuthien (2007), p. 7. Austrian doctrine seems to diverge from German principles. In fact, Sec. 1 para. 3 GenG refers explicitly to Art. 1 para. 3 SCE-R (which implies the object of a cooperative may also be the satisfaction of its members' social activities rather than their (personal) needs), with the result that the GenG acknowledges general interest cooperatives. Interestingly, it has been observed that Sec. 1 para. 3 GenG runs contrary to the description of a cooperative as self-help organisation. See Dellinger (2014), p. 32. These types of cooperatives are already extant in the Italian agricultural sector because of the adoption of specific laws and, thus, play an important role in agricultural activity. However, this study does not focus on these types of cooperatives; therefore, the issues arising in this regard will not be analysed here.

[63]I.e., by maximising returns on shares.

of its members (principle of double quality). Member involvement therefore becomes essential to defining what an agricultural cooperative is. It is therefore necessary to further explore what this so-called double quality principle legally means (also because the legal definitions analysed here are based on member involvement). However, the effective involvement of members ultimately depends on the actual scope of the activities. Involvement and scope go hand in hand. This study assumes that a cooperative is active in agricultural matters for the benefit of its members, who are farmers. This inevitably leads to the question of what, according to the law, constitutes agriculture or agricultural activities. It is therefore essential to clarify these concepts before proceeding to analyse the membership of an agricultural cooperative.

3.3 The Agricultural Cooperative and the SCE

Different approaches are used to legally determine what the terms agriculture or agricultural activities mean. This can be seen not only in the comparison of different national legal systems but also within a single legal system. For example, comparing the Italian civil law's definition of agricultural activities with that from Italian tax law reveals that the former is more qualitative (and therefore more open and flexible), while the latter applies quantitative and stricter criteria. It is therefore important to stress from the outset that the different national approaches are anchored in specific branches of law, which usually fulfil different objectives. Consequently, the same aspect—in this case, agriculture—could be partially delineated differently. Since all these different approaches can change (or develop) over time, the definitions linked to each approach are therefore not static.

We must remember that Article 8 para. 2 of the SCE-R does not preclude the application of national rules related to the nature of business carried out by an SCE,[64] i.e., the rules relating to the agricultural holding and the definition of agriculture and/or agricultural activities. Consequently, the SCE-R does not harmonise this field. Thus, we must first analyse both whether and how the national legislature defines an agricultural cooperative.[65] This is achieved primarily (with exceptions) by linking an agricultural activity to the activities of a cooperative.

Although the two national concepts analysed here differ to some extent, they both define agriculture as a multifunctional phenomenon. The framework for defining this notion is strongly influenced by EU law, which is also the basis for defining agricultural policy overall.[66] This policy determines not only the extent to which financial support can be granted for agricultural activities but also—and more

[64]See Sect. 2.4.

[65]As mentioned in the introductory part of this study, these analyses do not consider tax law.

[66]See Norer (2017b), p. 638 et seq.; Martinez (2016c), pp. 761 et seq. and 765. See also Vecchione (2009c), p. 353 et seq.; Costato (2004); Adornato (2007).

importantly—the framework that regulates which activities are exempt from competition rules and which are not. These rules emphasise entrepreneurialism as aspect of agricultural activity and establish agricultural law as a legal framework for a particular type of market in which producers of agricultural products meet consumers of those products.[67] Therefore, in order to give an SCE the scope of agricultural activity, this must undoubtedly be accomplished in accordance with national rules—but without neglecting how EU law understands agriculture: because it is EU law that ultimately creates the conditions for agricultural business activity and influences the content and concepts of national legislation.[68] In addition, EU Law has effects on practice by stimulating specific activities and behaviour and neglecting others. A relevant example is POs,[69] which demonstrate how national (cooperative) law can be applied in practice. Therefore, we must first discuss the two different national approaches (i.e., an agricultural cooperative under Italian or Austrian law) and then embed the results in the relevant EU agricultural law in order to discuss (and compare) the different legal solutions more comprehensively.

3.3.1 How to Create an Agricultural Cooperative as SCE: The Italian Approach . . .

According to the Italian legal system, the concept of an agricultural cooperative requires that an enterprise meets two criteria: (1) the criteria of a cooperative and (2) the criteria defining agricultural activities. According to legislative decree No. 228 (18 May 2001), natural persons can be considered as agricultural entrepreneurs/farmers, but so can companies (i.e., partnerships, companies and cooperatives) if certain conditions are met. This latter aspect presupposes that, apart from specific exceptions,[70] the undertaking in question almost exclusively carries out an agricultural activity as defined by law. Two legal norms are important here: (1) Article 2082 of the Italian Civil Code, which generally defines what an entrepreneur is, and

[67]See Germanò (2016), p. 10 et seq. See also Albisinni (2011a); Costato (2004), p. 121 et seq. Generally, the question concerning the notion of agricultural law was and is not easy to answer. What is agricultural law? It is, so to speak, the cardinal question in the history of scientific research of the special legal relationships attributable to agriculture and forestry in the broadest sense. Repeated attempts to answer these questions are manifold in their approaches and results, and are partly also subject to time-related developments. Compared with other legal disciplines that are well-established in jurisprudence, it is obviously difficult to provide a generally satisfactory definition of agricultural law that claims to be generally valid.

[68]See Martinez (2016c), p. 765.

[69]For details, see Sect. 3.3.4.

[70]E.g., the renting of buildings for residential use provided that revenues are marginal. See Art. 36 para. 8 legislative decree no. 179/2012.

(2) Article 2135 CC,[71] which specifically defines the agricultural entrepreneur and thus determines what agricultural activities are.

Art. 2082 CC broadly defines an entrepreneur as someone who professionally carries out an organised economic activity for the purpose of producing or exchanging goods or services.[72] Economic activity includes the risk to which the entrepreneur's resources are exposed by any value added activity.[73] According to Art. 2135 CC, an agricultural entrepreneur is a (natural or legal) person who carries out at least one of the following activities: (1) land management,[74] (2) forestry,[75] (3) animal

---

[71]See, among others, Germanò and Rook Basile (2011), p. 757 et seq.; Vecchione (2009a, b); Costato and Russo (2015), p. 324 et seq. In addition to the notion of agricultural entrepreneur, the Italian legal order also contains a definition of small farmer. Art. 2083 ZGB regulates the small entrepreneur, and as part of this definition, the small farmer (coltivatore diretto). Under this term, the legislature subsumes 'self-builders of real estate, craftsmen, small merchants and those who pursue a professional activity primarily based on their own work and the work of their family members'. With regard to the self-construction of real estate, this means that a farmer must carry out at least one-third of the agricultural activity himself or herself (in accordance with Art. 2135 ZGB). Family members also can meet this quantitative requirement. If the farmer has employees, the requirement, according to Art. 2083 ZGB, must be distinguished from managerial activity, which this does not cover. On this issue, see, among others, Germanò (2011), p. 801 et seq.

[72]Economic activity is an organised activity. Organisation of the entrepreneur's labour and capital is sufficient, but it is necessary to have a minimum of 'external organisation' (e.g., the use of external labour or capital). Professional means habitual and continuous, not occasional. As a rule, a single business transaction is insufficient unless it involves a large number of individual operations. Someone who only produces for his or her own needs is not deemed an entrepreneur (requirement of market orientation). See, among others, Cetra (2019); Rondinone (2017), p. 5 et seq. See also Rook Basile (1995), p. 87 et seq.; Galloni (1999), p. 15 et seq.; Lamanna Di Salvo (2003), p. 103 et seq.

[73]Therefore, this does not apply to freelancers or pure use of assets.

[74]Regarding the concept of land management, here are a few examples of the activities that may be mentioned: soil preparation; the use of technical aids/machinery; plant pruning; and the purchase of seeds or horticultural crops. Cultivation of the soil also includes rearing in greenhouses. Technical aids/machines are permitted if required by soil management (stretta relazione—The law refers here to a close relationship). It requires labour input that covers the entire growth cycle; therefore, mere harvesting of the fruit does not constitute cultivation of the soil. In civil law, garden centres also are regarded as agricultural holdings, whereas in tax law, differentiation must be made in this respect. The general criteria to be observed in plant breeding are the same as for mushroom growing. In principle, the term soil could lead one to think exclusively of fields, which would exclude greenhouses. However, this is not the case because soil management means that fruit/plants should be grown from the soil and that natural resources should be used. In other words, soil management means plant cultivation. Furthermore, dog breeding and/or a dog school is not sufficient, as this is not necessarily carried out on ground and soil, in the forest or near bodies of water. For details, see Germanò and Rook Basile (2011), p. 762 et seq.; Sciaudone (2005), p. 42; Petrelli (2007), p. 228; Vecchione (2009a), p. 238.

[75]This notion not only refers to logging, but also must take into account reforestation to meet the biological cycle's demands. Therefore, it is a matter of care, reproduction/development and conservation of the stock. This also includes the beating of timber. Thus, it is an economic activity to produce wood in accordance with the given reproductive cycles and through regular logging of wood plants. Additional activities are the care of trees and their renewal. The activity is subject to prior approval. It is also possible to speak of the care/processing of the forest soil. The forest not

farming[76] and (4) related activities. Numbers 1–3 refer to entrepreneurial activities that develop and maintain a biological cycle of a plant-based or animal-based nature or a necessary stage of such a cycle.[77] Whereas the older definition focused primarily on soil as the main component of agricultural activity, the new formula explicitly refers to the usage, or potential usage, of soil, forests and fresh, salt or sea water. This formulation assumes that the actual ownership of the land is no longer decisive and helps accommodate technical innovations.[78]

The relation of agricultural activities to the biological cycle is a special aspect that accounts for the development of modern agriculture. With this wording, the legislature has recognised that agricultural activity is oriented towards continuous

only produces wood, but also represents the environment and serves to protect the environment. It significantly affects the surrounding landscape, people, soil, water and air, as well as flora and fauna. These functions are so closely interconnected that their relationships were not understood until the twentieth century. The reasons for this increased awareness and the urge to understand include, among other things, decreasing land reserves, increased demand for clean drinking water, increased environmental pollution, an increasing need for recreation and the steady market demand for wood. Therefore, the forest has a utility function, protective function, recreational function and other special functions such as landscape conservation or nature conservation. Accordingly, Legislative Decree 227/2001 refers to these functions. It also contains a sustainability concept that regulates logging. Art. 2 Ld 227 distinguishes forestry from tree culture (arboricultura). This refers to tree cultivation that does not take place in forests (terreni non boscati), with the exclusive aim of producing wood and biomass. In this case, the forest is not managed. Forestry-related activities include debarking, logging and storage. For details, see Germanò and Rook Basile (2011), p. 767 et seq.; Petrelli (2007), p. 236; Vecchione (2009a), p. 251. See also Abrami (2005) and Bolognini (2011a).

[76]The term livestock has been replaced by the broader term animals, which overcomes restrictive judicial interpretations. Before this, livestock only included cattle, sheep, pigs, goats and horses (because the rearing of these animals traditionally is connected to the soil, in contrast to (small) farm animals such as poultry, bees, etc). The purpose of animal breeding must be to raise animals until they are fully developed, regardless of the fact that the animal's entire biological cycle does not take place on a single farm. For example, the concept refers to the following animals: rabbits; hares; pigeons; partridges; pheasants; frogs to be eaten; fish farming; shellfish farming; oyster farming; and the rearing of frogs, mollusks; crustaceans; and aquacultures (regardless of whether they live in fresh, salt or brackish water. Regarding fish farming, it should be noted that Italy never had classified hunting and fishing as an agricultural activity, as the rearing criterion was not met, whereas at the EU level, a different approach was adopted. In fact, in the Treaty of Rome (now Article 38 TFEU), the notion of agriculture was extended to fishing. As a result, Art. 2 LD 22672001 equates fishing with agricultural activity and requires appropriate authorisation. Finally, according to Law n 313/2004, beekeeping is an agricultural activity. See Petrelli (2007), p. 239; Vecchione (2009a), p. 256; Germanò and Rook Basile (2011), p. 768 et seq.

[77]Also see Casadei (2009), p. 328 et seq.; Costato (2006), p. 93 et seq.; Vecchione (2009d), p. 223 et seq.

[78]See also Salaris (2002), p. 54 et seq.; Costato (2001), p. 142 et seq.; Vecchione (2004), p. 67 et seq; Goldoni (2019), p. 380 et seq.; Iannarelli (2019), p. 218 et seq. Accordingly, such activities also can be carried out in seawater. For further information about the notion of agrarietà, see Sect. 1.2.2.

agricultural development.[79] For example, there are no agricultural activities if only individual activities, such as ploughing or sowing, are carried out.[80]

The phrase 'a necessary stage of the biological cycle' ('*una fase necessaria del ciclo stesso*')[81] refers to a phase of the production cycle. Here it concerns agricultural activity, provided that the requirements of Art. 2082 CC are given. Generally, one can consider a phase with a relevant minimum duration. The livestock dealer, who has to feed animals so that they can be resold, must therefore be excluded. It is necessary to feed the animals for a sufficient period of time so that one actually participates in the maintenance and development of the biological cycle. Monitoring the reproductive phase does not, therefore, have to be part of the biological cycle. Furthermore, the wording 'a necessary stage of the biological cycle' inevitably assumes that there is another necessary stage that is carried out by someone else; otherwise, the necessary stage would correspond to the whole biological cycle. This open definition makes it possible to describe an agricultural entrepreneur as one who is part of a production chain and who carries out one of the necessary stages in this chain.[82]

In addition to these main agricultural activities, Art. 2135 CC refers to related activities. These are commercial activities that, although not subsumable under paragraph 1, are classified as agricultural activities based on the criterion of connectivity of agricultural activity.[83] The law provides examples of activities, such as working, preserving, processing, marketing and/or refining production/products that were obtained principally from cultivating the land or forests and/or from animal farming.[84] These related activities must not be economically more significant than the main activity.[85] For example, a farmer—to a limited extent—can buy grapes in order to refine his own goods or to process them into wine. These different activities are therefore not the same, because the related activity interferes with the main activity: In other words, the related activity must be supportive, whether in the production phase or during the phase in which the products are used; it is supportive

[79]See also Casadei (2009), p. 328 et seq.; Galloni (1999), p. 11 et seq.; Vecchione (2004), p. 28 et seq.; Magno (2006), p. 89.

[80]It not only includes classical types of land cultivation, such as pasturing, but also flower growing, mushroom growing, tree nurseries and seed breeding. The same applies to plant products used to produce biogas or other energy.

[81]See Art. 2135 para. 2. CC.

[82]See also Albisinni (2011b), p. 286 et seq.; Albisinni (2014b), p. 6 et seq.; Casadei (2009), p. 334 et seq.; Albisinni (2003), p. 333 et seq. See also Vecchione (2004), pp. 44 et seq. and 54 et seq.

[83]For details, see Germanò and Rook Basile (2011), p. 775; Germanò and Rook Basile (2011), p. 775 et seq.; Sciaudone (2005), p. 56; Petrelli (2007), p. 248; Vecchione (2009b), p. 275; Vecchione (2004), p. 75 et seq. See also Goldoni (2019), p. 379 et seq.

[84]The list in paragraph 3 contains examples and also permits atypical activities. However, the application in this respect should be limited, as the rule is already very broad (examples could include preparatory work, such as levelling or ditch excavation). According to the cassation, the associated activity also may be carried out by a cooperative or a consortium.

[85]See Germanò and Rook Basile (2011), p. 776; Vecchione (2004), p. 86 et seq.

as it ultimately safeguards entrepreneurial profits. Furthermore, the law lays down binding requirements which are (1) subjective—i.e., the agricultural entrepreneur exercising the main activity must also exercise the related activity (criteria of *unisoggettività*)—and (2) objective—i.e., the related activities must be integrated into the organisation established to exercise the main activity (criteria of *uniaziendalità*). In other words, there is only one business.[86]

The law creates the relationship between agricultural activities as main activities and commercial activities as related activities by requiring that commercial products predominantly[87] arise from the main activity.[88] The question of what predominance might mean here is not easy to resolve. In principle, qualitative or quantitative assessments can be made. The clearer approach will probably be the application of quantitative criteria.[89] Ultimately, however, the agricultural operator concerned will look at tax law, which contains a number of categories that can pragmatically resolve the question of whether a product can or cannot be described as originating from a main activity.[90]

This notion of related activities also includes the provision of goods and services.[91] Two criteria must be observed here: the activity must be carried out through the predominant use of equipment and operating resources and must concern those items that are normally used to carry out agricultural activity. According to the law, these are, for examples activities that improve the soil and the land and forest resources and/or concern the accommodation and hospitality of guests in the manner specified by the legislature.[92]

To reiterate, the activity of an agricultural cooperative must be based on an activity within the meaning of Article 2135 CC. Now, on the basis of all these aspects that determine the various agricultural activities, scholars have developed three categories to better capture the diversity of agricultural cooperatives.[93] First are cooperatives that qualify as agricultural entrepreneurs. Here the cooperative members, who are agricultural entrepreneurs within the meaning of Art. 2135 CC, carry out the agricultural activity through the cooperative and for the cooperative. In this case, the cooperative acts as an entrepreneur and assumes all the associated risks.[94]

---

[86]See Germanò and Rook Basile (2011), p. 776 et seq. See also Casadei (2009), p. 345 et seq.

[87]Predominantly does not mean exclusively.

[88]It is emphasised that the activities concerned must relate primarily to the products and services of the holding concerned. As a result, the processing of agricultural products cannot take on industrial dimensions. Processing means that a new item is created, e.g., wine from grapes.

[89]On this issue, see, for example, Costato and Russo (2015), p. 348. See also Casadei (2009), p. 351 et seq.; Vecchione (2004), p. 88 et seq.

[90]In this regard, see Germanò and Rook Basile (2011), p. 780 et seq.

[91]One can see that the lines are blurring between industrial and service sectors.

[92]Another example would be an agricultural entrepreneur who helps farmers with agricultural activity (such as ploughing or harvesting) by providing machinery.

[93]See Cavanna (2014), p. 641 et seq.; Bonfante (1999), p. 213. In general, see Giuffrida (1981), Rossi (1979), Rook Basile (1981) and Carmignani (1999, 2011).

[94]See Cavanna (2014), p. 642 et seq.; Giuffrida (1981), p. 210.

Next are cooperatives that directly carry out certain production and marketing stages of their agricultural members' businesses.[95] Finally, there are agricultural cooperatives that operate as user companies/suppliers and provide specific services to their members, who in turn carry out an agricultural activity.[96]

Similarly, other scholars use the initial subdivision of cooperatives as described above[97] and divide agricultural cooperatives into workers' cooperatives, consumer cooperatives and service cooperatives. We note that, in agriculture, a workers' cooperative is based on the joint cultivation of the members' land or the joint rearing of the members' animals. Under Italian law, these activities comprise an agricultural enterprise by meeting the requirements of Article 2135 of the Italian Civil Code. The members of an agricultural consumer cooperative in turn use the services offered by the cooperative or buy goods from it (both are used to develop the biological cycle), which they also sell to non-members. Finally, a service cooperative processes the products of its members, as in the cases of social cellars, social oil mills and social cheese factories. The activities carried out in the latter two cases correspond to those referred to in Art. 2135 para. 3 CC and are therefore, in principle, commercial activities. In this context, it is useful to recall that the requirement of *unisoggettività*, as laid down in Art. 2135 of the Italian Civil Code, requires both activities—the cooperative activity (i.e., the processing service) and the activity of its members (i.e., the production of grapes, olives or milk)—to be carried out by the same subject.

Although these last two types of cooperatives (the agricultural consumer and agricultural service cooperative) may lack this requirement, their qualification as agricultural entrepreneurs is expressly recognised by the legislature on the basis of Art. 1 para. 2 of Legislative Decree No. 228 of 18 May 2001. It thus accounts for the fact that the agricultural cooperative is constituted and functions as a common body for individual farmers.[98] In fact, cooperatives are membership-based; as a rule, the legal personality of the cooperative cannot "hide" the persons of its members who join together to carry out the last phase of their business activity (this is called the principle of transparency).[99] In addition, the legislature requires the agricultural cooperative to predominantly engage with its members by using members' products or offering members services and/or goods. This, however, also implies that an

[95]See Cavanna (2014), p. 644 et seq.; Scordino (1970), p. 204 et seq.

[96]See Cavanna (2014), p. 647 et seq. Opposed to this approach, the cooperatives register only distinguishes between agricultural-worker cooperatives and cooperatives that manage the supply of agricultural products and conduct livestock farming, thereby excluding cooperatives that actually do not conduct agricultural activities, but merely deliver services to members who are agricultural entrepreneurs. See Cavanna (2014), p. 642.

[97]See Sects. 1.3.3 and 2.1.

[98]See Cavanna (2014), p. 645 et seq.; Carmignani (2013), p. 858; Carmignani (2011), p. 259. See also Casadei (2009), p. 347; Carmignani (2011), p. 860; Rook Basile (1981); Giuffrida (1981); Alessi (2006), p. 1248 et seq.

[99]See Carmignani (2013), p. 858 et seq. See also Costato and Russo (2015), p. 383 et seq.; Galloni (1999), p. 465. See also Vecchione (2009c), p. 367 et seq.

agricultural cooperative can process or transform products (e.g., turn olives into oil) supplied by non-members, albeit to a limited extent.

To conclude, the key factors for defining an agricultural cooperative are transparency and prevalence.[100] This prevalence criterion must be distinguished from those under Art. 2513 CC, which are explained in more detail below.[101] This latter concept may be useful for substantiating the prevalence criterion established by Legislative Decree No. 228/2001, which essentially defines the minimum activities (calculated according to the type of cooperative, i.e., according to consumption, labour costs, production costs or production value) to be carried out with members in cooperatives that are predominantly mutual (mainly mutual cooperatives).[102] There may also be agricultural cooperatives within the meaning of Legislative Decree No. 228/2001 that are not cooperatives with predominant mutuality.[103]

It has rightly been confirmed that the Italian legal framework strongly supports cooperation between farmers through cooperatives and confers on them the status of agricultural entrepreneur.[104] In addition, agricultural cooperatives may also be granted professional agricultural entrepreneur status (PAE), provided that at least one managing member (farmer) has these specific qualifications.[105] A PAE is the person who possesses professional knowledge and skills,[106] dedicates at least 50% of their total working time to agricultural activities[107] (directly or as a member of society) and earns at least 50% of their total income from those activities.[108] Fulfilling these requirements will allow agricultural cooperatives to receive specific support[109] in addition to the support granted to them because of their status as agricultural entrepreneurs.[110]

---

[100]Carmignani (2013), p. 863.

[101]See Sect. 3.4.1.

[102]See Carmignani (2013), p. 861 et seq.; Carmignani (2011), p. 259 et seq.

[103]These types of cooperatives must operate predominantly with members. For details, see Sect. 3.4.1.

[104]On this issue, in general, Germanò (2016), p. 4 et seq.; Costato and Russo (2015), p. 3 et seq. See also Sciaudone (2016). See also Zecchin (2017).

[105]On this issue, see, among others, Germanò (2011), p. 798 et seq. See also Carmignani (2013), p. 864; Sciaudone (2019); Rauseo (2018); Ferrara (2013); Vecchione (2009c), p. 359 et seq.

[106]In accordance with Article 5 of Regulation (EC) No 1257/1999 of the Council of 17 May 1999.

[107]As referred to in Article 2135 of the Civil Code.

[108]See Bolognini (2011b), p. 336 et seq. See also For the entrepreneur operating in the disadvantaged areas provided for by Art. 17 of EU Regulation no. 1257/1999, the requirements listed are reduced by 25%.

The Italian Legislation has introduced the figure of the 'professional agricultural entrepreneur' (PAE), who has replaced the former figure of 'main agricultural entrepreneur' for applying the legislation to the agricultural sector. For details, Costato and Russo (n 8), p. 375 et seq., Germanò (n 8), p. 118 et seq.

[109]They are eligible for further subsidies and tax relief.

[110]See Bolognini (2011b), p. 346. See also Rook Basile (1995), p. 77 et seq. and, in general, Lamanna Di Salvo (2003), p. 103 et seq.

3.3.2 ... Continues: The Austrian Approach

Similar to Italian law, it is necessary to analyse the rules enshrined in private law in order to understand what an agricultural cooperative is under Austrian law. The relevant norms for this discussion are contained in the *GewO*.[111] The Austrian approaches to the legal concept of agricultural activities and to determining agricultural cooperatives differs from those in Italian legal thinking. We must first clarify how agricultural activities are determined according to the Austrian legal system.[112]

The first difference relates to the conceptuality of the two concepts: While Italian law explicitly regards forestry as an agricultural activity, the Austrian legal system seems to distinguish between these two activities in so far as the different legal norms normally refer to agriculture and forestry, so that the two activities seem to stand side by side.[113] As we will see, the difference is only superficial, since the law that describes what agriculture and forestry actually are links these two activities together rather than distinguishing between them.

[111]See Holzer (2018), p. 38; Holzer (2017a), p. 22 et seq. It applies to all commercially exercised activities that are not prohibited by law if carried out independently, regularly and with the intention of realising a profit or other economic advantage.

[112]In addition to the notion of agricultural activities, the Austrian legal order also contains a definition of farmer, which can be found in the various Grundverkehrsgesetze (GVG) of the Länder, which comprises the various laws on the acquisition and sale of land (real estate law). It is important to stress that these laws regulate, generally speaking, the acquisition of land, as well as the acquisition of rights to agricultural or forestry land. Thus, the definitions contained therein must be read in conjunction with these laws' scope. Moreover, these laws do not define what agricultural activities are, but contain a definition of agricultural or forestry land, agricultural or forestry holding and farmer. This approach, which is not a specific definition of agricultural activities, is in line with the general approach followed by the Austrian legislature, which uses a negative differentiation criterion instead of providing a specific definition.

A legal definition of the term farmer can be found in the Grundverkehrsgesetze of Carinthia (§ 10 para. 4), Lower Austria (§ 10 para. 4), Salzburg (§ 4 para. 4), Styria (§ 8a para. 5), Tyrol (§ 2 para. 5) and Vorarlberg (§ 2 para. 3). Accordingly, a farmer is defined as a person who, alone or together with family members or his own agricultural workers, wishes to farm/cultivate an agricultural or forestry holding as an independent economic unit or to farm/cultivate land after it has been acquired, and who possesses the necessary skills to do so. The concerned laws of Carinthia, Lower Austria and Salzburg link the status of farmer to the additional criterion that the person concerned must at least, to a considerable extent, earn his living and that of his family from farming or wish to do so after land acquisition. Therefore, the decisive factor is the share of family income derived from the operation of agriculture and forestry according to the actual circumstances. However, the share of the concrete lifestyle's costs is irrelevant. In addition, legal persons are regarded as farmers on the condition that they are economically dominant in the society and are willing and able to manage the property themselves. As already explained, not only are those already engaged in farming deemed farmers, but also those who, after a planned land acquisition, seriously intend to produce agriculture oriented toward sustainable yields. They also must be able to substantiate this on the basis of certain circumstances (e.g., technical training, previous practical activity, business concept). GVG's openness to 'newcomers' is the necessary consequence of the fundamental prohibition on the creation of a privileged class of farmers already practising this profession.

[113]This has been a reality since the 1850s. See Holzer (2012a), p. 761. See also Norer (2005), p. 9.

Contrary to the Italian approach, the scope of agriculture and forestry, economically speaking, is not explicitly described in the Austrian legal system in the positive sense but can only be derived as a 'negative differentiation criterion' from the exception provisions of the *GewO*.[114] To put it simply, agriculture and forestry are exempted from the *GewO*.[115] At present, the *GewO* regulates the demarcation of agriculture and forestry as well as activities subject to the *GewO*: a corresponding activity therefore only exists if clearly defined characteristics are fulfilled. If this is not the case, then an activity is subject to the *GewO*.[116]

The activities in question—which are similar to commercial activities—are carried out with the intention of making a profit or securing other economic advantage. The Administrative Court (taking into account the fact that there is no legal definition of agriculture and forestry) has, in conjunction with planning law, not only examined whether the planned use of resources constitutes either the production and extraction of plant products by means of natural forces or the keeping of animals for breeding, fattening or the extraction of animal products, but also considered whether the planned use can be carried out in a sustainable manner (i.e., in principle, to generate income).[117] In other words, all these activities should ultimately lead to income generation. Italian law regulates this aspect with Art. 2082 CC.[118]

From the production of food in its unprocessed form to the delivery of classic farm products and processed products, no interference with commercial rights has ever been seen.[119] However, the scope of rights of farmers and foresters extends far beyond the actual production of goods; every producer should have the right to sell his products, unless this right is restricted by law. It was therefore not necessary to

---

[114]See Holzer (2012a), p. 760; Holzer (2018), p. 39.

[115]It is stressed that this is linked to a partially outdated historical demarcation between agriculture and forestry and the commercial sector. It has been argued that this does not do justice to the current economic and socio-political significance of multifunctional agriculture and forestry. Therefore, repeated recent calls have been made for an explicit constitutional anchoring of a contemporary concept of 'agriculture and forestry' or 'agricultural and forestry area'.

Already, the Kundmachungspaket of 20 December 1859 stipulated that the Gewerbeordnung was not to apply to agricultural and forestry production and its ancillary trades, in so far as these mainly concerned the processing of the company's own products.

[116]See also Holzer (2012a), p. 760 et seq.; Holzer (2018), p. 386.

[117]See decisions of the Administrative Court no. Ro 2014/05/0040 (27.04.2016) or no. 2013/05/0210 (05.03.2014). Consider also tax and social law: on these issues, Holzer (2018), p. 50 et seq.

[118]See Sect. 3.3.1.

[119]See Holzer (2018), p. 386. By 1859, it had been clarified that GewO was not to apply to 'agricultural production and its ancillary trades, in so far as they mainly involve the processing of their own products'. Also excluded from the GewO was the serving of one's own (agricultural) product. In the explanatory note it was explained that agriculture is not a trade in terms of language usage. This concerns both the extraction of a natural product and its processing, provided that the latter activity is so intimately connected with land cultivation that without it, the natural product cannot be brought into commerce at all, and provided that the persons involved belong to the actual agricultural population (e.g., dairy farmers, cheese makers, winemakers). See Holzer (2012a), p. 763.

expressly grant this right to farmers and foresters in the first place.[120] This statement in the explanatory note to the government bill of the *GewO* as amended in 1973 (*GewO* 1973) applies both to all agricultural products (original products) and to products from agricultural and forestry's ancillary trades. Farmers (and foresters) may therefore sell both their original products and their processed products to intermediaries and directly to end consumers without being subject to the *GewO*, i.e., without requiring a trade licence.[121]

How have these basic considerations and observations been put into legal provisions? To reiterate, the Austrian legislature adopts a negative formula stating in general that the *GewO* is not applicable to agriculture and forestry and the ancillary trades of agriculture and forestry,[122] and determining specific details concerning plant production, animal keeping, hunting and fisheries, servicing of horse/equine pensions, and related activities/ancillary trades.

In the field of primary plant production, agriculture and forestry include 'the production and extraction of plant products with the aid of natural forces, including viticulture and fruit-growing, horticulture and tree nurseries' and (under certain conditions) the purchase of such products. Therefore, exempted from the *GewO* are, for example, arable farming, meadow management, pasture farming, alpine farming and forestry as well as the specifically mentioned branches of viticulture, fruit-growing, horticulture and tree nurseries.[123] The exception for viticulture and fruit growing also includes the production (and sale) of wine and fruit wine (must) as well as the preliminary stages of producing grape and sweet must or grape and fruit storm.[124] The fact that wine is considered as a primary production can be used to compare the Austrian approach with the Italian approach, where wine production is not considered as a main activity but as a related activity. The Austrian approach integrates products that result from a transformative process into the notion of main/primary activity. One argument for this approach is that every producer should have the right to sell his products.[125]

---

[120]See Holzer (2012a), p. 760 et seq.; see also the statement in the explanatory note to the government bill of the GewO 1973, p. 111.

[121]See Holzer (2012a), p. 761.

[122]See Sec. 2 para. 1 GewO.

[123]Processing in the Buschenschank is also specifically excluded.

[124]See Holzer (2012a), p. 764; Holzer (2018), p. 39; Holzer (2017b), p. 22 et seq.; Holzer (2018), p. 387 et seq.

[125]See Holzer (2018), p. 386; see also the statement in the explanatory note to the government bill of the GewO 1973, p. 111. In the context of primary crop production, also the additional purchase of products is possible. Here the legislator determined rather strict quantitative criteria (see for example Sec. 2 para. 3 subpara. 1 GewO). See Holzer (2012a), p. 764; Holzer (2018), p. 388. It is clear that the Italian legal system—at least if one considers private law—will not deal with such issues, as it does not focus on product categories. However, Art. 2135 para. 3 CC shows that in this regard, the Italian legislature has adopted—under private law—a rather vague concept. An adequate answer regarding issues like this can be found in tax law.

Apart from these conceptual differences, the Austrian legislature, like its Italian counterpart, saw the need to draw up a legal framework to support agriculture and to make the content anchored therein flexible so as to serve the interest of competition. We see this in this phrase, 'production and extraction of plant products with the aid of natural forces', which clarifies that production need not be bound to the soil, but can either take place in containers or by using substrates (e.g., hydroponics).[126] This solution is comparable to the solution described in Art. 2135 CC. The Austrian formulation is also similar to the biological cycle prescribed by Italian law, because it emphasises the link between a plant product and its natural production cycle, thus linking the activity directly to the environment and making it dependent on it. Thus, similar to the Italian legal concept of agriculture, the activity is exposed to a natural risk,[127] which man can only influence to a limited extent.

The Austrian legal system too refers to a kind of biological cycle when it considers animal production. The *GewO* determines that agriculture includes 'the keeping of farm animals for breeding, fattening or production of animal products'. This implies that animal husbandry cannot be a single step in the production chain, but must at least include a necessary stage of a natural production (biological) cycle; otherwise, the breeding, fattening or production of products can hardly be carried out.[128] Animal farming is, therefore, an activity that consists of a set of cures to ensure that the animal reproduces. It refers to the birth, growth, shelter, care for, feed and cure from diseases. As an example one can consider the agricultural activity of fattening. It is stressed that in order to differentiate the fattening from the mere livestock trade, where the animals are kept for a few days and (of course) also fed, it is important to consider and evaluate the specific circumstances. Indications in favour of fattening (rearing) are, for example, a significant increase in weight, the supply of fodder from one's own (agricultural) production, as well as the appearance of the holding as an agricultural enterprise.[129] Moreover, similar to the Italian concept of animal farming, one does not have to own the animals. Essential characteristics are care and feeding.[130] Thus, various types of contract fattening (e.g., contracting out the fattening of animals) belong to agriculture.[131] In other

---

[126]See Holzer (2017b), p. 28; Holzer (2018), p. 387 fn 1492.

Thus, edible mushrooms, reeds and resins are considered to be vegetable primary products. Furthermore, it is not necessary for the farmer to bring in the harvest himself. For example, selling wood on the stick, selling a standing crop in the field or a buyer picking strawberries remain the seller's products (and the buyer does not become a farmer or forester).

[127]In this regard, see Lamanna Di Salvo (2003), p. 33 et seq.

[128]Here, too, no connection to soil and land is necessary, e.g., cattle fattening on a third-party feed basis is not a commercial operation under commercial law (in contrast to the tax field). See Holzer (2017b), p. 30; Holzer (2018), p. 388 et seq.

[129]See Holzer (2012a), p. 765 et seq.

[130]See Holzer (2012a), p. 765.

[131]See Holzer (2012a), p. 765 et seq.

words, what matters is not the ownership of the animals, but whether the animals have been bred and fattened or whether animal products have been produced.[132]

Next, farm animals include not only 'domestic animals', poultry of all kinds, bees, etc., but also those animals who are kept for breeding purposes and provide an economic benefit to the keeper.[133] Since Austrian farmers, like Italian farmers (generally speaking), produce for the same (common European) market, it is obvious that the Italian legislature addresses similar issues. Consequently, the Italian legal system, like the Austrian legal system, has also been made more flexible and no longer refers to the rather closed concept of livestock farming, but to that of animals.[134]

Since 2002, the *GewO* has included the authorisation and the obligation of the Federal Ministry of Economics, Family and Youth to determine,[135] which products manufactured by farmers and foresters qualify as primary agricultural and forestry production. The necessary regulation was only issued in 2008 after years of efforts to reach an agreement between the representatives of the interests of agriculture and trade and industry.[136] It lists those products that are part of agricultural and forestry primary production and breaks them down into the following product groups: (1) fish, meat, (2) milk, dairy products, (3) grain, straw, (4) fruit, vegetables, (5) drinks, (6) wood, forest products and (7) other products, such as eggs, honey, edible oil, etc.[137] The listed products can thus be produced by farmers without a trade licence and without being considered as a ancillary trade, even if several processing steps are required.[138]

This new approach helps to better take into account the traditional concepts of primary agricultural and forestry production. Before the adoption of this regulation,

---

[132]On the contrary, and similar to Italian law, keeping animals for other purposes, e.g., housing cats or dogs in a kind of 'animal shelter' during holidays for pet owners is a business practice. On this issue, see Germanò and Rook Basile (2011), p. 772; Costato and Russo (2015), p. 337 et seq.

[133]See Holzer (2018), p. 388; Holzer (2017b), p. 30.

[134]See Art. 2135 para. 1 CC. Also see Sect. 3.3.1.

[135]by Regulation and in agreement with the Federal Ministry of Agriculture, Forestry, Environment and Water Management, the Federal Ministry of Social Security and the Federal Ministry of Finance.

[136]It came into force on 1.1.2009. See https://www.ris.bka.gv.at/GeltendeFassung.wxe?Abfrage=Bundesnormen&Gesetzesnummer=20006095. Accessed 26 November 2019.

[137]The listing of products in primary product regulations that are considered to be primary products is also relevant for Social Security and tax assessment, although tax authorities do not recognise the products 'milled round wood, as well as raw boards and beams' as primary products. Italian tax law provides for a similar list-based system. See Art. 32 Testo Unico Imposte sui Redditi (TUIR, Italian Tax Law).

For a precise interpretation of individual products, it is possible to use the definitions contained in other laws (e.g., the Wine Act) or in the Austrian Food Code (Codex Alimentarius Austriacus).

[138]See Holzer (2017b), p. 31 et seq. The production of these primary products must be carried out by farmers, but it is irrelevant where this happens and whether the farmer produces it himself or has it produced by another farmer as part of an ancillary service activity. Exceptions are made for pressing edible oil and processing wine into sparkling wine, which an authorised trader must carry out. See Holzer (2012a), p. 768.

it was common practice to draw the line between primary agricultural and forestry products and products of the ancillary processing industry, at the point where a marketable product was manufactured for the first time.[139] For example, alpine cheese has been classified as a primary product, because the milk produced on the mountain pasture was not marketable in any other way. The authorisation in Sec. 2 para. 3a *GewO* now stipulates that when one determines what are primary agricultural and forestry products, he or she has to consider aspects, like old origin, years of practice, the customer's expectations for the form and condition of the product offering as well as changing views of marketability and other requirements, such as guaranteeing local supply in rural areas.[140]

In summary, these analyses show that the overall approach of the Austrian legislature to agriculture and agricultural activities contains elements that approximate the concept of the biological cycle as determined by Italian law. Yet, the Austrian approach does not explicitly focus on this concept, but uses a multi-faceted concept that is influenced/directed not only by traditional production techniques but also by customer expectations. Also for these reasons, the Austrian approach, compared to the Italian solution, seems to be more blurred and vague.[141] Ultimately, therefore, the approach focuses on outcomes rather than the activities themselves. Theoretically, the content of this list-based approach could be quickly adapted to new market developments; however, as reality shows, in the end this does not have to be the case, considering that it took several years of negotiations to adopt the current list of products. This category or list-based approach differs from the Italian approach,[142] but, as will be explained below,[143] it is similar to the approach adopted at European level.

Another difference is that the Italian legislature describes agricultural activities in order to define the agricultural entrepreneur, thus establishing a relationship between subject and activity. Oppposed to this, the Austrian *GewO* does not mention the aspect of entrepreneur at all. To define an agricultural entrepreneur, therefore, other norms have to be taken into account, in particular, the *Grundverkehrsgesetze* of the Austrian *Länder*, i.e., the various federal laws that generally refer to the use of agricultural land.[144] It is useful to add that this concept of the agricultural entrepreneur is also applied to enterprises and cooperatives.[145]

---

[139]See decision of the Administrative Court no. 2005/08/0140 (26.04.2006); see also Holzer (2018), p. 387.

[140]See also Holzer (2012a), p. 767; Holzer (2018), p. 389; Holzer (2017b), p. 31 et seq.

[141]It seems that the legislature preferred to use certain categories of activities and products instead of developing an abstract and generally applicable definition of agricultural activities.

[142]Which uses such an approach only under taw law. See Sect. 3.3.1.

[143]See Sect. 3.3.3.

[144]For example, Sec. 2 para. 5 Tiroler Grundverkehrsgesetz. Interestingly, the various notions of farmer contained therein refer to an agricultural activity conducted primarily by the farmer (or members of the farmer's family). Therefore, the concept appears to be similar to the concept of direct farmer, as determined by Art. 2083 CC. See fn 71 and 112. See also Sec. 10 para. 4 Kärtner Grundverkehrsgesetz. See also Holzer (2012b), p. 688 et seq.; Holzer (2018), p. 409 et seq.

[145]The Italian legal system offers a similar solution.

In addition to these various types of primary production, the Austrian legal system, like Art. 2135 para. 3 of the Italian Civil Code, acknowledges the ancillary trade of agriculture and forestry, which are commercial activities (and not agricultural and forestry activities). They are excluded from the scope of the *GewO*, because they are so closely related to agriculture and forestry that they are not suitable for regulation under trade law.[146]

Sec. 2 para. 4 *GewO* exhaustively lists the types of ancillary trades,[147] including the processing and treatment/working of the farmer's own natural product, the exploitation of his own soil substance, ancillary services, haulage services, the hiring of mounts (including horse pension activities), the hiring of agricultural and forestry equipment, the operation of certain facilities for the production and supply of heat from biomass and the Alpine buffet.[148]

This approach, which largely sticks to categories instead of criteria, results from a development that was initiated decades ago. E.g., the 1973 *GewO* limited ancillary trade mainly to the treatment and processing of its own natural product until a product was obtained that was usually marketed by farmers and foresters. It was essential that the activity of treatment and processing remained economically subordinate to the activity of the production of the natural product.[149]

With the *GewO* amendment of 1997, these restrictions, which were noticeable in daily practice for all direct marketing farmers, were considerably loosened. On the one hand, the permissible scope of the additional purchase of raw materials was extended insofar as the word 'main' was replaced by 'predominantly' (this implies a share of more than 50% of own raw materials). On the other hand, the 'standard linkage' to conventional machined or processed products was deleted. Now it is only a matter of preserving the 'character of the farm as an agricultural and forestry enterprise' during the production of processed products. As a result, the product range is no longer limited to classic farm products—such as bacon, butter, etc.—but is open to all innovations, including convenience products (semi-finished and whole-farm products).[150] Whether the character of an agricultural and forestry enterprise is (still) preserved has to be assessed on the basis of the following criteria: land management, the usual branches of agriculture and forestry, the existence of corresponding agricultural and forestry buildings, local proximity between agriculture and the processing site, as well as self-management (with the participation of the

[146]See Holzer (2017b), p. 36 et seq.; Gfrerer (2007), p. 199 et seq.; Holzer (2010), p. 171 et seq.; Holzer (2018), p. 390.

[147]For details, see, among others, Holzer (2018), p. 394 et seq.; Holzer (2010).

[148]The level of capital employed for investments in ancillary trades is not relevant. In addition, the 1997 amendment made it possible for an authorised trader (e.g., butcher, miller, baker) to carry out processing in the respective branch of industry on a contract basis. This is mandatory even when processing wine into sparkling wine.

[149]See Holzer (2018), p. 394 et seq.; see also Holzer (2017b), p. 43.

[150]With the abolition of the standard linkage, the production of biogas as an ancillary trade also was permitted.

operator/manager).[151] These aspects—in particular, the need for self-management—make it possible to bring the Austrian approach to related activities closer to the Italian approach. The consequence is that the relation between main and related activity can be described in a more structured way. As mentioned,[152] the Italian approach seems to be clearer by applying the principles of *unisoggettività* and *uniaziendalità*.

Despite the typification of individual ancillary trades in the *GewO*, there are—according to the case law of the Administrative Court[153]—two specific criteria decisive for determining ancillary activities. The first is from an organisational point of view, which asserts that the form of appearance must be closely connected/related to agriculture and forestry. The second is the economic subordination of the ancillary commercial activity to the main agricultural and forestry activity.[154] As mentioned above,[155] the Italian approach applies the connectivity criteria based on organisational characteristics and economic subordination. In other words, the related activities must be integrated into the organisation established to exercise the main activity and all activities must be carried out by the same agricultural entrepreneur.

The 1997 amendment to the *GewO* abolished the special requirement of economic subordination of the ancillary trade to the primary production, and, instead of this restriction, it is now important that the character of the respective enterprise as an agricultural and forestry enterprise is preserved. This does, however, not change the fact that the economic subordination criterion—derived from the term 'ancillary trade' itself—continues to apply unchanged to the other types of ancillary trade listed in Sec. 2 para. 4 *GewO*, whereas the criteria 'character of the farm' works as a substitute or replacement for the criteria of subordinance.[156] Yet, jurisprudence does not provide any concrete information as to where the limits of this economic subordination of ancillary commercial activities are. It only shows that economic indicators—such as the extent of value added, the amount of revenue and costs as well as labour costs and working hours—have to be taken into account when examining economic subordination (although without indicating a quantitatively calculable demarcation).[157]

---

[151]See Holzer (2017b), p. 43; Holzer (2018), p. 394.

[152]See Sect. 3.3.1.

[153]See decision of the Administrative Court no. 2007/07/0117 (25.09.2008).

[154]See also Holzer (2010), p. 171 et seq.; Holzer (2018), p. 40; Holzer (2017b), p. 28 et seq.

[155]See Sect. 3.3.1.

[156]See decision of the Administrative Court no. Ro 2014/04/0051 (14.10.2015).

[157]See also Holzer (2018), p. 393; Holzer (2010), p. 187 et seq.; Holzer (2012a), p. 768 et seq. In 2008, the Administrative Court, with reference to older findings, has argued that the economic subordination of an auxiliary agricultural activity to primary agricultural and forestry production is only given if it is slight (in terms of volume and economic significance). See decision of the Administrative Court no. 2008/07/0117 (25.09.2008).

Therefore, it seems advisable to refer to tax law to determine the relation between main and related activities or primary and ancillary production, as this is basically also valid for the Italian context.

Now that agricultural activities have been defined, however, nothing has been said about what is necessary to qualify a cooperative as an agricultural cooperative. The approach adopted here differs from that of the Italian legal system. The Austrian legislature, like its Italian counterpart, links agricultural activities directly to cooperatives, but it also uses a system of terminological categories; an approach also used by the European legislature.

For a better understanding of how Austrian agricultural cooperatives are defined, it is helpful to mention that until 1933, the question of how to treat agricultural and forestry cooperatives under trade law was controversial. In 1993 cooperatives were in principle subordinated to the *GewO*, and yet, certain activities of agricultural and forestry cooperatives were excluded from its scope of application. The 'cooperative question' also became a central problem during the negotiations over the *GewO* 1973. The solution consisted of including the purchasing and sales cooperatives (warehouse cooperatives) in the *GewO* 1973 and continuing to exempt certain activities of agricultural and forestry cooperatives from the trade law regime.[158]

Currently, according to Sec. 2 para. 1 subpara. 4 of the *GewO* (as amended in 1994), the following activities of agricultural and forestry cooperatives are excluded from the *GewO*'s scope of application[159]: (a) the operation of sawmills, mills, dairies, distilleries, wine presses and other (traditional) branches for processing agricultural and forestry products (so-called processing cooperatives); (b) the mediation of the purchase and sale as well as the auction of breeding cattle (e.g., cattle breeding cooperatives and pig breeding cooperatives); (c) the sale of unprocessed plant products—with the exception of cereals and potatoes—as well as piglets, fish, poultry, eggs and honey, also by auction (sales cooperatives, such as fruit and vegetable processing cooperatives and beekeepers' cooperatives); (d) the purchase, in connection with the activities referred to in character c, of packaging and wrappings for the products referred to in that character; (e) the breeding, propagation, processing, exploitation and procurement of seeds (so-called seed cooperatives); (f) the use of agricultural and forestry land and fixed agricultural and forestry facilities, provided that this activity serves the production and extraction of plant products (para. 3 no. 1) or the keeping of livestock (para. 3 no. 2) (e.g., alpine, pasture and breeding cooperatives), as well as the use of cooling facilities—provided that these are (exclusively) used for the members' own consumption (so-called cooling cooperatives); and (g) the exercise of the members' rights with regard to utilization within the meaning of the *Grundsatzgesetz* (Basic Act) of 1951 on the treatment of forest utilization rights and pasture utilization rights as well as special field servitudes.[160] Thus, cooperatives conducting one of these activities are

[158]As well as the clarification concerning the admissibility of a limited non-member business. See Holzer (2012a), p. 782; Massauer (1978), p. 82 et seq.

[159]For details, see Massauer (1978), p. 82 et seq.

[160]Also excluded are cooperatives whose activities include the operation of banking businesses (credit cooperatives such as Raiffeisenkassen, land credit and land acquisition cooperatives, and agricultural construction and machinery credit cooperatives). Purchasing cooperatives and sales cooperatives ('warehouse cooperatives') are not exempt from the GewO's application scope, as

considered agricultural cooperatives, to the extent that the business activities of these cooperatives essentially promote their *members' business* and personal activities

The situation described by character (f) contains, as *lex specialis*,[161] a special list of agricultural activities exempted from the *GewO* and carried out by agricultural cooperatives. With regard to the primary agricultural activity,[162] this list is partly narrower[163] and partly broader[164] than the general definition of agriculture and forestry. Apart from this specific aspect, this situation is therefore similar to the one described in Art. 2135 para. 1 CC. In these cases, a cooperative is already an agricultural cooperative because its scope of activity aligns with the Italian principle of *unisoggettività*: that is, the cooperative produces the agricultural products itself. Conversely, the other types of agricultural cooperatives, as specified by the *GewO*, offer their members a service rather than managing agricultural primary production. These types of agricultural cooperatives, then, essentially serve their members' businesses. Essentiality implies that the promotion of members is paramount, while business conducted with non-members is subordinate.[165]

The term 'member business' refers to independent entrepreneurs who normally belong to the same sector, e.g., dairy farmers in dairies or winegrowers in winegrowers' cooperatives.[166] The content of the member business is then determined according to the negative criteria specified by the *GewO*. Thus the Austrian solution—similar to Italian law, which recognises exceptions to the principle of *unisoggettività*—acknowledges that the status of agricultural activity can also be conferred by a specific legal rule and not by the activity itself. Apart from these common features, the essential differences between these two approaches cannot be overlooked. Under Austrian law, the primary activity—i.e., the activity of the members—is also determined by a list of categories, whereas under Italian law, all the main activities explicitly refer to a biological cycle, according to Article 2135 CC. This is a clear consequence of integrating the concept of *agrarietà* into Italian law, as described in Sect. 1.2.2, and represents the demarcation line. In fact, the Italian and Austrian concepts are similar, which seems logical given that they both share the same natural and social phenomenon, but under Italian law, the aspect of the biological cycle is the central one.

While Italian law emphasises the content of agricultural activities by placing the notion of a biological cycle at the centre of the debate, the Austrian legislature

---

they completely converged toward commercial operations in terms of appearance and operating form. See also Holzer (2012a), p. 782 et seq.

[161] lex specialis in respect of the general exemption provisions referred to in Sec. 2 para. 1 Nr. 1 in conjunction with Sec. 2 para. 3 of the GewO.

[162] As determined by Sec. 2 para. 1 in conjunction with Sec. 2 para. 3 GewO.

[163] The following activities mentioned in § 2 para. 3 are not covered by § 2 para. 1 no. 4: (a) the purchase of plant products, (b) hunting and fishing; and (c) the hiring of mounts (to be understood as primary production since the amendment of 2017).

[164] E.g. use of cooling systems for the members' own needs.

[165] See Sect. 3.4.1.

[166] See Dellinger (2014), p. 32.

refrains from creating a precise definition; instead, it uses a combination of approaches (also including aspects of a biological cycle). Yet, ultimately it appears to be more result-oriented, as the list-based approach illustrates. Similar to the Italian legislature, he distinguishes between primary or main activities and ancillary trade or related activities, but has solved the question of when the ancillary trade is (or is not) a commercial activity in a different way. However, even if Austrian law is based upon clear categories, which may make superfluous a discussion about whether a particular activity is related to another activity, this is ultimately not correct. As the Administrative Court points out, in order to fully comprehend the substance of ancillary trade, criteria similar to those in Article 2135 para. 3 CC must be taken into account. Moreover, there are other conceptual similarities, such as how the legal systems deal with cooperatives carrying on a related activity or an ancillary trade. Here, both legal systems use a legal provision to assign the status of the agricultural cooperative.

Although the Austrian legal approach to the concept of agriculture refers to similar activities and therefore overlaps with Italian ideas and approaches, the concepts of terms and structure between the two legal systems differ (yet, they differ less in content). However, this seems inevitable as Italian law fixes primary production to the biological cycle and thus makes a rather sharp distinction between the production of the natural product and the processed product because of ancillary activities. Thus, compared to the Italian legal system, the Austrian approach integrates two perspectives: one on activities and one on products. This integration is due to the list-based approach, which is similar to the method applied at the European level.[167] This mixed approach is also used to define the concept of an agricultural cooperative. The Austrian approach (like the Italian system) refers here to agricultural cooperatives that not only provide services to their farmers but also carry out agricultural activities.

A reason for the differences between the two legal systems might also be found in the different approaches used to determine agricultural law. The Italian legal system anchors its rules to the positively determined concept of agricultural activities, including the concept of the biological cycle, which adopts a strict distinction between main activities[168] and other activities that are somehow linked (related) to the former. Conversely, the Austrian legal system pursues a so-called functional approach. This means considering as part of agricultural law any norm that has functionally affects agriculture. In other words, one must analyse whether a given norm has a special function with respect to agriculture. This system is open in its systematic references, implying that the boundaries are blurred and movable. One could argue that such an open concept corresponds to today's modern necessities. But as one can see, the Italian approach is also weakened to a certain extent—and not strict. This is necessary to adapt agricultural activities to modern, internationalised

---

[167]See Sect. 3.3.3.

[168]Typical farm activities.

production cycles that require flexibility and efficiency to keep such activities innovative and ultimately competitive.

In both jurisdictions, all these activities aim at generating economic revenue, as they are entrepreneurial activities. Both jurisdictions also take into account the ecological component of agricultural activities and, consequently, the farmer as a producer of public goods (e.g., activities focusing on the preservation of the landscape).[169] This is not a market activity for which a farmer can generate income, but is rather a non-market activity supported by a public authority. Due to the different approaches adopted by the two legal systems, such an activity is, as will be explained below,[170] a related activity under Italian Law, which means that the production of public goods supports the main activity. Under Austrian Law, it is considered to be a (primary) agricultural activity that is therefore located within a different level of activity. This is in line with the functional approach, which considers the function of a norm in relation to agriculture—in this particular case, the preservation of the landscape and thus the preservation or better enablement of the activity: this ultimately indicates, in my opinion, a supportive activity that is similar to the Italian approach.

It has already been anticipated that the list-based approach is a central—but not the only—feature of the EU legal system that determines what agriculture legally means. In order to better understand the Italian and Austrian legal systems and hence, to better comprehend the two national agricultural SCEs, it seems useful to examine how EU law deals with the concept of agriculture. EU Law defines the general framework for agricultural activities and thus impacts national legal systems. Accordingly, the national legal systems must also be considered in the light of these effects in order to understand whether these systems need to be adapted[171] or whether the national concepts are flexible enough to include new issues raised at the EU level. It is also important to analyse how EU legislation contributes to anchoring environmental considerations in any agricultural activity. As will be seen, there are also some aspects that help to design an agricultural entrepreneur similar to the Italian approach. Finally, EU law opens up new possibilities that influence the implementation of national law. One example is POs. Since this type of organisation can be particular important for cooperatives, it will be explained in more detail in Sect. 3.3.4.

[169] On these issues see, among many, Norer (2005), p. 485; Holzer (2018), p. 139 et seq.; Germanò (2016), p. 295; Costato and Russo (2015), p. 340 et seq. In general, Balestrino (1994), Abler (2004), Vatn (2002), Beintema et al. (2009) or Organisation for Economic Co-operation and Development (2001), Potter (2015) and Manservisi (2014). See also Rook Basile (1995), p. 77 et seq.; Galloni (1999), p. 29 et seq.; Vecchione (2004), p. 134 et seq.; Vecchione (2009b), p. 327 et seq.; Alessi (2006), p. 1253 et seq.; Iannarelli (2007), p. 480; Magno (2006), p. 103 et seq.; Adornato (2004), p. 6; Costato (2008), p. 458 et seq.

[170] At the end of this sub-chapter.

[171] Here one can refer to the question of whether fishing is an agricultural activity or not. On this issue, see, among others, Germanò and Rook Basile (2014), p. 115 et seq.; Germanò and Rook Basile (2011), p. 773 et seq.; Holzer (2018), p. 53.

3.3.3 The European Definition of Agriculture: A Platform for Discussing National Solutions for Agricultural Cooperatives

In European law, the concept of agriculture was, from the outset, based on political compromises, which were and are ultimately guided by national interests. Moreover, from the outset, the EU concept of agriculture was positioned in relation to the market—more specifically, the internal market, where agriculture occupies a special and rather protected position. Protectionism here aligned with national interests that focused on the need to produce food for one's national population.[172] Thus, it is no wonder that agriculture,[173] has a prominent position in the 'internal policies and measures of the Union'.

The scheme contained in the *TFEU* has a framework character and sets vague guidelines for the development and final design of the CAP. Article 38 *TFEU*, which is the basic norm of the CAP, is based on the principle that the internal market includes agriculture, fisheries and trade in agricultural products.[174] While agriculture is not defined, 'agricultural products' are defined as 'products of the soil, of stock farming and of fisheries and products of first-stage processing directly related to these products'.[175] To be more specific, agricultural products are the products listed in Annex I pursuant to Art. 38 para. 3 *TFEU* (list-based approach). Thus, the specific legal regime that defines a particular internal market for agriculture, as set out in Arts. 39 to 44 *TFEU*, only applies to these products. The conclusion that agriculture within the meaning of the Treaty covers the production of these products is obvious.[176] Activities that are not aimed at the production of certain agricultural products, such as forestry or landscape management, would then not be covered by the concept of agriculture. However, they can be the subject of agricultural schemes if

[172]See Bieber (2016), p. 543 et seq.; McMahon (2007), p. 37 et seq.; Norer (2017b), pp. 636 et seq., 643 et seq.; Martinez (2016c), p. 757 et seq.; Iannarelli (2009); Costato (2009); Germanò (2015).

[173]EU agricultural law is rightly regarded as probably the most complex structure of the Community legal order, whose positive knowledge (by those subject to it and by the authorities) is made considerably difficult by its casuistry, technical nature and short-lived nature. Because of the Union's broad competence in agriculture (including fisheries) and the economic policies adopted on a large scale, the bulk of all Union legislation adopted still concerns agricultural policy. However, many provisions are merely periodic reassessments of levies or subsidies, purchase and selling prices, levies, refunds, etc. whose scope is limited in time and substance and whose structure and content are largely standardised. Whereas in the past almost half of the EU's legislative acts concerned agriculture, the share of agricultural legislation has been declining steadily for a number of years. In September 2009, about 17% of the legal catalogue in the Directory of the applicable Union law was still attributable to the agricultural sector. In terms of case law, the agricultural sector constitutes about 18% of all previous judgements of the European courts. See Norer (2017b), pp. 636 et seq., and 643 et seq.; Holzer (2018), p. 153 et seq.; Martinez (2016c), p. 757 et seq.

[174]See Bieber (2016), p. 543 et seq.

[175]See also Norer (2017b), p. 638; Martinez (2016c), p. 762 et seq.

[176]See Bieber (2016), p. 544 et seq.; McMahon (2007), p. 4 et seq.; Norer (2017b), p. 638 et seq.; Martinez (2016c), p. 764 et seq.; Germanò (2016), p. 24.

they directly serve agricultural objectives. Currently, these issues are dealt with as specific subjects by pillar two of the CAP.[177]

According to Art. 38 TFEU, the internal market includes agriculture, fisheries and trade in agricultural products, so the applicable rules cover not only the methods of producing agricultural products, but also trade in those products.[178] Thus, agricultural products are to be distinguished from industrial products, which results in differentiating their respective markets. The principle that agricultural products and fisheries are to be compared with and distinguished from industrial products and services runs through the whole body of rules in the *TFEU* dedicated to the agricultural market. These rules, taken as a whole, are characterised not only by the fact that they contain essential exceptions to the rules governing the internal market (i.e., essential exceptions to the principle of free competition),[179] but also by norms that determine the structure and policy of the agricultural market, which is to be distinguished from other markets.[180]

But how do these aspects define agriculture? Two observations can be made. First, one can affirm that a peculiarity results from a systematic approach. A second observations concerns the contents of Annex 1 to the *TFEU*, namely, the list of agricultural products to which the exceptions to free competition apply. The specificity of EU agricultural legislation is that a particular market has been created for the products listed in this Annex, where the priority of free competition rules is limited. The focus on products might lead to the conclusion that the approach chosen in European law refers to the product and not to the agricultural activity.[181] Yet, the EU legal framework also contains provisions that do exactly the opposite.[182] Here, one can consider the provisions of Directive No. 59 of 1972, which defines the figure of the agricultural entrepreneur as one who primarily (from a temporal point of view) exercises an agricultural activity. Then, one can refer to Regulation No. 1782 of 2003 and the succeeding Regulation No. 73 of 2009, both of which contain a

[177]See Holzer (2018), p. 164; Martinez (2016c), p. 766.

[178]See Bieber (2016), p. 544; Germanò (2016), p. 23. In this regard, see also Costato (2011).

[179]See Art. 42 TFEU. See also, among others, Martinez (2016b).

[180]These legal but also the economic peculiarities of agriculture and the agricultural market make it clear that this is an independent legal system. See Germanò (2016), p. 24. See also Norer (2017b), p. 641 et seq.; Martinez (2016c), p. 760 et seq.

Conversely, it is also true that the determination of such a topic must always be seen in connection with a specific legal discipline that requires a separate analysis. It follows from this difference that the special European legal standards dealing with agriculture do not only indicate that a separate consideration may be opportune, but rather that such a separate consideration may quasi be required.

[181]This approach is highlighted by the two judgments:. See Case T-61/89 (Dansk Pelsdyravlerforening v Commission of the European Communities), Judgment of 2 July 1992 and Case C-164/97 (European Parliament v. Council of the European Union), judgment of 25 February 1999.

[182]See Germanò and Rook Basile (2014), p. 111 et seq.

definition of agricultural activity (albeit only used to apply these regulations).[183] With the help of these provisions, these concepts have been introduced into the European set of rules dedicated to agriculture *and* agricultural activity.[184]

This activity, nowadays, not only concerns the production of agricultural products—i.e., foodstuffs—but also the protection of the environment and the territory. This is the result of a continuing development of the CAP in which environment and territory—both considered crucial for agricultural activities—have become more and more relevant. The norms dealing with agriculture that are contained in Art. 38 et seq. *TFEU* do not include explicit references to the meanwhile shifted accents in the objectives of the CAP, such as environmental or consumer protection.[185] Environmental issues are thus linked to agriculture because of other norms of the *TFEU*.[186] For example, Art. 11 *TFEU* requires to integrate environmental protection requirements into the definition and implementation of the CAP, with a view to promoting sustainable development. As a result, boundaries between agricultural and environmental policy appear to be blurred. Legal acts of environmental policy based on Art. 192 TFEU may also be relevant under agricultural law.[187] The same

---

[183]Accordingly, 'agricultural activity' means the production, rearing or growing of agricultural products including harvesting, milking, breeding animals and keeping animals for farming purposes, or maintaining the land in good agricultural and environmental condition as established in Article 6 (of Reg. 73/2009). See Art. 2 letter c Reg. 73/2009 (OJ L 30/06). See also McMahon (2007), p. 2 et seq.

[184]See also Norer (2017b), p. 639 et seq.; Martinez (2016c), p. 765; Martinez (2016d), p. 772 et seq.; Germanò and Rook Basile (2014), p. 112 et seq.; Albisinni (2014a), p. 973 et seq.

[185]See Norer (2017b), p. 643 et seq.; Holzer (2018), p. 1553 et seq.; Norer (2017c), p. 656 et seq.

With regard to the content of the agricultural policy itself, Articles 40 to 42 TFEU provide only indications as to which measures are intended to achieve these objectives. The central instrument is the common organisation of agricultural markets (Art. 4 para. 1 letter c TFEU), but also agricultural structural policy, various measures such as vocational training or sales promotion (Art. 41 TFEU) and the consideration of agriculture in the competitive sector (Art. 42 TFEU). Today, three pillars of the CAP have emerged: the Common Market Organisation, rural development and legal harmonisation. The fundamental principles of the CAP are market unity, Union preference (priority for production in the internal market) and financial solidarity (Union financing). Their validity as political guidelines is undisputed, but their importance and scope as legal principles—possibly directly applicable—appear doubtful. See Holzer (2018), p. 185 et seq.; Bieber (2016), pp. 545 et seq. and 547 et seq.; Norer (2017b), p. 647 et seq.

[186]In addition to the integration of agriculture into the internal market, Article 38 para. 4 of the TFEU lays down the CAP's application scope. The purpose of designing a CAP is to develop an internal market for agricultural products and make it work. Both must 'go hand in hand'. Art. 39 TFEU lists the CAP's objectives, taking into account the particular characteristics of agriculture and its close links with member states' economies in their entirety. This list of objectives includes increasing productivity, ensuring a fair standard of living for the agricultural population, stabilising markets, securing supplies and supplying consumers at reasonable prices. A powerful trend in the CAP and common agricultural law can be seen under the keywords of coherence and integration in a networked, integrated view and in consideration of all affected policy areas. This applies particularly to the integration of environmental policy. See Bieber (2016), p. 545 et seq.; Norer (2017c), p. 652 et seq.; Holzer (2018), pp. 171 et seq. and 176 et seq.

[187]See Norer (2017b), p. 636 et seq.; Bieber (2016), p. 545; Epiney (2016), p. 623 et seq.

applies to numerous other norms of the *TFEU* that address such issues as trade (Art. 207 *TFEU*), health protection (Art. 168 *TFEU*), consumer protection (Art. 169 *TFEU*) and/or development cooperation (Art. 209 *TFEU*).[188] European agricultural law is therefore not exclusively set within the framework of the CAP.[189] From this it follows that, in principle, agricultural products are the main object or reference point of the norms of the Treaty that address agriculture. However, one must also point out that agricultural activity is ultimately the subject of any agricultural policy. This activity is characterised by its relation to land and no longer solely by production (i.e., an activity with which products are to be made). It is therefore an activity that serves to make a agricultural product that has a relation to and originates from the environment.

This conclusion can also be drawn by considering Art. 4 of Regulation No. 1307 of 2013, which addresses agricultural activity. The approach contained in regulation is rather particular, since the definition contained therein includes a further and additional activity that focuses on preserving and safeguarding the land. Accordingly, agricultural activity also means maintaining land in an agricultural state in which it can maintain its production capacity. Thus, it is no longer just a question of seeing land as an instrument of production, but of looking at the activity itself and how it is performed in this context. Two things follow: First, one must consider the connection between human activity and the environment, and second, the land is the part of the environment with which agricultural products will be produced. The term 'land' is here defined as an 'agricultural area', which 'means any area taken up by arable land, permanent grassland and permanent pasture, or permanent crops'.[190] This area must be capable of producing one of the products listed in Annex I of the *TFEU*. Thus, land has become relevant for defining agricultural activity.[191]

The environmental aspect in Italian and Austrian agricultural law is not only part of a specific set of rules—i.e., environmental protection laws—but also an integral part of the two specific (national) concepts of agricultural activity, which refer to the biological cycle, on the one hand, and the use of natural forces and cycles, on the other. In fact, both set of rules relate to the various activities to nature and make them dependent on it. Even if none of these concepts contains an explicit commitment to protect the environment, the activities must therefore be carried out in an environmentally sound manner in order to be able to carry them out in the long term. This

---

[188]See Bieber (2016), p. 544 et seq.

[189]See Martinez (2016d), p. 772 et seq., Legal acts based on legal sources other than those in Articles 38 to 44 TFEU are constantly gaining in importance for agriculture: provisions of environmental protection law and nature conservation, structural and regional policy, state aid law, veterinary and public health law, as well as international agreements, legal acts and the setting of standards to implement the internal market, can have wide-ranging effects.

[190]See Art. 4 para. 1 letter e Reg. 1307/2013 (OJ L 347/608).

[191]See Germanò (2016), p. 25; Germanò and Rook Basile (2014), p. 114 et seq. See also Albisinni (2014a), pp. 976 et seq. and 984; Costato (2011), p. 123 et seq. Nevertheless, the list of agricultural products in Annex 1 is still essentially important, as it allows for specifying exemptions from competition law.

last aspect is part of the entrepreneurial feature, which both concepts of agricultural activity include. This criterion of sustainable behaviour must be taken into account in cases where an agricultural entrepreneur wants to run his activities in the long term or where the same entrepreneur wants to give up and sell his business. It is also important in this latter case that the activity has been carried out in an environmentally friendly way; otherwise, the value of the resource used for the agricultural activity diminishes.

Thus, the definition of agriculture from a European legal point of view means that the definition of the relevant terms may refer to the activities themselves or to the products. However, they must all take account of the environment as an essential production resource. Comparing the Italian, Austrian and European concepts one can conclude that the fundamental difference is therefore how this interrelationship between the environment and activity is designed and described. The reason for these different approaches lies in their path dependency. While the national approaches have to be considered in accordance with their scientifically and legally developed concepts, the EU approach—and this is true for many EU policies—is based on a pragmatism that tries to reflect different (often national) theoretical ways of thinking. I argue that the EU approach is not so different from the national one, especially when the content is considered and formalities are pushed into the background.

Now that the notions of agriculture and agricultural activity under EU law have been conceived, we must consider whether there are provisions under EU law that define exactly what a farmer—or agricultural entrepreneur—is. As agricultural activity is an entrepreneurial activity, it seems useful to first assess how, in general, the concept of entrepreneur is addressed by EU law.

As the Treaty of Rome does not contain a definition of enterprise,[192] the ECJ had to define this notion in regard to competition law in order to make competition rules more effective. This not only made it possible to better implement the rules that deal with competition, but also to identify the legal entity to which the provisions apply. Accordingly, an enterprise is any entity engaged in an economic activity, regardless of its legal status and the way in which it is financed.[193] The ECJ thus pursues a functional approach, in which the content of the term is therefore not determined by institutional or organisational criteria, but by the activity of the potential norm addressees (since it is a matter of controlling behaviour that is relevant to competition). Thus, in order to establish whether an entity constitutes an undertaking, the fact that it does not seek to make a profit is not decisive. An economic activity is any activity consisting in offering goods and services on a market. Non-profit entities can

[192]Neither in terms of commercial activity, nor in terms of agricultural activity. See Germanò and Rook Basile (2014), p. 140.

[193]Judgment of the ECJ of 23 April 1991 (Höfner and Elser v. Macrotron GmbH). See European Court reports 1991, Page I-01979.

also offer goods and services on a market.[194] There is no doubt that this rather broad definition includes both the Italian and the Austrian approaches: Both consider agricultural activities as entrepreneurial activities that must be economically efficient and generate reasonable income.[195]

The Treaty of Rome does not contain the concept of farmer, but rather, the term producer.[196] Regarding the definition of farmer, one can refer to Article 2 of Regulation No. 1782 of 2003 (and its successors, Regulation No. 73 of 2009 and Regulation No. 1307 of 2013), which provides a definition that is applicable to the implementation of the rules concerning direct payments.[197] Accordingly, farmer 'means a natural or legal person, or a group of natural or legal persons, regardless of the legal status granted to such group and its members by national law, whose holding is situated within the territorial scope of the Treaties, as defined in Article 52 *TEU* (Treaty on European Union) in conjunction with Articles 349 and 355 *TFEU*, and who exercises an agricultural activity'. This definition provides two essential criteria: on the one hand, the concept of a holding and, on the other hand, the expression 'exercises an agricultural activity'. The concept of agricultural activity has already been discussed above.[198] The concept of a holding is addressed by Art. 4 of the Reg. 1307/2013, which stipulates that it refers to 'all the units used for agricultural activities and managed by a farmer situated within the territory of the same Member State'.[199] It follows that, under the CAP, a farmer is a person who is entitled to use property that establishes a holding with which an activity is carried out with the aim of producing the products listed in Annex 1.[200]

The two national legal systems also contain definitions of farmer or agricultural entrepreneur, but they differ from each other by including different functions. While EU law uses this concept to determine the eligible subject, the national systems, in principle, use this concept—apart from tax issues—(1) to identify a particular type of entrepreneur as a particular subject of private law (who thus holds corresponding special obligations under private law) and (2) to regulate the acquisition and sale of agricultural land (real estate law).

We must also consider the farmer as a person who produces for the market. Here, the European legislature has established criteria to be fulfilled for getting financial support. Similar to the national approaches that require entrepreneurial efficiency, the European legislature established the figure of a professional farmer, who, in turn,

---

[194]See Judgment of the ECJ of 16 June 1987, Commission v. Italy (C-118/85), Judgement of the ECJ of 18 June 1998, Commission v. Italy (C-35/96), Judgment of the ECJ of 12 September 2000, Pavlov and Others, Joined Cases C-180/98 to C-184/98.

[195]See also Germanò and Rook Basile (2014), p. 140 et seq.; Alessi (2006), p. 1237 et seq.

[196]However, here, too, there is no definition. See Germanò and Rook Basile (2014), p. 141 fn 29. See also McMahon (2007), p. 2 et seq.

[197]See Germanò and Rook Basile (2014), p. 142.

[198]See first part of this chapter.

[199]See also McMahon (2007), p. 3 et seq.

[200]See Germanò and Rook Basile (2014), p. 142.

is at the centre of the CAP and must possess adequate occupational skills and competence. This concept demands that the entrepreneur is able to run an agricultural business in a professional manner and thus to make profits.[201]

Since 1999, obtaining financial support from the European Union has, in fact, not only been a question of creating a certain level of work performance or a certain agricultural added value and yield, but also of the farmer himself managing the farm professionally to achieve profits and to be competitive on the market.[202] Farmers who receive financial support from the European Union must ensure that the food they produce is safe, healthy and of an appropriate quality. They must also ensure that the environment is protected—including public health, plant health and animal health—and they must commit to protecting not only the countryside but also the cultural heritage of the rural areas in which they operate. The concept of decoupling, which has separated the production volume from the subsidies granted, no longer requires farmers to align their production exclusively on the level of subsidies, but enables them to base their production on what the market actually demands. These conditions are the basic prerequisites that a farmer must meet to receive public subsidies.[203]

Moreover, farmers can choose to merely keep the land in good agricultural and environmental condition. This aspect of decoupling unmistakably shows how the (production-oriented) concept of the farmer has been broadened in scope to include protecting the environment. This not only highlights the link between the farmer and his original function of food production, but also illustrates the farmer's function as a producer of public goods (healthy environment, etc.). Both aspects are clearly related to the activity of cultivating land, which is the classical function of the farmer.[204] The production of agricultural products and public goods results from the development of concepts that must also be oriented towards political development and are therefore subject to continuous development of policies.

It is clear that the development of the CAP has strongly influenced the definition of farmer (from a European law point of view). In doing so, the European legislature has been guided by pragmatism. This does not mean, however, that no uniform approach is visible. On the contrary, the European legislature has always kept current economic and social problems in mind. He tried to solve them in an appropriate and situation-related way, as shown by the fact that reference has always

---

[201]This reorientation moved away from the general objective of maximising production toward economic management, in line with the necessities for being competitive in the market. Furthermore, the aim or basic idea is to keep the rural population on the spot—and to give them a future in agricultural activities. See Holzer (2018), p. 172 et seq.; Norer (2017c), p. 652 et seq. See also Vecchione (2009c), p. 353 et seq. and in general Iannarelli (2007).

[202]See Vecchione (2009c), p. 353 et seq.; Alessi (2006), p. 1258 et seq.; Germanò and Rook Basile (2014), p. 143 et seq.

[203]See Martinez (2016a), p. 793 et seq.; Norer (2017a), p. 670 et seq.; Germanò and Rook Basile (2014), pp. 208 et seq. and 256 et seq.

[204]See Germanò and Rook Basile (2014), p. 146 et seq. See also Casadei (2009), p. 336 et seq.; Vecchione (2009c), p. 353 et seq.

been made to special economic categories, which, by their very nature differ from legal categories found in the jurisdictions of the EU member states.[205] These national categories are more clearly distinguishable, but, at the same time, relatively immovable.[206] Conversely, in European law we find a more flexible concept, which goes hand in hand with the factuality of the sources or is conditioned by them.

This static approach applies to the Italian legal system, while the Austrian legislature—in line with the functional approach of Austrian agricultural law—applies a multi-faceted concept that is based on less a clear definition of agriculture or agricultural activities and appears similar to the European approach. This is one of the main differences: the Italian approach is always based on a clear definition, while the other two approaches are influenced by changing ideas, interests and policies. Of course, this influence also exists in the Italian legal system, but these 'external forces' are absorbed by the clear and flexible definition based on the concept of the biological cycle. This cycle requires us to think about entrepreneurial activity, which is (in this case) agricultural activity, and to consider nature as an indispensable basis for agriculture.

While conceptual development is clearly visible in the Italian legal order, the European legislature reveals its pragmatic tendencies by adopting a product-oriented approach, which has been extended by various aspects, such as entrepreneurial thinking (efficiency and professionalism) and environmental initiatives that align with the requirements of changing policies. We should recall that the European approach primarily aims to define the scope of the competition rules and to distinguish the agricultural sector from other sectors, while the national solution does not focus on this perspective but must be considered in conjunction with specific branches of law (private law, commercial law, tax law and so on). The European approach is flexible and dynamic to accommodate the needs of agricultural policy, which today as we can see, goes beyond mere food production and strongly considers agricultural activities in context with the production of public goods.

Since agricultural activity is ultimately based on the environment—which requires being aware of changing environmental conditions and acting sustainably to maintain production capacity—the Italian legislature has also had to incorporate dynamic elements into its definition of agricultural activity. The dynamism of these activities is reflected in the concept of the biological cycle, which not only describes a lasting production phase, but also the vulnerability of agricultural activities since they depend on a sound environment. The Austrian approach to agricultural activity contains similar elements, e.g., when it relates agricultural activities to natural forces and thus to the environment, or when it refers to the keeping of livestock for breeding, fattening or production of animal products.

To sum up: European law provides the framework for an economic activity that must be constantly adapted to changing interests, nowadays in the fields of

---

[205] See Germanò and Rook Basile (2014), p. 142 et seq.

[206] This is also due to the fact that these are categories of terms that require clear definitions so that they can be interpreted.

environment and health. It establishes a system that must be constantly balanced between free competition and agricultural and environmental interests and needs. This flexible system shapes and reshapes the concepts and approaches to agriculture as they are contained in the various legal systems of the individual EU member states. The openness of this system is also reflected in the specific types of farmers (as regulated by EU law), such as young farmers,[207] small farmers[208] and, above all, active farmers[209] (and in the near future the genuine farmer?[210]). All these notions have their meaning for direct payments, but each focuses on a different aspect. The first lays down criteria for providing targeted support to young people in the exercise of an agricultural activity. Young people are encouraged to set up businesses and provide services to the community, such as the production of food and public goods. The second seeks to reduce the bureaucratic burden on small farmers, and the last notion aims to ensure that the system of direct payments is not exploited by identifying activities that do not fall within the scope of the regulation on direct payments.

It is crucial to understand the European framework for two reasons. First, it allows agricultural entrepreneurs to receive financial support for their activities. Second, the interaction between free competition and a managed market economy influences the often vague content of national provisions and concepts. One good example of this interaction is the provisions of EU law that allow farmers to be subsidised "only" for maintaining soil only in good environmental conditions.[211] For a person conducting an agricultural activity as defined by Italian or Austrian law, these provisions, in principle, do not have a major practical impact, since, according to the Italian CC and the Austrian *GewO*, the subject in question only carries out an activity which, since

[207]See Art. 50 Reg. 1307/2013. For details, see, among others, Germanò and Rook Basile (2014), p. 218 fn 33; Holzer (2018), p. 55.

[208]See title V Reg. 1307/2013. For details, see, among others, Germanò and Rook Basile (2014), p. 149; Holzer (2018), p. 55 et seq.

[209]See Art. 9 Reg. 1307/2013. For details, see, among others, Germanò and Rook Basile (2014), p. 149 et seq.; Albisinni (2014a), p. 979 et seq.; Holzer (2018), p. 54 et seq.

[210]See Proposal for a Regulation of the European Parliament and of the Council establishing rules on support for strategic plans to be drawn up by Member States under the Common agricultural policy (CAP Strategic Plans) and financed by the European Agricultural Guarantee Fund (EAGF) and by the European Agricultural Fund for Rural Development (EAFRD) and repealing Regulation (EU) No 1305/2013 of the European Parliament and of the Council and Regulation (EU) No 1307/2013 of the European Parliament and of the Council, COM(2018) 392 final (01.06.2018). Art. 4 para. 1 letter d states: 'genuine farmers shall be defined in a way to ensure that no support is granted to those whose agricultural activity forms only an insignificant part of their overall economic activities or whose principal business activity is not agricultural, while not precluding from support pluri-active farmers. The definition shall allow to determine which farmers are not considered genuine farmers, based on conditions such as income tests, labour inputs on the farm, company object and/or inclusion in registers.'

[211]Here, the production of public goods (i.e., biodiversity, water regulation, land-scape, erosion control, resilience to floods and climate change mitigation)—where there are currently no markets—is essential. See also Casadei (2009), p. 339 et seq. In general, Iannarelli (2007). See also Magno (2006), p. 89 and, on these issues, Albisinni (2014a).

no marketable product is produced, cannot be, in principle, classified as an agricultural activity. But what happens if a farm worker who works for a farmer on the basis of a dependent employment relationship carries out this activity?

Taking into account the definitions contained in the CC and the *GewO*, a farm worker who carries out an activity that is not at all agricultural could be carrying out an activity that does not fall within the scope of his employment contract. In order to prevent this, in 2002 the Austrian legislature amended the concept of agricultural activities in the *Landarbeitsrecht*, i.e., the law on the activity of agricultural workers. Accordingly, landscape protection, which serves the preservation of the cultural landscape, is equated with agricultural and forestry production, provided that the activity is subsidised and that this support is granted for the preservation of the cultural landscape.[212] In Italy, this situation is generally regulated by Article 2135 para. 3 CC, which defines activities aimed at improving the soil (or the land and forest resources) as related activities.[213] We should recall that under Italian law, the related activities are not agricultural activities. Thus, the Italian approach differs from EU law and also from Austrian law.[214]

To conclude the discussion, which should help us to deepen our understanding of how an SCE can define agriculture as its scope of business, we must address the issue of POs.[215] In addition to the notions of farmers and agriculture or agricultural activities, EU law also offers specific organisational structures that can be used to keep an agricultural activity competitive. Like its national counterpart, the European legislature has supported the horizontal and vertical integration of the production chain through POs, among other things.[216] These generally share some characteristics with cooperatives; interestingly, studies have shown that POs are mainly organised through cooperatives.[217]

---

[212]For details, see Holzer (2018), p. 433 et seq.; Holzer (2018), p. 41 et seq.

[213]For details, see Germanò and Rook Basile (2011), p. 775 et seq. See also Casadei (2009), p. 336 et seq.; Sgarbanti (2009).

[214]This issue is also regulated by the relevant Italian collective agreement, which governs employment relationships between enterprises engaged in agricultural activities, as well as related activities—including enterprises engaged in the creation, development and maintenance of public and private green areas—and the agricultural workers employed by them.

[215]On this issue, see, among others, Canfora (2008). See also Costantino (2013), Albisinni (2013, 2014b), Sepe (2013) and Iannarelli (2008b, 2011).

[216]A producer organisation (PO) is a strategic tool developed by the European Commission, and this is fully in line with the broader objective of reforming the Common Agricultural Policy (introduced by Art. 11 of Reg. (EC) No. 2200/96 and confirmed by Reg. (EC) No. 1234/2007 and Reg. 1308/2013 (OJ L 347/671). See also Iannarelli (2008a).

[217]Studies have revealed that POs are mostly organised by means of cooperatives. See Van der Sangen (2012), p. 101. Also consider Ecorys and Wageningen Economic Research (2018), pp. 15 and 27. According to the specific Italian legal framework, these entities can be organised as a joint-stock company, agricultural cooperative and its consortia and/or consortium societies. See Art. 3 para. 1 legislative decree no. 102/2005.

3.3.4 European Producer Organisations as Entities Created by Farmers and Agricultural Food Producers in the Legal Form of a Cooperative

A producer organisation (PO) can be defined as a legal entity that is created voluntarily by farmers and agricultural food producers.[218] It allows several farmers to be brought into a single sectoral organisation and aims to achieve economic equilibrium in the agri-food chain by regulating production prices.[219] POs enable participating individual units (farmers) to reduce costs through economies of scale and can therefore be financially supported by EU policies.[220] Art. 152 Reg. 1308/2013 lists specific objectives,[221] of which at least one must be met. These cover topics, such as production planning, concentration of supply, optimising production costs, research initiatives and marketing initiatives. In the fruit and vegetable sectors, the law allows for the implementation of an operational programme aimed at improving product quality, conducting production planning and promotion

[218]See Art. 152 para. 1 letter b Reg. 1308/2013. In the PO, the decision of 'what, how and how much to produce' results from the sum of multiple free individual decisions, which are not shattered into disjointed entrepreneurial behaviours but contained in a collective will capable of orienting those behaviours.

[219]See Art. 152 para. 1 Reg. 1308/2013. See also Holzer (2018), p. 192; Germanò and Rook Basile (2014), p. 154 et seq.; Germanò (2016), p. 132; Costantino (2013), p. 1449; Alessi (2006), p. 1271 et seq.; Norer (2017a), p. 667 et seq.

[220]See Art. 32 Reg. 1308/2013. Concerning the economic functioning of POs, see Ecorys and Wageningen Economic Research (2018), p. 9 et seq.; Amat et al. (2019), p. 145 et seq.; Ajates Gonzalez (2018), p. 22 et seq. See also Alessi (2006), p. 1271 et seq.

[221]The objectives are: (1) ensuring that production is planned and adjusted to demand, particularly in terms of quality and quantity; (2) concentration of supply and the placing on the market of the products produced by its members, including through direct marketing; (3) optimising production costs and returns on investments in response to environmental and animal welfare standards, and stabilising producer prices; (4) carrying out research and developing initiatives on sustainable production methods, innovative practices, economic competitiveness and market developments; (5) promoting, and providing technical assistance for, the use of environmentally sound cultivation practices and production techniques, and sound animal welfare practices and techniques; (6) promoting, and providing technical assistance for, the use of production standards, improving product quality and developing products with a protected designation of origin, with a protected geographical indication or covered by a national quality label; (7) the management of by-products and of waste in particular to protect the quality of water, soil and landscape and preserving or encouraging biodiversity; (8) contributing to a sustainable use of natural resources and to climate change mitigation; (9) developing initiatives in the area of promotion and marketing; (10) managing of the mutual funds referred to in operational programmes in the fruit and vegetables sector referred to in Article 31(2) of this Regulation and under Article 36 of Regulation (EU) No 1305/2013, (11) providing the necessary technical assistance for the use of the futures markets and of insurance schemes. See Art. 152 para. 1 letter c Reg. 1308/2013.

initiatives, etc. These programmes, which are supported by different financial means,[222] must be approved by the member states.[223]

POs must be recognised by one of the member states, which confirms that a PO meets the legal criteria and can therefore fulfil the tasks laid out in the regulation. For recognition, however, POs must prove that they have a certain degree of market strength.[224] Accordingly, it is necessary for POs to have a minimum number of members and/or cover a determined minimum volume (or value) of marketable production.[225]

Since the last CAP reform, this type of organisation must be mutually recognised in multiple sectors—including fruit and vegetables, olive oil and table olives, silkworms, hops as well as milk and milk products—while in other sectors, the recognition of POs is voluntary.[226]

If recognised, POs may conclude volume and price agreements—in order to achieve the objectives of the CAP—and, in particular, strengthen the market position of producers vis-à-vis their customers.[227] The position of the PO is furthermore strengthened by Art. 153, para. 1 letters b and c, which stipulate that farmers may join only one PO for a specific product and obliges them to provide information to their PO for statistical purposes.

Essentially, a PO as solves two functions: On the one hand, there is a normative function, according to which a PO is to give the affiliated members (a) specifications with regard to rearing and soil cultivation, and (b) specifications with regard to the products which are to be sold later by the PO. On the other hand, they carry out an operational activity by marketing the products. These two tasks can include optional requirements for the members, but also binding ones. One possible example is that

[222] See Art. 32 Reg. 1308/2013.

[223] Art. 33 para. 1 subpara. 2 Reg. 1308/2013. In addition, specific support may be granted for the establishment of a PO under the rural development programme of a Member State.

[224] See Art. 154 para. 1 letter b and c Reg. 1308/2013. POs may also ask the member states to lay down binding rules for the supply of certain products (cheese and ham) bearing a protected designation of origin or a protected geographical indication. See Art. 150 and Art. 172 Reg. 1308/2013.

[225] See Art. 154 para. 1 letter b Reg. 1308/2013. Moreover, according to Art. 154 para. 1 letter c the PO must provide sufficient evidence that it can carry out its activities properly, both over time and in terms of effectiveness, provision of human capital, material and technical support to its members, and as appropriate concentration of supply. See also Germanò and Rook Basile (2014), p. 157; Holzer (2018), p. 192. See also Amat et al. (2019).

In general, the EU encourages farmers to set up POs.

[226] See Art. 159 Reg. 1308/2013. The importance of this collaboration vehicle is also demonstrated by the fact that recognised POs' rules also may be extended to non-members. See Art. 164 Reg. 1308/2013.

[227] See Holzer (2018), p. 192, Here the specific link between agricultural activities and the mechanisms of the free market is evident.

members may be required to sell their products exclusively through the PO, as happens in the fruit and vegetable sector.[228]

In addition, Chap. 3, Section 5 of Reg. 1308/2013 provides for a specific contractual system.[229] Accordingly, POs active in the olive oil, beef and veal and/or arable crops sectors may negotiate contracts on behalf of their members for the supply of all or part of their production.[230] This activity, in contrast to marketing activities, seems to consist of the facts that the concentration of supply is only indirect and that the contracts themselves are ultimately concluded between producers and purchasers.[231]

In practice, POs have been set up mostly by cooperatives, perhaps because POs are economic organisations with similar characteristics to cooperatives.[232] In particular, POs, like cooperatives, should have a democratic decision-making mechanism (i.e., one member, one vote) and be controlled by their members.[233] It is similar perhaps, but definitely different from a legal point of view for at least three reasons.[234]

A first difference results from the purpose of the two organisational models. In fact, the purpose and activities of POs are more strictly regulated than those of cooperatives. Examples of a strict regulation that affects the relationship between the organisation and its members include the concentration of supply, the marketing of members' production, the adaptation of production to market requirements, and the improvement of the product and the rationalisation of mechanising production.

The next point concerns derogations from competition law. These will only be granted if certain conditions are met.[235]

The third difference concerns the legal form: POs do not have to be organised in the legal form of a cooperative; the aim is to find an appropriate legal form to achieve

[228]See Germanò and Rook Basile (2014), p. 158; Germanò (2016), p. 132; Costato and Russo (2015), p. 162. In general, Costantino (2013).

[229]See Arts. 168 et seq. Reg. 1308/2013.

[230]See Arts. 169 et seq. Reg. 1308/2013.

[231]See Costato and Russo (2015), p. 162 et seq.

[232]These similarities also are shown by acknowledging that POs can be the first step to a formation of a cooperative, and cooperatives may comprise several POs recognised for different agricultural sectors. The introduction of POs has been endorsed by the European Union as part of its policy to ensure that farmers remain competitive and have the bargaining power to do so. See Van der Sangen (2012), p. 18 et seq.; Ecorys and Wageningen Economic Research (2018), p. 105 et seq. As already mentioned, bargaining power is also created by agricultural cooperatives and is one of their factors for success. See Sect. 1.3.3.

[233]See Art. 153 para. 2 letter c Reg. 1308/2013. The fact that different implementation models exist in this respect is illustrated in a 2012 study. See Van der Sangen (2012), p. 18 et seq.

[234]See also Ajates Gonzalez (2018), p. 23 et seq.

[235]See Arts. 152, 222, 209 and 149 Reg. 1308/2013. Yet, POs must offer the possibility of integrating members' activities in other ways, with the aim of producing efficiency gains that, in turn, should compensate for the possible negative effects of joint selling. See van Herck (2014), p. 14. On this issue, see also Albisinni (2013), p. 12.

the purpose of a PO. It is only important that these objectives are met.[236] The choice of legal form takes a back seat.

These rules inevitably lead to certain peculiarities. The specific nature of their activities leads POs to concentrate on quality products and regional specialities. Another practical difference between a cooperative and a PO is that the latter is generally very much geared to the joint sale of agricultural products. Consequently, since POs are primarily concerned with selling products to consumers, they are usually at the forefront of the production and sales chain, i.e., POs are primarily involved in negotiating with consumers rather than processing agricultural products.

Could these findings be significant for an agricultural SCE? The fact that POs are often formed by cooperatives shows not only the practical significance for an agricultural SCE, but also the perspective from which an agricultural SCE should additionally be considered. Organising an agricultural SCE as a PO leads to the non-application of competition law; this type of organisation can therefore considerably influence the function of an agricultural SCE. Moreover, the application of this set of rules may significantly determine how cooperative governance and financing can be handled. In the second part of this study, I address these issues.[237] In this way, the provisions for the PO shape the internal structure of a cooperative: For example, the rules can oblige the members of the agricultural SCE to produce exclusively for it.

Applying these provisions can influence the format of an agricultural SCE, but this does not imply that the application of these schemes will ultimately lead to a harmonised legal framework. Interestingly, the European legislature has issued special provisions for POs that conduct multinational business (that is, the member producers' holdings are located in more than one Member State).[238] Of course, at this point, one can heretically question whether this specific arrangement has made the legal form of an SCE obsolete, at least in the agricultural sector.

These results show that the discussion on questions of agricultural cooperatives requires many things. We must not only understand the multifunctional approach, which the European legislature is (continuously) developing,[239] but also the organisational instruments of European law.

---

[236]See Art. 154 para. 1 Reg. 1308/2013; in particular Art. 154 para. 1 letter a in conjunction with Art. 152 para. 1 letter c Reg. 1308/2013. On this issue, see also Ecorys and Wageningen Economic Research (2018), p. 9 et seq.

[237]Which are primarily anchored in private law.

[238]See Commission delegated Regulation (EU) 2016/232 of 15 December 2015 supplementing Regulation (EU) No. 1308/2013 of the European Parliament and of the Council with regard to certain aspects of producer cooperation (OJ L 44/1).

[239]And this will probably become even clearer if one considers that modern agri-food production is a not insignificant driver of anthropogenic climate change and that the European legislature can take this circumstance into account, among other things, through the instrument of cross-compliance.

3.4 Insights on the Topic of the Agricultural Cooperative as SCE: On Members' Involvement

The involvement of members is essential to the definition of a cooperative and depends upon the scope of activity, which (for our purposes) is an agricultural activity. Having analysed what this latter term implies, according to the different legal systems analysed here, we can now investigate how membership in an agricultural cooperative can be conceived from a legal point of view.

We begin with a detailed analysis of what the so-called principle of double quality could legally mean to better understood how—from a legal point of view—an agricultural SCE can transact with its members. However, describing the relationship between an (agricultural) cooperative and its members also requires distinguishing between those transactions that the cooperative concludes with non-members. Similarly, the legal systems considered here also deal with members who are not primarily interested in concluding business transactions, but rather in achieving economic added value. This type of members is comparable with shareholders of a capitalist-oriented company. Here, the different legal systems have developed concepts that differ more in their terminology, but less in their content.[240] After these more general considerations, we must examine how the different legal systems adequately define the composition of the membership base of an Italian or Austrian SCE in order to ensure that the interests of the members and the scope of the SCE's activities are consistent with each other. This requires us to look at membership requirements and admission procedures.

3.4.1 *The Principle of Double Quality of Cooperative's Members and Its Exemptions Under Reg. 1425/2003 and the Italian and Austrian Legal Systems*

As the SCE is member-focused, every provision in the SCE-R that governs conditions of membership, members' rights and duties and/or loss of membership must be considered relative to the specific nature of this corporate form. The relationship between an SCE and its members is therefore particularly governed by its main aim, as described by Art. 1 para. 3 SCE-R.[241] This relationship is primarily directed

[240]This chapter analyses the position of members within an SCE. It does not analyse specific rights and obligations, except where necessary to understand the issues. This focus is saved for the chapters on the general meeting and financing issues.

[241]Art. 1 para. 3 SCE-R states: "An SCE shall have as its principal object the satisfaction of its members' needs and/or the development of their economic and social activities, in particular through the conclusion of agreements with them to supply goods or services or to execute work of the kind that the SCE carries out or commissions. An SCE may also have as its object the satisfaction of its members' needs by promoting, in the manner set forth above, their participation in

towards fulfilling a supportive or serving purpose and not maximising profits.[242] Thus, SCEs *must* be member-oriented, not investor-oriented.[243]

This provision spells out the principle of double quality when it states that 'an SCE shall have as its principal object the satisfaction of its members' needs and/or the development of their economic and social activities, in particular through the conclusion of agreements with them to supply goods or services or to execute work of the kind that the SCE carries out or commissions'. Thus, an SCE achieves its main purpose by either meeting members' needs through providing goods or services and/or promoting the activity of its members. The term 'principal object' implies that an SCE may have other goals.[244] Accordingly, members can be supported in their economic activities and their social commitments.[245]

The determination to conduct member-oriented business does not explicitly obligate the SCE to conclude transactions with its members, either with in-kind contributions or through the use of its services. Such an obligation could, however, be derived from Art. 1 para. 3 SCE-R, which describes the object of the SCE.[246] Similarly, Recital 10 points out that the activities of the SCE 'should be conducted for the mutual benefit of its members' needs' with the result that 'each member benefits from the activities of the SCE in accordance with his/her participation'.[247]

The members of the SCE should be its 'customers, employees or suppliers or should be otherwise involved in the activities of the SCE'.[248] Due to this involvement, members of an SCE are 'user members'. This involvement is based on statutory provisions defining the circle of persons whose needs shall be satisfied; it will be discussed in more detail in the next chapter.[249] Yet, this concept of

economic activities, in one or more SCEs and/or national cooperatives. An SCE may conduct its activities through a subsidiary." For general information, see Sect. 3.2. On this issue, see also Pönkä (2018).

[242]Like public limited-liability companies.

[243]See Lehner (2007), p. 148; Lehner (2009), p. 99 et seq. Also consider Schöpflin (2018a), p. 1241 et seq.; Bianca and Zanardo (2016), p. 204 et seq.; Racugno (2006), pp. 317; Chirico and Troianiello (2007), p. 43; Alfandari and Piot (2004), p. 80. See also Pönkä (2018), p. 43 et seq.

[244]They do not have to refer to the members' needs, but may be described as secondary goals. See Schöpflin (2018a), p. 1241 et seq.

[245]Thus, ideal aims can be promoted. It is important to stress that an SCE may not focus solely on remuneration of the capital subscribed by its members via conducting business with third parties. See Schöpflin (2018a), p. 1241 et seq. Also consider Lutter et al. (2012), p. 1586; Albamonte (2008), p. 298 et seq.

[246]See Alfandari and Piot (2004), p. 80.

[247]See Recital 10 bullet 1 SCE-R.

[248]See Recital 10 bullet 2 SCE-R. Also consider Albamonte (2008), p. 304.

[249]This does not imply that ultimately a single user member wants his needs to be satisfied. See Schöpflin (2018e), p. 1270 et seq. As a result of admission to an SCE, and in accordance with the principle of double quality, customers become members. Their position when transacting with a cooperative is changed from a mere voluntary relation to something more, even though the specifics of this involvement under Recital 10 are vague. See Münkner (2014), p. 52. Also consider Fici (2012), p. 9; Alfandari and Piot (2004), p. 80. Generally, Birchall (2011), p. 3 et seq. In general, the obligation to participate is based on agreeing to the statutes. See Alfandari and Piot (2004), p. 80.

'involvement' is rather vague, and—in addition to the position of members as contracting partners—it can differ in practice according to their degree of participation in the activities or management of the SCE. For instance, in a consumer cooperative, members can generally influence both marketing campaigns and the selection of new products or suppliers.[250] Moreover, the SCE-R does not require SCEs to directly promote their members' needs; instead, promotion may be achieved by an SCE's participation in other national cooperatives or SCEs, provided that this participation serves the SCE's purpose of promotion. Art. 1 para. 3 sent. 3 SCE-R thus allows indirect promotion, which may be achieved via a holding cooperative.[251] This SCE-R's flexibility concerning the determination of the membership base is reflected in the provisions, which stipulate that legal bodies (including associations of persons) may also be user members of an SCE, even if their members and not the bodies themselves are promoted.[252] Similarly, as the recitals repeatedly state, employees may become members of an SCE.[253] In this case, the requirements of the principle of double quality is fulfilled as soon as an employee acquires a share in the SCE.[254] Given the different ways to participate, the level of participation is ultimately determined by the statutes or the contracts concluded.[255]

These initial analyses show that an agricultural SCE can be organised as (1) a workers' cooperative, based on the joint cultivation of member land and/or the joint breeding of member animals, (2) a consumer cooperative, in which its members use the services offered to them or purchase goods supplied by the cooperative and (3) a service cooperative. In the latter case, for example, the agricultural SCE processes the members' products.

The principle of double quality is therefore not only typical of cooperatives, but ultimately indispensable for their functioning. This is why both the SCE-R and Italian and Austrian law deal with this issue in their respective cooperative legal traditions.[256] They have developed different ways of describing the interaction between a cooperative and its members.[257] Compared to the approach outlined by the SCE-R, the Italian legal system uses a slightly different approach that does not explicitly refer to a purpose of promotion but uses the concept of mutual scope. As

[250] See Alfandari and Piot (2004), p. 80.

[251] See Schöpflin (2018a), p. 1241 et seq.

[252] In this sense, Art. 14 para. 1 subpara. 3 SCE-R states that members who are legal bodies shall be deemed users members by virtue of the fact that they represent their own members, provided the members are themselves users. These members have to be natural persons. In other words, this provision is not applicable if the members are legal persons. Thus members of the legal persons need not necessarily be members of the SCE. In fact, the provisions states "are users", and subpara. 3 should make membership superfluous. See Schöpflin (2018e), p. 1270 et seq.

[253] See Recitals 9 and 10 bullet 2 SCE-R.

[254] See Alfandari and Piot (2004), p. 82. Generally, Schöpflin (2018a), p. 1242 et seq; Schöpflin (2018c), p. 1250 et seq.

[255] Between the SCE and its members. See Alfandari and Piot (2004), p. 80.

[256] See Sect. 2.1.

[257] See Sect. 3.2.

has been seen, this concept may have an external and even systemic character. To the contrary, the formula used in the *GenG* is similar to that used by the SCE-R. Here, the principal object of a cooperative is promoting its members' business and personal activities. This can also be achieved through participation in legal entities, although only in a subordinated manner. Since 2008, Austrian law explicitly allows social aims.[258]

The principle of equal treatment is a corollary to the principle of double quality: cooperatives in both jurisdictions must observe this principle when conducting business with their members. The SCE-R, however, is rather vague: Recital 10 refers to the prohibition of artificial restrictions on membership. This requirement can be seen as part of equal treatment, but only reflects one aspect.[259] However, this issue impacts those persons who can apply for membership (for example, only farmers from one territory to the detriment of farmers from another territory or all farmers). It will become apparent that such issues can be resolved by applying national law in accordance with Article 8 para. 1 letter c SCE-R (on the grounds that there is a gap to be filled by national law). Regarding the principle of equal treatment, the Italian legal system contains a specific provision in its Civil Code. Austrian doctrine and jurisprudence also recognise this principle, even if the law—like the SCE-R—does not explicitly mention it.

The principle of double quality—which is closely linked to the purpose of a cooperative—is therefore an essential component of the concept of cooperative. But there is no rule without an exception, and there are two: (1) transactions conducted with non-members (third parties) and (2) transactions conducted with non-user members.[260]

Bearing in mind the function of the principle of double quality, one might conclude that cooperatives must conduct their business exclusively with their members. However, this is often not efficient for economic reasons.[261] In some cases, certain processing capacities cannot be fully utilised because of poor harvests. One possible solution is to make an agricultural SCE more flexible if part of the members' harvest has been destroyed by hail, even though their cooperative has already concluded concrete supply contracts. As a result, various ways to conduct business with non-members have been developed. Art. 1 para. 4 SCE-R clearly states that, as a general rule, non-members generally cannot benefit from the activities of an SCE nor participate in its business,[262] but explicitly allows statutes to provide

[258]The basic rule in this context is contained in Sec. 1 GenG, referring to the promotion purpose of a cooperative, which must be specified by the statutes.

[259]See Art. 2516 CC. Also consider Hirte (2007), p. 2216.

[260]Other questions regarding specific rights and duties will be dealt with in the chapters on financing. See Sect. 5.3.

[261]See Laurinkari (1990), p. 403. Also consider Chirico and Troianiello (2007), p. 43.

[262]It states: "An SCE may not extend the benefits of its activities to non-members or allow them to participate in its business, except where its statutes provide otherwise."

otherwise.[263] In this latter case, the SCE-R does not require prioritising transactions with members over transactions with non-members.[264] The SCE-R, in fact, does not contain any explicit indication in this respect.

The second exemption to the principle of double quality relates to non-user members. This special class of members are not primarily interested in the principal object of the cooperative but instead consider it worthwhile to invest in the SCE. Thus, non-user members attempt to gain a monetary advantage because of the capital they subscribe, not by concluding business transactions. The SCE-R expressly links this possibility to the national legal order. In fact, according to the SCR R, the statutes can provide for the admission of investing or non-user members, as long as the applicable national law provides for such a possibility.[265] Note that non-user members often provide risk capital that user members of agricultural cooperatives are unwilling to invest for reasons closely related to the cooperative model, as the economic analysis shows.[266]

The formula used by the SCE-R requires some comments. According to Art. 14 para. 1 subpara. 2 SCE-R, the statutes may contain a provision according to which 'persons who do not expect to use or produce the SCE's goods and services may be admitted as investor (non-user) members'. This assumes that the laws of the member state in which the SCE has its registered office permits the admission of non-user members. It has been observed that the wording, 'who do not expect to', is rather restrictive and thus limits the circle of investing members,[267] and it seems that persons who are user members cannot be admitted as non-user members.[268] They could, however, conduct certain transactions as non-members (for example, purchase securities issued according to Art. 64 SCE-R[269]). There is general concern that provisions allowing investing members might weaken the cooperative's goal to promote the needs of (user) members. Recital 8 of the SCE-R preamble addresses such concerns with the principle of the primacy of the individual (and their needs). Similarly, Recital 9 explains that the admission of investing or non-user members

[263]The relevant feature here is that the customer is not obliged to subscribe capital. The same is true for cooperatives which offer their services to disabled people (e.g., cooperative sociali in Italy or société coopérative d'intérêt collectif in France). See Alfandari and Piot (2004), p. 81. Also consider Schöpflin (2018a), p. 1241 et seq. In general, Laurinkari (1990).

[264]See Greda (2014), p. 835 et seq. Also consider Chirico and Troianiello (2007), p. 43. Critical, Beuthien (2007), p. 7.

[265]See Art. 14 para. 1 subpara. 2 SCE-R.

[266]For details see Sects. 3.5.2 and 5.6.

[267]See Alfandari and Piot (2004), p. 81.

[268]And vice versa. See Schöpflin (2018e), p. 1270 et seq.

[269]The SCE-R refers to both members, and third parties in the context of investors. In fact, Art. 64 para. 1 sent. 1 SCE-R allows the formulation of a statutory provision, according to which an SCE may issue "securities other than shares, or debentures the holders of which are to have no voting rights." They may be subscribed by both members and non-members, although they do not confer member status. See Alfandari and Piot (2004), p. 81 et seq.; Albamonte (2008), p. 309; Bianca and Zanardo (2016), p. 206.

must be limited.[270] These issues can be solved with a precise definition of admissions policy as well as by various national legal rules.

How do the Italian and Austrian legal systems deal with the principle of double quality? These findings are important for two reasons. First, the SCE-R refers partly to national law. Second, the implementation of this principle depends upon the scope of an SCE's activities, including the question of whether these activities can be conducted with non-members. Therefore, in order to understand how an Italian or Austrian SCE functions, it is necessary to first analyse the national provisions that deal with the involvement of members and regulate non-member business.[271] There are some specific features related to agricultural cooperatives.

The *Italian legal system* not only applies (in part) different notions but also contains many more (default) provisions. According to the Italian legal term of mutuality, the status of a member primarily provides someone with the opportunity to transact with the cooperative. These opportunities or cooperative advantages may have different content, depending on the object of the cooperative. This mutual advantage consists of providing specific benefits to the advantage of the member. According to Italian cooperative theory, the economic activity exercised by the cooperative is not limited to serving the interests of its members; it may also satisfy the interest of the community (external mutuality and/or systemic mutuality).[272]

Moreover, the Italian legal system contains a specific provision on equal treatment, which supplements the implementation of the principle of double quality. The provisions of this principle apply to an Italian (agricultural) SCE.[273] Accordingly, this principle must be observed not only in the constitution of mutual relations, but also in their exercise.[274] This principle refers to equal treatment in a formal sense (i.e. the rights and obligations relating to the relationship of mutuality), as well as broad equal treatment (i.e., concerning the effective use of the advantages offered by the cooperative/SCE).[275] Moreover, as it refers to the mutual relationship between a member and the cooperative (SCE), it thus refers to the services provided by the cooperative which members may use, which are those services that help realise the mutual purpose of the cooperative.[276]

Similar to the solution offered by the SCE-R, this does not imply that a member has a right to obtain any advantage offered by a cooperative. This would counteract the characteristic of a cooperative as an enterprise. Thus, a member has no subjective

---

[270]See Greda (2014), p. 834.

[271]See Iengo (2006), p. 9 et seq.

[272]See Paolucci (2012a), p. 99 et seq.; Paolucci (2019a), p. 29 et seq.; Tatarano (2011), p. 69; Paolucci (2012b), p. 4 fn 7. Also consider de Giorgi and Vaciago (2011), p. 192 et seq.

[273]Due to Art. 8 para. 1 letter c SCE-R.

[274]I.e., when the agricultural SCE transacts with its members.

[275]See Giorgi (2018a), p. 3207 et seq.; Cuomo (2014), p. 109 et seq. Generally, Cuomo (2013). Also see Paolucci (2019b), p. 51 et seq.; Santagata (2017), p. 811.

[276]See Art. 2527 CC. Also consider Paolucci (2019b), p. 51 et seq.; Tonelli (2003), p. 49 et seq.; Giorgi (2018a), p. 3207 et seq. Also Cuomo (2014), p. 100; Santagata (2017), p. 811.

right to use the service offered by the cooperative (SCE) but, if ever, a type of expectation.[277] This implies that the statutes contain rules about carrying out mutualistic activity, whereas activity with third parties is a mere faculty, and hence must be explicitly provided for by statutes.[278] This provision not only refers to abusive behaviour by social entities, but also to abusive behaviour conducted by members infringing the obligations of solidarity connected to transactions conducted with a cooperative (SCE).[279]

The Italian legal system operates similar to the SCE-R when it addresses the exemptions to the principle of quality, determining that cooperatives may include non-members, as long as the statutes provide for this.[280] There is an important distinction between 'mainly mutual cooperatives' and 'other cooperatives'.[281] The activities of 'mainly mutual cooperatives' with non-members are subject to limitations, implying that these types of cooperatives must operate predominantly with members.[282] In order to implement this requirement, the Italian legislature has adopted a number of provisions that lay down clear criteria for an agricultural cooperative.[283] Their application—meaning compliance with the criteria—gives an agricultural SCE preferential tax treatment.

The Italian law contains provisions that determine whether the concept of predominant activity with members has been fulfilled. There are different requirements for different types of cooperative:

1. Consumer cooperatives must have sales proceeds from members' consumption that exceed 50% of total sales.
2. Worker cooperatives must pay more than 50% of total labour costs for members' jobs.
3. Production cooperatives should incur manufacturing costs for goods and services provided by members that are greater than 50% of total manufacturing costs.

In addition, para. 3 of Art. 2513 CC determines, in respect to agricultural cooperatives' transforming and selling products of their farmer-members, that the

[277]A right to obtain services could jeopardise the economic success or even survival of the cooperative. The same is true for patronage refunds, where members also do not have rights. See Paolucci (2019b), pp. 51 et seq. and 54; Giorgi (2018a), p. 3207 et seq. Also consider Cuomo (2014), pp. 100 et seq., 114, 121; Santagata (2017), p. 809 et seq.

[278]See Paolucci (2019b), p. 52. Also consider Art. 2521 para. 2 CC.

[279]See Giorgi (2018a), p. 3207 et seq.; Schirò (2008a), p. 43; Santagata (2017), p. 811.

[280]See Art. 2521 para. 2 CC.

[281]The 2003 company law reform introduced a distinction between mainly mutual cooperatives and other cooperatives. For general observations consider Paolucci (2019l), p. 52 et seq.; Bonfante (2014), p. 132 et seq.; Marano (2014), p. 72 et seq.; Marasà (2004), p. 50 et seq.; Bassi and Passalacqua (2014), p. 13 et seq. Also consider Marasà (2013), p. 847. See also Paolucci (2019a), p. 29 et seq.; Santagata (2017), p. 813 et seq.

[282]See Art. 2512 CC. According to Art. 2513 CC, the status of this condition must be reported in the balance sheet.

[283]See Arts. 2513 and Art. 2514 CC. For details, see Sects. 5.3 and 5.4.

quantity or value of the products delivered by members must exceed 50% of the total quantity or value of the products.[284] With regard to this latter specification, Article 111 Septies prov. impl. CC explains that cooperatives that carry on an activity within the meaning of Article 2135 CC are predominantly mutual when they fulfil the conditions laid down in Article 2513 para. 3 CC. This general reference to Art. 2135 CC means that related activities also fall within the scope of Art. 2513 CC.

In other words, it is discussed whether agricultural cooperatives must apply the criteria only as determined by para. 3, or alternatively, also may apply criteria contained in para. 2. This second approach is preferable because, as has been correctly stated,[285] it better corresponds to a reality in which the price of raw materials can suddenly change. Such a shift is typical for agricultural production and entails the risk that the general requirements for production cooperatives will not be met. Thus, this second interpretation helps to widen the scope of service cooperatives so that the characteristic of predominant mutuality can be determined by cost as well as yield.[286]

The regime applicable to mainly mutual cooperatives implies that particular asset restrictions must be considered.[287] This means that this type of cooperatives can only remunerate both subscribed capital and the financial instruments of user members to a limited extent, may not distribute their reserves to user members and must allocate the residual assets of the cooperative to mutual funds in the event the cooperative is dissolved. These restrictions apply to a limited extent to other types of cooperatives.[288] Specifically, other cooperatives are not subject to this limitation when it comes to activities it conducts with non-members, implying that they may transact predominantly with non-members. Compared to mainly mutual cooperatives, 'other cooperatives' are, however, only eligible for limited tax benefits.[289]

---

[284]See Art. 2513 para. 3 CC.

[285]See Rocchi (2007), p. 45 et seq., Similar, Marano (2014), p. 75 et seq.; Carmignani (2011), p. 259 et seq. Partially different, Di Ronza (2010), p. 34.

[286]See Rocchi (2007), p. 45 et seq. Similar, Marano (2014), p. 75 et. seq. This provision must be viewed as an exception to the former three, which delineate the general framework on how to calculate mutuality, whereas here, the legislature has determined ad hoc criteria for a specific type of agricultural cooperative.

[287]See Art. 2514 para. 1 CC. See Sects. 5.3, 5.5 and 5.6.

[288]See Sects. 5.3, 5.4 and 5.5.

[289]See Ingrosso (2013), Sect. 3.

Art. 2520 para. 2 CC refers to special laws for cooperatives, stating that special laws can allow founding cooperatives that aim to promote the needs of special categories of persons, even though they are not members. In this context, law no. 381/1991, which governs social cooperatives, is important. It is important to stress that the Italian legislator primarily fostered what Italian cooperative theory defines as "internal mutuality", whereby cooperatives must favour the promotion of their members' needs. See Bonfante (2014), p. 149. See also Santagata (2017), p. 813 et seq. For the differentiation between internal, external and systemic mutuality, see Sect. 3.2, Sects. 5.3 and 5.5 fn 306. Regarding the agricultural sector, here one can refer to social farming. As mentioned, this study does not further deal with this specific issue.

How can the concept of a mainly mutual cooperative be implemented by an Italian agricultural SCE? When we compare the provisions of the SCE-R[290] with the outlined Italian solution, communication 9203 correctly states that an SCE may be incorporated under Italian law as a mainly mutual cooperative or a so-called 'other cooperative'.[291] According to Art. 1 para. 4 SCE-R, the statute's drafters may determine whether the SCE can conduct business with non-members, creating an SCE of the 'other' type. As mentioned above, the SCE-R does not explicitly require a precedence for transactions with member. In addition, the statutes may make the cooperative mainly mutual, giving the SCE various tax benefits.[292] Given the importance of mainly mutual cooperatives in the agricultural sector, this option is very important if one wishes to set up an agricultural SCE under Italian law.

In addition to establishing provisions that determine the relationship between member and non-member businesses, the Italian legal system provides for some concepts concerning non-user businesses who interact with an Italian agricultural SCE. As a general rule, Italian law permits the admission of non-user members, thus fulfilling the requirement as determined by Art. 14 para. 1 subpara. 2 SCE-R. There are, however, some relevant differences between the rules applicable to an Italian SCE and those applicable to an Italian cooperative.

Italy adopted specific provisions in 1992. The adoption of law no 59/1992 introduced a new type of member, the investor member (*soccio sovventore*), focusing on remuneration of capital subscribed rather than mutual advantage.[293] Note that the Italian legislature did not introduce the investor member as a specific figure, but instead introduced equity for investor members. As a result, it is possible that a single person may be both a traditional member and an investor member, albeit with conflicting interests.[294] This concept was absorbed by the reforms of 2003,[295] and currently the main pillar of the new financing system established for cooperatives is based on Art. 2526 CC. This provision states that as long as a specific statutory provision provides accordingly, a cooperative may issue both participation- and debt-based financial instruments. In these cases, the specific rules determined for an *spa* must be applied.[296]

It has been observed that, to favour the capitalisation of cooperatives, the position of investor members[297] (and their rights to cooperative financial instruments) seems

---

[290] Art. 1 para. 4 SCE-R.

[291] See Ministry for economic development (2006), Art. 1; Fici and Strano (2010), p. 674. Also see Sect. 2.5.

[292] By applying the clauses contained in Art. 2514 CC. See Ministry for economic development (2006), Art. 1; Chirico and Troianiello (2007), p. 35.

[293] See Bonfante (2014), p. 186 et seq. Also consider Tatarano (2011), p. 86; Galgano (1993), p. 38 et seq.; Marasà (1992), p. 369. In general, Ragazzini (1992).

[294] See Rocchi (2006), p. 97 et seq.; Mazzoli and Rocchi (1996), p. 117 et seq.

[295] See Bonfante (2014), p. 186 et seq.

[296] See Bonfante (2014), p. 291 et seq.

[297] Or non-members, as Art. 2526 CC applies regardless of whether a person is a member or not.

stronger than that of user members.[298] Art. 2526 CC addresses the fear that investor members might become too influential by requiring that investor members be smaller in number than user members. This restricts their power to influence the management of the cooperative, and stresses the mutualistic aims. Offering a wide range of statutory autonomy should help provide a structure that best fits cooperatives' individual needs.[299] This provision establishes the principle that investor members rank second to user members, as non-user members are never mandatory. A specific legal framework has thus been determined for these non-user members, as distinguished from provisions that apply to user members.[300]

These observations hold true for non-user members of an SCE, as these groups of members are optional.[301] The SCE-R contains specific provisions safeguarding the interests of user members,[302] prioritising their interests over those of non-user members. Even though the Italian legal system allows user members to subscribe shares issued to investor members—and thus expand their specific range of duties and rights—this possibility does not apply to Italian SCEs, for the reasons given above. Thus, the SCE-R is less flexible in this regard. For example, a statute provision could generally stipulate that non-user members may be admitted to agricultural cooperatives (with reference to law no. 59, 31 January 1992). The statutes may also specify that they may not hold more than a certain (e.g. 10%) share of the capital with voting rights. Furthermore, and this applies in the specific case where the agricultural SCE is also a PO in the fruit and vegetables sector, the statutes may provide that voting rights in decisions concerning the operational fund are excluded in all cases. Statutes may also provide that non-user members may not benefit from measures financed by the European Union. Lastly, it should also be possible to include a non-competition clause that is similar to that for members (see next chapter).

Having analysed how the Italian legal system deals with the principle of double quality, I now turn to the *Austrian legal system* and the specific provisions contained in the *GenG*. The *GenG*'s formulation regarding involvement of members is similar

---

[298]The only real limit defined for financial instruments is contained in para. 2 of Art. 2526 CC, according to which the privileges of allocation of profits or reimbursement of capital, do not include the indivisible reserves determined by Art. 2545 ter CC. Consider in this context, Sect. 5.5.

The specific characteristics of financial instruments issued by a cooperative, will depend on the statutes. Hence, a cooperative may issue a variety of financial instruments such as equity financial instruments (admitting investor members), bonds or hybrids (participative bonds). See Lamandini (2007), p. 214 et seq.; Cusa (2006), p. 25 et seq.; Rescigno (2007), p. 932.

[299]See Lolli (2012), p. 151; Paolucci (2019f), p. 85 et seq. The law gives a wide range of freedom to draft the statutes in this context. Accordingly, statutes may define the financial and administrative rights of the holder of financial instruments. See Lamandini (2007), p. 214.

[300]E.g., voting rights. Non-user members are ultimately an optional minority group with regards to user members. They are considered instrumental in relation to traditional user members. See Bonfante (2014), p. 186 et seq. Also consider Marasà (2012), p. 202.

[301]See Art. 1 para. 4 SCE-R.

[302]See Art. 39 para. 3 SCE-R, Art. 59 para. 3 SCE-R or Art. 61 para. 3 subpara. 2 SCE-R. Also consider Lutter et al. (2012), p. 1601 et seq.; Münkner (2006), p. 22.

to that in the SCE-R, stating, in general terms, that the principal object of a cooperative is promoting its members' business and personal activities.[303] In addition, the law allows the pursuit of social aims.[304] Opposed to the Italian legislature, Austria did not adopt further legislation to promote social farming.

Of particular importance for the discussion as conducted here is Sec. 11 *GenG*. Accordingly, the legal relationship between members and a cooperative is primarily governed by the statutes. These may only differ from the provisions contained in the *GenG* if expressly authorised by the *GenG*. Thus, if no specific legal provisions have been determined by the legislature, these issues may be regulated by statutory provisions, but only on the condition that commonly acknowledged principles, like the principle of equal treatment, are observed.[305] When implementing this principle, an Austrian SCE must consider national law, as the SCE-R only contains little references to this principle in its recitals.

Under the Austrian legal system, this principle is not a written legal norm, but doctrine and case law have both acknowledged it.[306] It must be observed when regulating the relation between a cooperative (agricultural SCE) and its members. The principle states that, *ceteris paribus,* all members must be treated equally. In other words, all members must be assigned the same rights and duties if conditions are equal. However, unequal or differentiated treatment is permissible when based on factual or objective reasons.[307] When different situations arise, differentiation is permitted.[308] For example, it could be generally stated that all members are entitled to use all cooperative facilities in accordance with the provisions and to make use of the services offered by the agricultural cooperative.

Moreover, the principle of equal treatment is binding for all organs in a cooperative (here, an agricultural SCE). As a result, a member cannot be denied the right to use the cooperative without an objective reason.[309]

In this context, fiduciary duties are discussed. Assuming that members are normally also customers, I assert that this arrangement is based on relationships

[303]As seen, this can also be achieved through subscription of shares in legal entities, although only in a subordinated manner.

[304]The basic rule in this context is contained in Sec. 1 GenG, referring to the promotion purpose of a cooperative, which must be specified by the statutes.

[305]See Astl and Steinböck (2014a), p. 180; also consider Zahn (1963), p. 37; Holthaus and Lehnhoff (2016), p. 223 et seq.

[306]See Kastner et al. (1990), p. 17 et seq.; Keinert (1988), p. 111; OGH 07.04.1987, 5 Ob 29/86 SZ60/62.

[307]For instance, consider the discussion on investor members. See Astl and Steinböck (2014a), p. 180 et seq.; Keinert (1988), p. 150.

[308]In this context one may refer to it as relative equal treatment. See Astl and Steinböck (2014a), p. 181; Keinert (1988), p. 111. In addition, absolute equal treatment exists for certain matters. Consider, e.g., the right of resignation. See Astl and Steinböck (2014a), p. 181. If the equal treatment is not absolute, unjustified discrimination is permitted provided the affected person consents. See Astl and Steinböck (2014a), p. 181.

[309]See Astl and Steinböck (2014a), p. 181 et seq.; OGH 07.04.1987, 5 Ob 29/86 SZ60/62.

built on trust, leading to so-called fiduciary duties. These duties can be considered from two different points of view: (1) the duty of the cooperative (SCE) with respect to its members and (2) the duty of the members in respect to the cooperative and, thus, other members. From the latter perspective, members must act in the interests of the cooperative. This can require that they accept certain measures connected to this interest, provided these measures are in line with a member's individual circumstances and specific interests. In other words, it must be objectively acceptable for the member to support a specific measure. In principle, this duty requires a member to conduct those transactions which are in line with the object of the cooperative (SCE). However, it is also argued that these transactions must not be concluded with the cooperative (SCE) if they can be conducted under better economic conditions with other enterprises or companies. There is ultimately no obligation for a member to transact with his own cooperative.[310]

In line with the SCE-R, the Austrian legal order deals with exceptions to the principle of double quality, which must be understood in the context of an Austrian SCE, particularly because tax law[311] uses specific terms (also used in the *GenG*) that apply to an Austrian agricultural SCE.

Concerning non-member businesses, the solution applicable to an Austrian cooperative is slightly different than the one applicable to an Austrian SCE. Of particular importance is the set of notions developed by Austrian doctrine and law. Similar to Art. 1 para. 4 SCE-R, Sec. 5a para. 1 *GenG* contains a specific opening clause. Accordingly, the statutes of an Austrian cooperative must contain a specific clause that allows for expanding the business goals.[312]

In an ideal case, the members of the cooperative would be identical with the business partners, that is, only farmer-members would deliver their products to their agricultural cooperative.[313] Depending on the aim of the cooperative, its members are thus either producers, workers or consumers. Doctrine and law (Sec. 5a *GenG*) refer to these transactions as *Zweckgeschäfte*, literally 'purpose transactions'. These *Zweckgeschäfte* must be distinguished from other transactions a cooperative may conduct.[314] Yet, while the *GenG* explicitly refers to the *Zweckgeschäfte*, it does not specify the other types of transactions which must be understood in this context[315]—

[310]The cooperative (SCE) must also observe those fiduciary duties whose best manifestation is the principle of equal treatment. See Astl and Steinböck (2014a), p. 184; Holthaus and Lehnhoff (2016), p. 236.

[311]See Bundesministerium für Finanzen (2013).

[312]Genossenschaftsvertrag.

[313]The so-called "principle of identity".

[314]See Dellinger (2014), p. 23; Bundesministerium für Finanzen (2013), nt15–nt 18, findok.bmf.gv.at/findok?execution=e1s1 (13.02.2017).

[315]Also consider Bundesministerium für Finanzen (2013), nt 15- nt 18 and Schöpflin (2018a), p. 1241 et seq.

that is, counter transactions,[316] supporting or auxiliary transactions[317] and sideline transactions.[318] These three categories are not bound to membership and hence can be conducted with anybody.[319] In an agricultural cooperative, one can think of the milk sold by the dairy cooperative as a counter transaction, the employment of staff or the purchase of office equipment as supporting or auxiliary transaction, and the letting of dwellings to non-operators as sideline transactions.

Sec. 5a para. 1 *GenG* requires statutes to refer to the restriction of Sec. 1 para. 1 *GenG*; hence, the promotion of members is paramount, while business conducted with non-members is subordinate.[320] Sec. 1 para. 1 *GenG* refers to the criterion of essentiality. To reiterate, this criterion is also important to determining what an agricultural SCE is, according to the *GewO*. This criterion implies that cooperatives have to promote their members' businesses and personal economic activities. This does not imply, however, that cooperatives cannot do business with non-members, but only that transactions shall be concluded mainly with members.[321]

It is not quite clear, however, whether non-member business may be conducted if the required restriction is not mentioned by the statutes. In such circumstances, it seems advisable to determine a statutory provision that allows non-member business, at least in cases of emergency.[322] Art. 1 para. 4 SCE-R, opposed to the Austrian solution, explicitly requires such a statutory provision.

Determining how non-member business has to be conducted must be outlined via a statute. For instance, statutes can limit non-member businesses to specific groups of persons or determine a specific body that must approve the transaction (in addition to the managing organ).[323] This does not require setting a ratio of member-businesses to non-member businesses, as long as the latter is subordinate to the

[316]Counter transactions are those necessary to conduct primary main transactions. For example, in a credit cooperative whose aim is to offer loans to its members a typical counter transaction would be the deposit business. Another example would be a consumer cooperative which purchases its goods from a producer. Dellinger (2014), p. 23 et seq.; also consider Bundesministerium für Finanzen (2013), nt 16.

[317]Auxiliary transactions are necessary to transact both the primary and counter transactions, e.g., hiring employees or renting a shop. See Dellinger (2014), p. 24; also consider Bundesministerium für Finanzen (2013), nt 17.

[318]Sideline transactions are all other types of transactions, e.g., those conducted to achieve social or idealistic goals but which are not covered by the promotion purpose of the cooperative. In this context, one can refer to privilege of sideline aims (Nebenzweckprivileg). See Dellinger (2014), p. 24; also consider Bundesministerium für Finanzen (2013), nt 18.

[319]See Dellinger (2014), p. 23.

[320]See Astl and Steinböck (2014e), p. 160.

[321]See Dellinger (2014), p. 23; Nowotny (2008), nt 5/13; Frotz (1977), p. 59.

[322]See Astl and Steinböck (2014e), p. 160; also consider Pramer and Pfaffenzeller (1976), p. 6; Kastner (1986), p. 137. If non-member business is conducted without a specific statutory provision, the transaction is still effective, but the management organ could be liable for any damage sustained. See Astl and Steinböck (2014e), p. 160. Also consider Sec. 23 GenG.

[323]See Astl and Steinböck (2014e), p. 160.

former.[324] For instance, the criterion is fulfilled if the earnings from non-member business at least indirectly benefit the members, as when a consumer cooperative increases its transaction volume to gain better purchasing prices. Likewise, an agricultural cooperative is allowed to purchase agricultural products from non--members—in certain cases, such as crop—to ensure its own capacity utilisation and the continuity of the business operations.[325] Ultimately, cooperatives are enterprises that must compete on the market and generate profits to remain competitive in the long run. Thus, a balance must be struck between profit-seeking and the promotion of members. The law does not contain a strict prohibition against maximising profits; however, *Zweckgeschäfte* should be regulated so that the cooperative places more emphasis on benefiting members rather than maximising profits.[326]

In summary, compared to this concept of promotion based on the criterion of essentiality, the SCE-R seems to be more open towards non-member activity. Art. 1 para. 4 SCE-R does not contain a restriction similar to that in Sec. 5a para. 1 *GenG* (referring to Sec. 1 para. 1 *GenG*).[327] Yet, since the 2013 directives for the corporation income tax also refer to the concepts and notions that concern activities that go beyond *Zweckgeschäfte*,[328] these concepts must still be considered—and understood—even though an Austrian agricultural SCE need not apply Sec. 5a para. 1 *GenG*.

A next observation concerns non-user members. Due to Art. 14 para. 1 subpara. 2 SCE-R, the Austrian legislature not only introduced the distinction between user and non-user members by applying a specific law for an Austrian SCE,[329] but went even further and introduced this distinction for national cooperatives by amending the *GenG*.[330] All three provisions contained therein are formulated identically.

The relevant provision of the *GenG* is contained in Sec. 5a para. 2 no 1, which replicates this phrase from the SCE-R: 'persons who do not expect to use or produce'. It has been observed that this reference to non-user members does not

---

[324]See Dellinger (2014), p. 33. There are no limits on transactions conducted to fulfil the purpose of the cooperative, including counter transactions and auxiliary transactions. See Astl and Steinböck (2014e), p. 160; also consider Keinert (1988), p. 88 et seq.; Pramer and Pfaffenzeller (1976), p. 6 et seq.

[325]See Dellinger (2014), p. 33.

[326]Also Nowotny (2008), nt 5/9; Dellinger (2014), p. 28. A further distinguishing feature of the Zweckgeschäfte results from how benefits are distributed among members. Unlike companies, which distribute their benefits after the fact in the form of dividends, cooperatives distribute their benefits directly by conducting business with their members. As a result, the conditions of the purpose transactions must be calculated based on the benefit to the members, not the cooperative. Thus, the promotion purpose aims to ensure that members who conclude transactions with the cooperative gain an economic advantage. See Dellinger (2014), p. 24.

[327]See Greda (2014), p. 835 et seq.

[328]Bundesministerium für Finanzen (2013).

[329]Sec. 3 SCEG.

[330]See Greda (2014), p. 835.

automatically preclude the possibility that user members may also subscribe shares offered to non-user members.[331] As the *GenG* only regulates the concept of non-user members in a rudimentary way, a statutory provision dealing with this issue is necessary. Thus, provided that the statutes do not prohibit this possibility, a member of an Austrian cooperative may have various rights and duties, depending on the different shares subscribed. Consequently, it must be clear which of the shares a member holds relate to user business and which ones concern investor business.[332]

For several reasons, this interpretation must be viewed with caution, at least in relation to Austrian SCEs. First, it has been observed with respect to Sec. 8 para. 2 German *GenG*—which uses the same wording as Sec. 5a para. 2 sent. 1 *GenG*—that this provision does not focus on potential members and their desires to be promoted by the cooperative, but on whether these persons can be admitted as user members if a cooperative cannot satisfy or support their needs.[333] Moreover, the SCE-R, unlike the *GenG*, contains robust regulations for non-user members. In addition to Art. 14 para. 1 subpara. 2 sent. 1 SCE-R,[334] the SCE-R contains specific provisions dealing with the competent body empowered to approve applications for non-user membership,[335] voting rights[336] and decision taking during the general meeting,[337] along with the possibility that non-user members may appoint members to the supervisory organ.[338] These are important arguments suggesting that farmers, as members, can only additionally finance 'their' SCE by subscribing securities and debentures, as determined by Art. 64 SCE-R.

In summary, it can be stated that both Austrian and Italian law deal with the principle of double quality and allow exceptions to this principle. Although they have developed different descriptions of the interaction between a cooperative and its members, the basic concepts[339] are similar.[340] The starting point is Art. 1 para. 3 SCE-R, which specifies that the principal object of an SCE is to satisfy its members needs and/or further their economic and social activities. This must then be further

[331]See Astl and Steinböck (2014e), p. 162.

[332]See Astl and Steinböck (2014e), p. 162.

[333]See Kober (2008), p. 47 et seq.

[334]This only requires national law to permit the admission of non-user members without making further national rules applicable. In addition, other articles of the SCE-R dealing with the admission of members in general are applicable to non-user members. See Art. 4 para. 7 sent. 1 SCE-R, Art. 14 SCE-R para. 1 subpara. 4 or para. 2 SCE-R.

[335]Art. 14 para. 1 subpara. 2 sent. 2 SCE-R.

[336]Art. 59 para. 3 SCE-R, which defers almost everything about voting rights granted to non-user members to national law.

[337]Art. 61 para. 3 SCE-R.

[338]Art. 39 para. 3 SCE-R.

[339]Promotion purpose and internal mutual purpose.

[340]Especially since the enactment of the URÄG 2008. See Sect. 3.2.

The mutual purpose does not substantially differ from the purpose which the SCE-R assigns to an SCE according to Art. 1 para. 3 SCE-R. See Fici and Strano (2010), p. 682.

specified by the statutes (statement of the objects[341]) of the agricultural SCE and may include, for example, the acceptance, processing and utilisation of agricultural products (e.g., milk and other dairy products, eggs and poultry) as well as trade in such products, the production of food and beverages as well as the trade in these and other products, and/or the procurement of operating materials, machines, motor vehicles and consumer goods at reduced prices. But also, more general activities are possible, such as the representation and promotion of common interests in the dairy sector (or wine sector, etc.), as well as cooperation with other agricultural organisations for the purpose of advice, storage, processing and marketing of agricultural products.

When it comes to member involvement, in general, no member has the right to obtain the services provided by an SCE.[342] This aspect is determined in both legal systems by the principle of equal treatment, which also covers fiduciary duties. As the SCE-R does not contain a specific provision in this regard, national rules must be applied,[343] which requires understanding of what provisions help to make an agricultural SCE work. The observation of this principle is also requested by the PECOL,[344] which specify that the principle of equal treatment must be observed in the conclusion and execution of cooperative transactions. I emphasise that this principle is necessary for the proper functioning of a mutual cooperative.[345] Note that, in accordance with Art. 15 para. 1 bullet 2 SCE-R, a member may be expelled if he or she acts contrary to the interests of his SCE. Thus, the principle of double quality is given concrete form by a legal framework based on pressure (from the SCE) and necessities (by the member) instead of obligation. For example, the statutes of an agricultural SCE could specify that a member may be excluded (by the competent body) if he or she has seriously breached obligations derived from the law, the statutes (including, where appropriate, rules of procedure), business relations or the decisions of the bodies of agricultural cooperatives (or, where appropriate, the PO).

As the SCE-R does not contain further provisions explaining how member involvement should be adopted in practice, it is necessary to understand how national provisions deal with the involvement of members and regulate non-member business.[346] The two legal systems use different concepts to describe the same thing: While Austrian law uses the concept of purpose of promotions, which is then put into practice via a set of specific transaction categories, the Italian

---

[341]Art. 5 para. 4 SCE-R.

[342]In this context, Recital 10 points out that the members should naturally be involved in the activities of the SCE, for instance as customers, employees or suppliers. In addition, the opening clause of Art. 1 para. 4 SCE-R states that third parties who are not members of the SCE, may not take advantage of its activities unless the statutes provide otherwise.

[343]These prevent unequal treatment, unless based on objective reasons. Thus, ultimately differentiations can be made.

[344]Sec. 1.4 para. 2 PECOL.

[345]See Fici (2017), p. 41.

[346]See Iengo (2006), p. 9 et seq.

legal system uses a very open concept of mutuality, which—without considering social cooperatives—helps distinguish between transactions with members and non-members. In general, the Italian legal system seems more regulated, whereas the Austrian legal system relies strongly on statutory freedom. Ultimately, apart from the conceptual differences and specific tax issues, the results are basically the same.

In practice, member involvement is made concrete, for example, by the statements of the chief purpose of the agricultural SCE; accordingly, the statutes can stipulate that the SCE's object is, among other things, the takeover of, for example, grapes, wine and grape products produced by the members (on their own land).

It is important to be aware of a set of notions when dealing with non-member businesses. The Austrian concept refers to different categories of transactions. *Zweckgeschäfte* (purpose transactions) must be concluded with members, meaning that non-member business must fulfil an auxiliary function.[347] The law determines that the *Zweckgeschäfte* have to be concluded essentially with members. In other words, cooperatives must conduct transactions mainly but not exclusively with members.[348] Austrian tax law also uses these categories, which therefore have legal implications for an Austrian agricultural SCE.

Italian law differs in this respect. It acknowledges two types of cooperatives: mainly mutual cooperatives and other cooperatives. The former are more regulated when it comes to non-member business, and the law explicitly determines the relationship between non-member and member businesses. This approach is (also) based on tax benefits,[349] which SCEs are not granted under Austrian law. Thus, if an Italian agricultural SCE wants to benefit from these tax breaks, the specific provisions designed for mainly mutual cooperatives must be observed.[350]

The solutions proposed by the PECOL[351] are similar to those from the Italian approach, which uses general notions or concepts to differentiate between types of cooperatives (instead of focusing on cooperatives' basic activities). Accordingly, Sec 1.4 para. 1 PECOL determines that so-called mutual cooperatives shall pursue their objective mainly through transactions with user members. The concept of being 'mainly' mutual limits both activity with non-members and extra-cooperative

[347]Doctrine and the law have developed the category of Zweckgeschäft. Members must be promoted via these types of transaction. Other categories of transaction have also been developed by doctrine, including counter transactions, supporting transactions and sideline transaction. These are not bound to membership and, thus, can be conducted with anybody. Counter transactions and supporting transactions are conducted to fulfil the purpose of the cooperative. Hence they can be conducted without limits.

[348]This does not require to set a ratio between member business and non-member business, as long as the non-member business is in the minority.

[349]To enjoy tax benefits and thus become a mainly mutual cooperative, cooperatives must opt in via statutory provision, as determined by Art. 2514 CC.

[350]Crucially, the SCE-R does not contain any information on the relation between members and non-members. Thus it seems to propose a rather flexible approach, which would allow the adoption of either model outlined in the Italian legal system. Yet, the SCE-R does not require the criterion of essentiality, meaning it differs from the model of an Austrian cooperative.

[351]See Sec. 1.4 para. 1 PECOL.

activities, i.e., activities that differ from those conducted with members.[352] Moreover, the PECOL set criteria to help put the idea of transactions with non-members into practice while simultaneously safeguarding the identity of a mutual cooperative.[353] In this context, it requires the statutes to contain a provision defining member business and, in particular, setting a minimum extent for the transactions to be carried out in this context.[354]

Concerning non-user members[355] (investor members)—which are a category exempted from the principle of double quality—there are strong arguments that SCE user members cannot be admitted as non-user members, whereas both national legal systems provide for the opposite concerning the national cooperatives. In this regard, both Austrian and Italian SCEs are less flexible than Austrian or Italian cooperatives. The SCE-R's approach seems to align with the PECOL's, which explicitly defines non-user members as members who do not engage in cooperative transactions but who are interested in pursuing the cooperative's objective.[356] This arrangement refers to a farmer who, as a member, e.g., delivers olives to his agricultural cooperative (in order to obtain an economic advantage) without being given the opportunity to obtain further purely monetary advantage from the cooperative, at least not in his role as a member. However, he or she could subscribe to debentures if his agricultural SCE were to issue them.

---

[352]The PECOL use the term "cooperative transactions", and similar concepts are applied under Italian law. In fact this relates to mutual relationships. Similarly, German and Austrian scholars use the term Zweckgeschäfte (purpose transactions) for the typical transactions with members. See Fici (2017), p. 41.

[353]Section 1.5 of PECOL deals with transactions with non-members. It acknowledges that activities with non-members are necessary, but requires them to be limited (but not prohibited), at least for mutual cooperatives (General interest cooperatives may conduct business with third parties without restrictions.). It is stressed that this is necessary to preserve the distinct identity of mutual cooperatives. Clearly, non-member business in mutual cooperatives may be prohibited via statute. See Sec. 1.5 para. 2 PECOL, Fici (2017), p. 43 et seq. Interestingly, the approach contained in Art. 1 para. 4 SCE-R works the other way around, as the basic rule is that non-member business is not allowed unless the statutes provide otherwise. Thus, it can be argued that the general model of the PECOL is based on the assumption that non-member business in mutual cooperatives is the norm, rather than the exception. As mentioned above, a further difference is that the SCE-R does not try to regulate the relationship between members and non-members, either in terms of numbers or quality. This is linked to the fact that Art. 1 para. 4 SCE-R does not differentiate between satisfying members needs and developing social activities. This latter refers to social cooperatives which provide services in the general interest instead of focusing primarily on its members' needs.

[354]See Sec. 1.4 para. 3 PECOL. Then Sec. 1.5 para. 3 PECOL explicitly specifies that non-members may be allowed to become members. It also requires the revenue from non-member cooperative transactions to be allocated to indivisible reserves (Sec 1.5 para. 5 PECOL). These last two provisions are to prevent the abuse of the cooperative legal form. See Fici (2017), p. 43 et seq. As will be seen (Sect. 5.3), the Italian legal system requires indivisible reserves on a mandatory basis, whereas the Austrian legal system simply allows indivisible reserves as a faculty.

[355]Here the PECOL (Sec. 1.3 para. 3 PECOL) specifically stress that these members shall support the cooperative via their contributions. E.g., voluntary work or capital. See Fici (2017), p. 39.

[356]See Fici (2017), p. 43 et seq. In addition, Sec. 1.3 para. 5 PECOL requires specific statutory provisions to admit non-user members.

After analysing the legal rules that define the relationship between farmers and agricultural cooperatives—which helps us understand how an agricultural SCE can work with its members—this study examines how an agricultural SCE can determine its membership base through membership requirements and admissions procedures. The relevant rules ensure that members' interests and scope of business are balanced.

3.4.2 The Membership Base as a Determining Factor When Defining an Agricultural Cooperative and an Agricultural SCE

Members of an SCE are 'user members' because of their involvement in the SCE business as customers, employees or suppliers. This raises the question of *how* such involvement can be put into practice. As seen, involvement is based on statutory provisions that define the circle of persons whose needs shall be satisfied. The second question to be asked is: *who* concretely should be allowed to benefit from the advantages of the cooperative?[357] In principle those who benefit should be those whose personal interests are addressed by the purpose of the cooperative and, thus, the services it offers. But does this mean that every interested person can become a member? In fact, admission to a cooperative is governed by the open-door principle (or principle of open membership[358]), which implies that a cooperative should—at least in theory—admit all those persons who are willing and able to use the services provided by the cooperative.

This assertion might sound theoretically appealing, but it may actually be economically questionable. A cooperative is a company and must therefore meet economic requirements and run its business efficiently. The need that any application be approved can lead to a number of members that can ultimately be counterproductive. Think, for example, of an agricultural cooperative with processing capacities for farmers' products. These capacities determine the maximum number of products that can physically be processed. Thus, when the capacity is fully utilised, it can be difficult and even counterproductive to accept new members. Such aspects can be addressed by defining membership requirements prior to establishing an admissions process.

The SCE-R does not provide a specific group of provisions that deal with the membership requirements for an SCE. Instead, binding rules result from the provisions for forming SCEs and admitting members.[359] For example, Art. 2 SCE-R covers forming an SCE and determining membership eligibility. Further

[357]See Bonfante (2014), p. 199.

[358]See Sect. 2.1.

[359]These provisions are contained in Chap. 1, which outlines general provisions. See also Alfandari and Piot (2004), p. 77.

preconditions can be determined via statutes.[360] As will be seen, various provision indicate a certain flexibility while raising the question of who—under the law—is actually entitled to become a member of an Austrian or Italian SCE and whether there are any restrictions in this regard. In this context, the SCE contains some provisions that will be analysed here as a first step.

According to Art. 2 para. 1 SCE-R[361] and Art. 14 para. 1 subpara. 4 SCE-R, **natural persons and legal bodies may apply for membership**. Legal bodies must be formed under the law of a member state and may be governed by public or private law.[362] In addition, an SCE may be formed by companies and firms within the meaning of Art. 54 para. 2 *TFEU*.[363] These are 'companies or firms constituted under civil or commercial law, including cooperative societies, and other legal persons governed by public or private law, save for those which are non-profit-making'.[364] Even though certain types of companies, like the Dutch *Vennootschap onder firma* or the Italian *società semplice*, are not considered legal persons under their national legal systems, these types of company fall within the meaning of Art. 54 *TFEU*.[365] In addition, non-profit companies, which are able to conduct an

---

[360]See Alfandari and Piot (2004), p. 78; Bianca and Zanardo (2016), p. 208. According to Art. 5 para. 4 SCE-R, the statutes must include not only "the conditions and procedures for the admission, expulsion and resignation of members," but also "the rights and obligations of members, and the different categories of members, if any, and the rights and obligations of members in each category." In this context, see Art. 14 para. 1 subpara. 4 SCE-R, Art. 14 para. 2 SCE, Art. 4 para. 1 subpara. 2 SCE-R or Art. 1 para. 4 SCE-R.

[361]Art. 2 para. 1 bullets 1–3 state:

> An SCE may be formed as follows:
> — by five or more natural persons resident in at least two member states,
> — by five or more natural persons and companies and firms within the meaning of the second paragraph of Article 48 of the Treaty and other legal bodies governed by public or private law, formed under the law of a Member State, resident in, or governed by the law of, at least two different member states,
> — by companies and firms within the meaning of the second paragraph of Article 48 of the Treaty and other legal bodies governed by public or private law formed under the law of a Member State which are governed by the law of at least two different member states.

[362]Art. 2 para. 1 bullets 2 and 3 SCE-R. If provided for by national law, a local authority can also become a member of an SCE. As a result, an SCE can also try to satisfy public needs. See Alfandari and Piot (2004), p. 78; Schöpflin (2018b), p. 1244 et seq.

[363]Former Art. 48 para. 2 ECT. See Art. 2 para. 1 bullets 2 and 3 SCE-R.

[364]See Art. 54 para. 2 TFEU.

This is based on the right of establishment, as contained in Art. 49 para. 2 TFEU. This right of establishment is interpreted broadly. See Alfandari and Piot (2004), p. 78.

[365]See Alfandari and Piot (2004), p. 78. Also consider Schöpflin (2018b), p. 1244 et seq; Iengo (2006); Chirico and Troianiello (2007), p. 68. Generally, Lutter et al. (2012), p. 64 et seq.

Even though Art. 14 para. 1 subpara. 4 SCE-R only refers to natural persons and legal bodies, it has been correctly observed that it would not make sense to allow such associations of persons to form a new SCE, only to deny them membership at a later stage. See Schöpflin (2018e), p. 1270. The same is true for companies prior to registration, and therefore also cooperatives prior to registration. See Schöpflin (2018e), p. 1270 et seq.

economic activity, may refer to Art. 54 *TFEU* and apply for membership.[366] In any case, statutes may deny membership to legal bodies as well as foster it.[367] This results from the general provision contained in Art. 5 para. 4 bullet 5 SCE, which determines that the statutes shall include the conditions for admitting members. SCEs thus have a wide range of statutory freedom.[368]

In agricultural secondary cooperatives, we generally find companies and cooperatives as members. The latter are called primary cooperatives and have mostly natural persons as members. In this context, both the Italian and Austrian legal systems contain some provisions that are worth taking into account, even if not all of them apply to an Italian or Austrian SCE (but only to its national counterpart). Yet, some of them can be implemented because of statutory freedom. As will be seen, comparison of these rules reveals similarities and differences, and helps to better understand the provisions of the SCE-R, since it also shows what an agricultural SCE cannot do.

The *Italian legal system* allows both natural and legal persons to become members of a cooperative. However, as cooperative law and political circumstances have evolved, the question of whether legal persons should be admitted as members, has been addressed in different ways.[369] The current situation, which was introduced by the reform of 2003, definitively allows companies to be members of cooperatives. Art. 2538 para. 3 CC allows, albeit indirectly, any legal person to become a member

---

[366]See Alfandari and Piot (2004), p. 78 et seq.; Schöpflin (2018b), p. 1244 et seq.

If an SCE's membership is exclusively made up of cooperatives, it is called a "secondary" or "second-degree" cooperative. See Recital 9. Also consider Alfandari and Piot (2004), p. 78 et seq.; Schöpflin (2018b), p. 1244 et seq.

[367]See Schöpflin (2018e), p. 1270 et seq.; Alfandari and Piot (2004), p. 78 et seq.

[368]See Recital 9, which states: "Cooperatives have a share capital and their members may be either individuals or enterprises. These members may consist wholly or partly of customers, employees or suppliers. Where a cooperative is constituted of members who are themselves cooperative enterprises, it is known as a 'secondary' or 'second-degree' cooperative. In some circumstances cooperatives may also have among their members a specified proportion of investor members who do not use their services, or of third parties who benefit by their activities or carry out work on their behalf."

[369]While these issues can be considered settled due to the 2003 company law reform, it was previously ignored. This might be linked to the economy, which at that time was not well developed. A different situation applied during the Fascist period. At that time, cooperatives were increasingly seen as an instrument for achieving political goals. As a result, representatives of the state were admitted as members to act as a guardian for the Fascist regime and provide financial resources. As a result, the old version of Art. 2532 para. 3 CC expressly allowed legal persons to be members of a cooperative. More precisely, statutory provisions could grant up to five voting rights to legal persons depending on their quota and the number of members. Nowadays, a similar provision can be found in Art. 2538 para. 3 CC. See Bonfante (2014), p. 206 et seq. Also consider Racugno (2014), p. 196 et seq.; Paolucci (2019e), p. 81 et seq.

It has been discussed whether companies might also be admitted. During the period immediately following the Second World War, it was argued that companies could not be members of cooperatives because the promotion purpose at the heart of the cooperative system cannot be reconciled with the goals of a capitalistic society. Especially public limited-liability companies. However, during the early 1960s the discussion changed.

of a cooperative.[370] In addition, Art. 2525 para. 4 CC not only admits legal persons, but also allows persons who are not legal entities (with its reference to non-natural persons).[371] Regarding the content, this approach is close to that contained in the SCE-R.[372]

It has been discussed whether legal entities should be admitted as members of a cooperative and if the members of these legal entities are able to take advantage of the promotions offered by the cooperative.[373] An example of this approach is Art. 14 para. 1 subpara. 3 SCE-R, which states that 'members, who are legal bodies shall be deemed to be users by virtue of the fact that they represent their own members provided that their members who are natural persons are users'. However, this requires that the members of the legal entity meet the requirements to become a member (requirements to be determined according to Art. 2527 CC).[374] This observation should also be true for an SCE, as subpara. 3 explicitly describes the natural persons as users.

The next issue concerns entrepreneurs. Italian law previously excluded their membership in cooperatives, but the current legal framework allows it, provided that specific conditions are met.[375] Art. 2527 para. 2 CC states that persons engaging in economic activity, which competes with the activity of the cooperative, cannot become members. Conversely, entrepreneurs engaging in economic activity that does not compete with the activity of the cooperative might be allowed membership.[376] Membership of entrepreneurs is also permitted if this membership is instrumental to the development of the cooperative.[377] However, the conditions of Art. 2527 CC have to be observed. This implies that membership requirements must conform to the mutual purpose and economic activity of the cooperative. This is a mandatory provision that must be observed by an Italian cooperative, whereas, the

[370]Para. 3 determines that the statutes may assign any member that is a legal entity up to five votes, either in relation to the capital held or the number of its members. It does not explicitly address the question of who may become a member.

[371]Which hence do not have the status of a legal person. See Bonfante (2014), p. 208; Racugno (2014), p. 198. Also consider Marasà (1992), p. 368.

[372]But not regarding the somewhat cumbersome formula.

[373]In this case scholars refer to "indirect" mutuality (mutualità mediata). See Bonfante (2014), p. 151.

[374]Art. 2527 para. 1 CC states that membership requirements must be determined via statutes and must agree with the object of the cooperative (its mutualistic aim) and its economic activity. It is also required that they be defined according to non-discriminatory criteria.

Special legislation often allows membership of legal entities based on instrumental grounds. See Bonfante (2014), p. 208; also consider Chieffi (2007), p. 230; Paolucci (2019g), p. 88 et seq.

[375]The legislative framework has also been changed to allow freelancers to form a cooperative. See law no 266/1997 and law no 183/2011 and decree no 1/2012). See Bonfante (2014), p. 210.

[376]See Bonfante (2014), p. 209; there is also nothing restricting this option to small- or medium-sized enterprises. See Bonfante (2014), p. 210; Marasà (1984), p. 309; Oppo (1992), p. 404. The law on social cooperatives allows membership to be granted to public or private entities who are interested in developing the activity of the social cooperative, along with voluntary or disadvantaged workers. See Art. 11 law No 381/1991.

[377]Consider, for instance, the specific provisions regarding social cooperatives.

situation is different for Italian SCEs, which, in principle, have a wider range of statutory freedom. This also implies that an SCE may, by applying Art. 14 para. 2 bullet 2 SCE-R, adopt a specific statutory provision to ensure their members do not compete with their activities. The members of an (agricultural) SCE can be expelled if they act contrary to the SCE's interests.[378]

How does *Austrian law* deal with the question of who may become a member of a cooperative? Compared to Austrian SCEs, Austrian cooperatives are regulated slightly differently; however, certain provisions are mandatory for Austrian SCEs. Under the Austrian legal system, both natural and legal persons can become members of cooperatives. Legal bodies may be regulated by both private and public law. The result is that only cooperatives, *GmbH*,[379] *AG*,[380] *OG*[381] and *KG*,[382] may apply for membership in an Austrian cooperative. Civil law companies or silent partnerships may not, as they are not legal entities.[383] As seen, this limitation does not affect SCEs that are more open because of their ability to extend membership to civil law partnerships under Art. 54 para. 2 *TFEU*. In general, however, Austrian SCEs and cooperatives both have a wide range of statutory freedom. The limitations applicable to an SCE may stem from special legislation whose aim exceeds the scope of the SCE-R.[384]

After having clarified (1) which legal entities can become members of an Italian or Austrian agricultural SCE and (2) whether there are legal restrictions in this regard, it is now possible to examine which rules link the membership criteria with the agricultural scope of an SCE in order to determine which competence, abilities and other characteristics members are supposed to have.

As a general rule, the **conditions for membership** in an SCE are determined by statutes.[385] According to Art. 4 para. 7 SCE-R, the first condition is subscription of a minimum number of shares.[386] The SCE must set an adequate threshold here to

---

[378]Art. 15 para. 1 bullet 2 SCE-R.

[379]Gesellschaft mit beschränkter Haftung, private limited-liability company.

[380]Aktiengesellschaft, public limited-liability company.

[381]Offene Gesellschaft, general partnership.

[382]Kommanditgesellschaft, limited partnership.

[383]See Astl and Steinböck (2014d), p. 128; also consider Kastner (1986), p. 130; Keinert (1988), p. 269.

[384]See Art. 8 para. 2 SCE-R. Also consider Schröder (2010), p. 186 et seq. Other areas not covered by the SCE-R must be determined according to international private law. Schöpflin (2018d), p. 1262 et seq. The legal form of cooperatives is generally not available to freelancers, as employment law restricts which legal forms of incorporation they can choose. Consider, for instance, the Austrian professional law for lawyers Sec. 1a Rechtsanwaltsordnung. See Miribung and Reiner (2013), p. 236.

[385]Art. 5 para. 4 bullet 5 SCE-R determines that statutes shall include the conditions for admission of members.

[386]See Schöpflin (2018e), p. 1270 et seq.; Alfandari and Piot (2004), p. 79; Albamonte (2008), p. 308.

ensure it will not be closed to new applicants.[387] Then, according to Art. 14 para. 2 SCE-R,[388] the statutes can indicate other conditions of membership, including subscription of a minimum amount of capital[389] and conditions that specifically refer to the object of the SCE.[390] As seen, the statutes can also provide for the admission of investing or non-user members.[391] As a result, the founders and members of an agricultural SCE can define its membership base. For example, statutory provisions might restrict membership to cooperatives, associations or other legal persons. Or, an agricultural SCE could be formed as a worker cooperative, defining via statute that only natural persons who are employees of the agricultural SCE may apply for membership.[392] (One can think of the example of a workers' cooperative based on the joint cultivation of the members' land and the joint breeding of the members' animals.) Thus, the range of possible members is at the discretion of the body drafting the statutes.[393]

In general, the statutes will contain the basic principles, which must be adopted by the general meeting. For example, the statutes can determine the specific number of shares to be subscribed. A specific number of shares could be linked to the estimated number of transactions that will be conducted with the new member.[394] Such mechanisms are mainly used by large agricultural cooperatives, as they help to better link the member's financial contribution with the expected benefits.

A limitation of statutory freedom is provided by Art. 4 para. 7 sent. 2 SCE-R, which refers to an SCE whose statutes (1) stipulate that the majority attending the general meeting must be members who are natural persons and (2) determine a subscription requirement for members wishing to take part in the SCE's activities. In this case, statutes may not make membership subject to subscription for more than one share. This provision aims to foster admission of natural persons with limited

---

[387]See Rocchi (2006), p. 111. Also consider Bianca and Zanardo (2016), p. 205.

[388]Art. 14 para. 2 SCE-R states:

"Unless the statutes provide otherwise, membership of an SCE may be acquired by natural persons or legal bodies. The statutes may make admission subject to other conditions, in particular: (a) subscription of a minimum amount of capital, (b) conditions related to the objects of the SCE." For the minimum number and value of shares, see Sect. 5.2.

[389]Art. 4 para. 7 SCE-R refers to a minimum number of shares which must be subscribed to qualify as a member, while Art. 14 para. 2 SCE-R refers to the subscription of a minimum amount of capital or contribution in kind, greater than the threshold determined by the former norm. See Alfandari and Piot (2004), p. 79.

[390]Art. 14 para. 2 bullet 2 SCE-R refers to the possibility and readiness for promotion. This can be based on a special company goal, a specific number of employees, social needs or services for or within the SCE. See Schöpflin (2018e), p. 1269 et seq. Also consider Lutter et al. (2012), p. 1602.

[391]As long as the applicable national law provides for such a possibility. See Art. 14 para. 1 subpara. 2 SCE-R.

[392]See Alfandari and Piot (2004), p. 78 et seq.; Schöpflin (2018e), p. 1269 et seq.; Lehner (2007), p. 150.

[393]Of course, the relevant statutory provisions may be altered by applying the normal amendment procedure. See Lehner (2007), p. 150. Also consider Art. 61 para. 4 SCE-R.

[394]See Alfandari and Piot (2004), p. 79.

capital; however, these same members can obtain further shares on a voluntary basis. This provision certainly supports the cooperative principle, which gives priority to persons rather than capital. For example, such a provision could be adopted in worker-cooperatives, allowing legal persons to acquire shares while reserving the actual control of the SCE for its employees.[395]

The *Italian legal system* contains provisions that deal with conditions of membership. One contained in Art. 2527 para. 1 CC states that membership requirements must be determined via statutes and must agree with the object of the cooperative (its mutualistic aim) and its economic activity. This helps identify those persons who may have a potential interest in the services provided by the cooperative.[396] It is also required that they be defined according to non-discriminatory criteria.

Even though it is not explicitly stated by the SCE-R, the solution adopted by the Italian legislature which links membership requirements with the object of the cooperative is similar to that contained in the SCE-R. We can draw this conclusion by recognizing that Art. 5 para. 4 bullet 5 SCE-R and Art. 14 para. 2 SCE-R must be read in conjunction with Art. 1 para. 3 SCE-R. As mentioned, the former two clauses determine that the statutes must include the conditions for admitting members, while the latter states that the principal object of an SCE is either the satisfaction of its members' needs or the development of their economic and social activities. Every provision in the statutes must agree with the object of the SCE and support this object's realisation. Thus, a link between the conditions for membership and the object of an SCE must exist. Nevertheless, there should be some discretion, because Art. 14 para. 2 SCE contains an option, whereas Art. 2527 para. 1 CC is a mandatory provision.[397]

A further interesting provision that an agricultural SCE may apply can be found in Art. 2527 para. 3 CC, which states that the statutes may allow the admission of a special category of user members. Such members may only be admitted if they

---

[395]See Alfandari and Piot (2004), p. 79 et seq.; Schöpflin (2018c), p. 1250 et seq.

If a SCE is formed through a merger between two (or more) existing cooperatives through converting a cooperative formed under the law of a particular member state, the members of the founding cooperatives become members of the SCE ipso iure. See Alfandari and Piot (2004), p. 79 et seq.

[396]Art. 2527 para. 1 CC is fundamentally important for developing the concept of a cooperative's mutual purpose. It is described as a tool for putting the promotion purpose into practice. It considerably simplified the former legal discipline. See Bonfante (2014), p. 202 et seq.; Capo (2014a), p. 227 et seq.; Bonfante (2004a), p. 2494. See also Paolucci (2019g), p. 88 et seq. Depending on the object of the cooperative, the requirements for admission must consider the specific requirements contained in special laws. Consider, for instance, social cooperatives or cooperative banks. The specific provisions concerning cooperative banks determine that members must reside (or have a registered office or operate continuously) in the territory where the bank operates (see Art. 34 para. 2 legislative decree 385/1993).

[397]The more open formulation of Art. 14 para. 2 SCE-R prevails. See Art. 14 para. 2 SCE-R prevails due to Art. 8 para. 1 letter b SCE-R. A specific aim of Art. 2527 CC—in combination with Art. 2528 CC—is to make the open door principle more concrete and applicable. See Paolucci (2019g), p. 88 et seq.; Paolucci (2019h), p. 90 et seq.

receive training or are otherwise integrated into the cooperative. These user members may not make up more than one third of the total membership. After a maximum period of 5 years, these members must have all the same rights that are assigned to other members. A similar solution should be adoptable under Art. 14 para. 2 SCE-R and Art. 5 para. 4 bullets 4 and 5 SCE-R, which requires an SCE's statutes to include the rights and obligations of every category of members.

The *Austrian legal system* uses a rather general approach to determine the criteria that members shall fulfil. According to Sec. 5 para. 1 no. 4 *GenG*, the statutes must determine the conditions for accepting cooperative members. This provision is mandatory. The conditions, however, cannot be used to fix the number of members, which would contravene Sec. 1 para. 1 *GenG*.[398] This general observation is also true for an Austrian (agricultural) SCE. On the other hand, a statutory provision that only permits the owner and employees of a particular company to apply for membership does not contradict the principle of an indeterminate number of members. The same is true for a provision that only admits natural persons or excludes specific legal forms (e.g., companies).[399] In this regard, the *GenG* is as flexible as the SCE-R, with the exception of Art. 4 para. 7 SCE-R.[400]

Moreover, according to Austrian law, statutes can be used to admit persons whose membership is in the interest of the cooperative. A typical example is a person who may become a member of one of the organs. It is argued that these persons should be admitted, because they can make a useful contribution to the cooperative,[401] and according to the *GenG*, only members of the cooperative may become members of its organs (according to the principle of *Selbstorganschaft*).[402] As will be explained below,[403] this observation does not apply to an SCE, as the SCE-R does not apply the *principle of Selbstorganschaft*. In any case, the open approach of both the Austrian legal system and the SCE-R allows membership to be linked to personal and practical conditions via statutes.

To reiterate, determining the appropriate membership base is not only a matter of determining the membership requirements, but also needs to be discussed in the context of the **admission procedure**, as this appears to potentially create hurdles that may limit the application of new members. The relevant provisions are contained in Art. 14 SCE-R. According to para. 1 subpara. 1 sent. 1, the request for membership requires the approval of the management or administrative organ. This approval is a

[398]See Astl and Steinböck (2014d), p. 128; Keinert (1988), p. 267; Kastner (1986), p. 139; Zahn (1963), p. 24.

[399]See Astl and Steinböck (2014d), p. 129; also consider Kastner (1986), p. 139; Keinert (1988), p. 269.

[400]Dealing with the minimum number of shares.

[401]See Astl and Steinböck (2014d), p. 129.

[402]See Sec. 15 and Sec. 24 GenG.

[403]See Sect. 4.2.1.3.

contractual acceptance of the application for membership.[404] As already mentioned,[405] Art. 14 para. 2 SCE-R allows the statutes to make admission subject to other conditions. For example, the statutes could require the approval of the general meeting.[406] Such a provision can increase the influence of farmers, especially in a small (in terms of number of members) agricultural SCE, where personal relationships between individual farmers are essential. To the contrary, if investor/non-user members are admitted, the competence to admit new members is, in principle, assigned to the general meeting, but can be delegated to any other organ.[407]

The SCE-R does not contain explicit information about whether the reasons must be given for declining membership applications. Since the SCE-R does allow the decision to be appealed to the general meeting, which would require the general meeting to be informed about the grounds of non-acceptance, it could be argued that a justification must be provided.[408] In fact, the aim of the appeal is to control the competent organ's exercise of discretion: the general meeting may send the application back to the deciding organ to be reprocessed.[409] Similarly, one can refer to recital 10 bullet 6 for this argumentation, which forbids an SCE from imposing artificial restrictions on membership. This implies that the decision must not reference the applicant's race, gender or religious affiliation.[410] In order to determine whether such artificial restrictions have been imposed, the grounds for non-acceptance must certainly be disclosed.

An issue related to the admission procedure concerns the application of an 'entry fee'. It is quite common in agricultural cooperatives for applicants to have to pay such a fee, which may be collected via a surcharge. This aspect is not considered by the SCE-R, but, as there is no provision prohibiting this, one could be based on Art. 14 para. 2 SCE-R.[411] Such a requirement could involve either a surcharge or an admission fee to cover the expenses of processing the admission application.

[404]In principle, membership is acquired via a stipulation of contract or by transfer or purchase of shares. See Schöpflin (2018e), p. 1269 et seq. Also consider Alfandari and Piot (2004), pp. 79, 83; Korte (2012), p. 335. The prerequisite of entry to the contract is not explicitly laid down in the SCE-R, but it can be derived from the fact that membership (according to Art. 4 para. 7 SCE-R) is accompanied by the subscription of capital. See Alfandari and Piot (2004), p. 79.

According to Art. 5 para. 4 bullet 5 SCE-R, the statutes of an SCE must include the conditions and procedures for admitting new members.

[405]Specifically, the regulation refers to the subscription of a minimum amount of capital and to conditions related to the object of the SCE. In contrast, the minimum number of shares which must be subscribed for in order to qualify for membership, must be determined by the body stipulating the statutes (Art. 4 para. 7 SCE-R).

[406]See Schöpflin (2018e), p. 1270 et seq. Also consider Alfandari and Piot (2004), p. 83.

[407]Via statutes or the general meeting. See Art. 14 para. 1 subpara. 2 SCE-R.

[408]This must be at the first general meeting held following the application for membership.

[409]See Schöpflin (2018e), p. 1270 et seq. Different opinion Alfandari and Piot (2004), p. 83. Critical, Bonfante (2006), p. 9.

[410]See Alfandari and Piot (2004), p. 83; Schöpflin (2018e), p. 1270.

[411]See Rocchi (2006), p. 111.

The last point concerns the moment when the (positive) decision on membership takes effect. Art. 14 paras. 4 et seq. SCE-R requires an SCE to keep an alphabetical index of all its members[412] and determines that this registration has constitutive effect.[413] In fact, para. 6 and para. 5 together explicitly determine that transactions—which affect the manner in which the capital is ascribed or allotted, or increased or reduced—only have an effect on the condition that they are entered in the mentioned index.

The *Italian legal system* contains specific provisions concerning the admission procedure, which provisions help to properly address the law applicable to an Italian agricultural SCE. Under Italian law, the admission of members is regulated by Arts. 2527 and 2528 CC. Accordingly, the statutes must determine both the requirements and the procedures for admitting new members, as based on non-discriminatory criteria and consistent with the aims of the cooperative.[414] Art. 2516 CC, which contains the principle of equal treatment, must also be observed. Similarly, the SCE-R states that 'there should be no artificial restrictions on membership',[415] so the decision must be made without reference to an applicant's race, gender or religious affiliation.[416] Like the SCE-R, the competence to decide on admission is assigned to the members of the management or administrative organ. Under Italian law, they must justify any refusal within 60 days of application. The applicant then has 60 days to appeal to the general meeting.[417]

---

[412]This index must contain the address of every member and the number and class of shares they hold. It requires that members shall be registered in a specific alphabetical index.

[413]See Schöpflin (2018e), p. 13271; Lutter et al. (2012), p. 1604.

[414]See Art. 2527 para. 1 CC. For applicants to be admitted as members, they should generally be able to carry out activity with the cooperative (user members). In other words, a person cannot be admitted as a member without the requisite qualities for conducting said activity. The law does not determine what these might be, but requires them to be set via the statutes, taking into account the mutual purpose and economic activity of the cooperative. See Art. 2521 para. 1 no 6 CC and Art. 2527 para. 1 CC. See Capo (2014a), p. 229 et seq.; Schirò (2008b), p. 95 et seq., Santagata (2017), p. 811. See also Paolucci (2019d), p. 68; Paolucci (2019g), p. 88 et seq.

The law on social cooperatives allows admitting public or private entities who are interested in developing the activity of the social cooperatives, as well as voluntary and disadvantaged workers. See Arts 2 and 11 l no 381/91.

The specific provisions regarding cooperative banks state that members must reside (or have a registered office or operate continuously) in the territory where the bank operates (see Art. 34 para. 2 legislative decree 385/1993, TUB).

[415]See Recital 10 bullet 4 SCE-R.

[416]See Schöpflin (2018e), p. 1270. As mentioned above, the law allows the admittance of non-user members.

[417]See Art. 2528 paras 1, 3 and para. 4 CC. This approach means the open-door principle is not fully implemented by Italian law, as it does not recognise a right to admission. However, to a certain extent the law protects the interests of candidates wishing to become members. See Capo (2014b), p. 237 et seq.; Mazzoni (2007), p. 770; Bonfante (2004b), p. 2501. Also consider Chirico and Troianiello (2007), p. 39; Paolucci (2019h), p. 90 et seq.

The rules contained in Art. 2527 para. 1 CC and Art. 2528 paras. 1, 3 and 4 CC are,[418] however, not binding for Italian (agricultural) SCEs, as the SCE-R regulates both the approval and appeals processes.[419] The time limits in Art. 2528 CC must also not be applied to an Italian SCE. In fact, the SCE-R's provisions are generally less stringent in this regard, containing only one rather vague requirement that the appeal be dealt with by the general meeting following the application for membership. Yet, in order to make this right applicable, one can argue that the management or administrative organ must make a decision within a reasonable timeframe.[420]

Next, like the SCE-R, Italian law does not explicitly require a written membership application, although the statutes may instruct otherwise.[421] It is unclear under Italian law about whether membership is acquired because of the decision by the competent organ or whether it is necessary for the membership to be registered in the members' book.[422] Some Italian legal scholars stress that, even though the formal decision of admission can be considered a precondition to becoming a member of the cooperative, the procedure of admission is concluded only by means of registration in the members' book.[423] This approach would be similar to that contained in the SCE-R.

Of essential importance for an Italian agricultural SCE is Art. 2545 sexiesdecies last para. CC, which authorises the supervisory authority to warn the cooperative if it detects irregularities in the admission procedure. If the cooperative does not address these irregularities, the supervisory authority may remove the members of the administrative, management or supervisory organ. The cooperative must then be run by a provisional director.[424] This provision, which deals with forms of control by a supervisory authority, is fully applicable to an Italian agricultural SCE.[425]

---

[418]The principle of self-regulation is limited by these safeguards with regards refusal, the right to appeal, the requirement to communicate within 60 days and the need to illustrate the reason for the decision on the balance sheet. See Paolucci (2012a), p. 107; Paolucci (2019g), p. 88 et seq.; Schirò (2008b), p. 102.

[419]Details of the admissions procedure can be determined via statute. See Art. 14 para. 2 SCE-R.

[420]The principle determined by Recital 10 bullet 6 SCE-R, which prohibits artificial restrictions on membership, also refers to the admissions procedure.

[421]Due to Art. 2527 para. 1 CC.

[422]See Cass Civ sez I 26.05.2006 no 12627 (07.02.2017, iusexplorer.it); Tatarano (2011), p. 303; Grosso (2011), p. 2149. Different opinion Bassi and Passalacqua (2014), p. 296. See also Paolucci (2019h), p. 91.

[423]Neither with the written minutes of the decision by the deciding organ, nor with the subscription or the deposit of one part of the quota or share. The admissions procedure has always started with a contractual proposal (a formal application for membership filed by a person) and continued with the acceptance or non-acceptance of the application. See Bonfante (2014), p. 221 fn 221, Bassi and Schlesinger (1988), p. 296. Also consider Sect. 4.4.3.

One scholar refers to this as a contract with an open structure, characterised by the possibility of new admissions. See Tatarano (2011), p. 302.

[424]See Paolucci (2012a), p. 108. For details Cusa (2014b), p. 616 et seq.; Paolucci (2019j).

[425]Due to Art. 8 para. 2 SCE-R, which provides accordingly.

Austrian law handles admission procedures with Sec. 3 para. 2 and Sec. 5 para. 1 no. 4 *GenG*. They are relevant, because they contain the details of formal requirements. Similar to provision contained in Art. 14 para. 1 SCE-R, gaining membership in an Austrian cooperative is not a unilateral legal act. In addition to a applicant's declaration of intent, the cooperative must also declare a manifestation of will. In other words, the declaration of intent must be accepted by the cooperative for an applicant to become a member.[426] Sec. 3 para. 2 *GenG* requires new members to be admitted via a written declaration that must unequivocally present the intention of submission. Oral declarations are insufficient.[427] These provisions must also be observed by an Austrian agricultural SCE. In fact, the SCE-R is silent when it comes to the formalities of applying for membership,[428] even though a reference regarding a possible written application could—arguably—be found in Art. 4 para. 7 SCE-R, requiring that membership be obtained only on the condition of the subscription of shares, which results in some kind of written declaration of membership.[429]

Similar to the SCE-R, Sec. 5 para. 1 letter 4 *GenG* requires the statutes to include the conditions and procedures for accepting new members. This procedure consist of two steps: the declaration and its acceptance. Furthermore, the statutes must determine which organ is entitled to accept the declaration; if no specific statutory provision is given, this competence is assigned to the management organ.[430] As seen, Art. 14 SCE-R is more precise in this regard.

Regarding membership confirmation, the Austrian legal system not only allows explicit but also conclusive confirmation. For instance, it is possible for the statutes to contain a provision according to which the applicant automatically becomes a member if the competent organ does not act within a specific timeframe.[431] To the contrary, a similar statutory provision cannot be applied by an Austrian agricultural

[426]See Astl and Steinböck (2014e), pp. 128, 130; Kastner (1986), p. 139.

[427]The same is true for implied actions like paying a deposit. This does not imply that this intention has to be described as such, nor is it required that the declaration must be a specific request for admission. However, a written declaration which unequivocally describes the signatory's intention to become a member of the cooperative is required. See Astl and Steinböck (2014c), p. 113. Also consider OGH 20.01.1954, 2 Ob 568/53 HS 2274/42 and Keinert (1988), p. 271.

[428]Schöpflin emphasises that the acquisition of membership could also be conducted via the conclusion of a formless contract. See Schöpflin (2018e), p. 1269.

[429]Similar to the declaration required by Sec. 3 para. 2 GenG. See Lehner (2007), p. 151 et seq.

[430]See Astl and Steinböck (2014d), p. 130; also consider Keinert (1988), p. 277; Kastner (1986), p. 139; Kastner et al. (1990), p. 459.

[431]See Astl and Steinböck (2014d), p. 130; also consider OGH 23.02.2005, 9 Ob 77/04w; Keinert (1988), p. 275. The statutes can also provide for a condition according to which the member can only exercise his rights if specific conditions are fulfilled. However, it is not possible to limit the length of membership. See Astl and Steinböck (2014d), p. 130 et seq.

SCE because of Art. 14 para. 6 SCE-R. According to the Austrian legal system, registering membership is only declaratory in nature.[432]

If membership in an Austrian cooperative is refused, it is usually not possible for the refused candidate to contest this decision, even if the candidate fulfils every criteria that is required by the statutes.[433] It is, however, possible to provide an appeals process via the statutes.[434] The approach adopted by the SCE-R is more stringent, as it explicitly assigns this competence to the general meeting. Even though there might be small differences in practice, applicants are legally better protected under the SCE-R.

The last aspect that shall discussed here regards the **number of members**. The SCE-R generally states that the number of members must be variable.[435] What is clear, though, is that the members must be from at least two member states. In fact, the SCE-R aims to develop the internal market; hence, cross-border cooperation is mandatory. This need not be demonstrated, but simple cross-border business activity is not sufficient.[436] A study shows that there are some very successful cross-border agricultural cooperatives in the European Union, but none of them had used the legal form of SCE at the time the study was conducted.[437]

These two basic principles are limited by the provisions contained in Art. 2 SCE-R. If an SCE is formed entirely of natural persons, there must be at least five members. If an SCE is formed of a combination of natural persons and companies and/or firms (within the meaning of Art. 54 para. 2 TFEU) and/or other legal bodies,[438] only two members are required. Even though not specifically determined, it does not seem possible to drop below the threshold of five natural persons after forming the SCE. It would not make sense to only require this number at the outset. It is also impossible to form a one-member SCE, even after formatting the SCE, by transferring all shares to a single member.[439]

[432]See Astl and Steinböck (2014b), p. 187. Austrian law does not contain any obligation to admit new members. The statutes frequently determine certain individual requirements new members have to fulfil (e.g., a particular profession or residence in a certain area). However, even if these requirements are met, the authorising organ does not have to accept their application (unless the statutes provide otherwise). These observations are also valid for an Austrian SCE. Under the Austrian legal system, it is not necessary to provide grounds for refusing membership. In practice, however, the statutes often provide otherwise. See Astl and Steinböck (2014d), p. 131; Dellinger (2014), p. 21 et seq.; Keinert (1988), p. 278; Keinert (1988), p. 81; Kastner (1986), p. 139.

[433]Joining an auditing federation is different. Consider Sec. 19 para. 2 no 2 GenRevG, which defines an entitlement for acceptance. See Astl and Steinböck (2014d), p. 131; Keinert (1988), p. 81.

[434]E.g., to the general meeting. See Astl and Steinböck (2014d), p. 131; Keinert (1988), p. 277.

[435]Art. 1 para. 2 subpara. 2 SCE-R.

[436]For instance to supply a good to another member state. See Schöpflin (2018b), p. 1244 et seq; Ebers (2004), p. 46.

[437]For details, see Van der Sangen (2012), p. 114.

[438]Governed by public or private law.

[439]According to Art. 15 para. 1 bullet 3 SCE-R.

See Schöpflin (2018b), p. 1244 et seq. Also consider Chirico and Troianiello (2007), p. 64; Münkner (2006), p. 18.

If there has been a breach of Art. 2 para. 1 SCE-R, the SCE must be dissolved.[440] This provision exclusively refers to the moment of formation. Therefore, if the number of members of an agricultural SCE drops below the required minimum number after formation has occurred,[441] and as the SCE-R does not contain a provision that addresses this situation, national law has to be applied. If the SCE does have to be closed, Art. 72 SCE-R has to be considered, which refers to the relevant national law.

Now to examine how the two legal systems deal with this issue and to determine if they contain provisions that an *Italian* or Austrian SCE must also comply with. The provisions of the former legal system differ to some extent from those in the SCE-R; however, some provisions can and must be applied. First, it contains a provision according to which a cooperative must have a certain minimum number of members. This provision expresses that a cooperative must be open to the specific needs of a fixed category of persons.[442] In this context, Art. 2522 CC determines that at least nine members are needed to form a cooperative.[443] Thus, Italian law is more stringent (than the provision contained in the SCE-R),[444] but must not be observed by an Italian agricultural SCE.

Next, para. 3 states that if membership falls below this minimum number, and the minimum number is not restored within a year, the cooperative must be dissolved.[445] As seen, the SCE-R only considers a situation in which an SCE is formed in breach of the requirements determined by Art. 2 para. 1 SCE-R[446]; thus, national law must be applied if the number of members later falls below this threshold after formation of the SCE.[447] Thus, Art. 2522 para. 3 CC is applicable to an Italian agricultural

[440] Art. 73 para. 1 SCE-R.

[441] Art. 2 para. 1 SCE-R specifies that an SCE may be formed by at least five natural persons who are resident in at least two member states. A similar rule applies to legal persons or companies and firms within the meaning of Art. 54 para. 2 TFEU and formed under the law of a member state. In this case, the members have to be "resident in, or governed by the law of at least two different member states." See Alfandari and Piot (2004), p. 79. Also consider Schöpflin (2018b), p. 1244 et seq; Ebers (2004), p. 46.

[442] See Bonfante (2014), p. 188.

[443] This limit refers to user rather than non-user members. See Bonfante (2014), p. 188; Cusa (2006), p. 51 et seq.

[444] In addition, if an Italian cooperative adopts the provisions for an srl instead of those for an spa, the minimum is three members (Art. 2522 para. 2 CC). Special laws may determine other limits for particular types of cooperatives Art. 2522 para. 4 CC. Examples include credit cooperatives, which must have at least 200 members or cooperatives consortiums, which must have at least three members.

[445] If the cooperative adopts the framework for an spa and membership falls below the minimum of nine members, the cooperative can still amend its statutes and adopt the provisions determined for an srl. See Bonfante (2014), p. 189.

[446] Minimum number of members, when the SCE is formed. See Art. 73 SCE-R.

[447] Due to Art. 8 para. 1 letter c SCE-R.

SCE; this implies that the SCE must be dissolved. In this case, national provisions must be applied.[448]

These analyses show that both the provisions of the SCE-R and those of Italian law provide for a minimum number of members. Even though the *Austrian legal system* does not contain any such specifications, at least two founding members are needed to establish a new cooperative. An Austrian cooperative that fails to do so must be dissolved.[449] Under Austrian law, one can draft statutory provisions to set a minimum and/or a maximum number of members. There is no contradiction between the principle of variable membership[450] and such a statutory provision, as the number of members remains flexible within the two limits.[451] Such a solution should also be valid for an Austrian agricultural SCE.

Both the Italian and the Austrian solutions align with the solution proposed by Sec. 1.3 para. 4 PECOL. Accordingly, a cooperative must have at least two members.[452] In the case of a mutual cooperative, both members must be user members. The PECOL require that a cooperative be dissolved if only one member remains.[453]

Austrian law does not contain a specific provision governing the dissolution procedure. It is discussed whether the remaining members must adopt a specific decision or whether the cooperative is closed automatically.[454] This second approach seems better, as it ensures that the cooperative does not continue to exist because of a delay of the remaining members.[455] This must also be considered by an Austrian agricultural SCE because of Art. 72 SCE-R.[456]

To conclude, both Italian and Austrian agricultural SCEs have a wide range of statutory freedom to determine who is entitled to become a member. Both natural and legal persons or bodies can apply, along with companies and firms that are not considered legal persons according to the relevant national legal system.[457] This could be important since, in both legal systems, the *società semplice* and the *Gesellschaft bürgerlichen Rechts* play a significant role in the agricultural

---

[448]See Art. 72 SCE-R.

[449]See Astl and Steinböck (2014c), p. 109; also consider Kastner (1986), p. 136; Nowotny (2008), nt 5/39; Keinert (1988), pp. 41 et seq. and 96 et seq.

[450]The criterion of an "indeterminate number of members" is provided by Sec. 1 GenG.

[451]See Dellinger (2014), p. 21; Kastner (1986), p. 122; Keinert (1988), p. 80. Different opinion Pramer and Pfaffenzeller (1976), p. 5. Sec. 6 para. 1 WGG sets a minimum of 60 members for building associations organised as cooperatives.

[452]Unlike Art. 2 para. 1 SCE-R, the PECOL do not differentiate between natural persons and legal or other persons.

[453]See Fici (2017), p. 39.

[454]See Astl and Steinböck (2014c), p. 109; Dellinger (2001), p. 29.

[455]See Astl and Steinböck (2014c), p. 109.

[456]Consider Art. 72 SCE-R.

[457]See Sec. 1.3 PECOL only refers to natural or legal persons here. See also Fici (2017), p. 38 et seq.

business.[458] Apart from very specific details found primarily in the Italian legal system,[459] all the different approaches to membership requirements (and possible statutory freedom granted in this context) align with para. 6 of Sec. 1.3 PECOL, which generously allows the statutes to determine the requirements for membership and simultaneously provides a mechanism to prevent cooperatives from abusing this faculty; it adds that these requirements cannot be based on gender, social, ethnic, racial, political or religious characteristics or contain artificial restrictions on membership.[460] Recital 10 bullet 6 SCE-R also refers to this principle of non-discrimination. A similar provision must be observed by Italian cooperatives,[461] whereas the *GenG* does not contain such a prohibition or a similar provision, even though—as outlined above—the general principle of non-discrimination must still be observed.

Comparing the admission procedures of Italian and Austrian agricultural SCEs reveals that differences stem primarily from different formality requirements; however, many aspects are directly regulated by the SCE-R and are thus harmonized. Austrian law specifically requires a written declaration to become a member. This declaration must be unequivocal in the intent of submission. Hence oral declarations are insufficient. By contrast, an applicant to an Italian SCE need not file a written application for membership. As a general rule, registration in the members' book of an agricultural SCE is constitutive in nature. When it comes to the right to appeal, both Austrian and Italian agricultural SCEs must observe Art. 14 para. 1 subpara. 1 last sent. SCE-R instead of their national rules.

The notion that there should be no artificial restrictions on membership prevents existing members from increasing their value at the expense of potential new members. This notion informs Sec. 2.2 para. 1 PECOL, which determines that a cooperative must, in principle, be open to all persons able and willing to accept the responsibilities of membership. According to para. 2, the statutes must ensure that: (1) the applications are processed in a reasonable time, (2) a reason is provided if an application is declined, (3) appeals are permitted and (4) applicants have a right to be heard before a decision is made on the appeal. Lastly, the PECOL explicitly acknowledge that no person has a right to join a particular cooperative.[462] Thus, considering the legal framework that both Austrian and Italian agricultural SCEs must observe, it seems particularly advisable to implement requirements 1, 2 and 4, whereas requirement 3 is already addressed by the SCE-R. As it can be argued that an appeal can only be exercised on the condition that the reasons for refusal have been communicated properly, and as the SCE-R is rather vague about the first requirement, a specific statutory provision could be helpful, but is not necessary.

---

[458]However, freelancers are handled differently, with the Austrian legal system being more restrictive here.

[459]E.g., Art. 2527 para. 3 CC.

[460]See Fici (2017), p. 40.

[461]See Art. 2516 CC.

[462]Sec. 2.2 para. 3 PECOL. See also Snaith (2017), p. 49.

Thus, different degrees of rights are possible. Basic statutory provisions, which, for example, stipulate that only those persons can be admitted who are in a position to contribute to the realisation of the agricultural SCE's purpose and are therefore in a position to comply with specific production guidelines, could thus be softened for a transitional period.

In general, membership will be restricted to a specific group of people, e.g., people in a specific profession, people residing in a specific territory or people of the same profession in a specific territory. Statutes for an agricultural SCE may restrict membership to farmers carrying on activities, such as fruit growing or viticulture, in the area of activity that is precisely defined by the SCE. Such a provision helps ensure that members of the SCE have similar economic interests, something that cooperatives shall promote.[463]

The minimum number of members of an agricultural SCE must fall into one of two categories, according to the SCE-R. If these numbers drop after formation,[464] national law has to be applied. If, as a result, the SCE has to be closed up, Art. 72 SCE-R has to be considered (referring to the relevant national law).

3.5 An Economic Understanding of Agricultural Cooperatives: Benefits and Costs

3.5.1 Setting the Stage: Agricultural Cooperatives in Economic Theory

A key feature of a business organisation is ownership, which is, from an economic perspective,[465] the right to control and receive the firm's residual assets. In the case of a cooperative, this is granted to the patrons of the firm,[466] who are those persons that transact with the firm or enterprise, like its suppliers, workers or customers. Unlike owners of investor firms, these patrons not only supply equity but also fulfil one of the cooperative's functions. For example, in an agricultural cooperative, they might supply their apples. In order to eliminate or, at least, reduce possible conflicts between these two functions, investor interest is eliminated or at least superseded in order to prioritise the members' shared interest in maximising their return as

[463] See Astl and Steinböck (2014d), p. 128; also consider Kastner (1986), p. 122 et seq.

[464] Art. 2 para. 1 SCE-R specifies that an SCE may be formed by at least five natural persons who are resident in at least two member states. A similar rule applies to legal persons or companies and firms within the meaning of Art. 54 para. 2 TFEU and formed under the law of a member state. In this case, the members have to be "resident in, or governed by the law of at least two different member states." See Alfandari and Piot (2004), p. 79. Also consider Schöpflin (2018b), p. 1244 et seq; Ebers (2004), p. 46.

[465] According to new institutional economics.

[466] See Sect. 1.3.3.

patrons.[467] This return is called 'patronage refund'.[468] For example, the statutes may specify that they may not hold more than a certain (e.g., 10%) share of the capital with voting rights. Similarly, their right to appoint the members of the organs could be limited to a certain number of members.

NIE describes cooperatives as being a type of business organization between a firm and the market. In this context, firms are defined as unified structures based on a hierarchy, while markets are bilateral structures based on the autonomy of the parties involved.[469] Accordingly, cooperatives can be considered hybrids, as their members have autonomy, but they also have unified structures that include a degree of hierarchy.[470] Clearly, from a legal point of view, cooperatives are firms or corporations, which implies that they have members and organs. Both are assigned rights and duties.[471]

From an economic perspective, agricultural cooperatives essentially provide vertical or horizontal integration between actors in the markets.[472] Depending on the type of cooperative, this integration may be upstream (i.e., integrating the production chain) or downstream (i.e., integrating consumers). The profits that normally accrue from these processes are captured by the cooperative rather than other actors, such as marketing firms or suppliers.[473]

---

[467]See Molk (2014), p. 910 et seq.; Royer (1992), p. 82 et seq.; Lehmann (2014), p. 42; Zoppini (2004), p. 442; Preite (1988), p. 274. Also consider Sykuta and Cook (2001), p. 1276; Szabó (2007). Generally, Ortmann and King (2007), p. 49 et seq.; Eschenburg (1988).

[468]See Fici (2013a), p. 40 et seq.; Henrÿ (2012), p. 78.

[469]See Williamson (1998), p. 75 et seq.

[470]See Lehmann (2014), p. 39; Søgaard (1994), p. 71; Kräkel (2012), p. 350. Also consider Bonus (1986), p. 311 et seq.; Szabó (2004); Ménard (2007).

[471]See Lehmann (2014), p. 39.

[472]In this context, Lehman explains: They can serve as an instrument of vertical integration. In the winemaking example, all economic functions, from the production of grapes to their processing, can be integrated into one unit. Thus, the problems related to asset-specific investments and the risk of exploitation by the contractual counterparty can be resolved. Note that competition among the producers of wine will be diminished through the cooperative. But that is not unwelcome. One of the important lessons learned from the application of NIE is precisely that the elimination of competition may, under certain circumstances, lead to increased efficiency. The need for vertical integration is a powerful explanation for the existence of cooperatives. On the other hand, it is not the only reason for which cooperatives exist. There are many other purposes that can be pursued. For instance, the cooperative form might be used to create a countervailing power against a dominant market actor, such as farmers facing a monopoly from a big retail company, for instance. In this case, a horizontal integration between the actors of the supply side takes place. The cooperative also allows for the horizontal integration of the demand side, as the Scandinavian consumer co-operatives illustrate. In addition, cooperatives may be used to administer common goods, like creating sanctioned fishing grounds to prevent excessive fishing." See Lehmann (2014), p. 42.

[473]See Lehmann (2014), p. 42; Molk (2014), p. 912. Also consider Kyriakopoulos (2000), p. 28 et seq.; Szabó (2007), p. 9. Generally Birchall (2011), p. 31 et seq.; Hoyt (2004), p. 268 et seq.; Ortmann and King (2007), p. 42 et seq.

But under what circumstances can cooperative ownership lead to advantages? Whereas a public limited-liability company must contract on the market for all of its interactions with one of the groups of actors mentioned above,[474] cooperatives do not have to contract with their patrons, as they are the owners. Cooperative can thus reduce market contracting costs, which in certain circumstances can be very high. From an economic perspective, cooperatives arise in situations where there is imperfect market contracting: There are information asymmetries between actors, which one party uses to exploit another party by using its market power. Here, cooperatives come into play, because they help reduce this opportunistic behaviour.

In general, if a firm has market power over a group of patrons, this can be reduced or eliminated completely if these patrons own the firm.[475] A typical example is an agricultural cooperative that sells its members' products to large retailers who, because of their market power (which includes the advantage of possessing specific market information), would have a significant advantage over an individual farmer during the negotiating process. Moreover, cooperatives can also generate positive externalities[476] for their owners and bring about desirable activity from patrons. One example is a worker cooperative; because the workers own their employer, they are spurred to better performance.[477]

In addition to these general observations about what a cooperative is and does, economic observations about the characteristics of cooperatives as enterprises help to organise the results of the legal analyses in a structured and coherent way. To reiterate,[478] ownership of capital or investor ownership is one of the fundamental features of a corporation. This is not true for cooperatives, at least not in this strict sense[479]; nevertheless, in order to better grasp the functioning of a cooperative and the specific features of its membership, it seems useful to consider this fundamental attribute of a corporation.

---

[474]Suppliers, workers, customers.

[475]See Molk (2014), pp. 912, 922 et seq. Also consider Szabó (2007), p. 9; Royer (1999), p. 53 et seq.; Egerstrom (2004), p. 80 et seq.; Hansmann (1996), p. 122 et seq.; Adams (1991), p. 22. Also consider Milgrom and Roberts (1992), p. 562 et seq. Generally Birchall (2011), p. 31 et seq. For a specific example, see Hernandez-Espallardo et al. (2013), p. 239.

[476]Positive externalities arise due to decisions (made by an individual or a firm) where the decision maker does not receive the full benefit of his decision. Instead, some benefit goes to external actors who do not provide adequate compensation. "External" implies that the effects of the decision are not sufficiently compensated by the market. See Kräkel (2012), p. 46. Also consider Mattei (1987), p. 9 et seq.; Adams (1991), p. 56 et seq.; Bortoleto and Rogerio de Moura Costa (2012).

[477]See Molk (2014), pp. 912 et seq. and 922; Hansmann (1996), p. 69 et seq. In general Pérotin (2013); Denozza (2002), p. 28 et seq.

[478]See Sect. 1.3.2.

[479]The opposite can also be argued, albeit in an abstract fashion. In fact, Hansmann conceptualises a public limited-liability company as a special type of cooperative, the capital cooperative. See Hansmann (1996), p. 13 et seq. Also consider Armour et al. (2009b), p. 15; Hansmann (2011, 2014); Ortmann and King (2007), p. 54 et seq.

To determine the ownership of a firm from an economic perspective, it is necessary to define two key elements[480]: the right to control the firm and the right to receive the firm's net earnings (cost of risk bearing).[481] Both rights are normally granted in proportion to the amount of capital subscribed and serve to maximise shareholders' financial returns.[482] If there is more than one class of owner, the transaction costs are particularly high; in fact, the costs may exceed the savings generated from avoiding contracting in the markets (and the associated costs). Therefore, in general, firms have one group of owners with fairly homogeneous interests. Typically, investors of capital in public limited-liability companies have highly homogeneous interests, because it is in their common interest to maximise returns, which reduces potential conflicts and costs.[483] Thus, homogeneous interests are a key feature of success; this clear prerogative also applies to agricultural cooperatives. However, in practice, agricultural cooperatives are far from having a homogeneous membership base, a typical effect associated with the growth of the agricultural cooperative. In a cooperative's first years, the needs and interests of its members are rather homogeneous. Heterogeneity increases with the development of the cooperative, the development of the business of the members and the development of the market. However, there are specific legal instruments that can, to a certain extent, help to solve the problems resulting from heterogeneity.[484]

Another characteristic of ownership is transferability of shares, which allows a corporation to conduct its business without interruption, even if the identity of its owners changes. This makes the investments of the shareholders more liquid and allows shareholders to diversify their investment portfolios more easily. Through diversification, shareholders can reduce the risks they incur from holding shares by employing different investment strategies to ultimately maximise their earnings. Shares that are freely tradeable, therefore, maximise the liquidity of shareholdings and the ability of shareholders to diversify their investments. These mechanisms also make corporations more flexible when they need to raise capital.[485] The transferability of shares is also linked to the concepts of limited liability and liquidation protection, both of which are safeguards to protect a firm's assets. In fact, because of

[480]This concept of ownership differs from that normally used by law. See Sect. 1.3.2.

[481]See Sect. 1.3.2.

[482]See Schäfer and Ott (2012), p. 701 et seq.; Armour et al. (2009b), p. 14 et seq. Also consider Ribstein and Kobayashi (1999), p. 81 et seq.; Fama and Jensen (1983).

[483]See Easterbrook and Fischel (1998), p. 35 et seq.; Armour et al. (2009b), p. 15; Hansmann (1996), p. 53 et seq.; Holmstrom (1999), p. 407 et seq.

[484]For details, see Sect. 3.5.2.

[485]See Armour et al. (2009b), p. 11 et seq.; Easterbrook and Fischel (1998), p. 41 et seq.; Bolten et al. (2007), p. 846. Also consider Schäfer and Ott (2012), p. 699 et seq. Corporations whose shares are freely tradeable are therefore also treated as open or public corporations rather than closed or private corporations, where the transferability of shares is restricted. See Armour et al. (2009b), p. 12.

liquidation protection, shareholders cannot withdraw their shares at will, and personal creditors cannot foreclose on shares in the firm's assets.[486]

Now, what do these general findings mean for agricultural cooperatives? As already mentioned,[487] a fundamental characteristic of a cooperative is that ownership—in the economic sense—is given, in principle, to persons who are more interested in maximising earnings by conducting transactions with the cooperative rather than maximising the remuneration of capital subscribed. By its very nature, a cooperative is a collective enterprise whose basic aim is to integrate personal economies.[488] Consequently, a cooperative aims to maximise the median earnings assignable to each user-member.[489] This is rather unlike a company. Thus not only is a cooperative an alternative to a company, but its benefits are also completely different. In fact, the benefits a member can receive from the cooperative are both monetary (patronage refunds[490]) and high quality goods and services.[491] As a result, the members assess the performance of the management or administrative organ by evaluating the financial returns as well as the quality of goods and services provided by the cooperative.[492]

These dynamics are illustrated in this study through the example of an agricultural cooperative, which is a specific type of producer cooperative. In producer cooperatives, the owners produce goods via the activity of the cooperative. So in an agriculture cooperative, farmers might supply fruit to their cooperative, which then processes and sells them. These types of cooperative are often created in response to potential or actual market power. For example, buyers of apples can dictate the terms of trade because of information asymmetries. Typically, many small farmers will have to trade with a large single buyer (monopsony buyer[493]). To avoid being taken advantage of, the farmers concentrate the selling activity in a cooperative in order to counterbalance the external buyer. An investor-owned business would exploit this market power by pursuing the maximum financial returns for its investors, instead of maximising patronage refunds (which is here the price obtained for the fruits sold by

---

[486]See Armour et al. (2009b), p. 12; Kershaw (2012), p. 18 et seq. For further details, see Sect. 5.6. Limited liability shields the owners (i.e., the shareholders) and their assets from the corporation's creditors. As a result, the creditworthiness of the corporation does not depend on the creditworthiness of its shareholders. If this were not the case, it would be very difficult to determine the value of shares for potential purchases. See Armour et al. (2009b), p. 12.

[487]See Sect. 1.3.2.

[488]In an SCE there must be at least two members, or five if the SCE is made up exclusively of natural persons.

[489]See Zoppini (2004), p. 442 et seq. Also consider Preite (1988), p. 274; Hansmann (1996), p. 13 et seq. It has been criticised that cooperatives disincentivise production as they maximise the median rather than total earnings of each member. See Zoppini (2004), p. 445. For general information Kräkel (2012), p. 350 et seq.

[490]Art. 66 SCE-R uses the term "dividends".

[491]See Hansmann (1999), p. 398; Kyriakopoulos (2000), p. 30; Torgerson et al. (1998); Lehmann (2014), p. 39 et seq.; Henrÿ (2012), p. 37 et seq.

[492]See Hansmann (1999), p. 398. Also consider Kräkel (2012), p. 353 et seq.; Alho (2015), p. 5.

[493]See Delbono (1994); Wall et al. (2010), p. 199. See also Hansmann (1996), p. 122 et seq.

the cooperative). But a cooperative does not exercise its market power, as it is controlled by the ones who supply the input. Thus the cooperative can exploit economies of scale without wielding market power. As a result, farmers who conduct their business with an agricultural cooperative can capture these economies of scale without paying the full expense of monitoring because of the risk of market power (thus reducing monitoring costs).[494] A prerequisite for this is homogeneity in the membership base: the more homogeneous, the better it works.

Evidence shows that it is in the interests of a farmer[495] to safeguard his own production business, which is a strong incentive to monitor the management efficiently.[496] In addition, it has been shown that agricultural cooperatives often provide secondary benefits—for instance, from research and development—that can help a farmer improve the quality of his inputs. This improved production leads to higher earnings. Positive externalities are also created.[497]

However, cooperatives have been criticised as being inefficient because of vaguely defined property rights. Unlike (investor-owned) companies, the right to obtain residual earnings and the transferability of shares is limited (locked-in),[498] if not excluded. In other words, members of a cooperative have no individual ownership, to put it in economic terms.[499]

Moreover, because of cooperatives' particular reserve systems, members often have no claim to residual earnings. In fact, a fundamental feature of cooperatives is that 'the co-operative society normally also has some unallocated capital, i.e., collectively owned and subject to collective decision-making'.[500] The SCE-R refers

[494]See Hansmann (1996), pp. 123 et seq. and 141 et seq.; Molk (2014), p. 913 et seq. Also consider Youde and Helmberger (1966), p. 33. Kislev/Peterson, Economies of Scale in Agriculture: A Reexamination of the Evidence, in Antle/Sumner (Ed), Papers in honor of D. Gale Johnson (1996) 156, 156 et seq.; Schroeder (1992); Hetherington (1991), p. 129; Kräkel (2012), p. 350 et seq.; Nilsson (1999), p. 460; Valentinov (2005), p. 141 et seq. Generally, Birchall (2011), p. 155 et seq.

[495]The same is less true if one considers cooperative banks, for example, who act on a market which is more open and competitive, allowing many more alternatives to purchase banking products, in comparison to agricultural cooperatives, which are often necessary to protect and safeguard its members' businesses. See Hansmann (1996), p. 246 et seq. Also consider Birchall (2011), p. 147 et seq.

[496]See Hansmann (1996), p. 134 et seq. Other opinion Iliopoulos (2015), p. 11.

[497]See Molk (2014), p. 915 et seq.; Hansmann (1996), p. 133 et seq. Also consider Aviram and Tor (2004), p. 264 et seq. In general, Szabó (2004); Hanisch (2006), p. 301 et seq.; Gios and Santuari (2002).

[498]See Sect. 1.3.2.

[499]See Nilsson (2001), p. 334; Vitaliano (1983), p. 1079; Nilsson (1999), p. 458; Furubotn and Pejovich (1972), pp. 1141 et seq. and 1154; Fama and Jensen (1983), p. 302 et seq. Also consider Sect. 1.3.2.

"They simply own the monetary value of shares in the co-operative society, which are generally redeemable at par value." See Nilsson (2001), p. 334. Also consider Nilsson (1999), p. 455.

[500]See Nilsson (2001), p. 336. See also Royer (1999), p. 56, Ortmann and King (2007), p. 57; Gentzoglanis (2007), p. 158. Also consider Henrÿ (2012), p. 35 et seq.; Fajardo (2012), p. 5; Costi (2001), p. 129 et seq.

to the principle of disinterested distribution here. This implies that after an agricultural SCE is closed up, the net assets and reserves should be distributed either to another cooperative that pursues similar aims or to general interest purposes.[501] Yet, as this principle runs completely contrary to the fundamental feature of a corporation (as given above), it is argued that, as a result, members often lack the incentive to efficiently monitor and control their cooperative.[502]

From an economic perspective, this combination of rules creates vaguely defined property rights. As a result, specific problems linked to the separation of ownership and control are accentuated in cooperatives, leading to conflicts over residual claims and decision control. Agency theory helps describe these problems (which are also typically discussed in agricultural cooperatives), which are categorised as follows[503]: (1) the problem of shared ownership, also called the free-rider problem; (2) the horizon problem; (3) the portfolio problem[504]; (4) the follow-up problem, also called the control problem; and (5) the decision-making problem, also called the influence-costs problem.[505]

First, the problem of shared ownership arises when a new member joins an agricultural cooperative. As a result of the open door principle, this new member has access to assets that have been accumulated by previous and existing members. This is also called the (insider) free-rider problem.[506] It occurs 'when property rights are not tradable or not sufficiently well-defined and enforced to ensure that individuals bear the full cost of their actions or receive the full benefits they create'.[507] As new members often only pay a small entrance fee to join a cooperative, the share of the existing members is diluted while the increase in capital is low. Therefore, members are often reluctant to invest in their cooperative, as others can gain access to these investments without paying accordingly. However, when a member wants to resign (or is expelled), he or she generally does not have access to the assets

[501] In this context, cooperatives have been described as "ownerless capital". See Nilsson (2001), p. 342. Also consider Costi (2001), p. 128 et seq.; Consiglio nazionale del notariato (2006), p. 4.

[502] This will be discussed in detail in Sects. 3.5.2 and 4.4.6.

[503] See Nilsson (2001), p. 336; Royer (1999), p. 53 et seq. Also consider Tortia et al. (2013), p. 30; Egerstrom (2004), p. 73 et seq.

[504] The first three concern disincentives to contribute risk capital. They may come up due to vaguely defined property rights. See Iliopoulos (2015), p. 7. Also consider Cook (1995) and Cook and Iliopoulos (2000).

[505] The last two regard costs of monitoring management and costs of collective decision-making. See Iliopoulos (2015), p. 7. Also consider Hansmann (1996), p. 35 et seq.; Iliopoulos and Hendrikse (2009).

[506] See Nilsson (2001), p. 337; Royer (1999), p. 56; Tortia et al. (2013), p. 30. Also consider Schäfer and Ott (2012), p. 700.

[507] See Royer (1999), p. 56.

accumulated during his period of membership.[508] This will be discussed further in the chapters dealing with disinterested distribution.[509]

The external free-rider problem results from the common use of resources. It has been shown that cooperative property rights are not well placed to ensure that acting members or non-members bear the full cost of their actions or obtain the full benefit that they derive from their activities. This situation occurs, in particular, in open cooperatives. The generally cited example is that of a tomato processing producer who refuses to join a tomato distribution cooperative but uses its negotiated trading conditions.

The next problem is the so-called horizon problem. In general, it is assumed that members of an agricultural cooperative have a limited planning horizon; that is, they plan until the time they resign. As a result, the so-called horizon problem arises. This problem can be caused by many things, including the inability of residual rights to be transferred when a member resigns, the different planning horizons of the cooperative's members[510] and the different planning horizons of the members of the organs. Planning horizons generally depend on the age of the member. These inconsistencies make it difficult to make optimal investment decisions.[511] The severity of this problem is exacerbated by investments in research and development, advertising and other intangible assets. There is, therefore, pressure on the board of directors and management to increase the proportion of the cooperative's cash flow used for current payments to members in proportion to their investment. Pressure also arises to accelerate the repayment of equity, to the detriment of retained earnings. This leads to serious problems in the supply of risk capital by members.

In general, it is beneficial to diversify assets between different operations; this reduces the investor's risk. Yet, this requires the ability to purchase and sell shares freely.[512] This risk is exacerbated when a 'member's investment in the cooperative represents a high proportion of his off-farm investment and to the extent that his farming risks are positively correlated with the risks associated to the cooperative'.[513] It has been stressed that this mechanism (diversification) does not work in

[508] See Nilsson (2001), p. 337; Royer (1999), p. 56; Vitaliano (1983), p. 1078 et seq.; Chukwu (1990), p. 153 et seq.; Cook and Iliopoulos (2000), p. 336; Nilsson (1999), p. 460 et seq.; Iliopoulos (2015), p. 7. Also consider Ostrom (2007), p. 1 et seq. and in particular 182 et seq.; Hardin (1968), p. 1244 et seq.; Williamson (1973), p. 321 et seq.

[509] See Sects. 5.3 and 5.5.

[510] The horizon problem arises in particular when a member's residual claim to the net income generated by an asset is shorter than the period during which that asset can be used. This is due to restrictions on the transferability of residual claimant rights and a lack of liquidity, as there is no secondary market for the transfer of such rights.

[511] See Nilsson (2001), p. 338; Jensen and Meckling (1979), p. 484; Vitaliano (1983), p. 1082; Royer (1999), p. 55; Tortia et al. (2013), p. 31; Cook and Iliopoulos (2000), p. 336. Also consider Furubotn and Pejovich (1970). Critically, Olesen (2007) and Fahlbeck (2007).

[512] See Nilsson (2001), p. 338 et seq.; Iliopoulos and Cook (2013), p. 4; Minguez-Vera et al. (2010), p. 914; Cook (1995), p. 1157; Royer (1999), p. 55; Vitaliano (1983), p. 1082.

[513] See Ortmann and King (2007), p. 58.

a cooperative (the portfolio problem); thus, it is not possible to reduce risk effectively by this means, as members have different opinions about their risk preferences, the value of capital and other variables.[514] This dynamic is particularly noticeable when members leave the cooperative. As a result, members hold suboptimal portfolios: those who are forced to take more risk than they actually want will therefore put pressure on cooperative decision-makers to restructure the cooperative's investment portfolio, even though a low-risk portfolio will probably generate lower-than-expected returns.

The last two problems refer to control and decision making. As already seen, members' inputs do not necessarily match their reward (the output of the cooperative). For example, cooperatives often do not set an entrance fee equivalent to a new member's share of assets; new members may become free-riders.[515] As a result, members often act in a way that does not serve their best interests, as the presence of free-riders can reduce their motivation to become involved in the decision-making process. The result is that the control mechanism assigned to the owners does not work, putting the management in a position to promote its own interests.[516] Furthermore, the lack of a secondary market for cooperative residual claims makes it difficult to monitor agents. Even more challenging is the fact that subgroups of member patrons have the tendency to develop heterogeneous preferences over time, so that the cooperative's objectives may become unclear. Nevertheless, members (at least in some types of agricultural cooperatives) may still be in a good position to effectively monitor management, because income received from the cooperative represents their major income source.[517]

The decision-making problem, as mentioned,[518] refers to costs that inevitably arise in any enterprise when decisions affect the distribution of assets (or other benefits) among members of the enterprise, and the individuals (or groups of individuals) concerned attempt to influence decisions to their advantage during the decision-making process. In such a situation, one prioritizes one's own selfish interests to the detriment of the common interest. Legally, this could lead to cases where minorities are oppressed. Since a number of important decisions can lead to the distribution of wealth among members, with the consequent risk of selfish influence, such problems can lead to inefficiencies in agricultural cooperatives. Examples of such decisions are the allocations of overhead, quality assessments of

[514]See Nilsson (2001), p. 338 et seq.; Kräkel (2012), p. 356.

[515]This is an expression of distorted market signals. See Nilsson (2001), p. 339.

[516]See Nilsson (2001), p. 339; Cook (1995), p. 1157; Royer (1999), p. 55. Also consider Iliopoulos and Cook (1999), p. 80; Boettcher (1980), p. 89 et seq.; Alchian and Demsetz (1972), p. 789 et seq. Also consider Sect. 4.4.6.

[517]See Hansmann (1996), p. 134 et seq.; see also Iliopoulos (2014), p. 165; Iannarelli (2008a), p. 367 et seq.

[518]Consider costs of collective decision-making, Sect. 1.3.3. "Several crucial decisions entail the distribution of wealth among member-patrons and thus may provoke and influence attempts by members. The allocation of overhead costs, the assessment of members' product quality and the geographical location of a new investment" are some examples. See Iliopoulos (2015).

members' products or the geographical location where a new investment should be made. Moreover, it can be difficult for the management organ to know how to assess members' opinions, because members often have different opinions concerning investments or yields. This can lead to a situation in which those managing the cooperative may completely lose the ability to satisfy the members' needs.[519]

Now that we understand what the characteristics and dynamics of an agricultural cooperative are from an economic point of view, we proceed with an economic evaluation of the most important findings that are gleaned from a discussion of what an agricultural cooperative is from a legal perspective. The findings obtained here are also important for discussing the results of the legal analyses in Chaps. 4 and 5,[520] in which I focus on the portfolio problem, and monitoring and decision-making issues.

3.5.2 The Agricultural SCE from an Economic Perspective: Evaluation of the Key Aspects

One key feature of a successful cooperative is a homogeneous membership base 'where the patrons involved all have essentially identical interests – for example, where they all transact with the firm under similar circumstances for similar quantities of a single homogeneous commodity, as in the case of the farmers cheese cooperative (...) – the costs associated with the collective decision-making are naturally small'.[521] There is evidence that this can reduce the problem of shared ownership. Even though new members can join without paying a fee or by paying a small fee, this can still be beneficial for other existing members, as the new member provides an increase in volume. This helps harness economies of scale. While members, when they leave the cooperative, cannot withdraw the wealth to which they have contributed, they will still have benefited from their membership as they had access to new markets.[522]

As already mentioned, there are strong indications that in modern agricultural cooperatives the requirement of homogeneity is becoming blurred and the membership structure is becoming heterogeneous. Many reasons for this lie in the radical and dynamic changes that occur in the business environment. Therefore, it is crucial to develop policies—embedded in a legal framework—that foster homogeneity or, if

[519]See Nilsson (2001), p. 340; Royer (1999), p. 56; in general Cook (1995), p. 1153. Also consider Iliopoulos and Hendrikse (2009); Bolten et al. (2007), p. 845; Egerstrom (2004), p. 76.

[520]See in particular, Sects. 4.4.6 and 5.6.

[521]See Hansmann (1988), p. 278. Also consider Kräkel (2012), p. 356; Milgrom and Roberts (1992), p. 563; Holmstrom (1999), p. 407; Svendsen (2007), p. 116. Generally, Santoro (2014), p. 18 et seq. Rebelo and Caldas analyse the efficiency of Portuguese Agricultural Cooperatives. See Rebelo and Caldas (2015).

[522]See Nilsson (2001), p. 344; Nilsson et al. (2012), p. 196. For a specific example, see Arcas-Lario et al. (2014).

this is not possible, to develop policies that accept this fact while focusing on the heterogeneity problem.

One strategy is to improve retention through specific programs. This strategy assumes that the members share relatively common economic interests in the activities of their agricultural cooperative and that the differences in the preferences of the members are (still) compatible with each other. Such an approach can include binding cultivation contracts, the introduction of special membership programmes (such as exclusive marketing measures), measures to promote the image of the agricultural cooperative (including emphasis on the development and history of the cooperative) or training schools for members and establishing high costs in connection with the resignation of members.[523] If, however, the heterogeneity of the members exceeds a certain level—causing fractions, friction and extremely high collective decision costs—then the agricultural cooperative should redefine its limits and its orientation.[524] The rules of the PO are particularly helpful in this respect, since they contribute, as shown, to the control of the production process by permitting delivery obligations, to the definition of quality characteristics and to specific marketing and sales measures.

The basic legal instrument that addresses these issues is a cooperative's statutes. In this regard, Austrian and Italian SCEs both have a wide range of statutory freedom to set membership requirements and to foster a coherent membership base, which can ultimately safeguard homogeneity. These provisions must be counterbalanced by Recital 10 of the SCE-R.[525] For example, it is possible for SCEs to circumscribe the geographical scope of their activities (e.g., processing wine from a specific valley), or to restrict the membership base because of limited processing capacities.[526] However, it is not possible to completely close off an agricultural SCE, and thus it is not possible to introduce limited membership.[527]

One of the general ways to involve members is through fiduciary duties, which apply in both legal systems. Fiduciary duties can be used to set standards of conduct

---

[523]See Iliopoulos (2014); Iliopoulos and Valentinov (2018), p. 7; Cook and Iliopoulos (2016), p. 22. On these issues, see also Blome-Drees et al. (1998), p. 213 et seq.; Seuster (1990), p. 581 et seq.

[524]See Iliopoulos and Valentinov (2018), p. 8. See also Cook and Iliopoulos (2016); Hansmann (1996), p. 136 et seq.

[525]Bullet 6: "there should be no artificial restrictions on membership."

[526]See Giorgi (2018b), p. 3220 et seq.; Astl and Steinböck (2014d), p. 128. Also consider Santoro (2014); Conte and Vannini (2008), p. 149 et seq.

[527]As will be seen in Sect. 5.6, a New Generation Cooperative (NGC) cannot adopt the legal form of an SCE. An NGC is an agricultural cooperative model developed in the USA to make cooperatives more efficient. See Cook and Iliopoulos (2000); Nilsson (1999), p. 457. Chaddad and Cook identify different cooperative models in order to define and assign ownership rights to cooperative stakeholders. See Cook and Chaddad (2004). Also consider Chaddad and Cook (2004). However, one must accept the criteria developed to determine a European Cooperative Identity to provide, on the meta-level, the required choice between different standard legal entities (see Sect. 1.3.1). It has been correctly observed that "if open membership involved a societal or legal norm to accept any applicant, the principle could easily interfere with the economic need of the cooperative." See Van der Sangen (2012), p. 23.

for members.[528] Economic theory suggests that this duty is primarily a reaction to long-term contracts, especially since such contracts cannot cover every eventuality.[529] In fact, there is a danger of *ex post* opportunistic dealings. For example, the majority could make a decision that disadvantages the minority. As a result, a general principle has been established to resolve these potential problems before they occur. It aims to manage the expectations of all shareholders or members (*ex ante*) when it comes to possible unexpected situations (*ex post*). Thus, fiduciary duties are used as guiding principles for making future decisions in respect of unpredicted conflict (thus, they also help to reduce the costs of collective decision making). These are concretized on a case-by-case basis.[530] In this context, the statutes of an agricultural SCE may also generally require members to participate actively in achieving the common objectives and to refrain from any activity that is contrary to those objectives and to the interests of the agricultural cooperative.

As seen,[531] both natural and legal persons can apply for membership in an SCE.[532] The typical example for this second possibility is an agricultural SCE that

---

[528]See Fleischer (2014), p. 53; Fleischer (2000), p. 4 et seq. Also consider Easterbrook and Fischel (1998), p. 90 et seq. There are different theoretical approaches here. One describes loyalty as an element inherent to every association, functioning as a corollary to a relationship based on trust between the various partners. See Hueck (1947), p. 12 et seq. Others conceptualise these duties as a necessary counterpart to the decision-making power which majority shareholders hold. See Zöllner (1963), p. 342 et seq.

[529]See Sect. 1.3.2.

[530]See Fleischer (2000), p. 4 et seq.; Moll (2001–2002), p. 754; Fleischer (2014), p. 55. Also consider Furubotn and Richter (2000), p. 179; Easterbrook and Fischel (1998), p. 91 et seq.; Cooter and Freedman (1991), p. 1051; MacNeil (1974), p. 753.

From an economic perspective, there are different opinions for how to protect reasonable shareholder expectations. On the one hand, it is argued that courts should only enforce those contractual agreements which have been specifically agreed upon, otherwise shareholders will not be motivated to formalise a balance between minority protection and flexibility. See Easterbrook and Fischel (1998), p. 27; O'Kelley (1992), p. 247. On the other hand, it is argued that the court should also include informal agreements, previous contractual practice and the expectations of minority shareholders, where reasonable. It is argued that this will lead to increased investment by minorities. See Johnston (1992), p. 333 et seq.; Eisenberg (1989), p. 1465 et seq.

It is stressed that shareholders rarely include contractual provisions referring to potential future events when the statutes are written. Indeed, such provisions may often be counter-productive and erode mutual trust between the parties. Next, informal agreements among members hold members to their own contractual expectations. If the statutes contain a reference to initial mutual understandings and expectations, the courts cannot later impose their own understanding of fairness, at least not easily. On the other hand, protecting minority shareholders in this way cannot be used to safeguard vague hopes and one-sided expectations. Instead, the minority must provide credible evidence that there were informal agreements established to supplement the statutes. In this context, however, it has been criticised that such an approach may also lead to a significant increase in procedural costs, as it would require considering the entire history of the relationship between the majority and minority members. See Fleischer (2014), p. 56 et seq. Also consider Davies et al. (2012), p. 725 et seq.

[531]See Sect. 3.4.2.

[532]Austrian legal restrictions should in practice not affect agricultural cooperatives.

acts as a second degree cooperative, which means that its members are (primary) cooperatives. Art. 14 para. 1 subpara. 3 SCE-R provides another interesting possibility: members who are legal bodies shall be deemed to be users by virtue of the fact that they represent their own members, provided that their members who are natural persons are users. This makes SCEs more flexible and allows for new developments that harness the specific features of the legal person, for example, asset partitioning and entity shielding.[533]

In principle, members of Austrian or Italian SCEs do not have the right to obtain services from their SCE. In practice, it seems to work the other way around. In fact, studies show that many Italian agricultural cooperatives oblige their members to deliver all their products—which also means that they have the right to delivery, provided that the quality of the products corresponds to the agreed-upon quality. This is necessary, as the productive capacity of the cooperative is strongly connected to the products that members deliver.[534] A closer look shows that these cooperatives are organised as POs and thus take advantage of the extensive possibilities offered by European legislatures in this respect. Recognised POs shall have statutes that require the cooperative's members to be members of only one PO.[535] It should also be stipulated that all products (for which the PO has recognition) must be sold through that PO.[536] In addition, Art. 153 para. 1 letter a Reg. 1308/2013 states that the PO's rules regarding production, marketing and environmental protection must be complied with.[537] These criteria allow a PO to reduce heterogeneity and enhance the decision-making process, thus leading to reduced agency costs.[538]

By providing EU co-financing,[539] with POs a process of spreading new farming methods and advanced production techniques with less environmental impact will be promoted. Another objective is to support production planning, calculated on the basis of supply and demand, in order to prevent any product from remaining unsold.[540]

---

[533]See Hansmann et al. (2006). Also consider Cheffins (2012), p. 499 et seq.; Armour and Whincop (2001), p. 994 et seq.

[534]See Bono (2012), p. 38. Further evidence shows that, for example, not only supply obligations but also agreed-upon planning might help reduce the free rider problem. It is necessary to invest in member-commitment and reduce dependency on non-member supply. See Ton and Gábor (2012), pp. 15 and 18.

[535]See Art. 153 para. 1 letter b Reg. 1308/2013.

[536]See Art. 153 para. 1 letter b in conjunction with Art. 152 para. 1 letter c (ii) Reg. 1308/2013. See also Art. 160 Reg. 1308/2013 (Producer organisations in the fruit and vegetables sector).

[537]Under certain conditions, member states may make the rules and financial contributions that apply to members of a representative producer organisation compulsory for all producers of the products concerned, even if they are not members.

[538]On these issues, see also Saija (2013), p. 53 et seq.; Rook Basile (2017), p. 446 et seq.; Albisinni (2014b), p. 6 et seq.; Belliggiano (2009), p. 44.

[539]See Sect. 3.3.4.

[540]For details, Costato and Russo (2015). 386 et seq. and Gottfried Holzer, Agrarrecht (Studium & Praxis, 4th edn NWV, Wien 2018). 191 et seq.

Of particular importance for this study is the fact that the regulation establishing the PO requires farmers to comply with a statute that regulates the placing of products on the market; apart from possible exemptions, this must be done through the organisation.[541] As a result, POs can jointly negotiate contracts and set common prices for their members.

Yet, information asymmetries are created, which favour the position of an agricultural cooperative recognised as a PO relative to its farmer-members. In the case of achieving economic success, the agricultural cooperative represents a value, per se, that must be separated from the individual entrepreneurial objectives of each farmer. This shows the double effect of cooperatives: to support the individual interests of their members and to operate successfully on the market.[542] The power of POs vis-à-vis their members is reinforced by the requirement that the statutes provide penalties (e.g., written reprimands, fines and/or exclusion) for the infringements of statutory obligations (in particular, the non-payment of financial contributions or non-compliance with the PO's rules). Similarly, the position of the PO is reinforced by the definition of a minimum period of membership (implying the risk of locked-in) and the obligation for members to provide the information requested by their PO are also important. It is important to stress that some of these aspects do not apply to POs active in the dairy sector.

The next aspect of membership requirements specifically concerns the (internal) free-rider problem. To mitigate it, statutes may correspondingly be adjusted. The Italian provision contained in Art. 2527 para. 3 CC provides a good example, allowing for the allocation of full benefits to new members only after a certain period of time.[543] It can be argued that new members and the input they provide is often less than the input provided by long-standing members. This economic effect could disincentivise the admission of new members; yet, admittedly, this ultimately depends on the fact that there is a measurable difference in the quality of services provided by the new member.[544] This is quite possible in an agricultural SCE, which is tasked with processing the member's products, as the new member will need to adapt his goods to meet the required standards.[545] Another possibility is to introduce an entrance fee corresponding to the advantages that new members gain from participating in existing assets.[546] Similarly, Austrian cooperatives—and Austrian

[541] See Arts. 152 et seq. Reg. 1308/2013 and in particular Arts 152 para. 1 letter c (i) and (ii) and 153 para. 1 letter b.

[542] See Kramer (2006), p. 126; Fici (2017), p. 23 et seq.; Fici (2013a), p. 21 et seq.

[543] The statutes may allow the admission of a special category of user members. Such members may only be admitted if they receive training or are otherwise integrated into the cooperative. See Art. 2527 para. 3 CC.

[544] This is hardly conceivable in a consumer corporative, for instance. See Zoppini (2004), p. 449. Also consider Kräkel (2012), p. 354 et seq.

[545] Based on expertise and sophisticated means of production means.

[546] See Zanotti (2013), p. 227. Also consider Sect. 5.6.

agricultural SCEs—can introduce these fees via the statutes in certain circumstances, such as when an agricultural cooperative has made specific investments.[547]

As seen above, an SCE may conduct business with non-members. In principle, the SCE-R provides a rather flexible framework in this regard, as it does not set even vague criteria determining a relation between transactions conducted with members and non-members.[548] Thus, economies of scale can be increased more easily,[549] as conducting business with non-members is generally flexible. However, it is argued that a feature of essentiality—similar to that contained in the *GenG*—is needed to strengthen cooperative identity.[550] This aspect is fostered by Italian law, where Italian SCEs can enjoy substantial tax benefits if the statutes requiring that business must be conducted mainly with user-members are formed accordingly.[551]

As mentioned above,[552] both jurisdictions allow SCEs to also accept investors as non-user members in order to better attract risk capital. A consequence of this openness is that varying degrees of conflict can arise in SCEs between user and non-user members. The degree and impact of these conflicts[553] depends to a certain extent on the prioritisation of these two aims.[554] In this regard, Italian cooperative law subordinates non-user members' investments to the mutualistic aim of the cooperative. This is partly because non-user members are a minority in the decision-making process,[555] and partly because the legislature has established a hierarchy of different types of reserves.[556] As will be explained,[557] the SCE-R

---

[547]See Kühl (2012), p. 36.

[548]See Sect. 3.4.1.

[549]To guarantee the promotion of members' needs, which was basically the principle goal, the concept of promotion must be partly conceded to introduce mechanisms which allow increased earnings by conducting business with non-members. See Ortmann and King (2007), p. 60 et seq.; Astl and Steinböck (2014e), p. 162; Ragazzini (1992), p. 835 et seq. In general, Birchall (2011), p. 161 et seq.; Grosskopf (1990), p. 105 et seq.

[550]See Sect. 3.4.1.

[551]In this context it has been stressed that one explanation for the presence of (or absence of problems in) cooperatives is the public support they enjoy. This can lead to low taxes, subsidised interest rates, protective markets (allowing cooperatives to exploit their market power and providing technical assistance). However, as has been correctly observed, cooperatives differ from each other, so it is not easy to analyse and comment upon them. Next, public support may also encourage inefficiency, to the detriment of national economy. However, this support can also contribute to efficient production. See Nilsson (2001), p. 340 et seq.; Iliopoulos (2013). Also consider, Sexton and Iskow (1993); Molk (2014), p. 945 et seq.

[552]See Sect. 3.4.1.

[553]And their impact on costs of collective decision-making.

[554]In general, corporate law deals with conflicts between majority and minority members. See Armour et al. (2009a), p. 36. For details Enriques et al. (2009), p. 89 et seq.

[555]Ultimately, only user members may direct the cooperative. See Art. 2526 para. 2 CC. On this issue, see Conte and Vannini (2008), p. 152. See also Paolucci (2019f), p. 85 et seq.

[556]See Zoppini (2004), p. 450. For example, according to Art. 2545 quarter CC, indivisible reserves may only be used to cover losses if divisible reserves have already been used.

[557]See Sect. 5.3.

contains similar mechanisms that prioritise the interests of user members. However, such a rule does not imply that user members cannot decide to give priority to the (monetary) interests of non-user members. In practice, an agricultural SCE that is short of capital could arguably be tempted do this. To reiterate, a single person cannot be both a user and a non-user member. This principle mitigates heterogeneity and thus reduces potential conflicts (and the costs of collective decision making), as it ensures that each person can vote coherently. *Iliopoulos* presents the various possibilities found in practice on an axis, whereby the more the organisational structure moves away from the traditional model, the stronger the position of the investor (non-user member) becomes; investor strength occurs at the expense of the (user) member.[558]

The admissions procedure also serves to guarantee a fair decision about whether a person is admitted to an SCE. In principle, this decision should be based on efficiency grounds, i.e., the new member's potential to increase economies of scale. As this is of general interest to any SCE whose economic object is to reduce transaction costs, it is necessary to provide a specific procedure to help attain this aim. The basic steps of this procedure are already determined by the SCE-R, with the details to be determined via statutes. As a result, rational participants should be able to provide an efficient solution: This should include the possibility of appealing to the general meeting (if membership has been denied) rather than a legal court; this would considerably reduce procedural costs.[559]

The admissions procedure should help foster homogeneity of members' interests, which is an essential feature of a successful cooperative. However, this alone is not sufficient. Problems can arise as members enter and exit the agricultural SCE at different times. As seen, this can lead to a heterogeneity of interests that disrupt the cooperative's ability to function (the horizon problem). This problem is particularly acute when a member wants to exit the cooperative, for example, when a farmer retires from the farming business.[560] As will be discussed below,[561] one particular issue here is whether the capital subscribed will be refunded and when. On the other hand, one can argue that in agricultural businesses, the business undertaken by the cooperative is often closely related to the business of its own members. This fact creates uncomplicated and stable relations. An example is harvesting and processing raw materials. These types of activity do not tend to change much over time, which mitigates the horizon problem.[562] In addition, as homogeneous membership helps establish strong social and economic interdependencies, members tend to have longer time horizons, reducing the problem. Farmers, in particular, strive to make

[558]See Iliopoulos (2014), p. 162 et seq.

[559]On this issue, see for example Welser (2013). Also consider Armour and Whincop (2004), p. 89; Schwartz (1992).

[560]See Hansmann (1999), p. 399. Also consider Svendsen (2007), pp. 119 and 132.

[561]See Sect. 5.4.

[562]See Nilsson (2001), p. 345. Also consider Hansmann (1996), p. 136 et seq.

their cooperative stronger in the long run, as they know their children will take over the farm.[563]

3.6 Cross-Border Activities as a Prerequisite for the Establishment of the SCE

3.6.1 The Principle of Multi Nationality

The adoption of the SCE-R is intended to help cooperatives carry out cross-border activities. In this regard, one can refer to recital 2, where it states 'that the structures of production should be adapted to the Community dimension. For that purpose it is essential that companies of all types the business of which is not limited to satisfying purely local needs should be able to plan and carry out the reorganisation of their business on a Community scale.' Similarly, recital 3 argues that 'the legal framework within which business should be carried on in the Community is still based largely on national laws .... That situation forms a considerable obstacle to the creation of groups of companies from different Member States.' Therefore, the characteristic of cross-border activities is of central importance for the discussion on the functioning of the SCE as an agricultural cooperative and will be analysed here as a final step in identifying the agricultural SCE.

The SCE-R does not contain that much information in this regard, in which German doctrine mentions the principle of *Mehrstaatlichkeit* (multiple nationality), which is also a characteristic of an SE. This principle is an expression of the requirement of a cross-border relationship and is constitutive for the application of EU law.[564]

The principle of multiple nationality has found its legal basis in Art. 2 of the SCE-R, according to which the establishment of an SCE requires the participation of natural or legal persons from different member states. Accordingly, an SCE only can be formed if the founding members, i.e., natural or legal persons, are residents of or governed by the laws of at least two different member states. As mentioned, if natural persons are involved in the founding process, then the minimum number of members is five; otherwise, the minimum is two.[565] The requirement of multiple nationality also applies in the case of the merger or conversion of cooperatives.[566]

The cross-border criteria must be met at the time of registration in the commercial register, but must these criteria also be fulfilled during an SCE's existence? Two

---

[563]See Nilsson (2001), p. 344 et seq. Also consider Conte and Vannini (2008), p. 151.

[564]See Schöpflin (2018b), p. 1244 et seq. For the SE see Lutter (2015), p. 81 et seq.; Oechsler and Mihaylova (2014), p. 50 et seq.

[565]For details, see Sect. 3.4.2.

[566]Member states may provide that a legal body that does not have its head office in the Community also may participate in the formation of an SCE. For details, see Art. 2 para. 2 SCE-R.

opposing considerations seem possible here. On one hand, it can be argued that an SCE, by its very nature,[567] must have members in at least two member states, as an SCE first should do business with its members. However, if an SCE does business only with members from one member state, it is doubtful that the main concern—the promotion of cross-border activities—still will be met. The question then arises as to whether, in this case, the SCE should be converted into a national cooperative and, if this is not the case, whether it should be dissolved.

On the other hand, it also can be argued that such a rigid approach definitely would hamper strategic business decisions. In fact, cross-border activities over a period of time could be a valuable strategic decision, but the circumstances could change and make cross-border activities less attractive. It should be noted that doing business in several member states also means having to reconcile business transactions with different tax systems. Therefore, it may be the case that business activity in a particular member state loses its economic attractiveness due to a change in the tax environment. Moreover, one also can refer to a scenario in which a secondary SCE's founding cooperatives become subject to the laws of one and the same member state.

So, what are the legal consequences? Does the SCE need to be (a) converted, which entails administrative and other costs, (b) dissolved, or (c) could it continue to operate as an SCE, even though the cross-border activities criterion is no longer met? The answer is that the SCE can continue. In fact, the multiple-nationality criterion must be met only when an SCE is founded.[568]

This interpretation is based on Art. 73 SCE-R, which only requires the dissolution of an SCE if there has been a breach of Art. 2 para. 1 and/or Art. 3 para. 2 SCE-R and in the cases covered by Art. 34. The latter concerns merger, whereas the other two provisions refer to the minimum number of *founding* members and minimum capital. If there has been a breach, the SCE shall be dissolved. Thus, if multiple nationality later ceases to apply, this has no particular consequences for the SCE—in contrast to European Economic Interest Grouping, which, in this case, must be dissolved in accordance with Art. 31 para. 3 EEIG Reg.[569] One also may refer to Art. 72 SCE-R, which regulates the winding-up by stating that, in this regard, national provisions fully apply. Therefore, national law also governs the question of under which

[567]See, e.g., recital 2 SCE-R, which states that "it is essential that companies of all types the business of which is not limited to satisfying purely local needs should be able to plan and carry out the reorganisation of their business on a Community scale."

[568]See Schöpflin (2018b), p. 1244 et seq.; Greda (2014), p. 837; Ebers (2004), p. 43 et seq.; Korte (2012), p. 330. However, a preliminary draft of the SCE regulation provided for a de facto cross-border activity. See Art. 9 para. 2 draft march 1992, requiring that the SCE is "carrying on genuine and effective cross-border activities." For the SE, see Lutter (2015), p. 82; Hirte (2002), p. 10. See also Merkt (1992), p. 655.

[569]For the SE, see Lutter (2015), p. 82.

conditions and with what consequences can the dissolution of an SCE occur?[570] It seems clear that a national legal order will not (and indeed cannot) establish cross-border activities as a condition for non-dissolution, as this would go beyond the national market that a national legislature can regulate. This would go beyond the powers of a national legislature. Moreover, neither Art. 1 para. 3, nor Art. 5 para. 4 bullet 2 SCE-R links the object of the SCE to the principle of multiple nationality. This finding holds important practical consequences for an SCE, particularly for how membership requirements must be concretised. Even though Art. 1 para. 3 SCE-R refers to agreements with members for supplying goods or services, or the execution of works, this does not necessarily imply that these must be from different member states. As a consequence, the SCE-R does not require explicitly that activities must be conducted on a cross-border basis. Neither recital 10, which provides details about how an SCE's object should be concretised, nor recital 11 supports such an assumption. Instead, the combination of all these norms must be understood in line with recital 6 SCE-R, stressing the necessity to 'ensure a supportive environment in which cooperatives can participate on an equal footing with other forms of enterprise'. Requiring the application of the multiple-nationality principle after an SCE's formation would put this type of enterprise at a severe disadvantage with respect to the SE. As far as the SE is concerned, there is no doubt that the multiple-nationality criterion needs to be fulfilled only during an SE's establishment stage.[571] Therefore, concerning the SCE, this principle only plays a role during the foundation phase. Once the SCE has been formed, the question of who owns its shares no longer plays a role (and with this the question, whether or not the cooperatives' activities in the sense of Art. 1 para. 3 SCE-R are conducted on a cross-border basis).[572]

Apart from these observations, one also may question how, from a legal perspective, consumer cooperatives, worker cooperatives and service cooperatives may conduct cross-border activities. In this regard, one should remember that recital 10, bullet 2, requires that members also should be customers, employees or suppliers. Similarly, Art. 1 para. 3 SCE-R refers to agreements with members to supply goods or services, or execute works. In theory, this means that a farmer either works for an SCE, buys its products or supplies his or her own products to the SCE to process them.

---

[570]For the SE, see Hirte (2002), p. 10.

[571]The multiple-nationality principle has become the subject of increasing criticism. Some extant literature even calls for its abolition as part of a revision of the SE regulation. However, one must keep in mind that it will be difficult to reach a political consensus on this issue. Thus, cross-border activities are relevant when forming an SCE, but not for its later existence. For the SE, see Lutter (2015), p. 82; Oechsler and Mihaylova (2014), p. 80 et seq.

[572]Recitals 6, 11 or 12 of the SCE-R also may be invoked. They refer to a supportive environment that facilitates cross-border activities, but this does not mean that an SCE is obligated to do so.

3.6.2 How to Conceive Cross-Border Activities in the Three Types of Agricultural Cooperatives

Considering the classification as established by Italian doctrine in respect to agricultural activities, I will, as a final step for determining an agricultural SCE, make some specific comments that will help better understand how the cross-border activities criterion should be considered with respect to workers' cooperatives, consumer cooperatives and service cooperatives. Just a reminder: The first model refers to joint cultivation of members' land or the joint rearing of members' animals. In this case, the cooperative is an agricultural entrepreneur because the organisation itself carries out the agricultural activity, while in the other two cases, the cooperative sells and buys goods to and from members and non-members or processes its members' products (e.g., social wine cellars, social oil mills and social cheese factories). In these latter cases, the cooperative is granted the status of agricultural entrepreneur by law, even if the organisation itself does not carry out any agricultural activity.

Let us take a closer look at these agricultural cooperatives, organised as SCEs, which carry out cross-border activities. What is, of course, common to them is the aspect that they can become cross-border cooperatives by having members in two or more countries. However, what this means for practical implementation is difficult to say because currently, few studies have been conducted on the internationalisation of cooperative membership, even though the number of cross-border cooperatives in the EU has increased over the past decade.[573]

So, how do cooperatives actually operate across borders? Nilsson and Madsen (2007) identify four different strategies for cooperatives to operate across borders.[574] First, a national cooperative can seek members in a neighbouring country. Second, a cooperative can take over a foreign company, then recruit the acquired company's suppliers to be members. Third, farmers from different countries can set up a new cross-border cooperative. Fourth, cooperatives can merge, i.e., a cooperative from one country can merge with a cooperative from another country.

Concerning Strategy 1, one can add that members from a neighbouring country often are recruited when economies of scale in processing and/or marketing are important, and the cooperative must tie foreign farmers to its own processing and marketing activities. For example, it is not unusual for farmers in border regions to be members of foreign cooperatives, especially if the countries (or some regions in a country) have similar cultural features (especially language). The distance to the foreign cooperative often can be less than the distance to a home cooperative. Such

[573]The results from recent research show that few cooperatives choose to internationalise their memberships. Cross-border cooperatives are primarily a North-West European phenomenon. See Van der Sangen (2012), p. 82 et seq.

[574]See Nilsson and Madsen (2007).

examples can be found in Belgium and in the Netherlands,[575] but also on the border between Austria and Italy (dairy cooperative in Sterzing-Vipiteno).

Strategy 2 presents a different picture: The acquisition of a capitalistic foreign processing company seldom results in a cross-border cooperative. The suppliers of this foreign company supply the new owner, but experience shows that they rarely are invited to become members of this cooperative. Similarly, cooperatives also could acquire all assets from a foreign cooperative. In the next step, they then could offer membership to members of this foreign cooperative.[576]

Strategy 3 is also hardly applied. The formation of a new cross-border cooperative is rare, with exceptions occurring only in the fruit and vegetable industry (F&V), in which the use of EU subsidies under CMO Regulation for F&V have supported creation of cross-border producer organisations.[577]

Finally, regarding Strategy 4, examples exist of transnational cooperatives resulting from a cross-border merger between two or more dairy cooperatives.[578]

In addition to these four categories, one can design cross-border cooperative models that do not necessarily fit into these categories, e.g., different types of federal (or semi-federal) structures that are partly the result of takeovers or cooperation with companies/cooperatives from different member states. These cooperatives are often active in the supply business, in which the link between members' supplies and use of their own cooperative services is not very strong.[579]

Thus, in practice, examples exist that help better understand an agricultural SCE's functioning, yet they mainly seem to correspond to the service-cooperatives model, as described by Italian doctrine. In principle, it, indeed, should not be a problem for an agricultural service cooperative to provide its services to farmers in different member states. Thus, considering the examples mentioned in Sect. 3.3.1, no major problems should surface if a social cheese factory, social wine cellar or social oil factory offers its services to producers of milk, grapes and oil who produce their products in different member states. Similarly, consumer cooperatives also should not have any big problems selling agricultural products (produced by their members) to members and non-members domiciled or situated in different member states. However, at least at first glance, more complexity would be involved should a workers' cooperative attempt to conduct cross-border activities. As explained in Sect. 3.3.1, this refers to a cooperative in which the organisation itself conducts a typical or traditional agricultural activity. A detailed analysis must be made of whether or not the land or real estate (stable) used may be located in only one member state. For example, specific tax questions need to be answered: What if a cooperative based in Italy leases land in Austria? In this case, a substantial part of the biological cycle must be carried out in the seat state so that the activity can be

[575] See Nilsson and Madsen (2007), p. 27 et seq. See also Bijman et al. (2014), p. 170.

[576] See Nilsson and Madsen (2007), p. 28. See also Bijman et al. (2014), p. 170 et seq.

[577] See Nilsson and Madsen (2007), p. 28. See also Bijman et al. (2014), p. 171.

[578] See Nilsson and Madsen (2007), p. 28. See also Bijman et al. (2014), p. 171.

[579] See Bijman et al. (2014), p. 171.

classified as an agricultural activity. If, for example, in the case of animal breeding, there are only a few pastures and no farm building on the spot, it is unlikely that the activity would be deemed an agricultural activity.[580]

Another limitation will result from the application of the seat theory. Here it will be necessary to verify to what extent the activity of soil cultivation can be separated from the criterion that the registered office of the company must be located where the management is effectively carried out.

These results reflect the findings from aforementioned studies on agricultural cooperatives operating on a cross-border basis. The examples found that in practice, too, agricultural cooperatives mainly operate as service cooperatives, but not as workers' cooperatives.

Moreover, from these studies, we learn that some important aspects must be considered when an agricultural cooperative operates across borders, e.g., an agricultural SCE: Going transnational often implies increasing decision costs due to differences in culture, membership traditions, language etc. Moreover, this also often leads to a dilution of existing members' control and income rights. Basically, cross-border activities foster heterogeneity of membership. As mentioned in Sect. 3.4.2, this is an essential aspect to be considered when developing an agricultural SCE's proper governance and finance structures. These issues will be discussed in the second part of this study.

References

Abler D (2004) Multifunctionality, agricultural policy, and environmental policy. Agric Resour Econ Rev 33:8–17. https://doi.org/10.1017/S1068280500005591

Abrami A (2005) Manuale di diritto forestale e dell'ambiente territoriale: con appendice legislativa. Giuffrè, Milano

Adams M (1991) Eigentum, Kontrolle und beschränkte Haftung, 1st edn. Wirtschaftsrecht und Wirtschaftspolitik, vol 113. Nomos, Baden-Baden

Adornato F (2004) Di cosa parliamo quando parliamo di agricoltura. Agricoltura Istituzioni Mercati:5–9

Adornato F (2007) Agricoltura a cinquant'anni dal trattato di Roma. Agricoltura Istituzioni Mercati:5–9

Ajates Gonzalez R (2018) Farmers' cooperatives and sustainable food systems in Europe. Earthscan Food and Agriculture Ser. Routledge, Milton

Albamonte D (2008) Lo statuto della società cooperativa europea. In: Capriglione F (ed) La nuova disciplina della società europea. Cedam, Padova, pp 295–320

Albisinni F (2003) Nuove regole di impresa nel sistema europea di diritto alimentare. Rivista di diritto agrario:326–344

[580]Similarly, for example, according to Italian tax law, an agricultural entrepreneur's cultivated land must be located within the territory of Italy; otherwise, the earnings gained from activities conducted on it cannot be considered farm income, but must be classified as other income. This implies that the cultivated land cannot be classified as agricultural land, i.e., the concerned activity cannot be considered agricultural activity.

Albisinni F (2011a) Il diritto agrario europeo dopo Lisbona fra intervento e regolazione: i codici europei dell'agricoltura. Agricoltura-Istituzioni-Mercati:29–52
Albisinni F (2011b) Le peculiarità giuridiche dell'impresa agricola in Italia oggi. In: Accademia dei Georgofili (eds) Le nuove missioni dell'impresa agraria: Giornata di studio, pp 275–293
Albisinni F (2013) La nuova OCM ed i contratti agroalimentari. Rivista di diritto alimentare:4–14
Albisinni F (2014a) La definizione di attività agricola nella nuova PAC, tra incentivazione e centralizzazione regolatoria. Rivista Italiana di Diritto Pubblico Communitario XXIV:967–990
Albisinni F (2014b) Mercati agroalimentari e disciplina di filiera. Rivista di diritto alimentare:4–9
Alchian AA, Demsetz H (1972) Production, information costs, and economic organization. Am Econ Rev 62:777–795
Alessi R (2006) L'impresa agricola. In: Alessi R, Contaldi L, Corapi D, de Donno B (eds) Impresa e società nel diritto comunitario, 2nd edn. Giappichelli, Torino, pp 1234–1274
Alfandari E, Piot B (2004) Die Mitgliedschaft in der SCE. In: Schulze R (ed) Europäische Genossenschaft SCE: Handbuch, 1st edn. Nomos, Baden-Baden, pp 77–90
Alho E (2015) Farmers' self-reported value of cooperative membership: evidence from heterogeneous business and organization structures. Agric Food Econ 3:5. https://doi.org/10.1186/s40100-015-0041-6
Amat L, Chlebicka A, Ferreira I, Montanari F, Sorrentino A, Szabo GG, Traon D, Russo C (2019) Study of the best ways for producer organisations to be formed, carry out their activities and be supported: final report. OPL, Luxembourg
Arcas-Lario N, Martín-Ugedo JF, Mínguez-Vera A (2014) Farmers' satisfaction with fresh fruit and vegetable marketing Spanish cooperatives: an explanation from agency theory. Int Food Agribus Manage Rev:127–146. https://doi.org/10.22004/ag.econ.163357
Armour J, Whincop MJ (2001) An economic analysis of shared property in partnership and close corporations law. J Corp Law:73–92. https://doi.org/10.1093/acprof:oso/9780199264353.003.0003
Armour J, Whincop MJ (2004) An economic analysis of shared property in partnership and close corporations law. In: McCahery J, Raaijmakers MJGC, Vermeulen EM (eds) The governance of close corporations and partnerships: US and European perspectives. Oxford University Press, Oxford, pp 73–92
Armour J, Hansmann H, Kraakman RH (2009a) Agency problems and legal strategies. In: Kraakman RH, Armour J, Davies P, Enriques L, Hansmann H, Hertig G, Hopt K, Kanda H, Rock E (eds) The anatomy of corporate law: a comparative and functional approach, 2nd edn. Oxford University Press, Oxford, pp 35–53
Armour J, Hansmann H, Kraakman RH (2009b) What is corporate law. In: Kraakman RH, Armour J, Davies P, Enriques L, Hansmann H, Hertig G, Hopt K, Kanda H, Rock E (eds) The anatomy of corporate law: a comparative and functional approach, 2nd edn. Oxford University Press, Oxford, pp 1–34
Astl H, Steinböck G (2014a) § 11. In: Dellinger M (ed) Genossenschaftsgesetz samt Nebengesetzen: Kommentar, 2nd edn. LexisNexis ARD Orac, Wien, pp 180–184
Astl H, Steinböck G (2014b) § 14. In: Dellinger M (ed) Genossenschaftsgesetz samt Nebengesetzen: Kommentar, 2nd edn. LexisNexis ARD Orac, Wien, pp 186–188
Astl H, Steinböck G (2014c) § 3. In: Dellinger M (ed) Genossenschaftsgesetz samt Nebengesetzen: Kommentar, 2nd edn. LexisNexis ARD Orac, Wien, pp 108–115
Astl H, Steinböck G (2014d) § 5. In: Dellinger M (ed) Genossenschaftsgesetz samt Nebengesetzen: Kommentar, 2nd edn. LexisNexis ARD Orac, Wien, pp 122–158
Astl H, Steinböck G (2014e) § 5a. In: Dellinger M (ed) Genossenschaftsgesetz samt Nebengesetzen: Kommentar, 2nd edn. LexisNexis ARD Orac, Wien, pp 159–167
Aviram A, Tor A (2004) Overcoming impediments to information sharing. Ala Law Rev:231–279. https://doi.org/10.2139/ssrn.435600
Baer S (2011) Rechtssoziologie: Eine Einführung in die interdisziplinäre Rechtsforschung, 1st edn. Nomos-Lehrbuch, Nomos, Baden-Baden

Balestrino A (1994) Beni pubblici. In: Zamagni S (ed) Politica economica II. UTET libreria, Torino, pp 45–48
Barton DG (1989) What is a cooperative. In: Cobia DW (ed) Cooperatives in agriculture. Prentice-Hall, Englewood Cliffs, pp 1–20
Bassi A, Passalacqua P (2014) Art. 2511. In: Santosuosso DU (ed) Delle società, dell'azienda, della concorrenza. UTET, Torino, pp 3–66
Bassi A, Schlesinger P (1988) Delle imprese cooperative e delle mutue assicuratrici: Artt. 2511 - 2548. Il codice civile - commentario, / dir. da Piero Schlesinger. Giuffrè, Milano
Beintema N, Bossio D, Dreyfus F, Fernandez M, Gurib-Fakim A, Hurni H, Izac A-M, Jiggins J, Kranjac-Berisavljevic G, RRB L, Ochola W, Osman-Elasha B, Plencovich C, Röling N, Rosegrant M, Rosenthal E, Smith L (2009) Global summary for decision makers, international assessment of agricultural science and technology for development. https://www.researchgate.net/publication/269395240_Global_Summary_for_Decision_Makers_International_Assessment_of_Agricultural_Science_and_Technology_for_Development. Accessed 29 Nov 2019
Belliggiano A (2009) Percezione della sicurezza alimenatare e nuovi modelli di organizzazione della produzione. Rivista di diritto alimentare:42–44
Beuthien V (2007) Die Europäische Genossenschaft als gesellschaftsrechtliche Herausforderung: Was muss ein Genossenschaftsgesetz leisten? Zeitschrift für das gesamte Genossenschaftswesen 57:3–16. https://doi.org/10.1515/zfgg-2007-0102
Beyer J (2005) Pfadabhängigkeit ist nicht gleich Pfadabhängigkeit! Wider den impliziten Konservatismus eines gängigen Konzepts. Zeitschrift für Soziologie 34:5–21. https://doi.org/10.1515/zfsoz-2005-0101
Bianca M, Zanardo A (2016) La Società Europea e la Società Cooperativa Europea. In: Pederzini E (ed) Percorsi di diritto societario europeo, 3rd edn. Giappichelli, Torino, pp 177–214
Bieber R (2016) § 23 Landwirtschafts- und Fischereipolitik. In: Bieber R, Epiney A, Haag M, Kotzur M (eds) Die Europäische Union: Europarecht und Politik. Nomos, Baden-Baden, pp 543–544
Bijman J, Pyykkönen P, Ollila P (2014) Transnationalization of agricultural cooperatives in Europe. Dovenschmidt Q 2:168–178. https://doi.org/10.5553/DQ/221199812014002004005
Birchall J (2011) People centred businesses: co-operatives, mutuals and the idea of membership. Palgrave Macmillan, Basingstoke
Blome-Drees J, Zerche J, Schmale I (1998) Einführung in die Genossenschaftslehre: Genossenschaftstheorie und Genossenschaftsmanagement. Oldenbourg Wissenschaftsverlag, München
Boettcher E (1980) Die Genossenschaft in der Marktwirtschaft: Einzelwirtschaftliche Theorie der Genossenschaften. Schriften zur Kooperationsforschung, vol 1. Mohr, Tübingen
Bolognini S (2011a) Il bosco e la disciplina forestale. In: Costato L, Germanò A, Rook Basile E (eds) Trattato di diritto agrario: II. UTET, Torino, pp 81–134
Bolognini S (2011b) Organizzazione individuale, familiare o collettiva d'impresa, e tutele differenziate. Rivista di diritto agrario:330–350
Bolten P, Becht M, Röell A (2007) Corporate law and governance. In: Polinsky AM, Shavell S (eds) Handbook of law and economics: volume 2, 1st edn. North Holland, Amsterdam, pp 829–944
Bonfante G (1999) Delle imprese cooperative: Art. 2511-2545. Commentario del Codice civile Scialoja-Branca. Libro quinto, Del lavoro, art. 2511-2545. Zanichelli, Bologna, Roma
Bonfante G (2004a) Art. 2527. In: Cottino G, Bonfante G, Cagnasso O, Montalenti P (eds) Il nuovo diritto societario III: Commento al D. lgs. 17 gennaio 2003, n. 6, D. Lgs. 17 gennaio 2003, n. 5, D. lgs. 11 aprile 2002, n. 61 (art. 1). 3. Artt. 2484-2548 c.c. norme di attuazione, disciplina processuale, artt. 2621-2641 c.c., 1st edn. Zanichelli, Bologna, pp 2496–2499
Bonfante G (2004b) Art. 2528. In: Cottino G, Bonfante G, Cagnasso O, Montalenti P (eds) Il nuovo diritto societario III: Commento al D. lgs. 17 gennaio 2003, n. 6, D. Lgs. 17 gennaio 2003, n. 5, D. lgs. 11 aprile 2002, n. 61 (art. 1). 3. Artt. 2484-2548 c.c. norme di attuazione, disciplina processuale, artt. 2621-2641 c.c., 1st edn. Zanichelli, Bologna, pp 2500–2508

Bonfante G (2006) La società cooperativa europea. In: Galletti D, Fici A (eds) La società cooperativa europea: Quali prospettive per la cooperazione italiana? Universita degli Studi di Trento, Trento, pp 3–12

Bonfante G (ed) (2014) La società cooperativa. Trattato di diritto commerciale, vol 5,3. Cedam, Padova

Bono P (2012) Country report: Italy. In: Van der Sangen G, Pyykkönen POP, Iliopoulus C, Kühl R, Hagedorn K, Hanisch M, Judis R, Gijselinckx C, Hendrikse G, Hak T, Poppe K, Bijman J (eds) Support for farmers' cooperatives. Wageningen, pp 1–65

Bonus H (1986) The cooperative association as a business enterprise: a study in the economics of transactions. J Inst Theor Econ (JITE)/Zeitschrift für die gesamte Staatswissenschaft 142:310–339

Bortoleto FC, Rogerio de Moura Costa D (2012) The importance of cooperatives' corporate social responsibility to the loyalty of members. J Rural Coop:198–216

Bundesministerium für Finanzen (2013) nt15–nt18. https://findok.bmf.gv.at/findok?execution¼e1s1. Accessed 13 Feb 2017

Canfora I (2008) Il quadro normativo nazionale e comunitario sulle organizzazioni dei produttore. Rivista di diritto agrario:374–382

Capo G (2014a) Art. 2527. In: Santosuosso DU (ed) Delle società, dell'azienda, della concorrenza. UTET, Torino, pp 226–236

Capo G (2014b) Art. 2528. In: Santosuosso DU (ed) Delle società, dell'azienda, della concorrenza. UTET, Torino, pp 236–247

Carmignani S (1999) La società in agricoltura. Quaderni di "Studi Senesi", vol 90. Giuffrè, Milano

Carmignani S (2011) Le società agricole. In: Costato L, Germanò A, Rook Basile E (eds) Trattato di diritto agrario: I. UTET, Torino, pp 231–262

Carmignani S (2013) Art. 2135 (L'imprenditore agricolo cooperativa). In: Cagnasso O, Vallebona A (eds) Dell'impresa e del lavoro: Artt. 2118-2187. UTET, Torino, pp 858–873

Casadei E (2009) La nozione di impresa agricola dopo la riforma del 2001. Rivista di diritto agrario:309–358

Cavanna M (2014) Le cooperative agricole. In: Bonfante G (ed) La società cooperativa. Cedam, Padova, pp 641–649

Cetra A (2019) La nozione d'impresa. In: Cian M (ed) Manuale di diritto commerciale, 3rd edn. G. Giappichelli, Torino, pp 11–20

Chaddad FR, Cook ML (2004) Understanding new cooperative models: an ownership-control rights typology. Rev Agric Econ 26:348–360

Cheffins BR (2012) Corporations. In: Tushnet M, Cane P (eds) The Oxford handbook of legal studies. Oxford University Press, Oxford, pp 485–509

Chieffi A (2007) 2527. In: Presti G (ed) Società cooperative: Artt. 2511-2548. EGEA; Giuffrè, Milano, pp 227–240

Chirico S, Troianiello P (2007) La società cooperativa europea: Regolamento CE n. 1435/2003. Cooperative e consorzi. IPSOA, Milano

Chukwu SC (1990) Economics of the co-operative business enterprise. Theory and practice of self-help promotion Ser. A, Monographs and textbooks, vol 2. Marburg Consult für Selbsthilfeförderung, Marburg

Codini A (2007) Le cooperative sociali: Assetti di governance e aspetti di gestione. Economia Ricerche, vol 604. Angeli, Milano

Consiglio nazionale del notariato (2006) Brevi considerazioni sul problema della trasformazione di società cooperativa in società lucrativa contestuale alla perdita della mutualità prevalente. http://www.notariato.it/sites/default/files/7.pdf. Accessed 25 Oct 2017

Conte L, Vannini R (2008) Istituzioni e Governance Cooperativa. Department of Economics University of Siena. Studi e Note di Economia:139–155

Cook ML (1995) The future of U.S. agricultural cooperatives: a neo-institutional approach. Am J Agric Econ 77:1153–1159. https://doi.org/10.2307/1243338

Cook ML, Chaddad FR (2004) Redesigning cooperative boundaries: the emergence of new models. Am J Agric Econ 86:1249–1253. https://doi.org/10.1111/j.0002-9092.2004.00673.x
Cook ML, Iliopoulos C (2000) Ill-defined property rights in collective action: the case of US agricultural cooperatives. In: Ménard C (ed) Institutions, contracts and organizations. Edward Elgar Publishing, Cheltenham, pp 335–348
Cook ML, Iliopoulos C (2016) Generic solutions to coordination and organizational costs: informing cooperative longevity. J Chain Netw Sci 16:19–27. https://doi.org/10.3920/JCNS2016.x001
Cooter RD, Freedman BJ (1991) The fiduciary relationship: its economic character and legal consequences. N Y Univ Law Rev:1045–1075
Costantino L (2013) L'integrazione verticale per contratto nel settore agro-alimentare: fattispecie giuridica e disciplina applicabile. Contratto e impresa:1446–1471
Costato L (2001) L'imprenditore agricolo e il mercato. Rivista di diritto agrario:131–143
Costato L (2004) Dal diritto agrario al diritto agroalimentare. Un percorso ricostruttivo. Agricoltura Istituzioni Mercati:119–130
Costato L (2006) L'imprenditore agricolo: novità codicistiche e polemiche retro. Rivista di Diritto Civile:89–100
Costato L (2008) Attività agricole, sicurezza alimentare e tutela del territorio. Rivista di diritto agrario:451–463
Costato L (2009) La PAC come filo conduttore del travaglio europeo. Rivista di diritto agrario:246–253
Costato L (2011) Il nuovo titolo dedicato all'agricoltura nel TFUE. Rivista di diritto agrario:119–127
Costato L, Russo L (2015) Corso di diritto agrario italiano e comunitario, 4th edn. Giuffrè, Milano
Costi R (2001) Proprietà e impresa cooperative nella riforma del diritto societario. Giurisprudenza Commerciale:128–132
Cotronei G (2009) Cooperative sociali. Buffetti, Roma
Cuomo P (2013) Gestione mutualistica e parità di trattamento nelle cooperative. Rivista delle società:905–931
Cuomo P (2014) Art. 2516. In: Santosuosso DU (ed) Delle società, dell'azienda, della concorrenza. UTET, Torino, pp 99–128
Cusa E (2006) Il socio finanziatore nelle cooperative. Quaderni di giurisprudenza commerciale, vol 286. Giuffrè, Milano
Cusa E (2014a) Art. 2545 quaterdecies. In: Santosuosso DU (ed) Delle società, dell'azienda, della concorrenza. UTET, Torino, pp 565–588
Cusa E (2014b) Art. 2545 sexiesdecies. In: Santosuosso DU (ed) Delle società, dell'azienda, della concorrenza. UTET, Torino, pp 616–622
Davies PL, Gower LCB, Worthington S, Micheler E (2012) Gower and Davies' principles of modern company law, 9th edn. Sweet & Maxwell, London
de Giorgi M, Vaciago G (2011) Le società cooperative: Tipi di cooperative, strumenti di tutela, aspetti civili, concorsuali, tributari e penali. Cedam, Padova
Delbono F (1994) Monopsonio. In: Zamagni S (ed) Economia politica I, 1. ed. italiana. UTET, Torino, pp 443–444
Dellinger M (2001) Rechtsfähige Personengesellschaften in der Liquidation. Manz, Wien
Dellinger M (2014) § 1. In: Dellinger M (ed) Genossenschaftsgesetz samt Nebengesetzen: Kommentar, 2nd edn. LexisNexis ARD Orac, Wien, pp 17–55
Denozza F (2002) Norme efficienti: L'analisi economica delle regole giuridiche. Giuffrè, Milano
Di Ronza N (2010) Art. 2513. In: Cendon P (ed) Artt. 2511-2554: Cooperative mutue assicuratrici associazioni in partecipazione. Giuffrè, Milano, pp 31–37
Easterbrook FH, Fischel DR (1998) The economic structure of corporate law, [Repr.]. Harvard University Press, Cambridge
Ebers M (2004) Die Gründung einer SCE. In: Schulze R (ed) Europäische Genossenschaft SCE: Handbuch, 1st edn. Nomos, Baden-Baden, pp 43–76

Ecorys, Wageningen Economic Research (2018) Study on producer organisations and their activities in the olive oil, beef and veal, arable crops sectors. https://ec.europa.eu/competition/publications/reports/kd0218732enn.pdf. Accessed 26 Nov 2019

Egerstrom L (2004) Obstacles to cooperation. In: Merrett CD, Walzer N (eds) Cooperatives and local development: theory and applications for the 21st century. Sharpe, Armonk, pp 70–91

Eichwald B, Lutz KJ (2011) Erfolgsmodell Genossenschaften: Möglichkeiten für eine werteorientierte Marktwirtschaft. Grundlagen, Werte und Prinzipien, Herausforderungen und Lösungen genossenschaftlicher Unternehmen und Verbände, genossenschaftliche Modelle auf fünf Kontinenten. Deutscher Genossenschafts-Verl., Wiesbaden

Eisenberg MA (1989) The structure of corporation law. Columbia Law Rev:1461–1525

Engelhardt WW (1977) Zur Frage der Betrachtungsweisen und eines geeigneten Bezugsrahmens der Genossenschaftsforschung. Zeitschrift für das gesamte Genossenschaftswesen:337–352

Enriques L, Hansmann H, Kraakman RH (2009) The basic governance structure: minority shareholders and non-shareholder constituencies. In: Kraakman RH, Armour J, Davies P, Enriques L, Hansmann H, Hertig G, Hopt K, Kanda H, Rock E (eds) The anatomy of corporate law: a comparative and functional approach, 2nd edn. Oxford University Press, Oxford, pp 89–114

Epiney A (2016) § 32 Umwelt. In: Bieber R, Epiney A, Haag M, Kotzur M (eds) Die Europäische Union: Europarecht und Politik. Nomos, Baden-Baden, pp 621–641

Eschenburg R (1988) Zur Anwendung der Anreiz-Beitrags-Theorie in Genossenschaften. Zeitschrift für das gesamte Genossenschaftswesen:250–262

Explanatory note to the government bill of the GewO 1973. https://www.parlament.gv.at/PAKT/VHG/XIII/I/I_00395/imfname_318784.pdf. Accessed 26 Nov 2019

Fahlbeck E (2007) The horizon problem in agricultural cooperatives – only in theory? In: Karantininis K, Nilsson J (eds) Vertical markets and cooperative hierarchies: the role of cooperatives in the agri-food industry. Springer, Dordrecht, pp 255–274

Fajardo G (2012) Cooperative finance and cooperative identity. SSRN Electron J:1–12. https://doi.org/10.2139/ssrn.2185328

Fama EF, Jensen MC (1983) Separation of ownership and control. J Law Econ 26:301–325

Fauceglia G (2019) Il futuro della società cooperativa: la fine dell'umanizzazione e la scelta dell'efficienza. Giurisprudenza Commerciale:567–582

Ferrara G (2013) Gli oneri documentali dell'imprenditore agricolo professionale nell'agevolazione per la formazione della piccola proprietà contadina ([Nota a sentenza] Cass. Sez. Trib. 26 giugno 2013, n.16072). Diritto e giurisprudenza agraria, alimentare e dell'ambiente 22:453–456

Fici A (2010) Italian co-operative law reform and co-operative principles. SSRN Electron J:1–27. https://doi.org/10.2139/ssrn.1615344

Fici A (2012) Cooperative identity and the law. SSRN Electron J. https://doi.org/10.2139/ssrn.2005014

Fici A (2013a) An introduction to cooperative law. In: Cracogna D, Fici A, Henrÿ H (eds) International handbook of cooperative law. Springer, Berlin, Heidelberg, pp 3–62

Fici A (2013b) Italy. In: Cracogna D, Fici A, Henrÿ H (eds) International handbook of cooperative law. Springer, Berlin, Heidelberg, pp 479–501

Fici A (2014) The essential role of cooperative law. Dovenschmidt Q 2:147–158. https://doi.org/10.5553/DQ/221199812014002004003

Fici A (2015) Cooperation among cooperatives in Italian and comparative law. JEOD 4:64–97. https://doi.org/10.5947/jeod.2015.011

Fici A (2017) Definition and objectives of cooperatives. In: Fajardo-García IG, Fici A, Henrÿ H, Hiez D, Meira DMMA, Münkner H-H, Snaith I (eds) Principles of European Cooperative Law: principles, commentaries and national reports. Intersentia, Cambridge, pp 19–45

Fici A, Strano C (2010) Italy. In: Fici A (ed) Study on the implementation of the Regulation 1435/2003 on the Statute for European Cooperative Society (SCE): Final Study Part II. National Reports. Report drawn up following call tender no ENTR/2009/021 of 23 April from the European Commission, pp 671–702

Fleischer H (2000) Grundfragen der ökonomischen Theorie im Gesellschafts- und Kapitalmarktrecht. Zeitschrift für Unternehmens- und Gesellschaftsrecht 30:1–32. https://doi.org/10.1515/zgre.2000.047

Fleischer H (2014) Shareholder conflicts in closed corporations. In: Bachmann G, Eidenmüller H, Engert A, Fleischer H, Schön W (eds) Regulating the closed corporation. De Gruyter, Berlin, pp 29–81

Frotz G (1977) Anmerkungen zur österreichischen Genossenschaftsgesetznovelle 1974: Vortrag geh. am 6.5.1976, Wien. Zeitschrift für das gesamte Genossenschaftswesen 27:53–61

Furubotn EG, Pejovich S (1970) Property rights and the behavior of the firm in a socialist state: the example of Yugoslavia. Zeitschrift für Nationalkonomie 30:431–454. https://doi.org/10.1007/BF01289247

Furubotn EG, Pejovich S (1972) Property rights and economic theory: a survey of recent literature. J Econ Lit 10:1137–1162

Furubotn EG, Richter R (2000) Institutions and economic theory: the contribution of the new institutional economics, [Repr.]. Economics, cognition, and society. University of Michigan Press, Ann Arbor

Galgano F (1993) Impresa cooperativa e gruppi di società. In: Le società cooperative negli anni Novanta: Problemi e prospettive: atti del convegno internazionale in memoria di Piero Verrucoli: 18-19 maggio 1990. Giuffrè, Milano

Galle RCJ (2006) The Societas Cooperativa Europea (SCE) and national cooperatives in comparative perspective. Eur Comp Law:225–260

Galloni G (1999) Lezioni sul diritto dell'impresa agricola e dell'ambiente. Manuali. Liguori, Napoli

Genco R (2014) Cooperative bancarie e obbligo di devoluzione in favore dei Fondi mutualistici per la promozione cooperativa. Giurisprudenza Commerciale:175–184

Gentzoglanis A (2007) Regulation, governance and capital structure in cooperatives. In: Karantininis K, Nilsson J (eds) Vertical markets and cooperative hierarchies: the role of cooperatives in the agri-food industry. Springer, Dordrecht, pp 151–167

Germanò A (2011) Le figure soggettive specifiche. In: Costato L, Germanò A, Rook Basile E (eds) Trattato di diritto agrario: I. UTET, Torino, pp 798–812

Germanò A (2015) L'allargamento dell'Unione Euroea: i Paesi della parte orientale del continente europeo (PECO) e l'agricoltura. Agricoltura Istituzioni Mercati:95–117

Germanò A (2016) Manuale di diritto agrario, 8th edn. Giappichelli, Turin

Germanò A, Rook Basile E (2011) L'impresa agricola. In: Costato L, Germanò A, Rook Basile E (eds) Trattato di diritto agrario: I. UTET, Torino, pp 757–797

Germanò A, Rook Basile E (2014) Manuale di diritto agrario comunitario, 3rd edn. Il diritto dell'alimentazione, dell'ambiente e dell'agricoltura. Giappichelli, Torino

Gfrerer H (2007) Entwicklungsgeschichte der Nebengewerbe der Land- und Forstwirtschaft. In: Österreichische Gesellschaft für Agrar- und Umweltrecht (ed) Agrarrecht im Lichte des öffentlichen Rechts: Festschrift für Univ.-Prof. Dr. Gottfried Holzer zum 60. Geburtstag. NWV, Wien, pp 199–210

Giorgi V (2018a) Art. 2516. In: Cian G (ed) Commentario breve al Codice civile: Commentato con dottrina e giurisprudenza, 13th edn. Wolters Kluver, Milano, Padova, pp 3207–3208

Giorgi V (2018b) Art. 2527. In: Cian G (ed) Commentario breve al Codice civile: Commentato con dottrina e giurisprudenza, 13th edn. Wolters Kluver, Milano, Padova, pp 3220–3222

Gios G, Santuari A (2002) Agricultural cooperatives in the County of Trento (Italy): economic, organizational and legal perspectives. J Rural Coop 30:3–12. https://doi.org/10.22004/ag.econ.60951

Giuffrida G (1981) Le cooperative agricole. Giuffré, Milano

Goldoni M (2019) L'art. 2135 del codice civile e le esigenze di un ripensamento sul piano sistematico della "specialità" dell'impresa agricola. Rivista di diritto agrario:353–400

Götz V (2012) Das Recht der Gemeinsamen Agrarpolitik - Kontinuität, Wandel, Systematik. In: Martinez J (ed) Die Gemeinsame Agrarpolitik vor neuen Herausforderungen: 50 Jahre Institut für Landwirtschaftsrecht, 1st edn. Nomos Verlagsgesellschaft mbH & Co. KG, Baden-Baden, pp 11–18

Greda C (2014) Statut der Europäischen Genossenschaft. In: Dellinger M (ed) Genossenschaftsgesetz samt Nebengesetzen: Kommentar, 2nd edn. LexisNexis ARD Orac, Wien, pp 829–854
Grosskopf W (1990) Genossenschaftliche Identität bei sich ändernden Rahmenbedinungen. In: Laurinkari J (ed) Genossenschaftswesen: Hand- und Lehrbuch. Oldenbourg, München, pp 102–112
Grosso P (2011) Art. 2528. In: Bonfante G, Corapi D, de Angelis L, Napoleoni V, Rordorf R, Salafia V (eds) Codice commentato delle società: Società di persone, società di capitali, cooperative, consorzi, reati societari: aggiornato con le nuove norme in tema di revisione legale, esercizio dei diritti degli azionisti di società quotate e costituzione delle Spa, 3rd edn. IPSOA, Assago, pp 2146–2153
Hanisch M (2006) Eine Theorie genossenschaftlichen Wandels. In: Münkner H-H (ed) Zukunftsperspektiven für Genossenschaften: Bausteine für typgerechte Weiterentwicklung: [Beiträge zum Kolloquium "Elemente von Strategiekonzepten der Zukunftssicherung genossenschaftlicher Kooperation", Marburg 2005], 1st edn. Haupt, Bern, Stuttgart, Wien, pp 297–323
Hansmann H (1988) Ownership of the firm. J Law Econ Organ 4:267–304
Hansmann H (1996) The ownership of enterprise, 1st edn. Belknap Press of Harvard University Press, Cambridge
Hansmann H (1999) Cooperative firms in theory and practice. Liiketaloudellinen aikakauskirja LTA - Finn J Bus Econ:387–403
Hansmann H (2011) Firm ownership: the legacy of Grossman and Hart. SSRN Electron J. https://doi.org/10.2139/ssrn.2635719
Hansmann H (2014) All firms are cooperatives – and so are governments. J Entrep Organ Divers 2:1–10. https://doi.org/10.5947/jeod.2013.007
Hansmann H, Kraakman RH, Squire RC (2006) Law and the rise of the firm. Harv Law Rev 119:1333–1403
Hardin G (1968) The tragedy of the commons. Science 162:1243–1248. https://doi.org/10.1126/science.162.3859.1243
Henrÿ H (2012) Guidelines for cooperative legislation, 3rd edn. International Labour Organization, Geneva
Hernandez-Espallardo M, Arcas-Lario N, Marcos-Matas G (2013) Farmers' satisfaction and intention to continue membership in agricultural marketing co-operatives: neoclassical versus transaction cost considerations. Eur Rev Agric Econ 40:239–260. https://doi.org/10.1093/erae/jbs024
Hetherington JAC (1991) Mutual and cooperative enterprises: an analysis of customer-owned firms in the United States. University Press of Virginia, Charlottesville
Hiez D (2017) Introduction. In: Fajardo-García IG, Fici A, Henrÿ H, Hiez D, Meira DMMA, Münkner H-H, Snaith I (eds) Principles of European Cooperative Law: principles, commentaries and national reports. Intersentia, Cambridge, pp 1–15
Hirte H (2002) Die Europäische Aktiengesellschaft. Neue Zeitschrift für Gesellschaftsrecht:1–9
Hirte H (2007) Das neue Genossenschaftsrecht (Teil II). DStR:2215–2219
Holmstrom B (1999) The future of cooperatives: a corporate perspective. Liiketaloudellinen aikakauskirja LTA - Finn J Bus Econ:404–417
Holthaus J, Lehnhoff DJ (2016) § 18. In: Lehnhoff DJ, Holthaus J (eds) Lang/Weidmüller Genossenschaftsgesetz: Gesetz, betreffend die Erwerbs- und Wirtschaftsgenossenschaften mit Erläuterungen zum Umwandlungsgesetz und zur Europäischen Genossenschaft (SCE), 38., neu bearbeitete Auflage. De Gruyter, Berlin, pp 222–243
Holzer G (2010) Nebengewerbe der Land- und Forstwirtschaft im Lichte der Rechtssprechung des Verwaltungsgerichtshofes. In: Norer R, Holzer G (eds) Agrarrecht: Jahrbuch 2010. Neuer Wissenschaftlicher Verlag, Wien, pp 171–184
Holzer G (2012a) Gewerberecht. In: Norer R (ed) Handbuch des Agrarrechts, 2. Aufl. Verlag Österreich, Wien, pp 759–784

Holzer G (2012b) Grundverkehrsrecht. In: Norer R (ed) Handbuch des Agrarrechts, 2. Aufl. Verlag Österreich, Wien, pp 673–702

Holzer G (2017a) Bäuerliche Direktvermarktung, 2nd edn. Praxis. NWV, Wien, Graz

Holzer G (2017b) Gewerberecht. In: Holzer G (ed) Bäuerliche Direktvermarktung, 2nd edn. NWV, Wien, Graz, pp 21–54

Holzer G (2018) Agrarrecht, 4th edn. Studium & Praxis. NWV Verlag, Wien, Graz

Hoyt A (2004) Consumer ownership in capitalist economies: applications of theory of consumer cooperation. In: Merrett CD, Walzer N (eds) Cooperatives and local development: theory and applications for the 21st century. Sharpe, Armonk, pp 265–289

Hueck A (1947) Der Treuegedanke im modernen Privatrecht. Verlag der Bayerischen Akademie der Wissenschaften, München

Iannarelli A (2001) Il diritto dell'agricoltura nell'era della globalizzazione. Cacucci, Bari

Iannarelli A (2007) Pluralismo definitorio dell'attività e dell'impresa agricola tra diritto comunitario e diritto interno. Studi sull'integrazione europea:469–495

Iannarelli A (2008a) Cooperazione e conflitto nel sistema agro-alimentare. Rivista di diritto agrario:328–382

Iannarelli A (2008b) I contratti dall'impresa agricola all'industria di trasformazione: Problemi e prospettive dell'esperienza italiana. Rivista di diritto alimentare II:5–13

Iannarelli A (2009) La concorrenza e l'agrarietà nell'attuale esperienza europea: una relazione "speciale". Rivista di diritto agrario:515–566

van Diepenbeek WJJ (2007) Cooperatives as a business organization: lessons from cooperative organization history. Universiteit Maastricht, Maastricht

Iannarelli A (2011) Contractual relationships and inter-firm co-operation in the agri-food sector. Rivista di diritto alimentare:4–10

Iannarelli A (2019) La parabola della "specialità" dell'impresa agricola dopo il d.lgs. sulle crisi di impresa: considerazioni critiche. Rivista di diritto agrario:197–238

Iengo M (2006) Gli Studi del CNN - Società cooperativa europea - Analisi delle norme applicabili ai sensi dell'articolo 8 del regolamento n. 1435/2003 - Casi e materiali di diritto comunitario di interesse notarile: le società - e.library - Fondazione Italiana del Notariato. Studio n. 9-2006/I. http://elibrary.fondazionenotariato.it/approfondimento.asp?app=21/studiCNN/mi_9_2006_I&mn=3&tipo=3&qn=6. Accessed 21 Nov 2019

Iliopoulos C (2013) Public support for agricultural cooperatives: an organizational economics approach. Ann Public Coop Econ 84:241–252. https://doi.org/10.1111/apce.12012

Iliopoulos C (2014) Ownership, governance and related trade-offs in agricultural cooperatives. Dovenschmidt Q 2:159–167. https://doi.org/10.5553/DQ/221199812014002004004

Iliopoulos C (2015) Ownership and governance in agricultural cooperatives: an update. https://www.researchgate.net/publication/274064574_Ownership_and_Governance_in_Agricultural_Cooperatives_An_Update. Accessed 29 Nov 2019

Iliopoulos C, Cook ML (2013) Property rights constraints in producer-owned firms: solutions as prerequisites for successful collective entrepreneurship

Iliopoulos C, Cook ML (1999) The internal organization of the cooperative firm: an extension of a new institutional digest? J Coop:77–85

Iliopoulos C, Hendrikse G (2009) Influence costs in agribusiness cooperatives. Int Stud Manage Organ 39:60–80. https://doi.org/10.2753/IMO0020-8825390404

Iliopoulos C, Valentinov V (2018) Member heterogeneity in agricultural cooperatives: a systems-theoretic perspective. Sustainability 10:1271. https://doi.org/10.3390/su10041271

Ingrosso M (2013) Le cooperative e le nuove agevolazioni fiscali: Profili civilistici, contabili, comunitari, 2nd edn. Giappichelli, Torino

Jensen MC, Meckling WH (1979) Rights and production functions: an application to labor-managed firms and codetermination. J Bus 52:469–506. https://doi.org/10.1086/296060

Johnston JS (1992) Opting in and opting out: bargaining for fiduciary duties in cooperative ventures. Wash Univ Law Q:291–340

Kastner W (1986) Österreichisches Genossenschaftsrecht. In: Patera M (ed) Handbuch des österreichischen Genossenschaftswesens. Orac, Wien, pp 117–232

Kastner W, Doralt P, Nowotny C (1990) Grundriss des österreichischen Gesellschaftsrechts, 5th edn. Manzsche Kurzlehrbuch-Reihe, vol 2. Manz, Wien

Keinert H (1988) Österreichisches Genossenschaftsrecht: Lehr- und Handbuch. Manz, Wien

Kershaw D (2012) Company law in context: text and materials, 2nd edn. Oxford University Press, Oxford

Kober R (2008) Investierende Mitglieder: einfallende Heuschrecken oder Chance für die Genossenschaft. In: Brazda J, Kühl R, Rößl R (eds) Beiträge zur genossenschaftswissenschaftlichen Forschung: Proceedings der XIII. Nachwuchswissenschaftler-Tagung der Arbeitsgemeinschaft genossenschaftswissenschaftlicher Institute (AGI) e. V., 18./19. März 2008 in Wien, Wien, pp 43–62

Korte O (2012) Die Europäische Genossenschaft (SCE): Analyse der mangelnden Verbreitung dieser supranationalen Rechtsform. In: Baudenbacher C (ed) Aktuelle Entwicklungen des europäischen und internationalen Wirtschaftsrechts. Helbing et Lichtenhahn, Basel, München [u.a.], pp 323–349

Kräkel M (2012) Organisation und Management, 5th edn. Neue ökonomische Grundrisse. Mohr Siebeck, Tübingen

Kramer JW (2006) Was kennzeichnet eine "erfolgreiche" Genossenschaft. In: Münkner H-H (ed) Zukunftsperspektiven für Genossenschaften: Bausteine für typgerechte Weiterentwicklung: [Beiträge zum Kolloquium "Elemente von Strategiekonzepten der Zukunftssicherung genossenschaftlicher Kooperation", Marburg 2005], 1st edn. Haupt, Bern, Stuttgart, Wien, pp 126–151

Krimphove D (2010) Brauchen wir die Europäische Genossenschaft? EuZW:892–897

Kühl R (2012) Country report: Austria. In: Van der Sangen G, Pyykkönen POP, Iliopoulus C, Kühl R, Hagedorn K, Hanisch M, Judis R, Gijselinckx C, Hendrikse G, Hak T, Poppe K, Bijman J (eds) Support for farmers' cooperatives, Wageningen, pp 1–51

Kyriakopoulos K (2000) The market orientation of cooperative organizations: learning strategies and structures for integrating cooperative firm and members. Van Gorcum, Assen

Lamandini M (2007) Art. 2526. In: Presti G (ed) Società cooperative: Artt. 2511-2548. EGEA; Giuffrè, Milano, pp 203–225

Lamanna Di Salvo D (2003) La gestione aziendale nelle rilevazioni in partita doppia. WIP, Bari

Laurinkari J (1990) Entwicklungstypen. In: Laurinkari J (ed) Genossenschaftswesen: Hand- und Lehrbuch. Oldenbourg, München, pp 403–412

Lehmann M (2014) Cooperatives as governance mechanisms. Eur Comp Financ Law Rev 11:31–52. https://doi.org/10.1515/ecfr-2014-0031

Lehner JH (2007) Die Europäische Genossenschaft mit Sitzstaat Österreich. Wien, Univ., Diss., 2008

Lehner JH (2009) Verschmelzungsvarianten einer Europäischen Genossenschaft (SCE). In: Haslinger M, Kanonier A, Zehetner S (eds) Ein Jurist im Spannungsfeld von Wirtschaft, Technik und Recht: Festschrift für Franz Zehetner zum 60. Geburtstag. NWV, Wien, pp 97–110

Leyens PC (2003) Deutscher Aufsichtsrat und U.S.-Board: ein- oder zweistufiges Verwaltungssystem?: Zum Stand der rechtsvergleichenden Corporate Governance-Debatte. Rabels Zeitschrift fuer auslaendisches und internationales Privatrecht:57–105

Lolli R (2012) I mezzi propri delle cooperative e i bilanci. In: Paolucci LF (ed) Le società cooperative. UTET giuridica, Torino, pp 147–179

Lombardo S, Pasotti P (2004) The Societas Europaea: a network economics approach. Eur Comp Financ Law Rev 1:169–205. https://doi.org/10.1515/ecfr.2004.1.2.169

Lutter M (2015) Art. 1. In: Lutter M, Hommelhoff P, Teichmann C (eds) SE-Kommentar, 2nd edn. Verlag Dr. Otto Schmidt, Köln, pp 78–89

Lutter M, Schmidt J, Bayer W (2012) Europäisches Unternehmens- und Kapitalmarktrecht: Grundlagen, Stand und Entwicklung nebst Texten und Materialien, 5th edn. Zeitschrift für Unternehmens- und Gesellschaftsrecht. Sonderheft, T. 1. De Gruyter, Berlin

MacNeil IR (1974) The many futures of contracts. South Calif Law Rev:691–816

Magno P (2006) Sul diritto agrario "modernizzato". Rivista di diritto agrario:76–115

Manservisi S (2014) Il principio dello sviluppo sostenibile: da Rio+20 al diritto dell'Unione europea e il suo fondamentale ruolo nel diritto agrario. In: Sgarbanti G, Borghi P, Germanò A (eds) Il divenire del diritto agrario italiano ed europeo tra sviluppi tecnologici e sostenibilità: Convegno organizzato in onore del Prof. Ettore Casadei, in occasione del suo 70° compleanno: atti del Convegno IDAIC, Bologna-Rovigo, 25-26 ottobre 2012. Giuffrè, Milano, pp 175–224

Marano P (2014) Artt. 2512-2514 c.c., 2545 octies c.c. In: Santosuosso DU (ed) Delle società, dell'azienda, della concorrenza. UTET, Torino, pp 66–93

Marasà G (1984) Le società senza scopo di lucro. Giuffré, Milano

Marasà G (1992) La disciplina della legge n 59 del 1992. Rivista di Diritto Civile:365

Marasà G (ed) (2004) Le cooperative prima e dopo la riforma del diritto societario. Cedam, Padova

Marasà G (2012) Lucro, mutualità e solidarietà nelle imprese. (Riflessioni sul pensiero di Giorgio Oppo). Giurisprudenza Commerciale:197–219

Marasà G (2013) L'odierno significato della mutualità prevalente nelle cooperative. Giurisprudenza Commerciale:847–862

Martinez J (2016a) 40. In: Calliess C, Ruffert M (eds) EUV/AEUV: Das Verfassungsrecht der Europäischen Union mit Europäischer Grundrechtecharta: Kommentar, 5. Auflage. C.H. Beck, München, pp 774–806

Martinez J (2016b) 42. In: Calliess C, Ruffert M (eds) EUV/AEUV: Das Verfassungsrecht der Europäischen Union mit Europäischer Grundrechtecharta: Kommentar, 5. Auflage. C.H. Beck, München, pp 807–814

Martinez J (2016c) Art. 38. In: Calliess C, Ruffert M (eds) EUV/AEUV: Das Verfassungsrecht der Europäischen Union mit Europäischer Grundrechtecharta: Kommentar, 5. Auflage. C.H. Beck, München, pp 756–768

Martinez J (2016d) Art. 39. In: Calliess C, Ruffert M (eds) EUV/AEUV: Das Verfassungsrecht der Europäischen Union mit Europäischer Grundrechtecharta: Kommentar, 5. Auflage. C.H. Beck, München, pp 768–774

Massauer E (1978) Die Land- und Forstwirtschaft in der GewO einschließlich der Erwerbs- und Wirtschaftsgenossenschaften. In: Rill H-P (ed) Gewerberecht: Beiträge zu Grundfragen der GewO 1973. Orac, Wien, p 27

Mattei U (1987) Tutela inibitoria e tutela risarcitoria: Contributo alla teoria dei diritti sui beni. Studi di diritto privato, vol 54. Giuffrè, Milano

Mazzoli M, Rocchi E (1996) La finanza delle cooperative: Profili economici e giuridici. Liocorno, Roma

Mazzoni A (2007) La porta aperta delle cooperative tra premesse ideologiche e nuovo diritto positivo. In: Abbadessa P, Portale GB (eds) Scioglimento, trasformazione, fusione, scissione, società cooperative. UTET, Torino, pp 763–804

McMahon JA (2007) EU agricultural law. Oxford University Press, Oxford

Ménard C (2007) Cooperatives: hierarchies or hybrids? In: Karantininis K, Nilsson J (eds) Vertical markets and cooperative hierarchies: the role of cooperatives in the agri-food industry. Springer, Dordrecht, pp 1–18

Merkt H (1992) Europäische Aktiengesellschaft: Gesetzgebung als Selbstzweck? BB:652

Milgrom PR, Roberts J (1992) Economics, organization and management. Prentice Hall, Englewood Cliffs

Minguez-Vera A, Martín-Ugedo JF, Arcas-Lario N (2010) Agency and property rights theories in agricultural cooperatives: evidence from Spain. Span J Agric Res 8:908–924. https://doi.org/10.5424/sjar/2010084-1384

Ministry for economic development (2006)e Communication no 9203, 30 June 2006, GU no 171 25.07.2006.

Miribung G (2014) Über das genossenschaftliche Eigentum in der italienischen Rechtsordnung. In: Laurinkari J (ed) Genossenschaftswissenschaft zwischen Theorie und Geschichte: Festschrift für Prof. Dr. Johann Brazda zum 60. Geburstag. EHV Academicpress, Bremen, pp 779–791
Miribung G, Reiner E (2013) Austria. In: Cracogna D, Fici A, Henrÿ H (eds) International handbook of cooperative law. Springer, Berlin, Heidelberg, pp 231–250
Molk P (2014) The puzzling lack of cooperatives. Tulane Law Rev:889–958
Moll DK (2001–2002) Shareholder oppression and reasonable expectations: of change, gifts, and inheritances in close corporation disputes. Minn Law Rev:717–790
Münkner H-H (2006) Europäische Genossenschaft (SCE) und Europäische Genossenschaftstradition. Vorträge und Aufsätze des Forschungsvereins für Genossenschaftswesen, vol 30. Eigenverlag des FOG, Wien
Münkner H-H (2014) Ten lectures on co-operative law, 1st edn. LIT, Zürich
Münkner H-H (2015) Co-operative principles and co-operative law, 2nd edn. Lit Verlag GmbH, Zürich
Nilsson J (1999) Co-operative organisational models as reflections of the business environments. Liiketaloudellinen aikakauskirja LTA - Finn J Bus Econ:449–470
Nilsson J (2001) Organisational principles for co-operative firms. Scand J Manage 17:329–356. https://doi.org/10.1016/S0956-5221(01)00010-0
Nilsson J, Madsen O (2007) Issues in cross-border mergers between agricultural co-operatives. J Coop Stud 40:27–38
Nilsson J, Svendsen GLH, Svendsen GT (2012) Are large and complex agricultural cooperatives losing their social capital? Agribusiness 28:187–204. https://doi.org/10.1002/agr.21285
Norer R (2005) Lebendiges Agrarrecht: Entwicklungslinien und Perspektiven des Rechts im ländlichen Raum. Springer, Wien
Norer R (2017a) 40 AEUV. In: Pechstein M, Nowak C, Häde U (eds) Frankfurter Kommentar zu EUV, GRC und AEUV. Mohr Siebeck, Tübingen, pp 661–690
Norer R (2017b) Art. 38 AEUV. In: Pechstein M, Nowak C, Häde U (eds) Frankfurter Kommentar zu EUV, GRC und AEUV. Mohr Siebeck, Tübingen, pp 633–650
Norer R (2017c) Art. 39 AEUV. In: Pechstein M, Nowak C, Häde U (eds) Frankfurter Kommentar zu EUV, GRC und AEUV. Mohr Siebeck, Tübingen, pp 651–660
Nowotny C (2008) Genossenschaft. In: Kalss S, Nowotny C, Schauer M, Kastner W, Doralt P (eds) Österreichisches Gesellschaftsrecht: Systematische Darstellung sämtlicher Rechtsformen: in Fortführung des von Walther Kastner begründeten und in der letzten Auflage von Walther Kastner, Peter Doralt und Christian Nowotny bearbeiteten Lehr- und Handbuchs "Grundriss des österreichischen Gesellschaftsrechts". Manz, Wien, 5/1–5/182
Oechsler J, Mihaylova L (2014) Art. 3. In: Goette W, Habersack M, Kalss S (eds) Münchener Kommentar zum Aktiengesetz, 4th edn. C.H. Beck; Verlag Franz Vahlen, München, pp 49–54
O'Kelley CRT (1992) Filling the gaps in the close corporation contract: a transaction cost analysis. Northwest Univ Law Rev:216–253. https://doi.org/10.2139/ssrn.1548652
Olesen HB (2007) The horizon problem reconsidered. In: Karantininis K, Nilsson J (eds) Vertical markets and cooperative hierarchies: the role of cooperatives in the agri-food industry. Springer, Dordrecht, pp 245–253
Oppo G (ed) (1992) Scritti giuridici: Diritto delle società. Cedam, Padova
Organisation for Economic Co-operation and Development (2001) Multifunctionality: towards an analytical framework. OECD, Paris
Ortmann GF, King RP (2007) Agricultural cooperatives I: history, theory and problems. Agrekon 46:40–68. https://doi.org/10.1080/03031853.2007.9523760
Ostrom E (2007) Governing the commons: the evolution of institutions for collective action, 20th edn. Political economy of institutions and decisions. Cambridge University Press, Cambridge
Paolucci LF (2012a) I soci. In: Paolucci LF (ed) Le società cooperative. UTET giuridica, Torino, pp 95–124

Paolucci LF (2019a) Art. 2511. In: Paolucci LF (ed) Codice delle cooperative 2019: Aggiornato con le novità del D.Lgs. n. 14/2019. Maggioli, Santarcangelo di Romagna, Rimini, pp 29–40

Paolucci LF (2019b) Art. 2516. In: Paolucci LF (ed) Codice delle cooperative 2019: Aggiornato con le novità del D.Lgs. n. 14/2019. Maggioli, Santarcangelo di Romagna, Rimini, pp 51–54

Paolucci LF (2019c) Art. 2518. In: Paolucci LF (ed) Codice delle cooperative 2019: Aggiornato con le novità del D.Lgs. n. 14/2019. Maggioli, Santarcangelo di Romagna, Rimini, pp 55–57

Paolucci LF (2019d) Art. 2521. In: Paolucci LF (ed) Codice delle cooperative 2019: Aggiornato con le novità del D.Lgs. n. 14/2019. Maggioli, Santarcangelo di Romagna, Rimini, pp 65–75

Paolucci LF (2019e) Art. 2525. In: Paolucci LF (ed) Codice delle cooperative 2019: Aggiornato con le novità del D.Lgs. n. 14/2019. Maggioli, Santarcangelo di Romagna, Rimini, pp 81–84

Paolucci LF (2019f) Art. 2526. In: Paolucci LF (ed) Codice delle cooperative 2019: Aggiornato con le novità del D.Lgs. n. 14/2019. Maggioli, Santarcangelo di Romagna, Rimini, pp 85–87

Paolucci LF (2019g) Art. 2527. In: Paolucci LF (ed) Codice delle cooperative 2019: Aggiornato con le novità del D.Lgs. n. 14/2019. Maggioli, Santarcangelo di Romagna, Rimini, pp 88–89

Paolucci LF (2019h) Art. 2528. In: Paolucci LF (ed) Codice delle cooperative 2019: Aggiornato con le novità del D.Lgs. n. 14/2019. Maggioli, Santarcangelo di Romagna, Rimini, pp 90–94

Paolucci LF (2019i) Art. 2545-quaterdecies. In: Paolucci LF (ed) Codice delle cooperative 2019: Aggiornato con le novità del D.Lgs. n. 14/2019. Maggioli, Santarcangelo di Romagna, Rimini, pp 164–165

Paolucci LF (2019j) Art. 2545-sexiesdecies. In: Paolucci LF (ed) Codice delle cooperative 2019: Aggiornato con le novità del D.Lgs. n. 14/2019. Maggioli, Santarcangelo di Romagna, Rimini, pp 173–177

Paolucci LF (2019k) Art. 45 Cost. In: Paolucci LF (ed) Codice delle cooperative 2019: Aggiornato con le novità del D.Lgs. n. 14/2019. Maggioli, Santarcangelo di Romagna, Rimini, pp 13–25

Paolucci LF (2019l) Artt. 2512-2514. In: Paolucci LF (ed) Codice delle cooperative 2019: Aggiornato con le novità del D.Lgs. n. 14/2019. Maggioli, Santarcangelo di Romagna, Rimini, pp 41–49

Paolucci LF (2012b) Definizione e aspetti caratterizzanti. In: Paolucci LF (ed) Le società cooperative. UTET giuridica, Torino, pp 1–23

Pedri S (2017) Social-cooperatives in Italy. In: Michie J, Blasi JR, Borzaga C (eds) The Oxford handbook of mutual, co-operative, and co-owned business, 1st edn. Oxford University Press, Oxford, pp 308–320

Pérotin V (2013) Worker cooperatives: good, sustainable jobs in the community. J Entrep Organ Divers 2. https://doi.org/10.5947/jeod.2013.009

Petrelli L (2007) Studio sull'impresa agricola. Pubblicazioni dell'Istituto di diritto agrario internazionale e comparato di Firenze. Nuova serie, vol 53. Giuffrè, Milano

Piras A (2017) Le società cooperative. In: de Angelis L, Bertacchini E (eds) Diritto commerciale II. Wolters Kluwer; Cedam, Milano, Padova, pp 107–132

Pönkä V (2018) The legal nature of cooperative membership. JEOD 7:39–61. https://doi.org/10.5947/jeod.2018.009

Potter C (2015) Agricultural multifunctionality, working lands and public goods: contested models of agri-environmental governance under the Common Agricultural Policy. In: McMahon J, Cardwell MN (eds) Research handbook on EU agriculture law. Edward Elgar Publishing Limited, Cheltenham, pp 113–124

Pramer L, Pfaffenzeller W (1976) Die Genossenschaft in Recht und Steuer. Hollinek, Wien

Preite D (1988) La destinazione dei risultati nei contratti associativi. Studi di diritto privato, vol 55. Giuffrè, Milano

Racugno G (2006) La società cooperativa europea. Rivista del diritto commerciale:315–321

Racugno G (2014) Art. 2525. In: Santosuosso DU (ed) Delle società, dell'azienda, della concorrenza. UTET, Torino, pp 190–207

Ragazzini G (1992) Mutualità interna ed esterna nella riforma cooperativa. Contratto e impresa:833–880

Rauseo N (2018) L'equiparazione dell'imprenditore agricolo professionale al coltivatore diretto. Diritto e giurisprudenza agraria, alimentare e dell'ambiente 27:1–4

Rebelo J, Caldas J (2015) The economic role of the Portuguese agricultural cooperatives. Revista de Economia e Sociologia Rural 53:91–102. https://doi.org/10.1590/1234-56781806-94790053s01007

Rescigno M (2007) Strumenti finanziari emessi da società cooperative. In: Abbadessa P, Portale GB (eds) Scioglimento, trasformazione, fusione, scissione, società cooperative. UTET, Torino, pp 923–946

Ribstein LE, Kobayashi BH (1999) Choice of form and network externalities. William Mary Law Rev:79–140. https://doi.org/10.2139/ssrn.163832

Ringle G (2007) Genossenschaftliche Prinzipien im Spannungsfeld zwischen Tradition und Modernität. Wismarer Diskussionspapiere. Hochsch. Fachbereich Wirtschaft, Wismar

Rocchi E (2006) La struttura finanziaria della SCE. In: Galletti D, Fici A (eds) La società cooperativa europea: Quali prospettive per la cooperazione italiana? Universita degli Studi di Trento, Trento, pp 87–114

Rocchi E (2007) Artt. 2512 - 2514; 2545 octies. In: Presti G (ed) Società cooperative: Artt. 2511-2548. EGEA; Giuffrè, Milano, pp 27–73

Roe MJ (2004) Some differences in corporate structure in Germany, Japan, and the United States. In: Geest GD, van den Bergh R (eds) Comparative law and economics, vol III. Elgar, Cheltenham, pp 3–79

Rondinone N (2017) L'imprenditore, l'impresa e la concorrenza. In: de Angelis L, Bertacchini E (eds) Diritto commerciale I. Wolters Kluwer; Cedam, Milano, Padova, pp 1–45

Rook Basile E (1981) La coltivazione dei terreni in società nell'esperienza giuridica italiana e francese. Giuffré, Milano

Rook Basile E (1995) Introduzione al diritto agrario. Trittico giuridico. Sezione introduzioni / Collana coordinata da U. De Siervo, G. Iudica, F. Palazzo. Giappichelli, Torino

Rook Basile E (2017) Sicuezza e responsabilità nella filiera alimentare. Contratto e impresa:432–450

Rossi R (1979) La cooperativa di conduzione agraria. Jovene, Napoli

Royer J (1999) Cooperative organizational strategies: a neo-institutional digest. J Coop:44–67

Royer JS (1992) Cooperative principles and equity financing: a critical discussion. J Agric Coop 7

Saija R (2013) Standards e contratti di certificazione. Rivista di diritto alimentare:47–55

Salaris F (2002) Autonomia e globalità dell'azienda agraria. Rivista di diritto agrario:54–75

Santagata R (2017) Le società cooperative. In: Cian M (ed) Diritto commerciale: III. Diritto delle società. G. Giappichelli, Torino, pp 807–843

Santoro V (2014) Amministratori di cooperative e interessi dei soci. Odcc:15–30. https://doi.org/10.4478/77170

Schäfer H-B, Ott C (2012) Grundstrukturen und -probleme des Unternehmensrechts. In: Schäfer H-B, Ott C (eds) Lehrbuch der ökonomischen Analyse des Zivilrechts. Springer, Berlin, pp 697–729

Schaschko M (2010) Neugründungen von Genossenschaften in Österreich. Wiener Studien des Forschungsvereins für Genossenschaftswesen, vol 18. Eigenverlag des FOG, Wien

Schirò S (2008a) Art. 2516. In: Ceccherini A, Schirò S (eds) Società cooperative e mutue assicuratrici: (artt. 2511-2548 c.c.), 2nd edn. Giuffré, Milano, pp 37–44

Schirò S (2008b) Art. 2527. In: Ceccherini A, Schirò S (eds) Società cooperative e mutue assicuratrici: (artt. 2511-2548 c.c.), 2nd edn. Giuffré, Milano, pp 93–102

Schöpflin M (2018a) Art. 01. In: Beuthien V, Schöpflin M (eds) Genossenschaftsgesetz: Mit Umwandlungs- und Kartellrecht sowie Statut der Europäischen Genossenschaft, 16th edn. Beck, München, pp 1240–1243

Schöpflin M (2018b) Art. 02. In: Beuthien V, Schöpflin M (eds) Genossenschaftsgesetz: Mit Umwandlungs- und Kartellrecht sowie Statut der Europäischen Genossenschaft, 16th edn. Beck, München, pp 1243–1246

Schöpflin M (2018c) Art. 04. In: Beuthien V, Schöpflin M (eds) Genossenschaftsgesetz: Mit Umwandlungs- und Kartellrecht sowie Statut der Europäischen Genossenschaft, 16th edn. Beck, München, pp 1247–1252

Schöpflin M (2018d) Art. 08. In: Beuthien V, Schöpflin M (eds) Genossenschaftsgesetz: Mit Umwandlungs- und Kartellrecht sowie Statut der Europäischen Genossenschaft, 16th edn. Beck, München, pp 1259–1263

Schöpflin M (2018e) Art. 14. In: Beuthien V, Schöpflin M (eds) Genossenschaftsgesetz: Mit Umwandlungs- und Kartellrecht sowie Statut der Europäischen Genossenschaft, 16th edn. Beck, München, pp 1268–1272

Schröder A (2010) Art. 9. In: Manz G, Mayer B, Schröder A (eds) Europäische Aktiengesellschaft SE: SE, 2nd edn. Nomos, Baden-Baden, pp 179–204

Schroeder TC (1992) Economies of scale and scope for agricultural supply and marketing cooperatives. Rev Agric Econ 14:93–103. https://doi.org/10.2307/1349610

Schulze R (2004) Einführung: Die Verordnung über das Statut der Europäischen Genossenschaft. In: Schulze R (ed) Europäische Genossenschaft SCE: Handbuch, 1st edn. Nomos, Baden-Baden, pp 1–18

Schwartz A (1992) Relational contracts in the courts: an analysis of incomplete agreements and judicial strategies. J Leg Stud 21:271–318

Sciaudone A (2005) L'impresa agricola: Profili di qualificazione. Pubblicazioni della Scuola di ateneo per l'alta formazione europea Jean Monnet della Seconda universita degli studi di Napoli. Quaderni, vol 0010. Edizioni scientifiche italiane, Napoli

Sciaudone A (2016) L'azienda agricola tra esigenze della proprietà e sviluppo dell'impresa: Il potenziamento delle strutture agricole e la promozione dell'azienda tra politiche europee e dinamiche interne. Rivista di diritto agrario:402–443

Sciaudone A (2019) Il nuovo "IAP". In: Cristiani E, Di Lauro A, Sirsi E (eds) Agricoltura e Costituzione: Una Costituzione per l'agricoltura: in onore di Marco Goldoni. Pisa University Press, Pisa, pp 313–334

Scordino F (1970) La società cooperativa. Jovene, Napoli

Sepe G (2013) Il controllo del potere di mercato nella filiera agroalimentare: profili concorrenziali e ruolo dell'AGCM. Rivista di diritto alimentare:35–39

Seuster H (1990) Die Genossenschaften im ländlichen Berich: In der Marktwirtschaft. In: Laurinkari J (ed) Genossenschaftswesen: Hand- und Lehrbuch. Oldenbourg, München, pp 576–584

Sexton RJ, Iskow J (1993) The competitive role of cooperatives in market oriented economies: a policy analysis. In: Csáki C, Kislev Y (eds) Agricultural cooperatives in transition. Westview Press, Boulder, pp 55–84

Sgarbanti G (2009) Definizione di attività agricola nel diritto comunitario e obblighi di coltivare nel diritto interno. Atti del XXXVII Incontro di Studio (Ferrara). Aestimum:93–100. https://doi.org/10.13128/AESTIMUM-3244

Snaith I (2017) Cooperative governance. In: Fajardo-García IG, Fici A, Henrÿ H, Hiez D, Meira DMMA, Münkner H-H, Snaith I (eds) Principles of European Cooperative Law: principles, commentaries and national reports. Intersentia, Cambridge, pp 47–72

Søgaard V (1994) Farmers, cooperatives, new food products, 1st edn. MAPP monograph. MAPP, Århus

Svendsen SV (2007) Lock-in of farmers in agricultural cooperatives. In: Karantininis K, Nilsson J (eds) Vertical markets and cooperative hierarchies: the role of cooperatives in the agri-food industry. Springer, Dordrecht, pp 113–135

Sykuta ME, Cook ML (2001) A new institutional economics approach to contracts and cooperatives. Am J Agric Econ 83:1273–1279

Szabó G (2004) New institutional economics and agricultural co-operatives: a Hungarian case study. In: Karafolas S, Spear R, Stryjan Y (eds) Local society & global economy: the role of co-operatives: ICA international research conference; Naoussa 2002. Hellin, Athēna, pp 357–378

Szabó G (2007) "Co-operative identity": a theoretical concept for economic analyis of practical co-operation dynamics. Stud Agric Econ:5–22. https://doi.org/10.22004/ag.econ.107648

Tatarano MC (2011) La nuova impresa cooperativa, Nuova ed. de L'impresa cooperativa di Giovanni Tatarano. Trattato di diritto civile e commerciale / già diretto da Antonio Cicu, Francesco Messineo, Luigi Mengoni. Giuffrè, Milano

Ton G, Gábor S (2012) Organisational mechanisms to solve collective action challenges in vegetables marketing: case study report. In: Van der Sangen G, Pyykkönen POP, Iliopoulus C, Kühl R, Hagedorn K, Hanisch M, Judis R, Gijselinckx C, Hendrikse G, Hak T, Poppe K, Bijman J (eds) Support for farmers' cooperatives, Wageningen, pp 1–19

Tonelli E (2003) Art. 2516. In: Sandulli M, Santoro V (eds) La riforma delle società: Società cooperative Artt. 2511-2548 cod.civ. Giappichelli, Torino, pp 47–51

Torgerson RE, Reynolds BJ, Gray TW (1998) Evolution of cooperative thought, theory, and purpose. J Coop

Tortia E, Valentinov V, Iliopoulos C (2013) Agricultural cooperatives. J Entrep Organ Divers:23–36. https://doi.org/10.5947/jeod.2013.002

Valentinov V (2005) The organizational nature of agricultural cooperatives: a perspective from the farm problem theory. J Rural Coop:139–151

Van der Sangen G (2012) EU synthesis and comparative analysis report: legal aspects. In: Support for farmers' cooperatives, Wageningen, pp 1–50

van Herck K (2014) Assessing efficiencies generated by agricultural producer organisations. Publications Office, Luxembourg

Vatn A (2002) Multifunctional agriculture: some consequences for international trade regimes. Eur Rev Agric Econ 29:309–327. https://doi.org/10.1093/eurrag/29.3.309

Vecchione A (2004) L'imprenditore agricolo. Quaderni del Dipartimento di studi internazionali, Università degli studi di Salerno, Facoltà di giurisprudenza, vol 4. Edizioni scientifiche italiane, Napoli

Vecchione A (2009a) Le attività agricole principali. In: Iannarelli A, Vecchione A (eds) L' impresa agricola. Giappichelli, Torino, pp 233–274

Vecchione A (2009b) Le attività connesse. In: Iannarelli A, Vecchione A (eds) L' impresa agricola. Giappichelli, Torino, pp 275–332

Vecchione A (2009c) L'imprenditore agricolo nelle fonti speciali e figure professionali ad esso equiparate. In: Iannarelli A, Vecchione A (eds) L' impresa agricola. Giappichelli, Torino, pp 353–386

Vecchione A (2009d) L'impresa agricola nella realtà virtuale. In: Iannarelli A, Vecchione A (eds) L' impresa agricola. Giappichelli, Torino, pp 209–232

Vitaliano P (1983) Cooperative enterprise: an alternative conceptual basis for analyzing a complex institution. Am J Agric Econ 65:1078–1083. https://doi.org/10.2307/1240424

Wall N, Lines D, Martin B, Marcousé I (2010) Economics & business studies, 4th edn. A-Z handbook. Philip Allan Updates, Deddington

Welser I (2013) Efficiency - today's challenge in arbitration proceedings. In: Austrian yearbook on international arbitration. Manz, Vienna, pp 151–166

Williamson O (1973) Markets and hierarchies: some elementary considerations. Am Econ Rev 63:316–325

Williamson OE (1998) The economic institutions of capitalism: firms, markets, relational contracting. Free Press, New York

World Co-operative Monitor 2018. https://monitor.coop/en/media/library/research-and-reviews/world-cooperative-monitor-2018en. Accessed 9 Dec 2019

Youde JG, Helmberger PG (1966) Marketing cooperatives in the U.S.: membership policies, market power, and antitrust policy. J Farm Econ 48:23–36. https://doi.org/10.2307/1236316

Zahn J (1963) Handbuch für Genossenschaften, 2nd edn. Österreichischer Genossenschaftsverband

Zanotti A (2013) La governance societaria: Società per azioni e cooperative a confronto: una interpretazione economica. Rubbettino, Soveria Mannelli

Zecchin F (2017) La tutela del produttore agroalimentare fra tentativi di riequilibrio del potere contrattuale e misure di sostegno. Europa e Diritto Privato:1407–1465

Zöllner W (1963) Die Schranken mitgliedschaftlicher Stimmrechtsmacht bei den privatrechtlichen Personenverbänden. Institut fuer Wirtschaftsrecht (Koeln, Univ.):Schriften. Bd15. Beck, München

Zoppini A (2004) Il nuovo diritto delle società cooperative: un'analisi economica. Rivista di Diritto Civile:439–450

Part II
Analysing Some Specific SCE Issues Comparing Relevant Italian and Austrian Legal Rules

Chapter 4
Issues Concerning the Governance of SCEs

4.1 Introduction

The considerations set out in the previous chapters are insufficient to provide a complete picture of the SCE and its discipline. These rules are the basis for national SCEs and, thus, for an agricultural cooperative organised as an SCE. Therefore, it is necessary to examine some relevant issues, such as governance, always bearing in mind that the rules considered are valid, *mutatis mutandis*, for agricultural cooperatives with cross-border activities and, as such, for SCEs. However, in the concluding part of each (sub)chapter, specific references are made to agricultural SCEs or cooperatives because in this context, it seems helpful, **for a better understanding**, to associate the results obtained specifically with agricultural cooperatives. The same applies to the chapters in which the findings of the legal assessment are considered from an economic perspective. As already noted, from an economic perspective, agricultural cooperatives have some particularities, follow specific dynamics and, as such, are a specific object of research.

The SCE is a member-oriented enterprise in the sense that it promotes the needs of its members. In order to safeguard that members have a central role to play in the SCE, the SCE-R contains rules to ensure that cooperatives are ultimately controlled by their members.[1] This necessity does not impede, however, that specific functions and powers are distributed among a number of bodies, such as governing bodies or managers. Such aspects of governance can be linked to the values anchored in the ICA's definition. These values are both operational (personal responsibility, democracy, equality, justice and solidarity) and ethical; they represent an important aspect of decision making in cooperative institutions.[2] I reiterate the importance of the

[1] See Sect. 3.4.

[2] See Snaith (2017), p. 48.

G. Miribung, *The Agricultural Cooperative in the Framework of the European Cooperative Society*, Economic Analysis of Law in European Legal Scholarship 8,
https://doi.org/10.1007/978-3-030-44154-8_4

principle of autonomy and, in this context, the need for different governance structures. This diversity is necessary to account for the diversity of cooperatives. The requirements for the different types of cooperatives (e.g., consumer, producer, employee) are different, as are the needs of cooperatives with large or small numbers of members or of cooperatives with members from a wide or limited geographical area. The nature and scope of the cooperative's economic activity, as well as the number of employees, will also affect the governance structure—and with it, the autonomy of the concerned cooperative.[3]

These initial findings provide a basis for discussing various issues in the context of cooperative governance. They range from aspects of classic company law—such as management and supervisory issues, information rights and transparency requirements—to specific aspects that are clearly linked to the specific role that members must play in an agricultural SCE. As already mentioned, the interests of the members—which ultimately determine the possible role of the member within a cooperative—may today vary not only because there are different objectives in an agricultural SCE, but also because there are multiple meanings communicated by the term 'member', including both the classical user member and the non-user member. It is therefore not surprising that the SCE-R also has to address these issues. In this regard, one must consider its Chapt. 3, and specifically, Articles 36–63 of the SCE-R, which determine the structure of an SCE.[4] Certain rules cover the functions, composition and working methods of the general meeting and the various organs. In addition to the specific provisions for the one- and two-tier systems, Chap. 3 Sec. 3 SCE-R[5] also contains general rules applicable to both systems. These rules concern the term of office, conditions of membership,[6] power of representation and liability of the SCE,[7] operations requiring authorisation,[8] confidentiality,[9] conduct of the business organs[10] and civil liability.[11]

Even though Arts. 45–51 SCE-R contain rules common to both governance systems, certain questions arise that need to be discussed in the context of each system. Such an approach provides a better understanding of the two governance

[3]For example, consider an agricultural secondary cooperative that is responsible for selling the products on the international market, delivered by the primary cooperatives' members. See also Sect. 3.3.4.

[4]Chap. III (provisions regarding the structure of the SCE) begins by outlining specific rules and ends with general rules. The first two sections contain specific rules regarding the two- and one-tier systems, respectively, whereas the third and fourth sections contain rules to be observed by both systems.

[5]See Arts 45–51 SCE-R.

[6]See Art. 46 SCE-R.

[7]See Art. 47 SCE-R.

[8]See Art. 48 SCE-R.

[9]See Art. 49 SCE-R.

[10]See Art. 50 SCE-R.

[11]See Art. 51 SCE-R.

systems.[12] The aspect of the term of office is of little relevance for this study. For the sake of completeness, it should be noted that[13] the SCE-R determines a maximum period and the possibility of reappointment, both of which can be regulated further via statutory provisions.[14]

Art. 36 SCE-R lays down the basic structure of the governance system of each SCE. It states that an SCE must have a general meeting and provides two models for the administration of the cooperative.[15] The first, based on an Anglo-American approach, provides for a single administrative organ encompassing administrative and controlling powers (one-tier system), while the second (two-tier system) adds two additional organs to the general meeting: a management organ exercising management functions and a supervisory organ exercising controlling functions.[16]

[12]This is particularly true in this study, since its comparison of the Italian and Austrian legal systems makes these discussions even more complex.

[13]The standardised rules first refer to the term of office for members of the organs, which by law cannot exceed 6 years. The specific term of office must be laid down in the statutes (see Art. 45 SCE-R). This obligation excludes any application of national law and lets the drafters determine the specific term of office. It should also be possible to delegate the definition of the exact period to the body that elects the organ. A so-called "staggered board" seems possible. For the SE, see Egermann and Heckenthaler (2004), p. 263 et seq.; Teichmann (2015e), p. 728 et seq.; Hoffmann-Becking (2004), p. 364; Manz (2010h), p. 605 et seq.; Frodermann and Jannott (2005), p. 2251. Then, according to Art. 45 para. 2 SCE-R, members may also be re-appointed, although the statutes can restrict or even exclude re-appointment. However, the provisions clearly refer to an election mechanism, and automatic re-appointment is not permitted. For the SE, see Manz (2010h), p. 606; Teichmann (2015e), p. 730 et seq. It has been observed that re-appointment helps preserve the cooperative's knowledge, experience and self-government. See Schöpflin (2018l), p. 1309. Also consider Schulze (2004a), p. 105. The SCE-R does not contain any indication of when re-appointment occurs. Hence, it is argued that national provisions apply. For the SE, see Manz (2010h), p. 606 et seq. However, it is also argued that this can be determined by the statutes, as Art. 45 SCE-R does not contain any reference to national law, instead stipulating a framework the drafters of the statutes may complete. For the SE, see Schmidt (2006), p. 494 et seq. This interpretation seems better as Art. 45 para. 2 SCE-R not only refers to the possibility to restrict re-appointment, but in general states that the period shall be determined by statutes. This necessarily implies the moment when (re)appointment occurs and when organ membership expires. Although the SCE-R exhaustively regulates the issue of term of office, it is helpful to consider national law in particular, as the provisions contained therein may be used as examples for drafting specific statutory provisions of an SCE.

[14]Statutory freedom includes issues like when reappointment occurs or when the term of office ultimately terminates.

[15]This shows that the European legislator aimed to provide founders with far-reaching freedom to self-regulate important issues like governance structure. See Schulze (2004a), p. 91 et seq. For the SE, see Bianca and Zanardo (2016), p. 193 et seq.

Art 36 SCE-R only determines the compulsory organs and thus cannot be considered final. However, the statutes cannot grant competences to other organs, which must be assigned to these compulsory organs. As a result, these other organs mostly conduct preparatory and consulting activities. See Schöpflin (2018c), p. 1298 et seq.

[16]See Schulze (2004a), p. 91 et seq.; Greda (2014), p. 846 et seq. For the SE, see Costa and Bilreiro (2003), p. 61; Sarcina (2006), p. 741 et seq.; Teichmann (2015a), p. 459 et seq. In general, Leyens (2003).

By considering both systems, the SCE-R tries to reflect the different traditions of corporate governance within EU member states. However, at the time the SCE-R was enacted, certain member states such as Austria only offered one of the two systems. As neither approach is clearly better and both had to be considered, the European legislature allowed both systems and left the actual choice to the drafters of the statutes.[17] Both systems can be used for any kind of business activity without legal restriction. Neither the size of a cooperative nor its volume of business affect the choice of governance system. In practice, however, practical considerations might influence which one is chosen.[18]

The competence to choose the governance structure is assigned to individual SCEs and not, as a former draft[19] stipulated, to member states. This right is exercised by means of a statutory provision[20] and is therefore a mandatory part of the statutes. This implies that an SCE can change this provision, switching from one governance system to the other.[21]

For jurisdictions that had previously only provided a single governance system, this provision significantly increased the freedom of self-regulation with regards to the functioning of an SCE. In fact, the introduction of this choice at the EU level prompted national legislatures to adopt appropriate measures.[22] Yet, Art. 36 et seq. SCE-R adds limits to this freedom of self-regulation by determining what the basic structure of an SCE is, including the relation between the normative requirements and the freedom of self-regulation.[23] In addition, certain provisions grant the possibility to introduce further provisions at the national level.[24] Other provisions require the application of national provisions enacted for national cooperatives (e.g., Art. 37 para. 1 sent. 2 SCE-R).

According to Art. 37 para. 5 SCE-R and Art. 42 para. 4 SCE-R, a member state may adopt appropriate measures if the existing national legal system does not contain provisions covering either the two-tier or the one-tier systems. Interestingly, these provisions are not mandatory, according to their wording.[25] It is argued that if a national legislature does not adopt provisions to amend the existing national legal

[17]See Schulze (2004a), p. 91. Also consider Lehner (2009), p. 102. For specific details Jungmann (2006).

[18]See Lehner (2007), p. 113.

[19]Art. 30 draft SCE-R.

[20]According to Art. 36 letter b SCE-R, the statutes must contain the relevant provision.

[21]An SCE can switch between governance systems by amending the statutes. See Schöpflin (2018c), p. 1298 et seq.; Alfandari and Piot (2004), p. 91 et seq.

[22]According to Art. 37 para. 5 SCE-R and Art. 42 para. 4 SCE-R. For the SE see Thoma and Leuering (2002), p. 1451; Teichmann (2015a), p. 458 et seq.; Bungert and Beier (2002), p. 3; Hopt (2002), p. 1; Kalss (2004), p. 121.

[23]See Schulze (2004a), p. 92.

[24]Consider, e.g. Art. 37 para. 4 SCE-R, Art. 39 para. 4 SCE-R or Art. 42 para. 1 sent. 2 SCE-R. See also Sect. 2.4.

[25]According to Art. 37 para. 5 and 42 para. 4 SCE-R, member states may but are not obliged to adopt measures governing SCEs.

framework, the adoption of a governance system not explicitly regulated by national law could be based on statutory provisions.[26] Such an interpretation seems to be problematic, though, inasmuch as Art. 8 para. 1 letter b SCE-R allows the adoption of statutory provisions only where the regulation expressly grants authorisation.[27] In fact, Art. 36 letter b SCE-R only authorises the drafters of the statutes to choose between one of the two different systems, whereas the SCE-R explicitly authorises the national legislatures to adopt appropriate further measures. The provisions contained in the SCE-R that regulate the functioning of the two governance systems do not contain sufficient detail.[28] Considering these options as an authority rather than an obligation could *de facto* lead to the denial of the right of option if a member state did not adopt the measures necessary to introduce one of these governance systems. The doctrine of *effet utile* thus makes it necessary to view these options as obligations.[29]

We now consider how the Italian and Austrian legislatures have responded to this issue. As mentioned above,[30] the *Italian legislature* did not amend the existing legal system in order to implement the SCE-R, instead asserting with communication no. 9203 that their existing legal system was already in line with the SCE-R's provisions. The Italian legislature argued that the company law reform accomplished in 2003 had already introduced particular features of the SCE into the Italian legal system, especially the one- and two-tier systems.[31] Rather interestingly, according to

---

[26]For the SE, see Ferrarini (2004), p. 82; Artmann (2002), p. 191; Manz (2010a), § 38 p. 485.

[27]See Sect. 2.4.

[28]For the SE, see Teichmann (2015a), p. 468; Lind (2004), p. 20; Mahi (2004), p. 82.

[29]For the SE, see Thoma and Leuering (2002), p. 1451; Teichmann (2015a), p. 469; Bungert and Beier (2002), p. 3 fn 25; Hopt (2002), p. 1; Kalss (2004), p. 121; Drygala (2015a), p. 500. Also consider Alfandari and Piot (2004), p. 92; Lind (2004), p. 127. Different opinion Korte (2012), p. 339.

[30]See Sect. 2.5.

[31]See Ministry for economic development (2006), premessa and sezione III. Generally, Ghezzi and Malberti (2008). See also Mirone (2017a).

The reformed legislative framework now grants the possibility to choose among three different systems of administration: the traditional system, a two-tier and a one-tier system. However, most provisions have not been specifically enacted for cooperatives. Instead, due to specific references, provisions governing the spa must be applied (see Art. 2519 CC). As a default rule for national cooperatives, the traditional system applies. This is based on three bodies: the general meeting, the board of directors and the board of statutory auditors. The members of these latter two organs are appointed and removed by the general meeting. This competence, as well as the competence to approve the annual balance sheets, is one of the main functions of the general meeting. The directors are in charge of managing the cooperative. This implies that they may perform all the acts necessary to implement the cooperative's social object (see Art. 2380 bis para. 1 CC). According to Art. 2542 para. 3 CC, the majority of members of the board of directors must be members of the cooperative. This implies that the other directors can be non-members. The board of statutory auditors must verify the duties performed by directors, observance of the legal and statutory rules which govern their actions and their general good faiths. The law specifies that only registered auditors, registered professionals and law or economics professors may be appointed. At least one member must be a registered auditor. In addition, a cooperative must appoint at least one registered external auditor for

communication no. 9203, nothing impedes the application of the traditional Italian corporate governance system[32]: this is an interpretation that does not hold. As a matter of fact, national legislation can only be applied in a residual way, on the condition that either an explicit reference is contained in the SCE-R or Art. 8 para. 1 letter c SCE-R is applied.[33] In this context, it is helpful to consider Art. 36 SCE-R, which only refers to the one- and two-tier systems. Hence, there is no gap that could be filled, according to Art. 8 para. 1 letter c SCE-R. In addition, applying the traditional Italian corporate governance system clearly would not help to apply the SCE-R as uniformly as possible.[34]

The *Austrian legal system*, which traditionally employs the two-tier system, was amended by *GenRÄG* 2006 to introduce the one-tier system *ex novo*. The Austrians' ability to choose between two different governance systems can be considered a step towards increased freedom of self-regulation.[35] As a consequence, compared to Austrian national cooperatives, SCEs can be organised with greater structural flexibility and wider scope.

4.2 The Two-Tier System

The characteristic element of the two-tier system is the strict separation between the management and supervisory organs.[36] This separation has been described by scholars as the strength of this model. At least, theoretically, a clear distinction between management and supervision is the ideal basis for efficiently and independently supervising the management.[37] On the other hand, a 'distorted' flow of information between the two organs could prove to be a weakness of the model.[38]

---

the specific task of auditing the annual accounts. If the board of supervisors is entirely formed of registered auditors, this particular function can be fulfilled by the board of supervisors. Small cooperatives are not obliged to appoint a supervisory organ or external auditor.

[32]See Ministry for economic development (2006), sezione III.

[33]See Sect. 2.4.

[34]See Chirico and Troianiello (2007), p. 67. For the SE, see Bianca and Zanardo (2016), p. 195 et seq. Different opinion Arnò et al. (2007), p. 77 et seq. Also consider Presti (2006), p. 83 et seq.

[35]See Lehner (2007), p. 101; Fici (2013c), p. 147; Greda (2014), p. 846 et seq.

[36]See Lutter et al. (2012), p. 1609.

[37]The separation between management and supervisory functions should guarantee an objective supervisory function. See Schöpflin (2018d), p. 1300. Also consider Schulze (2004a), p. 91.

For the SE, see Artmann (2002), p. 195; Fleischer (2004), p. 526; Henssler (2003), p. 208; Slagter (2004), p. 37.

[38]For the SE, see Fleischer (2004), p. 526; Schiessl (2003), p. 241.

Art. 37 para. 1 SCE-R and Art. 39 para. 1 SCE-R define the functional separation between these two organs. While 'the management organ shall be responsible for managing the SCE',[39] 'the supervisory organ shall supervise the duties performed by the management organ'.[40] The separation in personnel between the two organs is defined by Art. 37 para. 3 SCE-R.[41] Accordingly, no one may simultaneously be a member of both organs.

If there is a (temporary) vacancy within the management organ, the supervisory organ can nominate one of its members to fill this vacancy.[42] This exceeds the duties and powers of the supervisory organ, resulting from the member's change in roles. The member must suspend their function within the supervisory organ. The SCE-R does not set a time limit in this respect, but allows national legislatures to impose one.[43] Neither the Austrian nor the Italian legislatures have exercised this option.[44]

---

[39]See Art. 37 para. 1 SCE-R. It states: "The management organ shall be responsible for managing the SCE and shall represent it in dealings with third parties and in legal proceedings. A Member State may provide that a managing director is responsible for the current management under the same conditions as for cooperatives that have registered offices within that Member State's territory."

[40]See Art. 39 para. 1 SCE-R.

This separation of functions requires specific legal instruments to ensure the supervisory duties are properly fulfilled. Art. 40 SCE-R determines specific rights to information granted to the supervisory organ and its members. See Schulze (2004a), p. 93. Also consider Sect. 4.2.2.1.

Art 39 para. 1 SCE-R states: "The supervisory organ shall supervise the duties performed by the management organ. It may not itself exercise the power to manage the SCE. The supervisory organ may not represent the SCE in dealings with third parties. It shall represent the SCE in dealings with the management organ, or its members, in respect of litigation or the conclusion of contracts."

[41]Art. 37 para. 3 SCE-R states: "No person may at the same time be a member of the management organ and of the supervisory organ of an SCE. The supervisory organ may, however, nominate one of its members to exercise the function of member of the management organ in the event of a vacancy. During such period, the functions of the person concerned as member of the supervisory organ shall be suspended. A Member State may impose a time limit on such a period."

[42]See Art. 37 para. 3 SCE-R.

[43]See Schulze (2004a), p. 96. For the SE, see Drygala (2015a), p. 495 et seq.; Manz (2010b), p. 500 et seq.

[44]See Fici (2010), p. 64 et seq. The approach adopted by the SCE-R here is different to that adopted by the Italian legislator. Art. 2409 novies para. 6 CC determines that if one or more members of the management organ leaves their post during the financial year, the supervisory organ must promptly provide for their replacement. This provision is different to that for the traditional Italian corporate governance system, as Art. 2386 CC allows co-optation by the administrative organ. In contrast, under the two-tier system the supervisory organ is only obliged to act promptly. The difference stems from the fact that, under the traditional system, the members of the administrative organ are appointed by the general meeting, an organ which only holds meetings periodically (in general once a year) and when called. Having to fulfil these conditions would definitely impede replacing members of the management organ. On the other hand, under the two-tier system, the members of the management organ are appointed by the supervisory organ, who can react promptly. In addition, under Italian law members of the management organ cannot be substituted by members of the supervisory organ, even temporarily. See Miotto (2018c), p. 2904.

Having briefly outlined the link between the two organs, this study now turns to analyse the two systems in detail. The main sections[45] analyse several issues grouped according to the following key aspects: functions of the organ, composition of the organ, appointment and removal of the members of the organ, internal organisation of the organ and civil liability. Finally, the results are considered from an economic perspective.

4.2.1 The Management Organ

4.2.1.1 Function 1: Managing the SCE

Art. 37 para. 1 SCE-R lays out the two functions of the management organ: (1) responsibility for managing the SCE and (2) representation in dealings with third parties and in legal proceedings. While the first function concerns management and conducting transactions, the second function, representation, concerns the extent to which the activities of the organs establish rights and duties for the SCE with respect to third parties.[46]

In principle, the members of the management organ are authorised to act jointly,[47] and as a result, must jointly manage the SCE.[48] These duties fall exclusively under the competence of the management organ, which should not, at least in principle, receive instructions from either the supervisory organ or the general meeting.[49] Yet, the ultimate extent of this competence depends on the competence of the general meeting, which can be altered by national law under Art. 52 SCE-R and through the application of Art. 48 SCE-R, which deals with operations authorised by either the supervisory organ or the general meeting.[50] Moreover, Art. 37 para. 1 sent. 2 SCE-R authorises a member state to delegate current management to a managing director under the same conditions as those for cooperatives with registered offices within that member state's territory. This faculty is limited, though, as the management organ remains responsible for the overall management of the agricultural SCE.[51]

In general, the management's duty comprises conducting business with members and third parties (non-members). In addition, the management organ may act in

The Austrian legal system provides another solution to this problem. If one or members leaves the management organ of a Austrian cooperative, a court must appoint an interim manager until the vacancy is filled. See Strommer (2014a), p. 194.

[45] Sections 4.2.1 and 4.2.2.

[46] For the SE, see Manz (2010b), p. 491 et seq.

[47] Art. 47 para. 1 sent. 1 SCE-R.

[48] See Schöpflin (2018d), p. 1300.

[49] For the SE, see Manz (2010b), pp. 492 and 495; Mayer (2010a), p. 651; Drygala (2015a), p. 478 et seq. Also consider Schöpflin (2018d), p. 1300.

[50] For the SE, see Drygala (2015a), p. 481 et seq.; Bianca and Zanardo (2016), p. 194.

[51] For the SE, see Manz (2010b), p. 492 et seq.; Drygala (2015a), p. 487.

matters related to membership, e.g., claiming membership fees or notifying members about holding a general meeting.[52] Ultimately, the specific powers assigned to the management organ strongly depend on the SCE's purpose and can vary accordingly.

The regulation does not contain further provisions that define and limit the term 'management', as contained in Art. 37 SCE-R.[53] Any additional definition of this term must occur through doctrine and jurisdiction. In principle, this term must evolve uniformly, because neither the wording nor intent of the provisions indicate that these issues have only been partly regulated, such that national law could be applied according to Art. 8 para. 1 letter c SCE-R. Even though the SCE-R (Art. 37 para. 1 sent. 2 SCE-R) considers the possibility that a managing director may be appointed to current management under the same conditions as 'national' cooperatives, it is argued that this specific provision—along with the requirements contained in Art. 47 para. 1, para. 2 subpara. 2 and para. 4 SCE-R—implies that the SCE-R regulates the management function on the community level, with only the issues specified in Art. 37 SCE-R being regulated on the national level.[54]

In any case, it is useful to discuss the meaning of management within the Italian and Austrian legal systems. It is probable that when actually determining the competence of the management organ of an SCE, national provisions and practice will be considered, at least as guidelines or first references. The following analyses also consider the possibility of delegating current management, as provided for by Art. 37 para. 1 sent. 2 SCE-R.[55]

As previously mentioned, the *Italian legal system* contains specific provisions referring to the management organ, which must be supplemented by the provisions adopted for the traditional governance system.[56] Clearly, in addition and prior to these provisions, the provisions specifically adopted for cooperatives must be observed to determine the complete nature of the tasks the management organ must fulfil. A short overview of all these competence is used to create a proper structure for determining the competence of an Italian SCE.

According to Art. 2409 novies para. 1 CC, management under the two-tier system is exclusively entrusted to the management organ, which may enter into any transactions necessary to achieve the corporate purpose.[57] Moreover, this task is linked to

---

[52]See Schulze (2004a), p. 93.

[53]The same as for Art. 42 SCE-R; for specific observations regarding the power of representation, see Sect. 4.2.1.2. Apart from these provisions, the SCE-R does not contain any further rules referring to the content and limits of the power of representation.

[54]See Schulze (2004a), p. 94. Also consider Drygala (2015a), p. 481.

[55]Art. 37 para. 1 sent. 2 SCE-R states: "A Member State may provide that a managing director is responsible for the current management under the same conditions as for cooperatives that have registered offices within that Member State's territory."

[56]Due to references, most of the provisions adopted for the traditional administrative organ must be applied to the management board. See Paolucci (2012), p. 142. See also Mirone (2017a), p. 562 et seq.

[57]See Del Sole (2010c), p. 326 et seq.; also consider Breida (2004b), p. 1129. See also Romano (2017u), p. 3003 et seq.; Mirone (2017a), p. 573.

the duty to establish organisational, administrative and accounting structures appropriate to the nature and size of the business; these structures must be appropriate also in relation to the timely detection of the business crisis and the loss of business continuity.[58]

In principle, this exclusive entitlement does not prohibit from delegating certain functions to one or more members of the management organ.[59] The management function may also be influenced via a supervisory organ, which under certain circumstances can authorise specific management tasks (or influence the decision making of the management organ). In addition, the law determines a wide range of functions the management organ must fulfil, including calling the general meeting,[60] challenging invalid resolutions made by the general meeting,[61] constituting dedicated assets,[62] drafting financial statements[63] and drafting management reports annexed to the financial statements.[64] These reports must contain detailed information about how the mutualistic purpose of the cooperative was met.[65] The issues of calling the meeting and the various reporting duties of the management organ of an SCE are discussed in later chapters.[66]

Art. 2365 para. 2 CC specifies that the management organ can be authorised to create or eliminate secondary offices, as long as the statutes provide accordingly. It may also specify which members of the management organ have the power to represent the cooperative.[67] The aim of this provision is to enhance self-regulation

---

[58]See Art. 2086 para. 2 CC. This obligation is not an end in and of itself, but is also connected to the timely detection of the company's crisis and the loss of business continuity.

[59]See Cariello (2012), p. 250. See also Mirone (2017a), p. 573.

[60]Art. 2366 para. 1 CC.

[61]Art. 2377 CC. Applicable due to Art. 53 SCE-R or Art. 8 para. 1 letter c SCE-R.

[62]Art. 2447 ter para. 2 CC. It must also keep statutory books and other account books regarding assets dedicated to specific business activities (Art. 2447 sexies CC).

[63]Art. 2423 CC. Consider in this context Art. 68 SCE-R.

[64]Art. 2428 CC.

[65]Art. 2545 CC. Other competencies include preparing a final report if the business activity to which a pool of business assets was dedicated is terminated or becomes impossible to pursue (Art. 2447 novies CC) and, if provided for by the statutes, the necessary resolutions regarding mergers as determined by Art. 2505 and Art. 2505 bis CC In this context, the specific provisions of the SCE-R must first be observed. There are also further provisions which can be considered due to Art. 2380 para. 3 CC and 223 septies prov. impl. CC. This requires that nothing else has been otherwise established and that these provisions are compatible with the two-tier system. See Del Sole (2010c), p. 328. Also consider Guaccero (2004a), p. 881; Rufini (2005), p. 1131.

[66]See Sects. 4.4.2 and 4.2.2.1.

[67]Further competencies can be assigned in matters related to mergers or transfer of the registered office within the national territory. See Art. 2365 para. 2 CC.

When specifying which members of the organ have the power to represent the cooperative, this provision only refers to those members of the organ who were appointed after the founding of the company. See Santi (2010), p. 65; Maffezzoni (2008), p. 52. Consider in this context Art. 2328 CC and Art. 2521 CC. See also Romano (2017b).

and encourage entrepreneurial dynamics.[68] These competence are regulated according to Art. 52 subpara. 2 SCE-R.[69]

Moreover, the Italian legal system allows for either strong or weak cooperation between the management and supervisory organs, thus influencing the competence of the management organ. According to Art. 2409 terdecies para. 1 letter f-bis CC, the statutes can allow the supervisory organ to decide upon the strategic transactions and industrial and financial plans drafted by the management organ. This is a specific issue also dealt with by the SCE-R, and will be discussed in detail later.[70]

Next, the Italian legal system contains specific provisions that cooperatives, in general, have to observe when delegating powers: Art. 2409 novies para. 1 CC contains rules regarding the delegation of powers. Accordingly, the management organ may delegate its functions to one or more of its members (specifically, paras. 3, 4 and 5 of Art. 2381 CC have to be observed).[71] This delegation of powers can be carried out in the absence of a specific statutory provision, as there is no reference to Art. 2381 para. 2 CC.[72] However, the management organ cannot delegate some or all of its powers to an executive committee.[73] Art. 2381 para. 4 CC lists the specific functions that cannot be delegated. Lastly, Art. 2544 CC determines a limitation concerning the management organ of a cooperative: accordingly, it cannot delegate its competence governing the admission, resignation and expulsion of members or decisions that affect the mutuality relationship with members.[74]

[68]See Santi (2010), p. 63; Santosuosso (2003), p. 104.

[69]See Sect. 4.4.1.

[70]See Cariello (2012), p. 253; Cariello (2009), p. 253 et seq. See Sect. 4.2.2.1.

[71]Art 2381 paras 3 to 5 CC deal with the delegation of powers, functions which cannot be delegated and specific duties the delegated bodies must fulfil. See Usai (2010b), p. 490 et seq. See also Romano (2017g), p. 2944 et seq.; Sanfilippo (2017a), p. 491 et seq.

[72]It states that if the statutes or the shareholders' meeting permit, the board of directors can delegate its functions to an executive committee consisting of certain of its members, or of one or more of its members.

[73]See Del Sole (2010c), p. 329; Breida (2004b), p. 1122. See also Sanfilippo (2017a), p. 492. On the other hand, it is argued that there are no grounds to prevent such a delegation, which can be governed by specific statutory provisions. See Rufini (2005), p. 1130. Some scholars have observed that there can be both executive and non-executive members within the management organ. See Del Sole (2010c), p. 329; Panzironi (2007), p. 27. Such a solution could be based on Art. 2381 para. 3 CC, which states that the content, limits and procedures for exercising the delegated powers are set by the management organ. According to this paragraph, the management organ may also give directives to the delegated bodies and advocate transactions falling within this delegation to itself. The delegated bodies must also ensure that the organisational, administrative and accounting structures are adequate to the nature and size of the company. In this context, the managing directors must report to the management organ. Consider Art. 2381 para. 5 CC.

[74]In this context, it is argued that the wording refers to the establishment, modification and termination of the transactions of mutual purpose in general. On the other hand, it is argued that only decisions relating to the modification and termination of transactions cannot be delegated. Indeed, the mutual transactions must be established for decisions to refer to them. This second interpretation seems to be the one which meets the legislator's intent. See Giorgi (2018b), p. 3243; Bonfante (2004b), p. 2596 et seq. See also Paolucci (2019g), p. 139 et seq.

All these mentioned rules define the basic framework an Italian cooperative must observe when delegating competence of the management organ. In this context, communication no. 9203 argues that the provisions mentioned in Art. 2544 CC and 2381 CC apply to an Italian SCE.[75] However, exercising the option to nominate a managing director must be done with caution. In fact, a legislative act is needed to apply the option in Art. 37 para. 1 SCE-R. Here, it is helpful to remember that communication no. 9203 has been criticised for failing to be binding.[76] It seems that an Italian SCE cannot delegate current management to a managing director.

What makes the discussion more tricky is the fact that Art. 37 para. 1 sent. 2 SCE-R contains no equivalent wording between the German and Italian versions of the SCE-R. Where the German version uses the term '*Geschäftsführer*', which refers to a managing director who can be—but is not necessarily—a member of the management organ, the Italian version is stricter, as it refers to an '*amministratore delegato*', who can only be a member of the organ. Without debating which term is correct, it seems the Italian version of Art. 37 SCE-R does not refer to the possibility that a managing director be outside the body. Accepting this interpretation, however, it remains unclear whether competence can be delegated to an outside managing director, by arguing that the Italian version of the SCE-R contains a gap here, thus opening the door for Art. 8 para. 1 letter c (ii) or (iii) SCE-R.

There are debates about whether a two-tier system under Italian law can have a so-called general manager. It has been observed that the provisions explicitly dealing with the two-tier system do not contain a specific reference to Art. 2396 CC—which contains provisions regarding general managers—with the result that this provision is not applicable.[77] Nevertheless, as the appointment procedure contained in Art. 2396 CC cannot be considered exclusive,[78] it is possible to appoint a general manager via a different procedure.[79] If this is true, an Italian SCE could theoretically be structured to have an external managing director with delegated competence, although the possibility of delegating competence to an internal managing director would be precluded. Yet, allowing an organ to only delegate its competence externally, which severely restricts the possibility of structuring the organ according to its own needs, produces a rather inconsistent outcome, especially as it runs counter to the principles of self-regulation. This rather strict interpretation ultimately depends on the fact, whether one accepts the above outlined interpretation of Art. 37 para. 1 last sent. SCE-R.

[75] See Ministry for economic development (2006), Art. 37.

[76] As discussed in Sect. 2.5.

[77] Nor can it be applied due to Art. 223 sexies prov. impl. CC. See Cariello (2012), p. 271.

[78] See Cass Civ sez II 30.10.2006 no 23329 (07.02.2017, iusexplorer.it).

[79] More precisely, this article states that the provisions governing the liability of the directors (of the administrative organ) also apply to the general managers appointed by the shareholders' meeting or via a specific statutory provision. It has been observed that liability issues can also be based on the provisions governing the working relationship. Cariello (2012), p. 271.

Having discussed the managerial function of the management organ of an Italian agricultural SCE, this study now considers the *Austrian legal system* and the relevant Austrian norms which are important here. This analysis roughly outlines the competence of an Austrian cooperative, which shall be used as a framework for describing the competence of an Austrian SCE.

Whereas representation[80] of an Austrian cooperative, as a task of the management organ,[81] is specifically regulated by Sec. 17 *GenG*, the *GenG* does not contain an explicit provision regarding other competence of the management organ. However, according to the *ratio legis*, it can be argued that the management organ must be empowered to manage the cooperative and conclude the necessary transactions; otherwise, the power of representation would be meaningless.[82] In this respect, the SCE-R is more precise.[83]

In addition to this general (management) task, the law specifies various functions and responsibilities the management organ must fulfil, including being responsible for accounting,[84] preparing accounts[85] and the management report,[86] reporting duties, such as (annual) reporting to the supervisory organ about basic issues of future business policy and the development of net assets and the financial position[87] or (quarterly) reporting to the supervisory organ about the development of business.[88] Next, the organ must draw up a special report as requested by Sec. 22 para. 3 *GenG*. Finally, under Austrian law,[89] the management organ must convene the general meeting.[90]

In general, the organ must observe the fulfilment of the purpose of promotion as a guiding principle, as well as the cooperative's object, as determined by the statutes. Then, according to Secs. 19 and 34 *GenG*, the management organ is obliged to monitor and execute the decisions of the general meeting.[91] This implies that the general meeting can instruct the management organ according to its competence and,

---

[80]See Sect. 4.2.1.2.

[81]According to Sec. 26 SCEG, the management organ is called "Vorstand" and the supervisory organ "Aufsichtsrat". Hence, the SCEG uses the same terminology as the GenG.

[82]See Strommer (2014b), p. 206. Also consider Keinert (1988), p. 163.

[83]See Art. 37 para.1 sent. 1 SCE-R.

[84]Sec. 22 GenG. Consider in this context Art. 68 SCE-R.

[85]Financial statements or other statement of accounts. Consider in this context Art. 68 SCE-R.

[86]See Sec. 22 para. 2 GenG.

[87]See Sec. 22 para. 3 GenG.

[88]Also by considering future development (Sec. 22 para. 3 GenG).

[89]See Sec. 28 GenG. This study discusses the reporting system and the power to convene the general meeting in Sects. 4.2.2.1 and 4.4.2; however, accounting issues and liquidation are not considered further.

[90]These latter competences and the reporting duties are discussed in detail in one of the following chapters.

[91]See Strommer (2014b), p. 207. Also consider Keinert (1988), p. 164.

in case of doubt, in all matters that have not been assigned, by law or by statutes, to the management organ or any other organs.[92] It is unclear whether the general meeting's option to adopt such directives holds for Austrian SCEs. While the German and Italian versions of the SCE-R provide further details, the English version does not: Both the German and Italian versions declare that this management task must be fulfilled on its own responsibility.[93] Various scholars[94] have correctly observed that the general meeting, therefore, cannot give any instructions to the management organ; Austrian SCEs differ from Austrian cooperatives in this regard.

Finally, the 2008 amendment of the *GenG* introduced a catalogue containing specific transactions that must be agreed upon by the supervisory organ of an Austrian cooperative.[95] This issue is discussed in detail in Sect. 4.2.2.1.[96]

As previously mentioned, Art. 37 para. 1 sent. 2 SCE-R permits national legislatures to allow the delegation of current management to a managing director. The German[97] text of the SCE-R allows national law to determine whether a managing director must be a member of the organ or whether he or she can be appointed from outside.[98] However, the Austrian legislature did not exercise this option.[99] In fact, the SCEG does not contain a specific provision in this regard, meaning that Sec. 26 *GenG* does not apply. This latter contains a specific provision to be observed when appointing an external managing director. Note that this cannot be introduced by applying Art. 8 para. 1 letter c (ii) SCE-R, because there is no gap.[100] Thus, Austrian cooperatives are more flexible in this regard than Austrian SCEs.

To conclude, as the regulation does not provide any further provisions defining the management task, it is first necessary to define the competence of the other organs to contextualise these management tasks. Then, we use the national legal systems as guidelines to determine the content of the management's functions. The analysis showed that both legal systems conceptualise this function in similar ways. In addition, specific limits to this competence are given by competence assigned to other organs, especially, the supervisory organ and the general meeting. Finally, Austrian law allows the general meeting to give directives to the management organ,

---

[92]See Siebenbäck (2014a), p. 337 et seq. Also consider Kastner (1986), p. 152; Manz (2010k). These directives can be challenged, as provided for by secs 196, 197 and 199 AktG Strommer (2014b), p. 208.

[93]"in eigener Verantwortung" and "sotto la propria responsabilità".

[94]See Greda (2014), p. 848; Schöpflin (2018d), p. 1300. For discussion regarding the administrative organ of an Austrian SE consider Kalss (2014), nt 31, Kalss (2008), nt 3/1098; Egermann and Heckenthaler (2004), p. 260 et seq.; Rauter (2010), p. 502 et seq. For discussion regarding the management organ of an Italian SE consider Donativi in Capriglione, p. 185 et seq.

[95]See Sect. 4.2.2.1. For details consider Zehetner (2014c), p. 321 et seq.

[96]See Sect. 4.2.2.1.

[97]Section 1.2.1 stresses that interpretive issues arise due to the different wordings in the German and Italian versions of the SCE-R.

[98]See Schöpflin (2018d), p. 1300; Schulze (2004a), p. 93.

[99]See Fici (2010), p. 64.

[100]See Lehner (2007), p. 106 et seq. For a dissenting opinion, see Greda (2014), p. 848.

but this cannot be applied to an Austrian SCE. Otherwise, there would be a significant difference in competence.

In this regard, PECOL Sec. 2.5 para. 1 determines three functions for the organs of a cooperative: executive management, representation and supervision. Then, para. 3 determines that executive management and representation are allocated to the management organ.[101] Even though the PECOL use a different term, one can assume that 'executive management' corresponds to the function determined by Art. 37 para. 1 SCE. Accordingly, it encompasses all powers not reserved for another organ. This very broad definition fully aligns with the concepts considered by both Austrian and Italian SCEs.

Accordingly, the statutes of an *agricultural cooperative* will include a requirement that managers have extensive powers to manage the cooperative. The limits of the management competence then result from clarification that only those powers are excluded which are expressly reserved for the general meeting. With regard to the transactions to be carried out, the management organ should be allowed to decide on the purchase and sale of real estate or on the encumbrance of the same. It may also decide on the construction of buildings, including their financing. In general, it can carry out all activities aimed at achieving the cooperative's purpose. For example, the statutes may generally stipulate that the purpose of the cooperative is to provide its members with comprehensive support in the production, storage, processing and marketing of the agricultural products that they deliver to the cooperative. From this, additional powers can be given to the management organ; for example, it must ensure that the products of the members are taken over and subsequently processed and stored, that it markets the products accordingly in the wholesale trade or that it produces further products from these delivered products. In addition, the management organ will also be authorised to represent and promote common interests or to improve general production techniques and to train members and employees accordingly.

In the case of a PO, the management organ's field of activity will include those activities that result from the activity of a PO, such as optimising production costs and stabilising producer prices, or promoting environmentally sound production methods, cultivation techniques or waste management techniques. If an operational programme has been drawn up, the management organ will also have to ensure that the resulting requirements for improving the quality of the member products are complied with.

Finally, neither the Austrian nor Italian legislatures exercised the option contained in Art. 37 para. 1 sent. 2 SCE-R. As a result, it does not seem possible to delegate current management to a managing director, even though the analysis referring to the Italian legal system brought up some doubts in this regard. By contrast, the PECOL explicitly offer the possibility to allocate these powers to one or more directors and managers.[102] In addition, the PECOL acknowledge in Sec. 2.5

[101]Or to the administrative organ in the one-tier system.

[102]See Sec. 2.5 para. 3 subpara. 2 PECOL.

para. 3 subpara. 2 that these powers may, in principle, be delegated by the organ on which these powers have been conferred. According to the PECOL, exceptions to this rule are only permitted if the statutes provide otherwise. Thus, the PECOL call for a wide range of discretion to be used when delegating powers, also allowing restrictions on representation.[103] It is suggested that the rules applicable to Austrian and Italian SCEs should be changed accordingly.

4.2.1.2 Function 2: Representing the SCE

According to Art. 37 para. 1 SCE-R, the management organ not only manages the SCE, but also represents it in dealings with third parties and in legal proceedings; accordingly, this organ directly creates rights and obligations for the SCE. Procedural acts accomplished by the management organ directly impact the SCE.[104]

Art. 47 SCE-R contains further provisions regarding the content and limits of this power of representation.[105] Art. 47 para. 1 SCE-R regulates the power of representation between third parties and members of the management organ.[106] If the organ has more than one member, in principle, the members exercise power collectively.[107] As collective representation is the general rule for multi-member management, declarations with legal relevance (i.e., the acceptance of an offer) must always be made by all members of the organ to be binding. However, neither the wording nor the intent of this rule request members to act simultaneously or require each member to make an explicit declaration. As a result, approval via concluding behaviour or successive declaration should be admissible.[108] If only one member remains, the collective representation is substituted with individual representation.[109]

It is not clear whether Art. 47 para. 1 sent. 1 SCE-R refers exclusively to making a declaration *vis-à-vis* third parties[110] or includes a situation in which a third party

[103]See also Snaith (2017), p. 68 et seq.

[104]See Schulze (2004a), p. 83 et seq. Also consider Schöpflin (2018d), p. 1300.

[105]These apply to both the two-tier and the one-tier systems. See Schulze (2004a), p. 94.

[106]Or the administrative organ.

Art 47 para. 1 SCE-R states: "Where the authority to represent the SCE in dealings with third parties, in accordance with Articles 37(1) and 42(1), is conferred on two or more members, those members shall exercise that authority collectively, unless the law of the Member State in which the SCE's registered office is situated allows the statutes to provide otherwise, in which case such a clause may be relied upon against third parties where it has been disclosed in accordance with Articles 11(5) and 12."

[107]This requirement for collective decision making must also be fulfilled if a member is absent for a longer period through no fault of his own (e.g., due to sickness). The obligation for participation only stops with the termination of membership of the organ. From then on, the remaining members of the organ act as collective representatives. See Schulze (2004a), p. 107 et seq. Also consider Schöpflin (2018d), p. 1300.

[108]Without prejudice to any formal requirements for a specific legal transaction.

[109]See Schulze (2004a), p. 107 et seq.

[110]Active representation.

makes a declaration to the SCE.[111] However, such a wide interpretation could raise serious problems for everyday businesses and make interactions with third parties too complicated. Hence, it is preferable to refuse to apply Art. 47 para. 1 SCE to third-party declarations: a declaration made to one of the members of the management organ[112] should be sufficient. However, the chosen approach must align with national law.[113]

Next, Art. 47 para. 1 SCE-R offers the possibility to deviate from collective representation, provided that such a solution is permitted by national law and determined by the statutes. Such a rule must be disclosed in accordance with Art. 11 para. 5 and Art. 12 SCE-R; otherwise, it will not be effective when it comes to third parties. In agricultural SCEs of a certain size, this solution might be more practical than collective representation as it seems less burdensome.[114]

It might be possible to allow systems other than collective representation for certain types of transactions (business types) or liabilities worth a certain amount of money. Again, such a solution must align with the relevant national law. Within the restrictions of national law, the statutes of an SCE may consider a variety of options. For instance, the authority of individual representation may be granted to all members on an individual basis or to specific members of the organ (e.g., the chairman).[115]

Next, according to Art. 47 para. 4 sent. 1 SCE-R,[116] a member state can determine that the general power of representation may be conferred on a single person or on several persons acting jointly. This must be based on a statutory provision. This provision can further broaden the options for regulating the power of representation, which thus allows representation by persons who are not members of the management organ.[117] A mixed system, in which the SCE is represented by a member of the management organ[118] in addition to an external person, could also be possible.[119]

However, the prerequisite for these solutions is that the law in the member state must provide for validity of such a statutory provision *vis-à-vis* third parties.[120]

---

[111]Passive representation.

[112]Or administrative organ.

[113]See Schulze (2004a), p. 108. Such a provision makes the operational management of an SCE much more flexible than would be possible with collective representation, especially if business volumes are low. Schöpflin stresses that Art. 47 para. 1 SCE-R does not refer to passive representation. See Schöpflin (2018n), p. 1311 et seq.

[114]See Schulze (2004a), p. 108; Schöpflin (2018n), p. 1311 et seq.

[115]It also seems possible to modify collective representation such that the SCE is represented by a fixed number of members or by the chairman together with a member responsible for a specific business activity. See Schulze (2004a), p. 108.

[116]It states: "A Member State may stipulate that the power to represent the SCE may be conferred by the statutes on a single person or on several persons acting jointly."

[117]Authorised signatory.

[118]Or administrative organ.

[119]See Schulze (2004a), p. 109; Schöpflin (2018n), p. 1311 et seq.

[120]See Schulze (2004a), p. 109; Schöpflin (2018n), p. 1311 et seq.

Specifically, only general representation may be regulated, not extraordinary representation.[121]

As already seen, Art. 37 para. 1 SCE-R, Art. 42 para. 1 SCE-R and Art. 47 paras. 1 and 4 SCE-R regulate who can use a declaration to bind and entitle the SCE against third parties (power of representation). In addition, Art. 47 para. 2 SCE-R[122] defines the limits within which the SCE can thus be obliged. Outside of these limits, the authorised representatives lack the power of authorisation, with the result that declarations exceeding these limits can neither oblige nor entitle an SCE.[123]

These limits are rather broad, however. Acts performed by an organ of the SCE are binding with respect to third parties, even if the act concerned does not correspond to the object of the SCE (e.g., if the management organ buys a yacht for a credit union). Stricter limits may result only from a relevant national law, either directly from the law or via a statutory provision, if the relevant law allows for this possibility.[124] If an organ of the SCE exceeds these limits, the SCE cannot be effectively obliged against third parties. These limits can vary between member states, because the SCE-R does not offer any criteria with which to better determine these limits.[125]

In addition to these various constraints, Art. 47 para. 2 subpara. 2 SCE-R[126] deviates from the principle to bind the SCE, even if the acts performed by an organ fall outside the SCE's purpose. Art. 47 para. 2 subpara. 2 SCE-R lets member states regulate that an SCE acting outside its objects cannot be bound,[127] if it proves that the third party knew or at least could not be unaware (in the circumstances) that the act exceeded the limit as set by the objects. The disclosure of the statutes alone is not sufficient proof.[128] (Neither the Austrian nor the Italian legislatures exercised this option.[129]) This final clarification follows from the rule contained in Art. 47 para.

[121] See Art. 48 para. 4 sent. 2 SCE-R. Also consider Schöpflin (2018n), p. 1311 et seq. In this context, the provisions regarding publication of documents, contained in Art. 12 SCE-R, must be observed. See Art. 48 para. 4 sent. 3 SCE-R. Also consider Schulze (2004a), p. 109.

[122] It states: "Acts performed by an SCE's organs shall bind the SCE vis-à-vis third parties, even where the acts in question are not in accordance with the objects of the SCE, providing they do not exceed the powers conferred on them by the law of the Member State in which the SCE has its registered office or which that law allows to be conferred on them."

[123] See Schulze (2004a), p. 109; Schöpflin (2018n), p. 1311 et seq.

[124] See Schulze (2004a), p. 109; Schöpflin (2018n), p. 1312.

[125] See Schulze (2004a), p. 109 et seq. In this context also consider Art. 51 SCE-R, which determines how liability can be asserted. See Sect. 4.2.1.6.

[126] It states: "member states may, however, provide that the SCE shall not be bound where such acts are outside the objects of the SCE, if it proves that the third party knew that the act was outside those objects or could not in the circumstances have been unaware of it; disclosure of the statutes shall not of itself be sufficient proof thereof."

[127] Ultra vires doctrine. While the principle enshrined in para. 2 subpara. 1 reflects legal traditions typical for continental Europe, common law systems follow the ultra vires doctrine, which in principle prohibits obligating a company outside of its mandate. See Schulze (2004a), p. 110.

[128] See Art. 47 para. 2 subpara. 2 SCE-R. Also consider Schulze (2004a), p. 110.

[129] See Fici (2010), p. 64 et seq.

3 SCE-R,[130] which states that statutory limits on the powers of the organs cannot be relied on against third parties, even if these limits have been disclosed according to Art. 12 SCE-R. This is even more true if the limits on powers simply arise from a decision by the competent organs. Such statutory provisions or decisions would only effect the internal relationship of the SCE's organ, never the external relationship with a third party and an SCE.[131]

As seen, the SCE-R contains options for representation that allow member states to integrate their national solutions into the legal framework established for an SCE. Thus it is necessary to analyse how the Italian and Austrian legislatures have used these options. In line with the general approach, the *Italian legislature* did not adopt a law to implement specific options of the SCE-R; instead, one must refer to specific rules contained in the CC in order to apply Art. 47 SCE-R.

In principle, under the Italian legal system, the management organ must act as a collegial organ.[132] However, it is possible to assign the power of representation to an individual member. According to Art. 2521 para. 2 no. 10 CC, the statutes must determine which member of the management organ will be delegated the power of representation. Accordingly, the power of representation can be assigned to one or more members of this organ. Thus, the possibility contained in Art. 47 para. 1 sent. 2 SCE-R can be applied.[133] Next, in line with the overall approach adopted by the Italian legislature, the option contained in Art. 47 para. 4 SCE-R has not been exercised.[134] This implies that an Italian SCE cannot confer the general power of representation to non-members of the organ.

As mentioned in this chapter, the limits of the power of representation, as determined by Art. 47 para. 2 subpara. 1 SCE-R, are regulated by reference to national law. In this context, it is necessary to refer to Art. 2409 undecies para. 1 CC in combination with Art. 2384 CC. According to para. 1 of this article, the powers of

---

[130]It states: "The limits on the powers of the organs of the SCE, arising under the statutes or from a decision of the competent organs, may never be relied on as against third parties, even if they have been disclosed."

[131]See Schulze (2004a), p. 110.

[132]This conclusion can be drawn from different provisions contained in the civil code: first, Art. 2409 novies para. 2 CC states that the management organ must consist of no less than two members; next, Art. 2409 octies CC determines that the management shall be carried out by a management organ, while Art. 2409 novies para. 1 CC states the management of the business is exclusively entrusted to the management; finally, Art. 2409 novies or undecies CC, which do not refer to Art. 2380 bis para. 3 CC, which considers (indirectly) the possibility of having an organ with only one member. See Cariello (2012), p. 281; Calandra Buonaura (2007), p. 666. See also Mirone (2017a), p. 573.

[133]Thus, not all members have or must have the power of representation. See Usai (2010d), p. 529.

[134]See Fici (2010), p. 65. The same is true for an Italian cooperative, where general representation cannot be conferred to third parties. Even though some scholars favour the opposite. See Sandei (2018c), p. 2821.

representation are general in nature[135] and are granted by either statutes or the appointment resolution. As these powers are general in nature, they encompass all acts carried out in the company's name.[136] The provision in para. 1 cannot be derogated, but is granted to safeguard third parties. Para. 2 states that the limitations of the power of representation cannot be invoked against third parties.[137] The only exception is if it is proved that the third party intentionally acted to the detriment of the company. In other words, the limitations referred to in Art. 2384 para. 2 CC can be opposed to third parties only if they acted with intent. Such actions must go beyond simple 'bad faith'.[138] This limitation is applicable to an Italian SCE because of Art. 47 para. 2 SCE-R.[139]

Contrary to the Italian legislature, the *Austrian legislature* adopted provisions to apply Art. 47 SCE-R. As a general rule, members who represent an Austrian SCE must collectively exercise the power of representation. One can raise the question about whether this collective power must also be considered for a third-party declaration referring to the SCE. Unlike the provisions for the one-tier system,[140] the SCEG does not contain any information in this regard. As the SCE-R arguably contains a gap in this context,[141] Sec. 17 para. 2 last sent. *GenG* would apply. As a result, it is sufficient to make a declaration to a single member of the management

[135]See Usai (2010d), p. 524 et seq. See also Sanfilippo (2017a), p. 510 et seq. Furthermore, the fact that this power is general in nature must be considered if specific representative acts have been completed without a specific decision being made by the management organ (representative act made by the chairman due to his specific competence). See Usai (2010d), p. 525; Bonelli (2004), p. 80; Cass Civ sez I 26.01.2006 no 1525 (07.02.2017, iusexplorer.it). The representation power which links the members of the organ to the company is defined as an organic representation power. For further information, see Usai (2010d), p. 524. On these issues, see also Romano (2017i), p. 2949 et seq.; Sanfilippo (2017a), p. 509 et seq.

[136]This article contains no reference to the object of a company or cooperative. As a result, management powers and powers to represent are divided. The management powers assigned to individual members are only relevant internally. See Sandei (2018d), p. 2819. See Sanfilippo (2017a), p. 510 et seq. Also consider Usai (2010d), p. 525 et seq., see also Romano (2017i), p. 2949 et seq. Due to this general representation, the empowered member may confer the power to represent the cooperative for one or more individual transactions to third parties, as long as the statutes do not provide otherwise. See Usai (2010d), p. 528 et seq.; Mosco (2004a), p. 614.

[137]Set forth in the statutes or by decision of the competent organs, even if published. The term "competent organs" refers to the founding members, the ordinary general meeting and the supervisory organ. See Sandei (2018d), p. 2821. See also Romano (2017i), p. 2949 et seq.; Sanfilippo (2017a), p. 513.

[138]See Usai (2010d), p. 530 et seq.; Bonelli (2004), p. 91; Cass Civ sez I 08.11.2000 no 14509 (07.02.2017, iusexplorer.it). Also consider Calandra Buonaura (2007), p. 664 et seq.; Sanfilippo (2017a), p. 513 et seq.

[139]Art. 2384 CC, however, only applies to members assigned this power. If a member without this power conducts such acts, the general provisions regarding representation (Art. 1387 et seq. CC) must be applied (see, especially, Art. 1398 CC representation without power). See Usai (2010d), p. 529. See also Romano (2017i), p. 2949 et seq.

[140]Sec. 27 para. 1 sent. 2 SCEG.

[141]See Schöpflin (2018n), p. 1311 et seq.

organ.[142] Next, Sec. 27 para. 1 SCEG allows the statutes to determine that the management organ[143] can delegate individual members to represent the SCE with respect to certain transactions or certain types of transactions, thus deviating from the principle of collective power of representation. As a result, the drafters of the statutes can define specific areas of business and transfer the responsibility to individual members of the organs.[144]

The Austrian legislature also adopted a specific provision via the SCEG to empower a single person or several persons acting jointly to represent the SCE, albeit in a restrictive way. Sec. 27 para. 2 SCEG determines[145] that a single member of the management organ[146] may represent the SCE alone. Representation can also be exercised jointly with an authorised signatory. Thus, the latter cannot represent the SCE alone. An Austrian SCE can therefore only be represented with the participation of at least one member of the management organ.[147]

Finally, Art. 47 para. 2 subpara. 1 SCE-R and Sec. 19 *GenG* together refer to a possible scenario for acts that do not bind an Austrian SCE, for instance, if a member of the management organ and a business partner collude to damage the SCE. Acts are also not binding if a third party, without any intention of causing damage, knew or at least could have known (as it was quite evident) of such an intent of a member of the management organ.[148]

Similar to Art. 47 para. 2 subpara. 1 SCE-R, Sec. 18 *GenG* defines the effect and extent of the power of representation. Accordingly, the management organ may authorise and bind the cooperative via legal transactions which the former concludes. It is not relevant whether the transaction has been concluded expressly on behalf of the cooperative or not; it is sufficient if the circumstances indicate that it has been concluded on behalf of the cooperative. Para. 2 of Sec. 18 determines that the power of representation extends to all transactions, which, according to the

[142]According to the Austrian legal system, the management organ acts as a collegial organ. Specific tasks can be delegated to one or more of its members or to specific committees, on the condition the statutes provides accordingly. According to Sec. 17 para. 2 GenG, the management organ can authorise individual members of the organ to transact (or to fulfil certain categories of transactions). See Strommer (2014b), p. 204. Also consider Kastner (1986), p. 154.

[143]Or the administrative organ.

[144]As mentioned above, such a provision can only be relied upon against third parties where it has been disclosed in accordance with Art. 11 para. 5 and 12 SCE-R.

[145]If a specific statutory provision provides accordingly.

[146]Or the administrative organ.

[147]When it comes to the participation of an authorised signatory in the representation of the SCE, Sec. 2 para. 2 SCEG specifies that the representation of the cooperative must be granted even without his participation. As explained, the provisions contained in Art. 12 SCE-R must be observed to make such a provision reliable against third parties.

The general rule is contained in Sec. 17 para. 1 GenG. Accordingly, a cooperative is represented by the management organ in and out of court. The cooperative is represented by the organ in all areas not explicitly assigned to another organ by law. See Strommer (2014b), p. 208.

[148]See Strommer (2014d), p. 216. Also consider Kastner et al. (1990), p. 103; OGH 19.04.1978, 8 Ob 505/78; OGH 25.06.1996, 4 Ob 2078/96h.

provisions of the *Allgemeines bürgerliches Gesetzbuch* (*ABGB*), require a special power of attorney. The management organ is obliged to comply with the restrictions on the power of representation, as provided for by either the statutes or the decisions of the general meeting.[149] Similar to Art. 47 para. 3 SCE-R, Sec. 19 *GenG* determines that restrictions on the power of representation have no legal power over third parties. Some examples that are applicable to an Austrian SCE include situations where the power of representation only refers to certain transactions (or types of transactions), or to certain circumstances, places or times. The same is true for transactions that require the approval of the general meeting, the supervisory organ or any other organ.[150]

To sum up, representation, as a task of the management organ of an *agricultural SCE*, is regulated by Art. 47 SCE-R, which also contains references to national law and offers two options: collective representation or representation by individual members of the organs. Both legal systems allow individual representation. Whereas Italian law treats the power of representation as general in nature, the Austrian legislature has adopted a more flexible approach by empowering individual members to represent the SCE for certain transactions or types of transactions. These transactions include all those activities that have an external impact, such as the conclusion of supply contracts, the conclusion of contracts for the construction of buildings, the conclusion of contracts to strengthen the market position through targeted marketing measures, the conclusion of contracts for strategic cooperation within the framework of federations, or the conclusion of financing contracts.

With regards to the general power of representation, the Austrian legal system allows this power to be exercised by an authorised signatory. However, the latter cannot represent the *agricultural SCE* alone, but most do so with the participation of at least one member of the management organ. In this context, Sec. 2.5 para. 2 PECOL determines, as a general definition, that representation must be understood as an authority who represents the cooperative in dealings with third parties and legal proceedings.[151] In addition, subpara. 2 explicitly requires that this power may be delegated by those on whom it is conferred. Exceptions are only possible via statutory provisions. Thus, the PECOL advocate for a wide range of statutory freedom, in this regard. As seen from the analyses, both legal systems differ from this proposal to a certain extent.[152]

Finally, according to Art. 47 para. 2 SCE-R, the acts performed by an SCE's organs bind the SCE *vis-a-vis* third parties if these acts are not in line with the object of the SCE. Both legal systems contain a limit that must be observed in this context. Under the Austrian legal system, certain acts are not binding if the third party, without any intent to damage, knew or at least could have known of the intent to

[149] Also consider Strommer (2014c), p. 214.

[150] Also consider Strommer (2014c), p. 215.

[151] Under the PECOL, this function is assigned to the management or administrative organ or to one or more directors or managers. See also Snaith (2017), p. 68.

[152] See also Snaith (2017), p. 68.

damage by the member of the organ. However, the Italian legal system only allows derogation from the provision contained in the SCE-R, if it is proved that the third party intentionally acted to the detriment of the company. Neither legal system adopts the *ultra vires* doctrine.

4.2.1.3 Composition of the Management Organ

The regulation addresses two main factors that impact how a management organ should be composed: the conditions of membership and the number of members. The concerned rules are contained in Chapt. III, Sect. 3 of the SCE-R, thus referring to both the two-tier and one-tier systems. Moreover, these rules are applicable not only to the management organ but also to the supervisory organ. Thus, the following analyses are important with respect to the supervisory organ and the administrative organ.

Starting from the assumption that members of the organs are generally natural persons, Art. 46 para. 1 SCE-R expands membership to companies within the meaning of Art. 54 TFEU. Companies may be members of the organs if both the applicable national law[153] does not state otherwise and the statutes contain a corresponding provision.[154] According to the wording of Art. 46 para. 1 SCE-R, national law cannot explicitly exclude this possibility, but neither is it explicitly required to permit it.[155]

As it is not possible for a company to take action within the organ of the SCE, it must designate a natural person as its representative to exercise its functions. The regulation does not require this person to hold a specific position within the designating company; it only specifies that the representative must be subject to the same conditions and obligations as if this person was personally a member of the organ.[156]

In *Italy*, there are discussions that favour allowing legal entities to become members of companies in general, including cooperatives. Even before the 2003 reform, it had been discussed whether persons other than natural persons might be

[153]The law applicable to cooperatives in the member state in which the SCE's registered office is situated.

[154]Art. 46 para. 1 SCE-R states: "The statutes of an SCE may permit a company within the meaning of Article 48 of the Treaty to be a member of one of its organs, provided the law applicable to cooperatives in the member state in which the SCE's registered office is situated does not provide otherwise. That company shall designate a natural person as its representative to exercise its functions on the organ in question. The representative shall be subject to the same conditions and obligations as if they were personally a member of the organ."

[155]See Alfandari and Piot (2004), p. 105. For the SE, see Manz (2010i), p. 609; Teichmann (2015f), p. 732.

[156]See Alfandari and Piot (2004), p. 106. Also consider Art. 37 para. 3 sent. 1 SCE-R. For the SE, see Teichmann (2015f), p. 732.

appointed as members of the administrative organ of an *spa*.[157] The legal system did not and still not does provide a clear answer to this issue.[158] While the reform did not help to clarify this discussion, in general, it did allow for an interpretation that seems to admit the admission of legal entities.[159] It is argued that the mandatory provisions that are applicable to natural persons and that refer to the functions of the administrative organ can also be fully applied to legal entities.[160]

Regarding Italian cooperatives, one must consider Art. 2542 para. 3 CC, which deals with the appointment of members to the administrative organ of a cooperative.[161] This provision states that only the majority of members must be chosen from user members or from a range of persons nominated by the members who are legal entities. In this context, it has been observed that, even if one accepts that the majority of the members of these organs cannot be legal entities, this interpretation does not prevent legal entities from being appointed as members of these organs (albeit in minority positions). It has been noted that this article does not prohibit members who are legal entities from nominating other legal entities. It has also been observed that this article can be interpreted to mean that legal entity members may decide whether to be elected as user members or to nominate a third party.[162] However, these observations are mostly hypothetical. I conclude that Art. 46 para. 1 SCE-R cannot be applied to an Italian SCE.

Like the Italian legal system, the *Austrian legal system* does not allow the possibility to appoint legal entities. Until 2008 in Austria, it was a matter for discussion whether the representatives of legal persons could be directly appointed as members of the supervisory organ. The prevailing opinion required the representatives to become members of the cooperative to be qualified for membership in one of the two organs, with the consequence that legal persons would be in a worse position than natural persons.[163]

Even though the law at that time did not explicitly provide for such a solution, it was argued that representatives could become members of the organs because of the fact that the legal person, as a member of the cooperative, is someone who acts by

[157] See Cetra (2008), p. 680; Cetra (2010), p. 114 et seq.; Stella Richter (2004), p. 293; Breida (2009), p. 677.

[158] In contrast, consider the German AktG, which explicitly states that only natural persons can be appointed as members of the management organ (see Sec. 76 para. 3 AktG).

[159] As this discussion is rather complex, only a few arguments will be illustrated. For a detailed discussion on this issue, see for example Cetra (2008), p. 680; Cetra (2010), p. 115 et seq. Critical Rescio (2003), p. 973. See also Sanfilippo (2017a), p. 472 et seq.; Romano (2017h), p. 2947; Sanfilippo (2017a), p. 472 et seq.

[160] See Stella Richter (2004), p. 293 et seq. This should be true for the criterion of independence, which, too, seems to be applicable to legal entities. See Cariello (2012), p. 289; Cetra (2010), p. 121 et seq. Also consider Art. 147 ter para. 4 TUF and Art. 147 quarter TUF.

[161] This provision is also applicable to the management organ. For details, see Paolucci (2019e), p. 131 et seq.

[162] See Pescatore (2009), p. 1167 et seq. See also Cusa (2004c), p. 179.

[163] Because legal persons cannot become members of an organ. See Zehetner (2014b), p. 268 et seq.

means of the cooperative's organs and, hence, by means of its representatives. It had been observed that members of a cooperative were traditionally natural persons, whereas it is now generally accepted that legal persons can become members of a cooperative. The *URÄG* 2008 clarified these doubts by modifying Sec. 24 *GenG*. Accordingly, the law now states that supervisory organ members are elected from among (a) the members of the cooperative and (b) their organ members, in the event that a cooperative member is a legal entity. Interestingly, Sec. 15 *GenG*, also modified by the *URÄG* 2008, is more stringent, referring to members of organs who are authorised to represent.[164] The materials annexed to the government bill for the *URÄG*[165] explicitly state that the aim of this amendment is not to allow legal persons to become members of an organ, but to carefully expand the circle of persons who can be elected. Therefore, the personal responsibility of the elected natural person remains.

Apart from the question of whether companies might become members of the management organ of an SCE, Art. 46 addresses the **conditions of membership of a personal nature**, as well as other impediments to membership. These rules apply to the management, supervisory and administrative organs. However, different conditions must be observed for each organ, so this issue must be analysed separately for each. In addition, Art. 46 para. 3 SCE-R contains a provision that only applies to the administrative organ.

Art. 46 para. 2 SCE-R[166] indicates specific conditions denying interested candidates membership status. According to para. 2, bullet 1,[167] a person may be disqualified from becoming an organ's member[168] according to the law of the member state in which the SCE has its registered office. In addition, para. 2, bullet 2 of Art. 46 SCE-R considers the impediments that arise from a judicial or administrative decision delivered in any member state. As a result, such decisions have a Europe-wide effect,[169] with the result that the same impediments apply to the members of the management organ of both Austrian and Italian agricultural SCEs. Indeed, any judicial or administrative decision in any member state leads to inadmissibility of membership. Whether this decision has legal force must be determined according to the law of the relevant member state. However, it is sufficient that a

[164]See Zehetner (2014b), p. 268 et seq. These observations are also valid for the management organ. See Strommer (2014a), p. 193.

[165]See ErläutRV 467 BlgNR 23. GP 467 39.

[166]It states: "No person may be a member of any SCE organ or a representative of a member within the meaning of paragraph 1 who: - is disqualified, under the law of the Member State in which the SCE's registered office is situated, from serving on the corresponding organ of a cooperative governed by the law of that State, or - is disqualified from serving on the corresponding organ of a cooperative governed by the law of a Member State owing to a judicial or administrative decision delivered in a Member State."

[167]Preconditions of a personal nature.

[168]Or representative of a company (within the meaning of Article 48 of the Treaty) who is a member of an organ.

[169]In those European countries, in which the SCE-R must be applied.

person cannot become a member of the organ as the result of a decision in any member state.[170]

Due to the limitations outlined in the introduction, this study focuses on preconditions of a personal nature.[171] Therefore, it continues by analysing the consequences of bullet 1 from the perspective of the Italian and Austrian legal systems and by providing specific examples to be considered when applying Art. 46 para. 2 bullet 1 SCE-R. The *Italian legal system* contains provisions that need to be considered when applying Art. 46 para. 2 SCE-R. First, as a general rule, under Italian law a member of an organ must have full legal capacity. Thus, for instance, it is not possible to appoint a minor.[172] Next, various laws determine the specific grounds upon which membership of an organ becomes unfeasible, for example, if the applicant is a stockbroker.[173] In addition, according to Art. 2387 para. 2 CC, the provisions contained in special laws relating to the exercise of specific activities must also be observed.[174] Then, like Art. 37 para. 3 SCE-R, Italian law determines that members of the supervisory organ cannot be appointed members of the management organ.[175]

Concerning the conditions of membership in the management organ, one has to refer to Art. 2382 CC, which is of particular importance for an Italian SCE.[176] It lists the specific reasons for ineligibility (and forfeiture of office) and determines that the following persons may not be appointed as members of the management organ: (1) interdicted and banned persons, (2) disqualified persons, (3) bankrupt persons, (4) persons who have been sentenced to a penalty entailing a ban, even temporary, from public office or (5) persons who have been sentenced to a penalty entailing the inability to exercise managerial functions. If these persons are appointed, they forfeit their office.[177]

Then, it must be determined whether the provisions contained in Art. 2542 para. 3 CC apply. It refers to the traditional corporate governance system and states that

---

[170]As considered in Art. 46 para. 2 bullet 2 SCE-R, this member state is therefore not necessarily the same as the seat state. For the SE, see Manz (2010i), p. 610 et seq.; Teichmann (2015f), p. 733 et seq. Also consider Schulze (2004a), p. 106.

[171]See Sect. 1.1.

[172]See Usai (2010c), p. 506; Mosco (2004c), p. 604; Romano (2017h), p. 2946 et seq.

[173]See Art. 1 Royal Decree-Law no 222/1925; for further examples consider Sandei (2018a), p. 2815 and Sanfilippo (2017a), p. 470 fn 42. For a list of specific reasons for ineligibility, see e.g. Usai (2010c), p. 506. See also Sanfilippo (2017a), p. 470.

[174]Especially businesses in the banking and financial sectors. See Usai (2010e), p. 557; Mosco (2004b), p. 626; see also Romano (2017k), p. 2954 et seq.; Sanfilippo (2017a), p. 470.

[175]For specific requirements for listed companies, see e.g., See Cariello (2012), p. 304 et seq.

[176]Reference determined by Art. 2409 undecies para. 1 CC. For the SE, see Donativi in Capriglione 201.

[177]This reasons for ineligibility cannot be derogated by the statutes, as they are considered an expression of public order. These reasons are effective from the moment the judgment ascertaining the existence of the conditions as determined by Art. 2382 CC is published. See Usai (2010c), p. 505 et seq. For details consider Bonelli (2004), p. 55.

the majority of administrators must be chosen from user members. Here, it must first be decided whether this provision also applies to the two-tier system, even though the law explicitly refers to administrators who are members of the administrative organ, but not to members of the management organ. Some have argued that this paragraph does not apply, thus favouring a solution with a management organ without user members.[178] In this context, it has been recognized that the main organ under the two-tier system is the supervisory organ, whereas the management organ basically executes the strategic decisions of the supervisory organ. As a result, it is argued that user members need not be members of the management organ.[179] However, if one considers Art. 2528 CC[180] and Art. 2533 CC,[181] the central role of the management organ becomes clear. It might be difficult to argue that these decisions should be made without explicitly involving user members. In favour of the argument that Art. 2542 para. 3 CC also applies to the two-tier system, it must be remembered that member participation in the management organ is a fundamental principle of cooperative systems.[182] Moreover, it is clear from Art. 2519 CC, which refers to the provisions governing the *spa*, that these provisions only have to be applied to the extent that they can.

This is definitely true for an Italian cooperative. But, does it necessarily hold for an Italian SCE? Communication no. 9203 states that, even though there are no coordinating rules regarding the administrative organ under the traditional system and the management organ under the two-tier system, the majority of the members of the management organ must reflect the interests of the user members.[183] Thus, it is possible to appoint members who are not user members or are not chosen among the persons indicated by legal persons (who are user members), as long as the requirements contained in Art. 2542 para. 3 and 5 CC and Art. 2544 para. 2 CC[184] are fulfilled. In other words, other members (i.e., those not chosen from this group) must be in the minority.[185]

This argument, while reaching a true conclusion, needs further clarification. First, Art. 46 para. 2 bullet 1 SCE-R refers to reasons for exclusion and only contains prohibitions, whereas Art. 2542 para. 5 CC is a provision containing an order. As a

[178]See Cariello (2012), p. 135 et seq.

[179]See Bonfante (2014a), p. 343 et seq.

[180]This article deals with admission of members. For further details, see Sect. 3.4.2.

[181]This article deals with the expulsion of members. For further details, see Sect. 5.4.

[182]See Bonfante (2014a), p. 343 et seq.; Cusa (2006), p. 376 et seq.

[183]The supervisory organ must ensure that the given limits are applied.

[184]This article states that non-user members may not appoint more than 1/3 of the members of the management organ.

[185]See Ministry for economic development (2006), Art. 37.

result, these latter cannot be subsumed under Art. 46 para. 2 SCE-R.[186] Then, if one analyses the complete SCE-R, one finds that it only contains two specific provisions regarding the composition of organs. The first of these is contained in Art. 39 para. 3 SCE-R and Art. 42 para. 2 last sent. SCE-R. It determines that not more than one quarter of the posts available in the supervisory or administrative organ may be filled by non-user members. This does not, however, imply that the other three quarters has to be filled with user members. It is argued that a national law cannot require that all the members of an organ be members of the cooperative.[187] Thus, it seems that these two provisions are an exemption to a general rule[188]; one can argue that the SCE-R determines, as a general rule, that members as well as non-members may be elected into the management organ.[189] The SCE-R contains only one exemption to this general rule.

The other provision regarding the composition of the organs is contained in Art. 39 para. 4 SCE-R, which contains an option empowering the member states to stipulate the composition of the supervisory organ.[190]

The SCE-R does not contain any other provisions in this regard. Nor can statutes determine specific conditions because of Art. 8 para. 1 letter b SCE-R, as the SCE-R does not contain a specific reference to statutes. This could, however, be problematic, especially as statutes should include the powers and responsibilities of the members of the organs, whereas the SCE-R does not explicitly grant the drafters of the statutes the option to determine specific conditions for membership deemed necessary in order to exercise the required powers and responsibilities. Therefore, one can argue that a gap exists and needs to be closed, according to Art. 8 para. 1 letter c SCE-R. This assertion is supported by the fact that Art. 46 para. 2 SCE only refers to prohibitions, excluding other rules. As a result, Art. 2542 para. 3 CC has to be applied to an Italian SCE.[191]

---

[186] See Hoeffler (2013), p. 157 et seq. According to the wording of Art. 46 para. 2 SCE-R, the application of national law is limited to those conditions required for every member of an organ, but not to those conditions which have been determined in respect of the complete or overall composition of an organ. As a result, Art. 2542 para. 3 CC does not seem to apply. See Presti (2006), p. 78. This argument, however, neglects the fact that Art. 46 para. 2 bullet 1 SCE-R refers to provisions containing a prohibition and not an order.

Then, some arguments foster the assumption that the SCE-R acknowledges the possibility of appointing non-SCE members as members of the organs. It is argued that a national law cannot require that all the members of an organ be members of the cooperative. Considering Art. 2542 para. 3 CC, this is, however, not required in this case. See the discussion in this chapter concerning the application of the principle on Selbstorganschaft.

[187] See Schulze (2004b), p. 190.

[188] Also consider Presti (2006), p. 78.

[189] This general rule is also valid for the supervisory and administrative organs.

[190] Also consider Sect. 4.2.2.2.

[191] Although not due to Art. 46 para. 2 bullet 1 SCE-R.

Art 5 para. 4 bullet 9 SCE-R requires that the statutes determine the powers and responsibilities of the members of each of the governing organs. As a consequence, it can be argued that the drafters of the statutes are empowered to, and actually must, determine what the members of the organs

Let us now address a valid situation for an *Austrian SCE*. As mentioned above, Art. 46 para. 2 SCE-R must be read in conjunction with national law to be applicable. According to the Austrian legal system, only natural persons who have full legal capacity may be appointed as members of the management organ.[192] What is complicated is the question of whether it is necessary to be a member of the cooperative in order to be a member of the management organ. The cooperative law of certain member states, such as Austria[193] and Germany, state that only members of a cooperative can become members of the organ (the principle of *Selbstorganschaft*). However, the SCE-R does not contain a similar provision.[194]

As explained, Art. 46 para. 2 bullet 1 SCE-R thus implies that persons who may not become members of the organs of a cooperative according to national law equally cannot become members of an organ in an SCE. Under the Austrian legal system, the members of the management organ[195] must be members of the cooperative; thus, it might be argued that the members of the organs of an Austrian SCE must be members of the cooperative. *Schulze*[196] observes that such an interpretation goes beyond the scope of this provision.

Moreover, there are other arguments that deny the application of the principle of *Selbstorganschaft*. First, as argued above, Art. 46 para. 2 SCE-R only refers to provisions that contain the reasons for exclusion. Thus, according to this reasoning, Sec. 15 para. 1 and Sec. 24 para. 1 *GenG* cannot be subsumed under Art. 46 para. 2 bullet 1 SCE-R. Next, when analysing the SCE-R in detail, it becomes clear that the regulation does not leave room for the application of the principle of *Selbstorganschaft*. According to Art. 58 para. 2 SCE-R, members of the SCE's organs may attend the general meeting without voting rights, while para. 1 confers to every member of an SCE a right to attend general meeting. Therefore, it can be argued that the particular provision contained in para. 2 refers to members of the organs who are not members of the SCE, with the result that this principle must not be applied to Austrian SCEs. Nor is there a gap to be closed by Art. 8 para. 1 letter c SCE-R, as the regulation already addresses this question, albeit indirectly.[197] Thus, there are good arguments for denying the mandatory application of the principle of

---

ultimately must do. This at least indirectly requires the drafters of the statutes to know what the capacities must be, in order that the powers assigned can be properly fulfilled. Hence, it is necessary for the drafters of the statutes to also determine the conditions for membership.

This also depends on how Art. 5 para. 4 SCE-R is interpreted. Does it grant a power to the general meeting to establish specific statutory provisions in respect of the listed items, thus making them applicable? Or does para. 4 only determine which items the statutes must contain, without granting such a power?

[192]See Strommer (2014a), p. 193. Also consider Kastner (1986), p. 149, referring to § 75 Abs 2 AktG.

[193]See Sec. 15 and Sec. 24 GenG.

[194]See Schulze (2004a), p. 107. Also consider Münkner (2006), p. 19.

[195]As well as the supervisory organ.

[196]See Schulze (2004b), p. 190.

[197]See Wiese (2006), p. 172.

Selbstorganschaft. It will be discussed below whether such conditions can be implemented via statutory provisions.

Finally, Sec. 24 para. 1 *GenG* determines that members of the supervisory organ cannot be appointed members of the management organ. This parallels Art. 37 para. 3 SCE-R.

Apart from these findings, the *GenG* does not contain any impediments that prevent a person from becoming a member of the management organ of an Austrian SCE.

The analyses conducted up to this point addressed impediments that are based on specific national rules; yet, nothing has been said about whether it is possible to adopt **statutory provisions regarding the conditions of membership**. According to Art. 46 para. 3 SCE-R, this is possible for SCEs adopting the one-tier system. Similarly, the SE-R[198] determines that statutes may, in accordance with the relevant national law,[199] lay down special eligibility conditions for members who represent the shareholders. However, as seen above, the SCE-R only partially regulates this issue. Hence, national provisions can be applied on the basis of Art. 8 para. 1 letter c (iii) SCE-R. If national law does not provide for a corresponding solution, such issues cannot be regulated via statutes. Hence, the drafters of the statutes cannot themselves define the criteria that determines who can join the management organ.[200]

According to *Italian law*, this gap can be closed by means of Art. 2387 CC,[201] which allows the statutes to set requirements for integrity, professionalism and independence. These may also refer to the requirements in the codes of conduct, which codes were drafted by the professional associations.[202] Here, integrity means no previous convictions, while professionalism refers to specific professional capacities.[203] Finally, independence refers to family relations as well as cooperative employees or members of the management organ of a controlled company or cooperative.[204] Art. 2387 CC must not be interpreted in a restrictive way, but in a manner in which the statutes can determine further requirements.[205]

The *Austrian legal system*, like Italian law, allows an SCE to use statutes to determine eligibility criteria. Accordingly, the *GenG* requires the statutes to include

---

[198]See Art. 47 para. 3 SE-R.

[199]"In accordance with the law applicable to public limited-liability company companies in the member states in which the SE's registered office is situated."

[200]Or the supervisory organ. Also consider Art. 9 SCE-R.

[201]Art. 2387 CC is applicable to the two-tier system due to the reference contained in 2409 undecies para. 1 CC.

[202]Or the management companies of regulated markets. See Art. 2387 CC.

[203]Documented by registration into specific professional registers.

[204]See Sandei (2018e), p. 2828 et seq. See also Romano (2017k), p. 2954 et seq.; Sanfilippo (2017a), p. 471 et seq.

[205]See Cariello (2012), p. 287; Comitato interregionale dei consigli notarili delle Tre Venezie (2011), H.D.5. E.g., time limits to be observed before a former member of the supervisory organ can become a member of the management organ. See also Sanfilippo (2017a), p. 469.

the terms of composition of the management organ. This implies that, under the Austrian legal system, it is possible to adopt qualification criteria.[206] In addition, it has been correctly observed that the principle of *Selbstorganschaft* can be inserted into the statutes.[207] Within the limits of this principle,[208] the statutes might determine that all or a specific number of members of one or all organs must be members of the cooperative. Yet, while this principle might be advantageous in terms of self-administration, internal decision making and the cooperative's identity, it might also carry disadvantageous consequences: these include low levels of expertise and professionalism, which are factors that strongly influence effectiveness and efficiency.[209]

The last issue concerning the composition of the management organ regards the **number of the organ's members**. According to the SCE-R, the management organ can consist of one or more members.[210] Thus, an SCE does not necessarily have to have a collegial management organ.[211] The number of members must be determined in the statutes. According to Art. 37 para. 4 SCE-R, the statutes must provide either a fixed number of members or the rules for determining this number.[212] This approach clearly reflects the notions of self-responsibility and self-regulation[213] by granting flexibility and freedom to adopt statutes. Self-regulation is in line with different traditions in the member states. As a result, the founders and members of the SCE can define the solution that best suits their needs.[214]

If the statutes contain rules for determining the number of members of the management organ, rather than setting a fixed number of members, it will be easier to adjust the number of members to ensure effective and efficient management. This number should be in line with the total number of members in the agricultural SCE and/or its growing business.[215] However, this flexible statutory freedom can be

[206]See Astl and Steinböck (2014), p. 148. Also consider Gruber (2012), nt 25.

[207]See Schulze (2004a), p. 107.

[208]And without prejudice to the specific rules regarding employee participation.

[209]See Schulze (2004a), p. 107.

[210]See Art. 37 para. 2 SCR R. Art. 37 para. 4 SCE-R states: "The number of members of the management organ or the rules for determining it shall be laid down in the SCE's statutes. However, a Member State may fix a minimum and/or maximum number."

[211]See Schulze (2004a), p. 94; Schöpflin (2018e), p. 1301.

[212]For instance, the statutes could determine whether and how the number of members must change in accordance with the volume of transactions or the number of members. See Schulze (2004a), p. 94 et seq. Less clear Schöpflin (2018e), p. 1301.

For the SE, see Drygala (2015a), p. 497 et seq.

[213]On these issues, see Fici (2013a), p. 49 et seq.

[214]Schulze favours the adoption of a management organ with at least two members in order to ensure that representation is guaranteed if member is absent. It is argued that such a solution could also satisfy the four-eyes principle, with the result that members can not only provide mutual assistance but also supervise and control each other. On the other hand, a management organ with only one member might be more suitable for an SCE with few members or a specialised or limited area of business. See Schulze (2004a), p. 95.

[215]See Schulze (2004a), p. 95.

restricted by national legislation because of Art. 37 para. 4 sent. 2 SCE-R, which allows a minimum and/or a maximum number of members to be fixed.[216] As an example, member states might provide for an organ with at least two or not more than five members. Considering the wording of the provision, a member state cannot set a fixed number of members. In other words, the minimum and maximum numbers cannot be identical. Such a provision would undermine the principle of self-regulation. The same is true for a national provision that would allow the statutes to fix the number of members, but not the rules for setting this number.[217] Provisions that specifically regulate the number of members in national cooperatives only apply to SCEs if a member state expressly declares as much.[218]

Neither Austria nor Italy have exercised the option contained in Art. 37 para. 4 sent. 2 SCE-R[219]; thus, cooperatives in these jurisdictions apply a legal regime that may somehow differ from the framework determined by the SCE-R. In fact, the *Italian legal system* applies a different approach to the SCE-R, in terms of both the minimum number of members and the mandatory content of the statutes. Art. 2542 para. 2 CC determines, in general, that the administrative organ must consist of no fewer than three members.[220] In addition, Art. 2409 novies para. 3 CC holds that the statutes must determine specific limits to the number of members. This implies that the statutes must set a minimum or maximum number.[221] Compared to the method advocated in Art. 37 para. 4 SCE-R, the Italian approach is less flexible.

In the *Austrian legal system*, Sec. 15 para. 2 *GenG* offers the options of a single- or multi-headed organ; this section basically corresponds to Art. 37 para.

[216]Interestingly, Art. 37 para. 4 SCE-R does not specifically determine that the authority granted to member states only refers to an SCE with registered offices within that member state's territory. Nevertheless, it is argued that this authority must be considered as such, in accordance with the general rules. See Schulze (2004a), p. 95.

[217]See Schulze (2004a), p. 95. Also consider Schöpflin (2018e), p. 1301. For the SE, see Manz (2010b), p. 501.

[218]For the SE, see Manz (2010b), p. 501.

[219]See Fici (2010), p. 65. In contrast, the German legislator considered this option and provided that the management organ has to contain at least two members. The statutes may adopt a higher number. See Sec. 14 SCEAG.

[220]This provision is applicable to an Italian cooperative adopting the two-tier system. See Paolucci (2019e), p. 131 et seq. Similarly, Art. 2409 novies para. 2 CC determines, in general, that the management organ must consist of no fewer than two members. See Del Sole (2010c), p. 330 et seq. The minimum of two members, as requested by para. 2, has been criticised because diverging opinions will lead to decision making being blocked (due to a tie). One approach is to assign the chairman a casting vote. It has also been suggested to increase the minimum number to at least three members, amending para. 2 as follows: "The management board consists of no less than three members". Rufini (2005), p. 1131.

[221]On this issue, see Miotto (2018c), p. 2409 novies 2903 et seq.; Del Sole (2010c), p. 330.

2 SCE-R.[222] In both cases, the number of members in the management organ is ultimately determined via statute,[223] reflecting the principle of statutory freedom.[224] Under Austrian law, the statutes may determine a fixed number, a minimum number, a maximum number or a combination of both.[225] These statutory provisions can also be applied to an Austrian SCE.

In this chapter, a comparison of the two legal systems has shown that in Austria it is not possible for legal entities to become members of the organs. This is in line with the prevailing Italian legal doctrine.[226] In this context, Sec. 2.5 para. 6 PECOL mentions that the majority of members of the organs in mutual cooperatives must be user members. Sec. 1.3 para. 2 PECOL states that user members may be either natural or legal persons. The PECOL do not contain any further information or limitations in this regard. Hence, it can be concluded that the PECOL support admitting legal persons as members of the organs.[227]

Then, regarding the composition of the management organ, and, in particular, the factors that influence the conditions of membership and the number of members, the analysis showed that an Italian *agricultural SCE* is more regulated, whereas both national legal systems allow the adoption of eligibility criteria by statutory provisions. Moreover, the majority of members of the management organ in an Italian SCE must be user members, whereas an Austrian SCE must not obey the principle of *Selbstorganschaft* and thus leaves the decision, to what extent this principle shall be applied, to the drafters of the statutes. As mentioned above, the PECOL require that the majority of members appointed to the management organ of mutual cooperatives must first be members of the cooperative.[228] This requirement is in line with Italian law and is therefore consistent with the rules that an Italian SCE must follow. If the PECOL are accepted as guidelines for establishing a common European cooperative identity, the SCEG should be amended in this regard.

Sec. 2.5 para. 7 letter e PECOL determines that the qualifications of the management organ's members should not unduly limit the democratic right of the general meeting to appoint members to the organ. In addition, the PECOL acknowledge that the law or statutes may provide grounds for disqualification. Some provisions might refer to the membership of the cooperative or contain a requirement of service to a different organ such as a regional committee.[229] Next, Sec. 2.5 para. 9 PECOL refers to cooperative training and experience. It requires members to have or acquire professional qualifications that comply with the particularities of cooperatives.[230]

[222]Determining that the management organ can be formed by one or more members.

[223]Also consider Sec. 5 para. 1 no 7 GenG.

[224]See Lehner (2007), p. 103 et seq.

[225]See Strommer (2014a), p. 190. Also consider Keinert (1988), p. 156; Kastner (1986), p. 148.

[226]Although a minority of Italian scholars support the opposite position.

[227]Also consider Snaith (2017), p. 69.

[228]See Snaith (2017), p. 69.

[229]See Snaith (2017), p. 70 et seq.

[230]See Snaith (2017), p. 71.

In addition, Sec. 2.5 para. 7 letter c PECOL requires the law or statutes to lay down any requirements for gender balance.[231] These recommendations can be based on statutory provisions and are therefore applicable to both Austrian and Italian agricultural SCEs.

Depending on the geographical area (which is the catchment area of an agricultural cooperative) or the hierarchical structure (as in the case of a secondary cooperative), further requirements may be contained in the statutes, which the members of the management organ must fulfil in order to qualify for their offices. Accordingly, not only technical competence but also geographical affiliation can be taken into account. This second aspect, in particular, is important helping farmer-members to feel suitably represented. Furthermore, it can also be specified that the chairman of the secondary cooperative must also be the chairman of a member cooperative.

Finally, neither the Austrian nor the Italian legislatures exercised the option contained in Art. 37 para. 4 SCE-R to establish a minimum and/or maximum number of members. Thus, neither Austrian nor Italian rules are relevant here, although they can be used as examples for drafting the statutes of an *agricultural SCE*. Moreover, in line with the SCE-R, it is possible to have organs with only a single member. In this regard, Sec. 2.5 para. 7 PECOL stresses that the organ must be both small enough to operate effectively and large enough to represent a range of members. This aspect can be crucial in multi-stakeholder or general interest cooperatives, because interests may diverge. The PECOL do not specify figures here; it only requires the law or statutes to lay down the maximum and minimum number of members for each organ.[232] This approach is more stringent than the one determined by the SCE-R's provision. However it is not clear why such stringency is required. The approach advocated by the SCE-R is better, as it allows the general meeting to be flexible when deciding upon membership numbers.[233]

The actual number of members serving on the management organ will probably ultimately be influenced by whether the members of an agricultural primary cooperative come from different municipalities, or whether an agricultural secondary cooperative unites different cooperatives with perhaps partly different orientations. Here, too, consideration will have to be given to the various interests involved. It is therefore necessary to take into account different local needs.

---

[231] There are legal initiatives to make this last requirement mandatory for listed companies. On this issue, see, e.g., Bruno et al. (2018).

[232] See Snaith (2017), p. 69 et seq.

[233] See Art. 37 para. 4 SCE-R, which refers to the rules for determining the number of members.

4.2.1.4 Appointment and Removal of Members of the Management Organ

The SCE-R contains provisions regarding the **appointment** and removal of the members of the management organ. According to Art. 39 para. 2 SCE-R, the general meeting regularly appoints the members of the supervisory organ, which in turn appoints the members of the management organ.[234] This rule can be amended by national legislation, inasmuch as the competence to appoint the management organ is assigned to the general meeting. Such a provision can be adopted by the statutes, as long as the same conditions apply to (national) cooperatives with registered offices within the member state's territory.[235]

In principle, the SCE-R thus creates a multi-stage system for appointing members to the various organs. The general meeting first appoints the members of the supervisory organ, which in turn appoints the members of the management organ. The intermediary role of the supervisory organ can be disposed of via national law, thus empowering the general meeting to appoint the members of the management organ. Art. 37 para. 2 subpara. 2 SCE-R provides for two different methods here: it can be determined directly by national law, or national law can permit to draft a statutory provision, increasing statutory freedom. In both cases, competence can be assigned to the general meeting under the same conditions as for cooperatives with registered offices within the territory of the member state. In other words, national cooperatives must also have this possibility.[236] It is assumed that these possibilities can be used only if the member state at issue adopts an appropriate legal act.[237]

The *Italian legislature* did not exercise this option, with the result that members of the management organ can only be appointed by the supervisory organ. This lines up with the set of provisions an Italian cooperative must observe. According to Art. 2409 novies para. 3 CC and Art. 2409 terdecies para. 1 letter a CC, the appointment of the members to the management organ is entrusted to the supervisory organ.[238]

---

[234] Art. 37 para. 2 subpara. 1 SCE-R.

[235] See Art. 37 para. 2 subpara. 2 SCE-R. It states: "The member or members of the management organ shall be appointed and removed by the supervisory organ.

However, a Member State may require or permit the statutes to provide that the member or members of the management organ are appointed and removed by the general meeting under the same conditions as for cooperatives that have registered offices within its territory."

[236] See Schulze (2004a), p. 96; Schöpflin (2018d), p. 1300. For the SE, see Manz (2010b), p. 499; Drygala (2015a), p. 494 et seq. Also consider Artmann (2002), p. 192; Brandt (2002), p. 993 et seq.; Kübler (2003), p. 232 et seq.

[237] See Fici (2013c), p. 148 fn 125 and in general 135 et seq.

[238] In this context it has been discussed whether, similar to the traditional governance system, the general meeting may also appoint the members of the management organ under the two-tier system. Especially as Art. 2519 CC, by referring to the provisions regarding the spa, makes these latter provisions applicable insofar as possible. In favour Tatarano (2011), p. 461 et seq. Different opinion Bonfante (2014a), p. 342 et seq. See also Mirone (2017a), p. 573.

Italian scholars have discussed whether the contract linking the managers to the company might be considered a contract regulated by Art. 1703 CC, a contract for work and services or a

Apart from these provisions, the Italian legal system contains other provisions that should be analysed in this context. Even though they do not apply to an Italian SCE, they are worth mentioning as they help to better understand the content of the SCE-R. According to Art. 2544 para. 2 CC, the holders of financial instruments can directly elect the members of the management organ and of the supervisory organ.[239] This provision is, however, not applicable to an SCE, as the SCE-R only refers to national law with respect to the admissibility of non-user members, whereas all the other relevant details are regulated by the SCE-R.[240]

The SCE-R provides an alternative mechanism to protect the interests of non-user members. According to Art. 39 para. 3 SCE-R, 25% of the supervisory organ can be made up of non-user members. Thus, non-user members can directly influence the composition of the management organ. Admittedly, such discussions are only theoretically relevant. In practice, if an SCE wants to be attractive to non-user members, it must provide adequate instruments that allow them to protect their interests; the SCE-R is flexible enough to guarantee this.[241] An additional requirement determining a specific number or proportion of seats in the management organ would not only be cumbersome, but may also contradict the criteria of professionalism to be fulfilled by the members of this organ.

Contrary to the Italian legislature, the *Austrian legislature* increased statutory freedom[242] by exercising the option given in Art. 37 para. 2 subpara. 2 SCE-R,[243] Thus, the management organ may be appointed by either the supervisory organ or the general meeting. An Austrian cooperative is less flexible. Interestingly, until the *URÄG* 2008, Sec. 15 para. 1 *GenG* did not explicitly determine which organ had to

management contract. Nowadays, the general opinion is that one of the two latter answers is correct. As determined by Art. 1703 CC, the manager does not only conclude one or more juridical acts; they have an autonomous position, even in respect of the general meeting (to a certain extent). The fulfilment of their tasks is supervised by different internal and external control mechanisms. It can be argued that these are not compatible with the type of contract provided for by Art. 1703 CC. It is stressed that this type of contract cannot be considered subordinated work. See Usai (2010a), p. 484. See also Sanfilippo (2017a), p. 470 et seq.

[239]Within the limits according to Art. 2544 para. 2 CC. This has been criticised, as this right has been denied to user members. The favoured position of holders of financial instruments becomes even more evident if one compares their rights with the rights Art. 2351 CC assigns to the holders of financial instruments of an spa, who can elect only one member of the supervisory organ. Moreover, it is not quite clear yet, whether the supervisory organ may dismiss the members elected by the holder of financial instruments. See Giorgi (2018b), p. 3243 et seq. Also consider Bonfante (2004b), p. 2599.

[240]See Cusa (2004c), p. 178 et seq.

[241]See Sects. 4.2.2.2, 4.4.4 and Sect. 5.3.

[242]As already mentioned, the option given by the regulation would also permit such an obligation.

[243]See Sec. 22 SCEG.

appoint the members of the management organ. However, there was no doubt that this competence belonged to the general meeting.[244]

The act of appointing members of the management organ normally also leads to the question of their **remuneration**. In this regard, the SCE-R does not contain a specific provision,[245] but solely states that the supervisory organ represents the SCE in dealings with the members of the management organ, including the conclusion of contracts.[246] This includes the conclusion of employment or management contracts.[247] But does this also include the corresponding negotiation process, during which contracts shall be concluded? This process, when linked to the duty of the supervisory organ to appoint the members of the management organ, basically relates to two issues: (1) accepting responsibilities to manage the SCE and (2) receiving appropriate remuneration. As a result, the supervisory organ should be empowered to include remuneration in the negotiation procedure. This, however, does not prevent the general meeting from adopting a remuneration policy by specifying guidelines the supervisory organ must consider during the negotiation process. As will be seen, the two legal systems provide for different solutions. The specific comments in this regard are helpful to better understand this issue.

In contrast to the SCE-R,[248] the *Italian civil code* explicitly deals with the issue of remuneration. According to Art. 2409 terdecies para. 1 letter a CC, an Italian cooperative may choose between two possibilities. As a default rule, the supervisory organ[249] sets the remuneration of the members of the management organ. Alternatively, the general meeting can set it. This latter approach allows competence to be shared between the two organs and must be based on a specific statutory

---

[244]In addition, it was discussed whether the other organs of the cooperative would be authorised to appoint the management organ. See Strommer (2014a), p. 190 et seq. Also consider Kastner (1986), p. 148. Other opinion Keinert (1988), p. 152 et seq.

According to Austrian (and German) legal doctrine, membership in an organ can be considered from two perspectives: one can distinguish between the functions as a member of the management organ and the contractual relation of the member with the cooperative. For instance, Sec. 15 para. 2 GenG states that the members may be paid or unpaid. This provision clearly refers to the contractual relationship between the member and the cooperative. Appointment as a member of the management organ is not sufficient to establish this contractual relationship; a specific contract is necessary which establishes this obligation. This obligation must be concluded by the organ which appointed the member of the management organ. If this function is fulfilled on a honorary basis, a mandate can still be given, albeit only implicitly. In this way, the members of the organ can put forward their claims for compensation of costs. If this function is fulfilled on a paid basis, it is necessary to decide whether this relation should be considered an employment contract or a freelance activity. As the general meeting, as the superior organ of the cooperative, is empowered to issue binding directives, it is argued that the relationship must be considered an employment contract. See Strommer (2014a), p. 197 et seq. As will be seen in Sect. 4.4.1, this competence is not assigned to the general meeting of an Austrian SCE.

[245]See Chirico and Troianiello (2007), p. 66.

[246]See Art. 39 para. 1 sent. 4 SCE-R.

[247]See Schöpflin (2018f), p. 1302.

[248]And the Austrian legal system.

[249]It appoints the members of the management organ.

provision.[250] A corresponding provision could be applied to an Italian SCE because of Art. 52 subpara. 2 SCE-R.

Regarding the important issue of remuneration, interestingly, the *Austrian legal system*, like the SCE-R, does not contain a specific provision. In this context, *Binder* and *Lengauer* have observed that the supervisory organ seems more suited to represent the cooperative in dealings with the management organ, even though (in general) the general meeting appoints and removes the members of the management organ.[251] This comment is particularly true regarding remuneration for members of the management organ, a topic not suited for discussion at the general meeting.[252] This observation is also valid for an SCE.

In addition to the appointment procedure, Art. 37 para. 2 SCE-R refers to the **removal of members** of the management organ, regulating both in the same way. In principle, these competences belong to the supervisory organ; they can be shifted to the general meeting under the described circumstances. Apart from Art. 45 para. 1 SCE-R,[253] the regulation does not provide for any rules determining or limiting reasons for removal.[254]

Discussion centres on whether a member of an SCE can be removed freely or only with good cause. This is an important question, because the answer ultimately decides the extent of power of the supervisory organ. If the supervisory organ can remove members of the management organ at any time, its powers are considerable, allowing the removal of members who do not share the supervisory organ's views.

The SE-R contains the same provisions in this respect. It is argued that Art. 39 para. 2 SE-R regulates the competence of removal is based on the principle to freely remove members of the management organ. This argument is based on the wording of the paragraph, which neither bases the power to remove upon further conditions nor obliges member states to establish specific rules.[255] However, this argument is not convincing, as the final version of the SE-R does not contain any reference in this regard.[256] It is also argued that Art. 46 para. 1 SE-R, by defining a fixed term of office (like the SCE-R), completely excludes free removal.[257] However, this interpretation is also unconvincing, as Art. 46 para. 1 SE-R refers to the term of office and not the power of removal.[258] Thus the SE-R does not exhaustively regulate this issue.[259] These observations are also valid for an SCE. The content of

[250] See Del Sole (2010d), p. 359. Also consider Breida (2004c), p. 1177. See also Romano (2017v), p. 3006 et seq.

[251] See Sec. 15 para. 1 GenG, which provides for both possibilities.

[252] See Binder and Lengauer (2014b), p. 332.

[253] A specific reason for terminating office can be found in Art. 45 para. 1 SCE-R. It determines that membership in the management organ expires with the term of office expires.

[254] See Schulze (2004a), p. 97.

[255] For the SE, see Lange (2003), p. 305 et seq.; Gutsche (1994), p. 81 et seq.

[256] See Artmann (2002), p. 192.

[257] For the SE, see Hirte (2002), p. 5.

[258] For the SE, see Manz (2010b), p. 498.

[259] For the SE, see Manz (2010b), p. 498; Artmann (2002), p. 192.

this right to removal must therefore be understood by applying national laws, in accordance with Art. 8 para. 1 letter c SCE-R.[260]

As far as removal of the members of the management organ is concerned, the *Italian legal system* contains specific provisions that must be observed by an Italian SCE, because of the aforementioned gap. According to Art. 2409 novies para. 5 CC, the members of the management organ may be removed by the supervisory organ at any time.[261] If membership is revoked without cause, the affected member of the management organ can exercise their right to compensation of damages, which is not prejudiced.[262] The legislature's intent here was to give the supervisory organ strong influence over the management organ. There is no question that the supervisory organ may remove the members of the management organ *ad nutum* if there are diverging opinions (between the management organ and the supervisory organ) about strategic decisions.[263] In addition, this authority holds both the cooperative and the members of the supervisory organ who decide upon the removal liable for damages. Consequently, we argue, the actual exercise of this authority will be modest.[264]

Let us now turn to consider the *Austrian situation*. According to Sec. 15 para. 2 *GenG*, the organ responsible for appointing members of the management organ

[260]Remember that the EU legislator has conceived of the SCE-R as based on a subsidiary applicability of national law and not as an exhaustive regulation. For the SE, see Manz (2010b), p. 498. Also consider Drygala (2015a), p. 493 et seq.

[261]Even if appointed by the statutes. Similarly, Art. 2409 terdecies para. 1 CC determines that the supervisory organ removes the members of the management organ.

[262]In case of revocation without cause, the removed member has a right to compensation.

[263]If the statutes provide for this possibility according to Art. 2409 terdecies para. 1 letter f-bis CC. For further details, see Sect. 4.2.2.1.

[264]See Fortunato (2003), p. 879 et seq. Scholars have described this power as the mechanism to activate the split between the shareholders' property and the power of the organs of the company. See Breida (2004c), p. 1177; Del Sole (2010d), p. 359. See also Romano (2017v), p. 3007.

Further specific cases dealing with revocation are contained in Art. 2449 para. 2 CC and Art. 2409 para. 4 CC. Then, according to Art. 2385 CC (applicable due to Art. 2409 undecies CC) a member may resign his office. In this case, the member has to give written notice thereof to the management organ and the chairman of the supervisory board. Art. 2385 CC specifies that resignation is effective either immediately, on the condition a majority of members remains in office or otherwise from the time when the majority has been reappointed (as a result of the acceptance of the new members). It is not necessary to motivate resignation. In this context it is discussed whether resignation without good cause may held the resigning member liable for damages. See Sandei (2018d), p. 2824. See also Romano (2017j), p. 2951 et seq. Moreover, two hypothesis of automatic removal can be considered in this context. Art. 2409 decies para. 1 CC determines that an action for liability against the members of the management organ may be brought by the company or the shareholders (pursuant to articles 2393 and 2393 bis civil code), leading if certain conditions are met, to the removal of the concerned/respective member of the management organ. Next, Art. 2409 decies para. 2 CC determines that the action of liability may also be brought further pursuant to a resolution of the supervisory organ.

may revoke this membership at any time. The law grants a right of compensation if removal would damage the interests of the person whose membership is revoked.[265] This general rule is applicable to an Austrian SCE, whether the management organ has been appointed by either the supervisory organ or the general meeting. The same is true for the rules contained in Sec. 15 para. 3 sent. 1 and sent. 2 *GenG*. Accordingly, para. 3 sent. 1 determines that it may only be possible to revoke membership with good cause, provided these conditions are met: (1) the statutes assign the competence for revocation to the supervisory organ, (2) the statutes determine a fixed term of office for the members of the management organ, and (3) the statutes determine that membership can only be revoked with good cause. The legislature introduced these provisions, as it is often difficult to find people with appropriate management qualifications.[266]

In addition, para. 3 last sent. determines that the general meeting cannot be deprived of its right to revoke membership at any time. It is argued that the general meeting, as the supreme organ of a cooperative, should not be obliged to advance arguments in the case of a loss of confidence. Accordingly, para. 3 last sent. determines that the general meeting may always reserve the right to revoke membership, even if a statutory provision, as required by para. 3 sent. 1, exists.[267] This provision contained in para. 3 last sent. is based on the assumption that the general meeting of an Austrian cooperative may give instructions to all organs, because of its special role. However, as already mentioned,[268] the general meeting of an Austrian SCE does not have such a competence; therefore, this provision does not apply. This interpretation would line up with the basic structure of an SCE, which gives to the supervisory organ the competence to remove members of the management organ.[269] The general meeting's right to remove the members of the management organ can thus be based exclusively on Sec. 15 para. 2 *GenG*.[270]

---

[265]See Strommer (2014a), p. 194. Revocation however, does not affect the contractual relation with a professional management organ. In order to dissolve this relationship, further steps are necessary. See Strommer (2014a), p. 194. Also consider Keinert (1988), p. 157; Kastner (1986), p. 151, OGH 29.03.2001, 8 Ob A 44/01 et seq.

[266]See Strommer (2014a), p. 194. Revoking membership without good cause is provisionally effective, as long as the court has not made a legally binding decision to the contrary.

[267]If the general meeting is entitled to revoke, the agenda must contain a specific item. See Strommer (2014a), p. 194 et seq.

[268]See Sect. 4.2.1.1.

[269]See Art. 37 para. 2 subpara. 1, in contrast to subpara. 2 SCE-R.

[270]Under the Austrian legal system, resignation of office is further grounds for termination. In case of doubts, the contractual relationship is not affected by this act. If the office was accepted for an indeterminate period, resignation of office can occur without good cause. In addition, revocation by mutual agreement is possible at any time and also if there is neither good cause nor a specific deadline. If a member of the management organ resigns without good cause, the cooperative may have a right to compensation. In addition, if the function has been accepted for a specific period of time, resignation of office is only possible for good cause. If this is not given, the resignation is still effective, but the former member can be held liable for damages. In this case revocation of membership by mutual agreement is possible. It is not quite clear to whom the member must declare his resignation. It is argued that the supervisory organ is the best choice here. See Strommer (2014a), p. 195.

This section has analysed the appointment and removal procedures that Italian and Austrian SCEs must observe. In principle, members are appointed and removed by the supervisory organ, in accordance with the SCE-R. Compared to the Italian rules applicable to an SCE, the Austrian agricultural SCE has increased statutory freedom, as the legislature allows a statutory provision that states that the members are appointed by the general meeting.

According to the SCE-R, the supervisory organ is empowered to negotiate remuneration for the members of the management organ. The *GenG* does not contain a similar provision, but it is argued that the supervisory organ—instead of the general meeting—should negotiate this issue. In contrast, the Italian legal system specifically addresses this issue, determining that, by default, the supervisory organ can set remuneration. Alternatively, this task can be transferred to the general meeting. This solution seems applicable to an Italian agricultural SCE.

The PECOL acknowledges the variety of remuneration models used in Europe without providing specific recommendations on which model to apply.[271] However, Sec. 2.5 para. 10 PECOL explicitly requires that remuneration must be decided upon by the general meeting, which must account for the nature of the cooperative and its specific features. More precisely, it requires that any remuneration must be decided on or approved by the general meeting.[272] This should also imply that the general meeting sets remuneration policies that a supervisory organ must observe. As already seen, this possibility is in line with the rules determined by the SCE-R.

For limits on the reasons for removal, it is necessary to consider national law. Both legal systems allow the removal of the members of the management organ at any time. In both jurisdictions, the removed member may exercise a right to compensation for damages. In addition, the Austrian legal system allows membership to be revoked for good cause, provided that specific conditions are met.

4.2.1.5 Internal Organisation of the Management Organ

Regarding the internal organisation of the management organ, Sect. 1 of Chapt. III SCE-R contains provisions about two things: (1) the chairmanship and (2) the calling of meetings. Section 3 of Chapt. III SCE-R adds further provisions dealing with the decision-making process, representation when decisions are made and other similar issues. Art. 38 SCE-R specifically addresses the chairmanship of the management

[271] As a general rule, Sec. 2.4 para. 6 letter c states that the members' meeting shall elect and remove the members of an elected board or committee. Then, para. 2 letter b acknowledges that governance can be divided between the general meeting and one or more boards or committees. The PECOL acknowledge that such separated structures are not suitable for small cooperatives. Without giving further information, the PECOL acknowledge that the members of the management organ may be elected by either the supervisory organ or the general meeting. The same is true for removal. In this context, PECOL also refers to the relevant provisions of the SCE-R. See Snaith (2017), p. 68 et seq.

[272] See Snaith (2017), p. 71.

organ.[273] It contains provisions governing the election of the chairman and the calling of meetings, but does not consider further issues, especially with respect to the chairman's duties. Accordingly, national law must be considered.[274]

According to Art. 38 para. 1 SCE-R, the management organ must elect a chairman from among its members, in accordance with the statutes. It is correctly emphasised that it is not possible to divide the **chairmanship** post between two or more members of the organ.[275] Statutes can determine the period of office, the election procedure and the procedural competence of the chairman. If the statutes do not contain this information, the management organ can autonomously decide these things.[276]

The right to elect the chairman is a power of the management organ. A statutory provision shifting this right to the general meeting or the supervisory organ would contradict the law. Similarly, only members of the management organ have the right to stand as a candidate.[277]

The SCE-R identifies the duty to call the meeting of the organ as a specific task assigned to the chairman. According to Art. 38 para. 2 SCE-R,[278] the conditions detailed in the statutes must be observed here. The meeting can be called at the initiative of the chairman or at the request of any member. In the latter case, the requesting member must indicate his reasons for calling the meeting. If this condition is fulfilled, the chairman must call the meeting within 15 days. If this time expires without any action having been taken, the meeting can be called by the requesting member.[279] In addition, the statutes may include an obligation to call a meeting; such an obligation is given if it is in the interests of the SCE.[280] Finally, according to Art. 50 para. 2 SCE-R, the chairman has the casting vote in the case of a tie.[281]

---

[273]In contrast, the SE-R does not provide any rules in this respect. Art. 38 SCE-R states: "The management organ shall elect a chairman from among its members, in accordance with the statutes."

[274]Applying thus Art. 8 para. 1 letter c SCE-R.

[275]See Schulze (2004a), p. 97.

[276]See Schöpflin (2018e), p. 1301.

[277]Another solution (e.g., the election of an external chairman) would be contrary to the wording "among its members". External advice can be obtained by nominating a managing director. See Schulze (2004a), p. 97. As mentioned in Sect. 4.2.1.1, according to Art. 37 para. 1 sent. 2 SCE-R, such a provision can be given by national law.

[278]It states: "The chairman shall call a meeting of the management organ under the conditions laid down in the statutes, either on his own initiative or at the request of any member. Any such request shall indicate the reasons for calling the meeting. If no action has been taken in respect of such a request within 15 days, the meeting of the management organ may be called by the member(s) who made the request."

[279]See Schulze (2004a), p. 97; Schöpflin (2018e), p. 1301.

[280]See Schöpflin (2018e), p. 1301. Compared to German cooperative law, the SCE-R grants wider minority rights, as it does not determine a specific quorum or require a juridical authorisation. See Schöpflin (2018e), p. 1301.

[281]Provided there is no relevant provision in the statutes.

As the SCE-R does not contain further information regarding the competence of the chairman, the necessary details must be determined by national law.[282] According to *Italian law*, details about such competence are determined by Art. 2381 para. 1 CC.[283] Even though neither Art. 2409 novies para. 1 CC nor Art. 2409 undecies CC explicitly refer to this provision, it seems indirectly applicable, because of Art. 223 septies prov. impl. CC.[284] Accordingly, the chairman calls the meeting of the management organ, sets its agenda, coordinates the work and makes sure adequate information about the matters on the agenda is provided to all the members of the management organ.[285] The chairman thus has the competence to safeguard the function of the management organ.[286] These findings also applicable to the chairman of an Italian agricultural SCE.

The chairman primarily focuses on the efficient functioning of the management organ. Thus, the tasks he or she must fulfil can never be considered exhaustive, even if they are specifically determined by statutory provisions. He or she must carry out all tasks necessary for making the management organ functional.[287] Even though Art. 2381 para. 1 CC does not grant management powers, in practice, such powers are frequently granted to the chairman via statutory provisions.[288] In this case, the chairman also acts as a managing director. By not exercising the option contained in Art. 37 para. 1 SCE-R,[289] the Italian legislature precluded such a provision from being adopted by an Italian SCE.

Contrary to both the SCR R and the Italian legal system, the *Austrian legal system* does not contain a provision dealing with the chairman. Therefore, information about the possible competence of the chairman comes from real-life examples.

General matters concerning the management organ—such as election, composition of the organ and so on—are determined by the statutes, in accordance with Sec. 5 para. 1 no. 7 *GenG*. In practice, if the management organ is constituted by more than one person, the statutes may provide for the possibility to elect the chairman.[290] In contrast, this aspect is specifically regulated by the SCE-R. Next, under Austrian

[282] According to Art. 8 para. 1 letter c SCE-R. Also consider Schöpflin (2018e), p. 1301.

[283] Art. 2380 bis para. 5 CC (Art. 2409 undecies para. 1 CC refers to it.) states that the management organ selects the chairman from among its members, as long as the chairman is not appointed by the general meeting. See Del Sole (2010c), p. 331. However, as seen above, this latter possibility is not open to an Italian SCE.

[284] See Guaccero (2004a), p. 879; Cariello (2012), p. 326 et seq.; Rufini (2005), p. 1134; Mirone (2017a), p. 574.

[285] See Del Sole (2010c), p. 331.

[286] However, the statutes may provide for a different solution. Finally, the chairman of the management organ frequently chairs the general meeting. See Usai (2010b), p. 491. See also Romano (2017g), p. 2944 et seq.; Sanfilippo (2017a), p. 484 et seq.

[287] See Usai (2010b), p. 490 et seq.; Bonelli (2004), p. 38; Sanfilippo (2017a), p. 485 et seq.

[288] Critical Bonelli (2004), p. 41.

[289] See Sect. 4.2.1.1.

[290] See Strommer (2014b), pp. 205; 148. Also consider Kastner (1986), p. 154; Keinert (1988), p. 156.

law, the role of chairman can best be described as *primus inter pares* (first among equals), with competence ultimately determined by the statutes.[291] Thus, the chairman of the management organ of an Austrian SCE could exercise a similar role.

Unlike the supervisory organ,[292] the *GenG* does not contain a legal provision that addresses the need to call meetings of the management organ. Normally, however, the chairman both calls and chairs the meeting.[293]

According to the Austrian legal system, a precondition for decision making is that every member of the management organ must be invited to the meeting, in line with the provisions contained in the statutes or rules of procedure. The provisions referring to the general meeting—which regulate how to convene it, the agenda and the decision-making process—cannot be applied by analogy. As a result, if neither the statutes nor the rules of procedure contain specific provisions, it is argued that the notification can be submitted without indicating the agenda.[294] This solution can also be applied by an Austrian SCE in one of two situations: (1) if the chairman calls the meeting or (2) the meeting is convened as requested by a member of the organ. Here, Art. 38 para. 2 SCE-R only requires that the request (directed to the chairman) indicates the reasons for calling the meeting, whereas the SCE-R is silent in regards to the content of the notification. Therefore, an Austrian SCE, when considering the issue of chairmanship, must first consider the SCE-R and then adopt statutory provisions. The *GenG* contains no further provisions to be applied in this context. Compared to an Austrian cooperative, individual members of the management organ in an Austrian SCE are better able to make their voices heard.

The SCE-R's provisions concerning chairmanship and the calling of the meetings of the management organ are complemented by Art. 50 SCE-R, which contains rules regarding the **decision-making process**. This article is part of Chap. 3 Sec. 3 SCE-R, which contains rules common to the one- and two-tier systems. The following analysis thus also refers to the supervisory and administrative organs.[295] These rules prevail over national rules. However, apart from Art. 50 para. 1 subpara. 2 SCE-R, they can be amended by statutory provisions. An exception arises if the regulation provides a solution contrary to Art. 50 SCE-R.[296]

---

[291]See Strommer (2014b), p. 205. Also consider Keinert (1988), p. 156.

[292]See Sec. 24 letter d GenG.

[293]See Strommer (2014b), p. 205. The management organ normally makes its decisions in dedicated meetings. The calling of these meetings and how they are conducted is in principle regulated by the statutes. However, such provisions can also be determined by rules of procedure, as long as the statutes contain this possibility. See Strommer (2014b), p. 204 et seq.

[294]See Strommer (2014b), p. 205 et seq. Also consider Nowotny (2008a), nt 5/75.

[295]Specific details can be found in Sects. 4.2.2.4 and 4.3.4.

The only organs governed by Art. 50 SCE-R are those mentioned in Art. 37 para. 1 sent. 1 SCE-R, Art. 39 para. 1 sent. 1 SCE-R and Art. 42 para. 1 sent. 1 SCE-R. See Schöpflin (2018q), p. 1315. Art. 61 and Art. 58 para. 3 SCE-R contain specific provisions relating to the decision making process of the general meeting. These provisions are analysed in Sects. 4.4.4 and 4.4.5.

[296]For the SE, see Teichmann (2015i). Also consider Donativi in Capriglione 204.

Para. 1[297] determines the rules for quorums and decision making, which the management organ[298] must observe. These rules are valid unless the SCE-R or the statutes provide otherwise.[299] The statutes may establish relatively strict rules governing the quorum, but they may only set stricter rules for majority requirements.[300] The SCE-R requires a quorum of at least 50% of members with voting rights. The SCE-R requires the majority of these members to vote in favour of a decision for it to pass.[301] In addition, absent members can either authorise another member of the organ to take part in decisions or take part via alternate members. These must be appointed at the same time as the authorising members.

Though nothing is explicitly said in the SCE-R about the formalities of decision making,[302] two approaches seem possible. First, if the rule determined by Art. 50 para. 1 letter b SCE-R applies, then national law must arguably be applied, as required by Art. 8 para. 1 letter c SCE, since the SCE-R does not contain further details on formalities. As mentioned above, the rule contained in letter b only applies if the statutes do not provide otherwise.[303] Thus, depending on national law, decisions can be made via email, a show of hands or video conference, among others. However, national provisions cannot introduce decision making via circular resolutions, as this practice runs counter to letter b, which refers to members present or represented.

The second approach relates to the possibility of establishing formalities by means of statutory provisions, which means that the rule contained in Art. 50 para. 1 letter b SCE-R is amended. This provision allows for two interpretations: First, it can imply that the possibility of adopting statutory provisions for quorums and decision making (as granted by Art. 50 para. 1 SCE-R) only refers to 'half of the members' (this formulation relates to quorum, as determined by letter a) and the 'majority of the members' (this formulation relates to decision-making, as determined by letter b). if this interpretations applies, statutory provisions only may

[297] Art. 50 para. 1 SCE-R states: "Unless otherwise provided by this Regulation or the statutes, the internal rules relating to quorums and decision taking in SCE organs shall be as follows:

- quorum: at least half of the members with voting rights must be present or represented;
- decision-taking: a majority of the members with voting rights present or represented.

Members who are absent may take part in decisions by authorising another member of the organ or the alternate members who were appointed at the same time to represent them."

[298] Along with the supervisory and administrative organs.

[299] See Schulze (2004a), p. 112.

[300] See Schöpflin (2018q), p. 1315 et seq. For the SE, see Hirte (2002), p. 5; Manz (2010l), p. 630. Critically, Teichmann (2015i), p. 758.

[301] Abstentions and invalid votes are not counted. See Schöpflin (2018r), p. 1316. For the SE, see Manz (2010l), p. 630 et seq.; Teichmann (2015i), p. 763.

[302] See Schöpflin (2018r), p. 1316. For the SE, see Manz (2010l), p. 631; Teichmann (2015i), p. 763.

[303] On the other hand, this means that the statutes may determine the decision-making process in the event that the rule contained in letter (b) is amended. The formulation of Art. 50 para. 1 SCE is particularly clear and strict in this regard.

determine a quantitative criterion. Second, the possibility of amending Art. 50 para. 1 letter b SCE-R can imply that this also refers to those members who are 'present or represented'. In other words, the question is, may statutory provisions alter this second formulation? This second approach is the better interpretation, because it is more coherent.[304] The stricter approach, i.e., the first approach, could have been introduced by a simple reference to majority and quorum requirements,[305] instead of referring to the various elements of the entire decision-making process.[306] Therefore, as long as the statutes amend the rule contained in letter b, statutory provisions could allow decisions to be made via email, a show of hands and circular resolutions, among others. As mentioned above, decision making via circular resolutions requires that the wording 'members present or represented' be amended.[307]

As mentioned above, Art. 50 para. 2 SCE-R[308] addresses what happens in the event of a tie. In this case, the chairman of the management organ[309] has the casting vote. However, this provision must only be applied if the statutes do not contain a relevant provision in this regard.[310] It is therefore possible that the chairman has a casting vote even if the organ only has two members.[311] However, the chairman cannot have exclusive decision-making power, even in specific matters. Such a wide interpretation would run contrary to the joint responsibility of all members of the organ.[312]

Having analysed how the SCE-R permits the management organ to make decisions, it is now important to understand those provisions of national law that regulate issues that emerge from the decision-making process. This not only helps to better grasp the content of the SCE-R's provisions, but also helps to understand which

[304] See also Schöpflin (2018r), p. 1316. Also consider Mahi (2004), p. 90 et seq.

[305] Like, for example, Art. 5 para. 4 bullet 11 SCE-R does.

[306] Similarly, both the German and Italian versions of the SCE-R distinguish between "Mehrheit- und Beschlussfähigkeitsregeln" as opposed to "interne Regeln für die Beschlussfähigkeit und Beschlussfassung" and "regole che disciplinano le maggioranze e i quorum" as opposed to "norme interne in materia di quorum e di presa di decisioni".

[307] It has been correctly observed that the statutes may also determine the type of decision making, e.g., meetings, circular resolutions, telephone or video conferences, email, etc. See Manz (2010l), p. 632; Teichmann (2015i), p. 758.

[308] It states: "Where there is no relevant provision in the statutes, the chairman of each organ shall have a casting vote in the event of a tie. There shall be no provision to the contrary in the statutes, however, where half of the supervisory organ consists of employees' representatives. Where employee participation is provided for in accordance with Directive 2003/72/EC, a Member State may provide that the supervisory organ's quorum and decision-making shall, by way of derogation from the provisions referred to in paragraphs 1 and 2, be subject to the rules applicable, under the same conditions, to cooperatives governed by the law of the Member State concerned."

[309] As well as of the supervisory and administrative organs.

[310] Para 2 specifies that a different statutory provision cannot be applied, where half of the supervisory organ consists of employees' representatives.

[311] See Schöpflin (2018q), p. 1315 et seq. For the SE, see Manz (2010m), p. 633; Teichmann (2015i), p. 765.

[312] See Schöpflin (2018q), p. 1315 et seq.

national rules must be applied because of Art. 8 para. 1 letter c SCE-R. According to *Italian law*, the provisions for the decision-making process, as undertaken by the management organ of an Italian cooperative, are determined by Art. 2409 undecies para. 2 CC, which refers to Art. 2388 CC.[313] Art. 2388 CC contains provisions on the validity of resolutions. The law here requires the presence of a majority (quorum) and grants the option of requiring a larger number of members to be present via the statutes. As seen above, the SCE-R is more flexible in this regard.

Resolutions are passed by an absolute majority of those present.[314] However, the statutes may determine a different (but higher) majority. This approach is the same as that contained in the SCE-R. Like the SCE-R, a casting vote is also possible.[315]

A marked difference for an Italian SCE is that, in Italian cooperatives, votes cannot be cast by proxy, according to an explicit provision contained in Art. 2388 para. 3 CC.[316] Nor is it possible to make decisions via correspondence, as the law requires the presence of members.[317] As a result, decisions cannot be made by circular resolutions.

Next, according to Art. 2388 para. 1 last sent. CC, the statutes may determine that a member can attend the meetings of the management organ via telecommunications devices. As the SCE-R does not contain any information about how members must attend meetings, this paragraph is thus also applicable to an Italian SCE, on the condition that Art. 50 para. 1 letter b SCE-R is applied, with the consequence that national rules on formalities must fill a gap.[318] Yet, as seen, in case letter b has been altered, then the national rules cannot be applied, according to Art. 50 para. 1 SCE-R, as this article generally refers to the internal rules for quorums and the decision-making process. These internal rules can then be drafted via the statutes.[319]

[313]In addition, the Italian legal system specifically regulates the possibility to challenge these resolutions (consider Art. 2388 para. 4 CC). The provisions dealing with conflict of interests are also applicable. See Art. 2391 CC and Sect. 4.2.1.6, dealing with duty of loyalty. Art. 2409 undecies para. 2 CC specifies that the right to challenge also pertains to the supervisory organ.

[314]Art. 2388 para. 2 CC.

[315]Due to freedom of self-regulation, as determined by Art. 2388 CC. See Cariello (2012), p. 329. See also Sanfilippo (2017a), p. 484.

[316]Consider Art. 50 para. 1 subpara. 2 SCE-R.

[317]See Sandei (2018f), p. 2831; Facchin (2009a), p. 501; Comitato interregionale dei consigli notarili delle Tre Venezie (2011), H.C.8. See also Romano (2017l), p. 2955 et seq.; Sanfilippo (2017a), p. 484.

[318]As explained above.

Art 2388 para. 4 CC states that resolutions taken by the management organ that are not in compliance with the law or statutes are challengeable. A specific right is assigned to the supervisory organ, as well as to the members of the management organ, who were not present at the meeting when the decision was taken or dissented. Also, members or shareholders may challenge a decision on the condition that their rights are harmed; further provisions are contained in Arts. 2377 and 2378, to the extent that they are compatible. For the procedure for challenging, see Art. 2378 CC, where compatible.

[319]Either directly, inasmuch as they contain detailed information, or indirectly, inasmuch as they assign a specific competency to the general meeting to draft internal rules.

As letters a) and b) of Art. 50 para. 1 SCE-R refer to 'members represented', the internal rules may also implicitly determine how members may authorise other members to represent them in the meeting. This alternate member should be appointed in the same way as the first member. In fact, this provision requires both to be appointed at the same time by the supervisory organ.[320]

Italian law does not explicitly provide for provisions that deal with procedural rules, but such rules can be adopted,[321] which also would enable the voting procedure's details to be determined. This finding also applies to an Italian SCE.[322] Finally, the management organ of both Italian cooperatives and Italian SCEs must keep a register of the meeting and the resolutions.[323]

Now we can consider what can be learned from the *Austrian legal order* concerning the decision-making process of an SCE. The *GenG* does not contain a specific provision dealing with the quorum.[324] In principle, the statutes regulate how meetings of the management organ are held. However, such provisions can be determined via the procedural rules, as long as the statutes provide for this.[325] Thus, the quorum is normally determined via the statutes.[326] As already explained in this chapter, to make valid decisions, all members must have been notified, as determined by the statutes or procedural rules. However, if all members are present, the quorum is met even if no notification was made.[327] Yet, this possibility does not seem compatible with the SCE-R,[328] which explicitly requires that statutes determine the conditions that must be observed when calling a meeting. It seems that, in any case, some type of notification is necessary to regularly convene the meeting. However, this does not preclude a specific statutory provision which regulates the case where no notification was made.[329]

The law does not contain a provision specifically dealing with how the management organ must make its decisions.[330] Hence, there is also no provision that explicitly requires decisions to be made via meetings. Thus, circular resolutions are admissible, provided that neither the statutes nor the rules of procedure prohibit

[320]Or alternatively by the general meeting.

[321]See Cariello (2012), p. 328.

[322]If Art. 50 para. 1 letter b SCE-R applies.

It also seems possible to adopt internal committees due to Art. 2381 para. 3 CC, as referred to by Art. 2409 novies para. 1 CC. See Cariello (2012), p. 329.

[323]Consider Art. 2421 para. 1 no 4 CC, which is applicable due to Art. 8 para. 1 letter c SCE-R. Also consider Del Sole (2010c), p. 328; Sanfilippo (2017a), p. 488.

[324]See Strommer (2014b), p. 205 et seq.

[325]See Strommer (2014b), p. 204 et seq. Also consider OGH 29.10.2009, 9 ObA 100/08h.

[326]Or rules of procedure.

[327]See Strommer (2014b), p. 205 et seq.

[328]Art. 38 para. 2 SCE-R.

[329]Because the SCE-R grants statutory freedom here.

[330]Unlike the supervisory organ.

this.[331] In contrast, if the management organ of an Austrian SCE wants to adopt circular resolutions, the statutes must explicitly allow this.

The statutes[332] normally contain a provision dictating which minutes must be taken.[333] In any case, it is advised (for liability purposes) that proper minutes be taken.[334] This observation applies to an Austrian SCE, because of Art. 8 para. 1 letter c (iii) SCE-R.

Statutes may also allow members of the management organ to appoint representatives. The statutes can determine the election procedure and the means for legitimising representation.[335] As argued above, this also applies to an Austrian SCE, because of Art. 8 para. 1 letter c SCE-R, on the condition that Art. 50 para. 1 letter b SCE-R is applied. Similar to the provision contained in Art. 50 para. 2 SCE-R, the statutes and the procedural rules can grant a casting vote to the chairman.[336]

The results here refer to the internal organisation of the management organ, particularly (1) the chairman, (2) calling meetings and (3) the decision-making process. It has been shown that the provisions governing the chairman are primarily determined by the SCE-R. The Austrian legal system does not contain a specific provision dealing with this issue, instead relying on statutory freedom. By contrast, the Italian legal system provides specific provisions that can be used as examples for statutory provisions.[337] Taken together, both legal systems provide significant statutory freedom. The PECOL do not contain any specific information in this regard.

The decision-making process of the management organ was also analysed. The SCE-R contains provisions for quorums, majorities, proxy voting and the chairman's casting vote. Internal rules about the formalities of the decision-making process can be based on statutory provisions, provided the rules contained in Art. 50 para. 1 letters a and/or b SCE-R are altered. Otherwise, national provisions determine the necessary formalities. Accordingly, the management organs of both Austrian and Italian SCEs may adopt rules of procedure. Only Italian *agricultural SCEs* are obligated to take minutes,[338] whereas Austrian *agricultural SCEs* may adopt a specific statutory provision.

---

[331] If, however, at least one member of the management organ requires a meeting, circular resolutions cannot be employed. Strommer (2014b), p. 205.

[332] Or rules of procedure.

[333] Again, there is no explicit provision, unlike for the supervisory organ. Consider Sec. 24c GenG.

[334] See Strommer (2014b), p. 204 et seq.

[335] See Astl and Steinböck (2014), p. 149.

[336] Similar to Sec. 70 para. 2 AktG. As seen, according to Art. 50 para. 2 SCE-R, the casting vote must not be based on a statutory provision. The GenG does not contain a specific provision in this regard. Therefore, this type of casting vote is not the same as the one contained in Sec. 33 para. 1 GenG. See Strommer (2014b), p. 205.

[337] The Italian provisions are default rules.

[338] To be more precise, the law requires a register of the meetings and resolutions to be kept.

The internal rules of the management organ of an *agricultural SCE* can, for example, determine that a qualified majority is required for certain items on the agenda. Such a rule can also be designed in such a way that a resolution is not passed if a certain number of dissenting votes, totalling less than the majority, is cast. This may concern, for example, certain points, such as the introduction of new quality parameters, changes to the existing quality guidelines or member awareness of certain new agricultural products. These are issues that significantly impact how members produce. Accordingly, a qualified majority seems advisable.

4.2.1.6 Civil Liability

The final issue concerns the civil liability of the organ members.[339] The whole issue is rather complex, and analysing it in details would go beyond the scope of this research; so this study aims to provide a concise overview of the concept contained in the SCE-R by showing how it is applied by the two legal systems. This analysis only deals with the relationship between an SCE and its organ members and does not address the liability of these members (or the SCE) relative to third parties. This issue is regulated by Art. 47 paras. 2 and 3 SCE-R. These rules are analysed in the chapters on the representation of the SCE.[340] Furthermore, it is helpful and necessary to briefly describe the duty of confidentiality contained in Art. 49 SCE-R, because it is linked to civil liability. A deeper analysis will not be conducted. Then, two major aspects of civil liability will be analysed: the preconditions for civil liability law and the assertion of claims. It will be shown that there are interesting differences between the two national legal systems that arise from the fact that liability concerns organs of cooperatives.

According to Art. 51 SCE-R, a precondition for liability is for the members of the organs to breach the legal, statutory or other obligations inherent in their duties.[341] The SCE-R contains a provision regarding the duty of confidentiality. Other duties can be determined according to the tasks assigned to the organs by the SCE-R. The normative framework for both governance systems is regulated by the SCE's regulation itself (Art. 37 et seq.). The competence of the management, supervisory

[339]Similar to the provisions regarding decision making, Art. 51 SCE-R is also contained in Sec. 3, and thus applies to the management, supervisory and administrative organs.

Art 51 SCE-R states: "Members of management, supervisory and administrative organs shall be liable, in accordance with the provisions applicable to cooperatives in the Member State in which the SCE's registered office is situated, for loss or damage sustained by the SCE following any breach on their part of the legal, statutory or other obligations inherent in their duties."

[340]See Sects. 4.2.1.2 and 4.3.1.

For further issues concerning liability (e.g., claims by third parties or members) one must refer to national law.

[341]See Art. 51 SCE-R. Also consider Schulze (2004a), p. 112. For the SE, see Manz (2010m), p. 639; Hirte (2002), p. 5; Hoffmann-Becking (2004), p. 363 et seq.; Teichmann (2015j), p. 771 et seq.

and administrative organs of an SCE established therein create specific obligations for the members of the organs; I analyse these in the relevant chapters.[342] Additional duties can then be determined according to national law.[343] Thus, the specific duties required for the exercise of an office are determined by combining European and national law.

The breach of duties must result in loss or damage that is sustained by the SCE. The law requires a causal link between the breach of obligations and the damage incurred.[344] For further preconditions (e.g., negligence), the SCE-R refers to national law.[345] This is also true for determining the damage or loss sustained (e.g., non-material damage).[346] Thus, according to Art. 51 SCE-R, members of the management organ of an Austrian SCE are fully liable under Austrian law, while organ members of an Italian SCE are liable under Italian law. As a result, the concrete definition of damage and causality is governed by the law of the Member State, as are questions of the burden of proof, evidence and fault. Finally, in case of litigation, the SCE-R[347] explicitly confers the power to represent the SCE to the supervisory organ. This power results from the characteristic division of powers on which the two-tier system is based.

Regarding the duty of confidentiality, Art. 49 SCE-R obliges every member of an SCE's organ to maintain confidentiality.[348] This principle must be observed both

---

[342] See, first of all, Sects. 4.2.1.1 and 4.2.1.2. Moreover, passivity towards the task assigned by law would be just as much a breach of duty as the careless exercise of the competence.

[343] For the SE, see Manz (2010m), p. 639.

[344] See Art. 51 SCE-R. Also consider Schulze (2004a), p. 112. For the SE, see Manz (2010m), p. 639; Teichmann (2015j), p. 772. For a comparative view, see Gallo (1998a), p. 381 et seq.

[345] Member state in which the SCE's registered office is located. Also consider Teichmann (2015j), p. 772.

[346] See Art. 51 SCE-R. Also consider Schulze (2004a), p. 112. For the SE, see Manz (2010m), p. 638.

Whereas former draft of the SCE-R still contained specific regulations on civil liability (Art. 47 draft SCE-R), the final version does not contain any in rule which deals in detail with this issue. In fact, Art. 47 draft SCE-R, determined in a general way that the members of the organs are liable for loss or damages resulting from breach of obligations. Then, it contained provisions regarding joint and severally liability of the members as well as the exemption thereto. Art. 47 draft SCE-R then dealt with the proceedings on behalf of the SCE in order to claim compensation for damages. Accordingly, the general meeting was entitled thereto; furthermore, Art. 47 draft SCE-R also contained minority rights.

[347] Art. 39 para. 1 last sent. SCE-R.

[348] Art. 49 SCE-R states: "The members of an SCE's organs shall be under a duty, even after they have ceased to hold office, not to divulge any information which they have concerning the SCE the disclosure of which might be prejudicial to the cooperative's interests or those of its members, except where such disclosure is required or permitted under national law provisions applicable to cooperatives or companies or is in the public interest."

during the period they hold office and during the period after they cease to hold office. Art. 49 SCE-R does not determine a precise temporal limit on this duty.[349] The duty only expires if the conditions on which it is based cease to exist, for instance, if damage to the SCE is no longer possible.[350]

The obligation for confidentiality exists towards third parties as well as individual members of the cooperative, but not towards other members of the organs. This would be contrary to Arts. 40 and 43 SCE-R.[351] The duty of confidentiality enshrines all the information concerning the SCE, which might be prejudicial to the interests of the cooperative or its members if it were disclosed.[352] Due to this wording, this duty already exists if the interests of the cooperative or its members might be compromised.[353] The content of this duty includes knowledge obtained outside the activity that a person conducts as a member of an organ of the SCE. This duty not to divulge any information refers to the means of information sharing (oral, written, gestures, etc.).[354]

If the duty of confidentiality is violated, civil liability, as determined by Art. 51 SCE-R, might result. In addition, penal law could be violated or infringed, depending on the relevant national legal system.[355]

Art. 49 determines an exception to this rule. The prohibition on disclosing information does not apply if such disclosure is either required or permitted under the applicable national law[356] or is in the public interest. Hence, the exact content of this duty may vary between one national legal system and another. The option to disclose information because of public interest can arise if it is necessary to prosecute or prevent the commission of a crime.[357] However, the concept of public interest must be interpreted narrowly.[358]

[349]Thus, it does not stop when a member ceases to hold office. See Schulze (2004a), p. 111. For the SE, see Manz (2010k), p. 625; Teichmann (2015h), p. 753. One can argue that this duty of confidentiality also refers to managing directors. Sec. 3 as a whole (rules common to the one- and two-tier systems) refers to secs 2 and 3 and thus to Arts 37 and 42 SCE-R. Regarding the SE, see Manz (2010k), p. 625 et seq.; Teichmann (2015h), p. 752.

[350]For the SE, see Manz (2010k), p. 625; Teichmann (2015h), p. 752.

[351]See Schöpflin (2018p), p. 1314. For the SE, see Manz (2010k), p. 626; Teichmann (2015h), p. 752.

[352]See Schulze (2004a), p. 111. An example of a cooperative interest is the capacity to satisfy members' needs. Examples of members' interests include their entrepreneurial or domestic activities. See Schöpflin (2018p), p. 1314. In line with the nature of a cooperative, the SCE-R explicitly also refers to the interests of its members, whereas the SE-R only refers to the interests of the company. For details, See Manz (2010k), p. 625; Teichmann (2015h), p. 753 et seq.

[353]See Manz (2010k), p. 625.

[354]See Schöpflin (2018p), p. 1314. For the SE, see Manz (2010k), p. 625.

[355]For the SE, see Manz (2010k), p. 626; Teichmann (2015h), p. 753. Also consider Schöpflin (2018p), p. 1314.

[356]Applicable to cooperatives or companies.

[357]The same is true for ascertaining public claims, for example, because of tax law.

[358]For the SE, see Manz (2010k), p. 626. In this context, one can also consider Art. 52 TFEU and its use of the terms "public policy" and "security". For the SE, see Manz (2010k), p. 626; Schröder (2010b), p. 164 et seq.; Teichmann (2015h), p. 754.

Having analysed the rules of the SCE-R, it is now important to consider how the concerned national legal systems deal with civil liability. As mentioned, this issue is explicitly subject to national law. In this regard, the *Italian legal system* contains specific provisions that are applicable, because of Art. 51 SCE-R.

Art. 2392 para. 1 CC determines the liability for the members of the management organ.[359] Accordingly, they must fulfil their duties as required by law and the statutes and are jointly liable for damages that result from the non-observance of these duties.[360] In addition, specific provisions contained in the civil code refer to self-dealing,[361] corporate opportunities[362] and prohibition of competition.[363]

However, the Italian civil code does not explicitly address duties of confidentiality. In general, it can be argued that the duty of confidentiality forms part of the general duty of loyalty, as determined by law.[364] In addition, the civil code contains a specific provision that must be considered when we analyse duties of confidentiality.[365] According to Art. 2391 para. 5 CC, a member of the management organ is liable for damages arising from the use of data, information or business opportunities in connection with his office.[366] The law specifies that this use must be made for his own benefit or for the benefit of third parties. With respect to these duties of confidentiality, national law sets specific limits. For example, one can refer to the competence of auditors in requiring information necessary to fulfil their tasks.[367]

According to Art. 2392 para. 1 CC, the duties of organ members must be fulfilled with the diligence required by the nature of their appointment and their specified tasks and duties. Diligence in this context does not refer to medium or generic diligence,[368] but to diligence that is required by the nature of the task, as determined according to Art. 1176 para. 2 CC. This relates to the level of care one might expect from a reasonable manager in a similar position. However, this type of diligence

[359]Applicable due to a reference contained in Art. 2409 undecies para. 1 CC.

[360]The management organ remains liable for its own acts, even when applying Art. 2409 terdecies para. 1 letter f-bis CC, which allows cooperation with the supervisory organ in strategic transactions and industrial and financial plans. See Cariello (2012), p. 353. Also consider Schiuma (2007), p. 674; Cariello (2012), p. 255; Romano (2017v), p. 3007. Also consider Sect. 4.2.2.1.

[361]See Art. 2391 CC. Members must inform the other members and the supervisory organ of any interest they have on their own behalf or for third parties in a specific transaction the cooperative intends to conclude. This article is directly applicable. Cariello (2012), p. 343 fn 507; Guaccero (2004a), p. 879.

[362]See Art. 2391 para. 5 CC. For details Enriques and Pomelli (2005), p. 758 et seq.; Baracchini (2007), p. 605 et seq. See also Romano (2017m), p. 2961 et seq.

[363]See Art. 2390 CC.

[364]Due to 2392 para. 1 CC. See Facchin (2009b), p. 513. Generally, Auletta and Salanitro (2009), p. 178 et seq.; Sanfilippo (2017a), p. 515 et seq.

[365]This provision also applies to the management organ due to Art. 2409 undecies para. 2 CC.

[366]This concept refers to so-called corporate opportunities doctrine. For details Baracchini (2007), p. 605 et seq.

[367]See Art. 14 legislative decree no 39 2010.

[368]As determined by Art. 1176 para. 1 CC.

does not imply that standardised criteria can be applied. Instead, the required diligence depends on the position assigned.[369] For example, consideration must be given to the reasons for appointing the member to an organ, to this member's competence[370] and whether he or she is assisted by a general manager.[371] Diligence is, therefore, a subjective duty. Judges must consider what the members of the management organ actually think about the interests of a company, which must be safeguarded when taking a management decision. As a result, courts cannot review such decisions on different grounds. In addition, the courts must consider the time and circumstances when a decision was made.[372]

Next, managers are required to make well-informed decisions that are rooted in their own knowledge and give consideration to any associated risk.[373] The specific provisions that apply in this context are Art. 2381 para. 6 CC, which states that members are required to act in an informed way, and Art. 2392 para. 2 CC, which requires members to do everything in their power to prevent harmful acts and/or eliminate or reduce their harmful consequences.[374] The standard used to determine whether a member has complied is gross negligence.[375] This implies that the court will consider whether a transaction was substantially legitimate.[376]

As mentioned above, the members of the management organ are jointly liable. The law provides exceptions if functions are assigned exclusively to one or more members of the organ.[377] In any case, they are jointly liable if they were aware of harmful acts but did not do everything in their power to prevent them or did not try to eliminate or reduce the harmful consequences of these harmful acts.[378] Personal liability can be excluded as long as a member—being without fault—dissented from

[369]See Perrone (2018a), p. 2851; Sandulli (2003), p. 473 et seq.; de Nicola (2005), p. 555; Facchin (2009c), p. 518 et seq. See also Romano (2017n), p. 2964 et seq.; Sanfilippo (2017a), p. 515 et seq.

[370]Required for a company in crisis, for instance.

[371]See Ricci (2010a), p. 697. See also Sanfilippo (2017a), p. 516 et seq. There is minor dissent in this regard, favouring a strictly objective approach. Ricci (2010a), p. 697 et seq.

[372]See Facchin (2009c), p. 518 et seq.; de Nicola (2005), p. 555 et seq. See also Romano (2017n), p. 2964 et seq.

[373]See Perrone (2018a), p. 2851 et seq.; Santosuosso (2003), p. 147; Facchin (2009c), p. 518. See also Romano (2017n), p. 2964 et seq.; Sanfilippo (2017a), p. 516 et seq.

[374]See Cariello (2012), p. 343 et seq. For details Facchin (2009c), p. 519 et seq.; de Nicola (2005), p. 561 et seq.; Perrone (2018a), p. 2852 et seq. See also Romano (2017n), p. 2964 et seq.; Sanfilippo (2017a), p. 516 et seq.

[375]"manifestamente imprudente o irrazionale". See Facchin (2009c), p. 518; Ricci (2010a), p. 693 et seq. Also consider Cesiano (2013), p. 948.

[376]See Facchin (2009c), p. 518 et seq.; Bonelli (2004), p. 163 et seq. It is acknowledged that courts are moving towards business judgement rule. See Perrone (2018a), p. 2851; Sanfilippo (2017a), p. 517; Cesiano (2013). For a critical assessment of implementing this concept into the Italian legal system, see Miribung (2017).

[377]See Art. 2392 para. 1 CC.

[378]See Art. 2392 para. 2 CC.

specific acts or omissions.[379] The law requires that dissent be recorded, without delay, in the management organ's meeting and resolution book and that the concerned member gives immediate notice to the chairman of the supervisory organ.[380]

Lastly it is important to understand how the breach of duties can be asserted. According to Italian law, various bodies can bring an action of liability[381]: that is the general meeting, the members of the cooperative[382] and the supervisory organ.[383] These provisions are applicable because of Art. 51, when taken in conjunction with Art. 8 SCE-R and Art. 52 subpara. 2 SCE-R. To be more specific, Art. 2393 CC determines that the action for liability may be exercised upon the decision of the general meeting.[384] Next, Art. 2393 bis para. 1 CC, which refers to minority shareholders,[385] states that action may be taken by members representing at least 20% of the number of members[386] or a different percentage (when specified by the

---

[379]See Art. 2392 para. 3 CC. For details Ricci (2010a), p. 701 et seq.; Facchin (2009c), p. 519; Perrone (2018a), p. 2851 et seq. See also Romano (2017n), p. 2964 et seq.; Sanfilippo (2017a), p. 519 et seq.

[380]See Art. 2392 para. 3 CC.

[381]See Cariello (2012), p. 346.

Also, if specific conditions are met, creditors of the cooperative according to Art. 2394 CC, the bankruptcy receiver, the receiver and the special receiver according to Art. 2394 bis CC. According to Art. 2395 CC, individual members or third parties can take also action against the members of the management organ. See Cariello (2012), p. 346. A further but slightly different possibility is granted by Art. 2409 CC (applicable due to Art. 2409 terdecies para. 1 letter e CC). Accordingly, the supervisory organ may report to the court if there is a well-founded suspicion that the managers have committed serious irregularities in managing the company, in violation of their duties. This violation must be detrimental to the company or to one or more of its subsidiaries. It is argued that this option is also granted to a minority of members due to Art. 223 septies prov. impl. CC, on the condition that they represent 10% of the corporate capital or 5% of the corporate capital on the capital market. See Cariello (2012), p. 355. Unlike Art. 2392 CC, a report can be filed to the court as long as damage is possible. Further investigations may require the removal of members of the management organ. It is then possible to bring action for liability against them according to Art. 2393 CC.

[382]According to Art. 2409 decies para. 1 CC, which refers to Art. 2393 CC (Corporate action for liability) and Art. 2393 bis CC (Company actions for liability for shareholders). If the resolution is adopted by members holding at least 20% of the capital, the members of the management organ are removed. In this case, the shareholders' (or general) meeting provides for their replacement, in accordance with Art. 2393 para. 5 CC.

[383]According to Art. 2409 decies para. 2 CC and Art. 2409 terdecies para. 1 letter d CC. These provisions are similar to Art. 39 SCE-R.

[384]For details Perrone (2018b), p. 2854 et seq.; Facchin (2009d), p. 521 et seq.; Picciau (2005), p. 569 et seq.; Ricci (2010b), p. 707 et seq. See also Romano (2017o), p. 2967 et seq.; Sanfilippo (2017a), p. 522.

In this context, Art. 2409 decies para. 5 CC provides that a waiver for the action by the company or the supervisory organ does not prevent the exercise of the actions set forth in Art. 2393 bis CC (Company action for liability by shareholders), Art. 2394 CC (Liability to company creditors) and Art. 2394 bis CC (Liability actions within settlement proceedings).

[385]Or members in case of a cooperative.

[386]Art. 2393 bis CC refers to company capital. Consider Sect. 4.4.4.

statutes).[387] Then, Art. 2409 decies para. 2 CC determines that action may also be brought pursuant to a resolution of the supervisory organ.[388] This resolution must be adopted by the majority of the members of the supervisory organ. If adopted by a majority of two thirds of its members, the members of the management organ against whom the action is brought are automatically removed from office.[389] The plaintiff needs to prove those points demonstrating that duties have not been observed and that the incurred damage results from the behaviour of the members of the management organ. These members must then prove that they acted in accordance with their duties.[390]

Concerning an *Austrian SCE*, the legal provision to be observed in this context is contained in Sec. 23 *GenG*. Accordingly, members of the management organ who act beyond the limits of their authority or against the provisions of the *GenG* or the statutes are jointly and severally (personally) liable for any damage sustained by the cooperative. In particular, they are held liable if (1) they exceed the restrictions on their power of representation, as determined by Sec. 19 *GenG*, (2) they act beyond the limits of their authority or against the provisions of cooperative law or the statutes, (3) they act against another provision of law, or (4) the management organ does not execute the decisions taken by the general meeting.[391]

As a general rule, the members of the management organ are obliged to observe duties of legality, compliance and expediency.[392] The typical duty is the proper professional management of the cooperative.[393] Their obligation to act in the interests of the cooperative requires their loyalty to the cooperative as well as their silence about any transactions that would damage the cooperative if these information were disclosed. Thus, the duties also refer to the duty of confidentiality,[394] as

---

[387]And in any case no higher than a third. So called derivative action. For details, see Perrone (2018c), p. 2857 et seq.; Facchin (2009e), p. 523 et seq.; Picciau (2005), p. 569 et seq.; Ricci (2010c), p. 721 et seq. See also Romano (2017p), p. 2970 et seq.; Sanfilippo (2017a), p. 525 et seq.
Art 2393 bis para. 2 CC contains provisions governing companies which resort to the capital markets.

[388]This authority is also recognised by means of Art. 2409 terdecies para. 1 letter d CC. For details Del Sole (2010a), p. 335 et seq.; Facchin (2009f), p. 662 et seq.; Miotto (2018a), Art. 2409 decies 2905 et seq. See also Romano (2017s); Mirone (2017a), p. 572.

[389]At the same time, they are replaced by the supervisory organ. According to para. 3 of Art. 2409 decies CC, this action may be brought by the supervisory organ within 5 years from the removal of the director of the office.

[390]The responsibility of the members of the management organ is contractual in nature; it is in line with Art. 1218 CC. See Ricci (2010a), p. 703 et seq.; Facchin (2009c), p. 518 et seq. For further details de Nicola (2005), p. 545 et seq.

[391]A decision taken in accordance with the statutes (Sec. 34 GenG). See Strommer (2014e), p. 251.

[392]See Strommer (2014b), p. 207; also consider Kastner (1986), p. 152 and Sec. 5 para. 1 GenRevG.

[393]See Strommer (2014e), p. 253. Also consider Harrer (1990), p. 16 et seq. or Koppensteiner and Rüffler (2007), § 25 nt 10; Kraus (2014), p. 242 et seq. Because the management organ is frequently appointed on a honorary basis, this duty implies the appointment of a professional managing director, capable of fulfilling the required tasks (culpa in eligendo). (Note that an Austrian SCE cannot appoint a managing director.) See Strommer (2014e), p. 253.

[394]See Strommer (2014e), p. 253.

determined by Art. 49 SCE-R. Under the Austrian legal system, this duty implies that a member of the management organ may not divulge a cooperative's secrets or act in competition with the cooperative, inasmuch as this behaviour would damage the interests of the cooperative.[395] However, the *GenG* does not contain specific provisions regarding confidentiality. Therefore, it is argued that the rules pertaining to companies (and the principles contained therein) must be applied by analogy.[396] This duty of confidentiality does not apply where the personal interests of the members of the management organ[397] are concerned or where the duty would be unreasonable.[398] Even though the *GenG* does not contain a provision prohibiting competition, members of the management organ may not act in a disloyal manner. For example, they may not abuse business opportunities provided by the cooperative.[399]

When fulfilling these duties, the members must use the ordinary diligence of a member of a management organ, as determined by the ABGB.[400] As a result, diligence is determined according to objective criteria.[401] Here, it must be noted that the members of the management organ of an Austrian cooperative normally fulfil their duties on an honorary basis and are appointed from among the cooperative members.[402] Hence, they are not usually professional experts. As already seen in this chapter, however, this must not be valid for the management organ of an Austrian SCE, to which external experts can be appointed. If a person appointed to become a member of the management organ does not have the capacities to duly fulfil his duties (for instance, because of lack of specific knowledge), they cannot accept the appointment. If they accept regardless, they may be held liable.[403]

As mentioned at the outset, under the *GenG*,[404] members are severally (personally) and jointly liable.[405] The degree of fraud is not important,[406] except in the

[395]See Strommer (2014e), p. 253; also Nowotny (2008a), nt 5/79. If the members of the management organ are employees, the prohibition of competition as determined by Sec. 7 AngG applies.

[396]See Kastner (1986), pp. 176; 157. According to Sec. 84 AktG, confidential information must be kept secret.

[397]Or the supervisory or administrative organ. For the SE, see Manz (2010k), p. 628.

[398]For the SE, see Manz (2010k), p. 628.

There are specific cases, regulated by law, which permit disclosure, e.g., the information right of the member in the general meeting or the duty to information in respect of the auditor. In this context, see Sect. 4.4.3 and GenRevG.

[399]Contracts concluded with professional members of the management organ normally contain clauses dealing with prohibition of competition. Strommer (2014e), p. 253.

[400]Allgemeines Bürgerliches Gesetzbuch.

[401]By analogy to Sec. 1299 ABGB. Consider Strommer (2014e), p. 252; Nowotny (2008a), nt 5/81; also consider Riss (2008).

[402]See Sect. 4.2.1.4.

[403]See Strommer (2014e), p. 252. Also consider Kastner (1986), p. 160.

[404]Sec. 23 GenG.

[405]See Lehner (2007), p. 130 et seq.

[406]For instance, even slight negligence can trigger liability. See Strommer (2014e), p. 251. Also consider Kastner (1986), p. 160.

internal relationship between the various members of the management organ. Members can take recourse against other members.[407] In addition, the liability of the members of the management organ is strict. The business risk must be borne by the cooperative itself.[408]

Finally, not participating in a meeting of the management organ is not sufficient to avoid liability for a decision taken by the majority. Instead, the member of the organ must immediately take every reasonable measure to avoid the threatened damage. Hence, the member of the organ must participate in the meeting and voice his particular concerns. In addition, he or she must ensure that his objections are recorded in the minutes, must notify the supervisory organ, must vote against the decision and must request to convene an extraordinary general meeting.[409]

Concerning the possibility of bringing an action of liability, the *GenG*[410] determines that the supervisory organ is authorised (by the general meeting) to conduct any lawsuits against members of the management organ.[411] The plaintiff must prove the damage, and also that this damage occurred because of an act or omission by a member of the management organ.[412] In addition, he or she must disclose all facts that support the assertion that the member did not fulfil their duties. The members of the management organ can discharge themselves from liability if they can prove their behaviour showed the required diligence.[413]

The general meeting may decide by majority not to pursue a lawsuit.[414] In this case, the minority has no way to force the pursuit of a claim. This is applicable to an

---

[407]See Strommer (2014b), p. 206. Also consider Kastner (1986), p. 160.

[408]See Zehetner (2014c), p. 326. Also consider OGH 31.10.1973, 1 Ob 179/73 SZ 46/113 and 26.02.2002, 1 Ob 144/01k. The criteria of the doctrine of business judgment rule are applied. Note that in 2015 the AktG was amended to formalise this approach, however without amending the GenG. This has rightly been criticised. See Schima (2015). For a critical assessment of implementing this concept into the Austrian legal system, see Told (2015).

[409]See Strommer (2014e), p. 254; also consider Nowotny (2012), nt 22. Also consider Art. 38 para. 2 SCE-R.

[410]Sec. 25 para. 1 GenG.

[411]It is argued that this competence includes passive legitimation. See Binder and Lengauer (2014b), p. 331.

In general, claims for damages expire within 3 years from the time of discovering the damage. Strommer (2014e), p. 256.

[412]These lawsuits only refer to the activity of the member of the management organ. Hence, the management organ as such cannot be party to the case. Binder and Lengauer (2014b), p. 333. Also consider Riss (2008).

[413]See Strommer (2014e), p. 253 et seq.; OGH 24.06.1998, 3 Ob 34/97i. Also consider Kastner (1986), p. 161; Nowotny (2008a), nt 5/81. Also consider Sec. 12 para. 1 GenVG and Sec. 33 letter a para. 2 GenG.

[414]This indirect reduction of liability is connected to the fact that cooperatives appoint the members of its organs from among its members. They normally fulfil their duties on a honorary basis. As a result, the legislator grants the possibility to reduce liability, provided the majority agrees. See Strommer (2014e), p. 255.

Austrian SCE because of Art. 52 SCE-R.[415] An exception occurs if the decision taken by the general meeting can be appealed.[416] An individual member of a cooperative has no individual right of claim, but only has the option to engage as an intervening party.[417]

In this chapter, we found that civil liability is, foremost, a national issue. Thus, in this context, the relevant national law has to be taken into consideration. In addition, the SCE-R contains a specific provision regarding the duty of confidentiality. Then, other duties can be determined according to the tasks assigned to the organs by the SCE-R.

The analysis has shown that both national legal systems refer to a similar concept of civil liability inasmuch as the members of the organs are liable for the damage sustained if they act outside the limits set by the norms or if they do not show due diligence as a general standard of conduct. In addition, both legal frameworks have provisions for duties of confidentiality (i.e., organ members cannot divulge secrets, nor act in competition to the cooperative inasmuch such behaviour could damage its interests).

Both legal systems refer, in principle, to an objective standard and consider the specific responsibilities to be fulfilled as well as the general context in which these responsibilities have to be fulfilled. A significant difference lies in the fact that the Austrian legal order acknowledges that the members of the management organ normally fulfil their duties on an honorary basis. Both legal frameworks acknowledge the criteria of the business judgement rule. Interestingly, under Austrian law, a liability is triggered by a slight failure or negligence, whereas gross negligence is required in the Italian legal framework.

In other words, the Austrian legal system considers a farmer, who as a member of an *agricultural cooperative*, acts as a member of the management organ for his cooperative on an honorary basis, whereas, according to Italian law, a similar farmer must have appropriate professional management skills in order to qualify for this office. What the definitive difference could be shall not be clarified here, but it seems useful to emphasize that there probably will not be such big differences: On the one hand, the diligence of the persons who act on an honorary basis, and are therefore not equated with professional staff, is considered. In this case, the duty of care is already violated in the event of slight failure or negligence. On the other hand, we refer to professional managers—even if in practice they are not really professionals—who are only liable if they are found to be grossly negligent. Moreover, it is useful to

[415] Due to Art. 51 SCE-R; also consider Art. 52 subpara. 2 SCE-R. According to the prevailing doctrine, Sec. 84 para. 5 AktG can be applied by analogy, thus allowing creditors to claim for damages in respect of members of the management organ, on the condition that the cooperative is not able to satisfy their claims. See Strommer (2014e), p. 254.

[416] E.g., due to violation of voting prohibition.

[417] According to Sec. 25 para. 3 GenG, every member of the cooperative is entitled to act as an intervening party in a lawsuit against a member of the management organ at is own expense.

It is not possible to provide a minority right by analogy to company law. See Strommer (2014e), p. 255. Also consider OGH 31.01.2002, 6 Ob 313/01z.

highlight in this context that, according to the SCE-R, non-members of an *agricultural SCE* can become members of the management organ and, perhaps, enhance the organ's professionalism. This professionalism could be fostered by the fact that the members of an SCE must come from different member states. This criterion is likely to require more professionals and fewer volunteers in order to gain and increase trust between the members of the SCE.

In this context, the PECOL not only require members of the management organ to comply with the law, the cooperative's statutes, and their duties of honesty, loyalty, good faith, care and skill, but it also explicitly stresses the need to establish an obligation to adhere to the defining values, principles and practices of cooperatives. The PECOL refer here to the universally recognised cooperative values and principles as defined by the ICA.[418] Clearly, these are matters that cannot be determined in full by law—especially where values are concerned—and must be clarified by an SCE's internal social responsibility policies. This issue will therefore not be discussed further, but these principles and values could be relevant, in practice, for better determining the content of due diligence.

Specific differences between the Italian and Austrian legal system are notable regarding the enforcement of liability. Austrian law authorises the supervisory organ to launch a lawsuit and provides for the possibility that a lawsuit cannot be initiated if the general meeting decides not to do so. To the contrary, the Italian legal framework not only designates various bodies that can start a liability action, but also defines minority rights in this regard, which will enhance the constraints on the members of the management organ.

4.2.2 The Supervisory Organ

4.2.2.1 Functions

The analyses regarding the supervisory organ of an SCE start with its function. This procedure resembles those we undertook to analyse the management organ. To begin with, I analyse Art. 39 SCE-R, which states that the primary function of the supervisory organ is supervising the management organ; as will be seen, under certain circumstances, the supervisory organ may also represent the SCE. Next, Art. 48 SCE-R allows a procedure of co-determination for the supervisory organ to authorise specific transactions to be conducted by the management organ. The chapter concludes by analysing the right to information assigned to the supervisory organ, which is the main instrument for implementing its primary functions.

According to Art. 39 para. 1 SCE-R,[419] the primary duty of the supervisory organ is **supervising** the actions performed by the management organ. It has both the

[418]Sec. 2.5 para. 8 PECOL; also consider See Snaith (2017), p. 71.

[419]It states: "The supervisory organ shall supervise the duties performed by the management organ. It may not itself exercise the power to manage the SCE. The supervisory organ may not represent the SCE in dealings with third parties."

authority and the obligation to do this. This power of supervision concerns the management in general and thus relates to all areas of management. Specifically, this power is not restricted to legal issues; it also oversees the management organ's organisation of the SCE, such that the principal object[420] can be achieved effectively and efficiently.[421] This power implies advisory tasks.[422]

In the two-tier system, the task of supervising the management is strictly separated from management tasks. Consequently, the supervisory organ cannot carry out any management tasks. This implies that it cannot give orders to the management organ, but rather, only non-binding recommendations.[423] This strict division of powers is outlined by Art. 37 para. 3 SCE-R, which requires that the functions of a member of the supervisory organ must be suspended in the exceptional case where this member must also exercise the functions of a member of the management organ. As a further consequence of this division of power, the supervisory organ cannot give orders to employees or reprimand them.[424]

The supervisory organ can use various instruments to fulfil these duties. It can appoint and remove the members of the management organ[425] and employ the right to information. In addition, the SCE-R deals with operations requiring authorisation from the supervisory organ, which increases this organ's power. The SCE-R does not contain any provisions stating whether the supervisory organ can have further competence assigned to it via statutes; however, neither does the regulations prohibit this. As a result, it should be possible as long as national law provides accordingly.[426]

Similar to the provisions referring to the management function of the management organ,[427] the SCE-R does not specify the content of the term 'supervision'. Hence, it seems useful to analyse this term as used by both the Austrian and *Italian legal systems*. In practice, it is likely that these rules will be considered as guidelines

[420]See Art. 1 para. 3 SCE-R. It states: "An SCE shall have as its principal object the satisfaction of its members' needs and/or the development of their economic and social activities, in particular through the conclusion of agreements with them to supply goods or services or to execute work of the kind that the SCE carries out or commissions. An SCE may also have as its object the satisfaction of its members' needs by promoting, in the manner set forth above, their participation in economic activities, in one or more SCEs and/or national cooperatives. An SCE may conduct its activities through a subsidiary."

[421]See Schulze (2004a), p. 98; Schöpflin (2018f), p. 1302 et seq. For the SE, see Manz (2010c), p. 516; Drygala (2015b), p. 503.

[422]For the SE, see Manz (2010c), p. 516; Drygala (2015b), p. 503.

[423]This task must be performed by the management organ.

[424]See Schulze (2004a), p. 98; Schöpflin (2018f), p. 1302 et seq. Also consider Lutter et al. (2012), p. 1610 et seq. For the SE, see Manz (2010c), p. 516; Drygala (2015a), p. 496; Drygala (2015b), p. 504.

[425]See Sect. 4.2.1.4.

[426]By applying Art. 8 para. 1 letter c SCE-R. See Schöpflin (2018f), p. 1302 et seq. For the SE, see Manz (2010c), p. 517.

[427]See Sect. 4.2.1.1. Also consider Presti (2006), p. 80. For the SE, see Bianca and Zanardo (2016), p. 195.

or first references. To determine the content of the supervisory task according to Italian law, one must analyse different provisions from the civil code. In general, according to Art. 2409 octies CC, the supervisory organ must supervise the management carried out by the management organ.[428] As the supervisory organ appoints the management organ, it also determines the future direction of the company (cooperative).[429] In addition, the supervision of the management organ influences the decisions of the latter. As will be explained below, specific statutory provisions may grant a power of co-decision.[430]

Art. 2403 para. 1 CC[431] is of particular relevance for determining the content of duties that belong to the supervisory function of an Italian SCE, as it sets forth specific functions. Thus, the supervisory organ supervises compliance with the law, the statutes, the principles of proper management and, especially, the adequacy and operation of the organisational, administrative and reporting structures.[432]

---

[428]As seen in Sect. 4.2.1.4 under Italian law, the supervisory organ may appoint and remove members of the management organ. It also fixes their remuneration, unless the relevant powers are attributed to the shareholder's meeting by the statutes. For further details Cariello (2012), p. 359 et seq.

[429]Known as strategic supervision. See Magnani (2005b), p. 137 et seq.

[430]See Art. 2409 terdecies para. 1 letter f-bis CC, which underlines the importance of this organ's function. The Italian legal system thus allows establishing a supervisory function which is either weakly or strongly administrative. In the latter case, the power of co-decision must be implemented, as determined by Art. 2409 terdecies letter f-bis CC. See Cariello (2012), p. 359 et seq. See also Art. 2365 para. 2 CC. See Magnani (2005b), p. 136 et seq. See also Romano (2017v), p. 3007; Mirone (2017a), p. 568 et seq.

[431]These are the duties the board of statutory auditors must fulfil under the traditional Italian corporate governance system. The statutory audit of the accounts is excluded, however. According to Art. 2409 bis CC, which is referred to by Art. 2409 quinquiesdecies CC, the statutory audit of the accounts must be carried out by an auditor or an audit firm enrolled in the dedicated register.

[432]As seen in Sect. 4.2.1.6, the supervisory organ can promote an action of liability against the members of the management organ and file the complaint to the court provided for in Art. 2409 CC. It also reports, in writing, to the general meeting at least once a year about its activities, omissions and censurable facts assessed. Further provisions can be found in Art. 2406 CC, which deals with omissions by the members of the management organ which oblige the supervisory organ to convene a shareholders' meeting, and Art. 2408 CC, which deals with complaints filed by the shareholders to the supervisory organ.

The supervisory organ, unlike the traditional board of statutory auditors, not only has supervisory powers, but also has essential administrative powers such as appointing and removing members of the management organ, promoting the action of liability or approving financial statements. Thus the competences of the supervisory organ are significantly expanded compared to the traditional board of statutory auditors. See Paolucci (2012), p. 142; Magnani (2005b), p. 136 et seq.; Paolucci (2019f), p. 137 et seq. See also Romano (2017v), p. 3007; Mirone (2017a), p. 564 et seq.

Accordingly, the financial statements drafted by the management organ are approved by the supervisory organ.[433]

All these tasks are typical for a supervisory organ. These same tasks are found in *Austrian law*. In fact, the Austrian legal system, like the SCE-R, states that the supervisory organ must supervise the management organ.[434] In rough terms, the supervisory organ behaves similar to an auditor by supervising the legality, expediency and economic efficiency of the management organ.[435] The newly introduced Sec. 24e *GenG* determines the main tasks of the supervisory organ, which can be grouped according to the following headings and which may also be used as references to put into practice the supervisory tasks determined by the SCE-R: (1) auditing financial statements,[436] (2) supervising past and future management, (3) authorising operations, (4) suspending and removing members of the management organ,[437] (5) convening the general meeting[438] and (6) conducting lawsuits against members of the management organ (Sec. 25 para. 1 *GenG*). In addition, specific duties may arise during a crisis of the cooperative and in case of insolvency.[439]

The supervisory organ must consider how accounting tasks are to be fulfilled.[440] The *URÄG* 2008 introduced a provision requiring the compulsory appointment of an audit committee if the criteria in Sec. 24c *GenG* are met.[441] In this case, the auditor

---

[433]See Art. 2409 terdecies para. 1 letter b CC (and Art. 2363 bis CC), applicable due to Art. 68 SCE-R and Art. 52 SCE-R. The supervisory organ may also decline to approve the financial statements; however, it is not clear what the consequences would be if the statutes to do not provide accordingly. Art. 2409 terdecies para. 2 CC states that the competence to approve the financial statements can only be attributed to the general meeting if the statutes provide accordingly. See Paolucci (2012), p. 143; Mucciarelli (2003), p. 203 et seq.; Magnani (2005b), p. 146 et seq. See also Romano (2017v), p. 3007.

[434]See Sec. 24e para. 1 GenG. According to Austrian law, a cooperative is obliged to have a supervisory organ either because the law requires or due to a specific statutory provision. Sec. 24 GenG defines the criteria according to which a cooperative is obliged to have a supervisory organ by law. Other legal sources can provide similarly.

The law is based on the presumption that the management organ is supervised by the supervisory organ. However, in practice things can be different. The management organ often fulfils its tasks on a honorary basis, including supervising day-to-day management, which is performed by one or more managing directors (or at least two managing directors in cooperative banks). These are supervised by both the management organ and the supervisory organ. The division of tasks between these two organs is determined by the statutes. See Zehetner (2014c), p. 320 et seq.; Dellinger (2016), p. 1375 et seq.

[435]These criteria must be fulfilled when the management organ undertakes its tasks. Consider Sec. 1 para. 1 GenRevG. Also consider OGH Ob 306/76 EvBl 1978/4.

[436]Consider in this context Art. 68 SCE-R.

[437]For details, see Sect. 4.2.1.4.

[438]For details, see Sect. 4.4.2.

[439]Consider in this context Art. 72 SCE-R.

[440]Considering economic efficiency and expediency, status and progress of assets and liabilities, profits and losses. See Sec. 1 GenRevG. Also Zehetner (2014c), p. 316. Also consider OGH 26.02.2002, 1 Ob 144/01k and OGH 22.05.2003, 8 Ob 262/02s.

[441]See Sec. 24c para. 6 GenG. For details Dellinger and Steinböck (2014), p. 296 et seq.

must be consulted in all committee meetings about auditing the financial statements and reporting on the audit. Next, the supervisory organ must examine the accounting for the relevant business periods, particularly the annual accounts, the balance sheets and the proposals for distributing profits. It must then report on these to the general meeting.[442] As will be explained in this chapter, in addition to its accounting competence, the supervisory organ can supervise the management via a specific right to information.

All these single tasks are under the umbrella of the primary task, which is to supervise the management organ. In addition, the position of the supervisory organ is fostered by empowering it to **authorise specific operations** the management organ aims to set. This is because certain transactions can strongly influence the conduct of business; hence, it is important to ensure that the management organ cannot conduct these transactions without authorisation from the supervisory organ. These dealings may be important because of their particular strategic importance, large volume or high risk, for example. These authorisation acts are key instruments for preventative supervision.[443]

Art. 48 para. 1 SCE-R[444] requires the statutes to list the specific transactions that must be authorised by either the supervisory organ or the general meeting. Art. 48 para. 2 SCE-R specifies that the provisions contained in para. 1 are without prejudice to Art. 47 SCE-R. This implies that the statutory limitations adopted according to Art. 48 para. 1 SCE-R may not be relied on against third parties.[445]

Para. 1 requires the statutes to contain a minimum number of operations requiring authorisation.[446] The particular operations must be determined according to the principle of self-regulation. These authorisation requirements cannot circumvent the separation of powers on which the two-tier system is based, as the management organ cannot be at the mercy of the supervisory organ. In addition, as the types of transactions can be determined by applying the principle of self-regulation, the required catalogue of operations is not limited to extraordinary transactions.[447] In principle, approval must be given in advance. Only in select cases can authorisation

[442]See Sec. 22 para. 2 GenG, Sec. 24e para. 4 GenG. Also consider Zehetner (2014c), p. 316 et seq.

[443]See Schulze (2004a), p. 110 et seq. Also consider Presti (2006), p. 80 et seq. For the SE, see Manz (2010j), p. 617; Teichmann (2015g), p. 743.

[444]This provision outlines two different authorisation mechanisms, depending on the governance structure. Under the two-tier system, the management organ must be either authorised by the general meeting or by the supervisory organ. Meanwhile, the one-tier system requires the administrative organ to adopt an express decision or acquire authorisation from the general meeting. Art. 48 para. 1 SCE-R states: "SCE's statutes shall list the categories of transactions (a) under the two-tier system, authorisation from the supervisory organ or the general meeting to the management organ, (b) under the one-tier system, an express decision adopted by the administrative organ or authorisation from the general meeting."

[445]See Schulze (2004a), p. 110 et seq. Also consider Schöpflin (2018o), p. 1313.

[446]For the SE, Teichmann (2015g), p. 744.

[447]See Schöpflin (2018o), p. 1313. For the SE, see Manz (2010j), p. 617. Also consider Teichmann (2015g), p. 744 et seq.

be granted in retrospect. A lack of authorisation can lead to civil liability, as determined by Art. 51 SCE-R.[448]

Art. 48 para. 3 SCE-R[449] contains an option allowing member states to curb the statutory freedom used to determine these operations. Accordingly, member states can set minimum categories, which the statutes must list, and determine which organ may be empowered to authorise. Member states can alternatively allow that the supervisory organ determine these categories itself.[450]

The *Italian legislature* did not exercise this option and, thus, did not restrict the rule contained in Art. 48 para. 1 SCE-R. However, the Italian norms that must be considered when determining the function of the relationship between the management and supervisory organs contain a feature that is worth mentioning in this context. Specifically, Art. 2409 terdecies para. 1 letter f-bis CC provides for the possibility to adopt a statutory provision that enables the supervisory organ to adopt resolutions concerning strategic transactions and the industrial and financial plans of the cooperative drafted by the management organ.[451]

The Italian legislature thus has not developed a specific catalogue of operations that must be authorised by the supervisory organ—even for Italian cooperatives[452]—instead preferring to extend the freedom of self-regulation, which provides, in principle, for two types of supervision: with or without co-decision power.[453] These provisions allow for a specific form of shared decision making. Yet, even though Italian law explicitly states that these decisions and the specifics of their implementation remain the exclusive competence of the management organ,[454] it is more than probable that these final decisions will be strongly linked with the resolutions taken by the supervisory organ.[455] This approach is similar to that contained in the SCE-R, with neither one eroding the clear distinction between management and supervision.

[448]See Schöpflin (2018o), p. 1313. For the SE, see Manz (2010j), p. 621.

[449]It states: "However, a Member State may determine the minimum categories of transactions and the organ which shall give the authorisation which must feature in the statutes of SCEs registered in its territory and/or provide that, under the two-tier system, the supervisory organ may itself determine which categories of transactions are to be subject to authorisation."

[450]See Schulze (2004a), p. 111. Also consider Schöpflin (2018o), p. 1314.

[451]For details Cariello (2012), p. 364 et seq. Here, Art. 2365 para. 2 CC empowers the extraordinary general meeting to shift decision making for specific matters to the supervisory organ. Art. 48 SCE-R does not refer to Art. 2365 para. 2 CC, inasmuch as Art. 48 SCE-R is based on an interplay between the management organ and the supervisory organ, whereas Art. 2365 para. 2 CC exclusively empowers the supervisory organ. See Cian (2018b), p. 2777. Also consider Montagnani (2004b); Romano (2017b), p. 2908 et seq.; Mirone (2017a), p. 565.

[452]As opposed to Sec. 24e para. 3 GenG.

[453]Here, Art. 2409 terdecies para. 1 letter f-bis CC highlights the primacy of the function this organ could fulfil. Both transactions and plans must be drafted by the management organ in advance. For details Cariello (2012), p. 364 et seq.; Magnani (2005b), p. 155 et seq.

[454]See Art. 2409 terdecies para. 1 letter f-bis CC. Also consider Cariello (2012), p. 253; Mirone (2017a), p. 565.

[455]See Del Sole (2010d), p. 360 et seq.; Magnani (2005b), p. 158.

But what are the limits to this power of co-decision, especially given that, according to Art. 2409 novies para. 1 CC, the management of the business is exclusively entrusted to the management organ? The supervisory organ cannot interfere with or modify the strategic transactions or the industrial and financial plans of the cooperative beyond their duty to approve or reject them. However, the statutes may oblige to reveal the grounds for rejection or confer the authority to make a proposal according to which strategic transactions or industrial/financial plans might be approved. Even though such proposals ultimately would not be binding, the management organ, nevertheless, would need to consider them, as otherwise (arguably), this organ might be obliged to refrain from the business operation in question.[456] If the option in Art. 2409 terdecies para. 1 letter f-bis CC were applied,[457] the two-tier system would require strong cooperation between the management and supervisory organs. However, this does not imply that the supervisory organ can interfere with management decisions.[458] This approach can also be applied by an Italian SCE, as Art. 48 does not state how this authorisation process should be structured. Based on the assumption that Art. 48 SCE-R will help improve management and, therefore, foster cooperation between the two organs, it can be argued that a two-step procedure (management organ's proposal and supervisory organ's counter-proposal) could be appropriate in this regard.

Like Italy, *Austria* did not exercise the option contained in Art. 48 para. 3 SCE-R. However, the amendment to Austrian cooperative law in 2008 (*URÄG*) introduced a catalogue of transactions that must be authorised by the supervisory organ.[459] It has to be analysed whether an Austrian SCE must comply with it. The transactions

[456] See Del Sole (2010d), p. 361.

[457] Specific provisions have been enacted here concerning banks.

[458] See Del Sole (2010d), p. 361; Magnani (2005b), pp. 158 and 164. Also consider Miotto (2018e), p. 2908 et seq.; Schiuma (2007), p. 706; Bonelli (2004), p. 238. See also Romano (2017v), p. 3007; Mirone (2017a), p. 565. For this reason, some scholars define the two-tier system as a variant of the traditional Italian corporate governance system, simply with different names for the organs. It is argued that the major difference is that under the traditional system the administrative organ is appointed by the general meeting, whereas under the two-tier system the management organ is appointed by the supervisory organ. It is argued that the major difference between the two corporate governance systems lies in the power to decide on other matters assigned by law to the shareholder's meeting, as well as on authorisations which may be required by the statues for directors' initiatives, without prejudice to the directors' liability for their actions and deeds, which is only assigned to the ordinary shareholders' meeting of a company adopting the traditional system (see Art. 2364 para. 1 no 5 CC). As a result, the exclusivity of the management power as assigned to the management organ under the two-tier system is much stronger than the exclusivity assigned to the administrative organ under the traditional system. See Del Sole (2010c), p. 327; Caselli (2003), p. 259.

[459] See Sec. 24e para. 3 GenG. This list may be expanded by the general meeting or the supervisory organ.

are[460]: (1) the acquisition or sale of shares and the acquisition, sale and liquidation of companies and enterprises; (2) the acquisition, sale and encumbrance of real estate, unless part of ordinary business operations; (3) the establishment or closure of branch offices; (4) investments that exceed certain acquisition costs during the financial year, in particular and *in toto*; (5) the raising of bonds, loans and credits in excess of a certain amount in the fiscal year, in particular and *in toto*; (6) the granting of loans and credits, unless part of ordinary business operations; (7) the acquisition and closing down of branches and manufacturing processes; (8) the definition of general principles of business policy; (9) the definition of principles for the participation in profits or in sales and the granting of pension commitments to executive employees; (10) the granting of procuration; (11) the appointment of business managers in accordance with Sec. 2 no. 1 letter b *BWG*, if the statutes of the cooperative provide for an appointment by the management board; (12) the conclusion of contracts with members of the supervisory organ, by which they commit themselves[461] outside of their tasks and outside the objects by which the cooperative intends to promote a service to its members, *vis a vis* the cooperative or any of its subsidiaries. This also applies to contracts with companies in which a member of the supervisory board has a considerable economic interest; (13) the acceptance of an executive position in the cooperative by the annual auditor, the group auditor, the annual auditor of a significant affiliated company or the auditor signing the audit certificate and anyone working for him who has exercised a decisive role in managing the audit,[462] if this is not prohibited by Sec. 271c *Unternehmensgesetzbuch* (UGB).[463]

Here, one can raise the question about whether this catalogue should be applied, either because of Art. 48 SCE-R or alternatively because of Art. 8 para. 1 letter c SCE-R. This list was introduced in 2008 without amending the SCEG; this would have been necessary to exercise the option contained in Art. 48 para. 3 SCE-R. The SCE-R addresses the issue of operations requiring authorisation exhaustively and only allows the amendment of the rules contained in Art. 48 para. 1 SCE-R.[464] Therefore, as there is no gap, Art. 8 para. 1 letter c SCE-R cannot be applied. Thus, an Austrian SCE must not adopt this list of transactions, meaning that Austrian SCEs

[460]The law specifies that for the transactions mentioned in 1 and 2, the statutes or the supervisory organ may set limits, whereas for the transactions in numbers 4, 5 and 6, the statutes or the supervisory organ must set them. For details Zehetner (2014c), p. 322 et seq. If these transactions have been conducted without consent, the transactions are not void. However, if this duty is not observed, the management organ might be removed and/or be responsible for damages. See Zehetner (2014c), p. 321. Thus, the consequences are similar to those determined by the SCE-R according to Art. 47 SCE-R, Art. 48 SCE-R and Art. 51 SCE-R.

[461]Against more than a minimal charge.

[462]Within 2 years of after signing the audit certificate.

[463]Austrian Corporate Code.

[464]Art. 48 para. 3 SCE-R contains an authorisation to adopt a specific provision, which must be adopted to make it applicable. Thus national law is not automatically applicable. For the SE, see Manz (2010j), p. 623.

are granted a higher degree of self-regulation here than national cooperatives. One reason for this might be to keep the SCE as an attractive option for conducting cross-border transactions. However, Sec. 24e *GenG* could be used as a model for defining the list required by Art. 48 para. 1 SCE-R.

The next task assigned to the supervisory organ is the **representation in dealings with the management organ**. In general, the strict limitations on the functions of the supervisory organ implies that, in principle, members of the supervisory organ are not allowed to represent the SCE in dealings with third parties. However, a different situation arises if these dealings involve the management organ or its members. In these cases, the members of the management organ obviously cannot represent the SCE.[465] Hence, Art. 39 para. 1 last sent. SCE-R[466] explicitly determines that when concluding contracts[467] with members of the management organ, the SCE shall be represented by the members of the supervisory organ. To better grasp the content of this provision, this research briefly analyses how the Italian and Austrian legal systems handle this issue. This proves helpful, because the national solutions differ to some extent; hence, this specific duty contains different limits, depending on whether one refers to SCEs or national cooperatives.

The *Italian legal system* contains two provisions that need to be considered here. First, Art. 2409 terdecies para. 1 letter a CC states that the supervisory organ appoints and removes the members of the management organ and determines their remuneration.[468] Second, according to Art. 2409 undecies para. 2 CC, Art. 2391 CC must be applied to resolutions taken by the management organ. This latter article states that members of the management organ must inform the other organ members of any interest they may have in a company transaction. This rather vague description also encompasses the conclusion of contracts between a member of the management organ and the cooperative.[469] Para. 2 then states that the resolution adopted by the management organ must adequately justify the transaction. Thus, under Italian law, the competence to conclude these contracts is primarily assigned to the management organ,[470] whereas, for Italian SCEs, this competence is clearly assigned to the supervisory organ.

Let us now consider *Austrian law*. It was argued above[471] that the supervisory organ can generally represent an Austrian cooperative in lawsuits against members

[465] See Schulze (2004a), p. 98; Schöpflin (2018f), p. 1302 et seq.

[466] It states: "The supervisory organ may not represent the SCE in dealings with third parties. It shall represent the SCE in dealings with the management organ, or its members, in respect of litigation or the conclusion of contracts."

[467] Including remuneration when appointing a member of the management organ or litigation. In this context see Sect. 4.2.1.6.

[468] As seen in Sect. 4.2.1.4, Italian law allows this task to be shifted to the general meeting.

[469] See Cian (2018i), p. 2845; Patroni Griffi (2003), p. 462 et seq.; Guizzi (2004), p. 654. See also Romano (2017m), p. 2961 et seq.; Mirone (2017a), p. 573.

[470] Clearly, the content of the "management contract" is at least partly influenced by the supervisory organ. For the nature of this contract, see fn 238.

[471] See Sect. 4.2.1.4.

of the management organ. It is thus legitimised both actively and passively. The same is true for representing a cooperative in dealings with the management organ. As a result, it has been suggested that the supervisory organ be empowered to represent the cooperative via a statutory provision.[472] This is admissible under Austrian law.[473] However, as already seen, when compared to the SCE-R, the *GenG* is rather flexible in this regard.[474]

The last task assigned to the supervisory organ is the **right to information**. This is elementary, because it helps to ensure that the supervisory organ can effectively pursue its supervisory duties. The specific provisions are contained in Art. 40 SCE-R. The right to information is a vital part of the two-tier system.[475] According to the SCE-R, the management organ is obliged to report to the supervisory organ at specific intervals and in important circumstances. In addition, the supervisory organ can actively pursue its supervisory function and request all information needed to exercise its duties and arrange any necessary investigations.

Art. 40 para. 1 SCE-R[476] states that the management organ must inform the supervisory organ on a regular basis (at least every 3 months). This duty includes the progress and foreseeable developments of the business of the SCE[477] and must consider information relating to the undertakings controlled[478] by the SCE, inasmuch as they may significantly affect the progress of its business. The duty to provide detailed reports at regular intervals applies to all SCEs, without exception.[479]

The SCE-R does not state whether these reports must be submitted in writing or can be delivered orally. It also does not contain a provision allowing this to be determined via the statutes.[480] It has been observed that the management organ, as the reporting organ, can determine the form of the report.[481] This implies that, if the management organ decides to deliver the report orally, it can autonomously decide to

---

472 See Binder and Lengauer (2014b), p. 332.

473 See Strommer (2014d), p. 217; Zahn (1963), p. 49.

474 See Sect. 4.2.1.4.

475 See Schulze (2004a), p. 100. For the SE, see Manz (2010d), p. 530; Sailer-Coceani (2015), p. 517.

476 It states: "The management organ shall report to the supervisory organ at least once every three months on the progress and foreseeable developments of the SCE's business, taking account of any information relating to undertakings controlled by the SCE that may significantly affect the progress of the SCE's business."

477 For details, see Sailer-Coceani (2015), p. 519 et seq.

478 The SE-R does not refer to this latter aspect. This difference may be because outsourcing business activities may endanger the cooperative's goal to focus on its members' needs. See Schulze (2004a), p. 100 fn16.

479 It has been criticised that such an extensive information system may be burdensome due to increased costs. See Schulze (2004a), p. 100.

Regarding content of this duty, see also Manz (2010d), p. 531.

480 According to Art. 8 para. 1 letter b SCE-R.

481 For the SE, see Manz (2010d), p. 531.

participate in the meetings of the supervisory organ. This participation can be justified because of the fact that the management organ is obliged to report.[482]

In addition, the management organ must provide information if circumstances arise that could have an appreciable effect on the SCE (extraordinary reports).[483] Unlike the wording of Art. 40 para. 1 SCE-R, which strictly refers to the progress of an SCE, an 'appreciable effect' can involve any part of the SCE. Such information extends to any information that can be promptly communicated. Thus, the communication must occur without any appreciable delay.[484]

Next, the supervisory organ may request any information that it needs to exercise its supervisory duties.[485] For example, it might request an outline of entire lines of business or ask for detailed information about certain aspects of the SCE's business.[486] However, if not specifically provided for by the statutes or allowed by the management organ, Art. 40 para. 3 SCE-R does not allow a request to participate in a meeting of the management organ. Without the right to self-administration, the management organ could not manage and be responsible for the SCE, as required by Art. 37 SCE-R.[487]

In principle, the supervisory organ as a whole is entitled to this right to information. This right does not extend to its individual members. Decisions about which rights to assert are therefore made by the entire organ.[488] Yet, according to para. 3 last sentence, a national legislature may assign this right to each member of the supervisory organ. The provision does not, however, specify whether an individual member can request this information for himself or only for the supervisory organ as a whole. Even though the wording suggests that the requesting member might also be the recipient of the information, such an interpretation would probably be

[482]See Sect. 4.2.2.4.

[483]See Art. 40 para. 2 SCE-R. It states: "In addition to the regular information referred to in paragraph 1, the management organ shall promptly communicate to the supervisory organ any information on events likely to have an appreciable effect on the SCE."

"Appreciable effect" also implies that the supervisory organ must also be informed in case of an extremely positive business development. See Schöpflin (2018g), p. 1304 et seq. For the SE, see Manz (2010d), p. 532.

[484]See Schulze (2004a), p. 100 et seq. For the SE, see Sailer-Coceani (2015), p. 522 et seq.

[485]Art. 40 para. 3 SCE-R. It states: "The supervisory organ may require the management organ to provide information of any kind, which it needs to exercise supervision in accordance with Article 39(1). A Member State may provide that each member of the supervisory organ also be entitled to this facility."

[486]See Schulze (2004a), p. 101. For the SE, see Manz (2010d), p. 533. Also consider Sailer-Coceani (2015), p. 524 et seq.

[487]See Schulze (2004a), p. 101.

[488]See Schulze (2004a), p. 101; Schöpflin (2018h), p. 1305 et seq. For the SE, see Manz (2010d), p. 534; Sailer-Coceani (2015), p. 525.

detrimental to the other members, who might be excluded from the information flow. Thus, a better solution would be to grant this option to the organ as a whole.[489] This necessity is acknowledged by Art. 40 para. 5 SCE-R, which states that every member is entitled to examine all information that is submitted to the supervisory organ.

Next, para. 4[490] grants the supervisory organ the right to undertake or arrange for any investigation necessary to perform its duties. This right cannot be interpreted as a general right to access the documents and data of the management organ, but must be considered,[491] in the context of the supervisory duty, as determined by Art. 39 para. 1 SCE-R.[492] Thus, the right to investigate includes the right to inspect all written documents (including minutes), books, the cash desk, stocks of goods and operational facilities. According to Art. 40 para. 4 SCE-R, the supervisory organ can 'arrange for' an investigation; thus, it seems possible to involve other persons, particularly external experts.[493] However, the organ can only rely on them in specific circumstances.[494]

Finally, para. 5[495] outlines the far-reaching internal right to information, which entitles every member to examine all information submitted to the supervisory organ. This right cannot be limited by the statutes or national legislature such that it disadvantages an individual member or groups of members.[496]

Art. 40 SCE-R does not exhaustively regulate the information flow to the supervisory organ and the reporting system contained therein. It has been correctly observed that, in line with national law, information must be provided in case the supervisory organ must decide on a specific issue.[497] In fact, the right to information, guaranteed by Art. 40 para. 3 SCE-R, is explicitly linked to the supervisory tasks, as determined by Art. 39 para. 1 SCE-R, and not to operations requiring authorisation, as determined by Art. 48 SCE-R. Specific examples in this regard are Sec. 24e para.

---

[489] See Schulze (2004a), p. 101 et seq. Also consider see Manz (2010d), p. 534. For a different solution, see Reg 63 of The European Public Limited-Liability Company Regulations 2004. It states: "Each member of the supervisory organ is entitled to require the management organ to provide to that member information of a kind which the supervisory organ needs to exercise supervision in accordance with Article 40(1)."

[490] Art. 40 para. 4 states: "The supervisory organ may undertake or arrange for any investigations necessary for the performance of its duties."

[491] Similar to para. 3.

[492] For the SE, see Manz (2010d), p. 535; Sailer-Coceani (2015), p. 527.

[493] See Schulze (2004a), p. 101. For the SE, see Manz (2010d), p. 535; Sailer-Coceani (2015), p. 528.

[494] See Schöpflin (2018g), p. 1304 et seq.

[495] Art. 40 para. 5 states: "Each member of the supervisory organ shall be entitled to examine all information submitted to it."

[496] This is also true for employee's representatives, who can be part of the supervisory organ according to Art. 39 para. 2 SCE-R, or representatives of non-user members, who can be members of this organ according to Art. 39 para. 3 SCE-R. See Schulze (2004a), p. 102. Also consider Manz (2010d), pp. 536 and 534; Sailer-Coceani (2015), p. 528 et seq.

[497] For the SE, see Manz (2010d), p. 530; Sailer-Coceani (2015), p. 518. Other opinion, Galletti (2006), p. 65.

3 *GenG* or Art. 2409 terdecies para. 1 letter f-bis CC. Due to the rather vague wording, it is useful to also consider national provisions. Determining which ones do and do not align with the SCE-R helps create guidelines to put the vague wording of the SCE-R into practice.

The procedure for information procurement determined by *Italian legal system* differs from the procedure established by the SCE-R. Italian law does not contain a specific provision conferring a duty on the management organ to regularly submit reports to the supervisory organ.[498] Instead, the Italian legal system establishes a system that, in general, obliges the management organ to provide information to the supervisory organ on a regular basis. Even though this may lead to the same result,[499] different provisions must be considered.

According to Art. 2409 terdecies para. 4 CC, the individual members of the supervisory organ may attend the meetings of the management organ. It is not clear whether Art. 2405 para. 2 CC applies. Neither Art. 2409 terdecies CC nor Art. 2409 quaterdecies CC explicitly refer to Art. 2405 para. 2 CC, according to which statutory auditors (or members of the supervisory organ under the two-tier system) who do not attend the shareholders' meeting without a justifiable reason or who fail to attend two meetings of the administrative organ (or the management organ) during a financial year shall forfeit their office.[500] However, it has been correctly observed that para. 4 is completed by Art. 2409 terdecies para. 3 CC, which generally states that the members of the supervisory organ must fulfil their duties with the diligence required by the nature of the office and are jointly and severally liable with the members of the management organ for acts or omissions of the latter, provided the damage would not have occurred if they had fulfilled the duties of their office.[501]

---

[498]See Presti (2006), p. 82.

According to Art. 2428 para. 1 CC, the management organ must provide a report analysing the company's position, development and business results. This analysis must include every sector in which the company or cooperative operates (Also through controlled undertakings. The law requires that costs, revenues and investments must be considered, along with the risks and uncertainties which the cooperative may incur). For details Santini (2018), Art. 2428, p. 2951 et seq.; Balzarini (2006), p. 596 et seq. See also Romano (2017w), p. 3051 et seq. This report must be submitted with the financial statements, which (according to Art. 2409 terdecies para. 1 letter b CC) have to be approved by the supervisory organ. Whereas according to Sec. 22 para. 2 GenG, the supervisory organ of an Austrian cooperative "only" audits a similar report, which then must be approved—together with the financial statements—by the general meeting. See Zehetner (2014a), p. 234. Note that, according to Art. 68 para. 1 SCE-R, the preparation of annual accounts, including the annual report accompanying them, is subject to national law. Thus, this report is not covered by Art. 40 para. 1 SCE-R.

[499]See Art. 40 para. 1 and 2 SCE-R.

[500]See Cariello (2012), p. 410 et seq.

[501]See Cariello (2012), p. 411; Magnani (2005b), p. 171; Breida (2004c), p. 1193 et seq.; Miotto (2018e), p. 2910; Guaccero (2004a), p. 894; Romano (2017v), p. 3007; Mirone (2017a), p. 567. Also consider Sect. 4.2.2.5.

This implies that if the management organ takes decisions which are against the law, the statutes or the principles of proper management, or are clearly rash, the members of the supervisory organ must express their disapproval, to be put into the minutes. If the decision is taken despite this

Then, similar to Art. 40 para. 3 SCE-R, the Italian legal system contains provisions enabling the supervisory organ to require information from the management organ. According to Art. 2403 bis para. 2 CC,[502] the supervisory organ may request information from the management organ about the company's operations or specific business transactions. This information can also relate to the company's subsidiaries.[503]

The supervisory organ can also exchange information with the corresponding bodies of the subsidiaries. This information can relate to management and supervisory systems and the general course of the company's business.[504] Even though it is not specified, it seems clear that the supervisory organ may request information from the management organ at any time that it deems necessary. The members of the management organ cannot obstruct the exercise of the supervisory function, as determined by the law.[505]

This right to information can only be exercised on a collegial basis. In this context, it has been criticised that granting the right to information to the individual members of the supervisory organ would grant more autonomous powers to these members.[506] Hence, the Italian legal system does not contain a provision in line with a provision allowed by Art. 40 para. 3 last sent. SCE-R.[507] It establishes a system that has been described as 'circular disclosure', in which the information from the management organ is conveyed both to and from the supervisory organ.[508]

While the right to information determined by Art. 40 para. 3 SCE-R can be found in similar provisions within the Italian legal system, the same is not true for the reporting system outlined in Art. 40 para. 1 and 2 SCE-R. Yet, such a reporting system can be established upon the powers assigned to the supervisory organ. Nothing prevents the supervisory organ from requesting information on a regular basis if the supervisors have previously informed the management organ about their intentions. In particular, participating in the meetings of the management organ will

---

disapproval, the members of the supervisory organ must evaluate this behaviour to remove the members of the management organ, exercise the action for liability or report to the court. See also Sect. 4.2.1.6.

[502]Applicable due to a reference contained in Art. 2409 quaterdecies CC. For details Crescentini (2010), p. 63 et seq.; Magnani (2005b), p. 166 et seq.; Simone (2009a), p. 554 et seq.; Ambrosini (2004), p. 905 et seq. See also Romano (2017q), p. 2988 et seq.; Mirone (2017a), p. 567.

[503]Unlike the former Art. 2403 para. 3 CC, the new para. 2 also refers to the company's subsidiaries.

[504]This is particularly relevant, because the supervisory organ of the holding may directly request information from the controlling organ of one of the subsidiaries. See Crescentini (2010), p. 64; Ambrosini (2004), p. 904.

[505]See Crescentini (2010), p. 64; Benatti (2005), p. 942; Simone (2009a), p. 554. See also Romano (2017q), p. 2988 et seq.

[506]See Crescentini (2010), p. 63; Ambrosini (2004), p. 905 et seq., Romano (2017q), p. 2988 et seq.; Mirone (2017a), p. 567 et seq.

[507]In line with the overall approach, the Italian legislator did not exercise the option contained in Art. 40 para. 3 last sent. SCE-R. See Fici (2010), p. 65.

[508]See Pollio and Papaleo (2007), p. 884; Crescentini (2010), p. 64.

automatically keep the supervisory organ informed about the past and future development of the cooperative.

As mentioned above,[509] a specific statutory provision must confer the right to participate in the meetings of the management organ of an SCE. While this right is needed to acquire appropriate information under the Italian legal system, the SCE-R adopts a different approach by drawing a broader and more distinct separation between the two organs, which significantly increases the duties of the management organ.[510]

As to the question of whether reports have to be submitted in writing or orally, it has been observed that the duty of the delegated bodies to inform the administrative organ[511] requires these bodies to submit supporting documentation to the administrative organ during its meeting. This duty relates to the traditional corporate governance system, in which the members of the controlling body—i.e., the board of statutory auditors—must participate in the meetings of the administrative organ.[512] Similarly, the supervisory organ of an Italian SCE with the right to participate in the management organ's meeting can obtain the report from the management organ via oral submission with supporting documentation. However, if such a joint meeting is not possible, the report must be submitted entirely in writing.

Next, as mentioned, Art. 40 para. 4 SCE-R considers the possibility of conducting investigations. Art. 2403 bis para. 1 CC similarly allows the members of the board of statutory auditors (traditional corporate governance system) to perform inspections and supervisory acts at any time and, like Art. 40 para. 4 SCE-R, allows them to be aided by their assistants (and employees of the company/cooperative)[513]; Art. 2403 bis para. 1 CC, however, does not seem to apply to an Italian cooperative that adopts the two-tier system.[514]

Cooperation with an external auditor of accounts is possible. In fact, Art. 2409 septies CC[515] requires the supervisory organ and the auditor to promptly exchange any information relevant to the performance of their respective duties.

In summary, comparing the provisions that Italian cooperatives and Italian SCEs must observe shows that two different approaches have been adopted, which, taken in isolation, provide a consistent set of rules, with both guaranteeing a regular and immediate flow of information. However, the systems differ on the subject of

[509]In this chapter.

[510]Under Italian law, the duty to actively submit information is limited.

[511]See Art. 2381 para. 5 CC.

[512]See Sandei (2018a), p. 2812 et seq.; Ambrosini (2003a), p. 64; Romano (2017g), p. 2944 et seq.

[513]The wording "their own" implies that these persons must be third parties. See Crescentini (2010), p. 66.

[514]See Cariello (2012), p. 411; Riolfo (2013), p. 729 et seq. Also consider Magnani (2005b), p. 165; Breida (2004c), p. 1186.

[515]This applies due to the reference contained in Art. 2409 quaterdecies CC, which contains rules on the exchange of information between the board of statutory auditors and the persons entrusted with the statutory accounting audit.

involving external expertise, with the supervisory organ of an Italian SCE having more options.

The various Italian legal norms governing information procurement and delivery may help clarify the right to information contained in Art. 40 SCE-R, but no equivalent to para. 4 exists to help put this provision into practice, at least when it comes to the powers assigned to the supervisory organ of an Italian cooperative. Yet, it can be argued that the possibilities outlined by Art. 2403 bis CC relating to external assistance similarly apply to Italian SCEs, as asserted by Art. 40 para. 4 SCE-R, whereas these competence are precluded for Italian cooperatives.

We now consider the *Austrian legal perspective*. This helps to better understand (and interpret) the right to information derived from Art. 40 SCE-R. Austrian law provides a process of information procurement that is similar to that given by the SCE-R. It likewise provides different instruments for gathering information: (1) the management organ must submit different reports,[516] including annual, quarterly, immediate communications and special reports; (2) a right to information, granted to the supervisory organ; (3) a right to conduct inspections and examinations; and (4) a right to be supported by external specialists and auditors.

According to Sec. 22 para. 3 *GenG*, the management organ must report at least once a year to the supervisory organ about the future business policy of the cooperative, including the future development of the net assets, its financial position and, if contained in the financial statements, its financial position via a preview account (annual report).[517] The yearly report must be presented in writing and accompanied by oral commentary, if the supervisory organ asks for it.[518]

In addition, the management organ must report at least quarterly about the development of the business and the cooperative's situation relative to the preview account. This quarterly report must consider future development of the cooperative. The management organ must immediately inform the chairman of the supervisory organ about important circumstances. Information must be provided promptly about such circumstances that could significantly affect the profitability or the liquidity of the cooperative (special report).[519] Unlike the annual report, the management organ can choose whether quarterly and special reports are submitted in writing or orally.[520]

While the *GenG* outlines the reporting system in more detail, the contents of these reports are ultimately similar to those prescribed by the SCE-R. Both sets of rules refer to past and future developments. The SCE-R, however, specifies that this

[516]Sec. 22 para. 2 GenG refers to a report containing details on the business development and financial position of the cooperative or about changes to the number of members. This report is audited by the supervisory organ but given to the general meeting. This report is not covered by Art. 40 para. 1 SCE-R.

[517]So-called small cooperatives are exempted from the duty to report on the financial position by means of a preview account. See Zehetner (2014a), p. 230; ErläutRV 467 BlgNR 23. GP 40 et seq.

[518]Also consider Zehetner (2014c), p. 320; Zehetner (2014a), p. 230.

[519]See Zehetner (2014c), p. 320; Zehetner (2014a), p. 230.

[520]See Zehetner (2014a), p. 231.

information must also relate to controlled undertakings.[521] The management organ of an Austrian SCE can deliver its reports in writing or orally. This depends upon whether joint meetings are possible. If not, the reports must be submitted in writing.

As the wording contained in the SCE-R is rather broad and vague, it seems worthwhile to use the provisions of the *GenG* as guidelines to concretize the actual reporting system. This is also true for the annual report. Even though the SCE-R does not explicitly require such a report, it seems possible to require one based on Art. 40 para. 3 SCE-R. In fact, according to this provision, the supervisory organ may require the information used for both the annual report and additional oral comments.

Similar to Art. 40 para. 3 SCE-R, Sec. 24e para. 1 *GenG* explicitly states that the supervisory organ can ask the management organ for a report on the cooperative's affairs at any time. This report must include the cooperative's links to a group company. This right to information also applies on an individual basis. In other words, every member of the supervisory organ has an explicit right to information. Here, the law states that an individual member can request a report; however, this report must be given to the supervisory organ as a whole. The management organ is not obliged to deliver the information. If it refuses the request, the requesting member of the supervisory organ can only insist on obtaining this information if another member of the supervisory organ supports their request. The law grants an exception to the chairman of the supervisory organ, who may request a report without support from another member.[522] This latter provision is the same as that adopted for an Austrian SCE.[523] The Austrian legislature has thus exercised the option contained in Art. 40 para. 3 SCE-R, albeit with a specific limitation. Both Sec. 23 SCEG and Sec. 24e para. 1 *GenG* explicitly state that the information requested by an individual[524] must be delivered to the supervisory organ as a whole.

Akin to Art. 40 para. 4 SCE-R, the Austrian legal system[525] grants the possibility of inspecting and examining a cooperative's books, communications and assets (i.e., its stocks of money, securities and commodities). The law specifies that the supervisory organ can either entrust this inspection and examination to two or more members or allocate certain tasks to experts.[526] As already seen, Art. 40 para. 4 SCE-R states that the supervisory organ can request any kind of external and professional support needed to examine the information submitted to it. This implies that it can ask for assistance from specialist advisers or external auditors.[527] Here,

[521]See Art. 40 para. 1 SCE-R.

[522]Also consider Zehetner (2014c), p. 320.

[523]Consider Sec. 23 SCEG.

[524]Accordingly, a member can require information about specific issues as well as entire business areas. Thus, unlike the first step in the procedure (filing a request of information), the information must be communicated to the supervisory organ and not an individual member. This approach is line with Art. 40 para. 5 SCE-R, according to which each member of the supervisory organ is entitled to examine all information submitted to it.

[525]See Sec. 24e para. 1 last sent. GenG.

[526]Also consider Zehetner (2014c), p. 320.

[527]See Schöpflin (2018g), p. 1304 et seq.

Austrian law states that the supervisory organ[528] must be assisted by an auditory organ. This is also valid for an Austrian SCE.[529] The auditory organ audits the cooperative's facilities, accounting and management to determine the legality, compliance and expediency of such facilities. In particular, it focuses on fulfilling the purpose of promotion and economic efficiency. The auditory organ also audits the expediency, status and progress of the company's assets and liabilities, financial position and profits or losses.[530]

To sum up, the supervisory organ (of an *agricultural SCE*) generally has the duty to supervise the tasks performed by the management organ. These supervisory tasks cover all management areas; one specific example is determining whether the management organ has organised the SCE to achieve its principal object. The basic provisions regarding the function are determined by the SCE-R.[531] In order to better understand the term supervision, it has proven useful to analyse the Austrian and Italian legal systems. Even though the two legal systems refer to different terms or different concepts to a certain degree, it seems that there are no major differences regarding duties and obligations. Thus, generally speaking, supervision implies to supervise compliance with the law, the statutes and the principles of proper management, along with the adequacy of the organisational, administrative and reporting structures and their actual operations. Similarly, according to the PECOL, supervision relates to the economic and social performance of a cooperative. This implies monitoring executive directors and managers, along with a general level of internal oversight.[532]

Next, regarding operations authorised by the supervisory organ, as determined by Art. 48 SCE-R, the SCE-R requires that statutes contain a list with these specific transactions. This allows the organ to strongly influence the conduct of business. These authorisation acts are an important instrument for *ex ante* supervision. This authorisation cannot override the separation of power; however, it is vital that the management cannot be at the mercy of the supervisory organ. These provisions are without prejudice to Art. 47 SCE-R.

Neither the Italian nor the Austrian legal systems implemented the option provided by Art. 48 SCE-R, which allows to determine minimum categories to be contained in the statutes. This implies that the Austrian SCE is more flexible with

[528]And if necessary the management organ, working on a honorary basis. The law is based on the presumption that the management organ is supervised by the supervisory organ. However, in practice things can be different. The management organ often fulfils its tasks on a honorary basis, including supervising day-to-day management, which is performed by one or more managing directors (or at least two managing directors in cooperative banks). These are supervised by both the management organ and the supervisory organ. The division of tasks between these two organs is determined by the statutes. See Zehetner (2014c), p. 320 et seq.; Dellinger (2016), p. 1375.

[529]See Art. 71 SCE-R.

[530]See Zehetner (2014c), p. 321. For details Perkounigg and Kessler (2014), p. 556 et seq. Also consider Zehetner (1999), p. 282 et seq.; Dellinger (2016), p. 1375 et seq.

[531]On the condition that specific conditions are met, the SCE-R allows to exceptionally exercise the function of a member of the management.

[532]See Sec. 2.5 para. 4 PECOL; see also Snaith (2017), p. 69.

respect to its Austrian counterpart (Austrian cooperative). By contrast, the Italian legal system contains no such list at all. A legal solution to be mentioned in this context is, however, contained in Art. 2409 terdecies para. 1 letter f-bis CC; it could be used as an example of how to implement the procedure as determined by Art. 48 SCE-R. The same is true for the aforementioned list contained in the *GenG*. Among the examples that could be adopted by a statutory provision are, for instance, a provision requiring the supervisory organ to reveal the grounds for rejecting a proposal. Whatever the final solution will be, this authorisation task will be particularly relevant in case strategic reorientation is necessary or the long-term strategy of the *agricultural SCE* or substantial investments (such as the purchase of new production facilities or storage towns) need to be considered. Furthermore, one can think of new sales opportunities, the taking up of financing or, in general, the further development of business policy.

The SCE-R specifically addresses the supervisory organ's work to represent the SCE in dealings with the management organ, including the conclusion of management contracts (such as remuneration). Austrian law allows a similar approach, albeit a more flexible one. By contrast, Italian cooperatives that apply the two-tier system must adopt a different approach, as Italian SCEs have to follow the requirements established by Art. 39 SCE-R.

The final issue is the right to information that is assigned to the supervisory organ. The SCE-R establishes a procedure for reporting, which is based on regular reporting, reporting when circumstances require, the right to request information from the management organ and the option to conduct or arrange investigations. In general, the members of the supervisory organ of an *agricultural SCE* will have to form an opinion about how the management organ intends to achieve the quality characteristics set out in the statutes, to which the *agricultural SCE* commits, and how the management organ intends to monitor compliance with these characteristics. Such assessments concern the functioning of the internal control system and require knowledge of both the production methods and the products (notably with regard to the quality and hygiene requirements laid down by law).

The contents of the reports are determined by the SCE-R, albeit rather vaguely. Extraordinary reports concern the SCE as a whole and may also include positive business developments. The right to obtain information of any kind is very broad, but it does not imply a right to participate in the meeting of the management organ. Such a right must be granted by the management organ itself. In this context, Art. 40 para. 3 SCE-R contains an option allowing member states to provide that each member of the supervisory organ be entitled to request information. While the Austrian legislature adopted this option in a limited way, this is not an option under Italian law. Finally, Art. 40 para. 5 SCE-R specifies that each member is entitled to examine all information submitted to the supervisory organ. Thus, except for issues surrounding the formalities of reporting, as determined by para. 1, the issue of the right to information is exhaustively regulated by the SCE-R. As a result, national provisions cannot be applied. However, in order to put the rather vague terms contained in the SCE-R into practice, it is useful to consider both legal systems. The analysis showed that the Austrian legal system adopts an approach similar to that contained in the SCE-R, whereas the Italian legal system adopts an approach based on the potential to request information.[533] However, the Italian legal system also permits a similar approach to that contained in the SCE-R. Both national regimes allow oral and written reports. The most significant difference here is that the supervisory organ of Italian cooperatives that adopt the two-tier system can only use external expertise in a limited fashion, whereas Italian SCEs are more flexible in this regard.

The PECOL do not propose any significant additions to this right to information, but simply stress that this right to information may be exercised by either the members collectively or the supervisory or auditory organs that act on behalf of the members.[534]

4.2.2.2 Composition of the Supervisory Organ

Having analysed the function of the supervisory organ, we now turn to the composition of this organ. This requires us to investigate two issues: the first concerns the conditions of membership, and the second addresses the number of members. When we analysed the management organ, we touched on the provisions contained in Art. 46 para. 2 SCE-R, which govern the conditions of membership; these provisions, as seen, concern preconditions of a personal nature and impediments that result from judicial or administrative decisions.[535] For example, equal to members of the management organ, also members of the supervisory organ must have full legal capacity.[536]

From the analysis that we conducted, one can see that, first, it is not necessary for all the members of the supervisory organ to be members of the SCE, and second, that the provisions concerning the impediments that result from a judicial or administrative decision apply equally to members of the supervisory organs of both Austrian and Italian SCEs. As already seen,[537] a decision adopted in one of the 30 member states of the European Economic Area creates an obstacle to becoming a member of

---

[533]Rather than formalising a duty for the management organ to deliver it.

[534]See Sec. 2.6 PECOL. These information rights are an application of the ICA value of transparency of member control. In other words, members must have sufficient information to properly control their cooperative. See Snaith (2017), p. 72. It also specifically acknowledges that the members of the supervisory organ work together with cooperative auditors (external auditors). In this context, a special form of audit is needed due to the goal of promoting members. Because of the unique characteristics of cooperatives, an approximation to a company audit is insufficient. See Münkner (2017), p. 92 et seq. 92 and in general, Chap. 4 PECOL. As already mentioned, this study does not concentrate on this issue.

[535]See Sect. 4.2.1.3.

[536]For Italy, see Art. 2382 CC, which is applicable due to a reference contained in Art. 2409 duodecies para. 10 letter a CC, making thus fully applicable the reasons for ineligibility contained therein. Specific details have already been discussed in Sect. 4.2.1.3. Also consider Del Sole (2010b), p. 352 et seq.

[537]See Sect. 4.2.1.3.

a supervisory organ. We will explore these general conclusions more deeply in the following analysis of the Italian and Austrian legal systems.

The *Italian legal system* contains several provisions to be read in conjunction with Art. 46 para. 2 SCE-R. Concerning the possibility of appointing legal entities as members, the legal system does not provide a clear answer, at least for an *spa*.[538] For cooperatives, it has been observed that Art. 2544 para. 2 CC requires that members of the supervisory organ be chosen either from the user members or from a range of persons nominated by those members who are legal entities. This latter criterion is used as an argument to prevent legal persons from becoming members of the supervisory organ.[539]

Next, according to Art. 2409 duodecies para. 4 CC, at least one acting member of the supervisory organ of an Italian cooperative must be selected from among the statutory auditors enrolled in the dedicated register.[540] The question is, does this provision apply to an Italian SCE? Based on the discussion above,[541] this provision should not be addressed by Art. 46 para. 2 bullet 1 SCE-R, because it is not worded as a prohibition.[542] As seen above,[543] it seems possible to integrate this provision with Art. 8 para. 1 letter c (ii) SCE-R. Interestingly, according to Art. 39 para. 4 SCE-R, Italian law could have determined the composition of the supervisory organ. However, the Italian legal system did not exercise any of the relevant options.[544]

Art. 2409 duodecies para. 10 CC adds that specific persons cannot be appointed as members of the supervisory organ.[545] It refers to (1) members of the management organ or (2) persons connected to the company, to companies controlled by the

[538]See Cariello (2012), p. 463. As explained in Sect. 3.2, fn 26, Italian cooperatives are not regulated by a single act, but by a set of rules that also include rules adopted for companies (spa).

[539]See Cariello (2012), p. 463 fn 791.

[540]This provision cannot be derogated, at least for Italian cooperatives.

Art 2409 duodecies para. 4 CC is less stringent than Art. 2397 para. 2 CC. In fact, the provisions regarding the board of statutory auditors (in the traditional Italian corporate governance system) require the members not enrolled in the register to be chosen from those persons registered in the professional registers determined by decree of the Ministry of Justice, or among university professors with tenure in economic or legal disciplines. See Cariello (2012), p. 453. Also consider Cariello (2012), p. 56 et seq.; Del Sole (2010b), p. 351 et seq.

[541]See Sect. 4.2.1.3.

[542]Presti stresses that Art. 46 para. 2 SCE refers to every member of an organ, with the result that provisions of national law which only consider individual members are not covered by this article. See Presti (2006), p. 78.

[543]See Sect. 4.2.1.3.

[544]See Fici (2010), p. 65.

The SE-R does not refer to the composition of the supervisory organ, only to the number of its members. See Art. 40 para. 3 SE-R.

[545]If so elected, they will forfeit their office. It is argued that under the two-tier system, the members of the management organ, who cannot be re-elected, may be elected to become members of the supervisory organ. See Giorgi (2018b), p. 3243; Marano (2003), p. 153 et seq. See also Mirone (2017a), p. 566.

company or to companies subject to joint control because of either a work relationship, an ongoing consultancy relationship or a remunerated professional service that may compromise their independence. This provision is fully applicable because of Art. 46 para. 2 bullet 1 SCE-R.[546]

Unlike the management organ, the law states that members of the supervisory organ of an Italian cooperative can only be chosen from user members or persons who have been nominated by members who are legal entities.[547] However, as argued in Sect. 4.2.1.3, this provision does not apply to an Italian SCE, as this provision contains an order and is therefore not covered by Art. 46 para. 2 SCE-R.[548] In addition, the SCE-R is based on the assumption that the members of the organs may also be non-members of the SCE. The only exception to this general rule can be found in both Art. 39 para. 3 SCE-R and Art. 42 para. 2 last sent. SCE-R.

Finally, like Art. 2409 undecies CC (in the context of the management organ), Art. 2409 duodecies para. 10 CC refers to Art. 2382 CC and states that interdicted and banned persons, disqualified or bankrupt persons, persons sentenced to a penalty entailing a ban[549] from public office or persons unable to exercise managerial functions cannot be appointed as members of the supervisory organ.[550] As seen, this provision applies to an Italian SCE.

Austrian law addresses the conditions of membership (as set out in Art. 46 para. 2 SCE-R) in the *GenG*. Like the SCE-R, Sec. 24 para. 1 *GenG* states that members of the management organ cannot be members of the supervisory organ.[551] The *GenG* does not contain any other preconditions. Nevertheless, because of a similar provision in Italian law, which has been analysed above, it is useful to briefly mention one particular feature of Sec. 24c para. 6 subpara. 1 *GenG*, which requires cooperatives that fulfil certain characteristics[552] to appoint an auditing committee.[553] The law states that at least one member of this committee must be a financial expert

[546]It has been discussed whether the blood relatives and in-laws of the members of the management organ may become members of the supervisory organ. This seems possible due to the missing reference to Art. 2399 para. 1 letter b CC. In fact, Art. 2409 duodecies para. 10 CC determines the same causes of ineligibility and forfeiture as Art. 2399 CC (regarding the Italian traditional corporate governance system), excluding, however, the grounds contained in Art. 2399 para. 1 letter b CC. Therefore the causes of ineligibility and forfeiture to be considered under the two-tier system are less stringent than in the traditional corporate governance system. See Del Sole (2010b), p. 352 et seq.; Miotto (2018b), p. 2908. See also Romano (2017t) and Mirone (2017a), p. 564.

[547]See Art. 2544 para. 2 CC; Paolucci (2012), p. 143. Also consider Bonfante (2004b), p. 2599 et seq. For another opinion on Art. 2544 para. 2 CC, see Presti (2006), p. 78.

[548]Different opinion Presti (2006), p. 81.

[549]Even a temporary ban.

[550]If so elected, they will forfeit their office. Also consider Sect. 4.2.1.3. See also Del Sole (2010b), p. 352 et seq.; Mirone (2017a), p. 566.

[551]Membership of an Austrian cooperative is conferred as soon as the member of the organ is appointed. The status of cooperative member must only be given during the term of office. This implies that they become members by means of appointment. See Zehetner (2014b), p. 268.

[552]Specific public interest entities and large cooperatives.

[553]Also consider Sect. 4.2.2.4.

who possesses knowledge and practical experience in finance, accounting and reporting that comply with the requirements of the company.[554] For the reasons stated above,[555] this provision applies because of Art. 8 para. 1 letter c SCE-R.[556] One example of a specific obstacle outside the *GenG* is found in Sec. 28a *BWG*, which states that the chairman of the supervisory organ may be excluded from office because of Sec. 13 paras. 1–3, 5 and 6 *GewO* or as a result of undergoing bankruptcy proceedings. In addition, he or she must be in a sound economic situation with no doubts about his reliability. The law also requires him to possess the necessary professional qualifications.

Then, the analyses regarding the management organ reveals that there are not only conditions set by law, but as explained,[557] there are also good grounds to allow **statutory provisions** to set further eligibility conditions if national law provides accordingly. This approach is based on Art. 8 para. 1 letter c (iii) SCE-R. *Italian law* contains two provisions that allow the statutes to set further eligibility requirements.[558] According to Art. 2409 duodecies para. 6 CC, the statutes[559] can base membership in the supervisory organ on special integrity requirements, professional capability and independence. For example, the additional requirements mentioned in Art. 2397 para. 2 CC could be mandated via a specific statutory provision.[560] Next, because of Art. 2409 duodecies para. 11 CC, the statutes can provide for further causes of ineligibility and forfeiture,[561] along with causes of incompatibility as well as restrictions and criteria for holding more than one office.[562] These solutions apply to an Italian SCE as well.

Opposed to this, the *Austrian GenG* does not contain a provision explicitly dealing with this issue. In general, however,[563] the members of the supervisory organ must be able and ready to demonstrate concern for the interests of the cooperative and to attend training or to receive further education. Thus, members of the supervisory organ or a cooperative can possess fewer capabilities than their

[554]This provision is also an exception to the general principle that members of the supervisory organ of an Austrian cooperative must be members of the cooperative. However, in practice these financial experts usually become members. See Zehetner (2014b), p. 268. Also consider Dellinger (2016), p. 1383.

[555]When analysing the corresponding Italian provision (Art. 2409 duodecies para. 4 CC).

[556]Sec. 24e para. 6 GenG primarily governs internal committees, which, as will be explained in Sect. 4.2.2.4, are not dealt with by the SCE-R and hence can be integrated by means of Art. 8 SCE-R.

[557]See Sect. 4.2.1.3.

[558]For details Cariello (2012), p. 452 et seq. Also consider Cariello (2012), p. 56 et seq.

[559]Without prejudice to that considered by special provisions of law in connection with the exercise of specific activities.

[560]See Cariello (2012), p. 452 et seq. For the specific requirements for cooperative banks, see Art. 26 TUB.

[561]In addition to the impediments determined by Art. 2409 duodecies para. 10 CC.

[562]Also consider Del Sole (2010b), p. 352 et seq.

[563]As will be discussed in Sect. 4.2.2.5.

counterparts in a company.[564] It is recognised that members of the supervisory organ are chosen from members of the cooperative and normally fulfil unpaid duties.[565] Therefore, as only members of the cooperative may be appointed as members of the supervisory organ, one can argue that, ultimately, the general meeting may decide who—from among the potential candidates—has the best prerequisites.

The next issue concerns the **number of members** of the supervisory organ. As for the management organ,[566] the number of members must be determined via statute. Hence, the principle of statutory freedom applies. As the SCE-R refers to members, it can be argued that the supervisory organ must be formed of at least two members.

According to Art. 39 para. 4 SCE-R,[567] the statutes can either directly set the number of the members or provide the rules for determining this number. Member states can limit these rules, an authority that goes further than that conferred regarding the management organ: Not only can they set the minimum and/or maximum number of members, but they also can stipulate the specific number. In addition, the SCE-R sets a specific limit for statutory provisions to protect user members from non-user members. According to Sec. 39 para. 3 SCE-R, no more than 25% of posts in the supervisory organ may be filled by non-user members.[568] Thus, they can appoint non-user members, as well as external persons or user members, if they consider them trustees who will protect their interests. In the event that they appoint external individuals or user members, the SCE-R's limits clearly must not be observed.

The *Italian legislature* did not exercise the option contained in Art. 39 para. 4 SCE-R, making Italian SCEs more flexible and granting them a higher degree of self-regulation than their national counterparts. For national cooperatives, the civil code states that the supervisory organ must have a minimum of three members.[569] The statutes can either increase this number or set the exact number of members.[570]

---

[564] They must not necessarily be above the level of an average businessman.

[565] See Zehetner (2014c), p. 327 et seq. Also consider Dellinger (2016), p. 1376 et seq. Different opinion Riss (2008), p. 768.

[566] See Art. 37 para. 4 SCE-R.

[567] It states: "The statutes shall lay down the number of members of the supervisory organ or the rules for determining it. A Member State may, however, stipulate the number of members or the composition of the supervisory organ for SCEs having their registered office in its territory or a minimum and/or a maximum number."

[568] See Schulze (2004a), p. 99; Schöpflin (2018f), p. 1302 et seq. Also consider Lutter et al. (2012), p. 1611 et seq.; Albamonte (2008), p. 310.

[569] See Art. 2409 duodocies para. 1 CC.

[570] The law does not determine whether this greater number needs to be odd or even. It is argued that an odd number helps foster decision making, it prevents the possibility of a tie. This could be particularly important for certain competences the supervisory organ has to fulfil, such as approving the financial statements, exercising the action of liability and reporting to the courts. As seen when analysing the management organ, the regulation explicitly assigns a casting vote to the chairman, unless there is no relevant provision in the statutes. See Del Sole (2010b), p. 347; Breida (2004a), p. 1157 et seq.; Magnani (2005a), p. 110. Also consider Mirone (2017a), p. 565. Miotto (2018b), p. 2907.

The *Austrian legislature* also favoured statutory freedom and flexibility by not exercising the option contained in Art. 39 para. 4 SCE-R.[571] As a result, an Austrian cooperative is bound by stricter limits than an Austrian SCE. Austrian cooperative law states that the supervisory organ must have a minimum of three members, unless the statutes do not provide for a higher number.[572] This provision only refers to the members appointed by the general meeting. If there is a work council, further members are appointed.[573]

This part of the study concerned the supervisory organ's composition and the number of its members. Many observations that were made when we analysed the management organ also apply here: for example, members must have full legal capacity.[574] The results are similar to those for the management organ,[575] but two issues need further consideration: (a) personal impediments, and (b) the question of whether special conditions for eligibility can be determined via the statutes.

For Austrian SCEs that are of public interests and are considered as being large SCEs, the provisions contained in Sec. 24c para. 6 *GenG* apply. Specific limitations can be found in the *BWG*. The Italian approach is more regulatory, even though many provisions are formulated as default provisions. Various examples demonstrate the more stringent approach, e.g., an Italian *agricultural SCE* must select one member from statutory auditors enrolled in a specific register, as an Italian cooperative does, whereas a similar provision contained in Sec. 24c para. 6 *GenG* only applies to specific Austrian SCEs. Another provision of the Italian civil code deals with conflicts of interest.[576] This provision also applies.

Next, we determined whether the requirement that members of the supervisory organ be chosen from among user members also applies to an Italian SCE. For similar reasons as for members of the management organ of an Austrian SCE, this provision does not apply. Finally, Art. 2382 CC applies to the supervisory organ of an Italian SCE.

---

[571] See Fici (2010), p. 64. Instead, the German legislator set a minimum number of members of the supervisory organ, which must have at least five members. If the SCE has 20 members of fewer, this minimum is three. Consider Sec. 19 para. 1 SCEAG.

[572] As mentioned in fn 434, if it is not compulsory to adopt a supervisory organ, the adoption of this organ may be provided for by the statutes of the cooperative. Interestingly, para. 3 does not refer to the minimum number of members contained in para. 1. As a result, if para. 3 is applied, the supervisory organ may also have less than three members. See Zehetner (2014b), p. 266; Kastner (1986), p. 169 et seq.; Keinert (1988), p. 171. Different opinion OLG Innsbruck 30.11.2004, 3 R 180/04a. It is strongly recommended to appoint more than the minimum number of members, in case members leave during their term of office. See Binder and Lengauer (2014a), p. 273.

[573] See Sec. 110 ArbVG. Also consider Zehetner (2014b); Dellinger (2016), p. 1380 et seq.

[574] Furthermore, it is not necessary for every member of the supervisory organ to be a member of the SCE. For impediments owing to a judicial and administrative decision, see the chapter dealing with the management organ.

[575] Members must have full legal capacity, but they do not need to be members of the SCE.

[576] Art. 2409 duodecies para. 10 CC.

The Italian legal system allows for further eligibility conditions to be determined through the statutes, whereas according to the Austrian legal system, a concrete decision on whether interested members are suitable candidates is made at the general meeting when appointing the supervisory organ's members.

Neither the Italian nor Austrian legislatures exercised the option in the SCE-R to set the specific number of members of the supervisory organ (including a minimum and/or a maximum number); the number of members can therefore be determined via statutes. There must be at least two. Then, in order to protect user members against non-user members, the SCE-R requires that no more than a quarter of the posts available in the supervisory organ be filled by non-user members.

In this context, the PECOL determine, in a rather general way, that laws or statutes shall lay down the maximum and minimum number of members of the supervisory organ, requirements for gender balance and qualifications for membership. These qualifications must not unduly limit the possibility of cooperative members being elected members of the organ.[577] While the SCE-R specifically regulates the first requirement, by law, the latter two should be based on specific statutory provisions of an *agricultural SCE*. Similarly, the PECOL require the majority of the members of the supervisory organ of (mutual) cooperatives to be user members.[578] This requirement must be based on a statutory provision, as the SCE-R only hinders the full application of the principle of *Selbstorganschaft*.[579]

In general, it can be said that it is ultimately the task of the general meeting to pay attention to the appropriate professional and social competence that the members of the supervisory organ of an *agricultural SCE* should have. Thus, it is upon the farmer-members to define adequate supervisory functions, (this shows the importance of the general meeting in this context).

4.2.2.3 The Appointment and Removal of Members

Similar to Art. 37 para. 2 SCE-R, which refers to the management organ, the SCE-R contains provisions dealing with the **appointment** and removal of members of the supervisory organ. Accordingly, the members of the supervisory organ are appointed by the general meeting. The only exception is for members of the first supervisory organ, who can be appointed via the statutes.[580] As mentioned in the previous chapter, para. 3[581] specifies that no more than 25% of the available posts can be

---

[577] See Sec. 2.5 para. 7 PECOL; Snaith (2017), p. 69 et seq.

[578] See Sec. 2.5 para. 6 PECOL; Snaith (2017), p. 69.

[579] See Sect. 4.2.1.3.

[580] Also consider Schulze (2004a), p. 99; Schöpflin (2018f), p. 1302 et seq.

Art 39 para. 2 states: "The members of the supervisory organ shall be appointed and removed by the general meeting. The members of the first supervisory organ may, however, be appointed in the statutes. This shall apply without prejudice to any employee participation arrangements determined pursuant to Directive 2003/72/EC."

[581] It states: "Of the members of the supervisory organ, not more than one quarter of the posts available may be filled by non-user members."

filled by non-user members. The composition of the supervisory organ can also depend on employee participation, with particular features determined by the directive on the involvement of employees.[582] The methods for appointing employee representatives are determined according to the specific regulations for employee participation, which are stipulated for individual SCEs.[583]

The SCE-R does not contain further provisions about the appointment procedure. As a result, the relevant national provisions must be applied in accordance with Art. 53 SCE-R.[584] Remuneration and contractual issues that regulate the relationship between the SCE and the members of the supervisory organ must also be addressed via national law,[585] as the SCE-R does not contain any specific provisions here.[586]

Under the *Italian legal system*, the provisions dealing with the appointment of members to the supervisory organ are contained in Art. 2409 duodecies para. 2 CC and Art. 2544 para. 2 CC. The Italian provisions are similar, but not identical, to Art. 39 para. 2 SCE-R; they state that the first members are appointed by the statutes, with all other members appointed by the general meeting.[587] Unlike the SCE-R, this rule is mandatory in Italian law. Then, according to Art. 2400 para. 4 CC,[588] the election must be accepted.[589] This provision also applies to Italian SCEs, as the SCE-R is silent in this regard.

According to Art. 2544 para. 2 CC, holders of financial instruments may appoint no more than a third of the members of the supervisory organ. Thus, the limit for Italian SCEs is stricter than for Italian cooperatives.[590] A further difference involves employee participation, as referred to by Art. 39 para. 2 last sent. SCE-R. It has been discussed whether Art. 2409 duodecies CC allows the introduction of specific

[582]Schulze (2004a), p. 99.

[583]For comments, see Fici (2006) and Snaith (2006). Also consider Marhold (2008) and Ales (2008).

[584]For the SE, see Drygala (2015b), p. 505.

Art 53 states: "Without prejudice to the rules laid down in this section, the organisation and conduct of general meetings together with voting procedures shall be governed by the law applicable to cooperatives in the Member State in which the SCE's registered office is situated."

[585]By applying Art. 8 para. 1 letter c SCE-R.

[586]Austrian law does not contain a specific legal provision dealing with this issue but it seems coherent for the general meeting to deal with it. In contrast, the Italian civil code determines in Art. 2364 bis para. 1 no 2 CC that the general meeting fixes the remuneration due to the members of the supervisory organ, unless it is determined by statutes. According to Italian law, when determining remunerations it is possible to consider the various tasks different members must fulfil (e.g., chairman, members of internal committees). See Cariello (2012), p. 470.

[587]See Art. 2409 duodecies para. 2 CC. For details Del Sole (2010b), p. 347 et seq.; Miotto (2018b), p. 2906 et seq.; Magnani (2005a), p. 113 et seq. See also Romano (2017t), p. 3005 et seq.

[588]As referred to by Art. 2409 quaterdecies para. 1 CC.

[589]See Miotto (2018b), p. 2907; Magnani (2005a), p. 114; Cariello (2012), p. 459. Acceptance implies that resignation is possible. See Cariello (2012), p. 465.

[590]See Art. 39 para. 3 SCE-R. While the Italian legal system focuses on the right to appoint (active legitimacy), the SCE-R focuses on the members to be appointed (passive legitimacy). See Presti (2006), p. 78.

statutory provisions guaranteeing the representation of employees in the supervisory organ, which could be in line with European legislation. However, it is argued that the law excludes such a possibility, according to Art. 2409 duodecies para. 10 letter c CC, which corresponds to Art. 2399 para. 1 letter c CC. According to this latter provision, persons connected to the company[591] cannot be elected as members of the supervisory organ.[592]

Art. 2409 duodecies para. 4 CC contains a reference to effective members. Due to Art. 2409 duodecies paras. 1 and 7 CC,[593] it seems there is no obligation to appoint non-effective members. In addition, Art. 2409 quaterdecies para. 1 CC does not contain a reference to Art. 2397 CC, which states that the board of statutory auditors is composed of three or five acting members. This provision also states that two alternate auditors must be appointed. In any case, the appointment of alternate members to the supervisory organ of an Italian cooperative can be determined by a specific statutory clause,[594] whereas the SCE-R explicitly allows such a solution by law.[595]

Like the SCE-R, *Austrian law* states that the members of the supervisory organ are appointed by the general meeting.[596] Even though not specifically determined by law, this decision must be accepted by the person elected.[597] This is also true for an Austrian SCE.

In contrast to the laws dealing with the *AG*[598] and the *GmbH*,[599] the *GenG* does not contain a provision dealing with restricting the mandate. For an SCE, this aspect is regulated by Art. 45 para. 2 SCE-R, which grants statutory freedom in this regard.

Then, unlike the SCE-R,[600] the *GenG* does not allow the members of the supervisory organ to be chosen via the statutes instead of being elected by the general meeting,[601] nor does it contain a provision similar to Art. 39 para. 3 SCE-R.[602]

Sec. 24a *GenG* deals with judicial appointments and refers to a supervisory organ that (1) must be constituted on a mandatory basis (on the condition that the

---

591 Or to the companies controlled by it or companies subjected to joint control by them due to a work relationship, an ongoing consultancy relationship or remunerated professional service.

592 See Guaccero (2004a), p. 887. Different opinion Breida (2004a), p. 1157. Also consider Del Sole (2010b), p. 348 et seq.

593 And as compared to Art. 2401 para. 1 CC.

594 See Cariello (2012), p. 459 et seq.; Guaccero (2004a), p. 888; Corapi (2011), p. 1098; Cariello (2012), p. 20 et seq. Different opinion Salafia (2003), p. 8.

595 Art. 50 para. 1 subpara. 2.

596 See Sec. 24 para. 1 GenG.

597 See Zehetner (2014b), p. 269.

598 Sec. 86 AktG.

599 Sec. 30a GmbHG.

600 See Art. 39 para. 2 SCE-R.

601 See Zehetner (2014b), p. 269. See also Sec. 88 AktG.

602 It states that "not more than one quarter of the posts available may be filled by non-user members."

requirements contained in Sec. 24 para. 1 *GenG* are met) or (2) does not have at least three members.[603] If the members of the supervisory organ are not appointed, the company register court sets (*ex officio*) a period of 3 months for appointing or completing it. After this period has elapsed, the court can nominate the required members.[604] These members remain in office until replacements are appointed by the general meeting. But do these provisions apply to an Austrian SCE? According to the wording of Art. 39 SCE-R, the right to appoint is assigned to the general meeting. However, nothing is said about the specific circumstances referred to by Sec. 24a *GenG*,[605] nor does the SCE-R allow a statute to deal with this issue. As a result, it can be argued that national rules can be integrated because of Art. 8 para. 1 letter c SCE-R.

Finally, a labour law provision contained in the *Arbeitsverfassungsgesetz* (*ArbVG*)[606] specifically deals with employment participation and the opportunity to appoint work council members to the supervisory organ.[607] As mentioned, the issue of employment participation is specifically regulated by dir 2003/72/EC. The present study does not address this issue.

As the provisions referring to the appointment of the members of the supervisory organ are regulated in a fragmentary way, so is the provision that governs the **removal of the members** in Art. 39 para. 2 SCE-R, which only mentions that the members of the supervisory organ are removed by the general meeting.[608] Consequently, it can be argued that regulatory a gap needs to be filled, according to Art. 8 para. 1 letter c SCE-R.[609] Alternatively, Art. 53 SCE-R applies. Basically, the national rules determine the required majority and whether removal *ad nutum* is possible.[610]

[603]The provision only refers to cooperatives with a duty to appoint a supervisory organ, not those which appoint a supervisory organ on a faculty basis. See Binder and Lengauer (2014a), p. 272. Sec. 24 para. 1 GenG also contains a specific provision concerning the promotion of the number of women on supervisory bodies.

[604]The period must be set by the commercial register. See Sec. 24 a para. 1 GenG. See Binder and Lengauer (2014a), p. 272 et seq. Italian law does not contain a provision granting courts the power to appoint the members of the supervisory organ.

[605]Art. 37 para. 3 SCE-R contains a different solution for the management organ.

[606]See Sec. 110 ArbVG.

[607]See Zehetner (2014b), p. 267.

[608]See Schulze (2004a), p. 99; Schöpflin (2018f), p. 1302 et seq.

[609]See Lutter et al. (2012), p. 1612.

[610]The same is true for further reasons of termination. The SCE-R only determines that the term of office terminates with the expiration of the period as determined by the SCE-R (Art. 45 para. 1 SCE-R). In addition, both the Austrian and Italian legal systems deal with the resignation of office by the member or the cessation of personal preconditions. According to the Austrian legal system, a member can resign his office at any time without providing reasons. However, resignation at the worst possible time can lead to compensation for damages. See Zehetner (2014b), p. 270.

The majority requirement that an *Italian SCE* must follow is contained in Art. 2409 duodecies para. 5 CC. It states that the members of the supervisory organ may be removed by the general meeting at any time.[611] This requires that a resolution be adopted by votes controlling at least 20% of the company's capital, thereby granting special protection to minority shareholders (Art. 2393 para. 5 CC).[612] This seems to be in contrast with the principle 'one member one vote'; yet, linking the voting right to the shares held and deviating from this principle both align with the Italian legislature's approach to the appointment of the controlling organ. In this regard, statutes may make voting rights, be in proportion to the shares held.[613] As a result, the majority requirement adopted by Art. 2393 para. 5 CC must be based on a specific statutory provision; otherwise, this majority is calculated based on the number of cooperative members.[614] If the removal occurs without cause, the removed members have a right to compensation.[615] Members of the management organ who are also shareholders cannot participate in votes on the removal of members of the supervisory organ.[616] These provisions apply to an Italian SCE.

Interestingly, the members of the traditional board of statutory auditors are better protected than the members of the supervisory organ. According to Art. 2400 para. 2 CC, statutory auditors may only be removed from office with just cause. In addition, removal must be approved by a court decree after hearing from the statutory auditor. By contrast, membership in the supervisory organ can be revoked *ad nutum*.[617] The two-tier system's aim is, in principle, to strengthen the supervisory organ by giving it major autonomy with respect to the general meeting. However, as the members of the supervisory organ can be removed without cause and without further control by a court authority, this aim has been undermined. It has been criticised that legal provisions allow the influence of the general meeting to become too strong here.[618] Conversely, it has been asserted that, even though the law allows

---

[611] Similarly, according to Art. 2364 bis para. 1 CC, the shareholders' meeting appoints and revokes the members of the supervisory organ. Also consider Presti (2006), p. 82.

[612] This provision also applies if the members were appointed via the statutes. Also consider Del Sole (2010b), p. 350.

It has been discussed whether this reference also refers to "at least". If so, this would imply a more stringent threshold would be possible. See Cariello (2012), p. 468.

[613] See Art. 2543 para. 2 CC.

[614] See Sect. 4.4.5; Cusa (2014a), p. 340; Bonfante (2014a), p. 310. See also Paolucci (2019b), p. 121 et seq.

[615] For instance, if they did not participate at the general meetings, stood in office even though there are causes for incompatibility, personal situations which are in contrast with the regular fulfilment of the function of a member of the supervisory organ. See Del Sole (2010b), p. 350.

[616] See Del Sole (2010b), p. 350. See also Mirone (2017a), p. 565 fn 9. Furthermore, Art. 2449 para. 2 CC states that membership appointed by the state or public entities can be revoked only by these entities.

[617] See Miotto (2018b), p. 2908; Magnani (2005a), p. 116; Bonelli (2004), p. 254; Cariello (2012), p. 468. See also Sanfilippo (2017b), p. 548.

[618] See Santi (2005a), p. 1161 et seq.

removal *ad nutum*, the right to obtain compensation should prevent a majority in the general meeting from removing a member on mere instrumental grounds.[619]

Concerning the removal of the members of the supervisory organ, the *Austrian legal system* does not contain much detail. In this regard, an Austrian SCE must observe Sec. 24 para. 1 *GenG*, which states that membership in the supervisory organ can be revoked by the general meeting at any time by a simple majority.[620] Unlike the law on the *AG*, the *GenG* does not contain a specific provision dealing with the protection of minority positions of members.[621]

Assessing the various details concerning the appointment of members of the supervisory organ (of an *agricultural SCE*), one can **conclude** the SCE-R deals with these issues modestly. Except for the competence (which is assigned to the general meeting),[622] the appointment procedure is determined by national law. Both legal systems require the elected person to accept their role. One difference is that Sec. 24a *GenG* contains a mechanism for judicial appointments that is not found in the Italian legal system.

Similarly, the SCE-R assigns the competence to remove members of the supervisory organ to the general meeting. Further provisions must be determined by national law in accordance with Art. 8 para. 1 letter c SCE-R. Both legal systems allow the general meeting to revoke membership at any time. The Italian legal system provides specific minority rights which are not given by the Austrian legal system.

4.2.2.4 The Internal Organisation of the Supervisory Organ

The SCE-R contains specific provisions governing the internal organisation of the supervisory organ. They concern electing the chairman, calling meetings and making decisions. National provisions must also be observed in this context, as determined by Art. 8 para. 1 letter c SCE-R. This sub-chapter deals with these issues in the following order: chairmanship (including calling meetings, which is one of his competence), decision making and committees.

Like the management organ, the supervisory organ elects a **chairman** from among its members.[623] In cases where half of the organ's members are appointed

[619]See Breida (2004a); Del Sole (2010b), p. 351.

[620]Opposed to this, the laws referring to the AG and the GmbH require a qualified majority. Consider Sec. 87 para. 8 AktG and Sec. 30b para. 3 GmbHG. Also consider Zehetner (2014b), p. 270.

[621]According to Sec. 87 para. 10 AktG and Sec. 30b para. 5 GmbHG, a minority of shareholders (10%) can apply to the competent court to remove a member of the supervisory organ as long as good cause is given.

[622]Apart from the members of the first supervisory organ, which may be determined by the statutes. For employee participation refer to the relevant literature. See fn 583.

[623]See Art. 41 para. 1 SCE-R. It states: "The supervisory organ shall elect a chairman from among its members. If half of the members are appointed by employees, only a member appointed by the general meeting may be elected chairman."

by employees,[624] the chairman must be elected from among the members appointed by the general meeting. The aim of this provision is to prevent complete co-determination.[625]

The SCE-R states that the chairman is responsible for calling meetings, with the details laid down in the statutes.[626] Thus, the statutes determine when a meeting must be called, either at (a) the initiative of the chairman or (b) by request. The chairman can call a meeting if it is necessary to ensure the proper supervision of the management organ.[627] For the second option, the SCE-R states that requests must be submitted by at least a third of the members of the supervisory or management organs, with the reasons for calling the meeting outlined in the request. Because the members of the organ are jointly liable, they should be able to convene it.[628] In addition, the right to call a meeting is assigned to the management organ because of its duty to report, as determined by Art. 40 para. 1 and, especially, para. 2 SCE-R. Thus, this organ must be empowered to seek the necessary support of the supervisory organ. This is particularly necessary for extraordinary management activities. As a result, the supervisory organ cannot impede such meetings.[629]

Next, Art. 41 para. 2 last sent. SCE-R states that the chairman must act within 15 days of receiving the request; otherwise, the meeting can be called by those who submitted it. As mentioned above, calling meetings is the only competence assigned to the chairman by the SCE-R. Thus, further competence or tasks must be determined in accordance with the relevant national law. The same is true for holding meetings.[630]

It is shown that an SCE must observe specific national provisions when dealing with chairmanship. According to *Italian law*, and in contrast to Art. 39 para. 2 SCE-R, Art. 2409 duodecies para. 8 CC states that the chairman of the supervisory organ of an Italian cooperative must be appointed by the general meeting. As Italian law does not explicitly regulate the role of the chairman's representative,[631] it can be

[624]As determined by directive 2003/72/EC.

[625]See Schöpflin (2018h), p. 1305 et seq.

[626]See Art. 41 para. 2 SCE-R. It states: "The chairman shall call a meeting of the supervisory organ under the conditions laid down in the statutes, either on his/her own initiative, or at the request of at least one third of its members, or at the request of the management organ. The request shall indicate the reasons for calling the meeting. If no action has been taken in respect of such a request within 15 days, the meeting of the supervisory organ may be called by those who made the request."

[627]See Schöpflin (2018h), p. 1305 et seq.

[628]See Schöpflin (2018h), p. 1305 et seq.

[629]See Schöpflin (2018h), p. 1305 et seq. Also consider Sect. 4.2.2.1.

[630]By applying Art. 8 para. 1 letter c SCE-R. For the SE, see Manz (2010e), p. 540.

[631]Art. 2409 quaterdecies CC does not contain a reference to Art. 2401 para. 2 CC. This latter provision states that if the chairman is replaced, the oldest member must act as chairman until the next shareholders' meeting. If this article does not apply—either by analogy or due to article 223 septies prov. impl. CC—another approach can be found in Art. 2409 duodecies para. 7 CC, which states that the general meeting must provide for a replacement without delay. This paragraph refers to members in general. See Cariello (2012), p. 491.

argued that if necessary, an Italian SCE's supervisory organ must replace the chairman in accordance with Art. 41 para. 1 SCE-R.

Next, the statutes must set the powers of the chairman of the supervisory organ.[632] It is argued that, if no specific statutory provision is adopted, the competence contained in Art. 2381 para. 1 CC apply.[633] This provision sets minimum powers and include the chairman's competence to call the meeting of the organ, set its agenda, coordinate the work and ensure that adequate information about the issues on the agenda is provided to all the members of the supervisory organ.[634] These issues must be considered when determining the competence of the chairman of the supervisory organ of an Italian SCE, as the SCE-R does not contain further details in this regard.

Under Italian law, if a statutory provision provides, every member of the supervisory organ of an Italian cooperative can request that a meeting be called. This request must be addressed to the chairman. As Art. 2409 quaterdecies para. 1 CC does not contain an explicit reference to Art. 2403 bis para. 1 CC, which assigns specific powers to individual members, it can be argued that this option is not available without a specific statutory provision, at least for Italian cooperatives.[635] The SCE-R is quite precise in this regard. The same is true for the chairman's power to convene the meeting. Thus, in both cases, the statutes of an Italian SCE need not contain a specific provision.[636]

Next, para. 1 Art. 2404 CC determines the frequency of meetings. The supervisory organ must meet at least every 90 days,[637] although this time period can be shortened via statutory provisions.[638] It also seems possible to require the organ to meet in extraordinary circumstances.[639] This can be based on Art. 41 para. 2 SCE-R. However, as seen,[640] the SCE-R generally grants statutory freedom in this regard. Therefore, an Italian SCE is not obliged to define such specific rules.

Art. 2404 CC[641] governs the function of the meeting without containing further provisions for calling it. According to the Italian legal system, any means can be employed to call the meeting. The law does not contain provisions governing the

[632]See Art. 2409 duodecies para. 9 CC.

[633]See Cariello (2012), p. 492; Cariello (2012), p. 92 fn 20; Magnani (2005a), p. 129 et seq.

[634]Specific powers of the chairman may also cover the inter-organ relationship with the management organ and general meeting. See Del Sole (2010b), p. 349; Zamperetti (2006), p. 1198; Cariello (2012), p. 493 et seq.

[635]See Cariello (2012), p. 507 et seq.

[636]The SCE-R requires the conditions under which a meeting must be called to be defined via the statutes, whereas it explicitly empowers the chairman to convene the meeting.

[637]Unlike the former provision, which determined the necessity to meet every 3 months, the current provision determines that the organ must meet at least every 90 days.

[638]According to para. 4, external persons can also participate in meetings, depending on the topics to be discussed.

[639]See Serraino (2010a), p. 69; Ambrosini (2004), p. 902; Magnani (2005a), p. 132 fn 64.

[640]See Art. 41 para. 1 sent. 1 SCE-R.

[641]Applicable by reference contained in Art. 2409 quaterdecies para. 1 CC.

agenda[642] or where the meeting must be held. However, it seems possible to meet outside the cooperative's registered office.[643] In this regard, the SCE-R grants statutory freedom.

Finally, like the SCE-R, Italian law does not contain a specific obligation to attend the meetings.[644] However, it could be argued that Art. 2409 terdecies para. 3 CC, which obliges members of the supervisory organ to fulfil their duties with the diligence required by the nature of the office, makes it necessary to attend.[645] These observations are also valid for an Italian SCE.

Like the Italian legal system, the *Austrian legal system* contains specific provisions regulating chairmanship. Yet, not all of them are applicable to an Austrian SCE. Like the SCE-R, the *GenG*[646] requires that a chairman be elected from among the members of the supervisory organ. Thus, every member can be appointed chairman. In addition, the *GenG* mandates the election of at least one representative, again from among the members of the organ. As the SCE-R does not contain any information about a representative, this provision should also apply to Austrian SCEs.[647] Then, according to the Austrian legal system, election becomes effective at the moment of acceptance. Finally, the supervisory organ can remove (without good cause) the chairman and the representative.[648] Both rules must be followed by Austrian SCEs.[649]

The *GenG* states that the chairman of the supervisory organ must convene the meetings. In addition, any member of the organ can ask the chairman to convene the

---

[642]If the agenda is not provided, this does not imply a reason to invalidate calling the meeting. On the other hand, the agenda helps members prepare themselves for the meeting. As a result, if a member is not properly informed about an issue to be discussed during the meeting, the member can oppose these specific issues being discussed. See Serraino (2010a), p. 69 et seq. See also Sanfilippo (2017b), p. 550.

[643]See Serraino (2010a), p. 69.

[644]Neither due to explicit nor indirect reference to Art. 2404 para. 2 CC. According to this latter provision, an auditor who fails to attend two meetings of the board of auditors during the company financial year without good cause shall forfeit his office.

[645]See Magnani (2005a), p. 133.

[646]Sec. 24c para. 1 GenG. The 2008 reform introduced specific provisions dealing with several aspects of the internal organisation of the supervisory organ. Sec. 24c GenG contains provisions regarding the chairman, the minutes, committees, decision making, control committee and the representation of members of the supervisory organ. These factors must be considered even if a cooperative has voluntarily adopted a supervisory organ. The specific details can be regulated by rules of procedure. In practice, the statutes oblige the supervisory organ to adopt these. See Dellinger and Steinböck (2014), p. 278 et seq.

[647]See Art. 8 para. 1 letter c SCE-R. According to Art. 24c para. 1 GenG, if the statutes provide accordingly the general meeting can provide for the election. This approach cannot be adopted by an Austrian SCE due to the stringent formulation of Art. 41 para. 1 SCE-R.

[648]See Dellinger and Steinböck (2014), p. 279; Kalss (2012), nt 32 and nt 36; Strasser (2011a), nt 11.

[649]Due to Art. 8 para. 1 letter c SCE-R. However, it can also be argued that the competence to revoke membership is, implicitly assigned to the supervisory organ, as both competences are connected with each other.

meeting, although they must state their reasons for calling the meeting. The meeting must take place within 2 weeks of being called.[650] There are differences from the SCE-R: Under the *GenG*, any member may make a request to call a meeting, whereas the SCE-R sets a minimum of at least one-third of the members for making such a request. Thus, the *GenG* is more flexible here.[651]

In general, the chairman must manage and coordinate the activity of the supervisory organ. In addition to calling the meeting, he or she is responsible for organising it; this activity includes drafting the agenda and preparing the meeting. He or she also chairs the meetings and is responsible for drafting and signing the minutes, along with supervising the execution of the decisions.[652] The chairman additionally communicates with the management organ and, if necessary, the general meeting. He or she receives all reports addressed to the supervisory organ. In practice, the rules of procedure contain specific details governing the competence of the chairman.[653] These findings are also relevant for an Austrian SCE, as they help to better describe the role of the chairman.

Unlike the SCE-R, Sec. 24d para. 3 *GenG* states that the supervisory organ must hold a meeting at least quarterly.[654] In this regard, the SCE-R grants statutory freedom.

Next, every member of the supervisory organ can participate in its meetings and has the right to comment on every item on the agenda. Regarding possible joint meetings with the management organ, Sec. 6 *GenRevG*[655] states that both organs must discuss the report in a joint meeting. Yet, the rules of procedure can also set further items to be discussed in joint meetings.[656] These findings are also valid for Austrian SCEs.

When **making decisions**, Italian and Austrian SCEs must both observe the provisions in Art. 50 para. 1 SCE-R.[657] As already mentioned,[658] these are default

---

[650]See Sec. 24d GenG.

[651]The SCE-R (Art. 41 para. 2 SCE-R) and GenG (Art. 24 para. 2 GenG) both provide a solution if no action is taken in response to such a request.

[652]See Dellinger and Steinböck (2014), p. 280.

[653]If the chairman or his representatives are members of a committee they automatically chair it. In practice, the statutes or the rules of procedure can assign a casting vote. See Dellinger and Steinböck (2014), p. 279 et seq.

[654]The provision refers to cooperatives which must have a supervisory organ due to Sec. 24 para. 1 GenG.

[655]Applicable to an Austrian SCE due to Art. 71 SCE-R.

[656]See Dellinger and Steinböck (2014), p. 283.

[657]It states: "Unless otherwise provided by this Regulation or the statutes, the internal rules relating to quorums and decision taking in SCE organs shall be as follows (a) quorum: at least half of the members with voting rights must be present or represented; (b) decision-taking: a majority of the members with voting rights present or represented.

Members who are absent may take part in decisions by authorising another member of the organ or the alternate members who were appointed at the same time to represent them."

[658]See Sect. 4.2.1.5.

provisions and prevail over national law. Accordingly, the whole decision-making procedure may be regulated by the statutes. In case no statutory provisions are determined, the national law applies for gap filling.

In brief, para. 1 contains provisions regarding quorums, majorities and representation. As already seen,[659] the chairman can have a casting vote, which, in principle, can be regulated by the statutes. Art. 50 para. 2 SCE-R explicitly states that a different statutory provision cannot be applied to the supervisory organ if half of the members are employee representatives.[660]

Like the SCE-R, the *Italian legal system* contains specific provisions dealing with quorums and majorities, which apply in case gap filling is necessary. As already seen, Art. 50 para. 1 SCE-R provides statutory freedom for quorums and majorities. Italian law is slightly vague here. Due to explicit references in Art. 2409 quaterdecies para. 1 CC, two provisions must be observed: Art. 2388 paras. 1 and 2 CC, which must be adopted by the administrative organ,[661] and Art. 2404 para. 4 CC, which regulates the meetings of the board of statutory auditors.[662] As the wording between these two provisions is not identical, problems can occur when actually applying the rules.[663]

Unlike Art. 50 para. 2 SCE-R, Italian law does not contain a provision for tied votes. However, it is argued that it is possible to adopt a specific statutory provision.[664]

Next, according to Italian law,[665] meetings can be held via telecommunications devices.[666] The statutes must specify the instruments which may be used.[667] As

---

[659]See Sect. 4.2.1.5.

[660]Neither Austria nor Italy exercised the option contained in Art. 50 para. 3 SCE-R. See Fici (2010), p. 64 et seq.

[661]Traditional corporate governance system.

[662]Traditional corporate governance system.

[663]Whereas both require the presence of a majority of members and an absolute majority of those present to pass a resolution, Art. 2388 CC differs inasmuch as it allows to provide otherwise by statutes. Considering the wording of the two articles, it is clear that there might be inconsistencies. In order to overcome these inconsistencies, it is argued that Art. 2404 CC and the provisions contained therein have priority, as this article is a typical provision for a controlling organ. On the other hand, it is argued that the provisions contained in Art. 2388 CC must be applied to a decision relating to the competences of high administration (due to Art. 2409 terdecies para. 1 letter f-bis CC). See Cariello (2012), p. 509; Cariello (2012), p. 41 et seq.; slightly different opinion Magnani (2005a), p. 131 et seq.

[664]See Art. 2409 duodecies para. 9 CC; also consider Del Sole (2010b), p. 349; Miotto (2018b), p. 2907; Magnani (2005a), p. 130.

[665]See Art. 2404 para. 1 CC.

[666]As long as the statutes provide accordingly.

[667]For details see Serraino (2010a), p. 69 et seq. See also Sanfilippo (2017b), p. 550. Basically, the rules of procedure may contain all the provisions necessary to safeguard the functioning of the meetings. Due to an explicit reference contained in Art. 2409 quaterdecies para. 1 CC, Art. 2404 para. 3 CC (dealing with the minutes of the meeting) applies. The minutes must be taken and signed by the attendances and be recorded in the corporate book as mentioned in Art. 2421 para. 1 no 5 CC. See Cariello (2012), p. 512.

already mentioned,[668] this provision only applies to an Italian SCE if Art. 50 para. 1 letter b SCE-R also applies; otherwise, such an approach (i.e., virtual meetings) can be adopted in accordance with Art. 50 para. 1 SCE-R (in other words, by adopting a specific statutory provision; in this latter case, the legal source is the SCE-R and not Italian Law). A similar solutions applies to the minutes: the law[669] requires minutes to be taken and signed by the participants in the meeting.

As seen above,[670] the Italian legal system does not allow proxy voting, unlike the SCE-R. Nor can the supervisory organ of an Italian cooperative make decisions remotely, which prevents making decisions by circular resolutions. Finally, as mentioned,[671] it is possible to adopt rules of procedure, which can contain details on voting procedures.[672] This applies to Italian SCEs in cases where national law is used for gap filling.[673]

Having explained the Italian situation, I turn to the *Austrian legal system*, which equally contains specific provisions that are applicable to an Austrian SCE. Under the Austrian legal system, decisions are taken during meetings. However, according to Sec. 24c para. 3 *GenG*, decisions can also be taken outside of meetings if the statutes permit and no member objects. No specific formalities have to be observed here, so it is not necessary for members to actively allow decisions to be made outside of meetings. The primary aim of this provision is to allow circular resolutions.[674] As mentioned above,[675] for SCEs, the adoption of circular resolutions must be based on Art. 50 para. 1 SCE-R.

The law does not restrict decision making, when it occurs outside of meetings, to written decisions; because of the general wording of para. 3, other methods such as telephone voting are also allowed.[676] As already seen,[677] if an Austrian SCE wants to adopt this approach, it must be based on Art. 50 para. 1 SCE-R, provided that letter b is amended. Otherwise, national law applies.

The law requires at least half of the members to attend the meeting in order for a decision to be made.[678] This criterion includes those members who participate via

---

[668]See Sect. 4.2.1.5.

[669]Art. 2404 para. 1 CC., applicable due to reference as contained in Art. 2409 quaterdecies para. 1 CC.

[670]See Sect. 4.2.1.5.

[671]When analysing the provisions that apply to the management organ. See Sect. 4.2.1.5.

[672]See Cariello (2012), p. 502.

[673]As long as Art. 50 para. 1 letter b SCE-R applies.

[674]See Dellinger and Steinböck (2014), p. 283. Also consider Kalss (2012), nt 99.

[675]See Sect. 4.2.1.5.

[676]There are good arguments for including presence via communication devices in the definition of "meeting". Voting without participating in the meetings (e.g., video conference but also written or telephone votes) are admissible as long as the statutes or the rules of procedure provide accordingly. Furthermore, para. 3 determines that decisions outside meetings are only permitted if no member objects to this procedure. See Dellinger and Steinböck (2014), p. 282. Also consider Schärf (2002), p. 200; Kalss (2012), nt 110.

[677]See Sect. 4.2.1.5.

[678]Sec. 24c para. 4 GenG.

telecommunications devices. The statutes, the general meeting or the supervisory organ may increase this limit, but it is not possible to reduce it.[679] In this respect, Austrian law differs from the SCE-R. In addition, the statutes of an Austrian SCE can require the chairman or his representative to be present.[680] Next, according to Sec. 24c para. 4 *GenG*, decisions require a simple majority of votes cast.[681] In this context, however, the specific provisions of the SCE-R must be observed.[682]

Then, Sec. 24c para. 4 sent. 2 *GenG*, which applies to Austrian SCEs,[683] states that each member has one vote. This does not exclude multiple voting in the event that one member of the supervisory organ represents other members. However, votes cannot be weighted.[684]

According to Sec. 24c para. 7 *GenG*, the members' duties of representation can only be exercised on a strictly personal basis, and representation must be based on a specific statutory provision. This is not valid for an SCE, where representation is based on Art. 50 para. 1 subpara. 2 SCE-R.

According to Sec. 24c para. 7 *GenG*, a written notice is necessary to entrust representation to another member. This representation only lasts for one meeting and can only be granted to another member of the organ.[685] This applies to Austrian SCEs as long as the internal rules in Art. 50 para. 1 are not altered.[686] The same is true for the voting procedure. According to the Austrian legal system, the voting procedure[687] can be defined via the statutes or the rules of procedure. Otherwise, the chairman decides in this regard.[688]

---

[679]See Dellinger and Steinböck (2014), p. 285 et seq.

[680]In this regard see Dellinger and Steinböck (2014), p. 286; Kalss (2012), nt 127; Koppensteiner and Rüffler (2007), § 30g nt 8. Different opinion Strasser (2011a), nt 57.

[681]It is not clear whether this provision is dispositive in nature, with the result that qualified majorities can be established. Sent. 4 of this paragraph states that "the statutes of the cooperative, the general meeting or the supervisory organ may set a higher number." It is not clear whether this sentence refers to sent. 3 or also to sent. 1. Sent. 3 states that the organ can only satisfy the quorum, if at least half of its members attend the meeting. As a result, sent. 4 could refer exclusively to the quorum and not to the majority. On the other hand, it can be argued that, as the provisions regarding the AG and the GmbH allow qualified majorities, it is appropriate to extend the meaning of sentence 4 to sentence 1. As a result, qualified majorities can be determined via the statutes and probably also via the rules of procedure. It is, however, necessary to safeguard the functioning of the supervisory organ. In other words, qualified majorities must not obstruct decision making. See Dellinger and Steinböck (2014), p. 284; Strasser (2011a), nt 86.

[682]Art. 50 para. 1 letter b SCE-R refers to a majority of the members with voting rights present or represented.

[683]Due to Art. 8 para. 1 letter c SCE-R.

[684]See Dellinger and Steinböck (2014), p. 285.

[685]See Dellinger and Steinböck (2014), p. 289; Strasser (2011b), nt 83 et seq.; Koppensteiner and Rüffler (2007), § 30j nt 27; Eckert and Schopper (2014b), p. 340.

[686]See Sect. 4.2.1.5.

[687]E.g., a show of hands or oral or written voting.

[688]See Dellinger and Steinböck (2014), p. 285. Also consider Strasser (2011a), nt 60; Kalss (2012), nt 81 et seq.

The issue of conflicts of interests (e.g., when an item on the agenda affects a member of the supervisory organ or one of his close relatives) is only regulated by national law; the relevant national provisions must be applied by an Austrian SCE. Thus, the affected member cannot take part in the decision-making process. Whether this conflict of interest also prevents them from taking part in the discussion is unclear and must ultimately be decided by the chairman. In any case, the rules of procedure can contain a specific provision dealing with this issue.[689]

Finally, Austrian agricultural SCEs must observe the rules on taking minutes. According to Sec. 24c para. 2 *GenG*, all discussions and decisions must be recorded. The minutes must be signed by the chairman or one of his representatives. Minutes must be taken for both regular meetings and teleconferences. It is the duty of the chairman to ensure that minutes are properly taken.[690]

The last issue pertaining to the internal organisation of the supervisory organ concerns the constitution of **committees**. As will be seen, the constitution of committees is a typical instrument used to enhance the efficiency and effectiveness of the supervisory organ. In this regard, the SCE-R does not contain any specific provisions; therefore, the national provisions must be observed in accordance with Art. 8 para. 1 letter c SCR R.[691]

According to *Italian law*, the supervisory organ acts collegially. Thus, powers cannot be delegated to individual members or groups of members.[692] However, it seems possible to delegate specific tasks to committees.[693] This is in line with the

[689]See Dellinger and Steinböck (2014), p. 285. Also consider Strasser (2011a), nt 65; Kalss (2012), nt 87 et seq.

[690]See Dellinger and Steinböck (2014), p. 288; Kalss (2012), nt 56. The rules of procedure can set the minimum content of the minutes. See Dellinger and Steinböck (2014), p. 288; Strasser (2011a), nt 36; Kalss (2012), nt 59. Under the Austrian legal system, decision making can be defective for several reasons. For instance, the decision might violate the law or statutes. Next, errors can relate to the provisions regulating the procedural rules, e.g., missing quorum or circular resolutions despite opposition by members, etc. However, the GenG does not consider how defective resolutions should be dealt with. Approaches vary wildly here. Violating the law or statutes invalidates the decision. Examples include decisions which are not covered by the competences of the supervisory organ. The possibility to claim invalidity can be temporarily limited. If procedural rules are violated, a decision can be void if the application of specific provision cannot be waived. A further condition is that violating the specific provision is relevant to the outcome of the decision. Specific deficiencies do not lead to the inefficiency, if all members are present with no objection raised to decision taking. Finally, infringements may be against simple procedural rules (participation of third parties or regarding minutes). Deficiencies like this do not lead to ineffectiveness. The declaration of invalidity can be promoted according to Sec. 228 ZPO. In any case, the members of the supervisory and management organs are actively legitimised. Members of the cooperative are only actively legitimised if they are affected by the invalid decision. See Dellinger and Steinböck (2014), p. 286 et seq.; Kalss (2012), nt 116 et seq.; Koppensteiner and Rüffler (2007), §30g nt 14. Also consider Strasser (2011a), nt 72 and Eckert and Schopper (2014a), p. 318.

[691]For the SE, see Manz (2010c), p. 519; Teichmann (2015i), p. 764. Also consider Mahi (2004), p. 85; Artmann (2002), p. 193; Hirte (2002), p. 6.

[692]See Cariello (2012), p. 450 et seq.; Riolfo (2013), p. 619. See also Mirone (2017a), p. 565.

[693]See Cariello (2012), p. 504 et seq.; Riolfo (2013), p. 619 et seq.; Comitato interregionale dei consigli notarili delle Tre Venezie (2011), H.D.19.

general expression of the principle of self-regulation. It is not possible to limit this power by either the statutes or other organs in the cooperative. However, limits imposed by the law must be observed.[694] Thus, it is possible to assign advisory tasks, for example.[695] In any case, the supervisory organ remains responsible for decisions taken by its committees.[696] These findings apply to an Italian SCE because of Art. 8 para. 1 letter c SCE-R.

Concerning the *Austrian legal system*, one has to consider the portion on committees in Sec. 24c para. 5 *GenG*, which states that the supervisory organ may elect one or more committees from among its members.[697] These committees are particularly useful for preparing negotiations to be conducted by the supervisory organ, preparing decisions to be taken by this organ, or for monitoring the implementation of these decisions. Committees may also take decisions themselves. Depending on the tasks to be fulfilled, committees can be formed temporarily or permanently.[698] This approach is in line with Art. 50 para. 1 SCE-R, which grants a wide range of statutory freedom in this regard. As seen, committees may be integrated because of Art. 8 para. 1 letter c SCE-R. This is valid for the obligation, determined by Sec. 24 c para. 6 GenG, to appoint an audit committee either if the cooperative fulfils the criteria from Sec. 189a para. 1 letter a and d UGB or if the cooperative can be classified as a 'big cooperative'.[699]

This chapter has analysed the three key aspects of the internal organisation of the supervisory organ (of an *agricultural SCE*)[700]: chairmanship, decision making and the constitution of internal committees. It has been shown that the provisions of the SCE-R must be completed by national provisions. In fact, the regulation basic provisions for electing the chairman and calling meetings. Other competences of the chairman must be determined by national provisions. Here, the results have shown that one difference between Austrian and Italian law is that the former requires the election of representatives, whereas the latter does not mention this figure at all.

---

[694] See Cariello (2012), p. 504 et seq. The law also indicates specific committees which must be formed, e.g., as required by Consob regulation no 17221/2010 or the TUB.

[695] See Comitato interregionale dei consigli notarili delle Tre Venezie (2011), H.D.19.

[696] See Riolfo (2013), p. 621.

[697] The constitution of committees can be mandatory, for example if the supervisory tasks are too complex. See Dellinger and Steinböck (2014), p. 290 et seq.; Kalss (2012), nt 155; Rauter (2014), p. 61. Also consider Eckert and Schopper (2014a), p. 316.

[698] See Sec. 24c para. 5 GenG. Also consider Dellinger and Steinböck (2014), p. 291 et seq.; Rauter (2014), p. 76 et seq.; Dellinger (2016), p. 1382 et seq., Eckert and Schopper (2014a), p. 316.

[699] In brief, this audit committee must monitor the financial reporting process and the effectiveness of the internal control system. In addition, where appropriate it must monitor the cooperative's internal auditing and risk management systems. It must also monitor the audit of financial statements and consolidated financial statements, review the financial statements, the proposal for distributing profits and the management report, in addition to submitting the report on the review results to the supervisory organ. If necessary, it also reviews the audit of the consolidated financial statements and consolidated management reports and the submission of the report on the audit results to the supervisory organ of the parent company. See Sec. 24c para. 6 subpara. 4 GenG.

[700] The PECOL do not contain any specific information in this regard.

Hence, if the chairman can no longer fulfil his duties, he or she must be replaced in accordance with Art. 41 para. 1 SCE-R. Both legal systems take similar flexible approaches to determine further competence of the chairman.

The SCE-R grants statutory freedom when it comes to the frequency of meetings, whereas the two legal systems, in this regard, set specific timeframes for their national cooperatives. Neither legal system creates a duty to attend the meeting; however, such a duty could result from the fact that the members of the supervisory organ are jointly and severally liable. Finally, while Italian law allows joint meetings by permitting the supervisory organ to attend meetings of the management organ, the Austrian legal system explicitly allows this only when the revision report is being discussed.

This sub-chapter also discussed decision making by the supervisory organ. The basic provisions to be observed are contained in the SCE-R. For circular resolutions or specific voting procedures, see the analysis on the management organ.[701]

Finally, this sub-chapter analysed committees. As the SCE-R does not contain specific provisions here, national provisions must be observed. Both legal systems, though flexible, outline specific committees that must be established.

How the supervisory organ of an *agricultural SCE* is ultimately structured depends on the size and structure of the agricultural cooperative, including whether it is a primary cooperative or a secondary cooperative and whether it is a PO. The more complex the whole, the more complex the monitoring structure: this inevitably affects the organisation of the information gathering process and what kind of committees are used. In this context, one can think of committees for preparing decisions, for independent monitoring, for making renumeration deals with members of the management organ and so on. The concrete implementation of the internal organisation is ultimately determined by the existing circumstances.

4.2.2.5 Civil Liability

When analysing the provisions concerning the management organ, we saw that, because of Art. 51 SCE-R, the civil liability of the members of the management, administrative and supervisory organs is determined according to national law.[702] This sub-chapter deals with those issues regarding the civil liability of members of the supervisory organ.[703]

According to *Italian law*, 2409 terdecies para. 3 CC, the members of the supervisory organ of an Italian SCE must fulfil their duties with the diligence required by the nature of their offices. Moreover, they are jointly and severally liable with the

[701] See Sect. 4.2.1.5.

[702] As mentioned in Sect. 4.2.1.6.

[703] For general information regarding confidentiality—as a duty to be observed by the members of the supervisory organ—one may consider the analysis of civil liability in the context of the management organ. See Sect. 4.2.1.6.

members of the management organ for their acts or omissions if the damage would not have occurred if they had supervised in compliance with the duties of their office.[704]

In practice, liability depends on the specific duties and obligations that the supervisory organ must fulfil. The actual scope of the tasks depends on how Art. 2409 terdecies para. 1 letter f-bis CC is applied.[705] Thus, in this context, three entitlements of liability exist[706]: (1) liability with respect to the supervisory function[707]; (2) liability with respect to a 'high administrative' power to approve strategic, industrial or financial plans[708]; and (3) liability without this specific power (what can be referred to as weak administrative power).[709] As Art. 48 SCE-R grants a similar power of co-decision, similar liabilities also impact Italian SCEs.[710]

The concept of liability, as determined by Art. 2409 terdecies para. 3 CC, is similar to that contained in Art. 2407 CC, which refers to the board of statutory auditors. Whereas Art. 2407 CC refers to the professionalism required by the nature of the office when determining how the duties must be fulfilled, this aspect is not contained in Art. 2409 terdecies para. 3 CC. This difference does not imply that the members of the supervisory organ must fulfil their duties with any less diligence. Both systems analysed here[711] require at least one member to be enrolled in a register for statutory auditors; moreover, Art. 2409 duodecies para. 6 CC provides for the possibility that the statutes may subordinate the appointment to the fulfilment

[704]This implies that, if the members of the supervisory organ consider that decisions taken by the management organ contravene the law, the statutes or the principles of proper management or are an example of clear rashness, they must express their disapproval in the minutes. If the decision is taken despite this disapproval, the members of the supervisory organ must evaluate this behaviour to remove the members of the management organ, exercise the action for liability or to report to the court. See Balzarini (2007), p. 880; Magnani (2005b), p. 181; Serraino (2010c), p. 89. See also Romano (2017r), p. 2992 et seq. For details Del Sole (2010d), p. 363 et seq.; Magnani (2005b), p. 180 et seq.; Miotto (2018e), p. 2910; Facchin (2009g), p. 667 et seq.

[705]See Sect. 4.2.2.1, analysing Art. 2409ter f-bis CC.

[706]See Cariello (2012), p. 518. Also consider Santi (2005b), p. 1171 et seq.; Breida (2004c), p. 1191 et seq.; Magnani (2005b), p. 180 et seq.; Riolfo (2013), p. 793 et seq. See also Mirone (2017a), p. 572.

[707]Based on the duties as contained in Art. 2403 para. 1 CC. See Sect. 4.2.2.1. A specific case of liability arises because the supervisory organ approves the yearly financial statements (and, if drafted, the consolidated accounts). Due to Art. 223 septies prov. impl. CC, it is argued that Art. 2434 CC can be applied, with the consequence that approving the financial statements does not imply the discharge of the managers appointed with drafting accounting documents or the members of the supervisory organ from the liabilities accrued in the corporate management. See Cariello (2012), p. 516.

[708]See Fici (2013b), p. 494.

[709]See Cariello (2012), p. 518. See Sect. 4.2.2.1.

[710]Based on Art. 48 SCE-R. See Sect. 4.2.2.1.

[711]One referring to the traditional corporate governance system, the other one referring to the two-tier system.

of special professional requirements.[712] To reiterate an early point,[713] Italian SCEs require a statutory auditor.

Art. 2407 CC contains a provision dealing with confidentiality. Even though the set of rules in the civil code, as adopted for the two-tier system, does not contain an explicit reference in this regard, it is argued that this provision is applicable because of 223 septies prov. impl. CC, as the supervisory organ also fulfils the monitoring task in a manner similar to the board of statutory auditors.[714] This conclusion is also valid for an Italian SCE.

In general terms, the members of the supervisory organ must display the diligence required by Art. 1176 para. 2 CC. Liability of the members of the supervisory organ is thus regulated in the same way as for members of the management organ.[715] To set the criteria of diligence and professionalism, one may refer to the requirements in the codes of conduct that are drafted by the professional associations. These codes can be instruments used to verify the degree of diligence displayed by the members of the supervisory organ.[716] In addition, the reference to the nature of the office (as required by Art. 2407 para. 1 CC) implies that it is necessary to consider a company's size, organisational structure and purpose.[717]

In case of infringements of the organ's duties, the general meeting decides on the liability of the members of the supervisory organ, according to Art. 2364 bis para. 1 no. 3 CC.[718] Even though there is no explicit reference to Art. 2392 paras. 2 and 3 CC, one can argue that these provisions could be used to exclude or restrict liability. As already in Sect. 4.2.1.6, this article contains two possible exceptions to the principle of joint liability. Accordingly, the members are jointly liable if they were aware of the harmful effects, but did not do everything in their power to either prevent the occurrence of the infringement or to eliminate—or at least reduce—the harmful consequences.[719] For burden of proof, one may refer the analysis conducted

[712]See Del Sole (2010d), p. 363 et seq.; Santi (2005b), p. 1172. Also consider Magnani (2005b), p. 183; Miotto (2018b), p. 2908. See also Sanfilippo (2017b), p. 552 et seq.

[713]See Sect. 4.2.2.2.

[714]See Ferrucci and Ferrentino (2012), p. 778. See also Sanfilippo (2017b), p. 552 et seq.

[715]See Serraino (2010c), p. 87; Ferrucci and Ferrentino (2012), p. 788; Miotto (2018e), p. 2910; Romano (2017r), p. 2992 et seq. Also consider Paolucci (2012), p. 143.

[716]See Domenichini (2004), p. 767; Serraino (2010c), p. 87. See also Romano (2017r), p. 2992 et seq.; Sanfilippo (2017b), p. 552.

[717]See Serraino (2010c), p. 87 et seq.; Domenichini (2004), p. 768; Simone (2009b), p. 566; Romano (2017r), p. 2992 et seq.

[718]In addition, it is discussed whether the action for liability can also be exercised by a minority of members or creditors. Even though there is no explicit reference to the specific articles, some scholars argue they can be applied due to the general reference contained in Art. 223 septies prov. impl. CC. Others argue that this is not possible, as it would require a direct reference. See Bonelli (2004), p. 262; Santi (2005b), p. 1172 et seq.; Riolfo (2013), p. 820. Critical Cariello (2012), p. 522 et seq.

[719]For details Ricci (2010a), p. 701 et seq. Also consider Cariello (2012), p. 516 fn 902. See also Romano (2017n), p. 2964 et seq.

when discussing the civil liability of the management organ,[720] as the same observations apply.[721]

Under *Austrian law*, the civil liability of the members of the supervisory organ of an Austrian SCE is primarily regulated by Sec. 24e para. 6 *GenG*, which states that members are liable for damages caused by their failure to fulfil their obligations. This provision is based on the same model of liability as Sec. 23 *GenG*.[722] Obviously, these two provisions differ on the various responsibilities the organs have.

In brief, the duties or tasks a member of the supervisory organ must fulfil are limited to (a) monitoring of the management, (b) specific duties if the cooperative is in crisis, (c) specific collaboration when opening insolvency proceedings and (d) examining the annual financial statements.[723] These tasks must be undertaken with the diligence required of an ordinary member of a supervisory organ of a cooperative.[724]

The *GenG* does not contain a specific provision for the duties of confidentiality that the members of the supervisory organ must observe. Such a duty, however, derives from the general provision in Sec. 24e para. 6 *GenG*, which refers to the duties of the supervisory organ. It is furthermore argued that the specific duties outlined in the Sec. 84 *Aktiengesetz* (*AktG*, Stock Corporation Act) apply to the members of the supervisory organ, requiring them to keep confidential information secret[725]; this results from a reference contained in Sec. 99 AktG.

The members are jointly liable for any damages caused, regardless of their degree of fault. This requires personal fault; otherwise, no liability can be provided. Different degrees of fault are only relevant when recourse is taken against the other members of the supervisory organ.[726]

The Austrian legal system determines that members of the supervisory organ must compensate for damages because of slight negligence.[727] A member's degree of diligence must be determined according to objective normative criteria (i.e., by the economic activity of the cooperative and by other factors, such as size or market position of the cooperative). As a result, the supervisory organ's members will be liable because of a lack of due diligence that, in specific circumstances, may be required from an ordinary organ member.[728]

It must be recognised that the members of the supervisory organ must be chosen from the members of the cooperative. As cooperatives are self-help organisations

---

[720] See Sect. 4.2.1.6.

[721] See Miotto (2018e), p. 2910. Different opinion Magnani (2005b), p. 186.

[722] See Sect. 4.2.1.6.

[723] See Sect. 4.2.2.1.

[724] See Zehetner (2014c), p. 326 et seq. Also consider Dellinger (2016), p. 1377.

[725] See Kastner (1986), p. 177.

[726] See Zehetner (2014c), p. 326; Kastner (1986), p. 176 et seq.

[727] This, however, does not imply strict liability. See Zehetner (2014c), p. 326. Also consider OGH 31.10.1973, 1 Ob 179/73 SZ 46/113 and OGH 26.02.2002, 1 Ob 144/01k.

[728] See Zehetner (2014c), p. 326 et seq.; OGH 26.02.2002, 1 Ob 144/01k.

that focus on the needs of (in general, economically) disadvantaged groups, it would not make sense to require the representatives of this group to possess specific economic knowledge greater than that possessed by an average businessperson. The legislature has given the cooperative audit a particular role to counterbalance this deficit.[729] In addition, it must be remembered that members of the supervisory organ normally fulfil the function unpaid. This criteria must be considered when determining which degree of diligence to apply. As a result, the members of the supervisory organ of a cooperative need *not* have above-average economic knowledge and experience.[730] However, they must be able and ready to demonstrate concern for the interests of the cooperative, to attend training or receive further education and to attend meetings.[731]

Regarding the assertion of an infringement, Sec. 25 para. 2 *GenG* determines that a cooperative is represented by authorised persons who are elected by the general meeting. As already seen,[732] according to para. 3, every member of the cooperative is entitled to engage in these lawsuits[733] as an intervening party at his own expense. Yet, the members of the cooperative or SCE have no specific minority rights.[734] Next, as the lawsuits referred to by Sec. 25 *GenG* only relate to the activity of a member of the supervisory organ,[735] the supervisory organ as a whole cannot be party to the case.[736]

In these lawsuits, the member of the supervisory organ carries the burden of proof and must demonstrate that he or she has exercised the necessary diligence. In addition, the member must prove either that the damage would have occurred in any event or that he or she would not have been able to meet the diligence requirements and, thus, cannot be blamed. Conversely, the cooperative must prove a causal link between the breach of obligations and the damage incurred and substantiate that a behaviour shows lack of diligence.[737]

This last chapter analysing the supervisory organ (of an *agricultural SCE*) addressed civil liability, adding specific details based on national law.[738] Both

---

729 See Dellinger (2016), p. 1377.

730 According to judge-made law, the members of a company's supervisory organ must have specific capacities greater than those of an average businessperson. Otherwise, effective monitoring would be impossible. See OGH 26.02.2002, 1 Ob 144/01k; Ob 306/76 EvBl 1978/4. However, the principles developed for companies cannot easily be transferred to cooperatives.

731 See Zehetner (2014c), p. 327 et seq. Different opinion Riss (2008), p. 768; Nowotny (2008a), nt 5/91. Also consider Sec. 1 para. 1 GenRevG; for details Perkounigg and Kessler (2014). Specific requirements are set for banks. See Sec. 28a para. 5 BWG.

732 See Sect. 4.2.1.6.

733 Lawsuits against members of the management and supervisory organs.

734 On this issue, see Sect. 4.2.1.6.

735 E.g., legal regress.

736 See Binder and Lengauer (2014b), p. 331 et seq.

737 See Zehetner (2014c), p. 329. Also consider OGH 26.02.2002, 1 Ob 144/01k; OGH 24.06.1998, 3 Ob 34/97i; and OGH 08.05.1980, 8 Ob 505/80 HS 11.465.

738 For general observations linked to the provisions of the SCE-R one may consider the analysis from the relevant chapter on the management organ.

legal systems set specific duties,[739] along with diligence criteria to be observed when fulfilling these duties. One difference is that the Italian legal system primarily refers to professional diligence, as determined by the law, whereas the Austrian legal system acknowledges that no specific economic expertise is necessary. The fact that (*agricultural*) cooperatives are self-help organisations whose members normally fulfil their function unpaid is also considered; therefore, less diligence is required than for a company. Cooperative audit helps mitigate this shortcoming. Moreover, members of the supervisory organ must be ready to attend training and pursue further education, to use their individual experience to promote the interests of the cooperative and to generally provide for the benefit of the cooperative. Austrian law refers to the diligence of an ordinary member of the supervisory organ of a cooperative.

The concepts of diligence adopted by the Italian and Austrian national legislatures allow diligence to be considered in the context of the general framework within which the duties must be fulfilled.[740] Generally, diligence requires one to consider the members of the cooperative, the organisational structure or the corporate purpose. A significant difference between the two legal systems is that the Austrian legal system allows reduced diligence, as it is acknowledged that cooperatives are self-help organisations and that the members of the organs normally fulfil their functions without pay. By contrast, the Italian legal system primarily refers to the general criteria of professional diligence. In this context, the PECOL require that the duties of the members of the supervisory organ include an obligation to adhere to universally recognised values and principles.[741] For specific observations on the differences found, consider the corresponding analyses related to the management organ.

The analysis, then, revealed significant differences arising from the fact that Austrian law only allows the general meeting to conduct a lawsuit against a member of the supervisory organ, whereas Italian law is more flexible and also allows a minority of members to exercise the action of liability. Last, both legal systems take a similar approach to the burden of proof.

4.2.3 The Two-Tier System from an Economic Perspective

In principle, the management organ has three functions[742]: (1) it manages the SCE upon delegation (i.e., the general meeting can delegate management to qualified[743]

[739]See Sect. 4.2.2.1.

[740]E.g., the size of the cooperative.

[741]See Sec. 2,5 para. 8 PECOL; Snaith (2017), p. 71. Also consider Sect. 4.2.1.6.

[742]See Engert (2014), p. 85 et seq.; Bolten et al. (2007), pp. 836 and 842.

[743]It is stressed that actual effectiveness will depend on the quality of the members of the various organs. See Van der Sangen (2012), p. 22. Then, it has been observed that the managers of Italian agricultural cooperatives have developed specific managerial capabilities, allowing them to add value to their members' agricultural products. See Bono (2012), p. 37.

individuals), (2) it serve as the primary organ for conducting business and (3) it acts as the primary locus of specific legal duties to be performed on behalf of the minority stakeholders, among others. Therefore, as an additional organ to the general meeting, the central aims of the management organ are the assumption of specific tasks related to decision making and the implementation of decisions made by the general meeting.

This division of labour leads to advantages. In practice, many issues, especially those arising during day-to-day business, do not need the involvement of all members. There may also be a need to specialise.[744] In economic terms, this means that the problems involved in collective decision making lead to increasing costs, which can be decreased by a group of individual managers.[745] Specialisation is even more relevant for agricultural SCEs used as secondary cooperatives, because it brings together different cooperatives with each other's members (and their specific needs), which is likely to increase the problem of collective decision making.[746] In addition, delegating tasks to a management organ reduces the risk from so-called shareholder deadlock or shareholder passivity.[747]

A separate management organ can, furthermore, mediate in case there is a conflict of interests between various stakeholders. In fact, there are diverging interests not only between members—and here it is useful to remember what has been said about homogeneity and heterogeneity of the membership base[748]—but also between them and third parties. This latter conflict may result in management taking a decision that runs contrary to the will of the majority of members. Thus, the managers are not simply agents who act on behalf of the members, but they act for the company or cooperative as a whole.[749] Moreover, they can also be required to take a specific action (or abstain from a specific action) in the interest of a minority of members or

[744]See , 86; Armour et al. (2009c), p. 12 et seq.; Easterbrook and Fischel (1998), pp. 4 et seq. and 11. Also consider Fleckner (2010), p. 47 et seq.; Marchetti (2007), p. 308.

[745]See Engert (2014), p. 86; Hansmann (1996), p. 136 et seq.; Stout (2007), p. 792 et seq.; Rebelo and Caldas (2015), p. 100; Cools (2014), p. 272 et seq.; Armour and Whincop (2001), p. 991.

As collective decision making by majority is legally required for companies, a separate management organ also can provide institutional advantages.

[746]See Nilsson (2001), p. 346; Ortmann and King (2007), p. 59; Royer (1999), p. 56. Also consider Schäfer and Ott (2012), p. 700.

[747]See Engert (2014), p. 86; Armour et al. (2009c), p. 13. Also consider Ortmann and King (2007), p. 54 et seq.

[748]See Sect. 3.5.2.

[749]See Armour et al. (2009a), p. 36; Engert (2014), p. 87. Discussions about whether managers must act in the interests of third parties or minority shareholders implies issues like corporate objective functions, corporate social responsibility or corporate interests as interests to be distinguished from those of the members. See Keay (2008), p. 667 et seq. Also consider Klöhn (2008); Kräkel (2012), p. 287 et seq.; Tirole (2006), p. 56 et seq.

creditors.[750] As will be seen, the Italian legal system contains specific minority rights to better protect their interests, whereas under Austrian law, such rights are less pronounced.

Of particular relevance is the fact that the SCE-R deals with specific rights assigned to non-user members, whose interests must be subordinated to those of user members, and employee representation. It has been observed that all members benefit in the long run if the managers safeguard the interests of the minority or third parties; this represents an institutional guarantee that the interests of these groups will not be sacrificed for the sake of short-term profits. Thus, the minority group may remain in the cooperative or third parties may continue to conduct business in the long run.[751] In this context, one shall remember[752] that members of agricultural cooperatives tend to focus on the long-term existence of the cooperative, as this depends upon the existence of individual member's farms.

However, it is difficult to completely regulate in advance which decisions should be taken, including what exactly should be delegated to the management organ.[753] Even though managers are inevitably permitted a certain amount of discretion,[754] the legal framework can influence how the management organ exercises this discretion. For instance, the law can provide for a right of instruction or supervision rights granted to other persons to direct or guide the managers.[755] Here, the two-tier system establishes a supervisory organ to fulfil this task.[756] In addition, specific incentives foster decision making in the interest of the cooperative. Examples of such incentives include performance-based remuneration (positive incentive) or removal from office (negative incentive).[757]

It is clear that the organisational structure of the agricultural cooperative way is defined by how the decision-making powers are divided between the general meeting and the management organ. This division of tasks is not only a question of heterogenous membership base and complexity of business requiring external experts as

---

[750]See Engert (2014), p. 88; Armour et al. (2009b), p. 123 et seq. Examples favouring minority positions or third parties include: the obligation to maintain a shareholders' record, to keep the books, grant individual right of inspection and especially to treat members or shareholders equally. One specific protection mechanism for creditors is the obligation to not distribute specific assets to members or initiate insolvency proceedings unless necessary. Such duties may also stem from a general duty of care. See Engert (2014), p. 88; Enriques et al. (2009b), p. 94. Also consider Bolten et al. (2007), p. 895 et seq.

[751]See Engert (2014), p. 89 et seq.; Blair and Stout (2006), p. 488 et seq. Also consider Stout (2007), p. 794 et seq.; Schmidt and Weiß (2010), p. 171 et seq.

[752]See Sect. 3.5.2.

[753]E.g., which suppliers should be chosen, which business opportunities should be pursued or abundant, or the amount of risk to be taken when conducting transactions.

[754]See Engert (2014), p. 89; Enriques et al. (2009a), p. 79 et seq. Also consider Roe (2002), p. 242 et seq.; Leyens (2006), p. 16; Schäfer and Ott (2012), p. 700; Fleischer (2000), p. 24; Armour and Whincop (2001), p. 989.

[755]See Engert (2014), p. 89.

[756]See Sect. 4.2.2.1.

[757]See Kräkel (2012), p. 301.

managers, but, for the sake of transparency, including legal certainty, the management organ should be the sole representatives in respect of third parties.[758] In fact, a major reason for installing a separate management organ is to allow the cooperative to act at any time. The analysis showed that an Austrian agricultural SCE is more flexible here, as the legal system offers more options for the members of the SCE to choose from. However, this flexibility does not impede an approach that allows members of the cooperative to impose internal limits on the organ's decision-making power[759]; generally, this freedom shall be restricted inasmuch as it is in the interests of the minority or other stakeholders.[760] This restriction may, for example, concern large investments in the general interest, which can be specified either by fixing a certain amount of money (static approach) or by using a percentage (dynamic approach), such as 15% of the average total turnover from the last two fiscal years. If these thresholds are exceeded, the decision is displayed in the competence of the general meeting. Examples of large investments are the financing of intangible fixed assets (such as production facilities and machinery) and tangible or financial assets. Decisions to extend the agricultural SCE's scope also can be mentioned here.[761]

Assessing the two-tier system from an economic point of view—which necessitates evaluating the management and supervisory organs and their respective interplay—one sees that, generally, the way that national legal systems regulate aspects of agricultural cooperatives, such as the structure of their organs or their responsibilities, does not produce significant inefficiencies.[762] By analysing how the SCE-R's legal provisions deal with this governance system, one can generally observe that efficiency is enhanced by statutory freedom. Here, the Italian legal system, in particular, contains various default provisions that help to lower transaction costs[763]: for example, Art. 2409 terdecies para. 1 letter f-bis CC and Art. 2527 para. 3 CC can be referred to. Conversely, the legal framework of an Austrian SCE

[758]See Engert (2014), p. 94; Enriques et al. (2009a), p. 56 et seq. Ferrarini and Ungureanu give an overview of trends in regulation on executive remuneration. See Ferrarini and Ungureanu (2014).

[759]Tied member control.

[760]See Engert (2014), p. 94. Also consider Schäfer and Ott (2012), p. 700 et seq.; Cools (2014). Generally, Armour and Whincop (2001), p. 992.

These are specific observations concerning the interplay between the management and supervisory organs, yet as this issue of separation of competencies between these two organs also concerns the general meeting, it is discussed further in that chapter.

[761]These decisions are normally part of statutes amendments and must be decided by the general meeting anyway.

[762]See Van der Sangen (2012), p. 21. Bijman, Hendrikse and Van Oijen discuss different corporate governance models applied in practice. See Bijman et al. (2013). Also consider Chaddad and Iliopoulos (2013), p. 6 et seq.

[763]See Sect. 1.3.1.

The SCE-R also contains provisions regarding the terms of office. This is necessary because the "one member, one vote" may prevent members of the management organ from leaving, reducing effective and efficient control. In fact, the managers might use their position to obtain opinions and decisions in their favour and thus impede effective control. See Zoppini (2004), p. 449. Also consider Zoppini (2000), pp. 354 and 358.

allows more areas to be regulated by statutes.[764] In these specific cases, Austrian law is more efficient, as it allows negotiation to occur between the actors involved.

A cornerstone of the two-tier system is the fact that the management task is specifically juxtaposed with a supervisory function, that is, the management organ is monitored by the supervisory organ.[765] Thus, the competence of the organs are interlinked and, therefore, must be considered in parallel. As seen above,[766] the supervisory organ, as the representative of the SCE's members, is provided with two specific tools for monitoring the management organ: (1) the right to information and (2) the authorisation procedure (as determined by Art. 48 SCE-R).

From an economic perspective, one can generally affirm that the proper fulfilment of the monitoring task requires specific incentives. Not only does the agent (management organ) have to be incentivised, but also the supervisory organ. Incentives[767] (for instance, performance-related remuneration or removal[768]) and adequate monitoring instruments may then lead to effective monitoring.[769] It has been correctly observed that, if there is an efficient incentive plan,[770] management tasks do not have to be conducted in an improper way.[771] Thus, if the supervisory organ is involved in the decision-making process (i.e., because of Art. 48 para. 1 SCE-R defining an authorisation procedure), this involvement will result in the assistance of the management organ in evaluating the information with the aim of ensuring proper decision making.[772] Such an approach can be based on Art. 40 para. 3 SCE-R and should improve the quality of decisions. With this approach, monitoring costs are reduced and planning security for the management organ enhanced. Yet, this involvement also bears the risk that the management organ's decisions can be amended, with the consequence that remuneration may be reduced and its members removed. As a result, the members of the management organ will tend to only

---

[764] E.g., appointing the management organ via the general meeting, reduced impediments to becoming a member of the organs or removal of office.

[765] See Kräkel (2012), p. 137. Generally Tirole (1986). The general meeting delegates monitoring to the supervisory organ. This allows specific advantages like specialisation, time-saving for the principal (members of the SCE) and so on. See Kräkel (2012), p. 292. Also consider Strausz (1997).

[766] See Sect. 4.2.2.1.

[767] The effectiveness of incentives also depends on whether the members of the supervisory organ pursue homogenous or heterogeneous interests. See Kräkel (2012), p. 293.

[768] See Kräkel (2012), p. 294.

[769] See Kräkel (2012), pp. 138 and 288. Generally Tirole (1986); Strausz (1997). Also consider Marchetti (2007), p. 306 et seq.; Santoro (2014), p. 24 et seq.

[770] E.g. performance-linked remuneration. See Enriques et al. (2009a), p. 75 et seq.; Armour et al. (2009a), p. 42 et seq. Also consider Kräkel (2012), p. 24 et seq.; Fleischer (2000), p. 9; Bolten et al. (2007), p. 862 et seq. Generally, Milgrom and Roberts (2005), pp. 567 et seq. and 617 et seq.; Tirole (2006), p. 20 et seq.

[771] See Cooter and Freedman (1991), p. 1056 et seq.; Leyens (2006), p. 27 et seq.; Eisenberg (1989), p. 1472 et seq.; Kräkel (2012), p. 307. Generally Tirole (1986) and Strausz (1997).

[772] See Leyens (2006), p. 37. Also consider Theisen (1996), p. 21 et seq.; Leyens (2007b), p. 24; Potthoff et al. (2003), p. 17.

disclose information related to completed decisions.[773] In order to solve this dilemma, the supervisory organ of an agricultural SCE should delegate this task to a member of the supervisory organ (or to a specific committee) not directly involved in decisions regarding remuneration and supervision.[774]

In an ideal scenario, the management has more incentive to share information rather than withhold it. Yet, in order to foster cooperation with the supervisory organ from the outset, joint responsibility should be defined for certain tasks.[775] Due to agency costs (monitoring costs),[776] this approach should be used sparingly.[777] Thus, only specific co-decision rights of the supervisory organ should be defined and linked to acts of high economic importance.[778] Such a solution is required by Art. 48 para. 1 SCE-R, which implies that the supervisory organ must monitor future decisions. Both the Austrian and the Italian legal system contain provisions that can put Art. 48 para. 1 SCE-R into practice. Consequently, it is necessary for the supervisory organ to advise the management organ if important business decisions need to be taken. As operations requiring authorisation[779] can lead to shared responsibility, this mechanism should enhance the necessary information flow. In this regard, it is helpful to define both when reports must be given and their content.[780] Art. 40 para. 3 SCE-R provides the necessary legal rule here.

An important aspect of the interplay between the management organ and the supervisory organ concerns business planning. In this regard, cooperation between the two organs from an early stage can be achieved via authorisation, which, however, can run contrary to the agricultural SCE's interests by keeping specific decisions secret. To remedy this problem of secrecy, the supervisory organ can, for example, delegate the preparation of the supervisory report and supervisory tasks during the year to a specific committee within the supervisory organ. This can lead to better information sharing between the supervisory and management organs. In addition, trust can be increased by requiring that only limited material be made available in writing to the members of this committee.[781] As seen, both legal systems allow the establishment of specific committees, such as committees for preparing the negotiations and decisions to be taken by the supervisory organ, others for monitoring the implementation of its decisions, and still others for overseeing remuneration.

---

[773] See Leyens (2006), pp. 36 et seq. and 426.

[774] See Leyens (2006), pp. 45 et seq. and 426. Also consider Bainbridge (2001), p. 42 et seq.; Klein et al. (2010), p. 135.

[775] Consider in this context Art. 48 para. 2 SCR and Art. 51 SCE-R.

[776] See Sect. 1.3.3.

[777] See Leyens (2006), p. 21. Also consider Ruffner (2000), p. 132; Tombari (2008), p. 410 et seq.

[778] See Leyens (2006), pp. 36 et seq. and 426. Also consider Potthoff et al. (2003), p. 17.

[779] See Art. 48 para. 1 bullet 1 SCE-R.

[780] See Leyens (2006), pp. 37 et seq. and 427. Also consider Adams and Ferreira (2007).

[781] See Leyens (2006), p. 427. Also consider Marchetti (2007), p. 316 et seq.

These solutions increase information processing in the supervisory organ; they also help to optimise the use of individual members' capabilities.[782]

In addition to this shared information, the supervisory organ needs to consider information independent from the management organ. Such an approach can be based on Art. 40 para. 4 SCE-R and helps to improve the supervision of the management organ by better detecting management errors and conflicts. From an economic perspective, it is necessary to obtain information independent from the management organ. It is assumed that the information provided by the management organ is incomplete, because the management only provides limited information and subjective reports in which errors are likely; thus, the supervisory organ can only partially assess whether the provided information is complete and correct.[783] Information gathered independently of the management helps to verify the information delivered by the management, giving the management organ an incentive to freely provide correct information. Possible information conflicts can be reduced via regular and independent information sharing. Due to monitoring costs, however, this only makes sense in certain circumstances. Ultimately, it is the task of the supervisory organ to assess the optimal amount of information sharing. It is important that this independently gathered information is not of an extraordinary nature and that this process of information procurement is fully transparent. This will increase trust between the two bodies and therefore reduce monitoring costs.[784]

A particular feature of delegating management is that, generally, the management organ has a large margin of discretion when taking its decisions. In order to counterbalance this competence, the law grants shareholders or members specific monitoring and controlling rights to ensure the management organ's interests are in line with theirs. These rights include a right of instruction and, particularly, the right to appoint and remove the members of the management organ.[785] Having the management organ be appointed by the supervisory organ, as determined by Art. 39 para. 2 SCE-R, helps involve external expertise[786] and precludes shareholder (member) conflicts from impairing the selection process. It also allows non-member interests to be represented. Moreover, the statutes can determine the specific details of these appointment rights, for instance, that only members of the agricultural SCE may become managers to keep their interests in line with the members.[787]

---

[782]See Leyens (2006), p. 44. Also consider Leyens (2007b), p. 25; Klein et al. (2010), p. 134 et seq. Also consider Scarpa (2014), p. 165 et seq.

[783]See Leyens (2006), p. 40 et seq.; Roth and Wörle (2004), p. 616; Leyens (2007b), p. 24 et seq. Similarly, Scarpa (2014), p. 164. Also consider Bamberg et al. (2013), p. 166 et seq.

[784]See Leyens (2006), p. 43 et seq.; Nowak and McCabe (2003), p. 301 et seq. Also consider Theisen (1987), p. 280; Fleischer (2001), p. 170 et seq.; Leyens (2007b), p. 26 et seq.

[785]See Enriques et al. (2009a), pp. 58 et seq. and 72 et seq.; Armour et al. (2009a), p. 42; Engert (2014), p. 106. In order to keep this election procedure simple, the default rule is for simple majority to apply. In order to save time and costs, members of the management organ remain in office until they are replaced. See Engert (2014), p. 106. This is also true for the supervisory organ, which is appointed and removed by the general meeting.

[786]E.g., with the help of external advisors.

[787]Consider in this context Liang and Hendrikse (2013), p. 23.

The analysis showed that—in line with the PECOL—the majority of members of the management organ in an Italian SCE must be user members. Even though this approach restricts flexibility and statutory freedom, it can be argued that this feature of cooperative identity helps to properly define the menu of corporate forms, which ultimately fosters competition.[788] However, one should acknowledge that, in order to improve efficiency, it is necessary to involve professionals in decision making.[789] Thus, with increasing organisational complexity and the need for more efficient decision making, the cooperative is moving from traditional to so-called extended traditional, then to managerial and lastly to corporate governance models. As will be discussed further in one of the following chapters,[790] at the same time, the cooperative's members are losing more and more formal and probably real control over the agricultural SCE.

An important area of conflict relates to the costs of monitoring and collective decision making. As cooperatives increasingly adopt non-traditional governance, the cost of collective decision making is said to be decreasing. However, this result can occur at the expense of higher costs for management monitoring. If agency costs in agricultural cooperatives are relatively low, this hypothetical lost of control by members should not threaten agricultural cooperatives seriously. On the one hand, the argument is put forward that farmers are in a relatively good position to effectively monitor the management effectively, as the income received from the cooperative is their main source of income.[791] Yet, others argue that farmer-members are in a weak position to effectively monitor management, because they lack the expertise, are not supported by a secondary market mechanism and face a serious free-rider problem when monitoring the management. The result could then be that the cooperative is ultimately unable to meet the long-term needs of its members.[792] Whatever solution is adopted should allow the members of the cooperative to have the final competence to recover the competence, e.g., by amending the statutes.[793] The analysis showed that only Austrian SCEs can shift the appointment and removal competence from the supervisory organ to the general meeting, thus strengthening its position.

In addition to appointment, removal and monitoring, other incentives like remuneration can ensure the interests of the members of the management organ support the goals of the agricultural SCE.[794] Statutes or employment contracts could regulate

---

[788]See Sect. 1.3.1.

[789]See Iliopoulos (2015), p. 10. Also consider Conte and Vannini (2008), p. 149; Hanisch (2006), p. 317.

In this context, different governance approaches are discussed. See Chaddad and Iliopoulos (2013) and Bijman et al. (2013, 2014). Also consider Tombari (2008), p. 405 et seq.

[790]See Sect. 4.4.6.

[791]See Hansmann (1996), p. 134.

[792]See Iliopoulos (2014), p. 165. In general, Iliopoulos and Cook (2013).

[793]See Engert (2014), p. 106 et seq. Also consider Ventoruzzo (2011); Cools (2011), p. 199.

[794]See Engert (2014), p. 109; Armour et al. (2009a), p. 42 et seq. Also consider Williamson (1998), p. 137 et seq.; Holmstrom and Milgrom (1994).

how management performance is rewarded. In practice, there are many ways to define business success. Therefore it is not advisable for a legislature to set a default rule in this regard.[795] Both legal systems provide for an open approach. Admittedly, determining the actual success of the cooperative will often be difficult, because of its complex goal orientation.[796] It will, however, be expedient if the general meeting has a say in determining the remuneration, which allows it to award special bonuses for exceptional services.

In addition to incentives, the law typically contains specific conduct duties and indirect incentives to control the behaviour of the members of the two organs and to ensure that the cooperative runs its business in the interest of its members. In addition, the law also considers the interests of all other stakeholders.[797] The specific conduct duties can either be derived from the general duty of care or be imposed by statutes; the behaviour of members of the organ can be influenced via the duty of loyalty.[798] If the liabilities, which stem from this set of rules and obligations, are infringed upon, the acting person can be held liable. The central question is whether the organ's members, as agents, believed that what they were doing was in the best interest of the principal, i.e., the interests of the agricultural SCE. In this regard, Art. 51 SCE-R refers to inside liability towards the SCE and, thus, protects the owners/members against the misbehaviour of their agents. These liabilities can be conceived as a strategy for constraining the agents' behaviour, and they aim to maintain good behaviour ex ante.[799]

The general duty of care imposed on members of the management organ benefits cooperative members as a whole, because they are the first to be affected by profits and losses. Normally, entrepreneurial activity entails great uncertainty. For example, when deciding to enter a new market, there is no way to know whether this will ultimately be worthwhile for the agricultural cooperative (or SCE). Therefore, it does not make sense to subject business decisions to unlimited legal scrutiny. In fact, when the decision is taken, it is impossible to foresee ex ante whether this decision will be considered a breach of duty. As a result, even if the organ behaves carefully, they always possess a considerable risk of liability. Furthermore, unlimited legal scrutiny could prevent the management organ from considering worthwhile ventures

[795]See Engert (2014), p. 109. For specific details, see Hueth and Marcoul (2009).

[796]In general, Iliopoulos and Valentinov (2018).

[797]Like third parties.

[798]See Engert (2014), p. 96; Enriques et al. (2009a), p. 79; Fleischer (2000), p. 24 et seq.; Di Gaspare (2012), p. 7 et seq. Also consider Fleckner (2010), p. 79 et seq.; Schäfer and Ott (2012), p. 702 et seq.; Fleischer (2000), p. 7 et seq. Gelter and Helleringer specifically address the issue of fiduciary duties. See Gelter and Helleringer (2015). Also consider Sitkoff (2011). See also Mathis (2019), p. 96 et seq.

The duty of loyalty helps avoid conflicts of interest, as in practice there are too many different forms of conflicts which cannot be properly regulated via the statutes. It tries to prevent decisions which run counter to the interests of the cooperative. It is suggested to determine general provisions on conflicts of interests via the statutes. See Engert (2014), p. 109. For details, Hopt (2013).

[799]See Enriques et al. (2009a), p. 79 et seq.

and innovations. In addition, the members of the organs would try to reduce their personal liability risk at the expense of the agricultural SCE, and capable persons would be less willing to accept membership in the organs. Moreover, such an overstretched duty of care cannot be offset by benefits for the cooperative's members. In fact, because of their rights to directly or indirectly appoint and remove members of the management organ by means of the supervisory organ, the cooperative's members can themselves punish poor entrepreneurial behaviour. With the right to instruct the organ, they can monitor business development and the organ's decisions. In addition, specific incentives like performance-related remuneration can foster better entrepreneurial behaviour. Due to these various aspects, the members of the organ should have a wide range of discretion under the so-called business judgement rule,[800] as it favours entrepreneurial decision making.

Similar observations can be made about the supervisory organ: compared to executive tasks, non-executive tasks are not so easy to judge in court. It is already difficult to question business decisions on the basis of ex ante information; a reassessment of which supervisory measures would have prevented or mitigated negative outcomes is even more prone to retrospective bias, including misinterpretations of facts and legal errors.

The analysis showed that both legal systems are moving towards such a solution.[801] The duties laid down by the two legal systems are basically similar, but there are interesting differences that emerge from a comparison of the used concepts of due diligence. While under Austrian law, slight fault is sufficient to trigger liability, the Italian legal system requires gross negligence.[802] As a result, under Austrian law, the members of a cooperative's governing organs who are less qualified than the members of the governing bodies of an incorporated company must act very carefully in accordance with their lack of qualifications, whereas under Italian law, the organ member is a professional manager who must have the appropriate qualifications and is, therefore, more capable and empowered to take risks.

Farmers who are members of an agricultural SCE are not often actually trained as professional managers or members of a supervisory organ, but may nevertheless become members of an SCE's organ. On the one hand, Austrian farmers must act with due caution, because they are considered to be less qualified. Italian farmers, on the other hand, will have to acquire the appropriate qualifications; otherwise, they will not be able to properly perform their duties. Though both legal systems thus exert pressure on the acting persons to avoid liability, the Italian system promotes

---

[800]See Engert (2014), p. 97 et seq.; Fleischer (2011), pp. 521, 522 et seq.; Myers (1977), p. 157; Fleischer (2002b), p. 829 et seq.; Easterbrook and Fischel (1998), p. 93 et seq. Also consider Hommelhoff (1988), p. 168 et seq.; Denozza (2002), p. 92 et seq.; Leyens (2007a), p. 1064; Velasco (2015). Regarding fiduciary duties, see Schäfer and Ott (2012), p. 704.

[801]For details, see Lutter (2007), Schima (2015), p. 288; Kalss (2015); Told (2015); Tallia (2013); Coropatri (2010); Piscitello (2012); Di Gaspare (2012), p. 7 et seq.; Marchetti (2007), p. 317; Miribung (2017).

[802]For a specific analysis, see Cooter et al. (1999), p. 391 et seq. Gallo briefly discusses aspects of fault. See Gallo (1998b), p. 75 et seq. Also consider Grechenig et al. (2005).

professionalisation more strongly. This should lead to efficiency gains. Yet it is also true that the organ can be professionalised with the appointment of external experts.[803]

Concerning the assertion of liability, the analysis showed that the Italian legal system defines specific minority rights, which enhances pressure on the management organ. This may, however, lead to a hold-up problem, because a small group of shareholders might be tempted to frivolously use this instrument and prompt the threat of unjustified suits, thus increasing the risk-aversion of managers.

Overall, the flexibility that the two legal systems offer make it possible to account for different aspects and needs in the specific design of the interaction between the management organ and the supervisory organ. Efficiency can ultimately be increased and optimised if the various instruments and strategies are effectively combined. Excessive reliance on only one method is unlikely to pay off. Thus, in both jurisdictions, the drafters of the statutes of an agricultural SCE must consider constraints (liability), rewards (remuneration), and decision making (approval by the general meeting and independent supervision). These observations also apply to the one-tier system, which will be analysed in the next chapter.

4.3 The One-Tier System

The SCE-R allows a one-tier structure for SCEs without restricting them to a specific type of cooperative or branch of business.[804] The drafters of the statutes can decide which system they want to adopt. In this context, the regulation contains specific provisions (Arts. 42–44 SCE-R) concerning the functions, the appointment of members and the internal organisation of the administrative organ. Even though structural differences exist in the provisions for the one-tier structure versus provisions for the two-tier system, the rules share a number of functional similarities.[805] Thus, where appropriate, the following analysis will refer to the analysis of the two-tier system and its results. As a result, a similar structure is used, addressing the following key aspects: the functions and composition of the organ, the appointment and removal of the members of the administrative organ, the internal organisation of the administrative organ and, finally, civil liability.

It is important to note at the outset that the PECOL do not contain specific provisions covering the one-tier system; they only state that governance shall be divided between a structure or organ and one or more boards or committees, which are responsible for the current management and are accountable to the members. Clearly, all these conditions are met. In this context, the PECOL state that 'a classic

[803] See Kräkel (2012), p. 294. Also consider Marchetti (2007), p. 308 et seq.; Schäfer and Ott (2012), p. 702 et seq.

[804] See Schulze (2004a), p. 102.

[805] See Schulze (2004a), p. 102.

dichotomy is provided by the SCE-R which furnishes a choice between a unitary board (administrative organ) and a two-tier board consisting of the supervisory board and the management board'.[806]

4.3.1 Functions

Three specific issues pertaining to functions are analysed. The first two—responsibility for management and representation—follow the structure adopted when analysing the management organ, while the third—operations requiring authorisation—follows the structure adopted when analysing the supervisory organ. As will be seen, there are two types of authorisation procedures. One concerns internal authorisation and could, therefore, also be analysed in the chapter 'Internal organisation of the administrative organ'. However, for clearer comparison, an approach similar to that which analyses the supervisory organ has been chosen.

In an SCE structured according to the one-tier system, the administrative organ fulfils the same functions as the **management** organ in the two-tier system: it manages the SCE and represents it in dealings with third parties and in legal proceedings.[807] As has already been seen,[808] the ultimate extension of this competence depends on the competence of the general meeting. Furthermore, the exercise of these competence may be influenced by statutes or law because of Art. 48 SCE-R, which deals with operations requiring authorisation.[809] In addition, it is argued that the content of the management has to be determined by EU law.[810] National provisions can help us understand what management might entail.

The SCE-R only provides rules regarding the management and representation of the SCE, and does not define a specific supervisory function.[811] According to Art. 42 para. 4 SCE-R, the member states can adopt specific rules in this context, with the condition that the relevant legal system does not contain a provision for a one-tier

[806] See Sec. 2.4 para. 2 PECOL; Snaith (2017), p. 60 et seq.

[807] See Art. 42 para. 1 SCE-R. It states: "The administrative organ shall manage the SCE and shall represent it in dealings with third parties and in legal proceedings. A Member State may provide that a managing director shall be responsible for the current management under the same conditions as for cooperatives that have registered offices within that Member State's territory."

For details, see Schöpflin (2018i), p. 1307 et seq.; Schulze (2004a), p. 103. For the SE, see Eder (2004), p. 544 et seq.; Teichmann (2004), p. 120 et seq.; Kalss and Greda (2004), p. 103 et seq.; Manz (2010f), p. 543; Nagel (2004), p. 834; Reichert and Brandes (2003), p. 788 et seq.; Brandt (2003), p. 1212; Hirte (2005), p. 701; Teichmann (2004), p. 120 et seq.

[808] See Sect. 4.2.1.1. Also consider Teichmann (2015b), p. 542.

[809] See Sect. 4.2.2.1.

[810] For information about management in general, see Sect. 4.2.1.1. Also consider Teichmann (2015b), p. 542 et seq.

[811] For the SE, see Bianca and Zanardo (2016), p. 197.

system. Thus, national law could provide for an internal audit committee, for example.[812]

Under the one-tier system, the current management—and only the current management[813]—may be delegated to one or more managing directors.[814] The SCE-R does not explicitly determine that these managing directors have to be members of the administrative organ.[815] It would be possible either to assign different functions or areas of responsibility to different members or to structure the relationship between the chairman and the other members accordingly.[816] The rules contained in Art. 47 paras. 1[817] and 4 SCE-R could be helpful here.[818] If a managing director is appointed, the administrative organ can adopt a supervisory function with respect to the managing director's performance; their relationship is similar to the one between the managing and supervisory organs in the two-tier system.[819] Last, in order to fulfil their function, Art. 43 para. 2 SCE-R empowers the members of the administrative organ to examine all reports, documents and information submitted to it.[820]

These are the provisions regarding the management function of an SCE. However, they have to be read in conjunction with the relevant national provisions.

The *Italian legal system* lodges its national provisions in the civil code.[821] These rules determine specific aspects of the one-tier system while utilizing the norms of the traditional corporate governance system; such rules are similar to the rules adopted for the two-tier system. Art. 2544 CC determines that a cooperative may also adopt the one-tier system. This was introduced with the 2003 corporate law reform. As a result, the Italian legal system already contained provisions for a one-tier system, as requested by Art. 42 para. 4 SCE-R.

---

[812]See Schöpflin (2018i), p. 1307 et seq.; Schulze (2004a), p. 103. For the SE, see Manz (2010f), p. 553; Arnò et al. (2007), p. 79. Different opinion, Presti (2006), p. 84.

[813]For details, see Teichmann (2015b), p. 543 et seq.

[814]Art. 42 para. 1 sent. 2 SCE-R. For observations on the wording "under the same conditions as", see Teichmann (2015b), p. 548 et seq.

[815]See Schöpflin (2018i), p. 1307 et seq. For the SE, see Manz (2010f), p. 546; Teichmann (2015b), p. 543 et seq.

[816]See Schulze (2004a), p. 103. Also consider Teichmann (2015b), p. 543 et seq.

[817]It states: "Where the authority to represent the SCE in dealings with third parties, in accordance with Articles 37(1) and 42(1), is conferred on two or more members, those members shall exercise that authority collectively, unless the law of the Member State in which the SCE's registered office is situated allows the statutes to provide otherwise, in which case such a clause may be relied upon against third parties where it has been disclosed in accordance with Articles 11(5) and 12."

[818]See Sect. 4.2.1.2.

[819]See Schulze (2004a), p. 103. Also consider Münkner (2006), p. 19. For the SE, see Manz (2010f), p. 547; Teichmann (2015b), p. 543 et seq. Also consider Leyens (2007a), p. 1065.

[820]Granting thus an internal right to information as opposed to the right to information granted to the members of the supervisory organ. See Sect. 4.2.1.1. Also consider Schulze (2004a), p. 104; Schöpflin (2018k). For the SE, see Manz (2010g), p. 599; Teichmann (2015c), p. 719.

[821]The Italian civil code contains four provisions specifically dealing with the one-tier system: Art. 2409 sexiesdecies CC, Art. 2409 septiesdecies CC, Art. 2409 octiesdecies CC and Art. 2409 noviesdecies CC.

Under Italian law,[822] the one-tier system only provides for a single organ that exercises both the management and supervisory functions. Within it, a committee must be formed to fulfil the supervisory function. The management function's tasks are similar to those in the traditional system.[823] More precisely, the references to almost all provisions[824] regulating the administrative organ under the traditional system make the rules for the management powers more or less identical. One exception is the role of the independent administrator.[825]

For competence, Art. 2409 sexiesdecies CC generally determines that the statutes may provide for management and supervision to be exercised respectively by the administrative organ and a committee formed within it. In addition, Art. 2409 septiesdecies CC specifies that management of the company is the exclusive purview of the administrative organ. Management under the one-tier system includes the duty to establish an organisational, administrative and accounting structure that must be appropriate to the nature and size of the business.[826] In addition to this general function, the CC determines a wide range of functions the administrative organ must fulfil.[827]

As explained, the SCE-R sketches a one-tier system in which the administrative organ manages and represents the SCE, but the SCE-R omits discussion of the control or supervisory function. However, the Italian legal system also requires this function. Italian SCEs must abide by this, as the SCE-R leaves the ultimate structure of the one-tier system up to the national legislature. In fact, Art. 42 para. 4 SCE-R only requests that a provision be made for a one-tier system. It does not define a particular system.[828]

---

[822]Bonfante observes that the one-tier system, as conceptualised by the Italian CC, is very flexible and similar to the traditional Italian corporate governance structure. See Bonfante (2014a), p. 334. For general observations, see Cottino, Il nuovo diritto societario nella dottrina e nella giurisprudenza (2009), p. 741. This structure is also called the Latin corporate governance system. See Riolfo (2010), p. 26 et seq. See also Mirone (2017a), p. 575 et seq.; Abriani (2019).

[823]See Paolucci (2012), p. 143 et seq.

[824]See Art. 2409 noviesdecies CC. Applicable are thus Art. 2380 bis CC (management of the company), Art. 2381 CC (chairman, executive committee and managing directors), Art. 2382 CC (reasons for ineligibility and forfeiture), Art. 2383 CC (appointment and dismissal of directors), Art. 2384 CC (powers of representation), Art. 2385 CC (cessation of office of directors), Art. 2386 CC (replacement of directors), Art. 2387 CC (requirements of honour, professionalism and independence), Art. 2388 CC (validity of the board resolutions), Art. 2389 CC (payment of directors), Art. 2391 CC (prohibition on competition), Art. 2392 CC (liability to the company), Art. 2393 CC (corporate action for liability), Art. 2393 bis CC (company action for liability by shareholders), Art. 2394 CC (liability to company by creditors), Art. 2394 bis CC (liability actions with settlement proceedings) and Art. 2395 CC (individual action by a shareholder and third party).

[825]See Riolfo (2010), p. 27 et seq. Also consider Ghezzi (2005), p. 222.

[826]Also in relation to the timely detection of the business crisis and the loss of business continuity. See Art. 2086 para. 2 CC.

[827]Consider, for example, Art. 2366 CC, Art. 2377 CC, Art. 2447 ter para. 2 CC, Art. 2423 CC or 2428 CC.

[828]Similar Schöpflin (2018j), p. 1308. For the SE, see Teichmann (2015a), p. 471. Different opinion Presti (2006), p. 84.

The main functions of the internal control committee can be summarised in the CC as follows. Art. 2409 octiesdecies para. 5 letters b and c and para. 6 CC determine the function of the management control committee. According to letter b, the committee monitors the company's organisational structures, the internal auditing system, the administration and accounting systems as well as the representation of the management's activities.[829] It must report to the administrative organ and the general meeting.[830] Next, according to Art. 2409 CC (in particular, para. 7),[831] the management control committee may file a petition to the court and report that certain administrators have committed serious irregularities when managing the company.[832] According to Art. 2405 para. 1 CC, the committee must attend the meetings of the administrative organ and the general meeting.[833] Last, the administrative organ may assign further competence to the committee,[834] which also concerns the relationship with the person entrusted with the statutory accounting audit.[835]

The civil code does not contain any provisions about the powers of information and the powers of inspection assigned to the management control committee. In fact, there is no explicit reference to Art. 2403 bis CC or Art. 2409 septies CC.[836] As the members of the management control committee are also administrators, and because the control committee is formed within the administrative organ, it could be argued that the members of the committee should receive information directly from the managing administrators. In fact, any information that management has acquired must be shared with the members of the control committee, because these committee members are also administrators. As a result, all members are informed to the same extent.[837] This solution is in line with Art. 43 para. 2 SCE-R.

In addition, it can be argued that, when exchanging information with the person entrusted to perform the statutory accounting audit,[838] the committee has an obligation to give all the information required to the auditor, and the committee can demand all the information necessary to carry out its functions.[839]

---

[829]For a definition of organisational structure consider Riolfo (2010), p. 130 et seq.

[830]Consider in this latter case Art. 223 septies prov. impl. CC, Art. 2408 CC, Art. 2391 bis para. 2 CC and Art. 2446 para. 1 CC.

[831]Provisions regarding the complaint to the board of statutory auditors.

[832]This report can be filed on the condition that there is a well-founded suspicion and that the irregularities may be detrimental either to the company or to one or more of its subsidiaries.

[833]See Riolfo (2010), p. 130 et seq.

[834]Due to Art. 2409 octiesdecies para. 5 letter c CC.

[835]Art. 2409 bis CC.

[836]See Mirone (2017a), p. 579.

[837]See Riolfo (2010), p. 143; Ghezzi and Rigotti (2005), p. 311. See also Mirone (2017a), pp. 576 and 520.

[838]Art. 2409 septies CC.

[839]See Riolfo (2010), p. 143; Ghezzi and Rigotti (2005), p. 311. See also Mirone (2017a), p. 579.

The management control committee (and individual members) can exercise powers of inspection without a specific legal provision. In fact, every member of the committee has the obligation to monitor the management. This obligation requires taking action based on proper information. While decisions must be taken by the committee as a whole, the powers of inspection may be exercised by individual members.[840] In any case, it seems advisable to adopt clear and specific statutory provisions.[841] This solution is in line with Art. 43 para. 2 SCE-R, which entitles each member to examine all reports, documents and information submitted to the administrative organ. This, however, implies that the members of the management control committee must forward all the information they possess to the managing members.

According to Italian law, and by the permission of the statutes or the general meeting, the administrative organ can delegate its functions either to an executive committee that is comprised of some of its members or to one or more of its members (thus, not constituting an executive committee).[842] As a result, day-to-day business is delegated to a limited number of individuals, whereas the entire administrative organ fulfils the function of the strategic supervision of the management.[843] The administrative organ must evaluate the adequacy of the cooperative's organisational, management and accounting structures. In addition, it reviews drafts of the company's strategic, industrial and financial plans. Finally, the organ must evaluate the general trends of management, based on reports by any delegated bodies.[844] This solution is contained in the Italian CC; however, it does not seem applicable to Italian SCEs. As already observed,[845] a legislative act is needed to apply the option in Art. 42 para. 1 SCE-R, whereas communication no. 9203 is non-binding.

In contrast to the Italian legal system, the *Austrian legal system* had to be explicitly amended to make the one-tier system applicable. The SCEG contains specific provisions dealing with competence of the administrative organ, which have to be combined with those contained in the SCE-R.

According to Sec. 24 para. 1 SCEG,[846] an SCE generally has to observe the provisions regarding the management and supervisory organs (as organs of the

---

[840]See Riolfo (2010), p. 143 et seq.; Ghezzi and Rigotti (2005), p. 313; Fortunato (2003), p. 889. See also Mirone (2017a), p. 579.

[841]See Riolfo (2010), p. 144.

[842]See Art. 2381 para. 2 CC. The suitability of these solutions depends on the size of the cooperative. The administration can thus adopt different internal structures. See Riolfo (2010), p. 75. Also consider Galgano (2003), p. 264.

[843]See Riolfo (2010), p. 76; Galgano (2003), p. 264.

[844]See Art. 2381 para. 3 CC. Art. 2381 para. 4 CC determines specific functions, by references to other articles, which cannot be delegated.

The strategic management tasks must be distinguished from the monitoring tasks the management control committee must fulfil. See Art. 2409 octiesdecies para. 5 letter b CC. See Riolfo (2010), p. 77 et seq. Also consider Ambrosini (2003b), pp. 308, 312 et seq.; Mirone (2017a), p. 578.

[845]See Sect. 4.2.1.1.

[846]The Law adapting and implementing the one-tier system into the Austrian legal system.

two-tier system).[847] According to para. 2, the rights and obligations of the management and supervisory organs are conferred to the administrative organ, provided they are not conferred to a managing director. Briefly, this implies a general responsibility to conclude all necessary transactions, and also further functions and responsibilities determined by law, such as preparing accounts or performing other specific information functions.[848] As the law requires the fulfilment of supervisory tasks,[849] it is necessary to split the two different functions within the administrative organ to properly supervise the management. This separation necessarily affects the number of members of this organ.[850] However, the division of tasks could alternatively be achieved by delegating the management functions to a/an (external) managing director.

Sec. 24 paras. 1 and 2 SCEG help determine the position of the administrative organ. It must determine the basic principles of the cooperative and may appoint qualified managing directors. As mentioned above, the current management can be delegated to directors, while the administrative organ supervises them. This model is called the structured one-tier system[851] and will be further illustrated below.

The right to information, as outlined by Art. 43 para. 2 SCE-R, is strengthened by the SCEG. It expands this competence by explicitly assigning certain duties and rights of the supervisory organ to the administrative organ.[852] This implies, according to the *GenG*, specific rights of information and in particular those contained in Sec. 24e *GenG*.[853] Under Art. 43 para. 2 SCE-R, information must be accessible to all members of the administrative organ, not just those fulfilling a supervisory function.[854]

---

[847]Also consider Sec. 39 SEG, which contains details regarding the duties and rights of the administrative organ of an Austrian SE. For details Kalss (2008), nt 3/1097 et seq.; Kalss and Greda (2004), p. 100 et seq.; Kalss (2014), nt 30; Rauter (2010), p. 500. Critical Egermann and Heckenthaler (2004), p. 258 et seq. For information about whether the general meeting can adopt directives relating to the administrative organ, see fn 94.

[848]See Sect. 4.2.1.1.

[849]E.g., auditing of financial statements, supervision of management. See Sect. 4.2.2.1.

[850]See Sect. 4.3.2.

[851]See ErläutRV 1421 BlgNR 22. GP 21.

[852]See Sec. 24 para. 1 and 2 SCEG.

[853]Consider Sect. 4.2.2.1.

[854]The administrative organ determines the direction of activities and supervises their implementation. See Schöpflin (2018i), p. 1307 et seq.

According to Sec. 18 SCEAG (German law), the administrative organ manages the SCE, defines its activities and monitors their implementation. In addition, the administrative organ is responsible for convening the general meeting if it is in the interest of the SCE. It is also responsible for keeping the necessary books and monitoring the liquidity of the cooperative. The law explicitly refers to the monitoring competence of the administrative organ and determines that the administrative organ may, in a collegial way, examine the SCE's books, documents, etc. These monitoring duties can be fulfilled by a single member of the organ, appointed accordingly. Para 3 contains specific provisions to be observed in the case of losses.

Also consider Sec. 58 SEG, which contains details on information to be delivered by the managing directors to the administrative organ. This could be used as an example for statutory provisions dealing with this issue. See Kalss (2008), nt 3/1103 and nt 3/1105; Kalss (2014), nt 36.

As enabled by the SCE-R, according to Sec. 25 SCEG, the current management can be delegated to managing directors, thus distinguishing between management and supervisory tasks and creating a structure similar to the two-tier system. However, a crucial difference remains. The competence of the managing directors can only be derived from the administrative organ; in other words, they are awarded by a legal transaction.[855] As a result, a managing director would never have more competence then a member of the administrative organ.[856] Moreover, according to Sec. 24 para. 2 SCEG, the administrative organ, when supervising the managing directors, has all the competence of the supervisory organ.[857]

The administrative organ is responsible for determining its structure and, thus, the structure of the one-tier system that the concerned SCE applies. In fact, it is their responsibility to delegate certain tasks to managing directors.[858] In any case, binding provisions can be determined by statutes.[859] As a result, the ultimate responsibility for designing the governance structure lies with the members of the SCE. In other words, the one-tier system can be defined by the statutes within the given limits (as determined by legal provisions) in order to best match the scope of the SCE.[860]

The legal basis for appointing one or more managing directors is Art. 42 para. 1 sent. 2 SCE-R. Accordingly, a member state may provide that a managing director is responsible for the current management under the same conditions as for cooperatives with registered offices within that member state's territory. As already seen, the Austrian legislature decided to introduce a specific provision in the SCEG, which explicitly allows the appointment of managing directors. According to Sec. 25 para. 1 SCEG, the members of the administrative organ can be appointed as managing directors, on the condition that the majority of members are non-managing directors; the law explicitly denies this opportunity to the chairman.[861]

Sec. 26 GenG, too, deals with the managing directors' role, but this provision neither contains restrictions on specific groups of people, nor does it refer to provisions other than those of civil law. Accordingly, the conditions that determine the

[855] Their competences stem exclusively from administrative organ's delegation and hence are based on a contract governed by the relevant national laws.

[856] See Lehner (2007), p. 114. On this issue, see Kalss and Schauer (2006), p. 138 et seq.

[857] See Sect. 4.2.2.1. Also consider Sec. 58 SEG.

[858] See Sec. 25 para. 1 SCEG.

[859] See Sec. 25 para. 2 SCEG.

[860] See Lehner (2007), p. 115. Also consider Sec. 56 SEG, stating that tasks specifically assigned by law to the administrative organ cannot be delegated to a managing director.

[861] The German SCEAG determines that members of the administrative organ may be appointed as managing directors provided the majority of the administrative organ is made up of non-managing members (Sec. 22 para. 1 SCEAG). The managing directors are appointed by the administrative organ, unless statutes do not provide otherwise (Sec. 22 para. 1 SCEAG). In principle, management can only be exercised on a collective basis (Sec. 22 para. 2 SCEAG). Every managing director is independent from both the general meeting and the administrative organ. Moreover, the provisions concerning managing directors also apply to their representatives (Sec. 22 para. 7 SCEAG). Next, German law expounds details regarding representation (passive and mixed, See Sec. 23 SCEAG). Also consider Schöpflin (2018i), p. 1307 et seq.

relationship to the managing director must be determined according to civil law, in other words, according to the rules of authorisation (mandate).

In addition to the management function, which—and this is the particular feature of the one-tier system—allows to integrate a supervisory function within the administrative organ, this organ, equal to the management organ under the two-tier system, **represents the SCE** in legal proceedings and dealings with third parties.[862] In other words, it creates rights and obligations for the SCE. In this context, Art. 47 SCE-R contains further details that must be observed. They have been analysed when dealing with the management organ.[863] Basically, it defines collective representation as the general rule, with scope for deviation if provided by national law. Representation may also be granted to external persons. It defines the limits within which an SCE can be obligated to third parties. We must understand how these provisions have to be combined with national law, because certain national provisions may add some particular features to the one-tier system, as defined by the SCE-R.

The particular structure of the one-tier system, as sketched by the CC, requires detailed analysis of the *Italian legal norms* that address representation in order to determine how they must be combined with the relevant provisions of the SCE-R. According to it, representation is assigned to the administrative organ. In this regard, Art. 2409 noviesdecies CC refers to Art. 2384 CC, which determines the powers of representation in the traditional corporate governance system. Accordingly, this competence is general in nature and is, in principle, assigned to all administrators.[864] The question arises as to whether this implies that members of the managing control committee may represent a cooperative or an Italian SCE, especially as Art. 2409 noviesdecies CC makes Art. 2384 CC applicable insofar as it is compatible. Even though it has been affirmed that these members are also administrators, there are some arguments that seem to deny the power of representation. In fact, the traditional corporate governance system assigns the power of representation to the managers of the cooperative, whereas a board of statutory auditors monitors the administrative organ and thus cannot represent the cooperative. As mentioned above, the solution given for the one-tier system is quite close to the traditional corporate governance system. In addition, Art. 2409 octiesdecies CC clearly defines the competence of the managing control committee without referring to any kind of representation (Art. 2409 octiesdecies para. 6 CC connects this committee to the board of statutory auditors). Hence, there are strong arguments to deny the committee their power of representation.

Putting the power of representation into practice involves similar observations to those made in the chapter dealing with the management organ.[865] Thus, it is possible to assign representation to individual members[866] by allowing the possibilities

[862]See Art. 42 para. 1 SCE-R.

[863]For a detailed analysis of Art. 47 SCE-R, see Sect. 4.2.1.2.

[864]See Sect. 4.2.1.2.

[865]See Sect. 4.2.1.2.

[866]Art. 2521 para. 2 no 10. Note that these members cannot be members of the management control committee.

provided by Art. 47 para. 1 sent. 2 SCE-R. However, the general power of representation cannot be conferred to non-members (as governed by Art. 47 para. 4 SCE-R). Due to the general nature of the power of representation and its limits,[867] all acts accomplished for the SCE are covered. It is not possible to invoke limitations against third parties. The only exception occurs when third parties act to the detriment of the company,[868] as covered by Art. 47 para. 2 SCE-R.

The *Austrian* SCEG likewise contains specific provisions that supplement the relevant provisions of the SCE-R. In line with Art. 47 SCE-R, Sec. 27 para. 1 SCEG determines that the statutes may grant the power of sole representation. In fact, the administrative organ may delegate the representation of individual business transactions or types of business to individual members of the organ. Then, with respect to passive representation, Sec. 27 para. 1 SCEG explicitly states that a declaration of intent by third parties must not be granted to all the members of the organ who have the power of representation; it is sufficient to grant it to one member or to the managing director.

Sec. 27 para. 2 SCEG states that a single member of the administrative organ may represent the SCE, provided a specific statutory provision allows it. Representation can also be exercised jointly with an authorised signatory. This implies that the signatory alone cannot represent the SCE.

As Art. 47 SCE-R does not contain a provision for managing directors, the Austrian legislature introduced a provision to fill this gap. As a result, Sec. 25 para. 2 SCEG determines that the SCE shall be represented in both legal and extra-legal proceedings by both the administrative organ and the managing directors.[869] In other words, the members of the administrative organ and the managing directors can only exercise this authority collectively, unless the statutes provide otherwise.[870]

It is unclear whether Sec. 24 SCEG can limit the representation assigned to the members of the administrative organ, as it also requires adopting the provision for the management and supervisory organs in the general sense. According to the *GenG* and SCEG, only the management organ may represent an Austrian SCE; thus, one can argue that, under the one-tier system, only the members of the administrative organ who exercise management functions should be empowered to represent the SCE. Even though the SCEG does not explicitly favour this approach,[871] a statutory provision can implement such a division of tasks because of Sec. 27 para. 2 SCEG. Unlike Sec. 25 SCEG, here a supervisory committee is constituted within the administrative organ.[872]

[867] Art. 47 para. 2 subpara. 1 SCE-R.

[868] Art. 2384 para. 2 CC.

[869] On the condition that managing directors have been appointed. Also consider Sec. 25 para. 1 SCEG.

[870] For the effect and extent of the power of representation, see Sect. 4.2.1.2.

[871] Consider in this context Sec. 24 para. 3 SCEG.

[872] Similar to the Italian approach.

The last function assigned by the SCE-R to the administrative organ is called '**operations required authorisations**'. According to Art. 48 para. 1 SCE-R, the statutes must list all the categories of transactions[873] that either require an express decision by the administrative organ or are authorised by the general meeting. Here, 'express decision' means that the decision clearly refers to a specific case.[874] Both types of authorisation are important instruments for *ex ante* supervision: conducted, in the latter case, by the general meeting. Without authorisation, the administrative organ cannot conduct the transaction.[875] In addition, these provisions are without prejudice to Art. 47 SCE-R. In other words, these statutory limitations may not be relied upon against third parties.[876] Finally, according to Art. 48 para. 3 SCE-R, the member states may determine (1) the minimum categories that the statutes must list and (2) the organ empowered for authorisation. This raises the question, how have the Italian and Austrian legislature reacted with respect to this option?

The *Italian legislature* did not implement it, with the result that this aspect is, first of all, regulated by the SCE-R. Yet, it is useful to add that the provision concerning authorisation, contained in Art. 2409 terdecies para. 1 letter f-bis CC, can be used to formulate a specific statutory provision, as requested by Art. 48 para. 1 bullet 2 SCE-R. No specific problems should arise in this context. Note that the members of the managing control committee are part of the decision process of the administrative organ, as requested by Art. 48 para. 1 bullet 2 SCE-R. As seen, the position of the general meeting can thus be strengthened.

Likewise, the *Austrian legislature* did not implement this option.[877] Nor is it obligatory for an Austrian SCE to apply the list contained in Sec. 24e *GenG*. This list, however, can be used as a model to generate the list required by Art. 48 para. 1 SCE-R.[878] As mentioned, the administrative organ of an Austrian SCE must fulfil both management and supervisory tasks.[879] This implies that task division (executive and non-executive) needs to be distributed among different members of the organ. If specific decisions have to be authorised by the whole organ, both executive members and non-executive members of the administrative organ are involved. This increases *ex ante* supervision, especially if members are appointed as managing directors, as in this case the majority of members of the organ must be non-executives, with the result that they strongly influence the transactions established in Art. 48 para. 1 SCE-R.

---

[873] As seen in Sect. 4.2.2.1. Also consider Presti (2006), p. 83 et seq.; Teichmann (2015g), p. 744.

[874] See Schöpflin (2018o), p. 1313. For the SE, see Manz (2010j), p. 620; Teichmann (2015g), p. 743.

[875] A lack of authorisation leads to civil liability, as determined by Art. 51 SCE-R. Also consider Teichmann (2015g), p. 746.

[876] See also Sect. 4.2.2.1.

[877] Also consider Sec. 37 SEG, which requires a specific list to be used if an Austrian SE adopts the one-tier system.

[878] See also Sect. 4.2.2.1.

[879] See Sec. 24 SCEG.

To conclude, one can assert that, according to the SCE-R, the administrative organ manages the *agricultural SCE* and represents it in dealings with third parties and legal proceedings. These functions are further enlarged by the two national legal systems, giving the administrative organ some particular (national) features. In fact, according to Art. 42 para. 4 SCE-R, the member states can adopt appropriate measures, if the relevant legal system does not contain a provision for a one-tier system. It is argued that the specific type of one-tier system determined by the national legal system has to be used. In other words, the provisions of the SCR R are supplemented and even widened conceptually if the national legal system provides. Both legal systems introduce a specific supervisory function in the one-tier system. This means that monitoring is carried out within the organ to ensure both compliance with the law and efficiency of management of the agricultural SCE. In addition, the adequacy of the organisational structure of an *agricultural SCE*, its internal control system, its accounting system and its administrative system, in general, will be reviewed. The execution of the monitoring tasks should relate to the extent to which business transactions of the *agricultural SCE* are suitably presented.

The approach adopted by the Austrian legal system follows the two-tier system adopted by the *GenG*. Austrian SCEs must observe the provisions concerning the management and supervisory organs in the general sense. Therefore, it can be argued that the administrative organ must split its functions to put supervision of management into practice. Concerning the supervisory function, the Italian legal system requires the management control committee to be established within the administrative organ. Next, whereas the Austrian legislature allows current management to be delegated to a managing director, the Italian legislature has not adopted this option, as determined by Art. 42 para. 1 SCE-R. Similar to the Austrian approach, the Italian approach determines a wide range of information sharing; it considers the supervisory function, specifying the content of Art. 43 para. 2 SCE-R.

In this context, PECOL Sec. 2.5 para. 1 explicitly acknowledge that the functions of the organs include executive management, representation and supervision. It then adds that all three functions may be performed by the administrative organ. In line with Art. 42 para. 2 SCE-R, the PECOL explicitly acknowledge that the executive management may be allocated to managing directors.[880] This option was adopted by the Austrian legislature, but not the Italian legislature. We propose that the Italian legal framework be amended.

Representation is also specifically regulated. The SCE-R contains references to national law as well as two options. In principle, representation is exercised collectively and by individual members of the organs. Both legal systems allow this.

The Italian solution refers to general representation; it is argued that only members who exercise a management function (as opposed to a supervisory function) may represent the *agricultural SCE*. The Italian legal system also provides the opportunity to assign representation to a single member, but general power cannot

[880] Also consider Snaith (2017), p. 68.

be conferred to non-members, because of a lack of implementation of the option contained in Art. 47 para. 4 SCE-R.

Contrary to the Italian solution, the Austrian legal system allows individual members to represent the *agricultural SCE* for certain types of transactions (typically strategic investments, or, for example, specific aspects related to POs). According to Austrian law, an authorised signatory may exercise the power of representation, but only with the participation of at least one member of the management organ. If the decisions do not fulfil the object of the SCE, they still bind the organs *vis a vis* third parties. Both legal systems have limits in this regard.

The SCE-R also contains specific provisions for operations that must be authorised either by the general meeting or by the entire administrative organ. Neither the Austrian nor Italian legislature exercised the option contained in Art. 48 para. 3 SCE-R, but both legal systems contain examples that can be used to define the list of categories of transactions that require authorisation. For express decisions by the administrative organ,[881] the SCEG, which assigns management and supervisory functions to the administrative organ, in practice, also empowers the supervisors to make these decisions, implying that *ex ante* supervision is increased. The same is true for the members of the management control committee, as determined by Italian law.

If an *agricultural SCE* chooses the one-tier system of governance, in practical terms there will probably be minor differences between this system and the two-tier system. The actual differences will ultimately be structural and organisational, but the general objectives are similar or identical, namely putting in place an agricultural activity that serves a management function and as a control task over this function. This is demonstrated by the fact that, while both systems rely on a clear separation of powers (separation between management and supervision), there are overlaps in this division when the non-executive managers (or members of the managing control committee) both carry out the control activity and participate in the management of the *agricultural SCE*. The differences are, therefore, structural and organisational; they do not stem from content. Accordingly, reference can essentially be made to what has been said in this regard in the chapter on the two-tier system, with respect to examples.

4.3.2 The Composition of the Organ

The next topic concerning an SCE's administrative organ is its composition, which refers to two broad issues: the **conditions of membership** and the number of members. The study conducted on the management and supervisory organs under the two-tier system is relevant, as many results also apply to the administrative organ. As seen above,[882] Art. 46 para. 2 SCE-R indicates specific reasons denying

[881] See Art. 48 para. 1 bullet 2 SCE-R.

[882] For a detailed analysis, see Sect. 4.2.1.3.

interested candidates membership of an organ of an SCE. Accordingly, a person may be disqualified from becoming a member or representative of a member either according to the law of the member state, in which the SCE's registered office is situated, or according to a judicial or administrative decision delivered in a member state. Specific aspects regarding the two mentioned issues, because of the particular features of the one-tier system (as determined by national law) need further analyses, which will be conducted in this part of the study.

As seen, the conditions of membership are determined either by law or by statutes. *Italian law* contains certain provisions that apply to the criteria of eligibility, as requested by Art. 46 para. 2 SCE-R. According to the law,[883] persons who fulfil the following requirements cannot be appointed as organ's members and must forfeit their office if appointed: (1) interdicted and banned persons, (2) disqualified persons, (3) bankrupt persons, (4) persons who have been sentenced to a penalty entailing a ban, even temporary, from public office or (5) persons who have been sentenced to a penalty entailing the inability to exercise managerial functions.[884] This implies that minors cannot be appointed. In addition, non-natural persons cannot be appointed. Moreover, various laws determine the grounds that makes membership incompatible.[885]

As a general rule, members of the administrative organ (fulfilling either management or controlling tasks) may be shareholders or non-shareholders.[886] Art. 2542 para. 3 CC contains an exception that requires the majority of administrators to be chosen from user members. It is argued that this provision is applicable to an Italian SCE, based on Art. 8 para. 1 letter c SCE-R rather than Art. 46 para. 2 SCE-R.[887]

Additionally, when an Italian SCE wants to apply the one-tier system, at least one third of the members of the organ must meet the requirements of independence, as determined by Art. 2399 para. 1 CC.[888] The members of the management control committee must then be chosen from these independent members.[889] This does not

[883]Art. 2382 CC, applicable due to the reference in Art. 2409 noviesdecies para. 1 CC.

[884]See Riolfo (2010), p. 38 et seq.

[885]See Riolfo (2010), p. 58. According to Art. 2387 para. 2 CC, the provisions contained in special laws relating to the exercise of specific activities apply. See Riolfo (2010), p. 38 et seq. Also consider Sect. 4.2.1.3.

[886]See Riolfo (2010), p. 38.

[887]For further information, see Sect. 4.2.1.3.

[888]Due to a reference contained in Art. 2409 septiesdecies para. 2 CC. Art. 2399 para. 1 CC determines the following criteria (causes of ineligibility and forfeiture): those who are in the conditions contemplated in Art. 2382, the spouse, blood relatives and in-laws of the directors of the company up to the fourth degree, the spouse, blood relatives and in-laws up to the fourth degree of the directors of the company's subsidiaries or of the directors of the company's controlling entities or of companies under joint control, those connected with the company or with its subsidiaries or its controlling entities or companies under joint control by an employment relationship, or a continuous remunerated relationship of consultancy or other remunerated services or works, or other relationships of an economic nature which would comprise their independency. Different opinion Presti (2006), p. 84.

[889]If a member no longer meets the requirements, they must leave office. See Riolfo (2010), p. 109. See also Mirone (2017a), p. 576.

prevent other independent members, who are not appointed as members of the committee, from becoming members of the administrative organ. In fact, at least a third of them must be independent members,[890] the actual members of the committee being determined by the administrative organ itself (apart from the exception in Art. 2409 octiesdecies para. 1 sent. 2 CC). Therefore, not every independent member need be part of the committee.[891]

Finally, according to Art. 2409 octiesdecies para. 3 CC, at least one member must be selected from among the statutory auditors enrolled in the dedicated register.[892] This provision must be applied by an Italian SCE, for reasons previously outlined.[893]

The *Austrian legal system* contains specific rules that have to be considered when one analyses the conditions that the potential members of an administrative organ must fulfil. According to Austrian law, members of the administrative organ must be natural persons and have full legal capacity.[894] However, they need not be members of the SCE. In fact, the SCE-R does not follow the principle of *Selbstorganschaft.*[895]

The *GenG* does not list any preconditions for becoming a member of the organs, except those given by Sec. 24c para. 6 *GenG*, which refers to cooperatives fulfilling the characteristics listed in Sec. 189a para. 1 letter a and d UGB or cooperatives classified as a 'big cooperative'. Here, the law requires an auditing committee to be appointed within the supervisory organ, of which at least one member must be a financial expert. This implies that this person must have knowledge of and practical experience in finance, accounting and reporting. A similar provision is applicable to the administrative organ on the basis of Sec. 24 para. 4 SCEG[896]; this is consistent with Sec. 24 para. 1 SCEG, which determines that some members of the administrative organ must fulfil supervisory tasks.

Conversely, it can be argued that the impediments in Sec. 28a *BWG* need not be observed, as the chairman of an SCE's administrative organ primarily fulfils the function of chairman of an organ similar to the management organ, rather than an organ similar to the supervisory organ. This is clear from the SCE-R, which defines the administrative organ as having management competence. The SCEG adds

[890] These persons may not be members of the executive committee or have been delegated powers or specific offices. They cannot perform any functions relating to the management of the company's business or the companies which control it or are under control by it, not even de facto. See Riolfo (2010), p. 104. See also Mirone (2017a), p. 576.

[891] See Riolfo (2010), p. 59; Riolfo (2010), p. 107; Ghezzi and Rigotti (2005), p. 262. Under the two-tier system, members of the management organ who cannot be re-elected may be elected to become members of the supervisory organ. However, under the one-tier system, members of the administrative organ who cannot be re-elected may not become members of the controlling committee, as the members of the controlling committee must be elected members of the administrative organ. See Giorgi (2018b), p. 3243.

[892] See Riolfo (2010), p. 109.

[893] See Sect. 4.2.2.2.

[894] See Sect. 4.2.1.3.

[895] See Sect. 4.2.1.3.

[896] However, it refers to Sec. 51 para. 3a SEG.

supervisory functions, but cannot alter the nature of the administrative organ, as defined by the SCE-R. Therefore, the *BWG*'s impediments, which refer to the chairman of the supervisory organ, need not be observed. This solution seems applicable on the condition that management tasks are not delegated to the managing directors because of Sec. 25 SCEG. In this case, the chairman of the administrative organ explicitly cannot exercise management tasks.

In addition to these legally determined conditions for membership (and contrary to the provisions referring to the two-tier system), Art. 46 para. 3 SCE-R[897] expressly determines that the **statutes may establish eligibility requirements for membership** in the administrative organ, provided these rules align with the relevant national provisions.[898] It is unclear why the SCE-R grants this option to the administrative organ but not to the organs of an SCE that adopts the two-tier system.[899] One reason might be that, as the members of the administrative organ (especially, those empowered for representation) are not supervised by another organ of the SCE, it is desirable to allow further eligibility conditions to be determined by statutes. It must be stressed that the general meeting cannot fully supervise the members of the administrative organ. This bears some risk, as members who represent the SCE have a high degree of responsibility for its activities. One can therefore argue that the SCE-R allows the statutes to contain special requirements, for instance, a requirement of technical expertise.[900]

As mentioned, this opportunity to enhance statutory freedom is explicitly linked to national law, which raises the question, how do the Italian and Austrian legal systems address this issue? As required by Art. 46 para. 3 SCE-R, *Italian law* contains specific provisions allowing the statutes to determine the criteria of eligibility. Art. 2409 noviesdecies para. 1 CC makes Art. 2387 CC applicable and determines that statutes may define the requirements of integrity, professionalism and independence.[901] A further point of reference may be the requirements provided by the codes of conduct that are drafted by professional associations or management companies in regulated markets.[902]

Next, Art. 2409 octiesdecies para. 2 CC states that the statutes require members of the management control committee to fulfil the integrity and professionalism requirements.[903] When defining these requirements, the statutes can refer to the

897 It states: "An SCE's statutes may, in accordance with the law applicable to cooperatives in the Member State, lay down special conditions of eligibility for members representing the administrative organ."

898 See Schulze (2004a), p. 107; Schöpflin (2018m), p. 1310.

899 See Sects. 4.2.1.3 and 4.2.2.2 and, where it is argued that statutory provisions can be adopted based on Art. 8 para. 1 letter c (iii) SCE-R.

900 See Schöpflin (2018m), p. 1310. Also consider Lutter et al. (2012), p. 1607.

901 For further information, see Sect. 4.2.1.3.

902 See Art. 2409 septiesdecies para. 2 CC.

903 See Riolfo (2010), p. 109; Ghezzi and Rigotti (2005), p. 269; Stella Richter (2004), p. 201; Fortunato (2003), p. 887; Guaccero (2004b), p. 916. Some scholars argue that statutes not necessarily must require integrity and professionalism requirements. See Bonelli (2004), p. 190 et seq. See also Mirone (2017a), p. 576.

requirements for statutory auditors, for example. They can also provide for a different solution, determined according to the cooperative's size or business activity. In addition, integrity and professionalism requirements may differ between members.[904]

The *Austrian legal system* contains similar provisions that make Art. 46 para. 3 SCE applicable. According to Sec. 24 para. 1 SCEG, the provisions governing the management and supervisory organs must be applied if the SCE adopts the one-tier system. With this, the SCEG widens the set of rules that must be observed. In terms of eligibility criteria, the widening of applicable rules raises the question of whether this implies that specific provisions linked to the supervisory function must be observed. In this context, the Austrian legal system allows the qualification criteria for the management organ to be set via the statutes, whereas with regard to the members of the supervisory organ, the members of the cooperative ultimately decide on the suitability of a particular candidate when appointing the members of that organ.[905] This aligns with the approach adopted by the SCE-R, in which the tasks of the administrative organ are primarily those of the management organ. Thus, no specific doubts should arise when applying the provision contained in Art. 46 para. 3 SCE-R to an Austrian SCE.

The next issue, which regards the composition of the administrative organ, concerns the **number of members** of the organ. In general, the statutes determine the number of members of the administrative organ, its composition and/or the rules for determining these.[906] However, the member states can set a minimum and (in certain cases) a maximum number of members. Comparing the phrasing with that contained in Art. 37 para. 4 SCE-R,[907] it is clear that a member state may generally set a minimum number of members.[908] A member state may also adopt a maximum limit, but only where necessary. It has been observed that this formula implies that the national legislature is not obliged to also set a maximum limit. This approach is thus equivalent to the one adopted for the management organ.[909]

---

[904] See Riolfo (2010), p. 109 et seq.; Ghezzi and Rigotti (2005), p. 267.

[905] See Sects. 4.2.1.3 and 4.2.2.2.

[906] See Sect. 4.2.1.3, where it is argued that this second solution allows a more flexible approach, which might better satisfy the changing requirements of members or the SCE.

Art 42 para. 2 states: "The number of members of the administrative organ or the rules for determining it shall be laid down in the statutes of the SCE. However, a Member State may set a minimum and, where necessary, a maximum number of members. Of the members of the administrative organ, not more than one quarter of the posts available may be filled by non-user members. The administrative organ shall, however, consist of at least three members where employee participation is regulated in accordance with Directive 2003/72/EC."

[907] Dealing with the number of members of the management organ.

[908] Member states cannot set an exclusive number of members, as this would be in contrast to the clear wording of Art. 42 para. 2 sent. 2 SCE-R. See Manz (2010f), p. 549.

[909] For the SE, see Manz (2010f), p. 549; Teichmann (2015b), p. 551.

Unlike for the management organ, the SCE-R refers to 'members', i.e., multiple people.[910] As a specific condition, Art. 42 para. 2 subpara. 2 SCE-R adds that, if employee participation is regulated according to 2003/72/EC, the administrative organ must have at least three members.[911] This suggests that two members is sufficient in other cases. Still, the administrative organ must be a collegial organ. Like the two-tier system, non-user members may not make up more than a quarter of the members of the organ. As argued above,[912] this implies that non-user members and their interests can be represented by external persons, user members or by a limited number of non-user members. Ultimately, this issue is strongly influenced by national law, which, as argued above, strongly influences the final structure of the one-tier system. It is therefore necessary to consider the national solutions.

In Italy, the exact determination of the minimum numbers of members is influenced by the structure of the *Italian one-tier system*. A specific set of rules must be observed. First, Art. 2380 bis para. 4 CC[913] allows the number of members of the administrative organ to be determined by statutes.[914] Moreover, Art. 2409 septiesdecies para. 2 CC states that a third of the members must meet independence requirements. Other rules refer to the members of the management control committee. According to Art. 2409 octiesdecies para. 1 CC, the responsibility for determining the number of members of the management control committee lies with the administrative organ, unless otherwise required by the statutes. In addition, this paragraph states that the control committees of companies listed in the capital markets must have at least three members. For other companies, it is unclear whether the minimum number is two or three. However, there are strong arguments that support the latter. With only two members, it would be necessary for all members to be present to meet the majority requirement[915]; furthermore, giving the chairman the casting vote would contradict the primary function of the committee, which is to discuss and compare different options. Thus, in a two-member committee, the non-chairing member would have no power.[916] Then, as the members of the control committee must meet the independence requirement, and at least a third of the members of the administrative organ must also meet these requirements, it follows that the administrative organ must have at least four members (or at least seven if one

[910]See Art. 42 para. 3 SCE-R, which determines that the members must be appointed by the general meeting, as opposed to Art. 37 para. 2 SCE-R, which provides for the possibility to appoint a member. Similarly, Art. 44 para. 1 SCE-R requires the organ to elect a chairman from among its members. Also consider Art. 43 para. 3 SE-R and in this context Teichmann (2015d), p. 724.

[911]For the SE, see Manz (2010f), p. 549.

[912]Also consider Schulze (2004a), p. 103 et seq.; Schöpflin (2018i), p. 1307 et seq.

[913]Applicable due to a reference contained in Art. 2409 noviesdecies para. 1 CC.

[914]If the statutes only set a minimum and maximum number, the general meeting may decide on the number of members.

[915]See Art. 2404 para. 4 CC (applicable due to a reference contained in Art. 2409 octiesdecies para. 6 CC).

[916]See Riolfo (2010), p. 101; Ghezzi and Rigotti (2005), p. 255 et seq. Different opinion Bonelli (2004), p. 181. See also Mirone (2017a), p. 576 et seq.

follows the argument that executive members should not be in a minority position).[917] These requirements must be met by Italian SCEs; otherwise, the one-tier system, as designed by the Italian legislature, could not be meaningfully adopted.[918]

Let us now consider the *Austrian solution*. The Austrian legislature did not exercise the option, contained in Art. 42 para. 2 sent. 2 SCE-R, to restrict statutory freedom.[919] Instead, Austrian law determines a framework that ultimately provides for a minimum number of members and that is primarily based on how the supervisory role, which is assigned to the administrative organ of an Austrian SCE, is fulfilled. Such a division of tasks necessarily affects the number of members of this organ. If the organ appoints managing directors from among its members, the SCEG[920] explicitly requires that non-executives must make up the majority of the organ. As a result, the administrative organ must include at least three members; (otherwise, no majority-voting is possible). If external persons are appointed as managing directors or no managing directors are appointed, the general rule determined by the SCE-R requiring a minimum of two members applies. If necessary, the restriction contained in Art. 42 para. 2 subpara. 2 SCE-R must be observed, requiring the organ to have at least three members if employee participation is regulated in accordance with dir. 2003/72/EC.

Overall, these analyses considering the provisions that govern the composition of the administrative organ[921] have again shown that Austrian *agricultural SCEs* can adopt a generally flexible approach, although there are exceptions based on the preconditions determined by Sec. 24 para. 4 SCEG. They must not be members of the SCE, as the SCE-R does not follow the principle of *Selbstorganschaft*.

Compared to the Austrian solution, the Italian approach is stricter. Under Italian law, the majority of the members of the administrative organ must be user members.[922] This approach is in line with PECOL Sec. 2.5 para. 6, and it is argued in Sect. 4.2.1.3 that the SCEG should be amended accordingly. Additionally, at least one third of the members of the organ must meet the independence requirements laid out in Art. 2399 para. 1 CC. Art. 2382 CC applies to the administrative organ of an Italian *agricultural SCE*. In addition, various laws determine the criteria that preclude membership. To reiterate, Sec. 2.5 para. 7 letter c and para. 9 PECOL require specific qualifications for membership. As already observed,[923] these recommendations can be based on statutory provisions and can apply to both Austrian and Italian SCEs.

---

[917]See Ghezzi (2005), p. 222; Riolfo (2010), p. 27 et seq. See also Mirone (2017a), p. 577.
In this case ¾ of the members of the organ are independent members. All of them are members of the committee, whereas one member fulfils the management tasks.

[918]Due to Art. 42 para. 4 SCE-R.

[919]In contrast, the German legislator requires a minimum of five members for the administrative organ, reduced to three if an SCE has 20 or fewer members. See Sec. 19 SCEAG.

[920]Sec. 25 para. 1 sent. 2 SCEG.

[921]That is, preconditions of a personal nature and the number of members, and what implies integrating specific national provisions into rather general provisions contained in the SCE-R.

[922]Or chosen from those persons, determined by members who are legal persons.

[923]See Sect. 4.2.1.3.

No specific doubts should arise when applying the provision from Art. 46 para. 3 SCE-R. In this regard, the Italian legal system allows for statutes that determine the integrity and professionalism requirements for the members of the management control committee.

Then, we analysed the issue of the number of members. The SCE-R determines that the number of members or the rules for determining this number must be laid down in the statutes. The PECOL contain a more stringent approach.[924] The Austrian legislature did not exercise the option contained in Art. 42 para. 2 sent. 2 SCE; therefore, a greater number may be determined by the statutes. If the organ appoints managing directors from amongst its members, the minimum number is three; if either external persons are appointed as managing directors or no managing director is appointed, the minimum number is two. In opposition to this, it is argued that the administrative organ of an Italian SCE must have at least four members because of the structure of its one-tier system.[925]

In practice, the drafters of the statutes of an *agricultural SCE* may require certain requirements in addition to the legal requirements. Such qualities as technical skills and professional experience can bring the skill level of the members of the administrative organ into line with the specific needs of their SCE. A primary agricultural cooperative or a secondary cooperative has different needs. A geographical link could also be a criterion. In sum, all these characteristics should contribute to ensuring that the farmer-members feel adequately represented and that the cooperative can fulfil its objectives effectively and efficiently.

4.3.3 The Appointment and Removal of the Members of the Administrative Organ

The SCE-R contains specific provisions for **appointing the members** of the administrative organ. Contrary to the solution offered for the two-tier system, it does not explicitly refer to their removal. According to Art. 42 para. 3 SCE-R,[926] the general meeting appoints members of the administrative organ and any alternate members that the statutes allow. Appointing alternate members ensures that an SCE with a one-tier system remains fully capable of acting.[927] As the drafter of the statutes, the general meeting ultimately decides, in case of a vacancy, whether it is necessary to appoint alternates or whether it is better to convene a general meeting. As with the

924 See Sect. 4.2.1.3.

925 Independent members, executive members and members of the management control committee.

926 It states: "The members of the administrative organ, and, where the statutes so provide, their alternate members, shall be appointed by the general meeting. The members of the first administrative organ may, however, be appointed by the statutes. This shall apply without prejudice to any employee participation arrangements determined pursuant to Directive 2003/72/EC."

927 See Schöpflin (2018i), p. 1307 et seq.

supervisory organ under the two-tier system, the first members can be appointed by the statutes without prejudice to employee participation, as provided for by dir 2003/72/EC.[928]

As already observed for the management and supervisory organs, the SCE-R does not contain further provisions regarding the appointment procedure or other related issues that may arise. Therefore, national law has to be applied per Art. 53 SCE-R and/or Art. 52 SCE-R.

The *Italian legal system* provides a similar solution to that given in Art. 42 para. 3 SCE-R. The issues not dealt with by the SCE-R are regulated by national law. Here one must refer to the Art. 2364 CC, which is fully applicable to a one-tier system[929]; accordingly, the general meeting appoints and dismisses the members.[930] The position must be accepted by the new members.[931] Then, according to Art. 2364 para. 1 no. 3 CC, the general meeting defines the remuneration for the members of the administrative organ, unless the statutes provide otherwise.[932] These findings apply to an Italian SCE.

As previously seen,[933] some members of the administrative organ can be appointed by the general meeting as potential members of the management control committee despite not being chosen by the administrative organ. These members hold a position of attendance.[934] This observation is also valid for an Italian SCE.

Art. 2544 para. 3 CC determines that only a third of the members of the administrative organ may be elected by those who hold financial instruments. This condition must not be observed by an Italian SCE, as the SCE-R already contains an applicable provision.[935] However, the provision is important for an Italian SCE, because it states that the members of the administrative organ, who were elected by the holders of financial instruments, cannot be assigned operative tasks or be members of the executive committee.[936] Thus, in theory, the management control committee of an Italian SCE could be exclusively made up of members elected by the holders of financial instruments.[937]

[928]See Schulze (2004a), p. 104.

[929]See Riolfo (2010), p. 29.

[930]Similarly, under Art. 2383 CC, all members of the organ are appointed at the shareholders meeting, the first being appointed in the statutes. This article is applicable due to the reference contained in Art. 2409 noviesdecies para. 1 CC. See Riolfo (2010), p. 29 et seq.

[931]See Sandei (2018b), p. 2816. Also consider Bonelli (2004), p. 74.

[932]See Art. 2389 CC.

[933]See Sect. 4.3.2.

[934]It seems they cannot fulfil any management tasks and still be a candidate for appointment to the management control committee. Of course, it is not certain they would ever obtain this position. See Riolfo (2010), p. 33.

[935]See Art. 42 para. 2 sent. 2 SCE-R.

[936]The provision is applicable due to Art. 8 para. 1 letter c SCE-R.

[937]See Giorgi (2018b), p. 3243. Also consider Presti (2007), p. 1001.

Unless otherwise provided in the statutes, the administrative organ appoints (and removes) the members of the management control committee.[938] It has been discussed whether the statutes of a cooperative adopting the one-tier system may contain a specific clause about appointing administrators. For example, such a statutory provision might require the administrative organ to appoint a representative of a particular category of shareholders to the management control committee. In addition, the statutory provisions may fix the size of the management control committee and establish further independence requirements. On the other hand, if no specific statutory provision has been adopted, the administrative organ has no restrictions on its decisions.[939] The various solutions can be applied by an Italian SCE because of Art. 8 para. 1 letter c SCE-R.

Some difficulties may arise over the power to appoint members of the committee because of the possibility of assigning this power to other bodies, such as the general meeting. Empowering the general meeting to appoint the members of the management control committee could make the latter even more independent of the members who manage the cooperative. In general, some members may be appointed by the minorities or by a particular category of shareholders.[940] These findings are important for an Italian SCE, because Art. 52 subpara. 2 SCE-R refers to the competence of the general meeting (as regulated by Italian law).

The *Austrian* SCEG lacks specific provisions and only generally determines that the provisions adopted for the management and supervisory organs must be observed.[941] Accordingly, new members must accept the new position. It also seems possible to apply Sec. 24a *GenG* for the reasons stated above.[942] Remuneration must be determined by the general meeting, as there is no other organ that can deal with this issue.

As mentioned above,[943] the SCE-R does not contain any provision concerning the **removal of the members of the administrative organ**. Arguing ad *actus contrarius*, the provisions for appointing members would apply.[944] On the other

[938]See Art. 2409 octiesdecies para. 1 CC. Some Italian scholars have criticised the fact that the supervisors are appointed by those who they must supervise. On the other hand, members identify supervisors through their primary role as administrators. In favour of this governance system, it is argued that it helps circulate information between administrators and supervisors, as both are part of the same body. This seems to make it more effective. In addition, it is argued that effectiveness is increased by the fact that a one-tier system must undergo both internal and external audit. See Ghezzi (2005), p. 210 et seq.; Miotto (2018d), p. 2911; Guaccero (2004b), p. 913; Bonelli (2004), p. 268. See also Mirone (2017a), p. 577.

[939]See Riolfo (2010), p. 31 et seq. Also consider Galgano (2003), p. 246.

[940]See Riolfo (2010), p. 102 et seq.; Fortunato (2003), p. 886. Also consider Ghezzi and Rigotti (2005), p. 259.

[941]See Sec. 24 para. 1 SCEG. Consider in this context Sects. 4.2.1.4 and 4.2.2.3.

[942]See Sect. 4.2.2.3. The Austrian legislator has adopted a specific provision relating to Austrian SEs adopting the one-tier system and appointment by the court. See Sec. 47 SEG. Gesetz über das Statut der Europäischen Gesellschaft (Societas Europaea—SE), BGBl I 2004.

[943]For the SE, Teichmann (2015b), p. 554 et seq.

[944]See Schulze (2004a), p. 104; Lehner (2007), p. 117.

hand, removal must be determined by national law, as the SCE-R contains a gap.[945] However, the relevant national legal system might not contain such a provision. This can lead to a situation in which the members of the administrative organ cannot be legally removed. In this case, the only solution would be to assign this competence to the appointing organ.[946] Then, it could also be a competence that the SCE-R generally assigns to a specific organ on the condition that national law provides accordingly.

This latter solution can apply to an Italian SCE. In fact, the *Italian legal system* assigns the task of removing members to the general meeting; the relevant provision is thus applicable to an Italian SCE because of Art. 52 subpara. 2 SCE-R.[947] According to Art. 2383 para. 3 CC, the members of the administrative organ can be removed by the general meeting at any time. They have the right to compensation for damages if the removal occurs without just cause. This provision must be applied to every member of the administrative organ of an Italian SCE[948] and, hence, also to those who must be appointed as potential members of the management control committee. The general meeting thus retains the complete power to remove members of the organ, independent of the function they fulfil.[949]

---

[945]See Art. 8 para. 1 lettec SCE-R. Also consider Schöpflin (2018j), p. 1308. For the SE, Manz (2010f), p. 551.

[946]Next, it is argued that members of the supervisory organ cannot be removed at all. The mandate concludes as stipulated in Art. 45 SCE-R. For the SE, see Teichmann (2015b), p. 555.

[947]It states that "the general meeting shall decide on matters for which responsibility is given to the general meeting of a cooperative governed by the law of the Member State in which the SCE's registered office is situated, either by the law of that Member State or by the SCE's statutes in accordance with that law."

[948]Due to Art. 8 para. 1 letter c SCE-R and Art. 9 SCE-R.

[949]See Riolfo (2010), p. 33. See also Mirone (2017a), p. 577.

In this context, it is highlighted that the specific Italian provisions do not determine who may have the power to revoke the members of the committee. As such, revocation is a rather complex and problematic issue, as it may condition independence (with respect to decisions to be made and exercising powers). Two solutions are discussed: the power to revoke is attributed to the general meeting or it is attributed to the administrative organ. In the first case, the committee could be considered more independent, as, in this case, those who are controlled could not revoke the controllers. It is argued that, as a consequence, the controlling body would be more stable and more autonomous. It is stressed that the establishing moment of the committee is the moment in which the general meeting appoints the independent administrators. As known, the members of the committee have to be chosen among these. (This solution would be in line with arguments that consider the committee as a single organ.) Moreover, such an argument could also be based on Art. 2409 noviesdecies CC, which refers to Art. 2383 para. 3 CC, and according to which the members of the administrative organ can be removed by the general meeting. In fact, from a technical point of view, the members of the committee are members of the organ. On the other hand, applying general principles, the members of the committee could be revoked by the administrative organ, which, at least from a technical point of view, appoints the members of the committee. In this case, the relation between the administrative organ and committee could be described as relation between a delegating body and the delegates (mandate). In this case, the revoked member would remain a member of the administrative organ. Still, the general meeting could revoke the board of directors as such. Especially if one considers the fact that in the second case, revocation without cause would be possible. See Riolfo (2010), p. 111 et seq. Also consider Ghezzi and Rigotti (2005), p. 269; Fortunato (2003), p. 887. The second solution is in line with the SCE-R, as it does not identify further organs.

Determining who is empowered to remove the members of the administrative organ of an *Austrian SCE* is quite sophisticated. Art. 42 para. 4 SCE-R requires national legislatures to take appropriate measures, provided the relevant national legal system does not contain a provision governing the one-tier system.[950] One can therefore argue that removal that occurs in an Austrian SCE is regulated by Sec. 24 para. 1 SCEG, which refers to the provision for the management and supervisory organs. As a result, Sec. 15 para. 2 *GenG* in conjunction with Sec. 24 para. 1 *GenG*, explicitly assigns the power of removal to the general meeting. This organ may revoke membership at any time.[951] This solution aligns with Art. 52 subpara. 2 SCE-R.

Comparing the respective provisions that Italian and Austrian *agricultural SCEs* must apply to the appointment and removal of the members of the administrative organ, one can see that the members of the administrative organ are both appointed and removed by the general meeting. The SCE-R does not specifically deal with removal; hence, national provisions apply, provided that the national legal system contains a specific provision in this regard. Under both legal systems, removal is explicitly assigned to the general meeting. The general meeting may also negotiate remuneration. If vacancies appear, they may be filled by either alternate members who become members of the organ or the general meeting.

From a conceptual point of view, the Italian legal system provides a specific set of rules necessary to observe, whereas the Austrian legal system only generally refers to the provisions governing the two-tier system.

In Italian *agricultural SCEs*, where there must be a distinction between independent and other members, the general meeting can influence who will become an independent member when appointing members of the administrative organ. Unless otherwise provided in the statutes, the administrative organ of an Italian *agricultural SCE* appoints (and removes) the members of the management control committee. The provision in 2544 para. 3 CC that regards the holders of financial instruments must not be observed. In fact, the SCE-R contains its own provision for such instances. Moreover, it is possible for the management control committee to be exclusively made up of members elected by the holders of financial instruments. According to Italian law, the holders of financial instruments cannot be assigned operative tasks or serve as members on an executive committee. This provision is applicable to an SCE.

According to both legal systems, membership may be revoked at any time without just cause.

---

[950] Art. 42 para. 4 SCE-R states that member states may adopt appropriate measures if the existing national legal system does not contain a provision concerning the one-tier system. Interestingly, the German legislator was more explicit in this context. According to Sec. 20 SCEAG, membership may be revoked at any time with the majority of three quarters of the general meeting. In contrast, the managing directors can have their position revoked through a simple majority, unless the statutes provide otherwise (notwithstanding claims for compensation of damages) (Sec. 22 para. 4 SCEAG). See Schöpflin (2018i), p. 1307 et seq.

[951] See Strommer (2014a), p. 194; Zehetner (2014b), p. 270.

4.3.4 The Internal Organisation of the Administrative Organ

We now consider the internal organisation of the administrative organ. The SCE-R contains provisions that address chairmanship, calling meetings, the interval between meetings and the right to information. Items necessary for conducting business (the quorum, decision taking and the casting vote) are regulated by Art. 50 SCE-R, which contains provisions applicable to organs from both the two-tier and one-tier systems. Thus, the following analysis will only briefly sketch the results obtained when analysing the management and supervisory organs. However, the complexity of Italian law requires a deeper analysis.

The following discussion is divided between three key aspects[952]: chairmanship, decision making and committees.

The rules for the **chairman** are contained in Art. 44 SCE-R, which basically repeats the provisions from Art. 41 that refer to the supervisory organ.[953] In contrast to this latter provision, no other organ may call a meeting. Not even the general meeting has the right to convene a meeting of the administrative organ.[954]

This provision declares that the chairman must be elected by the administrative organ from among its members.[955] If half the members are appointed by the employees, the chairman has to be elected by the general meeting.[956] The SCE-R only determines the chairman's competence and duties to the extent that he or she may and must call a meeting. Further duties must be determined according to national law.

Meetings can be called either by the chairman or at the request of at least one third of the members. As mentioned above,[957] the second option is necessary, because the members are jointly liable with the other members of the administrative organ and therefore must have an agreed means to call a meeting in order to be properly informed about the conduct of business. The members calling the meeting must include their reasons for calling it in their request. To strengthen their position, Art. 44 para. 2 last sent. SCE-R explicitly determines that the requesting members may call the meeting on the condition that the chairman does not take action within 15 days of the request.

---

[952] And is again based on the structure used when analysing the management or supervisory organ.

[953] See Schulze (2004a), p. 104.

[954] See Schöpflin (2018k), p. 1309.

[955] For the SE, see Teichmann (2015d), p. 722.

[956] Art. 44 para. 1 SCE-R states: "The administrative organ shall elect a chairman from among its members. If half of the members are appointed by employees, only a member appointed by the general meeting may be elected chairman."

[957] See Sect. 4.2.2.4.

Next, the SCE-R[958] determines that meetings must be held according to the conditions laid down in the statutes and at least once every 3 months.[959] In principle, the administrative organ should meet at regular intervals since it manages the SCE. An interval of 3 months should be enough time when a managing director is responsible for the day-to-day business. Here, the non-managing members may supervise the managing directors on a regular basis.[960]

The regulation determines specific subjects for discussion at the meetings, in particular the progress of the SCE and its foreseeable development. This discussion must account for any information about the undertakings controlled by the SCE that may significantly affect the progress of its business. The provisions governing both the subjects and the interval of the meetings correspond to the duty of information as determined for the management organ of the two-tier system.[961] This solidifies the responsibility of every member of the administrative organ to inform themselves about the progress and development of the business.[962] Moreover, each member is obliged to submit information that he or she obtains to the other members.[963]

This responsibility is further fostered by para. 2 of Art. 43 SCE-R,[964] which confers upon every member the right to examine all the reports, documents and information submitted to the administrative organ, irrespective of whether a meeting is called. As every member is a member of the administrative organ (executives and non-executives), there is no organisational barrier[965] inhibiting the inspection and examination of documents.[966]

As already seen, the *Italian legal system* determines the features of the one-tier system, which an Italian SCE must comply with. The following analysis considers the relevant Italian norms by also describing the similarities and differences between the rules that an Italian cooperative must apply. This helps us to better understand the applicable rules dealing with chairmanship.

---

[958] Art. 43 para. 1 SCE-R. It states: "The administrative organ shall meet at least once every three months, at intervals laid down in the statutes, to discuss the progress of and foreseeable development of the SCE's business, taking account, where appropriate, of any information relating to undertakings controlled by the SCE that may significantly affect the progress of the SCE's business."

[959] Schulze (2004a), p. 104. Also consider Egermann and Heckenthaler (2004), p. 263; Teichmann (2015c), p. 717.

[960] See Schöpflin (2018j), p. 1308. For this reason, para. 1 of Art. 43 SCE-R is formulated similarly to Art. 40 para. 1 SCE-R. See Schöpflin (2018j), p. 1308. Also consider Manz (2010g), p. 599 et seq.; Teichmann (2015c), p. 718 et seq.

[961] See Schulze (2004a), p. 104; Schöpflin (2018k), p. 1309. Also consider Manz (2010g), p. 599; Teichmann (2015c), p. 717.

[962] See Schöpflin (2018j), p. 1308. For the SE, see Teichmann (2015c), p. 718.

[963] For the SE, see Manz (2010g), p. 599.

[964] It states: "Each member of the administrative organ shall be entitled to examine all reports, documents and information submitted to it."

[965] See Greda (2014), p. 850. As a result it is not necessary to further define the right to information, as for instance Art. 40 SCE-R does.

[966] For the SE, see Manz (2010g), p. 599.

Italian law contains provisions similar to those in the SCE-R. From the civil code, Art. 2380 bis para. 5 CC. determines that the administrative organ selects the chairman from among its members, unless the chairman is appointed by the general meeting. However, this latter option contradicts the SCE-R and therefore does not apply to an Italian SCE.

Then, the law requires the members of the organ to determine the rules that define the internal structure and function of the organ.[967] This obligation also applies to an Italian SCE. It is unclear whether an independent member who is not a member of the management control committee may be appointed as chairman. It can be argued that the criteria of independence could foster impartiality when managing the organ. It seems that an independent member can become chairman as long as statutory provisions do not appoint him with executive tasks.[968] In addition, a chairman who is elected from the independent members could be considered a safeguard for minorities and third parties.[969] This solution aligns with Art. 44 para. 1 SCE-R, which only states that the organ shall elect a chairman from among its members. Moreover, the applicable one-tier system is that proposed by a national legislature, to be integrated into the loosely defined one-tier system adopted by the SCE-R.[970]

Next, according to Art. 2381 CC, the chairman calls the meeting of the organ, sets its agenda, coordinates the work and ensures that adequate information about the matters on the agenda is provided to all members of the administrative organ. Statutes may provide otherwise.[971] According to Art. 44 para. 2 SCE-R, such details are regulated by statute.

Then, Art. 2404 paras. 1, 3 and 4 CC[972] contain provisions that determine the management control committee's internal structure. The meeting has to be convened by its chairman, who also has limited discretionary powers over setting the agenda. If specific items are requested by a managing member, the chairman is bound accordingly. He or she can refuse, however, if there are justifications for this decision.[973] These provisions are applicable to an Italian SCE[974]; in fact, the SCE-R only contains general provisions about the administrative organ. The same is true for the requirement to hold meetings at least every 90 days. Note that the control

[967] See Art. 2380 bis para. 1 CC.

[968] See Riolfo (2010), p. 74 et seq.; Galgano (2003), p. 262. See also Mirone (2017a), p. 576. According to Art. 2381 paras 2, 3 and 4 CC, the board of directors can delegate its functions to one of its members.

[969] See Riolfo (2010), p. 75.

[970] See Sect. 4.3.1.

[971] See also Sect. 4.2.1.5.

[972] These provisions are applicable due to the reference contained in Art. 2409 octiesdecies para. 6 CC.

[973] See Riolfo (2010), p. 110.

[974] Due to Art. 8 para. 1 letter c SCE-R.

committee's meetings must be held separately from those of the administrative organ.[975]

The *Austrian rules* can lead one to ascertain that the SCEG only specifies that the chairman cannot simultaneously be the managing director. According to the law, one must consider the provisions that are generally applicable to the management and supervisory organs of an Austrian SCE.[976] Previous analyses[977] reveal that the chairman acts as *primus inter partes*; statutes can determine his specific competence. The chairman is responsible for organising meetings and executing decisions. Finally, the chairman's position may be revoked by the administrative organ.

Also the **decision-making** process needs to be discussed in the context of the administrative organ's internal organisation. As with all organs of the SCE, the decision-making process is determined by Art. 50 para. 1 SCE.[978] As long as the statutes do not provide otherwise, the administrative organ may make decisions if at least half of the members with voting rights are present (including representatives). Decisions are then taken by a majority of the members with voting rights who are present or represented. Certain transactions that are determined by Art. 48 SCE-R must be authorised either by the general meeting or expressly by the administrative organ. The chairman has a casting vote unless the statutes provide otherwise.[979] As previously shown,[980] the formalities of decision making can be determined by either national law[981] or statute.[982] The former applies when the criteria determined by Art. 50 SCE-R are not altered. In this case, it might be necessary to refer to national law to fill any gaps.

The *Italian legal* system contains specific provisions concerning decision making which are relevant. These rules are similar to the provisions of the SCE-R. Like Art. 50 para. 1 SCE-R, Italian law provides in Art. 2388 CC that the administrative organ makes decisions according to the principle of majority. The organ is validly

[975]It is argued that, in order to prevent pressure or undesired mixing, it is necessary to prevent members of the management organ from participating in committee meetings. One exception might be if they have been explicitly invited to provide information on items on the agenda. See Riolfo (2010), p. 110. Also consider Ghezzi and Rigotti (2005), p. 270.

[976]See Sec. 24 SCEG.

[977]See Sects. 4.2.1.5 and 4.2.2.4. For the SE, see Teichmann (2015d), p. 723 et seq.

[978]It explicitly refers to the decisions taken in accordance with Art. 42 para. 1 sent. 1 SCE-R.

It states: "Unless otherwise provided by this Regulation or the statutes, the internal rules relating to quorums and decision taking in SCE organs shall be as follows

- quorum: at least half of the members with voting rights must be present or represented;
- decision-taking: a majority of the members with voting rights present or represented.

Members who are absent may take part in decisions by authorising another member of the organ or the alternate members who were appointed at the same time to represent them."

[979]See Art. 50 para. 2 SCE-R.

[980]See Sect. 4.2.1.5.

[981]If Art. 50 para. 1 letter b SCE-R is not amended.

[982]If Art. 50 para. 1 letter b SCE-R is amended.

constituted if the majority of members in office is present. Resolutions are valid if the majority of members are present. However, the statutes may require a larger number of members to be present. As seen, these issues are regulated by Art. 50 para. 1 SCE-R.

Next, the voting procedures for the administrative organ (and the management control committee) are the same as those for the management organ under the two-tier system and are regulated by Art. 2388 CC.[983] For a specific analysis, refer to the relevant chapters of this study.[984] It is discussed whether independent members are counted among those present. There is no question that independent members who are not a member of the management control committee have to be counted when determining the constitutive or deliberative majority of the administrative organ. But what about those independent members who are members of the management control committee? They are still members of the administrative organ, even though they monitor the members who manage the cooperative. Is it therefore necessary to consider their presence? This depends ultimately on the nature of the management control committee. Is it an independent organ or not? There are arguments supporting both approaches.[985] However, it does not seem possible to consider the management control committee as an independent organ when following the provisions of the SCE-R, which only defines a single organ for the one-tier system. This does, however, not prevent management and monitoring tasks from being differentiated if explicitly requested by a national legal system.

As already seen,[986] the *Austrian legal system* provides different solutions for the decisions taken by the management and supervisory organs. This influences the decision-making process in an Austrian SCE for two reasons. First, national law must be observed if Art. 50 para. 1 letter b SCE-R is not amended, and, second, Sec. 24 para. 1 SCEG refers to the provisions for both the management and supervisory organs. Finally, Sec. 24 para. 2 SCEG determines that the administrative organ of an Austrian SCE must observe the rights and duties of the management and supervisory organs. Both sets of rules allow the adoption of statutory provisions in this regard. There are no substantial differences.[987]

Our final topic in this section is **committees**, which the administrative organ might use to make or prepare its decisions and to better fulfil its tasks. The SCE-R does not contain any provisions dealing with committees, so national provisions have to be applied.[988]

According to *Italian law*, the administrative organ may constitute other committees in addition to the management control committee, which is required by law. In

[983]Art. 2409 noviesdecies CC refers to Art. 2388 CC. See Sect. 4.2.1.5.

[984]See Sects. 4.2.1.5 and 4.2.2.4.

[985]See Riolfo (2010), p. 78 et seq.; Riolfo (2010), p. 84 et seq.; Ghezzi and Rigotti (2005), p. 249 et seq.; Montalenti (2002), p. 830; Montalenti (2005), p. 300; Ambrosini (2003b), p. 329.

[986]See Sects. 4.2.1.5 and 4.2.2.4.

[987]For further details, see Sects. 4.2.1.5 and 4.2.2.4. Also consider Sec. 51 para. 1 and 2 SEG.

[988]See Greda (2014), p. 852. For the SE, see Manz (2010f), p. 553.

this context, para. 5 of Art. 2381 CC states that the delegated bodies have the duty to ensure that the organisational, administrative and accounting structures are adequate to the nature and size of the company. They also have a duty to inform the administrative organ and the management control committee[989] about many topics: the general trend of management, its expected development and transactions of major significance. The criteria for this last point are based on the size and character of the company and its subsidiaries. In any case, the delegated bodies have to report at least every 6 months, although a more regular reporting frequency can be established by the statutes.

The *Austrian legal system* contains references to committees, which can help to better organise the tasks of the administrative organ. The first legal reference is found in Sec. 24 para. 1 SCEG, which makes the provisions for the management and supervisory organs applicable. Under Austrian law, it is possible to determine specific tasks that need to be fulfilled by the individual members of the management organ. Such a determination occurs with statutes or a decision taken by the general meeting. Therefore, it should be possible to constitute committees.[990] Provisions regarding the supervisory organ are Sec. 24c para. 5 *GenG* and Sec. 24 para. 4 SCEG.[991] The correct approach depends on whether the administrative organ is structured as an administrative organ that monitors directors responsible for the day-to-day business or as an administrative organ that fulfils both supervisory and management tasks. In this latter case, it seems useful to establish a committee with supervisory function within the organ.[992]

This sub-chapter analysed the internal organisation of the administrative organ of an *agricultural SCE* and addressed three key topics: chairmanship, decision making and committees. Most provisions that concern chairmanship (the election of the chairman, the calling of meetings, the topics on the agenda) are in the SCE-R; other aspects must necessarily be taken from national law. The SCE-R states that meetings must be held a minimum of every 3 months; this period can be shortened via statute. A 3-month interval could be significant if a managing director has been appointed and non-managing members are supervising him. Next, the SCE-R determines specific subjects that must be discussed during meetings. The first is the progress of the SCE and its foreseeable development. This obligates members to inform themselves about the progress and development of the business. These information duties are further fostered by Art. 43 para. 2 SCE-R.

---

[989]The provision refers to the statutory board of auditors, which it is argued can also be interpreted as the management control committee. See Riolfo (2010), p. 76 fn 143.

[990]See Strommer (2014d), p. 218. Also consider Keinert (1988), p. 174 et seq.; Nowotny (2008a), nt 5/107; Kastner (1986), p. 186 et seq.

[991]Also consider Sec. 51 para. 3 and 3bis SEG, Kalss (2008), nt 3/1094.

[992]According to German law (Sec. 19 para. 4 SCEAG), the administrative organ may appoint an audit committee formed of non-managing members of the administrative organ. This audit committee supervises the financial reporting process and the effectiveness of the internal control, risk management and auditing systems. Also consider Schöpflin (2018i), p. 1307 et seq.

The Austrian and Italian legal systems similarly determine that the chairman's role is *primus inter pares*. Then, the Italian legal system also refers to independent members, determining that one of them can become chairman on the condition that he or she does not undertake managerial tasks. Similarly, the Austrian SCEG contains provisions stating that an individual cannot simultaneously hold the roles of chairman and managing director.

The SCE-R determines chairman's duty to call meetings. The details are determined by statute. The Italian legal system also contains provisions regarding the chairman and his duty to call meetings of the management control committee.[993]

The SCE-R determines the basic provisions of decision making. If the internal rules determined by Art. 58 para. 1 SCE-R are not amended, further details can be integrated according to national law.[994]

Finally, we discussed committees, concluding that both legal systems allow the constitution of specific committees.

Thus, Italian and Austrian provisions on the internal organisation of an *agricultural SCE* contain sufficient flexibility for adapting the SCE concerned to the actual situation. This applies to specific decisions that require qualified majorities, for example, decisions that influence the quality of production and thus the production methods of the members of an *agricultural SCE*. Since the administrative organ also performs supervisory functions, the various rules need to provide sufficient flexibility to ensure a well-functioning supervisory process. Agricultural cooperatives can vary in scope, size and hierarchy (consider, for example, an agricultural SCE as a secondary cooperative). If the *agricultural SCE* operates as a PO, the organisation of the administrative organ's various tasks must account for the PO's increased competence as compared to an agricultural cooperative: this is not only a question of the personal requirements to be met by the individual members of the administrative organ, but also a question of the appropriate distribution of tasks and, consequently, the appropriate definition of the processes for obtaining information, which reflect the role of the PO within an internationalised food production chain.

4.3.5 Civil Liability

As already discussed in the context of the management and supervisory organs, Art. 51 SCE-R deals with civil liability. It also applies to the members of the administrative organ. Civil liability is determined according to national law, including Italian and Austrian law. The relevant norms are basically the same as those governing the management and supervisory organs. Therefore, I only offer a brief analysis.[995]

---

[993]In this context, discussions defining the committee as independent organ were briefly mentioned.

[994]For further details, one may consider the analyses of the management and supervisory organs.

[995]For further details, please refer to the chapters on the liability of the management and supervisory organs. See Sects. 4.2.1.6 and 4.2.2.5. See also Mancuso (2017).

In the *Italian legal system*, there seem to be no problems in interpreting the responsibilities of the members of the administrative organ, as the general provisions have to be applied.[996] This implies that the members must fulfil their duties with the diligence required by the nature of their office and by their specified tasks and duties (which are determined by law or statute).[997] Diligence is determined according to Art. 1176 para. 2 CC, and the standard for diligence is primarily based on gross negligence. Members are jointly liable with the other members of the administrative organ, so they are liable for damages if monitoring is not performed and actions are not taken on an informed basis.[998] The same is true for independent members, as they are still members of the organ even though they have to fulfil independence requirements.[999]

An action of liability is governed by Art. 2393 CC, Art. 2393 bis CC, Art. 2394 CC, Art. 2394 bis CC and Art. 2395 CC.[1000] The traditional corporate governance system provides the option for the board of statutory auditors to bring liability actions against the members of the administrative organ; the power to challenge the resolutions taken by the organ is attributed, in the case of the one-tier system, to the management control committee.[1001]

Austrian law addresses civil liability differently from the German legislature.[1002] The Austrian legislature did not provide an explicit provision referring to the responsibilities and obligations that the members of the administrative organ in the one-tier system must exercise with due care. The starting point of this brief analysis is thus Sec. 24 paras 1 and 2 SCEG, which explicitly connect the duties and rights of the members of the administrative organ to those determined by the *GenG* for the management and supervisory organs. Given that both link the liability of the organs members and the applicable standard of care with the tasks actually performed, the duties and tasks that a member of an administrative organ actually fulfils must first be considered. Then either Sec. 23 *GenG* or Sec. 24 para. 7 *GenG* applies.[1003]

---

[996] In this context, Art. 2409 noviesdecies para. 1 CC refers to Art. 2392 CC (liability to the company), Art. 2393 CC (corporate action for liability), Art. 2393 bis CC (company action for liability by shareholders), Art. 2394 CC (liability to company creditors), Art. 2394 bis CC (liability actions within settlement proceedings) and Art. 2395 CC (individual action by a shareholder and third party). In the same way, Art. 2390 CC (prohibition on competition) and Art. 2391 CC (interests of the directors) are applicable.

[997] See Art. 2392 CC.

[998] See Sect. 4.2.1.6.

[999] See Riolfo (2010), p. 80 et seq. See also Mirone (2017a), pp. 580 and 576.

[1000] See Sect. 4.2.1.6.

[1001] See Riolfo (2010), p. 79 et seq.

[1002] By introducing Sec. 21 into the SCEAG, the German legislator provides an explicit link to Sec. 34 of the German GenG. This latter paragraph determines the obligations of due care and the responsibilities of the members of the management organ.

[1003] If an SCE has its registered office in Austria, the applicable norms are Sec. 23 of the GenG for members of the management organ and Sec. 24 para. 7 GenG for members of the supervisory organ. Also consider Sec. 55 SEG, which explicitly links the duty of care and responsibility of the members of the administrative organ of an Austrian SE to Sec. 84 AktG (Duty of care and responsibility of the members of the management organ) and Sec. 99 AktG (Duty of care and responsibility of the members of the supervisory organ). See Kalss (2008), nt3/1099.

Thus, these analyses show that the tasks to be fulfilled influence how civil liability in Austrian law is governed. Either Sec. 23 *GenG* or Sec. 24 para. 7 *GenG* apply, depending on whether the member fulfils a management or a supervisory role. Italian law also contains specific provisions.[1004] Both legal systems consider the specific tasks and duties to be undertaken when determining liability.[1005] Yet, while the Italian legal system requires gross negligence to trigger liability, Austrian law only requires slight negligence. Thus, a distinction is made between the scale of liability between a farmer who is a member of an *agricultural cooperative* and works there on a honorary basis, whereas, in Italy, a similar farmer must have professional management experience in order to qualify for his position. However, the appointment of non-members can compensate for any shortfalls because of insufficient professionalisation.

4.3.6 The One-Tier System from an Economic Perspective

Many provisions that must be considered when adopting the one-tier system are similar, if not identical, to those an Austrian or Italian agricultural SCE must observe if they adopt the two-tier system. The central economic question focuses on the interplay between management tasks and supervisory tasks. Hence, an economic evaluation of these provisions might revisit the economic observations made about the two-tier system. In general, the options to monitor and discipline are similar: hence, the strategies and instruments to increase efficiency are applicable to the same extent.[1006] Yet, it is necessary and helpful to add the following remarks.

Under the one-tier model defined by the SCE-R, all members are responsible for management. This is also true when specific tasks are delegated to one or more members; still, the overall responsibility belongs to the whole organ. They must all participate in meetings. Thus, the chairman's efforts to prepare for the meeting may be crucial to putting responsibility into practice. It is also important that the chairman be independent, as this makes him better able to understand what information is needed.[1007]

The independence of certain members of the administrative organ is particularly important here (and this observation also applies to the overall approach to the one-tier system), as it is intended to separate supervisory and management tasks. It is the general criterion for making the decision-making process more efficient, which

---

[1004]See Art. 2392 CC following.

[1005]For further information, also refer to the chapters on liability of the management and supervisory organs.

[1006]See Sect. 4.2.3.

For general observations see Kräkel (2012), p. 295 et seq. Also consider Leyens (2007b), p. 21. For specific observations regarding the Italian model, see Bianchi (2016), p. 28 et seq.

[1007]See Leyens (2006), pp. 426 et seq. and 42. Also consider Kräkel (2012), p. 298.

decreases agency costs. In addition, the authorisation procedure, as determined by the SCE-R, shall be regarded as a decision-making strategy that ensures the proper decision making of managers who, under delegated management, control the SCE's assets.[1008] The targeted use of authorisation rights provides a mechanism for resolving or mitigating conflicts of interest rather than preventing profitable transactions.

As seen, both legal systems require a separation between management and supervisory tasks.[1009] Even though the Italian legal system better articulates the important role of independent directors, in practice, there should be no significant difference in Austrian law, as determined by Sec. 24 para. 1 and para. 2 and Sec. 25 para. 1 SCEG. These provisions clearly separate monitoring tasks from managerial functions.[1010] The most important prerequisite for the successful implementation of this approach is the timely provision of targeted and meaningfully comprehensive information. The separation of the management and supervisory tasks enables monitoring, on the one hand, but leads to an information problem, on the other. Governance strategies and instruments (such as constraints, rewards, veto and trusteeship) can only be properly implemented if the non-executive supervising members have adequate information. In this context, Article 43 para. 2 SCE-R is essential, because it provides that any member of an organ may examine all information submitted to the administrative organ.

From a legal point of view, the assignment of tasks is similar but not identical. Austrian agricultural SCEs must differentiate between management tasks and supervisory tasks as determined for an Austrian cooperative, while Italian law requires two things: first, that the administrative organ is formed of independent members, and second, that a committee must be established within the administrative organ to supervise the managers. The committee basically fulfils the same functions as the board of statutory auditors (from the traditional corporate governance system). Other independent members who are not members of this committee must also fulfil supervisory tasks. Overall, when compared with the Austrian solution, the assignment of tasks is similar, even though they have to be structured differently. One particular difference is that Austrian law is more flexible about member numbers, while Italian law requires the administrative organ to have at least four members, which clearly increases monitoring costs. Moreover, the Austrian legal system allows the current management task to be delegated to a managing director, making the overall approach more flexible; this, too, helps with designing an efficient structure.

As information that is independent of the management is especially important when supervisory tasks have to be fulfilled, the members must cooperate with

[1008]See also Sect. 4.2.3.

[1009]See Leyens (2006), p. 20 et seq.; Armour et al. (2009c), p. 13. Also consider Hopt and Leyens (2004), p. 160 et seq.; Kräkel (2012), p. 137 et seq.; Marchetti (2007), p. 311 et seq. Generally Tirole (1986) and Strausz (1997). Mallin, Melis and Gaia discuss the effect of remuneration on independent directors. See Mallin et al. (2015).

[1010]These provisions clearly separate monitoring tasks from managerial functions.

external auditors and internal auditing.[1011] Both legal systems provide options for obtaining external advice in the provisions for the board of statutory auditors and the supervisory organ. Specific rules also consider cooperation with external auditors.

The ultimate aim is to find the right mix of applicable strategies and methods to reduce the principal agent conflict: both legal systems offer specific instruments and flexibility with which to define functioning governance structures. Empirical evidence suggests that agricultural cooperatives with a more heterogeneous membership base tend to move from the traditional corporate governance structure—which is significantly based on the interests of a specific group of members—to governance structures that account for the interests of non-user members. These conflicting interests raise important questions about cooperative identity and efficiency. These and other issues will be addressed in the next chapter.

4.4 The General Meeting

According to Art. 36 SCE-R, every SCE must have a general meeting. Its competence, functions, composition and rights to information are regulated by Sect. 4, Chapt. III SCE-R.[1012] It also contains provisions for sectoral or section meetings,[1013] which can precede the general meeting and help organise the cooperative democratic decision-making process, if provided for by the relevant national law. This can be useful, especially in big cooperatives.[1014] Yet, this study does not specifically address the issue[1015]; however, both legal systems allow the establishment of such assemblies in an agricultural SCE.[1016]

[1011] See Leyens (2006), pp. 45 and 429. Also consider Kräkel (2012), p. 297 et seq.

[1012] Arts 52–62 SCE-R.

[1013] Art. 63 SCE-R.

[1014] See Schulze (2004a), p. 113; Schöpflin (2018ak), p. 1330 et seq. Also consider Lutter et al. (2012), p. 1620.

[1015] Every member is entitled to attend the general meeting, to speak and vote on the points included in the agenda (Art. 58 para. 1 SCE-R). The general meeting is based on the assumption that the members attending the meeting want to participate in the process of cooperative decision making. However, if an SCE conducts different activities, operates in more than one territory, has many establishments or a high number of members, trying to make decisions in a single place can be cumbersome. In such situations, an organisation model with different stages and based on representation rather than direct democracy may help. See Schulze (2004a), p. 120. Also consider Holthaus and Lehnhoff (2016c), p. 50. If the relevant national law provides for it, the SCE-R allows sectoral or section meetings as offshoots of the general meeting. This must be established explicitly by the statutes. Similarly, only the general meeting may abolish the sectoral or section meetings. The statutes cannot allow simultaneous sectoral or section meetings, as their contents overlap. See Schöpflin (2018ak), p. 1330 et seq.

[1016] In this sense, see also Sec. 2.4 para. 4 PECOL. Both the Austrian and Italian legal systems contain specific provisions in this regard. By adopting Sec. 29 SCEG, the Austrian legislator directly provides for the possibility to hold sectoral or section meetings. The Italian concept of separate meetings is stricter than that proposed by the SCE-R, which ultimately must be adopted by Italian SCEs. See Art. 2540 CC.

Art. 53 SCE-R is essential to the organisation of the general meeting, as it contains a special general reference to national law about the conduct of the general meeting. Consequently, this reference takes priority over the general one in Art. 8 para. 1 letter c SCE-R.[1017] According to Art. 53 SCE-R, the organisation and conduct of the general meeting and its procedures are governed by national law,[1018] albeit in a subsidiary fashion. This can be concluded from the phrase 'without prejudice in the rules laid down' in Sect. 4.[1019] In addition, Art. 52 SCE-R defines its own hierarchy of competence norms by also referring to national law.

We will address three key topics. First, the competence of the general meeting as assigned to Italian and Austrian SCEs. Next, the organisation and conduct of the general meeting. Finally, the decision-making process As always, the final section adds the economic evaluation.

4.4.1 Competence

The general meeting is the highest decision-making organ of the SCE. It decides on items related to the cooperative's economic basis or existence.[1020] Art. 8 SCE-R and Art. 52 SCE-R are similar[1021]; the latter provision contains a conflict rule defining a hierarchy of provisions that help determine the competence of the general meeting. This includes four levels[1022]: (1) competence according to the SCE-R,[1023] (2) competence according to national legislation implementing directive 2003/72/EC,[1024] (3) national provisions that define competence,[1025] and (4) statutory provisions, if they align with national law.[1026] The competence of the general meeting is thus harmonized at the highest level, where they are explicitly determined by the SCE-R.

[1017]For the SE, see Mayer (2010b), p. 658.

[1018]Which is applicable to cooperatives in the member state where the SCE's registered office is situated.

[1019]For the SE, see Mayer (2010b), p. 658. Also consider Schöpflin (2018ab), p. 1318.

[1020]Basic decisions about the development of the SCE are determined by statutory amendments, which fall under the competence of the general meeting. See Schöpflin (2018aa), p. 1317. Also consider Schulze (2004a), p. 113 et seq. For the SE, see Mayer (2010a), p. 649.

[1021]It states: "The general meeting shall decide on matters for which it is given sole responsibility by: (a) this Regulation; or (b) the legislation of the Member State in which the SCE's registered office is situated, adopted under Directive 2003/72/EC. Furthermore, the general meeting shall decide on matters for which responsibility is given to the general meeting of a cooperative governed by the law of the Member State in which the SCE's registered office is situated, either by the law of that Member State or by the SCE's statutes in accordance with that law."

[1022]See Lutter et al. (2012), p. 1617 et seq. For the SE, see Spindler (2015a), p. 778.

[1023]Art. 52 letter a SCE-R.

[1024]Art. 52 letter b SCE-R.

[1025]Art. 52 subpara. 2 SCE-R.

[1026]Art. 52 subpara. 2 SCE-R.

The daily management of the SCE is the sole responsibility of the management organ or administrative organ.[1027] The general meeting can restrict their management competence via statutory provisions, particularly by mandating that specific transactions be authorised by the general meeting,[1028] but the general meeting may not be assigned the authority to issue such directives, which influences the management's competence of these organs beyond the limits determined by Art. 48 SCE-R. This authority would counteract the principle of responsibility expressed in Art. 37 and Art. 42 SCE-R.[1029]

But on which matters can the general meeting decide? With the exception of the second level (as neither the Austrian nor Italian legislature determined specific competence in this context),[1030] the SCE-R's references require the general meeting of either an Italian or Austrian SCE to be responsible for[1031]: (1) determining capital,[1032] (2) increasing capital,[1033] (3) changing the nominal value of shares,[1034] (4) transferring the registered office,[1035] (5) approving the terms of a merger,[1036] (6) approving the draft terms of conversion into an SCE,[1037] (7) appointing and removing members of the supervisory and administrative organs,[1038] (8) amending the statutes,[1039] (9) approving the annual accounts and allocation of profits,[1040] (10) converting the SCE into a cooperative,[1041] (11) considering appeals from candidates who are refused membership,[1042] and (12) handling appeals against the decisions to expel a member of the SCE.[1043]

Then, other competence either can be assigned to the general meeting or are already assigned to the general meeting but can be delegated to other organs: (1) appointing and removing members of the management organ,[1044] (2) appointing

1027 See Art. 37 para. 1 sent. 1 and Art. 42 para. 1 sent. 1 SCE-R.

1028 See Art. 48 para. 1 SCE-R.

1029 See Schöpflin (2018aa), p. 1317 et seq. For the SE, see Mayer (2010a), p. 649.

1030 On this issue, see Marhold (2008) and Ales (2008).

1031 It is discussed whether winding up, liquidation and similar procedures (see Art. 72 SCE-R) are explicit competences of the general meeting. In favour Schulze (2004a), p. 113; Schöpflin (2018aa), p. 1357. For the SE, see Spindler (2015a), p. 788. Other opinion, and more convincing, see Schröder (2010a), p. 752.

1032 Art. 4 para. 8 SCE-R.

1033 Art. 4 para. 8 subpara. 2 SCE-R.

1034 Art. 4 para. 9 and para. 10 SCE-R.

1035 Art. 7 para. 4 SCE-R.

1036 Art. 27 SCE-R.

1037 Art. 35 para. 6 SCE-R.

1038 See Art. 39 para. 2 SCE-R and Art. 42 para. 3 SCE-R.

1039 Art. 61 para. 4 SCE-R.

1040 Art. 54 para. 3 SCE-R and Art. 67 para. 2 SCE-R. Also consider Cusa (2004a), p. 149 et seq.

1041 Art. 76 para. 6 SCE-R.

1042 Art. 14 para. 1 SCE-R.

1043 Art. 15 para. 3 SCE-R.

1044 Art. 37 para. 2 subpara. 2 SCE-R, if a member State has adopted a specific provision.

alternates to the members of the administrative organ,[1045] (3) agreeing to the transfer of shares,[1046] and (4) admitting non-user members.[1047]

Further competence can be found in the provisions of the SCE-R, which allows specific issues to be determined by statutory provisions, and hence, by the general meeting.[1048]

Last, the general meeting may decide on matters that national law allocates to national cooperatives or that can be determined via statutory provisions.[1049]

[1045] Art. 42 para. 3 SCE-R, if the statutes provide so.

[1046] Art. 4 para. 11 SCE-R; this competence can be delegated to other organs.

[1047] Art. 14 para. 1 subpara. 2 SCE-R; this competence can be delegated to other organs.

[1048] The following list refers to aspects which can be determined by statute, as specified in provisions of the SCE-R: Liability: Art. 1 para. 2 subpara. 3 SCE-R; non-member business: Art. 1 para. 4 SCE-R; minimum capital if members leave the SCE: Art. 3 para. 4 SCE-R; class of shares: Art. 4 para. 1 subpara. 2 SCE-R; nominal value of shares: Art. 4 para. 3 sent. 3 SCE-R; the period within which shares issued for cash must be paid in: Art. 4 para. 4 SCE-R; minimum numbers of shares: Art. 4 para. 7 SCE-R; non-user members: Art. 14 para. 1 subpara. 2 sent. 1 SCE-R; types of members: Art. 14 para. 1 subpara. 4 SCE-R; conditions for acquiring membership: Art. 14 para. 2 SCE-R; applications for a supplementary stake in capital: Art. 14 para. 3 SCE-R; loss of membership: Art. 15 para. 1 bullets 3 and 7 SCE-R; procedures and conditions for exercising the right to resign, repayment: Art. 16 para. 3 SCE-R; structure of the organs: Art. 36 para. 1 letter b SCE-R; number of members of the management organ or rules for determining this: Art. 37 para. 4 sent. 1 SCE-R; election of the chairman of the management organ: Art. 38 para. 1 SCE-R; calling meetings of the management organ: Art. 38 para. 2 SCE-R; appointing the first members of the supervisory organ: Art. 39 para. 2 sent. 2 SCE-R; number of members of the supervisory organ or rules for determining this: Art. 39 para. 4 sent. 1 SCE-R; number of members of the administrative organ or rules for determining this and its composition: Art. 42 para. 2 sent. 1 SCE-R; alternate members of the members of the administrative organ: Art. 42 para. 3 sent. 1 SCE-R; appointment of the first members of the administrative organ: Art. 42 para. 3 sent. 1 SCE-R; frequency with which the administrative organ must meet: Art. 43 para. 1 SCE-R; calling of the meetings of the administrative organ: Art. 44 para. 2 SCE-R; term of office: Art. 45 para. 1 SCE-R; reappointing members of the organs: Art. 45 para. 2 SCE-R; companies as members of the organs: Art. 46 para. 1 subpara. 1 SCE-R; special conditions of eligibility for members representing the administrative organ: Art. 46 para. 3 SCE-R; non-collective representation: Art. 47 para. 1 SCE-R; power to represent the SCE conferred on a single or several persons: Art. 47 para. 4 sent. 1 SCE-R; operations requiring authorisation: Art. 48 paras 1 and 3 SCE-R; Conduct of the business of organs: Art. 50 para. 1 sent. 1 SCE-R; casting vote assigned to the chairman of each organ: Art. 50 para. 2 sent. 1 SCE-R; competences of the general meeting: Art. 52 subpara. 2 SCE-R; meetings called by a minority of members: Art. 55 para. 1 sent. 2 SCE-R; notice of meeting: Art. 56 para. 1 sent. 1 SCE-R; additions to the agenda: Art. 57 sent. 2 SCE-R; attending the general meeting: Art. 58 para. 2 SCE-R; proxies: Art. 58 para. 3 SCE-R; postal or electronic voting: Art. 58 para. 4 SCE-R; plural voting: Art. 59 para. 2 and para. 3 SCE-R; participation of employee representatives: Art. 59 para. 4 sent. 1 SCE-R; quorum and majorities when amending statutes: Art. 61 para. 3 SCE-R; sectoral or section meetings: Art. 63 para. 1 SCE-R; issue of shares conferring special advantage: Art. 64 SCE-R; allocation of profits: Art. 65 para. 1 and Art. 67 para. 2 SCE-R; legal reserves: Art. 65 para. 2 SCE-R; patronage refunds: Art. 66 SCE-R; prohibition of distributing available surplus: Art. 67 para. 3 SCE-R; distribution of net assets: Art. 75 para. 1 sent. 1 SCE-R.

[1049] Subpara 2 thus repeats what has already been determined by Art. 8 para. 1 letter c SCE-R. See Schöpflin (2018aa), p. 1318. For the SE, see Spindler (2015a), p. 788.

According to Art. 52 subpara. 2 SCE-R, this expressly relates to decisions; the aim of this provision suggests that this allocation of competence should also apply to consulting and other similar activities of the general meeting.[1050] However, national law can only determine competence if no SCE-R provision has done so.[1051] National provisions, in this sense, can refer to unwritten competence or judge-made law.[1052]

Both the SCE-R's provisions and the national provisions must be observed. To begin with, I focus on an *Italian SCE*.[1053] To get a complete picture, it is therefore necessary to consider other provisions in the CC.[1054] Italian law allows the general meeting to be organised in its ordinary and extraordinary forms while constituting the same organ. The different meaning implies that different provisions apply to competence, the quorum and keeping minutes.[1055]

Due to the general reference in Art. 2519 CC, three general provisions must be observed. First, for ordinary meetings, Art. 2364 CC[1056] provides rules for the one-tier system, while (second) Art. 2364 bis CC[1057] does so for the two-tier system. Third, for extraordinary meetings, both the one- and two-tier systems must observe Art. 2365 CC.[1058] Art. 2364 CC and 2364 bis CC contain a non-exhaustive list of tasks. According to these provisions, the general meeting exclusively decides on those matters defined by law.

In addition to the competence determined by the SCE-R, the general meeting of an Italian SCE that adopts the one-tier system must also[1059]: (1) decide on the

[1050]See Schulze (2004a), p. 114.

[1051]For the SE, see Mayer (2010a), p. 651.

[1052]See Schöpflin (2018aa), p. 1358. For the SE, see Mayer (2010a), p. 651. Also consider Mahi (2004), p. 94.

[1053]The relevant chapter of the CC only has four provisions specifically dealing with cooperatives' general meetings. Art. 2538 CC contains rules referring to voting rights, quorums and voting by correspondence. Art. 2539 CC contains provisions regarding proxy voting. Art. 2540 CC deals with separated meetings. Finally, Art. 2541 CC contains provisions regarding special meetings of holders of financial instruments.

[1054]See Paolucci (2012), p. 129; Di Cecco (2003), p. 115.

[1055]See Bonfante (2014a), p. 302. See also Mirone (2017b), p. 400.

[1056]Ordinary shareholders meeting of companies without a supervisory organ.

[1057]Ordinary shareholders meeting of companies with a supervisory organ.

[1058]Extraordinary shareholders meeting.

[1059]Art. 2364 CC also determines that the general meeting approves the financial statements and appoints and dismisses the members of the administrative organ, appoints the statutory auditors and the chairman of the board of statutory auditors and, where foreseen, the persons entrusted with the statutory accounting audit (Art. 2409 bis CC). It has been criticised that adopting one of the alternative governance systems could weaken the general meeting. For instance, the general meeting might be relieved from approving the report on the criteria adopted by the management to fulfil the mutual propose. This would run contrary to the need to verify an essential item stemming from the social contract, something which should be verified by the members. Hence, it is argued that a systematic interpretation of the norms requires defining the general meeting as the competent organ to approve the balance sheet. This is necessary to safeguard the particular features of the cooperative system. See Giorgi (2018b), p. 3243. However, the wording, along with the implementation of the two-tier system into the Italian legal system, ultimately seems to exclude the possibility of assigning this competence to the general meeting. See Giorgi (2018b), p. 3243.

liability of the members of the administrative organ, (2) decide on other matters assigned by law to the general meeting, and (3) approve, where applicable, the regulations for the meeting agenda.

For an Italian SCE adopting the two-tier system, Art. 2364 bis CC adds the following tasks[1060]: (1) deciding on the liability of the members of the supervisory organ and (2) entrusting persons with the statutory accounting audit.[1061] Even though Art. 2364 bis CC does not refer to competence generally assigned by law, it is assumed that this provision is valid under the two-tier system.[1062]

Art. 2365 CC states that the extraordinary shareholders meeting decides on amendments to the statutes,[1063] the appointment, replacement and powers of liquidators[1064] and other matters expressly granted to it by law.[1065] If the extraordinary general meeting exceeds its competence, the relevant decisions are void.[1066]

These provisions collectively comprise the starting point for defining the competence of the general meeting; however, the particular features of a cooperative require significant amendments. There are provisions that particularly apply to Italian SCEs[1067]; for example, the competence to approve the regulation of the relationship between the cooperative and its members is based on a proposal made by the management or administrative organ.[1068] There is also the right to inspect the company's registers (Art. 2422 CC or Art. 2545 bis CC), according to which 10% of members (or 5% for cooperatives with over 3000 members) have the right to examine the register of the meeting and the resolutions of the administrative or management organ.[1069] The members may be assisted by a professional. Art. 2545 bis CC enhances the general meeting's function as the sovereign of the cooperative; however, this sovereignty is illusory, given the absolute determination of the competence, which excludes any interference with the management's competence of the

[1060]Art. 2364 bis CC also determines that the general meeting appoints and revokes the members of the supervisory organ, fixes the remuneration due to them, unless this is set out in the statutes, and decides on the distribution of profits.

[1061]See Art. 2409 bis CC.

[1062]See Cian (2018a), p. 2776; Petrazzini (2004), p. 481. See also Romano (2017a).

[1063]Regulated by Art. 61 para. 4 SCE-R.

[1064]See Art. 72 SCE-R.

[1065]Also consider Art. 52 subpara. 2 SCE-R.

[1066]See Bonfante (2014a), p. 302. See also Mirone (2017b), p. 404 et seq.

[1067]Whereas other specific competences are explicitly regulated by the SCE-R. e.g., Art. 2433 CC (distribution of profits) and, referring to cooperatives, also Art. 2545 sexies CC, dealing with patronage refunds. Next, according to Art. 2528 para. 4 CC, candidates refused membership can appeal to the general meeting.

[1068]Art. 2521 last para. CC. According to para. 1 Art. 2544 CC, the decision implementing this regulation falls under the competence of the members of the administrative or management organs.

[1069]Even though Art. 2545 bis CC does not explicitly mention the management organ, it should also apply if the two-tier system is adopted.

management (or administrative) organ. This clearly cannot be changed, as a different approach would impede entrepreneurial efficiency.[1070]

In addition to these mandatory activities, the general meeting of an Italian SCE may also define the remuneration for the members of the supervisory organ[1071] and authorise initiatives established by the administrative organ.[1072] This latter rule, however, does not seem to be applicable in the two-tier system.[1073] Finally, Italian law permits the statutes and, as a result, the general meeting to explicitly determine further items. These will be illustrated in this study as necessary.[1074]

Overall, the Italian legal system only allows the exercise of those powers that it permits to be assigned to the general meeting. The law clearly determines the competence of the general meeting, leaving all other powers to the management (and supervisory) or administrative organ.[1075]

The *Austrian legal system* contains specific provisions that must be considered when determining the competence of an Austrian SCE. Accordingly, the general

---

[1070]Worker cooperatives are an exception in this context. See Bonfante (2014a), p. 302 et seq.

[1071]Art. 2364 bis para. 1 no 2 CC. The general meeting of an Italian cooperative may also determine remuneration for the members of the management organ.

[1072]Without prejudice to the liability for their actions and deeds. See Bonfante (2014a), p. 302; This provision has to be read in conjunction with Art. 48 SCE-R.

[1073]See Mirone (2017a), p. 570.

[1074]The following list is not exhaustive and refers to an Italian cooperative, but also applies to an Italian SCE if it does not contradict Art. 52 SCE-R: requirements of mainly mutual cooperatives (Art. 2514 CC), object of the cooperative (Art. 2521 CC), the subscribed capital of each member and the nominal value of the shares, the paid in capital (Art. 2521 CC), the requirements and conditions for the admission of members (Art. 2521 CC), the conditions for resignation and expulsion of members (Art. 2521 CC), rules on the distribution of surplus and criteria for distributing patronage refunds (Art. 2521 CC), the governance structure of the cooperative (Art. 2521 CC), the power of representation of the members of the administrative or management organs (Art. 2521 CC), regulation regarding mutual activity (Art. 2521 CC), increasing capital (Art. 2524 CC), excluding or limiting the option right (Art. 2524 CC), the maximum number of shares, if certain conditions are met (Art. 2525 CC), the issue of financial instruments (Art. 2526 CC), the requirements for admitting new members (Art. 2527 CC), the acquisition of individual shares (Art. 2529 CC), prohibiting the sale of shares (Art. 2532 CC), resignation of members (Art. 2532 CC), expulsion of members (Art. 2533 CC), the possibility that heirs might become members of a cooperative (Art. 2534 CC), liquidating shares (Art. 2535 CC), voting rights linked to financial instruments offered to user members (Art. 2538 CC), voting rights assigned to legal persons (Art. 2538 CC), voting rights in case of Art. 2538 para. 4 CC, quorum and majorities for general meetings (Art. 2538 para. 5 CC), voting systems by means of telecommunication devices (Art. 2538 para. 6 CC), separate assemblies (Art. 2540 CC), composition of the administrative organ (Art. 2542 paragraph 4 CC), voting rights regarding the controlling organ (Art. 2543 para. 2 CC), composition of the controlling organ (Art. 2543 CC), indivisible reserves (Art. 2545ter CC), distribution of surplus (Art. 2545 quater CC), distribution of dividends to user members (Art. 2545 quinquies CC), distribution of divisible reserves (Art. 2545 quinquies CC), distribution of patronage refunds (Art. 2545 sexies CC), amendment of statutes (Art. 2545 novies CC), transformation in capitalistic companies (Art. 2545 decies and Art. 2545 undecies CC), winding up (Art. 2545 duodecies CC).

[1075]As mentioned in Sect. 4.2.1.4, under Italian law the general meeting cannot appoint the members of the management organ. Consider in this context Art. 37 para. 2 subpara. 2 SCE-R.

meeting empowers the members to exercise the rights assigned to them by the *GenG* and the statutes. Thus, the following competence can be added to those powers set out in Art. 52 letter a SCE-R[1076]: (1) deciding on reports from the management organ,[1077] (2) deciding on lawsuits against members of the other organs,[1078] (3) appointing representatives to lawsuits against a member of the supervisory organ,[1079] (4) making decisions on the dissolution of the cooperative (free dissolution),[1080] (5) formally approving the actions of the management and supervisory organs (as members of these organs),[1081] and (6) deciding on the audit report.[1082]

Other legal provisions allow the general meeting to exercise other powers, for instance, appointing and removing the members of other organs[1083] (as long as this competence is not assigned to the management or supervisory organs) or appointing and removing liquidators.[1084]

Due to the *Holzmüller* and *Gelatine* judgements adopted by the German Federal Supreme Court (*Bundesgerichshof, BGH*), Austrian scholars started to discuss the question of whether the general meeting might also have unwritten powers.[1085] Even

[1076]Other competencies of the general meeting assigned according to the GenG (or other laws) are specifically regulated by the SCE-R. They include: appointment and removal of the members of the supervisory organ (Sec. 24 GenG), approval of the financial accounts, which are prepared by the management organ and controlled by the supervisory organ (Sec. 27a GenG), decisions on profits and losses (Sec. 27a GenG), decisions on amendments to the statutes (Sec. 33 GenG), decisions on mergers (Sec. 2 GenVG), appointment and removal of members of the management organ, unless the statutes do not provide for this (Sec. 15 GenG). In addition, the statutes can provide to elect the chairman of the supervisory organ by the general meeting Sec. 24 letter c para. 1 GenG.

[1077]Secs 27a and 22 para. 2 GenG. According to Sec. 27a GenG, the general meeting decides on the financial statements, the report by the management organ, deprivation of profits and the formal approval of the actions of the management and supervisory organs, within the first 8 months of each financial year for the previous financial year. In this context, Sec. 22 para. 2 GenG, determines that the management organ must prepare the accounts (financial statements or other statement of accounts, within the first 5 months of each financial year for the past financial year). In addition, the management organ must draw up a report including details about the business development and financial position of the cooperative, changes in the number of members, the cooperative shares and the guaranteed liability allotted thereto and about the amounts already paid in. In addition, the accounts must be submitted to the supervisory organ for audit and, afterwards, for transmission to the general meeting. The report must also address the fulfilment of the cooperative's object. In this context, the supervisory organ does not decide on the accounts, but it does monitor the various documents. See Zehetner (2014d), p. 353.

[1078]Sec. 25 GenG.

[1079]Sec. 25 GenG.

[1080]Sec. 36 GenG.

[1081]Sec. 27a GenG.

[1082]Sec. 6 GenREVG.

[1083]Sec. 19 GenG.

[1084]Sec. 41 GenG.

[1085]See Siebenbäck (2014a), p. 338 et seq. It has been discussed whether a cooperative might have similar unwritten competences as the GmbH. Consider Nowotny (2008b), nt 4/178.

though the Austrian Supreme Court (*Oberster Gerichtshof, OGH*)[1086] has not explicitly decided on this issue, unwritten competence might be assigned, especially where particularly drastic steps must be taken. In such cases, the management cannot decide without a specific decision by the general meeting.[1087] This approach is valid for an Austrian SCE, as it does not contradict Art. 37 para. 1 SCE-R and can be implemented because of Art. 8 para. 1 letter c SCE-R.

Next, the law does not distinguish between ordinary and extraordinary general meetings. However, a general meeting to decide on the financial statements for the previous year that occurs within the first 8 months of each financial year is an ordinary general meeting, with all others being extraordinary.[1088]

To conclude, the Austrian legal system considers the general meeting to be the highest organ of an Austrian cooperative, as illustrated by the fact that it may require any other organ to report on any issue and may issue binding instructions on any issue. Here,[1089] the general meeting of an Austrian SCE lacks such a competence, with respect to either the management organ or the administrative organ.[1090]

These analyses have shown that the powers of the general meeting of an *agricultural SCE* are determined primarily by the SCE-R and secondarily by national law. To distinguish between types of tasks, both legal systems use the terms ‘ordinary’ and ‘extraordinary’ general meeting, albeit in different ways: in Italy, the distinction is based on legal norms, while in Austria, on accepted practice. The competence is generally in line with the PECOL,[1091] with an exception to the role of the general meeting. According to Austrian doctrine, the general meeting of a cooperative may have an unwritten competence[1092] if there is a situation in which drastic steps must be taken. This should also be valid for an Austrian agricultural SCE. The *Holzmüller* doctrine is not recognised by Italian law. Overall, Austrian law seems more flexible than Italian law, and the Austrian approach makes the general meeting the sovereign of the cooperative.[1093] Interestingly, the general meeting of an

---

[1086]See OGH 11.03.1996, 1 Ob 566/95 and OGH 09.10.2014, 6 Ob 77/14p.

[1087]See Siebenbäck (2014a), p. 340. Also consider Keinert and Keinert-Kisin (2013), p. 999.

[1088]See Siebenbäck (2014a), p. 340.

[1089]See Sect. 4.2.1.1.

[1090]Consider in this context Sec. 24 para. 1 SCEG.

[1091]Sec. 2.4 paras 5 and 6 PECOL determine the competence of the general meeting. First, it has the power to appoint and remove the members of the organs. Next, it must have the power to make fundamental decisions, for example about restructuring or dissolving the cooperative. These decisions also include statute amendments, establishing subsidiaries or participating in legal entities or groups. Then, para. 6 list as specific competences the power to acquire information about economic and cooperative performance, along with the activity and results of companies in which the cooperative participates. It also appoints and removes auditors and members of the organs and has all the competences determined by the law or statutes. Also consider Snaith (2017), p. 69.

[1092]This sub-chapter also concluded that, unlike an Austrian cooperative, the general meeting of an Austrian SCE may not give binding instructions on every issue.

[1093]According to Sec. 2.4 para. 3 PECOL, “the powers of the decision-making organs of a cooperative are either (a) fixed by law or cooperative statutes, or (b) can be delegated by the members’ meeting on a basis of revocable delegation.”

Italian cooperative is also considered to be sovereign, but this sovereignty is criticised for being illusory. As a result, the Austrian approach seems to adopt a very extensive interpretation of the ICA principle that calls for basic democracy.[1094]

In this context, Sec. 2.4 para. 1 of the PECOL determines that 'cooperative governance structures must ensure that the members democratically control the cooperative and can actively participate in policy making and major decisions'. This passage distinguishes between a model based on collective decision making and one in which the general meeting controls one or more boards, committees or councils that are responsible for current management. The collective model is thus described as the purest form of member control. However, this model is limited to small cooperatives.[1095] Both legal systems can be subsumed under the second type of model, although the norms that an Austrian SCE must observe also contain an element of the collective model.[1096]

The following duties of an agricultural cooperative could be listed in the statutes: the decision on the appropriation of profits, whether shares will be issued to non-user members (including how many shares) and whether voting rights are associated with these shares (including how many). On the other hand, specific decisions must be made about the members of the various organs (the management and supervisory organs or, alternatively, the administrative organ, external auditor, etc.). In the case of an *agricultural SCE* recognised as a PO, a decision will be taken on adopting rules about production notification, on the production of the products to be delivered, on their marketing and on environmental protection.[1097] Typically, the general meeting of a PO (in the fruit and vegetables sector) also deals with the establishment of an operational fund to be used for the implementation of operational programmes. In particular, operational programmes aimed at improving the quality of member products and promoting product marketing must be approved by the general meeting.

4.4.2 Preparing the General Meeting

The SCE-R contains several provisions about organising and conducting general meetings. These provisions refer to holding the general meeting, calling meetings by a minority of members, providing notice of the meeting, making additions to the agenda, regulating attendance and proxies, voting rights, detailing the right to

[1094] See Sect. 2.1.

[1095] The PECOL add that most laws require a model based on a strict separation of powers, hence the use of boards or committees in addition to the general meeting. See Snaith (2017), p. 60 et seq. See also Pönkä (2018), p. 51 et seq.

[1096] This type is even more visible within Austrian cooperatives, where the general meeting may give binding instructions for every issue.

[1097] See Art. 153 para. 1 letter a Reg. 1308/2013.

information, making decisions and taking minutes. These provisions are supplemented by national law. In fact, Art. 53 SCE-R contains a general remit that governs how to apply the national laws of the state where the SCE has its registered office.[1098] These topics can be included under three headings: the preparatory stage of the general meeting; the conduct of the general meeting and related questions; the structure of the organisational process; and, finally, the decision-making process.

Analysing the provisions for the preparation of the general meeting, one must consider Arts. 54–57 SCE-R, which specifically deals with holding the general meeting. A distinction can be drawn between a regular meeting and one called by a minority of members. Further details must then be determined by the relevant national law, including these issues[1099]: the **frequency of meetings**, entitlement, formalities and minority rights. According to the SCE-R, the general meeting is regularly held at least once per calendar year and within 6 months of the end of the financial year. The relevant national law may allow or require more frequent meetings. Art. 54 para. 1 last sent. SCE-R permits a member state to allow the SCE to hold its first general meeting at any time in the 18 months following its incorporation.[1100] Neither Austria nor Italy have implemented this option.[1101]

The *Italian legal system*'s solution differs from the solution in the SCE-R; however, tax reasons require us to understand the Italian provisions, as well. They require convening a general meeting to approve the financial statements from the previous financial year.[1102] This meeting must be called no later than 120 days prior to the end of the financial year.[1103] The Italian rule thus differs from the SCE-R's, which allows a longer timeframe for convening the general meeting. Despite being less strict, the SCE-R applies here, as Art. 54 para. SCE-R exhaustively regulates this issue. However, this rule must be coordinated with tax law, specifically, Art. 17 of the president of the republic's decree no. 435/2001, which determines that taxes must be paid by the last day of the sixth month after the closure of the financial year. In addition, para. 2 allows this date to be postponed for 30 days; under these

[1098]See Schulze (2004a), p. 115; Schöpflin (2018ab), p. 13518. For the SE, see Mayer (2010b), p. 658; Spindler (2015b), p. 800.

[1099]Art. 53 SCE-R.

[1100]Art. 54 para. 1 SCE-R states: "An SCE shall hold a general meeting at least once each calendar year, within six months of the end of its financial year, unless the law of the Member State in which the SCE's registered office is situated applicable to cooperatives carrying on the same type of activity as the SCE provides for more frequent meetings. A Member State may, however, provide that the first general meeting may be held at any time in the 18 months following an SCE's incorporation." Also consider Schulze (2004a), p. 115; Schöpflin (2018ac), p. 1319. For the SE, see Mayer (2010c), p. 681 et seq.; Spindler (2015c), p. 818 et seq.

[1101]See Fici (2010), p. 64 et seq.

[1102]Arts 2364 para. 2 CC and 2364 bis para. 2 CC.

[1103]If the companies are required to provide consolidated financial statements, the statutes can provide for a longer time limit, although this cannot exceed 180 days. This option can also be exercised if there are special needs related to the structure and purpose of the company. In these cases, the members of the administrative or management organ must indicate the reasons for delay in the report stipulated by Art. 2428 CC (annual management report).

circumstances, the tax cost increases by 0.40%. This latter rules applies, if an Italian agricultural SCE convenes its meeting on the evening of the last day of the sixth month after the closure of the financial year, which is in line with Art. 54 SCE-R.

The *Austrian legal system* contains some peculiarities that must be understood. Differences over the frequency of meetings arise between an Austrian SCE and an Austrian cooperative. According to Sec. 27a *GenG*, the general meeting of an Austrian cooperative must generally decide on the financial statements for the previous financial year within the first 8 months of each year. This provision contradicts the SCE-R, which refers to a shorter period of time.[1104] Thus, Austrian SCEs must abide by this shorter time frame.

An important question is, **who may convene** the meeting. According to the SCE-R, the general meeting can be convened at any time by the management, administrative or supervisory organs[1105] as well as by any other organ of the SCE or competent authority in accordance with national law.[1106] It has been correctly observed that 'at any time' does not require a reason to be given, but simply that it is possible to convene further meetings beyond the regular ones.[1107]

No precise criteria are laid down for determining the reasons that must be given for convening a general meeting; it seems that informing the general meeting about a particular issue could be sufficient.[1108] In addition, the phrasing 'in accordance with the national law applicable to cooperatives' is somewhat ambiguous; it is not clear

[1104]Specific provisions must be considered for cooperative banks, according to which the financial statements must be submitted to the FMA (Finanzmarktaufsicht, financial market authority) and OeNB (Österreichische Nationalbank, Austrian National Bank) at the latest 6 months after the close of the business year. The law states: "Credit institutions and the branches of foreign credit institutions must submit audited annual financial statements, annual reports, consolidated financial statements and consolidated annual reports pursuant to Sec. 59 BWG and Sec. 59a BWG, as well as the audit reports on the financial statements, annual reports, consolidated financial statements and consolidated annual reports pursuant to Sec. 59 BWG and Sec. 59a BWG, including the annex to the audit report on the annual financial statements (prudential report) indicated in Sec. 63 para. 5 BWG, to the FMA and the OeNB at the latest within six months after the close of the business year. In addition, credit institutions must submit the data from annual financial statements and consolidated financial statements pursuant to Sec. 59 BWG and Sec. 59a BWG, including the annex to the audit report on the annual financial statements (prudential report) mentioned in Sec. 63 para. 5 BWG and disclosures regarding hidden reserves, to the FMA and the OeNB electronically and in a standardised format at the latest within six months after the close of the business year." FMA, Federal Banking Act (Sec. 44 para. 1).

[1105]Depending on the governance structure chosen by the SCE.

[1106]Applicable to cooperatives in the member states in which the SCE's registered office is located. Also consider Schulze (2004a), p. 115; Schöpflin (2018ac), p. 1319.

Art 54 para. 2 SCE-R states: "General meetings may be convened at any time by the management organ or the administrative organ, the supervisory organ or any other organ or competent authority in accordance with the national law applicable to cooperatives in the Member State in which the SCE's registered office is situated. The management organ shall be bound to convene a general meeting at the request of the supervisory organ."

[1107]See Schöpflin (2018ac), p. 1319. For the SE, see Mayer (2010c), p. 683; Spindler (2015c), p. 824.

[1108]For the SE, see Mayer (2010c), p. 683 et seq.

whether it refers to the management, administrative and/or supervisory organs. If it did refer to these organs, the legislature would not have introduced this list, as the sense of such a provision could easily be determined by the general reference contained in Art. 53 SCE-R.[1109]

Next, the supervisory organ may require the management organ to convene a general meeting.[1110] In addition, the general meeting has a right to decide during a meeting to convene a further meeting. In this case, the general meeting sets the date and the agenda.[1111] Art. 55 SCE-R grants a specific minority right in this context, which will be addressed at the end of this sub-chapter.

There are some occasions when a general meeting must or can be convened. Art. 54 para. 3 SCE-R[1112] states that the general meeting held after the end of the financial year must cover at least two items: the approval of the annual accounts and the allocation of profits. However, it does not specify which organ must convene this meeting. Hence, it must be determined according to Art. 53 SCE-R.[1113] Other provisions contain further reasons for convening a general meeting.[1114] Further obligations to convene can also result from the applicable national law.[1115]

Apart from some exceptions, the following legal norms apply to an *Italian SCE*. According to Art. 2366 para. 1 CC, the general meeting can only be convened with a decision by the management or administrative organ. This provision applies to an Italian SCE when it convenes a general meeting to approve the annual accounts and decide on the allocation of profits.[1116]

If the general meeting is convened by a single member, this is considered an irregularity, and the decision must be cancelled.[1117] An exception is allowed if a member of the administrative or management organs has been duly authorised.[1118] This seems to apply for Italian SCEs, as it is based on an authorisation of the competent organ.[1119]

[1109]For the SE, see Mayer (2010c), p. 682 et seq. Also consider Spindler (2015c), p. 822.

[1110]See Art. 54 para. 2 last sent. SCE-R. Also consider Schöpflin (2018ac), p. 1319.

[1111]See Art. 54 para. 4 SCE-R. It states: "The general meeting may in the course of a meeting decide that a further meeting be convened and set the date and the agenda." Also consider Schöpflin (2018ac), p. 1320.

[1112]It states: "The agenda for the general meeting held after the end of the financial year shall include at least the approval of the annual accounts and the allocation of profits."

[1113]See Schöpflin (2018ac), p. 1319. For the SE, see Spindler (2015c), p. 821.

[1114]These include those which explicitly require a decision to be made by the general meeting.

[1115]See Lutter et al. (2012), p. 1618 et seq. For the SE, see Mayer (2010c), p. 684.

[1116]See also Paolucci (2019h), p. 144 et seq.

[1117]See Bonfante (2014a), p. 306; Balzano (2004), p. 539.

[1118]See Mirone (2017b), p. 408 et seq. See also Paolucci (2019b), p. 122 et seq. It is unclear whether a properly called meeting may subsequently be called off. It is argued that the competent organ which convened the meeting should also be allowed the corresponding competence to call it o et seq. See Bonfante (2014a), p. 306; Montagnani (2004a), p. 437.

[1119]It should therefore align with Art. 54 para. 2 SCE, which prohibits the general meeting from being convened by a single person.

According to the Italian civil code, the general meeting must be convened by the supervisory organ if the management organ fails to do so or there is an unjustifiable delay. It can also be convened if it encounters censurable or serious events that require urgent action.[1120] This competence cannot be assigned to the management control committee under the one-tier system.[1121] The latter reason for convening the general meeting does not assign the competence in place of the management organ, but instead consists of an order to convene in case of urgency or serious events.[1122] Thus, Italian law is stricter than the provisions contained in the SCE-R, as it links the power to convene to specific grounds and limits the competence of the organs. I stress that these conditions refer to obligations, which implies that the general meeting is obliged to address specific items. This is particularly true for the obligation to convene the general meeting in case of omission or unjustified delay by the management organ. These obligations apply to an Italian SCE because of Art. 52 and Art. 53 SCE-R.[1123]

Furthermore, specific provisions entitle liquidators,[1124] judicial administrators[1125] or tribunals[1126] to convene the general meeting. These provisions are encompassed by Art. 54 para. 2 SCE-R.

The *Austrian legal system* also addresses the issue of who is entitled to convene the general meeting. Yet, not all of the *GenG*'s provisions can be applied by an Austrian SCE. The Austrian legal system follows provisions that are similar to those in the SCE-R, which allows different organs and bodies to call a general meeting,[1127] which meeting can then only be cancelled by the organ that convened it.[1128] The general rule is contained in Sec. 28 *GenG*. Accordingly, the management organ is empowered with the duty to convene the general meeting,[1129] provided this competence is not assigned to other persons by the *GenG* or the statutes.[1130] As seen, the

[1120] Art. 2406 CC.

[1121] With the exception contained in Art. 2367 para. 2 CC. See Cian (2018c), p. 2777. Different opinion Riolfo, see Riolfo (2010), p. 138.

[1122] See Serraino (2010b), p. 80; Benatti (2005), p. 953; Ambrosini (2004), Art. 2406 907.

[1123] It states that "the general meeting shall decide on matters for which responsibility is given to the general meeting of a cooperative governed by the law of the Member State in which the SCE's registered office is situated . . ."

[1124] Art. 2489 CC.

[1125] Art. 2409 CC.

[1126] Art. 2482 para. 2 CC in order to appoint the liquidator, Art. 2367 CC at the request of a minority of members (consider in this context Sect. 4.4.2) and Art. 2409 para. 4 CC (in this context also consider Art. 2545 quinquiesdecies CC).

[1127] As already mentioned, in practice, the ordinary general meeting decides on the financial statements within the first 8 months of each financial year for the previous financial year, whereas a general meeting which decides on other issue is called an extraordinary general meeting. See Siebenbäck (2014a), p. 337 et seq.

[1128] See Siebenbäck (2014b), p. 363.

[1129] As a collegial organ, it must adopt a specific resolution. This latter refers to the convocation and to the agenda of the general meeting.

[1130] See Siebenbäck (2014b), p. 363.

SCE-R regulates the general authorisation to convene a meeting. Therefore, in this regard, Sec. 28 *GenG* does not apply.

Next, Sec. 24e paras. 2 and 5 *GenG* determine the obligations that are imposed on the supervisory organ to convene a meeting. These provisions apply to an Austrian SCE on the basis of Art. 52 subpara. 2 SCE-R and Art. 53 SCE-R.[1131] These obligations have to be considered by the administrative organ on the basis of Sec. 24 para. 2 SCEG.

Then, if specific requirements are met, the competence to convene a general meeting is assigned to the liquidators[1132] and auditors.[1133] The range of persons who may convene a general meeting, according to Art. 54 para. 2 SCE-R, is thus extended.

Next, as Art. 54 para. 2 SCE-R refers to organs, it does not seem possible to entitle single persons to convene a general meeting.[1134] On the other hand, the statutes of national cooperatives may authorise persons to convene the general meeting. For instance, this power could be assigned to the chairman of the administrative or management organs, the representative of the chairman or the chairman of the supervisory organ.[1135]

The SCE-R does not specify which organ must convene the general meeting to approve the annual accounts and allocation of profits. This must be determined according to national law. According to the *GenG*, this competence is assigned, in principle, to the management or administrative organ,[1136] but can also be assigned to other organs if the statutes provide accordingly.

In addition to the grounds for convening the meeting given in the SCE-R, others may be determined according to national law, for example, by statutory provisions.[1137] Sec. 29 *GenG* states that the general meeting must be convened if deemed necessary for the interests of the cooperative. This might arise if specific decisions must be taken by the general meeting, at least, according to the opinion of those convening the meeting. Some examples include motioning to remove some or all the members of an organ or making an important change (for instance, amendments to the statutes, merger or dissolution).[1138]

One addition issue is the **formalities** that must be considered when convening a general meeting. According to the SCE-R, a general meeting can only be convened

[1131]For the SE, see Spindler (2015c), p. 824 et seq.

[1132]Sec. 49 GenG.

[1133]Sec. 7 GenREVG.

[1134]Under the Austrian legal system, if the general meeting is convened by an organ which is not entitled to do so, the general meeting is not effective. See Siebenbäck (2014b), p. 363.

[1135]Despite these possibilities, the statutes cannot completely exclude the competence of the management organ to convene the assembly. For instance, a statutory provision could be admissible according to which the supervisory organ may convene the assembly but if it does not act promptly the competence may be shifted to the management organ. See Siebenbäck (2014b), p. 363.

[1136]Due to Sec. 24 para. 1 SCEG.

[1137]Sec. 29 GenG.

[1138]See Siebenbäck (2014c), p. 365. Also consider Sec. 84 GenG.

after written notice is sent to every person entitled to attend. The statutory provisions can allow every available written means (e.g., fax). It is sufficient to publish this notice in the SCE's official internal publication.[1139] As determined by Art. 56 para. 1 SCE-R,[1140] those entitled to attend the meeting include the members of the SCE, the members of the organs, the holders of securities (according to Art. 64 SCE-R) and all persons permitted under national law.[1141]

The notice calling the meeting must include the following information[1142]: (1) the name and registered office of the SCE, (2) the venue, date and time of the meeting, (3) the type of general meeting (where appropriate) and (4) the agenda, including the subjects to be discussed and the proposals for decisions. The agenda for the regular general meeting held after the end of the financial year must include the approval of the annual accounts and the allocation of profits.[1143]

The SCE-R requires a period of at least 30 days between dispatching the notice and opening the meeting. In urgent cases, this period can be reduced to 15 days. If the statutes have to be amended according to Art. 61 para. 4 SCE-R, the time between the first and second meetings can be reduced if the relevant national law provides accordingly and the agenda is not amended.[1144]

The first two sentences of Art. 56 para. 3 SCE-R refer to the period between dispatching the notice and opening the meeting, whereas sentence 3 refers to the period between the two meetings, which can be shortened if national law provides accordingly. It is unclear how this second period is determined. One can argue that the explicit reference to the second meeting would be superfluous if only national law applied. Moreover, sentence 3 connects the option to reduce the period to national law, but not the period as such. Therefore, it seems necessary to determine this period using the provisions contained in the SCE-R.

[1139]The notice must be written. In fact the wording sent by any available means refers to sent and hence regards the form of transmission. See Schöpflin (2018ae), p. 1321. Also consider Schulze (2004a), p. 116.

[1140]It states: "A general meeting shall be convened by a notice in writing sent by any available means to every person entitled to attend the SCE's general meeting in accordance with Article 58 (1) and (2) and the provisions of the statutes. That notice may be given by publication in the official internal publication of the SCE."

[1141]See Schöpflin (2018ae), p. 1321. Also consider Art. 58 para. 1 and 2 SCE-R.

[1142]Minimum requirement. See Lutter et al. (2012), p. 1619.

Art 56 para. 2 SCE-R. It states: "The notice calling a general meeting shall give at least the following particulars: - the name and registered office of the SCE, - the venue, date and time of the meeting, - where appropriate, the type of general meeting, - the agenda, indicating the subjects to be discussed and the proposals for decisions."

[1143]See Art. 54 para. 3 SCE-R.

[1144]See Art. 56 para. 3 SCE-R. It states: "The period between the date of dispatch of the notice referred to in paragraph 1 and the date of the opening of the general meeting shall be at least 30 days. It may, however, be reduced to 15 days in urgent cases. Where Article 61(4) is applied, relating to quorum requirements, the time between a first and second meeting convened to consider the same agenda may be reduced according to the law of the Member State in which the SCE has its registered office." Also consider Schulze (2004a), p. 116; Schöpflin (2018ae), p. 1321.

One solution could be to use the same period as that between the date of dispatch and the first meeting. If one assumes that the notice is sent the day after the first meeting, the second meeting cannot be held sooner than 30 days later. For Art. 56 para. 3 last sent. SCE-R to apply, the national law must allow a change to the date of dispatch if a second meeting is necessary. In addition, when considering Art. 54 para. 2 SCE in conjunction with Art. 56 para. 2 bullet 2 SCE-R, it seems that the SCE-R not only determines the organs that may convene a general meeting, but also grants discretion over the date of the second meeting, as the organ convening the meeting is empowered to determine this at its own discretion. Therefore, in principle, the convening organ may determine the date of the second meeting at its own discretion. It must, however, observe the required period, as determined by Art. 56 para. 3 sent. 1 SCE-R. This minimum period may be adapted to a reduced period in accordance with Art. 56 para. 3 last sent. of the SCE-R.

The SCE-R does not contain any provisions for situations when the meeting is not duly convoked. As a result, national law has to be applied.[1145] In this context, the *Italian legal system* refers to provisions adopted for cooperatives and, in addition, to provisions adopted for an *spa*. The following analysis discusses these provisions and their implications for an Italian SCE.

According to Art. 2521 para. 1 no. 9 CC, statutes may determine the formalities of convening the general meeting by derogating legal rules. In cases where statutes do not provide accordingly, the legal rules have to be applied.[1146] The legislature thus allows a simplified procedure, as compared to the procedure for an *spa*. With respect to the latter, Art. 2366 para. 2 CC determines a procedure that starts with a notice calling the meeting,[1147] specifying the day, time, place and agenda. This notice must be published in the *Official Journal of the Italian Republic* or at least one daily newspaper. The statutes must indicate the newspaper to be used.

It has been observed that statutes can derogate how (form) the general meeting of an Italian cooperative should be convened and which time periods have to be observed, whereas statutes cannot derogate other details that are determined by law—for example, who may convene or the rules concerning the content of the instrument of notification. Derogation is thus only possible with respect to the specific details of Art. 2366 para. 2 CC. It must be guaranteed that the form used is suitable for informing the members of the convened meeting.[1148] Whereas both methods of publication (as determined by para. 2) can be considered written notice (as determined by Art. 56 para. 1 last sent. SCE-R),[1149] ultimately, neither Italian cooperatives[1150] nor Italian SCEs are required to use these media.[1151]

[1145] See Schöpflin (2018ae), p. 1322.

[1146] See Cusa (2007), p. 301.

[1147] Art. 2366 CC, formalities for calling the meeting.

[1148] See Balzano (2004), p. 534 et seq.; Cusa (2004b), p. 854. Also consider Bassi (1995), p. 246.

[1149] Similarly Schöpflin (2018ae), p. 1321.

[1150] Due to Art. 2521 no 9 CC.

[1151] According to Art. 56 para. 1 convening procedure is determined by statutes. Different opinion Schöpflin (2018ae), p. 1321.

Art. 2366 para. 2 CC also contains specific (derogable[1152]) time limits. Accordingly, the notice must be published at least 15 days prior to the date set for the general meeting. Companies that do not use the capital markets, which are, more or less, all cooperatives, can call the meeting by notifying members only 8 days prior to the meeting, provided the method used guarantees receipt of the notification,[1153] such as a registered letter or faxed acknowledgement of receipt.[1154] The statutes must outline the rules to be observed, which in turn must agree with the provisions contained in Art. 2366 CC.[1155] Thus the obligations of an Italian SCE are similar to those in the CC. However, the SCE-R is less strict about proving receipt of notice and determining how the written notice is sent. The notice period set by the SCE-R is longer and hence less flexible, especially when compared to the reduced notice period of 8 days.

Next, the Italian civil code contains a provision about the reference in Art. 56 para. 3 last sent. SCE-R. The notice usually also determines the date for calling the second meeting, which is necessary if the first fails to meet the necessary quorum.[1156] According to Art. 2369 para. 2 CC,[1157] the earliest the second meeting can take place is the day after the first. If the date for the second meeting is not specified in the notice, the meeting must be called within 30 days of the first meeting. In this case, the time period set out in Art. 2366 para. 2 CC for publishing the notice in a newspaper[1158] is reduced to 8 days. This is the time period that Italian SCEs must observe. However, unlike Italian cooperatives, Italian SCEs are not obligated to call the second meeting within 30 days of the first. Art. 56 para. 3 SCE-R refers to the time by which the notice must be sent to (indirectly) determine the minimum period between the first and second meetings, with the date for the second ultimately determined according to Art. 56 para. 2 bullet 2 SCER in combination with Art. 54 para. 2 SCE-R, which does not differentiate between the two meetings and therefore applies in both cases.[1159] In addition, it seems possible to set the date for the second meeting in the notice for the first, as determined by Art. 2369 para. 2 sent. 1 and sent. 2 CC. This is because the SCE-R does not consider this possibility and hence contains a regulatory gap that needs to be closed, according to Art. 53 SCE-R.

Finally, if the formalities for calling the meeting are not duly observed, the meeting is deemed to have been duly constituted only if the entire company capital

---

[1152] Statutory provision must guarantee that the members are informed on time. See Tatarano (2011), p. 425 et seq.

[1153] See Art. 2366 para. 3 CC.

[1154] See Bonfante (2014a), p. 305; Trimarchi (2005), p. 648.

[1155] See Bonfante (2014a), p. 305; Tatarano (2011), p. 425.

[1156] Required by the statutes or by law. See Bonfante (2014a), p. 305. Also consider Serra (2007), p. 60 et seq.

[1157] Second and subsequent calls.

[1158] Which is defined as 15 days.

[1159] According to Art. 56 para. 2 bullet 2 SCE-R, the notice must also contain the date the meeting will be convened.

is represented. In addition, the majority of the members of the administrative and audit bodies must be present. The law determines that any participant may object to discussing topics about which they have not been adequately informed.[1160] In addition, the decisions must be communicated in a timely fashion to those members of the administrative and controlling bodies not present.[1161] These findings are valid for an Italian SCE.

The *Austrian legal system* contains some rules that are similar to the Italian laws dealing with the formalities that need to be observed when a general meeting is convened. It is important for an Austrian SCE to understand to what extent they must be applied. Sec. 30 *GenG*, which deals with the formalities of convening the general meeting, is of central importance here. Accordingly, the statutes must determine how the general meeting has to take place. In this context, Sec. 5 para. 1 no. 8 *GenG* determines that the statutes must include the relevant particulars (i.e., the notice and convocation periods). The statutes may determine that the meeting must be convened via public announcement, for example, affixing the notice to a noticeboard or publishing it in a newspaper.[1162] Thus, it is not necessary for the notice to be sent to all entitled persons, and the Austrian legal system is more flexible in this regard than the SCE-R.

The same is true for the convening period, which Austrian law (unlike the SCE-R) determines by statute. These periods are binding and must be set to facilitate member participation in the meeting. A maximum period is often determined. It is also possible to set different convening periods for different agenda items.[1163] The ability to shorten the convocation period for a second meeting (as dealt with by Art. 56 para. 3 last sent. SCE-R) should, in principle, be determined via statutory autonomy. This aligns with the general approach of the *GenG* and must be considered by an Austrian SCE.[1164]

As mentioned above, the SCE-R does not contain the details about what to do if the formalities are not duly observed, causing national law to be applied. In this case, mistakes can be rectified under the condition that all members of the cooperative participated at the general meeting that was not properly convoked and agreed with the decisions to be taken. In principle, decisions taken by a general meeting that was not duly convoked are invalid[1165]; however, they become valid if 3 years have passed since their registration in the commercial register (by analogy to Sec. 200 AktG).[1166]

The last topic in our discussion about the preparatory stage of the general meeting of an SCE is **minority rights**. The SCE-R provides two provisions: Art. 55 SCE-R

[1160] See Art. 2366 para. 4 CC.

[1161] Art. 2366 para. 5 CC.

[1162] Siebenbäck (2014d), p. 368 et seq.

[1163] See Siebenbäck (2014d), p. 369.

[1164] As required by Art. 56 para. 3 SCE-R.

[1165] By analogy to Sec. 199 AktG.

[1166] See Siebenbäck (2014d), p. 369.

determines the preconditions for a minority of members to convene a meeting, and Art. 57 SCE-R offers rules for putting additional items on the agenda.

According to Art. 55 SCE-R,[1167] a minority of members has the right to require the SCE to convene a general meeting. They can also set the agenda. This request must be brought by at least 5000 members or 10% of the total number of votes, whichever is smaller. These limits can be reduced by statute, but more stringent requirements cannot be applied.[1168] It is not necessary to specify the reasons for convening the meeting. However, because of fiduciary duties, this right cannot be misused.[1169] Interestingly, the English version of the SCE-R states that the request to convene a general meeting must be addressed to the SCE and hence to the organ representing it. The German and Italian versions do not explicitly address the SCE and do not contain any reference to a possible addressee.[1170] As a result, one can argue that national law applies.[1171]

In addition to Art. 55 SCE-R, Art. 57 SCE-R determines that a minority can require that more items be put on the agenda of any general meeting. The conditions for doing so are the same as those elaborated upon in Art. 55 SCE-R.[1172] Unlike the draft SCE-R,[1173] Art. 57 SCE-R does not refer exclusively to general meetings that have already been convened and whose agendas have already been drafted.[1174] Instead, it contains the general wording 'any general meeting'. Again, no reasons have to be stated.[1175] If this minority right is exercised for a general meeting that has already been convened and for which the agenda has already been drafted, the convening organ must notify every person entitled to attend the meeting about the additional item, in accordance with the formalities determined by Art. 56 para.

[1167]It states: "Members of the SCE who together number more than 5 000, or who have at least 10 % of the total number of the votes, may require the SCE to convene a general meeting and may draw up its agenda. The above proportions may be reduced by the statutes."

[1168]See Schulze (2004a), p. 115 et seq.; Schöpflin (2018ad), p. 1320. Also consider Alfandari and Piot (2004), p. 85. For the SE, Spindler (2015d), p. 833 et seq.

[1169]For the SE, see Mayer (2010d), p. 696; Spindler (2015d), p. 837 et seq. The draft SCE-R still contained this obligation. See Art. 19 draft SCE-R. Schöpflin has a different opinion, stressing that the reasons must also be indicated. See Schöpflin (2018ad), p. 1320.

[1170]The German version states: "Die Einberufung der Generalversammlung und die Aufstellung ihrer Tagesordnung können von mindestens 5000 Mitgliedern der SCE oder von Mitgliedern, die mindestens zehn Prozent der Stimmrechte halten, verlangt werden."

The Italian version states: "La convocazione dell'assemblea generale e la fissazione dell'ordine del giorno della medesima possono essere richieste, congiuntamente, da oltre 5000 soci della SCE o da soci della SCE che costituiscano almeno il 10 % dei diritti di voto."

[1171]For the SE, see Mayer (2010d), p. 696. Different opinion Spindler (2015c), p. 835.

This also applies if the competent SCE organ does not convene the general meeting in due time. In this case Art. 51 SCE-R applies. For the SE, see Spindler (2015d), p. 838. See also Art. 55 para. 3 SE-R.

[1172]See Schulze (2004a), p. 115 et seq.

[1173]See Art. 20 draft SCE-R.

[1174]In this context, see Mayer (2010e), p. 703; Spindler (2015e), p. 851 et seq.

[1175]Consider the analysis referring to Art. 55 SCE-R.

1 SCE-R. In this case, however, the shorter period determined by Art. 56 para. 3 sent. 2 SCE-R applies, because it counts as an 'urgent case'.[1176] As for Art. 55, statutes may set lower requirements without including an obligation to observe the specific national provisions, hence, favouring the principle of self-regulation.[1177]

The *Italian legal system* grants rights to a minority of shareholders enabling them to convene a general meeting; Art. 2367 para. 1 CC addresses these rights. A group of members holding at least 10% of the available votes may bring a motion to convene a general meeting.[1178] The statutes may reduce these figures, akin to Art. 55 SCE-R. The minority must declare the issues to be dealt with in its request. National cooperatives must therefore follow an approach markedly similar to that of the SCE-R, except that the latter, alternatively, requires a minimum number of 5000 members.

If the competent management or administrative organ does not provide accordingly, it is the obligation of the controlling body (the supervisory organ or management control committee) to convene the general meeting. If these do not act accordingly, the calling members may require the judiciary authority to convene the general meeting.[1179] These provisions are applicable to an Italian SCE because of Art. 54 para. 2 SCE-R and Art. 53 SCE-R.

The law then provides for two specific grounds that prevent the exercise of this right. Art. 2367 para. 3 CC asserts that it is not possible to file this request for matters that the meeting must resolve (pursuant to law) at the request of the members of the administrative or management organ or according to a plan or report prepared by them. These provisions apply to an Italian SCE because of Art. 53 SCE-R. Similarly, abusing the system can prevent the exercise of this right.[1180] This finding is also valid for an Italian SCE.

Unlike for meetings called by a minority and unlike Art. 57 SCE-R, the law does not explicitly deal with adding items to the agenda. However, such a right could presumably be assigned to the minority members, if the statutes provide accordingly.[1181]

The provisions contained in the *Austrian legal system* differ to some extent from the provisions in the SCE-R. Comparing these provisions helps us to better

[1176]See Schöpflin (2018af), p. 1322.

[1177]See Art. 56 SE-R. It states: "... the SE's statutes or national legislation may provide for a smaller proportion under the same conditions as those applicable to public limited-liability companies." Also consider Mayer (2010e), p. 704.

[1178]See Bonfante (2014a), p. 305 et seq.

[1179]Art. 2367 para. 2 CC. Bonfante (2014a), p. 305 et seq. See also Mirone (2017b), p. 408. The court will order the meeting if it finds the refusal to proceed unjustified. The court must hear the members of the administrative and supervisory bodies and can then enact a corresponding decree (Art. 2367 para. 2 CC).

[1180]See Cian (2018d), p. 2780. Also consider Fiorio (2004), p. 515. See also Romano (2017c), p. 2912 et seq.; Mirone (2017b), p. 408.

[1181]See Cian (2018d), p. 2780.

determine the content of the applicable rules. In addition, certain national rules must be applied, as the SCE-R does not completely regulate the issue of minority rights.

The issue of minority rights is addressed by Sec. 29 para. 2 *GenG*, which states that a general meeting must be convened immediately if at least 10% of members request this via a signed application, which must state reasons for calling the meeting. This right can be linked to a different proportion of members, if the statutes provide accordingly.[1182] Austrian law thus focuses on 10% of members, whereas the SCE-R focuses on a large number of members or at least 10% of voting rights. This latter criteria should be the easiest to achieve, assuming that plural voting rights have been assigned.

Unlike for the SCE, the members of an Austrian cooperative must state their reasons for convening the general meeting. They must also specify why the general meeting must be convened immediately and why the proposed measures cannot be decided upon by the next ordinary general assembly.[1183] Thus, Austrian SCEs face less strict requirements.

The SCE-R does not contain provisions for what happens if the competent organ does not comply with a request. National law must be considered in these cases. According to Sec. 29 para. 3 *GenG*, the persons obliged to convene the meeting can be compelled to do so by the commercial court (with fines up to 3500 EUR) if requested by the applicants. This request can only be rejected if the request is not based on legal preconditions or refers to issues that do not fall within the scope of the general meeting. It is also possible to reject a request that abuses the procedure, for example, if the previous general meeting already decided upon the issue, and there are no specific grounds to deal with it again.[1184] As seen above,[1185] this right cannot be misused because of fiduciary duties. Thus, it is necessary to decide on a case-by-case basis whether abuse has occurred or not.

Finally, the *GenG* does not contain provisions dealing with additions to the agenda. In principle, the agenda is determined by the person who convenes the meeting; in practice, the statutes allow further items to be added. By analogy to Sec. 29 *GenG*, minorities can supposedly add items to the agenda.[1186]

We now **summarise** our results for the preparatory stage of a general meeting of an Italian *agricultural SCE* and its Austrian counterpart. The basic rules determined by Art. 54 para. 1 SCE-R require the general meeting to be held at least once per calendar year[1187] and within 6 months of the end of the financial year.[1188] While under Austrian law there should be nothing further to consider when applying this

[1182]See Siebenbäck (2014c), p. 365.

[1183]See Siebenbäck (2014c), p. 365. Also consider Bachner (2012), nt 40. Moreover, the management organ can add further items to the agenda. See Siebenbäck (2014c), p. 366.

[1184]See Siebenbäck (2014c), p. 365 et seq. Also consider Bachner (2012), nt 48.

[1185]See Sect. 3.4.1.

[1186]See Siebenbäck (2014d), p. 369.

[1187]Also consider Sec. 2.4 para. 13 PECOL.

[1188]Neither Austria nor Italy exercise the option contained in Art. 54 para. 1 last sent. SCE-R.

norm, an Italian *agricultural SCE* must be aware that it must pay taxes by the last day of the sixth month after the closure of the financial year. Tax law grants the option to increase the tax burden if this deadline is extended for 30 days. For example, this option applies when the general meeting is held on the evening of the last day of the 6-month period.

The SCE-R considers various possibilities for which organs can convene the general meeting. The flexibility of the SCE-R is apparent in the reasons for convening a general meeting, for which no strict demands are required. The SCE-R only asserts that approving the annual accounts and allocating profits is necessary. Then, the SCE-R also allows so-called competent authorities to convene the general meeting, if national law provides. Both legal systems determine specific authorities who may convene the general meeting, and they also detail the obligations of the supervisory organ of an Austrian or Italian SCE to convene a general meeting.

Overall, the legal framework for an Austrian SCE seems more flexible, as it allows for the adoption of statutory provisions that determine the obligations for convening a general meeting. On the other hand, the general clause that determines the obligation to convene if it is in the interests of the cooperative may make this obligation overly common. This follows the definition of the general meeting as the sovereign of the cooperative; thus, it should be easy to convene. Italian law seems more stringent here.

The PECOL acknowledge the different approaches by different member states. In addition to the annual meeting, Sec. 2.4 para. 13 PECOL states it is possible to convene extraordinary general meetings. The power to do so is assigned to the designated organ. In addition, extraordinary meetings must be convened if other organs are empowered to do so by law or the statutes or the audit entity require one to be convened. This in line with Art. 54 SCE-R and Art. 55 SCE-R.[1189]

Next, the SCE-R contains provisions governing the formalities for convening the general meeting. This issue is primarily regulated by the SCE-R, which lays out a fairly open legal framework that contains provisions for the notice required when convening the meeting and the content of this notice.[1190] Finally, we briefly discussed general meetings not duly convoked, acknowledging that both legal systems determine different means to remedy the resulting errors.

Of practical importance are those requirements that force the convening of a meeting in cases of urgency. Thus, the statutes of *agricultural SCEs* may provide the option to convene the general meeting by the administrative or management organ at any time if the latter deems necessary. Furthermore, those provisions are conceivable that strengthen minority rights, i.e., if a minority of members submits a request for convening a meeting, this request should have to be followed immediately. In an

[1189] See Snaith (2017), p. 66.

[1190] Here, Sec. 2.4 para. 11 PECOL only stresses the importance of providing adequate notice of the agenda, giving members the opportunity to attend. The same is true for giving notice of the time and place of meetings. In this context, Arts 56 and 57 SCE-R are mentioned as examples. See Snaith (2017), p. 66.

agricultural SCE recognised as a PO, the farmer-members are particularly bound by the requirements of the PO; minority rights can be of great importance if the farmer-members do not see that their personal interests safeguarded because of an actual information gap between the administrative or management organ and the farmer-members. The importance of minority rights is also acknowledged by the PECOL, which contain provisions similar to those in the SCE-R that specifically deal with the issue of minority rights and grant a specific right to convene the general meeting.[1191] If the competent organ does not comply with a request, the consequences are determined by national law. Both legal orders systems lay out specific procedures here.

4.4.3 The Conduct of the General Meeting

Unlike the SE-R, the SCE-R contains specific provisions on how a general meeting must be conducted. These refer to attendance, the right to speak, the right to information and taking minutes. Other issues, such as the chairman(ship), must be determined by applying Art. 53 SCE-R and, thus, the relevant national rules. This next sub-chapter deals with these topics in the following order: attendance, chairman, the right to information and, finally, the minutes of the general meeting.

The general meeting primarily serves as a meeting of the members of an SCE during which, in principle, every member has the **right to participate**. This right includes the authority to speak and vote on the points on the agenda.[1192] Persons with voting rights are also entitled to appoint a proxy to represent them at the meeting, as long as the statutes expressly allow this. The statutes must set the maximum number of persons for whom a proxy may act, along with the procedure to be followed.[1193] Only persons entitled to vote may appoint a proxy.[1194] The statutes may declare proxies inadmissible for certain discussion topics and decisions.[1195] The issue of proxies will be discussed when we analyse voting rights in Sect. 4.4.4.

[1191]See Sec. 2.4 para. 13 PECOL. Also consider Sec. 2.3 para. 5 letter c PECOL.

[1192]See Schulze (2004a), p. 114; Schöpflin (2018ag), p. 1323. Also consider Art. 58 para. 1 SCE-R. It states: "Every member shall be entitled to speak and vote at general meetings on the points that are included in the agenda."

[1193]See Schulze (2004a), p. 114; Schöpflin (2018ag), p. 1323. Also consider Albamonte (2008), p. 312 et seq.

[1194]Art. 58 para. 3 of the German version of SCE-R refers to members entitled to vote ("stimmberechtigte Mitglieder"), suggesting that there may be also members without voting rights. However, the Italian text uses the formula "gli aventi diritto al voto" which is similar to the English version of the SCE-R, which refers to persons entitled to vote.

Art 58 para. 3 SCE-R states: "A person entitled to vote shall be entitled to appoint a proxy to represent him/her at a general meeting in accordance with procedures laid down in the statutes. The statutes shall lay down the maximum number of persons for whom a proxy may act."

[1195]This could happen by amending the statutes. See Schöpflin (2018ag), p. 1323.

Other persons without voting rights may attend the general meeting.[1196] This type of attendance does not exclude the right to speak.[1197] The SCE-R directly refers to two groups of persons here: members of the SCE's organs[1198] and holders of securities other than shares and debentures (within the meaning of Art. 64 SCE-R). Finally, the SCE-R extends the group of people without voting rights to those who may attend according to the relevant national law, if the statutes allow.[1199]

Last, Art. 59 para. 4 SCE-R lays down conditions for employee representatives, who can participate in the general meeting as persons entitled to vote. According to this provision, this right must be granted as soon as the SCE-R is enacted by the member state where the SCE has its registered office.[1200] The statutes must provide for this accordingly. Employee representatives cannot control more than 15% of voting rights. If the SCE transfers its seat to a member state which does not provide for such participation, this right ceases to apply.[1201] As explained in the introduction, this study does not concentrate on these issues.

The *Italian legal system* contains various provisions referring to attendance.[1202] Some of them differ to some extent from the provisions in the SCE-R, whereas others must be observed by an Italian SCE.

Specific provisions determine who may attend a cooperative's general meeting. The starting point is Art. 2538 CC. Accordingly, only members who have been registered in the members' book for at least 90 days have voting rights. Only members with voting rights may intervene (participate) at a general meeting[1203]; members who do not fulfil this registration requirement may not attend.[1204] Yet, as

[1196]See Art. 58 para. SCE-R: "Members of the SCE's organs and holders of securities other than shares and debentures within the meaning of Article 64 and, if the statutes allow, any other person entitled to do so under the law of the State in which the SCE's registered office is situated may attend a general meeting without voting rights."

[1197]See Schöpflin (2018ag), p. 1323.

[1198]Consider in this context see Sect. 4.2.1.3, discussing whether these persons must be members of the SCE.

[1199]Also consider Schöpflin (2018ag), p. 1323.

[1200]It does not seem possible to grand this right after that. See Schulze (2004a), p. 114.

[1201]See Schulze (2004a), p. 114 et seq.

[1202]Regarding attendence, Italian law uses the phrasing "right of intervention." This right of intervention allows both assisting in the work of the general meeting and participating in the discussion by means of the right to obtain information. See Bonfante (2014a), p. 307.

[1203]Art. 2538 CC linked to Art. 2370 para. 1 CC due to the general reference contained in Art. 2519 CC. According to Art. 2370 CC, only the person(s) entitled to vote may attend the meeting. See Bonfante (2014a), p. 307 et seq. See also Santagata (2017), p. 830.

[1204]See Bonfante (2014a), p. 307; Cusa (2014a), p. 330; Tatarano (2011), p. 431. See also Santagata (2017), p. 831. In this context, various scholars have discussed the link between Art. 2538 CC and Art. 2370 para. 1 CC (due to Art. 2519 CC). Art. 2370 CC confers a right of intervention exclusively to those members having voting rights, what is in line with Art. 2538 CC. However, specific doubts have been raised based on cooperative principles, which require members to actively participate in the business of the cooperative via specific transactions. It is argued that this is a

this issue is expressly regulated by the SCE-R, this provision is not valid for an Italian SCE.[1205]

The law contains exceptions to the general rule of attendance. For instance, Art. 2541 last para. CC states that the representative of those holders of financial instruments who do not have voting rights may assist at the general meeting.[1206] In addition, Art. 2540 para. 4 CC states that members who have attended a separate meeting[1207] may also attend the general meeting. Another exception can be found in Art. 2418 CC.[1208] These provisions apply because of Art. 58 para. 2 SCE-R.

Lastly, Art. 2539 CC specifically deals with proxy voting, stating that only members may act as proxies. As will be explained below,[1209] SCEs are more flexible in this regard as they also allow proxy voting by non-members.

Under *Austrian law*, the provisions concerning the right to attend are generally regulated by Sec. 27 GenG. It states that members' rights in matters affecting the cooperative are exercised via the general meeting. This implies the right to attend and the right to vote. According to prevailing Austrian doctrine, the right to attend includes the right to speak, the right to file an application and the right to information. The right to attend is granted to every member,[1210] from the beginning of their membership until the end. Legal persons have their respective representatives, who may exercise these rights.[1211]

According to the Austrian legal system, it is also possible for members to be represented by other persons.[1212] The chairman can decide whether non-members—such as consultants, journalists or honoured guests—may attend the meeting.[1213] This is also valid for an Austrian SCE, if the statutes provide accordingly. Thus, the essential content of the right to attend is equivalent to that proposed by the SCE-R. One difference is that the chairman of an Austrian cooperative has more leeway to

---

specific difference from capitalistic companies, where shareholders do not specifically transact with the company to gain an advantage. In fact, this runs contrary to the concept of shareholders, which is focused on the remuneration of capital. Thus, it is argued that new members should be allowed to participate in the general meeting, even though they do not have voting rights. This would help integrate new members into the business activity of the cooperative. See Di Cecco (2003), p. 115; Bonfante (2014a), p. 308; Marano (2013a), p. 2735.

1205 Also consider Presti (2006), p. 74.

1206 See Bonfante (2014a), p. 307 et seq.

1207 Sectoral or section meetings as determined by Art. 63 SCE-R.

1208 Common representative of bondholders. Also consider Cusa (2014a), p. 328.

1209 See Sect. 4.4.4.

1210 User and non-user members. See Siebenbäck (2014a), p. 340 et seq.

1211 See Siebenbäck (2014a), p. 340 et seq.

1212 For further information on proxy voting, see Sect. 4.4.4.

1213 See Siebenbäck (2014a), p. 341 et seq. Also consider Keinert (1988), p. 143; Holthaus and Lehnhoff (2016a), p. 576. A member may, however, require the general meeting to decide on the presence of a specific non-member. See Siebenbäck (2014a), p. 342.

admit third parties, whereas an Austrian SCE requires a specific statutory provision.[1214]

The topic, the role of the **chairman**, is acknowledged by the SCE-R, which does not give further details about this role.[1215] As a result, national provisions must be applied, as required by Art. 53 SCE-R.

An *Italian SCE* must consider Art. 2371 CC. Accordingly, the statutes normally determine the person who chairs the meeting. If they do not, the chairman may be elected by the general meeting. Third parties may also be elected.[1216] With the support of a secretary, the chairman must verify the regularity of the meeting, check the identity of the members present and their right of intervention, direct the discussion and validate the results of the votes. According to Art. 2371 CC, both the chairman and the secretary must sign the minutes.[1217] As Art. 62 para. 4 SCE-R specifically addresses this, the Italian provision must not be observed by an Italian SCE; however, the other findings hold for an Italian SCE.

The *Austrian GenG* does not contain information about the chairman.[1218] In principle, the person convening the meeting also chairs it. However, in practice, statutes quite often determine specific provisions for the chairman. For instance, if the cooperative is managed by a professional management organ, the chairman of the supervisory organ often chairs the meeting. Thus, the chair is transferred to a neutral person in case there is a conflict of interest. As the chairman conducts the general meeting, he or she is responsible for the quick resolution of the items on the agenda.[1219] These findings and observations also apply to Austrian SCEs.

The **right to information** granted to the members of an SCE is particularly important to the function of the general meeting. Art. 60 SCE-R regulates members' rights to information and thus provides the basis for effective decision making. The right to information should be considered a further control mechanism for supervising the management or administrative organ.[1220]

The basis for decision making in the general meeting is comprehensive information about the SCE's business. In this respect, the SCE-R grants two types of the right to information.[1221] First, to prepare for participation in the general meeting that decides on the annual accounts, every member has the right to examine the relevant (business) documents. These are the balance sheet, the profit-and-loss account and

---

[1214] Art. 58 para. 2 SCE-R.

[1215] See Art. 62 para. 4 SCE-R: "The minutes shall be signed by the chairman of the meeting."

[1216] See Cian (2018g), p. 2786; Laurini (2008a), p. 159. See also Romano (2017e), p. 29; Mirone (2017b), p. 425 et seq.

[1217] See Bonfante (2014a), p. 331 et seq. Also consider Barbarito (2004), p. 586 et seq.; Cass Civ sez I 30.05.2008 no 14554 (07.02.2017, iusexplorer.it). See also Romano (2017f), p. 2925 et seq.; Mirone (2017b), p. 426.

[1218] See Keinert (1988), p. 146; Siebenbäck (2014a), p. 350.

[1219] See Siebenbäck (2014a), p. 350 et seq. Also consider Schöpflin (2018a), p. 12855; Holthaus and Lehnhoff (2016b), p. 116 et seq.

[1220] See Schulze (2004a), p. 118; Schöpflin (2018ai), p. 1327.

[1221] See Schulze (2004a), p. 118 et seq.

the notes thereon, the management report, the conclusion of the audit of the accounts by the responsible party and, if the prerequisites are met, the consolidated accounts.[1222] This right is granted to every member and can be exercised within the 10 days preceding the general meeting required to decide on the end of the financial year.[1223] However, the SCE-R does not state the particulars of how this right can be exercised. Accordingly, national law has to be applied because of Art. 53 SCE-R.

In addition, every member has a right to obtain information from the management or administrative organ about items that the general meeting must decide upon. This includes items placed on the agenda by a minority of members.[1224] The SCE-R does not require that the request for information be justified.[1225] This right of information is not granted to the holders of securities, as determined by Art. 64 SCE-R.[1226]

Art. 60 para. 1 SCE-R only refers to information on items that the general meeting must decide on. This is necessary, as proper information is the basis for making good decisions.[1227] However, the SCE-R does not regulate whether members may obtain information about other issues.[1228] Whereas para. 2 refers to an exhaustive list, the formulation used in para. 1 does not. This gap must be closed according to Art. 53 SCE-R. Potentially, as members already have the right to speak on points

---

[1222]On the condition that the SCE is a parent company within the meaning of dir. 83/349/EEC.

[1223]See Art. 60 para. 4 SCE-R. It states: "Within the 10 days preceding the general meeting required to decide on the end of the financial year, members may examine the balance sheet, the profit-and-loss account and the notes thereon, the management report, the conclusion of the audit of the accounts by the person responsible and, where a parent company within the meaning of Directive 83/349/EEC is concerned, the consolidated accounts."

[1224]According to Art. 61 para. 1 sent. 2 SCE-R and Art. 57 SCE-R. As mentioned in Sect. 4.4.2, a minority of members can place items on the agenda and thus require the responsible organ to give information.

Art 60 para. 1 SCE-R states: "Every member who so requests at a general meeting shall be entitled to obtain information from the management or administrative organ on the affairs of the SCE arising from items on which the general meeting may take a decision in accordance with Article 61(1). In so far as possible, information shall be provided at the general meeting in question." Also consider Schulze (2004a), p. 119; Schöpflin (2018ai), p. 1327; Schöpflin (2018aj), p. 1328.

[1225]See Schulze (2004a), p. 119; Schöpflin (2018ai), p. 1327.

[1226]See Schöpflin (2018ai), p. 1327.

[1227]In this context, it is necessary to mention the specific rights of information if an SCE is formed via merger. As this study does not specifically deal with the formation of an SCE, this issue will not be analysed further. According to Art. 25 para. 1 SCE-R, members are entitled to inspect the following documents: the draft terms of the merger, the annual accountants and management report of the merging co-operatives for the three preceding financially years, the expert report on the value of shares to be distributed in exchange for the assets for the merging co-operatives or the share exchange ratio, the report from the co-operatives administrative or management organs, an accounting statement (if required). In addition, every member may request to obtain (free of charge) a full copy of these documents or at least an extract. See Alfandari and Piot (2004), p. 84 et seq.

[1228]For a different opinion, see Schöpflin (2018ai), p. 1327.

included on the agenda,[1229] they could have the option to request information. Thus, the members of the management or administrative organ should supply information, even though they are not obligated to respond, as refusal to provide information could reduce the trust between the general meeting and the members of the organs.

Next, the relevant organ must provide the members with information during the appropriate general meeting. This implies that the SCE-R does not contain individual information rights; in other words, this provision does not assign a means for exclusive information.[1230]

There is no fixed time within which a request must be made. As a result, the request can be placed before or even during the general meeting. However, only requests made in good time oblige the (questioned) organ to conduct a full investigation, because of the phrasing of 'in so far as possible'.[1231] This wording also suggests that if it is not possible to supply the information at the general meeting, it must be supplied afterwards.[1232]

The management or administrative organ has the right to refuse to supply information in two situations.[1233] The first occurs when the supply or content of the information could seriously compromise the SCE. This might involve confidential information about a new product in development or a new technology not yet protected by patent.[1234] The regulation does not require that these consequences caused by the provision of information actually occur. It is sufficient that it is possible.[1235] Thus, it is possible to refuse to disclose secret business information if such disclosure could lead to severe economic losses. However, the aim of these rules is not to prevent the disclosure of information that could lead to the loss of reputation on the part of the management or administrative organ.[1236] Second, it is possible to refuse to disclose information if the disclosure would violate a legal obligation of confidentiality.[1237]

Art. 60 SCE-R only partially regulates the consequences of a refusal to supply information. According to Art. 60 para. 3 SCE-R, a member to whom information was refused may require that his questions and grounds for refusal be entered into the minutes of the meeting. The SCE-R does not deal with further rights that can be exercised in case there is a unjustified refusal of information; these must be

---

[1229]This right is contained in Art. 58 SCE-R.

[1230]See Schöpflin (2018ai), p. 1327.

[1231]See Schulze (2004a), p. 119.

[1232]See Schöpflin (2018ai), p. 27. Also consider Lutter et al. (2012), p. 1620.

[1233]See Art. 60 para. 2 SCE-R. It states: "The management or administrative organ may refuse to supply such information only where: - it would be likely to be seriously prejudicial to the SCE, - its disclosure would be incompatible with a legal obligation of confidentiality."

[1234]See Schulze (2004a), p. 119.

[1235]See Schöpflin (2018ai), p. 1327.

[1236]See Schulze (2004a), p. 119.

[1237]In this context, also consider the specific duties of confidentiality determined by Art. 49 SCE-R.

determined according to national law.[1238] For example, one consequence of applying national law could be an appeal against a decision if the refused information was important for taking that decision. In addition, national law could determine whether members other than the one to whom information was refused may appeal.[1239] Thus, the SCE-R contains gaps that require closure by Art. 53 SCE-R.

The *Italian legal system* contains specific provisions that address the right to information. Art. 2429 para. 3 CC determines that a copy of the financial statements[1240] must be filed at the registered seat of the cooperative during the 15 days preceding the general meeting and until their approval. This grants members the opportunity to examine these documents. The reports by the administrative or management organ, the supervisory organ and the auditor of the accounts must also be filed with the financial statements. Apart from the longer period, the content of this provision is similar to that in Art. 60 para. 3 SCE-R. The observations made above apply to the report by the supervisory organ.

According to Italian law, members who participate[1241] in the general meeting have the right to speak about the items on the agenda and the right to obtain information about items that must be decided upon. They also have the right to obtain information about the development of the cooperative.[1242] This right to information, however, is limited in several ways. First, it pertains to the items on the agenda, but not exclusively to the items that require decisions. This latter finding is also valid for an Italian SCE. Next, the delivery of information cannot be prejudicial to the cooperative[1243]; this observation aligns with Art. 60 para. 2 SCE-R. Provided the statutes determine his competence, the chairman is usually tasked with deciding to exercise the right to information,[1244] which decision is influenced by the potential prejudice caused by the disclosure of information. On the other hand, the member has the right to obtain sufficient information[1245] to

[1238] Art. 53 SCE-R and Art. 8 para. 1 letter c SCE-R. See Schulze (2004a), p. 119; Schöpflin (2018ah), p. 1325.

[1239] See Schulze (2004a), p. 119 et seq.

[1240] Together with the copies of the latest financial statements of each controlled company with a sheet summarising the essential figures of the latest financial statements of each affiliated company. According to Art. 2423 CC, the financial statements comprise the balance-sheet, the profit and loss account and the integrative note on the account.

[1241] In this context, the CC uses the phrase "right to intervene," which means be present. See Mirone (2017b), p. 421 et seq; Cian (2018f), p. 2784. According to Art. 2370 para. 1 CC, any person entitled to the voting right may intervene at the shareholder's meeting, provided they are actually present.

[1242] The right to information is described as an instrument by which the administrative or management organ can be indirectly urged to enforce the principle of democracy. See Cusa (2014a), p. 330. See also Paolucci (2019b), p. 121 et seq.; Mirone (2017b), p. 421 et seq.

[1243] See Cusa (2014a), p. 330. See also Mirone (2017b), p. 427 et seq.

[1244] See Cusa (2014a), p. 330. Also consider Cass Civ sez I 30.05.2008 no 14554 (07.02.2017, iusexplorer.it).

[1245] If it is not prejudicial to the cooperative.

anticipate uncertainties. It is the court's role to determine whether these criteria have been met.[1246] This latter solution applies because of Art. 53 SCE-R.

The *Austrian GenG* does not determine that there is a general right to information. As a result, Sec. 118 AktG grants the right to information for every aspect of the cooperative. (We determine this by analogy.) This is based on the assumption that the general meeting, as the highest organ of the cooperative, has the right to instruct all the other organs. To exercise this right, the general meeting must acquire correct information. Thus, the members' right to information must be interpreted extensively.[1247] As seen,[1248] the law applicable to an Austrian SCE differs here, as it contains no general right to give instructions. The influence of an SCE's general meeting on the actions of the management or administrative organ is primarily determined by Art. 60 SCE-R and Art. 61 SCE-R.

The Austrian legal system asserts that access to information can only be refused if the interests of the cooperative or its associated companies are seriously endangered. Consequently, this threat extends to the interests of the members themselves.[1249] Other reasons for refusing access to information include the protected interests of the members of the management organ, the managing director or individual members. The same is true if disclosing information would violate data protection laws.[1250] In cases of unjustified refusal, Austrian law grants members of an Austrian SCE the option to appeal in court,[1251] as the regulation does not govern this issue.[1252]

The provision in the SCE-R differs in two ways: first, by intertwining the right to information with the requirement that the general meeting must take a decision on the relevant items. Thus, Art. 60 SCE-R seems to preclude information about those issues on which no decision will be made. However, as mentioned above, the need to obtain information about other items added to the agenda[1253] creates a gap that national law can close. The applicable Austrian Sec. 118 AktG is wider in scope and allows to acquire information on those items for which no decision shall be made. Second, the Austrian provision differs on the right to refuse information, as determined by Art. 60 para. 2 SCE-R. As there is an exhaustive list of grounds, the personal interests of individuals such as members of the organs are not protected, unless this protection is not based on a legal obligation of confidentiality, as determined by Art. 60 para. 2 bullet 2 SCE-R.

[1246] See Cass Civ sez unita 21.02.200 no 27 (07.02.2017, iusexplorer.it). See also Mirone (2017b), p. 425.

[1247] See Siebenbäck (2014a), p. 345 et seq.

[1248] See Sect. 4.4.1.

[1249] Sec. 118 para. 3 AktG requires the refusal to be based on a reasonable business judgement. Also consider Kastner (1986), p. 177; Patera (1986), p. 542; Zacherl (1981), p. 233.

[1250] See Siebenbäck (2014a), p. 346.

[1251] See Bydlinski and Potyka (2018).

[1252] Due to Art. 8 para. 1 letter c SCE-R and/or Art. 53 SCE-R.

[1253] On which no decision shall be taken but which are supplied for informational purposes.

Contrary to Art. 58 para. 1 SCE-R, the Austrian legal system does not contain specific provisions about the members' right to speak.[1254] In principle, this right is governed by the chairman, as he or she must give the floor to each speaker.[1255] This solution must also be adopted by Austrian SCEs. Yet, the rights of individual members of Austrian SCEs are better protected, as they are assigned by law.

Next, the *GenG* does not contain a specific provision covering the members' rights to information preceding the general meeting. Sec. 35 *GenG* only states that the management is obliged to hand over a copy of the approved accounts and balance sheets.[1256] Neither does Sec. 27 *GenG* grant rights to information preceding the general meeting. Austrian company law and private limited company law contain provisions for this right to information. Comparable rules should be developed by analogy to close this gap,[1257] and the right to information should be given within the convening period, as determined by statute. This prerequisite guarantees proper decision taking about the financial statements and the distribution of the surplus. Alternatively, these documents can be disclosed on the cooperative's website.[1258] These findings are valid for an Austrian SCE, as the SCE-R does not determine how the right to information must be put into practice.

Though it is unclear which documents must be disclosed, such documents could include the financial statements, the management's report,[1259] the proposal for distributing the surplus and the report of the supervisory organ. In addition, Sec. 6 para. 3 *GenReVG* requires that an abstract of the audit report be made available to cooperative members during the cooperative's ordinary business hours.[1260] Taken together, this solution, which is based on analogy, and the approach offered by the *GenReVG* are similar to the provisions in Art. 60 para. 4 SCE-R. Unlike the Austrian solution, the SCE-R determines the earliest time when the documents are available for examination. However, the regulation does not refer to the report by the supervisory organ. This may be integrated by applying Art. 53 SCE-R, which addresses the organisation of the general meeting.

[1254] A specific right to speak is conferred to the auditor, who, according to Sec. 6 para. 3 GenREVG, is entitled, together with the auditing association, to participate as a consultant. A similar right is contained in the Austrian BWG, given to the federal commissioner and the state commissioner. See Siebenbäck (2014a), p. 344; also consider Kastner (1986), p. 181.

[1255] The right to speak is linked to the issue on the agenda. See Siebenbäck (2014a), p. 344; also consider Holthaus and Lehnhoff (2016a), p. 579.

[1256] For reimbursement of costs. However, this provision only relates to a right to information after the balance sheets have been approved.

[1257] For example Sec. 108 para. 3 AktG.

[1258] See Zehetner (2014d), p. 358 et seq.

[1259] Also the consolidated financial statements and the consolidated management report.

[1260] See Zehetner (2014d), p. 360; Zehetner (1999), p. 332.

The last issue that we must address is the requirement to take **minutes** at every general meeting, which requirement is in Art. 62 SCE-R.[1261] These minutes must contain, at a minimum, the venue and the date of the meeting, the resolutions passed and the results of any votes. The minutes[1262] must be kept for at least 5 years. Every member has the right to obtain a copy of the minutes.[1263] Other opportunities to examine the minutes must be determined according to Art. 53 SCE-R or other national rules whose content is not regulated by the SCE-R. The same applies to documents that are annexed to the minutes, which include the attendance list, documents about convening the general meeting and the reports that were submitted to the members about the agenda. The SCE-R does not provide legal consequences for the failure to take minutes; thus, national law has to be observed. As will be seen, the two national legal systems apply different approaches.

Italian law[1264] mandates that the minutes contain the date of the meeting, the identities of the participants and the capital that they each represent.[1265] The minutes must also contain the procedures and the results of any votes, including identifying how members voted (i.e., in favour of, against, abstained from or dissented). The members who make statements about the agenda can request that the minutes summarise these statements. According to Art. 2375 para. 3 CC, the minutes must not be recorded during the meeting but, rather, should be recorded within the filing or publication requirements.[1266] Next, the minutes of the resolutions must be signed by the chairman and the secretary. If an extraordinary assembly has been convened, the minutes must be signed by a notary.[1267] If the minutes are not recorded, the resolutions become void and may be challenged (Art. 2379 para. 1 CC). Art. 2379 para. 3 CC provides a remedy for this deficiency. These provisions must be applied by an Italian SCE, as the SCE-R is silent in this regard. Italian SCEs must also observe Art. 2375 para. 3 CC; otherwise, Art. 2379 para. 1 CC cannot be applied. Art. 2375 para. 3 CC contains parameters that can be used to determine when the minutes have failed to be recorded.[1268] Finally, Italian law permits third parties such

[1261]It states: "Minutes shall be drawn up for every general meeting. The minutes shall include at least the following particulars: - the venue and date of the meeting, - the resolutions passed, - the result of the voting. The attendance list, the documents relating to the convening of the general meeting and the reports submitted to the members on the items on the agenda shall be annexed to the minutes. The minutes and the documents annexed thereto shall be preserved for at least five years. A copy of the minutes and the documents annexed thereto may be obtained by any member upon request against defrayal of the administrative cost."

[1262]Which must be signed by the chairman.

[1263]Against defrayal of the administrative cost.

[1264]See Art. 2375 CC.

[1265]The identity of the participants can also be contained in an attachment.

[1266]See Bonfante (2014a), p. 332. Also consider Cian (2018h), p. 2792; Romano (2017f), p. 2925 et seq.; Mirone (2017b), p. 433.

[1267]See Art. 2375 para. 1 CC. Bonfante (2014a), p. 332; Barbarito (2004), p. 586 et seq.; Romano (2017f), p. 2925 et seq.; Mirone (2017b), p. 432.

[1268]See Bonfante (2014a), p. 332. Also consider Cottino and Cagnasso (2011), p. 357 et seq.

as auditors to examine the minutes.[1269] As shown above, these provisions must be considered by an Italian SCE.

The provisions in Art. 2375 and Art. 62 SCE-R have similar content, although some aspects are more precise, particularly, the identity of the participants or the results of the vote. These additional details do not contradict Art. 62 SCE-R and thus sharpen rather than prejudice its content; such details must be applied because of Art. 53 SCE-R. Art. 62 SCE-R only defines the minimum contents for the minutes.[1270]

The Austrian approach differs from the Italian approach. When referring to the term 'minutes' *Austrian law* distinguishes between the minute book and the minutes of the general meeting, which typically include the main contents of the meeting. According to Sec. 34 para. 2 *GenG*, the decisions of the general meeting must be recorded in the minute book, which contains the resolutions that were made.[1271] In practice, however, there is no separation between the two documents. The law only requires that the decisions be recorded in the minute book; it does not mandate that any other content be included. Among other things, it does not seem necessary to sign it. However, it is necessary to record the date on which the decisions are made.[1272] Every member of the cooperative may access the minute book, but third parties need authorisation to do so.[1273]

Comparing Sec. 34 para. 2 *GenG* and Art. 62 SCE-R reveals that the Austrian approach is less strict, even though the practical result is identical, at least in terms of content. One difference is the lack of a mandate that requires someone to sign the minute book. Austrian law gives authorised persons access to the minutes, a provision that must also be observed by Austrian SCEs.[1274]

For Austrian cooperatives and SCEs the resolutions are still effective even if the minutes are not drawn up. Austrian law requires that the minutes be primarily drawn up for evidence reasons. An exception is given for amending the statutes. These resolutions must be registered in the commercial register to be effective,[1275] something that must also be observed by Austrian SCEs. If Sec. 34 para. 2 *GenG* is not observed, the offending organ may be fined according to Sec. 87 *GenG*.[1276] This is also valid for an Austrian SCE.

[1269] Consider in this context, Art. 2375 para. 3 CC and Art. 2409 bis CC.

[1270] Without allowing the integration of further aspects via statutory provision. Also consider Lutter et al. (2012), p. 1620.

[1271] In practice, its contents are determined by statute.

[1272] See Siebenbäck (2014h), p. 385. Also consider Koppensteiner and Rüffler (2007), § 40 nt 4.

[1273] E.g., auditors. In this context Art. 71 SCE-R applies. According to Sec. 4 para. 1 GenRevG, the auditor is entitled to examine the books and records of the cooperative as well as the assets and debts; to this end all information and evidences necessary for a thorough audit shall be given to him. See Siebenbäck (2014h), p. 386 et seq.

[1274] Gap to be closed according to Art. 8 para. 1 letter c SCE-R.

[1275] Consider in this context Art. 5 para. 2 SCE-R. See Siebenbäck (2014h), p. 386; OGH 30.05.1973, 6 Ob 104/73 SZ 46/59; Koppensteiner and Rüffler (2007), § 40 nt 5.

[1276] See Siebenbäck (2014h), p. 387.

To summarise, the right to attend is regulated by the SCE-R, which assigns members the rights to speak and vote.[1277] They may be represented by a proxy. Some details are regulated by statute, while others must be determined by national law. Both legal systems address this issue, specifying that third parties may attend the general meeting. The chairman of the general meeting of an Austrian *agricultural SCE* has some discretion over admitting third parties. There are no significant differences between the rules applicable to Italian and Austrian SCEs with regard to the content of the right to attend.[1278] Members of an Italian *agricultural SCE*[1279] must not be registered for at least 90 days in the members' book in order to be allowed to attend the general meeting. The Italian legal system regulates the attendance of the holders of financial instruments who do not possess voting rights; the application of this provision is linked to Art. 58 para. 2 SCE-R.

Yet, considering a cooperative's needs, the right to attend is more accurately a requirement: Sec. 2.3 para. 1 letter c PECOL requires requires members to participate in the governance of the cooperative at a minimum level. One such requirement could be a minimum level of attendance at general meetings, with non-attendance leading to expulsion. This approach seems applicable to SCEs on the basis of Art. 14 para. 2 SCE-R. The PECOL define attendance as an individual right, which is similar to the definition in the SCE-R; the PECOL also allow members to attend via a proxy.[1280]

In principle, a member of an agricultural cooperative must actively work to attain the common objectives; they must thus refrain from any activity that contradicts the interests of the agricultural cooperative.[1281]

The member's commitment to an agricultural cooperative that is recognised as a PO is very strong, and the member will demonstrate their own initiative and interest in the PO by participating in the general meeting. Recall that the members of a PO are required to be members of only one PO.[1282] This pressures the members to participate in the general meeting: the strong link created by the PO means that the economic development of both the members' agricultural enterprises and the PO are intertwined. For instance, the members are obligated to sell all their products through the same PO. The members must also comply with PO's rules for production reporting, production, marketing and environmental protection. The combination of these various rules leads the member to have strong self-interest in exercising his right to attend the general meeting.

[1277]Other persons with no voting rights may attend the general meeting, particularly members of the SCE organs and holders of shares and debentures may. The SCE-R extends this group of people to those listed in the relevant national law. In this case, the statutes have to provide accordingly.

[1278]If ever a different wording is used to describe the same content.

[1279]Contrary to the legal solution applicable to an Italian cooperative.

[1280]See Sec. 2.3 para. 4 letter b PECOL; Snaith (2017), p. 56.

[1281]Not least also because of the fiduciary duties. See Sect. 3.3.1.

[1282]For any given product of the agricultiural holding. See Art. 153 para. 1 letter b Reg. 1308/2013.

The role of the chairman of the general meeting is rudimentarily regulated by the SCE-R.[1283] Thus, national provisions have to be considered because of Art. 53 SCE-R. The main difference here is that Austrian law does not contain a provision for the chairman's duties; in practice, statutes often contain specific provisions. In certain cases, third parties can chair the meeting. In general, the chairman conducts the meeting and must ensure that the items on the agenda are appropriately processed. An Italian *agricultural SCE* must observe similar provisions in the law.[1284] Accordingly, the chairman can be determined via the statutes or elected by the general meeting (after it is formed).

The SCE-R grants the right of information to the members of an SCE, which they can use to prepare for the general meeting[1285] or to request information during the general meeting. Both legal systems determine that the supervisory organ's report should be disclosed in advance. These provisions apply because of Art. 53 SCE-R.

Members may request information about items on the agenda and those items that do not require a decision. Though the SCE-R does not explicitly refer to this second possibility, it is indirectly provided by Art. 58 SCE-R[1286] or national law, if the latter so provides. Both the Austrian and Italian legal systems adopt a broad concept of the right of information. This approach is in line with the PECOL,[1287] which generally determine that the members of the organs must provide the members of the cooperative with the necessary information to control the cooperative, which includes setting its business, defining the promotion of members or participating in elections. Members need proper information to change the statutes or to reorganise the cooperative's structure.[1288]

This requirement is important to POs in the fruit and vegetables sector, given that members must approve operational programmes in general meetings and set up the operational fund. If they lack sufficient information, important strategic instruments cannot be adopted. This is similar to when the general meeting of an agricultural cooperative has the opportunity to decide on strategic investments; in this situation, it is essential for all the members to have sufficient information.

The SCE-R contains the option to refuse the requested information. The analyses have shown that the chairman of an Austrian SCE has the power to enact the right of information while balancing the interests of the members and the interest of cooperative to refuse specific information. Italian law provides a similar solution. Both

[1283]The PECOL do not consider this issue.

[1284]Art. 2371 CC.

[1285]In this context, Sec. 2.6 para. 2 PECOL refers to the annual accounts published to members, including an annual report and audit reports, as determined by law. It is specifically stressed that these documents must be available to the public. See Snaith (2017), p. 72.

[1286]The relevant member of the organ can be urged to supply information to guarantee trust between the organs and members.

[1287]Sec. 2.6 PECOL. Also consider Sec. 2.3 para. 5 letter a PECOL.

[1288]See Snaith (2017), p. 72.

legal systems allow the concerned member to appeal to a court when there is an unjustified refusal to supply information.

Our final topic is taking minutes, which is extensively regulated by the SCE-R. Yet, specific details about the legal consequences for failing to record the minutes are determined by national law, according to Art. 53 SCE-R. The two national legal systems differ over the contents of the minutes and the ability to challenge decisions when minutes are not taken.

4.4.4 Decision Making I: Quorums, Voting Rights and Proxy Voting ...

Art. 61 SCE-R contains several provisions that detail the general meeting's decision-making procedure. Art. 53 SCE-R determines that voting procedures are governed by national law,[1289] with the result that Austrian and Italian SCEs might have different voting procedures. The following 2 sub-chapters structure our comparison of the following issues: (1) the quorums necessary to constitute a general meeting, (2) voting rights, (3) proxy voting, (4) voting procedures and (5) majorities necessary to decide on specific issues. National law is useful for several purposes: to better conceptualise the provisions of the SCE-R, to apply these provisions, and to provide examples for possible statutory provisions.

According to Art. 61 para. 3 subpara. 1 SCE-R, the statutes complement and clarify the provisions of the SCE-R by establishing the **quorum** and the majority requirements for the general meeting.[1290] The statutes may, in principle, freely determine the quorum, with the exception in para. 4 of this article that refers to the amendment of the statutes.[1291] This statutory freedom is extended to both ordinary and extraordinary general meetings[1292]; however, this freedom is reduced if the statutes allow the admission of non-user members.[1293] To protect the user members,

---

[1289] Hence, the principal norm to be referenced is Art. 53 SCE-R and not Art. 8 SCE-R. See Schöpflin (2018ab), p. 1318. For the SE, see Mayer (2010b), p. 658.

[1290] See Schulze (2004a), p. 116. Art. 50 para. 1 SCE is not applicable. For the SE, see Mayer (2010f), p. 707.

Art 61 para. 3 subpara. 1 SCE-R states: "The statutes shall lay down the quorum and majority requirements which are to apply to general meetings."

[1291] See Schöpflin (2018aj), p. 1329.

[1292] See Schöpflin (2018aj), p. 1329.

[1293] See Art. 61 para. 3 subpara. 2 SCE-R. It states: "Where the statutes provide for the possibility of an SCE to admit investor (non-user) members, or to allocate votes according to capital contribution in SCEs involved in financial or insurance activities, the statutes shall also lay down special quorum requirements with relation to members other than investor (non-user) members or members that have voting rights according to capital contribution in SCEs involved in financial or insurance activities. Member states shall be free to set the minimum level of such special quorum requirements for those SCEs having their registered office in their territory."

the statutes must contain specific rules regarding the quorum.[1294] Ultimately, however, it is irrelevant whether or not the SCE actually has admitted non-user members.[1295]

Special rules must be adopted if the SCE conducts financial or insurance activities. If the statutes allow votes to be allocated according to capital contributions, specific rules must be adopted to protect those members whose voting rights are not allocated this way. Member states are authorised to set minimum levels of such special quorum requirements for SCEs with the registered office in their territory.[1296] Art. 61 para. 3 subpara. 2 SCE-R prevents non-user members from controlling the SCE, which members (according to Art. 59 para. 3 SCE-R) may not hold more than 25% of the total voting rights, if only the latter group of members is present at the meeting. The second rule contained in this provision, which considers voting rights in relation to capital contributions, has the same aim.[1297]

For decisions that amend the statutes, the SCE-R limits the quorum.[1298] This must be applied at a general meeting that is convened for the first time. In this case, the members present or represented must comprise at least half the total number of members on the date that the general meeting is convened. This creates a requirement that the statutes cannot be amended without due process. In other words, this legitimises the amendment of the statutes.[1299] However, if the general meeting is convened for a second time with the same agenda, no quorum needs to be met.[1300] This provision ensures that the decision-making process is not paralysed and does not restrict the functionality of the SCE.[1301]

Italian provisions contain requirements for both quorums and majorities that must be determined by the statutes and must be calculated according to the number of

---

[1294]If the statutes provide for the admission of non-user members.

[1295]See Schulze (2004a), p. 116 et seq. Also consider Schöpflin (2018aj), p. 1328 et seq.; Lutter et al. (2012), p. 1622 et seq.

[1296]See Art. 61 para. 3 subpara. 1 SCE-R. Also consider Schulze (2004a), p. 116 et seq.

[1297]See Schöpflin (2018aj), p. 1329.

[1298]See Art. 61 para. 4 SCE-R. It states: "A general meeting may amend the statutes the first time it is convened only if the members present or represented make up at least half of the total number of members on the date the general meeting is convened, and the second time it is convened on the same agenda no quorum shall be necessary. In the cases referred to in the first subparagraph, at least two thirds of the votes cast validly must be cast in favour, unless the law applicable to cooperatives in the Member State in which the SCE's registered office is situated requires a greater majority." This norm prevails over corresponding national provisions.

Amending the statutes implies any formal and material amendment. It refers, for instance, to measures regarding minimum capital, or mergers the SCE. For the SE, see Mayer (2010h), p. 732.

[1299]See Schöpflin (2018aj), p. 1329; Schulze (2004a), p. 117.

[1300]See Art. 61 para. 4 SCE-R.

[1301]See Schöpflin (2018aj), p. 1329.

votes attributed to the members.[1302] This approach grants the freedom to set the necessary quorums, thus facilitating the decision-making process as much as possible. However, this does not imply unlimited statutory freedom: the provisions must align with those that govern the function of the *spa*. It is not possible to apply provisions that either require unanimous decisions or fix a quorum for extraordinary general meetings that is lower than that set for ordinary general meetings. However, it is possible to set an identical quorum for both.[1303]

Apart from the mandatory provision in Art. 61 para. 4 SCE-R, the Italian legislature adopts a solution for its national cooperatives that is basically the same as that established by the SCE-R. However, Italian cooperatives are not obligated to determine specific quorum requirements for situations in which non-members are admitted or where the cooperative is involved in financial or insurance activities. The Italian legislature did not exercise the option in Art. 61 para. 3 subpara. 2 last sent. SCE-R.

The quorum that an *Austrian cooperative* must observe is regulated by Sec. 31 *GenG*. Accordingly, at least 10% of members must be present or represented, unless otherwise stated by the statutes. In practice, the statutes frequently establish a higher quorum, and so, too, does the law.[1304] In specific cases, at least a third of members need to be present or represented.[1305]

[1302]Art. 2538 para. 5 CC. Until 2003, it was possible to derogate the majorities indicated by Art. 2368 CC and Art. 2369 CC via statutory provisions. According to Art. 2368 CC, a shareholders' meeting is validly convened if at least half of the share capital is represented. . . . The meeting adopts resolutions by means of absolute majority, unless a larger majority is required. . . . The extraordinary shareholders' meeting adopts resolutions with the favourable vote of more than half of the capital, unless a larger majority is required by the statutes. Art. 2369 para. 3 CC determines that the ordinary shareholders' meeting resolves on the matters which should have been dealt with at the first call, regardless of what portion of capital is represented; in turn, the extraordinary shareholders' meeting is validly constituted with the presence of more than one third of the share capital and adopts resolutions with the favourable vote of at least two thirds of the capital represented at the meeting.

[1303]See Bonfante (2014a), p. 308 et seq. Also consider Di Cecco (2003), p. 124; Cusa (2011a), p. 2207 et seq.; Cusa (2007), p. 306; Marano (2013a), p. 2735. See also Paolucci (2019b), p. 121 et seq.

[1304]For example, when decisions must be made about converting between types of liability or reducing the number of shares. See Sect. 5.1.

[1305]See Siebenbäck (2014e), p. 374. Also consider Keinert (1988), p. 146; Reischauer (1976), p. 11; Kastner et al. (1990), p. 471. It is not quite clear whether minority rights are bound to the presence of a determined number of members or, if the statutes determine majority voting rights, on the presence of 10% (according to Sec. 31 GenG or two thirds according to Sec. 33 para. 3 GenG) of the votes. Based on the wording, it is the number of members that counts. See Keinert (1988), p. 146.

Comparing the approaches in the SCE-R and the *GenG* reveals similar results, although the Austrian provision is a default rule (with an opt-out clause); both sets of rules allow a meeting to be convened for a second time without observing a quorum. However, Austrian cooperatives are not obliged to set special quorum requirements if either non-user members are admitted or a cooperative conducts financial or insurance activities, in which case the votes are allocated according to capital contributions.

Sec. 32 *GenG* refers to a waiting period. Accordingly, if there is no quorum, the general meeting may decide on the agenda's items, regardless of the number of members present or represented, once half an hour has elapsed, unless the statutes do not provide otherwise.[1306] To be valid, this waiting period must have been mentioned during the notification of the meeting. This provision makes a second meeting superfluous if no quorum is set. Members' protected interests are not violated, because they always have the opportunity to participate at the meeting. The waiting period allows members who are late to participate during the general meeting.[1307] Such a provision is not considered by the SCE-R, but can be introduced via statute. In fact, as the general meeting of an Austrian SCE can be convened without a quorum,[1308] it should be possible to adopt a provision that requires a quorum and establishes a waiting period to offset it. Last, according to Art. 61 para. 3 subpara. 2 SCE-R, member states may set minimum quorum requirements. However, the Austrian legislature did not exercise this option.[1309]

Voting rights, our second topic, is regulated by Art. 59 SCE-R,[1310] which considers different categories of members and their connections to an SCE. However, these rules must be supplemented by national provisions.

[1306]These provisions are also applied when changing the type of liability or reducing the number of cooperative shares. Consider Sec. 33 para. 3 GenG.

[1307]See Siebenbäck (2014f), p. 375; Dellinger and Oberhammer (1996), p. 160. A waiting period can only be applied if the statues do not preclude it, in which case, a second general meeting must be convened. For this second meeting, the quorums determined by the law (or statutes) must again be applied. The facts necessary to evaluate the quorum must be recorded in the minutes. This implies that, in practice, the chairman must open the meeting at the predefined time and ascertain that the required quorum is not met. This fact must be recorded in the minutes. It seems possible to discuss items on the agenda during these 30 min, provided no decision is taken. See Siebenbäck (2014f), p. 375 et seq.

[1308]Clearly, an exception applies when amending the statutes.

[1309]See Fici (2010), p. 64 et seq.

[1310]The SCE-R does not deal with the issue of voting rights in case of conflict of interests (ban of votes); hence national provisions have to be taken into consideration as required by Art. 53 SCE-R. As opposed to the laws on private and public limited-liability companies, the GenG does not consider the aspect of voting right preclusions/legal bans on voting. According to the main doctrine, the voting right of a member is precluded if a decision has to be taken on issues regarding the member himself. Moreover, also controlled companies cannot exercise their voting rights at the general meeting of the cooperative. The same is true for cooperatives that hold own shares (the voting right has to be put on hold. It is discussed whether holding own shares is permissible). An exception is the voting right regarding elections: In analogy to the laws on the GmbH and the AG, a member of a cooperative may vote also in case he or she has to be appointed to be a member of an

The principle of democratic control is fundamental to cooperatives and thus agricultural SCEs. A member's allocated voting rights are independent of the number of shares that they hold.[1311] This right cannot be excluded by the statutes, although exceptions are allowed.[1312] Under certain conditions, the law of the member state in which the agricultural SCE has its registered office allows multiple voting rights.[1313]

First, the number of votes may be determined according to the member's participation in the cooperative's activity.[1314] However, limits must be observed. In fact, it cannot exceed five votes per member or 30% of total voting rights, whichever is lower.[1315]

Another exception to the principle of 'one member, one vote' can be found in Art. 59 para. 2 subpara. 2 SCE-R, which concerns SCEs that conduct financial or insurance activities.[1316] The statutes may provide that the number of votes be

organ. See Siebenbäck (2014a), p. 343 et seq. Considering the Italian legal system, one has to take into consideration the provisions as adopted for the spa (according to Art. 2519 CC), as the provisions directly referring to cooperatives do not contain any specific details in this regard. Specific provisions regarding conflict of interests are contained in Art. 2373 CC determining the procedure in case of invalidity of resolutions. In fact, para. 1 determines that resolutions approved with the deciding vote of members having a direct conflict of interest may be challenged in accordance with Art. 2377 CC on the condition that the decision could harm the company. In this context, it has been highlighted that the items discussed and decided have to refer directly the member. See Tatarano (2011), p. 433 fn 42.

1311 Art. 59 para. 1 SCE-R states that each member of an SCE shall have one vote, regardless of the number of shares he or she holds.

1312 This is commonly referred to as the principle of "one member, one vote", a democratic and participatory tradition of the cooperative system. See Schulze (2004a), p. 117; Alfandari and Piot (2004), p. 85. Also consider Henrÿ (2012), p. 85; Lehner (2009), p. 101; Bianca and Zanardo (2016), p. 211; Korte (2012), p. 337; Galle (2006), p. 258. For general observations on the evolution of voting rights, see Hansmann and Pargendler (2013).

1313 See Alfandari and Piot (2004), p. 85; Lutter et al. (2012), p. 1621; Holthaus and Lehnhoff (2016c), p. 49 et seq.

1314 Unlike a company, the decisive factor in a cooperative is participation other than by making a capital contribution. See Sect. 3.3.1.

1315 See Art. 59 para. 2 subpara. 1 SCE-R. It states: "If the law of the Member State in which the SCE has its registered office so permits, the statutes may provide for a member to have a number of votes determined by his/her participation in the cooperative activity other than by way of capital contribution. This attribution shall not exceed five votes per member or 30 % of total voting rights, whichever is the lower." Secondary cooperatives are particularly likely to take advantage of this. See Alfandari and Piot (2004), p. 85.

1316 These cooperatives normally need a considerable amount of capital. See Schöpflin (2018ah), p. 1325; Lutter et al. (2012), p. 1621. Also consider Alfandari and Piot (2004), p. 86.

determined by each member's participation in the cooperative's activity, including participation in the capital of the SCE. However, this attribution cannot exceed five votes per member or 20% of the total voting rights, whichever is lower.[1317]

Next, the SCE-R refers to SCEs in which the majority of members are cooperatives.[1318] In this case, the regulation does not determine any limit on voting rights. The statutes can require that the number of votes be determined in accordance with each member's participation, including participation in the capital of the SCE, and/or by the number of members of each entity. The relevant national law must permit this accordingly.[1319]

Finally, Art. 59 para. 3 SCE-R determines that the voting rights of non-user members are governed by the law of the state of registration.[1320] However, non-user members may not hold more than 25% of the total voting rights,[1321] including plural voting rights.[1322] If the national legislator allows the admission of non-user members, he can determine if and how the statutes of an SCE connect plural voting rights to capital participation; thus, he can, ultimately, set a more stringent limit than that established by Art. 59 para. 3 SCE-R.[1323] Furthermore, the 25% limit is based on the assumption that these categories of members *per definitionem* have interests that

[1317] Art. 59 para. 2 subpara. 2 SCE-R states: "If the law of the Member State in which the SCE has its registered office so permits, SCEs involved in financial or insurance activities may provide in their statutes for the number of votes to be determined by the members' participation in the cooperative activity including participation in the capital of the SCE. This attribution shall not exceed five votes per member or 20 % of total voting rights, whichever is the lower."

[1318] In this case, the SCE has the function of a secondary cooperative. See Schöpflin (2018ah), p. 1325 et seq. Also consider Alfandari and Piot (2004), p. 86; Lutter et al. (2012), p. 1621.

[1319] Art. 59 para. 2 subpara. 3 SCE-R states: "In SCEs the majority of members of which are cooperatives, if the law of the Member State in which the SCE has its registered office so permits, the statutes may provide for the number of votes to be determined in accordance with the members' participation in the cooperative activity including participation in the capital of the SCE and/or by the number of members of each comprising entity."

[1320] See Lutter et al. (2012), p. 1622.

[1321] It states: "As regards voting rights which the statutes may allocate to non-user (investor) members, the SCE shall be governed by the law of the Member State in which the SCE has its registered office. Nevertheless, non-user (investor) members may not together have voting rights amounting to more than 25 % of total voting rights."

[1322] See Schöpflin (2018ah), p. 1326. Also consider Alfandari and Piot (2004), p. 86. This voting right is thus not assigned by a statutory provision; it is assigned on the basis of membership, assuming that the statutes allow it. Hence, it is a specific feature of this type of membership. See Schöpflin (2018ah), p. 1326.

[1323] See Schulze (2004a), p. 118. Also consider Alfandari and Piot (2004), p. 81; Ebers (2004), p. 47.

conflict with the interests of user members.[1324] However, investor members do not automatically pursue a speculative purpose or expect particular dividends on their investments; the SCE-R does not consider the option of statutory provisions granting special financial privileges. Hence, these types of members ultimately concentrate on the promotion of the user-members' needs.[1325]

To summarise, applying plural voting rights depends on national law, which requires us to compare the national solutions with those offered by the SCE-R. This comparison helps us to better evaluate the content of the latter. In principle, the *Italian legal system* adopts the rule of 'one member, one vote',[1326] with some exceptions to this rule that result in a rather complex framework. Under Italian law, the principle of 'one member, one vote' can only be derogated if a specific legal provision provides accordingly.[1327] In addition, the statutes must specify the chosen derogation. Clearly, the way voting rights are calculated has important consequences for the principle of democracy, one of the pillars of the cooperative movement. Until 1992, the number of votes more or less coincided with the number of members; after 1992, the situation changed.[1328]

Art. 2538 para. 2 CC thus determines that each member has one vote in the general meeting, no matter the amount of subscribed capital. Voting power is thus linked to membership itself.[1329] The article contains the first reference to plural

---

[1324]This provision ensures that basic cooperative principles are not weakened too much. Admitting only non-user members would give the SCE a pure capitalistic approach. With such a statutory provision, the promotion would no longer focus on business transactions with the members but on the allocation of dividends based on how many shares a member holds. See Greda (2014), p. 835 et seq. Also consider Lutter et al. (2012), p. 1622. Also consider Corapi and de Donno (2006), p. 1323.

[1325]See Rocchi (2006), p. 98.

[1326]This principle is probably the most iconic. While the nature and importance of other principles like solidarity or providing services can differ, the principle of "one member, one vote" is a constant of cooperative law all over the world. With the adoption of law no 59 in 1992, this principle was partly amended. Whereas these amendments were initially made for non-user members, they have also been introduced for user members. In 2003 the company law reform amended this principle to increase participation of risk capital. See Bonfante (2014a), p. 311 et seq.

As seen in Sect. 4.4.3, voting rights can be exercised by members of an Italian cooperative on the condition that they have been registered in their members' book for at least 90 days.

[1327]Cooperative banks cannot derogate this principle. See Art. 30 para. 1 TUB and Art. 34 para. 3 TUB.

[1328]The concept of non-user members was introduced into the Italian legal system in 1992. See Bonfante (2014a), p. 312.

Specific problems may arise, because the legal system contains criteria that governs both the number of votes (see Art. 2538 para. 5 CC) and the number of members (See Art. 2541 para. 2 CC, Art. 2545 bis CC and Art. 135 and 157 of the TUF). Also consider Bonfante (2014a), p. 309.

[1329]This reflects the democratic principle of administration, whereas a link to the amount of the subscribed capital would be in line with a capitalistic principle of administration. See Bonfante (2014a), p. 15 et seq.; Henrÿ (2012), p. 85 et seq.; Lehner (2009), p. 101; Corapi and de Donno (2006), p. 1323.

voting. Accordingly, the statutes determine the limits of voting rights related to financial instruments that are offered for subscription to user members. This provision helps overcome the uncertainties surrounding the possibility of a user member simultaneously holding shares and financial instruments, as well as doubts about voting methods. While it was previously argued that, in such situations, the member could only vote as an investor-member, the new law limits non-user members' voting rights via statutory provisions and generally allows members to cast a additional vote (in addition to the principle of 'one member, one vote'), because he or she holds a financial instrument.[1330] By contrast,[1331] the SCE-R seems to exclude such 'double' voting.

Art. 2526 para. 2 CC contains safeguards for user members. This provision limits the voting rights of the holders of financial instruments to a third of the total number of voting rights that are granted to members (present or represented) in each general meeting.[1332] Unless the statutes provide otherwise, voting rights must be calculated in proportion to the capital subscribed rather than according to the principle of 'one member, one vote'.[1333] In any case, the maximum limit of a third of the total votes in each general meeting must be observed.[1334]

The SCE-R differs from Italian law in two ways. First, it defines a threshold of 25%. Second, it refers to total voting rights and not to votes assigned to members (present or represented) in each general meeting. As will be seen below, these different approaches to limits can lead to different results. I argue that an Italian SCE may use statutes to require that the limit of 25% be linked to those members actually present at the general meeting, as long as the limit set by Art. 59 para. 3 sent. 2 SCE-R is not exceeded. To reiterate, Art. 61 para. 3 subpara. 2 SCE-R requires the statutes to provide safeguards for user members. This implies that the statutes must regulate the presence of these two types of members.[1335] One possibility is to establish a link to those members actually present, specifying that the lower limit must be applied. Voting rights that are granted to financing members can hence be determined according to various criteria.[1336]

[1330] See Bonfante (2014a), p. 312; Tatarano (2011), p. 435; Santagata (2017), p. 831. For a different opinion, see Cusa (2006), p. 427.

[1331] See Sect. 3.4.1.

[1332] Paolucci (2012), p. 130; Paolucci (2019a), p. 85 et seq.

[1333] See Bonfante (2014a), p. 310. For a different opinion, see Cusa (2006), p. 427. Further details, see Sect. 4.4.5. Also consider Marasà (2016), p. 4 et seq.

[1334] See Bonfante (2014a), p. 314. Consider in this context Sect. 4.4.5, where this argument is discussed in more detail. See also Santagata (2017), p. 831.

[1335] See Rocchi (2006), p. 100 et seq. Generally, Münkner (2006), p. 18.

[1336] Also consider Rocchi (2006), p. 100 et seq.

Next, the Italian legal system considers two cases that refer to Art. 59 para. 2 subpara. 1 SCE-R[1337]: first, cooperatives formed of members integrating their companies or parts of their companies (Art. 2538 para. 4 CC) and, second, members of the controlling body who are appointed according to proportional voting in relation to shares held or to participation in the mutual exchange (Art. 2543 para. 2 CC).

In the first case, Art. 2538 para. 4 CC states that the statutes may allocate votes in proportion to the transactions that occur between the members and the cooperative. This exception applies to cooperatives among entrepreneurs, however. More specifically, the law refers to cooperatives that are formed by integrating different companies or parts of companies.[1338] In this case, the statutes may create categories of members and limit the votes such that no member has more than 10% of the total votes in each general meeting. In addition, each category combined may not hold more than a third of the total votes in each general meeting.[1339]

A problem might arise, as the limit of 10% for each member must be combined with the overall threshold of a third of the total votes for each general meeting. As a result, the first limit will be compressed relative to the number of members in each category.[1340] Even though this provision is slightly ambiguous, no general principle has been introduced that allows for plural voting rights in proportion to the transactions that occur between the members and the cooperative. This possibility may be exclusively granted to consortia of cooperatives in which all members are entrepreneurs.[1341] On the other hand, scholars stress that Art. 2538 para. 4 CC not only refers to user-members, but also enables the founding of consortia that are open to non-user members.[1342] In addition, it is not easy to define a clear limit with which to create a category of preferred members who are ascribed plural voting rights. In fact, statutory provisions can be rather arbitrary. Further difficulties might arise from the fact that the membership in a specific category is based on how the members

[1337]Number of votes determined by participation.

[1338]It is not important whether these entrepreneurs are legal entities or natural persons. As opposed to Art. 2538 para. 3 CC, this possibility is not limited to secondary cooperatives and, moreover, the provision contains different limits.

[1339]See Bonfante (2014a), p. 313; Marano (2013a); Santagata (2017), p. 831. Also consider Cusa (2006), p. 427. It must be added that under the Italian legal system, plural voting does not replace the basic principle but must be added to it. Otherwise, those who collaborated most with the cooperative would always be in the minority as they could never hold more than a third of the votes. The aim of this provision is to favour those members who use the cooperative more. See Bonfante (2014a), p. 314.

[1340]Bonfante (2014a), p. 314. In this case, it appears the principle of "one member, one vote" has been interpreted such that the democratic principle only forbids the control of the cooperative by one member or category of members. It does not require each member to have equal voting rights. Voting in this context is linked to the degree of interest each member has in mutuality. Hence, it can be called a mutualistic criterion of vote assignment. See Fici and Strano (2010), p. 689. Also consider Lehner (2009), p. 101.

[1341]See Bonfante (2014a), p. 313.

[1342]See Cusa (2014a).

participate in mutual transactions, which may change over time. As a result, control mechanisms may be introduced to verify the use of services and may include procedures to admit and expel members from specific categories.[1343]

Communication no. 9203 from the ministry for economic development states that only the limits in Art. 2538 para. 4 CC apply. Some wrongly assume that the SCE-R refers exclusively to national law, which ignores the clear maximum levels set by the SCE-R.[1344] It can be debated whether national law must be combined with Art. 59 para. 2 subpara. 1 SCE-R, which requires the lower limit to be applied. However, doing so would make applying the provisions particularly cumbersome, as the following example shows.

In brief, Italian law determines a maximum limit per member of 10% of the votes in each general meeting, whereas the SCE-R limits votes to five per member. Next, Italian law sets a limit of a third of the votes of the members who are present or represented at each general meeting, whereas the SCE-R fixes the threshold at 30% of total voting rights. The SCE-R clearly sets a maximum limit that can be undercut by the national legislature. Comparing the SCE-R's provisions with Italian ones reveals that this is a complicated solution in practice:

1) Consider a cooperative with 100 members, in which all members are present at the general meeting. The limits are calculated as follows:

   - according to the SCE-R: 5 votes per member and 30 votes overall
   - according to Italian law: 10 votes per member and 33 votes overall

   Here the limits of the SCE-R, which sets maximum limits, must be observed, as they are lower.
2) Consider a cooperative with 100 members and 40 members present at the general meeting. Now the limits change significantly:

   - according to the SCE-R: 5 votes per member and 30 votes altogether.
   - according to Italian law: 4 votes per member and 13 votes altogether.

   Here the Italian provisions must be observed, as they set lower thresholds.

On the other hand, the provisions in Art. 59 para. 2 SCE-R could be interpreted as exclusively determining the limits and excluding further provisions from a national legislature. The structure of subpara. 1[1345] refers to national law, only requiring that national law must permit the voting calculation to be linked to member's participation in the cooperative's activity, while statutes can determine the number of votes. Therefore, the second sentence of Art. 59 para. 2 subpara. 1 SCE-R can be considered a specific rule adopted by the SCE-R that must take priority over divergent national law.[1346] As a result, only the limits of the SCE-R need to be applied.

[1343]See Bonfante (2014a), p. 314.

[1344]Ministry for economic development, Art. 59. Also consider Chirico and Troianiello (2007), p. 62.

[1345]And similarly subpara. 2.

[1346]See Art. 8 para. 1 letter b SCE-R.

The other provision that must be considered when trying to apply Art. 59 para. 2 subpara. 1 SCE to an Italian SCE is Art. 2543 para. 2 CC. Accordingly, the statutes may determine the voting rights for appointing members of the controlling body (supervisory organ) in proportion to mutual exchanges.[1347] This exception has been both praised as the solution to problems that result from heterogeneous membership and interpreted as an incentive that establishes a cooperative even under these conditions.[1348] This provision should not pose further interpretative problems. Clearly, the limits determined by the SCE-R must be observed. Note that this rule does not seem to apply under the one-tier system, as the management control committee is appointed by the administrative organ and not by the members.[1349]

Next, Art. 2538 para. 3 CC refers to the option to use an Italian SCE as a secondary cooperative.[1350] It determines that the statutes may assign any member that is a legal entity up to five votes, either in relation to the capital held or the number of its members. By contrast, an Italian SCE may regulate such limits by statute.

The exception in para. 3 results from adapting the democratic principle to the necessities of secondary cooperatives.[1351] However, this derogation seems to only apply to legal entities that are interested in using the service provided by the cooperative as a means to support their own members. This is allowed by the concept of indirect mutuality (*mutualità mediata*) that is introduced by the SCE-R.[1352]

Art. 2538 para. 3 CC may be applied in the context of Art. 59 para. 2 subpara. 2 SCE-R, which refers to SCEs involved in financial and insurance activities. An exception is given for cooperative banks, which cannot derogate from the principle of 'one member, one vote'.[1353] Communication no. 9203 from the ministry for economic development stresses that the limits in Art. 2538 para. 3 CC must be applied. The doubts expressed about the binding nature of Communication no. 9203

[1347]Or in proportion to the capital held, which can only be applied by an Italian SCE according to para. 2 subparas 2 and 3. This exception differs from the previous ones, as it applies to all cooperatives, and not only to those made up of entrepreneurs. It applies to the appointment of the supervisory organ and, interestingly, the criterion to determine the voting power may also be a capitalistic one (as it refers to the amount of capital held).

[1348]This exception admittedly represents a departure from the principle of democracy. However, as it only applies to the election of the supervisory organ, one can argue that this reduces risk of undermining the social function of a cooperative. See Fici and Strano (2010), p. 689.

[1349]Unless otherwise provided in the statutes. See Art. 2409 octiesdecies para. 1 CC. For further details on Art. 2543 CC, Giorgi (2018a), p. 3241 et seq.; Bonfante (2004a), p. 2592 et seq.; Paolucci (2019f), p. 137 et seq.

[1350]See Art. 59 para. 2 subpara. 3 SCE-R.

[1351]See Fici and Strano (2010), p. 689.

[1352]See Bonfante (2014a), p. 313. Also consider Sect. 3.4.2; Bonfante (2006), p. 12; Racugno (2014); Iengo (2006).

[1353]See Art. 30 para. 1 testo unico bancario (TUB, Consolidated Law on Banking) and Art. 34 para. 3 TUB. See also Cusa (2004c), p. 180.

are also valid in this context.[1354] The better solution would be to exclusively apply the limits that are determined by the SCE-R.

Austrian law fully implemented Art. 59 para. 2 subpara. 1 SCE-R into Sec. 28 para. 1 subpara. 1 SCEG. The same is true for subparas. 2 and 3 as well as for Art. 59 para. 3 SCE-R.[1355] The main provisions of the *GenG* help us to comprehend the complete approach used under Austrian law. In fact, the option for plural voting is already contained in the *GenG*. According to Sec. 5 para. 1 no. 9 *GenG*, the statutes must determine the conditions of the voting rights and the form in which they are to be exercised. The law gives cooperatives an almost free rein here. As a basic rule, every member must have at least one vote during the general meeting.[1356] However, the open formulation of Sec. 5 para. 1 no. 9 *GenG* makes it possible to determine the voting rights in relation to the shares held.[1357]

Statutory provisions can limit plural voting. In addition, voting rights can be determined according to transactions that are conducted with the cooperative.[1358] The regulations governing voting rights must align with the principle of equality and be objectively justified.[1359] Thus, the *GenG* provides a fairly flexible framework that allows different approaches, which can probably go further than that determined by the SCE-R for an Austrian SCE, particularly given the limitations contained therein.

The next (third) subtopic of decision making is **proxy voting**. The SCE-R provides the option to represent members[1360] at the general meeting by means of a proxy, assuming the statutes expressly allow this. In addition, the statutes must

[1354]See Sect. 2.5.

[1355]The national implementing law uses the same wording as the German version of the SCE-R. Also consider Avsec (2009), p. 55.

[1356]Like the right to attend, also the right to vote are bound to the member. If legal persons are members, the voting right is exercised by their representatives. In case of natural persons who are legally incapable, the voting right is granted to the legal representatives. See Siebenbäck (2014a), p. 342. Also consider Sangiovanni (2005), p. 257 et seq.

[1357]See Siebenbäck (2014a), p. 342. In this case, the law requires a calculation of both the members present and the votes present, for each item to be decided. Consider, e.g., Sec. 33 GenG. For minority rights, the law normally considers the number of the members (Sec. 29 and 31 GenG). If the legal requirements are not mandatory and plural voting has been adopted, the statutes must determine (also by interpretation) whether the 10% criterion refers to members or votes. See Siebenbäck (2014a), p. 343.

[1358]For instance, in a production cooperative, the amount of transactions would be determined according to the products delivered. In this way, the member helps increase the turnover and thus the economic success of the cooperative, with the consequence that the promotion aim of the cooperative can be fulfilled in the best possible way.

[1359]See Siebenbäck (2014a), p. 343.

[1360]The English version of the SCE-R refers to this as persons entitled to vote. Also consider Sect. 4.4.3 fn 1194.

determine the necessary procedure for this purpose and the maximum number of persons for whom a proxy may act.[1361]

The wording here is rather unclear. While the English text describes the entitlement to appoint a proxy as being governed by the statutes,[1362] the German and Italian versions describe 'being represented' as the concept regulated by the statutes.[1363] Thus, the extent to which statutory provisions and other aspects can be applied via national law, according to Art. 53 SCE-R is unclear. The English translation seems stricter, as it focuses on the process of appointment, arguably excluding the person to be appointed. Conversely, the other two versions, especially the German version, focus on the possibility that a member be represented by a proxy, according to statutory provisions. It is unclear from the English text whether the statutes can also determine who may be a proxy, as this is not necessarily included in the process of appointment, at least if interpreted narrowly. In this case, national law clarifies what Art. 58 para. 3 SCE-R means by the word 'proxy'.

As this study analyses the application of the SCE-R in Austria and Italy, the more open interpretation is used. Thus, I argue both that the statutes could determine who may be appointed as a proxy and that proxies may be other members of the SCE, members of the administrative, management or supervisory organ or non-members.[1364] In addition, the statutes may determine when relevant formalities need to be observed, for instance, in cases where proxies may only be conferred in writing. The SCE-R does not contain a limitation in this regard.[1365]

At this point, comparing the solutions offered by the SCE-R the two national legal systems may help us to better determine the content of the proxy voting and how to apply it. The *Italian legal system* allows proxy voting, according to two provisions in Art. 2539 CC.

First, it offers the option to delegate the power to vote by appointing another member as a proxy to represent them at the general meeting.[1366] The law limits this delegation by specifying that each member may not represent more than 10 other members.[1367] Art. 58 para. 3 subpara. 2 SCE-R asserts that such limits must be

[1361]See Schulze (2004a), p. 114.

Art 58 para. 3 SCE-R states: "A person entitled to vote shall be entitled to appoint a proxy to represent him/her at a general meeting in accordance with procedures laid down in the statutes. The statutes shall lay down the maximum number of persons for whom a proxy may act."

[1362]"... shall be entitled ... in accordance with procedures laid down in the statutes." See Art. 58 para. 3 SCE-R.

[1363]German text: "... können sich in der Generalversammlung nach Maßgabe der Satzung von einem Bevollmächtigen vertreten lassen."; Italian version: "... possono farsi rappresentare all'assemblea generale da un mandatario secondo le modalità previste dallo statuto."

[1364]See Schöpflin (2018ag), p. 1323.

[1365]See Schöpflin (2018ag), p. 1323.

[1366]The provisions contained in Art. 2539 CC must be applied to every type of meeting (ordinary, extraordinary, separated or special meetings). See Bonfante (2014a), p. 321. See also Paolucci (2019c), p. 125 et seq.

[1367]This provision has been enacted to promote member participation. However, it only applies to cooperatives which are subject to the regulation of an spa. See Paolucci (2019c).

determined via the statutes. In addition, the Italian approach is stricter than the provisions contained in the SCE-R, as it only allows other members to act as proxies.[1368]

Second, when the member is an individual entrepreneur, they may delegate the power to vote to their spouse, relatives within the third degree and second-degree or closer relatives-in-law that work with the enterprise.[1369] It has been questioned whether Art. 2539 para. 1 CC can really eliminate the need for proxy voting to be based on a specific statutory provision, as was requested by the former norm.[1370] It is doubtful that every member *ex lege*[1371] has the opportunity to represent up to 10 members. Such an interpretation would be inconsistent with a cooperative that has relatively few members. The principles expressed in the delegating law[1372] require that proxy voting be adapted to the organisational structure and the mutual purpose of the cooperative.[1373] Yet, from a formal perspective, a specific statutory clause that authorises proxy voting does not seem to be obligatory. However, making a statutory provision obligatory seems inevitable to safeguard members' individual participation and to respect the principle of democracy.[1374]

Art. 2539 CC does not distinguish between user members and non-user members. This lack of distinction raises the questions of (a) whether non-user members also must observe the limit in para. 1 and (b) whether mixed delegation is possible, i.e., whether delegation without considering the two different member groups is allowed. To answer the first question, the formulation of Art. 2539 CC does not allow a distinction to be drawn between these two groups. As a result, this provision must be observed by all members, regardless of their membership type. To answer the second question, a mixed delegation of voting rights does not appear to be possible, as both member groups combine different rights and obligations, which can hardly be represented by the same vote.[1375] Both observations are significant for Italian SCEs, as Art. 58 para. 3 SCE-R refers to members (persons entitled to vote) without

---

[1368]This provision has been introduced to combat absenteeism at the general meeting. The previous limits have been extended to foster greater representation among members. See Bonfante (2014a), p. 319. Also consider Ceccherini (2008); Falcone (2003), p. 136; Di Cecco (2003), p. 127; Cusa (2011b), p. 2215 et seq.; Marano (2013b), p. 2741. See also Paolucci (2019c), p. 125 et seq.

[1369]For details Paolucci (2019c). Italian scholars have stressed that this provision derogates from the general principle, which determines that only members may vote at a meeting of a cooperative. For example, this exception is contained in the laws referring to family companies (Art. 14 law no 903/77). See Bonfante (2014a), p. 322.

[1370]See Cusa (2014b), p. 355.

[1371]If no specific statutory provision provides accordingly.

[1372]Law no 366 from 3 October 2001, enabling the government to reform company law.

[1373]A statutory clause could, for instance, set a limit lower than the one provided for by Art. 2539 para. 1 CC. Cusa (2014b), p. 355. Also consider Di Cecco (2003), p. 127; Bonfante (2014a), p. 320.

[1374]Which could be eroded by means of proxy voting, where ultimately only two members could represent the entire member structure in the general meeting. See Bonfante (2014a), p. 320. Different opinion Marano (2013b), p. 2743.

[1375]See Bonfante (2014a), p. 321.

distinguishing between user- and non-user member. In addition, mixed voting does not seem to apply to an Italian SCE, because of the argument advanced above.[1376]

The reference in Art. 2519 CC requires Art. 2372 CC to be observed, according to which a proxy must be conferred in writing. The relevant documents must be retained by the cooperative.[1377] In addition, the document must provide the name of their representative and a person who may substitute for the representative. This person must also be a member of the cooperative. The appointment procedure is regulated by statutory provisions; this provision is not applicable to Italian SCEs.[1378] However, it can be used as a guideline for drafting specific statutory provisions. According to Art. 2372 para. 2 CC, a proxy can be granted to more than one meeting on the condition that the cooperative does not use the risk capital market. This option can be exercised via statutory provision because of Art. 58 para. 3 subpara. 1 SCE-R.

Finally, a proxy to the general meeting of an Italian cooperative cannot be granted to members of the management or administrative organ, nor to members of the controlling body,[1379] which (under the two-tier system) is the supervisory organ. The same is true for the employees of a (non-worker) cooperative.[1380] The SCE-R demonstrates more flexibility by allowing these persons and third-parties to be proxies. Due to this flexibility and openness, the statutes of an Italian SCE can also contain a provision similar to para. 2 of Art. 2539 CC (which governs the members of an Italian cooperative who are individual entrepreneurs,[1381] but generally limits proxy voting to members).

Under the *Austrian legal system*, there is no dispute over whether members may be represented in the general meeting, because the law frequently uses the wording 'members present or represented'.[1382] On the other hand, the statutes regularly require natural persons to exercise their voting rights in person, which excludes representation. This is possible from a legal perspective, as the *GenG* allows representation but does not expressly require it.[1383] In addition, Sec. 5 para. 1 no.

[1376] See Sect. 3.4.1, where it is argued that user-members cannot be non-user members at the same time.

[1377] Art. 2372 para. 1 CC.

[1378] See Art. 58 para. 3 SCE-R.

[1379] Art. 2372 para. 5 CC.

[1380] Or for companies controlled by it, the members of the various organs or their employees. Art. 2372 para. 5 CC.

[1381] According to Italian law, he or she may delegate the vote to his spouse, relatives up to the third-degree, or to his in-laws, on the condition that they work together within the company.

It has been criticised that para. 2 only refers to cooperatives which conduct entrepreneurial activities for their members. For instance, this provision would not consider the situation of an entrepreneurial member in a credit cooperative, but instead only refer to production cooperatives, agricultural cooperatives and consortiums. See Bassi (2003), p. 265. However, it has been correctly argued that the wording of this provision would allow an extensive and general interpretation, with the result that this provision must be considered whenever a member is an individual entrepreneur, in whose company spouse, relatives and in-laws work together. See Bonfante (2014a), p. 322.

[1382] See Kastner (1986), p. 182 et seq.

[1383] See Siebenbäck (2014a), p. 341.

9 *GenG* only requires that the conditions, formalities and methods of exercising voting rights must be determined via the statutes, not what these should be.[1384] Accumulating proxies might be a way to circumvent the principle of 'one member, one vote' and give disproportionate influence to individual members. Therefore, I recommend that statutory provisions restrict proxy voting. However, excluding proxy voting completely would deprive members of their voting rights if, for example, they were ill or overseas.[1385] Finally, the proxy should be conferred in writing.[1386]

Comparing the provisions of the SCE-R and the *GenG* reveals that both foster flexibility, even where formalities are concerned. However, the SCE-R offers a stricter approach by explicitly requires that proxy voting be limited by the statutes.[1387]

Having clarified the issues of quorums, voting rights and proxy voting, all of which are particularly important to the decision-making process, we turn to the next chapter, which continues the analyses by addressing the voting procedure and the topic of majorities required to make a decision.

4.4.5 . . . Decision Making II: Voting Procedure and Majorities

According to Art. 58 para. 4 SCE-R,[1388] the statutes may allow electronic or postal voting. The statutes may then determine the necessary **voting procedures**. It is unclear whether para. 4 allows circular resolutions. As every member is entitled to speak at the general meeting, this right could only be asserted if the general meeting is actually convened.[1389] Due to the lack of further provisions, specific details about the voting procedure must be determined by national provisions, according to Art. 53 SCE-R.

Like the SCE-R's provisions, *Italian law* permits the statutes to determine the voting procedure[1390]; the Italian legal system contains some provisions that extend to an Italian SCE; others, as we shall see, can be used as examples for statutory provisions. First, Art. 2375 CC requires to identify the members voting in favour, against and those abstaining from voting. This provision also applies to an Italian

[1384]Sec. 43 para. 5 last sent. German GenG explicitly provides for the possibility to exclude representation entirely.

[1385]See Siebenbäck (2014a), p. 341 et seq.

[1386]See Kastner (1986), p. 183.

[1387]The necessity of this limitation is acknowledged by Austrian scholars.

[1388]It states: "The statutes may permit postal voting or electronic voting, in which case they shall lay down the necessary procedures."

[1389]See Schöpflin (2018ag), p. 1323 et seq.

[1390]See 2538 para. 5 CC.

SCE.[1391] Then, Art. 2538 para. 6 CC contains provisions for voting procedures that an Italian cooperative must observe.

Para. 6 deals with postal and electronic voting,[1392] stating that the statutes may allow voting via writing (by post or email) or other telecommunications devices[1393]; this provision applies to every type of general meeting and every kind of member.[1394] In all these voting systems, the notice calling the meeting must include the entire proposal.[1395] Italian SCEs must not apply these provisions, which refer to procedural aspects of postal of electronic voting, as Art. 58 para. 4 SCR R grants statutory freedom in this regard. However, Art. 2538 para. 6 CC provides technical details that could or should be used to determine the voting procedure.

Though para. 6 provides significant statutory freedom over the choice of voting methods, this provision fails to address the problem of determining the provenance of the vote. Thus, the statutes must define a distance voting system that allows for verifying that each vote actually comes from a specific member.[1396] It is advisable for Italian SCEs to adopt such a provision.

[1391] See Sect. 4.4.3.

[1392] It has been criticised that the problems related to distance voting and the practical use of distance voting have not been resolved by this provision. It has also been criticised that Art. 2538 para. 6 CC does not expressly deal with video meetings and different forms of distance participation by means of telecommunication devices. It is argued that meeting by video conference should be possible, similar to the provision contained in Art. 2370 para. 4 CC. See Cusa (2014a), p. 329. Also consider Bonfante (2014a), p. 315; Palmeri (2000). This is, in any case, only possible if the statutes provide accordingly. However, some scholars stress that the legislator has intentionally not adopted this solution because the ratio of the provision as contained in Art. 2370 CC (favouring participation of the shareholders) is, if one considers cooperatives, achieved by means of separate assemblies. Hence, participation via telecommunication devices is unnecessary. It has been questioned whether Art. 2370 para. 4 CC is really compatible with the provisions enacted for cooperatives. See Bonfante (2014a), p. 315 et seq. Next other discussions concern the legal qualification of the behaviour of a member who does not send his declaration or who sends his declaration without any express decision. In legal terms, the first situation can be determined as an abstention of vote and the second one can be qualified as absent member. See Bonfante (2014a), p. 317; Di Cecco (2003), p. 127. Also consider Cusa (2006), p. 309.

[1393] "espresso per corrispondenza, ovvero per altri mezzi di telecommunicazione".

For details, see Balzano (2004), p. 551; Marano (2013a), p. 2740.

[1394] There is wide range of statutory freedom allowing to introduce various procedures like conditional voting, voting limitations to specific issues, laddered voting (scalare), staggered voting (scallionato), etc. Bonfante (2014a), p. 314.

[1395] See Art. 2538 para. 6 CC. Also consider Di Cecco (2003), p. 126. Then, per Italian law, if the members must decide on proposals other than those contained in the notice, the votes expressed in writing (per corrispondenza) do not have to be calculated to determine the regular constitution of the general meeting. See Santagata (2017), p. 831.

[1396] See Bonfante (2014a), p. 316.

Art. 2375 CC seems to ban secret voting by stating that it must be possible to identify the shareholders who vote in favour of or against an item on the ballot and those who abstain from voting.[1397]

Austrian law regulates voting procedures far less than Italian law does. To determine the formalities of voting via the statutes, Sec. 5 para. 1 no. 9 *GenG* grants a significant amount of self-regulation. Thus, electronic voting should be allowed. The statues may employ additional methods, such as ballot papers, a show of hands or standing up. If the statutes determine different possibilities, the chairman can decide which is most feasible. The general meeting can determine the voting procedure if the statutes do not provide this information.[1398] In any case, the procedure must be the same for all members[1399] These observations also apply an Austrian SCE.[1400]

The last issue that impacts decision making in an SCE is the **majority requirements** for a decision taken by the general meeting. These requirements are determined by Art. 61 paras. 2–4 SCE-R. In brief, this provision distinguishes between those majorities that are required to amend the statutes and those majorities that are needed to make other decisions.

As a general rule, the general meeting can only decide upon the items on its agenda, which includes items that are requested by a minority of members.[1401] For a decision to be taken, the majority of the votes need to be validly cast by the members present or represented to support a specific proposal.[1402] The proposal fails in the

[1397]See Bonfante (2014a), p. 317. On the other hand, only secret voting can guarantee freedom of voting, which is especially important in elections. In this respect, the national notaries committee expressly favours secret voting, not only when used for elections, but also when nominating the delegates for the general assembly, or when board decisions referring to admission or expulsion of members have to be reviewed. Trimarchi (2005), p. 647 et seq. Also consider Presti (2007), p. 983; Cusa (2006), p. 275; Bonfante (2014b).

Italian agricultural SCEs that consider adopting a voting system with pre-printed ballots should know that the so-called 'voting referendum', in which the members must decide upon a single ballot that contains the names of the members of an organ, has been strongly criticised, because such a system requires agreements outside the general meeting, and this would have doubtful democratic value. This system has been reluctantly allowed on the condition that the members may expressly cancel or substitute the names on the ballot with others of their liking. See Bonfante (2014a), p. 318; Presti (2007), p. 984.

[1398]See Siebenbäck (2014g), p. 378; Keinert (1988), p. 145.

[1399]And should be specified to promote clarity and avoid disputes. See Astl and Steinböck (2014), p. 152; Pramer and Pfaffenzeller (1976), p. 12.

[1400]Details about the voting procedure must be determined by national provisions, according to Art. 53 SCE-R.

[1401]According to Art. 57 SCE-R. See Sect. 4.4.2. Also consider Schulze (2004a), p. 116.

Art 61 para. 1 SCE-R states: "A general meeting may pass resolutions on items on its agenda. A general meeting may also deliberate and pass resolutions concerning items placed on the agenda of the meeting by a minority of members in accordance with Article 57."

[1402]See Art. 61 para. 2 SCE-R. It states: "A general meeting shall act by majority of the votes validly cast by the members present or represented." Also consider Schulze (2004a), p. 116.

case of a tie. Similarly, abstaining from voting is equivalent to not participating in the voting procedure.[1403]

Art. 61 para. 3 subpara. 1 SCE-R requires the statutes to determine the majority requirements for the general meeting.[1404] The statutes both complement and define the provisions of the SCE-R.[1405] The general meetings thus make decisions with a simple majority, unless the conditions contained in paras. 3 and 4 are met. In this context, the valid votes count,[1406] not the number of members present or represented.[1407] The statutes may define more stringent majorities here, for example, by determining higher majority requirements for extraordinary resolutions or special resolutions.[1408] These provisions cannot be amended by national law, as they express the principle of SCE self-regulation (i.e., statutory freedom), as determined by Art. 8 para. 1 letter b SCE-R.

Finally, Art. 61 para. 4 subpara. 2 SCE-R requires a majority of at least two thirds of the valid votes to amend the statutes. The relevant national law can require an even greater majority.[1409] In cases where the statutes are amended, Art. 15 para. 2 SCE-R grants minority rights,[1410] including specific (extraordinary) rights to resign granted to members who oppose an amendment to the statutes at a general meeting. This right to resign is given if the statutory amendment (1) introduces new obligations for payments or other services, (2) substantially extends existing member obligations, or (3) extends the period of notice for resignation from the SCE to more than 5 years.[1411]

[1403]For a different opinion, see Schöplin, who stresses that in case of abstention from voting, national provisions must be applied according to Art. 53 SCE-R, which explicitly mentions voting procedures, whereas it is correct to consider national law to determine whether black papers have to be considered spoilt papers or not. Schöpflin (2018aj), p. 1327. Art. 58 SE-R provides for a different solution. See Mayer (2010g), p. 731.

[1404]Interestingly, the German text of the SCE-R refers to the ordinary general meeting (ordentliche Generalversammlung), but neither the Italian nor the English version of the SCE-R does likewise.

Art 61 para. 3 subpara. 1 SCE-R states: "The statutes shall lay down the quorum and majority requirements which are to apply to general meetings."

[1405]See Schulze (2004a), p. 116.

[1406]Consider in this context Mayer (2010g), p. 731.

[1407]See Schöpflin (2018aj), p. 1328 et seq.

[1408]See Lutter et al. (2012), p. 1623.

[1409]It states: "In the cases referred to in the first subpar (amendment of statutes), at least two thirds of the votes cast validly must be cast in favour, unless the law applicable to cooperatives in the Member State in which the SCE's registered office is situated requires a greater majority." Also consider Schulze (2004a), p. 117.

[1410]The SCE-R refers to these as minority members. Also consider Lutter et al. (2012), p. 1603; Galletti (2006), p. 57; Bianca and Zanardo (2016), p. 208; Korte (2012), p. 336; Albamonte (2008), p. 305.

[1411]Art. 7 para. 5 SCE-R contains a further specific right to resign related to a decision taken by the general meeting to transfer the SCE's registered office to another member state. Members who oppose this decision may resign. Art. 7 SCE-R specifies that resignation must be declared within 2 months of the general meeting's decision. These four specific cases are of particular interest, as these provisions may have more favourable conditions and legal consequences than rights to resign

The members of an SCE are, in principle, free to leave the SCE. However, the procedures—including the conditions for exercising the right to resign—that might be adopted may confer on the management or administrative organ a right of control that could delay the withdrawal. This is hardly possible in the case of a resignation, pursuant to Art. 15 para. 2 SCE-R, since the SCE-R stipulates this possibility as an exception to the general reasons for and the time of resignation. In fact, Art. 16 para. 3 SCE-R[1412] determines that the statutes of an SCE must lay out the procedures and conditions under which members can exercise their right to resign; these procedures and conditions specify that repayment of his/her part of the subscribed capital must occur within 3 years.[1413]

These general comments on majority requirements shall be read in conjunction with national law. In fact, our analysis of the two legal systems not only offers some good examples of the statutory provisions that SCEs could adopt, but also provides us with a better understanding of the provisions contained in the SCE-R as we compare them with national provisions. Under *Italian law*, the statutes determine the majorities that Italian cooperatives need to make a decision. These must be calculated according to the number of votes attributed to the members.[1414] This approach grants as much statutory freedom as possible to define these majorities; however, this freedom is still limited. For example, it is not possible to apply provisions that require unanimous votes.[1415]

To understand how the general meeting of an SCE functions, we must discuss how majorities are calculated. As discussed above,[1416] the law explicitly refers to the number of votes that are assigned to the members. If non-user members exist, the votes are calculated according to the methods that were defined when these financial instruments were issued. These must be determined via statutory provisions, with

---

determined via the statutes. See Alfandari and Piot (2004), p. 89. Admitting non-user members is not a valid reason for resignation, as these can only have limited influence on decision making. See Schöpflin (2018b), p. 1273 et seq.

While membership in cases one, two and four terminates at the end of the financial year in which the resignation is tendered, in case three membership terminates at the end of the period of notice which applied before the statutes were amended. Neither the amendment of the statutes, nor transfer of the registered office effect the resigning member. Resignation implies entitlement to repayment of shares. See Sect. 5.4.

[1412]It aims to protect members' right to resign and right to repayment. The resulting provisions must be determined autonomously, however, not without limits. See Rocchi (2006), p. 112 et seq. Also consider Galletti (2006), p. 56 et seq.

[1413]Additionally, the law provides that the SCE is not obliged to make a repayment less than 6 months after approval of the balance sheet issued following the loss of membership.

[1414]Art. 2538 para. 5 CC. Until 2003 it was possible to derogate the majorities via statutory provisions, as indicated by Art. 2368 CC and Art. 2369 CC. For a different approach consider for example Art. 2545 decies CC, which specifically deals with converting a cooperative into a company, requiring at least 50% of the members of the cooperative to agree.

[1415]See Bonfante (2014a), p. 308 et seq.; Bassi and Schlesinger (1988), p. 391; Di Cecco (2003), p. 124.

[1416]See Sect. 4.4.4.

different options being made available.[1417] In the absence of statutory provisions, it has been debated whether the method of assigning votes to non-user members (according to Art. 2526 CC) is identical to that for user members, or whether votes assigned to non-user members may also be calculated according to subscribed capital. This depends on whether non-user members are considered capitalistic members (like shareholders).[1418]

For example, one may discuss the methods for calculating the 5% of votes that are needed to challenge the decisions of the general meeting. Art. 2377 CC explicitly refers to shares that have a voting right of 5%. This provision is definitely more flexible than a criterion based on the number of members. Recognising a general criterion of minority protection that is connected to the number of members suggests that a similar criterion should be applied when challenging a decision of the general meeting. Of course, challenging a decision is not solely related to minority protection; it is also a proper function of the cooperative. These issues are rather complex, especially given that the criteria for minority protections in a cooperative are still being developed.[1419]

In our next example, Art. 2545 quinquiesdecies CC adopts a criterion of capital (in addition to numerical criteria), which allows the holders of 10% of the capital to challenge decisions. Even though this provision seems to refer to the members as the holders of financial instruments (non-user members), it also seems applicable to user members on two conditions: (1) they cannot represent more than 10% of the number of members and (2) they must hold more than 10% of the capital. This interpretation completely aligns with the 2003 reform, which aimed to foster investment in cooperatives.[1420] These issues must be observed by an Italian SCE, inasmuch as the voting rights of non-user members have to be calculated according to national law.[1421]

It seems that abstaining votes are counted.[1422] As mentioned above, the SCE-R provides for a different solution.

[1417]E.g., staggered voting.

[1418]It is important to decide whether votes cast by non-user members are calculated according to the principle of "one member, one share" or in proportion to the capital subscribed. The method used to determine the majority when considering non-user members must consider the method used to define their voting rights. If proportional criteria have to be applied (proportional vote according to the proportion of capital held), the provisions which refer to the spa must be applied. See Bonfante (2014a), p. 310 and 310 fn 44. A different argument claims the method for calculating the voting rights are identical for both types of members. See Cusa (2006), p. 427. For the sake of clarity, these two issues should be resolved via specific statutory provisions.

[1419]See Bonfante (2014a), p. 309 et seq.

[1420]See Bonfante (2014a), p. 311.

[1421]As determined by Art. 59 para. 3 SCE-R. Also consider Sect. 4.4.4.

[1422]See Cian (2018e), p. 2781; also consider Laurini (2008b), p. 86; Montagnani (2004c), p. 489 et seq. See also Romano (2017d), p. 2913 et eq.

Lastly, with respect to the chairman's casting vote, the Italian legal system aligns with the SCE-R, as it can be excluded that in the general meeting the clause of casting vote is admissible.[1423]

Austrian law contains provisions that are similar to those in the SCE-R, albeit with some differences about amending the statutes. According to Sec. 5 para. 1 no. 9 *GenG*, the statutes must determine the conditions of the voting rights and how they are exercised. According to Sec. 5 para. 1 no. 10 SCE-R, the statutes must determine those objects that cannot be decided by a simple majority; instead, such objects need a qualified majority or other particular voting procedures.

In principle, the law requires a simple majority for decisions to be valid.[1424] However, if the general meeting decides to amend the statutes[1425] or dissolve the cooperative,[1426] a majority of at least two thirds of the votes cast is required. The statutes may provide different options, but the requirements of the simple majority cannot be undercut.[1427] If the general meeting decides to change the cooperative's type of liability, reduce liability or reduce the cooperative's shares, the two-thirds majority is mandatory; however, the statutes can provide even stricter requirements.[1428] A two-thirds majority is also required for mergers.[1429] Apart from the specific cases determined by Sec. 33 para. 3 *GenG* and Sec. 2 para. 1 *GenVG*, the *GenG* is very flexible. Concerning the amendments of the statutes, the Austrian legal system does not require a greater majority than that determined by the SCE-R; thus, the reference in Art. 61 para. 4 subpara. 2 SCE-R (concerning amendment of the statutes) must not be observed.

According to the prevailing doctrine, the term 'votes cast' means valid votes cast. Abstained or invalid votes are therefore not counted.[1430] However, the statutes may provide a different solution, for instance, referring to the majority of the members present or represented.[1431] Art. 61 para. 2 SCE-R makes this solution unavailable to Austrian SCEs.

Last, similar to the provision contained in Art. 61 para. 1 SCE-R, under Austrian law, the general meeting cannot decide upon issues that have not been announced in the agenda.[1432] Finally, the freedom to form statutes permits an Austrian cooperative

[1423]See Bonfante (2014a), p. 314 et seq.

[1424]Sec. 33 para. 1 GenG. The chairman takes part in the vote. In the event of a tie, he or she has the casting vote, as long as the statutes do not preclude this. See Siebenbäck (2014f), p. 378.

[1425]According to Sec. 27 GenREVG, an amendment of the statutes concerning the subject of a cooperative (and also an SCE), which is a member of an auditing association, may be granted only on the condition that this association gives written approval of the amendment. Also consider Siebenbäck (2014f), p. 379.

[1426]Also consider in this context Art. 71 SCE-R.

[1427]See Siebenbäck (2014f), p. 379. In this sense, Sec. 5 para. 1 no 10 GenG.

[1428]See Siebenbäck (2014f), p. 377 et seq.

[1429]Sec. 2 para. 1 GenVG.

[1430]See Siebenbäck (2014f), p. 378; Keinert (1988), p. 146; Kastner (1986), p. 143; Schöpflin (2018j), p. 1308.

[1431]See Kastner (1986), p. 183.

[1432]See Siebenbäck (2014f), p. 379.

to set other criteria with which to make decisions for instance, double majority.[1433] An Austrian SCE should be able to adopt these solutions as long as the provisions in Art. 59 SCE-R are observed.

We conclude by asking, what is important about this interplay between European and national norms that aims to regulate the decision-making process of an *agricultural SCE*? Answering this question requires us to consider quorums, voting rights, voting procedure and majorities.

In principle, the SCE-R grants statutory freedom to quorums.[1434] However, this freedom is reduced if the statutes allow the admission of non-user members, in which case, the statutes must contain rules that protect user members. Neither the Austrian nor the Italian legislatures exercised the option in Art. 61 para. 3 subpara. 2 SCE-R. The Austrian legal system contains a provision for a waiting period that could be adopted by the statutes of an Austrian *agricultural SCE*. No further Italian provisions need be considered. Overall, Austrian and Italian SCEs must both apply the same basic set of rules, as determined by the SCE-R.

The next topic is the principle of 'one member, one vote and its exceptions. The SCE-R allows exceptions by setting limits on multiple voting rights. As a basic condition, the exceptions have to align with the relevant national law. No specific problems should arise for an Austrian SCE, because the SCEG fully implements the provisions contained in the SCE-R. However, the rules applicable to Italian SCEs are more difficult to interpret. The Italian legislature did not implement the SCE-R a legislative act but, rather, utilised the existing legal framework. Accordingly, the provisions of the SCE-R must be interpreted with certain provisions in the civil code. The Italian legal system defines specific voting rights for non-user members, for cases of participation other than by way of capital contribution[1435] and for secondary cooperatives[1436]; it also specifies specific limits to these voting rights. Unlike communication no. 9203 of the Ministry for economic development, we argue that only the limits determined by the SCE-R apply.

In the case of secondary agricultural cooperatives, it can be useful for the votes to be allocated in proportion to the paid-up shares or in proportion to the transactions conducted between a member and the SCE. The number of members in the primary cooperatives would thus be represented to some extent. Accordingly, the shares in the secondary cooperative would have to correspond to the number of members in the primary cooperative (i.e., the more members there are, the higher the number of shares and vice versa).

[1433]This is a majority according to members and also majority according to shares. See Siebenbäck (2014f), p. 379. Also consider Schmidt-Pachinger (2012), nt 15.

[1434]Sec. 2.4 para. 11 sent. 2 PECOL emphasizes in this context that quorums shall help to ensure that decisions represent membership.

[1435]See Art. 2538 para. 4 CC and Art. 2543 para. 2 CC.

[1436]For Italian SCEs which are secondary cooperatives, Art. 2538 para. 3 CC must be observed. This provision can be linked to Art. 59 para. 2 subpar 3 or subpar 2 SCE-R. The latter covers SCEs involved in financial or insurance activities. Again, these limits are determined by the SCE-R and not the Italian civil code. See also Fici (2015), p. 76 et seq.

Voting rights are addressed by Sec. 2.4 para. 7 PECOL, which acknowledges, as a general rule, that voting rights are based on the principle of 'one member, one vote'. In addition, para. 8 of Sec. 2.4 PECOL stresses that the statutes might need to confer plural voting rights if this is necessary for better functioning of the cooperative.[1437] The PECOL (Sec. 2.4 para. 10 sent. 2) deviate from this rule for non-user members, who may have multiple voting rights based upon the capital that they have subscribed. As seen above, neither the SCE-R nor the Austrian and Italian legal systems strictly observe this requirement. As the PECOL provide valuable guidelines with which to determine the essential features of a cooperative, Italian and Austrian law should be amended accordingly. The same reasoning is valid for the aspect, where the PECOL explicitly require that safeguards be implemented to keep non-user members (or a minority of user members) from controlling the cooperative. The PECOL also highlight the need to limit the assignment of multiple votes via specific percentages.[1438] These requirements are addressed by Art. 59 paras. 2 and 3 SCE-R and Art. 61 para. 3 subpara. 2 SCE-R. However, the approach of the SCE-R is less strict, as Art. 61 para. 3 sent. 2 SCE-R only refers to non-user members or members of an SCE who are involved in financial or insurance activities that have multiple votes assigned according to capital contribution, which excludes other situations in which a minority of user members might control an SCE.

Accordingly, the general meeting of an *agricultural SCE* could regulate the following aspects pertaining to the admission of non-user members: the total amount of the capital issued, the corresponding interest rate and the property rights in the event of withdrawal. So, too, the minimum duration of the contribution would seem to give the agricultural cooperative relative financial stability. Obviously, the resolution should determine the proportion of voting rights in relation to the capital contribution.

Regarding proxy voting, no specific issues should arise here; however, specific provisions from the Italian civil code can be used as examples for statutory provisions.[1439]

[1437]Interestingly, this shall be limited to cases that do not concern capital contributions. The PECOL mention as a particular example the possibility of granting multiple voting rights based on participation transactions. This is the most common exception to the general principle. This concept can be applied by either primary or secondary cooperatives. Next, Sec. 2.4 para. 8 letter b PECOL also acknowledges the possibility to assign multiple voting rights based on the number of members in particular subdivisions. This is an indirect reflection of the general principle of "one member, one vote". For secondary cooperatives, it is highlighted that this instrument can help balance the influence of their various primary (member) cooperatives. Of particular concern is the question of how votes in the different subdivisions can be assessed. In this context, the PECOL favour the solution adopted by Art. 59 para. 2 SCE-R, which allows statutory freedom in this regard. See Snaith (2017), p. 65 et seq.

[1438]See Sec. 2.4 para. 10 PECOL; Snaith (2017), p. 66.

[1439]For example proxy conferred in writing, a limitation in respect of persons who can act as proxies or a specific provision considering the situation of a member of an SCE, who is an individual businessman.

Then, the analysis switched to the voting procedure. The SCE-R determines that statutes may permit electronic or postal voting,[1440] and the statutes provide details about these voting systems. The regulation contains no further information about the voting procedure, so national law must be applied in accordance with Art. 53 SCE-R. The analysis showed that Austrian *agricultural SCEs* have substantial statutory freedom. Therefore, in practice various options are possible.[1441] The Italian legal system provides a similar flexible approach; however, it must be possible to identify which of the members voted in favour of or against an item on the ballot, abstained from voting or dissented against a proposition.

The basic requirements for decision-making are laid down by the SCE-R. In general, simple majority is enough; however, the statutes can set more stringent requirements. Sec. 2.4 para. 12 PECOL state that, in principle, decisions are taken by a simple majority of the votes cast. Para. 5 of this section adds that special majorities are necessary for making fundamental decisions; these decisions must be made according to the principle of 'one member, one vote'.[1442] This solution can be adopted via statutes.[1443] The SCE-R requires a majority of two thirds when amending the statutes, and the relevant national law can require an even greater majority. Neither the Austrian nor the Italian legal systems use this option.

One particular problem can arise in the Italian legal system when votes are calculated, particularly when non-user members vote, as it is not clearly specified whether these votes are calculated according to the capital subscribed or according to the method assigned to user members. A statutory provision should be adopted to address this issue. Overall, both Austrian and Italian *agricultural SCEs* have a wide range of statutory freedom; basically, SCEs in both jurisdictions must consider similar provisions.

4.4.6 The General Meeting from an Economic Perspective

Certain issues are noteworthy here. The first concerns the competence of the general meeting. To reiterate, the allocation of the decision-making powers between the general meeting and the various organs defines the organisational structure of the SCE. The law is required to provide a set of default rules that the statutes can then modify.[1444] Yet, it is uncertain what legal limits can be placed on the general meeting when the default rules are amended. Two approaches are possible: the

[1440] In respect of the technical devices, the PECOL stress that votes can be taken in meetings but also electronically or by post. See Sec. 2.3 para. 4 letter c PECOL.

[1441] E.g., via ballot paper, a show of hands or standing up.

[1442] For instance restructuring or dissolving the cooperative or amending its statutes. See Sec. 2.4 para. 5 PECOL.

[1443] According to the Art. 59 SCE-R.

[1444] See Sect. 1.3.1.

law can either (1) use a general standard or (2) define specific rules for select matters. The latter approach increases legal certainty. In general, the statutes should explicitly define the competence of the general meeting and assign the remaining decisions to the organs with a catch-all provision.[1445] This is the approach that an Italian SCE must adopt, whereas an Austrian SCE may apply a kind of residual competence that allows the general meeting to make decisions in cases where doubt arises.[1446]

Furthermore, competence that is related to a particular issue need not necessarily be assigned to a single organ; such competence can be divided, for instance, into competing competence, approval requirements or rights of instruction.[1447] The SCE-R contains a provision[1448] that allows the statutes to assign authorisation competence to the general meeting.[1449] This approach can be adopted within both the one-tier and the two-tier systems and helps managers to make proper decisions by solving or alleviating conflicts of interest instead of banning worthwhile deals. Typical examples are decisions on large or strategic investments (e.g., a new storage hall or a washing and sorting plant in a fruit cooperative). Deliberation on the operational programme (provided the agricultural SCE is recognised as a PO) is another related topic.[1450] Yet, exercising these different types of competence requires appropriate procedures for convening the general meeting, especially in urgent cases. The SCE-R provides specific minority rights; then, both the Italian and Austrian legal orders obligate the supervisory organ to convene the general meeting. These constraints put pressure on the management organ and help to better regulate principal-agent conflicts.

The next issue concerns the right to information that is granted to members. When the right to remove or to control is exercised (e.g., remuneration or suing for damages), the members of the cooperative need information about the SCE's business and general state of affairs. Thus, the SCE's members can use the right of instruction to acquire the requisite information. To protect confidential business information, statutory provisions should restrict these monitoring rights by delegating such tasks to the supervisory or administrative organ. However, information and inspection rights that are assigned to individual members or minorities can improve monitoring by safeguarding the coordination costs[1451] that occur between

[1445]See Enriques et al. (2009a), p. 72 et seq.; Engert (2014), p. 91 et seq.; Stout (2007), p. 798 et seq.; Tombari (2008), p. 418 et seq. Regarding the costs of member involvement, see e.g. Svendsen (2007), pp. 127 and 132.

[1446]See Sect. 4.4.1.

[1447]See Engert (2014), p. 93; Enriques et al. (2009a), p. 72 et seq. Also consider Armour and Whincop (2001), p. 991. Generally, Schäfer and Ott (2012), p. 697 et seq.

[1448]Art. 48 para. 1 SCE-R.

[1449]Members of Italian agricultural cooperatives are always involved in strategic decisions, although operational aspects are delegated to the management. E.g., mergers and acquisitions are carried out using controlling tools so the members can verify the quality of the management's choices. See Bono (2012), p. 37.

[1450]On this issue, see Sect. 3.3.4.

[1451]See costs of collective decision-making, Sect. 1.3.3.

members.[1452] The SCE-R explicitly assigns such a right to information to every member for every item that the general meeting decides. This improves minority protection, as it is not possible to determine in advance which decisions will be favoured and by whom.[1453] The analysis also showed that members of both Austrian and Italian SCEs may request more information than is indicated in the SCE-R. To promote proper decisions, the SCE-R grants the right to information for accounting documents.

It has been mentioned[1454] that supervising the managers requires the members of an agricultural SCE to know much more about the functioning of a cooperative and its businesses than shareholders in a company[1455]: for example, an important reason for becoming informed about the SCE's affairs is that the transactions conducted between a member and their cooperative often comprise a substantial part of the farmer-member's income. Consequently, members should obtain proper information about the development of their agricultural SCE, which helps them to reduce the costs of collective decision making. This fosters thoughtful participation in the decision-making process.[1456]

The members of both Austrian and Italian SCEs may request information that extends beyond the provision in Art. 60 SCE-R, which information may concern the development of their SCE. One must, however, be aware that members often are unable to evaluate the information provided by the SCE or to predict the development of the mutualistic relationship.[1457] They therefore strongly rely on the information provided by the management, supervisory or administrative organ.

However, asymmetric information is an issue not only in terms of information being provided by the cooperative's members to the managing and supervising organs (up-stream perspective), but also of information being provided by the latter to the cooperative's members (down-stream perspective). For managers to make good decisions, they must have sufficient accurate information about the members' needs, which ultimately must be satisfied by the goods or services provided by the agricultural cooperative.[1458] Member responsiveness is generally high, regardless of the size of the agricultural cooperative.[1459]

[1452]See Engert (2014), p. 108 et seq.

[1453]See Enriques and Volpin (2007), p. 126 et seq. Also consider Gentzoglanis (2007), p. 159.

[1454]See Sect. 4.2.3.

[1455]See Hansmann (1999), p. 398; Ortmann and King (2007), p. 59 et seq.; Royer (1999), p. 56 et seq.

[1456]See Hansmann (1999), p. 397. Also consider Royer (1999), p. 49; Ortmann and King (2007), p. 53 et seq.

[1457]See Zoppini (2004), p. 447 et seq. For general information Schäfer and Ott (2012), p. 700; also consider Fleischer (2000), p. 24.

[1458]See Hansmann (1999), p. 398. Also consider Ortmann and King (2007), p. 59 et seq.; Royer (1999), p. 56.

[1459]See Hansmann (1996), p. 134 et seq.; Iliopoulos (2014).

The rules for POs also deal with the problem of a possible information gap and oblige farmers to provide information for statistical purpose.[1460] This obligation is formulated in general terms and covers a range of different general and specific information. The members of the management or administrative organ are generally very well-informed about members' preferences and ideas, which results from the adoption of various techniques to promote responsiveness, such as the federated structure used by large cooperative banks or agriculture cooperatives. This federated structure helps large cooperatives remain responsive to local cooperatives, who in turn can be more responsive to their individual members.[1461] Both Austrian and Italian SCEs can adopt separate assemblies to help foster responsiveness to individual members and streamline the collective decision-making process.[1462]

From a legal perspective, issues concerning the decision-making process may sound rather simple; however, decision making appears to be a rather dynamic undertaking when examined from an economic perspective. There are various legal aspects to the function of the general meeting of an agricultural SCE, and these aspects include quorums, voting rights, majorities, etc. However, decision making in an agricultural SCE depends very much on the actual economic (and social) situation of the individual farmer, as this ultimately influences his behaviour. Therefore, the economic perspective provides some useful lessons for appropriate (efficient and effective) decision making.

Several factors need to be considered concerning the decisions taken by the general meeting of an SCE. It is shown[1463] that successful membership relies on the cooperative's ability to correct for market failures, which stimulates members to actively control the firm. Though other problems remain, such as costs that arise from vaguely defined property rights, such problems can be mitigated by the benefits provided by the cooperative.[1464] There is also evidence that social factors like trust are crucial to a cooperative's success cooperative, which fosters mutual understanding and creates both feelings of community and shared approaches to problems. The combination of all these aspects leads to low personal transaction costs between members, which is supports decision making.

These factors provide a common understanding of how an agricultural SCE should be run. However, these costs must be low enough for a shared position to be found when strategic decisions are made. Thus, the members of a well-functioning cooperative often share homogeneous characteristics—shared problem-solving, mutual understanding, trust and so on—that contribute to a sense

---

1460 See Art. 153 para. 1 letters a and c Reg. 1308/2013.

1461 See Hansmann (1999), p. 397; Royer (1999), p. 56 et seq.; Ortmann and King (2007), p. 59 et seq.

1462 See Hansmann (1999), p. 397. In this sense, see Cusa (2014c), p. 362 et seq.; Paolucci (2019d), p. 127 et seq.; Schöpflin (2018ak), p. 1330 et seq. Generally, Holmstrom (1999), p. 414 et seq.; Nilsson et al. (2012).

1463 See Sect. 3.5.

1464 See Nilsson (2001), p. 343. In general, Ortmann and King (2007), p. 56 et seq.; Gios and Santuari (2002), p. 6 et seq. Also consider Sect. 3.5.1.

of solidarity.[1465] Thus, the more that the characteristics of an agricultural SCE align with those of its members, the more efficient it will be.[1466]

An agricultural SCE recognised as a PO ties farmers' needs to the requirements of the PO and vice versa. On the other hand, members have various planning horizons because of certain factors, including differences in their age.[1467] As a result, it may be difficult to make optimal investment decisions.[1468] Section 3.5.1 stresses that decision making is influenced by the existence of free-riders. Members are reluctant to invest in their cooperative, as they must share this investment with others. It has been observed that 'in order to create incentives for members to contribute risk capital and combat the negative consequences of diachronically increased member interest heterogeneity, agricultural cooperatives may spend a considerable amount of time on experimenting with minor changes in statutes and organisational policies'.[1469]

It is beneficial to diversify the assets between different operations to reduce the risks for the investor. Yet, in general, this mechanism (asset diversification) hardly operates in a cooperative, as members have heterogeneous opinions about their risk preferences, the value of capital and other variables. In general, cooperatives' investment decisions follow the average preferences of the members, which average represents a wide range of individual preferences. As a consequence, the investment is then only optimal for a small number of members. Principles and agents may have different ideas about how a portfolio should be diversified. Again, further conflicts can arise and lead to economic inefficiency.[1470] Finally, as the involvement of the members is not reflected in the remuneration of capital, and major investments do not lead to an increase in decision-making power, it is difficult to provide incentives for investment.[1471] All these insights into agricultural cooperatives explain which aspects and circumstances influence the decision of a member, and thus they explain how decision-making costs are influenced (that is how they increase or decrease).

The principle of 'one member, one vote' eliminates transaction costs that would arise from the process of determining the extent to which each member contributed to the common aim by conducting transactions with the cooperative. This principle also helps to determine individual preferences by favouring median rather than marginal actors. More importantly, this principle helps to establish an internal market within the SCE, as it promotes members' business transactions rather than

---

[1465]See Nilsson (2001), p. 343. Also consider Holmstrom (1999), p. 414 et seq.

[1466]See Nilsson (2001), p. 345. Pozzobon and Zylbersztajn address the issue of member participation and its costs. See Pozzobon and Zylbersztajn (2013). Also consider Pozzobon et al. (2012), p. 119.

[1467]See Sect. 3.5.1.

[1468]See Nilsson (2001), p. 338; Zoppini (2004), p. 444 et seq.; Holmstrom (1999), p. 415. Also consider Sect. 3.5.1 (horizon problem).

[1469]See Iliopoulos (2015), p. 8.

[1470]See Nilsson (2001), p. 338 et seq. Also consider Sect. 3.5.1 (portfolio problem).

[1471]See Zoppini (2004), p. 445; Ortmann and King (2007), p. 57; Royer (1999), p. 56.

the remuneration of capital.[1472] However, there are negative aspects. This principle has been criticised for weakening control mechanisms within an agricultural cooperative, as it prevents control from being assigned to those who value it most. This is because governance mechanisms—as they are based on the principal of 'one member, one vote'—do not consider the capital subscribed by individuals.[1473] Voting rights that are assigned in proportion to transactions conducted can create incentives for efficient monitoring and decision making.[1474]

Other inefficiencies may arise from increasing the membership base. It has been criticised that the advantages linked to direct control are lost in these cases: For example, in a cooperative with tens of thousands of members, it is difficult to see both how members can control each other and the services they provide. Clearly, this can make decision making rather cumbersome.[1475]

The analysis has shown that both legal systems try to address these issues by allowing exceptions to the principle of 'one member, one vote'. Austrian agricultural SCEs are granted statutory freedom without providing default provisions.[1476] In contrast, the Italian legal system contains various default provisions[1477]: For example, one can refer to Art. 2538 para. 4 CC (dealing with voting rights linked to participation in the mutualistic relationship). This relates to cooperatives where the mutualistic aim is realised by integrating the members' enterprises or some parts of them. In this case, voting rights can be assigned with respect to the transactions conducted in participation of the mutual purpose. I stress that derogating the principle of 'one member, one vote' provides an incentive to integrate the economies of scale. This also makes it possible to more easily measure mutualistic transactions without leading to conflicts of interest between members.[1478] Voting rights that are proportional to the volume of transactions conducted with an agricultural cooperative correlates to the quality of members' supply. This type of voting right can also help prevent free-riding by small members.[1479]

Another example is given by Art. 2543 para. 2 CC, which assigns voting rights (in the election of the members of the controlling organ) in proportion either to shares subscribed or to participation in the mutual exchange. The legislature

[1472]See Zoppini (2004), p. 444. Also consider van Diepenbeek (2007), p. 38; Svendsen (2007), p. 119 et seq. For general observations, see Hansmann and Pargendler (2013).

[1473]See Zoppini (2004), p. 445. Also consider Ortmann and King (2007), p. 57 et seq.; Royer (1999), p. 54 et seq.

[1474]See Zoppini (2004), p. 445. Also consider Kräkel (2012), p. 299; Iliopoulos (2014), p. 164.

[1475]See Zoppini (2004), p. 445. Also consider Iliopoulos (2015), p. 11; Iliopoulos and Cook (2013); Cook and Chaddad (2004).

[1476]See Sec. 5 GenG. As mentioned, default provisions help lower transactions costs. See Sect. 1. 3.1.

[1477]In Italian agricultural cooperatives, the attribution of voting rights linked to capital contribution seems the most frequent exception to the principle of "one member, one vote". See Bono (2012), p. 38.

[1478]See Zoppini (2004), p. 448.

[1479]See Van der Sangen (2012), p. 23. Also consider Iliopoulos (2015), p. 10.

acknowledges that persons who participate in capital are more incentivised to control, and thus bear the costs linked with control. The same is true for those who participate more in mutual exchanges or relationships. Thus, not applying the principle of 'one member, one vote' in this case (when electing members of the controlling organ) makes the cooperative more efficient.[1480]

In an agricultural SCE, the majority, in principle takes the decisions,[1481] a process that differs from something like a negotiated contract, in which greater fairness can be guaranteed. In fact, the majority does not pass resolutions but, rather, issues orders. Therefore, legal limitations have been enacted to restrict the power of the majority. Now, a specific danger to minority rights arises from the fact that cooperatives mostly have broad discretion to design their statutes[1482]; qualified majority requirements must often be observed in these cases.[1483] This approach is also adopted by the SCE-R, which grants additional minority rights over the convening of the general meeting and provides a means to protect user members over non-user

[1480]See Zoppini (2004), p. 448.

[1481]For general observations, see Denozza (2002), p. 86 et seq.

[1482]See Fleischer (2014), p. 33; Enriques et al. (2009b), p. 93; Fleischer (2002a). Also consider Dyck and Zingales (2004); Nenova (2003); Svendsen (2007), p. 125 et seq. Unbalanced third-party transactions with the company are the most important exploitation strategies available to majority shareholders. Here, the majority enters into unfair transactions with his own company (appropriation of business opportunities and corporate resources). See Fleischer (2014), p. 37; Armour et al. (2009b), p. 115 et seq. Also consider Goshen (2003).

The typical remedies for minorities are a right to file an action (actions challenging the validity of resolutions by the general meeting), claims for compensation (direct action and derivative shareholder action) or exit right. Further measures include specific rights of information and inspection. (Right to information on company affairs, right to inspect the books and records. See Fleischer (2014), p. 63 et seq. For details Enriques et al. (2009b), p. 89 et seq. These problems can also be restricted by law, but also via so-called self-help mechanisms. For instance, when amending the statutes, it can be helpful to consider a menu of sample statutes and the use of formalised contract conclusion procedures involving independent expert advisers like notaries or lawyers. See Fleischer (2014), p. 41. Also consider Sneirson (2008) and Molitor (2009). On the other hand, the law can grant exit rights as a means to protect minorities, to be used as a last resort. This gives the minority some bargaining power. See Fleischer (2014), p. 66. Also consider Enriques et al. (2009b), p. 99. It is argued that the statutes must provide functioning exit mechanisms in order to keep the SCE attractive. Otherwise, no new members will apply for membership. Consider Sect. 3.5.2.

[1483]See Fleischer (2014), p. 44 et seq. Also consider Armour and Whincop (2001), p. 991; Svendsen (2007), p. 131. A good solution to preventing minority shareholders from preventing necessary changes is to have a qualified majority as a default rule with the duty of loyalty. However, this still has the potential to leave some minorities exposed. Fleischer (2014), p. 45; Enriques et al. (2009b), p. 96.

In contrast, there may also be a problem of ex-post opportunism by minority members. This problem arises when there is a statutory right of veto or when the majority do not have a sufficiently qualified majority to amend statutes. In this case there is the danger that the minority might abuse their veto right to further their own decisions. One remedy to restrict opportunistic minority behaviour is the duty of loyalty, which not only applies to majorities but also to minorities with blocking power. Other possible solutions are exclusion for good cause or squeeze out regulations. See Fleischer (2014), p. 71 et seq. Also consider Strohn (2015) and Fleischer (2002a). Generally, Armour and Whincop (2001), p. 992.

members when decisions are made. This protects the interests of user members, which in turn protects the homogeneity of interests. Yet, one must consciously safeguard the interests of a minority of user-members. 'If the suppressed members cannot exercise convincingly their voice option, they usually will leave the cooperative and may start a new collective entrepreneurship venture'.[1484] In practice, the statutes of an agricultural SCE will take these aspects into account; they may contain clauses that are stricter than the legislature's thresholds and, for example, stipulate that nonproducers (non-user members) may not hold more than, e.g., 10% of the voting capital of the cooperative. Both legal systems provide a rather flexible framework that should help to increase efficiency.[1485] As the Austrian legal system contains fewer default provisions, those in the Italian legal system might be used as examples for Austrian SCEs.

Members who are not satisfied may leave their SCE. Contrary to investor-owned companies, the management organ of an agricultural SCE is not constrained by the threat of a takeover. This risk arguably keeps the management honest, as takeovers normally cause a change in management.[1486] Yet, the threat of a takeover would require shares to be freely tradeable, which Art. 4 para. 11 SCE-R strongly restricts in an SCE: thus, either the general meeting or the management or administrative organ must agree upon the transfer of shares. Thus, in an agricultural SCE there is no takeover threat.[1487] Nevertheless, the exit mechanism established by the SCE-R may place similar pressure on the management.[1488] In this regard, the SCE-R provides statutory freedom for setting the procedures and conditions for resignation.[1489]

The efficiency of agricultural cooperatives is also affected by the unrestricted withdrawal by members. Yet, cooperatives who place onerous restrictions on leaving may distort competition and prevent potential members from joining the cooperative. Striking the right balance between the need for the cooperative to operate

[1484]See Iliopoulos (2015), p. 10.

[1485]"There must be exist a point of (temporary) equilibrium where the allocation of residual claim and control rights, the prevailing mentality of members (patron vs investor) and membership heterogeneity meet and result in an optimum result. Locating this point, though, is not possible through standard economic optimization techniques. On the contrary, it requires a trial-and-error effort and, in many cases, the adoption of second-best choice is the only feasible alternative." See Iliopoulos (2015), p. 11. It is necessary to conduct further research on these issues based on multidisciplinary and transdisciplinary approaches. See Iliopoulos (2015), p. 14.

[1486]See Sect. 1.3.2. Also Molk (2014), p. 926; Schneiberg (2002), p. 51 et seq. For general information Hirschman (1970); Armour et al. (2009a), p. 40 et seq.; Fama and Jensen (1983), p. 312 et seq.; Schäfer and Ott (2012), p. 711 et seq.

[1487]In this context, Eidenmüller advocates a default rule. See Eidenmüller (2014), p. 197 et seq.

[1488]See Molk (2014), p. 926 fn 118; Zanotti (2013), p. 252 et seq.; Svendsen (2007), pp. 116 and 130; Kräkel (2012), p. 352. Also consider Karantininis and Nilsson (2007). A study referring to Austrian agricultural cooperatives shows that the threat of withdrawing strongly influences the whole decision-making process. See Kühl (2012), p. 36.

[1489]The provisions regarding repayment of the subscribed capital are dealt with in Sect. 5.4. These provisions aim to counterbalance the members' intent to leave and the interests of the cooperative to avoid liquidity and financing problems.

efficiently on one hand and fairness for the resigning member on the other is not easy[1490]; however, this balance is crucial, because new members shall be informed about the resignation process from the outset to assess any possible risk of lock-in.[1491] With this, the farmer-member can decide to resign (in principle) at any time (rather than voice,[1492] which implies participation) if the exit costs and his loyalty towards the cooperative are sufficiently low.[1493]

Some problems may arise from Art. 15 para. 2 (i) SCE-R, which allows minorities to leave the cooperative if the period of notice for resignation from the SCE is extended to more than 5 years. This requirement may cause the problem of temporary lock-in if this period is extended from, for example, 2 years to a limit lower than 5 years, such as 4 years and 8 months. This can be exacerbated if the repayment of subscribed shares occurs a long time after the member's resignation. Three years is the maximum limit here, as determined by Art. 16 para. 3 SCE-R. Thus, in a worst case scenario, minority members would only be repaid the shares they subscribed after 7 years and 8 months.[1494] This problem can be counterbalanced by Art. 15 para. 2 bullet 2 SCE-R, which allows members to exit if existing obligations are substantially extended. The PECOL do not address minority rights in such cases but, instead, adopts a negotiation-based approach.[1495] However, taking into account the assumptions on which the concept of *homo oeconomicus* is based,[1496] this approach could lead to an efficient outcome, as the drafters of the statutes (hence, the general meeting) must consider appropriate minority rights to attract new members to the agricultural SCE.[1497] This should reduce the risk of lock-in and make exiting a more effective way to constrain the management bodies. This, in turn, should increase efficiency, which is in all members' interests. For example, statutes could provide that withdrawal from the agricultural SCE would take effect only at the end of the current financial year, provided that resignation is notified at least 6 months in advance. Furthermore, it will have to be stipulated that the repayment will be made on the basis of the balance sheet for the financial year in which the membership is terminated. The repayment itself can then be made within 180 days of the approval of the balance sheet.

On the other hand, minorities can exploit the qualified majority requirement in situations where their votes are needed to reach a qualified majority. Thus, a hold-up problem can arise when a minority of members blocks the development of an agricultural SCE. This could typically occur during a realignment of the cooperative, which requires the statutes of the agricultural SCE to change, which in turn can only

---

[1490] See Van der Sangen (2012), p. 24.

[1491] A study about Austrian agricultural cooperatives shows that, in general, a period of 3 months is applied. See Kühl (2012), p. 38.

[1492] See Hirschman (1970). Also consider Tirole (2006), p. 333 et seq.

[1493] The latter however is difficult to calculate objectively. See Zanotti (2013), p. 252 et seq.

[1494] 4 years 8 months + 3 years.

[1495] See Snaith (2017), p. 52.

[1496] For information about this concept, see Sect. 1.3.1.

[1497] See Holmstrom (1999), p. 416.

be carried out if, for example, two thirds of the members present (or represented) are in favour of the repositioning. Accordingly, to protect the SCE's interests,[1498] the SCE-R allows expulsion for good cause, i.e., if a member seriously breaches his obligations or acts contrary to the SCE's interests. The requirement of a good cause is usually met if the circumstances that are presented do not permit a trustworthy continuation of the business relationship with the member. A decision to expel must be adequately justified in order to explain why the requirements for membership in an agricultural cooperative are no longer met or how a central obligation under the statutes or resolution of an organ has not been satisfied. Expulsion in these cases favours the homogeneity of members' interests and thus strengthens the membership base, but should only be applied as an *ultima ratio.* Acting contrary to the SCE's interests violates the fiduciary duties that members must observe. Expulsion also reflects the 'general principle that longer-term legal relationships encroaching significantly on the daily lives of their members should be prematurely dissolved on demonstration of good cause'.[1499]

The principle of equal treatment can reduce opportunistic behaviour by the deciding organ. For Italian SCEs, Art. 2516 CC connects this principle to the execution of the mutualistic relationship and, arguably, also includes the termination of the mutualistic relationship. By contrast, the *GenG* does not contain a provision that governs expulsion. However, a cooperative needs a functioning exit mechanism to reduce or eliminate the free-rider problem.[1500] Although, in practice, appropriate contractual solutions seem to have been found, it would have been better to include a default provision in the *GenG*, as the negotiation process for finding an efficient exit mechanism incurs high transaction costs. However, the problem of transactions costs is mitigated by compulsory membership in an auditing association, which will provide the necessary expertise.

References

Abriani N (2019) Corporate governance e sistema monistico: linee evolutive. Rivista delle società:527–539

Adams RB, Ferreira D (2007) A theory of friendly boards. J Finance 62:217–250. https://doi.org/10.1111/j.1540-6261.2007.01206.x

Albamonte D (2008) Lo statuto della società cooperativa europea. In: Capriglione F (ed) La nuova disciplina della società europea. Cedam, Padova, pp 295–320

Ales E (2008) Italy. In: Study on the implementation of the Directive 2003/72/EC (employee involvement in the European cooperative society) in ten Member States. https://ec.europa.eu/social/main.jsp?catId=707&langId=en&intPageId=213. Accessed 21 Nov 2019

[1498]That is the interest of the majority of its members.

[1499]See Fleischer (2014), p. 73. Also consider Strohn (2015), nt 123 et seq. Easterbrook and Fischel (1998), p. 90 et seq.

[1500]See Kräkel (2012), p. 355.

Alfandari E, Piot B (2004) Die Mitgliedschaft in der SCE. In: Schulze R (ed) Europäische Genossenschaft SCE: Handbuch, 1st edn. Nomos, Baden-Baden, pp 77–90
Ambrosini S (2003a) La riforma delle società: Profili della nuova disciplina. Giappichelli, Torino
Ambrosini S (2003b) L'amministrazione e i controlli nelle spa. Giurisprudenza Commerciale:308
Ambrosini S (2004) Artt. 2403-2406. In: Cottino G, Bonfante G, Cagnasso O, Montalenti P (eds) Il nuovo diritto societario I: Commento al D. lgs. 17 gennaio 2003, n. 6, D. Lgs. 17 gennaio 2003, n. 5, D. lgs. 11 aprile 2002, n. 61 (art. 1). 1. Artt. 2325-2409 c.c, 1st edn. Zanichelli, Bologna, pp 892–909
Armour J, Whincop MJ (2001) An economic analysis of shared property in partnership and close corporations law. J Corp Law:73–92. https://doi.org/10.1093/acprof:oso/9780199264353.003.0003
Armour J, Hansmann H, Kraakman RH (2009a) Agency problems and legal strategies. In: Kraakman RH, Armour J, Davies P, Enriques L, Hansmann H, Hertig G, Hopt K, Kanda H, Rock E (eds) The anatomy of corporate law: a comparative and functional approach, 2nd edn. Oxford University Press, Oxford, pp 35–53
Armour J, Hertig G, Kanda H (2009b) Transactions with creditors. In: Kraakman RH, Armour J, Davies P, Enriques L, Hansmann H, Hertig G, Hopt K, Kanda H, Rock E (eds) The anatomy of corporate law: a comparative and functional approach, 2nd edn. Oxford University Press, Oxford, pp 115–152
Armour J, Hansmann H, Kraakman RH (2009c) What is corporate law. In: Kraakman RH, Armour J, Davies P, Enriques L, Hansmann H, Hertig G, Hopt K, Kanda H, Rock E (eds) The anatomy of corporate law: a comparative and functional approach, 2nd edn. Oxford University Press, Oxford, pp 1–34
Arnò G, Cancarini S, Romanelli F (2007) La società europea: La disciplina comunitaria e il suo recepimento in Italia e nei principali stati membri. EGEA, Milano
Artmann E (2002) Die Organisationsverfassung der Europäischen Aktiengesellschaft. Wirtschaftsrechtliche Blätter:189
Astl H, Steinböck G (2014) § 5. In: Dellinger M (ed) Genossenschaftsgesetz samt Nebengesetzen: Kommentar, 2nd edn. LexisNexis ARD Orac, Wien, pp 122–158
Auletta GG, Salanitro N (2009) Diritto commerciale, 17th edn. Giuffrè, Milano
Avsec F (2009) Die Europäische Genossenschaft innerhalb des europäischen Wirtschaftsraumes. Marburger Beiträge zum Genossenschaftswesen, vol 53. Universität Marburg, Institut für Genossenschaftswesen, Marburg
Bachner T (2012) § 105. In: Doralt W, Nowotny C, Kalss S (eds) Kommentar zum Aktiengesetz, 2nd edn. Linde, Wien, pp 1501–1531
Bainbridge SM (2001) Why a board? Group decisionmaking in corporate governance. Vanderbilt Law Rev 55:1–56
Balzano M (2004) L'assemblea. In: Marasà G (ed) Le cooperative prima e dopo la riforma del diritto societario. Cedam, Padova, pp 533–582
Balzarini P (2006) Art. 2428. In: Notari M, Bianchi LA (eds) Obbligazione bilancio: Artt. 2410-2435 -bis c.c. EGEA, Milano, pp 595–615
Balzarini P (2007) Responsabilità solidale e concorrente di amministratori e sindaci. Le società:875–881
Bamberg G, Coenenberg AG, Krapp M (2013) Betriebswirtschaftliche Entscheidungslehre, 15th edn. Vahlens Kurzlehrbücher. Vahlen, München
Baracchini F (2007) L'appropriazione delle corporate opportunities come fattispecie di infedeltà degli amministratori di s.p.a. In: Abbadessa P, Portale GB (eds) Assemblea, amministrazione, UTET, Torino, pp 603–656
Barbarito MC (2004) Art. 2375. In: Cottino G, Bonfante G, Cagnasso O, Montalenti P (eds) Il nuovo diritto societario I: Commento al D. lgs. 17 gennaio 2003, n. 6, D. Lgs. 17 gennaio 2003, n. 5, D. lgs. 11 aprile 2002, n. 61 (art. 1). 1. Artt. 2325-2409 c.c, 1st edn. Zanichelli, Bologna, pp 585–596
Bassi A (1995) Le società cooperative. Il diritto attuale, vol 20. UTET, Torino

Bassi A (2003) Le società cooperative. In: Bassi A, Buonocore V, Pescatore S (eds) La riforma del diritto societario: Commento ai d.lgs. n. 5-6 del 17 gennaio 2003. Giappichelli, Torino, pp 233–277

Bassi A, Schlesinger P (1988) Delle imprese cooperative e delle mutue assicuratrici: Artt. 2511 - 2548. Il codice civile - commentario, / dir. da Piero Schlesinger. Giuffrè, Milano

Benatti L (2005) Artt. 2397-2406. In: Maffei Alberti A (ed) Il nuovo diritto delle società: Commento sistematico al D. lgs. 17 gennaio 2003, n. 6, aggiornato al D. lgs. 28 dicembre 2004, n. 310. Cedam, Padova, pp 869–971

Bianca M, Zanardo A (2016) La Società Europea e la Società Cooperativa Europea. In: Pederzini E (ed) Percorsi di diritto societario europeo, 3rd edn. Giappichelli, Torino, pp 177–214

Bianchi LA (2016) Il modello monistico è più efficiente di quello tradizionale? Appunti per una ricerca. Analisi Giuridica dell'Economia:23–34. https://doi.org/10.1433/83783

Bijman J, Hendrikse G, van Oijen A (2013) Accommodating two worlds in one organisation: changing board models in agricultural cooperatives. Manag Decis Econ 34:204–217. https://doi.org/10.1002/mde.2584

Bijman J, Hanisch M, Van der Sangen G (2014) Shifting control?: The changes of internal governance in agricultural cooperatives in the EU. Ann Public Coop Econ 85:641–661. https://doi.org/10.1111/apce.12055

Binder R, Lengauer A (2014a) § 24a. In: Dellinger M (ed) Genossenschaftsgesetz samt Nebengesetzen: Kommentar, 2nd edn. LexisNexis ARD Orac, Wien, pp 272–273

Binder R, Lengauer A (2014b) § 25. In: Dellinger M (ed) Genossenschaftsgesetz samt Nebengesetzen: Kommentar, 2nd edn. LexisNexis ARD Orac, Wien, pp 331–333

Blair MM, Stout LA (2006) Specific investment and corporate law. Eur Bus Organ Law Rev 7:473–500. https://doi.org/10.1017/S1566752906004733

Bolten P, Becht M, Röell A (2007) Corporate law and governance. In: Polinsky AM, Shavell S (eds) Handbook of law and economics: volume 2, 1st edn. North Holland, Amsterdam, pp 829–944

Bonelli F (2004) Gli amministratori di spa dopo la riforma delle società. Giuffrè, Milano

Bonfante G (2004a) Art. 2543. In: Cottino G, Bonfante G, Cagnasso O, Montalenti P (eds) Il nuovo diritto societario III: Commento al D. lgs. 17 gennaio 2003, n. 6, D. Lgs. 17 gennaio 2003, n. 5, D. lgs. 11 aprile 2002, n. 61 (art. 1). 3. Artt. 2484-2548 c.c. norme di attuazione, disciplina processuale, artt. 2621-2641 c.c., 1st edn. Zanichelli, Bologna, pp 2590–2594

Bonfante G (2004b) Art. 2544. In: Cottino G, Bonfante G, Cagnasso O, Montalenti P (eds) Il nuovo diritto societario III: Commento al D. lgs. 17 gennaio 2003, n. 6, D. Lgs. 17 gennaio 2003, n. 5, D. lgs. 11 aprile 2002, n. 61 (art. 1). 3. Artt. 2484-2548 c.c. norme di attuazione, disciplina processuale, artt. 2621-2641 c.c., 1st edn. Zanichelli, Bologna, pp 2595–2600

Bonfante G (2006) La società cooperativa europea. In: Galletti D, Fici A (eds) La società cooperativa europea: Quali prospettive per la cooperazione italiana? Universita degli Studi di Trento, Trento, pp 3–12

Bonfante G (ed) (2014a) La società cooperativa. Trattato di diritto commerciale. Cedam, Padova

Bonfante G (2014b) L'inammissibilità del voto segreto nelle cooperative: una questione aperta. Le società:811–815

Bono P (2012) Country report: Italy. In: Van der Sangen G, Pyykkönen POP, Iliopoulus C, Kühl R, Hagedorn K, Hanisch M, Judis R, Gijselinckx C, Hendrikse G, Hak T, Poppe K, Bijman J (eds) Support for farmers' cooperatives. Wageningen, pp 1–65

Brandt U (2002) Überlegungen zu einem SE-Ausführungsgesetz. Neue Zeitschrift für Gesellschaftsrecht:991–996

Brandt U (2003) Der Diskussionsentwurf zu einem SE-Ausführungsgesetz. DStR:1208–1215

Breida MC (2004a) Art. 2409duodecies. In: Cottino G, Bonfante G, Cagnasso O, Montalenti P (eds) Il nuovo diritto societario II: Commento al D. lgs. 17 gennaio 2003, n. 6, D. Lgs. 17 gennaio 2003, n. 5, D. lgs. 11 aprile 2002, n. 61 (art. 1). 2. Artt. 2409 bis-2483 c.c., 1st edn. Zanichelli, Bologna, pp 1155–1171

Breida MC (2004b) Art. 2409novies. In: Cottino G, Bonfante G, Cagnasso O, Montalenti P (eds) Il nuovo diritto societario II: Commento al D. lgs. 17 gennaio 2003, n. 6, D. Lgs. 17 gennaio 2003, n. 5, D. lgs. 11 aprile 2002, n. 61 (art. 1). 2. Artt. 2409 bis-2483 c.c., 1st edn. Zanichelli, Bologna, pp 1117–1132

Breida MC (2004c) Art. 2409terdecies. In: Cottino G, Bonfante G, Cagnasso O, Montalenti P (eds) Il nuovo diritto societario II: Commento al D. lgs. 17 gennaio 2003, n. 6, D. Lgs. 17 gennaio 2003, n. 5, D. lgs. 11 aprile 2002, n. 61 (art. 1). 2. Artt. 2409 bis-2483 c.c., 1st edn. Zanichelli, Bologna, pp 1172–1194

Breida MC (2009) Il modello dualistico. In: Cottino G, Bonfante G, Cagnasso O, Montalenti P (eds) Il nuovo diritto societario nella dottrina e nella giurisprudenza: 2003-2009. Zanichelli, Bologna, pp 673–740

Bruno GSF, Ciavarella A, Linciano N (2018) Boardroom gender diversity and performance of listed companies in Italy. http://www.consob.it/documents/46180/46181/wp87.pdf/d733b58a-44b4-42de-98c7-3c89a82a0182. Accessed 12 Dec 2019

Bungert H, Beier CH (2002) Die Europäische Aktiengesellschaft. EWS - Europäisches Wirtschafts- und Steuerrecht:1–12

Bydlinski S, Potyka M (2018) § 118. In: Artmann E, Karollus M (eds) Kommentar zum Aktiengesetz 2: §§ 7–144, 6th edn. Manz'sche Verlags- und Universitätsbuchhandlung, Wien, pp 1–8

Calandra Buonaura V (2007) Il potere di rappresentanza degli amministratori di società per azioni. In: Abbadessa P, Portale GB (eds) Assemblea, amministrazione. UTET, Torino, pp 657–682

Cariello V (2009) Il sistema dualistico: Vincoli tipologici e autonomia statutaria, 2nd edn. Quaderni di banca, borsa e titoli di credito, vol 27. Giuffrè, Milano

Cariello V (2012) Il sistema dualistico. Diritto dei sistemi alternativi di amministrazione e controllo, vol 1. Giappichelli, Torino

Caselli G (2003) Elogio, con riserve, del collegio sindacale. Giurisprudenza Commerciale:251–266

Ceccherini A (2008) Art. 2539. In: Ceccherini A, Schirò S (eds) Società cooperative e mutue assicuratrici: (artt. 2511-2548 c.c.), 2nd edn. Giuffré, Milano, pp 159–162

Cecco D (2003) La governance nelle società cooperative: l'assemblea. In: Genco R (ed) La riforma delle società cooperative. IPSOA, Milano, pp 115–181

Cesiano D (2013) L'applicazione della "Business Judgment Rule" nella giurisprudenza italiana. Giurisprudenza Commerciale:941–965

Cetra A (2008) La persona giuridica amministratore di una società a responsabilità limitata o società per azioni nella massima n. 100 del Consiglio notarile di Milano. Rivista di diritto societario:676–693

Cetra A (2010) La persona giuridica amministratore nelle società. In: Amministrazione e controllo nel diritto delle società: Liber amicorum Antonio Piras. Giappichelli, Torino, pp 107–127

Chaddad F, Iliopoulos C (2013) Control rights, governance, and the costs of ownership in agricultural cooperatives. Agribusiness 29:3–22. https://doi.org/10.1002/agr.21328

Chirico S, Troianiello P (2007) La società cooperativa europea: Regolamento CE n. 1435/2003. Cooperative e consorzi. IPSOA, Milano

Cian M (2018a) Art. 2364 bis. In: Cian G (ed) Commentario breve al Codice civile: Commentato con dottrina e giurisprudenza, 13th edn. Wolters Kluver, Milano, Padova, p 2776

Cian M (2018b) Art. 2365. In: Cian G (ed) Commentario breve al Codice civile: Commentato con dottrina e giurisprudenza, 13th edn. Wolters Kluver, Milano, Padova, pp 2776–2777

Cian M (2018c) Art. 2366. In: Cian G (ed) Commentario breve al Codice civile: Commentato con dottrina e giurisprudenza, 13th edn. Wolters Kluver, Milano, Padova, pp 2777–2779

Cian M (2018d) Art. 2367. In: Cian G (ed) Commentario breve al Codice civile: Commentato con dottrina e giurisprudenza, 13th edn. Wolters Kluver, Milano, Padova, pp 2779–2780

Cian M (2018e) Art. 2368. In: Cian G (ed) Commentario breve al Codice civile: Commentato con dottrina e giurisprudenza, 13th edn. Wolters Kluver, Milano, Padova, pp 2780–2782

Cian M (2018f) Art. 2370. In: Cian G (ed) Commentario breve al Codice civile: Commentato con dottrina e giurisprudenza, 13th edn. Wolters Kluver, Milano, Padova, pp 2784–2786

Cian M (2018g) Art. 2371. In: Cian G (ed) Commentario breve al Codice civile: Commentato con dottrina e giurisprudenza, 13th edn. Wolters Kluver, Milano, Padova, pp 2786–2787
Cian M (2018h) Art. 2375. In: Cian G (ed) Commentario breve al Codice civile: Commentato con dottrina e giurisprudenza, 13th edn. Wolters Kluver, Milano, Padova, p 2792
Cian M (2018i) Art. 2391. In: Cian G (ed) Commentario breve al Codice civile: Commentato con dottrina e giurisprudenza, 13th edn. Wolters Kluver, Milano, Padova, pp 2845–2850
Comitato interregionale dei consigli notarili delle Tre Venezie (2011) Orientamenti del comitato triveneto dei notai in materia di atti societari. http://www.notaitriveneto.it/file/massime/41/1316098658_orientamenti_societari2011.pdf. Accessed 19 Nov 2019
Conte L, Vannini R (2008) Istituzioni e Governance Cooperativa. Department of Economics University of Siena. Studi e Note di Economia:139–155
Cook ML, Chaddad FR (2004) Redesigning cooperative boundaries: the emergence of new models. Am J Agric Econ 86:1249–1253. https://doi.org/10.1111/j.0002-9092.2004.00673.x
Cools S (2011) Europe's Ius Commune on director revocability. Eur Comp Financ Law Rev 8:199–234. https://doi.org/10.1515/ecfr.2011.199
Cools S (2014) The dividing line between shareholder democracy and board autonomy: inherent conflicts of interest as normative criterion. Eur Comp Financ Law Rev 11:258–296. https://doi.org/10.1515/ecfr-2014-0258
Cooter RD, Freedman BJ (1991) The fiduciary relationship: its economic character and legal consequences. N Y Univ Law Rev:1045–1075
Cooter R, Mattei U, Monateri PG, Pardolesi R, Ulen T (1999) Il mercato delle regole: Analisi economica del diritto civile. Il Mulino, Bologna
Corapi D (2011) Art. 2409 duodecies. In: Bonfante G, Corapi D, de Angelis L, Napoleoni V, Rordorf R, Salafia V (eds) Codice commentato delle società: Società di persone, società di capitali, cooperative, consorzi, reati societari: aggiornato con le nuove norme in tema di revisione legale, esercizio dei diritti degli azionisti di società quotate e costituzione delle Spa, 3rd edn. IPSOA, Assago, pp 1095–1106
Corapi D, de Donno B (2006) Le società in generale. In: Alessi R, Contaldi L, Corapi D, de Donno B (eds) Impresa e società nel diritto comunitario, 2nd edn. Giappichelli, Torino, pp 1275–1324
Coropatri M (2010) La business judgment rule in Italia e il privilegio amministrativo. Giurisprudenza Commerciale:129–143
Costa CTD, Bilreiro AdM (2003) The European company statute. European business law & practice series, vol 19. Kluwer Law International, The Hague
Cottino G, Cagnasso O (2011) Diritto societario, 2nd edn. Manuali di scienze giuridiche. Cedam, Padova
Crescentini G (2010) Art. 2403bis. In: Cendon P (ed) Artt. 2397-2420 ter: Società per azioni: [3] sindaci, controllo contabile, sistema dualistico e monistico, obbligazioni. Giuffrè, Milano, pp 61–66
Cusa E (2004a) Die Verwendung des Betriebsergebnisses. In: Schulze R (ed) Europäische Genossenschaft SCE: Handbuch, 1st edn. Nomos, Baden-Baden, pp 123–168
Cusa E (2004b) Il procedimento assembleare nella società cooperativa e il principio democratico. Giurisprudenza Commerciale:843–858
Cusa E (2004c) Zur Rechtslage in den Mitgliedsstaaten: Italien. In: Schulze R (ed) Europäische Genossenschaft SCE: Handbuch, 1st edn. Nomos, Baden-Baden, pp 176–183
Cusa E (2006) Il socio finanziatore nelle cooperative. Quaderni di giurisprudenza commerciale, vol 286. Giuffrè, Milano
Cusa E (2007) Art. 2538. In: Presti G (ed) Società cooperative: Artt. 2511-2548. EGEA; Giuffrè, Milano, pp 299–311
Cusa E (2011a) Art. 2538. In: Bonfante G, Corapi D, de Angelis L, Napoleoni V, Rordorf R, Salafia V (eds) Codice commentato delle società: Società di persone, società di capitali, cooperative, consorzi, reati societari: aggiornato con le nuove norme in tema di revisione legale, esercizio dei diritti degli azionisti di società quotate e costituzione delle Spa, 3rd edn. IPSOA, Assago, pp 2199–2214

Cusa E (2011b) Art. 2539. In: Bonfante G, Corapi D, de Angelis L, Napoleoni V, Rordorf R, Salafia V (eds) Codice commentato delle società: Società di persone, società di capitali, cooperative, consorzi, reati societari: aggiornato con le nuove norme in tema di revisione legale, esercizio dei diritti degli azionisti di società quotate e costituzione delle Spa, 3rd edn. IPSOA, Assago, pp 2215–2221

Cusa E (2014a) Art. 2538. In: Santosuosso DU (ed) Delle società, dell'azienda, della concorrenza. UTET, Torino, pp 326–351

Cusa E (2014b) Art. 2539. In: Santosuosso DU (ed) Delle società, dell'azienda, della concorrenza. UTET, Torino, pp 351–359

Cusa E (2014c) Art. 2540. In: Santosuosso DU (ed) Delle società, dell'azienda, della concorrenza. UTET, Torino, pp 360–375

de Nicola A (2005) Art. 2392. In: Ghezzi F (ed) Amministratori: Artt. 2380 - 2396 c.c, 1st edn. EGEA, Milano, pp 545–568

Del Sole V (2010a) Art. 2409 decies. In: Cendon P (ed) Artt. 2397-2420 ter: Società per azioni: [3] sindaci, controllo contabile, sistema dualistico e monistico, obbligazioni. Giuffrè, Milano, pp 335–342

Del Sole V (2010b) Art. 2409 duodecies. In: Cendon P (ed) Artt. 2397-2420 ter: Società per azioni: [3] sindaci, controllo contabile, sistema dualistico e monistico, obbligazioni. Giuffrè, Milano, pp 345–353

Del Sole V (2010c) Art 2409 novies. In: Cendon P (ed) Artt. 2397-2420 ter: Società per azioni: [3] sindaci, controllo contabile, sistema dualistico e monistico, obbligazioni. Giuffrè, Milano, pp 325–334

Del Sole V (2010d) Art 2409 terdecies. In: Cendon P (ed) Artt. 2397-2420 ter: Società per azioni: [3] sindaci, controllo contabile, sistema dualistico e monistico, obbligazioni. Giuffrè, Milano, pp 355–364

Dellinger M (2016) Besonderheiten des Aufsichtsrates in der Genossenschaft. In: Kalss S, Kunz P (eds) Handbuch für den Aufsichtsrat, 2nd edn. Facultas, Wien, pp 1367–1385

Dellinger M, Oberhammer P (1996) Entwurf eines Genossenschaftsgesetzes. Veröffentlichungen des Ludwig-Boltzmann-Institutes für Rechtsvorsorge und Urkundenwesen, vol 17. Manz, Wien

Dellinger M, Steinböck G (2014) § 24c. In: Dellinger M (ed) Genossenschaftsgesetz samt Nebengesetzen: Kommentar, 2nd edn. LexisNexis ARD Orac, Wien, pp 276–310

Denozza F (2002) Norme efficienti: L'analisi economica delle regole giuridiche. Giuffrè, Milano

Di Gaspare A (2012) Riflessioni su consiglio di amministrazione e board of directors nella gestione dei problemi di agenzia. http://www.comparazionedirittocivile.it:1–21

Domenichini G (2004) Art. 2407. In: Niccolini G, Stagno d'Alcontres A (eds) Società di capitali: Commentario. Jovene, Napoli, pp 767–775

Drygala T (2015a) Art. 39. In: Lutter M, Hommelhoff P, Teichmann C (eds) SE-Kommentar, 2nd edn. Verlag Dr. Otto Schmidt, Köln, pp 472–500

Drygala T (2015b) Art. 40. In: Lutter M, Hommelhoff P, Teichmann C (eds) SE-Kommentar, 2nd edn. Verlag Dr. Otto Schmidt, Köln, pp 501–516

Dyck A, Zingales L (2004) Private benefits of control: an international comparison. J Finance 59:537–600. https://doi.org/10.1111/j.1540-6261.2004.00642.x

Easterbrook FH, Fischel DR (1998) The economic structure of corporate law, [Repr.]. Harvard University Press, Cambridge

Ebers M (2004) Die Gründung einer SCE. In: Schulze R (ed) Europäische Genossenschaft SCE: Handbuch, 1st edn. Nomos, Baden-Baden, pp 43–76

Eckert G, Schopper A (2014a) § 30g. In: Torggler U (ed) GmbH-Gesetz: (GmbHG) Kurzkommentar. Manzsche Verlags- und Universitätsbuchhandlung, Wien, pp 310–318

Eckert G, Schopper A (2014b) § 30j. In: Torggler U (ed) GmbH-Gesetz: (GmbHG) Kurzkommentar. Manzsche Verlags- und Universitätsbuchhandlung, Wien, pp 328–341

Eder CJ (2004) Die monistisch verfasste Societas Europaea - Überlegungen zur Umsetzung eines CEO-Modells. Neue Zeitschrift für Gesellschaftsrecht:544–547

Egermann C, Heckenthaler S (2004) Der Verwaltungsrat in der Europäischen Gesellschaft (SE) österreichischer Prägung: Überlegungen zu §§ 38 ff SEG. GesRZ:256–266
Eidenmüller H (2014) Formation, management and transfer of shares. In: Bachmann G, Eidenmüller H, Engert A, Fleischer H, Schön W (eds) Regulating the closed corporation. De Gruyter, Berlin, pp 179–200
Eisenberg MA (1989) The structure of corporation law. Columbia Law Rev:1461–1525
Engert A (2014) The board of directors. In: Bachmann G, Eidenmüller H, Engert A, Fleischer H, Schön W (eds) Regulating the closed corporation. De Gruyter, Berlin, pp 85–121
Enriques L, Pomelli A (2005) Art. 2391. In: Maffei Alberti A (ed) Il nuovo diritto delle società: Commento sistematico al D. lgs. 17 gennaio 2003, n. 6, aggiornato al D. lgs. 28 dicembre 2004, n. 310. Cedam, Padova, pp 758–778
Enriques L, Volpin P (2007) Corporate governance reforms in continental Europe. J Econ Perspect 21:117–140. https://doi.org/10.1257/jep.21.1.117
Enriques L, Hansmann H, Kraakman RH (2009a) The basic governance structure: the interests of shareholders as a class. In: Kraakman RH, Armour J, Davies P, Enriques L, Hansmann H, Hertig G, Hopt K, Kanda H, Rock E (eds) The anatomy of corporate law: a comparative and functional approach, 2nd edn. Oxford University Press, Oxford, pp 55–88
Enriques L, Hansmann H, Kraakman RH (2009b) The basic governance structure: minority shareholders and non-shareholder constituencies. In: Kraakman RH, Armour J, Davies P, Enriques L, Hansmann H, Hertig G, Hopt K, Kanda H, Rock E (eds) The anatomy of corporate law: a comparative and functional approach, 2nd edn. Oxford University Press, Oxford, pp 89–114
Facchin N (2009a) Art 2388. In: Grippo G (ed) Commentario delle società. UTET, Torino, pp 501–504
Facchin N (2009b) Art 2391. In: Grippo G (ed) Commentario delle società. UTET, Torino, pp 510–514
Facchin N (2009c) Art 2392. In: Grippo G (ed) Commentario delle società. UTET, Torino, pp 518–521
Facchin N (2009d) Art 2393. In: Grippo G (ed) Commentario delle società. UTET, Torino, pp 521–523
Facchin N (2009e) Art 2393bis. In: Grippo G (ed) Commentario delle società. UTET, Torino, pp 523–524
Facchin N (2009f) Art 2409decies. In: Grippo G (ed) Commentario delle società. UTET, Torino, pp 662–663
Facchin N (2009g) Art 2409terdecies. In: Grippo G (ed) Commentario delle società. UTET, Torino, pp 666–669
Falcone G (2003) Art 2539. In: Sandulli M, Santoro V (eds) La riforma delle società: Società cooperative Artt. 2511-2548 cod.civ. Giappichelli, Torino, pp 136–138
Fama EF, Jensen MC (1983) Separation of ownership and control. J Law Econ 26:301–325
Ferrarini G (2004) Societas Europaea and the limits of harmonisation: a view from Italy. In: Baums T, Cahn A (eds) Die Europäische Aktiengesellschaft: Umsetzungsfragen und Perspektiven. De Gruyter, Berlin, pp 79–93
Ferrarini G, Ungureanu MC (2014) Executive remuneration: a comparative overview. http://papers.ssrn.com/sol3/papers.cfm?abstract_id=2509968##. Accessed 19 Nov 2019
Ferrucci A, Ferrentino C (2012) Le società di capitali, le società cooperative e le mutue assicuratrici, 2nd edn. Collana notarile. Giuffrè, Milano
Fici A (2006) Società cooperative europea e partecipazione dei lavoratori. In: Galletti D, Fici A (eds) La società cooperativa europea: Quali prospettive per la cooperazione italiana? Universita degli Studi di Trento, Trento, pp 137–155
Fici A (2010) Mapping of the relevant legislation implementing the SCE regulation in the EU Member States and EEA countries. In: Fici A (ed) Study on the implementation of the Regulation 1435/2003 on the Statute for European Cooperative Society (SCE): Executive

Summary and Part I: Synthesis and comparative report. Report drawn up following call tender no ENTR/2009/021 of 23 April from the European Commission, pp 33–80

Fici A (2013a) An introduction to cooperative law. In: Cracogna D, Fici A, Henrÿ H (eds) International handbook of cooperative law. Springer, Berlin, Heidelberg, pp 3–62

Fici A (2013b) Italy. In: Cracogna D, Fici A, Henrÿ H (eds) International handbook of cooperative law. Springer, Berlin, Heidelberg, pp 479–501

Fici A (2013c) The European Cooperative Society. In: Cracogna D, Fici A, Henrÿ H (eds) International handbook of cooperative law. Springer, Berlin, Heidelberg, pp 115–151

Fici A (2015) Cooperation among cooperatives in Italian and comparative law. JEOD 4:64–97. https://doi.org/10.5947/jeod.2015.011

Fici A, Strano C (2010) Italy. In: Fici A (ed) Study on the implementation of the Regulation 1435/2003 on the Statute for European Cooperative Society (SCE): Final Study Part II. National Reports. Report drawn up following call tender no ENTR/2009/021 of 23 April from the European Commission, pp 671–702

Fiorio P (2004) Art 2367. In: Cottino G, Bonfante G, Cagnasso O, Montalenti P (eds) Il nuovo diritto societario I: Commento al D. lgs. 17 gennaio 2003, n. 6, D. Lgs. 17 gennaio 2003, n. 5, D. lgs. 11 aprile 2002, n. 61 (art. 1). 1. Artt. 2325-2409 c.c, 1st edn. Zanichelli, Bologna, pp 507–521

Fleckner AM (2010) Antike Kapitalvereinigungen: Ein Beitrag zu den konzeptionellen und historischen Grundlagen der Aktiengesellschaft. Univ., Diss.—Regensburg, 2008. Forschungen zum Römischen Recht, vol 55. Böhlau, Köln

Fleischer H (2000) Grundfragen der ökonomischen Theorie im Gesellschafts- und Kapitalmarktrecht. Zeitschrift für Unternehmens- und Gesellschaftsrecht 30:1–32. https://doi.org/10.1515/zgre.2000.047

Fleischer H (2001) Informationsasymmetrie im Vertragsrecht: Eine rechtsvergleichende und interdisziplinäre Abhandlung zu Reichweite und Grenzen vertragsschlußbezogener Aufklärungspflichten. Univ., Habil.-Schr.-1999--Köln, 1998. Schriften des Instituts für Arbeits- und Wirtschaftsrecht der Universität zu Köln, vol 85. Beck, München

Fleischer H (2002a) Das neue Recht des Squeeze out. Zeitschrift für Unternehmens- und Gesellschaftsrecht 31. https://doi.org/10.1515/zgre.2002.026

Fleischer H (2002b) Die "Business Judgment Rule" im Spiegel von Rechtsvergleichung und Rechtsökonomie. In: Wank R (ed) Festschrift für Herbert Wiedemann zum 70. Geburtstag. C.H. Beck, München, pp 827–850

Fleischer H (2004) Der Einfluß der Societas Europaea auf die Dogmatik des deutschen Gesellschaftsrechts. Archiv für die civilistische Praxis 204:502–543

Fleischer H (2014) Shareholder conflicts in closed corporations. In: Bachmann G, Eidenmüller H, Engert A, Fleischer H, Schön W (eds) Regulating the closed corporation. De Gruyter, Berlin, pp 29–81

Fleischer H, Schmolke K, Ulrich ZD (2011) Verhaltensökonomik als Forschungsinstrument für das Wirtschaftsrecht. In: Fleischer H, Zimmer D, Altmann S (eds) Beitrag der Verhaltensökonomie (Behavioral Economics) zum Handels- und Wirtschaftsrecht. Recht und Wirtschaft, Frankfurt am Main, pp 9–62

Fortunato S (2003) I controlli nella riforma del diritto societario. Rivista delle società:863–894

Frodermann J, Jannott D (2005) Zur Amtszeit des Verwaltungs- bzw. Aufsichtsrats der SE. Zeitschrift für Wirtschaftsrecht:2251

Galgano F (2003) Il nuovo diritto societario. Trattato di diritto commerciale e di diritto pubblico dell'economia, / dir. da Francesco Galgano; 29. Cedam, Padova

Galle RCJ (2006) The Societas Cooperativa Europea (SCE) and national cooperatives in comparative perspective. Eur Comp Law:225–260

Galletti D (2006) La tutela delle minoranze nella SCE. In: Galletti D, Fici A (eds) La società cooperativa europea: Quali prospettive per la cooperazione italiana? Universita degli Studi di Trento, Trento, pp 48–66

Gallo P (1998a) Introduzione al diritto comparato Vol II: Istituti giuridici. Introduzione al diritto comparato. Giappichelli, Torino

Gallo P (1998b) Introduzione al diritto comparato Vol III: Analisi economica del diritto. Giappichelli, Torino

Gelter M, Helleringer G (2015) Lift not the painted Veil: to whom are directors' duties really owed? Univ Ill Law Rev:1069–1118

Gentzoglanis A (2007) Regulation, governance and capital structure in cooperatives. In: Karantininis K, Nilsson J (eds) Vertical markets and cooperative hierarchies: the role of cooperatives in the agri-food industry. Springer, Dordrecht, pp 151–167

Ghezzi F (2005) Sistemi alternativi di amministrazione e di controllo: Artt. 2409-octies - 2409-noviesdecies c.c. In: Ghezzi F (ed) Sistemi alternativi di amministrazione e di controllo: Artt. 2409-octies - 2409-noviesdecies c.c, 1st edn. EGEA, Milano

Ghezzi F, Malberti C (2008) The two-tier model and the one-tier model of corporate governance in the Italian reform of corporate law. Eur Comp Financ Law Rev 5:1–47. https://doi.org/10.1515/ecfr.5.1.1

Ghezzi F, Rigotti M (2005) Art 2409 octiesdecies. In: Ghezzi F (ed) Sistemi alternativi di amministrazione e di controllo: Artt. 2409-octies - 2409-noviesdecies c.c, 1st edn. EGEA, Milano, pp 247–322

Giorgi V (2018a) Art. 2543. In: Cian G (ed) Commentario breve al Codice civile: Commentato con dottrina e giurisprudenza, 13th edn. Wolters Kluver, Milano, Padova, pp 3241–3242

Giorgi V (2018b) Art. 2544. In: Cian G (ed) Commentario breve al Codice civile: Commentato con dottrina e giurisprudenza, 13th edn. Wolters Kluver, Milano, Padova, pp 3242–3244

Gios G, Santuari A (2002) Agricultural cooperatives in the County of Trento (Italy): economic, organizational and legal perspectives. J Rural Coop 30:3–12. https://doi.org/10.22004/ag.econ.60951

Goshen Z (2003) The efficiency of controlling corporate self-dealing: theory meets reality. Calif Law Rev:393–438. https://doi.org/10.15779/Z38T417

Grechenig K, Eckert G, Stremitzer A (2005) Ökonomische Analyse der Vorstandshaftung. In: Kalss S (ed) Vorstandshaftung in 15 europäischen Ländern. Linde, Wien, pp 95–163

Greda C (2014) Statut der Europäischen Genossenschaft. In: Dellinger M (ed) Genossenschaftsgesetz samt Nebengesetzen: Kommentar, 2nd edn. LexisNexis ARD Orac, Wien, pp 829–854

Gruber E (2012) § 17. In: Doralt W, Nowotny C, Kalss S (eds) Kommentar zum Aktiengesetz, 2nd edn. Linde, Wien, pp 332–353

Guaccero A (2004a) Art. 2409 octies - quinquiesdecies. In: Niccolini G, Stagno d'Alcontres A (eds) Società di capitali: Commentario. Jovene, Napoli, pp 865–907

Guaccero A (2004b) Art. 2409 sexiesdecies noviesdecies. In: Niccolini G, Stagno d'Alcontres A (eds) Società di capitali: Commentario. Jovene, Napoli, pp 908–927

Guizzi (2004) Art. 2391. In: Niccolini G, Stagno d'Alcontres A (eds) Società di capitali: Commentario. Jovene, Napoli, pp 652–675

Gutsche R (1994) Die Eignung der Europäischen Aktiengesellschaft für kleine und mittlere Unternehmen in Deutschland. Univ., Diss.—Heidelberg, 1993, 1st edn. Nomos, Baden-Baden

Hanisch M (2006) Eine Theorie genossenschaftlichen Wandels. In: Münkner H-H (ed) Zukunftsperspektiven für Genossenschaften: Bausteine für typgerechte Weiterentwicklung: [Beiträge zum Kolloquium "Elemente von Strategiekonzepten der Zukunftssicherung genossenschaftlicher Kooperation", Marburg 2005], 1st edn. Haupt, Bern, Stuttgart, Wien, pp 297–323

Hansmann H (1996) The ownership of enterprise, 1st edn. Belknap Press of Harvard University Press, Cambridge

Hansmann H (1999) Cooperative firms in theory and practice. Liiketaloudellinen aikakauskirja LTA - Finn J Bus Econ:387–403

Hansmann H, Pargendler M (2013) The evolution of shareholder voting rights: separation of ownership and consumption. Yale Law J:100–165

Harrer F (1990) Haftungsprobleme bei der GmbH. Univ., Habil.-Schr.—Salzburg, 1989. Orac, Wien
Henrÿ H (2012) Guidelines for cooperative legislation, 3rd edn. International Labour Organization, Geneva
Henssler M (2003) Unternehmerische Mitbestimmung in der Societas Europaea: neue Denkanstöße für die “Corporate Governance”-Diskussion. In: Habersack M (ed) Festschrift für Peter Ulmer zum 70. Geburtstag am 2. Januar 2003. De Gruyter, Berlin, pp 193–210
Hirschman AO (1970) Exit, voice, and loyalty: responses to decline in firms, organizations, and states. Harvard University Press, Cambridge
Hirte H (2002) Die Europäische Aktiengesellschaft. Neue Zeitschrift für Gesellschaftsrecht:1–9
Hirte H (2005) Die Europäische Aktiengesellschaft - ein Überblick nach In-Kraft-Treten der deutschen Ausführungsgesetzgebung (Teil II). DStR:700–705
Hoeffler J (2013) Die Gestaltungsfreiheit im deutschen und europäischen Genossenschaftsrecht. Europäische Hochschulschriften. Reihe II, Rechtswissenschaft, Band 5534. Peter Lang, Frankfurt
Hoffmann-Becking M (2004) Organe: Strukturen und Verantwortlichkeiten, insbesondere im monistischen System. Zeitschrift für Unternehmens- und Gesellschaftsrecht 33:355–382. https://doi.org/10.1515/zgre.2004.014
Holmstrom B (1999) The future of cooperatives: a corporate perspective. Liiketaloudellinen aikakauskirja LTA - Finn J Bus Econ:404–417
Holmstrom B, Milgrom P (1994) The firm as an incentive system. Am Econ Rev 84:972–991
Holthaus J, Lehnhoff DJ (2016a) § 43. In: Lehnhoff DJ, Holthaus J (eds) Lang/Weidmüller Genossenschaftsgesetz: Gesetz, betreffend die Erwerbs- und Wirtschaftsgenossenschaften mit Erläuterungen zum Umwandlungsgesetz und zur Europäischen Genossenschaft (SCE), 38., neu bearbeitete Auflage. De Gruyter, Berlin, pp 567–614
Holthaus J, Lehnhoff DJ (2016b) § 6. In: Lehnhoff DJ, Holthaus J (eds) Lang/Weidmüller Genossenschaftsgesetz: Gesetz, betreffend die Erwerbs- und Wirtschaftsgenossenschaften mit Erläuterungen zum Umwandlungsgesetz und zur Europäischen Genossenschaft (SCE), 38., neu bearbeitete Auflage. De Gruyter, Berlin, pp 112–122
Holthaus J, Lehnhoff DJ (2016c) Einf. In: Lehnhoff DJ, Holthaus J (eds) Lang/Weidmüller Genossenschaftsgesetz: Gesetz, betreffend die Erwerbs- und Wirtschaftsgenossenschaften mit Erläuterungen zum Umwandlungsgesetz und zur Europäischen Genossenschaft (SCE), 38., neu bearbeitete Auflage. De Gruyter, Berlin, pp 1–54
Hommelhoff P (1988) Die Konzernleitungspflicht: Zentrale Aspekte eines Konzernverfassungsrechts. Univ., Habil.-Schr.-1981--Bochum, 1980, Unveränd. Nachdr. [der Ausg. 1982]. Heymanns, Köln
Hopt K (2002) Europäische Aktiengesellschaft - per aspera ad astra? EuZW:1
Hopt KJ (2013) Conflict of interest, secrecy and insider information of directors, a comparative analysis. Eur Comp Financ Law Rev 10:167–193. https://doi.org/10.1515/ecfr-2013-0167
Hopt KJ, Leyens PC (2004) Board models in Europe – recent developments of internal corporate governance structures in Germany, the United Kingdom, France, and Italy. Eur Comp Financ Law Rev 1:135–168. https://doi.org/10.1515/ecfr.2004.1.2.135
Hueth B, Marcoul P (2009) Incentive pay for CEOs in cooperative firms. Am J Agric Econ 91:1218–1223. https://doi.org/10.1111/j.1467-8276.2009.01287.x
van Diepenbeek WJJ (2007) Cooperatives as a business organization: lessons from cooperative organization history. Universiteit Maastricht, Maastricht
Iengo M (2006) Gli Studi del CNN - Società cooperativa europea - Analisi delle norme applicabili ai sensi dell’articolo 8 del regolamento n. 1435/2003 - Casi e materiali di diritto comunitario di interesse notarile: le società - e.library - Fondazione Italiana del Notariato. Studio n. 9-2006/I. http://elibrary.fondazionenotariato.it/approfondimento.asp?app=21/studiCNN/mi_9_2006_I&mn=3&tipo=3&qn=6. Accessed 21 Nov 2019
Iliopoulos C (2014) Ownership, governance and related trade-offs in agricultural cooperatives. Dovenschmidt Q 2:159–167. https://doi.org/10.5553/DQ/221199812014002004004

Iliopoulos C (2015) Ownership and governance in agricultural cooperatives: an update. https://www.researchgate.net/publication/274064574_Ownership_and_Governance_in_Agricultural_Cooperatives_An_Update. Accessed 29 Nov 2019

Iliopoulos C, Cook ML (2013) Property rights constraints in producer-owned firms: solutions as prerequisites for successful collective entrepreneurship

Iliopoulos C, Valentinov V (2018) Member heterogeneity in agricultural cooperatives: a systems-theoretic perspective. Sustainability 10:1271. https://doi.org/10.3390/su10041271

Jungmann C (2006) The effectiveness of corporate governance in one-tier and two-tier board systems – evidence from the UK and Germany. Eur Comp Financ Law Rev 3:426–474. https://doi.org/10.1515/ECFR.2006.019

Kalss S (2004) Die geplante SE-Gesetzgebung in Österreich. In: Baums T, Cahn A (eds) Die Europäische Aktiengesellschaft: Umsetzungsfragen und Perspektiven. De Gruyter, Berlin, pp 106–131

Kalss S (2008) Societas Europea. In: Kalss S, Nowotny C, Schauer M, Kastner W, Doralt P (eds) Österreichisches Gesellschaftsrecht: Systematische Darstellung sämtlicher Rechtsformen: in Fortführung des von Walther Kastner begründeten und in der letzten Auflage von Walther Kastner, Peter Doralt und Christian Nowotny bearbeiteten Lehr- und Handbuchs "Grundriss des österreichischen Gesellschaftsrechts". Manz, Wien, 3/1091–3/1111

Kalss S (2012) § 92. In: Doralt W, Nowotny C, Kalss S (eds) Kommentar zum Aktiengesetz, 2nd edn. Linde, Wien, pp 1186–1252

Kalss S (2014) Österreich. In: Goette W, Habersack M, Kalss S (eds) Münchener Kommentar zum Aktiengesetz, 4th edn. C.H. Beck; Verlag Franz Vahlen, München, pp 871–888

Kalss S (2015) Organhaftung in Österreich - einige rechtspolitische Anmerkungen. GesRZ:159–167

Kalss S, Greda C (2004) Die Europäische Gesellschaft (SE) österreichischer Prägung nach dem Ministerialentwurf. GesRZ:91–107

Kalss S, Schauer M (2006) Die Reform des Österreichischen Kapitalgesellschaftsrechts: Gutachten. Verhandlungen des Sechzehnten Österreichischen Juristentages Zivilrecht, vol 1. Manz, Wien

Karantininis K, Nilsson J (eds) (2007) Vertical markets and cooperative hierarchies: the role of cooperatives in the agri-food industry. Springer, Dordrecht

Kastner W (1986) Österreichisches Genossenschaftsrecht. In: Patera M (ed) Handbuch des österreichischen Genossenschaftswesens. Orac, Wien, pp 117–232

Kastner W, Doralt P, Nowotny C (1990) Grundriss des österreichischen Gesellschaftsrechts, 5th edn. Manzsche Kurzlehrbuch-Reihe, vol 2. Manz, Wien

Keay A (2008) Ascertaining the corporate objective: an entity maximisation and sustainability model. Mod Law Rev 71:663–698. https://doi.org/10.1111/j.1468-2230.2008.00711.x

Keinert H (1988) Österreichisches Genossenschaftsrecht: Lehr- und Handbuch. Manz, Wien

Keinert H, Keinert-Kisin C (2013) Ungeschriebene Kompetenzen der Generalversammlung der Genossenschaft? ecolex:996

Klein WA, Coffee JC, Partnoy F (2010) Business organization and finance: legal and economic principles, 11 edn. Concepts and insights series. Foundation Press, New York

Klöhn L (2008) Interessenkonflikte zwischen Aktionären und Gläubigern der Aktiengesellschaft im Spiegel der Vorstandspflichten – Ein Beitrag zur Leitungsaufgabe des Vorstands gemäß § 76 AktG. Zeitschrift für Unternehmens- und Gesellschaftsrecht 37:110–158. https://doi.org/10.1515/ZGR.2008.37.1.110

Koppensteiner H, Rüffler F (2007) GmbH-Gesetz: Kommentar, 3rd edn. LexisNexis ARD Orac, Wien

Korte O (2012) Die Europäische Genossenschaft (SCE): Analyse der mangelnden Verbreitung dieser supranationalen Rechtsform. In: Baudenbacher C (ed) Aktuelle Entwicklungen des europäischen und internationalen Wirtschaftsrechts. Helbing et Lichtenhahn, Basel, München [u.a.], pp 323–349

Kräkel M (2012) Organisation und Management, 5th edn. Neue ökonomische Grundrisse. Mohr Siebeck, Tübingen

Kraus S-F (2014) § 25. In: Torggler U (ed) GmbH-Gesetz: (GmbHG) Kurzkommentar. Manzsche Verlags- und Universitätsbuchhandlung, Wien, pp 236–260
Kübler F (2003) Leitungsstrukturen der Aktiengesellschaft und die Umsetzung des SE-Statuts. Zeitschrift für das gesamte Handelsrecht und Wirtschaftsrecht (ZHR):222–234
Kühl R (2012) Country report: Austria. In: Van der Sangen G, Pyykkönen POP, Iliopoulus C, Kühl R, Hagedorn K, Hanisch M, Judis R, Gijselinckx C, Hendrikse G, Hak T, Poppe K, Bijman J (eds) Support for farmers' cooperatives, Wageningen, pp 1–51
Lange O (2003) Überlegungen zur Umwandlung einer deutschen in eine Europäische Aktiengesellschaft. EuZW:301–309
Laurini (2008a) Art. 2371. In: Picciau A (ed) Assemblea: Artt. 2363 - 2379-ter c.c. EGEA, Milano, pp 147–188
Laurini (2008b) Artt. 2368-2369 c.c. In: Picciau A (ed) Assemblea: Artt. 2363 - 2379-ter c.c. EGEA, Milano, pp 79–120
Lehner JH (2007) Die Europäische Genossenschaft mit Sitzstaat Österreich. Wien, Univ., Diss., 2008
Lehner JH (2009) Verschmelzungsvarianten einer Europäischen Genossenschaft (SCE). In: Haslinger M, Kanonier A, Zehetner S (eds) Ein Jurist im Spannungsfeld von Wirtschaft, Technik und Recht: Festschrift für Franz Zehetner zum 60. Geburtstag. NWV, Wien, pp 97–110
Leyens PC (2003) Deutscher Aufsichtsrat und U.S.-Board: ein- oder zweistufiges Verwaltungssystem?: Zum Stand der rechtsvergleichenden Corporate Governance-Debatte. Rabels Zeitschrift fuer auslaendisches und internationales Privatrecht:57–105
Leyens PC (2006) Information des Aufsichtsrats: Ökonomisch-funktionale Analyse und Rechtsvergleich zum englischen Board. Univ., Diss.—Hamburg, 2006. Mohr Siebeck, Tübingen
Leyens PC (2007a) Corporate Governance: Grundsatzfragen und Forschungsperspektiven. JuristenZeitung 62:1061–1072. https://doi.org/10.1628/002268807782717113
Leyens PC (2007b) Internal corporate governance in Europe: towards a more market-based approach. Kyoto J Law Polit:17–36
Liang Q, Hendrikse G (2013) Cooperative CEO identity and efficient governance: member or outside CEO? Agribusiness 29:23–38
Lind M (2004) Die Europäische Aktiengesellschaft: Eine Analyse der Rechtsanwendungsvorschriften. Univ., Diss.—Graz, 2003. Neue juristische Monografien, vol 26. NWV, Wien
Lutter M (2007) Die Business Judgment Rule in Deutschland und Österreich. GesRZ:79–89
Lutter M, Schmidt J, Bayer W (2012) Europäisches Unternehmens- und Kapitalmarktrecht: Grundlagen, Stand und Entwicklung nebst Texten und Materialien, 5th edn. Zeitschrift für Unternehmens- und Gesellschaftsrecht. Sonderheft, T. 1. De Gruyter, Berlin
Maffezzoni I (2008) Art. 2365. In: Picciau A (ed) Assemblea: Artt. 2363 - 2379-ter c.c. EGEA, Milano, pp 45–58
Magnani P (2005a) Art. 2409 duodecies. In: Ghezzi F (ed) Sistemi alternativi di amministrazione e di controllo: Artt. 2409-octies - 2409-noviesdecies c.c, 1st edn. EGEA, Milano, pp 107–134
Magnani P (2005b) Art. 2409 terdecies. In: Ghezzi F (ed) Sistemi alternativi di amministrazione e di controllo: Artt. 2409-octies - 2409-noviesdecies c.c, 1st edn. EGEA, Milano, pp 135–186
Mahi FE (2004) Die Europäische Aktiengesellschaft: Societas Europaea, SE. Fachhochschule, Dipl.-Arb.—Frankfurt am Main, 2003. Herchen + Herchen, Frankfurt am Main
Mallin C, Melis A, Gaia S (2015) The remuneration of independent directors in the UK and Italy: an empirical analysis based on agency theory. Int Bus Rev 24:175–186. https://doi.org/10.1016/j.ibusrev.2014.07.006
Mancuso F (2017) Il comitato per il controllo sulla gestione nel modello monistico: problemi in tema di responsabilità dei componenti e di invalidità delle decisioni. Rivista delle società:773–794
Manz G (2010a) Art. 38. In: Manz G, Mayer B, Schröder A (eds) Europäische Aktiengesellschaft SE: SE, 2nd edn. Nomos, Baden-Baden, pp 482–490

Manz G (2010b) Art. 39. In: Manz G, Mayer B, Schröder A (eds) Europäische Aktiengesellschaft SE: SE, 2nd edn. Nomos, Baden-Baden, pp 490–515
Manz G (2010c) Art. 40. In: Manz G, Mayer B, Schröder A (eds) Europäische Aktiengesellschaft SE: SE, 2nd edn. Nomos, Baden-Baden, pp 515–529
Manz G (2010d) Art. 41. In: Manz G, Mayer B, Schröder A (eds) Europäische Aktiengesellschaft SE: SE, 2nd edn. Nomos, Baden-Baden, pp 529–539
Manz G (2010e) Art. 42. In: Manz G, Mayer B, Schröder A (eds) Europäische Aktiengesellschaft SE: SE, 2nd edn. Nomos, Baden-Baden, pp 539–542
Manz G (2010f) Art. 43. In: Manz G, Mayer B, Schröder A (eds) Europäische Aktiengesellschaft SE: SE, 2nd edn. Nomos, Baden-Baden, pp 542–598
Manz G (2010g) Art. 44. In: Manz G, Mayer B, Schröder A (eds) Europäische Aktiengesellschaft SE: SE, 2nd edn. Nomos, Baden-Baden, pp 598–601
Manz G (2010h) Art. 46. In: Manz G, Mayer B, Schröder A (eds) Europäische Aktiengesellschaft SE: SE, 2nd edn. Nomos, Baden-Baden, pp 605–608
Manz G (2010i) Art. 47. In: Manz G, Mayer B, Schröder A (eds) Europäische Aktiengesellschaft SE: SE, 2nd edn. Nomos, Baden-Baden, pp 608–616
Manz G (2010j) Art. 48. In: Manz G, Mayer B, Schröder A (eds) Europäische Aktiengesellschaft SE: SE, 2nd edn. Nomos, Baden-Baden, pp 616–624
Manz G (2010k) Art. 49. In: Manz G, Mayer B, Schröder A (eds) Europäische Aktiengesellschaft SE: SE, 2nd edn. Nomos, Baden-Baden, pp 624–628
Manz G (2010l) Art. 50. In: Manz G, Mayer B, Schröder A (eds) Europäische Aktiengesellschaft SE: SE, 2nd edn. Nomos, Baden-Baden, pp 628–638
Manz G (2010m) Art. 51. In: Manz G, Mayer B, Schröder A (eds) Europäische Aktiengesellschaft SE: SE, 2nd edn. Nomos, Baden-Baden, pp 638–648
Marano P (2003) Art. 2544 c.c. In: Sandulli M, Santoro V (eds) La riforma delle società: Società cooperative Artt. 2511-2548 cod.civ. Giappichelli, Torino, pp 148–161
Marano P (2013a) Art. 2538. In: Alpa G, Mariconda V (eds) Codice civile, 3rd edn. Wolters Kluwer Italia; IPSOA, Assago
Marano P (2013b) Art. 2539. In: Alpa G, Mariconda V (eds) Codice civile, 3rd edn. Wolters Kluwer Italia; IPSOA, Assago
Marasà G (2016) Voto plurimo, voto maggiorato e cooperative. Banca, borsa, titoli di credito:1–14
Marchetti C (2007) Composizione e nomina degli organi sociali: ovvero, la missione dei consigli di gestione e di sorveglianza. Analisi Giuridica dell'Economia:301–320. https://doi.org/10.1433/25661
Marhold F (2008) Austria. In: Study on the implementation of the Directive 2003/72/EC (employee involvement in the European cooperative society) in ten Member States. https://ec.europa.eu/social/main.jsp?catId=707&langId=en&intPageId=213. Accessed 21 Nov 2019
Mathis K (2019) Effizienz statt Gerechtigkeit?: Auf der Suche nach den philosophischen Grundlagen der Ökonomischen Analyse des Rechts, 4th edn. Schriften zur Rechtstheorie, Band 223. Duncker et Humblot GmbH, Berlin
Mayer B (2010a) Art. 52. In: Manz G, Mayer B, Schröder A (eds) Europäische Aktiengesellschaft SE: SE, 2nd edn. Nomos, Baden-Baden, pp 648–657
Mayer B (2010b) Art. 53. In: Manz G, Mayer B, Schröder A (eds) Europäische Aktiengesellschaft SE: SE, 2nd edn. Nomos, Baden-Baden, pp 657–680
Mayer B (2010c) Art. 54. In: Manz G, Mayer B, Schröder A (eds) Europäische Aktiengesellschaft SE: SE, 2nd edn. Nomos, Baden-Baden, pp 681–695
Mayer B (2010d) Art. 55. In: Manz G, Mayer B, Schröder A (eds) Europäische Aktiengesellschaft SE: SE, 2nd edn. Nomos, Baden-Baden, pp 695–702
Mayer B (2010e) Art. 56. In: Manz G, Mayer B, Schröder A (eds) Europäische Aktiengesellschaft SE: SE, 2nd edn. Nomos, Baden-Baden, pp 702–706
Mayer B (2010f) Art. 57. In: Manz G, Mayer B, Schröder A (eds) Europäische Aktiengesellschaft SE: SE, 2nd edn. Nomos, Baden-Baden, pp 706–730

Mayer B (2010g) Art. 58. In: Manz G, Mayer B, Schröder A (eds) Europäische Aktiengesellschaft SE: SE, 2nd edn. Nomos, Baden-Baden, pp 730–731

Mayer B (2010h) Art. 59. In: Manz G, Mayer B, Schröder A (eds) Europäische Aktiengesellschaft SE: SE, 2nd edn. Nomos, Baden-Baden, pp 731–737

Milgrom PR, Roberts J (2005) Economia, organizzazione e management II, 2nd edn. Il Mulino, Bologna

Ministry for economic development (2006) Communication no 9203, 30 June 2006, GU no 171 25.07.2006

Miotto L (2018a) Art. 2409 decies. In: Cian G (ed) Commentario breve al Codice civile: Commentato con dottrina e giurisprudenza, 13th edn. Wolters Kluver, Milano, Padova, pp 2905–2906

Miotto L (2018b) Art. 2409 duodecies. In: Cian G (ed) Commentario breve al Codice civile: Commentato con dottrina e giurisprudenza, 13th edn. Wolters Kluver, Milano, Padova, pp 2906–2908

Miotto L (2018c) Art. 2409 novies. In: Cian G (ed) Commentario breve al Codice civile: Commentato con dottrina e giurisprudenza, 13th edn. Wolters Kluver, Milano, Padova, pp 2903–2905

Miotto L (2018d) Art. 2409 sexiesdecies. In: Cian G (ed) Commentario breve al Codice civile: Commentato con dottrina e giurisprudenza, 13th edn. Wolters Kluver, Milano, Padova, p 2911

Miotto L (2018e) Art. 2409 terdecies. In: Cian G (ed) Commentario breve al Codice civile: Commentato con dottrina e giurisprudenza, 13th edn. Wolters Kluver, Milano, Padova, pp 2908–2910

Miribung G (2017) Quale Business Judgment Rule?: Osservazioni dall'ordinamento giuridico italiano e austriaco. In: Schurr FA, Umlauft M (eds) Festschrift für Bernhard Eccher. Verlag Österreich, Wien, pp 709–722

Mirone A (2017a) I sistemi alternativi di amminstrazione e controllo: il sistema dualistico e il sistema monistico. In: Cian M (ed) Diritto commerciale: III. Diritto delle società. G. Giappichelli, Torino, pp 562–580

Mirone A (2017b) Il sistema tradizionale: l'assemblea. In: Cian M (ed) Diritto commerciale: III. Diritto delle società. G. Giappichelli, Torino, pp 398–460

Molitor MK (2009) Eat your vegetables (or at least understand why you should): can better warning and education of prospective minority owners reduce oppression in closely held businesses? Fordham J Corp Financ Law:491–596

Molk P (2014) The puzzling lack of cooperatives. Tulane Law Rev:889–958

Montagnani C (2004a) Art. 2363. In: Niccolini G, Stagno d'Alcontres A (eds) Società di capitali: Commentario. Jovene, Napoli, pp 436–445

Montagnani C (2004b) Artt. 2364-2364bis. In: Niccolini G, Stagno d'Alcontres A (eds) Società di capitali: Commentario. Jovene, Napoli, pp 446–459

Montagnani C (2004c) Artt. 2368-2369. In: Niccolini G, Stagno d'Alcontres A (eds) Società di capitali: Commentario. Jovene, Napoli, pp 486–494

Montalenti P (2002) Corporate governance, consiglio di amministrazione, sistemi di controllo interno: spunti di riflessione. Rivista delle società:803–839

Montalenti P (2005) I sistemi di controlli interni nelle società di capitali. Le società:294–302

Mosco GD (2004a) Art. 2384. In: Niccolini G, Stagno d'Alcontres A (eds) Società di capitali: Commentario. Jovene, Napoli, pp 607–614

Mosco GD (2004b) Art. 2387. In: Niccolini G, Stagno d'Alcontres A (eds) Società di capitali: Commentario. Jovene, Napoli, pp 623–626

Mosco GD (2004c) Artt. 2382-2383. In: Niccolini G, Stagno d'Alcontres A (eds) Società di capitali: Commentario. Jovene, Napoli, pp 602–606

Mucciarelli (2003) La governance delle società cooperative: gli amministratori. In: Genco R (ed) La riforma delle società cooperative. IPSOA, Milano, pp 183–210

Münkner H-H (2006) Europäische Genossenschaft (SCE) und Europäische Genossenschaftstradition. Vorträge und Aufsätze des Forschungsvereins für Genossenschaftswesen, vol 30. Eigenverlag des FOG, Wien
Münkner H-H (2017) Cooperative audit. In: Fajardo-García IG, Fici A, Henrÿ H, Hiez D, Meira DMMA, Münkner H-H, Snaith I (eds) Principles of European Cooperative Law: principles, commentaries and national reports. Intersentia, Cambridge, pp 97–118
Myers SC (1977) Determinants of corporate borrowing. J Financ Econ 5:147–175. https://doi.org/10.1016/0304-405X(77)90015-0
Nagel B (2004) Die Europäische Aktiengesellschaft (SE) in Deutschland - der Regierungsentwurf zum SE-Einführungsgesetz. Neue Zeitschrift für Gesellschaftsrecht:833–839
Nenova T (2003) The value of corporate voting rights and control: a cross-country analysis. J Financ Econ 68:325–351. https://doi.org/10.1016/S0304-405X(03)00069-2
Nilsson J (2001) Organisational principles for co-operative firms. Scand J Manage 17:329–356. https://doi.org/10.1016/S0956-5221(01)00010-0
Nilsson J, Svendsen GLH, Svendsen GT (2012) Are large and complex agricultural cooperatives losing their social capital? Agribusiness 28:187–204. https://doi.org/10.1002/agr.21285
Nowak MJ, McCabe M (2003) Information costs and the role of the independent corporate director. Corp Gov 11:300–307. https://doi.org/10.1111/1467-8683.00328
Nowotny C (2008a) Genossenschaft. In: Kalss S, Nowotny C, Schauer M, Kastner W, Doralt P (eds) Österreichisches Gesellschaftsrecht: Systematische Darstellung sämtlicher Rechtsformen: in Fortführung des von Walther Kastner begründeten und in der letzten Auflage von Walther Kastner, Peter Doralt und Christian Nowotny bearbeiteten Lehr- und Handbuchs "Grundriss des österreichischen Gesellschaftsrechts". Manz, Wien, 5/1–5/182
Nowotny C (2008b) Gesellschaft mit beschränkter Haftung. In: Kalss S, Nowotny C, Schauer M, Kastner W, Doralt P (eds) Österreichisches Gesellschaftsrecht: Systematische Darstellung sämtlicher Rechtsformen: in Fortführung des von Walther Kastner begründeten und in der letzten Auflage von Walther Kastner, Peter Doralt und Christian Nowotny bearbeiteten Lehr- und Handbuchs "Grundriss des österreichischen Gesellschaftsrechts". Manz, Wien
Nowotny C (2012) § 84. In: Doralt W, Nowotny C, Kalss S (eds) Kommentar zum Aktiengesetz, 2nd edn. Linde, Wien, pp 1072–1091
Ortmann GF, King RP (2007) Agricultural cooperatives I: history, theory and problems. Agrekon 46:40–68. https://doi.org/10.1080/03031853.2007.9523760
Palmeri M (2000) Diritto societario virtuale: la videoassemblea diventa realtà. Contratto e impresa:830–849
Panzironi V (2007) Il modello dualistico di amministrazione; aspetti critici. Diritto e pratica delle società:26–29
Paolucci LF (2012) Il governo delle società cooperative. In: Paolucci LF (ed) Le società cooperative. UTET giuridica, Torino, pp 125–146
Paolucci LF (2019a) Art. 2526. In: Paolucci LF (ed) Codice delle cooperative 2019: Aggiornato con le novità del D.Lgs. n. 14/2019. Maggioli, Santarcangelo di Romagna, Rimini, pp 85–87
Paolucci LF (2019b) Art. 2538. In: Paolucci LF (ed) Codice delle cooperative 2019: Aggiornato con le novità del D.Lgs. n. 14/2019. Maggioli, Santarcangelo di Romagna, Rimini, pp 121–125
Paolucci LF (2019c) Art. 2539. In: Paolucci LF (ed) Codice delle cooperative 2019: Aggiornato con le novità del D.Lgs. n. 14/2019. Maggioli, Santarcangelo di Romagna, Rimini, pp 125–126
Paolucci LF (2019d) Art. 2540. In: Paolucci LF (ed) Codice delle cooperative 2019: Aggiornato con le novità del D.Lgs. n. 14/2019. Maggioli, Santarcangelo di Romagna, Rimini, pp 127–129
Paolucci LF (2019e) Art. 2542. In: Paolucci LF (ed) Codice delle cooperative 2019: Aggiornato con le novità del D.Lgs. n. 14/2019. Maggioli, Santarcangelo di Romagna, Rimini, pp 131–136
Paolucci LF (2019f) Art. 2543. In: Paolucci LF (ed) Codice delle cooperative 2019: Aggiornato con le novità del D.Lgs. n. 14/2019. Maggioli, Santarcangelo di Romagna, Rimini, pp 137–139
Paolucci LF (2019g) Art. 2544. In: Paolucci LF (ed) Codice delle cooperative 2019: Aggiornato con le novità del D.Lgs. n. 14/2019. Maggioli, Santarcangelo di Romagna, Rimini, pp 139–140

Paolucci LF (2019h) Art. 2545-quater. In: Paolucci LF (ed) Codice delle cooperative 2019: Aggiornato con le novità del D.Lgs. n. 14/2019. Maggioli, Santarcangelo di Romagna, Rimini, pp 144–145

Patera M (ed) (1986) Handbuch des österreichischen Genossenschaftswesens. Orac, Wien

Patroni Griffi U (2003) Art. 2391. In: Sandulli M, Santoro V (eds) La riforma delle società: Società per azioni, Società in accomandita per azioni. Giappichelli, Torino, pp 461–469

Perkounigg A, Kessler J (2014) § 1 GenRevG. In: Dellinger M (ed) Genossenschaftsgesetz samt Nebengesetzen: Kommentar, 2nd edn. LexisNexis ARD Orac, Wien, pp 556–567

Perrone A (2018a) Art. 2392. In: Cian G (ed) Commentario breve al Codice civile: Commentato con dottrina e giurisprudenza, 13th edn. Wolters Kluver, Milano, Padova, pp 2850–2854

Perrone A (2018b) Art. 2393. In: Cian G (ed) Commentario breve al Codice civile: Commentato con dottrina e giurisprudenza, 13th edn. Wolters Kluver, Milano, Padova, pp 2854–2857

Perrone A (2018c) Art. 2393bis. In: Cian G (ed) Commentario breve al Codice civile: Commentato con dottrina e giurisprudenza, 13th edn. Wolters Kluver, Milano, Padova, pp 2857–2858

Pescatore G (2009) Società di capitali amministratrice di altra società di capitali. Giurisprudenza Commerciale:1158–1177

Petrazzini B (2004) Artt. 2364 - 2364 bis. In: Cottino G, Bonfante G, Cagnasso O, Montalenti P (eds) Il nuovo diritto societario I: Commento al D. lgs. 17 gennaio 2003, n. 6, D. Lgs. 17 gennaio 2003, n. 5, D. lgs. 11 aprile 2002, n. 61 (art. 1). 1. Artt. 2325-2409 c.c, 1st edn. Zanichelli, Bologna, pp 469–482

Picciau A (2005) Artt. 2393, 2393bis, 2394bis. In: Ghezzi F (ed) Amministratori: Artt. 2380 - 2396 c.c, 1st edn. EGEA, Milano, pp 569–649

Piscitello P (2012) La responsabilità degli amministratori di società di capitali tra discrezionalità del giudice e business judgement rule. Rivista delle società:1167–1183

Pollio M, Papaleo P (2007) Art. 2403 bis. In: Fauceglia G, Di Schiano Pepe G (eds) Codice commentato delle S.p.A: Artt. 2363-2435. UTET giuridica, Torino

Pönkä V (2018) The legal nature of cooperative membership. JEOD 7:39–61. https://doi.org/10.5947/jeod.2018.009

Potthoff E, Trescher K, Theisen MR (2003) Das Aufsichtsratsmitglied: Ein Handbuch der Aufgaben, Rechte und Pflichten, 6th edn. Handelsblatt-Bücher. Schäffer-Poeschel, Stuttgart

Pozzobon DM, Zylbersztajn D (2013) Democratic costs in member-controlled organizations. Agribusiness 29:112–132. https://doi.org/10.1002/agr.21324

Pozzobon DM, Zylbersztajn D, Bijman J (2012) How can cooperatives reduce democratic costs without incurring excessive agency costs? J Rural Coop:119–144

Pramer L, Pfaffenzeller W (1976) Die Genossenschaft in Recht und Steuer. Hollinek, Wien

Presti G (2006) Le fonti della disciplina e l'organizzazione interna della società cooperative europea. In: Galletti D, Fici A (eds) La società cooperativa europea: Quali prospettive per la cooperazione italiana? Universita degli Studi di Trento, Trento, pp 67–86

Presti G (2007) Amministrazione e controllo nelle cooperative. In: Abbadessa P, Portale GB (eds) Scioglimento, trasformazione, fusione, scissione, società cooperative. UTET, Torino, pp 965–1085

Racugno G (2014) Il governo delle società cooperative: Il voto, i patti parasociali, i covenants. Rivista delle società:153–159

Rauter RA (2010) Probleme der Umsetzung des monistischen Systems der SE-VO in Österreich – ungenutzte Freiheit? Wirtschaftsrechtliche Blätter 24:499–508. https://doi.org/10.1007/s00718-010-1716-0

Rauter RA (2014) § 30g. In: Straube M (ed) Wiener Kommentar zum GmbH-Gesetz: 1.- 69. Lieferung - Kommentar in Faszikeln. MANZ Verlag Wien, Wien, pp 1–86

Rebelo J, Caldas J (2015) The economic role of the Portuguese agricultural cooperatives. Revista de Economia e Sociologia Rural 53:91–102. https://doi.org/10.1590/1234-56781806-94790053s01007

Reichert J, Brandes SM (2003) Mitbestimmung der Arbeitnehmer in der SE: Gestaltungsfreiheit und Bestandsschutz. Zeitschrift für Unternehmens- und Gesellschaftsrecht 32. https://doi.org/10.1515/zgre.2003.031
Reischauer R (1976) Das Schicksal fehlerhafter Generalversammlungsbeschlüsse einer Genossenschaft. JBl:7
Rescio G (2003) La Società Europea tra diritto comunitario e diritto nazionale. Rivista delle società:965–995
Ricci R (2010a) Art. 2392. In: Cendon P (ed) Artt. 2363-2396: Società per azioni: [2] assemblea, amministratori. Giuffrè, Milano, pp 691–705
Ricci R (2010b) Art. 2393. In: Cendon P (ed) Artt. 2363-2396: Società per azioni: [2] assemblea, amministratori. Giuffrè, Milano, pp 707–719
Ricci R (2010c) Art. 2393bis. In: Cendon P (ed) Artt. 2363-2396: Società per azioni: [2] assemblea, amministratori. Giuffrè, Milano, pp 721–729
Riolfo G (2010) Il sistema monistico nelle società di capitali e cooperative. Cedam, Padova
Riolfo G (2013) Il sistema dualistico. Le monografie di Contratto e impresa, vol 0158. Cedam, Padova
Riss O (2008) Welche Sorgfalt schuldet der Genossenschaftsvorstand? RdW:768–770
Rocchi E (2006) La struttura finanziaria della SCE. In: Galletti D, Fici A (eds) La società cooperativa europea: Quali prospettive per la cooperazione italiana? Universita degli Studi di Trento, Trento, pp 87–114
Roe MJ (2002) Corporate law's limits. J Leg Stud 31:233–271. https://doi.org/10.1086/341989
Romano G (2017a) Art. 2364 bis. In: Di Marzio F (ed) Codice civile. Giuffrè, Milano, p 2908
Romano G (2017b) Art. 2365. In: Di Marzio F (ed) Codice civile. Giuffrè, Milano, pp 2908–2909
Romano G (2017c) Art. 2367. In: Di Marzio F (ed) Codice civile. Giuffrè, Milano, pp 2912–2913
Romano G (2017d) Art. 2368. In: Di Marzio F (ed) Codice civile. Giuffrè, Milano, pp 2913–2915
Romano G (2017e) Art. 2371. In: Di Marzio F (ed) Codice civile. Giuffrè, Milano, pp 2919–2920
Romano G (2017f) Art. 2375. In: Di Marzio F (ed) Codice civile. Giuffrè, Milano, pp 2925–2926
Romano G (2017g) Art. 2381. In: Di Marzio F (ed) Codice civile. Giuffrè, Milano, pp 2944–2946
Romano G (2017h) Art. 2382. In: Di Marzio F (ed) Codice civile. Giuffrè, Milano, pp 2946–2947
Romano G (2017i) Art. 2384. In: Di Marzio F (ed) Codice civile. Giuffrè, Milano, pp 2949–2951
Romano G (2017j) Art. 2385. In: Di Marzio F (ed) Codice civile. Giuffrè, Milano, pp 2951–2952
Romano G (2017k) Art. 2387. In: Di Marzio F (ed) Codice civile. Giuffrè, Milano, pp 2954–2955
Romano G (2017l) Art. 2388. In: Di Marzio F (ed) Codice civile. Giuffrè, Milano, pp 2955–2957
Romano G (2017m) Art. 2391. In: Di Marzio F (ed) Codice civile. Giuffrè, Milano, pp 2961–2963
Romano G (2017n) Art. 2392. In: Di Marzio F (ed) Codice civile. Giuffrè, Milano, pp 2964–2966
Romano G (2017o) Art. 2393. In: Di Marzio F (ed) Codice civile. Giuffrè, Milano, pp 2967–2970
Romano G (2017p) Art. 2393 bis. In: Di Marzio F (ed) Codice civile. Giuffrè, Milano, pp 2970–2972
Romano G (2017q) Art. 2403 bis. In: Di Marzio F (ed) Codice civile. Giuffrè, Milano, pp 2988–2989
Romano G (2017r) Art. 2407. In: Di Marzio F (ed) Codice civile. Giuffrè, Milano, pp 2992–2994
Romano G (2017s) Art. 2409 decies. In: Di Marzio F (ed) Codice civile. Giuffrè, Milano, p 3004
Romano G (2017t) Art. 2409 duodecies. In: Di Marzio F (ed) Codice civile. Giuffrè, Milano, pp 3005–3006
Romano G (2017u) Art. 2409 novies. In: Di Marzio F (ed) Codice civile. Giuffrè, Milano, pp 3003–3004
Romano G (2017v) Art. 2409 terdecies. In: Di Marzio F (ed) Codice civile. Giuffrè, Milano, pp 3006–3007
Romano G (2017w) Art. 2428. In: Di Marzio F (ed) Codice civile. Giuffrè, Milano, pp 3051–3052
Roth GH, Wörle U (2004) Die Unabhängigkeit des Aufsichtsrats Recht und Wirklichkeit. Zeitschrift für Unternehmens- und Gesellschaftsrecht 33:565–630. https://doi.org/10.1515/zgre.2004.027
Royer J (1999) Cooperative organizational strategies: a neo-institutional digest. J Coop:44–67

Ruffner M (2000) Die ökonomischen Grundlagen eines Rechts der Publikumsgesellschaft: Ein Beitrag zur Theorie der Corporate Governance. Schulthess, Zürich

Rufini D (2005) Art. 2409 novies. In: Maffei Alberti A (ed) Il nuovo diritto delle società: Commento sistematico al D. lgs. 17 gennaio 2003, n. 6, aggiornato al D. lgs. 28 dicembre 2004, n. 310. Cedam, Padova, pp 1129–1140

Sailer-Coceani V (2015) Art. 41. In: Lutter M, Hommelhoff P, Teichmann C (eds) SE-Kommentar, 2nd edn. Verlag Dr. Otto Schmidt, Köln, pp 516–532

Salafia V (2003) Il nuovo modello di società a responsabilità limitata. Le società:7–12

Sandei C (2018a) Art. 2382. In: Cian G (ed) Commentario breve al Codice civile: Commentato con dottrina e giurisprudenza, 13th edn. Wolters Kluver, Milano, Padova, pp 2813–2815

Sandei C (2018b) Art. 2383. In: Cian G (ed) Commentario breve al Codice civile: Commentato con dottrina e giurisprudenza, 13th edn. Wolters Kluver, Milano, Padova, pp 2815–2819

Sandei C (2018c) Art. 2384. In: Cian G (ed) Commentario breve al Codice civile: Commentato con dottrina e giurisprudenza, 13th edn. Wolters Kluver, Milano, Padova, pp 2819–2823

Sandei C (2018d) Art. 2385. In: Cian G (ed) Commentario breve al Codice civile: Commentato con dottrina e giurisprudenza, 13th edn. Wolters Kluver, Milano, Padova, pp 2823–2825

Sandei C (2018e) Art. 2387. In: Cian G (ed) Commentario breve al Codice civile: Commentato con dottrina e giurisprudenza, 13th edn. Wolters Kluver, Milano, Padova, pp 2828–2829

Sandei C (2018f) Art. 2388. In: Cian G (ed) Commentario breve al Codice civile: Commentato con dottrina e giurisprudenza, 13th edn. Wolters Kluver, Milano, Padova, pp 2829–2835

Sandulli M (2003) Art. 2392. In: Sandulli M, Santoro V (eds) La riforma delle società: Società per azioni, Società in accomandita per azioni. Giappichelli, Torino, pp 470–478

Sanfilippo PM (2017a) Gli amministratori. In: Cian M (ed) Diritto commerciale: III. Diritto delle società. G. Giappichelli, Torino, pp 461–537

Sanfilippo PM (2017b) Il controllo sulla gestione e contabile. In: Cian M (ed) Diritto commerciale: III. Diritto delle società. G. Giappichelli, Torino, pp 538–561

Sangiovanni V (2005) Il diritto di voto plurimo nella cooperativa tedesca: Cenni di comparazione con la riforma italiana. Le società:256–263

Santagata R (2017) Le società cooperative. In: Cian M (ed) Diritto commerciale: III. Diritto delle società. G. Giappichelli, Torino, pp 807–843

Santi E (2005a) 2409 duodecies. In: Maffei Alberti A (ed) Il nuovo diritto delle società: Commento sistematico al D. lgs. 17 gennaio 2003, n. 6, aggiornato al D. lgs. 28 dicembre 2004, n. 310. Cedam, Padova, pp 1157–1164

Santi E (2005b) 2409 terdecies. In: Maffei Alberti A (ed) Il nuovo diritto delle società: Commento sistematico al D. lgs. 17 gennaio 2003, n. 6, aggiornato al D. lgs. 28 dicembre 2004, n. 310. Cedam, Padova, pp 1165–1173

Santi F (2010) Art 2365. In: Cendon P (ed) Artt. 2363-2396: Società per azioni: [2] assemblea, amministratori. Giuffrè, Milano, pp 57–67

Santini R (2018) Art. 2428. In: Cian G (ed) Commentario breve al Codice civile: Commentato con dottrina e giurisprudenza, 13th edn. Wolters Kluver, Milano, Padova, pp 2951–2952

Santoro V (2014) Amministratori di cooperative e interessi dei soci. Odcc:15–30. https://doi.org/10.4478/77170

Santosuosso DU (2003) La riforma del diritto societario: Autonomia privata e norme imperative nei DD.Lgs. 17 gennaio 2003, nn.5 e 6. Prima interpretazione.Le nuove leggi civili. Giuffrè, Milano

Sarcina A (2006) La Societas Europaea e il consolidamento del sistema societario europea. Europa e Diritto Privato:729–754

Scarpa D (2014) Studio della organizzazione societaria della s.p.a. e analisi economica del diritto. Le monografie di Contratto e impresa, vol 160. Cedam, Padova

Schäfer H-B, Ott C (2012) Grundstrukturen und -probleme des Unternehmensrechts. In: Schäfer H-B, Ott C (eds) Lehrbuch der ökonomischen Analyse des Zivilrechts. Springer, Berlin, pp 697–729

Schärf G (2002) Aufsichtsratssitzungen über Videokonferenz? RdW:199

Schiessl M (2003) Leitungs- und Kontrollstrukturen im internationalen Wettbewerb – Dualistisches System und Mitbestimmung auf dem Prüfstand – ZHR 2003, S. 235. Zeitschrift für das gesamte Handelsrecht und Wirtschaftsrecht:235–257

Schima G (2015) Reform des Untreue-Tatbestandes und gesetzliche Verankerung der Business Judgement Rule im Gesellschaftsrecht. RdW:288–292

Schiuma L (2007) Il sistema dualistico. I poteri del consiglio di sorveglianza e del consiglio di gestione. In: Abbadessa P, Portale GB (eds) Assemblea, amministrazione. UTET, Torino, pp 683–731

Schmidt J (2006) "Deutsche" vs. "britische" Socictas Europaea (SE): Gründung, Verfassung, Kapitalstruktur. Jenaer Studien zum deutschen, europäischen und internationalen Wirtschaftsrecht, vol 8. Jenaer Wissenschaftlicher Verlag, Jena

Schmidt R, Weiß M (2010) Shareholder vs. Stakholer: Ökonomische Fragen. In: Hommelhoff P, Hopt KJ, Werder Av, Feddersen D, Pohle K (eds) Handbuch corporate governance: Leitung und Überwachung börsennotierter Unternehmen in der Rechts und Wirtschaftsprazis, 2nd edn. Dr. Otto Schmidt; Schäffer-Poeschel, Köln, Stuttgart, pp 161–184

Schmidt-Pachinger S (2012) § 121. In: Doralt W, Nowotny C, Kalss S (eds) Kommentar zum Aktiengesetz, 2nd edn. Linde, Wien, pp 1769–1781

Schneiberg M (2002) 2. Organizational heterogeneity and the production of new forms: politics, social movements and mutual companies in American fire insurance, 1900–1930. In: Lounsbury M, Ventresca MJ (eds) Social structure and organizations revisited, vol 19. Emerald, Bingley, pp 39–89

Schöpflin M (2018a) Art. 06. In: Beuthien V, Schöpflin M (eds) Genossenschaftsgesetz: Mit Umwandlungs- und Kartellrecht sowie Statut der Europäischen Genossenschaft, 16th edn. Beck, München, p 1255

Schöpflin M (2018b) Art. 15. In: Beuthien V, Schöpflin M (eds) Genossenschaftsgesetz: Mit Umwandlungs- und Kartellrecht sowie Statut der Europäischen Genossenschaft, 16th edn. Beck, München, pp 1272–1276

Schöpflin M (2018c) Art. 36. In: Beuthien V, Schöpflin M (eds) Genossenschaftsgesetz: Mit Umwandlungs- und Kartellrecht sowie Statut der Europäischen Genossenschaft, 16th edn. Beck, München, pp 1298–1299

Schöpflin M (2018d) Art. 37. In: Beuthien V, Schöpflin M (eds) Genossenschaftsgesetz: Mit Umwandlungs- und Kartellrecht sowie Statut der Europäischen Genossenschaft, 16th edn. Beck, München, pp 1299–1301

Schöpflin M (2018e) Art. 38. In: Beuthien V, Schöpflin M (eds) Genossenschaftsgesetz: Mit Umwandlungs- und Kartellrecht sowie Statut der Europäischen Genossenschaft, 16th edn. Beck, München, p 1301

Schöpflin M (2018f) Art. 39. In: Beuthien V, Schöpflin M (eds) Genossenschaftsgesetz: Mit Umwandlungs- und Kartellrecht sowie Statut der Europäischen Genossenschaft, 16th edn. Beck, München, pp 1301–1303

Schöpflin M (2018g) Art. 40. In: Beuthien V, Schöpflin M (eds) Genossenschaftsgesetz: Mit Umwandlungs- und Kartellrecht sowie Statut der Europäischen Genossenschaft, 16th edn. Beck, München, pp 1304–1305

Schöpflin M (2018h) Art. 41. In: Beuthien V, Schöpflin M (eds) Genossenschaftsgesetz: Mit Umwandlungs- und Kartellrecht sowie Statut der Europäischen Genossenschaft, 16th edn. Beck, München, pp 1305–1306

Schöpflin M (2018i) Art. 42. In: Beuthien V, Schöpflin M (eds) Genossenschaftsgesetz: Mit Umwandlungs- und Kartellrecht sowie Statut der Europäischen Genossenschaft, 16th edn. Beck, München, pp 1306–1308

Schöpflin M (2018j) Art. 43. In: Beuthien V, Schöpflin M (eds) Genossenschaftsgesetz: Mit Umwandlungs- und Kartellrecht sowie Statut der Europäischen Genossenschaft, 16th edn. Beck, München, p 1308

Schöpflin M (2018k) Art. 44. In: Beuthien V, Schöpflin M (eds) Genossenschaftsgesetz: Mit Umwandlungs- und Kartellrecht sowie Statut der Europäischen Genossenschaft, 16th edn. Beck, München, pp 1308–1309

Schöpflin M (2018l) Art. 45. In: Beuthien V, Schöpflin M (eds) Genossenschaftsgesetz: Mit Umwandlungs- und Kartellrecht sowie Statut der Europäischen Genossenschaft, 16th edn. Beck, München, p 1309

Schöpflin M (2018m) Art. 46. In: Beuthien V, Schöpflin M (eds) Genossenschaftsgesetz: Mit Umwandlungs- und Kartellrecht sowie Statut der Europäischen Genossenschaft, 16th edn. Beck, München, pp 1309–1311

Schöpflin M (2018n) Art. 47. In: Beuthien V, Schöpflin M (eds) Genossenschaftsgesetz: Mit Umwandlungs- und Kartellrecht sowie Statut der Europäischen Genossenschaft, 16th edn. Beck, München, pp 1311–1313

Schöpflin M (2018o) Art. 48. In: Beuthien V, Schöpflin M (eds) Genossenschaftsgesetz: Mit Umwandlungs- und Kartellrecht sowie Statut der Europäischen Genossenschaft, 16th edn. Beck, München, pp 1313–1314

Schöpflin M (2018p) Art. 49. In: Beuthien V, Schöpflin M (eds) Genossenschaftsgesetz: Mit Umwandlungs- und Kartellrecht sowie Statut der Europäischen Genossenschaft, 16th edn. Beck, München, p 1314

Schöpflin M (2018q) Art. 50. In: Beuthien V, Schöpflin M (eds) Genossenschaftsgesetz: Mit Umwandlungs- und Kartellrecht sowie Statut der Europäischen Genossenschaft, 16th edn. Beck, München, pp 1315–1316

Schöpflin M (2018r) Art. 51. In: Beuthien V, Schöpflin M (eds) Genossenschaftsgesetz: Mit Umwandlungs- und Kartellrecht sowie Statut der Europäischen Genossenschaft, 16th edn. Beck, München, p 1316

Schröder A (2010a) Art. 63. In: Manz G, Mayer B, Schröder A (eds) Europäische Aktiengesellschaft SE: SE, 2nd edn. Nomos, Baden-Baden, pp 751–759

Schröder A (2010b) Art. 8. In: Manz G, Mayer B, Schröder A (eds) Europäische Aktiengesellschaft SE: SE, 2nd edn. Nomos, Baden-Baden, pp 140–179

Schulze R (2004a) Die Struktur der SCE. In: Schulze R (ed) Europäische Genossenschaft SCE: Handbuch, 1st edn. Nomos, Baden-Baden, pp 91–121

Schulze R (2004b) Zur Rechtslage in den Mitgliedsstaaten: Deutschland. In: Schulze R (ed) Europäische Genossenschaft SCE: Handbuch, 1st edn. Nomos, Baden-Baden, pp 183–190

Serra A (2007) Il procedimento assembleare. In: Abbadessa P, Portale GB (eds) Assemblea, amministrazione. UTET, Torino, pp 36–76

Serraino G (2010a) Art. 2404. In: Cendon P (ed) Artt. 2397-2420 ter: Società per azioni: [3] sindaci, controllo contabile, sistema dualistico e monistico, obbligazioni. Giuffrè, Milano, pp 67–71

Serraino G (2010b) Art. 2406. In: Cendon P (ed) Artt. 2397-2420 ter: Società per azioni: [3] sindaci, controllo contabile, sistema dualistico e monistico, obbligazioni. Giuffrè, Milano, pp 77–81

Serraino G (2010c) Art. 2407. In: Cendon P (ed) Artt. 2397-2420 ter: Società per azioni: [3] sindaci, controllo contabile, sistema dualistico e monistico, obbligazioni. Giuffrè, Milano, pp 83–91

Siebenbäck H-J (2014a) § 27. In: Dellinger M (ed) Genossenschaftsgesetz samt Nebengesetzen: Kommentar, 2nd edn. LexisNexis ARD Orac, Wien, pp 337–351

Siebenbäck H-J (2014b) § 28. In: Dellinger M (ed) Genossenschaftsgesetz samt Nebengesetzen: Kommentar, 2nd edn. LexisNexis ARD Orac, Wien, pp 363–364

Siebenbäck H-J (2014c) § 29. In: Dellinger M (ed) Genossenschaftsgesetz samt Nebengesetzen: Kommentar, 2nd edn. LexisNexis ARD Orac, Wien, pp 365–367

Siebenbäck H-J (2014d) § 30. In: Dellinger M (ed) Genossenschaftsgesetz samt Nebengesetzen: Kommentar, 2nd edn. LexisNexis ARD Orac, Wien, pp 368–373

Siebenbäck H-J (2014e) § 31. In: Dellinger M (ed) Genossenschaftsgesetz samt Nebengesetzen: Kommentar, 2nd edn. LexisNexis ARD Orac, Wien, p 374

Siebenbäck H-J (2014f) § 32. In: Dellinger M (ed) Genossenschaftsgesetz samt Nebengesetzen: Kommentar, 2nd edn. LexisNexis ARD Orac, Wien, pp 375–376

Siebenbäck H-J (2014g) § 33. In: Dellinger M (ed) Genossenschaftsgesetz samt Nebengesetzen: Kommentar, 2nd edn. LexisNexis ARD Orac, Wien, pp 377–381
Siebenbäck H-J (2014h) § 34. In: Dellinger M (ed) Genossenschaftsgesetz samt Nebengesetzen: Kommentar, 2nd edn. LexisNexis ARD Orac, Wien, pp 385–387
Simone C (2009a) Art. 2403 bis. In: Grippo G (ed) Commentario delle società. UTET, Torino, pp 554–555
Simone C (2009b) Art. 2407. In: Grippo G (ed) Commentario delle società. UTET, Torino, pp 565–571
Sitkoff RH (2011) The economic structure of fiduciary law. Boston Univ Law Rev:1039–1049. https://doi.org/10.2139/ssrn.1782999
Slagter W (2004) Landesbericht Niederlande zum Begleitgesetz Europäische Gesellschaft. In: Baums T, Cahn A (eds) Die Europäische Aktiengesellschaft: Umsetzungsfragen und Perspektiven. De Gruyter, Berlin, pp 30–38
Snaith I (2006) Employee involvement in the European Cooperative Society: a range of stakeholders? Int J Comp Labour Law Ind Relat:213–230
Snaith I (2017) Cooperative governance. In: Fajardo-García IG, Fici A, Henrÿ H, Hiez D, Meira DMMA, Münkner H-H, Snaith I (eds) Principles of European Cooperative Law: principles, commentaries and national reports. Intersentia, Cambridge, pp 47–72
Sneirson JF (2008) Soft paternalism for close corporations: helping shareholders help themselves. Wis Law Rev:899–940
Spindler G (2015a) Art. 52. In: Lutter M, Hommelhoff P, Teichmann C (eds) SE-Kommentar, 2nd edn. Verlag Dr. Otto Schmidt, Köln, pp 776–799
Spindler G (2015b) Art. 53. In: Lutter M, Hommelhoff P, Teichmann C (eds) SE-Kommentar, 2nd edn. Verlag Dr. Otto Schmidt, Köln, pp 800–816
Spindler G (2015c) Art. 54. In: Lutter M, Hommelhoff P, Teichmann C (eds) SE-Kommentar, 2nd edn. Verlag Dr. Otto Schmidt, Köln, pp 816–829
Spindler G (2015d) Art. 55. In: Lutter M, Hommelhoff P, Teichmann C (eds) SE-Kommentar, 2nd edn. Verlag Dr. Otto Schmidt, Köln, pp 829–846
Spindler G (2015e) Art. 56. In: Lutter M, Hommelhoff P, Teichmann C (eds) SE-Kommentar, 2nd edn. Verlag Dr. Otto Schmidt, Köln, pp 846–855
Stella Richter M Jr (2004) Forma e contenuto dell'atto costitutivo della società per azioni. In: Colombo GE, Portale GB (eds) Trattato delle società per azioni I: Tipo - Costituzione - Nullità. UTET, Torino, pp 165–319
Stout LA (2007) The mythical benefits of shareholder control. Va Law Rev:789–809
Strasser P (2011a) §§ 92-94. In: Strasser P, Jabornegg R (eds) Kommentar zum Aktiengesetz, 5th edn. Manz, Vienna
Strasser P (2011b) §§ 95-97. In: Strasser P, Jabornegg R (eds) Kommentar zum Aktiengesetz, 5th edn. Manz, Vienna
Strausz R (1997) Collusion and renegotiation in a principal-supervisor-agent relationship. Scand J Econ 99:497–518. https://doi.org/10.1111/1467-9442.00078
Strohn L (2015) § 34. In: Fleischer H, Goette W (eds) Münchener Kommentar zum Gesetz betreffend die Gesellschaften mit beschränkter Haftung: (GmbHG) Bd.1 §§ 1-34, 2nd edn. Beck; Vahlen, München
Strommer M (2014a) § 15. In: Dellinger M (ed) Genossenschaftsgesetz samt Nebengesetzen: Kommentar, 2nd edn. LexisNexis ARD Orac, Wien, pp 189–200
Strommer M (2014b) § 17. In: Dellinger M (ed) Genossenschaftsgesetz samt Nebengesetzen: Kommentar, 2nd edn. LexisNexis ARD Orac, Wien, pp 204–213
Strommer M (2014c) § 18. In: Dellinger M (ed) Genossenschaftsgesetz samt Nebengesetzen: Kommentar, 2nd edn. LexisNexis ARD Orac, Wien, p 214
Strommer M (2014d) § 19. In: Dellinger M (ed) Genossenschaftsgesetz samt Nebengesetzen: Kommentar, 2nd edn. LexisNexis ARD Orac, Wien, pp 215–218
Strommer M (2014e) § 23. In: Dellinger M (ed) Genossenschaftsgesetz samt Nebengesetzen: Kommentar, 2nd edn. LexisNexis ARD Orac, Wien, pp 251–257

Svendsen SV (2007) Lock-in of farmers in agricultural cooperatives. In: Karantininis K, Nilsson J (eds) Vertical markets and cooperative hierarchies: the role of cooperatives in the agri-food industry. Springer, Dordrecht, pp 113–135

Tallia F (2013) Il dovere di diligenza e la business judgment rule. Il nuovo diritto delle Società:14–39

Tatarano MC (2011) La nuova impresa cooperativa, Nuova ed. de L'impresa cooperativa di Giovanni Tatarano. Trattato di diritto civile e commerciale / già diretto da Antonio Cicu, Francesco Messineo, Luigi Mengoni. Giuffrè, Milano

Teichmann C (2004) Germany. In: Teichmann C, Oplustil K (eds) The European company - all over Europe: a state-by-state account of the introduction of the European company. De Gruyter, Berlin, pp 109–131

Teichmann C (2015a) Art. 38. In: Lutter M, Hommelhoff P, Teichmann C (eds) SE-Kommentar, 2nd edn. Verlag Dr. Otto Schmidt, Köln, pp 452–471

Teichmann C (2015b) Art. 43. In: Lutter M, Hommelhoff P, Teichmann C (eds) SE-Kommentar, 2nd edn. Verlag Dr. Otto Schmidt, Köln, pp 537–715

Teichmann C (2015c) Art. 44. In: Lutter M, Hommelhoff P, Teichmann C (eds) SE-Kommentar, 2nd edn. Verlag Dr. Otto Schmidt, Köln, pp 716–721

Teichmann C (2015d) Art. 45. In: Lutter M, Hommelhoff P, Teichmann C (eds) SE-Kommentar, 2nd edn. Verlag Dr. Otto Schmidt, Köln, pp 721–725

Teichmann C (2015e) Art. 46. In: Lutter M, Hommelhoff P, Teichmann C (eds) SE-Kommentar, 2nd edn. Verlag Dr. Otto Schmidt, Köln, pp 727–731

Teichmann C (2015f) Art. 47. In: Lutter M, Hommelhoff P, Teichmann C (eds) SE-Kommentar, 2nd edn. Verlag Dr. Otto Schmidt, Köln, pp 731–741

Teichmann C (2015g) Art. 48. In: Lutter M, Hommelhoff P, Teichmann C (eds) SE-Kommentar, 2nd edn. Verlag Dr. Otto Schmidt, Köln, pp 741–751

Teichmann C (2015h) Art. 49. In: Lutter M, Hommelhoff P, Teichmann C (eds) SE-Kommentar, 2nd edn. Verlag Dr. Otto Schmidt, Köln, pp 751–755

Teichmann C (2015i) Art. 50. In: Lutter M, Hommelhoff P, Teichmann C (eds) SE-Kommentar, 2nd edn. Verlag Dr. Otto Schmidt, Köln, pp 755–768

Teichmann C (2015j) Art. 51. In: Lutter M, Hommelhoff P, Teichmann C (eds) SE-Kommentar, 2nd edn. Verlag Dr. Otto Schmidt, Köln, pp 768–776

The European Public Limited-Liability Company Regulations 2004. http://www.legislation.gov.uk/uksi/2004/2326/pdfs/uksi_20042326_en.pdf. Accessed 29 Dec 2019

Theisen MR (1987) Die Überwachung der Unternehmungsführung: Betriebswirtschaftl. Ansätze zur Entwicklung erster Grundsätze ordnungsmäßiger Überwachung. Univ., Habil.-Schr.—Regensburg, 1986. Betriebswirtschaftliche Abhandlungen, N.F., Bd. 70. Poeschel, Stuttgart

Theisen MR (1996) Grundsätze einer ordnungsmäßigen Information des Aufsichtsrats, 2., vollst. überarb. und erw. Aufl. Schriftenreihe Der Betrieb. Schäffer-Poeschel, Stuttgart

Thoma GF, Leuering D (2002) Die Europäische Aktiengesellschaft - Societas Europaea. Neue Juristische Wochenschrift:1449–1455

Tirole J (1986) Hierarchies and bureaucracies: on the role of collusion in organizations. J Law Econ Organ 2:181–214

Tirole J (2006) The theory of corporate finance. Princeton University Press, Princeton

Told J (2015) Business Judgment Rule und ihre Anwendbarkeit in Österreich. GES:60–72

Tombari U (2008) Governo dell'impresa e sistema dualistico nelle società cooperative. Analisi Giuridica dell'Economia:399–422. https://doi.org/10.1433/28532

Trimarchi G (2005) Questioni in tema di assemblea nelle società cooperative. In: Consiglio nazionale del notariato. (ed) Studi e materiali in tema di riforma delle società cooperative. Giuffrè, Milano, pp 647–654

Usai P (2010a) Art. 2380 bis. In: Cendon P (ed) Artt. 2363-2396: Società per azioni: [2] assemblea, amministratori. Giuffrè, Milano, pp 479–486

Usai P (2010b) Art. 2381. In: Cendon P (ed) Artt. 2363-2396: Società per azioni: [2] assemblea, amministratori. Giuffrè, Milano, pp 487–502

Usai P (2010c) Art. 2382. In: Cendon P (ed) Artt. 2363-2396: Società per azioni: [2] assemblea, amministratori. Giuffrè, Milano, pp 503–508
Usai P (2010d) Art. 2384. In: Cendon P (ed) Artt. 2363-2396: Società per azioni: [2] assemblea, amministratori. Giuffrè, Milano, pp 521–531
Usai P (2010e) Art. 2387. In: Cendon P (ed) Artt. 2363-2396: Società per azioni: [2] assemblea, amministratori. Giuffrè, Milano, pp 551–557
Van der Sangen G (2012) EU synthesis and comparative analysis report: legal aspects. In: Support for farmers' cooperatives, Wageningen, pp 1–50
Velasco J (2015) A defense of the corporate law duty of care. J Corp Law:647–703
Ventoruzzo M (2011) Empowering shareholders in directors' elections: a revolution in the making. Eur Comp Financ Law Rev 8. https://doi.org/10.1515/ecfr.2011.105
Wiese MH (2006) Die Europäische Genossenschaft im Vergleich zur eingetragenen Genossenschaft deutschen Rechts: Reformüberlegungen zum deutschen Genossenschaftsrecht. Münstersche Schriften zur Kooperation, vol 69. Shaker, Aachen
Williamson OE (1998) The economic institutions of capitalism: firms, markets, relational contracting. Free Press, New York
Zacherl U (1981) Zur Konzeption der genossenschaftlichen Förderbilanz. Zeitschrift für das gesamte Genossenschaftswesen:226
Zahn J (1963) Handbuch für Genossenschaften, 2nd edn. Österreichischer Genossenschaftsverband
Zamperetti GM (2006) Prime significative applicazioni del sistema dualistico. Le società:1193
Zanotti A (2013) La governance societaria: Società per azioni e cooperative a confronto: una interpretazione economica. Rubbettino, Soveria Mannelli
Zehetner J (1999) Rechnungslegung der Genossenschaften. Manz, Wien
Zehetner J (2014a) § 22. In: Dellinger M (ed) Genossenschaftsgesetz samt Nebengesetzen: Kommentar, 2nd edn. LexisNexis ARD Orac, Wien, pp 221–250
Zehetner J (2014b) § 24. In: Dellinger M (ed) Genossenschaftsgesetz samt Nebengesetzen: Kommentar, 2nd edn. LexisNexis ARD Orac, Wien, pp 258–271
Zehetner J (2014c) § 24e. In: Dellinger M (ed) Genossenschaftsgesetz samt Nebengesetzen: Kommentar, 2nd edn. LexisNexis ARD Orac, Wien, pp 313–330
Zehetner J (2014d) § 27a. In: Dellinger M (ed) Genossenschaftsgesetz samt Nebengesetzen: Kommentar, 2nd edn. LexisNexis ARD Orac, Wien, pp 352–362
Zoppini A (2000) Relazione introduttiva ad una proposta per la disciplina dell'"impresa sociale". Rivista Critica del Diritto Privato:335–392
Zoppini A (2004) Il nuovo diritto delle società cooperative: un'analisi economica. Rivista di Diritto Civile:439–450

Chapter 5
Issues About Financing SCEs

5.1 Introduction

As already mentioned, the Reg. 1435/2003 provisions are the basis for national SCEs and thus, for an agricultural cooperative organised as an SCE. When examining the SCE's financial aspects, it always should be kept in mind that the rules considered apply, *mutatis mutandis*, to agricultural cooperatives with cross-border activities and, therefore, to SCEs. However, both the concluding part of every sub-chapter and sub-chapter 5.6. specifically link the obtained results to agricultural SCEs or cooperatives.

The social purpose of the cooperative (which is closely tied to its mutualistic orientation) requires a financial structure that promotes the interests of its members, including satisfying their economic, social and cultural needs. In contrast to capitalist enterprises, the cooperative carries out economic activity that is not primarily profit-oriented but, instead, is mutualistic in nature. However, the mutual character of the cooperative does not mean that it works exclusively with its members, as it can also do business with non-members. The financial structure of cooperatives is therefore based on a logic of its own that results both from the specific characteristics of the cooperative's purpose and from the need to respect the cooperative's values and principles. The cooperative pursues its social objective in an organised and professional manner and, like all other companies, must use various management and financial instruments to better achieve its objectives. Therefore, cooperatives use different instruments as a financing source (e.g., stocks, bonds). However, they all must be compatible with the character of a cooperative and, thus, ultimately promote mutual exchange.

These particular aspects require specific provisions that meet the needs of cooperatives and that reflect the special role of members in financing the cooperative and in obtaining an advantage from it. In particular, certain issues—such as contributions of capital, liability and allocation of profits—need to be addressed. Since members

G. Miribung, *The Agricultural Cooperative in the Framework of the European Cooperative Society*, Economic Analysis of Law in European Legal Scholarship 8,
https://doi.org/10.1007/978-3-030-44154-8_5

are primarily interested in obtaining an advantage other than maximising shareholder value, the means by which this can be safeguarded needs to be determined. As we will see, the reserves play a special role here. All these interests, then, are partly counterbalanced by the interests of non-user members, whose role approximates that of the classic shareholder of a capitalist enterprise. It becomes clear that the topic of capital—in the broadest sense—is particularly important for cooperatives and thus for agricultural SCEs.

In this chapter, we will discuss certain issues concerning an SCE's capital and shares, along with other financial issues such as distribution of profits. We will also analyse the members' financial entitlements. There are some features (e.g., specific asset restrictions) that characterise the function of cooperatives and hence also the function of agricultural SCEs.

This chapter is divided into the following sub-sections: (1) capital, (2) allocation of profits, (3) financial entitlements in case of resignation or expulsion and (4) the rights of the members in case of dissolution. Each sub-section concludes by briefly summarising the main findings. The last part of this chapter compares the most important findings and considers them from an economic perspective. Some of these issues are directly connected to membership; our present discussion thus complements our earlier analyses. I do limit this study by choosing not to analyse Art. 64 SCE-R,[1] which addresses securities other than shares and debentures.

5.2 Capital

The capital[2] of an SCE influences several issues: minimum and variable capital, liability, shares, and operations on capital. To understand the legal problems involved, we must examine both the SCE rules and national law.

[1]The proposal on the SCE, as put forward in 1992, also contained similar provisions. Art. 49 draft SCE-R (holders of non-voting shares) provides the possibility to offer investor shares for subscription by interested parties. These shares do not convey any right to vote at general meetings. To offset these disadvantages, such shares may be given preferential financial entitlements either in the rules of the SCE or by agreement at the time they are issued. Finally, the rules must include provisions ensuring the interests of holders of non-voting shares can be represented and defended. In particular, they must provide for special meetings of such shareholders. Next, Art. 50 draft SCE-R allows admittance of members who do not expect to use the SCE's services but who are interested in the progress of the SCE. The number of these members is limited such that they may not hold more than one third of all votes. In addition, the rules may lay down special provisions for distributing surpluses which benefit such members. Finally, Art. 51 draft SCE-R allows an SCE to use all forms of financing in the member state in which it has its registered office under the same conditions as those applying to the legal entities which founded it. The proposal discussed at that time not only contained these financing mechanisms, which the most evolved cooperative laws contained, but also contained a general clause (Art. 51 draft SCE-R) in line with the flexibility of this supranational business form. Also consider Rocchi (2006), p. 95 et seq.

[2]In the sense of equity as determined by IAS 32. See Holthaus and Lehnhoff (2016), p. 47.

Minimum capital is governed by Art. 3 para. 4 SCE-R,[3] which determines that the statutes must set a sum below which subscribed capital may not fall as a result of repaying the shares of members who exit the SCE. This sum may not be less than the required minimum capital of 30,000 EUR,[4] although it can be increased via a statutory provision. The SCE-R thus contains a threshold of solidity,[5] which is in line with the principle of maintaining capital.[6]

Next, Art. 3 para. 5 SCE-R states that variations in the amount of the capital do not require (a) amendments to the statutes or (b) disclosure. In addition, Art. 1 para. 2 subpara. 2 SCE-R states that the number of members and the level of capital must be variable. We previously discussed a situation in which a cooperative theoretically has fixed capital[7]; it would be necessary to increase or reduce this level by amending the statutes every time a member joined or left the cooperative. Clearly, this approach would contradict the principle in Recital 10 para. 1 bullet 6 SCE-R.[8]

The regulation also provides a mechanism for determining the minimum number of shares that a member must subscribe (this number must be laid down in the statutes).[9] The SCE-R contains an exemption to this general rule.[10] Then, the statutes may differentiate between user and non-user members and hence set different

---

[3]It states: "The statutes shall lay down a sum below which subscribed capital may not be allowed to fall as a result of repayment of the shares of members who cease to belong to the SCE. This sum may not be less than the amount laid down in paragraph 2. The date laid down in Article 16 by which members who cease to belong to the SCE are entitled to repayment shall be suspended as long as repayment would result in subscribed capital falling below the set limit."

[4]See Art. 3 para. 2 SCE-R. It states: "The subscribed capital shall not be less than EUR 30,000."

According to Art. 1 para. 5 SCE-R, the SCE has legal capacity. As such, it can be subjected to obligations and exercise rights. More precisely, it has legal personality with capitalistic patterns. This is clear from the fact that the capital of the SCE is comprised of shares to be paid-in and must respect a minimum amount of at least €30,000 (Art. 3 para. 2 SCE-R and Art. 1 para. 2 SCE-R). In addition, Art. 1 para. 2 SCE provides for a non-mandatory joint liability, once again reflecting the SCE's capitalistic approach. It has been observed that under the Austrian legal system, the legal status of members without an obligation to make additional capital contributions is the same as that of a shareholder in a capital company. See Greda (2014), p. 834.

[5]See Rocchi (2006), p. 93. For different discussions referring to the function of a company's capital, consider for instance Di Sabato (2005), p. 152; Ginera (2011), p. 10; Figà-Talamanca (1997), p. 88; Ferri (2008), p. 750; Simonetto (1959), p. 262 et seq.; Kalss and Eckert (2005), p. 237 et seq.; Raiser and Veil (2006), p. 388; Lutter (1983), p. 166; Werner (2008), p. 58 et seq. For an overview Miribung (2015a), p. 142. Also consider Adams (1991), p. 29 et seq.

[6]See Schöpflin (2018a), p. 1246 et seq. Also consider Lutter et al. (2012), p. 1596 et seq. and 1599.

[7]See Sect. 3.2.

[8]In this context, Art. 4 para. 8 subpara. 1 SCE-R adds certain disclosure duties. See Schöpflin (2018a), p. 1246 et seq. Art. 4 para. 8 SCE-R states: "When it considers the accounts for the financial year, the annual general meeting shall by resolution record the amount of the capital at the end of the financial year and the variation by reference to the preceding financial year."

[9]Art. 4 para. 7 SCE-R. Also consider Sect. 3.4.2.

[10]See Sect. 3.4.2. Accordingly, subscription can be requested for no more than one share, provided the statutes (a) stipulate that the majority at general meetings must be made up of natural persons and (b) lay down a subscription requirement for members wishing to take part in the activities of the SCE. See Art. 4 para. 7 sent. 2 SCE-R. Also consider Rocchi (2006), p. 93.

minimum share amounts. Members may subscribe for more shares than the minimum number mandated by the statutes. However, these additional shares do not necessarily give them more voting rights.[11] In this case, the related voting right is suspended.[12]

The capital of an SCE clearly mixes features of variable and fixed capital, both of which determine the flow of an SCE's financial resources.[13] Yet, this particular approach differs, in part, from the solutions offered by the Italian and Austrian legal systems. *Italian law* determines that the variability of capital is a fundamental characteristic of a cooperative, according to the definition of a cooperative given in Art. 2511 CC[14] Applying this principle does not require one to amend the statutes when new members join or old members leave.[15] It is not possible to derogate from this principle, for instance, by setting a maximum membership limit.[16] This principle is not affected if those attending the general meeting decide to increase capital, either by admitting new members or offering new shares to existing members.[17] These observations are also valid for an Italian SCE.

[11]See Sect. 4.4.4. Also consider Art. 59 para. 1 SCE-R.

[12]See Schöpflin (2018b), p. 1250 et seq. In this context also consider Cusa (2004), p. 142.

[13]See Rocchi (2006), p. 94 et seq. Also consider Krimphove (2010), p. 894.

[14]It has been observed that this principle, together with the principle of "one member, one vote" is a fundamental feature of cooperatives. Similar provisions can be found in other legal systems like those of Portugal, Spain, France or Germany, and many others. See Bonfante (2014), p. 361; Grosso (2011), p. 2120. See also Paolucci (2019c), p. 79 et seq. Similar to the Austrian approach, this implies that a cooperative may admit new members without amending its statutes. Neither is it necessary to disclose or file with registered enterprises or other registries (according to Art. 2524 para. 2 CC). This is in line with the open nature of cooperatives, and indeed favours such openness. However, it is necessary to bear in mind that candidates do not have a right of admission. On these issues, see also Paolucci (2019a).

The variability of capital affects its function. Being variable, it may fluctuate, with the consequence that it cannot assume the function of credit protection in the same way as fixed capital. See Tatarano (2011), p. 220 et seq.; also consider Paolucci (2019c), p. 80. In addition, the capital is generally not relevant in terms of voting power, as the principle "one person, one vote" generally prevails. See Tatarano (2011), p. 433 et seq. Thus a cooperative's capital is different from that of other companies, both in terms of creditor protection and its organisational role among members.

[15]Amending statutes requires calling an extraordinary general meeting.

[16]See Bonfante (2014), p. 361 et seq.; Cusa (2009), p. 353.

[17]See Bonfante (2014), p. 362. It is discussed whether variability of capital also refers to shares subscribed by non-user members. From a traditional point of view, the latter are excluded. See Di Cecco (2012), p. 222 et seq. On the other hand, it is argued that this principle is fundamental to the whole cooperative model, without distinguishing between user and non-user members. As a result, Art. 2328 para. 2 No. 4 CC (according to which the statutes must specify the amount of share capital subscribed and paid-in) cannot be applied. See Cusa (2009), p. 355. Against this it is rather convincingly argued that—apart from the fact that this article is not applicable—the provisions require a resolution adopted by the general meeting to issues these instruments for a fixed amount of capital. These instruments are similar to shares of fixed capital rather than shares of variable capital. In addition, this type of capital is an exception rather than the general rule. See Bonfante (2014), p. 363.

A member's participation in a cooperative may be represented by shares or stock. Italian law does not specify when it is obligatory to use shares or quotas. Due to the general reference in Art. 2525 CC to both quotas and shares (in the sense of stock), participation in a cooperative with an *spa* structure must be represented by shares, with quotas required for an *srl* structure, at least in principle. However, it seems more convincing to assert that cooperatives applying the *spa* structure can use either shares or quotas. Participation by financing members can only be represented by shares.[18] Such questions have been appropriately answered by the SCE-R, at least with respect to Italian (agricultural) SCEs. It is necessary to consider Art. 4 SCE-R, which explicitly refers to shares in the sense of quotas and not shares in the sense of stock.[19]

Next, according to Art. 2525 CC, the value of each share or quota must lie between 25 and 500 EUR. Unless certain laws provide otherwise, no natural person may subscribe capital in excess of 100,000 EUR.[20] Exceptions are possible for members that are legal entities or non-user members.[21] If a cooperative has more than 500 members, this limit can be increased to up to 2% of the capital. The minimum limit strengthens the capital structure of the cooperative, while the maximum limit keeps the cooperative open by not pricing out new members.[22] As this provision only considers the nominal share value, no provision prevents members from making further unsecured contributions (*a fondo perduto*).[23] This approach clearly differs from that delineated in the SCE-R, which uses a minimum capital level to foster capital structure and thus grants statutory freedom over the nominal share value. Members of an SCE may subscribe more than one share and exceed the 100,000 EUR limit set by the CC. In addition, an SCE's statutes must determine the minimum number of shares to which a member must subscribe (whereas a provision

---

[18]Note that the shares issued or used by cooperatives cannot be fully compared to shares issued by an spa, in either content or function. See Bonfante (2014), p. 191; Genco (2003), p. 62; Chieffi (2007b), p. 183.

[19]Consider in this context Art. 4 of the German and Italian versions of the SCE-R, which are more precise.

Rocchi stresses that the possibility to use shares in the sense of stock could have been explicitly regulated by the national legislator. See Rocchi (2006), p. 91.

[20]According to Art. 223 sexies decies prov. impl. CC, the ministry for economic development must update this amount every 3 years to consider the evaluation of money.

[21]See Art. 2525 para. 4 CC. Also consider Tonelli (2003), p. 87 et seq.; Chieffi (2007a), p. 192. See also Santagata (2017), p. 821.

[22]These limits must naturally be considered in the context of the democratic structure of a cooperative. These limits help avoid a dominance of capitalistic aims. See Bonfante (2014), p. 192. However, these limits are not applied to investor members who have administrative rights or user members who are not natural persons. These limits also do not have to be observed for contributions in kind or contributions of credits when revaluating the quota by means of liquidation of divisible reserves (as determined by Art. 2545 quinqiuies CC) or patronage refunds (as determined by Art. 2545 sexies para. 3 CC). See Bonfante (2014), p. 192 et seq.

[23]See Bonfante (2014), p. 192. Also consider Paolucci (2012a), p. 95 et seq., Paolucci (2019d), p. 83.

determining a maximum limit can be determined by the statutes according to Art. 14 para. 2 SCE-R). The absence of a maximum limit does not necessarily weaken the open door principle, as the degree to which new members are admitted also depends on the economic needs of the cooperative.

Under *Austrian law*, Sec. 5a para. 2 no. 2 *GenG* regulates minimum and variable capital. Accordingly, the statutes may set a base level below which the subscribed capital may not fall, even if members leave.[24] This provision was introduced in 2006, because it was unclear whether shares should be considered shareholder capital (equity) or not. According to international accounting standards, cooperative shares cannot be considered as equity, as they can be resigned at any time because of the open door principle. As a result, it was necessary to introduce a mechanism to deny resignation, at least partially.[25] Yet, this minimum level can only be set if the statutes do not generally prohibit the transfer of cooperative shares or other credits attributed[26] to the members.[27] If members leaving the cooperative would cause capital to fall below the minimum requirements, repayment is suspended until the base level has been reached again.[28] This mechanism is similar to that proposed by the SCE-R.

As seen above, Art. 3 para. 4 SCE-R works as an instrument for maintaining capital, which is necessary because of the cooperative's capital-variability criteria. The minimum sum required in Art. 3 para. 2 SCE-R inevitably carries consequences for entitlement to repayment. The SCE-R suspends repayment[29] as long as such repayment would cause capital to fall below the required 30,000 EUR minimum.[30] The difference between the Austrian provision setting a base sum and SCE-R's provision determining the minimum capital is that the SCE-R sets an obligation, whereas the *GenG* contains a mere faculty.[31]

---

[24]The statutes must set the base amount. This may be an absolute value or a specific percentage, for example relative to the entire amount of shares from the previous financial year, which cannot be reduced. The base amount could also correspond to 100% of shares. See Astl and Steinböck (2014b), p. 164 et seq.; Hofinger and Zawischa (2007), p. 38 et seq. and 35; Beuthien and Jud (2007), p. 32 et seq.

[25]This base sum can be considered equity. Then, due to regulation 53/2009, the situation has changed, at least partially. If the conditions determined by IAS 32.16 a and IAS 32.16 b are met, cooperative shares can be considered entirely as equity, and not only the basic sum according to Sec. 5a para. 2 No. 2 GenG. It is argued that the criteria contained therein also apply to cooperatives. See Astl and Steinböck (2014b), p. 163 et seq. Also consider Dellinger (2006), p. 572; Hofinger and Zawischa (2007), p. 35 et seq.; Beuthien and Jud (2007), p. 32 et seq.

[26]Because of their membership.

[27]Sec. Astl and Steinböck (2014b), p. 166; Dellinger (2006), p. 572; Hofinger and Zawischa (2007), p. 36 et seq.; Beuthien and Jud (2007), p. 36.

[28]See Astl and Steinböck (2014b), p. 166.

[29]As determined by Art. 16 SCE-R.

[30]Suspension implies that the entitlement can still be ceased. See Schöpflin (2018b), p. 1250 et seq.

[31]The general meeting may, at a later stage, amend the respective statutory provision or completely abolish it. This does not require an application of the cancellation proceedings laid out in Sec. 33a GenG. See Astl and Steinböck (2014b), p. 165; also consider Dellinger (2006), p. 572.

Apart from these findings (and in contrast to the solution adopted by the SCE-R), there is no provision that refers to a cooperative's minimum capital.[32] The amount of capital is therefore determined according to the number of the shares issued and their value. Similar to an SCE, an Austrian cooperative can freely determine the nominal share value and the type of capital contribution. Sec. 5 para. 1 no. 5 *GenG* states that the statutes must include the nominal value of the shares that are subscribed by each member and the methods of raising these shares. Housing cooperatives are an exception, as Sec. 6 para. 1 *WGG* determines a minimum nominal share value of 218 EUR.[33]

According to Austrian law, every member (in principle) must subscribe to at least one share; statutes must explicitly exclude the option to subscribe to more than one share,[34] although there are also other opinions.[35] This confusion would appropriately be resolved via the statutes and also by determining whether members may or even must subscribe to more than one share. In the latter case, objective criteria must be used to identify when this provision applies.[36] The statutes may also determine the subscription of a minimum number of shares.[37] The Austrian approach, similar to the one determined by the SCE-R, maintains that it is always possible to subscribe to more shares (unless excluded by the statutes).[38] The statutes may also require the subscription of more than one share.[39] Under Austrian law, cooperatives thus have no specific mechanisms that guarantee capital adequacy. However, minimum capital can be viewed as a threshold that must be crossed to prevent economically unsustainable companies from being constituted.[40] The function of such a threshold in a cooperative is fulfilled by the economic forecast, which an auditing association

---

[32]See Astl and Steinböck (2014a), p. 141; Dellinger (2014b), p. 105. Also consider Sec. 5 para. 1 No. 5 BWG.

[33]See Sec. 2 para. 3 GenG regarding consumer cooperatives.

[34]See Astl and Steinböck (2014a), p. 141; Zahn (1963), p. 27.

[35]See Keinert (1988), p. 110 et seq.

[36]A member, at the moment they enter into the contract, must be able to completely determine the full amount of his obligation to pay in capital. See Astl and Steinböck (2014a), p. 141; Keinert (1988), p. 111; Zahn (1963), p. 28.

[37]Statutory provisions according to which only a specific member may subscribe more than one share are not permitted. See Astl and Steinböck (2014a), p. 141; Keinert (1988), p. 110 et seq.; Kastner (1986), p. 140; Zahn (1963), p. 27.

[38]Leaving the minimum share value and the minimum capital undetermined is also linked to the open door concept. Minimum capital levels can prevent members from leaving and being reimbursed.

[39]See Schöpflin (2018b), p. 1250 et seq.

[40]See Dellinger (2014b), p. 105 et seq. Also consider Miribung (2015a), p. 142 et seq. In general, Eidenmüller et al. (2006), p. 17 et seq.

requires when a new cooperative is founded.[41] This finding is also valid for an SCE, as Art. 71 SCE-R makes the national law fully applicable.

The next topic that concerns capital is **liability**. According to Art. 1 para. 2 subpara. 3 SCE-R,[42] the members of an SCE (in principle) can only be held liable for the amount they have subscribed. The statutes may provide otherwise, however. For instance, statutes may determine that liability is a multiple of the subscribed shares or define it as unlimited. It also seems possible to calculate liability according to the specific type of share issued.[43] The SCE-R does not distinguish between the different types of members. As a result, a statutory clause assigning unlimited responsibility to investor members might be possible.[44] In any case, it is not possible to fully exclude liability.[45] If liability is limited, the name of the SCE must end in 'limited'.[46]

The two legal systems approach liability differently The SCE-R allows the option to hold members liable for more than the amount subscribed. By contrast, *Italian legal provisions* that deal with cooperatives no longer provide for unlimited or multiple responsibility (on the amount of capital subscribed).[47] The previous liability system distinguished between (a) limited liability in the strict sense, (b) liability limited to a predetermined sum (setting a further predefined sum) and (c) unlimited liability.[48] (This system was similar to that described in Sec. 2 *GenG*.) The current set of rules seems to prohibit statutory provisions or decisions taken by the general

---

[41] According to Sec. 5 para. 1 GenRevG. See Dellinger (2014b), p. 106.

[42] It states: "Unless otherwise provided by the statutes of the SCE when that SCE is formed, no member shall be liable for more than the amount he/she has subscribed. Where the members of the SCE have limited liability, the name of the SCE shall end in 'limited'."

Art 1 para. 2 sent. 3 SCE-R explicitly refers to an SCE at the moment it is formed. This clearly implies the issue of limited or unlimited responsibility must be addressed when the SCE is founding. As a result, it is argued this specific feature can no longer be changed. This is unconvincing, as one can argue that the provision simply requires that persons forming an SCE must decide which liability regime shall be applied from the outset, which does not imply that the decision cannot changed at a later stage. Art. 1 para. 2 subpara. 3 does not contain any reference in this regard. See Rocchi (2006), p. 88 et seq.

[43] E.g., user members with unlimited liability and non-user members with limited liability. See Rocchi (2006), p. 88. Also consider Alfandari and Piot (2004), p. 88.

[44] See Rocchi (2006), p. 88.

While Art. 1 para. 2 subpara. 3 SCE-R deals with limited (default rule) and unlimited liability (to be based on a specific statutory clause), Art. 14 para. 3 SCE-R (referring to the acquisition of membership) states that statutes may require members to subscribe to a supplementary stake in the capital. The practical consequences of these rules may be roughly equivalent. However, the community legislature refers to distinct phenomena, at least from a technical point of view. See Rocchi (2006), p. 87.

[45] See Alfandari and Piot (2004), p. 88.

[46] See Art. 1 para. 2 subpara. 3 last sent. SCE-R.

[47] See Art. 2518 CC. Also consider Rocchi (2006), p. 87 et seq.; Rocchi (2007), p. 89 et seq.

[48] See Paolucci (2019b), p. 55 et seq.; Giorgi (2018a), p. 3208 et seq., Art. 2518; Schirò (2008a), p. 51 et seq.

meeting that require members to make additional capital contributions.[49] Thus, Italian SCEs are more flexible in this regard than Italian cooperatives by reintroducing into the Italian legal system the concepts of liability that were abolished in 2003.[50]

According to the *Austrian GenG*, cooperatives can be established with either unlimited or limited member liability.[51] In the latter case, the liability is limited to a specific sum. Next, Sec. 2 para. 3 *GenG* deals with liability limited to the cooperative's shares. This type of liability may only be adopted by cooperatives who have as their object the collective procurement of food and other goods for private households (in wholesale) and their sale (small-scale, consumer cooperatives). The law requires a minimum share value of 1 EUR. The statutes must also limit the distribution of goods to members. The same holds for consumer cooperatives that accept savings deposits.[52]

The distinction between different types of liability determines the structure of the *GenG*. Certain provisions explicitly refer to unlimited or limited liability while one provision refers to liability limited to cooperative shares (as provided for in para. 3).[53] According to Sec. 2 para. 2 *GenG*, unlimited liability means that members are jointly and severally liable for the liabilities of the cooperative with all their private assets. However, unlimited liability is subordinate to the liability of the cooperative. According to Sec. 53 para. 1 *GenG*, the members are only jointly and severally liable if the cooperative's assets are insufficient to cover its debts in cases of liquidation or bankruptcy. Thus, this type of liability is not unlimited in the strict sense, but rather consists of an internal obligation to contribute additional capital to the cooperative (indirect liability). In practice, unlimited liability has been completely replaced by limited liability.[54]

If a cooperative has limited liability, all members remain jointly and severally liable for the liabilities of the cooperative; however, this liability is limited to a predetermined sum. Here, the wording 'jointly and severally liable' is slightly misleading. In fact, members are liable only if the cooperative is liquidated or

---

[49]See Paolucci (2019b), p. 455; Giorgi (2018a), p. 3208 et seq. See also Santagata (2017), p. 820.

[50]See Chirico and Troianiello (2007), p. 42.

Art 2536 para. 2 CC determines that, if the cooperative becomes insolvent within 1 year of paying the quota or share in case of liquidation, these former members must refund the money. The same provision applies to the heirs of a deceased former member. For details, see Giorgi (2007), p. 294 et seq.; Delle Priscoli (2014), p. 321 et seq. This provision applies to an Italian SCE due to Art. 72 SCE-R.

[51]Sec. 2 para. 1 GenG.

[52]Consider in this context Sec. 95 para. 1 BWG. This provision, however, has never been of practical relevance, because a consumer cooperative would never limit the distribution of goods exclusively to its members. Dellinger (2014b), p. 103; Kastner (1986), p. 126; Nowotny (2008), nt 5/24.

[53]See Dellinger (2014b), p. 101 et seq.

[54]See Dellinger (2014b), p. 102; Kastner et al. (1990), p. 478; Dellinger (1995), p. 91 et seq.; Nowotny (2008), nt 5/22.

insolvent.[55] To be more specific, Sec. 76 *GenG* determines that every member of a cooperative is liable for its debts in cases of bankruptcy or liquidation.[56] Liability here extends not only to shares but also to a further amount equal to the shares subscribed by a member. The amount of an obligatory additional capital contribution is ultimately determined by the statutes and does not correspond to the subscribed capital. In general, it is therefore impossible to limit liability to the subscribed capital.[57] Contrary to this, for specific types of cooperatives para. 3 of Sec. 2 allows liability to be limited to shares.[58]

The most noticeable differences between the solutions in Austrian law and the SCE-R is the use of terms. According to the SCE-R, limited liability is limited to shares (default provision).[59] If an Austrian SCE wants to adopt limited liability, as conceptualised by the *GenG*, then the drafters of the statutes must adopt a specific statutory provision.[60] Moreover, as this issue is mostly regulated by the SCE-R, liability limited to shares[61] is not restricted to consumer cooperatives, but (in principle) may be applied to every type of cooperative. While liability in an SCE is primarily regulated by the SCE-R, an Austrian SCE must observe other provisions that subordinate liability to liquidation or insolvency. Art. 72 SCE-R explicitly refers to national law with respect to liquidation, insolvency and similar procedures.

The third issue related to capital is **shares**. The SCE-R rather strictly states that subscribed capital must be divided into shares.[62] Interestingly, the English version of the SCE-R refers to shares—which might suggest shares in the sense used by the SE-R–[63] while the German and Italian versions refer to *Geschäftsanteile*[64] and *quote*, respectively, both of which mean a share in the sense of a quota.

The SCE-R contains different provisions to outline the common features of a share in an SCE. According to Art. 4 para. 3 SCE-R, shares must be held by named persons. In addition, the nominal value of shares—to be laid down in the statutes—in a single class must be identical, excluding issued shares. To increase creditor

[55]In these two cases, liability is limited to a certain sum and considers only the internal relationship between the members and their cooperative.

[56]According to the GenIG, the internal liability has been transformed into a secondary liability. See Dellinger (2014b), p. 102 et seq.

[57]See Dellinger (2014b), p. 102 et seq.

[58]In this case, members cannot be obligated to contribute additional capital. In case of insolvency, they lose only the capital that they paid in.

[59]See Art. 1 para. 2 subpara. 3 SCE-R.

[60]See Art. 1 para. 2 subpara. 3 SCE-R. Also consider Art. 14 para. 3 SCE-R in this context. Also consider Hirte (2007), p. 2217.

[61]Sec. 2 para. 3 GenG.

[62]Art. 1 para. 2 SCE-R.

[63]See Art. 5 SE-R. Also consider Mayer (2010), p. 103.

[64]See Art. 1 para. 2 SE-R (English, German and Italian version) and Art. 1 para. 2 SCE-R (English, German and Italian version.) Also consider the Spanish and French versions, which refer to quotas rather than shares.

protection, the SCE-R states that shares may not be issued at a price lower than their nominal value.[65] The reference to 'single class' allows different nominal share values to be determined.[66] A class of shares is made up of those shares with identical entitlements.[67] Based on Art. 4 para. 1 subpara. 2 SCE-R,[68] the statutes can, for example, allow different classes of shares to confer different entitlements for the distribution of surpluses.[69] Next, according to Art. 66 SCE-R, an SCE may also allow the payment of a dividend to members in proportion either to their business or to the services they have performed for the SCE. These two options correspond to the notion of patronage refunds.[70] Taken together, these provisions allow for differentiation within the shares of user and non-user (investor) members regarding the rights attached thereto, e.g., by granting privileges based on the allocation of surplus.[71] An SCE may arguably issue different classes of shares, connecting the obligation to subscribe additional capital to some, but not all, types of shares.[72]

The shares acquired[73] by the members must have an economic value.[74] As this value is variable, it can be altered by either a write down or the complete or partial conversion of the reserves.[75] Thus different types of shares are possible, provided that the following conditions are met: (1) shares must be held by named persons; (2) shares must be capable of economic value; (3) shares must be issued at nominal value; and (4) the nominal value of shares in a single class must be identical. It thus seems possible to issue shares with different nominal values. A class of shares is made up of all shares with identical entitlements.

---

[65]See Schöpflin (2018b), p. 1250 et seq.

Art 4 para. 3 SCE-R states: "Shares shall be held by named persons. The nominal value of shares in a single class shall be identical. It shall be laid down in the statutes. Shares may not be issued at a price lower than their nominal value."

[66]See Rocchi (2006), p. 101. Also consider Schöpflin (2018b), p. 1250 et seq and Holthaus and Lehnhoff (2016), p. 47.

[67]Art. 4 para. 1 subpara. 2 last sent. SCE-R.

[68]The regulation states that more than one class of shares may be issued.

[69]See Rocchi (2006), p. 101 et seq. Also consider Albamonte (2008), p. 306 et seq.

[70]For details, see Sect. 5.3.

[71]See Rocchi (2006), p. 101.

[72]Such a provision would be fully in line with the principle of non-discrimination. See Greda (2014), p. 834.

[73]According to Art. 4 para. 11 SCE-R, they may be assigned or sold to a member or to anyone acquiring membership on the condition that the general meeting or the management or administrative organ approve. Also consider Sects. 5.2 and 5.4.

[74]Art. 4 para. 2 sent. 1 SCE-R. It states: "The capital may be formed only by assets capable of economic assessment."

According to Art. 4 para. 2 sent. 2 SCE-R, members' shares may not be issued for an undertaking to perform work or supply services. However, this provision does not prevent an SCE from obliging members to make such performances. See Schöpflin (2018b), p. 1250 et seq.

[75]See Alfandari and Piot (2004), p. 86 et seq. Also consider Art. 4 para. 8 subpara. 2 SCE-R and Schöpflin (2018b), p. 1251 et seq.

These more general observations on shares now lead us to focus on the main issues[76] related to shares: shares issued for cash and non-cash contributions. The SCE-R is rather strict about the obligation to pay **shares issued for cash**. In fact, on the day of subscription, no less than 25% of their nominal value must be paid for.[77] The obligation to pay 25% might be burdensome for specific cooperatives, like service cooperatives or worker cooperatives with a wide base of members, as these members often have limited economic means. However, the second sentence of Art. 4 para. 4 SCE-R allows the balance to be paid within 5 years, making such an investment easier.[78] It can even be argued that 25% is low, which makes capitalization easier, and the option to pay the balance serves as an instrument for the SCE itself to foster capitalization.[79] The (perceived) strictness of this provision ultimately depends on circumstances.

How does the national law address these aspects?

Italian legal norms for cooperatives do not define the specific forms of contribution that members must utilise; however, the provisions adopted for the *spa* apply because of the reference in Art. 2519 CC. Certain exemptions exist, for instance, the exemption of a contribution in cash of at least 25%, as determined by 2342 CC and 2329 CC.[80] While Art. 2342 CC and Art. 2329 CC both require subscribing at least 25% in cash as soon as a company is formed, Art. 2531 CC apparently does not consider this.[81] As seen above, the SCE-R adopts a different solution.

In Italy, the most common type of contribution is in cash,[82] for which specific limitations have to be observed. These limitations are determined by Art. 2525 CC and have been discussed at the beginning of this chapter. Lastly, Italian law makes it possible to set a surcharge.[83]

The *Austrian legal system* determines that, according to Sec. 5 para. 1 no. 5 *GenG*, the statutes must include the nominal value of the shares and the methods of raising these shares. Shares, as indicated by no. 5, refer to members' obligation to pay in.[84] According to the prevailing doctrine, the nominal share value must be the same for all members.[85] However, reconsideration of this thinking is urged by the newly introduced Sec. 5a, which considers the possibility of investor members. The

[76]As determined by the SCE-R.

[77]See Art. 4 para. 4 SCE-R. Also consider Rocchi (2006), p. 92; Schöpflin (2018b), p. 1250 et seq.

[78]See Rocchi (2006), p. 92 et seq.

[79]See Schöpflin (2018b), p. 1250 et seq.

[80]See Bonfante (2014), p. 367.

[81]See Bonfante (2014), p. 99 et seq.; Scordino (1970), p. 123; Bassi and Schlesinger (1988), p. 386; Pinna (2005), p. 2682.

[82]According to Art. 2342 para. 1 CC, contributions shall be made in cash, unless otherwise provided for in the statutes. See Bonfante (2014), p. 366 et seq.

[83]See Art. 2525 CC.

[84]This is directly linked with liability, entitlement to profits and eventually voting rights. See Astl and Steinböck (2014a), p. 141; Kastner (1986), p. 141.

[85]Kastner (1986), p. 140; Keinert (1988), p. 108 et seq.; Zahn (1963), p. 27.

GenG does not contain any provision that explicitly forbids shares with different nominal values. Thus, a different nominal value can be granted, provided that the principle of equality is not violated or that an objective justification for unequal treatment is given.[86] Differentiation seems particularly justified for investor members and includes specific provisions about the shares to be subscribed and their nominal value. It seems also justifiable to set a higher nominal value after a specific period.[87] Thus the SCE-R has satisfactorily resolved the doubts over the prevailing Austrian doctrine.

Austrian law permits the issuing of shares at a higher value than the nominal value (surcharge). The statutes must determine how this surcharge is set and which organ has the competence to set it. The statutes may also set an accession fee that does not form part of the share.[88] These solutions can be adopted by an Austrian SCE under Art. 14 para. 2 SCE-R.

The SCE-R not only regulates the issue of shares for cash, but also, as Art. 4 para. 5 SCE-R explains, deals with **shares issued other than for cash**. These must be fully paid for at the time of subscription. This requirement is essential, as in-kind contributions are only valuable if the SCE can use them immediately.[89] Art. 4 para. 2 SCE-R prohibits the issuing of shares to perform work or supply services. The SCE-R does not contain additional provisions in this regard, but merely specifies that when one values these type of shares, they must necessarily consider, by analogy, the relevant national law that is applicable to public limited-liability companies (this extends to appointing experts[90]).

Comparing these provisions with national law, we see some interesting aspects. Art. 2525 CC contains limitations on the maximum limit of shares to which a natural person may subscribe; these limits for cash contributions, however, do not apply to in-kind contributions. According to *Italian law*, the use of in-kind contributions is permitted, while generic property, future property and other people's property cannot form part of a contribution. The same is true for services and hence performances.[91] Art. 2342 CC states that shares corresponding to such contributions must be paid in full upon subscription. The concepts adopted by the Italian legislature

[86]Relative principle of equality.

[87]Consider, for instance, shares subscribed with a surcharge, and the possibility of reduce this surcharge or increasing the nominal value. See Astl and Steinböck (2014a), p. 141 et seq.

[88]See Astl and Steinböck (2014a), p. 142.

[89]See Schöpflin (2018b), p. 1250 et seq. Also consider Lutter et al. (2012), p. 1598.

[90]Of the member state where the SCE has its registered office. See Art. 4 para. 6 SCE-R. It states: "The law applicable to public limited-liability companies in the Member State where the SCE has its registered office, concerning the appointment of experts and the valuation of any consideration other than cash, shall apply by analogy to the SCE."

[91]Art. 2342 last para. CC. See Bonfante (2014), p. 367; Campobasso and Campobasso (2004), p. 42. Consider in this context also Art. 2342 CC and following. Art. 2342 para. 5 determines that, for contributions in kind, the provisions of Arts 2254 and 2255 must be applied. For accessory services consider in particular Art. 2345 CC.

align with the SCE-R. Finally, the procedure for the appraisal of in-kind contributions is determined by Art. 2343 CC.[92]

According to the prevailing *Austrian* doctrine, shares in a cooperative may also be acquired via in-kind contributions. This option can be determined by either the statutes or the general meeting.[93] An Austrian SCE is directly authorized by the SCE-R to issue shares of this type.

For Austrian cooperatives, the value of in-kind contributions is determined by Sec. 202 para. 1 UGB,[94] while the valuation of in-kind contributions for Austrian SCEs is determined by Art. 4 para. 6 SCE-R, according to Sec. 20 AktG.[95]

It is unclear whether the Austrian legal system permits services as part of in-kind contributions. In German cooperative law, services as in-kind contributions make sense because of the self-help nature of cooperatives. As a result, persons with less capital or fewer goods can become members, which inclusion fosters participation. Services as in-kind contributions are, in principle, acknowledged by company law,[96] and therefore Austrian cooperative law should also allow this option.[97] However, an Austrian SCE may not utilise this option, as Art. 4 para. 2 SCE-R prohibits the issuing of shares to perform work or supply services.[98]

After analysing minimum and variable capital, liabilities and shares, all of which are related to the capital of an SCE, we now address the final topic about **operations on capital**. When considering an SCE's capital operations, we must distinguish between operations concerning capital (in general) and those concerning minimum capital, as determined by the statutes.[99] Variations in capital do not, in principle, require disclosure or an amendment to the statutes.[100] However, these variations only become effective for SCEs and third parties if the transaction has been entered

[92]It requires the submission of a report, to be produced by an expert appointed by the court. The law contains provisions regarding the content of this report, liability of the expert and a verification procedure to be conducted by the members of the management or administrative organ. In addition, if specific conditions are met, no appraisal is needed for contributions of securities or financial instruments (Art. 2343 ter CC).

[93]Former doctrine excluded this possibility. Against this, it is argued that, due to Sec. 57 para. 2 GenG, contributions in kind seem possible. This provision deals with objects contributed to the cooperative by one of its members, which seems to include non-cash contributions. Consider in this context Sec. 12 para. 3 UMGRSTG and Astl and Steinböck (2014a), p. 143. Also consider Kastner (1986), p. 141; Keinert (1988), p. 110. Contributions in kind can include, for instance, movable and immovable goods, outstanding debt, intangible assets, companies, shares in companies, and so on. See Astl and Steinböck (2014a), p. 143; Ettel (2012), nt 12 et seq.

[94]See Astl and Steinböck (2014a), p. 143.

[95]See Greda (2014), p. 845.

[96]See § 1183 ABGB.

[97]See Astl and Steinböck (2014a), p. 144.

[98]See Greda (2014), p. 845.

[99]See Heilmeier (2010), p. 887. In general, Hirte (2007), p. 2217.

[100]See Art. 3 para. 5 subpara. 2 SCE-R.

into an index of members, as provided for by Art. 14 para. 4 SCE-R.[101] This alphabetical index must be kept at the SCE's registered office and record the addresses of each member, along with the number and the types[102] of shares that they hold. The index must also contain the nominal value of each share, because Art. 14 paras. 5 and 6 SCE-R require any change in capital to be entered into the index. This variation could result from the process of members joining or leaving the SCE as well as a change in the nominal value of entire classes of shares.[103] However, operations on minimum capital always require the statutes to be amended.[104]

Capital can be increased in various ways. For example, it can be increased by capitalising all or part of the reserves that are available for distribution.[105] The general meeting decides upon these issues after a proposal by the administrative or the management organ. The new shares must be awarded to the members in proportion to their shares in the previous capital.[106] Capital can also be increased when the general meeting takes a decision, according to Art. 67 para. 3 bullet 3 SCE-R, that pertains to a return on capital in which payment is made in shares. In this case, the decision cannot be made solely at the request of the management or administrative organ; it must be put on the agenda in line with Art. 61 para. 1 SCE-R.[107] Next, capital may also be increased by admitting new members or through additional subscriptions purchased by members,[108] which leads to the issue

[101]See Art. 14 para. 5 and 6 SCE-R. Art 14 paras 4–6 SCE-R state: "(4) An alphabetical index of all members shall be kept at the registered office of the SCE, showing their addresses and the number and class, if appropriate, of the shares they hold. Any party having a direct legitimate interest may inspect the index on request, and may obtain a copy of the whole or any part at a price not exceeding the administrative cost thereof. (5) Any transaction which affects the manner in which the capital is ascribed or allotted, or increased or reduced, shall be entered on the index of members provided for in paragraph 4 no later than the month following that in which the change occurs. (6) The transactions referred to in paragraph 5 shall not take effect with respect to the SCE or third parties having a direct legitimate interest until they are entered on the index referred to in paragraph 4."

[102]If appropriate.

[103]See Heilmeier (2010), p. 889.

[104]See Heilmeier (2010), p. 890.

[105]See Art. 4 para. 8 subpara. 2 SCE-R. This rule aims to conserve capital. As converting reserves in combination with repaying shares when members leave the cooperative may lead to a decrease in established capital, it is necessary for such decisions to be taken by a qualified majority. See Alfandari and Piot (2004), p. 86 et seq. Also consider Rocchi, who stresses that this specific quorum is a safeguard mechanism for members (not the cooperative) and leads to a free increase of capital. See Rocchi (2006), p. 109 et seq. Also consider Cusa (2004), p. 152.

[106]If new shares must be issued as a consequence of increasing capital, Art. 4 para. 8 subpara. 2 last sent. SCE-R determines that they shall be awarded to members in proportion to their shares in the previous capital.

[107]A minority of members may also require specific items be put on the agenda of the general meeting. See Sect. 4.4.2. Also consider Cusa (2004), p. 151 and Heilmeier (2010), p. 889.

[108]Art. 3 para. 5 SCE-R. It states: "5. The capital may be increased by successive subscriptions by members or on the admission of new members, and it may be reduced by the total or partial repayment of subscriptions, subject to paragraph 4." This does not require amendment of the statutes. See Art. 3 para. 5 subpara. 2 SCE-R. Also consider Schöpflin (2018b), p. 1249 et seq.

of new shares.[109] Even though it is not explicitly determined by the SCE-R, additional capital may be acquired by increasing the nominal value of a specific class of shares with an amendment to the statutes.[110] This requirement is essential, as Art. 4 para. 3 sent. 3 SCE-R requires the nominal value of the shares for a specific category of members to be determined via the statutes.[111] Then, it is not possible to increase capital by using dividends (patronage refunds)[112] to grant new shares. While Art. 67 para. 2 bullet 3 SCE-R explicitly allows returns to be made in shares,[113] Art. 66 SCE-R refers only to the payment of dividends to members in proportion to their business conducted with the SCE. Thus, Art. 66 SCE-R grants a financial allowance.[114] Finally, capital may be increased by raising the (statutory) minimum capital, as determined by Art. 3 paras. 2 and 4 SCE-R. A distinction must be drawn here between requalifying existing capital[115] and acquiring new capital.[116] When increasing (statutory) minimum capital above paid-in capital, it is necessary to distinguish between increases in capital that occur with existing shares (but not completely paid in) and with new ones, which can be accomplished similarly to increasing capital as described above. In any case, the new shares must be paid in to reach the statutory minimum capital.[117]

The national perspectives add significant details to these results. The *Italian legal system* contains provisions that serve as examples for statutory provisions. Thanks to the 2003 reform, changes in capital[118] are now practical rather than merely theoretically possible. The law permits an increase in capital because of (a) payment and (b) on a free basis.[119] For the former, a provision that deals with the increase in capital requires an amendment to the statutes.[120]

Art 3 para. 5 refers to variability of capital, whereas Art. 4 para. 8 subpara. 2 SCE-R refers to an increase in capital.

[109]The conditions determined by Art. 14 SCE-R have to be observed.

[110]It has been correctly observed that the possibility to take such a decision is not excluded by Art. 4 paras 9 and 10 SCE-R, as these provisions exclusively refer to variations in the nominal value of shares within the framework of existing capital. See Heilmeier (2010), p. 889.

[111]The effect of these transactions relies on them being entered into the index of members, as determined by Art. 14 para. 4 SCE-R. This provision must be given priority in respect of national law. Also consider Cusa (2004), p. 151; Heilmeier (2010), p. 889 et seq. and Genco (2006), p. 122 et seq.

[112]See Art. 66 SCE-R.

[113]See Schöpflin (2018an).

[114]See Heilmeier (2010), p. 890. In this context also consider Schöpflin (2018an). Different opinion Cusa (2004), p. 152 et seq. and Chirico and Troianiello (2007), p. 71.

[115]Shares completely paid in.

[116]Both decisions require observing the majority requirements determined by Art. 61 para. 4 subpara. 2 SCE-R.

[117]See Heilmeier (2010), p. 890.

[118]Increase of capital and reduction of capital.

[119]See Lolli (2012), p. 151. See also Paolucci (2019c), p. 80 et seq.

[120]According to Art. 2524 para. 3 CC, a cooperative may deliberate on the increase in capital by modifying the statutes. Such a decision must be taken by the extraordinary general meeting. See

The provisions in Art. 2438 CC and following apply to this situation and must be observed. With the new Art. 2524 CC, the legislature grants the power to decide to increase capital by asking the members to subscribe to new shares in proportion to the shares they already own. This initiative could be necessary in such cases where losses considerably reduce the amount of existing capital or new business must be financed.[121] As observed by the Italian High Court (*corte di cassazione*), members cannot be expelled if they do not subscribe to the new shares, even if a decision has been taken to increase the cooperative's minimum capital. Such a decision would be void.[122] If existing members will not subscribe to the issued shares, these shares can be offered to new members.[123]

Now, the SCE-R does not explicitly provide an option to subscribe to the issued shares to existing members if capital increases because new shares are being issued. Such a right could, however, be determined by the general meeting if it decides to issue new shares.[124] Moreover, one can argue that the SCE-R contains a gap that national law can fill.[125] Italian SCEs may be able to adopt a similar approach by considering Art. 2524 para. 4 CC, which states the option may be revoked or limited if it is authorised by the general meeting.[126] This option can be revoked, for example, if the new shares are issued for in-kind contributions. Of course, this must align with the effective interests of the cooperative.[127]

Next, any increase in capital that occurs from exercising an option must follow the limits in Art. 2525 CC. For instance, if the limit of 100,000 EUR is exceeded,

---

Bonfante (2014), p. 377 et seq. Even though the only method of increasing capital which requires a statutory amendment is payment, there is nothing to prevent amending the statutes anyway to provide more qualified information about the capital. See Lolli (2012), p. 154. Also consider Bonfante (2014), p. 375; Bonfante (1999), p. 387. It seems not convincing to argue that some kind of mixed system (fixed capital with variable capital) has been introduced. This provision, however, might be important for initiatives to enlarge the membership base. Separately, an increase in capital might also imply an invitation for existing members to subscribe further capital. See Bonfante (2014), p. 377 et seq.

[121] See Bonfante (2014), p. 375 et seq. Also consider Montagnani (2003), p. 81 et seq.; Paciello (2007a), p. 173 et seq.; Petroboni (2013), p. 2641 et seq. and Paolucci (2019c), p. 79 et seq.

[122] See Cass Civ sez I 22.08.2006 no 18218 (07.02.2017, iusexplorer.it).

[123] The new member must meet the requirements determined by the statutes. Consider Art. 2527 CC. See Bonfante (2014), p. 379. Also consider Rocchi (2005), p. 194 and Paolucci (2019e), p. 88 et seq.

[124] Also based on Art. 14 para. 2 SCE-R. Also consider Art. 4 para. 8 subpara. 2 SCE-R, dealing with increase of capital by capitalisation of the reserves.

[125] Based on Arts 8 and 52 SCE-R.

[126] Due to Art. 52 SCE-R. Such a decision must be based on a motivated proposal submitted by the administrators or managers. This will enlarge the membership structure. However, the subscribers must meet the necessary requirements to participate in the cooperative. As already seen, the admission of new members must be approved by the administrators or managers.

[127] See Bonfante (2014), p. 378 et seq.

these shares must first be reserved for the other members[128] and then offered to third parties.[129] An Italian SCE need not observe these limitations.

Art. 2526 CC provides another way to increase capital.[130] A cooperative's capital is variable, so normally the statutes do not have to be amended. However, amendments are necessary if a cooperative plans to give new members particular financial instruments with differing characteristics, rights and obligations. For instance, bonds that have already been issued may be subject to an increase of capital if they are converted into participative financial instruments. In this case, Art. 2420 bis CC[131] and Art. 2420 ter CC[132] seem to apply.[133] These solutions can apply to an Italian SCE, based on Art. 4 para. 1 subpara. 2 SCE-R and Art. 64 SCE-R.

Capital also may be raised at no cost. According to Art. 2545 quinquies CC, divisible reserves[134] may be attributed to the members by: (1) proportionally increasing the subscribed and paid-in quota or (2) issuing new shares. In these cases, the provisions in Art. 2525 CC can be derogated. In any case, the capital increase cannot exceed 20% of the original value, and this increase is possible as long as the relationship between the net assets and total debts is higher than 3:1. This latter condition helps foster stability and prevents a mass exodus of members.[135] An Italian SCE need not observe these provisions, as these issues is regulated by Art. 4 para. 8 subpara. 2 SCE-R, which states that the general meeting may only decide on proposals that are submitted by the administrative or management organs. Therefore, it is the bodies' responsibility to decide whether financial stability is safeguarded or not.

If an agricultural SCE that is organised as a mainly mutual cooperative wants to increase its capital at no cost, Art. 2514 para. 1 letter c CC must be observed; thus, the increase in capital can affect only non-user members and can be carried out only on the condition that divisible reserves have been created in their favour.[136]

---

[128]As a consequence, their option is expanded.

[129]See Bonfante (2014), p. 379. Also consider Rocchi (2005), p. 194. Different opinion Paciello (2007a), p. 175; Petroboni (2013), p. 2649.

[130]This increase in capital could be due to losses or initiating new business initiatives. It is discussed whether increasing capital by issuing financial instruments, as provided by Art. 2526 CC, is also regulated by Art. 2524 CC. It is argued that it is specifically regulated by Art. 2526 CC, hence Art. 2524 CC cannot be applied. See Bonfante (2014), p. 376; different opinion Petroboni (2013), p. 2641 et seq.

[131]Debentures convertible into shares.

[132]Delegation to the directors.

[133]See Lolli (2012), p. 154; Genco (2003), p. 108.

[134]In addition to divisible reserves, facultative or statutory reserves can also be used, provided they have been created to increase capital. Extra charge reserves can also be used to increase capital (Art. 2535 para. 2 CC), and if certain conditions are met, also legal reserves. See Lolli (2012), p. 151 et seq., see also Paolucci (2019i), p. 146 et seq.

[135]See Paolucci (2019i), p. 146.

[136]See Lolli (2012), p. 151 et seq.

Finally, according to Art. 2545 sexies CC, the general meeting may decide to allocate patronage refunds by increasing the capital in proportion to members' shares and by issuing new shares.[137] The SCE-R, I argue, does not support such an approach.

Whereas the Italian legal system contains certain rules that govern the increase in capital, the *Austrian legal system* is less detailed. In fact, Sec. 5a para. 2 no. 2 *GenG* is the only provision that must be observed; this provision deals with a base amount below which subscribed capital may not fall, even if members leave. As seen above, this aspect is regulated by the SCE-R.

Austrian law always allows the option to increase quotas. Increases in nominal value can be achieved by amending statutory provisions. In addition, statutes can allow shares to be increased by adding previously subscribed shares. Then, an increase in shares can be achieved with newly paid-in or existing capital.[138] These solutions partly follow those applicable under the SCE-R. Once again, it is not possible to increase capital via dividends (patronage refunds).

Finally, members may cancel their membership if the general meeting decides to increase the cooperative's shares, provided that they have raised objections against the decision or were neither present nor represented. This provision seems to be encompassed by Art. 15 para. 2 SCE-R.

The other facet of capital operations is the **reduction of capital**. The SCE-R marginally addresses this issue in provisions that govern a decrease in share value[139] and the automatic reduction of capital in cases where there is a loss of membership.[140] Capital can be reduced by a partial reduction of shares. However, this possibility is based on the assumption that the minimum number of shares necessary to obtain membership is not reduced.[141] It is not possible to subscribe or purchase own shares.[142]

The nominal value of shares can be reduced via statutory provisions, according to Art. 4 para. 3 sent. 3 SCE-R. In this context, the same arguments as put forward when analysing an increase in capital can be considered; similarly, the effects of these transactions must be registered in the alphabetical index of members.[143] Members' financial entitlements are regulated according to Art. 16 para. 4 SCE-R.[144]

---

[137]See Lolli (2012), p. 152, see also Paolucci (2019j), p. 147 et seq.

[138]In this case, only after-tax profits can be used. See Astl and Steinböck (2014a), p. 144; Bundesministerium für Finanzen (2005).

[139]See Art. 4 para. 3 SCE-R.

[140]See Art. 3 para. 5 subpara. 1 SCE-R, Art. 15 para. 1 SCE-R and Art. 16 SCE-R. Also consider Schöpflin (2018a), p. 1246 et seq; Schöpflin (2018d), p. 1276 et seq.; Heilmeier (2010), p. 890.

[141]See Art. 4 para. 7 SCE-R; also consider Art. 16 para. 4 SCE-R. Also consider Heilmeier (2010), p. 890.

[142]See Art. 4 para. 11 SCE-R. For details Schöpflin (2018b), p. 1251 et seq.

[143]See Art. 14 para. 4, 5 and 6 SCE-R. See Heilmeier (2010), p. 890.

[144]See Sect. 5.4.

In any case, the provisions that determine the minimum capital must be strictly observed. If the reduction in capital leads to a reduction in minimum capital, as determined by statutory provisions, it becomes necessary to reduce the statutory minimum capital by amending the statutes.[145] Finally, Art. 3 paras. 2 and 4 SCE-R place a specific limit on repayment, according to which the capital cannot fall below an amount established by the statutes. This sum cannot be lower than the minimum capital of 30,000 EUR.[146]

Italian law determines that capital may be reduced by (1) reducing the nominal share value, (2) reducing the number of shares or (3) acquiring shares on behalf of the managers and refunding the capital using profits or available reserves.[147] In the third case, the ratio between the cooperative's net assets and overall debts must be higher than 3:1.[148] This condition does not apply to an Italian SCE, as it contradicts Art. 4 para. 12 SCE-R.

Moreover, the law explicitly regulates the situation that arises if capital is reduced because of losses.[149] According to the law, if capital is reduced by less than a third, replenishment of losses is not mandatory.[150] Thus, in principle, losses can be carried over to following years. However, capital can also be reduced voluntarily. Then, if capital is reduced by more than a third, Art. 2446 CC must be applied, and the general meeting must be convened without delay to decide upon any necessary measures.[151] If the loss is not reduced to less than a third within the subsequent financial year, the capital must be reduced in proportion to the accrued losses.[152] Alternatively, members may recapitalise the cooperative.[153] These provisions also apply to an Italian SCE, as the SCE-R does not regulate situations when losses eat into capital.

Austrian cooperative law does not contain many provisions about reducing capital. First, capital can be reduced by reducing the nominal share value with an

---

[145]See Heilmeier (2010), p. 890. Also consider Bianca and Zanardo (2016), p. 205. While the SCE exists, the shares may be repaid completely or partially. See also Sect. 5.4.

[146]Minimum capital required by the SCE-R. Also consider Alfandari and Piot (2004), p. 87; Schöpflin (2018a), p. 1246 et seq.

[147]See Bonfante (2014), p. 380 fn 84; Cardarelli (2008), p. 471.

[148]See Art. 2545 quinquies para. 2 CC, which is expressly referred to by Art. 2529 CC.

[149]There is no reduction in capital due to losses if the losses can be covered by reducing net assets instead of capital. In this case, reduction of nominal capital is not permitted. See Bonfante (2014), p. 383.

Loss of capital only occurs if all net assets other than capital have been used and it is not possible to reduce losses via other methods, for example by paying in capital or forgoing claims the cooperative has against its members. See Bonfante (2014), p. 384.

[150]If it has been decided to reduce capital due to losses, it is necessary to refer to Art. 2446 CC, not Art. 2445 CC. The latter contains provisions concerning voluntary reduction of capital, whereas Art. 2446 CC contains mandatory provisions. See also Bonfante (2014), p. 383 et seq.

[151]See Bonfante (2014), p. 382. Also consider Cusa (2010), p. 477 et seq.

[152]See Art. 2446 papa 2 CC.

[153]See Bonfante (2014), p. 384.

amendment to the statutory provisions. Sec. 33a *GenG* must be observed,[154] according to which the value can only be reduced within specific legal limits[155] and only after executing cancellation proceedings. Accordingly, the decisions made during the general meeting that deal with reducing shares must be relayed by the management organ to the commercial register of the commercial court. The court then must make the decision public and declare that the cooperative is ready to satisfy all creditors' claims that exist on the day of the court's announcement. It must also state that creditors who do not give notice to the cooperative within a three-month period are considered to have consented to the general meeting's decision. Then, the law states that known creditors must be addressed directly by the cooperative.[156] Known creditors are those whose credit results directly from the account books (or directly in any other way). The cancellation proceedings also refer to completely unknown creditors, although the law does not require a specific form of communication here. As a result, any suitable form should be admissible.[157]

After the application period expires, the application to amend the statutes within the commercial register must be made by all the members of the management organ. At the same time, the members of the relevant organ must confirm that all known creditors have been informed according to the required procedure and that creditors who have contacted the cooperative are satisfied. It must also be declared if other creditors have not spoken up within the deadline.[158] The resolution that reduces shares only takes legal effect[159] if it has been registered with the commercial court; this implies that members have a claim to payment of the amount of money by which the capital has been reduced.[160]

Must an Austrian SCE observe this provision or not? Art. 14 para. 6 SCE-R protects the interests of third parties with a direct legitimate interest in the case of "any transaction which affects the manner in which the capital is ascribed or allotted, or increased or reduced" and determines that these transactions shall not take effect (with respect to the SCE or third parties having a direct legitimate interest) until they are entered on the index referred to in para. 4. This interest is clearly given in the case of creditor protection. However, it could be argued that Sec. 33a *GenG* provides a mechanism that is not offered by Art. 14 SCE-R, inasmuch as it specifically protects unknown creditors. In fact, Sec. 33a *GenG* provides an enhanced protection mechanism that is assigned exclusively to unknown creditors and that requires registration

[154]See Astl and Steinböck (2014a), p. 145.

[155]Sec. 2 para. 3 GenG and Sec. 76 GenG.

[156]Sec. 33a para. 2 GenG.

[157]See Siebenbäck (2014), p. 382.

[158]Sec. 33a para. 2 GenG.

[159]See Sec. 9 para. 3 GenG.

[160]See Siebenbäck (2014), p. 382 et seq.; also consider Müller (2000), § 22. Sec. 33a para. 2 GenG also considers the situation in which the members of the management did not directly contact the creditors or the declaration that other creditors have not spoken up is wrong. In these two cases they are collectively liable for the sustained damage to the creditors.

with the commercial court, whereas Art. 14 SCE-R grants a legal effectiveness once the transaction that reduces capital is entered into the index at the SCE's registered office. I argue that this latter provision can be integrated because of Art. 8 para. 1 letter c (rather than Art. 11 SCE-R), as the SCE-R does not completely regulate this issue.

We conclude by recognising that a peculiar characteristic of the SCE-R results from the mixture of the features of variable capital[161] and fixed **capital**. Sec. 3.2 para. 1 PECOL states that cooperatives should be established without minimum capital unless the law or the statutes provide otherwise. In line with ICA cooperative principles, it should be possible to form a cooperative without share capital, which means that cooperatives can completely rely upon reserves generated due to specific asset restrictions.[162] I stress that generally, as an acknowledged principle, share capital in a cooperative is instrumental in nature, as it allows a cooperative to fulfil its objective, i.e., to conduct economic transactions with its members. However, Sec. 3.2 para. 1 PECOL also acknowledges that law or statutes may provide otherwise. In other words, statutes or the law may require that a cooperative be established with minimum capital,[163] thus accepting the SCE-R's solution. Specific rules concern the minimum number of shares to be subscribed[164] and the option to suspend repayment of shares if the minimum level of capital is reached. It is possible to differentiate between user and non-user members and therefore to set different minimum numbers of shares. Overall, Italian and Austrian *agricultural SCEs* must both apply a similar set of rules.

Determining the value of shares can be done by establishing a fixed value or by using a more dynamic approach. For example, in an *agricultural SCE* that conducts a cellar cooperative, the amount of capital shall be calculated on the basis of the area to be managed by the member. Here, the general meeting could determine the amount to be paid according to certain parameters (e.g., the sizes of area). If the areas are expanded during the course of membership, the share must be recalculated. This

[161]The PECOL define variable capital as an essential feature of cooperatives. Variability makes entry and exit of members easier and is in line with open and voluntary membership. Moreover, Sec. 3.2 para. 3 PECOL explicitly acknowledges that variability of capital implies that statutes must not be amended nor amendments be disclosed. It is highlighted that variability implies variation in the amount of capital (primarily through changes in membership), which implies that variations in the amount of the capital do not require amendments to the statutes, provided the level of capital exceeds the minimum set by the statutes. See Fajardo and Meira (2017), p. 74 et seq.

[162]See Sects. 3.2 and 3.4.1. The PECOL mention the UK legal system as an example. See Fajardo and Meira (2017), p. 75.

[163]In this context, Sec. 3.2 para. 2 PECOL determines that a cooperative's statutes may fix a minimum share capital. The PECOL refer to this obligation as principle of determination. See Fajardo and Meira (2017), p. 76. The PECOL acknowledge that going below the minimum capital threshold may be grounds for dissolving the cooperative. Sec. 3.2 para. 4 PECOL.

[164]Sec. 3.3 para. 4 PECOL also requires the maximum amount of shares held by members to be limited by statutes. Such a provision ensures that user members with high capital participation cannot determine the decisions of the cooperative. See Fajardo and Meira (2017), p. 81. It is not clear, however, why this should be a consequence of excessive participation. As argued above, the restrictions on voting rights limit the risk of excessive influence.

recalculation can also result in a corresponding increase in the surcharge that must be paid.

Next, the SCE-R allows both limited and unlimited **liability**[165]; basically, Italian and Austrian *agricultural SCEs* must both apply the same basic set of rules to liability. Sec. 3.5 para. 2 PECOL determines that, in general, members are only liable up to the amount of shares subscribed.[166] However, the statutes may determine liability by guarantee, although this is subject to a cap. The PECOL tend to limit liability, even though it acknowledges that liability may be extended beyond the subscribed capital.[167] The solutions offered by the PECOL and Austrian and Italian law are all similar, whereas the provisions of the SCE-R, by additionally allowing unlimited liability, are not completely covered by the PECOL.

Two aspects of the **shares** (to be understood as quotas rather than stock) that are determined by the SCE-R include shares issued for cash and in-kind contributions.[168] These issues are additionally regulated by national rules, in this case, those rules that determine the procedure by which to assess the value of in-kind contributions.

The analysis showed that it is possible to issue different classes of shares and also to apply a surcharge and set an accession fee. Sec. 3.3 para. 3 PECOL acknowledges that the law may allow the statutes to obligate new members to contribute more capital or a higher contribution than the minimum.[169] The PECOL provide different examples for how to apply this provision. For instance, the higher contribution can compensate for the depreciation over time of previous members' contributions. It is also possible to require an admission fee to help cover the costs of admitting the new member or to offset (at least in part) the contributions made by existing members to the cooperative's shared assets. The obligation to give a larger contribution is balanced by the phrase 'in a reasonable manner', which helps to maintain the principle of voluntary and open membership and to limit the barriers to entry for new members.[170] Neither the SCE-R nor the two national legal systems explicitly

---

[165]Interestingly, the SCE-R reintroduces unlimited liability into the Italian legal system.

[166]The PECOL stress that "legal personality" implies full patrimonial autonomy. In other words, a cooperative has its own assets which can be used to fulfil the cooperative's goal and respond to its creditors. See Fajardo and Meira (2017), p. 87.

[167]See Fajardo and Meira (2017), p. 88.

[168]Similarly, the PECOL require that contributions in kind must be paid in full, whereas contributions in cash can be paid in part at the time of subscription. See Fajardo and Meira (2017), p. 75. Sec. 3.2 para. 2 PECOL determines that the statutes may fix the nature of members' contributions. Contributions can be made either in cash or in kind, but it is not possible to contribute services because it is difficult to assess their economic value (in this context, the PECOL refer to Art. 4 para. 2 SCE-R). See Fajardo and Meira (2017), p. 75 et seq.

[169]Sec. 3.3 para. 2 PECOL determines as a general rule that members must contribute equally to the cooperative's capital. However (para 3), it is also possible to determine other criteria (by statutes), for example contributions in line with participation in transactions. Also consider Fajardo and Meira (2017), p. 79 et seq.

[170]See Fajardo and Meira (2017), p. 80.

provide such a clause.[171] However, as setting an accession fee is ultimately determined by the general meeting, this common-sense criterion should arguably be considered when the general meeting decides upon such a fee. Explicit references to law seem unnecessary.

The last issue pertained to **operations on capital**. Art. 14 para. 5 SCE-R requires that these transactions, which do not require an amendment of the statutes, be entered into the index of members; accordingly, the transactions take effect with respect to the *agricultural SCE* and third parties. We identified different means by which to increase capital[172]; yet, we also recognised that it is not possible to increase capital via dividends (patronage refunds). Both Austrian and Italian SCEs can apply similar sets of rules, although Italian SCEs that adopt the mainly mutual cooperative model must observe specific limitations (e.g., Art. 2514 CC). Moreover, we discussed some Italian provisions that can be used as examples of statutory provisions.

The SCE-R contains few provisions for reducing capital (e.g., by decreasing the value of the shares). Capital is automatically reduced when membership terminates. Finally, it can be reduced through a partial reduction in the shares. Both the provisions that deal with the minimum number of shares necessary to obtain membership and the provisions that determine minimum capital must be strictly observed. In addition to the provisions in the SCE-R, Austrian *agricultural SCEs* must consider Sec. 33a *GenG*, which addresses a special cancellation proceeding that protects unknown creditors, while Italian *agricultural SCEs* must consider which provisions to apply, depending on whether the reduction is greater or less than a third of the total.

5.3 The Allocation of Profits

Like cooperatives in general, SCEs must consider provisions that govern the allocation and distribution of the surplus, including those provisions that affect the parts of net assets known as reserves.[173] The essential norms in the SCE-R refer to legal

[171] However, the principle of non-discrimination applies. See Recital 10 bullet 6 SCE-R.

[172] The PECOL (Sec. 3.2 para. 3 and Sec. 3.3) acknowledge that capital can be either increased or reduced by new contributions made by existing members, by applying surplus or reserves, or through the allocation of losses. For an increase in capital, the PECOL outline various possibilities: new contributions from existing members, new members joining the cooperative, voluntary contributions from existing members, allocating refunds to share capital and converting available reserves into share capital. Reductions in capital mainly occur when exiting members are allocated capital or due to losses. Sec. 3.3 PECOL also deals with operations regarding capital, stating that the share value must be fixed by the statutes. Some legal systems offer the possibility to increase the value of shares using available reserves. This helps offset depreciation over time. The same is true for reducing the share value, which can be achieved by charging losses. See Fajardo and Meira (2017), p. 79 et seq.

[173] This concept is contained in the principles established by the ICA and in various national cooperative laws. See Henrÿ (2012), pp. 35 and 92; see also Sect. 2.1. Also consider Rocchi

reserves, to provisions about dividends (known as patronage refunds) and to norms that address the allocation of the available surplus. These provisions determine the topics covered in the following chapter. Since the two national systems address these issues differently, it seems appropriate to discuss all these issues together, first from the perspective of European law and then from the perspective of the two national legal systems.

According to recital no. 7, an SCE's net profits for the financial year must be distributed equally among the members. The statutes determine which criteria to apply here.[174] We must not only consider the different classes of shares,[175] but also the relevant provisions in the SCE-R and the mandatory national laws.[176] According to Art. 65 para. 2 subpara. 1 SCE-R,[177] the statutes must determine that the surplus must first be used to establish a **legal reserve fund**. As long as the legal reserve is below the minimum capital that is required by law, at least 15% of the surplus for the financial year—after deducting any losses carried over—must be allocated to the legal reserve.[178] The rest can be used for other purposes.[179] According to Art. 65 para. 3 SCE-R,[180] members leaving the SCE have no claim against the sums allocated to the legal reserves. This suggests that exiting members might have claim to other parts of the net assets.[181] This is only possible if the statutes do not prohibit the distribution of any surplus.[182] In addition, specific reserves can be funded for user members and non-user members, and other reserves may be funded as specific assets for holders of financial instruments.[183]

(2006), p. 103; Bonfante (2006), p. 6; Holthaus and Lehnhoff (2016), p. 51; Lehner (2009), p. 100 et seq.

[174]Art. 67 para. 2 SCE-R. Also consider Schöpflin (2018an).

[175]Art. 4 para. 1 subpara. 2 SCE-R.

[176]Art. 65 para. 1 SCE-R states: "Without prejudice to mandatory provisions of national laws, the statutes shall lay down rules for the allocation of the surplus for each financial year." Also consider Cusa (2004), p. 128 and Lutter et al. (2012), p. 1600.

[177]It states: "Where there is such a surplus, the statutes shall require the establishment of a legal reserve funded out of the surplus before any other allocation."

[178]See Art. 65 para. 2 subpara. 2 SCE-R. It states: "Until such time as the legal reserve is equal to the capital referred to in Article 3 (2), the amount allocated to it may not be less than 15% of the surplus for the financial year after deduction of any losses carried over."

[179]See Alfandari and Piot (2004), p. 87. Also consider Schöpflin (2018an); Cusa (2004), p. 154; Bianca and Zanardo (2016), p. 213 and Albamonte (2008), p. 313 et seq.

[180]It states: "Members leaving the SCE shall have no claim against the sums thus allocated to the legal reserve."

[181]See Rocchi (2006), p. 113.

[182]See Art. 67 para. 3 SCE-R.

[183]See Art. 64 para. 2 SCE-R. It states: "Holders of securities or debentures referred to in paragraph 1 may be given special advantages in accordance with the statutes or the conditions laid down when they are issued."

Also consider Rocchi (2006), p. 113.

The next issue is **dividends or patronage refunds**. Art. 66 SCE-R[184] determines that the statutes[185] may allow the option to pay a dividend—which is commonly referred to as a patronage refund or patronage dividend[186]—to the members in proportion to the business that they conduct with the SCE. Alternatively, dividends may be paid in proportion to the services that members have performed for the SCE. Customers or suppliers who are not members may not receive a dividend.[187] Moreover as the dividends must be paid in proportion to the business that was transacted or the services that were performed, non-user members naturally cannot be entitled to a dividend.[188]

The last issue regards the **allocation of profits**,[189] which Art. 67 SCE-R addresses by stating that the profits that are available for distribution are the balance of the surplus after deductions and additions.[190] Deductions include (1) the allocation to the legal reserve (because of Art. 65 paras. 2 and 3 SCE-R), (2) any sums paid out in dividends (because of Art. 66 SCE-R) and (3) any losses carried over.[191] The additions are (1) any surpluses carried over and (2) any sums drawn from the reserves.

The surplus is allocated by the general meeting according to the relevant statutes.[192] The SCE-R gives examples here: the surplus can be carried forward, appropriated to a legal or statutory reserve fund[193] or used as a return on paid-up capital and quasi-equity. I stress that quasi-equity, as described in Art. 67 para. 2 bullet 3 SCE-R, refers to additional equity, as determined by national law.[194] (Thus, quasi-equity does not refer to securities and debentures as determined by Art. 64 SCE-R, as these are loan capital.) Whether interest should be paid and how much it should be is determined by the statutes or, if there are no statutory provisions, by the single resolution about allocating the surplus.[195]

---

[184]It states: "The statutes may provide for the payment of a dividend to members in proportion to their business with the SCE, or the services they have performed for it."

[185]Consider in this context Cusa (2004), p. 157.

[186]See Sect. 5.2. Also consider Fici (2013), p. 145 and Cusa (2004), p. 136.

[187]If the SCE is a workers' cooperative, the refunds must be calculated according to the work performed by its members. See Alfandari and Piot (2004), p. 87. Also consider Cusa (2004), p. 136 et seq.

[188]See Schöpflin (2018an), p. 1335; Cusa (2004), p. 137. Also consider Chirico and Troianiello (2007), p. 71.

[189]For details Cusa (2004), p. 134.

[190]For details Cusa (2004), p. 129.

[191]See Cusa (2004), p. 134.

[192]See Alfandari and Piot (2004), p. 87; Iengo (2006).

[193]In addition to the legal reserve fund, surplus can be appropriated to any other reserve funds. See Schöpflin (2018an), p. 1336. Also consider Cusa (2004), pp. 154 and 162.

[194]Due to Art. 8 para. 1 letter c SCE-R. E.g., silent partnerships. Consider in this context for instance Sec. 10 para. 4 German banking law. See Schöpflin (2018an), p. 1336. Also consider Cusa (2004), p. 158.

[195]See Schöpflin (2018an), p. 1336. Also consider Cusa (2004), p. 157.

The SCE-R has been criticised for not specifying a limit to the amount of the surplus that will be returned to the members, even though the provisions seem to suggest that a maximum limit exists.[196] This might risk the adoption of evasive solutions, for example, by introducing a clause which sets a limit of 99.9%.[197] In any case, the general meeting decides. To reiterate, the members' basic interest is, first of all, dividends (patronage refunds).[198]

The SCE-R does not limit pay-outs to investor members. If the statutes do not provide otherwise, it does not seem possible to differentiate between the reimbursement given to user and non-user members.[199] One might also ask whether there is a limit to the ratio between user and non-user members' capital. This question is usually raised with respect to non-user members because of the fear that an inappropriate number of these members might weaken the mutuality of the cooperative.[200] The SCE-R does not seem to limit the capital that is paid up by non-user members, because the attribute of variable capital from Art. 1 para. 2 sent. 2 SCE-R refers to capital in general—and thus includes capital brought in by non-user members.

But, is it possible to limit the different types of capital by statutory provisions? Such a limit could prove crucial when allocating any surplus to members, because capital that is strongly based on the resources that are brought in by non-user members could harm the user members' dividend expectations.[201] In order to solve this dilemma, statutes can determine that non-user members may only be admitted if their financial resources help foster the conclusion of agreements with user-members 'to supply goods or services or to execute work of the kind the SCE carries out or commissions'.[202] Another solution is to priorities the dividends of user members over those of non-user members. Note that Art. 67 para. 3 SCE-R states that the statutes can prohibit any distribution of surpluses.[203] Therefore, there is no explicit mechanism to safeguard the interests of non-user members. The SCE-R relies upon statutory provisions and thus negotiation. Ultimately, the extent to which it is necessary to make membership attractive to non-user members will depend on

---

[196] In fact, Recital 10 bullet 4 states there should be limited interest on loans and share capital.

[197] See Rocchi (2006), p. 106. Also consider Albamonte (2008), p. 313 et seq. and Iengo (2006). One approach might be to link these rules to the mutuality clauses contained in Art. 2514 CC. This provides tax relief if the specific provisions regarding mainly mutual cooperatives are adopted. See Rocchi (2006), p. 106. Also consider Cusa (2004), pp. 144 and 164.

[198] See Cusa (2004), p. 155.

[199] See Rocchi (2006), p. 107 et seq. Also consider Cusa (2004), p. 131.

[200] One solution is to limit voting rights.

[201] See Rocchi (2006), p. 107 et seq. Rocchi proposes to determine a total nominal value of financial equilibrium, similar to that contained in Art. 64 para. 3 SCE-R referring to securities other than shares and the debentures conferring special advantages. Such a financial equilibrium would focus on the complete financial resources of the SCE and strive to make user member shares attractive. See Rocchi (2006), p. 108.

[202] See Art. 3 par 3 SCE-R. See also Art. 14 para. 2 SCE-R.

[203] See Cusa (2004), p. 140. Also consider Münkner (2006), p. 22.

the SCE's economic circumstances. The SCE-R allows significant freedom to draft the appropriate statutes for this situation.[204] This also applies to the holders of financial instruments, for whom the statutes may define certain financial and administrative rights. In theory, there is no limit on the remuneration of these instruments.[205]

Both national legal systems contain provisions that one must consider when discussing the allocation of profits, because they regulate details that need to be added to the provisions of the SCE-R. This is particularly true for the Italian legal system. The national solutions are then compared with those offered by the SCE-R, which helps us better grasp the latter's content.

The *Italian legal system* contains certain provisions. Accordingly, all cooperatives must assign at least 30% of their annual total profits to a legal reserve fund. This obligation must be observed regardless of the amount of the legal reserve. In other words, the reserves have no limit.[206] This compulsory contribution aims to counterbalance the limited relevance of the capital[207] as well as to promote the solidarity of the cooperatives and their function to reinforce the non-distribution constraint.[208]

Next, Art. 2545 quarter para. 2 CC obliges all cooperatives to allocate a percentage (currently 3%)[209] of total annual profits to mutual funds to promote and finance the development of new cooperatives in various areas.[210] According to Art. 11 law no. 59/1992, these funds must be established and headed by the representative organisations of the cooperative movement. An additional measure that strengthens solidarity among cooperatives can be found in the obligation to dissolve the residual assets to these funds in case of dissolution. This is an aspect that mainly mutual cooperatives have to address. These reserves cannot be allocated to members. The obligation to dissolve the residual assets to these funds is a feature of the so-called 'systemic mutuality'[211] and seeks to strengthen the social function of the cooperative movement.[212] So-called 'other cooperatives' may also apply such a provision, in which case they must declare (part of) their reserves as indivisible.[213] According to

[204] See Schöpflin (2018an), p. 1335 et seq. Also consider Cusa (2004), p. 156.

[205] See Schöpflin (2018al), p. 1332 et seq. Also consider Cusa (2004), pp. 135 and 160 et seq.

[206] See Art. 2545 quarter para. 1 CC. See Bonfante (2014), p. 370; Rocchi (2006), p. 103 et seq. Also consider Art. 32 and Art. 37 TUB.

[207] Due to its variability, capital in cooperatives cannot function like fixed capital in companies. See Sect. 5.2.

[208] See Bonfante (2014), p. 370; Petrelli (2005), p. 223; Lolli (2012), p. 161. See also Paolucci (2019h), p. 144 et seq.

[209] See Santagata (2014a), p. 441 and Art. 11 para. 4 law no. 59/1992. See also Paolucci (2019h), p. 144 et seq.

[210] E.g., through participation in the capital as founders. Also consider Bosi (2012), p. 79 et seq. and 141 et seq. Generally, Ragazzini (1992).

[211] See Sects. 3.2 and 3.4.1.

[212] See Fici and Strano (2010), p. 686; Genco (2003), p. 74; Bosi (2012), p. 58 et seq.

[213] Art. 2545 ter para. 1 CC.

the law, this indivisibility is irreversible.[214] Therefore, the reserves are bonded during and beyond the lifetime of the cooperatives.[215]

Italian SCEs may adopt the rules for mainly mutual cooperatives.[216] The Italian legislature has connected the limited profit-making aspect of this model to specific tax relief.[217] If an Italian SCE wants to adopt the mainly mutual model, it must abide by specific obligations[218] that result from the general normative framework that Italian cooperatives must observe. This implies that reserves must not have a limit, which contrasts with the provision in Art. 65 para. 2 subpara. 2 SCE-R,[219] whereas the concept of indivisibility aligns with Art. 75 SCE-R, which refers to the principle of disinterested distribution, to be applied if the SCE is liquidated. In addition, the even more stringent Art. 67 para. 3 SCE-R, also allows for the introduction of statutory provisions that fully prohibit any distribution of the available surplus.[220]

Similarly, if an Italian SCE does not adopt the mainly mutual structure, Art. 2545 quarter CC supplies the limits on constituting legal reserves.[221] Art. 2545 quarter para. 2 CC must be applied, as the SCE-R does not contain a similar provision.[222]

Italian law draws a clear distinction between dividends and patronage refunds (*ristorni*). Art. 2514 CC considers a dividend to be remuneration for invested capital. On the other hand, Art. 2545 sexies para. 1 CC, defines a patronage refund as an amount of money calculated in proportion to the quantity or quality of the transactions that each member conducts with the cooperative. Therefore, patronage refunds are considered to be a restitution made to members for buying goods and services from their cooperative or as remuneration for working for or providing goods or services to their cooperative. The statutes must contain the criteria to apply this provision.

---

[214]See Lolli (2012), p. 160. See also Paolucci (2019k), p. 144.

[215]See Bonfante (2004c), p. 2609. Also consider Miribung (2015b), p. 4 et seq. See also Paolucci (2019k), p. 144.

[216]See Sect. 3.4.1. Also consider Iengo (2006).

[217]See Lolli (2012), p. 160. For details Ingrosso (2013), p. 143 et seq. See also Paolucci (2019l), p. 45 et seq.

[218]See Art. 2514 para. 1 CC. The obligations are: mainly mutual cooperatives may not distribute dividends on the subscribed capital which exceed the maximum interest on postal bonds plus 2.5%; they may not remunerate the financial instruments subscribed by user members more than the maximum interest on postal bonds plus 4.5%; they must dissolve residual assets to mutual funds for the promotion and development of co-operation in case of dissolution; they may not allocate reserves to user-members.

[219]As already seen, the SCE-R offers a different solution. Also consider Iengo (2006). According to Art. 65 para. 2 subpara. 2 SCE-R, this amount may not be less than 15% of the surplus until the legal reserve has reached the minimum capital of €30,000.

[220]See Rocchi (2006), p. 103 et seq. Also consider Bonfante (2006), p. 8.

[221]Due to Art. 65 para. 1 SCE-R. Also consider Iengo (2006) and Chirico and Troianiello (2007), p. 69.

[222]National rules must be considered as requested by Art. 65 para. 1 SCE-R. See Chirico and Troianiello (2007), p. 70.

The law does not limit the distribution of profits as patronage refunds.[223] However, only profits that remain after the deduction of compulsory allocations are eligible for refund. This raises the question of how to determine refunds when cooperatives transact with non-members in addition to members. Should only those profits that stem from transactions with members be refunded or should all profits? Ministerial communication no. 53/E of 18 June 2002[224] states: 'cooperative refund, the restitution to members of part of the prize paid for goods and services or the extra remuneration for work and in general good and service provision by members, is possible only if the balance of the activity performed by the cooperative with its members is positive. What may be refunded is only the documented surplus from transactions with members and not from those with non-members'.[225] In practice, it is difficult to calculate patronage refunds and to prevent them from being used as an instrument to distribute surplus based on transactions with third parties, thus circumventing the legal reserve. As patronage refunds must be considered a debt that the cooperative owes its members, it follows that the surplus should be allocated to the legal reserve after the patronage refunds have been paid.[226]

Therefore, it seems that the Italian legal system clearly sets a hierarchy for allocating earnings. By contrast, Art. 67 para. 1 SCE-R ranks the various options for allocating profits differently; this provisions first considers legal reserves and then considers patronage refunds. However, as the SCE-R does not touch on accountancy rules, the ranking established by Art. 67 para. 1 SCE-R is not mandatory.[227] Finally, both the SCR as well as the Italian legal system only apply dividends/patronage refunds (*ristorni*) if the statutes provide accordingly.[228]

Next, we discuss the allocation of profits as regulated by Italian law. The law outlines two different obligations for allocating the remaining profits, depending on whether the cooperative is mainly mutual or not. Mainly mutual cooperatives must follow the obligations of Art. 2514 CC, which provide numerous restrictions on profit distribution. Accordingly, mainly mutual cooperatives (1) may not distribute dividends on the subscribed capital that exceed the maximum interest on postal bonds plus 2.5% and (2) may not remunerate the financial instruments (to which user members subscribe) more than the maximum interest on postal bonds plus 4.5%. To the contrary, the statutes of other cooperatives are only obliged to determine the specific methods for allocating the surplus among their members and the maximum

[223]As an exception, the law on worker cooperatives sets a limit of 30% of the salary. See Art. 3 para. 2 law No 142/2001.

[224]In dealing with the specific treatment of cooperative refunds.

[225]See Fici and Strano (2010), p. 687 fn 114.

[226]See Lolli (2012), p. 158. Also consider Genco (2003), p. 89 et seq. Different opinion Bonfante (2004b), p. 2627 et seq. In this context also consider Münkner (2006), p. 21 and Paolucci (2019j).

[227]See Iengo (2006).

[228]Iengo correctly observes that, according to Art. 66 SCE-R, statutes provide for the payment of patronage refunds, whereas, according to Italian law, this possibility is at the discretion of the general meeting. See Iengo (2006).

percentage of the profits that may be distributed to the members.[229] Apart from the obligation (as previously mentioned) to (a) assign 30%[230] to the legal reserve funds and (b) 3% to mutual funds, other cooperatives are not subject to the same non-distribution constraints as mainly mutual cooperatives.[231] Both obligations must be observed by an Italian SCE, assuming that it does not voluntarily use the mainly mutual cooperative model. Remember that Art. 2514 CC applies here.[232]

The remaining available surplus may then be distributed by the general meeting according to statutory provisions that specify how this distribution should occur. Art. 2545 quinquies para. 2 CC prohibits the distribution of surplus and divisible reserves if the ratio between net assets and the total debt is higher than 3:1. This condition specifically does not apply to holders of financial instruments.[233] This provision, which aims to prevent too much liquidity from being absorbed because of a distribution of profits,[234] must be applied by an Italian SCE because of Art. 65 para. 1 SCE-R.

Last, it has been observed that the statutes may prohibit any distribution at all. This may indirectly result from the statutes, for example, if they fully allocate the surplus to the cooperative as a self-financing tool. Further limitations may result from statutory provisions that determine an allocation to the legal reserve that is higher than that requested by law or that require allocation for different purposes, with the result that no surplus remains for dividends (term as determined by Italian law, not by Art. 66 SCE-R).[235] An Italian SCE can adopt similar statutory provisions.

As mentioned, the two legal systems deal with these issues discussed in this sub-chapter differently. While Italian law contains specific provisions, an *Austrian SCE* considers an approach that is based on law, doctrine and practical implications. The starting point in this debate is the fact that cooperatives must generate profits in order to survive economically. According to the Austrian legal system, profits must be achieved relative to counter transactions.[236] The same is true for ancillary

[229]See Art. 2545 quinquies para. 1 CC. Also consider Falcone (2003), p. 176; Bonfante (2004a) and Paolucci (2019i), p. 145 et seq.

[230]This limit of 30% is increased to 70% for credit cooperatives. See Art. 37 TUB. However, distributing the surplus by means of dividends cannot lead to a percentage which neglects the concept of mutuality in favour of a shareholder-driven approach. See Lolli (2012), p. 156. Also consider Ciccarelli (2000), p. 143.

[231]This mandatory destination to mutualistic funds can be considered a withdrawal in respect of the final devolution of the patrimony. See Lolli (2012), p. 155.

[232]See Albamonte (2008), p. 313 et seq.

[233]See Lolli (2012), p. 157. Because these have not been designed as an instrument to safeguard the mutualistic aim but rather as an instrument to protect the interests of creditors. See Lolli (2012), p. 156 et seq.; Paolucci (2019i), p. 146. Also consider Chiusoli (2003), p. 45. See also Paolucci (2019i), p. 145 et seq.

[234]See Rocchi (2006), p. 110.

[235]See Lolli (2012), p. 157. See also Paolucci (2019h).

[236]See Sect. 3.4.1, where the different types of transactions are explained.

transactions. These transactions must both be guided by economic efficiency and expediency.[237] However, restrictions can emerge for those transactions that fulfil the purpose of the cooperative. These transactions must have member benefits as their primary goal, not profits. But promoting members' needs does not exclude optimising profits, and not every advantage that results from the cooperative's activity needs to be transferred to the members. In order to foster the cooperative's economic sustainability, these purpose transactions[238] must cover costs, and their profits will stock the reserves and provide means for the internal financing of future investments.[239]

Aligned with Sec. 5 para. 1 no. 6 *GenG*, promotion is achieved via profit distribution. To comply with the cooperative's principles, this must occur via patronage refunds. Accordingly, the actual distribution of profits depends on the volume of the transactions that were carried out between each member and the cooperative. A purely capitalistic distribution of profits[240] is not permitted; however, it is possible to distribute profits via returns on subscribed capital in addition to patronage refunds.[241] Sec. 5 para. 1 no. 6 *GenG* states that the statutes must include the principles according to which the profit is calculated.[242] In addition, the statutes must contain a provision on the distribution of profits and losses amongst a cooperative's members.

The statutes can supply detailed provisions along with a simple provision that determine the competence of the general meeting, which can decide the distribution of profits and losses.[243] These provisions must also be applied to any surplus that remains after covering the cooperative's debts and refunding shares to members.[244] For instance, profits can be used as follows[245]: (1) allocation to reserves, (2) return on subscribed capital, (3) patronage refunds[246] or (4) profit carried forward. A combination of these different types of profit distribution is also possible.[247]

[237] See Sec. 1 para. 1 GenRevG. See Dellinger (2014a), p. 28; Nowotny (2008), nt 5/9.

[238] See Sect. 3.4.1.

[239] See Dellinger (2014a), p. 28 et seq.; Nowotny (2008), nt 5/9.

[240] Distribution of profits in relation to the shares subscribed.

[241] See Sec. 5 para. 1 No 6 GenG and especially Sec. 5a para. 2 No 1 referring to investing members. See Dellinger (2014a), p. 28 et seq.

[242] This is an accounting issue, which this study does not discuss further.

[243] See Astl and Steinböck (2014a), p. 146; Keinert (1988), p. 186.

[244] See Sec. 48 para. 1 no. 3 GenG.

[245] See Astl and Steinböck (2014a), p. 146; Zehetner (1999), p. 327. Also consider Keinert (1988), p. 184 et seq.; Kastner (1986), p. 142.

[246] For information about tax issues surrounding patronage refunds, see Maurer (2014), p. 97.

[247] See Astl and Steinböck (2014a), p. 146 et seq. If the principle of equality is observed, distribution of profits can be pursued by membership numbers as well as shares subscribed. See Kastner (1986), p. 142. According to Sec. 27a GenG, the management organ must put forward a proposal for appropriating profits, upon which the general meeting has to decide. However, the general meeting is not bound by this proposal. This decision taken by the general meeting confers a right to payment on the member. In addition, specific provisions are contained in the law referring to housing

However, statutory provisions that specify a fixed return on subscribed shares are prohibited. In practice, profits are allocated to reserves.[248] Finally, losses can be covered by using the existing reserve funds; alternatively, losses can be carried forward if they are expected to be covered by future profits. Losses can also be covered by reducing the value of individual members' shares.[249]

In general, the provisions of both the SCE-R and the Austrian legal system provide a high degree of statutory freedom over the allocation of profits. The major difference between these provisions is the obligation to allocate parts of the surplus to a legal reserve fund, which is mandatory for an Austrian SCE but not for an Austrian cooperative. Interestingly, the SCE-R explicitly states that the statutes may prohibit any distribution of the available surplus. Last, Austrian SCEs must be familiar with the concept of 'purpose transactions':[250] This is also true for analysing the applicable law on the distribution of profits.

To conclude, the SCE-R contains basic provisions regarding the allocation of profits; these provisions specifically concern the aspects **legal reserves**,[251] **dividends (patronage refunds)** and the **allocation of available surplus**[252] and must be observed by both Austrian and Italian SCEs.

Overall, Italian SCEs must consider more legal norms than Austrian *agricultural SCEs*, which are embedded in a fairly flexible legal framework. This difference stems from the fact that the Italian legal system recognises two types of cooperatives: mainly mutual cooperatives and other cooperatives. If an Italian SCE adopts the first model, it must observe the stringent provisions in Art. 2514 CC.[253] However, a slightly different situation arises for an Italian SCE that adopts the second model. Here, Italian SCEs must observe the provisions contained in Art. 2545 quarter para. 1 CC. However, Art. 2545 quarter para. 2 CC seems to apply, as the SCE-R does not contain a similar provision. Thus, no matter which type of cooperative they adopt, Italian SCEs must allocate 3% of annual net profits to mutual funds for the

cooperatives, especially Sec. 10 para. 1 WGG and Sec. 14 para. 1 No 3 WGG. See Astl and Steinböck (2014a), p. 147. Also consider Zehetner (1999), p. 327.

[248] With the distribution of profits being an exception. See Astl and Steinböck (2014a), p. 147; Kastner (1986), p. 142.

[249] See Astl and Steinböck (2014a), p. 147; Keinert (1988), p. 193 et seq.; Zahn (1963), p. 30.

[250] See Sect. 3.4.1.

[251] Sec. 3.4 para. 4 PECOL determines ways to establish legal reserves: via a percentage of net annual surplus (subject to a cap by law or statutes), via a percentage of net annual profits (as determined by statutes) or via a percentage of other resources (as determined by statutes).

[252] The PECOL (Sec. 3.6 para. 4) explicitly acknowledge the need to distribute surpluses only on the condition they are not needed to cover existing losses. This helps ensure the solvency of the cooperative. Also consider Sec. 3.7 PECOL.

[253] For example, for dividends (patronage refunds), Italian SCEs adopting the mainly mutual cooperative model must observe stringent provisions, as determined by the civil code. In this context, the Italian legal system defines patronage refunds as a debt owed to the members. It is argued that the list given by Art. 67 para. 1 SCE-R and the ranking contained therein cannot therefore be mandatory. This is a general observation and therefore applies to both types of cooperative.

promotion and development of co-operation. The Austrian legal system does not contain similar provision. In practice, no particular problems should arise for Austrian SCEs; they have substantial statutory freedom to determine the provisions for allocating the profits. However, I emphasise that Austrian SCEs must be familiar with the different types of transactions that are defined by law and doctrine.

There may be problems with determining the exact calculation of profits to be achieved via purpose transactions in advance, e.g. before the end of the financial year.[254] Nevertheless, the statutes of an *agricultural SCE* may specify that payment is to be made in the form of payments on account (leaving it to the administrative organ or management organ to fix the dates for payment and to decide the amount of each payment on the basis of the available funds). This allows farmers to cover their own running costs (including the cost of living) without financing them with borrowed capital. The remaining payment and final settlement can then be made after the annual balance sheet has been drawn up at the end of the financial year. This means that, in the course of preparing the balance sheet, the administrative organ or management organ determines the final payment price for the products that are delivered by the members during the course of the financial year and then submits this price to the general meeting during the course of approving the balance sheet so that the SCE's members can decide on it.

The analyses have focussed on some provisions that could be amended in light of the PECOL. First, both the SCE-R and PECOL do not require allocations to legal reserves without limits, i.e., allocations are made until a certain percentage (as defined by law) has been met. In this regard, the Italian legal system is stricter[255]; accordingly, an amendment to the corresponding Italian provision can be considered. Second, the dividends (patronage refunds) may not be allocated via shares, according to the SCE-R. This contradicts the PECOL,[256] which explicitly permit different means of distributing refunds: cash, shares or other financial instruments. It thus seems advisable to amend the SCE-R.

Art. 67 SCE-R deals with the allocation of the available surplus and allows it to be distributed after the allocation to the legal reserve is deducted, any sums are paid out in dividends and any losses are carried over.[257] This final sum is then augmented by the surplus that is carried over and any sums that are drawn from the reserves. The resulting sum can be allocated as the statutes allow. In this regard, the SCE-R mentions three examples: carrying the surplus forward, appropriating it to other

[254]The PECOL explicitly refer to difficulties in determining the amount of patronage refunds, as it is only possible to receive goods or services at near cost at the end of the financial year. Hence, prices charged for goods or services or paid for goods or services are only provisional. See Fajardo and Meira (2017), p. 89 et seq.

[255]See Fajardo and Meira (2017), p. 85.

[256]See Sec. 3.6 para. 3 letter a PECOL.

[257]The PECOL (Sec. 3.6 para. 4) explicitly acknowledge the need to distribute surpluses only on the condition they are not needed to cover existing losses. This helps ensure the solvency of the cooperative. Also consider Sec. 3.7 PECOL.

reserve funds or using it as a return on paid-up capital and quasi-equity.[258] The statutes set the order and the proportions that must be considered when allocating a surplus. In other words, the statutes can determine the allocation of the available surplus. In my analysis, I argued that the statutes may provide clauses to protect the interests of user members with respect to their dividends (patronage refunds).[259] With respect to interest due on paid-up capital, Sec. 3.3 para. 5 PECOL acknowledges that statutes may allow this method for the allocation of profits. It adds that the interest rate may differ according to the nature of the contribution and of the category of members providing it. However, this rate must be 'reasonable', suggesting an amount of money sufficient to obtain and retain capital to operate the business.[260] Similarly, the SCE-R allows safeguards to be implemented to protect the interest of user members.

5.4 Financial Entitlements During Resignation or Expulsion

Art. 15 and Art. 16 SCE-R both contain provisions on resignation and expulsion. Art. 15 SCE-R lists the valid grounds for losing membership.[261] These are only the minimum requirements; SCEs have the statutory freedom to determine when membership must be revoked.[262] The right to resign can be limited in accordance with the object of the SCE. In fact, the resignation of certain members—for example, those holding specific possessions—could be unfavourable. As the SCE-R does not contain measures to mitigate such unfavourable effects, the right to resign may be limited via a statutory provision. Obviously, the complete exclusion of this right is prohibited.[263]

Art. 15 para. 1 bullet 2 SCE-R governs the option to expel a member of an SCE. Accordingly, a member can be expelled if they commit a serious breach of their

[258]See Sec. 3.6 para. 3 letters a and b and para. 4 PECOL.

[259]See Art. 14 para. 2 SCE-R.

[260]See Fajardo and Meira (2017), p. 80.

[261]These are: (a) for all members: upon resignation, expulsion, transfer of all shares (where authorised by the statutes; see Art. 15 para. 1 bullet 3 SCE-R.), bankruptcy and in any other situation provided for in the relevant national legislation. (b) for natural persons only: upon death, and (c) for legal persons only: upon winding up. Art. 15 para. 1 last bullet SCE-R. Also consider Schöpflin (2018c), p. 1273 et seq. and Korte (2012), p. 335 et seq. Also See Alfandari and Piot (2004), p. 88.

[262]Art. 16 para. 3 sent. 1 SCE-R determines that the statutes of an SCE must lay out the procedures and conditions for members to exercise their right to resign. It aims to protect members' right to resign and right to repayment. The resulting provisions must be determined autonomously, however, not without limits. See Rocchi (2006), p. 112 et seq. Also consider Galletti (2006), p. 56 et seq.

[263]See Alfandari and Piot (2004), p. 89. Also consider Schöpflin (2018d), p. 1276 et seq.

obligations or perform an act that is contrary to the interests of the SCE.[264] Such a serious breach may include a breach of important obligations whose content is determined by the statutes, on the condition that immediate expulsion is justified in light of the severity of the breach.[265] A common example of such an action that is contrary to the interests of the SCE would be the betrayal of commercial secrets.[266] The specific obligations in the case of an agricultural cooperative recognised as a PO should also be mentioned here.[267]

Moreover, Art. 16 SCE-R[268] contains provisions that govern the members' financial entitlements, which must be observed in the event of resignation or expulsion. First, para. 1 states that resignation entitles members to the repayment of their part of the subscribed capital. However, this subscribed capital may be reduced in proportion to any losses charged against the SCE's capital. Note that members are entitled to the repayment of their subscribed capital no matter what the reason is for the loss of membership.[269] The calculations must be determined according to the balance sheet for the financial year in which the entitlement to repayment arose.[270]

While the SCE is still running, the resigning members are not entitled to payment of legal reserves.[271] A resigning member may not require that losses shall be covered by legal or other reserves. One might wonder whether the resigning member is

[264]On expulsion, membership is completely terminated. Partial expulsion is not possible. See Schöpflin (2018c), p. 1273 et seq.

[265]Para 3 deals with the expulsion procedure. Accordingly, the decision on expulsion must be taken by the management or administrative organ after the member has been heard. The provisions also provide for the possibility to appeal against this decision to the general meeting. The expulsion decision must be communicated immediately. However, the SCE-R does not stipulate a specific form of communication. See Schöpflin (2018c), p. 1273 et seq. Also consider Alfandari and Piot (2004), p. 90. Every excluded member has the right to appeal to the ordinary judiciary. Expelled members have the same financial entitlements as resigning members. See Alfandari and Piot (2004), p. 90; Schöpflin (2018c), p. 1273 et seq.

[266]See Schöpflin (2018c), p. 1273 et seq. Also consider Alfandari and Piot (2004), p. 90 and Korte (2012), p. 336.

[267]See, for example, Art. 153 para. 2 letters b and d Reg. 1308/2013. See also Sect. 3.3.4.

[268]It states: "Financial entitlements of members in the event of resignation or expulsion: (1). Except where shares are transferred and subject to Article 3, loss of membership shall entitle the member to repayment of his/her part of the subscribed capital, reduced in proportion to any losses charged against the SCE's capital. (2). The amounts deducted under paragraph 1 shall be calculated by reference to the balance sheet for the financial year in which the entitlement to repayment arose. (3). The statutes shall lay down the procedures and conditions for exercising the right to resign and lay down the time within which repayment shall be made, which may not exceed three years. In any event, the SCE shall not be obliged to make the repayment less than six months after approval of the balance sheet issued following the loss of membership."

[269]See Schöpflin (2018d), p. 1276 et seq. This entitlement cannot be restricted by statutes nor by a decision taken by the general meeting. See Schöpflin (2018d), p. 1276 et seq. Generally, Rocchi (2006), p. 111 et seq.; Alfandari and Piot (2004), p. 89 et seq.

[270]Art. 16 para. 2 SCE-R.

[271]See Sect. 5.3.

entitled to other statutory reserves that were created for the benefit of resigning members or whether surcharge can be repaid.[272] Art. 16 SCE-R does not consider these possibilities and only refers to the capital subscribed to by the member. In this regard, recital 15 determines that references to capital only entail the subscribed capital and not undistributed equity capital. On the other hand, Art. 65 para. 3 SCE states that members leaving the SCE have no claim against the sums that are allocated to the legal reserves.[273] This suggests that exiting members might be entitled to other statutory reserves. In fact, Art. 67 para. 2 bullet 2 SCE-R allows statutes to create reserve funds, although, naturally, this is only possible if the statutes do not prohibit any distribution of the surplus.[274] Such reserves could be created for user or non-user members and may also be funded as assets for the holders of financial instruments.[275] Similar arguments should be valid with respect to the repayment of the surcharge. It is necessary for national law to allow such a solution.

According to Art. 16 para. 1 SCE-R, reference must be made to Art. 3 SCE-R, which considers the possibility that the minimum capital threshold prescribed by the SCE-R[276] may be crossed because of liquidation. As already mentioned,[277] this reference must be interpreted as a temporary suspension of the eligibility of the claim and not as a possibility of expulsion without repayment of the subscribed capital.[278]

The statutes must specify the time within which repayments must be made, which timeframe cannot exceed 3 years.[279] More precisely, the regulation states that an SCE is not obliged to make a repayment less than six months after the approval of the balance sheet that was issued following the loss of membership.[280] The SCE-R does not contain a provision that governs a period of notice for resignations. This period must be determined via the statutes.[281]

Finally, these provisions must be applied even if only a portion of a member's shareholdings must be repaid.[282] Unlike the case of full repayment, partial repayment does not lead to a loss of membership. Members can therefore bring their

272 Consider in this context Alfandari and Piot (2004), p. 90. Critically, Genco (2006), p. 126.

273 See Rocchi (2006), p. 113.

274 See Art. 67 para. 3 SCE-R.

275 See Art. 64 SCE-R and especially para. 2. Also consider Rocchi (2006), p. 113. Generally, Alfandari and Piot (2004), p. 90; Schöpflin (2018d), p. 1276 et seq. Cusa (2004), pp. 154 and 162 and Chirico and Troianiello (2007), p. 68 et seq. Also consider Sect. 5.3.

276 At least € 30,000.

277 See Sect. 5.2.

278 Indeed, the open door mechanism is suspended in such a case. See Rocchi (2006), p. 112.

279 Provision favouring members.

280 Provision favouring the cooperative. See Art. 16 para. 3 SCE-R. Also consider Alfandari and Piot (2004), p. 90; Schöpflin (2018d), p. 1276 et seq. and Galletti (2006), p. 62.

281 According to Art. 16 para. 3 SCE-R, "statutes shall lay down the procedures and conditions for exercising the right to resign . . ." Also consider Schöpflin (2018c), p. 1273 et seq.

282 Art. 16 para. 4 SCE-R.

amount of shares in line with the proportion of the business that is conducted with the SCE.[283]

But what are the national approaches to these issues? According to *Italian law*, different provisions must be considered for financial entitlements in case of resignation or expulsion.[284] Art. 2535 CC determines that the liquidation of shares or quotas must be based on the balance sheet from the financial year in which the resignation was filed.[285] Repayment must occur within 180 days of the approval of the balance sheet. The liquidation criteria must be determined by the statutes, including the amount to be repaid.[286] Non-profitability criteria must be observed.[287] However, in the case of a mainly mutual cooperative, this statutory freedom is limited by legal provisions.[288]

According to Art. 2535 para. 2 CC, repayment also includes any surcharge paid, on the condition that (1) the statutes do not provide otherwise, (2) it is part of the cooperative's assets and (3) it has not been allocated to free increase of capital.[289] This provision considers the member as both a user-member and a non-user member who should be reimbursed the amount he or she would have obtained by transferring his shares.[290] It is also possible to assign divisible reserves. These may be assigned by transferable financial instruments, on the condition that the statutes do not provide otherwise. This allocation is obligatory if the relation between the net assets and the overall indebtedness of the cooperative is less than 3:1.[291] Finally, statutory provisions may allow for repayment in instalments based on the values that are assigned

[283]See Alfandari and Piot (2004), p. 90. Also consider Schöpflin (2018d), p. 1276 et seq.; Galletti (2006), p. 60 et seq. and Chirico and Troianiello (2007), p. 40.

[284]Art 2532 para. 3 CC determines that the corporate relationship is terminated once resignation has been approved, whereas the relationship based on mutual exchange ends with the current financial year, provided the request has been communicated at the latest 3 months before the end of the financial year. Otherwise it finishes with the subsequent financial year. For details Paolucci (2012a), p. 113 et seq. See also Paolucci (2019f), p. 104 et seq. According to Art. 2536 CC, loss of membership does not automatically entail loss of liability. In fact, former members are still liable for non-paid up shares. This liability stops a year after termination of membership.

[285]If the resigning member believes the balance sheet to be falsified or inaccurate, they may contest the irregularity, even if the balance sheet has already been approved. See Paolucci (2012a), p. 123.

[286]See Art. 2525 para. 2 and para. 3 CC.

[287]See Giorgi (2018b), p. 3232; Galletti (2005), p. 2775; Schirò (2008b), p. 144. See also Paolucci (2019g), p. 115 et seq. and Santagata (2017), p. 830.

[288]See Art. 2514 CC. It is acknowledged that shares can only be redeemed at their nominal value. See Giorgi (2018b), p. 3232. Furthermore, reserves cannot be distributed. See also Santagata (2017), p. 830.

[289]According to Art. 2545 quinquies para. 3 CC.

[290]See Paolucci (2012a), p. 123.

[291]See Art. 2545 quinquies para. 4 CC. On this issue, also consider Giorgi (2018c), p. 3246 et seq.; Santosuosso (2003), p. 283; Ceccherini (2008), p. 204 et seq.; Stasio (2007), p. 420 et seq. See also Paolucci (2019i), p. 145 et seq. See also Santagata (2017), p. 837.

to the members because of Art. 2545 quinquies CC and Art. 2545 sexies CC.[292] Repayment in instalments should help curb liquidity outflow.[293]

As mentioned, the SCE-R contains a gap that national law can close. Therefore, not only the distribution of divisible reserves seems possible, but also the repayment of surcharges. Then, if an Italian SCE applies the mainly mutual cooperative model, the rather strict provisions determined for this type of cooperative must be observed. Finally, there are differences in repayment periods between the Italian provisions and those contained in the SCE-R. The wording of Art. 16 para. 3 SCE-R seems to permit repayment in instalments, as it merely states that repayment must be made within a specific period. This does not necessarily suggest that repayment must occur immediately. Indeed, the definition of a repayment period arguably makes repayment in instalments feasible.

The *Austrian legal system* determines, as a general rule, that resigning members lose all rights and can claim their subscribed capital only to the extent determined by Sec. 55 para. 3 *GenG*. This provision refers to cooperatives with unlimited liability, while Sec. 79 *GenG* provides a similar provision for cooperatives with limited liability. The main difference between these two provisions is that, in the latter case, a vesting period must be observed.

Accordingly, members are not entitled to the cooperative's reserve funds or other existing assets. Neither are they entitled to hidden assets. However, the statutes may provide otherwise, including a quota entitlement to the cooperative's capital or participation in the assets.[294] As mentioned, an Austrian SCE can repay surcharges or establish specific funds for resigning members. When Art. 65 para. 3 SCE-R is observed, other assets should be repayable. If the general rule applies,[295] former members are only entitled to claim their capital share redeemed one month after the approval of the accounts statement. The provision does not apply if the dissolution of the cooperative has been resolved or enacted.[296]

---

[292] Art. 2535 para. 3 CC.

[293] See Paolucci (2012a), p. 123. See also Paolucci (2019g), p. 118.

[294] See Zahn (1963), p. 94 et seq.; Dellinger and Steinböck (2014), p. 461; Kastner (1986), p. 142. Similarly, Sec. 79 para. 2 GenG determines that a resigned member is not entitled to reserve funds or any of the cooperative's other existing assets. However, the statutes may provide otherwise. In case of doubts, members are only entitled to claim that the cooperative share must be paid out after expiry of the vesting period determined by Sec. para. 1 GenG. See Dellinger (2014d), p. 499. Consider the limitations determined by Sec. 5a para. 2 GenG and Sec. 79 GenG. Also consider Sec. 10 para. 2 WGG.

[295] Sec. 55 para. 3 GenG.

[296] See Dellinger and Steinböck (2014), p. 461 et seq. This refers to the capital share shown by the statement of accounts for the year in which the member resigns. This provision cannot be amended by statutory provisions. In general, the cooperative share is set by the nominal value of the quota. The credit balance due to the resigning member must contain profits, even if not paid out yet, and any losses must be deducted. The claim to the credit balance cannot be restricted by statutes. If there are doubts (in other words no statutory provision explicitly deals with this issue), the term "cooperative share", as contained in Sec. 79 para. 1 GenG, does not entail any kind of surcharge or application fee. See Dellinger (2014d), p. 499 et seq. The limitation on the claim to the

During the vesting period implemented by Sec. 79 para. 1 *GenG*, the resigning member's share of the cooperative and any remaining credit that they have because of their membership may only be paid out 1 year after the end of the financial year in which the member resigned. This vesting period, which is mandatory, prevents the cooperative's assets from being undermined. This period applies irrespective of whether creditors are at risk or not.[297] Statutes may set a later starting point or extend the length of the vesting period.[298] The SCE-R defines a period within which repayment must be made, irrespective of whether the SCE has unlimited or limited liability.

To summarise, the third issue pertaining to cooperative finance is the financial entitlements of members who leave or are expelled from the cooperative. In principle, both national *(agricultural) SCEs* must apply similar provisions, because the SCE-R contains provisions that refer to the amount of money that is repayable, to the obligation to suspend entitlements if the minimum capital threshold is reached and to the redemption period. In this regard, Sec. 3.3 para. 7 PECOL subjects reimbursement to reasonable conditions, for example, to notice periods for members who wish to exit or to deferred redemption.[299]

I found that it is possible to create specific reserves (called revenue reserves) that may benefit members if they resign. These type of reserves can be created for both user and non-user members.[300] The analysis conducted for Italian SCEs suggests that SCEs in general can allow repayment in instalments. A different set of rules applies for Italian *agricultural SCEs* that adopt the mainly mutual model, which must observe stringent provisions.

5.5 Financial Entitlements During Dissolution

If an SCE is dissolved, Art. 75 SCE-R[301] states that the residual assets (net assets) must be distributed in accordance with the **principle of disinterested distribution**. The residual assets are those assets that remain after paying all amounts to creditors

cooperative share is also referred to as a cooperative's privilege of capital formation. See Dellinger (2014d), p. 500, Keinert (1988), p. 45.

[297] In case of bankrupty, the members participate in distributing the proceeds of liquidation. In case of insolvency, consider Sec. 3 GenIG and Sec. 1 para. 2 GenIG.

[298] See Dellinger (2014d), p. 496 et seq.; Kastner (1986), p. 202; different opinion Keinert (1988), p. 312 et seq. According to Sec. 80 GenG, the provisions contained in Sec. 78 GenG and Sec. 79 GenG also apply to the cancellation of individual cooperative shares, without resignation (consider Sec. 77 para. 2 GenG).

[299] See Fajardo and Meira (2017), p. 82.

[300] Also consider Sec. 3.3 para. 7 PECOL.

[301] It states: "Net assets shall be distributed in accordance with the principle of disinterested distribution, or, where permitted by the law of the Member State in which the SCE has its registered office, in accordance with an alternative arrangement set out in the statutes of the SCE. For the

and reimbursing members' capital contributions. According to recital 10, the principle of disinterested distribution requires that residual assets be transferred to another cooperative body that pursues similar aims or general interest purposes. However, the statutes may allow an alternative arrangement, provided that the law of the state of registration offers such an option.[302] Hence, one might ask whether user and non-user members have additional financial entitlements beyond the repayment of subscribed capital.[303] As will be seen, the two legal systems analysed here apply different approaches that must be considered because of the reference to national law in Art. 75 SCE-R.

As highlighted several times during the course of this study, *Italian cooperative theory* does not just consider the promotion of members' needs[304]; it also allows for a mutuality that directly relates to public utility. This second aspect[305] of mutuality clearly derives from Art. 2514 CC, which states that if a mainly mutual cooperative dissolves, the full residual assets that remain after capital and dividends have been deducted must be allocated to mutual funds.[306]

For so-called 'other cooperatives', i.e., those that are not mainly mutual, in principle, the exemption in Art. 75 SCE-R can be connected to Art. 2545 ter CC.[307] This suggests that the statute of other cooperatives must contain a provision that defines indivisible reserves to make disinterested distribution possible. However, this principle is limited to these specific, indivisible reserves. As a result, only an Italian SCE structured as other cooperative can adopt a statutory provision that limits the application of this disinterested distribution, or that completely prevents the application of this principle by the failure to adopt a provision, with the result that any remaining surplus be distributed among the members.[308]

Finally, I provide some remarks on transforming a cooperative that communicate certain features of dissolution and consider the principle of disinterested distribution. According to Art. 2545 decies CC, only other cooperatives can be converted into a company or other form of enterprise. As a result, a mainly mutual cooperative must first divest itself of the feature of being mainly mutual, either by simply modifying

---

purposes of this Article, net assets shall comprise residual assets after payment of all amounts due to creditors and reimbursement of members' capital contributions."

[302]Generally, Alfandari and Piot (2004), p. 87 et seq.; Schöpflin (2018ap), p. 1342 et seq.; Albamonte (2008), p. 314.

[303]See Rocchi (2006), p. 114.

[304]Internal mutuality. See Sect. 3.2.

[305]In this regard, see Sect. 3.2.

[306]External or systemic mutuality. This second aspect of mutuality highlights that the cooperative advantage is not limited to members; it benefits the entire cooperative movement. This second concept is definitely rather general in nature. See Paolucci (2012b), p. 9 et seq.; Bosi (2012), p. 58 et seq.; Tatarano (2011), p. 62 et seq.; Bonfante (2014), p. 149 et seq. See also Paolucci (2019a), p. 33 et seq.

[307]Art. 2545 ter CC contains provisions regarding indivisible reserves.

[308]See Rocchi (2006), p. 113 et seq. Also consider Iengo (2006) and Chirico and Troianiello (2007), p. 76. In general, Marasà (2013), p. 858. See also Santagata (2017), p. 836.

the statutes or by no longer meeting specific features that characterise a mainly mutual cooperative.[309] Consequently, all net assets must be appropriated to indivisible reserves. If a other cooperative wants to convert into another company, it must devolve its assets to mutual funds, with the option to subtract only the paid-up capital and any additional amount necessary to meet the minimum capital requirements for the company into which the cooperative is converted.[310] While such a conversion is possible from a legal perspective, the provision that regulates the conversion strongly discourages it.[311] These provisions must be applied to an Italian SCE because of Art. 72 SCE-R.

According to Sec. 48 of the *Austrian GenG*,[312] if the cooperative is dissolved, the members are entitled to be paid out the cooperative shares (after the creditors are satisfied). Then, any surplus that remains after settling debts and repaying cooperative shares[313] must be distributed among the members according to the provisions that govern the distribution of profits.[314] For instance, the statutes may determine that profits must be used for cooperative aims. As a result, this provision also must apply to the remaining surplus, which is quite common in practice.[315]

Next, if the liability of the cooperative is limited, the vesting period contained in Sec. 81 para. 1 *GenG*[316] must be considered. The law does not provide such a period for cooperatives with unlimited liability. Then, Sec. 83 *GenG* refers to any further credit appertaining to a cooperative member because of their relationship with the cooperative: Such credits rarely exist in practice because members normally withdraw profits when they are distributed and not allocated to the reserves.[317] The remaining surplus, as determined by Sec. 48 para. 1 no. 3 *GenG*, may be distributed

[309]See Art. 2514 CC and Art. 2545 octies CC.

[310]Art. 2545 undecies CC states that if an other cooperative is transformed into a capitalistic company, its assets must be allocated to mutual funds for the promotion and development of co-operation, after deducting the (re-evaluated) capital subscribed and any dividends not yet distributed. The law only permits increasing the amount of money required up to the limit necessary to found the new company. Consider in this context Racugno (2006), p. 321.

[311]See Paciello (2007b), p. 489 et seq.; Maltoni (2014), p. 536 et seq. See also Santagata (2017), p. 840 et seq.

[312]See Sec. 81 para. 1 GenG.

[313]See Sec. 48 para. 1 No 2 GenG states: After satisfaction of creditors, surplus shall be used to redeem the amounts paid on the cooperative shares. If the stock does not suffice for full redemption, the remaining sum shall be financially contributed in proportion to the amount of each credit, unless otherwise provided in the statutes.

[314]See Sec. 48 para. 1 No 3 GenG and Sec. 5 para. 1 No 6 GenG. Also consider in this context Sect. 5.3.

[315]See Dellinger (2014c), p. 429; Keinert (1988), p. 217; Kastner (1986), p. 201; see also Sec. 11 para. 1 WGG.

[316]According to Sec. 81 GenG, the redemption of paid-in cooperative shares (as well as the distribution of surplus to members) may not take place before a year has elapsed, counted from the day on which the third announcement was made.

[317]See Dellinger (2014c), p. 428 et seq.

among the members of an Austrian SCE.[318] As the SCE-R explicitly refers to an arrangement permitted by national law, the vesting period must apply to limited liability Austrian SCEs; otherwise distributing the surplus would not be permitted according to Austrian law.

Thus, the principle of disinterested distribution must be considered when a cooperative is dissolved. Art. 75 SCE-R provides a general rule that aligns with the PECOL,[319] which rule requires the residual assets to be distributed in accordance with the principle of disinterested distribution,[320] while alternative arrangements can be adopted if national law allows. Austrian law allows statutory freedom, with the consequence that any remaining surplus can be paid out to members.[321] Austrian *agricultural SCEs* with limited liability must also observe the vesting period that is determined by Sec. 81 para. 1 *GenG*.

Under Italian law, one must first consider whether the SCE is a mainly mutual cooperative or not. My analysis showed that, once again, an Italian agricultural SCE that is formed as a mainly mutual cooperative is rather limited, whereas an Italian SCE that is formed as other cooperative can adopt solutions that are similar to those in an Austrian *agricultural SCE*, which gives them a wide range of statutory freedom during dissolution.[322] Thus, Austrian SCEs, and Italian SCEs formed as 'other cooperatives', may both distribute legal reserves during dissolution. This contrasts with Sec. 3.4 para. 3 PECOL, which determines that the legal reserves are indivisible,[323] which suggests that these reserves cannot be distributed to members, even after dissolution. This indivisibility of reserves should help to increase creditworthiness and avoid speculative winding up (in order to share the assets that were generated by previous members). Indivisible reserves create a kind of common property that grants solidarity across generations.[324] Accepting the PECOL as an

[318]User members and non-user members.

[319]This is in line with Sec. 3.8 para. 1 PECOL, which determines that when a cooperative is liquidated, members are only entitled to receive the nominal value of shares and their portion of divisible reserves (on the condition the statutes provide accordingly). In addition, Sec. 3.8 para. 2 PECOL explicitly states that residual net assets must be distributed in line with the principle of disinterested distribution, i.e., distributed to the community or other associated cooperatives. Also consider Fajardo and Meira (2017), p. 94. Consider in this context principle number 3 ICA.

[320]This implies that assets must be transferred to another cooperative body pursuing similar aims or general interest purposes.

[321]Deducting the subscribed capital. Debts must also be covered.

[322]Specific provisions must be considered when a cooperative transforms into a company. In this case, the principle of disinterested distribution must be strictly applied. On this issue, see Consiglio nazionale del notariato. (2006).

[323]The same is true for reserves for education, training and information. According to Sec. 3.4 para. 8 PECOL, the "reserve for cooperative education, training and information is used for the technical and cultural education and training of members, members of the organs, managers and employees of the cooperative, and the provision of information about cooperatives to the general public."

[324]See Fajardo and Meira (2017), p. 84. For this reason, legal reserves cannot be used to increase share capital, as this would the violate principle of disinterested distribution upon winding up. Reserves cannot be incorporated using reserves whose funding includes results of

instrument that outlines the key features of a cooperative, the SCE-R should be amended to exclusively allow disinterested distribution.

5.6 The Economic Perspective

From an economic point of view, specific issues need to be addressed in the context of the financial structure of an SCE. These are limited capital, the variability of capital, the concept of disinterested distribution and problems that arise if a member leaves the cooperative.

Though limited liability is a successful model, the SCE-R goes beyond this by allowing unlimited liability as Austrian law does.[325] This contrasts with Italian law, which abolished unlimited liability some time ago. Limited liability provides an incentive for investors to invest a limited amount of their own assets, without becoming liable for all their assets. This is especially necessary for public limited-liability companies that are refinanced via the open capital market.[326] In the latter case, investors may be less influential than in an SCE, particularly as cooperatives often appoint members to the decision-making bodies.[327]

Limited liability is linked to the transferability of shares and protection from liquidation. Protection from liquidation means that shareholders cannot withdraw their shares of the firm's assets at will. If they could, a corporation would be forced to liquidate. Nor can personal creditors (shareholders' creditors) foreclose on the shares of the firm's assets.[328] Conversely, limited liability shields the owners (i.e., the shareholders) and their assets from the corporation's creditors.[329] As a result, the creditworthiness of the corporation does not depend on the creditworthiness of the shareholders. If it did, it would be very difficult to determine the value of the

non-member transactions and results from ownership of company shares or other assets. If this was allowed, user members would either end up with more shares or the same shares with higher nominal value. See Fajardo and Meira (2017), p. 85 et seq. Profits resulting from these non-member transactions must be allocated to indivisible reserves. Consider Sec. 1.5 para. 4 and Sec. 1.5 para. 2 PECOL.

[325]In addition to limited liability.

[326]See Fleischer (2000), p. 16 et seq. Also consider Schäfer and Ott (2012), p. 715 et seq.

[327]However, this does not provide grounds to debate the general necessity of limited liability. This model has been proved the most successful. See Schön (2014), p. 127 et seq.; Armour et al. (2009b), p. 9 et seq.; Fleischer (2000), p. 17 et seq. Also consider Blumberg (1985–1986), Kershaw (2012), p. 18; Hansmann et al. (2006), Schön (2012), Easterbrook and Fischel (1998), p. 44 et seq.; Adams (1991), p. 12 et seq. and 47.

[328]See Armour et al. (2009b), p. 7; Hansmann et al. (2006), p. 411 et seq.; Kershaw (2012), p. 18 et seq.; Schäfer and Ott (2012), p. 716 et seq.

[329]This reduces costs of risk bearing. See Sect. 1.3.3. On this issue, see Adams (1991), p. 33 et seq. and Schäfer and Ott (2012), p. 716.

shares for potential purchases.[330] We must remember that the SCE-R requires a minimum capital of 30,000 EUR, which can also be considered as a means of creditor protection, at least to a limited extent.[331] Whereas the SCE-R applies limited liability, it is rather strict about the transferability of shares. Art. 4 para. 11 SCE-R restricts the transferability of shares in several ways (which creates the problem of lock-in).[332] Aligned with the concept of variability of capital, these restrictions are, to some extent, counterweighted by those SCE-R provisions that provide an exit mechanism.

As seen, the concepts of the allocation of profits and disinterested distribution are identifying features of an SCE. In general, however, national laws allow the statutes to create tailor-made financing solutions. Favouring such an approach, one can argue that flexible solutions to distributing profits are required to enhance efficiency and provide incentives to new (user and non-user) members.[333] One such example would be the distribution of profits and obligations to participate in self-financing that is executed according to the principle of proportionality.[334] Where agricultural cooperatives are involved, the application of this principle implies that these factors are regulated according to the value of the products supplied or purchased by the member.

Profits can be distributed to members in proportion to their use of the cooperative via patronage refunds (the SCE-R uses the term 'dividends').[335] This requirement is important, as receiving a disproportionate share of the profits could allow individual

---

[330]See Armour et al. (2009b), p. 12; Halpern et al. (1980), p. 136 et seq.; Armour et al. (2009a), p. 130 et seq.; Adams (1991), p. 48 et seq.; Schäfer and Ott (2012), p. 717. Also consider Zoppini (2002), p. 569.

[331]Due to its low amount. Consider in this context Eidenmüller et al. (2006). Generally, Fleischer (2000), p. 12 et seq.

[332]See Sect. 1.3.3.

[333]See Van der Sangen (2012), p. 26; Cook and Chaddad (2004), Iliopoulos (2015), p. 9. It has been observed that "as organizational complexity increases, the cooperative distributes more and more clearly defined residual claimants rights to member-patrons. See Iliopoulos (2015), p. 10. Also consider the issue of costs of market power. See Sect. 1.3.3.

[334]See Cook and Chaddad (2004), p. 1250.

[335]Evidence shows that Austrian agricultural cooperatives often allocate net proceedings to the general reserves. In addition, equity is raised in proportion to the value of the transactions between the members and the agricultural cooperative. In other words, members participate in equity raising. Austrian agricultural cooperatives also distribute profits normally based on the level of turnover between the member and the cooperative, whereas remuneration of capital is not considered suitable for Austrian agricultural cooperatives. It is stressed that the legal system provides flexible solutions to financial incentives to attract new members and increase the loyalty of the existing members. See Kühl (2012), p. 37 et seq.

From an economic point of view, one may criticise the Italian cooperative model because it severely limits the distribution of profits (by defining a maximum threshold), prohibits the distribution of reserves to members while the cooperative still exists and requires the devolution of indivisible reserves to other mutualistic aims. If the cooperative is wound-up, members are only repaid the nominal value of their subscribed capital and any possible dividends. See Zoppini (2004), p. 445 et seq.

members to pursue market power or to exploit information asymmetries over other members. As a result, the interest on the latter's profits would shrink relative to their business.[336] This then could be an incentive for them to exploit any asymmetric information that they possess. As a result, the disproportionate increase in profits could break the commitment mechanism.[337] This risk and these dynamics must be kept in mind when drafting statutory provisions about patronage refunds.

Even though the SCE-R does not require the use of patronage refunds (the SCE-R uses the term 'dividends'), the importance of this mechanism lies in the regulation's norms. In fact, a specific provision (Art. 67 para. 1 SCE-R) explicitly deals with this phenomenon and ranks distributing patronage refunds (dividends) higher than other distributable profits,[338] such as the profits to be used as return on paid-up capital.[339] Thus, contrary to limited-liability companies that focus on the remuneration of capital, agricultural SCEs are limited in their distribution of profits, as they primarily focus on fostering business transactions with their members rather than on the remuneration of the subscribed capital.[340] A positive aspect of limiting the possibility to distribute profits is that this—in general, but also during resignation or expulsion—hinders capitalistic investments,[341] limits the discretion of managers and helps to promote further business transactions between the members and the cooperative.[342]

Moreover, as a user members favour those strategies that guarantee earnings during the membership period, some national legal systems, including the Italian one, urge mainly mutual cooperatives to create indivisible reserves. These are a kind of institutionalised destined patrimony that contribute to the continuation of the mutualistic cause.[343] Indivisible reserves, as a means of disinterested distribution, function as a shock absorber. Thus, a cooperative must have a certain amount of these reserves to help protect members' transaction-specific investments by considerably reducing the risk that the agricultural cooperative will suddenly fail.[344]

Yet, it has been criticised that capital linked to indivisible reserves—which can also be called unallocated capital—functions as a filter between the members and the

---

336 Because the dominant member gains at the expense of the other members.

337 See Molk (2014), p. 924. Also consider Berman (1967), p. 113; Greenberg (1984), p. 184 et seq.

338 Also consider Recital 10 bullet 5 SCE-R.

339 In this context member-investor cooperatives are discussed. Here, returns are distributed in proportion to shareholdings in addition to patronage. See Cook and Chaddad (2004), p. 1250; Iliopoulos (2015), p. 5.

340 It is stressed that cooperatives can be an answer to market inefficiencies and market failure. A cooperative is an anticyclical economic organisation which is most successful during a negative economic cycle. This helps explain why the members accept a remuneration of capital lower than that offered by capital markets. See Zoppini (2004), p. 447.

341 Practically, this implies the influence and number of non-user members is restricted.

342 See Zoppini (2004), p. 444.

343 See Zoppini (2004), p. 445 et seq. Generally, Miribung (2015b) and Costi (2001).

344 See Nilsson (2001), p. 344. Also consider Santagata (2014b), p. 427 et seq.; Lolli (2010), p. 10 et seq. and 164 et seq. See also Paolucci (2019k), p. 143 et seq.

firm, as the signals that the members want to send to the markets do not get through, because the market value of the agricultural cooperative cannot be clearly defined. It may not be clear what investments should be made and how the cooperative should be managed. As a result, cooperatives often have difficulties raising capital[345]; thus, the allocation of capital is frequently suboptimal. As a result, lenders might be cautious, as they do not know exactly how their capital will be invested; consequently, the costs of borrowing capital increase.[346] Moreover, a situation can arise in which the members want to get the most out of their cooperative but do not want to contribute accordingly. Under these circumstances, the agricultural cooperative is required to borrow capital rather than requiring investments from its members, which suggests that the burden of borrowed capital is ultimately borne by future generations of members.[347]

A further problem of disinterested distribution appears when the market conditions change and the members' needs to be promoted become weaker or even disappear. Because the unallocated capital is locked in indivisible or other reserves, a cooperative is hard to shut down.[348] Moreover, if the remaining assets are transferred to common funds (such as the Italian mutual funds, but also as practiced in Austria) in the event of a liquidation, there is no incentive to dissolve an inefficient cooperative as long as there are assets that can be used by the members.[349] Nor is it easy to redirect the cooperative towards new member needs, as it is generally difficult to modify the objective of the cooperative. This is caused by the free-riders problem, which suggests that there might be vague alternative common needs.[350]

Due to the problem of collectivity, which is caused by the unallocated capital itself and the fact that shares cannot be exchanged at market prices, many

---

[345]Consider in this context proportional investment cooperatives. Here, "members are expected to invest in proportion to patronage." See Cook and Chaddad (2004), p. 1250; Iliopoulos (2015), p. 5.

[346]See Nilsson (2001), p. 337. The costs of raising capital (equity) are higher for cooperatives than capitalistic or investor owned companies because (a) cooperatives only get equity from their members and (b) the pool of potential equity contributors is smaller. Therefore, capital costs rise. In addition, the equity contribution is tied to the member relationship by means of transactions, meaning the pool of contributors is less diversified. This latter phenomenon (poor diversity) increases costs of equity. Thus cooperatives will favour debt over equity and have high costs for borrowed capital, because low equity increases default risks. See Molk (2014), p. 926 et seq. In general, Tirole (2006), p. 158 et seq. and Berk et al. (2015).

[347]See Nilsson (2001), p. 337; Jensen and Meckling (1979), p. 484. A further problem of unallocated capital is that it is hard to move. This runs contrary to an important condition for a well-functioning market economy, which is based on mobile resources. See Nilsson (2001), p. 337.

[348]Nilsson stresses that "a cooperative firm, in which unallocated capital represents the dominating part of the equity, will not necessarily be shut down if the members' need for the firm disappears, or is it likely that operations will be redirected if the needs of the members change. See Nilsson (2001), p. 337.

[349]See Nilsson (2001), p. 338.

[350]See Nilsson (2001), p. 337 et seq.; Ortmann and King (2007), p. 57 and Royer (1999), p. 56. Also consider Furubotn and Pejovich (1972), p. 1151; in general LeVay (1983).

cooperatives have a substantial amount of unallocated capital. Yet, unallocated and non-transferable shares are arguably not fundamental characteristics of cooperatives, at least from an economic perspective. As mentioned, one definition of a cooperative states: 'A cooperative is a user-owned and user-controlled business that distributes the benefits on the basis of use'.[351] If one accepts this definition, then cooperatives may have transferable shares that can be appreciated by market prices (which weakens the problem of lock-in).[352]

This approach also allows for defined membership, legally binding delivery contracts and investment requirements. These are all features of the so-called 'New Generation Cooperatives' (NGCs), which essentially function like investor-owned firms. Here, ownership is limited to those who conduct transactions with the cooperative. These types of cooperatives can have both unallocated capital and shares that carry residual rights, which can be bought and sold at market prices. Members are generally more involved and seem willing to invest larger amounts of money, because their planning horizon is greater.[353] As seen, the concept of unallocated capital or indivisible reserves is applied by the SCE-R via the concept of disinterested distribution.[354] My analysis has shown, however, that both legal systems allow this concept to be weakened, even though it is a fundamental part of the cooperative identity that is advanced by the PECOL. Weakening this concept runs contrary to the idea of creating a menu of different corporate structures that foster competition. Therefore, the approach offered by the PECOL excludes the option to constitute agricultural SCEs as NGCs.

Other observations can be made about financial entitlements during resignation or expulsion. As previously mentioned,[355] the fact that members will enter and exit at different times can cause problems. The resulting heterogeneity of interests can disrupt the function of an agricultural SCE.[356] One example would be a farmer retiring from the farming business. In this situation, should the subscribed capital be refunded? If so, when? Different interests must be considered. First, the member who wants to leave almost certainly wants to receive his capital in full and probably immediately.[357] If immediate redemption is not possible, he or she probably expects

[351]See Barton (1989), p. 1 et seq. Also consider Ortmann and King (2007), p. 42. In other words: (a) The persons who own and finance the cooperative are those who use it. (b) The cooperative is controlled by those who use it. (c) The benefits of the cooperative are distributed to its users on the basis of their use. See Barton (1989), p. 1 et seq. Also consider Nilsson (2001), p. 341; Ortmann and King (2007), p. 42. Generally, Nilsson (1999).

[352]See also Sect. 1.3.3.

[353]See Nilsson (2001), p. 341 et seq. For details Nilsson (1997), van Dijk (1997). See also Costantino (2015).

[354]See Art. 65 paras 2 and 3 SCE-R and Art. 75 SCE-R.

[355]See Sect. 3.5.1.

[356]Consider in this context costs of lock-in and costs of collective decision-making. See also Sect. 1.3.3.

[357]In general, residual rights cannot be transferred when a member leaves. As a result, members' planning horizons are reduced. Members generally consider what membership immediately offers

to get paid a market rate of interest until the capital is redeemed. On the other hand, members who remain in the cooperative generally do not want this capital to be redeemed in full. Moreover, as immediate redemption can lead to liquidity problems, redemption often occurs after a specific period of time. Even then, the remaining members would prefer not to redeem in full or not to pay a market rate of interest. In fact, redemption in full can encourage opportunistic exits from the cooperative.[358] As explained above,[359] cooperatives normally depend on economies of scale. As a result, the cost per unit may rise if even one member leaves. This problem can be minimised by setting a redemption penalty, which corresponds to the externality that results from the exit of the member.[360] Equity that is not redeemed in full—including the non-payment of market interest—clearly serves the interests of the remaining members. In fact, the amount that is not redeemed can be considered a free capital contribution to be used by the remaining members at zero cost. In other words, any equity that is not redeemed is transferred to the remaining members.[361]

In the long run, making such a rule mandatory rather than letting it continue as the default rule will help keep the cooperative stable.[362] Otherwise there is a theoretical danger that those members who are close to retirement will favour a redemption policy that allows redemption in full, while the others will favour partial or even zero redemption.[363] However, successful cooperatives with no liquidity problems could implement redemption policies that foster or support the interests of retiring members. Thus, two solutions seem possible: (1) mandatory rules that limit redemption in full or (2) a default rule that requires redemption in full if an agricultural cooperative has not adopted an equity redemption policy that aligns with both the members' and the cooperative's needs.[364] The SCE-R adopts the first rule. Art. 16 para. 1 SCE-R states that, in case of the loss of membership, exiting members are only entitled to the

---

them, not what business would be useful in the long term. For investments, it has been observed that members who will no longer be members when the investment pays out, frequently oppose the investment. Thus potentially profitable investments are not made, capital growth is hindered and the value of the cooperative reduced. However, this problem may be reduced if the value of the cooperative is based on how well the cooperative is able to satisfy its members' needs. See Nilsson (2001), p. 338; Jensen and Meckling (1979), p. 484. In general, Royer (1999) and Ortmann and King (2007).

[358]See Hansmann (1999), p. 399.

[359]See Sect. 3.5.1.

[360]It has been observed that leaving-restrictions for members of Austrian agricultural cooperatives are considered to be in the interests of the cooperative, as they enable it to plan and invest better. See Kühl (2012), p. 38.

[361]See Hansmann (1999), p. 399.

[362]See Zanotti (2013), p. 228. On this issue see Miribung (2015b), p. 6 et seq.; Lolli (2010), p. 90. Also consider Münkner (2006), p. 22 et seq.

[363]See Hansmann (1999), p. 400. In practice, one must consider whether there are lawsuits in this regard.

[364]See Hansmann (1999), p. 401. However, it is also true that new members who start to participate with the existing assets will transfer their part of accumulated assets to future members when they leave the cooperative. Thus, the members have defined a process of wealth transfer called

repayment of their part of the subscribed capital. According to Art. 4 paras. 1 and 3 SCE-R, capital is represented by shares, and these have a nominal value according to the statutes; thus, exiting members are arguably entitled to the nominal value of their shares. Therefore, in principle, the value cannot be adjusted (by interest payments or to compensate for inflation). On the other hand, my analysis has also shown that an SCE may implement specific revenue reserves. Furthermore, the SCE-R explicitly prohibits immediate redemption: the corresponding provision helps to limit liquidation problems.[365]

References

Adams M (1991) Eigentum, Kontrolle und beschränkte Haftung, 1st edn. Wirtschaftsrecht und Wirtschaftspolitik, vol 113. Nomos, Baden-Baden

Albamonte D (2008) Lo statuto della società cooperativa europea. In: Capriglione F (ed) La nuova disciplina della società europea. Cedam, Padova, pp 295–320

Alfandari E, Piot B (2004) Die Mitgliedschaft in der SCE. In: Schulze R (ed) Europäische Genossenschaft SCE: Handbuch, 1st edn. Nomos, Baden-Baden, pp 77–90

Armour J, Hertig G, Kanda H (2009a) Transactions with creditors. In: Kraakman RH, Armour J, Davies P, Enriques L, Hansmann H, Hertig G, Hopt K, Kanda H, Rock E (eds) The anatomy of corporate law: a comparative and functional approach, 2nd edn. Oxford University Press, Oxford, pp 115–152

Armour J, Hansmann H, Kraakman RH (2009b) What is corporate law. In: Kraakman RH, Armour J, Davies P, Enriques L, Hansmann H, Hertig G, Hopt K, Kanda H, Rock E (eds) The anatomy of corporate law: a comparative and functional approach, 2nd edn. Oxford University Press, Oxford, pp 1–34

Astl H, Steinböck G (2014a) § 5. In: Dellinger M (ed) Genossenschaftsgesetz samt Nebengesetzen: Kommentar, 2nd edn. LexisNexis ARD Orac, Wien, pp 122–158

Astl H, Steinböck G (2014b) § 5a. In: Dellinger M (ed) Genossenschaftsgesetz samt Nebengesetzen: Kommentar, 2nd edn. LexisNexis ARD Orac, Wien, pp 159–167

Barton DG (1989) What is a cooperative. In: Cobia DW (ed) Cooperatives in agriculture. Prentice-Hall, Englewood Cliffs, pp 1–20

Bassi A, Schlesinger P (1988) Delle imprese cooperative e delle mutue assicuratrici: Artt. 2511 - 2548. Il codice civile - commentario, / dir. da Piero Schlesinger. Giuffrè, Milano

Berk J, DeMarzo P, Harford J (2015) Fundamentals of corporate finance, 3rd edn. The Pearson series in finance. Pearson Education, Boston

Berman KV (1967) Worker-owned plywood companies: an economic analysis. Washington State University Press, Pullman

Beuthien V, Jud W (2007) Genossenschaftsrechsänderungsgesetz 2006. FOG, Wien

Bianca M, Zanardo A (2016) La Società Europea e la Società Cooperativa Europea. In: Pederzini E (ed) Percorsi di diritto societario europeo, 3rd edn. Giappichelli, Torino, pp 177–214

Blumberg PI (1985–1986) Limited liability and corporate groups. J Corp Law:573–632

Bonfante G (1999) Delle imprese cooperative: Art. 2511-2545. Commentario del Codice civile Scialoja-Branca. Libro quinto, Del lavoro, art. 2511-2545. Zanichelli, Bologna, Roma

intergenerational mutuality. See Zanotti (2013), p. 227 et seq.; Zoppini (2015), p. 355. Also consider Münkner (2006), p. 22 et seq.

[365]The calculation of the amount to be repaid should be based on the current approved balance sheet.

Bonfante G (2004a) Art. 2545 quinquies. In: Cottino G, Bonfante G, Cagnasso O, Montalenti P (eds) Il nuovo diritto societario III: Commento al D. lgs. 17 gennaio 2003, n. 6, D. Lgs. 17 gennaio 2003, n. 5, D. lgs. 11 aprile 2002, n. 61 (art. 1). 3. Artt. 2484-2548 c.c. norme di attuazione, disciplina processuale, artt. 2621-2641 c.c., 1st edn. Zanichelli, Bologna, pp 2619–2622

Bonfante G (2004b) Art. 2545 sexies. In: Cottino G, Bonfante G, Cagnasso O, Montalenti P (eds) Il nuovo diritto societario III: Commento al D. lgs. 17 gennaio 2003, n. 6, D. Lgs. 17 gennaio 2003, n. 5, D. lgs. 11 aprile 2002, n. 61 (art. 1). 3. Artt. 2484-2548 c.c. norme di attuazione, disciplina processuale, artt. 2621-2641 c.c., 1st edn. Zanichelli, Bologna, pp 2623–2633

Bonfante G (2004c) Art. 2545 ter. In: Cottino G, Bonfante G, Cagnasso O, Montalenti P (eds) Il nuovo diritto societario III: Commento al D. lgs. 17 gennaio 2003, n. 6, D. Lgs. 17 gennaio 2003, n. 5, D. lgs. 11 aprile 2002, n. 61 (art. 1). 3. Artt. 2484-2548 c.c. norme di attuazione, disciplina processuale, artt. 2621-2641 c.c., 1st edn. Zanichelli, Bologna, pp 2608–2613

Bonfante G (2006) La società cooperativa europea. In: Galletti D, Fici A (eds) La società cooperativa europea: Quali prospettive per la cooperazione italiana? Universita degli Studi di Trento, Trento, pp 3–12

Bonfante G (ed) (2014) La società cooperativa. Trattato di diritto commerciale, vol 5,3. Cedam, Padova

Bosi G (2012) I fondi mutualistici: Un'analisi giuridica ed economica. Studi e ricerche. Diritto, vol 636. Il Mulino, Bologna

Bundesministerium für Finanzen (2005) Einkommenssteuerrichtlinien 2000

Campobasso GF, Campobasso M (2004) La riforma delle società di capitali e delle cooperative, 2nd edn. Il sistema giuridico italiano. UTET, Torino

Cardarelli MC (2008) Le variazioni del capitale. In: Cusa E (ed) La cooperativa srl tra legge e autonomia statutaria. Cedam, Padova

Ceccherini A (2008) Art. 2545 quinquies. In: Ceccherini A, Schirò S (eds) Società cooperative e mutue assicuratrici: (artt. 2511-2548 c.c.), 2nd edn. Giuffré, Milano, pp 201–206

Chieffi A (2007a) 2525. In: Presti G (ed) Società cooperative: Artt. 2511-2548. EGEA; Giuffrè, Milano, pp 181–202

Chieffi A (2007b) 2527. In: Presti G (ed) Società cooperative: Artt. 2511-2548. EGEA; Giuffrè, Milano, pp 227–240

Chirico S, Troianiello P (2007) La società cooperativa europea: Regolamento CE n. 1435/2003. Cooperative e consorzi. IPSOA, Milano

Chiusoli R (2003) La riforma del diritto societario per le cooperative. IPSOA, Assago (MI)

Ciccarelli (2000) Destinazione degli utili ai fondi mutualistici. Rivista della cooperazione

Cook ML, Chaddad FR (2004) Redesigning cooperative boundaries: the emergence of new models. Am J Agric Econ 86:1249–1253. https://doi.org/10.1111/j.0002-9092.2004.00673.x

Costantino L (2015) Agricoltura di gruppo: ruolo delle cooperative di nuova generazione negli USA. Rivista di diritto agrario:510–534

Costi R (2001) Proprietà e impresa cooperative nella riforma del diritto societario. Giurisprudenza Commerciale:128–132

Cusa E (2004) Die Verwendung des Betriebsergebnisses. In: Schulze R (ed) Europäische Genossenschaft SCE: Handbuch, 1st edn. Nomos, Baden-Baden, pp 123–168

Cusa E (2009) Partecipazioni e capitale nelle società cooperative. In: Antonio B (ed) Studi per Franco Di Sabato. Edizioni scientifiche italiane, Napoli, pp 341–361

Cusa E (2010) La riduzione di capitale nelle società cooperative. Rivista delle società:471–498

Delle Priscoli L (2014) Art. 2536. In: Santosuosso DU (ed) Delle società, dell'azienda, della concorrenza. UTET, Torino, pp 321–323

Dellinger M (1995) Aus aktuellem Anlaß: Zur Einlage- und Deckungspflicht der Genossenschafter bei Liquidation, Konkurs oder Ausgleich ihrer Genossenschaft. GesRZ:91–110

Dellinger M (2006) Was bringt das GenRÄG 2006? ecolex:570

Dellinger M (2014a) § 1. In: Dellinger M (ed) Genossenschaftsgesetz samt Nebengesetzen: Kommentar, 2nd edn. LexisNexis ARD Orac, Wien, pp 17–55

Dellinger M (2014b) § 2. In: Dellinger M (ed) Genossenschaftsgesetz samt Nebengesetzen: Kommentar, 2nd edn. LexisNexis ARD Orac, Wien, pp 101–107
Dellinger M (2014c) § 48. In: Dellinger M (ed) Genossenschaftsgesetz samt Nebengesetzen: Kommentar, 2nd edn. LexisNexis ARD Orac, Wien, pp 422–431
Dellinger M (2014d) § 79. In: Dellinger M (ed) Genossenschaftsgesetz samt Nebengesetzen: Kommentar, 2nd edn. LexisNexis ARD Orac, Wien, pp 496–505
Dellinger M, Steinböck G (2014) § 55. In: Dellinger M (ed) Genossenschaftsgesetz samt Nebengesetzen: Kommentar, 2nd edn. LexisNexis ARD Orac, Wien, pp 459–462
Di Cecco G (2012) Variabilità e modificazioni del capitale sociale nelle cooperative. Edicioni Scientifiche Italiane, Napoli
Di Sabato F (2005) Capitale e responsabilità interna nelle società di persone. Giuffrè, Milano
Easterbrook FH, Fischel DR (1998) The economic structure of corporate law, [Repr.]. Harvard University Press, Cambridge
Eidenmüller H, Grunewald B, Noack U (2006) Minimum capital in the system of legal capital. In: Lutter M (ed) Legal capital in Europe. De Gruyter, Berlin, pp 17–41
Ettel M (2012) § 20. In: Doralt W, Nowotny C, Kalss S (eds) Kommentar zum Aktiengesetz, 2nd edn. Linde, Wien, pp 375–392
Fajardo E, Meira DMMA (2017) Cooperative financial strucutre. In: Fajardo-García IG, Fici A, Henrÿ H, Hiez D, Meira DMMA, Münkner H-H, Snaith I (eds) Principles of European Cooperative Law: principles, commentaries and national reports. Intersentia, Cambridge, pp 73–95
Falcone G (2003) Art 2545 quinquies. In: Sandulli M, Santoro V (eds) La riforma delle società: Società cooperative Artt. 2511-2548 cod.civ. Giappichelli, Torino, pp 175–177
Ferri G (2008) Struttura finanziaria dell'impresa e funzioni del capitale sociale. Rivista del notariato:741–794
Fici A (2013) The European Cooperative Society. In: Cracogna D, Fici A, Henrÿ H (eds) International handbook of cooperative law. Springer, Berlin, Heidelberg, pp 115–151
Fici A, Strano C (2010) Italy. In: Fici A (ed) Study on the implementation of the Regulation 1435/2003 on the Statute for European Cooperative Society (SCE): Final Study Part II. National Reports. Report drawn up following call tender no ENTR/2009/021 of 23 April from the European Commission, pp 671–702
Figà-Talamanca G (1997) Bilanci e organizzazione dei poteri dispositivi sul patrimonio sociale. Università degli studi di Roma "Tor Vergata" / Pubblicazioni della Facoltà di Giurisprudenza. Sezione di Diritto e Procedura Civile, vol 4. Giuffrè, Milano
Fleischer H (2000) Grundfragen der ökonomischen Theorie im Gesellschafts- und Kapitalmarktrecht. Zeitschrift für Unternehmens- und Gesellschaftsrecht 30:1–32. https://doi.org/10.1515/zgre.2000.047
Furubotn EG, Pejovich S (1972) Property rights and economic theory: a survey of recent literature. J Econ Lit 10:1137–1162
Galletti D (2005) Art 2535. In: Maffei Alberti A (ed) Il nuovo diritto delle società: Commento sistematico al D. lgs. 17 gennaio 2003, n. 6, aggiornato al D. lgs. 28 dicembre 2004, n. 310. Cedam, Padova, pp 2774–2778
Galletti D (2006) La tutela delle minoranze nella SCE. In: Galletti D, Fici A (eds) La società cooperativa europea: Quali prospettive per la cooperazione italiana? Universita degli Studi di Trento, Trento, pp 48–66
Genco R (2003) La struttura finanziaria. In: Genco R (ed) La riforma delle società cooperative. IPSOA, Milano, pp 57–113
Genco R (2006) Le operazioni straordinarie ed il trasferimento di sede della SCE: (Regolamento n 1435/2003 del 22 luglio 2003). In: Galletti D, Fici A (eds) La società cooperativa europea: Quali prospettive per la cooperazione italiana? Universita degli Studi di Trento, Trento, pp 115–136
Ginera E (2011) Oltre il capitale sociale: Spunti di riflessione del dibattito sulla riforma della struttura finanziaria delle società di capitali. In: Abbadessa P, Balzano M, Bartalena A, Boggio L, Bonaiti A, Calvosa L, Cariello V, Centonze M, Cetra A, de Marchi G, Stasio Vd,

Ginera E, Malimpensa E, Marchetti P, Miola M, Mozzarelli M, Nobili R, Pisani L, Portale GB, Presti G, Regoli D, Rescio G, Santus A, Schneider U-H, Speranzin M, Spolidoro MS, Strampelli G, Stucchi L, Vanoni S, Zanarone G (eds) La struttura finanziaria e i bilanci delle società di capitali: Studi in onore di Giovanni E. Colombo. Giappichelli, Torino

Giorgi V (2007) Art. 2536. In: Presti G (ed) Società cooperative: Artt. 2511-2548. EGEA; Giuffrè, Milano, pp 293–295

Giorgi V (2018a) Art. 2518. In: Cian G (ed) Commentario breve al Codice civile: Commentato con dottrina e giurisprudenza, 13th edn. Wolters Kluver, Milano, Padova, pp 3208–3209

Giorgi V (2018b) Art. 2535. In: Cian G (ed) Commentario breve al Codice civile: Commentato con dottrina e giurisprudenza, 13th edn. Wolters Kluver, Milano, Padova, pp 3232–3233

Giorgi V (2018c) Art. 2545 quinquies. In: Cian G (ed) Commentario breve al Codice civile: Commentato con dottrina e giurisprudenza, 13th edn. Wolters Kluver, Milano, Padova, pp 3246–3247

Greda C (2014) Statut der Europäischen Genossenschaft. In: Dellinger M (ed) Genossenschaftsgesetz samt Nebengesetzen: Kommentar, 2nd edn. LexisNexis ARD Orac, Wien, pp 829–854

Greenberg E (1984) Producer cooperatives and democratic theory: the case of plywood firms. In: Jackall R, Levin HM (eds) Worker cooperatives in America. University of California Press, Berkeley [etc.], pp 171–218

Grosso P (2011) Art. 2524. In: Bonfante G, Corapi D, de Angelis L, Napoleoni V, Rordorf R, Salafia V (eds) Codice commentato delle società: Società di persone, società di capitali, cooperative, consorzi, reati societari: aggiornato con le nuove norme in tema di revisione legale, esercizio dei diritti degli azionisti di società quotate e costituzione delle Spa, 3rd edn. IPSOA, Assago, pp 2120–2126

Hansmann H (1999) Cooperative firms in theory and practice. Liiketaloudellinen aikakauskirja LTA - Finn J Bus Econ:387–403

Hansmann H, Kraakman RH, Squire RC (2006) Law and the rise of the firm. Harv Law Rev 119:1333–1403

Halpern P, Trebilcock M, Turnbull S (1980) An economic analysis of limited liability in corporation law. Univ Tor Law J 30:117–150

Heilmeier M (2010) Die Kapitalverfassung der Europäischen Genossenschaft (SCE). EuZW:887–892

Henrÿ H (2012) Guidelines for cooperative legislation, 3rd edn. International Labour Organization, Geneva

Hirte H (2007) Das neue Genossenschaftsrecht (Teil II). DStR:2215–2219

Hofinger H, Zawischa G (2007) Das Genossenschaftsrechts-Änderungsgesetz 2006: Eine Genossenschaftsreform mit neuen Möglichkeiten der Kapitalaufbringung. Gewerbliche Genossenschaft:30

Holthaus J, Lehnhoff DJ (2016) Einf. In: Lehnhoff DJ, Holthaus J (eds) Lang/Weidmüller Genossenschaftsgesetz: Gesetz, betreffend die Erwerbs- und Wirtschaftsgenossenschaften mit Erläuterungen zum Umwandlungsgesetz und zur Europäischen Genossenschaft (SCE), 38., neu bearbeitete Auflage. De Gruyter, Berlin, pp 1–54

Iengo M (2006) Gli Studi del CNN - Società cooperativa europea - Analisi delle norme applicabili ai sensi dell'articolo 8 del regolamento n. 1435/2003 - Casi e materiali di diritto comunitario di interesse notarile: le società - e.library - Fondazione Italiana del Notariato. Studio n. 9-2006/I. http://elibrary.fondazionenotariato.it/approfondimento.asp?app=21/studiCNN/mi_9_2006_I&mn=3&tipo=3&qn=6. Accessed 21 Nov 2019

Iliopoulos C (2015) Ownership and governance in agricultural cooperatives: an update. https://www.researchgate.net/publication/274064574_Ownership_and_Governance_in_Agricultural_Cooperatives_An_Update. Accessed 29 Nov 2019

Ingrosso M (2013) Le cooperative e le nuove agevolazioni fiscali: Profili civilistici, contabili, comunitari, 2nd edn. Giappichelli, Torino

Jensen MC, Meckling WH (1979) Rights and production functions: an application to labor-managed firms and codetermination. J Bus 52:469–506. https://doi.org/10.1086/296060
Kalss S, Eckert G (2005) Zentrale Fragen des GmbH-Rechts: Entwicklung - Perspektiven - Materialien. Linde Verlag Wien, Wien
Kastner W (1986) Österreichisches Genossenschaftsrecht. In: Patera M (ed) Handbuch des österreichischen Genossenschaftswesens. Orac, Wien, pp 117–232
Kastner W, Doralt P, Nowotny C (1990) Grundriss des österreichischen Gesellschaftsrechts, 5th edn. Manzsche Kurzlehrbuch-Reihe, vol 2. Manz, Wien
Keinert H (1988) Österreichisches Genossenschaftsrecht: Lehr- und Handbuch. Manz, Wien
Kershaw D (2012) Company law in context: text and materials, 2nd edn. Oxford University Press, Oxford
Korte O (2012) Die Europäische Genossenschaft (SCE): Analyse der mangelnden Verbreitung dieser supranationalen Rechtsform. In: Baudenbacher C (ed) Aktuelle Entwicklungen des europäischen und internationalen Wirtschaftsrechts. Helbing et Lichtenhahn, Basel, München [u.a.], pp 323–349
Krimphove D (2010) Brauchen wir die Europäische Genossenschaft? EuZW:892–897
Kühl R (2012) Country report: Austria. In: Van der Sangen G, Pyykkönen POP, Iliopoulus C, Kühl R, Hagedorn K, Hanisch M, Judis R, Gijselinckx C, Hendrikse G, Hak T, Poppe K, Bijman J (eds) Support for farmers' cooperatives, Wageningen, pp 1–51
Lehner JH (2009) Verschmelzungsvarianten einer Europäischen Genossenschaft (SCE). In: Haslinger M, Kanonier A, Zehetner S (eds) Ein Jurist im Spannungsfeld von Wirtschaft, Technik und Recht: Festschrift für Franz Zehetner zum 60. Geburtstag. NWV, Wien, pp 97–110
LeVay C (1983) Agricultural co-operative theory: a review. J Agric Econ 34:1–44. https://doi.org/10.1111/j.1477-9552.1983.tb00973.x
Lolli R (2010) Le riserve divisibili e indivisibili nelle società cooperative. Le monografie di Contratto e impresa, vol 132. Cedam, Padova
Lolli R (2012) I mezzi propri delle cooperative e i bilanci. In: Paolucci LF (ed) Le società cooperative. UTET giuridica, Torino, pp 147–179
Lutter M (1983) Vom formellen Mindestkapital zu materiellen Finanzierungsregeln im Recht der Kapitalgesellschaften. In: Riesenfeld S, Jayme E (eds) Ius inter nationes. C. F. Müller, Heidelberg
Lutter M, Schmidt J, Bayer W (2012) Europäisches Unternehmens- und Kapitalmarktrecht: Grundlagen, Stand und Entwicklung nebst Texten und Materialien, 5th edn. Zeitschrift für Unternehmens- und Gesellschaftsrecht. Sonderheft, T. 1. De Gruyter, Berlin
Maltoni M (2014) Art. 2545 undecies. In: Santosuosso DU (ed) Delle società, dell'azienda, della concorrenza. UTET, Torino, pp 535–545
Marasà G (2013) L'odierno significato della mutualità prevalente nelle cooperative. Giurisprudenza Commerciale:847–862
Maurer R (2014) Anhang II zu § 1 GenG: Grundzüge der Ertragsbesteuerung von Genossenschaften und ihren Mitgliedern. In: Dellinger M (ed) Genossenschaftsgesetz samt Nebengesetzen: Kommentar, 2nd edn. LexisNexis ARD Orac, Wien, pp 92–100
Mayer B (2010) Art. 5. In: Manz G, Mayer B, Schröder A (eds) Europäische Aktiengesellschaft SE: SE, 2nd edn. Nomos, Baden-Baden, pp 97–124
Miribung G (2015a) Die GmbH light nach italienischem Recht. In: Benecke M, Hausmann R, Peifer K-N, Gebauer M (eds) Arbeitsrecht, Erbrecht, Urheberrecht: 50 Jahre deutsch-italienische Juristenvereinigung. Müller, Heidelberg, pp 131–147
Miribung G (2015b) Riserve indivisibili nelle cooperative e patrimonio separato: spunti di riflessione. www.giustiziacivile.com
Molk P (2014) The puzzling lack of cooperatives. Tulane Law Rev:889–958
Montagnani C (2003) Art. 2524. In: Sandulli M, Santoro V (eds) La riforma delle società: Società cooperative Artt. 2511-2548 cod.civ. Giappichelli, Torino, pp 81–83
Müller K (2000) Kommentar zum Gesetz betreffend die Erwerbs- und Wirtschaftsgenossenschaften, 2nd edn. Gieseking, Bielefeld

Münkner H-H (2006) Europäische Genossenschaft (SCE) und Europäische Genossenschaftstradition. Vorträge und Aufsätze des Forschungsvereins für Genossenschaftswesen, vol 30. Eigenverlag des FOG, Wien

Nilsson J (1997) New generation farmer co-ops. Rev Int Coop:32–38

Nilsson J (1999) Co-operative organisational models as reflections of the business environments. Liiketaloudellinen aikakauskirja LTA - Finn J Bus Econ:449–470

Nilsson J (2001) Organisational principles for co-operative firms. Scand J Manage 17:329–356. https://doi.org/10.1016/S0956-5221(01)00010-0

Nowotny C (2008) Genossenschaft. In: Kalss S, Nowotny C, Schauer M, Kastner W, Doralt P (eds) Österreichisches Gesellschaftsrecht: Systematische Darstellung sämtlicher Rechtsformen: in Fortführung des von Walther Kastner begründeten und in der letzten Auflage von Walther Kastner, Peter Doralt und Christian Nowotny bearbeiteten Lehr- und Handbuchs "Grundriss des österreichischen Gesellschaftsrechts". Manz, Wien, 5/1–5/182

Ortmann GF, King RP (2007) Agricultural cooperatives I: history, theory and problems. Agrekon 46:40–68. https://doi.org/10.1080/03031853.2007.9523760

Paciello A (2007a) Art. 2524. In: Presti G (ed) Società cooperative: Artt. 2511-2548. EGEA; Giuffrè, Milano, pp 171–180

Paciello A (2007b) Artt. 2545 decies - 2545 undecies. In: Presti G (ed) Società cooperative: Artt. 2511-2548. EGEA; Giuffrè, Milano, pp 489–504

Paolucci LF (2012a) I soci. In: Paolucci LF (ed) Le società cooperative. UTET giuridica, Torino, pp 95–124

Paolucci LF (2019a) Art. 2511. In: Paolucci LF (ed) Codice delle cooperative 2019: Aggiornato con le novità del D.Lgs. n. 14/2019. Maggioli, Santarcangelo di Romagna, Rimini, pp 29–40

Paolucci LF (2019b) Art. 2518. In: Paolucci LF (ed) Codice delle cooperative 2019: Aggiornato con le novità del D.Lgs. n. 14/2019. Maggioli, Santarcangelo di Romagna, Rimini, pp 55–57

Paolucci LF (2019c) Art. 2524. In: Paolucci LF (ed) Codice delle cooperative 2019: Aggiornato con le novità del D.Lgs. n. 14/2019. Maggioli, Santarcangelo di Romagna, Rimini, pp 79–81

Paolucci LF (2019d) Art. 2525. In: Paolucci LF (ed) Codice delle cooperative 2019: Aggiornato con le novità del D.Lgs. n. 14/2019. Maggioli, Santarcangelo di Romagna, Rimini, pp 81–84

Paolucci LF (2019e) Art. 2527. In: Paolucci LF (ed) Codice delle cooperative 2019: Aggiornato con le novità del D.Lgs. n. 14/2019. Maggioli, Santarcangelo di Romagna, Rimini, pp 88–89

Paolucci LF (2019f) Art. 2532. In: Paolucci LF (ed) Codice delle cooperative 2019: Aggiornato con le novità del D.Lgs. n. 14/2019. Maggioli, Santarcangelo di Romagna, Rimini, pp 101–106

Paolucci LF (2019g) Art. 2535. In: Paolucci LF (ed) Codice delle cooperative 2019: Aggiornato con le novità del D.Lgs. n. 14/2019. Maggioli, Santarcangelo di Romagna, Rimini, pp 115–118

Paolucci LF (2019h) Art. 2545-quater. In: Paolucci LF (ed) Codice delle cooperative 2019: Aggiornato con le novità del D.Lgs. n. 14/2019. Maggioli, Santarcangelo di Romagna, Rimini, pp 144–145

Paolucci LF (2019i) Art. 2545-quinquies. In: Paolucci LF (ed) Codice delle cooperative 2019: Aggiornato con le novità del D.Lgs. n. 14/2019. Maggioli, Santarcangelo di Romagna, Rimini, pp 145–147

Paolucci LF (2019j) Art. 2545-sexies. In: Paolucci LF (ed) Codice delle cooperative 2019: Aggiornato con le novità del D.Lgs. n. 14/2019. Maggioli, Santarcangelo di Romagna, Rimini, pp 147–148

Paolucci LF (2019k) Art. 2545-ter. In: Paolucci LF (ed) Codice delle cooperative 2019: Aggiornato con le novità del D.Lgs. n. 14/2019. Maggioli, Santarcangelo di Romagna, Rimini, pp 143–144

Paolucci LF (2019l) Artt. 2512-2514. In: Paolucci LF (ed) Codice delle cooperative 2019: Aggiornato con le novità del D.Lgs. n. 14/2019. Maggioli, Santarcangelo di Romagna, Rimini, pp 41–49

Paolucci LF (2012b) Definizione e aspetti caratterizzanti. In: Paolucci LF (ed) Le società cooperative. UTET giuridica, Torino, pp 1–23

Petrelli G (2005) I profili patrimoniali e finanziari nella riforma delle società cooperative. In: Consiglio nazionale del notariato. (ed) Studi e materiali in tema di riforma delle società cooperative. Giuffrè, Milano

Petroboni G (2013) Art. 2524. In: Alpa G, Mariconda V (eds) Codice civile, 3rd edn. Wolters Kluwer Italia; IPSOA, Assago

Pinna (2005) Art. 2521. In: Maffei Alberti A (ed) Il nuovo diritto delle società: Commento sistematico al D. lgs. 17 gennaio 2003, n. 6, aggiornato al D. lgs. 28 dicembre 2004, n. 310. Cedam, Padova, pp 2671–2689

Racugno G (2006) La società cooperativa europea. Rivista del diritto commerciale:315–321

Ragazzini G (1992) Mutualità interna ed esterna nella riforma cooperativa. Contratto e impresa:833–880

Raiser T, Veil R (2006) Recht der Kapitalgesellschaften: Ein Handbuch für Praxis und Wissenschaft; Aktiengesellschaft, Kommanditgesellschaft auf Aktien, Gesellschaft mit beschränkter Haftung, Kapitalgesellschaft & Co., Umwandlungsrecht, Konzernrecht, internationales Gesellschaftsrecht, 4th edn. Vahlen, München

Rocchi E (2005) Capitale variabile e riserve divisibili nel finanziamento della cooperativa. In: Uckmar V, Graziano F (eds) La disciplina civilistica e fiscale della nuova società corporativa. Cedam, Padova, pp 177–211

Rocchi E (2006) La struttura finanziaria della SCE. In: Galletti D, Fici A (eds) La società cooperativa europea: Quali prospettive per la cooperazione italiana? Universita degli Studi di Trento, Trento, pp 87–114

Rocchi E (2007) Art. 2518. In: Presti G (ed) Società cooperative: Artt. 2511-2548. EGEA; Giuffrè, Milano, pp 89–122

Royer J (1999) Cooperative organizational strategies: a neo-institutional digest. J Coop:44–67

Santagata R (2014a) Art. 2545 quater. In: Santosuosso DU (ed) Delle società, dell'azienda, della concorrenza. UTET, Torino, pp 436–444

Santagata R (2014b) Art. 2545 ter. In: Santosuosso DU (ed) Delle società, dell'azienda, della concorrenza. UTET, Torino, pp 424–436

Santagata R (2017) Le società cooperative. In: Cian M (ed) Diritto commerciale: III. Diritto delle società. G. Giappichelli, Torino, pp 807–843

Santosuosso DU (2003) La riforma del diritto societario: Autonomia privata e norme imperative nei DD.Lgs. 17 gennaio 2003, nn.5 e 6. Prima interpretazione.Le nuove leggi civili. Giuffrè, Milano

Schäfer H-B, Ott C (2012) Grundstrukturen und -probleme des Unternehmensrechts. In: Schäfer H-B, Ott C (eds) Lehrbuch der ökonomischen Analyse des Zivilrechts. Springer, Berlin, pp 697–729

Schirò S (2008a) Art. 2518. In: Ceccherini A, Schirò S (eds) Società cooperative e mutue assicuratrici: (artt. 2511-2548 c.c.), 2nd edn. Giuffré, Milano, pp 51–54

Schirò S (2008b) Art. 2535. In: Ceccherini A, Schirò S (eds) Società cooperative e mutue assicuratrici: (artt. 2511-2548 c.c.), 2nd edn. Giuffré, Milano, pp 143–146

Schön W (2012) Der Anspruch auf Haftungsbeschränkung im Europäischen Gesellschaftsrecht. In: Erle B, Goette W, Kleindiek D, Krieger G, Priester H-J, Schubel C, Schwab M, Teichmann C, Witt C-H (eds) Festschrift für Peter Hommelhoff: Zum 70. Geburtstag. De Gruyter; Otto Schmidt, Berlin, Köln, pp 1037–1058

Schön W (2014) Creditor protection in the closed corporation. In: Bachmann G, Eidenmüller H, Engert A, Fleischer H, Schön W (eds) Regulating the closed corporation. De Gruyter, Berlin, pp 124–178

Schöpflin M (2018a) Art. 03. In: Beuthien V, Schöpflin M (eds) Genossenschaftsgesetz: Mit Umwandlungs- und Kartellrecht sowie Statut der Europäischen Genossenschaft, 16th edn. Beck, München, pp 1246–1247

Schöpflin M (2018b) Art. 04. In: Beuthien V, Schöpflin M (eds) Genossenschaftsgesetz: Mit Umwandlungs- und Kartellrecht sowie Statut der Europäischen Genossenschaft, 16th edn. Beck, München, pp 1247–1252

Schöpflin M (2018c) Art. 15. In: Beuthien V, Schöpflin M (eds) Genossenschaftsgesetz: Mit Umwandlungs- und Kartellrecht sowie Statut der Europäischen Genossenschaft, 16th edn. Beck, München, pp 1272–1276

Schöpflin M (2018d) Art. 16. In: Beuthien V, Schöpflin M (eds) Genossenschaftsgesetz: Mit Umwandlungs- und Kartellrecht sowie Statut der Europäischen Genossenschaft, 16th edn. Beck, München, pp 1276–1277

Scordino F (1970) La società cooperativa. Jovene, Napoli

Siebenbäck H-J (2014) § 33a. In: Dellinger M (ed) Genossenschaftsgesetz samt Nebengesetzen: Kommentar, 2nd edn. LexisNexis ARD Orac, Wien, pp 382–384

Simonetto E (1959) Responsabilità e garanzia nel diritto delle società. Cedam, Padova

Stasio Vd (2007) Art. 2545 quinquies. In: Presti G (ed) Società cooperative: Artt. 2511-2548. EGEA; Giuffrè, Milano, pp 415–431

Tatarano MC (2011) La nuova impresa cooperativa, Nuova ed. de L'impresa cooperativa di Giovanni Tatarano. Trattato di diritto civile e commerciale / già diretto da Antonio Cicu, Francesco Messineo, Luigi Mengoni. Giuffrè, Milano

Tirole J (2006) The theory of corporate finance. Princeton University Press, Princeton

Tonelli E (2003) Art. 2525. In: Sandulli M, Santoro V (eds) La riforma delle società: Società cooperative Artt. 2511-2548 cod.civ. Giappichelli, Torino, pp 84–88

Van der Sangen G (2012) EU synthesis and comparative analysis report: legal aspects. In: Support for farmers' cooperatives, Wageningen, pp 1–50

van Dijk G (1997) Implementing the sixth reason for co-operation: new generation co-operatives in agribusiness. In: Nilsson JE, Dijk GE (eds) Strategies and structures in the agro-food industries. Van Gorcum and Co, Assen, pp 94–110

Werner K (2008) Die Limited ante portas: Das Haftkapital der GmbH vor dem Hintergrund des Wettbewerbs der Rechtsordnungen: eine rechtliche und ökonomische Analyse. VDM Verlag Dr. Müller, Saarbrücken

Zahn J (1963) Handbuch für Genossenschaften, 2nd edn. Österreichischer Genossenschaftsverband

Zanotti A (2013) La governance societaria: Società per azioni e cooperative a confronto: una interpretazione economica. Rubbettino, Soveria Mannelli

Zehetner J (1999) Rechnungslegung der Genossenschaften. Manz, Wien

Zoppini A (2002) Autonomia e separazione del patrimonio nella prospettiva dei patrimoni separati della società per azioni. Rivista di Diritto Civile:549–575

Zoppini A (2004) Il nuovo diritto delle società cooperative: un'analisi economica. Rivista di Diritto Civile:439–450

Zoppini A (2015) La struttura finanziaria della società cooperativa. In: La riforma del diritto societario dieci anni dopo: Per i quarant'anni di giurisprudenza commerciale: Milano, 13-14 giugno 2014. Giuffrè, Milano, pp 343–361

Part III
One Agricultural SCE or Many Agricultural SCEs?

Chapter 6
Final Remarks

The SCE-R also is characterised by the fact that it does not lay down the complete body of rules from the European Cooperative Society, only the basic rules. Thus, it applies a legislative technique similar to that used by the European Union when adopting directives. In fact, Art. 8 SCE-R expressly provides that 'in the case of matters not regulated by this regulation or, where matters are partly regulated by it, of those aspects not covered by it', an SCE may be governed (among other sources) by 'the laws of member states, which would apply to a cooperative formed in accordance with the law of the member state in which the SCE has its registered office'. For this reason, in the introductory part of this study, I mentioned that at least as many different types of SCEs as there are EU members might exist. This affirmation relies on the fact that the SCE-R creates rules that rely heavily on national legislation, and it often is not easy to provide an answer to such a presumption. Thus, because of the different national laws on cooperative societies, there may be, within the territorial scope of the European Union and its single market, cooperative societies operating across national borders with their own distinct rules. This conclusion must be kept in mind when establishing an agricultural cooperative organised as an SCE, as here, too, its framework is provided for by the general EU rules on SCEs and specific national provisions on agricultural cooperatives.

There is no doubt that the different national legal systems that are united under the umbrella of the European Union differ in terms of approaches, concepts and notions. These arise from different historical developments in legal thinking and political influence. Yet, there are also many similarities, and one can often find similar content that is described with different notions or concepts. This also results from this work: The differences vary between mere formal ones and more substantial ones, and they concern concepts, formalities, applied approaches and the structure of the law: it is the extent of the differences that, in turn, determines the extent of the similarities.

In light of the above, I briefly reiterate possible differences and similarities between agricultural cooperatives with cross-border activities, i.e., agricultural

G. Miribung, *The Agricultural Cooperative in the Framework of the European Cooperative Society*, Economic Analysis of Law in European Legal Scholarship 8,
https://doi.org/10.1007/978-3-030-44154-8_6

SCEs, in Italy and Austria's legal systems in relation to the general provisions of Regulation (EC) No. 1435/2003 and, above all, the differences and similarities between Italian and Austrian agricultural cooperatives with transnational activities. As an example of purely formal differences, one can mention different formalities by which new members are admitted to an agricultural SCE. Other differences of practical and substantial importance concern, for example, the possibility of delegating the power of representation to a non-member of the management organ.

More substantial differences reside in how the two legal systems address the issue of the civil liability of the organs: different concepts are used to define due diligence and to trigger liability. It is difficult to assess whether there can ultimately be significant differences in practice, but the different approaches can be brought to a similar level of liability by defining professional competence requirements that must be met by the members of the organ.

Another example is how the two legal systems variously address the issue of minority rights. Minority rights in an Italian agricultural SCE are extended as compared to Austrian solution. The Austrian SCE, on the other hand, primarily has to apply the provisions determined by the SCE-R. These examples demonstrate that the interaction between EU law and national rules can expand rights by applying national law. A similar finding concerns the right to information that SCE members enjoy. Here, too, the possibilities offered by the SCE-R are extended, which helps to reduce information asymmetries and enhance efficiency.

Then, another significant difference results from the competence of the general meeting of an agricultural SCE. While in Austria the general meeting has a kind of residual competence for matters that are not specifically assigned to another organ, the Italian solution accounts for only those competencies that are clearly assigned to the general meeting. On the other hand, the Italian solution seems more efficient from a legal and economic point of view, since it uses a catch-all provision.

Another difference partly results from the strong reliance of the Austrian legal system on statutory freedom. This, ultimately, makes the Austrian SCE slightly more flexible than its Italian counterpart. For example, the members of the management organ are usually appointed and dismissed by the supervisory organ. According to Austrian law, this competence can also be transferred to the general meeting.

The SCE-R provides concepts and notions that are then put into practice by determining useful statutory provisions, without indicating where the limits of this statutory freedom should lie or how it could be practically applied. In such cases, the national provisions may serve as guidelines and examples for designing the statutory freedom that is granted by the SCE-R. A suitable example of this is those operations that require authorisation under Art. 48 SCE-R. This finding demonstrates the usefulness of a comparative approach, in which different legal systems are linked to one other but not yet fully reconciled. Examining the two legal systems can also clarify the sometimes vague concepts that reside in the SCE-R (for example, the term 'supervision').

Then there are clear differences that result from the interplay of cooperative theory, including the question of how these theoretical considerations can be translated into legal rules. Here the question arises: how did the different legal systems transfer the theoretical considerations into their legal systems? From a normative legal perspective, this is a question of terminology and legal concepts. There are considerable differences in terminology that Austrian and Italian agricultural SCEs have to take into account; the most important[1] results from the way in which the essential function of a cooperative—to offer services and benefits to its members—is conceived. Austrian law uses the concept of the purpose of promotion, while Italian law uses the concept of mutuality. The first concept is then implemented through a number of transaction categories, while the second helps to distinguish between transactions with members and non-members. Thus, the way in which the notions work differs in part.

The different application of concepts—here, mutuality on the one hand and the purpose of promotion on the other—is clearly visible when one looks at the Italian mainly mutual cooperatives and the so-called other cooperatives. This is a good example of the detailed formulation of legislation under Italian law. The Italian legislature has enacted many specific provisions that establish detailed procedures, while the Austrian legislature has adopted the principle of self-regulation, which allows statutory freedom. Now, the (Italian) strict approach may be a question of legal tradition, but it is also necessary to grant tax relief to cooperatives. In fact, Italy creates strong incentives for mainly mutual cooperatives.[2]

Apart from formalism and tax law issues, a particular difference is that Italian cooperatives can serve interest of the community (i.e., external mutuality and/or systemic mutuality) as well as the interest of their members. For examples that best illustrate the different approaches, one may consider how social cooperatives work or how the Italian legislature adopted the principle of disinterested distribution. According to the SCE-R, this principle has to be applied, but since the national provisions must also be observed, it can be weakened. For the Italian legal system, the main difference is whether an SCE is established as a mainly mutual cooperative or as other cooperative—and as mentioned, the former type is incentivised by the Italian legislature (and with it the application of the principle of disinterested dissolution).

The way in which the principle of disinterested distribution is applied is a central issue of cooperative theory; this has also been identified as an important feature of the PECOL. With economic theory, one can argue that the so-called indivisible reserves or unallocated capital—which are a corollary of the principle of disinterested distribution—protect specific investments of member transactions and function as shock absorbers. Similarly, the restriction on the allocation of profits helps foster to business transactions with members and limits managerial discretion. For this reason, the PECOL consider these mechanisms to be a feature of a cooperative's identity. Accordingly, Austrian law should be amended to enhance the possibility of choosing from different corporate forms, which ultimately promotes competition

[1]Because it determines the whole structure of the legal concept.

[2]It would therefore also be necessary to carry out specific studies on tax law to better show why certain rules are necessary.

and thus leads to efficiency. These amendments also need to focus on tax law (as the Italian approach shows).

Another important example of how the PECOL help to indicate whether provisions should be amended is the question of whether the members of an organ of an agricultural SCE should also be members of the SCE. The principle of *Selbstorganschaft*,[3] as determined by the Austrian legal system, cannot be applied, while another less restrictive solution applies to Italian SCEs, which aligns to the PECOL. The PECOL impose this requirement as a specific feature of cooperative identity. The non-application of the principle of *Selbstorganschaft* therefore creates to a substantial difference between an Austrian and an Italian agricultural SCE.

The PECOL have proved useful by highlighting the 'essential' differences. It helps to discuss the specific characteristics of cooperatives, to clarify relevant issues and to create an awareness of cooperative identity in other fields of law, like tax law and competition law. Yet, it has to be admitted that the identification of a common core, inevitably, always includes political considerations and evaluations; therefore, the development of rules is an expression of path dependency. This fact also illustrates how difficult it is to determine identifying features. This weakness in the methodology may be criticised, but it must be accepted, because legislation is a political act. The same is true for the PECOL, which, from an economic perspective, help us to define a menu of corporate forms that, as has already been argued, contributes to increasing efficiency.[4] The demand for a menu of different corporate forms is justified, because studies show that cooperatives, including agricultural cooperatives, are successful instruments of entrepreneurial activities and should therefore be protected legal structures.

Thus, there are particular differences between an Italian and Austrian agricultural SCE; yet, the overall evaluation of the differences shows that there are few that are truly relevant, at least not with relation to the issues discussed in this study. The Austrian legislature exercised few options, while Italy exercised none at all.[5] Accordingly, the two models are more harmonized than expected. Whereas the Austrian solution is strongly based on statutory freedom, the Italian law contains provisions (among them many default provisions) that regulate certain issues. The Italian mainly mutual cooperative is incentivised—and incentives require clear requirements to be applicable. Apart from this observation, a further positive aspect of the Italian approach is that default provisions help to reduce transactions cost. One can consider the provisions that deal with the principle of 'one member, one vote' and its exemption. Austrian law is vague, but this vagueness is counterbalanced by the obligation for Austrian cooperatives to join an association of cooperatives; these

---

[3]It states that only members of a cooperative can become members of the cooperative's organs.

[4]It can be argued that the features of cooperative identity help better design the menu of corporate forms, which ultimately fosters competition.

[5]As explained in Sect. 2.4, the SCE-R contains various options for member states, according to which they may adapt specific provisions of the SCE-R, if desired.

associations then helps to draft and amend statutes. Thus, the rules applied to Italian and Austrian agricultural SCEs yield practical results, that are not so different.

These observations, however, concern only one aspect of the study, which considers the SCE as an agricultural producer cooperative and how this type of cooperative is determined under the two different legal systems. I have considered a producer cooperative, specifically, agricultural cooperatives that process, transform and sell the products that their members supply. Examples can be found in the wine and fruit or milk sector.

Recalling what has been said in Sect. 3.3, it can be said that both legal systems, when determining what an agricultural cooperative is, focus on agricultural activities (conducted by a natural or legal person). Although they apply different approaches to determine the content of these activities, there are similarities and overlaps. The Italian legal system heavily focuses on the natural phenomenon (biological cycle), while the Austrian legal system takes a mixed approach that combines the natural phenomenon with lists of products and activities (list-based approach). I argue that the latter approach is necessary because, compared to the Italian approach, Austrian law does not refer so strictly to natural phenomenon; it also regards agriculture in its historical development and thus as a social phenomenon.

Some elements in the Austrian provisions consider agriculture in its social embeddedness. For example, this more open approach makes it possible to also include the product resulting from a transformation process in the concept of agricultural activity (i.e., wine, not only grapes). Every producer should have the right to sell his products. Another example is the definition of ancillary trades: the law requires that the agricultural character of the holding be maintained. Thus, compared to the Italian approach, the Austrian solutions seems to be more vague and to contain blurred boundaries. This is compensated by the list-based approach as the second element of the Austrian approach,; this enables a clearer delimitation. On the other hand, by identifying the notion of a biological cycle as an essential feature of agricultural activities, the Italian system reduces uncertainty (though not completely), so it does not need this list-based approach. Yet, clarifications were still needed also in the Italian approach: one can think of the entrepreneur who feeds the animals for a few days without actually carrying out an activity aimed at maintaining and developing the biological cycle of the animal.

If these activities are carried out by an SCE, it shall become an agricultural SCE. In this case, the SCE carries out this activity directly and must therefore be regarded as a farmer or agricultural entrepreneur; however, both legal systems also allow an SCE to provide certain services, such as processing, storage, sale, etc., for a group of farmers. These are not agricultural activities themselves, but supporting activities that are part of a production and distribution chain that is typical of industrial societies. Both legal regimes recognise this important aspect and, therefore, grant cooperatives (and SCEs) the status of an agricultural cooperative.

The analyses have shown that vagueness is also noticeable in European law, where a list-based approach constitutes the starting point for questions regarding what agriculture is or what an agricultural activity consists of. At the European level, this is a crucial issue, because, for political reasons agriculture is (strongly) incentivised. This has made it necessary to continuously develop an approach that encompasses all its inherent aspects and gives agriculture a suitable framework for development and adaption: this framework captures products and the needs of producers and consumers, and also considers agriculture as a producer of public goods. Given this combination of aspects, the notion of agriculture (and of agricultural activities) must be understood as an open concept, influenced by political considerations. This has an impact on the national legal concept of agriculture, because within the Common Market it is European law (and the CAP) that sets the stage, and not national law. As a consequence, it must be examined whether the national model is (still) capable of dealing appropriately with new European developments and legal requirements.

Thus, the study analysed three different legal approaches to agriculture, some of which overlap. The overlap lies not only in the natural phenomenon that necessarily determines the content of the legal term 'agriculture', but also in the integration into the European Union. This requires an appropriate examination and coordination of the different approaches, at least at the meta-level. The common core is the professional's care of plants and animals and the production not only of food, but also of public goods. These are activities that depend on the forces of nature and are therefore subject to a risk that cannot be fully controlled by the farmer or agricultural entrepreneur. I argue that all three legal approaches are based on this blunt statement: hence, it is not the content that makes the difference, but the concepts and notions.

The connection to forces of nature reveals the vulnerability of agricultural activities; probably also for this reason, agricultural cooperatives have some specific aspects to which the economic analyses point. This made it possible to specifically discuss legal provisions that relate to efficiency issues.[6] Evaluating the differences shows that there are few relevant differences between Austrian and Italian agricultural SCEs, at least where the topics of this study are concerned. The Austrian legislature has exercised few options, while Italy has exercised none at all. As a result, Austrian agricultural SCEs can apply provisions that are not allowed for an Italian SCE, so that under Austrian law, for example, the governing organ of an SCE can be structured in a more diverse way, which allows greater flexibility and efficiency. On the other hand, the Italian legal system offers a stricter approach. If we look at the competence of the governing organ of an agricultural SCE, the Italian solution seems more efficient from a legal-economic point of view, since it uses a general clause (catch-all provision).

Apart from these specific differences, both agricultural SCEs can use various instruments to increase efficiency, as the legal frameworks offer room to manoeuvre; the actual increase in efficiency is therefore a question of the application of the law. A crucial point in this context is the link with the interests of members. The more homogeneous the interests, the better. The cooperative sector is very heterogeneous, as the function of a cooperative depends on its members' needs, which in turn are

[6] At this point, we should remember that this study is anchored in law and therefore does not conduct a full efficiency analysis of agricultural SCEs.

closely linked to the type of cooperative. Therefore, understanding the dynamics of a cooperative depends upon knowing whether it is a consumer, worker or producer cooperative. This is necessary to better define the members' needs and thus explains how cooperatives work, at least from an economic point of view. The analyses have shown that this homogeneous membership base is attainable, since the various provisions offer statutory freedom. The involvement of members can make an agricultural SCE more stable and thus more efficient. On the other hand, specific problems may arise, for example, when members enter and leave at different times. This activity can lead to a heterogeneity of interests and ultimately disrupt the function of an agricultural SCE. One instrument that reduces this risk is pre-defined repayment periods. However, the provisions of the SCE-R that govern withdrawal can lead to a temporary lock-in. Thus, certain efficiency problems result if withdrawal is not properly regulated.

The vulnerability of the agricultural sector is being countered by the European legislator through the legal institution of POs, which is also applicable to an agricultural SCE. The application of these rules will enable an agricultural SCE to reconcile the interests of farmers with the entrepreneurial risks of his SCE, in particular, to resolve principal agent conflicts and thus to reduce agency costs. This reconciliation will make an agricultural SCE more efficient.

In general, rationalisation and homogeneity reduce transaction costs; homogeneity then also lowers the costs for resolving conflicts. An agricultural SCE must first account for certain details that arise from national law and that cannot be circumvented. The shape of other aspects of the statutory regulation, in which the legislature offers statutory freedom, can then be influenced by the provisions for POs, which addresses issues that are discussed in agricultural economics. This will increase efficiency and harmonise the statutory provisions to be applied.

Applying the provisions for POs is voluntary, yet, it's application shows that these rules make farmers more efficient and therefore better off. The development of this particular regime is based on political considerations that highlight the importance of agricultural production. One can critically add that the European approach to agriculture, which already started to consider these activities with respect to the public goods they produce, must be forced to consider this latter aspect in the coming years because of climate change. Thus, it could also be of great scientific value to consider how the provisions for POs should deal with this issue and what impact it should have upon notions of agriculture. In other words: shall POs have a particular role in combatting climate change and, if yes, how?

Thus, these analyses showed that agricultural SCEs are not so different, at least, if one considers the Italian and Austrian legal systems. This is, first, because certain options have not been implemented, which means that EU law applies, and, second, because both are granted a high degree of statutory freedom. Applying the rules for POs helps to organise the agricultural SCE efficiently. However, these findings lead to other questions and issues. For example, it might be interesting to analyse the extent to which there really are significant differences in practice between the statutes of agricultural cooperatives. This would require a legal empirical investigation of the different statutes as they are applied in practice. This might also lead to better a understanding of the extent to which tax law is relevant to the practice of drafting statutes in both Italy and Austria. In other words, a more open approach on the same subject—namely, the comparison of agricultural cooperatives and SCEs—could help to better understand why, in practice, certain rules are chosen instead of other rules.

The PECOL could be used as a useful guideline for conducting studies in the field of legal empirical research, e.g., for structuring interviews. In fact, as shown, most of the characteristics defined by the PECOL can be found in the different European legal systems, albeit in various forms. The PECOL could thus also be used as a valid model for thinking about a common core of European agricultural law. One central question could be: how do other legal systems conceptualise the fact that agricultural activities depend on natural forces?

Yet, nothing has been said about whether it is appropriate to talk about one or whether it is justified to talk about more/many SCEs: I argue that the latter is not the case. Rather, the SCE is a unique type of cooperative that is flexible enough to integrate different European legal approaches into a single entity, while at the same time allowing for formal and substantial differences. However, such possible differences between the Italian and Austrian legals systems are few. I, therefore, have the impression that the SCE-R is similar to what is typical of the European Union: unity in diversity.[7]

[7]Yet, maybe a set of rules not necessary anymore: here I repeat the heretical issues raised in Sect. 3.3.4. It should also be scientifically interesting to analyse whether POs that operate across borders do make the SCE-R obsolete, at least, if applied in the agricultural sector.

References

(2013) Körperschaftssteuerrichtlinien 2013: KStR

Abler D (2004) Multifunctionality, agricultural policy, and environmental policy. Agric Resour Econ Rev 33:8–17. https://doi.org/10.1017/S1068280500005591

Abrami A (2005) Manuale di diritto forestale e dell'ambiente territoriale: con appendice legislativa. Giuffrè, Milano

Abriani N (2019) Corporate governance e sistema monistico: linee evolutive. Rivista delle società:527–539

Adams M (1991) Eigentum, Kontrolle und beschränkte Haftung, 1st edn. Wirtschaftsrecht und Wirtschaftspolitik, vol 113. Nomos, Baden-Baden

Adams RB, Ferreira D (2007) A theory of friendly boards. J Finance 62:217–250. https://doi.org/10.1111/j.1540-6261.2007.01206.x

Adar Y, Sirena P (2013) Principles and rules in the emerging European contract law: from the PECL to the CESL, and beyond. Eur Rev Contract Law 9:1–37. https://doi.org/10.1515/ercl-2013-0001

Adornato F (2004) Di cosa parliamo quando parliamo di agricoltura. Agricoltura Istituzioni Mercati:5–9

Adornato F (2007) Agricoltura a cinquant'anni dal trattato di Roma. Agricoltura Istituzioni Mercati:5–9

Ajani G, Peruginelli G, Sartor G, Tiscornia D (eds) (2007) The multilanguage complexity of European law: methodologies in comparison. Workshop, 17 November 2006, European University Institute, Fiesole, Italy. Information and communications technology. European Press Acad. Publ, Florence

Ajates Gonzalez R (2018) Farmers' cooperatives and sustainable food systems in Europe. Earthscan Food and Agriculture Ser. Routledge, Milton

Akerlof GA (1970) The market for "lemons": quality uncertainty and the market mechanism. Q J Econ 84:488–500. https://doi.org/10.2307/1879431

Albamonte D (2008) Lo statuto della società cooperativa europea. In: Capriglione F (ed) La nuova disciplina della società europea. Cedam, Padova, pp 295–320

Albisinni F (2003) Nuove regole di impresa nel sistema europea di diritto alimentare. Rivista di diritto agrario:326–344

Albisinni F (2010) Istituzioni e regole dell'agricoltura: dopo il trattato di Lisbona. Rivista di diritto agrario:206–247

G. Miribung, *The Agricultural Cooperative in the Framework of the European Cooperative Society*, Economic Analysis of Law in European Legal Scholarship 8, https://doi.org/10.1007/978-3-030-44154-8

Albisinni F (2011a) Il diritto agrario europeo dopo Lisbona fra intervento e regolazione: i codici europei dell'agricoltura. Agricoltura-Istituzioni-Mercati:29–52
Albisinni F (2011b) Le peculiarità giuridiche dell'impresa agricola in Italia oggi. In: Accademia dei Georgofili (eds) Le nuove missioni dell'impresa agraria: Giornata di studio, pp 275–293
Albisinni F (2013) La nuova OCM ed i contratti agroalimentari. Rivista di diritto alimentare:4–14
Albisinni F (2014a) La definizione di attività agricola nella nuova PAC, tra incentivazione e centralizzazione regolatoria. Rivista Italiana di Diritto Pubblico Communitario XXIV:967–990
Albisinni F (2014b) Mercati agroalimentari e disciplina di filiera. Rivista di diritto alimentare:4–9
Alchian AA (1977) Some economics of property rights. In: Alchian AA, Coase RH (eds) Economic forces at work. Liberty Press, Indianapolis, pp 127–149
Alchian AA, Demsetz H (1972) Production, information costs, and economic organization. Am Econ Rev 62:777–795
Alchian AA, Woodward S (1987) Reflections on the theory of the firm. J Inst Theor Econ (JITE)/ Zeitschrift für die gesamte Staatswissenschaft 143:110–136
Ales E (2008) Italy. In: Study on the implementation of the Directive 2003/72/EC (employee involvement in the European cooperative society) in ten Member States. https://ec.europa.eu/social/main.jsp?catId=707&langId=en&intPageId=213. Accessed 21 Nov 2019
Alessi R (2006) L'impresa agricola. In: Alessi R, Contaldi L, Corapi D, de Donno B (eds) Impresa e società nel diritto comunitario, 2nd edn. Giappichelli, Torino, pp 1234–1274
Alessi R (2019) La ricerca della "specialità" dell'impresa agricola e l'inesorabile tramonto dell'art. 2135 cod. civ. Rivista di diritto agrario:182–196
Alfandari E, Piot B (2004) Die Mitgliedschaft in der SCE. In: Schulze R (ed) Europäische Genossenschaft SCE: Handbuch, 1st edn. Nomos, Baden-Baden, pp 77–90
Alho E (2015) Farmers' self-reported value of cooperative membership: evidence from heterogeneous business and organization structures. Agric Food Econ 3:5. https://doi.org/10.1186/s40100-015-0041-6
Altmann S, Falk A, Marklein F (2011) Eingeschränkt rationales Verhalten: Evidenz und Implikationen. In: Fleischer H, Zimmer D, Altmann S (eds) Beitrag der Verhaltensökonomie (Behavioral Economics) zum Handels- und Wirtschaftsrecht. Recht und Wirtschaft, Frankfurt am Main, pp 63–82
Amat L, Chlebicka A, Ferreira I, Montanari F, Sorrentino A, Szabo GG, Traon D, Russo C (2019) Study of the best ways for producer organisations to be formed, carry out their activities and be supported: final report. OPL, Luxembourg
Ambrosini S (2003a) La riforma delle società: Profili della nuova disciplina. Giappichelli, Torino
Ambrosini S (2003b) L'amministrazione e i controlli nelle spa. Giurisprudenza Commerciale:308
Ambrosini S (2004) Artt. 2403-2406. In: Cottino G, Bonfante G, Cagnasso O, Montalenti P (eds) Il nuovo diritto societario I: Commento al D. lgs. 17 gennaio 2003, n. 6, D. Lgs. 17 gennaio 2003, n. 5, D. lgs. 11 aprile 2002, n. 61 (art. 1). 1. Artt. 2325-2409 c.c, 1st edn. Zanichelli, Bologna, pp 892–909
Arcas-Lario N, Martín-Ugedo JF, Mínguez-Vera A (2014) Farmers' satisfaction with fresh fruit and vegetable marketing Spanish cooperatives: an explanation from agency theory. Int Food Agribus Manage Rev:127–146. https://doi.org/10.22004/ag.econ.163357
Arlen J, Spitzer M, Talley E (2002) Endowment effects within corporate agency relationships. J Leg Stud 31:1–37. https://doi.org/10.1086/324659
Armour J, Whincop MJ (2001) An economic analysis of shared property in partnership and close corporations law. J Corp Law:73–92. https://doi.org/10.1093/acprof:oso/9780199264353.003.0003
Armour J, Whincop MJ (2004) An economic analysis of shared property in partnership and close corporations law. In: McCahery J, Raaijmakers MJGC, Vermeulen EM (eds) The governance of close corporations and partnerships: US and European perspectives. Oxford University Press, Oxford, pp 73–92
Armour J, Hansmann H, Kraakman RH (2009a) Agency problems and legal strategies. In: Kraakman RH, Armour J, Davies P, Enriques L, Hansmann H, Hertig G, Hopt K, Kanda H, Rock E (eds) The anatomy of corporate law: a comparative and functional approach, 2nd edn. Oxford University Press, Oxford, pp 35–53

Armour J, Hertig G, Kanda H (2009b) Transactions with creditors. In: Kraakman RH, Armour J, Davies P, Enriques L, Hansmann H, Hertig G, Hopt K, Kanda H, Rock E (eds) The anatomy of corporate law: a comparative and functional approach, 2nd edn. Oxford University Press, Oxford, pp 115–152

Armour J, Hansmann H, Kraakman RH (2009c) What is corporate law. In: Kraakman RH, Armour J, Davies P, Enriques L, Hansmann H, Hertig G, Hopt K, Kanda H, Rock E (eds) The anatomy of corporate law: a comparative and functional approach, 2nd edn. Oxford University Press, Oxford, pp 1–34

Arnò G, Cancarini S, Romanelli F (2007) La società europea: La disciplina comunitaria e il suo recepimento in Italia e nei principali stati membri. EGEA, Milano

Arrow KJ (1973) Higher education as a filter. J Public Econ 2:193–216. https://doi.org/10.1016/0047-2727(73)90013-3

Artmann E (2002) Die Organisationsverfassung der Europäischen Aktiengesellschaft. Wirtschaftsrechtliche Blätter:189

Astl H, Steinböck G (2014a) § 11. In: Dellinger M (ed) Genossenschaftsgesetz samt Nebengesetzen: Kommentar, 2nd edn. LexisNexis ARD Orac, Wien, pp 180–184

Astl H, Steinböck G (2014b) § 14. In: Dellinger M (ed) Genossenschaftsgesetz samt Nebengesetzen: Kommentar, 2nd edn. LexisNexis ARD Orac, Wien, pp 186–188

Astl H, Steinböck G (2014c) § 3. In: Dellinger M (ed) Genossenschaftsgesetz samt Nebengesetzen: Kommentar, 2nd edn. LexisNexis ARD Orac, Wien, pp 108–115

Astl H, Steinböck G (2014d) § 5. In: Dellinger M (ed) Genossenschaftsgesetz samt Nebengesetzen: Kommentar, 2nd edn. LexisNexis ARD Orac, Wien, pp 122–158

Astl H, Steinböck G (2014e) § 5a. In: Dellinger M (ed) Genossenschaftsgesetz samt Nebengesetzen: Kommentar, 2nd edn. LexisNexis ARD Orac, Wien, pp 159–167

Auletta GG, Salanitro N (2009) Diritto commerciale, 17th edn. Giuffrè, Milano

Austrian Co-operative Act (unofficial translation), www.raiffeisenverband.at/wp-content/uploads/2014/10/GenG-eng_2016.pdf. Accessed 19 Nov 2019

Austrian Food Code (Codex Alimentarius Austriacus). http://www.lebensmittelbuch.at/. Accessed 26 Nov 2019

Aviram A (2006) A note on economic theories of the firm. SSRN J. https://doi.org/10.2139/ssrn.880435

Aviram A, Tor A (2004) Overcoming impediments to information sharing. Ala Law Rev:231–279. https://doi.org/10.2139/ssrn.435600

Avsec F (2009) Die Europäische Genossenschaft innerhalb des europäischen Wirtschaftsraumes. Marburger Beiträge zum Genossenschaftswesen, vol 53. Universität Marburg, Institut für Genossenschaftswesen, Marburg

Bachmann G (2008) Optionsmodelle im Privatrecht. JuristenZeitung 63:11–20. https://doi.org/10.1628/002268808783355591

Bachner T (2012) § 105. In: Doralt W, Nowotny C, Kalss S (eds) Kommentar zum Aktiengesetz, 2nd edn. Linde, Wien, pp 1501–1531

Bäck E (2012) Anerben- und Höferecht. In: Norer R (ed) Handbuch des Agrarrechts, 2. Aufl. Verlag Österreich, Wien, pp 717–734

Baer S (2011) Rechtssoziologie: Eine Einführung in die interdisziplinäre Rechtsforschung, 1st edn. Nomos-Lehrbuch, Nomos, Baden-Baden

Bainbridge SM (2001) Why a board? Group decisionmaking in corporate governance. Vanderbilt Law Rev 55:1–56

Balestrino A (1994) Beni pubblici. In: Zamagni S (ed) Politica economica II. UTET libreria, Torino, pp 45–48

Balzano M (2004) L'assemblea. In: Marasà G (ed) Le cooperative prima e dopo la riforma del diritto societario. Cedam, Padova, pp 533–582

Balzarini P (2006) Art. 2428. In: Notari M, Bianchi LA (eds) Obbligazione bilancio: Artt. 2410-2435 -bis c.c. EGEA, Milano, pp 595–615

Balzarini P (2007) Responsabilità solidale e concorrente di amministratori e sindaci. Le società:875–881

Bamberg G, Coenenberg AG, Krapp M (2013) Betriebswirtschaftliche Entscheidungslehre, 15th edn. Vahlens Kurzlehrbücher. Vahlen, München

Baracchini F (2007) L'appropriazione delle corporate opportunities come fattispecie di infedeltà degli amministratori di s.p.a. In: Abbadessa P, Portale GB (eds) Assemblea, amministrazione. UTET, Torino, pp 603–656

Barbarito MC (2004) Art. 2375. In: Cottino G, Bonfante G, Cagnasso O, Montalenti P (eds) Il nuovo diritto societario I: Commento al D. lgs. 17 gennaio 2003, n. 6, D. Lgs. 17 gennaio 2003, n. 5, D. lgs. 11 aprile 2002, n. 61 (art. 1). 1. Artt. 2325-2409 c.c, 1st edn. Zanichelli, Bologna, pp 585–596

Barney JB (1990) Organizational economics, 1st edn. The Jossey-Bass social and behavioral science series. Jossey-Bass, San Francisco

Barton DG (1989) What is a cooperative. In: Cobia DW (ed) Cooperatives in agriculture. Prentice-Hall, Englewood Cliffs, pp 1–20

Bassi A (1995) Le società cooperative. Il diritto attuale, vol 20. UTET, Torino

Bassi A (2003) Le società cooperative. In: Bassi A, Buonocore V, Pescatore S (eds) La riforma del diritto societario: Commento ai d.lgs. n. 5-6 del 17 gennaio 2003. Giappichelli, Torino, pp 233–277

Bassi A, Passalacqua P (2014) Art. 2511. In: Santosuosso DU (ed) Delle società, dell'azienda, della concorrenza. UTET, Torino, pp 3–66

Bassi A, Schlesinger P (1988) Delle imprese cooperative e delle mutue assicuratrici: Artt. 2511 - 2548. Il codice civile - commentario, / dir. da Piero Schlesinger. Giuffrè, Milano

Beintema N, Bossio D, Dreyfus F, Fernandez M, Gurib-Fakim A, Hurni H, Izac A-M, Jiggins J, Kranjac-Berisavljevic G, RRB L, Ochola W, Osman-Elasha B, Plencovich C, Röling N, Rosegrant M, Rosenthal E, Smith L (2009) Global summary for decision makers, international assessment of agricultural science and technology for development. https://www.researchgate.net/publication/269395240_Global_Summary_for_Decision_Makers_International_Assessment_of_Agricultural_Science_and_Technology_for_Development. Accessed 29 Nov 2019

Bellantuono G (2000) I contratti incompleti nel diritto e nell'economia. Dipartimento di scienze giuridiche, Università di Trento, vol 30. Cedam, Padova

Bellantuono G (2016) The comparative law and economics of energy markets. In: Eisenberg T, Ramello GB (eds) Comparative law and economics. Edward Elgar Publishing, Cheltenham, pp 236–261

Bellantuono G, Iamiceli P (2005) Analisi economica del diritto. UNI service, Trento

Belliggiano A (2009) Percezione della sicurezza alimenatare e nuovi modelli di organizzazione della produzione. Rivista di diritto alimentare:42–44

Benatti L (2005) Artt. 2397-2406. In: Maffei Alberti A (ed) Il nuovo diritto delle società: Commento sistematico al D. lgs. 17 gennaio 2003, n. 6, aggiornato al D. lgs. 28 dicembre 2004, n. 310. Cedam, Padova, pp 869–971

Berk J, DeMarzo P, Harford J (2015) Fundamentals of corporate finance, 3rd edn. The Pearson series in finance. Pearson Education, Boston

Berman KV (1967) Worker-owned plywood companies: an economic analysis. Washington State University Press, Pullman

Beuthien V (2007) Die Europäische Genossenschaft als gesellschaftsrechtliche Herausforderung: Was muss ein Genossenschaftsgesetz leisten? Zeitschrift für das gesamte Genossenschaftswesen 57:3–16. https://doi.org/10.1515/zfgg-2007-0102

Beuthien V (2018) Einleitung. In: Beuthien V, Schöpflin M (eds) Genossenschaftsgesetz: Mit Umwandlungs- und Kartellrecht sowie Statut der Europäischen Genossenschaft, 16th edn. Beck, München, pp 1–24

Beuthien V, Jud W (2007) Genossenschaftsrechsänderungsgesetz 2006. FOG, Wien

Beyer J (2005) Pfadabhängigkeit ist nicht gleich Pfadabhängigkeit! Wider den impliziten Konservatismus eines gängigen Konzepts. Zeitschrift für Soziologie 34:5–21. https://doi.org/10.1515/zfsoz-2005-0101
Bianca M, Zanardo A (2016) La Società Europea e la Società Cooperativa Europea. In: Pederzini E (ed) Percorsi di diritto societario europeo, 3rd edn. Giappichelli, Torino, pp 177–214
Bianchi LA (2016) Il modello monistico è più efficiente di quello tradizionale? Appunti per una ricerca. Analisi Giuridica dell'Economia:23–34. https://doi.org/10.1433/83783
Bieber R (2016) § 23 Landwirtschafts- und Fischereipolitik. In: Bieber R, Epiney A, Haag M, Kotzur M (eds) Die Europäische Union: Europarecht und Politik. Nomos, Baden-Baden, pp 543–544
Bieber R, Kotzur M (2016) § 4 Institutionelles System. In: Bieber R, Epiney A, Haag M, Kotzur M (eds) Die Europäische Union: Europarecht und Politik. Nomos, Baden-Baden, pp 101–127
Bijman J, Hanisch M (2012) Developing a typology of cooperatives and producer organisations in Europe. In: Van der Sangen G, Pyykkönen POP, Iliopoulus C, Kühl R, Hagedorn K, Hanisch M, Judis R, Gijselinckx C, Hendrikse G, Hak T, Poppe K, Bijman J (eds) Support for farmers' cooperatives. Wageningen
Bijman J, Hendrikse G, van Oijen A (2013) Accommodating two worlds in one organisation: changing board models in agricultural cooperatives. Manag Decis Econ 34:204–217. https://doi.org/10.1002/mde.2584
Bijman J, Hanisch M, Van der Sangen G (2014a) Shifting control?: The changes of internal governance in agricultural cooperatives in the EU. Ann Public Coop Econ 85:641–661. https://doi.org/10.1111/apce.12055
Bijman J, Pyykkönen P, Ollila P (2014b) Transnationalization of agricultural cooperatives in Europe. Dovenschmidt Q 2:168–178. https://doi.org/10.5553/DQ/221199812014002004005
Binder R, Lengauer A (2014a) § 24a. In: Dellinger M (ed) Genossenschaftsgesetz samt Nebengesetzen: Kommentar, 2nd edn. LexisNexis ARD Orac, Wien, pp 272–273
Binder R, Lengauer A (2014b) § 25. In: Dellinger M (ed) Genossenschaftsgesetz samt Nebengesetzen: Kommentar, 2nd edn. LexisNexis ARD Orac, Wien, pp 331–333
Birchall J (1997) The international co-operative movement. Manchester University Press, Manchester
Birchall J (2011) People centred businesses: co-operatives, mutuals and the idea of membership. Palgrave Macmillan, Basingstoke
Blair MM, Stout LA (2006) Specific investment and corporate law. Eur Bus Organ Law Rev 7:473–500. https://doi.org/10.1017/S1566752906004733
Blome-Drees J, Zerche J, Schmale I (1998) Einführung in die Genossenschaftslehre: Genossenschaftstheorie und Genossenschaftsmanagement. Oldenbourg Wissenschaftsverlag, München
Blumberg PI (1985–1986) Limited liability and corporate groups. J Corp Law:573–632
Bodiguel L, Cardwell M (2006) Nuove definizioni di "agricoltura" per un'agricoltura in evoluzione: Francia ed Inghilterra a confronto. Rivista di diritto agrario:149–173
Boettcher E (1980) Die Genossenschaft in der Marktwirtschaft: Einzelwirtschaftliche Theorie der Genossenschaften. Schriften zur Kooperationsforschung, vol 1. Mohr, Tübingen
Bolognini S (2011a) Il bosco e la disciplina forestale. In: Costato L, Germanò A, Rook Basile E (eds) Trattato di diritto agrario: II. UTET, Torino, pp 81–134
Bolognini S (2011b) Organizzazione individuale, familiare o collettiva d'impresa, e tutele differenziate. Rivista di diritto agrario:330–350
Bolognini S (2019) La "specialità" dell'impresa agricola nel registro delle imprese fra codice civile e legislazione di settore. Rivista di diritto agrario:279–308
Bolten P, Becht M, Röell A (2007) Corporate law and governance. In: Polinsky AM, Shavell S (eds) Handbook of law and economics: volume 2, 1st edn. North Holland, Amsterdam, pp 829–944
Bonelli F (2004) Gli amministratori di spa dopo la riforma delle società. Giuffrè, Milano
Bonfante G (1999) Delle imprese cooperative: Art. 2511-2545. Commentario del Codice civile Scialoja-Branca. Libro quinto, Del lavoro, art. 2511-2545. Zanichelli, Bologna, Roma

Bonfante G (2004a) Art. 2527. In: Cottino G, Bonfante G, Cagnasso O, Montalenti P (eds) Il nuovo diritto societario III: Commento al D. lgs. 17 gennaio 2003, n. 6, D. Lgs. 17 gennaio 2003, n. 5, D. lgs. 11 aprile 2002, n. 61 (art. 1). 3. Artt. 2484-2548 c.c. norme di attuazione, disciplina processuale, artt. 2621-2641 c.c., 1st edn. Zanichelli, Bologna, pp 2496–2499
Bonfante G (2004b) Art. 2528. In: Cottino G, Bonfante G, Cagnasso O, Montalenti P (eds) Il nuovo diritto societario III: Commento al D. lgs. 17 gennaio 2003, n. 6, D. Lgs. 17 gennaio 2003, n. 5, D. lgs. 11 aprile 2002, n. 61 (art. 1). 3. Artt. 2484-2548 c.c. norme di attuazione, disciplina processuale, artt. 2621-2641 c.c., 1st edn. Zanichelli, Bologna, pp 2500–2508
Bonfante G (2004c) Art. 2543. In: Cottino G, Bonfante G, Cagnasso O, Montalenti P (eds) Il nuovo diritto societario III: Commento al D. lgs. 17 gennaio 2003, n. 6, D. Lgs. 17 gennaio 2003, n. 5, D. lgs. 11 aprile 2002, n. 61 (art. 1). 3. Artt. 2484-2548 c.c. norme di attuazione, disciplina processuale, artt. 2621-2641 c.c., 1st edn. Zanichelli, Bologna, pp 2590–2594
Bonfante G (2004d) Art. 2544. In: Cottino G, Bonfante G, Cagnasso O, Montalenti P (eds) Il nuovo diritto societario III: Commento al D. lgs. 17 gennaio 2003, n. 6, D. Lgs. 17 gennaio 2003, n. 5, D. lgs. 11 aprile 2002, n. 61 (art. 1). 3. Artt. 2484-2548 c.c. norme di attuazione, disciplina processuale, artt. 2621-2641 c.c., 1st edn. Zanichelli, Bologna, pp 2595–2600
Bonfante G (2004e) Art. 2545 quinquies. In: Cottino G, Bonfante G, Cagnasso O, Montalenti P (eds) Il nuovo diritto societario III: Commento al D. lgs. 17 gennaio 2003, n. 6, D. Lgs. 17 gennaio 2003, n. 5, D. lgs. 11 aprile 2002, n. 61 (art. 1). 3. Artt. 2484-2548 c.c. norme di attuazione, disciplina processuale, artt. 2621-2641 c.c., 1st edn. Zanichelli, Bologna, pp 2619–2622
Bonfante G (2004f) Art. 2545 sexies. In: Cottino G, Bonfante G, Cagnasso O, Montalenti P (eds) Il nuovo diritto societario III: Commento al D. lgs. 17 gennaio 2003, n. 6, D. Lgs. 17 gennaio 2003, n. 5, D. lgs. 11 aprile 2002, n. 61 (art. 1). 3. Artt. 2484-2548 c.c. norme di attuazione, disciplina processuale, artt. 2621-2641 c.c., 1st edn. Zanichelli, Bologna, pp 2623–2633
Bonfante G (2004g) Art. 2545 ter. In: Cottino G, Bonfante G, Cagnasso O, Montalenti P (eds) Il nuovo diritto societario III: Commento al D. lgs. 17 gennaio 2003, n. 6, D. Lgs. 17 gennaio 2003, n. 5, D. lgs. 11 aprile 2002, n. 61 (art. 1). 3. Artt. 2484-2548 c.c. norme di attuazione, disciplina processuale, artt. 2621-2641 c.c., 1st edn. Zanichelli, Bologna, pp 2608–2613
Bonfante G (2006) La società cooperativa europea. In: Galletti D, Fici A (eds) La società cooperativa europea: Quali prospettive per la cooperazione italiana? Universita degli Studi di Trento, Trento, pp 3–12
Bonfante G (ed) (2014a) La società cooperativa. Trattato di diritto commerciale. Cedam, Padova
Bonfante G (2014b) L'inammissibilità del voto segreto nelle cooperative: una questione aperta. Le società:811–815
Bono P (2012) Country report: Italy. In: Van der Sangen G, Pyykkönen POP, Iliopoulus C, Kühl R, Hagedorn K, Hanisch M, Judis R, Gijselinckx C, Hendrikse G, Hak T, Poppe K, Bijman J (eds) Support for farmers' cooperatives. Wageningen, pp 1–65
Bonus H (1986) The cooperative association as a business enterprise: a study in the economics of transactions. J Inst Theor Econ (JITE)/Zeitschrift für die gesamte Staatswissenschaft 142:310–339
Bortoleto FC, Rogerio de Moura Costa D (2012) The importance of cooperatives' corporate social responsibility to the loyalty of members. J Rural Coop:198–216
Bosi G (2012) I fondi mutualistici: Un'analisi giuridica ed economica. Studi e ricerche. Diritto, vol 636. Il Mulino, Bologna
Brandt U (2002) Überlegungen zu einem SE-Ausführungsgesetz. Neue Zeitschrift für Gesellschaftsrecht:991–996
Brandt U (2003) Der Diskussionsentwurf zu einem SE-Ausführungsgesetz. DStR:1208–1215
Brandt U, Scheifele M (2002) Die Europäische Aktiengesellschaft und das anwendbare Recht. DStR:547–555
Breida MC (2004a) Art. 2409duodecies. In: Cottino G, Bonfante G, Cagnasso O, Montalenti P (eds) Il nuovo diritto societario II: Commento al D. lgs. 17 gennaio 2003, n. 6, D. Lgs. 17 gennaio

2003, n. 5, D. lgs. 11 aprile 2002, n. 61 (art. 1). 2. Artt. 2409 bis-2483 c.c., 1st edn. Zanichelli, Bologna, pp 1155–1171
Breida MC (2004b) Art. 2409novies. In: Cottino G, Bonfante G, Cagnasso O, Montalenti P (eds) Il nuovo diritto societario II: Commento al D. lgs. 17 gennaio 2003, n. 6, D. Lgs. 17 gennaio 2003, n. 5, D. lgs. 11 aprile 2002, n. 61 (art. 1). 2. Artt. 2409 bis-2483 c.c., 1st edn. Zanichelli, Bologna, pp 1117–1132
Breida MC (2004c) Art. 2409terdecies. In: Cottino G, Bonfante G, Cagnasso O, Montalenti P (eds) Il nuovo diritto societario II: Commento al D. lgs. 17 gennaio 2003, n. 6, D. Lgs. 17 gennaio 2003, n. 5, D. lgs. 11 aprile 2002, n. 61 (art. 1). 2. Artt. 2409 bis-2483 c.c., 1st edn. Zanichelli, Bologna, pp 1172–1194
Breida MC (2009) Il modello dualistico. In: Cottino G, Bonfante G, Cagnasso O, Montalenti P (eds) Il nuovo diritto societario nella dottrina e nella giurisprudenza: 2003-2009. Zanichelli, Bologna, pp 673–740
Brendel M (2011) Genossenschaftsbewegung in Deutschland - Geschichte und Aktualität. In: Allgeier M (ed) Solidarität, Flexibilität, Selbsthilfe. VS Verlag für Sozialwissenschaften, Wiesbaden, pp 1–36
Broeusseau É (2008) Contracts: from bilateral sets of incentives to the multi-level governance of relations. In: Brousseau E, Glachant J-M (eds) New institutional economics: a guidebook. Cambridge University Press, Cambridge, pp 37–66
Bruno GSF, Ciavarella A, Linciano N (2018) Boardroom gender diversity and performance of listed companies in Italy. http://www.consob.it/documents/46180/46181/wp87.pdf/d733b58a-44b4-42de-98c7-3c89a82a0182. Accessed 12 Dec 2019
Budzinowski R (2013) Il diritto agrario di fronte alle sfide contemporanee. Alcune riflessioni. Agricoltura Istituzioni Mercati:145–155
Budzinowski R (2018) Der Agrarrechtsbegriff aus Sicht der polnischen Agrarrechtswissenschaft. In: Martínez J (ed) Reichweite und Grenzen des Agrarrechts: Gedächtnisschrift für Dr. Wolfgang Winkler, 1st edn. Nomos Verlagsgesellschaft, Baden-Baden, pp 133–150
Bundesministerium für Finanzen (2005) Einkommenssteuerrichtlinien 2000
Bundesministerium für Finanzen (2013) nt15–nt18. https://findok.bmf.gv.at/findok?execution¼e1s1. Accessed 13 Feb 2017
Bungert H, Beier CH (2002) Die Europäische Aktiengesellschaft. EWS - Europäisches Wirtschafts- und Steuerrecht:1–12
Buonocore V (1997) Diritto della cooperazione. Strumenti. Diritto. Il Mulino, Bologna
Busse C (2018) Die Sonderrechtstheorie im Agrarrecht - Konzeptionelle Überlegungen zu ihrer Weiterentwicklung. In: Martínez J (ed) Reichweite und Grenzen des Agrarrechts: Gedächtnisschrift für Dr. Wolfgang Winkler, 1st edn. Nomos Verlagsgesellschaft, Baden-Baden, pp 19–62
Bydlinski S, Potyka M (2018) §118. In: Artmann E, Karollus M (eds) Kommentar zum Aktiengesetz 2: §§ 7--144, 6th edn. Manz'sche Verlags- und Universitätsbuchhandlung, Wien, pp 1–8
Calandra Buonaura V (2007) Il potere di rappresentanza degli amministratori di società per azioni. In: Abbadessa P, Portale GB (eds) Assemblea, amministrazione. UTET, Torino, pp 657–682
Campobasso GF, Campobasso M (2004) La riforma delle società di capitali e delle cooperative, 2nd edn. Il sistema giuridico italiano. UTET, Torino
Cane P, Kritzer HM (eds) (2013) The Oxford handbook of empirical legal research, reprint. Oxford University Press, Oxford
Canfora I (2008) Il quadro normativo nazionale e comunitario sulle organizzazioni dei produttore. Rivista di diritto agrario:374–382
Capizzano E (1991) Agricoltura, diritto agrario, società: Manuale per la ricerca e l'insegnamento. Cedam, Padova
Capo G (2014a) Art. 2527. In: Santosuosso DU (ed) Delle società, dell'azienda, della concorrenza. UTET, Torino, pp 226–236
Capo G (2014b) Art. 2528. In: Santosuosso DU (ed) Delle società, dell'azienda, della concorrenza. UTET, Torino, pp 236–247

Cardarelli MC (2008) Le variazioni del capitale. In: Cusa E (ed) La cooperativa srl tra legge e autonomia statutaria. Cedam, Padova

Cariello V (2009) Il sistema dualistico: Vincoli tipologici e autonomia statutaria, 2nd edn. Quaderni di banca, borsa e titoli di credito, vol 27. Giuffrè, Milano

Cariello V (2012) Il sistema dualistico. Diritto dei sistemi alternativi di amministrazione e controllo, vol 1. Giappichelli, Torino

Carmignani S (1999) La società in agricoltura. Quaderni di "Studi Senesi", vol 90. Giuffrè, Milano

Carmignani S (2011) Le società agricole. In: Costato L, Germanò A, Rook Basile E (eds) Trattato di diritto agrario: I. UTET, Torino, pp 231–262

Carmignani S (2013) Art. 2135 (L'imprenditore agricolo cooperativa). In: Cagnasso O, Vallebona A (eds) Dell'impresa e del lavoro: Artt. 2118-2187. UTET, Torino, pp 858–873

Carrozza A (1988) Lezioni di diritto agrario I: Elementi di teoria generale. Giuffrè, Milano

Carrozza A (2001a) Agricoltura (teoria generale). In: Massart A, Goldoni M, Sirsi E (eds) Scritti di diritto agrario. Giuffrè, Milano, pp 773–790

Carrozza A (2001b) Diritto agrario "1980". In: Massart A, Goldoni M, Sirsi E (eds) Scritti di diritto agrario. Giuffrè, Milano, pp 361–382

Carrozza A (2001c) La scienza di diritto agrario e il problema dell'oggetto. In: Massart A, Goldoni M, Sirsi E (eds) Scritti di diritto agrario. Giuffrè, Milano, pp 645–662

Carrozza A (2001d) L'autonomia del diritto agrario. In: Massart A, Goldoni M, Sirsi E (eds) Scritti di diritto agrario. Giuffrè, Milano, pp 287–306

Carrozza A (2001e) L'oggetto del diritto agrario. In: Massart A, Goldoni M, Sirsi E (eds) Scritti di diritto agrario. Giuffrè, Milano, pp 705–728

Casadei E (2009) La nozione di impresa agricola dopo la riforma del 2001. Rivista di diritto agrario:309–358

Caselli G (2003) Elogio, con riserve, del collegio sindacale. Giurisprudenza Commerciale:251–266

Casper M (2003) Der Lückenschluß im Statut der Europäischen Aktiengesellschaft. In: Habersack M (ed) Festschrift für Peter Ulmer zum 70. Geburtstag am 2. Januar 2003. De Gruyter, Berlin, pp 51–72

Cavanna M (2014) Le cooperative agricole. In: Bonfante G (ed) La società cooperativa. Cedam, Padova, pp 641–649

Ceccherini A (2008a) Art. 2539. In: Ceccherini A, Schirò S (eds) Società cooperative e mutue assicuratrici: (artt. 2511-2548 c.c.), 2nd edn. Giuffré, Milano, pp 159–162

Ceccherini A (2008b) Art. 2545 quinquies. In: Ceccherini A, Schirò S (eds) Società cooperative e mutue assicuratrici: (artt. 2511-2548 c.c.), 2nd edn. Giuffré, Milano, pp 201–206

Cecco D (2003) La governance nelle società cooperative: l'assemblea. In: Genco R (ed) La riforma delle società cooperative. IPSOA, Milano, pp 115–181

Cesiano D (2013) L'applicazione della "Business Judgment Rule" nella giurisprudenza italiana. Giurisprudenza Commerciale:941–965

Cetra A (2008) La persona giuridica amministratore di una società a responsabilità limitata o società per azioni nella massima n. 100 del Consiglio notarile di Milano. Rivista di diritto societario:676–693

Cetra A (2010) La persona giuridica amministratore nelle società. In: Amministrazione e controllo nel diritto delle società: Liber amicorum Antonio Piras. Giappichelli, Torino, pp 107–127

Cetra A (2019) La nozione d'impresa. In: Cian M (ed) Manuale di diritto commerciale, 3rd edn. G. Giappichelli, Torino, pp 11–20

Chaddad FR, Cook ML (2004) Understanding new cooperative models: an ownership-control rights typology. Rev Agric Econ 26:348–360

Chaddad F, Iliopoulos C (2013) Control rights, governance, and the costs of ownership in agricultural cooperatives. Agribusiness 29:3–22. https://doi.org/10.1002/agr.21328

Cheffins BR (2006) Company law: theory, structure, and operation. Clarendon Press, Oxford

Cheffins BR (2012) Corporations. In: Tushnet M, Cane P (eds) The Oxford handbook of legal studies. Oxford University Press, Oxford, pp 485–509

Cheng TK (2014) An economic analysis of limited shareholder liability in contractual claims. Berkeley Bus Law J:112–181

Chieffi A (2007a) 2525. In: Presti G (ed) Società cooperative: Artt. 2511-2548. EGEA; Giuffrè, Milano, pp 181–202
Chieffi A (2007b) 2527. In: Presti G (ed) Società cooperative: Artt. 2511-2548. EGEA; Giuffrè, Milano, pp 227–240
Chirico S, Troianiello P (2007) La società cooperativa europea: Regolamento CE n. 1435/2003. Cooperative e consorzi. IPSOA, Milano
Chiusoli R (2003) La riforma del diritto societario per le cooperative. IPSOA, Assago (MI)
Chukwu SC (1990) Economics of the co-operative business enterprise. Theory and practice of self-help promotion Ser. A, Monographs and textbooks, vol 2. Marburg Consult für Selbsthilfeförderung, Marburg
Cian G (1998) Hundert Jahre BGB aus italienischer Sicht. ZEuP:215–225
Cian M (2014) Appunti su scambi mutualistici e traslazioni del rischio d'impresa nelle società cooperative. In: Nappi P, Sgarbanti G, Borghi P, Russo L, Fioravanti C, Agostini C, Manservisi S, Borraccetti M, Rizzioli S (eds) Studi in onore di Luigi Costato: III. Jovene, Napoli, pp 165–174
Cian M (2018a) Art. 2364 bis. In: Cian G (ed) Commentario breve al Codice civile: Commentato con dottrina e giurisprudenza, 13th edn. Wolters Kluver, Milano, Padova, p 2776
Cian M (2018b) Art. 2365. In: Cian G (ed) Commentario breve al Codice civile: Commentato con dottrina e giurisprudenza, 13th edn. Wolters Kluver, Milano, Padova, pp 2776–2777
Cian M (2018c) Art. 2366. In: Cian G (ed) Commentario breve al Codice civile: Commentato con dottrina e giurisprudenza, 13th edn. Wolters Kluver, Milano, Padova, pp 2777–2779
Cian M (2018d) Art. 2367. In: Cian G (ed) Commentario breve al Codice civile: Commentato con dottrina e giurisprudenza, 13th edn. Wolters Kluver, Milano, Padova, pp 2779–2780
Cian M (2018e) Art. 2368. In: Cian G (ed) Commentario breve al Codice civile: Commentato con dottrina e giurisprudenza, 13th edn. Wolters Kluver, Milano, Padova, pp 2780–2782
Cian M (2018f) Art. 2370. In: Cian G (ed) Commentario breve al Codice civile: Commentato con dottrina e giurisprudenza, 13th edn. Wolters Kluver, Milano, Padova, pp 2784–2786
Cian M (2018g) Art. 2371. In: Cian G (ed) Commentario breve al Codice civile: Commentato con dottrina e giurisprudenza, 13th edn. Wolters Kluver, Milano, Padova, pp 2786–2787
Cian M (2018h) Art. 2375. In: Cian G (ed) Commentario breve al Codice civile: Commentato con dottrina e giurisprudenza, 13th edn. Wolters Kluver, Milano, Padova, p 2792
Cian M (2018i) Art. 2391. In: Cian G (ed) Commentario breve al Codice civile: Commentato con dottrina e giurisprudenza, 13th edn. Wolters Kluver, Milano, Padova, pp 2845–2850
Ciccarelli (2000) Destinazione degli utili ai fondi mutualistici. Rivista della cooperazione
Cigarini GP (1977) Agrarietà e territorio. Rivista di diritto agrario:688–697
Coase RH (1937) The nature of the firm. Economica 4:386–405. https://doi.org/10.2307/2626876
Codini A (2007) Le cooperative sociali: Assetti di governance e aspetti di gestione. Economia Ricerche, vol 604. Angeli, Milano
Cole GDH (1944) A century of co-operation. Georg Allen & Unwin Ltd
Comitato interregionale dei consigli notarili delle Tre Venezie (2011) Orientamenti del comitato triveneto dei notai in materia di atti societari. http://www.notaitriveneto.it/file/massime/41/1316098658_orientamenti_societari2011.pdf. Accessed 19 Nov 2019
Consiglio nazionale del notariato (2006) Brevi considerazioni sul problema della trasformazione di società cooperativa in società lucrativa contestuale alla perdita della mutualità prevalente. http://www.notariato.it/sites/default/files/7.pdf. Accessed 25 Oct 2017
Conte L, Vannini R (2008) Istituzioni e Governance Cooperativa. Department of Economics University of Siena. Studi e Note di Economia:139–155
Cook ML (1995) The future of U.S. agricultural cooperatives: a neo-institutional approach. Am J Agric Econ 77:1153–1159. https://doi.org/10.2307/1243338
Cook ML, Chaddad FR (2004) Redesigning cooperative boundaries: the emergence of new models. Am J Agric Econ 86:1249–1253. https://doi.org/10.1111/j.0002-9092.2004.00673.x
Cook ML, Iliopoulos C (1999) Beginning to inform the theory of the cooperative firm: emergence of the new generation cooperative. Finn J Bus Econ:525–535
Cook ML, Iliopoulos C (2000) Ill-defined property rights in collective action: the case of US agricultural cooperatives. In: Ménard C (ed) Institutions, contracts and organizations. Edward Elgar Publishing, Cheltenham, pp 335–348

Cook ML, Iliopoulos C (2016) Generic solutions to coordination and organizational costs: informing cooperative longevity. J Chain Netw Sci 16:19–27. https://doi.org/10.3920/JCNS2016.x001
Cools S (2011) Europe's Ius Commune on director revocability. Eur Comp Financ Law Rev 8:199–234. https://doi.org/10.1515/ecfr.2011.199
Cools S (2014) The dividing line between shareholder democracy and board autonomy: inherent conflicts of interest as normative criterion. Eur Comp Financ Law Rev 11:258–296. https://doi.org/10.1515/ecfr-2014-0258
Cooter RD, Freedman BJ (1991) The fiduciary relationship: its economic character and legal consequences. N Y Univ Law Rev:1045–1075
Cooter R, Mattei U, Monateri PG, Pardolesi R, Ulen T (1999) Il mercato delle regole: Analisi economica del diritto civile. Il Mulino, Bologna
COPA-COGECA (2015) Development of agricultural cooperatives in the EU in 2014. http://agricultura.gencat.cat/web/.content/de_departament/de02_estadistiques_observatoris/27_butlletins/02_butlletins_nd/documents_nd/fitxers_estatics_nd/2015/0165_2015_IA_Cooperatives_Cooperatives-UE.pdf. Accessed 5 Dec 2019
COPA-COGECA, History. https://copa-cogeca.eu/CogecaHistory.aspx. Accessed 19 Nov 2019
Corapi D (2011) Art. 2409 duodecies. In: Bonfante G, Corapi D, de Angelis L, Napoleoni V, Rordorf R, Salafia V (eds) Codice commentato delle società: Società di persone, società di capitali, cooperative, consorzi, reati societari: aggiornato con le nuove norme in tema di revisione legale, esercizio dei diritti degli azionisti di società quotate e costituzione delle Spa, 3rd edn. IPSOA, Assago, pp 1095–1106
Corapi D, de Donno B (2006) Le società in generale. In: Alessi R, Contaldi L, Corapi D, de Donno B (eds) Impresa e società nel diritto comunitario, 2nd edn. Giappichelli, Torino, pp 1275–1324
Corapi D, Pernazza F (2011) La Società europea: Fonti comunitarie e modelli nazionali. Giappichelli, Torino
Coropatri M (2010) La business judgment rule in Italia e il privilegio amministrativo. Giurisprudenza Commerciale:129–143
Costa CTD, Bilreiro AdM (2003) The European company statute. European business law & practice series, vol 19. Kluwer Law International, The Hague
Costantino L (2013) L'integrazione verticale per contratto nel settore agro-alimentare: fattispecie giuridica e disciplina applicabile. Contratto e impresa:1446–1471
Costantino L (2015) Agricoltura di gruppo: ruolo delle cooperative di nuova generazione negli USA. Rivista di diritto agrario:510–534
Costato L (2001) L'imprenditore agricolo e il mercato. Rivista di diritto agrario:131–143
Costato L (2004) Dal diritto agrario al diritto agroalimentare. Un percorso ricostruttivo. Agricoltura Istituzioni Mercati:119–130
Costato L (2006) L'imprenditore agricolo: novità codicistiche e polemiche retro. Rivista di Diritto Civile:89–100
Costato L (2008a) Attività agricole, sicurezza alimentare e tutela del territorio. Rivista di diritto agrario:451–463
Costato L (2008b) La lezione di Antonio Carrozza (e qualche possibile fraintendimento). Rivista di diritto agrario:15–24
Costato L (2009) La PAC come filo conduttore del travaglio europeo. Rivista di diritto agrario:246–253
Costato L (2011) Il nuovo titolo dedicato all'agricoltura nel TFUE. Rivista di diritto agrario:119–127
Costato L (2012) I nuovi confini del diritto agrario. Agricoltura Istituzioni Mercati:25–30
Costato L, Russo L (2015) Corso di diritto agrario italiano e comunitario, 4th edn. Giuffrè, Milano
Costi R (2001) Proprietà e impresa cooperative nella riforma del diritto societario. Giurisprudenza Commerciale:128–132
Cotronei G (2009) Cooperative sociali. Buffetti, Roma

Cottino G, Cagnasso O (2011) Diritto societario, 2nd edn. Manuali di scienze giuridiche. Cedam, Padova

Craswell R, Katz AW, Hermalin BE (2007) Contract law. In: Polinsky AM, Shavell S (eds) Handbook of law and economics, vol 1. Elsevier, Amsterdam, pp 3–138

Crescentini G (2010) Art. 2403bis. In: Cendon P (ed) Artt. 2397-2420 ter: Società per azioni: [3] sindaci, controllo contabile, sistema dualistico e monistico, obbligazioni. Giuffrè, Milano, pp 61–66

Cuomo P (2013) Gestione mutualistica e parità di trattamento nelle cooperative. Rivista delle società:905–931

Cuomo P (2014) Art. 2516. In: Santosuosso DU (ed) Delle società, dell'azienda, della concorrenza. UTET, Torino, pp 99–128

Cusa E (2004a) Die Verwendung des Betriebsergebnisses. In: Schulze R (ed) Europäische Genossenschaft SCE: Handbuch, 1st edn. Nomos, Baden-Baden, pp 123–168

Cusa E (2004b) Il procedimento assembleare nella società cooperativa e il principio democratico. Giurisprudenza Commerciale:843–858

Cusa E (2004c) Zur Rechtslage in den Mitgliedsstaaten: Italien. In: Schulze R (ed) Europäische Genossenschaft SCE: Handbuch, 1st edn. Nomos, Baden-Baden, pp 176–183

Cusa E (2006) Il socio finanziatore nelle cooperative. Quaderni di giurisprudenza commerciale, vol 286. Giuffrè, Milano

Cusa E (2007) Art. 2538. In: Presti G (ed) Società cooperative: Artt. 2511-2548. EGEA; Giuffrè, Milano, pp 299–311

Cusa E (2009) Partecipazioni e capitale nelle società cooperative. In: Antonio B (ed) Studi per Franco Di Sabato. Edizioni scientifiche italiane, Napoli, pp 341–361

Cusa E (2010) La riduzione di capitale nelle società cooperative. Rivista delle società:471–498

Cusa E (2011a) Art. 2538. In: Bonfante G, Corapi D, de Angelis L, Napoleoni V, Rordorf R, Salafia V (eds) Codice commentato delle società: Società di persone, società di capitali, cooperative, consorzi, reati societari: aggiornato con le nuove norme in tema di revisione legale, esercizio dei diritti degli azionisti di società quotate e costituzione delle Spa, 3rd edn. IPSOA, Assago, pp 2199–2214

Cusa E (2011b) Art. 2539. In: Bonfante G, Corapi D, de Angelis L, Napoleoni V, Rordorf R, Salafia V (eds) Codice commentato delle società: Società di persone, società di capitali, cooperative, consorzi, reati societari: aggiornato con le nuove norme in tema di revisione legale, esercizio dei diritti degli azionisti di società quotate e costituzione delle Spa, 3rd edn. IPSOA, Assago, pp 2215–2221

Cusa E (2014a) Art. 2538. In: Santosuosso DU (ed) Delle società, dell'azienda, della concorrenza. UTET, Torino, pp 326–351

Cusa E (2014b) Art. 2539. In: Santosuosso DU (ed) Delle società, dell'azienda, della concorrenza. UTET, Torino, pp 351–359

Cusa E (2014c) Art. 2540. In: Santosuosso DU (ed) Delle società, dell'azienda, della concorrenza. UTET, Torino, pp 360–375

Cusa E (2014d) Art. 2545 quaterdecies. In: Santosuosso DU (ed) Delle società, dell'azienda, della concorrenza. UTET, Torino, pp 565–588

Cusa E (2014e) Art. 2545 sexiesdecies. In: Santosuosso DU (ed) Delle società, dell'azienda, della concorrenza. UTET, Torino, pp 616–622

Danneman G (2019) Comparative law: study of similarities and differences? In: Reimann M, Zimmermann R (eds) The Oxford handbook of comparative law, 2nd edn. Oxford University Press, Oxford, pp 390–422

Davies PL, Gower LCB, Worthington S, Micheler E (2012) Gower and Davies' principles of modern company law, 9th edn. Sweet & Maxwell, London

de Giorgi M, Vaciago G (2011) Le società cooperative: Tipi di cooperative, strumenti di tutela, aspetti civili, concorsuali, tributari e penali. Cedam, Padova

de Nicola A (2005) Art. 2392. In: Ghezzi F (ed) Amministratori: Artt. 2380 - 2396 c.c, 1st edn. EGEA, Milano, pp 545–568

Del Sole V (2010a) Art. 2409 decies. In: Cendon P (ed) Artt. 2397-2420 ter: Società per azioni: [3] sindaci, controllo contabile, sistema dualistico e monistico, obbligazioni. Giuffrè, Milano, pp 335–342

Del Sole V (2010b) Art. 2409 duodecies. In: Cendon P (ed) Artt. 2397-2420 ter: Società per azioni: [3] sindaci, controllo contabile, sistema dualistico e monistico, obbligazioni. Giuffrè, Milano, pp 345–353

Del Sole V (2010c) Art 2409 novies. In: Cendon P (ed) Artt. 2397-2420 ter: Società per azioni: [3] sindaci, controllo contabile, sistema dualistico e monistico, obbligazioni. Giuffrè, Milano, pp 325–334

Del Sole V (2010d) Art 2409 terdecies. In: Cendon P (ed) Artt. 2397-2420 ter: Società per azioni: [3] sindaci, controllo contabile, sistema dualistico e monistico, obbligazioni. Giuffrè, Milano, pp 355–364

Delbono F (1994a) Adverse selection. In: Zamagni S (ed) Economia politica I, 1. ed. italiana. UTET, Torino, pp 5–6

Delbono F (1994b) Monopsonio. In: Zamagni S (ed) Economia politica I, 1. ed. italiana. UTET, Torino, pp 443–444

Delbono F (1994c) Moral hazard. In: Zamagni S (ed) Economia politica I, 1. ed. italiana. UTET, Torino, p 444

Delle Priscoli L (2014) Art. 2536. In: Santosuosso DU (ed) Delle società, dell'azienda, della concorrenza. UTET, Torino, pp 321–323

Dellinger M (1995) Aus aktuellem Anlaß: Zur Einlage- und Deckungspflicht der Genossenschafter bei Liquidation, Konkurs oder Ausgleich ihrer Genossenschaft. GesRZ:91–110

Dellinger M (2001) Rechtsfähige Personengesellschaften in der Liquidation. Manz, Wien

Dellinger M (2006) Was bringt das GenRÄG 2006? ecolex:570

Dellinger M (2014a) § 1. In: Dellinger M (ed) Genossenschaftsgesetz samt Nebengesetzen: Kommentar, 2nd edn. LexisNexis ARD Orac, Wien, pp 17–55

Dellinger M (2014b) § 2. In: Dellinger M (ed) Genossenschaftsgesetz samt Nebengesetzen: Kommentar, 2nd edn. LexisNexis ARD Orac, Wien, pp 101–107

Dellinger M (2014c) § 48. In: Dellinger M (ed) Genossenschaftsgesetz samt Nebengesetzen: Kommentar, 2nd edn. LexisNexis ARD Orac, Wien, pp 422–431

Dellinger M (2014d) § 79. In: Dellinger M (ed) Genossenschaftsgesetz samt Nebengesetzen: Kommentar, 2nd edn. LexisNexis ARD Orac, Wien, pp 496–505

Dellinger M (2016) Besonderheiten des Aufsichtsrates in der Genossenschaft. In: Kalss S, Kunz P (eds) Handbuch für den Aufsichtsrat, 2nd edn. Facultas, Wien, pp 1367–1385

Dellinger M, Oberhammer P (1996) Entwurf eines Genossenschaftsgesetzes. Veröffentlichungen des Ludwig-Boltzmann-Institutes für Rechtsvorsorge und Urkundenwesen, vol 17. Manz, Wien

Dellinger M, Steinböck G (2014a) § 24c. In: Dellinger M (ed) Genossenschaftsgesetz samt Nebengesetzen: Kommentar, 2nd edn. LexisNexis ARD Orac, Wien, pp 276–310

Dellinger M, Steinböck G (2014b) § 55. In: Dellinger M (ed) Genossenschaftsgesetz samt Nebengesetzen: Kommentar, 2nd edn. LexisNexis ARD Orac, Wien, pp 459–462

Demsetz H (2004) Toward a theory of property rights. In: Geest GD, van den Bergh R (eds) Comparative law and economics, vol I. Elgar, Cheltenham, pp 3–15

Denozza F (2002) Norme efficienti: L'analisi economica delle regole giuridiche. Giuffrè, Milano

Di Cecco G (2012) Variabilità e modificazioni del capitale sociale nelle cooperative. Edicioni Scientifiche Italiane, Napoli

Di Gaspare A (2012) Riflessioni su consiglio di amministrazione e board of directors nella gestione dei problemi di agenzia. http://www.comparazionedirittocivile.it:1–21

Di Lauro A (2007) Scienza, tecnica e diritto agrario: Dialoghi, regole, conflitti. Rivista di diritto agrario:568–587

Di Ronza N (2010) Art. 2513. In: Cendon P (ed) Artt. 2511-2554: Cooperative mutue assicuratrici associazioni in partecipazione. Giuffrè, Milano, pp 31–37

Di Sabato F (2005) Capitale e responsabilità interna nelle società di persone. Giuffrè, Milano

Dickstein C (1991) The promise and problems of worker cooperatives. J Plann Lit 6:16–33. https://doi.org/10.1177/088541229100600102
Domenichini G (2004) Art. 2407. In: Niccolini G, Stagno d'Alcontres A (eds) Società di capitali: Commentario. Jovene, Napoli, pp 767–775
Droit des sociétés coopératives (Acte uniforme OHADA du 15 décembre 2010), droit-afrique.com/upload/doc/ohada/Ohada-Acte-Uniforme-2010-societes-cooperatives.pdf. Accessed 18 Nov 2019
Drygala T (2015a) Art. 39. In: Lutter M, Hommelhoff P, Teichmann C (eds) SE-Kommentar, 2nd edn. Verlag Dr. Otto Schmidt, Köln, pp 472–500
Drygala T (2015b) Art. 40. In: Lutter M, Hommelhoff P, Teichmann C (eds) SE-Kommentar, 2nd edn. Verlag Dr. Otto Schmidt, Köln, pp 501–516
Dyck A, Zingales L (2004) Private benefits of control: an international comparison. J Finance 59:537–600. https://doi.org/10.1111/j.1540-6261.2004.00642.x
Easterbrook FH, Fischel DR (1985) Limited liability and the corporation. Univ Chic Law Rev:89–117
Easterbrook FH, Fischel DR (1998) The economic structure of corporate law, [Repr.]. Harvard University Press, Cambridge
Ebers M (2004) Die Gründung einer SCE. In: Schulze R (ed) Europäische Genossenschaft SCE: Handbuch, 1st edn. Nomos, Baden-Baden, pp 43–76
Ebert S (2003a) Das anwendbare Konzernrecht der Europäischen Aktiengesellschaft. Betriebs-Berater:1854–1860
Ebert S (2003b) The European company on the level playing field of the community. Eur Bus Law Rev:183–192
Ecchia G (1994a) Informazione assimetrica. In: Zamagni S (ed) Economia politica I, 1. ed. italiana. UTET, Torino, pp 328–329
Ecchia G (1994b) Teoria dell'impresa. In: Zamagni S (ed) Economia politica I, 1. ed. italiana. UTET, Torino, pp 301–309
Eckert G, Schopper A (2014a) § 30g. In: Torggler U (ed) GmbH-Gesetz: (GmbHG) Kurzkommentar. Manzsche Verlags- und Universitätsbuchhandlung, Wien, pp 310–318
Eckert G, Schopper A (2014b) § 30j. In: Torggler U (ed) GmbH-Gesetz: (GmbHG) Kurzkommentar. Manzsche Verlags- und Universitätsbuchhandlung, Wien, pp 328–341
Ecorys, Wageningen Economic Research (2018) Study on producer organisations and their activities in the olive oil, beef and veal, arable crops sectors. https://ec.europa.eu/competition/publications/reports/kd0218732enn.pdf. Accessed 26 Nov 2019
Eder CJ (2004) Die monistisch verfasste Societas Europaea - Überlegungen zur Umsetzung eines CEO-Modells. Neue Zeitschrift für Gesellschaftsrecht:544–547
Egermann C, Heckenthaler S (2004) Der Verwaltungsrat in der Europäischen Gesellschaft (SE) österreichischer Prägung: Überlegungen zu §§ 38 ff SEG. GesRZ:256–266
Egerstrom L (2004) Obstacles to cooperation. In: Merrett CD, Walzer N (eds) Cooperatives and local development: theory and applications for the 21st century. Sharpe, Armonk, pp 70–91
Eichwald B, Lutz KJ (2011) Erfolgsmodell Genossenschaften: Möglichkeiten für eine werteorientierte Marktwirtschaft. Grundlagen, Werte und Prinzipien, Herausforderungen und Lösungen genossenschaftlicher Unternehmen und Verbände, genossenschaftliche Modelle auf fünf Kontinenten. Deutscher Genossenschafts-Verl., Wiesbaden
Eidenmüller H (2005) Effizienz als Rechtsprinzip: Möglichkeiten und Grenzen der ökonomischen Analyse des Rechts. Univ., Diss.—München, 1994, 3rd edn. Die Einheit der Gesellschaftswissenschaften, vol 90. Mohr-Siebeck, Tübingen
Eidenmüller H (2014a) Analytical framework. In: Bachmann G, Eidenmüller H, Engert A, Fleischer H, Schön W (eds) Regulating the closed corporation. De Gruyter, Berlin, pp 5–27
Eidenmüller H (2014b) Formation, management and transfer of shares. In: Bachmann G, Eidenmüller H, Engert A, Fleischer H, Schön W (eds) Regulating the closed corporation. De Gruyter, Berlin, pp 179–200

Eidenmüller H, Grunewald B, Noack U (2006) Minimum capital in the system of legal capital. In: Lutter M (ed) Legal capital in Europe. De Gruyter, Berlin, pp 17–41
Eisenberg MA (1989) The structure of corporation law. Columbia Law Rev:1461–1525
Eisenhardt KM (1989) Agency theory: an assessment and review. Acad Manage Rev 14:57–74. https://doi.org/10.2307/258191
Engelhardt WW (1977) Zur Frage der Betrachtungsweisen und eines geeigneten Bezugsrahmens der Genossenschaftsforschung. Zeitschrift für das gesamte Genossenschaftswesen:337–352
Engelhardt WW (1990) Die Genossenschaftsidee als Gestaltungsprinzip. In: Laurinkari J (ed) Genossenschaftswesen: Hand- und Lehrbuch. Oldenbourg, München, pp 10–27
Engert A (2014) The board of directors. In: Bachmann G, Eidenmüller H, Engert A, Fleischer H, Schön W (eds) Regulating the closed corporation. De Gruyter, Berlin, pp 85–121
Englerth M (2012) Verhaltensökonomik. In: Towfigh EV, Petersen N (eds) Ökonomische Methoden im Recht: Eine Einführung für Juristen. Mohr Siebeck, Tübingen, pp 165–200
Enriques L, Pomelli A (2005) Art. 2391. In: Maffei Alberti A (ed) Il nuovo diritto delle società: Commento sistematico al D. lgs. 17 gennaio 2003, n. 6, aggiornato al D. lgs. 28 dicembre 2004, n. 310. Cedam, Padova, pp 758–778
Enriques L, Volpin P (2007) Corporate governance reforms in continental Europe. J Econ Perspect 21:117–140. https://doi.org/10.1257/jep.21.1.117
Enriques L, Hansmann H, Kraakman RH (2009a) The basic governance structure: the interests of shareholders as a class. In: Kraakman RH, Armour J, Davies P, Enriques L, Hansmann H, Hertig G, Hopt K, Kanda H, Rock E (eds) The anatomy of corporate law: a comparative and functional approach, 2nd edn. Oxford University Press, Oxford, pp 55–88
Enriques L, Hansmann H, Kraakman RH (2009b) The basic governance structure: minority shareholders and non-shareholder constituencies. In: Kraakman RH, Armour J, Davies P, Enriques L, Hansmann H, Hertig G, Hopt K, Kanda H, Rock E (eds) The anatomy of corporate law: a comparative and functional approach, 2nd edn. Oxford University Press, Oxford, pp 89–114
Epiney A (2016) § 32 Umwelt. In: Bieber R, Epiney A, Haag M, Kotzur M (eds) Die Europäische Union: Europarecht und Politik. Nomos, Baden-Baden, pp 621–641
Eschenburg R (1988) Zur Anwendung der Anreiz-Beitrags-Theorie in Genossenschaften. Zeitschrift für das gesamte Genossenschaftswesen:250–262
Ettel M (2012) § 20. In: Doralt W, Nowotny C, Kalss S (eds) Kommentar zum Aktiengesetz, 2nd edn. Linde, Wien, pp 375–392
European Commission (2012) Report from the Commission to the Council and the European Parliament, the European Economic and Social Committee and the Committee of the Regions. The application of Council Regulation (EC) No 1435/2003 of 22 July 2003 on the Statute for a European Cooperative Society (SCE), COM (2012) 72 final eur-lex.europa.eu/legal-content/EN/TXT/?uri=CELEX%3A52012DC0072. Accessed 29 Dec 2019
European Community of Consumer Cooperatives, Who we are. https://www.eurocoop.coop/about-us/Who-We-Are/. Accessed 19 Nov 2019
Explanatory note to the government bill of the GewO 1973. https://www.parlament.gv.at/PAKT/VHG/XIII/I/I_00395/imfname_318784.pdf. Accessed 26 Nov 2019
Fabbri F (ed) (1979) Il movimento cooperativo nella storia d'Italia, 1854-1975. Feltrinelli, Milano
Fabbri F (2011) L'Italia cooperativa: Centocinquant'anni di storia e di memoria 1861-2011. Ediesse, Roma
Facchin N (2009a) Art 2388. In: Grippo G (ed) Commentario delle società. UTET, Torino, pp 501–504
Facchin N (2009b) Art 2391. In: Grippo G (ed) Commentario delle società. UTET, Torino, pp 510–514
Facchin N (2009c) Art 2392. In: Grippo G (ed) Commentario delle società. UTET, Torino, pp 518–521
Facchin N (2009d) Art 2393. In: Grippo G (ed) Commentario delle società. UTET, Torino, pp 521–523

Facchin N (2009e) Art 2393bis. In: Grippo G (ed) Commentario delle società. UTET, Torino, pp 523–524
Facchin N (2009f) Art 2409decies. In: Grippo G (ed) Commentario delle società. UTET, Torino, pp 662–663
Facchin N (2009g) Art 2409terdecies. In: Grippo G (ed) Commentario delle società. UTET, Torino, pp 666–669
Fahlbeck E (2007) The horizon problem in agricultural cooperatives – only in theory? In: Karantininis K, Nilsson J (eds) Vertical markets and cooperative hierarchies: the role of cooperatives in the agri-food industry. Springer, Dordrecht, pp 255–274
Fajardo G (2012) Cooperative finance and cooperative identity. SSRN Electron J:1–12. https://doi.org/10.2139/ssrn.2185328
Fajardo E, Meira DMMA (2017) Cooperative financial strucutre. In: Fajardo-García IG, Fici A, Henrÿ H, Hiez D, Meira DMMA, Münkner H-H, Snaith I (eds) Principles of European Cooperative Law: principles, commentaries and national reports. Intersentia, Cambridge, pp 73–95
Falcone G (2003a) Art 2539. In: Sandulli M, Santoro V (eds) La riforma delle società: Società cooperative Artt. 2511-2548 cod.civ. Giappichelli, Torino, pp 136–138
Falcone G (2003b) Art 2545 quinquies. In: Sandulli M, Santoro V (eds) La riforma delle società: Società cooperative Artt. 2511-2548 cod.civ. Giappichelli, Torino, pp 175–177
Fama EF, Jensen MC (1983) Separation of ownership and control. J Law Econ 26:301–325
Fauceglia G (2019) Il futuro della società cooperativa: la fine dell'umanizzazione e la scelta dell'efficienza. Giurisprudenza Commerciale:567–582
Faust F (2019) Comparative law and economic analysis of law. In: Reimann M, Zimmermann R (eds) The Oxford handbook of comparative law, 2nd edn. Oxford University Press, Oxford, pp 826–851
Fehr E, Schmidt KM (1999) A theory of fairness, competition, and cooperation. Q J Econ 114:817–868
Fehr E, Klein A, Schmidt KM (2007) Fairness and contract design. Econometrica 75:121–154. https://doi.org/10.1111/j.1468-0262.2007.00734.x
Ferrara G (2013) Gli oneri documentali dell'imprenditore agricolo professionale nell'agevolazione per la formazione della piccola proprietà contadina ([Nota a sentenza] Cass. Sez. Trib. 26 giugno 2013, n.16072). Diritto e giurisprudenza agraria, alimentare e dell'ambiente 22:453–456
Ferrarini G (2004) Societas Europaea and the limits of harmonisation: a view from Italy. In: Baums T, Cahn A (eds) Die Europäische Aktiengesellschaft: Umsetzungsfragen und Perspektiven. De Gruyter, Berlin, pp 79–93
Ferrarini G, Ungureanu MC (2014) Executive remuneration: a comparative overview. http://papers.ssrn.com/sol3/papers.cfm?abstract_id=2509968##. Accessed 19 Nov 2019
Ferreri S (2010) Falsi amici e trappole giuridiche: Termini contrattuali anglofoni e difficoltà di traduzione. Giappichelli, Torino
Ferri G (2008) Struttura finanziaria dell'impresa e funzioni del capitale sociale. Rivista del notariato:741–794
Ferrucci N (2011) Il compendio unico. In: Costato L, Germanò A, Rook Basile E (eds) Trattato di diritto agrario: I. UTET, Torino, pp 465–476
Ferrucci A, Ferrentino C (2012) Le società di capitali, le società cooperative e le mutue assicuratrici, 2nd edn. Collana notarile. Giuffrè, Milano
Ficari L (2008) La partecipazione dei lavoratori nella società europea: Punto d'arrivo o di partenza? In: Capriglione F (ed) La nuova disciplina della società europea. Cedam, Padova, pp 207–234
Fici A (2006) Società cooperative europea e partecipazione dei lavoratori. In: Galletti D, Fici A (eds) La società cooperativa europea: Quali prospettive per la cooperazione italiana? Universita degli Studi di Trento, Trento, pp 137–155
Fici A (2010a) Italian co-operative law reform and co-operative principles. SSRN Electron J:1–27. https://doi.org/10.2139/ssrn.1615344

Fici A (2010b) Mapping of the relevant legislation implementing the SCE regulation in the EU Member States and EEA countries. In: Fici A (ed) Study on the implementation of the Regulation 1435/2003 on the Statute for European Cooperative Society (SCE): Executive Summary and Part I: Synthesis and comparative report. Report drawn up following call tender no ENTR/2009/021 of 23 April from the European Commission, pp 33–80

Fici A (2012) Cooperative identity and the law. SSRN Electron J. https://doi.org/10.2139/ssrn.2005014

Fici A (2013a) An introduction to cooperative law. In: Cracogna D, Fici A, Henrÿ H (eds) International handbook of cooperative law. Springer, Berlin, Heidelberg, pp 3–62

Fici A (2013b) Italy. In: Cracogna D, Fici A, Henrÿ H (eds) International handbook of cooperative law. Springer, Berlin, Heidelberg, pp 479–501

Fici A (2013c) Pan-European Cooperative Law: where do we stand? SSRN Electron J:1–12. https://doi.org/10.2139/ssrn.2198283

Fici A (2013d) The European Cooperative Society. In: Cracogna D, Fici A, Henrÿ H (eds) International handbook of cooperative law. Springer, Berlin, Heidelberg, pp 115–151

Fici A (2014) The essential role of cooperative law. Dovenschmidt Q 2:147–158. https://doi.org/10.5553/DQ/221199812014002004003

Fici A (2015) Cooperation among cooperatives in Italian and comparative law. JEOD 4:64–97. https://doi.org/10.5947/jeod.2015.011

Fici A (2017) Definition and objectives of cooperatives. In: Fajardo-García IG, Fici A, Henrÿ H, Hiez D, Meira DMMA, Münkner H-H, Snaith I (eds) Principles of European Cooperative Law: principles, commentaries and national reports. Intersentia, Cambridge, pp 19–45

Fici A, Strano C (2010) Italy. In: Fici A (ed) Study on the implementation of the Regulation 1435/2003 on the Statute for European Cooperative Society (SCE): Final Study Part II. National Reports. Report drawn up following call tender no ENTR/2009/021 of 23 April from the European Commission, pp 671–702

Figà-Talamanca G (1997) Bilanci e organizzazione dei poteri dispositivi sul patrimonio sociale. Università degli studi di Roma "Tor Vergata" / Pubblicazioni della Facoltà di Giurisprudenza. Sezione di Diritto e Procedura Civile, vol 4. Giuffrè, Milano

Fiorentini G (1994a) Diritti di proprietà. In: Zamagni S (ed) Politica economica II. UTET libreria, Torino, pp 163–167

Fiorentini G (1994b) Legge ed economia. In: Zamagni S (ed) Politica economica II. UTET libreria, Torino, pp 352–356

Fiorio P (2004) Art 2367. In: Cottino G, Bonfante G, Cagnasso O, Montalenti P (eds) Il nuovo diritto societario I: Commento al D. lgs. 17 gennaio 2003, n. 6, D. Lgs. 17 gennaio 2003, n. 5, D. lgs. 11 aprile 2002, n. 61 (art. 1). 1. Artt. 2325-2409 c.c, 1st edn. Zanichelli, Bologna, pp 507–521

Fischer T (1995) Die Europäische Genossenschaft. Univ., Diss.-1995--Münster (Westfalen), 1994. Kooperations- und genossenschaftswissenschaftliche Beiträge, Band 34. Institut für Genossenschaftswesen der Westfälischen Wilhelms-Universität, Münster

Fleckner AM (2010) Antike Kapitalvereinigungen: Ein Beitrag zu den konzeptionellen und historischen Grundlagen der Aktiengesellschaft. Univ., Diss.—Regensburg, 2008. Forschungen zum Römischen Recht, vol 55. Böhlau, Köln

Fleischer H (2000) Grundfragen der ökonomischen Theorie im Gesellschafts- und Kapitalmarktrecht. Zeitschrift für Unternehmens- und Gesellschaftsrecht 30:1–32. https://doi.org/10.1515/zgre.2000.047

Fleischer H (2001) Informationsasymmetrie im Vertragsrecht: Eine rechtsvergleichende und interdisziplinäre Abhandlung zu Reichweite und Grenzen vertragsschlußbezogener Aufklärungspflichten. Univ., Habil.-Schr.-1999--Köln, 1998. Schriften des Instituts für Arbeits- und Wirtschaftsrecht der Universität zu Köln, vol 85. Beck, München

Fleischer H (2002a) Das neue Recht des Squeeze out. Zeitschrift für Unternehmens- und Gesellschaftsrecht 31. https://doi.org/10.1515/zgre.2002.026

Fleischer H (2002b) Die "Business Judgment Rule" im Spiegel von Rechtsvergleichung und Rechtsökonomie. In: Wank R (ed) Festschrift für Herbert Wiedemann zum 70. Geburtstag. C.H. Beck, München, pp 827–850

Fleischer H (2004a) Der Einfluß der Societas Europaea auf die Dogmatik des deutschen Gesellschaftsrechts. Archiv für die civilistische Praxis 204:502–543

Fleischer H (2004b) Gesetz und Vertrag als alternative Problemlösungsmodelle im Gesellschaftsrecht. Zeitschrift für das gesamte Handelsrecht und Wirtschaftsrecht:673–707

Fleischer H (2010) Supranational corporate forms in the European Union: prolegomena to a theory on supranational forms of association. Common Mark Law Rev:1671–1717

Fleischer H (2011) Das unternehmerische Ermessen des GmbH-Geschäftsführers und seine GmbH-spezifischen Grenzen. Neue Zeitschrift für Gesellschaftsrecht:521–527

Fleischer H (2014) Shareholder conflicts in closed corporations. In: Bachmann G, Eidenmüller H, Engert A, Fleischer H, Schön W (eds) Regulating the closed corporation. De Gruyter, Berlin, pp 29–81

Fleischer H, Zimmer D (2008) Effizienzorientierung im Handels- und Wirtschaftsrecht: Einführung und Überblick. In: Fleischer H, Zimmer D (eds) Effizienz als Regelungsziel im Handels- und Wirtschaftsrecht. Verl. Recht und Wirtschaft, Frankfurt am Main, pp 9–42

Fleischer H, Schmolke K, Ulrich ZD (2011) Verhaltensökonomik als Forschungsinstrument für das Wirtschaftsrecht. In: Fleischer H, Zimmer D, Altmann S (eds) Beitrag der Verhaltensökonomie (Behavioral Economics) zum Handels- und Wirtschaftsrecht. Recht und Wirtschaft, Frankfurt am Main, pp 9–62

Fornasari M, Zamagni V (1997) Il movimento cooperativo in Italia: Un profilo storico-economico (1854-1992). Vallecchi, Firenze

Fortunato S (2003) I controlli nella riforma del diritto societario. Rivista delle società:863–894

Frodermann J, Jannott D (2005) Zur Amtszeit des Verwaltungs- bzw. Aufsichtsrats der SE. Zeitschrift für Wirtschaftsrecht:2251

Frotz G (1977) Anmerkungen zur österreichischen Genossenschaftsgesetznovelle 1974: Vortrag geh. am 6.5.1976, Wien. Zeitschrift für das gesamte Genossenschaftswesen 27:53–61

Fruehmann A, Nagy TR (2005) Aktiengesetz: the Austrian stock corporation act; Deutsch/Englisch, bilingual ed. Manz, Wien

Furubotn EG, Pejovich S (1970) Property rights and the behavior of the firm in a socialist state: the example of Yugoslavia. Zeitschrift für Nationalkonomie 30:431–454. https://doi.org/10.1007/BF01289247

Furubotn EG, Pejovich S (1972) Property rights and economic theory: a survey of recent literature. J Econ Lit 10:1137–1162

Furubotn E, Pejovich S (1974) The new property rights literature. In: Furubotn EG, Pejovich S (eds) Economics of property rights. Ballinger Publishing Co, S.l., pp 1–9

Furubotn EG, Richter R (2000) Institutions and economic theory: the contribution of the new institutional economics, [Repr.]. Economics, cognition, and society. University of Michigan Press, Ann Arbor

Galgano F (1993) Impresa cooperativa e gruppi di società. In: Le società cooperative negli anni Novanta: Problemi e prospettive: atti del convegno internazionale in memoria di Piero Verrucoli: 18-19 maggio 1990. Giuffrè, Milano

Galgano F (2003) Il nuovo diritto societario. Trattato di diritto commerciale e di diritto pubblico dell'economia, / dir. da Francesco Galgano; 29. Cedam, Padova

Galle RCJ (2006) The Societas Cooperativa Europea (SCE) and national cooperatives in comparative perspective. Eur Comp Law:225–260

Galletti D (2005) Art 2535. In: Maffei Alberti A (ed) Il nuovo diritto delle società: Commento sistematico al D. lgs. 17 gennaio 2003, n. 6, aggiornato al D. lgs. 28 dicembre 2004, n. 310. Cedam, Padova, pp 2774–2778

Galletti D (2006) La tutela delle minoranze nella SCE. In: Galletti D, Fici A (eds) La società cooperativa europea: Quali prospettive per la cooperazione italiana? Universita degli Studi di Trento, Trento, pp 48–66

Gallo P (1998a) Introduzione al diritto comparato Vol II: Istituti giuridici. Introduzione al diritto comparato. Giappichelli, Torino
Gallo P (1998b) Introduzione al diritto comparato Vol III: Analisi economica del diritto. Giappichelli, Torino
Gallo P (2001) Introduzione al diritto comparato Vol I: Grandi sistemi giuridici, 2nd edn. Introduzione al diritto comparato. Giappichelli, Torino
Galloni G (1999) Lezioni sul diritto dell'impresa agricola e dell'ambiente. Manuali. Liguori, Napoli
Galloni G (2014) L'ampliamento dei confini di diritto agrario: Diritto ambientale e alimentare nel pensiero di Luigi Costato. In: Nappi P, Sgarbanti G, Borghi P, Russo L, Fioravanti C, Agostini C, Manservisi S, Borraccetti M, Rizzioli S (eds) Studi in onore di Luigi Costato: I. Jovene, Napoli, pp 397–406
Gambaro A, Sacco R (2014) Sistemi giuridici comparati, 3rd edn. UTET, Torino
Garrouste P, Saussier S (2008) The theories of the firm. In: Brousseau E, Glachant J-M (eds) New institutional economics: a guidebook. Cambridge University Press, Cambridge, pp 23–36
Gelter M, Grechenig K (2007) Juristischer Diskurs und Rechtsökonomie. Journal für Rechtspolitik 15:30–41. https://doi.org/10.1007/s00730-007-0162-7
Gelter M, Helleringer G (2015) Lift not the painted Veil: to whom are directors' duties really owed? Univ Ill Law Rev:1069–1118
Genco R (2003) La struttura finanziaria. In: Genco R (ed) La riforma delle società cooperative. IPSOA, Milano, pp 57–113
Genco R (2006) Le operazioni straordinarie ed il trasferimento di sede della SCE: (Regolamento n 1435/2003 del 22 luglio 2003). In: Galletti D, Fici A (eds) La società cooperativa europea: Quali prospettive per la cooperazione italiana? Universita degli Studi di Trento, Trento, pp 115–136
Genco R (2014) Cooperative bancarie e obbligo di devoluzione in favore dei Fondi mutualistici per la promozione cooperativa. Giurisprudenza Commerciale:175–184
Gentzoglanis A (2007) Regulation, governance and capital structure in cooperatives. In: Karantininis K, Nilsson J (eds) Vertical markets and cooperative hierarchies: the role of cooperatives in the agri-food industry. Springer, Dordrecht, pp 151–167
Germanò A (2008) Le agevolazioni fiscali alle cooperative sono aiuti di stato oggetto di autorizzazione della Commissione? Diritto e giurisprudenza agraria, alimentare e dell'ambiente:413–418
Germanò A (2011) Le figure soggettive specifiche. In: Costato L, Germanò A, Rook Basile E (eds) Trattato di diritto agrario: I. UTET, Torino, pp 798–812
Germanò A (2015) L'allargamento dell'Unione Euroea: i Paesi della parte orientale del continente europeo (PECO) e l'agricoltura. Agricoltura Istituzioni Mercati:95–117
Germanò A (2016) Manuale di diritto agrario, 8th edn. Giappichelli, Turin
Germanò A (2017) L'istituto di diritto agrario internazionale e comparato. editoriale scientifica, Napoli
Germanò A (2019) Alle "soglie" della formulazione dell'art. 2153 del codice civile del 1942. Diritto agroalimentare:197–238
Germanò A, Rook Basile E (2011) L'impresa agricola. In: Costato L, Germanò A, Rook Basile E (eds) Trattato di diritto agrario: I. UTET, Torino, pp 757–797
Germanò A, Rook Basile E (2014) Manuale di diritto agrario comunitario, 3rd edn. Il diritto dell'alimentazione, dell'ambiente e dell'agricoltura. Giappichelli, Torino
Gfrerer H (2007) Entwicklungsgeschichte der Nebengewerbe der Land- und Forstwirtschaft. In: Österreichische Gesellschaft für Agrar- und Umweltrecht (ed) Agrarrecht im Lichte des öffentlichen Rechts: Festschrift für Univ.-Prof. Dr. Gottfried Holzer zum 60. Geburtstag. NWV, Wien, pp 199–210
Ghezzi F (2005) Sistemi alternativi di amministrazione e di controllo: Artt. 2409-octies - 2409-noviesdecies c.c. In: Ghezzi F (ed) Sistemi alternativi di amministrazione e di controllo: Artt. 2409-octies - 2409-noviesdecies c.c, 1st edn. EGEA, Milano

Ghezzi F, Malberti C (2008) The two-tier model and the one-tier model of corporate governance in the Italian reform of corporate law. Eur Comp Financ Law Rev 5:1–47. https://doi.org/10.1515/ecfr.5.1.1

Ghezzi F, Rigotti M (2005) Art 2409 octiesdecies. In: Ghezzi F (ed) Sistemi alternativi di amministrazione e di controllo: Artt. 2409-octies - 2409-noviesdecies c.c, 1st edn. EGEA, Milano, pp 247–322

Ginera E (2011) Oltre il capitale sociale: Spunti di riflessione del dibattito sulla riforma della struttura finanziaria delle società di capitali. In: Abbadessa P, Balzano M, Bartalena A, Boggio L, Bonaiti A, Calvosa L, Cariello V, Centonze M, Cetra A, de Marchi G, Stasio Vd, Ginera E, Malimpensa E, Marchetti P, Miola M, Mozzarelli M, Nobili R, Pisani L, Portale GB, Presti G, Regoli D, Rescio G, Santus A, Schneider U-H, Speranzin M, Spolidoro MS, Strampelli G, Stucchi L, Vanoni S, Zanarone G (eds) La struttura finanziaria e i bilanci delle società di capitali: Studi in onore di Giovanni E. Colombo. Giappichelli, Torino

Giorgi V (2007) Art. 2536. In: Presti G (ed) Società cooperative: Artt. 2511-2548. EGEA; Giuffrè, Milano, pp 293–295

Giorgi V (2018a) Art. 2516. In: Cian G (ed) Commentario breve al Codice civile: Commentato con dottrina e giurisprudenza, 13th edn. Wolters Kluver, Milano, Padova, pp 3207–3208

Giorgi V (2018b) Art. 2518. In: Cian G (ed) Commentario breve al Codice civile: Commentato con dottrina e giurisprudenza, 13th edn. Wolters Kluver, Milano, Padova, pp 3208–3209

Giorgi V (2018c) Art. 2527. In: Cian G (ed) Commentario breve al Codice civile: Commentato con dottrina e giurisprudenza, 13th edn. Wolters Kluver, Milano, Padova, pp 3220–3222

Giorgi V (2018d) Art. 2535. In: Cian G (ed) Commentario breve al Codice civile: Commentato con dottrina e giurisprudenza, 13th edn. Wolters Kluver, Milano, Padova, pp 3232–3233

Giorgi V (2018e) Art. 2543. In: Cian G (ed) Commentario breve al Codice civile: Commentato con dottrina e giurisprudenza, 13th edn. Wolters Kluver, Milano, Padova, pp 3241–3242

Giorgi V (2018f) Art. 2544. In: Cian G (ed) Commentario breve al Codice civile: Commentato con dottrina e giurisprudenza, 13th edn. Wolters Kluver, Milano, Padova, pp 3242–3244

Giorgi V (2018g) Art. 2545 quinquies. In: Cian G (ed) Commentario breve al Codice civile: Commentato con dottrina e giurisprudenza, 13th edn. Wolters Kluver, Milano, Padova, pp 3246–3247

Gios G, Santuari A (2002) Agricultural cooperatives in the County of Trento (Italy): economic, organizational and legal perspectives. J Rural Coop 30:3–12. https://doi.org/10.22004/ag.econ.60951

Giudici P (2008) La responsabilità civile nel diritto dei mercati finanziari. Il diritto della banca e della borsa, vol 44. Giuffrè, Milano

Giuffrida G (1981) Le cooperative agricole. Giuffré, Milano

Glenn HP (2019) Comparative legal families and comparative legal traditions. In: Reimann M, Zimmermann R (eds) The Oxford handbook of comparative law, 2nd edn. Oxford University Press, Oxford, pp 423–441

Göbel E (2002) Neue Institutionenökonomik: Konzeption und betriebswirtschaftliche Anwendungen. Grundwissen der Ökonomik Betriebswirtschaftslehre, vol 2235. Lucius & Lucius, Stuttgart

Goldoni M (2019) L'art. 2135 del codice civile e le esigenze di un ripensamento sul piano sistematico della "specialità" dell'impresa agricola. Rivista di diritto agrario:353–400

Gordon JN (1989) The mandatory structure of corporate law. Columbia Law Rev 89:1549–1598

Gorla G (1981) Diritto comparato e diritto comune europeo. Giuffré, Milano

Goshen Z (2003) The efficiency of controlling corporate self-dealing: theory meets reality. Calif Law Rev:393–438. https://doi.org/10.15779/Z38T417

Götz V (2012) Das Recht der Gemeinsamen Agrarpolitik - Kontinuität, Wandel, Systematik. In: Martinez J (ed) Die Gemeinsame Agrarpolitik vor neuen Herausforderungen: 50 Jahre Institut für Landwirtschaftsrecht, 1st edn. Nomos Verlagsgesellschaft mbH & Co. KG, Baden-Baden, pp 11–18

Grande E (2019) Development of comparative law in Italy. In: Reimann M, Zimmermann R (eds) The Oxford handbook of comparative law, 2nd edn. Oxford University Press, Oxford, pp 87–110

Graziadei M (2003) The functionalist heritage. In: Legrand P, Munday RJC (eds) Comparative legal studies: traditions and transitions. Cambridge University Press, Cambridge, pp 100–128

Grechenig K, Eckert G, Stremitzer A (2005) Ökonomische Analyse der Vorstandshaftung. In: Kalss S (ed) Vorstandshaftung in 15 europäischen Ländern. Linde, Wien, pp 95–163

Greda C (2014) Statut der Europäischen Genossenschaft. In: Dellinger M (ed) Genossenschaftsgesetz samt Nebengesetzen: Kommentar, 2nd edn. LexisNexis ARD Orac, Wien, pp 829–854

Greenberg E (1984) Producer cooperatives and democratic theory: the case of plywood firms. In: Jackall R, Levin HM (eds) Worker cooperatives in America. University of California Press, Berkeley [etc.], pp 171–218

Grillo M (2013) Competition rules and the cooperative firm: new wine in old bottles. J Entrep Organ Divers 2:36–53. https://doi.org/10.5947/jeod.2013.003

Grimm C, Norer R (2015) Agrarrecht, 4th edn. Studium und Praxis. C.H. Beck, München

Grossi P (2016) Fattualità del diritto pos-moderno: l'emersione di un diritto 'agrario' in Italia. Diritto agroalimentare:7–28

Grosskopf W (1990) Genossenschaftliche Identität bei sich ändernden Rahmenbedinungen. In: Laurinkari J (ed) Genossenschaftswesen: Hand- und Lehrbuch. Oldenbourg, München, pp 102–112

Grossman SJ, Hart OD (1986) The costs and benefits of ownership: a theory of vertical and lateral integration. J Polit Econ 94:691–719. https://doi.org/10.1086/261404

Grosso P (2011a) Art. 2524. In: Bonfante G, Corapi D, de Angelis L, Napoleoni V, Rordorf R, Salafia V (eds) Codice commentato delle società: Società di persone, società di capitali, cooperative, consorzi, reati societari: aggiornato con le nuove norme in tema di revisione legale, esercizio dei diritti degli azionisti di società quotate e costituzione delle Spa, 3rd edn. IPSOA, Assago, pp 2120–2126

Grosso P (2011b) Art. 2528. In: Bonfante G, Corapi D, de Angelis L, Napoleoni V, Rordorf R, Salafia V (eds) Codice commentato delle società: Società di persone, società di capitali, cooperative, consorzi, reati societari: aggiornato con le nuove norme in tema di revisione legale, esercizio dei diritti degli azionisti di società quotate e costituzione delle Spa, 3rd edn. IPSOA, Assago, pp 2146–2153

Grubel HG (1971) Risk, uncertainty and moral hazard. J Risk Insur:99–106

Gruber E (2012) § 17. In: Doralt W, Nowotny C, Kalss S (eds) Kommentar zum Aktiengesetz, 2nd edn. Linde, Wien, pp 332–353

Guaccero A (2004a) Art. 2409 octies - quinquiesdecies. In: Niccolini G, Stagno d'Alcontres A (eds) Società di capitali: Commentario. Jovene, Napoli, pp 865–907

Guaccero A (2004b) Art. 2409 sexiesdecies noviesdecies. In: Niccolini G, Stagno d'Alcontres A (eds) Società di capitali: Commentario. Jovene, Napoli, pp 908–927

Guarneri A (2003) Lineamenti di diritto comparato. Cedam, Padova

Guizzi (2004) Art. 2391. In: Niccolini G, Stagno d'Alcontres A (eds) Società di capitali: Commentario. Jovene, Napoli, pp 652–675

Gutsche R (1994) Die Eignung der Europäischen Aktiengesellschaft für kleine und mittlere Unternehmen in Deutschland. Univ., Diss.—Heidelberg, 1993, 1st edn. Nomos, Baden-Baden

Hagen-Eck R (1995) Die Europäische Genossenschaft. Duncker et Humblot, Berlin

Hanisch M (2006) Eine Theorie genossenschaftlichen Wandels. In: Münkner H-H (ed) Zukunftsperspektiven für Genossenschaften: Bausteine für typgerechte Weiterentwicklung: [Beiträge zum Kolloquium "Elemente von Strategiekonzepten der Zukunftssicherung genossenschaftlicher Kooperation", Marburg 2005], 1st edn. Haupt, Bern, Stuttgart, Wien, pp 297–323

Hansmann H (1988) Ownership of the firm. J Law Econ Organ 4:267–304

Hansmann H (1996) The ownership of enterprise, 1st edn. Belknap Press of Harvard University Press, Cambridge
Hansmann H (1999) Cooperative firms in theory and practice. Liiketaloudellinen aikakauskirja LTA - Finn J Bus Econ:387–403
Hansmann H (2003) The role of trust in nonprofit enterprise. In: Anheier HK, Ben-Ner A (eds) The study of the nonprofit enterprise. Springer US, Boston, pp 115–122
Hansmann H (2006) Corporation and contract. Am Law Econ Rev 8:1–19. https://doi.org/10.1093/aler/ahj007
Hansmann H (2010) The economics of nonprofit organizations. In: Hopt KJ, Hippel TV (eds) Comparative corporate governance of non-profit organizations. Cambridge University Press, Cambridge, pp 60–72
Hansmann H (2011) Firm ownership: the legacy of Grossman and Hart. SSRN Electron J. https://doi.org/10.2139/ssrn.2635719
Hansmann H (2014) All firms are cooperatives – and so are governments. J Entrep Organ Divers 2:1–10. https://doi.org/10.5947/jeod.2013.007
Hansmann H, Kraakman RH (1991) The uneasy case for limiting shareholder liability in tort. Yale Law J:1879–1934
Hansmann H, Pargendler M (2013) The evolution of shareholder voting rights: separation of ownership and consumption. Yale Law J:100–165
Hansmann H, Kraakman RH, Squire RC (2006) Law and the rise of the firm. Harv Law Rev 119:1333–1403
Halpern P, Trebilcock M, Turnbull S (1980) An economic analysis of limited liability in corporation law. Univ Tor Law J 30:117–150
Hardin G (1968) The tragedy of the commons. Science 162:1243–1248. https://doi.org/10.1126/science.162.3859.1243
Hardin R (1971) Collective action as an agreeable n-prisoners' dilemma. Behav Sci 16:472–481. https://doi.org/10.1002/bs.3830160507
Hardin R (2013) The free rider problem. In: Edward NZ (ed) The Stanford encyclopedia of philosophy, Spring 2013
Harrer F (1990) Haftungsprobleme bei der GmbH. Univ., Habil.-Schr.—Salzburg, 1989. Orac, Wien
Hart OD (1988) Incomplete contracts and the theory of the firm. J Law Econ Organ 4:119–139
Hart O, Moore J (1990) Property rights and the nature of the firm. J Polit Econ 98:1119–1158. https://doi.org/10.1086/261729
Heilmeier M (2010) Die Kapitalverfassung der Europäischen Genossenschaft (SCE). EuZW:887–892
Henrÿ H (2012) Guidelines for cooperative legislation, 3rd edn. International Labour Organization, Geneva
Henrÿ H (2013a) Public international cooperative law. In: Cracogna D, Fici A, Henrÿ H (eds) International handbook of cooperative law. Springer, Berlin, Heidelberg, pp 65–88
Henrÿ H (2013b) The contribution of the ILO to the formation of public international cooperative law. In: Kott S, Droux J (eds) Globalizing social rights. Palgrave Macmillan UK, London, pp 98–114
Henrÿ H (2017) Co-operative principles and co-operative law across the globe. In: Michie J, Blasi JR, Borzaga C (eds) The Oxford handbook of mutual, co-operative, and co-owned business, 1st edn. Oxford University Press, Oxford, pp 39–52
Henssler M (2003) Unternehmerische Mitbestimmung in der Societas Europaea: neue Denkanstöße für die "Corporate Governance"-Diskussion. In: Habersack M (ed) Festschrift für Peter Ulmer zum 70. Geburtstag am 2. Januar 2003. De Gruyter, Berlin, pp 193–210
Hernandez-Espallardo M, Arcas-Lario N, Marcos-Matas G (2013) Farmers' satisfaction and intention to continue membership in agricultural marketing co-operatives: neoclassical versus transaction cost considerations. Eur Rev Agric Econ 40:239–260. https://doi.org/10.1093/erae/jbs024

Hetherington JAC (1991) Mutual and cooperative enterprises: an analysis of customer-owned firms in the United States. University Press of Virginia, Charlottesville

Hiez D (2017) Introduction. In: Fajardo-García IG, Fici A, Henrÿ H, Hiez D, Meira DMMA, Münkner H-H, Snaith I (eds) Principles of European Cooperative Law: principles, commentaries and national reports. Intersentia, Cambridge, pp 1–15

Hiez D, Tadjudje W (2013) The OHADA cooperative regulation. In: Cracogna D, Fici A, Henrÿ H (eds) International handbook of cooperative law. Springer, Berlin, Heidelberg, pp 89–113

Hill CA, McDonnell BH (2012) Introduction: the evolution of the economic analysis of corporate law. In: Hill CA, McDonnell BH (eds) Research handbook on the economics of corporate law. Edward Elgar Publishing, Cheltenham, pp 1–13

Hirschman AO (1970) Exit, voice, and loyalty: responses to decline in firms, organizations, and states. Harvard University Press, Cambridge

Hirte H (2002) Die Europäische Aktiengesellschaft. Neue Zeitschrift für Gesellschaftsrecht:1–9

Hirte H (2005) Die Europäische Aktiengesellschaft - ein Überblick nach In-Kraft-Treten der deutschen Ausführungsgesetzgebung (Teil II). DStR:700–705

Hirte H (2007) Das neue Genossenschaftsrecht (Teil II). DStR:2215–2219

Hoeffler J (2013) Die Gestaltungsfreiheit im deutschen und europäischen Genossenschaftsrecht. Europäische Hochschulschriften. Reihe II, Rechtswissenschaft, Band 5534. Peter Lang, Frankfurt

Hoffmann EA (2006) Exit and voice: organizational loyalty and dispute resolution strategies. Soc Forces 84:2313–2330. https://doi.org/10.1353/sof.2006.0093

Hoffmann-Becking M (2004) Organe: Strukturen und Verantwortlichkeiten, insbesondere im monistischen System. Zeitschrift für Unternehmens- und Gesellschaftsrecht 33:355–382. https://doi.org/10.1515/zgre.2004.014

Hofinger H, Johler C (2002) Wettbewerb der genossenschaftlich-nationalen Rechtsformen in der SCE: Auftakt zur Diskussion um die Verweisnormen auf nationale Vorschriften und der Versuch einer attraktiven Gestaltung eines Ausführungsgesetzes für die Stärkung des Wirtschaftsstandorts Österreich. Ziller-Schriften, vol 3. Österr. Genossenschaftsverb. (Schulze-Delitzsch), Wien

Hofinger H, Zawischa G (2007) Das Genossenschaftsrechts-Änderungsgesetz 2006: Eine Genossenschaftsreform mit neuen Möglichkeiten der Kapitalaufbringung. Gewerbliche Genossenschaft:30

Holmstrom B (1999) The future of cooperatives: a corporate perspective. Liiketaloudellinen aikakauskirja LTA - Finn J Bus Econ:404–417

Holmstrom B, Milgrom P (1994) The firm as an incentive system. Am Econ Rev 84:972–991

Holthaus J, Lehnhoff DJ (2016a) § 18. In: Lehnhoff DJ, Holthaus J (eds) Lang/Weidmüller Genossenschaftsgesetz: Gesetz, betreffend die Erwerbs- und Wirtschaftsgenossenschaften mit Erläuterungen zum Umwandlungsgesetz und zur Europäischen Genossenschaft (SCE), 38., neu bearbeitete Auflage. De Gruyter, Berlin, pp 222–243

Holthaus J, Lehnhoff DJ (2016b) § 43. In: Lehnhoff DJ, Holthaus J (eds) Lang/Weidmüller Genossenschaftsgesetz: Gesetz, betreffend die Erwerbs- und Wirtschaftsgenossenschaften mit Erläuterungen zum Umwandlungsgesetz und zur Europäischen Genossenschaft (SCE), 38., neu bearbeitete Auflage. De Gruyter, Berlin, pp 567–614

Holthaus J, Lehnhoff DJ (2016c) § 6. In: Lehnhoff DJ, Holthaus J (eds) Lang/Weidmüller Genossenschaftsgesetz: Gesetz, betreffend die Erwerbs- und Wirtschaftsgenossenschaften mit Erläuterungen zum Umwandlungsgesetz und zur Europäischen Genossenschaft (SCE), 38., neu bearbeitete Auflage. De Gruyter, Berlin, pp 112–122

Holthaus J, Lehnhoff DJ (2016d) Einf. In: Lehnhoff DJ, Holthaus J (eds) Lang/Weidmüller Genossenschaftsgesetz: Gesetz, betreffend die Erwerbs- und Wirtschaftsgenossenschaften mit Erläuterungen zum Umwandlungsgesetz und zur Europäischen Genossenschaft (SCE), 38., neu bearbeitete Auflage. De Gruyter, Berlin, pp 1–54

Holzer G (1982) Zum Begriff und Standort des Agrarrechts in der österreichischen Rechtsordnung. Juristische Blätter:300–310

Holzer G (2010) Nebengewerbe der Land- und Forstwirtschaft im Lichte der Rechtssprechung des Verwaltungsgerichtshofes. In: Norer R, Holzer G (eds) Agrarrecht: Jahrbuch 2010. Neuer Wissenschaftlicher Verlag, Wien, pp 171–184
Holzer G (2012a) Gewerberecht. In: Norer R (ed) Handbuch des Agrarrechts, 2. Aufl. Verlag Österreich, Wien, pp 759–784
Holzer G (2012b) Grundverkehrsrecht. In: Norer R (ed) Handbuch des Agrarrechts, 2. Aufl. Verlag Österreich, Wien, pp 673–702
Holzer G (2017a) Bäuerliche Direktvermarktung, 2nd edn. Praxis. NWV, Wien, Graz
Holzer G (2017b) Der funktionale Agrarrechtsbegriff - Erfahrungen und Erkenntnisse. In: Norer R, Holzer G (eds) Agrarrecht: Jahrbuch 2017. Perspektiven des Agrarrechts. Festgabe für Manfried Welan, 1st edn. NWV Verlag, Wien, pp 131–168
Holzer G (2017c) Gewerberecht. In: Holzer G (ed) Bäuerliche Direktvermarktung, 2nd edn. NWV, Wien, Graz, pp 21–54
Holzer G (2018) Agrarrecht, 4th edn. Studium & Praxis. NWV Verlag, Wien, Graz
Hommelhoff P (1988) Die Konzernleitungspflicht: Zentrale Aspekte eines Konzernverfassungsrechts. Univ., Habil.-Schr.-1981--Bochum, 1980, Unveränd. Nachdr. [der Ausg. 1982]. Heymanns, Köln
Hommelhoff P (2003) Satzungsstrenge und Gestaltungsfreiheit in der Europäischen Aktiengesellschaft. In: Habersack M (ed) Festschrift für Peter Ulmer zum 70. Geburtstag am 2. Januar 2003. De Gruyter, Berlin, pp 267–278
Hommelhoff P, Teichmann C (2015) Art. 9. In: Lutter M, Hommelhoff P, Teichmann C (eds) SE-Kommentar, 2nd edn. Verlag Dr. Otto Schmidt, Köln, pp 172–193
Hopt K (2002) Europäische Aktiengesellschaft - per aspera ad astra? EuZW:1
Hopt KJ (2013) Conflict of interest, secrecy and insider information of directors, a comparative analysis. Eur Comp Financ Law Rev 10:167–193. https://doi.org/10.1515/ecfr-2013-0167
Hopt KJ (2016) Directors' duties and shareholders' rights in the European Union: mandatory and/or default rules? SSRN Electron J:1–23. https://doi.org/10.2139/ssrn.2749237
Hopt KJ, Leyens PC (2004) Board models in Europe – recent developments of internal corporate governance structures in Germany, the United Kingdom, France, and Italy. Eur Comp Financ Law Rev 1:135–168. https://doi.org/10.1515/ecfr.2004.1.2.135
Hoyt A (1996) And then there were seven: cooperative principles updated
Hoyt A (2004) Consumer ownership in capitalist economies: applications of theory of consumer cooperation. In: Merrett CD, Walzer N (eds) Cooperatives and local development: theory and applications for the 21st century. Sharpe, Armonk, pp 265–289
Hueck A (1947) Der Treuegedanke im modernen Privatrecht. Verlag der Bayerischen Akademie der Wissenschaften, München
Hueth B, Marcoul P (2009) Incentive pay for CEOs in cooperative firms. Am J Agric Econ 91:1218–1223. https://doi.org/10.1111/j.1467-8276.2009.01287.x
Ianes A (2013) Introduzione alla storia della cooperazione in Italia (1854-2011): Profilo storico-economico e interpretazione. Università. Rubbettino, Soveria Mannelli
Iannarelli A (2001) Il diritto dell'agricoltura nell'era della globalizzazione. Cacucci, Bari
Iannarelli A (2002a) Il diritto agrario tra profilo globale e profilo locale: spunti sul metodo e sull'oggetto della ricerca. Rivista di diritto agrario:729–753
Iannarelli A (2002b) L'impresa agricola nel sistema agro-industriale. Diritto e giurisprudenza agraria e dell'ambiente:213–219
Iannarelli A (2007) Pluralismo definitorio dell'attività e dell'impresa agricola tra diritto comunitario e diritto interno. Studi sull'integrazione europea:469–495
Iannarelli A (2008a) Cooperazione e conflitto nel sistema agro-alimentare. Rivista di diritto agrario:328–382
Iannarelli A (2008b) I contratti dall'impresa agricola all'industria di trasformazione: Problemi e prospettive dell'esperienza italiana. Rivista di diritto alimentare II:5–13
Iannarelli A (2009) La concorrenza e l'agrarietà nell'attuale esperienza europea: una relazione "speciale". Rivista di diritto agrario:515–566

Iannarelli A (2011) Contractual relationships and inter-firm co-operation in the agri-food sector. Rivista di diritto alimentare:4–10

Iannarelli A (2013) Il divenire del diritto agrario italiano ed europeo tra sviluppi tecnologici e sostenibilità. Rivista di diritto agrario:11–35

Iannarelli A (2019) La parabola della "specialità" dell'impresa agricola dopo il d.lgs. sulle crisi di impresa: considerazioni critiche. Rivista di diritto agrario:197–238

Ibáñez IE (2011) Law applicable to the European Cooperative Society: special reference to the European cooperative established in Spain. Eur Comp Financ Law Rev 8:30–46. https://doi.org/10.1515/ecfr.2011.30

Iengo M (2006) Gli Studi del CNN - Società cooperativa europea - Analisi delle norme applicabili ai sensi dell'articolo 8 del regolamento n. 1435/2003 - Casi e materiali di diritto comunitario di interesse notarile: le società - e.library - Fondazione Italiana del Notariato. Studio n. 9-2006/I. http://elibrary.fondazionenotariato.it/approfondimento.asp?app=21/studiCNN/mi_9_2006_I&mn=3&tipo=3&qn=6. Accessed 21 Nov 2019

Iliopoulos C (2013) Public support for agricultural cooperatives: an organizational economics approach. Ann Public Coop Econ 84:241–252. https://doi.org/10.1111/apce.12012

Iliopoulos C (2014) Ownership, governance and related trade-offs in agricultural cooperatives. Dovenschmidt Q 2:159–167. https://doi.org/10.5553/DQ/221199812014002004004

Iliopoulos C (2015) Ownership and governance in agricultural cooperatives: an update. https://www.researchgate.net/publication/274064574_Ownership_and_Governance_in_Agricultural_Cooperatives_An_Update. Accessed 29 Nov 2019

Iliopoulos C, Cook ML (2013) Property rights constraints in producer-owned firms: solutions as prerequisites for successful collective entrepreneurship

Iliopoulos C, Cook ML (1999) The internal organization of the cooperative firm: an extension of a new institutional digest? J Coop:77–85

Iliopoulos C, Hendrikse G (2009) Influence costs in agribusiness cooperatives. Int Stud Manage Organ 39:60–80. https://doi.org/10.2753/IMO0020-8825390404

Iliopoulos C, Valentinov V (2018) Member heterogeneity in agricultural cooperatives: a systems-theoretic perspective. Sustainability 10:1271. https://doi.org/10.3390/su10041271

Ingrosso M (2013) Le cooperative e le nuove agevolazioni fiscali: Profili civilistici, contabili, comunitari, 2nd edn. Giappichelli, Torino

International Co-operative Alliance, Guidance Notes to the Co-operative Principles (2015). https://www.ica.coop/en/media/library/research-and-reviews/guidance-notes-cooperative-principles?_ga=2.123262351.52726143.1574094684-1144315335.1574094684. Accessed 18 Nov 2019

International Co-operative Alliance, History of the cooperative movement. https://www.ica.coop/en/cooperatives/history-cooperative-movement. Accessed 18 Nov 2019

International Co-operative Alliance, What is a co-operative?. https://www.ica.coop/en/cooperatives/what-is-a-cooperative. Accessed 18 Nov 2019

International Labour Organisation, R193 - Promotion of Cooperatives Recommendation, 2002. ilo.org/dyn/normlex/en/f?p=NORMLEXPUB:12100:0::NO::P12100_INSTRUMENT_ID:312531 (18.11.2019)

Jaecks J, Schönborn AC (2003) Die Europäische Aktiengesellschaft, das Internationale und das deutsche Konzernrecht. Recht der Internationalen Wirtschaft:254–265

Jagschitz F, Rom S, Wiedey J (2015) Gemeinsame Geschichte Österreichischer Genossenschaftsverband (ÖGV) und Konsumverband. In: Brazda J, van Husen R, Rößl D (eds) Perspektiven für die Genossenschaftsidee: Festschrift zum 65. Geburtstag von Verbandsanwalt Professor DDr. Hans Hofinger. EHV Academicpress, Bremen, pp 58–68

Jensen MC, Meckling WH (1976) Theory of the firm: managerial behavior, agency costs and ownership structure. J Financ Econ 3:305–360. https://doi.org/10.1016/0304-405X(76)90026-X

Jensen MC, Meckling WH (1979) Rights and production functions: an application to labor-managed firms and codetermination. J Bus 52:469–506. https://doi.org/10.1086/296060

Johnston JS (1992) Opting in and opting out: bargaining for fiduciary duties in cooperative ventures. Wash Univ Law Q:291–340
Jungmann C (2006) The effectiveness of corporate governance in one-tier and two-tier board systems – evidence from the UK and Germany. Eur Comp Financ Law Rev 3:426–474. https://doi.org/10.1515/ECFR.2006.019
Kahan M, Kamar E (2002) The myth of state competition in corporate law. Stanford Law Rev 55:679. https://doi.org/10.2307/1229668
Kahneman 4D (1994) New challenges to the rationality assumption. J Inst Theor Econ (JITE)/ Zeitschrift für die gesamte Staatswissenschaft 150:18–36
Kahneman D (2012) Thinking, fast and slow. Penguin Books, London
Kalss S (2004) Die geplante SE-Gesetzgebung in Österreich. In: Baums T, Cahn A (eds) Die Europäische Aktiengesellschaft: Umsetzungsfragen und Perspektiven. De Gruyter, Berlin, pp 106–131
Kalss S (2008) Societas Europea. In: Kalss S, Nowotny C, Schauer M, Kastner W, Doralt P (eds) Österreichisches Gesellschaftsrecht: Systematische Darstellung sämtlicher Rechtsformen: in Fortführung des von Walther Kastner begründeten und in der letzten Auflage von Walther Kastner, Peter Doralt und Christian Nowotny bearbeiteten Lehr- und Handbuchs "Grundriss des österreichischen Gesellschaftsrechts". Manz, Wien, 3/1091–3/1111
Kalss S (2012) § 92. In: Doralt W, Nowotny C, Kalss S (eds) Kommentar zum Aktiengesetz, 2nd edn. Linde, Wien, pp 1186–1252
Kalss S (2014) Österreich. In: Goette W, Habersack M, Kalss S (eds) Münchener Kommentar zum Aktiengesetz, 4th edn. C.H. Beck; Verlag Franz Vahlen, München, pp 871–888
Kalss S (2015) Organhaftung in Österreich - einige rechtspolitische Anmerkungen. GesRZ:159–167
Kalss S, Eckert G (2005) Zentrale Fragen des GmbH-Rechts: Entwicklung - Perspektiven - Materialien. Linde Verlag Wien, Wien
Kalss S, Greda C (2004) Die Europäische Gesellschaft (SE) österreichischer Prägung nach dem Ministerialentwurf. GesRZ:91–107
Kalss S, Schauer M (2006) Die Reform des Österreichischen Kapitalgesellschaftsrechts: Gutachten. Verhandlungen des Sechzehnten Österreichischen Juristentages Zivilrecht, vol 1. Manz, Wien
Karantininis K, Nilsson J (eds) (2007) Vertical markets and cooperative hierarchies: the role of cooperatives in the agri-food industry. Springer, Dordrecht
Kastner W (1986) Österreichisches Genossenschaftsrecht. In: Patera M (ed) Handbuch des österreichischen Genossenschaftswesens. Orac, Wien, pp 117–232
Kastner W, Doralt P, Nowotny C (1990) Grundriss des österreichischen Gesellschaftsrechts, 5th edn. Manzsche Kurzlehrbuch-Reihe, vol 2. Manz, Wien
Keay A (2008) Ascertaining the corporate objective: an entity maximisation and sustainability model. Mod Law Rev 71:663–698. https://doi.org/10.1111/j.1468-2230.2008.00711.x
Keinert H (1988) Österreichisches Genossenschaftsrecht: Lehr- und Handbuch. Manz, Wien
Keinert H, Keinert-Kisin C (2013) Ungeschriebene Kompetenzen der Generalversammlung der Genossenschaft? ecolex:996
Kellerhals A, Truten D (2002) The creation of the European company. Tulane Eur Civ Law Forum:71–82
Kershaw D (2012) Company law in context: text and materials, 2nd edn. Oxford University Press, Oxford
Kirchner C, Painter RW, Kaal WA (2005) Regulatory competition in EU Corporate Law after inspire art: unbundling Delaware's product for Europe. Eur Comp Financ Law Rev 2:159–206. https://doi.org/10.1515/ecfr.2005.2.2.159
Kisker O (2006) Unternehmerische Mitbestimmung in der Europäischen Gesellschaft, der Europäischen Genossenschaft und bei grenzüberschreitender Verschmelzung im Vergleich. Recht der Arbeit:206–213
Klausner M (1995) Corporations, corporate law, and networks of contracts. Va Law Rev 81:757. https://doi.org/10.2307/1073499

Klein B, Crawford RG, Alchian AA (1978) Vertical integration, appropriable rents, and the competitive contracting process. J Law Econ 21:297–326

Klein WA, Coffee JC, Partnoy F (2010) Business organization and finance: legal and economic principles, 11 edn. Concepts and insights series. Foundation Press, New York

Klöhn L (2008) Interessenkonflikte zwischen Aktionären und Gläubigern der Aktiengesellschaft im Spiegel der Vorstandspflichten – Ein Beitrag zur Leitungsaufgabe des Vorstands gemäß § 76 AktG. Zeitschrift für Unternehmens- und Gesellschaftsrecht 37:110–158. https://doi.org/10.1515/ZGR.2008.37.1.110

Kober R (2008) Investierende Mitglieder: einfallende Heuschrecken oder Chance für die Genossenschaft. In: Brazda J, Kühl R, Rößl R (eds) Beiträge zur genossenschaftswissenschaftlichen Forschung: Proceedings der XIII. Nachwuchswissenschaftler-Tagung der Arbeitsgemeinschaft genossenschaftswissenschaftlicher Institute (AGI) e. V., 18./19. März 2008 in Wien, Wien, pp 43–62

Koke C (2005) Die Finanzverfassung der Europäischen Aktiengesellschaft (SE) mit Sitz in Deutschland. Univ., Diss.—Würzburg, 2004. Schriftenreihe zum deutschen und europäischen Gesellschafts- und Wirtschaftsrecht, vol 3. Peter Lang, Frankfurt am Main

Koppensteiner H, Rüffler F (2007) GmbH-Gesetz: Kommentar, 3rd edn. LexisNexis ARD Orac, Wien

Korte O (2012) Die Europäische Genossenschaft (SCE): Analyse der mangelnden Verbreitung dieser supranationalen Rechtsform. In: Baudenbacher C (ed) Aktuelle Entwicklungen des europäischen und internationalen Wirtschaftsrechts. Helbing et Lichtenhahn, Basel, München [u.a.], pp 323–349

Kräkel M (2012) Organisation und Management, 5th edn. Neue ökonomische Grundrisse. Mohr Siebeck, Tübingen

Kramer JW (2006) Was kennzeichnet eine "erfolgreiche" Genossenschaft. In: Münkner H-H (ed) Zukunftsperspektiven für Genossenschaften: Bausteine für typgerechte Weiterentwicklung: [Beiträge zum Kolloquium "Elemente von Strategiekonzepten der Zukunftssicherung genossenschaftlicher Kooperation", Marburg 2005], 1st edn. Haupt, Bern, Stuttgart, Wien, pp 126–151

Kraus S-F (2014) § 25. In: Torggler U (ed) GmbH-Gesetz: (GmbHG) Kurzkommentar. Manzsche Verlags- und Universitätsbuchhandlung, Wien, pp 236–260

Krimphove D (1998) Der Einsatz der ökonomischen Analyse des Rechts als notwendiges Instrument der Europäischen Rechtsvergleichung (Teil I): Dargestellt anhand des Erwerbes vom Nichtberechtigten in den Europäischen Rechtsordnungen. ZfRV:185–204

Krimphove D (2006) Das europäische Sachenrecht: Eine rechtsvergleichende Analyse nach der Komparativen Institutionenökonomik, 1st edn. Europäisches Wirtschaftsrecht (Lohmar, Germany), vol 1. Eul, Lohmar

Krimphove D (2010) Brauchen wir die Europäische Genossenschaft? EuZW:892–897

Kübler F (2003) Leitungsstrukturen der Aktiengesellschaft und die Umsetzung des SE-Statuts. Zeitschrift für das gesamte Handelsrecht und Wirtschaftsrecht (ZHR):222–234

Kühl R (2012) Country report: Austria. In: Van der Sangen G, Pyykkönen POP, Iliopoulus C, Kühl R, Hagedorn K, Hanisch M, Judis R, Gijselinckx C, Hendrikse G, Hak T, Poppe K, Bijman J (eds) Support for farmers' cooperatives, Wageningen, pp 1–51

Kyriakopoulos K (2000) The market orientation of cooperative organizations: learning strategies and structures for integrating cooperative firm and members. Van Gorcum, Assen

Lächler C, Oplustil K (2005) Funktion und Umfang des Regelungsbereichs der SE-Verordnung. Neue Zeitschrift für Gesellschaftsrecht:381–388

Lamandini M (2007) Art. 2526. In: Presti G (ed) Società cooperative: Artt. 2511-2548. EGEA; Giuffrè, Milano, pp 203–225

Lamanna Di Salvo D (2003) La gestione aziendale nelle rilevazioni in partita doppia. WIP, Bari

Lando O, Beale H, Prüm A, Clive E, Zimmermann R (2019) Principles of European Contract Law, Parts I - III: Student edition. Kluwer Law International, [S.l.]

Lange O (2003) Überlegungen zur Umwandlung einer deutschen in eine Europäische Aktiengesellschaft. EuZW:301–309
Langhein G (2015) § 68. In: Lutter M, Hommelhoff P, Teichmann C (eds) SE-Kommentar, 2nd edn. Verlag Dr. Otto Schmidt, Köln, pp 965–969
Laurini (2008a) Art. 2371. In: Picciau A (ed) Assemblea: Artt. 2363 - 2379-ter c.c. EGEA, Milano, pp 147–188
Laurini (2008b) Artt. 2368-2369 c.c. In: Picciau A (ed) Assemblea: Artt. 2363 - 2379-ter c.c. EGEA, Milano, pp 79–120
Laurinkari J (1990a) Einführung. In: Laurinkari J (ed) Genossenschaftswesen: Hand- und Lehrbuch. Oldenbourg, München, pp 1–10
Laurinkari J (1990b) Entwicklungstypen. In: Laurinkari J (ed) Genossenschaftswesen: Hand- und Lehrbuch. Oldenbourg, München, pp 403–412
Lehmann M (2014) Cooperatives as governance mechanisms. Eur Comp Financ Law Rev 11:31–52. https://doi.org/10.1515/ecfr-2014-0031
Lehner JH (2007) Die Europäische Genossenschaft mit Sitzstaat Österreich. Wien, Univ., Diss., 2008
Lehner JH (2009) Verschmelzungsvarianten einer Europäischen Genossenschaft (SCE). In: Haslinger M, Kanonier A, Zehetner S (eds) Ein Jurist im Spannungsfeld von Wirtschaft, Technik und Recht: Festschrift für Franz Zehetner zum 60. Geburtstag. NWV, Wien, pp 97–110
Leidwein A (2007) Die Internationalisierung des Agrarrechts. In: Österreichische Gesellschaft für Agrar- und Umweltrecht (ed) Agrarrecht im Lichte des öffentlichen Rechts: Festschrift für Univ.-Prof. Dr. Gottfried Holzer zum 60. Geburtstag. NWV, Wien, pp 33–48
LeVay C (1983) Agricultural co-operative theory: a review. J Agric Econ 34:1–44. https://doi.org/10.1111/j.1477-9552.1983.tb00973.x
Leyens PC (2003) Deutscher Aufsichtsrat und U.S.-Board: ein- oder zweistufiges Verwaltungssystem?: Zum Stand der rechtsvergleichenden Corporate Governance-Debatte. Rabels Zeitschrift fuer auslaendisches und internationales Privatrecht:57–105
Leyens PC (2006) Information des Aufsichtsrats: Ökonomisch-funktionale Analyse und Rechtsvergleich zum englischen Board. Univ., Diss.—Hamburg, 2006. Mohr Siebeck, Tübingen
Leyens PC (2007a) Corporate Governance: Grundsatzfragen und Forschungsperspektiven. JuristenZeitung 62:1061–1072. https://doi.org/10.1628/002268807782717113
Leyens PC (2007b) Internal corporate governance in Europe: towards a more market-based approach. Kyoto J Law Polit:17–36
Liang Q, Hendrikse G (2013) Cooperative CEO identity and efficient governance: member or outside CEO? Agribusiness 29:23–38
Lind M (2004) Die Europäische Aktiengesellschaft: Eine Analyse der Rechtsanwendungsvorschriften. Univ., Diss.—Graz, 2003. Neue juristische Monografien, vol 26. NWV, Wien
Lolli R (2010) Le riserve divisibili e indivisibili nelle società cooperative. Le monografie di Contratto e impresa, vol 132. Cedam, Padova
Lolli R (2012) I mezzi propri delle cooperative e i bilanci. In: Paolucci LF (ed) Le società cooperative. UTET giuridica, Torino, pp 147–179
Lombardo S, Pasotti P (2004) The Societas Europaea: a network economics approach. Eur Comp Financ Law Rev 1:169–205. https://doi.org/10.1515/ecfr.2004.1.2.169
Lutter M (1983) Vom formellen Mindestkapital zu materiellen Finanzierungsregeln im Recht der Kapitalgesellschaften. In: Riesenfeld S, Jayme E (eds) Ius inter nationes. C. F. Müller, Heidelberg
Lutter M (2007) Die Business Judgment Rule in Deutschland und Österreich. GesRZ:79–89
Lutter M (2015) Art. 1. In: Lutter M, Hommelhoff P, Teichmann C (eds) SE-Kommentar, 2nd edn. Verlag Dr. Otto Schmidt, Köln, pp 78–89

Lutter M, Schmidt J, Bayer W (2012) Europäisches Unternehmens- und Kapitalmarktrecht: Grundlagen, Stand und Entwicklung nebst Texten und Materialien, 5th edn. Zeitschrift für Unternehmens- und Gesellschaftsrecht. Sonderheft, T. 1. De Gruyter, Berlin

Macaulay S (1963) Non-contractual relations in business: a preliminary study. Am Sociol Rev:1–23

MacNeil IR (1974) The many futures of contracts. South Calif Law Rev:691–816

Maffezzoni I (2008) Art. 2365. In: Picciau A (ed) Assemblea: Artt. 2363 - 2379-ter c.c. EGEA, Milano, pp 45–58

Magnani P (2005a) Art. 2409 duodecies. In: Ghezzi F (ed) Sistemi alternativi di amministrazione e di controllo: Artt. 2409-octies - 2409-noviesdecies c.c, 1st edn. EGEA, Milano, pp 107–134

Magnani P (2005b) Art. 2409 terdecies. In: Ghezzi F (ed) Sistemi alternativi di amministrazione e di controllo: Artt. 2409-octies - 2409-noviesdecies c.c, 1st edn. EGEA, Milano, pp 135–186

Magno P (2006) Sul diritto agrario "modernizzato". Rivista di diritto agrario:76–115

Mahi FE (2004) Die Europäische Aktiengesellschaft: Societas Europaea, SE. Fachhochschule, Dipl.-Arb.—Frankfurt am Main, 2003. Herchen + Herchen, Frankfurt am Main

Mallin C, Melis A, Gaia S (2015) The remuneration of independent directors in the UK and Italy: an empirical analysis based on agency theory. Int Bus Rev 24:175–186. https://doi.org/10.1016/j.ibusrev.2014.07.006

Maltoni M (2014) Art. 2545 undecies. In: Santosuosso DU (ed) Delle società, dell'azienda, della concorrenza. UTET, Torino, pp 535–545

Mancuso F (2017) Il comitato per il controllo sulla gestione nel modello monistico: problemi in tema di responsabilità dei componenti e di invalidità delle decisioni. Rivista delle società:773–794

Manes P (1999) Il superamento della personalità giuridica: L'esperienza inglese. Le monografie di Contratto e impresa.Serie di diritto comparato, vol 1. Cedam, Padova

Manne HG (1965) Mergers and the market for corporate control. J Polit Econ 73:110–120. https://doi.org/10.1086/259000

Manservisi S (2014) Il principio dello sviluppo sostenibile: da Rio+20 al diritto dell'Unione europea e il suo fondamentale ruolo nel diritto agrario. In: Sgarbanti G, Borghi P, Germanò A (eds) Il divenire del diritto agrario italiano ed europeo tra sviluppi tecnologici e sostenibilità: Convegno organizzato in onore del Prof. Ettore Casadei, in occasione del suo 70° compleanno: atti del Convegno IDAIC, Bologna-Rovigo, 25-26 ottobre 2012. Giuffrè, Milano, pp 175–224

Manz G (2010a) Art. 38. In: Manz G, Mayer B, Schröder A (eds) Europäische Aktiengesellschaft SE: SE, 2nd edn. Nomos, Baden-Baden, pp 482–490

Manz G (2010b) Art. 39. In: Manz G, Mayer B, Schröder A (eds) Europäische Aktiengesellschaft SE: SE, 2nd edn. Nomos, Baden-Baden, pp 490–515

Manz G (2010c) Art. 40. In: Manz G, Mayer B, Schröder A (eds) Europäische Aktiengesellschaft SE: SE, 2nd edn. Nomos, Baden-Baden, pp 515–529

Manz G (2010d) Art. 41. In: Manz G, Mayer B, Schröder A (eds) Europäische Aktiengesellschaft SE: SE, 2nd edn. Nomos, Baden-Baden, pp 529–539

Manz G (2010e) Art. 42. In: Manz G, Mayer B, Schröder A (eds) Europäische Aktiengesellschaft SE: SE, 2nd edn. Nomos, Baden-Baden, pp 539–542

Manz G (2010f) Art. 43. In: Manz G, Mayer B, Schröder A (eds) Europäische Aktiengesellschaft SE: SE, 2nd edn. Nomos, Baden-Baden, pp 542–598

Manz G (2010g) Art. 44. In: Manz G, Mayer B, Schröder A (eds) Europäische Aktiengesellschaft SE: SE, 2nd edn. Nomos, Baden-Baden, pp 598–601

Manz G (2010h) Art. 46. In: Manz G, Mayer B, Schröder A (eds) Europäische Aktiengesellschaft SE: SE, 2nd edn. Nomos, Baden-Baden, pp 605–608

Manz G (2010i) Art. 47. In: Manz G, Mayer B, Schröder A (eds) Europäische Aktiengesellschaft SE: SE, 2nd edn. Nomos, Baden-Baden, pp 608–616

Manz G (2010j) Art. 48. In: Manz G, Mayer B, Schröder A (eds) Europäische Aktiengesellschaft SE: SE, 2nd edn. Nomos, Baden-Baden, pp 616–624

Manz G (2010k) Art. 49. In: Manz G, Mayer B, Schröder A (eds) Europäische Aktiengesellschaft SE: SE, 2nd edn. Nomos, Baden-Baden, pp 624–628

Manz G (2010l) Art. 50. In: Manz G, Mayer B, Schröder A (eds) Europäische Aktiengesellschaft SE: SE, 2nd edn. Nomos, Baden-Baden, pp 628–638

Manz G (2010m) Art. 51. In: Manz G, Mayer B, Schröder A (eds) Europäische Aktiengesellschaft SE: SE, 2nd edn. Nomos, Baden-Baden, pp 638–648

Manzini P (2006) Società Cooperativa Europea e diritto di stabilimento. In: Galletti D, Fici A (eds) La società cooperativa europea: Quali prospettive per la cooperazione italiana? Universita degli Studi di Trento, Trento, pp 27–48

Marano P (2003) Art. 2544 c.c. In: Sandulli M, Santoro V (eds) La riforma delle società: Società cooperative Artt. 2511-2548 cod.civ. Giappichelli, Torino, pp 148–161

Marano P (2006) La Società Cooperativa Europea nell'ambito delle politiche comunitarie in materia di reti e gruppi d'imprese. In: Galletti D, Fici A (eds) La società cooperativa europea: Quali prospettive per la cooperazione italiana? Universita degli Studi di Trento, Trento, pp 13–26

Marano P (2013a) Art. 2538. In: Alpa G, Mariconda V (eds) Codice civile, 3rd edn. Wolters Kluwer Italia; IPSOA, Assago

Marano P (2013b) Art. 2539. In: Alpa G, Mariconda V (eds) Codice civile, 3rd edn. Wolters Kluwer Italia; IPSOA, Assago

Marano P (2014) Artt. 2512-2514 c.c., 2545 octies c.c. In: Santosuosso DU (ed) Delle società, dell'azienda, della concorrenza. UTET, Torino, pp 66–93

Marasà G (1984) Le società senza scopo di lucro. Giuffré, Milano

Marasà G (1992) La disciplina della legge n 59 del 1992. Rivista di Diritto Civile:365

Marasà G (ed) (2004) Le cooperative prima e dopo la riforma del diritto societario. Cedam, Padova

Marasà G (2012) Lucro, mutualità e solidarietà nelle imprese. (Riflessioni sul pensiero di Giorgio Oppo). Giurisprudenza Commerciale:197–219

Marasà G (2013) L'odierno significato della mutualità prevalente nelle cooperative. Giurisprudenza Commerciale:847–862

Marasà G (2016) Voto plurimo, voto maggiorato e cooperative. Banca, borsa, titoli di credito:1–14

Marchetti C (2000) La "nexus of contracts" theory: Teorie e visioni del diritto societario. Studi di diritto privato, vol 88. Giuffrè, Milano

Marchetti C (2007) Composizione e nomina degli organi sociali: ovvero, la missione dei consigli di gestione e di sorveglianza. Analisi Giuridica dell'Economia:301–320. https://doi.org/10.1433/25661

Marchetti C (2014) Il silenzio del contratto: Gli implied terms nel diritto inglese. Giappichelli, Torino

Marcin I, Nicklisch A (2017) Testing the endowment effect for default rules. Discussion Paper Series of the Max Planck Institute for Research on Collective Goods 1:1–39

Marhold F (2008) Austria. In: Study on the implementation of the Directive 2003/72/EC (employee involvement in the European cooperative society) in ten Member States. https://ec.europa.eu/social/main.jsp?catId=707&langId=en&intPageId=213. Accessed 21 Nov 2019

Martinez J (2016a) 40. In: Calliess C, Ruffert M (eds) EUV/AEUV: Das Verfassungsrecht der Europäischen Union mit Europäischer Grundrechtecharta: Kommentar, 5. Auflage. C.H. Beck, München, pp 774–806

Martinez J (2016b) 42. In: Calliess C, Ruffert M (eds) EUV/AEUV: Das Verfassungsrecht der Europäischen Union mit Europäischer Grundrechtecharta: Kommentar, 5. Auflage. C.H. Beck, München, pp 807–814

Martinez J (2016c) Art. 38. In: Calliess C, Ruffert M (eds) EUV/AEUV: Das Verfassungsrecht der Europäischen Union mit Europäischer Grundrechtecharta: Kommentar, 5. Auflage. C.H. Beck, München, pp 756–768

Martinez J (2016d) Art. 39. In: Calliess C, Ruffert M (eds) EUV/AEUV: Das Verfassungsrecht der Europäischen Union mit Europäischer Grundrechtecharta: Kommentar, 5. Auflage. C.H. Beck, München, pp 768–774

Martínez J (ed) (2018) Reichweite und Grenzen des Agrarrechts: Gedächtnisschrift für Dr. Wolfgang Winkler, 1st edn. Schriften zum Agrar-, Umwelt- und Verbraucherschutzrecht, v.77. Nomos Verlagsgesellschaft, Baden-Baden

Massauer E (1978) Die Land- und Forstwirtschaft in der GewO einschließlich der Erwerbs- und Wirtschaftsgenossenschaften. In: Rill H-P (ed) Gewerberecht: Beiträge zu Grundfragen der GewO 1973. Orac, Wien, p 27

Mathis K (2019) Effizienz statt Gerechtigkeit?: Auf der Suche nach den philosophischen Grundlagen der Ökonomischen Analyse des Rechts, 4th edn. Schriften zur Rechtstheorie, Band 223. Duncker et Humblot GmbH, Berlin
Mattei U (1987) Tutela inibitoria e tutela risarcitoria: Contributo alla teoria dei diritti sui beni. Studi di diritto privato, vol 54. Giuffrè, Milano
Mattei U (1997) Comparative law and economics. University of Michigan Press, Ann Arbor
Mattei U (1999) Comparative law and economics. In: Bouckaert B, Geest GD (eds) Encyclopedia of law and economics. Edward Elgar, Cheltenham, pp 505–537
Mattei U (2001) The comparative jurisprudence of Schlesinger and Sacco: a study in legal influence. In: Riles A (ed) Rethinking the masters of comparative law. Hart Pub, Oxford, pp 240–256
Mattei U, Monti A (2001) Comparative law and economics: borrowing and resistance. Global Jurist Front 1:1535–1653. https://doi.org/10.2202/1535-1653.1038
Maul S (1998) Die faktisch abhängige SE (Societas Europaea) im Schnittpunkt zwischen deutschem und europäischem Recht. Univ., Diss.—Heidelberg, 1997. Europäisches Wirtschaftsrecht, vol 12. Beck, München
Maurer R (2014) Anhang II zu § 1 GenG: Grundzüge der Ertragsbesteuerung von Genossenschaften und ihren Mitgliedern. In: Dellinger M (ed) Genossenschaftsgesetz samt Nebengesetzen: Kommentar, 2nd edn. LexisNexis ARD Orac, Wien, pp 92–100
Mayer B (2010a) Art. 5. In: Manz G, Mayer B, Schröder A (eds) Europäische Aktiengesellschaft SE: SE, 2nd edn. Nomos, Baden-Baden, pp 97–124
Mayer B (2010b) Art. 52. In: Manz G, Mayer B, Schröder A (eds) Europäische Aktiengesellschaft SE: SE, 2nd edn. Nomos, Baden-Baden, pp 648–657
Mayer B (2010c) Art. 53. In: Manz G, Mayer B, Schröder A (eds) Europäische Aktiengesellschaft SE: SE, 2nd edn. Nomos, Baden-Baden, pp 657–680
Mayer B (2010d) Art. 54. In: Manz G, Mayer B, Schröder A (eds) Europäische Aktiengesellschaft SE: SE, 2nd edn. Nomos, Baden-Baden, pp 681–695
Mayer B (2010e) Art. 55. In: Manz G, Mayer B, Schröder A (eds) Europäische Aktiengesellschaft SE: SE, 2nd edn. Nomos, Baden-Baden, pp 695–702
Mayer B (2010f) Art. 56. In: Manz G, Mayer B, Schröder A (eds) Europäische Aktiengesellschaft SE: SE, 2nd edn. Nomos, Baden-Baden, pp 702–706
Mayer B (2010g) Art. 57. In: Manz G, Mayer B, Schröder A (eds) Europäische Aktiengesellschaft SE: SE, 2nd edn. Nomos, Baden-Baden, pp 706–730
Mayer B (2010h) Art. 58. In: Manz G, Mayer B, Schröder A (eds) Europäische Aktiengesellschaft SE: SE, 2nd edn. Nomos, Baden-Baden, pp 730–731
Mayer B (2010i) Art. 59. In: Manz G, Mayer B, Schröder A (eds) Europäische Aktiengesellschaft SE: SE, 2nd edn. Nomos, Baden-Baden, pp 731–737
Mazzoli M, Rocchi E (1996) La finanza delle cooperative: Profili economici e giuridici. Liocorno, Roma
Mazzoni A (2007) La porta aperta delle cooperative tra premesse ideologiche e nuovo diritto positivo. In: Abbadessa P, Portale GB (eds) Scioglimento, trasformazione, fusione, scissione, società cooperative. UTET, Torino, pp 763–804
McCahery JA, Vermeulen EPM (2008) Corporate governance of non-listed companies. Oxford University Press, Oxford
McMahon JA (2007) EU agricultural law. Oxford University Press, Oxford
Ménard C (2007) Cooperatives: hierarchies or hybrids? In: Karantininis K, Nilsson J (eds) Vertical markets and cooperative hierarchies: the role of cooperatives in the agri-food industry. Springer, Dordrecht, pp 1–18
Merkt H (1992) Europäische Aktiengesellschaft: Gesetzgebung als Selbstzweck? BB:652
Miceli TJ (2004) The economic approach to law. Stanford University Press, Stanford
Michaels R (2019) The functional method of comparative law. In: Reimann M, Zimmermann R (eds) The Oxford handbook of comparative law, 2nd edn. Oxford University Press, Oxford, pp 345–389

Michie J, Blasi JR, Borzaga C (2017) Introduction an overview. In: Michie J, Blasi JR, Borzaga C (eds) The Oxford handbook of mutual, co-operative, and co-owned business, 1st edn. Oxford University Press, Oxford, pp XXIII–XXXVI

MIHR (1982) http://aei.pitt.edu/62706/1/B2371.pdf. Accessed 25 Oct 2019

Milgrom PR, Roberts J (1992) Economics, organization and management. Prentice Hall, Englewood Cliffs

Milgrom PR, Roberts J (2005a) Economia, organizzazione e management I. Il Mulino, Bologna

Milgrom PR, Roberts J (2005b) Economia, organizzazione e management II, 2nd edn. Il Mulino, Bologna

Minguez-Vera A, Martín-Ugedo JF, Arcas-Lario N (2010) Agency and property rights theories in agricultural cooperatives: evidence from Spain. Span J Agric Res 8:908–924. https://doi.org/10.5424/sjar/2010084-1384

Ministry for economic development (2006) Communication no 9203, 30 June 2006, GU no 171 25.07.2006

Miotto L (2018a) Art. 2409 decies. In: Cian G (ed) Commentario breve al Codice civile: Commentato con dottrina e giurisprudenza, 13th edn. Wolters Kluver, Milano, Padova, pp 2905–2906

Miotto L (2018b) Art. 2409 duodecies. In: Cian G (ed) Commentario breve al Codice civile: Commentato con dottrina e giurisprudenza, 13th edn. Wolters Kluver, Milano, Padova, pp 2906–2908

Miotto L (2018c) Art. 2409 novies. In: Cian G (ed) Commentario breve al Codice civile: Commentato con dottrina e giurisprudenza, 13th edn. Wolters Kluver, Milano, Padova, pp 2903–2905

Miotto L (2018d) Art. 2409 sexiesdecies. In: Cian G (ed) Commentario breve al Codice civile: Commentato con dottrina e giurisprudenza, 13th edn. Wolters Kluver, Milano, Padova, p 2911

Miotto L (2018e) Art. 2409 terdecies. In: Cian G (ed) Commentario breve al Codice civile: Commentato con dottrina e giurisprudenza, 13th edn. Wolters Kluver, Milano, Padova, pp 2908–2910

Miribung G (2014) Über das genossenschaftliche Eigentum in der italienischen Rechtsordnung. In: Laurinkari J (ed) Genossenschaftswissenschaft zwischen Theorie und Geschichte: Festschrift für Prof. Dr. Johann Brazda zum 60. Geburstag. EHV Academicpress, Bremen, pp 779–791

Miribung G (2015a) Die GmbH light nach italienischem Recht. In: Benecke M, Hausmann R, Peifer K-N, Gebauer M (eds) Arbeitsrecht, Erbrecht, Urheberrecht: 50 Jahre deutsch-italienische Juristenvereinigung. Müller, Heidelberg, pp 131–147

Miribung G (2015b) Riserve indivisibili nelle cooperative e patrimonio separato: spunti di riflessione. www.giustiziacivile.com

Miribung G (2016) Genossenschaftliche Netzwerke in Südtirol - Versuch einer rechtssoziologischen Betrachtung. In: Ganner M, Voithofer C, Dahlvik J, Fritsche A, Fuchs W, Mayrhofer H, Pohn-Weidinger A (eds) Rechtstatsachenforschung - heute. Tagungsband 2016: Recht & Gesellschaft: Forschungsstand, Perspektiven, Zukunft, Innsbruck University Press, Innsbruck, pp 179–218

Miribung G (2017) Quale Business Judgment Rule?: Osservazioni dall'ordinamento giuridico italiano e austriaco. In: Schurr FA, Umlauft M (eds) Festschrift für Bernhard Eccher. Verlag Österreich, Wien, pp 709–722

Miribung G (2019) La disciplina dei masi chiusi: analisi delle modifiche apportate all'istituto dalla novella del 2018. Approfondimento del 26 aprile 2019. Giustiziacivile.com:1–13

Miribung G, Reiner E (2013) Austria. In: Cracogna D, Fici A, Henrÿ H (eds) International handbook of cooperative law. Springer, Berlin, Heidelberg, pp 231–250

Mirone A (2017a) I sistemi alternativi di amminstrazione e controllo: il sistema dualistico e il sistema monistico. In: Cian M (ed) Diritto commerciale: III. Diritto delle società. G. Giappichelli, Torino, pp 562–580

Mirone A (2017b) Il sistema tradizionale: l'assemblea. In: Cian M (ed) Diritto commerciale: III. Diritto delle società. G. Giappichelli, Torino, pp 398–460

Moccia L (2005) Comparazione giuridica e diritto europeo. Giuffrè, Milano
Molitor MK (2009) Eat your vegetables (or at least understand why you should): can better warning and education of prospective minority owners reduce oppression in closely held businesses? Fordham J Corp Financ Law:491–596
Molk P (2014) The puzzling lack of cooperatives. Tulane Law Rev:889–958
Moll DK (2001–2002) Shareholder oppression and reasonable expectations: of change, gifts, and inheritances in close corporation disputes. Minn Law Rev:717–790
Monateri PG (ed) (2012) Methods of comparative law. Research handbooks in comparative law series. Edward Elgar, Cheltenham
Montagnani C (2003) Art. 2524. In: Sandulli M, Santoro V (eds) La riforma delle società: Società cooperative Artt. 2511-2548 cod.civ. Giappichelli, Torino, pp 81–83
Montagnani C (2004a) Art. 2363. In: Niccolini G, Stagno d'Alcontres A (eds) Società di capitali: Commentario. Jovene, Napoli, pp 436–445
Montagnani C (2004b) Artt. 2364-2364bis. In: Niccolini G, Stagno d'Alcontres A (eds) Società di capitali: Commentario. Jovene, Napoli, pp 446–459
Montagnani C (2004c) Artt. 2368-2369. In: Niccolini G, Stagno d'Alcontres A (eds) Società di capitali: Commentario. Jovene, Napoli, pp 486–494
Montalenti P (2002) Corporate governance, consiglio di amministrazione, sistemi di controllo interno: spunti di riflessione. Rivista delle società:803–839
Montalenti P (2005) I sistemi di controlli interni nelle società di capitali. Le società:294–302
Morales Gutierrez AC (2004) A comparative synthesis of 20th century agricultural cooperative movements in Europe. J Rural Coop:47–65
Mosco GD (2004a) Art. 2384. In: Niccolini G, Stagno d'Alcontres A (eds) Società di capitali: Commentario. Jovene, Napoli, pp 607–614
Mosco GD (2004b) Art. 2387. In: Niccolini G, Stagno d'Alcontres A (eds) Società di capitali: Commentario. Jovene, Napoli, pp 623–626
Mosco GD (2004c) Artt. 2382-2383. In: Niccolini G, Stagno d'Alcontres A (eds) Società di capitali: Commentario. Jovene, Napoli, pp 602–606
Mucciarelli (2003) La governance delle società cooperative: gli amministratori. In: Genco R (ed) La riforma delle società cooperative. IPSOA, Milano, pp 183–210
Müller C, Tietzel M (1999) Property rights and their partitioning. In: Backhaus JG (ed) The Elgar companion to law and economics. Elgar, Cheltenham, pp 40–52
Müller K (2000) Kommentar zum Gesetz betreffend die Erwerbs- und Wirtschaftsgenossenschaften, 2nd edn. Gieseking, Bielefeld
Münkner H-H (1995) Chances of co-operatives in the future: contribution to the International Co-operative Alliance centennial 1895 - 1995. Papers and Reports/Institute for Co-operation in Developing Countries, vol 31. Marburg Consult für Selbsthilfeförderung eG, Marburg/Lahn
Münkner H-H (2006) Europäische Genossenschaft (SCE) und Europäische Genossenschaftstradition. Vorträge und Aufsätze des Forschungsvereins für Genossenschaftswesen, vol 30. Eigenverlag des FOG, Wien
Münkner H-H (2014) Ten lectures on co-operative law, 1st edn. LIT, Zürich
Münkner H-H (2015) Co-operative principles and co-operative law, 2nd edn. Lit Verlag GmbH, Zürich
Münkner H-H (2017) Cooperative audit. In: Fajardo-García IG, Fici A, Henrÿ H, Hiez D, Meira DMMA, Münkner H-H, Snaith I (eds) Principles of European Cooperative Law: principles, commentaries and national reports. Intersentia, Cambridge, pp 97–118
Murschitz K (2005a) Die Organstruktur der österreichischen Societas Europaea (SE) und Corporate Governance (CG) (Teil I). GesRZ:227
Murschitz K (2005b) Die Organstruktur der österreichischen Societas Europaea (SE) und Corporate Governance (CG) (Teil II). GesRZ:284
Myers SC (1977) Determinants of corporate borrowing. J Financ Econ 5:147–175. https://doi.org/10.1016/0304-405X(77)90015-0
Nagel B (2004) Die Europäische Aktiengesellschaft (SE) in Deutschland - der Regierungsentwurf zum SE-Einführungsgesetz. Neue Zeitschrift für Gesellschaftsrecht:833–839

Nenova T (2003) The value of corporate voting rights and control: a cross-country analysis. J Financ Econ 68:325–351. https://doi.org/10.1016/S0304-405X(03)00069-2
Nicklisch A, Petersen N (2012) Vertragstheorie. In: Towfigh EV, Petersen N (eds) Ökonomische Methoden im Recht: Eine Einführung für Juristen. Mohr Siebeck, Tübingen, pp 117–133
Nilsson J (1997) New generation farmer co-ops. Rev Int Coop:32–38
Nilsson J (1999) Co-operative organisational models as reflections of the business environments. Liiketaloudellinen aikakauskirja LTA - Finn J Bus Econ:449–470
Nilsson J (2001) Organisational principles for co-operative firms. Scand J Manage 17:329–356. https://doi.org/10.1016/S0956-5221(01)00010-0
Nilsson J, Madsen O (2007) Issues in cross-border mergers between agricultural co-operatives. J Coop Stud 40:27–38
Nilsson J, Svendsen GLH, Svendsen GT (2012) Are large and complex agricultural cooperatives losing their social capital? Agribusiness 28:187–204. https://doi.org/10.1002/agr.21285
Norer R (2005) Lebendiges Agrarrecht: Entwicklungslinien und Perspektiven des Rechts im ländlichen Raum. Springer, Wien
Norer R (2009) Agrarrecht und Recht des ländlichen Raumes: Orchideenfach oder Zukunftstrend? Zeitschrift für schweizerisches Recht:235–251
Norer R (2012) Agrarrecht: Eine Einführung. In: Norer R (ed) Handbuch des Agrarrechts, 2. Aufl. Verlag Österreich, Wien, pp 3–20
Norer R (2017a) 40 AEUV. In: Pechstein M, Nowak C, Häde U (eds) Frankfurter Kommentar zu EUV, GRC und AEUV. Mohr Siebeck, Tübingen, pp 661–690
Norer R (2017b) Agrarrechtliche Sonderrechtstheorie, funktionale Theorie und das Recht des ländlichen Raumes. In: Norer R, Holzer G (eds) Agrarrecht: Jahrbuch 2017. Perspektiven des Agrarrechts. Festgabe für Manfried Welan, 1st edn. NWV Verlag, Wien, pp 169–184
Norer R (2017c) Art. 38 AEUV. In: Pechstein M, Nowak C, Häde U (eds) Frankfurter Kommentar zu EUV, GRC und AEUV. Mohr Siebeck, Tübingen, pp 633–650
Norer R (2017d) Art. 39 AEUV. In: Pechstein M, Nowak C, Häde U (eds) Frankfurter Kommentar zu EUV, GRC und AEUV. Mohr Siebeck, Tübingen, pp 651–660
Norer R (2018) Agrarrechtliche Sonderrechtstheorie, funktionale Theorie und das Recht des ländlichen Raums. In: Martínez J (ed) Reichweite und Grenzen des Agrarrechts: Gedächtnisschrift für Dr. Wolfgang Winkler, 1st edn. Nomos Verlagsgesellschaft, Baden-Baden, pp 111–132
Nowak MJ, McCabe M (2003) Information costs and the role of the independent corporate director. Corp Gov 11:300–307. https://doi.org/10.1111/1467-8683.00328
Nowotny C (2008a) Genossenschaft. In: Kalss S, Nowotny C, Schauer M, Kastner W, Doralt P (eds) Österreichisches Gesellschaftsrecht: Systematische Darstellung sämtlicher Rechtsformen: in Fortführung des von Walther Kastner begründeten und in der letzten Auflage von Walther Kastner, Peter Doralt und Christian Nowotny bearbeiteten Lehr- und Handbuchs "Grundriss des österreichischen Gesellschaftsrechts". Manz, Wien, 5/1–5/182
Nowotny C (2008b) Gesellschaft mit beschränkter Haftung. In: Kalss S, Nowotny C, Schauer M, Kastner W, Doralt P (eds) Österreichisches Gesellschaftsrecht: Systematische Darstellung sämtlicher Rechtsformen: in Fortführung des von Walther Kastner begründeten und in der letzten Auflage von Walther Kastner, Peter Doralt und Christian Nowotny bearbeiteten Lehr- und Handbuchs "Grundriss des österreichischen Gesellschaftsrechts". Manz, Wien
Nowotny C (2012) § 84. In: Doralt W, Nowotny C, Kalss S (eds) Kommentar zum Aktiengesetz, 2nd edn. Linde, Wien, pp 1072–1091
Nuhanovic-Ribic S, Tortia EC, Valentinov V (2017) Agricultural co-operatives: struggle for identity. In: Michie J, Blasi JR, Borzaga C (eds) The Oxford handbook of mutual, co-operative, and co-owned business, 1st edn. Oxford University Press, Oxford, pp 158–170
Oechsler J, Mihaylova L (2014) Art. 3. In: Goette W, Habersack M, Kalss S (eds) Münchener Kommentar zum Aktiengesetz, 4th edn. C.H. Beck; Verlag Franz Vahlen, München, pp 49–54
O'Kelley CRT (1992) Filling the gaps in the close corporation contract: a transaction cost analysis. Northwest Univ Law Rev:216–253. https://doi.org/10.2139/ssrn.1548652

Olesen HB (2007) The horizon problem reconsidered. In: Karantininis K, Nilsson J (eds) Vertical markets and cooperative hierarchies: the role of cooperatives in the agri-food industry. Springer, Dordrecht, pp 245–253
Oppo G (ed) (1992) Scritti giuridici: Diritto delle società. Cedam, Padova
Organisation for Economic Co-operation and Development (2001) Multifunctionality: towards an analytical framework. OECD, Paris
Ortmann GF, King RP (2007) Agricultural cooperatives I: history, theory and problems. Agrekon 46:40–68. https://doi.org/10.1080/03031853.2007.9523760
Ostrom E (2007) Governing the commons: the evolution of institutions for collective action, 20th edn. Political economy of institutions and decisions. Cambridge University Press, Cambridge
Paciello A (2007a) Art. 2524. In: Presti G (ed) Società cooperative: Artt. 2511-2548. EGEA; Giuffrè, Milano, pp 171–180
Paciello A (2007b) Artt. 2545 decies - 2545 undecies. In: Presti G (ed) Società cooperative: Artt. 2511-2548. EGEA; Giuffrè, Milano, pp 489–504
Palmeri M (2000) Diritto societario virtuale: la videoassemblea diventa realtà. Contratto e impresa:830–849
Panzironi V (2007) Il modello dualistico di amministrazione; aspetti critici. Diritto e pratica delle società:26–29
Paolucci LF (2012a) I soci. In: Paolucci LF (ed) Le società cooperative. UTET giuridica, Torino, pp 95–124
Paolucci LF (2012b) Il governo delle società cooperative. In: Paolucci LF (ed) Le società cooperative. UTET giuridica, Torino, pp 125–146
Paolucci LF (2019a) Art. 2511. In: Paolucci LF (ed) Codice delle cooperative 2019: Aggiornato con le novità del D.Lgs. n. 14/2019. Maggioli, Santarcangelo di Romagna, Rimini, pp 29–40
Paolucci LF (2019b) Art. 2516. In: Paolucci LF (ed) Codice delle cooperative 2019: Aggiornato con le novità del D.Lgs. n. 14/2019. Maggioli, Santarcangelo di Romagna, Rimini, pp 51–54
Paolucci LF (2019c) Art. 2518. In: Paolucci LF (ed) Codice delle cooperative 2019: Aggiornato con le novità del D.Lgs. n. 14/2019. Maggioli, Santarcangelo di Romagna, Rimini, pp 55–57
Paolucci LF (2019d) Art. 2520. In: Paolucci LF (ed) Codice delle cooperative 2019: Aggiornato con le novità del D.Lgs. n. 14/2019. Maggioli, Santarcangelo di Romagna, Rimini, pp 64–65
Paolucci LF (2019e) Art. 2521. In: Paolucci LF (ed) Codice delle cooperative 2019: Aggiornato con le novità del D.Lgs. n. 14/2019. Maggioli, Santarcangelo di Romagna, Rimini, pp 65–75
Paolucci LF (2019f) Art. 2524. In: Paolucci LF (ed) Codice delle cooperative 2019: Aggiornato con le novità del D.Lgs. n. 14/2019. Maggioli, Santarcangelo di Romagna, Rimini, pp 79–81
Paolucci LF (2019g) Art. 2525. In: Paolucci LF (ed) Codice delle cooperative 2019: Aggiornato con le novità del D.Lgs. n. 14/2019. Maggioli, Santarcangelo di Romagna, Rimini, pp 81–84
Paolucci LF (2019h) Art. 2526. In: Paolucci LF (ed) Codice delle cooperative 2019: Aggiornato con le novità del D.Lgs. n. 14/2019. Maggioli, Santarcangelo di Romagna, Rimini, pp 85–87
Paolucci LF (2019i) Art. 2527. In: Paolucci LF (ed) Codice delle cooperative 2019: Aggiornato con le novità del D.Lgs. n. 14/2019. Maggioli, Santarcangelo di Romagna, Rimini, pp 88–89
Paolucci LF (2019j) Art. 2528. In: Paolucci LF (ed) Codice delle cooperative 2019: Aggiornato con le novità del D.Lgs. n. 14/2019. Maggioli, Santarcangelo di Romagna, Rimini, pp 90–94
Paolucci LF (2019k) Art. 2532. In: Paolucci LF (ed) Codice delle cooperative 2019: Aggiornato con le novità del D.Lgs. n. 14/2019. Maggioli, Santarcangelo di Romagna, Rimini, pp 101–106
Paolucci LF (2019l) Art. 2535. In: Paolucci LF (ed) Codice delle cooperative 2019: Aggiornato con le novità del D.Lgs. n. 14/2019. Maggioli, Santarcangelo di Romagna, Rimini, pp 115–118
Paolucci LF (2019m) Art. 2538. In: Paolucci LF (ed) Codice delle cooperative 2019: Aggiornato con le novità del D.Lgs. n. 14/2019. Maggioli, Santarcangelo di Romagna, Rimini, pp 121–125
Paolucci LF (2019n) Art. 2539. In: Paolucci LF (ed) Codice delle cooperative 2019: Aggiornato con le novità del D.Lgs. n. 14/2019. Maggioli, Santarcangelo di Romagna, Rimini, pp 125–126
Paolucci LF (2019o) Art. 2540. In: Paolucci LF (ed) Codice delle cooperative 2019: Aggiornato con le novità del D.Lgs. n. 14/2019. Maggioli, Santarcangelo di Romagna, Rimini, pp 127–129

Paolucci LF (2019p) Art. 2542. In: Paolucci LF (ed) Codice delle cooperative 2019: Aggiornato con le novità del D.Lgs. n. 14/2019. Maggioli, Santarcangelo di Romagna, Rimini, pp 131–136
Paolucci LF (2019q) Art. 2543. In: Paolucci LF (ed) Codice delle cooperative 2019: Aggiornato con le novità del D.Lgs. n. 14/2019. Maggioli, Santarcangelo di Romagna, Rimini, pp 137–139
Paolucci LF (2019r) Art. 2544. In: Paolucci LF (ed) Codice delle cooperative 2019: Aggiornato con le novità del D.Lgs. n. 14/2019. Maggioli, Santarcangelo di Romagna, Rimini, pp 139–140
Paolucci LF (2019s) Art. 2545-quater. In: Paolucci LF (ed) Codice delle cooperative 2019: Aggiornato con le novità del D.Lgs. n. 14/2019. Maggioli, Santarcangelo di Romagna, Rimini, pp 144–145
Paolucci LF (2019t) Art. 2545-quaterdecies. In: Paolucci LF (ed) Codice delle cooperative 2019: Aggiornato con le novità del D.Lgs. n. 14/2019. Maggioli, Santarcangelo di Romagna, Rimini, pp 164–165
Paolucci LF (2019u) Art. 2545-quinquies. In: Paolucci LF (ed) Codice delle cooperative 2019: Aggiornato con le novità del D.Lgs. n. 14/2019. Maggioli, Santarcangelo di Romagna, Rimini, pp 145–147
Paolucci LF (2019v) Art. 2545-sexies. In: Paolucci LF (ed) Codice delle cooperative 2019: Aggiornato con le novità del D.Lgs. n. 14/2019. Maggioli, Santarcangelo di Romagna, Rimini, pp 147–148
Paolucci LF (2019w) Art. 2545-sexiesdecies. In: Paolucci LF (ed) Codice delle cooperative 2019: Aggiornato con le novità del D.Lgs. n. 14/2019. Maggioli, Santarcangelo di Romagna, Rimini, pp 173–177
Paolucci LF (2019x) Art. 2545-ter. In: Paolucci LF (ed) Codice delle cooperative 2019: Aggiornato con le novità del D.Lgs. n. 14/2019. Maggioli, Santarcangelo di Romagna, Rimini, pp 143–144
Paolucci LF (2019y) Art. 45 Cost. In: Paolucci LF (ed) Codice delle cooperative 2019: Aggiornato con le novità del D.Lgs. n. 14/2019. Maggioli, Santarcangelo di Romagna, Rimini, pp 13–25
Paolucci LF (2019z) Artt. 2512-2514. In: Paolucci LF (ed) Codice delle cooperative 2019: Aggiornato con le novità del D.Lgs. n. 14/2019. Maggioli, Santarcangelo di Romagna, Rimini, pp 41–49
Paolucci LF (2012c) Definizione e aspetti caratterizzanti. In: Paolucci LF (ed) Le società cooperative. UTET giuridica, Torino, pp 1–23
Pardolesi P (2015) Profili comparatistici di analisi economica del diritto privato. Collana del Dipartimento jonico in sistemi giuridici ed economici del Mediterraneo, vol 13. Cacucci, Bari
Pargendler M (2012) The rise and decline of legal families. Am J Comp Law 60:1043–1074
Parisi F (1999) Coase theorem and transaction cost economics in the law. In: Backhaus JG (ed) The Elgar companion to law and economics. Elgar, Cheltenham, pp 7–39
Patera M (ed) (1986) Handbuch des österreichischen Genossenschaftswesens. Orac, Wien
Patroni Griffi U (2003) Art. 2391. In: Sandulli M, Santoro V (eds) La riforma delle società: Società per azioni, Società in accomandita per azioni. Giappichelli, Torino, pp 461–469
Pedri S (2017) Social-cooperatives in Italy. In: Michie J, Blasi JR, Borzaga C (eds) The Oxford handbook of mutual, co-operative, and co-owned business, 1st edn. Oxford University Press, Oxford, pp 308–320
Pellegrini M (2008) Gli antecedenti storici della società europea. In: Capriglione F (ed) La nuova disciplina della società europea. Cedam, Padova, pp 103–126
Perkounigg A, Kessler J (2014) § 1 GenRevG. In: Dellinger M (ed) Genossenschaftsgesetz samt Nebengesetzen: Kommentar, 2nd edn. LexisNexis ARD Orac, Wien, pp 556–567
Pernthaler P (2007) Land- und Forstwirtschaft als Verfassungsbegriff. In: Österreichische Gesellschaft für Agrar- und Umweltrecht (ed) Agrarrecht im Lichte des öffentlichen Rechts: Festschrift für Univ.-Prof. Dr. Gottfried Holzer zum 60. Geburtstag. NWV, Wien, pp 15–32
Pérotin V (2013) Worker cooperatives: good, sustainable jobs in the community. J Entrep Organ Divers 2. https://doi.org/10.5947/jeod.2013.009
Perrone A (2018a) Art. 2392. In: Cian G (ed) Commentario breve al Codice civile: Commentato con dottrina e giurisprudenza, 13th edn. Wolters Kluver, Milano, Padova, pp 2850–2854

Perrone A (2018b) Art. 2393. In: Cian G (ed) Commentario breve al Codice civile: Commentato con dottrina e giurisprudenza, 13th edn. Wolters Kluver, Milano, Padova, pp 2854–2857

Perrone A (2018c) Art. 2393bis. In: Cian G (ed) Commentario breve al Codice civile: Commentato con dottrina e giurisprudenza, 13th edn. Wolters Kluver, Milano, Padova, pp 2857–2858

Pescatore G (2009) Società di capitali amministratrice di altra società di capitali. Giurisprudenza Commerciale:1158–1177

Pestoff VA (2017) The social and political dimensions of co-operative enterprises. In: Michie J, Blasi JR, Borzaga C (eds) The Oxford handbook of mutual, co-operative, and co-owned business, 1st edn. Oxford University Press, Oxford, pp 76–94

Petrazzini B (2004) Artt. 2364 - 2364 bis. In: Cottino G, Bonfante G, Cagnasso O, Montalenti P (eds) Il nuovo diritto societario I: Commento al D. lgs. 17 gennaio 2003, n. 6, D. Lgs. 17 gennaio 2003, n. 5, D. lgs. 11 aprile 2002, n. 61 (art. 1). 1. Artt. 2325-2409 c.c, 1st edn. Zanichelli, Bologna, pp 469–482

Petrelli G (2005) I profili patrimoniali e finanziari nella riforma delle società cooperative. In: Consiglio nazionale del notariato. (ed) Studi e materiali in tema di riforma delle società cooperative. Giuffrè, Milano

Petrelli L (2007) Studio sull'impresa agricola. Pubblicazioni dell'Istituto di diritto agrario internazionale e comparato di Firenze. Nuova serie, vol 53. Giuffrè, Milano

Petroboni G (2013) Art. 2524. In: Alpa G, Mariconda V (eds) Codice civile, 3rd edn. Wolters Kluwer Italia; IPSOA, Assago

Piacentini V (2014) Codice civile italiano tradotto in inglese: Parte societaria (Artt. 2325-2510: società per azioni, società a responsabilità limitata, liquidazione, trasformazione, fusione, scissione), 3rd edn. IPSOA, Milano

Picciau A (2005) Artt. 2393, 2393bis, 2394bis. In: Ghezzi F (ed) Amministratori: Artt. 2380 - 2396 c.c, 1st edn. EGEA, Milano, pp 569–649

Picot A (1989) Zur Bedeutung allgemeiner Theorieansätze für die betriebswirtschaftliehe Information und Kommunikation: Der Beitrag der Transaktionskosten-und Principal-Agent-Theorie. In: Kirsch W, Picot A (eds) Die Betriebswirtschaftslehre im Spannungsfeld zwischen Generalisierung und Spezialisierung. Gabler Verlag, Wiesbaden, pp 361–381

Picot A, Dietl H (1993) Neue Institutionenökonomie und Recht. In: Ott C, Schäfer H-B (eds) Ökonomische Analyse des Unternehmensrechts: Beiträge zum 3. Travemünder Symposium zur Ökonomischen Analyse des Rechts. Physica., Heidelberg, pp 306–330

Pinna (2005) Art. 2521. In: Maffei Alberti A (ed) Il nuovo diritto delle società: Commento sistematico al D. lgs. 17 gennaio 2003, n. 6, aggiornato al D. lgs. 28 dicembre 2004, n. 310. Cedam, Padova, pp 2671–2689

Piras A (2017) Le società cooperative. In: de Angelis L, Bertacchini E (eds) Diritto commerciale II. Wolters Kluwer; Cedam, Milano, Padova, pp 107–132

Piscitello P (2012) La responsabilità degli amministratori di società di capitali tra discrezionalità del giudice e business judgement rule. Rivista delle società:1167–1183

Polinsky AM, Shavell S (eds) (2007) Handbook of law and economics: volume 2, 1st edn. Handbooks in economics, vol 27. North Holland, Amsterdam

Pollio M, Papaleo P (2007) Art. 2403 bis. In: Fauceglia G, Di Schiano Pepe G (eds) Codice commentato delle S.p.A: Artt. 2363-2435. UTET giuridica, Torino

Polo M (1994) Teoria dei contratti. In: Zamagni S (ed) Economia politica I, 1. ed. italiana. UTET, Torino, pp 133–141

Pönkä V (2018) The legal nature of cooperative membership. JEOD 7:39–61. https://doi.org/10.5947/jeod.2018.009

Posner EA (1996) Law, economics, and inefficient norms. Univ Pa Law Rev 144:1697–1744. https://doi.org/10.2307/3312637

Posner RA, Becker G (2014) The future of law and economics. Rev Law Econ 10:235–240. https://doi.org/10.1515/rle-2014-0056

Potter C (2015) Agricultural multifunctionality, working lands and public goods: contested models of agri-environmental governance under the Common Agricultural Policy. In: McMahon J,

Cardwell MN (eds) Research handbook on EU agriculture law. Edward Elgar Publishing Limited, Cheltenham, pp 113–124
Potthoff E, Trescher K, Theisen MR (2003) Das Aufsichtsratsmitglied: Ein Handbuch der Aufgaben, Rechte und Pflichten, 6th edn. Handelsblatt-Bücher. Schäffer-Poeschel, Stuttgart
Pozzo B, Timoteo M (2008) Europa e linguaggi giuridici. Le lingue del diritto, vol 3. Giuffrè, Milano
Pozzobon DM, Zylbersztajn D (2013) Democratic costs in member-controlled organizations. Agribusiness 29:112–132. https://doi.org/10.1002/agr.21324
Pozzobon DM, Zylbersztajn D, Bijman J (2012) How can cooperatives reduce democratic costs without incurring excessive agency costs? J Rural Coop:119–144
Pramer L, Pfaffenzeller W (1976) Die Genossenschaft in Recht und Steuer. Hollinek, Wien
Preite D (1988) La destinazione dei risultati nei contratti associativi. Studi di diritto privato, vol 55. Giuffrè, Milano
Presti G (2006) Le fonti della disciplina e l'organizzazione interna della società cooperative europea. In: Galletti D, Fici A (eds) La società cooperativa europea: Quali prospettive per la cooperazione italiana? Universita degli Studi di Trento, Trento, pp 67–86
Presti G (2007) Amministrazione e controllo nelle cooperative. In: Abbadessa P, Portale GB (eds) Scioglimento, trasformazione, fusione, scissione, società cooperative. UTET, Torino, pp 965–1085
Raaijmakers T (1999) The Statute for a European Company: its impact on board structures, and corporate governance in the European Union. Eur Bus Organ Law Rev 5:159–194. https://doi.org/10.1017/S1566752904001594
Rabbeno U (1915) Le società cooperative di produzione, Milano
Racugno G (2006) La società cooperativa europea. Rivista del diritto commerciale:315–321
Racugno G (2014a) Art. 2525. In: Santosuosso DU (ed) Delle società, dell'azienda, della concorrenza. UTET, Torino, pp 190–207
Racugno G (2014b) Il governo delle società cooperative: Il voto, i patti parasociali, i covenants. Rivista delle società:153–159
Ragazzini G (1992) Mutualità interna ed esterna nella riforma cooperativa. Contratto e impresa:833–880
Raiser T (1993) Die europäische Aktiengesellschaft und die nationalen Aktiengesetze. In: Bierich M (ed) Festschrift für Johannes Semler zum 70. Geburtstag am 28. April 1993: Unternehmen und Unternehmensführung im Recht. De Gruyter, Berlin, pp 277–298
Raiser T (2011) Beiträge zur Rechtssoziologie. Nomos, Baden-Baden
Raiser T (2013) Grundlagen der Rechtssoziologie, 6th edn. utb-studi-e-book, vol 2904. Mohr Siebeck, Tübingen
Raiser T, Veil R (2006) Recht der Kapitalgesellschaften: Ein Handbuch für Praxis und Wissenschaft; Aktiengesellschaft, Kommanditgesellschaft auf Aktien, Gesellschaft mit beschränkter Haftung, Kapitalgesellschaft & Co., Umwandlungsrecht, Konzernrecht, internationales Gesellschaftsrecht, 4th edn. Vahlen, München
Rasner H (1992) Die Europäische Aktiengesellschaft (SE) – ist sie wünschenswert? Zeitschrift für Unternehmens- und Gesellschaftsrecht 21:314–326. https://doi.org/10.1515/zgre.1992.21.3.314
Rauseo N (2018) L'equiparazione dell'imprenditore agricolo professionale al coltivatore diretto. Diritto e giurisprudenza agraria, alimentare e dell'ambiente 27:1–4
Rauter RA (2010) Probleme der Umsetzung des monistischen Systems der SE-VO in Österreich – ungenutzte Freiheit? Wirtschaftsrechtliche Blätter 24:499–508. https://doi.org/10.1007/s00718-010-1716-0
Rauter RA (2014) § 30g. In: Straube M (ed) Wiener Kommentar zum GmbH-Gesetz: 1.- 69. Lieferung - Kommentar in Faszikeln. MANZ Verlag Wien, Wien, pp 1–86
Rebelo J, Caldas J (2015) The economic role of the Portuguese agricultural cooperatives. Revista de Economia e Sociologia Rural 53:91–102. https://doi.org/10.1590/1234-56781806-94790053s01007

Reichert J, Brandes SM (2003) Mitbestimmung der Arbeitnehmer in der SE: Gestaltungsfreiheit und Bestandsschutz. Zeitschrift für Unternehmens- und Gesellschaftsrecht 32. https://doi.org/10.1515/zgre.2003.031
Reischauer R (1976) Das Schicksal fehlerhafter Generalversammlungsbeschlüsse einer Genossenschaft. JBl:7
Rescigno M (2007) Strumenti finanziari emessi da società cooperative. In: Abbadessa P, Portale GB (eds) Scioglimento, trasformazione, fusione, scissione, società cooperative. UTET, Torino, pp 923–946
Rescio G (2003) La Società Europea tra diritto comunitario e diritto nazionale. Rivista delle società:965–995
Retail Europe, About us. https://independentretaileurope.eu/en/about-us.html. Accessed 29 Dec 2019
Ribstein LE (1995) Statutory forms for closely held firms: theories and evidence from LLCs. Wash Univ Law Q:369–432
Ribstein LE, Kobayashi BH (1999) Choice of form and network externalities. William Mary Law Rev:79–140. https://doi.org/10.2139/ssrn.163832
Ricci R (2010a) Art. 2392. In: Cendon P (ed) Artt. 2363-2396: Società per azioni: [2] assemblea, amministratori. Giuffrè, Milano, pp 691–705
Ricci R (2010b) Art. 2393. In: Cendon P (ed) Artt. 2363-2396: Società per azioni: [2] assemblea, amministratori. Giuffrè, Milano, pp 707–719
Ricci R (2010c) Art. 2393bis. In: Cendon P (ed) Artt. 2363-2396: Società per azioni: [2] assemblea, amministratori. Giuffrè, Milano, pp 721–729
Richter R (2015a) Essays on new institutional economics. Springer, Cham
Richter R (2015b) The new institutional economics: its start, its meaning, its prospects. In: Richter R (ed) Essays on new institutional economics. Springer International Publishing, Cham, pp 1–35
Richter R (2015c) The role of law in the new institutional economics in comparison with the economic analysis of law. In: Richter R (ed) Essays on new institutional economics. Springer International Publishing, Cham, pp 77–96
Richter R, Furubotn EG, Streissler M (2003) Neue Institutionenökonomik: Eine Einführung und kritische Würdigung, 3rd edn. Neue ökonomische Grundrisse. Mohr Siebeck, Tübingen
Ringe G (2015a) Art. 7. In: Lutter M, Hommelhoff P, Teichmann C (eds) SE-Kommentar, 2nd edn. Verlag Dr. Otto Schmidt, Köln, pp 135–144
Ringe G (2015b) Art. 8. In: Lutter M, Hommelhoff P, Teichmann C (eds) SE-Kommentar, 2nd edn. Verlag Dr. Otto Schmidt, Köln, pp 145–172
Ringle G (2007) Genossenschaftliche Prinzipien im Spannungsfeld zwischen Tradition und Modernität. Wismarer Diskussionspapiere. Hochsch. Fachbereich Wirtschaft, Wismar
Riolfo G (2010) Il sistema monistico nelle società di capitali e cooperative. Cedam, Padova
Riolfo G (2013) Il sistema dualistico. Le monografie di Contratto e impresa, vol 0158. Cedam, Padova
Riss O (2008) Welche Sorgfalt schuldet der Genossenschaftsvorstand? RdW:768–770
Rocchi E (2005) Capitale variabile e riserve divisibili nel finanziamento della cooperativa. In: Uckmar V, Graziano F (eds) La disciplina civilistica e fiscale della nuova società corporativa. Cedam, Padova, pp 177–211
Rocchi E (2006) La struttura finanziaria della SCE. In: Galletti D, Fici A (eds) La società cooperativa europea: Quali prospettive per la cooperazione italiana? Universita degli Studi di Trento, Trento, pp 87–114
Rocchi E (2007a) Art. 2518. In: Presti G (ed) Società cooperative: Artt. 2511-2548. EGEA; Giuffrè, Milano, pp 89–122
Rocchi E (2007b) Artt. 2512 - 2514; 2545 octies. In: Presti G (ed) Società cooperative: Artt. 2511-2548. EGEA; Giuffrè, Milano, pp 27–73
Roe MJ (2002) Corporate law's limits. J Leg Stud 31:233–271. https://doi.org/10.1086/341989

Roe MJ (2004) Some differences in corporate structure in Germany, Japan, and the United States. In: Geest GD, van den Bergh R (eds) Comparative law and economics, vol III. Elgar, Cheltenham, pp 3–79
Romano G (2017a) Art. 2364 bis. In: Di Marzio F (ed) Codice civile. Giuffrè, Milano, p 2908
Romano G (2017b) Art. 2365. In: Di Marzio F (ed) Codice civile. Giuffrè, Milano, pp 2908–2909
Romano G (2017c) Art. 2367. In: Di Marzio F (ed) Codice civile. Giuffrè, Milano, pp 2912–2913
Romano G (2017d) Art. 2368. In: Di Marzio F (ed) Codice civile. Giuffrè, Milano, pp 2913–2915
Romano G (2017e) Art. 2371. In: Di Marzio F (ed) Codice civile. Giuffrè, Milano, pp 2919–2920
Romano G (2017f) Art. 2375. In: Di Marzio F (ed) Codice civile. Giuffrè, Milano, pp 2925–2926
Romano G (2017g) Art. 2381. In: Di Marzio F (ed) Codice civile. Giuffrè, Milano, pp 2944–2946
Romano G (2017h) Art. 2382. In: Di Marzio F (ed) Codice civile. Giuffrè, Milano, pp 2946–2947
Romano G (2017i) Art. 2384. In: Di Marzio F (ed) Codice civile. Giuffrè, Milano, pp 2949–2951
Romano G (2017j) Art. 2385. In: Di Marzio F (ed) Codice civile. Giuffrè, Milano, pp 2951–2952
Romano G (2017k) Art. 2387. In: Di Marzio F (ed) Codice civile. Giuffrè, Milano, pp 2954–2955
Romano G (2017l) Art. 2388. In: Di Marzio F (ed) Codice civile. Giuffrè, Milano, pp 2955–2957
Romano G (2017m) Art. 2391. In: Di Marzio F (ed) Codice civile. Giuffrè, Milano, pp 2961–2963
Romano G (2017n) Art. 2392. In: Di Marzio F (ed) Codice civile. Giuffrè, Milano, pp 2964–2966
Romano G (2017o) Art. 2393. In: Di Marzio F (ed) Codice civile. Giuffrè, Milano, pp 2967–2970
Romano G (2017p) Art. 2393 bis. In: Di Marzio F (ed) Codice civile. Giuffrè, Milano, pp 2970–2972
Romano G (2017q) Art. 2403 bis. In: Di Marzio F (ed) Codice civile. Giuffrè, Milano, pp 2988–2989
Romano G (2017r) Art. 2407. In: Di Marzio F (ed) Codice civile. Giuffrè, Milano, pp 2992–2994
Romano G (2017s) Art. 2409 decies. In: Di Marzio F (ed) Codice civile. Giuffrè, Milano, p 3004
Romano G (2017t) Art. 2409 duodecies. In: Di Marzio F (ed) Codice civile. Giuffrè, Milano, pp 3005–3006
Romano G (2017u) Art. 2409 novies. In: Di Marzio F (ed) Codice civile. Giuffrè, Milano, pp 3003–3004
Romano G (2017v) Art. 2409 terdecies. In: Di Marzio F (ed) Codice civile. Giuffrè, Milano, pp 3006–3007
Romano G (2017w) Art. 2428. In: Di Marzio F (ed) Codice civile. Giuffrè, Milano, pp 3051–3052
Rondinelli M (2016) L'armonizzazione nel diritto delle società: evoluzione e prospettive. In: Pederzini E (ed) Percorsi di diritto societario europeo, 3rd edn. Giappichelli, Torino, pp 43–94
Rondinone N (2017) L'imprenditore, l'impresa e la concorrenza. In: de Angelis L, Bertacchini E (eds) Diritto commerciale I. Wolters Kluwer; Cedam, Milano, Padova, pp 1–45
Rook Basile E (1981) La coltivazione dei terreni in società nell'esperienza giuridica italiana e francese. Giuffré, Milano
Rook Basile E (1995) Introduzione al diritto agrario. Trittico giuridico. Sezione introduzioni / Collana coordinata da U. De Siervo, G. Iudica, F. Palazzo. Giappichelli, Torino
Rook Basile E (2017) Sicuezza e responsabilità nella filiera alimentare. Contratto e impresa:432–450
Rose-Ackerman S (1997) L'inalienabilità e la teoria dei diritti di proprietà. In: Fabbri D, Fiorentini G, Franzoni LA (eds) L'analisi economica del diritto: Un'introduzione. La Nuova Italia Scientifica, Roma, pp 51–74
Ross SA (1973) The economic theory of agency: the principal's problem. Am Econ Rev 63:134–139
Rossi R (1979) La cooperativa di conduzione agraria. Jovene, Napoli
Rößl R, Reiner E (2010) Austria. In: Fici A (ed) Study on the implementation of the Regulation 1435/2003 on the Statute for European Cooperative Society (SCE): Final Study Part II. National Reports. Report drawn up following call tender no ENTR/2009/021 of 23 April from the European Commission, pp 325–342

Roth GH, WöRLE U (2004) Die Unabhängigkeit des Aufsichtsrats Recht und Wirklichkeit. Zeitschrift für Unternehmens- und Gesellschaftsrecht 33:565–630. https://doi.org/10.1515/zgre.2004.027
Royer J (1999) Cooperative organizational strategies: a neo-institutional digest. J Coop:44–67
Royer JS (1992) Cooperative principles and equity financing: a critical discussion. J Agric Coop 7
Ruffner M (2000) Die ökonomischen Grundlagen eines Rechts der Publikumsgesellschaft: Ein Beitrag zur Theorie der Corporate Governance. Schulthess, Zürich
Rufini D (2005) Art. 2409 novies. In: Maffei Alberti A (ed) Il nuovo diritto delle società: Commento sistematico al D. lgs. 17 gennaio 2003, n. 6, aggiornato al D. lgs. 28 dicembre 2004, n. 310. Cedam, Padova, pp 1129–1140
Ruggeri R (1994) Cooperative. In: Zamagni S (ed) Politica economica II. UTET libreria, Torino, pp 113–116
Sacco R (1991) Legal formants: a dynamic approach to comparative law (Installment I of II). Am J Comp Law 39:1–34. https://doi.org/10.2307/840669
Sacco R (1992) Che cos'è il diritto comparato. Lo Studio del Diritto, vol 2. Giuffrè, Milano
Sacco R (1994) Introduzione al diritto comparato, 5th edn. Trattato di diritto comparato. UTET, Torino
Sacconi L, Ottone S (eds) (2015) Beni comuni e cooperazione. Studi e ricerche. Il Mulino, Bologna
Saija R (2013) Standards e contratti di certificazione. Rivista di diritto alimentare:47–55
Sailer-Coceani V (2015) Art. 41. In: Lutter M, Hommelhoff P, Teichmann C (eds) SE-Kommentar, 2nd edn. Verlag Dr. Otto Schmidt, Köln, pp 516–532
Salafia V (2003) Il nuovo modello di società a responsabilità limitata. Le società:7–12
Salaris F (2002) Autonomia e globalità dell'azienda agraria. Rivista di diritto agrario:54–75
Sandei C (2018a) Art. 2382. In: Cian G (ed) Commentario breve al Codice civile: Commentato con dottrina e giurisprudenza, 13th edn. Wolters Kluver, Milano, Padova, pp 2813–2815
Sandei C (2018b) Art. 2383. In: Cian G (ed) Commentario breve al Codice civile: Commentato con dottrina e giurisprudenza, 13th edn. Wolters Kluver, Milano, Padova, pp 2815–2819
Sandei C (2018c) Art. 2384. In: Cian G (ed) Commentario breve al Codice civile: Commentato con dottrina e giurisprudenza, 13th edn. Wolters Kluver, Milano, Padova, pp 2819–2823
Sandei C (2018d) Art. 2385. In: Cian G (ed) Commentario breve al Codice civile: Commentato con dottrina e giurisprudenza, 13th edn. Wolters Kluver, Milano, Padova, pp 2823–2825
Sandei C (2018e) Art. 2387. In: Cian G (ed) Commentario breve al Codice civile: Commentato con dottrina e giurisprudenza, 13th edn. Wolters Kluver, Milano, Padova, pp 2828–2829
Sandei C (2018f) Art. 2388. In: Cian G (ed) Commentario breve al Codice civile: Commentato con dottrina e giurisprudenza, 13th edn. Wolters Kluver, Milano, Padova, pp 2829–2835
Sandulli M (2003) Art. 2392. In: Sandulli M, Santoro V (eds) La riforma delle società: Società per azioni, Società in accomandita per azioni. Giappichelli, Torino, pp 470–478
Sanfilippo PM (2017a) Gli amministratori. In: Cian M (ed) Diritto commerciale: III. Diritto delle società. G. Giappichelli, Torino, pp 461–537
Sanfilippo PM (2017b) Il controllo sulla gestione e contabile. In: Cian M (ed) Diritto commerciale: III. Diritto delle società. G. Giappichelli, Torino, pp 538–561
Sangiovanni V (2005) Il diritto di voto plurimo nella cooperativa tedesca: Cenni di comparazione con la riforma italiana. Le società:256–263
Santagata R (2014a) Art. 2545 quater. In: Santosuosso DU (ed) Delle società, dell'azienda, della concorrenza. UTET, Torino, pp 436–444
Santagata R (2014b) Art. 2545 ter. In: Santosuosso DU (ed) Delle società, dell'azienda, della concorrenza. UTET, Torino, pp 424–436
Santagata R (2017) Le società cooperative. In: Cian M (ed) Diritto commerciale: III. Diritto delle società. G. Giappichelli, Torino, pp 807–843
Santi E (2005a) 2409 duodecies. In: Maffei Alberti A (ed) Il nuovo diritto delle società: Commento sistematico al D. lgs. 17 gennaio 2003, n. 6, aggiornato al D. lgs. 28 dicembre 2004, n. 310. Cedam, Padova, pp 1157–1164

Santi E (2005b) 2409 terdecies. In: Maffei Alberti A (ed) Il nuovo diritto delle società: Commento sistematico al D. lgs. 17 gennaio 2003, n. 6, aggiornato al D. lgs. 28 dicembre 2004, n. 310. Cedam, Padova, pp 1165–1173

Santi F (2010) Art 2365. In: Cendon P (ed) Artt. 2363-2396: Società per azioni: [2] assemblea, amministratori. Giuffrè, Milano, pp 57–67

Santini R (2018) Art. 2428. In: Cian G (ed) Commentario breve al Codice civile: Commentato con dottrina e giurisprudenza, 13th edn. Wolters Kluver, Milano, Padova, pp 2951–2952

Santoro V (2014) Amministratori di cooperative e interessi dei soci. Odcc:15–30. https://doi.org/10.4478/77170

Santosuosso DU (2003) La riforma del diritto societario: Autonomia privata e norme imperative nei DD.Lgs. 17 gennaio 2003, nn.5 e 6. Prima interpretazione.Le nuove leggi civili. Giuffrè, Milano

Sarcina A (2006) La Societas Europaea e il consolidamento del sistema societario europea. Europa e Diritto Privato:729–754

Sarti A (2012) L'analisi della Corte di Giustizia sul regime fiscale delle cooperative di produzione a lavoro. Giurisprudenza Commerciale:605–615

Scarpa C (1994) Costi di transazione. In: Zamagni S (ed) Economia politica I, 1. ed. italiana. UTET, Torino, pp 147–148

Scarpa D (2014) Studio della organizzazione societaria della s.p.a. e analisi economica del diritto. Le monografie di Contratto e impresa, vol 160. Cedam, Padova

Schäfer H-B, Ott C (2012a) Grundstrukturen und -probleme des Unternehmensrechts. In: Schäfer H-B, Ott C (eds) Lehrbuch der ökonomischen Analyse des Zivilrechts. Springer, Berlin, pp 697–729

Schäfer H-B, Ott C (2012b) Homo Oeconomics, Behavioral Economics und Paternalismus. In: Schäfer H-B, Ott C (eds) Lehrbuch der ökonomischen Analyse des Zivilrechts. Springer, Berlin, pp 95–141

Schäfer H-B, Ott C (eds) (2012c) Lehrbuch der ökonomischen Analyse des Zivilrechts, 5. Aufl. 2012. Springer-Lehrbuch. Springer, Berlin, Heidelberg

Schäfer H-B, Ott C (2012d) Vom Vertrag zur Hierarchie. In: Schäfer H-B, Ott C (eds) Lehrbuch der ökonomischen Analyse des Zivilrechts. Springer, Berlin, pp 687–696

Schärf G (2002) Aufsichtsratssitzungen über Videokonferenz? RdW:199

Schaschko M (2010) Neugründungen von Genossenschaften in Österreich. Wiener Studien des Forschungsvereins für Genossenschaftswesen, vol 18. Eigenverlag des FOG, Wien

Schiessl M (2003) Leitungs- und Kontrollstrukturen im internationalen Wettbewerb – Dualistisches System und Mitbestimmung auf dem Prüfstand – ZHR 2003, S. 235. Zeitschrift für das gesamte Handelsrecht und Wirtschaftsrecht:235–257

Schima G (2015) Reform des Untreue-Tatbestandes und gesetzliche Verankerung der Business Judgement Rule im Gesellschaftsrecht. RdW:288–292

Schirò S (2008a) Art. 2516. In: Ceccherini A, Schirò S (eds) Società cooperative e mutue assicuratrici: (artt. 2511-2548 c.c.), 2nd edn. Giuffré, Milano, pp 37–44

Schirò S (2008b) Art. 2518. In: Ceccherini A, Schirò S (eds) Società cooperative e mutue assicuratrici: (artt. 2511-2548 c.c.), 2nd edn. Giuffré, Milano, pp 51–54

Schirò S (2008c) Art. 2527. In: Ceccherini A, Schirò S (eds) Società cooperative e mutue assicuratrici: (artt. 2511-2548 c.c.), 2nd edn. Giuffré, Milano, pp 93–102

Schirò S (2008d) Art. 2535. In: Ceccherini A, Schirò S (eds) Società cooperative e mutue assicuratrici: (artt. 2511-2548 c.c.), 2nd edn. Giuffré, Milano, pp 143–146

Schiuma L (2007) Il sistema dualistico. I poteri del consiglio di sorveglianza e del consiglio di gestione. In: Abbadessa P, Portale GB (eds) Assemblea, amministrazione. UTET, Torino, pp 683–731

Schlesinger RB, Mattei U, Ruskola T, Gidi A (2009) Schlesinger's comparative law: cases, text, materials, 7th edn. University casebook series. Foundation Press, New York

Schmidt J (2006) "Deutsche" vs. "britische" Societas Europaea (SE): Gründung, Verfassung, Kapitalstruktur. Jenaer Studien zum deutschen, europäischen und internationalen Wirtschaftsrecht, vol 8. Jenaer Wissenschaftlicher Verlag, Jena

Schmidt R, Weiß M (2010) Shareholder vs. Stakholer: Ökonomische Fragen. In: Hommelhoff P, Hopt KJ, Werder Av, Feddersen D, Pohle K (eds) Handbuch corporate governance: Leitung und Überwachung börsennotierter Unternehmen in der Rechts und Wirtschaftsprazis, 2nd edn. Dr. Otto Schmidt; Schäffer-Poeschel, Köln, Stuttgart, pp 161–184

Schmidtchen D (1998) Funktionen und Schutz von "property rights": Eine ökonomische Analyse. https://www.econstor.eu/bitstream/10419/23100/1/9804prop.pdf. Accessed 21 Nov 2019

Schmidt-Pachinger S (2012) § 121. In: Doralt W, Nowotny C, Kalss S (eds) Kommentar zum Aktiengesetz, 2nd edn. Linde, Wien, pp 1769–1781

Schneiberg M (2002) 2. Organizational heterogeneity and the production of new forms: politics, social movements and mutual companies in American fire insurance, 1900–1930. In: Lounsbury M, Ventresca MJ (eds) Social structure and organizations revisited, vol 19. Emerald, Bingley, pp 39–89

Schön W (2012) Der Anspruch auf Haftungsbeschränkung im Europäischen Gesellschaftsrecht. In: Erle B, Goette W, Kleindiek D, Krieger G, Priester H-J, Schubel C, Schwab M, Teichmann C, Witt C-H (eds) Festschrift für Peter Hommelhoff: Zum 70. Geburtstag. De Gruyter; Otto Schmidt, Berlin, Köln, pp 1037–1058

Schön W (2014) Creditor protection in the closed corporation. In: Bachmann G, Eidenmüller H, Engert A, Fleischer H, Schön W (eds) Regulating the closed corporation. De Gruyter, Berlin, pp 124–178

Schöpflin M (2018a) Art. 01. In: Beuthien V, Schöpflin M (eds) Genossenschaftsgesetz: Mit Umwandlungs- und Kartellrecht sowie Statut der Europäischen Genossenschaft, 16th edn. Beck, München, pp 1240–1243

Schöpflin M (2018b) Art. 02. In: Beuthien V, Schöpflin M (eds) Genossenschaftsgesetz: Mit Umwandlungs- und Kartellrecht sowie Statut der Europäischen Genossenschaft, 16th edn. Beck, München, pp 1243–1246

Schöpflin M (2018c) Art. 03. In: Beuthien V, Schöpflin M (eds) Genossenschaftsgesetz: Mit Umwandlungs- und Kartellrecht sowie Statut der Europäischen Genossenschaft, 16th edn. Beck, München, pp 1246–1247

Schöpflin M (2018d) Art. 04. In: Beuthien V, Schöpflin M (eds) Genossenschaftsgesetz: Mit Umwandlungs- und Kartellrecht sowie Statut der Europäischen Genossenschaft, 16th edn. Beck, München, pp 1247–1252

Schöpflin M (2018e) Art. 06. In: Beuthien V, Schöpflin M (eds) Genossenschaftsgesetz: Mit Umwandlungs- und Kartellrecht sowie Statut der Europäischen Genossenschaft, 16th edn. Beck, München, p 1255

Schöpflin M (2018f) Art. 07. In: Beuthien V, Schöpflin M (eds) Genossenschaftsgesetz: Mit Umwandlungs- und Kartellrecht sowie Statut der Europäischen Genossenschaft, 16th edn. Beck, München, pp 1256–1259

Schöpflin M (2018g) Art. 08. In: Beuthien V, Schöpflin M (eds) Genossenschaftsgesetz: Mit Umwandlungs- und Kartellrecht sowie Statut der Europäischen Genossenschaft, 16th edn. Beck, München, pp 1259–1263

Schöpflin M (2018h) Art. 14. In: Beuthien V, Schöpflin M (eds) Genossenschaftsgesetz: Mit Umwandlungs- und Kartellrecht sowie Statut der Europäischen Genossenschaft, 16th edn. Beck, München, pp 1268–1272

Schöpflin M (2018i) Art. 15. In: Beuthien V, Schöpflin M (eds) Genossenschaftsgesetz: Mit Umwandlungs- und Kartellrecht sowie Statut der Europäischen Genossenschaft, 16th edn. Beck, München, pp 1272–1276

Schöpflin M (2018j) Art. 16. In: Beuthien V, Schöpflin M (eds) Genossenschaftsgesetz: Mit Umwandlungs- und Kartellrecht sowie Statut der Europäischen Genossenschaft, 16th edn. Beck, München, pp 1276–1277

Schöpflin M (2018k) Art. 36. In: Beuthien V, Schöpflin M (eds) Genossenschaftsgesetz: Mit Umwandlungs- und Kartellrecht sowie Statut der Europäischen Genossenschaft, 16th edn. Beck, München, pp 1298–1299

Schöpflin M (2018l) Art. 37. In: Beuthien V, Schöpflin M (eds) Genossenschaftsgesetz: Mit Umwandlungs- und Kartellrecht sowie Statut der Europäischen Genossenschaft, 16th edn. Beck, München, pp 1299–1301
Schöpflin M (2018m) Art. 38. In: Beuthien V, Schöpflin M (eds) Genossenschaftsgesetz: Mit Umwandlungs- und Kartellrecht sowie Statut der Europäischen Genossenschaft, 16th edn. Beck, München, p 1301
Schöpflin M (2018n) Art. 39. In: Beuthien V, Schöpflin M (eds) Genossenschaftsgesetz: Mit Umwandlungs- und Kartellrecht sowie Statut der Europäischen Genossenschaft, 16th edn. Beck, München, pp 1301–1303
Schöpflin M (2018o) Art. 40. In: Beuthien V, Schöpflin M (eds) Genossenschaftsgesetz: Mit Umwandlungs- und Kartellrecht sowie Statut der Europäischen Genossenschaft, 16th edn. Beck, München, pp 1304–1305
Schöpflin M (2018p) Art. 41. In: Beuthien V, Schöpflin M (eds) Genossenschaftsgesetz: Mit Umwandlungs- und Kartellrecht sowie Statut der Europäischen Genossenschaft, 16th edn. Beck, München, pp 1305–1306
Schöpflin M (2018q) Art. 42. In: Beuthien V, Schöpflin M (eds) Genossenschaftsgesetz: Mit Umwandlungs- und Kartellrecht sowie Statut der Europäischen Genossenschaft, 16th edn. Beck, München, pp 1306–1308
Schöpflin M (2018r) Art. 43. In: Beuthien V, Schöpflin M (eds) Genossenschaftsgesetz: Mit Umwandlungs- und Kartellrecht sowie Statut der Europäischen Genossenschaft, 16th edn. Beck, München, p 1308
Schöpflin M (2018s) Art. 44. In: Beuthien V, Schöpflin M (eds) Genossenschaftsgesetz: Mit Umwandlungs- und Kartellrecht sowie Statut der Europäischen Genossenschaft, 16th edn. Beck, München, pp 1308–1309
Schöpflin M (2018t) Art. 45. In: Beuthien V, Schöpflin M (eds) Genossenschaftsgesetz: Mit Umwandlungs- und Kartellrecht sowie Statut der Europäischen Genossenschaft, 16th edn. Beck, München, p 1309
Schöpflin M (2018u) Art. 46. In: Beuthien V, Schöpflin M (eds) Genossenschaftsgesetz: Mit Umwandlungs- und Kartellrecht sowie Statut der Europäischen Genossenschaft, 16th edn. Beck, München, pp 1309–1311
Schöpflin M (2018v) Art. 47. In: Beuthien V, Schöpflin M (eds) Genossenschaftsgesetz: Mit Umwandlungs- und Kartellrecht sowie Statut der Europäischen Genossenschaft, 16th edn. Beck, München, pp 1311–1313
Schöpflin M (2018w) Art. 48. In: Beuthien V, Schöpflin M (eds) Genossenschaftsgesetz: Mit Umwandlungs- und Kartellrecht sowie Statut der Europäischen Genossenschaft, 16th edn. Beck, München, pp 1313–1314
Schöpflin M (2018x) Art. 49. In: Beuthien V, Schöpflin M (eds) Genossenschaftsgesetz: Mit Umwandlungs- und Kartellrecht sowie Statut der Europäischen Genossenschaft, 16th edn. Beck, München, p 1314
Schöpflin M (2018y) Art. 50. In: Beuthien V, Schöpflin M (eds) Genossenschaftsgesetz: Mit Umwandlungs- und Kartellrecht sowie Statut der Europäischen Genossenschaft, 16th edn. Beck, München, pp 1315–1316
Schöpflin M (2018z) Art. 51. In: Beuthien V, Schöpflin M (eds) Genossenschaftsgesetz: Mit Umwandlungs- und Kartellrecht sowie Statut der Europäischen Genossenschaft, 16th edn. Beck, München, p 1316
Schöpflin M (2018aa) Art. 52. In: Beuthien V, Schöpflin M (eds) Genossenschaftsgesetz: Mit Umwandlungs- und Kartellrecht sowie Statut der Europäischen Genossenschaft, 16th edn. Beck, München, pp 1316–1318
Schöpflin M (2018ab) Art. 53. In: Beuthien V, Schöpflin M (eds) Genossenschaftsgesetz: Mit Umwandlungs- und Kartellrecht sowie Statut der Europäischen Genossenschaft, 16th edn. Beck, München, p 1318

Schöpflin M (2018ac) Art. 54. In: Beuthien V, Schöpflin M (eds) Genossenschaftsgesetz: Mit Umwandlungs- und Kartellrecht sowie Statut der Europäischen Genossenschaft, 16th edn. Beck, München, pp 1318–1320

Schöpflin M (2018ad) Art. 55. In: Beuthien V, Schöpflin M (eds) Genossenschaftsgesetz: Mit Umwandlungs- und Kartellrecht sowie Statut der Europäischen Genossenschaft, 16th edn. Beck, München, p 1320

Schöpflin M (2018ae) Art. 56. In: Beuthien V, Schöpflin M (eds) Genossenschaftsgesetz: Mit Umwandlungs- und Kartellrecht sowie Statut der Europäischen Genossenschaft, 16th edn. Beck, München, pp 1320–1322

Schöpflin M (2018af) Art. 57. In: Beuthien V, Schöpflin M (eds) Genossenschaftsgesetz: Mit Umwandlungs- und Kartellrecht sowie Statut der Europäischen Genossenschaft, 16th edn. Beck, München, p 1322

Schöpflin M (2018ag) Art. 58. In: Beuthien V, Schöpflin M (eds) Genossenschaftsgesetz: Mit Umwandlungs- und Kartellrecht sowie Statut der Europäischen Genossenschaft, 16th edn. Beck, München, pp 1322–1324

Schöpflin M (2018ah) Art. 59. In: Beuthien V, Schöpflin M (eds) Genossenschaftsgesetz: Mit Umwandlungs- und Kartellrecht sowie Statut der Europäischen Genossenschaft, 16th edn. Beck, München, pp 1324–1326

Schöpflin M (2018ai) Art. 60. In: Beuthien V, Schöpflin M (eds) Genossenschaftsgesetz: Mit Umwandlungs- und Kartellrecht sowie Statut der Europäischen Genossenschaft, 16th edn. Beck, München, pp 1326–1327

Schöpflin M (2018aj) Art. 61. In: Beuthien V, Schöpflin M (eds) Genossenschaftsgesetz: Mit Umwandlungs- und Kartellrecht sowie Statut der Europäischen Genossenschaft, 16th edn. Beck, München, pp 1328–1329

Schöpflin M (2018ak) Art. 63. In: Beuthien V, Schöpflin M (eds) Genossenschaftsgesetz: Mit Umwandlungs- und Kartellrecht sowie Statut der Europäischen Genossenschaft, 16th edn. Beck, München, pp 1330–1331

Schöpflin M (2018al) Art. 64. In: Beuthien V, Schöpflin M (eds) Genossenschaftsgesetz: Mit Umwandlungs- und Kartellrecht sowie Statut der Europäischen Genossenschaft, 16th edn. Beck, München, pp 1331–1333

Schöpflin M (2018am) Art. 66. In: Beuthien V, Schöpflin M (eds) Genossenschaftsgesetz: Mit Umwandlungs- und Kartellrecht sowie Statut der Europäischen Genossenschaft, 16th edn. Beck, München, pp 1334–1335

Schöpflin M (2018an) Art. 67. In: Beuthien V, Schöpflin M (eds) Genossenschaftsgesetz: Mit Umwandlungs- und Kartellrecht sowie Statut der Europäischen Genossenschaft, 16th edn. Beck, München, pp 1335–1336

Schöpflin M (2018ao) Art. 73. In: Beuthien V, Schöpflin M (eds) Genossenschaftsgesetz: Mit Umwandlungs- und Kartellrecht sowie Statut der Europäischen Genossenschaft, 16th edn. Beck, München, pp 1340–1342

Schöpflin M (2018ap) Art. 75. In: Beuthien V, Schöpflin M (eds) Genossenschaftsgesetz: Mit Umwandlungs- und Kartellrecht sowie Statut der Europäischen Genossenschaft, 16th edn. Beck, München, pp 1342–1343

Schöpflin M (2018aq) Einl. SCE. In: Beuthien V, Schöpflin M (eds) Genossenschaftsgesetz: Mit Umwandlungs- und Kartellrecht sowie Statut der Europäischen Genossenschaft, 16th edn. Beck, München, pp 1230–1235

Schröder A (2010a) Art. 10. In: Manz G, Mayer B, Schröder A (eds) Europäische Aktiengesellschaft SE: SE, 2nd edn. Nomos, Baden-Baden, pp 204–206

Schröder A (2010b) Art. 63. In: Manz G, Mayer B, Schröder A (eds) Europäische Aktiengesellschaft SE: SE, 2nd edn. Nomos, Baden-Baden, pp 751–759

Schröder A (2010c) Art. 8. In: Manz G, Mayer B, Schröder A (eds) Europäische Aktiengesellschaft SE: SE, 2nd edn. Nomos, Baden-Baden, pp 140–179

Schröder A (2010d) Art. 9. In: Manz G, Mayer B, Schröder A (eds) Europäische Aktiengesellschaft SE: SE, 2nd edn. Nomos, Baden-Baden, pp 179–204

Schröder A (2010e) Vorbemerkungen. In: Manz G, Mayer B, Schröder A (eds) Europäische Aktiengesellschaft SE: SE, 2nd edn. Nomos, Baden-Baden, pp 21–49

Schroeder TC (1992) Economies of scale and scope for agricultural supply and marketing cooperatives. Rev Agric Econ 14:93–103. https://doi.org/10.2307/1349610

Schulz A, Geismair B (2001) Die Europäische Aktiengesellschaft - Eine kritische Bestandsaufnahme. DStR:1078–1085

Schulze R (2004a) Die Struktur der SCE. In: Schulze R (ed) Europäische Genossenschaft SCE: Handbuch, 1st edn. Nomos, Baden-Baden, pp 91–121

Schulze R (2004b) Einführung: Die Verordnung über das Statut der Europäischen Genossenschaft. In: Schulze R (ed) Europäische Genossenschaft SCE: Handbuch, 1st edn. Nomos, Baden-Baden, pp 1–18

Schulze R (2004c) Zur Rechtslage in den Mitgliedsstaaten: Deutschland. In: Schulze R (ed) Europäische Genossenschaft SCE: Handbuch, 1st edn. Nomos, Baden-Baden, pp 183–190

Schwartz A (1992) Relational contracts in the courts: an analysis of incomplete agreements and judicial strategies. J Leg Stud 21:271–318

Schwartz A (1997) Le teorie giuridiche dei contratti e i contratti incompleti. In: Fabbri D, Fiorentini G, Franzoni LA (eds) L'analisi economica del diritto: Un'introduzione. La Nuova Italia Scientifica, Roma, pp 97–126

Schwenzer I (2019) Development of comparative law in Germany, Switzerland and Austria. In: Reimann M, Zimmermann R (eds) The Oxford handbook of comparative law, 2nd edn. Oxford University Press, Oxford, pp 54–86

Sciaudone A (2005) L'impresa agricola: Profili di qualificazione. Pubblicazioni della Scuola di ateneo per l'alta formazione europea Jean Monnet della Seconda universita degli studi di Napoli. Quaderni, vol 0010. Edizioni scientifiche italiane, Napoli

Sciaudone A (2016) L'azienda agricola tra esigenze della proprietà e sviluppo dell'impresa: Il potenziamento delle strutture agricole e la promozione dell'azienda tra politiche europee e dinamiche interne. Rivista di diritto agrario:402–443

Sciaudone A (2019) Il nuovo "IAP". In: Cristiani E, Di Lauro A, Sirsi E (eds) Agricoltura e Costituzione: Una Costituzione per l'agricoltura: in onore di Marco Goldoni. Pisa University Press, Pisa, pp 313–334

Scordino F (1970) La società cooperativa. Jovene, Napoli

Scott RE (1987) Conflict and cooperation in long-term contracts. Calif Law Rev:2005–2054. https://doi.org/10.15779/Z38TF07

Senti R, Hilpold P (2017) WTO: System und Funktionsweise der Welthandelsordnung, 2nd edn. Schulthess, Zürich

Sepe M (2008) La cosituzione della società europea nel riferimento alle unità economico-giuridiche nazionali. In: Capriglione F (ed) La nuova disciplina della società europea. Cedam, Padova, pp 145–176

Sepe G (2013) Il controllo del potere di mercato nella filiera agroalimentare: profili concorrenziali e ruolo dell'AGCM. Rivista di diritto alimentare:35–39

Serra A (2007) Il procedimento assembleare. In: Abbadessa P, Portale GB (eds) Assemblea, amministrazione. UTET, Torino, pp 36–76

Serraino G (2010a) Art. 2404. In: Cendon P (ed) Artt. 2397-2420 ter: Società per azioni: [3] sindaci, controllo contabile, sistema dualistico e monistico, obbligazioni. Giuffrè, Milano, pp 67–71

Serraino G (2010b) Art. 2406. In: Cendon P (ed) Artt. 2397-2420 ter: Società per azioni: [3] sindaci, controllo contabile, sistema dualistico e monistico, obbligazioni. Giuffrè, Milano, pp 77–81

Serraino G (2010c) Art. 2407. In: Cendon P (ed) Artt. 2397-2420 ter: Società per azioni: [3] sindaci, controllo contabile, sistema dualistico e monistico, obbligazioni. Giuffrè, Milano, pp 83–91

Seuster H (1990) Die Genossenschaften im ländlichen Berich: In der Marktwirtschaft. In: Laurinkari J (ed) Genossenschaftswesen: Hand- und Lehrbuch. Oldenbourg, München, pp 576–584

Sexton RJ, Iskow J (1993) The competitive role of cooperatives in market oriented economies: a policy analysis. In: Csáki C, Kislev Y (eds) Agricultural cooperatives in transition. Westview Press, Boulder, pp 55–84

Sgarbanti G (2009) Definizione di attività agricola nel diritto comunitario e obblighi di coltivare nel diritto interno. Atti del XXXVII Incontro di Studio (Ferrara). Aestimum:93–100. https://doi.org/10.13128/AESTIMUM-3244

Shaffer J (1999) Historical dictionary of the cooperative movement. Historical dictionaries of religions, philosophies, and movements, vol 26. Scarecrow Press, Lanham

Siebenbäck H-J (2014a) § 27. In: Dellinger M (ed) Genossenschaftsgesetz samt Nebengesetzen: Kommentar, 2nd edn. LexisNexis ARD Orac, Wien, pp 337–351

Siebenbäck H-J (2014b) § 28. In: Dellinger M (ed) Genossenschaftsgesetz samt Nebengesetzen: Kommentar, 2nd edn. LexisNexis ARD Orac, Wien, pp 363–364

Siebenbäck H-J (2014c) § 29. In: Dellinger M (ed) Genossenschaftsgesetz samt Nebengesetzen: Kommentar, 2nd edn. LexisNexis ARD Orac, Wien, pp 365–367

Siebenbäck H-J (2014d) § 30. In: Dellinger M (ed) Genossenschaftsgesetz samt Nebengesetzen: Kommentar, 2nd edn. LexisNexis ARD Orac, Wien, pp 368–373

Siebenbäck H-J (2014e) § 31. In: Dellinger M (ed) Genossenschaftsgesetz samt Nebengesetzen: Kommentar, 2nd edn. LexisNexis ARD Orac, Wien, p 374

Siebenbäck H-J (2014f) § 32. In: Dellinger M (ed) Genossenschaftsgesetz samt Nebengesetzen: Kommentar, 2nd edn. LexisNexis ARD Orac, Wien, pp 375–376

Siebenbäck H-J (2014g) § 33. In: Dellinger M (ed) Genossenschaftsgesetz samt Nebengesetzen: Kommentar, 2nd edn. LexisNexis ARD Orac, Wien, pp 377–381

Siebenbäck H-J (2014h) § 33a. In: Dellinger M (ed) Genossenschaftsgesetz samt Nebengesetzen: Kommentar, 2nd edn. LexisNexis ARD Orac, Wien, pp 382–384

Siebenbäck H-J (2014i) § 34. In: Dellinger M (ed) Genossenschaftsgesetz samt Nebengesetzen: Kommentar, 2nd edn. LexisNexis ARD Orac, Wien, pp 385–387

Siems M (2014) Comparative law. Law in context. Cambridge University Press, Cambridge

Simone C (2009a) Art. 2403 bis. In: Grippo G (ed) Commentario delle società. UTET, Torino, pp 554–555

Simone C (2009b) Art. 2407. In: Grippo G (ed) Commentario delle società. UTET, Torino, pp 565–571

Simonetto E (1959) Responsabilità e garanzia nel diritto delle società. Cedam, Padova

Sitkoff RH (2011) The economic structure of fiduciary law. Boston Univ Law Rev:1039–1049. https://doi.org/10.2139/ssrn.1782999

Slagter W (2004) Landesbericht Niederlande zum Begleitgesetz Europäische Gesellschaft. In: Baums T, Cahn A (eds) Die Europäische Aktiengesellschaft: Umsetzungsfragen und Perspektiven. De Gruyter, Berlin, pp 30–38

Snaith I (2004) Das anwendbare Recht. In: Schulze R (ed) Europäische Genossenschaft SCE: Handbuch, 1st edn. Nomos, Baden-Baden, pp 19–42

Snaith I (2006) Employee involvement in the European Cooperative Society: a range of stakeholders? Int J Comp Labour Law Ind Relat:213–230

Snaith I (2017) Cooperative governance. In: Fajardo-García IG, Fici A, Henrÿ H, Hiez D, Meira DMMA, Münkner H-H, Snaith I (eds) Principles of European Cooperative Law: principles, commentaries and national reports. Intersentia, Cambridge, pp 47–72

Sneirson JF (2008) Soft paternalism for close corporations: helping shareholders help themselves. Wis Law Rev:899–940

Søgaard V (1994) Farmers, cooperatives, new food products, 1st edn. MAPP monograph. MAPP, Århus

Spence AM (1981) Market signaling: informational transfer in hiring and related screening processes, 2nd edn. Harvard economic studies, vol 143. Harvard University Press, Cambridge

Spindler G (2015a) Art. 52. In: Lutter M, Hommelhoff P, Teichmann C (eds) SE-Kommentar, 2nd edn. Verlag Dr. Otto Schmidt, Köln, pp 776–799

Spindler G (2015b) Art. 53. In: Lutter M, Hommelhoff P, Teichmann C (eds) SE-Kommentar, 2nd edn. Verlag Dr. Otto Schmidt, Köln, pp 800–816
Spindler G (2015c) Art. 54. In: Lutter M, Hommelhoff P, Teichmann C (eds) SE-Kommentar, 2nd edn. Verlag Dr. Otto Schmidt, Köln, pp 816–829
Spindler G (2015d) Art. 55. In: Lutter M, Hommelhoff P, Teichmann C (eds) SE-Kommentar, 2nd edn. Verlag Dr. Otto Schmidt, Köln, pp 829–846
Spindler G (2015e) Art. 56. In: Lutter M, Hommelhoff P, Teichmann C (eds) SE-Kommentar, 2nd edn. Verlag Dr. Otto Schmidt, Köln, pp 846–855
Staroßom H (2013) Informationsasymmetrie in der Finanzierung: Das Principal Agent-Problem. In: Staroßom H (ed) Corporate Finance Teil 1. Springer Fachmedien Wiesbaden, Wiesbaden, pp 97–114
Stasio Vd (2007) Art. 2545 quinquies. In: Presti G (ed) Società cooperative: Artt. 2511-2548. EGEA; Giuffrè, Milano, pp 415–431
Steinberg R (2010) Principal-agent theory and nonprofit accountability. In: Hopt KJ, Hippel TV (eds) Comparative corporate governance of non-profit organizations. Cambridge University Press, Cambridge, pp 73–126
Stella Richter M Jr (2004) Forma e contenuto dell'atto costitutivo della società per azioni. In: Colombo GE, Portale GB (eds) Trattato delle società per azioni I: Tipo - Costituzione - Nullità. UTET, Torino, pp 165–319
Stiglitz JE (1975) The theory of "screening," education, and the distribution of income. Am Econ Rev 65:283–300
Stiglitz JE (1989) Principal and agent. In: Eatwell J, Milgate M, Newman P (eds) Allocation, information and markets. Palgrave Macmillan UK, London, pp 241–253
Stiglitz JE (2009) Moving beyond market fundamentalism to a more balanced economy. Ann Public Coop Econ 80:345–360. https://doi.org/10.1111/j.1467-8292.2009.00389.x
Stout LA (2007) The mythical benefits of shareholder control. Va Law Rev:789–809
Strasser P (2011a) §§ 92-94. In: Strasser P, Jabornegg R (eds) Kommentar zum Aktiengesetz, 5th edn. Manz, Vienna
Strasser P (2011b) §§ 95-97. In: Strasser P, Jabornegg R (eds) Kommentar zum Aktiengesetz, 5th edn. Manz, Vienna
Strausz R (1997) Collusion and renegotiation in a principal-supervisor-agent relationship. Scand J Econ 99:497–518. https://doi.org/10.1111/1467-9442.00078
Strohn L (2015) § 34. In: Fleischer H, Goette W (eds) Münchener Kommentar zum Gesetz betreffend die Gesellschaften mit beschränkter Haftung: (GmbHG) Bd.1 §§ 1-34, 2nd edn. Beck; Vahlen, München
Strommer M (2014a) § 15. In: Dellinger M (ed) Genossenschaftsgesetz samt Nebengesetzen: Kommentar, 2nd edn. LexisNexis ARD Orac, Wien, pp 189–200
Strommer M (2014b) § 17. In: Dellinger M (ed) Genossenschaftsgesetz samt Nebengesetzen: Kommentar, 2nd edn. LexisNexis ARD Orac, Wien, pp 204–213
Strommer M (2014c) § 18. In: Dellinger M (ed) Genossenschaftsgesetz samt Nebengesetzen: Kommentar, 2nd edn. LexisNexis ARD Orac, Wien, p 214
Strommer M (2014d) § 19. In: Dellinger M (ed) Genossenschaftsgesetz samt Nebengesetzen: Kommentar, 2nd edn. LexisNexis ARD Orac, Wien, pp 215–218
Strommer M (2014e) § 23. In: Dellinger M (ed) Genossenschaftsgesetz samt Nebengesetzen: Kommentar, 2nd edn. LexisNexis ARD Orac, Wien, pp 251–257
Study Group on European Cooperative Law (2012) New study group on European Cooperative Law: "principles" project. https://www.euricse.eu/publications/wp-02412-new-study-group-on-european-cooperative-law-principles-project/. Accessed 21 Nov 2019
Svendsen SV (2007) Lock-in of farmers in agricultural cooperatives. In: Karantininis K, Nilsson J (eds) Vertical markets and cooperative hierarchies: the role of cooperatives in the agri-food industry. Springer, Dordrecht, pp 113–135
Sykuta ME, Chaddad F (1999) Putting theories of the firm in their place: a supplemental digest of the new institutional economics. J Coop:68–75

Sykuta ME, Cook ML (2001) A new institutional economics approach to contracts and cooperatives. Am J Agric Econ 83:1273–1279

Szabó G (2004) New institutional economics and agricultural co-operatives: a Hungarian case study. In: Karafolas S, Spear R, Stryjan Y (eds) Local society & global economy: the role of co-operatives: ICA international research conference; Naoussa 2002. Hellin, Athēna, pp 357–378

Szabó G (2007) "Co-operative identity": a theoretical concept for economic analyis of practical co-operation dynamics. Stud Agric Econ:5–22. https://doi.org/10.22004/ag.econ.107648

Tallia F (2013) Il dovere di diligenza e la business judgment rule. Il nuovo diritto delle Società:14–39

Tatarano MC (2011) La nuova impresa cooperativa, Nuova ed. de L'impresa cooperativa di Giovanni Tatarano. Trattato di diritto civile e commerciale / già diretto da Antonio Cicu, Francesco Messineo, Luigi Mengoni. Giuffrè, Milano

Teichmann C (2004) Germany. In: Teichmann C, Oplustil K (eds) The European company - all over Europe: a state-by-state account of the introduction of the European company. De Gruyter, Berlin, pp 109–131

Teichmann C (2015a) Art. 38. In: Lutter M, Hommelhoff P, Teichmann C (eds) SE-Kommentar, 2nd edn. Verlag Dr. Otto Schmidt, Köln, pp 452–471

Teichmann C (2015b) Art. 43. In: Lutter M, Hommelhoff P, Teichmann C (eds) SE-Kommentar, 2nd edn. Verlag Dr. Otto Schmidt, Köln, pp 537–715

Teichmann C (2015c) Art. 44. In: Lutter M, Hommelhoff P, Teichmann C (eds) SE-Kommentar, 2nd edn. Verlag Dr. Otto Schmidt, Köln, pp 716–721

Teichmann C (2015d) Art. 45. In: Lutter M, Hommelhoff P, Teichmann C (eds) SE-Kommentar, 2nd edn. Verlag Dr. Otto Schmidt, Köln, pp 721–725

Teichmann C (2015e) Art. 46. In: Lutter M, Hommelhoff P, Teichmann C (eds) SE-Kommentar, 2nd edn. Verlag Dr. Otto Schmidt, Köln, pp 727–731

Teichmann C (2015f) Art. 47. In: Lutter M, Hommelhoff P, Teichmann C (eds) SE-Kommentar, 2nd edn. Verlag Dr. Otto Schmidt, Köln, pp 731–741

Teichmann C (2015g) Art. 48. In: Lutter M, Hommelhoff P, Teichmann C (eds) SE-Kommentar, 2nd edn. Verlag Dr. Otto Schmidt, Köln, pp 741–751

Teichmann C (2015h) Art. 49. In: Lutter M, Hommelhoff P, Teichmann C (eds) SE-Kommentar, 2nd edn. Verlag Dr. Otto Schmidt, Köln, pp 751–755

Teichmann C (2015i) Art. 50. In: Lutter M, Hommelhoff P, Teichmann C (eds) SE-Kommentar, 2nd edn. Verlag Dr. Otto Schmidt, Köln, pp 755–768

Teichmann C (2015j) Art. 51. In: Lutter M, Hommelhoff P, Teichmann C (eds) SE-Kommentar, 2nd edn. Verlag Dr. Otto Schmidt, Köln, pp 768–776

Thaler R (1980) Toward a positive theory of consumer choice. J Econ Behav Organ 1:39–60. https://doi.org/10.1016/0167-2681(80)90051-7

The European Public Limited-Liability Company Regulations 2004. http://www.legislation.gov.uk/uksi/2004/2326/pdfs/uksi_20042326_en.pdf. Accessed 29 Dec 2019

Theisen MR (1987) Die Überwachung der Unternehmungsführung: Betriebswirtschaftl. Ansätze zur Entwicklung erster Grundsätze ordnungsmäßiger Überwachung. Univ., Habil.-Schr.—Regensburg, 1986. Betriebswirtschaftliche Abhandlungen, N.F., Bd. 70. Poeschel, Stuttgart

Theisen MR (1996) Grundsätze einer ordnungsmäßigen Information des Aufsichtsrats, 2., vollst. überarb. und erw. Aufl. Schriftenreihe Der Betrieb. Schäffer-Poeschel, Stuttgart

Thoma GF, Leuering D (2002) Die Europäische Aktiengesellschaft - Societas Europaea. Neue Juristische Wochenschrift:1449–1455

Thomas A (2004) The rise of social cooperatives in Italy. VOLUNTAS: Int J Volunt Nonprofit Org 15:243–263. https://doi.org/10.1023/B:VOLU.0000046280.06580.d8

Thomsen S (2014) Comparative corporate governance of non-profit organizations. Eur Comp Financ Law Rev 11:15–30. https://doi.org/10.1515/ecfr-2014-0015

Tietzel M (1981) Die Ökonomie der property rights: Ein Überblick. Zeitschrift für Wirtschaftspolitik 30

Tirole J (1986) Hierarchies and bureaucracies: on the role of collusion in organizations. J Law Econ Organ 2:181–214

Tirole J (2006) The theory of corporate finance. Princeton University Press, Princeton

Told J (2015) Business Judgment Rule und ihre Anwendbarkeit in Österreich. GES:60–72

Tomanek P (2014) Vor § 1 GenG. In: Dellinger M (ed) Genossenschaftsgesetz samt Nebengesetzen: Kommentar, 2nd edn. LexisNexis ARD Orac, Wien, pp 1–16

Tombari U (2008) Governo dell'impresa e sistema dualistico nelle società cooperative. Analisi Giuridica dell'Economia:399–422. https://doi.org/10.1433/28532

Ton G, Gábor S (2012) Organisational mechanisms to solve collective action challenges in vegetables marketing: case study report. In: Van der Sangen G, Pyykkönen POP, Iliopoulus C, Kühl R, Hagedorn K, Hanisch M, Judis R, Gijselinckx C, Hendrikse G, Hak T, Poppe K, Bijman J (eds) Support for farmers' cooperatives, Wageningen, pp 1–19

Tonelli E (2003a) Art. 2516. In: Sandulli M, Santoro V (eds) La riforma delle società: Società cooperative Artt. 2511-2548 cod.civ. Giappichelli, Torino, pp 47–51

Tonelli E (2003b) Art. 2525. In: Sandulli M, Santoro V (eds) La riforma delle società: Società cooperative Artt. 2511-2548 cod.civ. Giappichelli, Torino, pp 84–88

Torgerson RE, Reynolds BJ, Gray TW (1998) Evolution of cooperative thought, theory, and purpose. J Coop

Tortia E, Valentinov V, Iliopoulos C (2013) Agricultural cooperatives. J Entrep Organ Divers:23–36. https://doi.org/10.5947/jeod.2013.002

Towfigh EV (2012) Das ökonomische Paradigma. In: Towfigh EV, Petersen N (eds) Ökonomische Methoden im Recht: Eine Einführung für Juristen. Mohr Siebeck, Tübingen, pp 23–35

Trebilcock MJ (1997) The limits of freedom of contract, 2nd edn. Harvard University Press, Cambridge

Trechter DD, King RP, Cobia DW, Hartell JG (1997) Case studies of executive compensation in agricultural cooperatives. Rev Agric Econ 19:492–503. https://doi.org/10.2307/1349756

Trimarchi G (2005) Questioni in tema di assemblea nelle società cooperative. In: Consiglio nazionale del notariato. (ed) Studi e materiali in tema di riforma delle società cooperative. Giuffrè, Milano, pp 647–654

Tushnet M, Cane P (eds) (2012) The Oxford handbook of legal studies. Oxford University Press, Oxford

Urbani A (2008) La problematica della sede sociale e della sede effettiva. In: Capriglione F (ed) La nuova disciplina della società europea. Cedam, Padova, pp 321–342

Usai P (2010a) Art. 2380 bis. In: Cendon P (ed) Artt. 2363-2396: Società per azioni: [2] assemblea, amministratori. Giuffrè, Milano, pp 479–486

Usai P (2010b) Art. 2381. In: Cendon P (ed) Artt. 2363-2396: Società per azioni: [2] assemblea, amministratori. Giuffrè, Milano, pp 487–502

Usai P (2010c) Art. 2382. In: Cendon P (ed) Artt. 2363-2396: Società per azioni: [2] assemblea, amministratori. Giuffrè, Milano, pp 503–508

Usai P (2010d) Art. 2384. In: Cendon P (ed) Artt. 2363-2396: Società per azioni: [2] assemblea, amministratori. Giuffrè, Milano, pp 521–531

Usai P (2010e) Art. 2387. In: Cendon P (ed) Artt. 2363-2396: Società per azioni: [2] assemblea, amministratori. Giuffrè, Milano, pp 551–557

Valentinov V (2005) The organizational nature of agricultural cooperatives: a perspective from the farm problem theory. J Rural Coop:139–151

van Aaken A (2001) Vom Nutzen der ökonomischen Theorie des Rechts für die Rechtsvergleichung. In: Jud B (ed) Prinzipien des Privatrechts und Rechtsvereinheitlichung: Wiener Tagung, 13. - 16. September 2000. 11. Tagung der Gesellschaft Junger Zivilrechtswissenschaftler e.V. Boorberg, Stuttgart, pp 127–149

van Bekkum O-F, van Dijk G (eds) (1997) Agricultural co-operatives in the European Union: trends and issues on the eve of the 21st century. Onno-Frank van Bekkum, Gert van Dijk (eds); authors: Onno-Frank van Bekkum ... [et al.]. Van Gorcum, Assen, The Netherlands

Van der Sangen G (2012) EU synthesis and comparative analysis report: legal aspects. In: Support for farmers' cooperatives, Wageningen, pp 1–50
van Diepenbeek WJJ (2007) Cooperatives as a business organization: lessons from cooperative organization history. Universiteit Maastricht, Maastricht
van Dijk G (1997) Implementing the sixth reason for co-operation: new generation co-operatives in agribusiness. In: Nilsson JE, Dijk GE (eds) Strategies and structures in the agro-food industries. Van Gorcum and Co, Assen, pp 94–110
van Herck K (2014) Assessing efficiencies generated by agricultural producer organisations. Publications Office, Luxembourg
Vatn A (2002) Multifunctional agriculture: some consequences for international trade regimes. Eur Rev Agric Econ 29:309–327. https://doi.org/10.1093/eurrag/29.3.309
Vecchione A (2004) L'imprenditore agricolo. Quaderni del Dipartimento di studi internazionali, Università degli studi di Salerno, Facoltà di giurisprudenza, vol 4. Edizioni scientifiche italiane, Napoli
Vecchione A (2009a) Le attività agricole principali. In: Iannarelli A, Vecchione A (eds) L' impresa agricola. Giappichelli, Torino, pp 233–274
Vecchione A (2009b) Le attività connesse. In: Iannarelli A, Vecchione A (eds) L' impresa agricola. Giappichelli, Torino, pp 275–332
Vecchione A (2009c) L'imprenditore agricolo nelle fonti speciali e figure professionali ad esso equiparate. In: Iannarelli A, Vecchione A (eds) L' impresa agricola. Giappichelli, Torino, pp 353–386
Vecchione A (2009d) L'impresa agricola nella realtà virtuale. In: Iannarelli A, Vecchione A (eds) L' impresa agricola. Giappichelli, Torino, pp 209–232
Velasco J (2015) A defense of the corporate law duty of care. J Corp Law:647–703
Vella M (2010) Oltre il motivo del profitto: Storia, economia, gestione e finanza delle imprese cooperative italiane. Economia sociale, vol 51. Maggioli, Santarcangelo di Romagna, Rimini
Ventoruzzo M (2011) Empowering shareholders in directors' elections: a revolution in the making. Eur Comp Financ Law Rev 8. https://doi.org/10.1515/ecfr.2011.105
Vitaliano P (1983) Cooperative enterprise: an alternative conceptual basis for analyzing a complex institution. Am J Agric Econ 65:1078–1083. https://doi.org/10.2307/1240424
Wagner J (2002) Die Bestimmung des auf die SE anwendbaren Rechts. Neue Zeitschrift für Gesellschaftsrecht:985–990
Wall N, Lines D, Martin B, Marcousé I (2010) Economics & business studies, 4th edn. A-Z handbook. Philip Allan Updates, Deddington
Welan M (2017) Die Lehre des Rechts an der Universität für Bodenkultur. In: Norer R, Holzer G (eds) Agrarrecht: Jahrbuch 2017. Perspektiven des Agrarrechts. Festgabe für Manfried Welan, 1st edn. NWV Verlag, Wien, pp 105–130
Welser I (2013) Efficiency - today's challenge in arbitration proceedings. In: Austrian yearbook on international arbitration. Manz, Vienna, pp 151–166
Werlauff E (2003) The SE company – a new common European company from 8 October 2004. Eur Bus Law Rev:85–103
Werner K (2008) Die Limited ante portas: Das Haftkapital der GmbH vor dem Hintergrund des Wettbewerbs der Rechtsordnungen: eine rechtliche und ökonomische Analyse. VDM Verlag Dr. Müller, Saarbrücken
Wiese MH (2006) Die Europäische Genossenschaft im Vergleich zur eingetragenen Genossenschaft deutschen Rechts: Reformüberlegungen zum deutschen Genossenschaftsrecht. Münstersche Schriften zur Kooperation, vol 69. Shaker, Aachen
Williamson O (1973) Markets and hierarchies: some elementary considerations. Am Econ Rev 63:316–325
Williamson OE (1998) The economic institutions of capitalism: firms, markets, relational contracting. Free Press, New York

Winkler W (2018a) Agrarrecht - Umweltrecht: Gegensatz oder Ergänzung. In: Martínez J (ed) Reichweite und Grenzen des Agrarrechts: Gedächtnisschrift für Dr. Wolfgang Winkler, 1st edn. Nomos Verlagsgesellschaft, Baden-Baden, pp 211–248

Winkler W (2018b) Agrarrecht, agrarietà und Natur der Sache. In: Martínez J (ed) Reichweite und Grenzen des Agrarrechts: Gedächtnisschrift für Dr. Wolfgang Winkler, 1st edn. Nomos Verlagsgesellschaft, Baden-Baden, pp 159–210

World Co-operative Monitor 2018. https://monitor.coop/en/media/library/research-and-reviews/world-cooperative-monitor-2018en. Accessed 9 Dec 2019

Youde JG, Helmberger PG (1966) Marketing cooperatives in the U.S.: membership policies, market power, and antitrust policy. J Farm Econ 48:23–36. https://doi.org/10.2307/1236316

Zacherl U (1981) Zur Konzeption der genossenschaftlichen Förderbilanz. Zeitschrift für das gesamte Genossenschaftswesen:226

Zahn J (1963) Handbuch für Genossenschaften, 2nd edn. Österreichischer Genossenschaftsverband

Zamagni V (2017) A worldwide historical perspective on co-operatives and their evolution. In: Michie J, Blasi JR, Borzaga C (eds) The Oxford handbook of mutual, co-operative, and co-owned business, 1st edn. Oxford University Press, Oxford, pp 97–113

Zamagni V, Felice E (2006) Oltre il secolo: Le trasformazioni del sistema cooperativo Legacoop alla fine del secondo millennio. Storia e studi cooperativi. Il Mulino, Bologna

Zamperetti GM (2006) Prime significative applicazioni del sistema dualistico. Le società:1193

Zanotti A (2013) La governance societaria: Società per azioni e cooperative a confronto: una interpretazione economica. Rubbettino, Soveria Mannelli

Zecchin F (2017) La tutela del produttore agroalimentare fra tentativi di riequilibrio del potere contrattuale e misure di sostegno. Europa e Diritto Privato:1407–1465

Zehetner J (1999) Rechnungslegung der Genossenschaften. Manz, Wien

Zehetner J (2014a) § 22. In: Dellinger M (ed) Genossenschaftsgesetz samt Nebengesetzen: Kommentar, 2nd edn. LexisNexis ARD Orac, Wien, pp 221–250

Zehetner J (2014b) § 24. In: Dellinger M (ed) Genossenschaftsgesetz samt Nebengesetzen: Kommentar, 2nd edn. LexisNexis ARD Orac, Wien, pp 258–271

Zehetner J (2014c) § 24e. In: Dellinger M (ed) Genossenschaftsgesetz samt Nebengesetzen: Kommentar, 2nd edn. LexisNexis ARD Orac, Wien, pp 313–330

Zehetner J (2014d) § 27a. In: Dellinger M (ed) Genossenschaftsgesetz samt Nebengesetzen: Kommentar, 2nd edn. LexisNexis ARD Orac, Wien, pp 352–362

Ziliotti M (1994) Cooperativa, impresa. In: Zamagni S (ed) Economia politica I, 1. ed. italiana. UTET, Torino, pp 144–145

Zimmermann R (2019) Comparative law and the Europeanization of private law. In: Reimann M, Zimmermann R (eds) The Oxford handbook of comparative law, 2nd edn. Oxford University Press, Oxford, pp 557–598

Zöllner W (1963) Die Schranken mitgliedschaftlicher Stimmrechtsmacht bei den privatrechtlichen Personenverbänden. Institut fuer Wirtschaftsrecht (Koeln, Univ.):Schriften. Bd15. Beck, München

Zoppini A (2000) Relazione introduttiva ad una proposta per la disciplina dell'"impresa sociale". Rivista Critica del Diritto Privato:335–392

Zoppini A (2002) Autonomia e separazione del patrimonio nella prospettiva dei patrimoni separati della società per azioni. Rivista di Diritto Civile:549–575

Zoppini A (2004) Il nuovo diritto delle società cooperative: un'analisi economica. Rivista di Diritto Civile:439–450

Zoppini A (2015) La struttura finanziaria della società cooperativa. In: La riforma del diritto societario dieci anni dopo: Per i quarant'anni di giurisprudenza commerciale: Milano, 13-14 giugno 2014. Giuffrè, Milano, pp 343–361

Zweigert K, Kötz H (1996) Einführung in die Rechtsvergleichung auf dem Gebiete des Privatrechts, 3rd edn. Mohr, Tübingen

Zweigert K, Kötz H, Di Majo A, Gambaro A, Pozzo B (1998) Introduzione al diritto comparato, Rist. integrata con addenda. Giuffrè, Milano

The manufacturer's authorised representative in the EU is Springer
Nature Customer Service Centre GmbH, Europaplatz 3, 69115 Heidelberg,
Germany. If you have any concerns regarding our products, please
contact ProductSafety@springernature.com

Printed and bound by CPI Group (UK) Ltd, Croydon, CR0 4YY
30/09/2026
02225645-0020